W9-BFS-967

PLANNING AND CONTROL OF LAND DEVELOPMENT: CASES AND MATERIALS

EIGHTH EDITION

LexisNexis Law School Publishing Advisory Board

PLANNING AND CONTROL OF LAND DEVELOPMENT: CASES AND MATERIALS

EIGHTH EDITION

Daniel R. Mandelker
Howard A. Stamper Professor of Law
Washington University

Carol Necole Brown
Professor of Law
University of North Carolina School of Law

Stuart Meck
Associate Research Professor and Director, Center for Planning Practice, Edward J. Bloustein School of Planning and Public Policy
Rutgers, The State University of New Jersey, New Brunswick

Dwight H. Merriam
Robinson & Cole, LLP, Hartford, CT

Peter W. Salsich, Jr.
McDonnell Professor of Justice in American Society
Saint Louis University School of Law

Nancy E. Stroud
Lewis Stroud & Deutsch, P.L., Boca Raton, Florida

Julie A. Tappendorf
Ancel, Glink, Diamond, Bush, DiCianni & Krafthefer, P.C., Chicago, Illinois

ISBN: 978-1-4224-8163-9

Library of Congress Cataloging-in-Publication Data

Planning and control of land development : cases and materials / Daniel R. Mandelker ... [et al.]. -- 8th ed.
p. cm.
Includes bibliographical references and index.
ISBN 978-1-4224-8163-9 (hard cover)
1. Land use--Law and legislation--United States--Cases. 2. Real estate development--Law and legislation--United States--Cases. I. Mandelker, Daniel R.
KF5698.P584 2011
346.7304'5--dc22 2010051854

NOTE TO USERS

To ensure that you are using the latest materials available in this area, please be sure to periodically check the LexisNexis Law School web site for downloadable updates and supplements at www.lexisnexis.com/lawschool.

Editorial Offices
121 Chanlon Rd., New Providence, NJ 07974 (908) 464-6800
201 Mission St., San Francisco, CA 94105-1831 (415) 908-3200
www.lexisnexis.com

MATTHEW BENDER

(2011–Pub.3093)

Dedication

For all my children and grandchildren — D.R.M.

For Paul, and the late Allen and Valerie Brown — C.N.B.

For Jess — S.M.

For Professor Quintin Johnstone — D.H.M.

For Barbara — P.W.S.

For Carl — N.E.S.

For my family — J.A.T.

Preface

This Eighth Edition, of what has become a true classic in the field, is a sea change in several respects.

First, there are new Editors. John M. Payne, an Editor for several Editions and a Board of Governors distinguished service professor and Justice Frederick Hall scholar at Rutgers Law School, Newark, died on June 16, 2009. His scholarship lives on in this Edition. We have added four new Editors — Carol Necole Brown, Professor of Law at the University of North Carolina School of Law; Stuart Meck, FAICP, Associate Research Professor and Director, Center for Planning Practice, Edward J. Bloustein School of Planning at Rutgers; Dwight H. Merriam, FAICP, of Robinson & Cole LLP; and Julie A. Tappendorf of Ancel Glink Diamond Bush DiCianni & Krafthefer, P.C. in Chicago. We now have the most diverse and representative Editors of any land use law casebook ever — three law school professors, three practicing lawyers, and one of the nation's preeminent land use planners, and we note, not a lawyer.

Second, we have done some reorganizing to improve the flow and made Chapter 1 decidedly all about planning. It works, we are pleased with the result, and know you will be too.

Third, we have pushed at every turn to get the most recent issues, decisions, statutes and secondary materials into the text, many with web addresses — to the point of even inserting new material as we did the final proofreading. We will provide annual updates and are committed to maintaining our well-deserved reputation for being the most current and cutting edge of any land use law casebook.

Fourth, as before, there is a Teacher's Manual with supplemental CD-ROM and a supporting website. This will keep the material up-to-date on a near-daily basis. There will also be annual update letters.

Finally, Professor Mandelker, who brought us the First Edition of the casebook in 1979, will continue to be an active Editor of this casebook, but has decided with this Edition to shift the leadership responsibility to Dwight Merriam, who pledges with the new team of Editors to do everything possible to maintain the status of this casebook as the one without equal.

The Editors wish to acknowledge assistance in preparing this edition provided by Chester Hutchinson, J.D. Candidate, Saint Louis University, 2011, Shawna Shillair, J.D. Candidate, Saint Louis University, 2012, Priyanka Veerlapati, J.D. Candidate, Saint Louis University, 2012, Lauren Smith, J.D. Washington University 2010, Linda Lawder, J.D. Candidate, Saint Louis University 2012, and Katherine Asaro, University of North Carolina School of Law. Our thanks to them all.

Our editor at LexisNexis, Keith Moore, deserves special recognition for keeping us all on track and moving smoothly, on time, to completion of this Eight Edition.

Daniel R. Mandelker
Carol Necole Brown
Stuart Meck
Dwight H. Merriam
Peter W. Salsich, Jr.
Nancy E. Stroud
Julie A. Tappendorf

Acknowledgments

The American Planning Association, for permission to reprint from E. Kelly, Planning, Growth, and Public Facilities: A Primer for Local Officials, Planning Advisory Services Report No. 447 (1993). Copyright 1993 by the American Planning Association. Reprinted with permission.

The American Planning Association, and Taylor & Francis Group, www.informaworld.com, for permission to reprint from Tarlock, Euclid Revisited, 34 Land Use Law & Zoning Digest, No. 1 at 4, 6–8 (1982).

The American Planning Association, for permission to reprint from Daniel Mandelker, Planned Unit Developments, Planning Advisory Service Report No. 545 (2007). Copyright 2007 by The American Planning Association. Reprinted with permission.

The American Planning Association, for permission to reprint from Michael J. Meshenberg, *The Language of Zoning*, Planning Advisory Services Report No. 322, Figures 17A and 17B, pp 26–27. Chicago: American Planning Association. Copyright 1976.

The American Planning Association, for permission to reprint from Nelson, *Leadership in a New Era*, 72 J. Am. Plan. Ass'n 394, 398–399, 401–402 (2006). Copyright 2006.

The American Planning Association, for permission to reprint from Growing Smart Legislative Guidebook: Model Statutes for Planning and the Management of Change, pp. 4-11-4-14, ed. S. Meck. Copyright 2002 by The American Planning Assocition. Reprinted with permission.

Harvard Law Review, for permission to reprint from Hart, *Colonial Land Use Law and Its Significance for Modern Takings Doctrine*, 109 Harv. L. Rev. 1252, 1257, 1273–1281 (1996). Copyright 1996 by the Harvard Law Review Association.

Harvard Law Review, for permission to reprint from Michelman, *Property, Utility, and Fairness: Comments on the Ethical Foundations of Just Compensation Law*, 80 Harv. L. Rev. 1165, 1174–76 (1967). Copyright 1967 by the Harvard Law Review Association.

International City/County Management Association, for permission to reprint from S. Meck et al., Zoning and Subdivision Regulation, pp. 343, 362–369, in The Practice of Local Government Planning, ed. J. Hoch, L. Dalton & Frank S. So (2000).

Island Press, for material excerpted from Land Use and Society: Geography, Law and Public Policy by Rutherford Platt. Copyright 2004 by Island Press. Reprinted with permission of Island Press.

The Johns Hopkins University Press, for permission to reprint from Fischel, William A., The Economics of Zoning Laws: A Property Rights Approach to American Land use Controls pp. 4, 7–8, 18–19. Copyright 1985, The Johns Hopkins University Press. Reprinted with permission of The Johns Hopkins University Press.

Liverpool University Press, for permission to reprint from *The Laws of the Indies*, from *The City Planning Ordinances of the Laws of the Indies Revisited, I*, 48 Town Planning Review, pp. 251–258 (July 1977).

Missouri Coalition for the Environment, for permission to reprint from The State of Missouri's Floodplain Management Ten Years After the 1993 Flood 9-11 (2003). Copyright 2003 by Missouri Coalition for the Environment. All rights reserved.

Ohio State law Journal and Professor Mark Cordes, for permission to reprint from Mark Cordes,

Acknowledgments

Takings, Fairness and Farmland Preservation, 60 Ohio St. L.J. 1033 (1999). Originally published in 60 Ohio St. L.J. 1033 (1999).

Rutgers Center for Urban Policy Research, for permission to reprint from Eric Heikkila, The Economics of Planning (New Brunswick, N.J.: Center for Urban Policy Research). Copyright 2000 by Rutgers The State University of New Jersey. Reprinted with permission.

Washington University Law Quarterly, for permission to reprint from Mandelker, *Delegation of Power and Function in Zoning Administration*, 1963 Wash. U.L.Q. 60, 61, 63. Copyright 1963.

Wall Street Journal, for permission to reprint from Zimmerman, *Rival Chains Secretly Fund Opposition to Wal-Mart*, Wall Street Journal (June 7, 2010) available at http://tinyurl.com/254lb8h. Copyright 2010.

William & Mary Environmental Law & Policy Review, for permission to reprint from Daniel Mandelker, Managing Space to Manage Growth, 23 William and Mary Environmental Law and Policy Review 801 (1999). Copyright 1999 by The Marshal-Wythe School of Law College of William & Mary. Reprinted with permission.

A Note on the Text

Unless otherwise indicated in the text, the emphasis in all quoted materials is as in the original. Only selected footnotes from the cases are reproduced, but the original footnote numbering as it appeared in the source is retained. Ellipses are used within the cases only to indicate deleted text material. Internal citations to cases reproduced have sometimes been edited. Quoted statutes are not dated; all were current as of the date of publication of this edition of the casebook.

Notes on a Bibliography

Treatises. In addition to Professor Mandelker's one-volume treatise on Land Use Law (5th ed. 2003, with supplements), other one-volume books are J. Juergensmeyer & T. Roberts, Land Use Planning and Control Law, (2d ed. 2007), P. Salsich & T. Tryniecki, Land Use Regulation (2d ed. 2003), and B. Blaesser & A. Weinstein in Federal Land Use Law, which is updated annually. Juergensmeyer and Roberts also have a hornbook, Land Use Planning and Development Regulation Law, also published in 2003.

There are a number of multi-volume treatises. These include the late Professor Norman Williams' American Land Planning Law; P. Rohan, Zoning and Land Use Controls, presently edited by Professor Eric Kelly; Rathkopf's Law of Zoning and Planning, now periodically updated by Professor Ed Ziegler; and Professor Kmiec's Zoning and Planning Deskbook.

Journals and Periodic Publications. The Urban Lawyer, which is the official publication of the Urban, State and Local Government Law Section of the American Bar Association, and the Florida State University Journal of Land Use and Environmental Law, regularly contain articles on land use topics. The American Planning Association publishes a monthly periodical, Planning and Environmental Law. Each issue contains a lead article and digests of recent cases and statutes. APA also publishes Practicing Planner and Zoning Practice, which can carry useful articles on land use regulation topics.

ThomsonWest publishes a monthly Zoning and Planning Law Report that contains a lead article, case digests and reports on new developments. It also publishes an annual Land Use and Environment Law Review that reproduces leading articles published during the previous year and an annual Zoning and Planning Law Handbook that contains articles on land use topics. The Journal of the American Planning Association carries articles on land use planning and controls. Urban Land, published by the Urban Land Institute, occasionally has a section on regulatory problems that often covers land use issues. Land Development, a publication of the National Association of Homebuilders, is another useful publication.

The Journal of Planning Literature, edited at Ohio State University's planning school and published by Sage Publications, is a quarterly publication that contains bibliographies of articles on land use and related topics as well as abstracts of the more important articles. It also contains individual bibliographies and review articles on land use topics that are extremely helpful.

The American Planning Association also publishes a periodic Planning Advisory Service Report. Each issue is a report on a land use or planning topic. The reports often discuss land use control problems and techniques. The Advisory Service also includes periodic Quick Notes and the PASMemo, which can contain articles on land use regulation.

Some environmental law journals occasionally carry articles on land use law. These include the Environmental Law Reporter of the Environmental Law Institute, Ecology Law Quarterly, Environmental Law, the Harvard Environmental Law Review, and the Natural Resources Journal.

Web Sites. The casebook web site, at law.wustl.edu/landuselaw contains valuable materials that can be used in class, including comprehensive plans, recent cases, statutes, ordinances, law review articles and reports on land use issues. One section contains photos of all the Supreme Court cases included in the book. On the home page there are links to PowerPoint presentations and streaming videos. The annual update letter for the casebook will also be posted on the home page. Another section has links to numerous web sites that deal with land use questions. There is also a section on supplementary materials containing material from previous editions that has since been omitted.

There are two blogs devoted to land use topics. One, lawoftheland.wordpress.com/, is hosted by Dean Salkin at the Albany Law School and features daily postings of recent cases. For a land use law professors' blog go to http://lawprofessors.typepad.com/land_use/

TABLE OF CONTENTS

Chapter 1

AN INTRODUCTION TO LAND USE CONTROLS

A. WHY LAND USE CONTROLS?

Cities and other places don't just happen. The use of land requires the coming together of a complex set of social, economic and physical forces, joined together by a vision (sometimes inchoate) of the desired outcome. Planning for the use of land as we know it today began with the first European arrivals on the North American continent, and continues today. An example is "The Laws of the Indies" signed by King Phillip II of Spain that provided a sophisticated vision and direction for city planning in the New World. The laws were revised to their final form in 1573, and finally published as a book in 1681. In turn, the laws draw on Ten Books of Architecture, written by Vitruvius, a Roman architect and engineer in the 1st century BC. The impacts of these laws are reflected in the planning and the execution of Spanish settlements including St. Augustine and Pensacola, Florida; San Antonio, Texas; Galvez, Louisiana; Santa Fe, New Mexico; and the Mission San Luis Rey and the Presidio in California, among others. The first part of the laws, which has been omitted, covers the selection of sites for cities. The second part contains a series of detailed ordinances for city planning. Compare these ordinances with contemporary land use regulations.

THE LAWS OF THE INDIES

From the English translation by Axel I. Mundigo and Dora P. Crouch,
reprinted with permission from
The City Planning Ordinances of the Laws of the Indies Revisited, I,
48 Town Planning Review, pp. 251–258 (July 1977)

New Settlements

32. Before discoveries are duly recognized, no new population settlements are permitted, whether in the discovered areas or in those still to be discovered, but in those parts which are already discovered, pacified, and subjected to our mandate, population settlements, both of Spaniards and of Indians, should be ordered having permanence and giving perpetuity to both groups as specified in the fourth and fifth books [of the Laws of the Indies], especially in those parts dealing with population settlements and with land allotments. . . .

[Ordinances 35 and 36 address the desirability of fertile soil and adequate water for drinking and irrigation as well of the presence of Indians "to home we can preach the gospels" since this was a principal reason for Spanish colonization.]

37. And they should have good access and outlet by sea and by land, and also good roads and passage by water, in order that they may be entered and departed easily with commerce, while bringing relief and establishing defenses.

38. Once the region, province, county, and land are decided upon by the expert discoverers, select the site to build a town and capital of the province and its subjects, without harm to the Indians for having occupied the area or because they agree to it of good will.

39. The site and position of the towns should be selected in places where water is nearby and where it would be possible to demolish neighboring towns and properties in order to take advantage of the materials that are essential for building; and, [these sites and positions should be suitable] also for farming, cultivation, and pasturation, so as to avoid excessive work and cost, since any of the above would be costly if they were far.

40. Do not select sites that are too high up because these are affected by winds, and access and service to these are difficult, nor in lowlands, which tend to be unhealthy; choose places of medium elevation that enjoy good winds, especially from the north and south, and if there were mountains or hills, these should be in the west or in the east, and if there should be a need to build in high places, do it in areas not subjected to fogs; take note of the terrain and its accidental features and in case that there should be a need to build on the banks of a river, it should be on the eastern bank, so when the sun rises it strikes the town first, then the water.

41. Do not select sites for towns in maritime locations because of the danger that exists of pirates and because they are not very healthy, and because in these [locations] there are less people able to work and cultivate the land, nor is it possible to instill in them these habits. Unless the site is in an area where there are good and principal harbors, among these, select for settlement only those that are necessary for the entry of commerce and for the defense of the land. . . .

89. The persons who were placed in charge of populating a town with Spaniards should see to it that, within a specified term, assigned for its establishment, it should have at least thirty neighbors, each one with his own house, ten cows, four oxen or two oxen and two young bulls and a mare, and it should have [also] a clergyman who can administer sacraments and provide the ornaments to the church as well as the necessary implements for the divine service; if this is not accomplished, he should lose everything already built or formed and he will incur a fine of a thousand gold pesos.

90. The aforesaid stipulations and territory should be divided as follows:

Separate first the land that is needed for the house plots [solares] of the town, then allocate sufficient public land and grounds for pasture where the cattle that the neighbors are expected to bring with them can obtain abundant feed, plus another portion for the natives of the area.

The rest of the grounds and territory should be divided into four parts: one is for the person in charge of building the town, the other three should be subdivided into thirty lots for the thirty neighbors of the town.

91. Land and boundaries for the new settlement cannot be given nor taken at a seaport nor anywhere where it can ever be redundant and detrimental to the Crown nor to the country because such sites will be reserved for us. . . .

99. Those who have made a commitment to build the said town, who after having succeeded in carrying out its settlement, as an honor to them and to their descendants [and in] their laudable memory as founders, we pronounce them hijosdalgo [illustrious men of known ancestry]. To them and to their legitimate heirs, in whatever place they might reside or in any

other part of the Indies, they will be hijosdalgo, that is, persons of noble ascendancy and known ancestry.

100. Those who should want to make a commitment to building a new settlement in the form and manner already prescribed, be it of more or less than 30 neighbors, (know that) it should be of no less than twelve persons and be awarded the authorization and territory in accordance with the prescribed conditions.

101. If there is no person with the duty to select a site for a new settlement and there are enough married men who agree to create a new settlement wherever they are directed to locate it, as long as they are no less than ten married men they can do it and will be given land and boundaries accordingly and they will have the right to choose among themselves mayors and yearly councilmen.

[Ordinances 102 and 103 deal with the need to adhere to the regulations for town settlement and to write down everything concerning the distribution of city plots, grazing and farmlands, and that no settler is to receive more than five peonies and three caballarias (103). *A peonia* is a plot of 50 feet in width and 100 feet in depth (102) and a *caballeria* is a plot to build a house of 100 feet in width and 200 feet in depth (105). In addition to the plots, grains, cereals, and seeds were given to the settlers. These plots should be well delineated with clear and closed boundaries (106). Those who accept *caballerias* and *peonias* have an obligation to build a house, work the land, and acquire herds, grasslands, etc., within a particular time (107–108).]

109. The governor who authorizes the settlement of a new town or concedes rights for an existing town to be populated anew, by means of his own authority or by making a request, should ascertain that those who have made a commitment to settle in a new town comply with the taking of seat in a proper manner. This should be done with great diligence and care. Also, the magistrates and Council procurer should initiate due process against the settlers who are bound up by a specified term and who have not complied with it to make them meet the terms, and those who might have left should be prosecuted, seized, and brought back to the town in order that they comply with the terms of settlement, and if they were in another jurisdiction, a requisitioning order should be issued in order that justice be done under penalty of Our Lord.

110. Having made the discovery, selected the province, county, and area that is to be settled, and the site in the location where the new town is to be built, and having taken possession of it, those placed in charge of its execution are to do it in the following manner. On arriving at the place where the new settlement is to be founded — which according to our will and disposition shall be one that is vacant and that can be occupied without doing harm to the Indians and natives or with their free consent — a plan for the site is to be made, dividing it into squares, streets, and building lots, using cord and ruler, beginning with the main square from which streets are to run to the gates and principal roads and leaving sufficient open space so that even if the town grows, it can always spread in the same manner. Having thus agreed upon the site and place selected to be populated, a layout should be made in the following way:

111. Having made the selection of the site where the town is to be built, it must, as already stated, be in an elevated and healthy location; [be] with means of fortification; [have] fertile soil and with plenty of land for farming and pasturage; have fuel, timber, and resources; [have] fresh water, a native population, ease of transport, access and exit; [and be] open to the north wind; and, if on the coast, due consideration should be paid to the quality of the harbor and

that the sea does not lie to the south or west; and if possible not near lagoons or marshes in which poisonous animals and polluted air and water breed.

112. The main plaza is to be the starting point for the town; if the town is situated on the sea coast, it should be placed at the landing place of the port, but inland it should be at the center of the town. The plaza should be square or rectangular, in which case it should have at least one and a half its width for length inasmuch as this shape is best for fiestas in which horses are used and for any other fiestas that should be held.

113. The size of the plaza shall be proportioned to the number of inhabitants, taking into consideration the fact that in Indian towns, inasmuch as they are new, the intention is that they will increase, and thus the plaza should be decided upon taking into consideration the growth the town may experience. [The plaza] shall be not less that two hundred feet wide and three hundred feet long, nor larger than eight hundred feet long and five hundred and thirty feet wide. A good proportion is six hundred feet long and four hundred wide.

114. From the plaza shall begin four principal street: One [shall be] from the middle of each side, and two streets from each corner of the plaza; the four corners of the plaza shall face the four principal winds, because in this manner, the streets running from the plaza will not be exposed to the four principal winds, which would cause much inconvenience.

115. Around the plaza as well as along the four principal streets which begin there, there shall be portals, for these are of considerable convenience to the merchants who generally gather there; the eight streets running from the plaza at the four corners shall open on the plaza without encountering these porticoes, which shall be kept back in order that there may be sidewalks even with the streets and plaza.

116. In cold places, the streets shall be wide and in hot places narrow; but for purposes of defense in areas where there are horses, it would be better if they are wide.

117. The streets shall run from the main plaza in such manner that even if the town increases considerably in size, it shall not result in some inconvenience that will make ugly what needed to be rebuilt, or endanger its defense or comfort.

[Ordinances 118 to 135 describe the allocation of land for churches and related structures, government buildings, customs houses, and arsenals. Ordinance 133 directs that sites for slaughterhouses, fisheries, tanneries, "and other business which produce filth shall be so placed that the filth can easily be disposed of." Ordinance 126 declares that "shops and houses for the merchants should be built first, to which all the settlers of the town shall contribute, and a moderate tax shall be imposed on goods so that these buildings may be built" — an early form of development timing. Ordinance 129 provides that "[w]ithin the town, a commons shall be delimited, large enough that although the population may experience a rapid expansion, there will always be sufficient space where the people may go to for recreation and take their cattle to pasture without them making any damage" — an early example of parks and open space planning. Other ordinances deal with the manner in which lots would be distributed to settlers, the orientation of buildings, the quality of construction, and the need to build "quickly and at small cost . . . ." Ordinance 133 stipulates that housing be arranged "in such a way that they may serve as defense or barrier against those who may try to disturb or invade the town." Finally, Ordinances 136 through 148 address how the Spaniards were to engage and pacify the native Indian population and convert Indians to the Catholic faith.

Land use controls are often thought of as a phenomenon of the late 19th and early 20th centuries. However, Professor John Hart chronicles their use in colonial times for purposes related to community planning and securing public benefits, not just as devices to avoid nuisances. Colonial community planning and regulation limited the location of dwellings, the disposition of land, and the sequence of development, and controlled aesthetics and underutilization of land.

Hart, *Colonial Land Use Law and Its Significance for Modern Takings Doctrine*

109 Harv. L. Rev. 1252, 1257, 1273–1281 (1996)

. . . Contrary to the conventional image of minimal land use regulation, government in the colonial period often exerted extensive authority over private land for purposes unrelated to avoiding nuisance. Colonial lawmakers often regulated private landowners' usage of their land in order to secure public benefits, not merely to prevent harm to health and safety. Indeed, the public benefits pursued by such legislative action included some that consisted essentially of benefits for other private landowners. Legislatures often attempted to influence or control the development of land for particular productive purposes thought to be in the public good. Legislatures compelled owners of undeveloped land to develop it, beyond what was required by the original grants, and compelled owners of wetlands to participate in drainage projects. Owners risked losing preexisting mineral rights if they failed to conduct their mining with sufficient promptness. Owners of land suitable for iron forges risked losing their land if they declined to erect such forges themselves. In towns and cities, landowners were constrained by measures intended to channel the spatial pattern of development, to optimize the density of habitation, to promote development of certain kinds of land, and to implement aesthetic goals . . .

H. Community Planning and Regulation

1. Restrictions on Location and Disposition of Dwellings. — In order to shape the spatial configuration of local communities and to facilitate social control over inhabitants, public authorities sometimes dictated which private land might be used for residences. The General Court of Massachusetts Bay initially ordered that no dwelling be built more than half a mile from the meeting house in any town, without permission from the Court. Some towns resisted this policy, and after five years the General Court abandoned it. Yet other Massachusetts towns continued to follow the General Court's previous policy of restricting dwelling locations. A similar goal of maintaining social and spiritual order is suggested by the Plymouth colony's order prohibiting persons who had already been granted land from dwelling there if "such lands lye soe remote as the Inhabitants thereof can not ordinarily frequent any place of publicke worship." This prohibition was intended to promote "the settleing of New Plantations in an orderly way."

Many towns exercised the right to regulate the disposition of land within the township by approving sales or leases of land to outsiders. Connecticut imposed heavy fines on landowners who sold or rented land within townships to outsiders without first receiving such approval. The legislature complained that "Persons of ungoverned Conversation, thrust themselves into the Towns in this Colony," and "by . . . hiring Lands or Houses; or by purchasing the same, endeavour to become Inhabitants in such Towns." Similar restrictions were instituted elsewhere. A milder form of restriction required owners to offer their land for sale to townsmen before selling to any outsiders.

Other constraints on land use were incidental to regulating particular types of people already in the community. For example, in the Plymouth colony servants were entitled to receive land — at first from the colony, later from their masters — when their terms of indenture expired. An ordinance of the General Court qualified this right: servants would receive such land only "if they be fownd fit to occupie it for themselues in some convenient place." The Court also ordered that no servants "be allowed to be howsekeeps or build any Cottages or dwelling howses till such time as they be allowed by the Governor or some one or more [of the] Cowncell of Assistants." Similarly, a town ordinance in North Carolina prohibited inhabitants from renting "any Tenement to a Slave."

Some land use restrictions represented efforts to optimize the density of habitation in towns. Connecticut's building requirement sought to remedy "a great abuse in several Towns and Plantations in this Colony, of buying and purchasing Home lots, and laying them together, by means whereof great depopulation may follow." Conversely, other restrictions aimed to prevent overly dense habitation. Cambridge, Massachusetts prohibited building any new dwelling houses within the town without the consent of a majority of the townsmen. A New Jersey regulation prohibited owners of town lots from subdividing them by selling such lots "apart from his or their said house or houses." Brookline, Massachusetts ordered that "not above one dwelling house shall be built upon any one lot without the consent of the town's overseers." Brookhaven, New York ordered "that noe accomodations shall be sowld by peece-meales, but Intire, without the consent of the Overseeres and Constable . . . ." Restriction of location also took the form of dictating the sequence of urban development, as well as its ultimate form. The Director General and Council of New Netherland, "in order to promote the population, settlement, beauty, strength and prosperity" of the city of New Amsterdam, ordered that "no Dwelling-houses shall be built near or under the Walls or Gates of this City" until the lots in certain other areas designated for development had been "properly built on."

2. Aesthetic Restrictions. — The colonies commonly regulated the height of buildings and the choice of building materials to prevent the spread of fire in residential areas. Additional restrictions for the sake of orderliness or beauty were imposed in some communities. In the city of New Amsterdam, officials known as "surveyors" were directed "to condemn and in future to stop all unsightly and irregular Buildings, Fences, Palisades, Posts, Rails, etc." Citizens could not build on or enclose lands "within or near the city" without the prior approval of these surveyors. Similarly, the New York Assembly later authorized the city of New York to make "rules and orders for the better regulation[,] uniformity[,] and gracefulnesse of such new buildings as shall be Erected for habitations." The city government directed surveyors to ensure that "a Regular Order and Uniformity may be kept and observed in the Streets and Buildings." Virginia authorized town directors and trustees to make "such orders, rules, and directions, for the regular and orderly placing and building the houses . . . , as to them shall seem expedient." Connecticut ordered that "all dwelling or mansion houses . . . in any Plantation or Town within this Jurisdiction, shall be upheld, repaired and maintained sufficiently in a comely way."

3. Compelling Development of Urban Land. — An early Virginia statute addressed the problem of "antient proprietors" of land in James City "who neither build themselves nor suffer others." Persons who "built decent houses upon ground so deserted" were authorized to "take it upp for themselves" without hindrance from the prior owners. Later Virginia statutes

required owners of certain town lots to build houses on their lots or have the lots sold to new purchasers. Connecticut gave owners of home lots "not yet built upon" in any "Plantation or Town" twelve months to "build a house there fit for an Inhabitant to dwell in, if his Lot be one Acre and half, unless the Court upon knowledge of the case, finde cause to abate or give longer time for building, upon the penalty of twenty shillings per year." Rhode Island imposed a similar requirement, subject to a penalty of forfeiting the land to the town. South Carolina imposed a schedule of fines on landowners in a certain town who failed to build houses within a certain time.

Efforts to discourage underutilization of land have a long history in the city of New York, founded by the Dutch as New Amsterdam. The New Netherland government repeatedly tried to induce inhabitants of New Amsterdam to erect more buildings and to develop their land in accordance with official ambitions for the city. The problem, as one ordinance explained, was that:

> [M]any spacious and large Lots, even in the best and most convenient part of this City, lie and remain without Buildings and are kept by the owners either for greater profit, or for pleasure, and others are thereby prevented to build for the promotion of population and increase of Trade and consumption, as well as for the embellishment of this City, where unto many new comers would be encouraged in case they could procure a Lot at a reasonable price on a suitable location. . . .

The city government employed various measures to achieve a higher building density: first, forfeiture by lot owners who did not build by a certain date; then, conveyance of unimproved lots to new purchasers, allowing the present owners "a reasonable indemnity at the discretion of the Street Surveyors"; and finally, imposition of a tax on unimproved lots and fines against "obstinate" persons who refused to comply.

Using some of the same means, the English government continued the effort to promote more intensive utilization of private land in New York City. The common council noted that there were "Severall parcells and Lotts of vacant ground, convenient to build on within this Citty: and Severall persons being willing to build and Settle therein; but cannot gett houses, or ground to build on (the Owners of the Said grounds, refuseing to build or Sell)." There were also "Severall houses ruinated and decayed: The Owners whereof being either absent, or unwilling to build or repaire the Same." After a committee surveyed and valued "all the vacant Land convenient or fitt to build on: As alsoe all ruinated, decayed and untenentable houses . . . within this Citty," the New York Common Council ordered that all such property be sold "to any that will bee willing to pay the Purchase to the right Owners according to the apprizement." The prior owners could retain their land only if they themselves built "Sufficient dwelling howses" on the land within a year. We can infer that this intervention did not overcome a market failure. Perhaps the recalcitrant owners thought the land was worth more than anyone had offered to pay; perhaps they preferred to wait for the land to appreciate further in value — they were not monopolists. The point of this lawmaking was to ensure that the land be used, "for the better populating & Inhabiting" of the city and "for the generall good of this Citty." Landowners who failed to use their land in accordance with this community policy risked losing their land.

The province of West New Jersey provided a similar program of incentives for the town of Burlington, premised on the legislative finding that:

> [S]everal merchants, tradesmen and others, have been and are desirous to settle upon the said island, which might conduce to the great advantage, not only of the said island, but also to the said Province, and to those who are or may be concerned therein; and . . . that such persons as aforesaid, could not hitherto be accommodated with convenient lots of land in the said island whereupon to build, by reason whereof the said island, city or town of Burlington, hath been and would be rendered useless and unprofitable, either to the said Province, or others concerned therein . . .

Lands on the Island of Burlington that remained "unseated and unbuilt upon" for six months after this enactment could be sold by the town commissioners to "such person or persons, as will purchase the same, and build thereupon." A later statute referred to "the negligence of the generality of those who are concerned in the lots of land within the island of Burlington, in their building upon the same," which was a "great hindrance . . . in the promoting and encreasing the town of Burlington, to the great detriment of the country, and those interested therein."

4. Other Obligations of Urban Landowners. — Colonial governments often required owners of town lots to remove certain forms of vegetation. North Carolina, for example, directed lot-owners in the town of Salisbury to "grub, clear, Open, and inclose" their lots and "keep the same clean and open," and enacted comparable provisions for other towns. New York City ordered "that the poysonous and Stincking Weeds . . . before Every ones doore be forth with pluckt up," subject to a fine. Landowners in Charleston were required to cut down "all young pine trees or pine bushes, and by the roots dig up all other sorts of bushes, brushes, all weeds and under wood." A New Hampshire town ordinance required that "every man shall fall such trees as are in his lot being offensive to any other." Pennsylvania required that plants be added: "every owner or inhabitant of any and every house in Philadelphia, Newcastle and Chester" was to plant and maintain "one or more . . . shady and wholesome trees before the door of his, her or their house and houses, not exceeding eight feet from the front of the house . . . to the end that the said towns may be well shaded from the violence of the sun in the heat of summer and thereby be rendered more healthy." A Virginia statute required owners of marshlands in Alexandria to drain their land, based in part on the legislative finding that the land's marshy condition caused "delay of the further settlement and growth" of the town; the penalty for noncompliance was forfeiture of the land. This burden was retroactively imposed.

In the following excerpt, Professor Arthur C. Nelson calls on the planning profession to exert new leadership to replace the low-density suburbs that have emerged since the end of World War II with a different land development paradigm of higher densities and mixed uses. He predicts that this approach will be more sustainable and fiscally sound and will respond to changing demographics in the U.S.

Nelson, *Leadership in a New Era*

72 J. Am. Plan. Ass'n 394, 398–399, 401–402 (2006)

. . . America became a suburban nation during the last half of the 20th century: The share of Americans living in suburban areas rose from 27% in 1950 to 52% in 2000. The suburban population grew by 100 million, from 41 million to 141 million, and suburbia accounted for three-quarters of the nation's population change. The 21st century will be very different. In 1950 more than half of all households had children, single-person households accounted for slightly more than 10% of all households, and the average household included 3.4 persons. In 2000 only about a third of all households had children, one quarter were single-person households, and the average household contained 2.5 persons. . . . [B]y 2025 only about a quarter of all households will have children and nearly 30% will include only a single person, although the average household size will not change much. The needs of a society dominated by childless households, a growing share of which have only one person, will be different than those of the mid-20th century, when households with children were in the majority.

A growing body of evidence suggests that the very low density, single-use suburbs created in part based on [the planning approaches employed since the 1950s] have become less healthy than higher-density, mixed-use communities. An emerging body of work is also suggesting that higher-density, mixed-use developments are more economically and fiscally efficient land uses than segregated ones.

[Nelson predicts that most growth in the future will occur in the outer suburbs, but that cities and first-tier suburbs will be affected as well. He contends that the current approaches to planning are "ill-suited to meet future needs."]

What is at stake? Up to $30 trillion will be spent on development between 2000 and 2025. Half the structures I expect in 2025 did not exist in 2000. With so much change coming, now is the time for planners to craft a new template that meets the challenges of the next planning era. Planners are the only profession charged with shaping the built environment to preserve public goods, minimize taxpayer exposure, maximize positive land use interactions, distribute the benefits and burdens of change equitably, and elevate the quality of life. . . .

How can this be done? First, we must understand the nature of future demand across all land uses. Second, we must assess opportunities for redeveloping existing urbanized areas. Third, we must find ways to remove constraints on land use that are inconsistent with modern planning goals. And, fourth, we must champion the financial incentives and institutional changes that will make it possible to meet future needs. Other professions should join us in these endeavors, of course, but planners have the unique capacity to provide leadership in each of these areas. . . .

Emerging evidence suggests that the housing units existing in 2003 are unlikely to meet housing needs through the first quarter of the 21st century. The first several years after 2000 were characterized by record low home mortgage rates, inexpensive energy, and favorable construction prices. But now mortgage rates have begun to climb toward historically normal levels, energy prices have increased and prices for construction materials have risen due to greater global competition. These factors combined with changing demographic characteristics may influence the future demand for housing. . . .

To understand how telecommuting and the Internet will influence the need for nonresidential space in the future, consider that between 1992 and 2003, a period during which Internet hosts grew from fewer than 1 million to more than 150 million and reached most American households, per capita space for retail, office, medical, and service activities actually rose from 145 square feet to 149. [Two researchers] projected that there would be 25 million telecommuters by 2000, yet there were only about 9 million by 2005. Hence I assume these influences will not reduce future space demands significantly. . . .

Conservatively assuming nonresidential buildings will have average useful lives of 50 years I conclude that about 63 billion square feet of nonresidential space may require conversion to another use or replacement between 2000 and 2025. Thus to accommodate both the growth and replacement I expect, the United States will need about 78 billion square feet, or nearly as much again as existed in 2000. If my assumption of a nonresidential building's average useful life underestimates the frequency with which buildings are left vacant and become derelict, even more space will need to be constructed to meet future needs. . . .

. . . Although I expect over half of all development on the ground in 2025 will not have existed in 2000, even more important is that by 2025 much of society will have been spatially rearranged. An increasing number of empty-nesters, young professionals, and others will choose the city and first-tier suburban locations over outer suburban ones. According to [one author], they will drive up housing prices beyond the reach of many existing residents who may then be pushed to the suburban fringe and exurbs. Rising energy prices and declining demand for suburban homes on large lots may reduce the value of these homes, yielding important implications for the future.

First, the American dream of owning one's own home may result in millions of senior households living in autodependent suburban homes which have lost value compared to smaller homes in more central locations where many of their services will be located.

Second, as the value of large homes on large lots far from central locations erodes, they could become affordable housing for millions of households in the future. Many millions of these homes have more than 4,000 square feet of living area (U.S. Census Bureau, 2004) and may be easily subdivided internally to accommodate two, three, or more families. (If this were to happen on a large scale it could replace other sources of housing units.) This could cause fiscal stress in the localities where these homes are located (see below). And because those homes are not accessible to transit, low- and moderate-income households displaced to suburban fringe locations from central cities and first-tier suburbs may have greater difficulty reaching jobs than they do now.

Finally, such a scenario turns workforce housing and jobs-housing balance concerns upside down. . . . Past solutions included expanding job opportunities in central cities, improving accessibility to suburban employment centers, and changing zoning practices to allow a wider variety of housing options near those centers. In [one author's] scenario, empty-nesters, young professionals, and other affluent households move to cities and first-tier suburbs, where they outbid low- and moderate-income households for housing and enjoy the advantages of proximity to work and urbane leisure. This scenario actually exacerbates problems of proximity between jobs and housing because rather than being clustered, low- and moderate-income households are dispersed toward the suburban fringe, as in developing countries. This would also increase the risk of mortgage failure for homes on large lots, especially at the suburban fringe. If [this analysis] is correct, many millions of homes on large lots will lose value between now and 2025. Thus many households may come to owe more on their mortgages than their homes are worth, and some may choose to default rather than pay off these mortgages. Others may choose to ride out what they hope is a temporary cycle, deferring both relocation and reinvestment in their existing residences as a result. This could leave many millions of older homeowners in poorly maintained, suburban homes on large lots. Even a less extreme outcome like my midpoint scenario will have this effect on some households. Such scenarios cause the property tax base of suburban fringe jurisdictions to erode, and because low-density development is more expensive to maintain than higher density development, such jurisdictions are likely to become fiscally stressed in the future.

A similar phenomenon may occur for nonresidential development [due to lack of access to mass transit and other factors]. . . .

[To address these changes, Nelson proposes two templates for action, one for central cities and first tier suburbs, and a second for outer suburbs. In the first, the emphasis should be on redevelopment of existing downtowns, with improved linkages to mass transit. In the second, he emphasizes carefully projecting land use needs, realistically evaluating housing demand, and exploring redevelopment opportunities as well. He argues there is now a mismatch between what many suburban governments allow (single-family homes on large lots) and where the market is heading (attached homes and small-lot options)].

What can planners do? Several approaches seem to be gaining favor nationally. First, planners should question whether land uses need be separated at all. Some certainly may, but we are no longer in the 1920s [when Euclidian zoning, which emphasized separation of uses, arose].

Euclidian zoning needs to give way to zoning that favors mixed land uses. Second, innovations such as form-based codes, and conceptualized pre-platting (where general plan maps illustrate desired lot, street and public space configurations), permit a high quality built environment that anticipates change. Although they may not be applicable broadly, they can facilitate redevelopment of older areas facing economic decline. Third, communities should consider using financial incentives and concessions to encourage redevelopment they want in the long term, but whose rates of return would be insufficient to attract investors.

Tax abatement, fee waivers, tax-increment financing, below-market financing, and other techniques could be considered, all of which carry relatively low to modest risk to local governments. Fourth, when reviewing development proposals requiring land use decisions, communities should consider how easily the proposed development [can transition to other uses, as needs change, or as the proposed] use is no longer viable. . . . Planning in advance for such renewal is not common, but can make communities more resilient in the long term. . . .

NOTES AND QUESTIONS

1. *Motivation, vision, and contemporary relevance.* What was the motivation of Spain for the formulation of Laws of the Indies? Was it orderly growth? What kind of vision about community planning did the Laws of the Indies offer? Is that vision still relevant today? For an assessment of the impact of the Laws of the Indies on townsite design, see J. Reps, The Making of Urban America 26-55 (1965). Reps describes the Laws as "America's First Planning Legislation." Can you see any relationships between the Laws of the Indies, especially their design standards, and the New Urbanism, discussed in Chapter 3?

2. *City planning and Progressivism.* The American city planning movement has been characterized as an outgrowth of the Progressive movement in local government, which lasted from the 1890s into the early part of the 1920s, and a response to the rapid growth of cities during this period, which was the result of industrialization and immigration. Progressivism, according to historians Arthur S. Link and Richard L. McCormick, had three major characteristics: (1) "deep outrage against the worst consequences of industrialism"; (2) "faith in progress — in mankind's ability, through purposeful action, to improve the environment and conditions of life"; and (3) intervention "in economic and social affairs in order to control natural forces and impose a measure of order on them." A.S. Link & R.L. McCormick, Progressivism 21–22 (1983). One commentator has observed how the roots of planning in

Progressivism led to a value-free approach to the planning process, one that claimed to be above politics:

> The municipal reform arm of the Progressive Movement was one of the major forces shaping the new profession of planning. The Progressives had considerable faith in the capacity of professional expertise to solve problems ranging from environmental degradation caused by speculative resource extraction to the ugliness and disorder resulting from speculative urban development. But in adopting this paradigm, planners accepted the ideas that politics can be separate from planning or administration and that professionals would provide nonpartisan, expert advice to elected officials or municipal elites. This was the dominant image of professional planners into the period after World War II. [Howe, *Professional Roles and the Public Interest in Planning*, 6 J. Plan. Lit. 230, 231 (1992).]

Professor Claeys describes the main features of Progressive political theory as they apply to zoning as follows:

> First, in the Progressive understanding, "the general welfare" tends to elevate what the Progressives called "organic" goods and what we would now call collective, communitarian goods. It elevates order, community, homogeneity, financial security, and beauty, and subordinates more self-centered goods like freedom and individual expression in the use of land. Second, and conversely, Progressive theory reshapes how law and regulation conceive of property. Property is directed away from allocating to each owner a zone of non-interference within which to use her own property actively for her own peculiar purposes; instead, owners are transformed into stakeholders in the common civic, aesthetic, and property-value interests that unify everyone in the locality. Third, zoning expects that local majorities should be given free rein to express their own communal visions of community, security, and aesthetics. Last, zoning expects that these majority-driven community visions can be implemented by local planning experts, who bring them to life by promulgating a legislative pattern of use districts, by enforcing the districts, and by granting exceptions to them. [Claeys, *Euclid Lives? The Uneasy Legacy of Progressivism in Zoning*, 73 Fordham L.Rev. 101, 104–105 (2004). Compare with Haar & Wolfe, *Euclid Lives: The Survival of Progressive Jurisprudence*, 115 Harv. L. Rev. 2158 (2002)].

The planning movement (including the establishment of zoning) was part of a broader set of environmental reforms that included public health sanitary reform (the collection and treatment of domestic and industrial waste and the distribution and treatment of potable water), and housing and building reform (the construction of model tenements and the regulation of tenement housing). R.A. Mohl, The New City: Urban America in the Industrial Age, 1860-1920, ch. 9 (1985). See also H.J. Gans, *City Planning in America: A Sociological Analysis*, in People and Plans: Essays on Urban Problems and Solutions 57-77 (1968) (discussing the role of environmental determinism in early planning and the emphasis on the restoration of physical, social, and political order as the objectives of the reformers, who were threatened by the arrival of immigrants and the prospect of loss of cultural and political power). For a contemporaneous introduction to the thinking of the Progressives, see F.C. Howe, The City as the Hope of Democracy (1906). Are city planning and land use regulation still part of a reform movement and, if so, how would you describe that movement?

3. *Restricting nuisances and promoting segregation.* Early land use regulation in the U.S. was less concerned about achieving a pattern of orderly growth and more about regulating

nuisance-like activities and promoting or maintaining racial segregation. The earliest decisions from the U.S. Supreme Court involved Chinese laundries (*Barbier v. Connolly*, 113 U.S. 27 (1884); *Soon Hing v. Crowley*, 113 U.S. 703 (1885); *Yick Wo v. Hopkins*, 118 U.S. 356 (1886)), the creation of red light districts (*L'Hote v. City of New Orleans*, 177 U.S. 587 (1900)); height limitations (*Welch v. Swasey*, 214 U.S. 91 (1909)), cemetery burial (*Laurel Hill Cemetery v. City and County of San Francisco* 216 U.S. 358 (1910)); brick yards (*Hadacheck v. Sebastian*, 239 U.S. 394 (1915)); livery stables (*Reinman v. Little Rock*, 237 U.S. 171 (1915)); and oil and gas storage (*Pierce Oil Corp. v. City of Hope*, 248 U.S. 498 (1919)). For a discussion of *Welch v. Swasey*, see Stahl, *The Suburb as a Legal Concept: The Problem of Organization and the Fate of Municipalities in American Law*, 29 Cardozo L. Rev. 1193, 1233 (2008) (contending that "*Welch* completely altered the direction of the urban planning movement" and represented a "hijacking" of the movement by Progressives). Baltimore, Maryland (1910), Richmond, Virginia (1911), and other eastern and southern municipalities enacted racial zoning ordinances in the early decades of the 20th century. C. Silver, *The Racial Origins of Zoning: Southern Cities from 1910-40*, Planning Perspectives 189-205 (1991) (citing the adoption of racial zoning ordinances in Atlanta, Georgia; Indianapolis, Indiana; Norfolk, Virginia; Richmond, Virginia; New Orleans, Louisiana; Winston-Salem, North Carolina; Dallas, Texas; Charleston, South Carolina; Dade County, Florida; and Birmingham, Alabama). Although the U.S. Supreme Court struck down racial zoning in *Buchanan v. Warley*, 245 U.S. 60 (1917), it persisted into the 1950s, when Birmingham, Alabama's racial zoning was invalidated by a federal court. *City of Birmingham v. Monk*, 185 F.2d 859 (1951), affirming 87 F. Supp. 538 (1949). See C. Connerly, "The Most Segregated City in America": City Planning and Civil Rights in Birmingham, 1920–1980 (2005). Do you think that land use regulation is still used as a device to promote racial segregation? If so, in what way? See Pendall, *Local Land Use Regulation and the Chain of Exclusion*, 66 J. of the Am. Planning Ass'n 125 (2000) (finding that low density-only zoning, which restricts residential densities to fewer than eight dwelling units per acre, consistently reduced rental housing, which in turn limited the number of Black and Hispanic residents); Dubin, *From Junkyards to Gentrification: Explicating a Right to Protective Zoning in Low-Income Communities of Color*, 77 Minn. L. Rev. 739, 750, n. 49 (1993) (discussing persistence of racial zoning); Rothwell & Massey, *The Effect of Density Zoning on Racial Segregation in U.S. Urban Areas*, 44 Urb. Aff. Rev. 779 (2009) (finding that anti-density zoning increases black residential segregation in U.S. metropolitan areas by reducing the quantity of affordable housing in white jurisdictions). Is economic exclusion also racial and ethnic exclusion?

4. *Obstacles to change.* Do you think that local planning and land use regulation will change, as Professor Nelson recommends, to respond to social and economic changes underway in American society? What are the barriers? See W.A. Fischel, The Homevoter Hypothesis: How Home Values Influence Local Government Taxation, School Finance, and Land-Use Policies (2005). Professor Herbert J. Gans, a sociologist at Columbia University, in a lecture delivered in 2009 at the Edward J. Bloustein School of Planning and Public Policy at Rutgers, made the following predictions:

> Once the recession is over, and assuming it has not grown into a full scale depression, I imagine that customary patterns will resume. As young families grow in size and income, many will again become home owners and move to lower density settlements. And many of them will wind up in new subdivisions built on cheap land beyond the last previous zone of such construction.

Even so, larger percentages of new homeowners will choose or settle for higher density housing; more of the row and townhouses with which residents of the NY-NJ region are already familiar. I would expect popular and regionally variable new versions of New Urbanist planning all over the country.

Affluent people other than retirees will still move to bigger houses on larger lots in more prestigious suburbs as they become more affluent. Since heating costs can be expected to rise in the future, however, McMansions may be as out of date as Hummers.

At the same time, I would also expect urban and inner suburban gentrification to resume, at least in economically healthy metropolitan areas. In such areas, the now ongoing process of driving the poor into economically declining outer suburbs will speed up, and often the poor will be living very far from their previous residences.

Worse yet, they will be far away also from job opportunities as well as from the commercial, welfare and other support facilities they need. Many of the newly suburban poor are likely to be more concentrated and more surrounded by hostile neighboring communities than in the city. Helping agencies, including planners need to help them as much as possible, and they should be first in line for additional mass transit. [H.J. Gans, *Imagining the Suburban Future*, Robert A. Catlin Memorial Lecture, Edward J. Bloustein School of Planning and Public Policy (February 5, 2009), website: http://policy.rutgers.edu/news/events/Gans_remarks.pdf]

Examine these predictions in light of the materials you will study in your land use law course.

[1.] The Challenge of Land Use Policy

If successful land development and conservation ultimately require land use planning, land use planning in turn inevitably requires the formulation of land use policy. Not everyone wants to live in cities. (Frank Lloyd Wright, never one to mince words, observed that "[t]o look at the plan of any great city is to look at the cross section of some fibrous tumor." F.L. Wright, The Disappearing City 26 (1932)). Nor do we lack alternatives. The process of policy planning, for better or worse, produced the ubiquitous post-World War II pattern of dispersed homes, offices and shops, dependent on the automobile, now often criticized as "sprawl." This pattern, in turn, has in recent years produced its own reaction, the "smart growth" movement that emphasizes the preservation of farmland and open space by accommodating population growth in compact new developments or in revitalized, redeveloped cities, bringing land development back to something resembling patterns of old.

How is one to choose between these (and many more) possibilities? Even in a free-market society where most planning and policymaking is, by definition, assigned to the incremental decisions made by countless private individuals and groups, public planning and policymaking can play a significant role in determining the pattern of land uses. By what criteria should government act (or refrain from acting)? There are many possible answers to that question, some overlapping, some mutually exclusive. Some of these perspectives will be suggested in the remainder of this chapter. To start at the beginning, however, consider the two excerpts that follow, which consider the most basic of questions: how much land is available for use, are we in any danger of running out, and should we be concerned about controlling the land use decisions that private individuals make?

We begin with a puzzle good enough perhaps to be on the Law School Aptitude Test:

> Divide the current U.S. population into households of four persons and house them at the "suburban sprawl" density of one acre per household. (An acre is 1/640 of a square mile, or approximately the size of a football field without the end zones.) What percentage of the total land area of the contiguous forty-eight states would be taken up? [W. Fischel, The Economics of Zoning Laws: A Property Rights Approach to American Land Use Controls, pp. 1–2 (The Johns Hopkins University Press, 1985).]

Try to answer Professor Fischel's question before reading on.

R. Platt, Land Use and Society: Geography, Law and Public Policy, pp. 8–10, 24–26 (Island Press, Rev. Ed. 2004)

How Much Land Do We Have?

> In the United States, there is more land where nobody is than where anybody is. That is what makes America what it is. [Gertrude Stein, The Geographical History of America, 1936.]

In the early 1960s, resource economist Marion Clawson noted that the total land area of the United States, about 2.1 billion acres, theoretically amounted to a "share" of 12.5 acres for every living American at that time. In 1920, this figure stood at 20 acres per capita; it would further decline, in Clawson's estimate, to 7.5 acres in the year 2000. His prediction was stunning: In 2000, the actual ratio of land to population was 7.42 acres per capita! This ratio was still considerably higher than most other industrialized nations and many times higher than most of the rest of the world.

Acreage per capita, however, is not a very useful statistic. In the first place, it masks regional variation and is a poor measure of social well-being. At a state level, the citizens of Connecticut have one acre per capita (dividing its land area by its population) and New Jerseyites have only two-thirds of an acre each, whereas the 642,000 residents of North Dakota "claim" almost 70 acres apiece. Does that mean that the people of North Dakota are better off than those of Connecticut? In economic terms they clearly are not: in 2000, Connecticut ranked first in income per capita, whereas North Dakota was 38th among the fifty states. In terms of quality of life, that is a matter of personal judgment: windy grasslands and solitude of the Great Plains versus the crowding and culture of megalopolis.

Second, a large proportion of the nation's wealth of land resources is distant from the everyday habitat of most of us. Four-fifths of the U.S. population (225 million in 2000) live in the nation's 331 metropolitan statistical areas (MSAs) designated by the U.S. Bureau of the Census. . . . Those metropolitan areas occupy about 19 percent of the nation's land area and have an average density of 2.1 acres per capita. Yet even within MSAs, most of the population that does not live at the urban-rural fringe feels (and is) remote from "the country." . . .

A final limitation on the acres-per-capita measure of land wealth is the diversity of physical capacities and use categories into which land resources may be classified. Overall totals of land area reveal little about the sufficiency of land for particular purposes such as production of food and fiber, forest products, watershed functions, recreation, natural habitat, and urban uses. . . . Also, the growing importance of the global economy, the North American Free Trade Agreement (NAFTA), trade deficits, currency exchange rates, and multinational corporate ownership of land vastly complicate the task of appraising the adequacy of land resources in the United States or elsewhere.

. . . .

A clear dichotomy exists between rural land uses on the one hand and urban and built-up uses on the other. . . . Reversible conversion of rural land from one use to another is a normal response to changing economic circumstance. Irreversible transformation of productive rural land, either to a degraded condition (due to soil erosion, salinization, or inundation) or to an urban or built-up condition, poses important public policy issues.

The spatial growth of urban land is the mirror image of the loss of rural land to development. But the implications of such growth are not limited to the loss of productive or potentially productive rural land. Urbanization involves a spectrum of public issues including environmental quality, adequacy of water supply, equity in housing and economic opportunity, energy consumption, traffic congestion, visual blight, natural hazards, loss of biotic habitat and biodiversity, and rising public costs per capita for providing utilities and services to a vastly expanded region of urban habitation.

W. Fischel, The Economics of Zoning Laws: A Property Rights Approach to American Land Use Controls,

pp. 4, 7–8, 18–19 (The Johns Hopkins University Press, 1985)

A . . . measure of urban land is the Urbanized Area (UA). The UA is, roughly speaking, the built-up, contiguous part of an SMSA [Standard Metropolitan Statistical Area]. This does not mean just the central city of the SMSA; it includes surrounding suburbs. But its extent is based on population density rather than political boundaries. . . . The density criteria for being included in a UA are not too demanding: a suburban housing development that had one house for every two acres would be included so long as it was adjacent to the rest of the UA.

Urbanized Areas include about 60 percent of the U.S. population, and they take up only 1.2 percent of the land area. But this sanguine statistic does not address the concerns that many express about "suburban sprawl" or about development in smaller towns and rural areas.

Suburban sprawl data can be examined easily. It is true that suburban areas are less densely populated than central cities, but the difference is less than one might suspect. Since the problem of suburban sprawl most frequently focuses on the largest urban areas, I subtracted the population and land area of the central city (or cities, where there were two or more) of the twenty-five largest UAs and computed their gross-population density. It turns out to be 4.9 persons per acre. If we all lived at these 1970 suburban densities, we would take up less than 2.5 percent of the forty-eight states' land area.

. . . .

[T]here is no danger that development will impinge on the stock of land for nonurban uses. . . . [A]lthough land may not be crucial, *use* is.

Zoning and other land use controls influence the location and combination of labor and capital. They can have a far greater influence on economic and other social activity than might be indicated by the fraction of land affected or the share of rent in national income. Land *use* controls can affect the quality of the environment, the provision of public services, the distribution of income and wealth, the pattern of commuting, development of natural resources, and the growth of the national economy. The notion that zoning is just a matter of local concern is incorrect when the cumulative effect of these regulations is considered.

NOTES AND QUESTIONS

1. *Categories of land.* Professors Platt and Fischel agree that most Americans live in urbanized areas on a relatively small percentage of the country's total land, and that the supply of non-urban land for agriculture and related uses is, as Platt puts it, "abundant." Implicit in their discussions, moreover, is the assumption that land can, will, and perhaps should, migrate between one category and the other over time. The battleground of this process is sometimes characterized as the urban "fringe." The "can" and "will" of changing land uses is susceptible to objective study of historical trends and future projections although, by way of caution, note that by using different data units (MSA and SMSA, respectively) a decade apart, the two authors arrive at different absolute numbers about the extent of urbanization. When accepting claims of "objectivity," both planners and lawyers need to be alert to the nuances of data.

2. *Land use policy.* The "should" of land use change is the concern of policymakers. With respect to rural uses, Platt emphasizes principles of sustainability and reversibility, whereas for urbanized areas both he and Fischel note a long list of relevant factors: preserving some (unspecified) level of environmental quality, providing adequate public services (Platt is more specific), and encouraging social and economic equity. As to equity issues, Platt mentions "economic opportunity" while Fischel stresses economic growth; Platt singles out equity in housing, while Fischel highlights income equity. Fischel (but not Platt) mentions development of natural resources; Platt (but not Fischel) lists protection against visual blight and natural hazards. How would you change these lists of policy criteria, if at all?

3. *"Sprawl."* Land use policy makers have become increasingly concerned about low-density extensions of urbanized areas, or "sprawl." What can you glean from Platt's and Fischel's writings about sprawl? These issues are discussed in detail in Chapter 8, *infra.* For an interesting attempt to formulate and apply a multifactor definition for sprawl, see Galster et al., *Wrestling Sprawl to the Ground: Defining and Measuring an Elusive Concept*, 12 Hous. Pol'y Debate 681, 685 (2001). "Sprawl is a pattern of land use in an [urban area] that exhibits low levels of some combination of eight distinct dimensions: density, continuity, concentration, clustering, centrality, nuclearity, mixed uses and proximity." This article also reviews definitions of sprawl advanced by others. Compare with the State of Florida's definition of urban sprawl in its administrative rules for comprehensive planning, below:

> "Urban sprawl" means urban development or uses which are located in predominantly rural areas, or rural areas interspersed with generally low-intensity or low-density urban uses, and which are characterized by one or more of the following conditions: (a) The premature or poorly planned conversion of rural land to other uses; (b) The creation of areas of urban development or uses which are not functionally related to land uses which predominate the adjacent area; or (c) The creation of areas of urban development or uses which fail to maximize the use of existing public facilities or the use of areas within which public services are currently provided. Urban sprawl is typically manifested in one or more of the following land use or development patterns: Leapfrog or scattered development; ribbon or strip commercial or other development; or large expanses of predominantly low-intensity, low-density, or single-use development. [Florida Administrative Code § 9J-5.003 (134).]

4. *About density.* The term "density" refers to average number of persons, families, or dwelling units per areal unit of land. There are two types of densities: (1) net density (computed for the building site excluding streets, open space, and other publicly owned land; and (2) gross density (which includes streets and other publicly owned land). Zoning regulations typically regulate net densities in terms of dwelling units per net acre. S. Meck & K. Pearlman, Ohio Planning and Zoning Law § 5:7 (2010). A floor area ratio is a measure of intensity for both residential and non residential uses, the ratio between the sum of the area of all the floors of a building to the area of a lot. Thus, if the total floor area of a four-story building were 10,000 square feet and the lot area were 40,000 square feet, the floor area ratio would be 0.25.

Kevin Lynch and Gary Hack, two planning professors, present the following floor area and net density ranges for dwelling units as "reasonable . . . in normal practice," although there can be considerable variation from them. Single-family homes in suburban communities may be much lower, anywhere from 1-7 dwelling units per net acre, and even less:

Dwelling Unit Type	*Floor Area Ratio*	*Net Density*
Single-family	Up to 0.2	8 dwelling units/net acre
Zero lot-line detached	0.3	8-10
Two-family detached	0.3	10-12
Row houses	0.5	10-12
Stacked townhouses	0.8	16-24
Three-story walkup apartments	1.0	40-45
Six-story elevator apartments	1.4	65-75
Thirteen-story elevator apartments	1.8	85-95

K. Lynch & G. Hack, Site Planning 253 (3rd ed. 1984)
(adapted from Table 5, "Densities by Residential Type").

Density is important in land use planning because it affects the areal extent of the community (the higher the density for the same population, the lower the areal extent), because it has a relationship to the level of public services and facilities required, because it affects traffic through trip generation, because it is an element of the grain, character, or atmosphere of the community, and because it affects housing costs, among other factors. See generally N. Williams Jr. & J.M. Taylor, American Land Planning Law, Part 8, Subpart B (Control of Residential Density) (Rev. ed., 2010) (discussing policy implication of various density controls).

5. *Land use policy, taxation and public services.* Although our formal concern in this book is with land use controls, taxation (particularly property taxation at the local level) and the provision of public services are powerful determinants of land use. Recognition of these linkages can be seen in both the Platt and Fischel excerpts, and is elaborated upon in American Planning Association, Growing Smart Legislative Guidebook: Model Statutes for Planning and Management of Change pp. xlv-xlvi (S. Meck, gen. ed., 2002):

> The late Norman Williams, Jr., . . . observed, in two influential articles, that there is not one system of land-use control, but rather three, with each tending to work against the others. Williams noted that in most parts of the country, the property tax system supports major public services but does not bring in enough revenue to meet local needs. Inevitably, local officials are driven to take into account the revenue-raising capacities of various proposed land uses. This leads to a situation where "good ratables," such as industrial, most commercial, and high-value residential development

> — which bring in significant real property taxes and require little in the way of public services — are encouraged, but "bad ratables," such as quality affordable housing, are discouraged.
>
> The second system concerns the impact of major public services, particularly transportation facilities, such as highway interchanges, and those for sewage collection and disposal. Williams observed that, while the construction of some facilities, such as schools, depends primarily on the type and intensity of land use in the area, other public facilities, such as water and sewers, can have such a strong influence on adjacent land use that they actually may dominate the official set of controls.
>
> The third official system of land-use controls that Williams identified is comprised of zoning, subdivision control, official mapping, and other devices. Counter-intuitively, Williams pointed out that the official system may actually be the least important. If the first two systems work to produce unbalanced development in search of good ratables or development in the wrong place due to lack of forethought and coordination, the third system, in Williams' words, "comes out third best."

The two articles referred to by the American Planning Association are Norman Williams, Jr., *The Three Systems of Land Use Control*, 25 Rutgers L. Rev. 80 (1970), and *Planning Law in the 1980s: What Do We Know About It?*, 7 Vt. L. Rev. 205 (1982).

At least in the case of infrastructure, the interrelationship identified by Professor Williams can also work in reverse. For instance, to be cost-effective without unrealistically large public subsidies, public transportation needs high densities to provide sufficient ridership. Once land develops at low densities, it is increasingly difficult to apply mass transit solutions at a later date. See generally A. Downs, Still Stuck in Traffic: Coping with Peak Hour Congestion (Rev. ed., 2004).

6. *Utopia as policy.* Land use policymaking reaches its ultimate form in proposals for utopian alternatives to urban life, which invariably link planning to some overarching intellectual principle of social organization. While it would be an overstatement to say that land use planning has produced utopia in America, utopian ideas have nonetheless influenced the actual course of land use. In the twentieth century, perhaps the most famous, and also the most influential, was Ebenezer Howard's "Garden City," designed to reflect Howard's belief that relatively small communities organized around cooperative land ownership could mitigate the 19th century conflict between capital and labor. See E. Howard, Garden Cities of To-morrow (2010, Reprint of 1902 Edition).

This approach resulted in a compact village pattern surrounded and protected by a working greenbelt of fields, the prototype of which was constructed at Letchworth in England, beginning in 1903. See R. Fishman, Urban Utopias in the Twentieth Century 64-75 (1982). Letchworth in turn influenced the first wave of suburban-style development in the United States between the world wars, such as Radburn, New Jersey. Frank Lloyd Wright's utopian urban alternative, Broadacre City, fared less well in the 1930s. Wright followed Thomas Jefferson's agrarian belief that true democracy would reside in the virtues of a decentralized, self-sufficient, agrarian society of yeomen rather than capitalists; distrust of capitalism links Letchworth and Broadacre City. When adapted to the technology of the automobile age, however, Wright's design produced a far-flung, low density blanket of semi-urbanization. See Fishman, *id.*, at 122–134. No part of Broadacre City was ever built in anything resembling the form that Wright imagined F.L. Wright, The Disappearing City (1932).

7. *Changes in urban structure.* Urban geographers and others have tied changes in the pattern of land use in a city to the relationship of the city to its surrounding area, the type and extent of transport and changes in the nature of industries and the technologies they use. In an influential article written at the end of World War II, urban geographers Chauncy D. Harris and Edward J. Ullman focused on three generalized forms of internal city structure in the U.S.

In the first, the *concentric zone,* the city was described as a series of simple circular zones, with a central business district at the heart, and zones of successively less intensity emanating outward.

In the second, the city was seen as series of *sectors,* and growth takes place along main transportation routes and usually consisted of similar types of land use. Under this concept, for example, upper-end residential growth in the eastern quadrant of a city would tend to migrate outward, but always staying in the same quadrant.

In the third, the *multiple nuclei,* the land use pattern is not built around a single center, but around several discrete nuclei. This pattern reflects a combination of the need for specialized support facilities, such as access to ports, the benefits certain businesses obtain by being close to one another (such as law offices being near a court building), the undesirability of land use conflict (such as a prohibition of heavy industry near high-end residential uses), and the inability for certain businesses to pay high rents (such as wholesaling and storage businesses that require much horizontal space).

Harris and Ullman observed: "Most cities exhibit . . . aspects of the three generalizations of the land-use pattern." However, they noted that the concentric theory and the sector theory emphasize the general tendency of central residential areas to decline in value as new construction takes place on the outer edges, with the sector model being "more discriminating" in its analysis of that movement. Harris & Ullman, *The Nature of Cities*, 242 Annals Am. Acad. of Pol. & Soc. Sci. 16–17 (1945).

The impact of circumferential expressways and airports in the U.S. compelled Harris to formulate an additional theory of form, the *peripheral city,* to supplement the previous three models in an article published in 1997. Here, Harris described a peripheral model that differed from the concentric zone model "in that its patterns are defined with other parts of the peripheral zone, not in terms of distance to the central city but in its relation with other parts of the peripheral zone . . . ." The peripheral zone includes diverse clusters of economic activities in both new development and recently transformed older centers. It is tied together with a circumferential highway, large blocks of land for development and similar social, economic and housing characteristics. The area, according to Harris, is characterized by "the absence or lesser severity of problems of the inner city." Around this peripheral road are airports, airport-related businesses (such as motels and car rental agencies), regional shopping malls, distribution and warehouse clusters and well-landscaped office parks that are often home to national corporations. In addition, the area includes "large tracts of relatively homogenous private homes and some specialized communities offering well-advertised amenities such as hills, lakes, or woods with names such as 'country-club estate.' " Harris commented that the peripheral model did not exist when Ullman and he wrote their original article in 1945. Harris, *The Nature of Cities and Urban Geography in the Last Half Century*, 18 Urb. Geography 18–19 (1997); *see also* J. Garreau, Edge City: Life on the New Frontier (2001).

More recently — in part as a reaction to rising energy costs and the impacts of the national recession, including the subprime mortgage crisis, on real estate markets — some have questioned whether the outer edges of metropolitan areas will remain viable or turn into a depressed zones, and whether the next cycle of urban growth will be redirected at central cities. Leinberger, *The Next Slum?* The Atlantic, March 2008, http://www.theatlantic.com/doc/200803/subprime (maintaining that "much of the future decline is likely to occur on the fringes, in towns far away from the central city, not served by rail transit, and lacking any real core"). Do you agree with Leinberger that this will happen? Does this sound similar to the views of Professor Nelson, *supra*?

[2.] Conflict and Conflict Resolution in the Use of Land

The preceding materials demonstrate that the use of land necessarily involves the development, consciously or otherwise, of a land use policy. If this were all, there would be little need for the evolution of land use controls. Imagine, for instance, that each of us actually occupied the 7.5 acres that Rutherford Platt reports to be our statistical lot in the year 2000, and that we did so in complete isolation from our neighbors. Putting aside the obvious bleakness of a life lived this way, there would be no reason to interfere with each other's completely autonomous choices about how to use our allotted land. We would each have a land use "policy," but no matter.

Just the slightest relaxation of the assumption that we would live in *complete* isolation from our neighbors totally changes the picture, however. If I generate noxious fumes on my 7.5 acre island, for instance, the prevailing winds will blow them towards my neighbors just as, in the real world, smokestack pollution from the U.S. middle west ends up as toxic rain over New England forests. Inevitably, preferred land use policies can come into conflict with each other, as we seek to implement policies that maximize our own values. One function of the system of land use controls is to evolve policies that reduce the amount of conflict over land uses before conflict arises. Another is to provide a framework for resolving those conflicts that do occur.

Before beginning to introduce the prevailing system of land use controls in this country, based on comprehensive planning and local land use ordinances, the materials in this section invite you to notice that law is not always the best mechanism for resolution of land use disputes. Here, we will explore market mechanisms for resolution of land use controversies, as well as other forms of collective decisionmaking besides conventional zoning. It is true that regulation of the use of land has become pervasive in America, but only the most impassioned partisans will insist that either purely private or purely public control of land use decisionmaking will produce the best results. For thoughtful commentators, finding the proper balance between collective and individual decisionmaking, between "land use controls" on the one hand and "free markets" on the other, is the essence of the policy choice to be made.

It might be thought that posing this question is irrelevant at the start of a coursebook on the *law* of land use, for resort to law, by its very nature, suggests that the choice has already been made to collectivize the decisionmaking process. This is only partially true, however, for two interrelated reasons. Understanding the alternatives to the system of land use law (or to any particular law) is important because, as law students using this book already know, and others will soon come to realize, legal rules are often susceptible to multiple interpretations. Persuading decisionmakers to accept one interpretation and reject others is what lawyers do, and an understanding of how and why collective decisionmaking might or might not be preferable to private decisionmaking about a land use issue will sometimes be the key to effective analysis of an issue of land use law. And, for the same reasons, a persuasive critique might well convince legislators or administrators to add a law, amend a law, or repeal a law to make the system of land use work better.

To put these matters in perspective, consider the following problem, which is based on *PA Northwest Distributors, Inc. v. Township of Moon*, 584 A.2d 1372 (Pa. 1991). Relatively few land use disputes involve pornographic books, but Moon Township's commonplace decision to use "law" to resolve this community conflict over land use preferences is typical of the American way of land use practice. Do you agree with this approach? Is "law" the best way to resolve land use disputes? What are the alternatives?

PROBLEM

Blue owns property located on Beers School Road in the Township of Moon. Beers School Road is adjacent to the Greater Pittsburgh International Airport and is characterized by hotels, motels, restaurants, shopping centers, automobile dealerships, auto rental lots, gas stations, parking lots, and other commercial establishments. The zoning permits commercial uses, broadly defined. Blue leased the property to a tenant who opened an "adult" bookstore.

Four days later, the Moon Township Board of Supervisors published a public notice of its intention to amend the Moon Township Zoning Ordinance to regulate "adult commercial enterprises." On May 23, 1985, following a public hearing on the matter, the Moon Township Board of Supervisors adopted Ordinance No. 243, imposing extensive restrictions on the location and operation of "adult commercial enterprises." The bookstore, by definition, is an adult commercial enterprise under the ordinance, and it does not and cannot meet the locational restrictions set forth in the ordinance. Section 803 of the ordinance requires that no adult commercial enterprise can operate within 500 feet of a pre-existing school, hospital, nursing home, group care facility, park, church, establishment selling alcoholic beverages, or another adult commercial enterprise. Section 804 requires that no adult commercial enterprise can operate within 1,000 feet of an area zoned residential. Blue and his tenant contend that there is no site in Moon where the bookstore can operate legally.

The Zoning Officer of Moon Township has informed the bookstore that it is out of compliance with the ordinance and, as the ordinance requires, has ordered it to comply or move within 90 days. (After losing in various administrative and judicial proceedings, the Moon ordinance was invalidated by the Pennsylvania Supreme Court. The legal issues presented by the case are raised in Chapter 3, *infra*.)

A NOTE ON VARIOUS APPROACHES TO THE RESOLUTION OF LAND USE DISPUTES

Consider the range of ways that this conflict over the use of land in Moon Township might have been resolved. In doing so, we will put aside a world utterly without "law," land use or otherwise, where the disputants would simply square off and the one with superior force would win, at least until someone stronger came along. With the condition of minimal civility thus imposed, those who object to the sexually oriented business had at least three options available to them (can you think of others?):

Option 1. *Voluntary change.* Lawyers and politicians tend to overlook this option, because it doesn't normally require our services, but it is the option of choice for countless numbers of land use conflicts every day. Here, residents of Moon might have approached the owner of the bookstore and asked that he consider their preferences. If they did this early enough in the planning of the venture, the owner might have chosen to locate elsewhere, rather than face community opposition. Or, in a slightly less friendly approach to voluntary change, the community might have picketed the store once it opened, or picketed Blue's home or other business locations. Think of examples from your own experience where neighbors across the backyard fence or elevator lobby have resolved land use preferences either amicably or at least without resort to more formal mechanisms.

Option 2. *Purchase the right to change the offending use.* A well-heeled citizen might buy out the bookstore's lease, or buy the underlying fee from the landlord and evict the tenant, paying damages as necessary. Or a group of less affluent citizens might pool their resources to do the same. Why might an individual or a group of individuals be reluctant to do so, even if they could otherwise raise the money? Alternatively, the citizens could persuade Moon Township to use its power of eminent domain to "condemn" the lease or the underlying fee simple title, paying the lessee and lessor "just compensation" as necessary and putting the property to some other, public, purpose. Would this be more (or less?) effective than having private parties complete the buyout?

(Purchasing the right to change land uses need not be as confrontational as in the Moon Township example. Every time farm land is sold to a real estate developer for residential subdivision or for a suburban office park, the buyer is expressing a belief that the land can and should be put to better, or at least more lucrative, use than the farmer is making of it. A local government or the state acts similarly when it buys (through condemnation or otherwise) the land for an interstate highway, or a new community college.)

Option 3. *Compel the owner to change the offending use.* This is the approach taken in the actual case. Rather than persuasion (or after it had failed) and rather than outright purchase, the citizens of Moon expressed their preference that the land be used for something other than an adult bookstore by amending the zoning code (the form of regulation that dominates the field) to prohibit the offending use. Under some circumstances, the citizens of Moon might have resorted to the governmental power of the courts to compel the discontinuance of the offending use, rather than going to the local legislature. Consider, for instance, a state whose common law would recognize this type of use as a "public nuisance"; or perhaps the objectors get lucky and discover an enforceable covenant running with the land that restricts the use of the land to single-family residences. Judicial enforcement of unwritten common-law rules is every bit as compulsory as enforcement of legislation, and the rules are often sufficiently flexible to give the judge a good deal of discretion in deciding what range of land uses is permissible.

Of these possible strategies, the purest example of a "market" approach is to purchase the change of use, as suggested in Option Two. Note, however, that either a single private individual, a group of individuals acting privately but in concert, or the government acting on behalf of all the individuals in the community can pursue this strategy. Does it matter which individual or group acts, so long as "compensation" is paid?

Option One, informal negotiation, is similar to a market transaction except that inducements other than a cash price are used as the medium of exchange. Do these inducements qualify as "prices"? Note further that Option One does not include the government as one of the entities that could offer inducements to voluntary change. Is this omission appropriate? Why might we insist that governments act only through more formal mechanisms? Would it be appropriate to offer relocation assistance, maybe even to the next town (assuming the next town would be accommodating)?

Compelling change, the approach of Option Three, almost of necessity requires governmental involvement, because in our society, only government has legitimate access to the power to compel compliance under most circumstances. Note, however, that the nuisance and covenants approaches to compulsory change start with private decisionmaking and become coercive only when courts (which are agencies of government) are willing to enforce private norms or contracts. Indeed, an informal threat to bring a nuisance or covenant lawsuit may be sufficient to induce "voluntary" compliance, taking us full circle back to Option One.

We now turn to the specifics, beginning with the pros and cons of market-based strategies. These materials may help reinforce your intuitive sense of the strengths and weaknesses of the various options, they may suggest additional options, or they may cause you to rethink your views. There are no certifiably "correct" answers. When you are done with the chapter (or perhaps later in the semester), you may want to reread the Moon Township problem to see how, if at all, you would answer differently.

[a.] Efficiency and Equity: Government Intervention and Its Alternatives

In recent years, economists have offered powerful critiques of the existing system of land use controls, arguing that free markets operate best to resolve competition over the uses of land, and that the contemporary emphasis on land use *regulation* unduly interferes with this process. While not claiming that the private market, unaided, can resolve all land use conflicts, free market economists nonetheless advocate major changes to achieve a much less intrusive role for governments. What is the basis for the claim that free markets work best? Are there offsetting problems with the market approach that regulation might solve? How are we to know whether regulation is or is not appropriate in any given circumstance?

In the excerpt below, Eric Heikkila provides a justification for planning based on market failure but cautions that that regulation may raise more problems than it corrects.

E. Heikkila, The Economics of Planning, pp. 25–26, 37, 39 (Rutgers University, Center for Urban Policy Research, 2000)

To the economist, land use zoning is seen as an exercise in resource allocation, even if it may not normally be viewed in those terms by planners themselves. One of the most fundamental issues addressed by microeconomics [as it applies to land use markets. — Eds.] is how to allocate scarce resources in an efficient manner. If the quantity of land is fixed, as it is in most urban settings, then one is forced to make trade-offs. One more acre of land devoted to nonresidential uses, for example, results in one less acre devoted to residential use. From this perspective, zoning maps represent the planners' "solution" to the resource allocation problem. In preparing these plans (as zoning maps are sometimes called), planners must balance a range of considerations, among these economic efficiency. An efficient solution is defined as one that yields the greatest possible output (such as social benefit) for a given amount of input (such as land). An inefficient solution, by this same reasoning, is one that uses more inputs than necessary to achieve a given level of output. While there may be room for legitimate debate about what outputs are important (for example, whose benefits should count?), one would be hard pressed to argue in favor of an *inefficient* solution! After all, if we can receive more benefit from the same amount of land, why not do so?

. . . [U]nder certain conditions planners may expect the market to generate an allocation of land among competing uses in an efficient or benefit-maximizing manner. In other cases, such as in the case of externalities (effects that are not priced by the market), we may expect that the market solution is inefficient by the same definition. Where markets fail to generate optimal solutions there is the possibility that planning intervention may be warranted. Land use zoning represents a quantity-oriented mode of intervention, where zoning assigns each land use category a set quota of land as indicated by the land use maps referred to above.

Market Failure

The term market failure applies to any situation where the market outcome does not produce the maximum social benefit. . . . [T]he market demand curves provide the marginal valuation of each parcel of land from *the owner's perspective.* This should be apparent because the market demand curve registers willingness to pay, and . . . willingness to pay is the standard measure of individual benefit in cost-benefit analysis. If the owner of the good is the only one who is affected by its consumption, then the owner's benefit is equal to the overall social benefit. However, it is not rare to encounter situations where the benefits or costs of the use of a good extend beyond the owner of the good in question. This is particularly so in the case of land use, as is evidenced by all the attention given to land use issues in public hearings on parcel-specific rezoning issues. In many such cases the general public is quite affected by visual distractions, traffic noise, "undesirable elements," noxious fumes, quality-of-life issues, or other environmental impacts that are not encapsulated in the market price of the parcel in question. These and similar effects are not internalized in or reflected by market prices and so they are termed *externalities.* They are effects that are external to market prices.

. . . [Externalities] provide a potential justification for intervention by planners into the land use market. The market develops the "highest and best use" of properties from the owners' perspectives, but this may not coincide with the land use allocation that maximizes social benefit. However tempting it may be, as planners we must resist the temptation to leap in at this point with cries of "market failure!" as a justification for wanton intervention in land use markets by way of zoning [because] market failure does not preclude the possibility of even worse regulatory failure. . . .

NOTES AND QUESTIONS

1. *Who benefits?* Heikkila carefully qualifies his introduction to the efficiency principle by noting "legitimate debate" about which "outputs" should count. He gives examples of some things that individual consumers might value, but which cannot readily be reduced to a "price": "visual distractions, traffic noise, 'undesirable elements,' noxious fumes, quality-of-life issues, or other environmental impacts . . . ." Can you think of any others?

Many land use conflicts involve benefits that cannot be monetized easily, because there is no ready way to exclude any individual from enjoying the benefit at the same time as others. Economists call this kind of valuable asset a "public good"; the air we breathe is the classic example, because it can be shared without competition. Since supply is not affected by consumption, there can be no price in the conventional sense and no means to measure "willingness to pay." In theory, of course, it would be possible to determine the market price each of us places on, say, the existence of an unspoiled coastal view by asking us how much we would be willing to pay for it, but the diffused and widespread enjoyment of this "asset," and the fact that my coastal demand doesn't affect yours, makes it extremely unlikely that an accurate "price" could be determined. For one thing, the (immense) cost of finding out everyone's preference, which economists call a "transaction cost," has to be factored into the measure of whether a given allocation of resources is efficient; transaction costs are considered further in the following article. For another, each of us has an incentive to become what economists call a "free rider," concealing our true preference, knowing that we can get a "free ride" if someone else is foolish enough to fess up and pay.

2. *Perfect markets.* All responsible economists, Heikkila included, acknowledge freely that perfect markets are unobtainable, and that "market failure" may justify intervention in the form of public regulation. In a classic article, Frank Michelman explored (among many other things) why this might be so.

Michelman, *Property, Utility and Fairness: Comments on the Ethical Foundations of "Just Compensation" Law*,

80 Harvard Law Review 1165, 1174–1176 (1967)

[I]t will be useful to dwell briefly on the reasons why collective action should ever be necessary to the attainment of efficiency as above defined. For if an efficient change in the use of resources benefits gainers more than it costs losers, it might seem that gainers could be relied upon to make offers (directly to losers or indirectly through third-party enterprisers) which would suffice to induce losers to quit their objections to the change and, if they are in the way, to step aside. Conversely, if an inefficient change is one which costs losers more than it benefits gainers, it might seem that losers could be relied upon to make offers to induce gainers to abandon their proposal even if the losers could not directly block it.

This reasoning overlooks the extreme difficulty of arranging human affairs in such a way that each person is both enabled and required to take account of all the costs, or all the missed opportunities for mutual benefit, entailed by his proposed course of action before he decides whether he will embark on it. In addition, it overlooks the extreme difficulty of concluding voluntary arrangements to take account of such costs, or to exploit such opportunities, even after they become evident — a difficulty which stems from inertia, the expense (in time and effort) of bargaining, and strategic concealment. . . .

[A] government's regulatory activity may claim an efficiency justification. Consider an enactment requiring *A* to desist from operating a brickyard on land surrounded by other people's homes. The proposition implicit in the law (if we take efficiency to be its goal) is that *A*'s neighbors stand to gain more from *A*'s moving or altering his technology so as to reduce the nuisance than *A* or his customers would lose. It might, then, be argued that the measure is unnecessary because, if its premises are sound, we should expect the neighbors to offer *A* an acceptable sum in return for his agreement to cooperate. Conversely, the very fact that no such transaction has spontaneously evolved may be said to prove that *A*'s operation, granting that the neighbors are sustaining some of its costs, is efficient. Apparently, it is worth more to *A* to continue than it would be worth to the neighbors collectively to have him stop. The argument, however, is imperfect. A sufficient criticism, for present purposes, is that the failure of the neighbors to make an offer may indicate, not that it would not be worthwhile for each of them to contribute some sum to a fund whose total would be acceptable to *A* in exchange for his moving, but only that they are unable to arrive (except by the expenditure of more time and effort than it would be worth) at a settlement with *A*, and among themselves, about what the total price should be and how the burden should be distributed. The situation will be complicated by the impulse of each neighbor to be secretive about his true preferences because he hopes that others will take up the whole burden, thereby yielding him a free benefit. And *A*, dealing with a group instead of with an individual, may turn more than usually cagey himself. There will, in addition, be side costs of drafting agreements, checking on their legality, and so forth.

NOTES AND QUESTIONS

1. *The Coase Theorem.* Professor Michelman's discussion of transaction costs is in part a reply to another classic article, Coase, *The Problem of Social Cost*, 3 J.L. & Econ. 1 (1960). In a situation similar to the brickyard example that Michelman gives (using neighboring landowners, a cattle rancher and a farmer), Professor Coase argued that the two would voluntarily resolve this land use conflict by the one buying out part or all of the other's use until an "efficient" level of adjustment had been reached, one in which the benefits of the bargain are maximized for both parties. Coase's crucial insight, which supplies an important argument for a markets-based approach to land use policy, is that it doesn't matter whether the rancher or the farmer is given the initial legal entitlement to prevent the other's use. So long as the two are free to bargain, they will work themselves away from an initial all-or-nothing result to an economically "correct" solution.

At first glance, what has come to be called "the Coase Theorem" (a term Professor Coase did not use) might seem to have little practical applicability, since economists uniformly agree with Michelman that the transaction costs associated with the Coasean bargain are almost always too high to justify the effort. (Coase explicitly assumed zero transaction costs in his model, and acknowledged how limiting that assumption was.) In addition (as Professor Coase also recognized), we can only be indifferent to the initial allocation of rights under the "theorem" if both parties are similarly situated financially, i.e., that there is no "wealth effect." The wealth effect may not be as widespread as the transaction cost problem, but is a serious practical concern. Moreover, both problems — transaction costs and wealth effects — actually suggest ways to justify collective action. See also Macey, *Coasean Blind Spots: Charting the Incomplete Institutionalism*, 98 Geo. L.J. 863 (2010) (observing, at 865, that law and economics scholars' study of nuisance law and environmental protection "sidesteps a second set of transaction costs that arise from a proper understanding of Coase's broader concern with institutions").

2. *Entitlements.* Consider first a regime in which the *a priori* zoning rule is merely the starting point for bargaining between the farmer and rancher, or between the brickyard and the homeowners, rather than a fixed rule that can only be altered by formal legislative action. (The latter, of course, is the most typical situation in "the real world.") Wealth effects can be mitigated, or even eliminated altogether, by assigning the initial entitlement equitably so as to equalize the bargaining power of the two parties. Doing so, of course, requires a more subjective judgment about what is "fair" — something not within the four corners of classical microeconomic theory. Consider this further suggestion from Professor Michelman's article:

> But we cannot stand on the assumption that efficiency is the only goal. Few people any longer doubt that governments are properly engaged in controlling the distribution of wealth and income among members of society, as well as in controlling resource use so as to maximize the aggregate social product. . . . For the purposes of this essay I propose to rely on a proposition which will, I believe, command general and intuitive agreement. The proposition is that a designed redistribution by government action will

surely be regarded as arbitrary unless it has a general and apparent "equalizing" tendency — unless its evident purpose is to redistribute from the better off to the worse off. Progressive income taxes and social welfare programs are, of course, excellent examples of such measures. . . .

[M]easures such as the restriction on foundry operations in residential areas and the conversion of a neighborhood street into an arterial highway may be accompanied by accidental losses which, while not justified by any recognized distributional precept, are universally admitted to be noncompensable. It appears, then, that a redistribution which would have been unacceptable if undertaken for its own sake may be tolerated if it is the accidental consequence of a measure claiming the independent justification of efficiency. . . . [Michelman, *supra*, at 1183.]

3. *Collective markets.* Two other adaptations of the Coase Theorem become possible if we substitute collective action — the government — for one or both of the parties in the paradigmatic private market. First, as the representative of the community's welfare, the government could bargain with the adversely affected landowner for a shift from the initial entitlement represented by the zoning ordinance to a rule preferred by the landowner, by way of a variance, for instance, or a zoning amendment. By what mechanism would such a bargain be struck, it being contrary to accepted norms for the government to "sell" the right to develop? Would it matter how the initial entitlement was stated? Chapter 6, in addressing zoning amendments, suggests that local governments often enact regulation that allow reduced development of less profitable uses than the market dictates. This encourages land owners and developers to apply for changes and opens the door to bargaining for them. Informal dispute resolution mechanisms, also discussed in Chapter 6, further facilitate bargained-for solutions.

The other way in which the Coasean bargain can be adapted to collective action is to see the zoning ordinance (or other form of regulation) not as establishing the initial entitlement, but as the community's collective judgment about what it thinks the ultimate private bargain would have been, had the parties been able to surmount transaction costs and other barriers to the smooth functioning of the market. Of course, the question then becomes, can collective decision making adequately represent the myriad components of the private bargain and therefore reach a demonstrably "efficient" solution? Not all legislators can or do accurately gauge the public will (nor, on all occasions, should they, if The Federalist #10 is to be believed). Power and money influence governmental deliberations (a point that Heikkila emphasizes, *supra*). Do lessened transaction costs and wealth effects problems come at the expense of heightened subjectivity, exactly what the impersonal "market" ideally avoids? Even those sympathetic to collective action concede the problem: "Governmental regulation requires collectively agreeable land use policies whose formulation presents severe difficulties. These policies must be based on what economists call an interpersonal comparison of personal utility — the collective compromise of widely variant social preferences. These comparisons are difficult to make because they require subjective value judgments." D. Mandelker, Environment and Equity 6 (1981).

4. *Public choice theory.* "Public choice" theory, as it has been developed over the last half century, may suggest one way around this problem of subjective value judgments. Public choice posits that there is a market for citizens' votes, a market within which political representatives bargain for votes by offering the most acceptable packages of positions on public issues. See J. Buchanan & G. Tullock, The Calculus of Consent (1962). If a politician accurately discerns the mood of the public, he or she is returned to office by an objective majority that speaks in roughly the same way as the market's equilibrium price. Of course, it may take several rounds of "bargaining" for this consensus to emerge, but that is also true of market transactions, which do not necessarily arrive at the "efficient" solution immediately. For a variant on this, see Fischel, The Economics of Zoning Laws § 5.5 (1985), suggesting a "median voter" model, in which government officials act as if a public referendum were held on every public issue. Another variant argues that competition between *municipalities*, as opposed to individuals, might serve to maintain regulation at "efficient" levels. It has been suggested, for instance, that the ability of an individual or business to "exit" a jurisdiction or refuse to enter it, may make it less urgent for courts to review and possibly strike down regulations that are perceived as inefficient. Under some circumstances, other municipalities might simply "compete" for these "consumers" of regulations by offering them a more attractive regulatory environment. See Been, *"Exit" as a Constraint on Land Use Exactions: Rethinking the Unconstitutional Conditions Doctrine*, 91 Colum. L. Rev. 473 (1991). Are all actors equally able to exercise their right of "exit"? Similarly, are all actors equally able to "enter" a more favored jurisdiction? Is there a risk that market imperfections in the competition between municipalities might drive regulation to sub-optimal levels under some circumstances?

5. *Judicial review.* Is there a legitimate role for courts to play in seeing that initial entitlements are assigned in ways that facilitate efficient bargains? (Recall that in the Problem based on the *Moon Township* case, *supra*, one set of choices to be made was to invoke "collective action" in the form of the courts.) Later in these materials, you will encounter varying styles of deferential or non-deferential judicial review given to different types of land use controversies. In *Krause, infra* Chapter 3, for instance, a "garden variety" dispute between neighboring residential uses, the court gives substantial deference to the allocation of entitlements determined by the municipality. By contrast, in the celebrated *Mount Laurel* cases, *infra* Chapter 5, which involve claims that affordable housing is excluded from more affluent communities, the court requires municipalities to defend their allocations. The correctness of these decisions will be considered later; for now it suffices to see the linkage between such conventional legal techniques as burden of proof and the newer, transcendent themes of microeconomics.

6. *Tradeoffs.* Although freely noting that market failure could justify collective action, Heikkila still warns us that the "temptation" to "leap in" with "unwarranted regulation" must be resisted. The foregoing suggests that while his warning may be a bit too categorical, it correctly captures the tradeoffs that must be made between the self-executing virtues of the hypothetical free market on the one hand, and the potentially more equitable, but error-prone process of regulation on the other. At the very least, the free market critique of land use controls must give the proponent of such controls pause from time to time. Is this regulation truly necessary? Does it facilitate efficient results? If not, how securely can we articulate the justification for departing from what we think the market would do? Conversely, those who admire the objectivity and dispassion with which a smoothly operating market functions (particularly when graphed) must constantly remind themselves to take a reality check from time to time, especially when the market favors those with power and money over those without. On balance, does Professor Heikkila make a persuasive case for price-based intervention to address equity problems? How does Professor Michelman address this point?

Or is it a mistake to argue on the economist's terms? Some have suggested that we should simply reject the efficiency test as the basis for determining whether governmental regulation of land use is justified. Dean William Hines has written that the "ethical force" of an idea may provide a basis for governmental protection of natural resource areas even though the destruction of the resource area through development may be the efficient solution. Hines, *A Decade of Nondegradation Policy in Congress and the Courts: The Erratic Pursuit of Clean Air and Clean Water*, 62 Iowa L. Rev. 643 (1977):

> [U]nless restrained by some external force or internal command, mankind incessantly exploits and ultimately despoils or destroys natural environments. . . . [S]omewhere in the frenzied pursuit of more material possessions and a higher living standard it is morally necessary to think about what kind of world will be passed along to future generations. It is a sobering thought to reflect on the possibility that nature may not continue to exist as we know it. [*Id.* at 649.]

Hines was writing about programs in the national Clean Air and Clean Water Acts that protect "pure air" and "pure water" from further degradation. To what extent are his comments applicable to the land use conflict and control problems discussed in these notes? Consider that question throughout this book.

7. *Sources.* Richard Posner's treatise, Economic Analysis of Law (1998), now in its fifth edition, has heavily influenced this field for many years. For extensive collections of essays, see *Public Choice Theme Issue*, 6 Geo. Mason L. Rev. 709 (1998); *Symposium on Law and Economics of Local Government*, 67 Chi.-Kent L. Rev. 707 (1991); Smith, *Law and Economics: Realism or Democracy*, 32 Harv. J. L & Pub. Pol'y 127 (2009). See also Stearns, *The Misguided Renaissance of Social Choice*, 103 Yale L.J. 1219 (1994); Elhauge, *Does Interest Group Theory Justify More Intrusive Judicial Review?*, 101 Yale L.J. 31 (1991); Simon, *Social Republican Property*, 38 UCLA L. Rev. 1335 (1991); Hovenkamp, *Marginal Utility and the Coase Theorem*, 75 Cornell L. Rev. 783 (1990); Kelman, *On Democracy Bashing: A Skeptical Look at the Theoretical and "Empirical" Practice of the Public Choice Movement*, 74 Va. L. Rev. 199 (1988). For a set of earlier readings, see Economic Foundations of Property Law (B. Ackerman ed., 1975). Groves and Helland, *Zoning and the Distribution of Location Rents: An Empirical Analysis of Harris County, Texas*, 78 Land Economics 28 (2002), tests the Coase Theorem and concludes that zoning is distributive, with residential property gaining in value and commercial property losing value.

[b.] Other Private Ordering Solutions to Land Use Conflict Problems: Covenants and Nuisance

As the preceding materials demonstrate, totally private ordering of land use decision making through market mechanisms is not a realistic option, but at the same time, dissatisfaction with the results achieved by conventional zoning regulations has led to a steady stream of alternative proposals that embrace, to a greater or lesser extent, elements of private ordering. Some are described here. In addition, the evolution in recent years of alternative dispute resolution techniques, discussed in Chapter 6, *infra*, has added the possibility of "private order" dispositions even within the existing regulatory system. Note how these various devices fit into the framework of alternatives discussed in connection with the *Moon Township* case, *supra*. Consider, also, how well they should appeal to an enthusiast of market solutions, on the one hand, or of collective decision making on the other.

One of the best-known of the proposed alternatives to zoning was outlined by Professor Robert Ellickson in an extensive article, *Alternatives to Zoning: Covenants, Nuisance Rules, and Fines as Land Use Controls*, 40 U. Chi. L. Rev. 681, 713–14 (1973). Ellickson offers a trenchant critique of the zoning approach, and he makes a spirited case for a heavy infusion of private ordering, which he suggests could be based on venerable common-law concepts of covenants and nuisance:

> Existing property law provides for enforcement of many [private] agreements of this type, including covenants, leases, easements and defeasible fees. Covenants serve as a representative example of these consensual transactions between landowners; this category encompasses affirmative and negative obligations and is perhaps the most prevalent type of private agreement between neighbors.

Ellickson also notes that "[c]ovenants negotiated between landowners will tend to optimize resource allocation among them" because they "will enhance a developer's profit only if they increase his land values by more than the cost of imposing them. His land values will rise only if his home buyers perceive that the covenants will reduce the future nuisance costs they might suffer by an amount greater than the sum of their loss of flexibility in use and future administrative costs. . . . [A]ssuming equal bargaining power and information, consensual covenants will not involve inequitable gains or losses to any party."

He then suggests ways in which administration and judicial review could be modernized to better adapt devices such as covenants to modern conditions, but he also concludes that "[e]ven if covenant law were sensibly modernized, . . . covenants could play only a limited role in older established neighborhoods where land ownership is highly fractionated. Except for the simplest problems involving a few neighbors, land owners rarely meet as a group to draft agreements governing land use. . . . [T]he costs of organizing many people are apparently too high, and the risk of freeloaders too great, for private bargaining to take place." *Id.* at 718. Note the echoes of the Coase Theorem and its limitations.

To supplement covenants and other private ordering devices, Ellickson turns to nuisance rules in a modification of the Coase Theorem:

> In order to promote economically productive behavior that cannot easily be achieved by bargaining and to satisfy community desires to reward virtuous activities, legal rules should seek to transfer wealth from those whose actions have unusually harmful external impacts and to those whose actions are usually beneficial to others. [*Id.* at 729–30.]

He provides the following rule for nuisance liability:

> [A]n aggrieved landowner establishes a prima facie case for nuisance when he shows that his neighbor has damaged him by carrying on activities, or harboring natural conditions, perceived as unneighborly under contemporary community standards. [*Id.* at 733.]

Even without Ellickson's imaginative proposal, common law nuisance is a rich and fertile bed of doctrine from which much of contemporary land use law arises. As part of that evolution, its main outlines are traced in Chapter 2, sec. A, *infra*.

NOTES AND QUESTIONS

1. *Covenants and equity.* Elsewhere in his article, Professor Ellickson acknowledges that efficiency solutions do not guarantee equitable ones, and he takes care to argue that private ordering through devices such as covenants "usually" will not produce unfair gains or losses. Is his assumption of equal bargaining power a realistic one in the type of covenant situations he describes? Ellickson also points out, correctly, that covenants can be misused to enforce racial segregation, a problem of market failure that justifies governmental regulation. *Id.* at 714–15. But he argues that income-restrictive covenants are acceptable absent monopoly power, because income level, unlike race, is not necessarily a permanent condition, and he doubts that a sufficient number of private homeowners would agree to income restrictive covenants, "opting instead for freedom to devote their holdings to more dense residential developments in the future." *Id.* at 715. He then concludes, "Zoning is clearly more effective than restrictive covenants in achieving class exclusions." *Id.* These issues are considered at greater length in Chapter 5. Buntin, *Land Rush*, Governing, March 2006, at 25, describes an imaginative strategy to maintain affordable housing in a poor African-American neighborhood in Houston that was subject to rapid gentrification by using a quasi-public agency to buy land, restrict it to rental housing through deed covenants, and then resell it. See also Wiseman, *Public Communities, Private Rules*, 98 Geo. L.J. 697 (2010) (discussing the implementation of covenant-type "private" rules through zoning overlays, which place unusually detailed restrictions on individual property uses and, in so doing, have created new forms of "rule-bound" communities).

2. *Uncertainty as a problem.* Jan Krasnowiecki also agrees that zoning is unworkable but believes that Ellickson's solution would "be even more costly and chaotic than zoning." Krasnowiecki, *Abolish Zoning*, 31 Syracuse L. Rev. 719, 721 (1980). His concern is with the developer. "[O]ne of my complaints about zoning is that it does not offer assurances early enough or with sufficient finality to protect the developer from unexpected expenditures." *Id.* at 721–22. He does not believe that Professor Ellickson's expanded nuisance law would help with this problem. For another alternative, see Kmiec, *Deregulating Land Use: An Alternative Free Enterprise Development System*, 130 U. Pa. L. Rev. 28 (1981) (use of preestablished performance standards). See generally Nelson, *Zoning Myth and Practice — From Euclid into the Future*, Chapter 11, in Zoning and the American Dream: Promises to Keep (C.M. Haar and J.S. Kayden, eds., 1989) (review of proposals by Ellickson, Krasnowiecki, Kmiec, Siegan, and Fischel).

3. *Does private ordering work?* Houston, Texas, is an unzoned city, the largest urbanized place in America without conventional land use controls. Instead, covenants are widely used, thus offering a field test of at least part of Professor Ellickson's approach. In Land Use Without Zoning (1972), Bernard Siegan argued that zoning does not make a difference because housing prices in Houston were lower than in comparable zoned cities. His study is questionable. As Professor Fischel points out, *supra*, at Chapter 12, housing prices reflect a variety of housing attributes, including access to employment as well as the effect of an adjacent undesirable use. Lower transportation costs to employment may offset the price effect of the undesirable use. Lower house prices in Houston could actually indicate the presence of undesirable uses that zoning may have prevented. See Fischel, *supra* § 11.1. See also M. Goldberg & P. Horwood, Zoning: Its Costs and Relevance for the 1980s (1980) (reviewing the empirical studies and the Houston experience). Professor Siegan updated his argument and offered a Houston-Dallas comparison in Siegan, *Conserving and Developing the Land*, 27 San Diego L. Rev. 279, 295–304 (1990). See also MacDonald, *Houston Remains Unzoned*, 71 Land Econ. 137 (1995) (analyzing voting pattern in 1993 election in which Houston again rejected zoning proposal, and concluding that the "pattern of zoning suggests that the demand for zoning stems from its use as a device for excluding lower-income people from certain areas."). Compare with Berry, *Land Use Regulation and Residential Segregation: Does Zoning Matter?* 3 Am. Law. Econ. Rev. 251 (2001). This article compares patterns of residential segregation in Houston and Dallas. The

index of dissimilarity is used to measure segregation by race, tenure, and housing type, and a variation of the index is developed to measure segregation by income. No significant differences in residential segregation are evident between the two cities. These results, according to the author, suggest that, absent zoning, private voluntary institutions produce nearly identical patterns of residential segregation.

Despite its celebrity, there may be less than meets the eye in Houston's refusal to zone. Kapur, *Land Use Regulation in Houston Contradicts the City's Free Market Reputation*, 34 Envtl. L. Rep. 10045, 10057, 10063 (2004), argues that there is an "extensive patchwork of regulations in place in Houston" that are "strikingly similar to zoning authority exercised in other cities." The city, for instance, has a power unknown elsewhere to enforce the provisions of private covenants, and its subdivision regulations, building permit regulations, and transportation planning powers, among others, replicate many of the features otherwise found in zoning ordinances. Viewed this way, does Houston actually make the case for collective intervention in private land use markets, whether it is called "zoning" or something else? For a planner's take on Houston, see Neuman, *Do Plans and Zoning Matter?* Planning, December 2003, at 28.

4. *Does zoning work?* The Houston question can be reversed by asking whether there is any empirical evidence that zoning really works, as measured by its positive impact on housing prices. Earlier studies produced mixed results, and Fischel doubts their value, for the same types of reasons summarized in Note 3, above. More recently Pollakowski and Wachter, *The Effects of Land Use Constraints on Housing Prices*, 66 Land Econ. 315 (1990), found that zoning increased prices in Montgomery County, Md., particularly when combined with growth controls. See also McDonald & McMillen, *Land Values, Land Use, and the First Chicago Zoning Ordinance*, 16 J. Real Est. Fin. & Econ. 135 (1998) (ordinance had no effect on land values). Thorson, *An Examination of the Monopoly Zoning Hypothesis*, 72 Land Econ. 43 (1996), found higher prices in towns with monopoly power, but no clear evidence that it was used to limit housing production. Do Fischel's criticisms apply to these studies as well? In *Why Have Housing Prices Gone Up?* 95 Am. Econ. R. 329–333 (2005), economists Edward L. Glaeser, Joseph Gyourko, and Raven E. Saks found that between 1950 and 1970, the increase in housing prices reflected rising housing quality and construction costs. Since 1970, this rise reflects the increasing difficulty of obtaining regulatory approval for building new homes. The authors present a model for the regulatory approval process that suggests a number of explanations for this change including changing judicial tastes, decreasing ability to bribe regulators, rising incomes and greater tastes for amenities, and improvements in the ability of homeowners to organize and influence local decisions. Their preliminary evidence suggests that there was a significant increase in the ability of local residents to block new projects and a change of cities from urban growth machines to homeowners' cooperatives.

B. LAND USE CONTROLS: AN INTRODUCTION TO PLANNING

Beginning with Chapter 3, we will explore zoning, subdivision review, variances, and a host of other legal devices that directly and immediately implement collective decisions about competing land use. As you will see, often it is difficult to discern any consistent thread of social policy behind these piecemeal decisions, unless it is a "policy" of doing whatever one is doing at the moment. This does not have to be. It is possible to incorporate a broader and more thoughtful approach to land use policy-making into the regulatory process, by differentiating between a forward looking comprehensive planning process to make land use policy, implemented by zoning and other near term regulatory devices in ways that are consistent with long range policy goals. By *planning* first, the problems of implementation that inevitably arise (and which, as a practical matter, cannot be avoided altogether) are both minimized and, when they do arise, resolvable within a consistent and well-thought-out set of criteria and preferences.

"Planning" — the process of making plans by applying foresight to action — can occur at any level of government and can address either a specific concern or attempt comprehensive scope. At the dawn of the era of land use regulation in the 1920s, however, the emphasis was on local control of the overall process, encompassing both planning and zoning. A recent study found that 84.6% of the jurisdictions surveyed, covering 92.1% of the land area, had comprehensive plans. R. Pendall, R. Puentes & J. Martin, From Traditional to Reformed: A Review of the Land Use Regulations in the Nation's 50 Largest Metropolitan Areas 11, Table 2 (Brookings Institution, 2006). It is only in the last half century that regional and statewide planning has begun to play a major and increasingly important role. With this history in mind, we introduce the role that planning plays in land use regulation by first considering the local "comprehensive plan." This will be followed by consideration of state and regional planning issues.

[1.] The Local Comprehensive Plan

[a.] The Idea of Planning[1]

Some history. Model acts proposed by the U.S. Department of Commerce in the 1920s strongly influenced the pattern of state legislation adopted to authorize both planning and zoning at the municipal level. Logically (and with the benefit of hindsight), the Standard City Planning Enabling Act (SCPEA) should have been promulgated first as a model before any model zoning act, and adopted first by individual states, but strong political demand for legislation to authorize zoning led to publication of the Standard State Zoning Enabling Act (SSZEA) first. In a sense, planning has been trying to catch up to zoning ever since. (The SSZEA is discussed further in Chapter 3, *infra.*)

Several decisions made in the SCPEA continue to influence land use planning today. Remarkably, the SCPEA made planning optional rather than mandatory, and most states followed this model. Thus, a municipality could zone without having adopted a comprehensive plan, and many did. In addition, the Act was more about procedure than substance. It provided the legal authority to adopt a plan, and specified the role local agencies were to play in the plan adoption process, but other than general specification of the topics ("elements") that the plan was to address, it left the development of substantive planning policies to the local planning process.

The format of a plan. Comprehensive plans, sometimes known as "general" or "master" plans, have several common characteristics and elements. They plan for the physical development of the community to a future point in time (10 years, 20 years, etc.) or to some identified stage of growth. They cover all of the geographic area of the community, and sometimes the immediate extra-territorial area, and typically include all of the physical elements that determine future community development. Plan elements addressing future land use, needed community services and facilities, housing and transportation are found in virtually all plans. In theory, at least, the zoning ordinance, adopted to implement the

[1] This description is adapted from D. Mandelker, Land Use Law, Ch. 3 §§ 3.01–3.05 (5th ed. 2003).

comprehensive plan, would be based on all of these plan elements (and others as well in many cases) to permit, prohibit and regulate development to achieve the desired pattern of land use that is efficiently served by public facilities and transportation infrastructure.

Some states publish administrative rules or related guidance on the contents of comprehensive plans. These rules further detail the general descriptions contained in statutes. See, e.g., Fla. Admin. Code § 9J-5; Washington Dep't of Commerce, Administrative Rules Guiding Implementation of the Growth Management Act (February 19, 2010); Wash. Admin. Code §§ 365-190-010 et seq.; Rhode Island State Planning Council, Handbook on the Local Comprehensive Plan, Handbook No. 16 (2003), available at www.planning.ri.gov/comp/handbook16.pdf. See also L.T. Anderson, Guidelines for Preparing Urban Plans (1995).

Comprehensive plans usually have both text and maps. The text of the land use element, for instance, would describe the land use policies adopted by the municipality, and the plan map would indicate where development to implement the policies should occur. The comprehensive plan's future land use map is usually more generalized than the precise delineation of districts in the zoning map that is part of the implementing ordinance; the future land use plan map will show broad use categories, and may indicate densities (for residential uses) and intensities (for non-residential uses). The difference in the level of detail is justified because plan *policies* are usually broader and more flexible than zoning *regulations* and problems can arise when a too-detailed policy map is inappropriately used as if it were regulatory. To avoid this, some comprehensive plans contain only highly generalized maps.

The planning process. The well-established process that planners use to prepare comprehensive plans for community adoption has been called "rational planning" (see discussion below). This label underscores the traditional concern of the planning profession that the policies embodied in a comprehensive plan be supportable by objective data and analysis, rather than the subjective preferences of the planners or their local government clients. Rational planning therefore involves data collection, analysis of trends, careful projection of those trends over the period addressed by the plan, and the development of policies to address present and future needs. Although many kinds of data can be collected and analyzed, information about population and the economy is usually the most important, because it suggests what the community will need over time due to changes in the number and characteristics of residents and in jobs and the mix of businesses, what benefits and burdens it is likely to experience as change occurs, and what resources it will have available to keep pace with change. Data collection will also include an assessment of what is occurring and is likely to occur in the larger region of which the community is part, since those changes will influence the direction taken in the local plan. Consistent with the objective and expertise-based premise of rational planning, the process was traditionally vested in an independent and politically removed planning commission, at least partially insulated from the rough and tumble of everyday politics.

There is no standardized structure for presenting a comprehensive plan, but a common approach is to find three levels of textual statement, beginning with a highly generalized statement of planning "goals," which are then refined into more precise planning "objectives," which in turn provide the basis for a set of detailed planning "policies." (The actual labels used vary widely.) The housing element of the comprehensive plan provides an example. One of the community's broad "goals" might be to provide "adequate housing at reasonable cost" to all residents. This in turn might lead to an "objective" of providing a "balanced housing supply that offers a variety and choice of housing at different levels of cost." This in turn might result

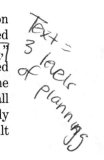

in a detailed planning "policy" or set of policies on where and under what conditions multi-family housing development should occur (for instance, a policy that such housing should be located at highway interchanges near non-residential developments or near transit stations or stops to minimize journeys to work, and a policy on density increases to make housing more affordable for lower income households).

Despite being anchored in a "rational" process of data collection and analysis, preparation and adoption of a comprehensive plan also engages the participatory democratic process at the local level. Planners usually develop more than one set of planning policies, which they test for feasibility and acceptability through public hearings, consultation with neighborhood leaders and single-issue advocates, and all of the usual mechanisms of local politics. Although the policies that emerge and form the basis for the adopted plan sometimes stray a bit from the rigorous objectivity implied by the "rational planning" label, defenders of the process argue that without such responsiveness to lay concerns, the plan could suffer a loss of legitimacy and public support that would make it more difficult to implement.

Criticisms of the planning process. Critics raise several objections to rational planning. Going to the heart of the premise that rational planning is rooted in objectivity, they attack on two fronts. First, they claim that the challenge of assembling complex data to support a *comprehensive* plan is beyond the capacity of the process. Limited intellectual capacity and resources, the interdependence between fact and value judgments, inadequate analytic systems, and the diversity of forms in which problems actually arise prevent successful comprehensive planning. See Lindblom, *The Science of Muddling Through*, 19 Pub. Admin. Rev. 79 (1959); Lindblom, *Still Muddling, Not Yet Through*, 39 Pub. Admin. Rev. 517 (1979). Second, critics claim forward-looking planning is inherently non-objective, because planners cannot control all of the factors that influence the land use context. For example, the planner cannot control changes in economic conditions, and such a change could prompt either much more or much less new residential or commercial activity than was projected before the change in the economy became known. For a case study that illustrates some of these issues, see Ryan, *Incomplete and Incremental Plan Implementation in Downtown Providence, Rhode Island, 1960-2000*, 5 J. Plan. Hist. 35 (2006).

Other criticisms of rational planning include the claim that the political process is incapable of specifying planning policies with sufficient precision, and the claim that rational planning ignores the non-physical consequences of community development, because the social impact of land use policy is difficult to measure and quantify. This can result in what has been called "partial planning" — the inability to integrate all of the necessary variables affected by community development into a comprehensive plan.

Planning practice today has overcome many of these criticisms. New consensus-building approaches through citizen participation can provide a source of information, secure feedback for planners and help define the public interest in planning more accurately. Related to this, the original apolitical "planning commission" model of planning has often been replaced by one in which the planning director is appointed by the mayor and the planning staff serves as advisors to political decisionmakers, with the role of the independent commission substantially reduced.

Concerns about the comprehensiveness of planning have been addressed by statutory changes in many states that have mandated the inclusion of additional elements in the plan, including such "social" concerns as housing and environmental elements that were lacking historically. New computer-based systems have dramatically expanded the ability of planners to manage complex data, test out development scenarios and impacts, and quickly respond to changed conditions. The inherent difficulty of predicting the future has been addressed by a new emphasis on so-called "middle range" plans that cover a shorter time frame and thus are less subject to planning errors arising from inaccurate projections. See Meyerson, *Building the Middle-Range Bridge for Comprehensive Planning*, in A Reader in Planning Theory, 127-139 (A. Faludi, ed., 1973). Finally, some communities have introduced more flexibility in planning by supplementing the comprehensive plan for the entire community with more detailed plans for sub-areas and even local neighborhoods. This allows planners to implement the plan in sequence and over time as development trends become clearer and projections are revised.

NOTES AND COMMENTS

1. *Rational planning and its critics.* The comprehensive plan has been characterized as "the translation of values into a scheme that describes how, why, when, and where to build, rebuild, or preserve the city." Hollander, Pollock, Reckinger & Beal, *General Development Plans, in* The Practice of Local Government Planning 60 (F. So & J. Getzels, eds., 2d ed. 1988). Market-oriented economists and planning critics naturally are skeptical that collective community decision making through planning can produce the necessary values for the scheme. They argue that plans may violate the market-based efficiency test and produce socially undesirable outcomes. The following excerpt from an article by Professor Dan Tarlock forcefully makes this point:

> The legitimacy of a planning choice rests on the assertion that collective intervention produces a net gain in society's aggregate welfare. The planner's claim is that his or her proposal will promote the most efficient allocation of available resources. A planning choice would be readily perceived as legitimate if, by curing market imperfections, it achieved an allocation equivalent to that produced by a perfectly competitive market. Too often, however, the aggregate gains of a planning choice cannot be demonstrated. The planning choice is not designed to force internalization of external costs, which are difficult enough to quantify, but is based upon the assumption that the planner's re-distributive values are superior to those of the market and will result in a net gain to the aggregate welfare.
>
> Planners assert that land use allocation is amenable to rational evaluation, that collective goals can be evaluated and welded into a single hierarchy of community objectives, and that planners can expertly resolve goal conflicts. The planner's choices derived from their overall perspective, however, risk being arbitrary since planners bear little responsibility for distribution of the costs or benefits of their activity. Furthermore, the choices are unlikely to rest upon a widespread consensus that would silence those adversely affected by short-term losses with the assurance of long-term efficiency gains. Thus the choices may be unacceptable to many members of the community because they appear unfair. The failure to consider the opportunity costs of the decision will make the planner's efficiency claims vulnerable to disproof. [Tarlock, *Consistency With Adopted Land Use Plans as a Standard of Review: The Case Against*, 9 Urb. L. Ann. 69, 75–76 (1975).]

2. *Beyond markets.* Professor Tarlock's critique judges planning by a market efficiency test. Is planning simply a response to market failure? As the following excerpt indicates, planning can seek to do much more than achieve an efficiency goal that cannot be achieved in the marketplace. Consider how it affects your view of the planning process.

> Some of the arguments offered in support of comprehensive land use planning — reducing conflicts between incompatible land uses, coordinating private development and public infrastructure, preserving open space, programming capital improvements, emphasizing long-range alternatives as a balance to the short time horizons of entrepreneurs and politicians — can be related to evidence of market failure. . . . The arguments are used, however, to justify the traditional methods of plan making rather than to seek the best ways for solving the problems. Reducing incompatibilities between adjacent land uses could be accomplished through regulation of the land market, but that would not require land use plans.
>
> When land use policy emphasizes comprehensive planning, it implicitly forces a choice between accepting the outcomes of land markets or replacing land market decisions with political ones. Because market failure can be corrected without land use plans, the plan-making method can only be justified as a policy instrument on the basis of public objectives that override market performance. [Lee, *Land Use Planning as a Response to Market Failure, in* The Land Use Policy Debate in the United States 149, 158–59 (J. deNeufville ed., 1981).]

Planning is also necessary because markets don't have proper time horizons to protect future generations. Markets emphasize the short term or the near future, not a future five to twenty years out.

3. *Types of plans.* Kaiser & Godschalk, *Twentieth Century Land Use Planning: A Stalwart Family Tree*, 61 J. Am. Plan. Ass'n 365 (1995), traces the evolution of planning and identify four prototypes of plans, although many communities blend them into hybrids. The traditional land use design plan emphasizes physical development, usually including action strategies and planning policies, and often proposing an "end-state" or a mapped depiction of where the community will be after a period of years. The "land use classification plan" is a more general map of growth policy areas rather than a detailed land use pattern, and is particularly useful for large jurisdictions that want to encourage urban growth in designated development areas and to discourage it in conservation or rural areas. Verbal or written policy plans focus "on written statements of goals and policy, without mapping specific land use patterns or implementation strategy." A development management plan "lays out a specific program of actions to guide development, such as a public investment program, a development code, and a program to extend infrastructure and services; and it assumes public sector initiative for influencing the location, type, and pace of growth."

As you read the zoning and other cases in this casebook, see if a comprehensive plan was involved and try to decide where it fits in this typology. Chapter 6 considers the requirement that land use regulations must be consistent with a comprehensive plan. How does the type of plan adopted affect the ability to have and demonstrate consistency?

4. *Values and variables.* In The City Planning Process, ch. 6 (1965), Professor Alan A. Altshuler points out that professionals are careful in selecting the variables that define their competence. The most successful professionals narrow the variables they claim to define their professional role. Highway engineers, for example, limit themselves to the solution of traffic engineering problems. Perhaps planners suffer because the range of variables they must consider is so wide.

Altshuler suggests that the selection of the variables professionals consider critical to professional competence implies a selection of the values they are attempting to implement. "In practical affairs . . . men easily slip into treating familiar variables as ultimate values." *Id.* at 337. Value judgment appears to be inherent, even in a rational planning process.

Altshuler also points out that the law has adopted a judicial decisionmaking process that does not claim legitimacy through the selection of a limited number of variables and is conducted under conditions of great value uncertainty. The judicial process avoids the problem of value selection by slipping around values, basing its credibility on a process of collective decisionmaking through incremental change. Is there a lesson here for planners? For a persuasive contemporary critique of Altschuler, see Innes, *Planning Through Consensus Building: A New View of the Comprehensive Planning Ideal*, 62 J. Am. Plan. Ass'n 460 (1996). In the City Planning Process, Altshuler challenged the legitimacy of comprehensive planning and of planners' expertise. He called on the profession to reinforce its theoretical arsenal. Professor Judith Innes contends that not only have practices now arisen that make comprehensive planning possible, but also political and social theory has evolved to provide its intellectual grounding. She argues that consensus building with stakeholders offers a model for planning that responds to each of Altshuler's critiques.

A NOTE ON THE RATIONAL MODEL AND ALTERNATIVES TO TRADITIONAL PLANNING APPROACHES

The Rational Model. In a classic essay, political scientist Edward Banfield described the elements of the rational planning model. "A course of action," Banfield wrote, "is a sequence of prospective acts which are viewed as a unit of action; the acts which comprise the sequence are mutually related as means to the attainment of ends." A plan is a "course of action which can be carried into effect, which can be expected to lead to the attainment of the ends sought, and which someone (an effectuating organization) intends to carry into effect." Plans that no one intends to carry into effect are "utopian schemes."

To Banfield, a plan is "comprehensive if it indicates the principal acts by which the most important ends are to be attained." Public planning "is planning to attain those ends of an organization which are substantively directives to attain the ends of some public." Community planning "is that special case of public planning in which the public is the whole community."

Banfield assumed that a planned course of action is selected rationally "when most likely to maximize the attainment of the relevant ends." In this sense, he wrote, "rational" planning and "efficient" planning are the same.

Banfield lists the following steps for rational decision making:

> . . . 1. The decision-maker considers all of the alternatives (courses of action) open to him; i.e., he considers what courses of action are possible within the conditions of the situation and in light of the ends he seeks to attain. 2. he identifies and evaluates all of the consequences which would follow from the adoption of each alternative; i.e., he predicts how the total situation would be changed by each course of action he might adopt; and 3. he selects that alternative the probable consequences of which would be preferable in terms of his most valued ends.

Banfield acknowledged that no decision can be "perfectly rational since no one can ever know all of the alternatives open to him at any movement or all of the consequences which would follow from any action." Still, he writes, decisions can be made with an approximation of alternatives, consequences, and ends. In this sense, "some decisions and some decision-making process [may be described] as more nearly rational than others." E. C. Banfield, *Note on a Conceptual Scheme*, in M. Meyerson & E.C. Banfield, Politics, Planning and the Public Interest, 312–315 (1964).

Alternatives to Rational Planning. A number of critics and commentators have proposed alternatives or adjuncts to a traditional rational planning. Some of these alternatives are discussed here.

Participatory planning. The War on Poverty programs of the 1960s required "citizen participation" in community development programs, which eventually led to the more general use of participatory techniques in many local planning programs. C. Hartman, Between Eminence and Notoriety: Four Decades of Radical Urban Planning (Rutgers Center for Urban Policy Research, 2002), captures the "radical" spirit of those times. Day, *Citizen Participation in the Planning Process: An Essentially Contested Concept?* 11 J. Plan. Lit. 421, 432 (1997), surveys current participation practices, concluding that the issue is "a very complex one." For a brilliant study of growth-management planning in Fairfax County, Virginia, which included a review of the citizen participation effort, see G. Dawson, No Little Plans (1977). Dawson concluded that active citizens organized in small groups and backed by their local politician could be effective in blocking unwanted development close to their homes, over the opposition of professional planners. "Ironically, the considerable citizen involvement was the major factor in the county's failure to channel growth." *Id.* at 110–11. Professor Burby's conclusion, based on a study of 60 plan-making processes, is more optimistic, finding that with greater "stakeholder" involvement, better plans emerged and were more likely to be implemented. Burby, *Making Plans That Matter: Citizen Involvement and Government Action*, 69 J. Am. Plan. Ass'n. 33 (2003). See also Anderson, *Doing the Impossible: Notes for a General Theory of Planning*, 25 Envt. & Plan. Bull. 667 (1998); Sager, *Deliberative Planning and Decision-making: An Impossibility Result*, 21 J. Plan. Educ. & Rsch. 367 (2002) (dialogue-based planning cannot ensure both consistency and democratic decision-making); Healey, *Collaborative Planning in Perspective*, 2 Planning Theory, no.2, at 104 (2003).

The "just city." This approach grows out of earlier arguments for "equity planning" as an antidote to the rigorous objectivity of rational planning. See Metzger, *The Theory and Practice of Equity Planning: An Annotated Bibliography*, 11 J. Plan. Lit. 112 (1996). Fainstein, *New Directions in Planning Theory*, 35 Urban Affairs Rev. 451 (2000), notes that just-city theory is based on a distributional concept of social justice that assumes there are criteria for judging better and worse. She recognizes the tendency of her model to "identify unfairness without positing what was fair," 35 Urb. Aff. Q. at 467, but she argues that one solution is to "judge results," *id.* at 470, by identifying and studying cities that have achieved relatively equitable societies. For a provocative argument that planning's "sinister dark side" is its capacity for use as a tool of social control and oppression, see Yiftachel, *Planning and Social Control: Exploring the Dark Side*, 12 J. Plan. Lit. 395 (1998).

One difficulty with theories of planning that are based on ethical precepts (and a persuasive explanation of why "objective" models such as "rational planning" have persisted for so long) is that it is very difficult to get from the normative to the real. Fainstein concedes that "[in] applying the just-city perspective, one must judge results." Still, she is vague about how one *plans* to achieve this outcome. Compare Knaap, *The Determinants of Residential Property Values: Implications for Metropolitan Planning*, 12 J. Plan. Lit. 267 (1998) (planning may have contributed to the problem of housing affordability, suggesting solutions).

Planning theory and cities. The process and equity approaches to planning described above have found particular expression in tackling the problems of densely settled places, so much so that a separate label — "urban planning" — has evolved. Professor Fainstein has cautioned against separating planning theory from urban planning, arguing that a concept such as "just city" theory cannot be isolated from its urban planning context. Fainstein, *Planning Theory and the City*, 25 J. Plan. Ed. & Rsch. 121 (2005). See also Judd, *Everything is Always Going to Hell: Urban Scholars as End-Times Prophets*, 41 Urb. Aff. Rev. 119 (2005) (estrangement of urban scholars from mainstream political science).

Can the future be planned? Symposium, *Putting the Future in Planning*, 67 J. Am. Plan. Ass'n 365 (2001), argues that the answer is yes, "despite the twin hazards of uncertainty and disagreement [that] form an essential context for planning's ambitions of shaping the future." See also S. Ames & E. Jensen, Putting Vision Into Action: An Oregon Community Makes Change Happen, PAS Memo, Oct. 2002, describing a "community visioning" process to "identify and articulate shared values [and] envision preferred futures for the first time." Avin and Dembner, *Getting Scenario Building Right*, Planning, November 2001, at 22, argue that business planning models can be adapted to long-range land use planning. See generally L. Hopkins & M. Zapata, Engaging the Future: Forecasts, Scenarios, Plans, and Projects (2007).

Planning or plan? In *Does Planning Need the Plan?* 64 J. Am. Plan. Ass'n 208 (1998), Michael Neuman notes the powerful criticisms of traditional planning theory, but asks rhetorically

> [C]an planning go plan-less, naked and exposed? If the latter, why not call our profession "ning" and leave out "plan" entirely? As it is, planning is blessed with an active verb for its name, a characteristic it shares with other professions that nurture and bring things into being: nursing, engineering, design. City planners bring cities to life and life to cities, and have done so for centuries using plans.

He argues that "persuasive plans possess the power of the dream [that] can stir minds, arouse hopes, and inspire action," and that plans serve as the "loci of conflict" to engage various participants in civic life to articulate their own visions for the community.

Sources. For additional reading on planning theory, see Sager, *Planning and the Liberal Paradox: A Democratic Dilemma in Social Choice*, 12 J. Plan. Lit. 16 (1997); Johnson, Urban Planning and Politics (1997); Shipley & Newkirk, *Visioning: Did Anybody See Where It Came From?* 12 J. Plan. Lit. 407 (1998); M. Branch, Comprehensive Planning for the 21st Century: General Theory and Principles (1998) (linking public and private planning processes); Beatley, Ethical Land Use (1994); Brody et al., *Mandating Citizen Participation in Plan Making*, 69 J. Am. Plan. Ass'n 245 (2003); Howe, *Professional Roles and the Public Interest in Planning*, 6 J. Plan. Lit. 230 (1992); Alexander, *The Public Interest in Planning: From Legitimation to Substantive Plan Evaluation*, 1 Plan. Theory 226 (2002); Sanyal, Planning's Three Challenges in The Profession of City Planning 312 (L. Rodwin & B. Sanyal eds., 2000); Haar and Wolf, *Planning and Law: Shaping the Legal Environment of Land Development and Preservation*, 40 Env. L. Rptr. 10419 (2010) (contending that "the modern land use attorney needs to have a healthy respect for planners and planning theory").

For a broad perspective on planning theory, see S. Campbell & S. Fainstein, eds., Readings in Planning Theory (2d ed. 2003). The American Planning Tradition: Culture and Policy (R. Fishman ed., 2000) provides a thoughtful overview of the twentieth century American experience. For a fascinating and well-written effort to develop a systematic theory of urban life, one aimed at ensuring opportunity and community, see L. Haworth, The Good City (1970).

On plan implementation and evaluation, see Forsyth, *Administrative Discretion and Urban and Regional Planners' Values*, 14 J. Plan. Lit. 5 (1999); Baer, *General Plan Evaluation Criteria: An Approach to Making Better Plans*, 63 J. Am. Plan. Ass'n 329 (1997); Talen, *Do Plans Get Implemented? A Review of Evaluation in Planning*, 10 J. Plan. Lit. 248 (1996); J. Grant, *On Some Public Uses of Planning "Theory,"* 66 Town Plan. Rev. 59 (1994) (Halifax, N.S. case studies); Hoch, *Evaluating Plans Pragmatically*, 1 Plan. Theory 53 (2002). H. Smith, Planning America's Communities: Paradise Found? Paradise Lost? (1991) is a readable collection of case studies and commentaries by a non-academic practicing planner. Silliman, *Risk Management for Land Use Regulations*, 49 Clev. St. L. Rev. 591 (2001), explores the day-to-day work of a municipal planner's office with the author's insights as a lawyer as well as a planner.

The "New Urbanist" approach mentioned above is explored further in Chapter 3.

[b.] Statutory Authorization for Comprehensive Planning

The Standard City Planning Enabling Act, described *supra*, provided a model for the state legislation needed to authorize local planning. Although the actual planning is carried out at the local level, this state enabling legislation sets the ground rules, as it were, and can have a significant influence on what cities and other local units of government actually do. As the importance of effective comprehensive planning at the local level has gradually become recognized, most states have found that the relatively simple form and procedures contemplated by the Standard Act of the 1920s requires modernization. The Rhode Island planning legislation that follows is an example of a well-drafted modern local planning enabling statute.

RHODE ISLAND COMPREHENSIVE PLANNING AND LAND USE ACT

§ 45-22.2-3 Legislative findings and intent — Statement of goals. —

(a) Findings. The general assembly recognizes these findings, each with equal priority and numbered for reference only, as representing the need to substantially revise present enabling legislation and, therefore, declares that:

(1) The absence of accurate technical information and comprehensive planning by municipal government as a rational basis for long-term physical development creates conflicting requirements and reactive land use regulations and decisions.

(2) Municipal government is responsible for land use, but lacks the technical information and financial resources to plan for orderly growth and development, and the protection and management of our land and natural resources.

(3) Land, water, and air are finite natural resources. Comprehensive planning must provide for protection, development, use, and management of our land and natural resources.

(4) Comprehensive planning and its implementation will promote the appropriate use of land. The lack of comprehensive planning and its implementation has led to the misuse, underuse, and overuse of our land and natural resources.

(5) The coordination of growth and the intensity of development with provisions for services and facilities is a proper objective of comprehensive planning.

(6) Comprehensive planning is needed to provide a basis for municipal and state initiatives to insure all citizens have access to a range of housing choices, including the availability of affordable housing for all income levels and age groups.

(7) Municipal comprehensive planning must recognize and address land uses in contiguous municipalities and encourage cooperative planning efforts by municipalities.

(8) Comprehensive planning will provide a basis for improved coordination so that local plans reflect issues of local, regional, and statewide concern. Comprehensive planning will insure that municipal government has a role in the formulation of state goals and policies.

(9) Improved coordination is necessary between state and municipal governments to promote uniform standards and review procedures as well as consistency in land use regulations.

(b) Intent. The general assembly declares it is the intent of this chapter to:

(1) Establish, in each municipality, a program of comprehensive planning that is implemented according to the standards and schedule contained in this chapter.

(2) Provide financial assistance for the formulation and implementation of the comprehensive plan.

(3) Provide financial assistance to establish a uniform data and technical information base to be used by state and municipal governments and their agencies.

(4) Establish standards and a uniform procedure for the review and approval of municipal comprehensive plans and state guide plans and their consistency with overall state goals, objectives, standards, applicable performance measures, and policies.

(5) Establish a procedure in comprehensive planning at state and municipal levels which will accommodate future requirements.

(c) Goals. The general assembly hereby establishes a series of goals to provide overall direction and consistency for state and municipal agencies in the comprehensive planning process established by this chapter.

The goals have equal priority and are numbered for reference only.

(1) To promote orderly growth and development that recognizes the natural characteristics of the land, its suitability for use, and the availability of existing and proposed public and/or private services and facilities.

(2) To promote an economic climate which increases quality job opportunities and overall economic well being of each municipality and the state.

(3) To promote the production and rehabilitation of year-round housing that achieves a balance of housing choices, for all income levels and age groups, which recognizes the affordability of housing as the responsibility of each municipality and the state and which facilitates economic growth in the state.

(4) To promote the protection of the natural, historic and cultural resources of each municipality and the state.

(5) To promote the preservation of the open space and recreational resources of each municipality and the state.

(6) To provide for the use of performance-based standards for development and to encourage the use of innovative development regulations and techniques that promote the development of land suitable for development while protecting our natural, cultural, historical, and recreational resources, and achieving a balanced pattern of land uses.

(7) To promote consistency of state actions and programs with municipal comprehensive plans, and provide for review procedures to ensure that state goals and policies are reflected in municipal comprehensive plans and state guide plans.

(8) To ensure that adequate and uniform data are available to municipal and state government as the basis for comprehensive planning and land use regulation.

(9) To ensure that municipal land use regulations and decisions are consistent with the comprehensive plan of the municipality, and to insure state land use regulations and decisions are consistent with state guide plans.

(10) To encourage the involvement of all citizens in the formulation, review, and adoption of the comprehensive plan.

(11) To preserve existing government subsidized housing for persons and families of low and moderate income and to increase the overall supply of year-round housing, including housing for low and moderate income persons and families. . . .

§ 45-22.2-5 Formulation of comprehensive plan by cities and towns. —

(a) There is established a program of local comprehensive planning to address the findings and intent and accomplish the goals of this chapter. Rhode Island's cities and towns, through the exercise of their power and responsibility pursuant to the general laws, applicable articles of the Rhode Island Constitution, and subject to the express limitations and requirements of this chapter, shall:

(1) Plan for future land use which relates development to land capability, protects our natural resources, promotes a balance of housing choices, encourages economic development, preserves and protects our open space, recreational, historic and cultural resources, and provides for orderly provision of facilities and services;

(2) Adopt, update, and amend comprehensive plans including implementation programs consistent with the provisions of this chapter;

(3) Conform its zoning ordinance and map with its comprehensive plan within eighteen (18) months of plan adoption and approval as provided for in § 45-22.2-9;

(4) Do all things necessary to carry out the purposes of this chapter.

(b) Each municipality shall prepare and adopt a comprehensive plan which is consistent with the goals, findings, intent, and other provisions of this chapter, or amend its existing comprehensive plan to conform with the requirements of this chapter.

(c) Each municipality shall submit its proposed comprehensive plan and existing land use regulation to the director [of administration of Rhode Island].

(d) Each municipality shall submit any amended comprehensive plan to the director [of administration of Rhode Island].

§ 45-22.2-6 Required elements of comprehensive plan. —
The comprehensive plan is a statement (in text, maps, illustrations, or other media of communication) that is designed to provide a basis for rational decision making regarding the long term physical development of the municipality. The definition of goals and policies relative to the distribution of future land uses, both public and private, forms the basis for land use decisions to guide the overall physical, economic, and social development of the municipality. The comprehensive plan must be internally consistent in its policies, forecasts, and standards, and include the following elements:

(1) Goals and policies statement. Identifies the goals and policies of the municipality for its future growth and development. The statement enumerates how the plan is consistent with the overall goals and policies of this chapter, the state guide plan, and related elements.

(2) Land use plan element. Designates the proposed general distribution and general location and interrelationship of land use for residential, commercial, industry, open space, recreation facilities, and other categories of public and private uses of land. The land use element is based upon the other elements contained in this section, and it relates the proposed standards of population density and building intensity to the capacity of the land and available or planned facilities and services. A land use plan map, illustrating the future strategy and land use policy of the municipality, as defined by the comprehensive plan, is required. The land use plan must contain an analysis of the inconsistency of existing zoning districts, if any, with the land use plan. The land use plan should specify the process by which the zoning ordinance and zoning map shall be amended to conform to the comprehensive plan.

(3) Housing element. Consists of identification and analysis of existing and forecasted housing needs and objectives including programs for the preservation, including, but not limited to, the preservation of federally insured or assisted housing, improvement, and development of housing for all citizens. The housing element enumerates local policies and implementation techniques to promote the production and rehabilitation of housing that achieves a balance of housing choices, recognizing local, regional, and statewide needs for all income levels and for all age groups, including, but not limited to, the affordability of housing and the preservation of federally insured or assisted housing. The element identifies specific programs and policies for inclusion in the implementation program necessary to accomplish this purpose and takes into account growth management and the need to phase and pace development in areas of rapid growth. The housing element includes an affordable housing plan that identifies housing needs in the community, including, but not limited to, the needs for low and moderate income housing, establishes goals and policies to address those needs, consistent with available resources and the need to protect public health, including drinking water supplies and safety and environmental quality. The affordable housing plan includes an implementation program of actions to be taken to effectuate the policies and goals of the affordable housing plan.

(4) Economic development element. Includes the identification of economic development policies and strategies, either existing or proposed by the municipality, in coordination with the land use plan element. These policies should reflect local, regional, and statewide concerns for the expansion and stabilization of the economic base and the promotion of quality employment opportunities and job growth. The policies and

implementation techniques must be identified for inclusion in the implementation program element.

(5) *Natural and cultural resources element.* Provides an inventory of the significant natural resource areas as water, soils, prime agricultural lands, natural vegetation systems, wildlife, watersheds, wetlands, aquifers, coastal features, flood plains, and other natural resources, and the policies for the protection and management of these areas. The element includes policies for the protection of the historic and cultural resources of the municipality and the state. The policies and implementation techniques must be identified for inclusion in the implementation program element.

(6) *Services and facilities element.* Provides an inventory of existing and forecasted needs for facilities and services used by the public as, but not limited to, educational facilities, public safety, water, sanitary sewers, libraries, and community facilities. The policies and implementation techniques must be identified for inclusion in the implementation program element.

(7) *Open space and recreation element.* Includes an inventory of recreational resources, open space areas, and recorded access to these resources and areas. The element must also contain an analysis of forecasted needs and policies for the management and protection of these resources and areas. The policies and implementation techniques must be identified for inclusion in the implementation program element.

(8) *Circulation element.* Consists of the inventory and analysis of existing and proposed major circulation systems, street patterns, and any other modes of transportation in coordination with the land use element. The policies and implementation techniques must be identified for inclusion in the implementation program element.

(i) A statement which defines and schedules for a period of five (5) years or more the specific public actions to be undertaken in order to achieve the goals and objectives of each element of the comprehensive plan. Scheduled expansion or replacement of public facilities, and the anticipated costs and revenue sources proposed to meet those costs reflected in a municipality's capital improvement program, must be included in the implementation program.

(ii) The implementation program identifies the public actions necessary to implement the objectives and standards of each element of the comprehensive plan that require the adoption or amendment of codes and ordinances by the governing body of the municipality.

(iii) The implementation program identifies other public authorities or agencies owning water supply facilities or providing water supply services to the municipality, and coordinates the goals and objectives of the comprehensive plan with the actions of public authorities or agencies with regard to the protection of watersheds as provided in § 46-15.3-1, et seq.

(iv) The implementation program must detail the timing and schedule of municipal actions required to amend the zoning ordinance and map to conform to the comprehensive plan.

NOTES AND QUESTIONS

1. *Optional and mandatory plan elements.* The Standard City Planning Enabling Act (SCPEA) of 1928, § 6, offered only vague generalities about what a comprehensive plan should include:

> Such plan, with accompanying maps, plats, charts, and descriptive matter shall show the commission's recommendations of said territory, including among other things, the general location, character and extent of streets, . . . parks, . . . grounds and open spaces, the general location of public buildings and other public property, and the general location and extent of public utilities and terminals, whether publicly or privately owned or operated; . . . as well as a zoning plan for the control of the height, area, bulk, location, and use of buildings and premises.

The Rhode Island legislation, by contrast, mandates inclusion of *all* of the elements specified in § 45-22.2-6. Pennsylvania also requires an "energy conservation plan element," describing the impact of each plan element on energy use and the measures to reduce energy consumption and promote the "effective utilization of renewable energy resources." Pa. Stat. Ann. tit. 53., § 10301.1. Expanded attention to environmental concerns is a feature of many modern planning enabling statutes. See, e.g., Breggin & George, *Planning for Biodiversity: Sources of Authority in State Land Use Laws*, 81 Va. Envtl. L.J. 81 (2003).

For a similar list of planning elements contained in the 1975 New Jersey Municipal Land Use Law, see N.J. Stat. Ann. § 40:55D-28. New Jersey also requires a housing element, a recreation element, a conservation element, a historic preservation plan, and "[a]n economic plan element considering all aspects of economic development and sustained economic vitality." Many states are less specific, however. The American Planning Association's Growing Smart Legislative Guidebook recommends that land use, housing, transportation and community facilities elements be mandatory, along with a statement of issues and opportunities, and a program for implementation. It would provide an "opting-out" procedure for elements dealing with economic development, critical and sensitive areas, and natural hazards, and it would make other elements (e.g., human services, community design, historic preservation) optional. See American Planning Association, Growing Smart Legislative Guidebook: Model Statutes for Planning and Management of Change 7-61 (S. Meck, gen. ed., 2002).

2. *Substantive plan requirements.* Notice that the Rhode Island legislation requires that the plan contain a "statement [that] enumerates how the plan is consistent with the overall goals and policies of this chapter [§ 45-22.2-3], the state guide plan, and related elements." The state guide plan, a state-formulated document, sets forth goals, policies, and plans or plan elements for the physical, economic, and social development of the state, adopted by a state planning council. Further, cities and towns must submit their plans to the state director of administration for review against the requirements of the act and state goals and policies. § 45-22.2-9. The SCPEA did not contain substantive policies for any of the elements for which it authorized planning, nor did it require any relationship to a regional or state plan or review by a state agency. What do you think would be the practical and legal consequences of such a requirement?

The substantive housing requirements in the Rhode Island planning legislation are an attempt to ensure that the plan forthrightly addresses the need for low- and moderate-income housing, which is one of the negative social consequences of the failure to provide substantive planning policies. This issue is discussed in Chapter 5, *infra*. Are there any other areas of planning concern where the statute should provide substantive policies? California requires a "local open-space plan for comprehensive and long-range preservation and conservation of open-space land within its jurisdiction." Cal. Gov't Code § 65563. Is this substantive? A Supreme Court case considered the taking problems raised by this uncommon planning requirement. See Ch. 2, *infra*.

3. *Internal consistency.* The Rhode Island legislation requires that the comprehensive plan "must be internally consistent in its policies, forecasts, and standards," § 45-22.2-6. California's planning legislation has a similar provision, which requires the general plan to "comprise an integrated, internally consistent and compatible statement of policies." Cal. Gov't Code § 65300.5. These provisions attempt to remedy the failure of the SCPEA to require plans to state an internally consistent planning policy. The California courts have applied this requirement to invalidate plans found to have internally inconsistent elements. See *Concerned Citizens of Calaveras County v. Board of Supvrs.*, 212 Cal. Rptr. 273 (Cal. App. 1985).

4. *Implementing the plan.* The Rhode Island statute requires a municipality to "[c]onform its zoning ordinance and map with its comprehensive plan within eighteen (18) months of plan adoption and approval . . . ." § 45-22.2-5(3). By contrast, Pennsylvania's planning statute provides that "Notwithstanding any other provision of this act, no action by the governing body of a municipality shall be invalid nor shall the same be subject to challenge or appeal on the basis that such action is inconsistent with, or fails to comply with, the provision of a comprehensive plan." Pa. Stat. Ann. tit. 53, § 10303(c). Citing this section, the court in *CACO Three, Inc. v. Board of Supervisors*, 845 A.2d 991, 995 (Pa. Commw. 2004), described the comprehensive plan as "a useful tool for guiding growth and development of the community," but one that requires only "intermediate and inconclusive steps" in the land use planning process. The court continued, "Unlike a specific and regulatory zoning ordinance, a comprehensive plan is, by its nature, an abstract recommendation as to desirable approaches to land utilization and development of the community. Consequently, any inconsistence with the comprehensive plan, standing alone, cannot justify disapproving the [developer's proposal]." (Internal citations deleted). Other states go farther. See, e.g., N.J.S.A. § 40:55D-62, which requires adoption of the land use and housing elements of the comprehensive plan as a condition of adopting *any* zoning ordinance, and further requires (albeit with some qualifications) that the zoning ordinance be "substantially consistent" with these plan elements. The relationships between planning and zoning and the consistency requirement are considered further in Chapter 6.

5. *The "zoning plan."* A puzzling provision in the SCPEA was that it authorized municipalities to prepare a "zoning plan" as well as other plan elements. SCPEA, § 6. The purpose of the zoning plan is not clear, and this provision no longer appears in state land use legislation. In light of the modern planning approaches described earlier, how would you differentiate between the SCPEA "zoning plan" and the "land use plan element" required by the Rhode Island statute?

6. *Improving planning legislation.* The American Planning Association's model enabling act for local planning is based on a series of important premises: that different types of communities (e.g., mature suburbs, developing areas) will require different types of plans; that planning must be done in a regional context and with citizen participation; that plan elements must be consistent with each other; and that planning must be an on-going process. The Guidebook also warns that plans must be drafted with realistic assumptions about local and regional land markets, and with due concern for constitutional takings limits. The American

Planning Association strongly recommends that local planning be mandated by the state, but it also acknowledges political constraints on some states' ability to do so. See generally American Planning Association, Growing Smart Legislative Guidebook: Model Statutes for Planning and Management of Change (S. Meck, gen. ed., 2002), pp. 7-61 to 7-67; *id.* pp. 7-54 to 7-61 (history of model acts).

For discussion of the organizational structure for planning, see *id.*, 7-9 to 7-18. The model act authorizes the creation of a local land planning agency, but its philosophy is that "the local government should be given as much discretion as possible in structuring the planning function." This follows a "tight-loose" philosophy adopted by the model act. It provides flexibility and options in organization for planning and land use regulation, but contains detailed prescription for issues such as the content of comprehensive plans.

7. *Planning and discretion.* Courts have begun to use plans to curb abuse of the freewheeling discretion that characterizes modern land use practice. This can have unintended but important consequences.

> One of the key issues that arises in the design of a planning system for local government is the tension between the need for flexibility to make decisions and the need to limit discretion. A city council, which must deal with a dynamic environment and must enter into a political bargaining process in which the final outcome is unpredictable, requires discretion to make decisions as problems and opportunities materialize. On the other hand there is pressure . . . [to] want the city council to adopt plans and stick to them. . . . Reduction of the city council's discretionary authority is intended to minimize capricious decisions. [Rider, *Local Government Planning: Prerequisites of an Effective System*, 18 Urb. Aff. Q. 271 (1982).]

One consequence of the use of planning to curb discretion is that policy decisions are pushed forward to the plan making stage, perhaps before true consensus has been reached, rather than delayed to the decision making stage. The plan may be overly generalized as a result. As Rider states, "[t]he adoption of a plan, far from signaling the arrival at a consensus . . . will more likely signal the opening of a new round of negotiations." *Id.* at 276. In a later article he urges "rejection of the plan as a standard and rejection of the related concept of 'consistency' which requires decisions to be consistent with a plan." Rider, *Planning as a Multicentric Process*, 57 Town Plan. Rev. 159, 161 (1986). Note that the rational planning model, with its emphasis on objectivity, may be most useful in limiting discretion. Is this an argument for or against rational planning?

8. *Sources.* For historical treatment of the SCPEA, see Black, *The Comprehensive Plan, in* Principles and Practice of Urban Planning at 349, 353-55 (W. Goodman & E. Freund eds., 1968). For additional background on the adoption of the SCPEA, see T.J. Kent, The Urban General Plan 28-38 (1964); Knack, Meck, & Stollman, *The Real Story Behind the Standard Planning and Zoning Acts of the 1920s*, Land Use Law & Zoning Dig., Feb. 1996, at 3.

For a modern treatment, see R. Burby & P. May, Making Governments Plan: State Experiments in Managing Land Use (1997). Comprehensive texts on planning include: P. Berke, D. Godschalk & E. Kaiser, with D. Rodriguez, Urban Land Use Planning (5th ed. 2006); E.D. Kelly, Community Planning: An Introduction to the Comprehensive Plan (2d ed. 2009); J.B. Cullingworth & R. Caves, Planning in the U.S.A.: Policies, Issues, and Processes (2008). W. Fulton & P. Shigley, Guide to California Planning (3d ed. 2005), provides an in-depth introduction to planning practices in a large state with extensive planning laws. S. Paul & S.

Meck, The Essential Planning Library Revisited, American Planning Ass'n, Planning Advisory Serv. Memo, Mar./Apr. 2007, is a useful bibliography.

[2.] State and Regional Planning

Many land use problems extend beyond local government boundaries. As such, they clearly generate serious externalities when observed from a local perspective, and just as clearly cannot be regulated effectively (using either an efficiency or an equity criterion) in a series of local plans and ordinances. At the same time, the tradition of home rule governance, which is particularly strong with respect to land use issues, has generated strong political resistance to the adoption of statewide or regional planning and zoning systems. English planner Peter Self explains:

> As the government framework widens, the planning of urbanization becomes theoretically and functionally more rational but tends to lose its political base and to become entangled with other policy issues. It seems that popular identification of a common metropolitan existence and set of interests declines steadily with distance from the main center, although this may be due to the political separatism of suburbanites rather than to their failure to recognize the existence of common problems. Few people, however, appear to recognize their membership of an entity called an urban or city region or to appreciate its functional importance except for transportation — and popular interest in that subject grows spottier as one moves outward. The influence of other regional interests of an economic or ethnic character will in some circumstances be perceived much more strongly. [P. Self, Planning the Urban Region 147 (1982).]

Many states have land use programs for environmental areas, such as coastal areas, but comprehensive state and regional planning and land use control programs that cover more than just environmental resources also have a long history. Regional planning, as opposed to state planning, usually refers to a component part of a state, such as a metropolitan area; regional planning on occasion also crosses state boundaries, as in the [Lake] Tahoe Regional Planning Agency. As used here, the term "state and regional" refers to planning and land use controls that are comprehensive in scope and not limited to environmental protection. These programs are explored in more detail in Chapter 8.

[a.] State Planning Agencies and Plans

State planning agencies and plans. State planning has a long history, and was modestly successful prior to World War II due to support by the federal government through the New Deal policies of President Franklin D. Roosevelt and by keeping to a narrow agenda that focused on conservation of natural resources. See M. Clawson, New Deal Planning: The National Resources Planning Board ch. 14 (1981). It waned thereafter. When it revived, beginning with pioneering efforts in Hawaii and New York in the late 1950s and early 1960s, the emphasis was broadened to comprehensive planning. The federal government also stimulated the creation of new state-level planning organizations with grants and what came to be known as the A-95 program, a regulation that gave state and regional agencies the ability to review federal grant applications for consistency with state and regional plans, goals and policies. Although these programs have dwindled, state-level planning is today perhaps at its historical peak, driven by the increasing recognition that failure to deal with externalities-based problems has burdened every level of government and every corner of society. Connecticut and New Jersey are among the states that have state-level plans with generalized land use designations that are mapped. The New Jersey plan is called the "State Development and Redevelopment Plan" and can be found at: www.state.nj.us/dca/divisions/osg/plan/.

For a good review of contemporary state development planning efforts, see Knaap & Lewis, A Primer on State Development Plans, a working paper for the Lincoln Institute of Land Policy, (2009), *available at:* https://www.lincolninst.edu/pubs/dl/1691_903_Knaap%20Lewis%20Working%20Final.pdf. Examining state development plans from Connecticut, Delaware, Florida, New Jersey, and Rhode Island, Knaap and Lewis found that they vary extensively in their structure, content, and horizontal and vertical linkages. Connecticut's plan is called the Conservation and Development Policies Plan. The plan is administered by the Office of Policy and Management (OPM), a staff agency for the governor that actually formulates and implements the plan, and the Legislative Continuing Committee on State Planning and Development. OPM formulates regulations on the criteria and process for initiating interim changes between the five year updates, and advises the legislature. The legislature adopts the plan after a public review process.

The plan text sets forth six plan goals, called "growth management principles," and a series of corresponding strategies. For example, one principle is "[c]oncentrate development around transportation nodes and along major transportation corridors to support the viability of transportation options." A strategy to carry this out is "[p]romote intensive development near the Stamford, New Haven and New London stations that provide high-speed rail passenger service between Boston and New York." OPM, Intergovernmental Policy Division, Conservation and Development Policies Plan for Connecticut, 2005-2010, 41, 43 (2005), *available at:* http://www.ct.gov/opm/cwp/view.asp?A=2990&Q=385378.

The plan contains a Locational Guide Map whose purpose is to provide a geographical or spatial interpretation of the state's conservation and development policies. The map defines two broad land management categories, conservation elements and development elements, "prioritized according to their characteristics and suitability for various state actions." *Id.*, at 5. "Conservation areas include existing preserved open space, preservation areas, conservation areas, and rural lands . . . . Development areas include regional centers, neighborhood conservation areas, growth areas, and rural community centers, and the state prioritizes spending in these areas in this order. Additionally, Aquifer Protection Areas and Historic Areas overlays appear on the map." Knaap & Lewis, *supra*, at 7–8. "The primary purpose of the plan is to provide context and direction for state agencies and to assure that state agency plans and actions are consistent with state growth management principles." *Id.* at 7. In essence, the plan is attempting to channel state investments in areas that are most suitable, and away from areas that are not.

"Although the [Connecticut plan] strives to achieve a high degree of consistency with municipal and regional plans of conservation and development and local zoning regulations, only state agency actions are required to be consistent with the Plan. Municipalities must consider the [p]lan and note any inconsistencies when they update their own plans, but they are not required to reconcile any differences." OPM *supra*, at 2.

While maintaining they hold considerable promise for addressing climate change issues and, reducing greenhouse gas emissions, Knaap and Lewis contend these plans are likely to need strengthening in their design detail, their horizontal and vertical linkages, and in their stability over changes in gubernatorial administrations. Among their recommendations is a state planning commission whose appointed members have longer than three-year terms and with the terms systematically overlapping state administrations.

American Planning Association, Growing Smart Legislative Guidebook: Model Statutes for Planning and the Management of Change,
pp. 4-11-4-14 (S. Meck, gen. ed., 2002)

TWO STATE PLANNING MODELS

Two general approaches in state planning have emerged and pose useful paradigms for drafting legislation. One has been called the *"civic model"* and is derived from the heritage and assumptions of city planning. The second has been termed the *"management model"* and draws its orientation and techniques from the science of organization management. Under the civic model, the state would engage in a goal-setting process, develop an inventory of resources and an appraisal of existing conditions that affect the ability to achieve those goals, identify a set of alternative actions, and compile a list of implementing measures. The civic model would produce plans affecting land use and critical areas management or addressing functional topics like transportation, water, and economic development. The plans would have regulatory impact and/or affect the programming of infrastructure to support particular growth strategies. . . .

[T]he purpose of the management model is to ensure that state agencies operate in an efficient and coordinated manner consistent with the priorities of the chief executive. Under the management model, the governor, who is the state's chief executive, implements policies and measures enacted by the state legislature and uses the planning system to exert administrative control over state agencies by establishing operational guidelines and directions for them. . . .

> Five main approaches to state land-use planning programs have been identified . . .
>
> *State planning* — the state plans and zones land, develops and maintains a statewide land-use plan, and implements the plan through permits and regulations (Hawaii is the only state that comes close to this model).
>
> *State-mandated planning* — the state sets mandatory standards, some of which apply to regional agencies and local governments, for those aspects of land use planning and control that involve state interests (e.g., Oregon, Florida).
>
> *State-promoted planning* — the state sets guidelines for those aspects of planning that involve state interests, establishing incentives for local governments to meet the guidelines (e.g., Georgia).
>
> *State review* (the "mini-NEPA system") — the state requires environmental impact reports for certain types of development, thus superimposing a second tier of review on the traditional local planning model. The state agency reviews the reports for conformance with state standards (e.g., California, Washington).
>
> *State permitting* — the state requires permits for certain types of development, thus preempting local review and permitting for those types of development (e.g., Vermont).

NOTES AND QUESTIONS

1. *From state planning to state regulation.* As the Growing Smart commentary indicates, only Hawaii has come even close to following up state planning with direct state regulation of land uses. See Callies, *Land Use Planning in the Fiftieth State*, in State and Regional Comprehensive Planning 125 (P. Buchsbaum & L. Smith eds., 1993). Everywhere else, the thrust of the state planning process is to guide decisions made by the tangle of state, regional and local agencies that have pre-existing jurisdiction over various aspects of the land use process. See also D. Callies, Regulating Paradise: Land Use Controls in Hawaii (2d ed., 2010).

Several exceptions to this generalization are evolving, however, in which direct state involvement is becoming greater. These are: undesirable or controversial facilities that serve a broad area, sometimes called LULUs (Locally Unwanted Land Uses); areas of critical state concern, often (but not necessarily) environmentally sensitive areas; and developments that have a regional impact, or DRIs. A common thread is that local governments, where the authority to regulate is commonly placed, have little if any incentive to recognize either the positive or negative benefits that result outside their boundaries when these types of decisions are made. Unless control is shifted to a higher level to capture these externalities in the decision making process, sub-optimal results are likely to occur. See generally American Planning Association, Growing Smart Legislative Guidebook ch. 5 (S. Meck, gen. ed., 2002).

2. *Areas of state concern.* Some states have created regional planning agencies with significant regulatory powers over critical natural resource areas. The extensive 1.1 million-square mile Pinelands in southeast New Jersey is an example. The transfer of development rights program for this area is described in Chapter 4, *infra*. In 1979, the state created a Pinelands Commission, which prepared a comprehensive management plan for the area, covering portions of seven counties and all or parts of 56 municipalities. N.J. Stat. Ann. §§ 13:18A-8, -9. Local master plans and land use ordinances must conform to the Commission's comprehensive management plan, § 13:18A-12, and the Commission may disapprove any development not in compliance with the plan. § 13:18A-15. The approach has survived judicial scrutiny. See Hovsons, Inc. v. Secretary of Interior, 519 F. Supp. 434 (D.N.J. 1981), *aff'd on other grounds*, 711 F.2d 1208 (3d Cir. 1983). Appraisals include Collins, *How Is the Pineland Program Working?*, *in* Protecting the New Jersey Pinelands 274, 278-280 (B. Collins & E. Russell eds., 1988); R. Mason, Contested Lands 191 (1992). The Commission maintains an informative website at www.state.nj.us/pinelands/ which includes, inter alia, the most recent annual report. See also N.J. Pinelands Comm., The Pinelands Development Credit Program (1996). New Jersey has two other regional planning bodies, the Meadowlands Commission and the Highlands Council. They are described below:

The New Jersey Meadowlands Commission (NJMC) oversees development in the New Jersey Meadowlands, a 30.4-square-mile district located five miles west of New York City in North Jersey, with 14 municipalities in two counties, Bergen and Hudson. Prior to the establishment of the Commission in 1969, the Meadowlands, an environmentally sensitive area, had suffered from industrial abuse and neglect. The legislation establishing the Meadowlands (N.J.S.A. 13:17-1 *et seq.*) recognized the wetlands area as an "incalculable resource" that would provide jobs and housing to the Meadowlands communities. The intent was to overcome three main obstacles to development: governmental fragmentation, local planning and land use controls, and competition for ratables. Among the commission's responsibilities and powers (N.J.S.A. 13:17-6 *et seq.*) include the following:

• Developing, adopting, and promulgating a master plan for the physical development of the lands within the district;

• Adopting codes and standards to carry out the master plan;

• Entering into cooperative agreements with other governmental agencies for the reclamation of the Meadowlands, determine the existence of renewal areas, and undertake redevelopment projects;

• Functioning as a local planning agency by undertaking projects necessary to reclaim, develop, redevelop, and improve land within the district;

• Reviewing and regulating all subdivisions within the district; and

• Operating an inter-municipal tax sharing account in order that the financial benefits of the district are clearly and equitably distributed among all the constituent municipalities.

The NJMC has adopted a master plan and zoning regulations for the district. These may be accessed at its website: www.njmeadowlands.gov/.

The Highlands Region is a 1,250-square- mile area in the northwest part of the state noted for its scenic beauty and environmental significance, especially its groundwater resources which supply much of New Jersey. It includes 88 municipalities. To protect the area, the Highlands Water Protection and Planning Act was enacted in 2004 (N.J.S.A. 13:20-1 *et seq.*). The act establishes a fifteen-member Highlands Water Protection and Planning Council. The Highlands Council is charged with carrying out the provisions of the act, including the development of a regional master plan for the Highlands Region, which it did in 2008. The plan may be accessed at its website: http://www.highlands.state.nj.us/.

Each municipality within the Highlands Region must revise its municipal master plan and development regulations, as applicable to the development and use of land in the "preservation area" designated by the Highlands Act. The preservation area is deemed to be the most environmentally sensitive by the act, and local plans and regulations must conform to the regional master plan as it applies to the preservation area. After receiving and reviewing the revisions, the council is to approve, reject, or approve with conditions the revised plan and development regulations, as it deems appropriate, after a public hearing. Similar provisions apply to county master plans and associated regulations. The New Jersey Department of Environmental Protection also reviews major Highlands developments in the preservation area. In addition, the Highlands Council operates a transfer of development rights program through the Highlands Development Credit Bank.

If any municipality or county fails to adopt or enforce an approved revised master plan, development regulations or other regulations — including any condition imposed by the council — the council shall adopt and enforce such rules and regulations as are necessary to implement the minimum standards contained in the regional master plan as they apply to any municipality or county within the preservation area. (This discussion has been adapted from S. Meck & J. Zelinka, Planning and Zoning in New Jersey: A Manual for Planning and Zoning Board Members 12-14 (2007).)

Because of restrictions on development in the preservation area and the lack of compensation for these restrictions, the Highlands Act has been controversial. Nonetheless, a New Jersey appeals court upheld the constitutionality of the Highlands Act in *County of Warren v.*

State, 978 A.2d 312 (N.J. App. Div. 2009).

New York has a similar system for the 9,375-square-mile Adirondack Park area in the northern part of the state, which was upheld against objections that it violated local home rule. *Wambat Realty Corp. v. State*, 362 N.E.2d 581 (N.Y. 1977), noted, 16 Urb. L. Ann. 389 (1979). See R. Liroff & G. Davis, Protecting Open Space: Land Use Control in the Adirondack Park 68–73 (1981), reviewed in 70 Cornell L. Rev. 361 (1985). See also Melewski, *Reforming the Adirondack Park Agency Act: A New Blueprint for the Blue Line*, 15 Envtl. L. in N.Y. 67, 89 (2004) (Part 1 of 2). For studies of special management areas that include the Pinelands and Adirondack Park, see Managing Land Use Conflicts (D. Brower & D. Carol eds., 1987). Legislation in some states also provides for state designation of natural resource areas as areas of critical state concern, and a state agency is then authorized to adopt regulations for these areas that must be implemented by local governments. Critical areas are discussed in Chapter 4.

Massachusetts has established two regional planning and regulatory agencies to protect popular coastal areas, the Cape Cod Commission, which covers Barnstable County (which is all of Cape Cod) and its 15 towns (website: www.capecodcommission.org) and the Martha's Vineyard Commission, which covers Dukes County (including all of Martha's Vineyard and the Elizabeth Islands) and its seven towns (website: /www.mvcommission.org). Both are responsible for preparing regional plans, regulating developments of regional impact, and creating or recommending the creation of districts of critical state planning concern, among other functions.

Norton, *More and Better Local Planning*, 71 J. Am. Plan. Ass'n 55 (2005), describes the limited success of state-mandated local planning intended to provide collectively for regional growth management in coastal North Carolina. See also Brody & Highfield, *Does Planning Work? Testing the Implementation of Local Environmental Planning in Florida*, 71 J. Am. Plan. Ass'n 159 (2005).

3. *Sources.* American Planning Association, Growing Smart Legislative Guidebook, *supra*, 4-7 through 4-11, contains an excellent short summary of the evolution of state and regional planning programs. On early state planning, see Wise, *History of State Planning — An Interpretive Commentary* (Washington: Council of State Planning Agencies, 1977). The classic description of the rebirth of state planning, whose title has given a name to the modern movement, is F. Bosselman & D. Callies, The Quiet Revolution in Land Use Control (1971). See also Callies, *The Quiet Revolution Redux: How Selected Local Governments Have Fared*, 20 Pace Envtl. L. Rev. 277 (2002); Wickersham, *Note, The Quiet Revolution Continues: The Emerging New Model for State Growth Management Statutes*, 18 Harv. Envtl. L. Rev. 489 (1994). Deyle & Smith, *Local Government Compliance with State Planning Mandates: The Effects of State Implementation in Florida*, 64 J. Am. Plan. Ass'n 457 (1998), finds highly variable compliance, attributable to weakness in implementation at the state level. State programs that regulate land use are considered in Chapter 8, *infra*.

A NOTE ON ENVIRONMENTAL JUSTICE

What is it? "Environmental justice" is a term of imprecise meaning that nevertheless has had a growing impact on both state and local planning in recent decades. In its narrowest and clearest sense, the "environmental justice" movement calls attention to and challenges the disproportionate siting of environmentally hazardous activities in communities of color. An early controversy that attracted widespread public attention, for instance, involved a landfill accepting PCBs in Warren County, North Carolina, a primarily African-American community. Warren County v. North Carolina, 528 F. Supp. 276 (E.D.N.C. 1981) (holding that county failed to prove that decision of the EPA to approve the site was arbitrary, capricious or otherwise not in accordance with law and that county ordinance totally forbidding disposal of PCBs in the county was void as conflicting with the purposes and objectives of Congress under the Toxic Substances Control Act). See R. Bullard, Dumping in Dixie: Race, Class and Environmental Quality (3d. ed. 2000); L. Cole & S. Foster, From the Ground Up: Environmental Racism and the Rise of the Environmental Justice Movement (2001). Executive Order 12898, signed by President Clinton in 1994, describes environmental justice more broadly as involving "disproportionately high and adverse human health or environmental effects . . . on minority populations and low-income populations in the United States." Arnold, *Planning for Environmental Justice*, Planning & Envtl. L., March 2007, at 3, says that "[a]t its core, the concept of environmental justice is about the impacts of environmental and land use policies on low-income communities of color." Broadly defined, the concept of environmental justice merges with other equity issues in land use law and planning, such as "exclusionary zoning." Some of these issues are treated in detail in Chapter 5. For a discussion of the Warren County case and the executive order, see Franzen, *The Time Is Now for Environmental Justice: Congress Must Take Action by Codifying Executive Order 12898*, 17 Penn State Env. L. Rev. 379 (2009).

Nonadversarial and adversarial strategies. Concerns about environmental justice are often worked out through community organizing and direct advocacy, with the purpose of defeating a particular proposal or reversing a decision that has already been made. Recall the description earlier in this Chapter of the different ways in which a land use controversy can be resolved. Which is best suited to environmental justice concerns? The American Planning Association's Planning Advisory Service (PAS) has proposed a series of measures to incorporate environmental justice into local planning. These include: (1) broad participation in the preparation of the local comprehensive plan; (2) training of planning commissions and zoning boards in environmental justice issues; (3) modifying zoning ordinances to prohibit environmentally hazardous land uses in minority and low-income neighborhoods; (4) ensuring more diverse membership on planning and zoning boards; and (5) eliminating nonconforming uses in minority or low-income neighborhoods that pose health and environmental problems. *Environmental Justice and Land Use Planning*, PAS Quicknotes, no. 26 (2010). See also University of California Hastings College of the Law Public Law Research Institute. Environmental Justice for All: A Fifty-State Survey of Legislation, Policies, and Initiatives (4th ed. 2010), website: http://www.uchastings.edu/centers/public-law/docs/ejreport-fourthedition.pdf; National Academy of Public Administration, *Addressing Community Concerns: How Environmental Justice Relates to Land Use Planning and Zoning*, prepared for the U.S. Environmental Protection Agency (2003), available at www.napawash.org/Pubs/EJ.pdf. For an interesting example of an environment justice statute from Connecticut, see P.A. 08-95 (2008), which requires a specialized "environmental justice participation plan" for certain types of facilities (e.g., sewage treatment plants, incinerators, electrical generating plants) proposed in certain distressed areas and authorizes "community benefit agreements" to mitigate adverse impacts from such facilities.

There have been litigation successes. In *Chester Residents Concerned for Quality Living v. Seif*, 132 F.3d 925 (3d Cir. 1997), plaintiffs used federal civil rights theories to challenge the state's approval of multiple waste sites in their community. The case was ultimately resolved in plaintiffs' favor by settlements and by the state denying permits for additional facilities. See 524 U.S. 974 (1998) (decision vacated and remanded as moot). Just across the river in Camden, New Jersey, however, plaintiffs were less fortunate. In *South Camden Citizens in Action v. New Jersey Dept. of Envtl. Prot.*, 2006 U.S. Dist. LEXIS 45765 (D.N.J. 2006), which involved a state permit to build a "granulated blast furnace slag grinding facility," *id.* at *1-2, the court rejected both private nuisance and federal civil rights theories: nuisance because the plaintiffs had not shown a unique harm and civil rights because they had not shown a pattern of discrimination. Nuisance is discussed further in Chapter 2. Intentional discrimination is treated in Chapter 5B. Professor Arnold concludes:

> Litigation is a reactive, remedial approach to environmental justice issues. It offers very few effective tools to stop the proliferation of intensive land uses in low income and minority neighborhoods once they exist or are well on their way to receiving regulatory permits. . . . In contrast, land use planning and regulation are proactive, prospective, preventative and participatory methods of defining a neighborhood's desired land use and environmental conditions. . . . The starting point for equitable land use regulation, though, is equitable planning. [Arnold, *supra*, at 6.]

Dubin, *From Junkyards to Gentrification: Explicating a Right to Protective Zoning in Low-Income Communities of Color*, 77 Minn. L. Rev. 739 (1993), is somewhat more enthusiastic about litigation strategies. He canvasses theories of judicial enforcement and argues for a right to "protective zoning." For an assessment of the environmental justice movement, see Power, Justice, and the Environment: A Critical Appraisal of the Environmental Justice Movement (D. N. Pellow & R.J. Brulle, eds., 2005); Environmental Law and Justice in Context (J. Ebbesson & P. Okowa, eds., 2009). Hiskes, *Missing the Green: Golf Course Ecology, Environmental Justice, and Local "Fulfillment" of the Human Rights to Water*, 32 Human Rights Q. 326 (May 2010), describes the right to water as an "emergent" basic right that "uniquely connects present and future generations into a relationship of justice involving reciprocity." This right would suggest that a golf course, a "profligate" user of water, might be a "legitimate focus of human rights litigation and advocacy." For a fascinating analysis of environmental justice impacts in Baltimore, Maryland, see Lord and Norquist, *Cities as Emergent Systems: Race as a Rule in Organized Complexity*, 40 Envtl. L. 551 (2010) (finding that the zoning system in Baltimore distributed unwanted land uses — here, certain conditional uses — on the basis of race and not a postsiting market dynamic).

State planning. The American Planning Association's Legislative Guidebook at 5-8 through 5-11 recommends shifting responsibility for regulating so-called "locally unwanted land uses" (LULUs) to the state level. How likely is it that state regulators will be more sensitive to environmental justice concerns than local officials? The *Chester* and *Camden* cases, *supra*, do not bode well for concerned neighborhoods. But see *Colonias Dev. Council v. Rhino Envtl. Services*, 117 P.3d 939 (N.M. 2005), where the combination of a state environmental law plus implementing regulations afforded the New Mexico Supreme Court the basis for reversing a permit that had been granted without hearing and without considering the community's environmental justice concerns such as the cumulative impact of siting decisions. See Fisher, *The Rhino in the Colonia: How Colonias Development Council v. Rhino Environmental Services, Inc. Set a Substantive State Standard for Environmental Justice*, 39 Env. L. 397 (2009).

Recall also Professor Arnold's observation that equitable regulation begins with equitable planning. California now requires that the state's general plan guidelines include a section encouraging localities to adopt environmental equity provisions. Cal. Govt. Code § 65040.12(c) through (e); see Cal. Gov. Off. of Plan. & Rsch., General Plan Guidelines 22-28 (2003), available at www.opr.ca.gov/planning. As will be discussed later in Chapter 6, the importance of plan provisions, even relatively modest ones such as California's, is that they can provide a policy basis for judicial enforcement, thus mitigating some of the limitations of environmental justice litigation mentioned above.

Local planning. Professor Arnold advocates a different, locally focused strategy:

> The next frontier for both the movement and the focus of environmental justice scholarship, however, is land use planning by communities of color and low-income communities. Local neighborhoods can use land use planning to articulate visions for what they want their communities to be, and negotiate land use regulations to implement these visions. In other words, they would not be merely late participants in using existing rules to stop (or attempt to stop) current proposals for unwanted land uses, but also pre-siting participants in developing the rules that will determine what will and will not go in their neighborhoods. . . . [T]he law is about more than litigation, rights, courts, and jurisprudence. The law is about problem-solving, policy making, participation, and regulation, all of which are part of the land use regulatory model. [Arnold, *Planning Milagros: Environmental Justice and Land Use Regulation*, 76 Denv. U. L. Rev. 1 (1998).]

Arnold, *Planning for Environmental Justice*, *supra* at 7, lists 18 planning principles that advance environmental justice concerns. For a case study, which explores how environmental justice concerns can stimulate the interest of minority communities in broader issues of "smart growth" planning, see Rast, *Environmental Justice and the New Regionalism*, 25 J. Plan. Ed. & Rsch. 249 (2006) (urban-suburban coalition in northwestern Indiana).

Sources. Planning & Envtl. L., March 2007, at 9-12, contains a bibliography of leading articles. For a careful but controversial study questioning some of the premises of the environmental justice movement, see Been, *What's Fairness Got to Do With It? Environmental Justice and the Siting of Locally Undesirable Land Uses*, 78 Cornell L. Rev. 1001 (1993). See also *Addressing Community Concerns: How Environmental Justice Relates to Planning and Zoning* (report by a panel of the National Academy of Public Administration for the U.S. Environmental Protection Agency, July 2003). On the important relationship between environmental justice and transportation planning, see T. Sanchez & J. Wolf, Environmental Justice and Transportation Equity: A Review of Metropolitan Planning Organizations (Brookings Institution, 2005), available at mi.vt.edu/uploads/SanchezWolf.pdf.

[b.] Regional Planning Agencies and Plans

Regional planning also has a respectable history, although many of the notable early efforts were privately sponsored (including the landmark New York City Regional Plan of the 1920s). As with state plans, the New Deal had some success encouraging the adoption of regional plans, but the real era of growth began in the 1950s and 1960s, when Congress added regional planning requirements to a number of federal assistance programs, such as housing, transportation, and environmental protection, and when federal funding became available. During its first term, the Reagan Administration substantially dismantled the federal programs that funded regional planning, because of the administration's emphasis on increasing the responsibilities of state governments. Federally mandated regional planning survives, but now concentrates almost entirely on transportation planning for transportation projects funded under federal legislation. Like state plans (and for the same reasons), regional plans became an increasingly important factor in land use regulation in the 1990s, particularly in larger states where there was political value in recognizing distinct sub-areas of the jurisdiction.

American Planning Association, Growing Smart Legislative Guidebook: Model Statutes for Planning and the Management of Change
6-5-6-6 (S. Meck, gen. ed., 2002)

WHAT IS REGIONAL PLANNING?

Regional planning is planning for a geographic area that transcends the boundaries of individual governmental units but that shares common social, economic, political, natural resource, and transportation characteristics. A regional planning agency prepares plans that serve as a framework for planning by local governments and special districts.

Throughout the United States, there are regional planning agencies that are either voluntary associations of local government or mandated or authorized by state legislation (e.g., the Metropolitan Council in the Twin Cities or the Metropolitan Services District in Portland, Oregon). These exist for purposes of: undertaking plans that address issues that cut across jurisdictional boundaries; providing information, technical assistance, and training; coordinating efforts among member governments, especially efforts that involve federal funding; and providing a two-way conduit between member governments and the state and federal agencies. Regional planning agencies may also serve as a forum to discuss complex and sometimes sensitive issues among member local governments and to try to find solutions to problems that affect more than one jurisdiction. Sometimes these organizations have direct regulatory authority in that they not only prepare plans, but also administer land-use controls through subdivision review and zoning recommendations, review proposals for major developments whose impacts may cross jurisdictional borders, and review and certify local plans. And in some cases, they directly implement the regional plan, as in the operation of regional transit systems.

States authorize the establishment of these regional planning agencies in different ways. In some parts of the country, the regional agencies take their structure from general enabling legislation (e.g., for regional planning commissions or councils of government). In other places, they are the product of intergovernmental or joint powers agreements, as in California, or interstate compacts, as with the Delaware Regional Planning Commission in the Philadelphia, Pennsylvania/Camden, New Jersey area, or the Tahoe Regional Planning Agency in Nevada and California. In some states, regional agencies are created by special state legislation that applies only to one particular agency (e.g., . . . the Cape Cod Commission in Massachusetts). In still others, they may exist as private, voluntary organizations that seek to provide a regional perspective through independently prepared plans and studies. Examples of such agencies are the Regional Plan Association in New York City and Bluegrass Tomorrow in the Lexington, Kentucky area.

NOTES AND QUESTIONS

1. *Defining regions.* State plans, by definition, follow existing state boundaries, but sub-state (regional) plans require choices. McDowell offers general criteria and examples:

> The region . . . should have a clear organizing concept which sets the theme for planning. A metropolitan area and a river basin are good examples. The former is a continuously urbanized community cut by numerous local jurisdictional boundaries but struggling to function as a single entity for many purposes. The second is a large interdependent land and water resource — also cut by many local jurisdictional boundaries as well as state lines — whose long-term preservation and productivity depends heavily upon its management as a single system. The stronger the organizing concept, the clearer will be the purposes of the region — and the benefits to be planned for. [McDowell, *Regional Planning Today, in* The Practice of State and Regional Planning 133, 151, 152 (F. So, I. Hand & B. McDowell eds., 1986).]

Note that McDowell's examples generate different regions for different purposes (a river basin may extend beyond a metropolitan area, for instance, or the latter may sprawl across more than one basin). Functional regions may also exert reciprocal influences on each other. For example, a housing region will be defined in part by how long it takes to travel to work, while a transportation region will be defined in part by where people live and at what densities. How are overlapping functional regions to coordinate their planning?

2. *Councils of Government and Metropolitan Planning Organizations.* In the 1960s and 1970s most of the old-style regional planning commissions, dominated by private citizens who were community leaders, gave way to Councils of Governments (COGs) made up of elected, politically accountable officials of local governments in the region. Instead of enabling powerful leaders to collectively make significant policy commitments and back them up with action, often just the opposite occurred, as political tensions in the COGs led to logrolling and timid or no action on regional plans. By the late 1970s, there were 39 federal programs that required or supported COGs, and many states established counterpart statewide systems for state programs. A reduction in federal aid has led to a substantial drop in the number of regional councils. For a discussion of regional planning, see D. Rothblatt & A. Sancton, Metropolitan Governance Revisited (1998).

3. *Transportation planning.* The importance of transportation facilities, such as highways, to land use and development and the availability of federal funding has made transportation planning the most important planning function regional agencies exercise today. Beginning in the 1970s, the federal government required state and regional planning as a precondition to the receipt of federal grants, and it provided funds to carry out the required planning. For the current form of this requirement, see 23 U.S.C. §§ 134 (regional planning), 135 (state planning).

An important issue, long-debated, is the connection between transportation and land use. This question is extensively analyzed in T. Moore et al., The Transportation/Land Use Connection, American Planning Ass'n, Planning Advisory Serv. Rep. Nos. 546/547 (2007). The report identifies the connection, but also finds a lack of balance between the two because land use policy is fragmented and transportation decisions are more centralized. It concludes that "land-use and transportation planning have to happen together. . . . The transportation system creates a structure to which land use must conform, so transportation planning should be done with consideration of the implications for land use . . . as well as for transportation when it sets that structure." *Id.* at 125, 126. The report makes a number of suggestions for carrying out that recommendation, but regional structures are not strong enough in most of the country to accomplish this change. Examples of coordination between transportation planning and land use are programs for planning for transit-oriented development and the preservation of highway corridors, both discussed in Chapters 3 and 8. For an interesting discussion of how the organizational structure of metropolitan planning agencies, which have responsibility for transportation planning in urban areas, affects priorities for mass transit, see Nelson *et al. Metropolitan Planning Organization Voting Structure and Transit Investment Bias: Preliminary Analysis with Social Equity Implications*, Transportation Research Record: Journal of the Transportation Research Board No. 1895, 1–7 (2004).

4. *Metropolitan agencies with land use powers.* Two metropolitan areas, the Twin Cities in Minnesota and Portland, Oregon, have metropolitan planning agencies that have land use powers over local governments. The Minnesota legislation requires the Metropolitan Council, which is an appointed body, to prepare a development guide and to "review the comprehensive plans of local government units . . . to determine their compatibility with each other and conformity with metropolitan system plans." Minn. Stat. Ann. § 473.175. The Council has teeth. See *City of Lake Elmo v. Metropolitan Council*, 674 N.W.2d 191 (Minn. App. 2003) (requiring changes in the City's plan because it had a substantial impact on, and departed from, the Council's metropolitan plan); *BBY Investors v. City of Maplewood*, 467 N.W.2d 631 (Minn. App. 1991) (applying the consistency requirement to uphold a city's rejection of a conditional use permit). But see Note, *Other Rising Legal Issues: Land Use Planning — The Twin Cities Metropolitan Council: Novel Initiative, Futile Effort*, 27 Wm. Mitchell L. Rev. 1941 (2001). On metropolitan planning generally, see J. Pack, ed., Sunbelt/Frostbelt: Public Policies and Market Forces in Metropolitan Development (2005).

The powers of the Portland agency, which are exercised under the state land use program, are even more extensive. See Chapter 8, *infra*.

5. *Emergency planning.* Apart from any other planning lessons that it may have taught, Hurricane Katrina provided the nation in 2005 with a powerful and tragic reminder that the need to create plans may be thrust upon us suddenly, within *ad hoc* planning regions determined by nature as much as logic or political choice. For a thoughtful description of post-Katrina planning efforts along the Gulf Coast, see Swope, *Mississippi's Urbanist Odyssey*, Governing, Sep. 2006, at 36. On equity and environmental justice issues, see D. Troutt, ed., After the Storm: Black Intellectuals Explore the Meaning of Hurricane Katrina (2006).

Sources: Some examples of regional or metropolitan development plans include: Chicago Metropolitan Agency for Planning, *GO* TO 2040: Metropolitan Chicago's official comprehensive regional plan, *available at:* www.goto2040.org/about.aspx.; Metro (Portland, OR), *2040* Growth Concept. *available at*:www.oregonmetro.gov/index.cfm/go/by.web/id=29882; Metro, Regional Framework Plan, *available at*: www.oregonmetro.gov/index.cfm/go/by.web/id=432/level=3; Sacramento Area Council of Governments, *Sacramento Region Blueprint: Transportation and Land Use Plan, available at:* www.sacregionblueprint.org.

Chapter 2

THE CONSTITUTION AND LAND USE CONTROLS: ORIGINS, LIMITATIONS AND FEDERAL REMEDIES

Scope of Chapter

This chapter traces, roughly in chronological order, the origins and changing treatment of land use law pursuant to the federal Constitution. We begin, however, with a brief review of the common law of nuisance, because it is the critical legal antecedent for land use regulation, federal and otherwise. As you read these nuisance cases, consider how they deal with the market/regulation and rationality/values dichotomies that were explored in Chapter 1.

A. NUISANCE LAW

BOVE v. DONNER-HANNA COKE CO.

236 App. Div 37, 258 N.Y.S. 229 (1932)

EDGCOMB J.:

The question involved upon this appeal is whether the use to which the defendant has recently put its property constitutes a private nuisance, which a court of equity should abate.

In 1910 plaintiff purchased two vacant lots at the corner of Abby and Baraga streets in the city of Buffalo, and two years later built a house thereon. The front of the building was converted into a grocery store, and plaintiff occupied the rear as a dwelling. She rented the two apartments on the second floor.

Defendant operates a large coke oven on the opposite side of Abby street. The plant runs twenty-four hours in the day, and three hundred and sixty-five days in the year. Of necessity, the operation has to be continuous, because the ovens would be ruined if they were allowed to cool off. The coke is heated to a temperature of around 2,000 degrees F., and is taken out of the ovens and run under a "quencher," where 500 or 600 gallons of water are poured onto it at one time. This is a necessary operation in the manufacture of coke. The result is a tremendous cloud of steam, which rises in a shaft and escapes into the air, carrying with it minute portions of coke, and more or less gas. This steam and the accompanying particles of dirt, as well as the dust which comes from a huge coal pile necessarily kept on the premises, and the gases and odors which emanate from the plant, are carried by the wind in various directions, and frequently find their way onto the plaintiff's premises and into her house and store. According to the plaintiff this results in an unusual amount of dirt and soot accumulating in her house, and prevents her opening the windows on the street side; she also claims that she suffers severe headaches by breathing the impure air occasioned by this dust and these offensive odors, and that her health and that of her family has been impaired, all to her very great discomfort and annoyance; she also asserts that this condition has lessened the rental value of

her property, and has made it impossible at times to rent her apartments.

Claiming that such use of its plant by the defendant deprives her of the full enjoyment of her home, invades her property rights, and constitutes a private nuisance, plaintiff brings this action in equity to enjoin the defendant from the further maintenance of said nuisance, and to recover the damages which she asserts she has already sustained.

As a general rule, an owner is at liberty to use his property as he sees fit, without objection or interference from his neighbor, provided such use does not violate an ordinance or statute. There is, however, a limitation to this rule; one made necessary by the intricate, complex and changing life of today. The old and familiar maxim that one must so use his property as not to injure that of another (*sic utere tuo ut alienum non laedas*) is deeply imbedded in our law. An owner will not be permitted to make an unreasonable use of his premises to the material annoyance of his neighbor if the latter's enjoyment of life or property is materially lessened thereby. This principle is aptly stated by Andrews, Ch. J., in *Booth v. R., W. & O.T.R.R. Co.* (35 N.E. 592, 594, N.Y.) as follows:

> "The general rule that no one has absolute freedom in the use of his property, but is restrained by the co-existence of equal rights in his neighbor to the use of his property, so that each in exercising his right must do no act which causes injury to his neighbor, is so well understood, is so universally recognized, and stands so impregnably in the necessities of the social state, that its vindication by argument would be superfluous. The maxim which embodies it is sometimes loosely interpreted as forbidding all use by one of his own property, which annoys or disturbs his neighbor in the enjoyment of his property. The real meaning of the rule is that one may not use his own property to the injury of any legal right of another."

Such a rule is imperative, or life to-day in our congested centers would be intolerable and unbearable. If a citizen was given no protection against unjust harassment arising from the use to which the property of his neighbor was put, the comfort and value of his home could easily be destroyed by any one who chose to erect an annoyance nearby, and no one would be safe, unless he was rich enough to buy sufficient land about his home to render such disturbance impossible. When conflicting rights arise, a general rule must be worked out which, so far as possible, will preserve to each party that to which he has a just claim.

While the law will not permit a person to be driven from his home, or to be compelled to live in it in positive distress or discomfort because of the use to which other property nearby has been put, it is not every annoyance connected with business which will be enjoined. Many a loss arises from acts or conditions which do not create a ground for legal redress. *Damnum absque injuria* is a familiar maxim. Factories, stores and mercantile establishments are essential to the prosperity of the nation. They necessarily invade our cities, and interfere more or less with the peace and tranquility of the neighborhood in which they are located.

One who chooses to live in the large centers of population cannot expect the quiet of the country. Congested centers are seldom free from smoke, odors and other pollution from houses, shops and factories, and one who moves into such a region cannot hope to find the pure air of the village or outlying district. A person who prefers the advantages of community life must expect to experience some of the resulting inconveniences. Residents of industrial centers must endure without redress a certain amount of annoyance and discomfiture which is incident to life in such a locality. Such inconvenience is of minor importance compared with the general good of the community. . . .

Whether the particular use to which one puts his property constitutes a nuisance or not is generally a question of fact, and depends upon whether such use is reasonable under all the surrounding circumstances. What would distress and annoy one person would have little or no effect upon another; what would be deemed a disturbance and a torment in one locality would be unnoticed in some other place; a condition which would cause little or no vexation in a business, manufacturing or industrial district might be extremely tantalizing to those living in a restricted and beautiful residential zone; what would be unreasonable under one set of circumstances would be deemed fair and just under another. Each case is unique. No hard and fast rule can be laid down which will apply in all instances. . . .

The inconvenience, if such it be, must not be fanciful, slight or theoretical, but certain and substantial, and must interfere with the physical comfort of the ordinarily reasonable person. . . .

Applying these general rules to the facts before us, it is apparent that defendant's plant is not a nuisance *per se*, and that the court was amply justified in holding that it had not become one by reason of the manner in which it had been conducted. Any annoyance to plaintiff is due to the nature of the business which the defendant conducts, and not to any defect in the mill, machinery or apparatus. The plant is modern and up to date in every particular. It was built under a contract with the Federal government, the details of which are not important here. The plans were drawn by the Kopperas Construction Company, one of the largest and best known manufacturers of coke plants in the world, and the work was done under the supervision of the War Department. No reasonable change or improvement in the property can be made which will eliminate any of the things complained of. If coke is made, coal must be used. Gas always follows the burning of coal, and steam is occasioned by throwing cold water on red hot coals.

The cases are legion in this and other States where a defendant has been held guilty of maintaining a nuisance because of the annoyance which he has caused his neighbor by reason of noise, smoke, dust, noxious gases and disagreeable smells which have emanated from his property. But smoke and noisome odors do not always constitute a nuisance. I find none of these cases controlling here; they all differ in some particular from the facts in the case at bar.

It is true that the appellant was a resident of this locality for several years before the defendant came on the scene of action, and that, when the plaintiff built her house, the land on which these coke ovens now stand was a hickory grove. But in a growing community changes are inevitable. This region was never fitted for a residential district; for years it has been peculiarly adapted for factory sites. This was apparent when plaintiff bought her lots and when she built her house. The land is low and lies adjacent to the Buffalo river, a navigable stream connecting with Lake Erie. Seven different railroads run through this area. Freight tracks and yards can be seen in every direction. Railroads naturally follow the low levels in passing through the city. Cheap transportation is an attraction which always draws factories and industrial plants to a locality. It is common knowledge that a combination of rail and water terminal facilities will stamp a section as a site suitable for industries of the heavier type, rather than for residential purposes. In 1910 there were at least eight industrial plants, with a total assessed valuation of over a million dollars, within a radius of a mile from plaintiff's house.

With all the dirt, smoke and gas which necessarily come from factory chimneys, trains and boats, and with full knowledge that this region was especially adapted for industrial rather than residential purposes, and that factories would increase in the future, plaintiff selected this locality as the site of her future home. She voluntarily moved into this district, fully aware of the fact that the atmosphere would constantly be contaminated by dirt, gas and foul odors; and that she could not hope to find in this locality the pure air of a strictly residential zone. She evidently saw certain advantages in living in this congested center. This is not the case of an industry, with its attendant noise and dirt, invading a quiet, residential district. It is just the opposite. Here a residence is built in an area naturally adapted for industrial purposes and already dedicated to that use. Plaintiff can hardly be heard to complain at this late date that her peace and comfort have been disturbed by a situation which existed, to some extent at least, at the very time she bought her property, and which condition she must have known would grow worse rather than better as the years went by.

To-day there are twenty industrial plants within a radius of less than a mile and three-quarters from appellant's house, with more than sixty-five smokestacks rising in the air, and belching forth clouds of smoke; every day there are 148 passenger trains, and 225 freight trains, to say nothing of switch engines, passing over these various railroad tracks near to the plaintiff's property; over 10,000 boats, a large portion of which burn soft coal, pass up and down the Buffalo river every season. Across the street, and within 300 feet from plaintiff's house, is a large tank of the Iroquois Gas Company which is used for the storage of gas.

The utter abandonment of this locality for residential purposes, and its universal use as an industrial center, becomes manifest when one considers that in 1929 the assessed valuation of the twenty industrial plants above referred to aggregates over $20,000,000, and that the city in 1925 passed a zoning ordinance putting this area in the third industrial district, a zone in which stockyards, glue factories, coke ovens, steel furnaces, rolling mills and other similar enterprises were permitted to be located.

One has only to mention these facts to visualize the condition of the atmosphere in this locality. It is quite easy to imagine that many of the things of which the plaintiff complains are due to causes over which the defendant has no control. At any rate, if appellant is immune from the annoyance occasioned by the smoke and odor which must necessarily come from these various sources, it would hardly seem that she could consistently claim that her health has been impaired, and that the use and enjoyment of her home have been seriously interfered with solely because of the dirt, gas and stench which have reached her from defendant's plant.

It is very true that the law is no respecter of persons, and that the most humble citizen in the land is entitled to identically the same protection accorded to the master of the most gorgeous palace. However, the fact that the plaintiff has voluntarily chosen to live in the smoke and turmoil of this industrial zone is some evidence, at least, that any annoyance which she has suffered from the dirt, gas and odor which have emanated from defendant's plant is more imaginary and theoretical than it is real and substantial.

I think that the trial court was amply justified in refusing to interfere with the operation of the defendant's coke ovens. No consideration of public policy or private rights demands any such sacrifice of this industry.

Plaintiff is not entitled to the relief which she seeks for another reason.

Subdivision 25 of section 20 of the General City Law gives to the cities of this State authority to regulate the location of industries and to district the city for that purpose. Pursuant to such authority the common council of the city of Buffalo adopted an ordinance setting aside the particular area in which defendant's plant is situated as a zone in which coke ovens might lawfully be located.

After years of study and agitation it has been found that development in conformity with some well-considered and comprehensive plan is necessary to the welfare of any growing municipality. The larger the community the greater becomes the need of such plan. Haphazard city building is ruinous to any city. Certain areas must be given over to industry, without which the country cannot long exist. Other sections must be kept free from the intrusion of trade and the distraction of business, and be set aside for homes, where one may live in a wholesome environment. Property owners, as well as the public, have come to recognize the absolute necessity of reasonable regulations of this character in the interest of public health, safety and general welfare, as well as for the conservation of property values. Such is the purpose of our zoning laws.

After due consideration the common council of Buffalo decreed that an enterprise similar to that carried on by the defendant might properly be located at the site of this particular coke oven. It is not for the court to step in and override such decision, and condemn as a nuisance a business which is being conducted in an approved and expert manner, at the very spot where the council said that it might be located. A court of equity will not ordinarily assume to set itself above officials to whom the law commits a decision, and reverse their discretion and judgment, unless bad faith is involved. No such charge is made here. . . .

I see no good reason why the decision of the Special Term should be disturbed. I think that the judgment appealed from should be affirmed.

All concur.

Judgment affirmed, with costs.

NOTES AND QUESTIONS

1. *The nature of a nuisance action.* The late William L. Prosser, the dean of American tort scholars, metaphorically threw up his hands when he reached the topic of nuisance in his influential treatise: "There is perhaps no more impenetrable jungle in the entire law than that which surrounds the word 'nuisance.' " W. Page Keeton, ed., Prosser and Keeton on Torts § 86 (5th ed. 1984). Fortunately, for the purpose of understanding zoning and planning law, we need not fully penetrate that jungle (at least until we reach the *Lucas* case, *infra*). We offer the briefest sketch of nuisance law in these notes; the reader is cautioned that a wonderful web of intricate detail lies beneath the surface and must be mastered through study of other sources if nuisance figures prominently in any particular case or problem. The summary which follows draws on the Prosser and Keeton treatise.

Nuisances may be private or public. A private nuisance is one that affects the use or enjoyment of land, and normally is privately enforced through a tort action for damages. A public nuisance affects the public at large, need not be connected to land, and is normally enforceable by public officials, although the same conduct may give rise to a parallel private nuisance if private lands are also affected. Prosser and Keeton on Torts § 86. See *Connecticut v. Am. Elec. Power Co.*, 582 F.3d 309 (2d Cir. 2009) (standing recognized for states, municipalities, and private parties bringing federal common law public nuisance claims alleging that power companies' release of carbon dioxide contributes to global warming); Beuscher & Morrison, *Judicial Zoning Through Recent Nuisance Cases*, 1955 Wis. L. Rev. 440 (concluding that the distinction between public and private nuisance is illusory when an activity affects the property of a large number of individuals). Some, but not all, nuisance actions may support an injunction instead of, or in addition to, damages. Prosser & Keeton, § 87 at 623. Nuisance is distinguishable from trespass (often tenuously) in that the latter affects the exclusive possession of land, rather than use and enjoyment. *Id.* at 622. Private nuisance rules, which seek to adjust the relationship between adjoining land users, are of primary interest to zoning lawyers.

The plaintiff in a private nuisance action must show intentional conduct, actual interference with use and enjoyment (although the interference may not have been intended), and substantial harm (normally including provable reduction in value of the property). Most importantly, it must be shown that "[t]he interference that came about under such circumstances was of such a nature, duration or amount as to constitute unreasonable interference with the use and enjoyment of the land." *Id.* at 623. While classic examples of private nuisance involve physical interference with the plaintiff's land, the smoke and grit in the principal case, for instance, physical or mental harm to the occupants of the land may also support an action, provided that it meets the requisites of intent, substantiality and unreasonableness; in practice, this means that if the harm is of a type that would offend a person of average sensibility and is of a continuing nature, it would adversely affect the value of the land itself, and a nuisance may be found. *Id.* at § 88. The maintenance of a structure or the carrying on of an activity that offends the plaintiffs' aesthetic sense may, in fact, reduce the value of their property as well as cause mental discomfort, but most courts have refused to find a nuisance because of the difficulty of establishing generally acceptable aesthetic standards. See, e.g., *Rankin v. FPL Energy, LLC*, 266 S.W.3d 506, 512 (Tex. App. 2008) ("an emotional reaction to the sight of . . . [lawful] wind turbines" was an insufficient basis for a nuisance claim). The leading case recognizing the possibility of an aesthetic nuisance is *Parkersburg Bldrs. Material Co. v. Barrack*, 191 S.E. 368 (W. Va. 1937). See also *Burch v. NedPower Mount Storm, LLC*, 647 S.E.2d 879, 889 (W. Va. 2007) (receipt of a siting certificate from the state Public Service Commission for a wind power electric generating facility did not preclude consideration of a common law nuisance claim "[b]ecause the rights of nearby landowners are not a primary consideration in the PSC's siting determinations"); *Allison v. Smith*, 695 P.2d 791 (Colo. App. 1984) (accumulation of junk and obnoxious debris on property bordering plaintiffs' amounted to a private nuisance). For a discussion of the cases and an argument that "[j]udicial recognition of aesthetic nuisances is long overdue," see Dodson, *Rethinking Private Nuisance Law: Recognizing Aesthetic Nuisance in the New Millennium*, 10 S.C. Envtl. L.J. 1, 21 (2002). Aesthetic regulation is considered further in Chapter 9 *infra*.

Most nuisance cases involve recurrent activity rather than an isolated wrongful act, because the latter conduct is less likely to meet the substantial interference test. Recurrent activity is also usually necessary before injunctive relief can be obtained by the plaintiff. And if the harm was neither foreseeable in the first instance nor a result of ultra-hazardous activity, some continuance of the defendant's activity is necessary to establish his fault and consequent liability. Moreover, the duration or frequency of the invasion of the plaintiff's interest certainly has a bearing on the reasonableness of his conduct. For contemporary reviews of nuisance law, see Gifford, *Public Nuisance as a Mass Products Liability Tort*, 71 U. Cin. L. Rev. 741 (2003); Nagle, *Moral Nuisances*, 50 Emory L.J. 265 (2001); Halper, *Untangling the Nuisance Knot*, 26 B.C. Envtl. Aff. L. Rev. 89 (1998).

2. *Courts, markets and planners.* Ultimately, the utility of the defendant's conduct depends upon the social value the courts attach to it. In an earlier edition of his treatise, Prosser observed that

> [t]he plaintiff must be expected to endure some inconvenience rather than curtail the defendant's freedom of action, and the defendant must so use his own property that he causes no unreasonable harm to the plaintiff. The law of private nuisance is very largely a series of adjustments to limit the reciprocal rights and privileges of both. In every case the court must make a comparative evaluation of the conflicting interests according to objective legal standards, and the gravity of the harm to the plaintiff must be weighed against the utility of the defendant's conduct. [Prosser, Torts 596 (4th ed. 1971).]

If the defendant's conduct has little or no social value, or is a result of pure malice or spite, should there be liability for causing a nuisance although the harm to the plaintiff is relatively slight? Most courts answer yes.

Note that it is *judges* who are making these decisions. Could they equally well be made in the free market, without the assistance of law? Are there impediments to bargained-for solutions between neighbors (are the trespassing cows in Coase's famous theorem, discussed in Chapter 1, a nuisance)? How would rational planners and the critics of rational planning handle nuisance-type problems? Some commentators argue that parties to a nuisance suit will bargain as Coase predicts after a court judgment fixing liability, but one study found this did not occur. Farnsworth, *Do Parties to Nuisance Cases Bargain After Judgment? A Glimpse Inside the Cathedral*, 66 U. Chi. L. Rev. 373 (1999). Animosity between the parties as a result of litigation, rather than transaction costs, was the problem.

3. *Judicial zoning.* Modern society requires factories, smelters, oil refineries, chemical plants, power stations, and use of explosives for blasting. Such activities may not be nuisances even though they cause substantial discomfort or inconvenience to neighboring landholders, if they are carried on in suitable localities and the adverse impact upon neighboring landholders is avoidable only at prohibitive expense. This led to the judicially developed doctrine during the first half of the 20th century that some activities are *per se* unreasonable in certain localities. Courts came to recognize that certain localities, because of their physical character or the pattern of community development (or both) are properly and primarily devoted to certain activities and that the introduction of incompatible activities must be deemed unreasonable. In short, to the extent that adjudication on a case-by-case basis permits, courts have engaged in "judicial zoning." See Beuscher & Morrison, *Judicial Zoning Through Recent Nuisance Cases*, 1955 Wis. L. Rev. 440.

Once most cities adopted comprehensive zoning ordinances and established administrative agencies to enforce them, courts "have shown an inclination to leave the problem of the appropriate location of certain types of activities, as distinguished from the way in which they are carried on, to the administrative agencies." *South Camden Citizens in Action v. New Jersey Dep't of Environmental Protection*, 254 F. Supp. 2d 486, 506–07 (D.N.J. 2003) (quoting Comment f of the Restatement (Second) of Torts § 821B). In dismissing a claim of public nuisance against the operator of a cement grinding facility, the *South Camden* court noted that the cement grinding facility was located in an area zoned for industrial uses and had received permits to discharge gases into the air from the New Jersey Department of Environmental Protection. The court distinguished a New Jersey state court case, *James v. Arms Tech., Inc.*, 820 A.2d 27, 49–52 (N.J. App. 2003) (handgun manufacturers may be liable for a public nuisance by fostering an illegal secondary gun market even though their conduct is legal under existing law because their activities are not closely regulated).

4. *The limits of nuisance.* Nuisance theory is of limited use in the areas in which it could be most valuable — slum and mixed fringe areas in which the patterns of land use are less than desirable and do not provide an acceptable measure against which an intruding and offensive use may be judged. Moreover, even where the nuisance *per se* approach allows a court to concentrate on the character of the neighborhood involved, the result of a litigated case is difficult to predict. In part, this is because there is no universally accepted standard of social value or suitability; hence different courts will necessarily vary in their appraisal of the reasonableness of particular land uses in particular localities. And in part, the difficulty of prediction results from uncertainty as to the availability of injunctive relief. This uncertainty exists both in cases where the plaintiff seeks to enjoin a proposed new land use on the ground that it will be a nuisance and in cases where the court finds that an established land use is a nuisance.

5. *Nuisance law and code enforcement.* A common technique associated with code enforcement is the demolition of derelict buildings. Statutes and ordinances authorizing local governments to take such action typically couch the authorization in public nuisance language. For example, the Dallas, Texas Minimum Urban Rehabilitation Standards Code defines serious non-compliance with the Code that "could reasonably cause injury, damage, harm, or inconvenience to a considerable portion of the community in the use and enjoyment of property" as an "urban nuisance." Dallas, Tex., Code, ch. 27, art. I, §§ 27-3(23), 27-11. Failure of the owner to make necessary repairs within a stipulated time following a hearing and a resultant "urban nuisance" designation can lead to buildings being placed in receivership or demolished by the city. Dallas, Tex., Code, ch. 27, art. II, § 27-8. The "urban nuisance" technique can be controversial. See, e.g., *James v. City of Dallas*, 254 F.3d 551 (5th Cir. 2001) (certification of due process class action against city and HUD for demolishing single family homes in predominantly minority neighborhood affirmed); *Freeman v. City of Dallas*, 242 F.3d 642, 644–45 (5th Cir. 2001) (city is not required to obtain a warrant before seizing property declared a nuisance through established police power procedures); *Wheeler v. New Times, Inc.*, 49 S.W.3d 471, 476 (Tex. App. 2001) (newspaper article criticizing Dallas' use of the "urban nuisance" technique did not defame a landlord who benefitted from allegedly unequal treatment of landowners in West Dallas).

6. *Injunctive relief.* As was the case in *Bove*, the plaintiff in a nuisance case usually seeks injunctive relief. As Professor Robert Ellickson has observed,

> [c]ommentators have traditionally offered four primary rationales for injunctions. First, since market values do not reflect the subjective losses a plaintiff suffers and since those losses are hard to monetize by any other means, the remedy of damages is said to be inadequate. . . . A second justification for . . . [the injunctive remedy] is the moral assertion that a landowner should not be able in effect to exercise a private power of eminent domain and force others to exchange basic property rights for damages. . . . The third rationale used for injunctions is that damages are inadequate when the defendant is judgment-proof.
>
> . . . A fourth justification for . . . injunctions is that administrative factors can make granting an injunction more efficient than awarding damages. [Ellickson, *Alternatives to Zoning: Covenants, Nuisance Rules, and Fines as Land Use Controls*, 40 U. Chi. L. Rev. 681, 739–42 (1973).]

Most courts will not enjoin a proposed land use in advance of its establishment unless it can be shown that it will constitute a nuisance per se at the locus in quo. If the plaintiff waits to sue until an offensive land use is established nearby, however, the court may deny injunctive relief on the basis of estoppel. More important, even if the court determines that the defendant is causing a nuisance, most courts will try to "balance the hardship," and will refuse to grant an injunction if there is a great disparity between the economic consequences of the nuisance and the injunction — i.e., if the plaintiff's economic loss is small in comparison to the economic loss that the injunction would visit upon the defendant and upon the community at large. See, e.g., *City of Harrisonville v. W.S. Dickey Clay Mfg. Co.*, 289 U.S. 334 (1933); *Koseris v. J.R. Simplot Co.*, 352 P.2d 235 (Idaho 1960) (over 1,000 employees); *Dundalk Holding Co. v. Easter*, 137 A.2d 667 (Md. 1958); *Antonik v. Chamberlain*, 78 N.E.2d 752 (Ohio Ct. App. 1947) ("life and death of a legitimate and necessary business"); *Storey v. Central Hide & Rendering Co.*, 226 S.W.2d 615 (Tex. 1950) (only plant in county).

7. *Priority in time.* Some courts consider priority in time as an important factor in nuisance cases and may hold against a plaintiff who "came to a nuisance." Is there an economic rationale for this doctrine? Did the plaintiff in the *Bove* case "come" to the nuisance? If not, why did she lose?

The Prosser and Keeton text argues that to award an injunction or damages to a plaintiff who came to a nuisance would confer "a windfall capital gain to which he is not entitled." Prosser & Keeton on Torts § 88B at 635 (5th ed. 1984). The reason is that the plaintiff would have purchased the property at a depressed value and then would have increased its value by enjoining the nuisance. But the authors conclude that:

> The prevailing rule is that in the absence of a prescriptive right, the defendant cannot condemn the surrounding premises to endure his operation, and that the purchaser is entitled to a reasonable use and enjoyment of his land to the same extent as any other owner, so long as he buys in good faith and not for the sole purpose of a vexatious lawsuit. [*Id.*]

For an analysis of this problem that "focuses on the efficiency of market activities as they unfold through time, rather than on static allocative effects," see Cordato, *Time Passage and the Economics of Coming to the Nuisance: Reassessing the Coasean Perspective*, 20 Campbell L. Rev. 273 (1998).

8. *The Boomer case and injunctive relief.* From an early date, some American courts have held that whenever the damage resulting from a nuisance is substantial, the plaintiff is entitled to injunctive relief as a matter of right. See, e.g., *Hulbert v. California Portland Cement Co.*, 118 P. 928 (Cal. 1911); *Sullivan v. Jones*, 57 A. 1065 (Pa. 1904). When the *Bove* case was decided, the New York courts adhered to the rule that injunctive relief is a matter of right once the court determines that the defendant is maintaining a nuisance. See, e.g., *Whalen v. Union Bag & Paper Co.*, 101 N.E. 805 (N.Y. 1913). Do you think the court would have been more likely to find that Donner-Hanna was maintaining a nuisance in the *Bove* case if New York had adopted the balancing approach to the question whether injunctive relief should be granted?

The New York Court of Appeals abandoned the rule that injunctive relief is a matter of right in an important case, *Boomer v. Atlantic Cement Co.*, 257 N.E.2d 870 (N.Y. 1970), where the loss to the defendant cement company if the operation of its cement plant were enjoined would apparently have been in excess of $45,000,000, while the amount required to compensate all the plaintiffs for their permanent loss (if the injunction were refused) would clearly be less than $1,000,000. The New York court expressly adopted the rule that a court should exercise its equitable discretion to refuse injunctive relief when there is a gross disparity between the economic consequences of the nuisance and the injunction. In addition, the court said,

> Effective control of air pollution is a problem presently far from solution even with the full public and financial powers of government. In large measure adequate technical procedures are yet to be developed and some that appear possible may be economically impracticable.
>
> It seems apparent that amelioration of air pollution will depend on technical research in great depth; on a carefully balanced consideration of the economic impact of close regulation; and of the actual effect on public health. It is likely to require massive public expenditure and to demand more than any local community can accomplish and to depend on regional and interstate controls.
>
> A court should not try to do this on its own as a by-product of private litigation, and it seems manifest that the judicial establishment is neither equipped in the limited nature of any judgment it can pronounce nor prepared to lay down and implement an effective policy for the elimination of air pollution. This is an area beyond the circumference of one private lawsuit. It is a direct responsibility for government and it should not thus be undertaken as an incident to solving a dispute between property owners and a single cement plant — one of many — in the Hudson River valley. [*Id.* at 871.]

The New York court ordered the trial court to "grant an injunction which shall be vacated upon payment by defendant of such amounts of permanent damage to the respective plaintiffs as shall for this purpose be determined by the court." One judge dissented, contending that the award of permanent damages instead of an injunction would amount to an inverse condemnation that "may not be invoked by a private person or corporation for private gain or advantage" and should "only be permitted when the public is primarily served in the taking or impairment of property," because the New York Constitution forbids the taking of private property when it is not to be put to a public use.

9. *What happened in Boomer.* After *Boomer* was remanded for further proceedings, two of the plaintiffs (including Boomer) settled with the defendant cement company; the trial court then undertook to determine the permanent damages to be awarded to the remaining plaintiff, Kinley, who owned a 238-acre dairy farm. The court received testimony that the defendant had converted the primary fuel of its plant from coal to oil, had added a spray system to the apparatus used to convey raw material from the quarry to the plant, and had replaced the multiclone dust collectors on the clinker cooler with a fiberglass bag type collector, all at a total cost of $1,600,000. The court then fixed Kinley's permanent damages at $140,000 after finding that the value of his farm without the nuisance was $265,000 and that its value with the nuisance would be only $125,000. 340 N.Y.S.2d 97 (Sup. Ct. 1972).

The appellate division affirmed the trial court's judgment. *Kinley v. Atlantic Cement Co.*, 349 N.Y.S.2d 199 (App. Div. 1973). A majority of the panel agreed that the proper measure of permanent damages in a nuisance case is "the difference between the market value of the property before and after the nuisance." One judge, in a concurring opinion, took a different view. He asserted that, although the before and after measure of damages is proper in eminent domain cases, it is not necessarily proper in private nuisance cases where

> it would be unrealistic to assume that the defendant could acquire a servitude of the present nature simply by paying the price which a willing seller could accept. . . . While the public interest may dictate that the defendant be afforded an opportunity to

> acquire a servitude, there is no apparent reason to assume that the purchase is being made either by or on behalf of the public and, accordingly, the value of the servitude should reflect the private interest of the parties to this lawsuit [*Id.* at 202.]

The concurring opinion then concluded that defendants in such cases should be required to pay the holdup price required to persuade an unwilling landowner to sell an "easement to pollute." Do you think the judge who wrote the concurring opinion would have taken a different view if the air pollution produced by the defendant's cement plant had been considered a public nuisance? Was the concurring judge applying the Coase Theorem?

10. *Change in circumstances post-judgment.* Suppose that the defendant paid Kinley the permanent damages of $140,000 and that the defendant were later able to reduce or eliminate the air pollution found to constitute a nuisance, or that a state or federal air pollution control agency later closed down or substantially curtailed the operation of the defendant's cement plant. Would the defendant then be entitled to restitution of some part of the permanent damages it paid to Kinley? Or, do the facts that the law generally seeks finality and that Tort law in particular has accepted the idea that the risk of erroneous estimation should be borne by the wrongdoer argue against restitution? Could the problem of determining the amount of restitution be avoided by awarding Kinley, instead of permanent damages, a right to recover on a periodic basis all damages up to the time of suit? The latter would result, in substance, in the defendant being required to pay a periodic "rent" for its "easement to pollute."

11. *Compensated injunctions.* Another possible alternative in cases like *Boomer* would be to enjoin the nuisance and require the plaintiff to compensate the defendant for its financial loss by paying money damages. The leading case adopting this position is *Spur Industries, Inc. v. Del E. Webb Development Co.*, 494 P.2d 700, 707–708 (Ariz. 1972). The court in *Spur Industries* acknowledged the general rule that in a "coming to the nuisance" case, a new residential landowner was not entitled to relief "if he knowingly came into a neighborhood reserved for industrial or agricultural endeavors and [was] damaged thereby." But the unusual circumstances of a "new city . . . spring[ing] up, full blown, alongside [an agricultural] feeding operation" led the court to order a lawful feed lot operation to move in order to abate the public harm that residents of the new city were suffering, and to order the developer to indemnify the feedlot operator for its costs in moving or ceasing operation. For an application of the Coase Theorem that can lead to the same result, see Calabresi & Melamed, *Property Rules, Liability Rules, and Inalienability: One View of the Cathedral*, 85 Harv. L. Rev. 1089 (1972) (adding a fourth alternative, injunction coupled with damage award to compensate the defendant for losses occasioned by the injunction, to the three traditional results of nuisance actions, finding no nuisance, finding nuisance and granting an injunction, or finding nuisance and awarding only damages).

12. *Effect of zoning.* In *Bove*, the zoning ordinance allowed the defendant's use. What effect did the court give to the ordinance? The majority rule is that a zoning ordinance cannot legalize the creation of a nuisance, although most courts mean by this that the ordinance cannot preclude a court from holding a use a *nuisance per accidens* (a nuisance in fact). See, e.g., *Armory Park Neighborhood Ass'n v. Episcopal Community Serv.*, 712 P.2d 914 (Ariz. 1985). Is this correct? Some courts will give some effect to the uses allowed by a zoning ordinance in nuisance actions. *Harrison v. Indiana Auto Shredders Co.*, 528 F.2d 1107 (7th Cir. 1976). Why should land use regulations adopted by a municipality be allowed to affect a trial court judgment in a nuisance case? Is the question really whether courts or local legislatures are better able to deal with the market failure aspects of nuisance law?

13. *An economic model.* We might now try to develop an economic model of nuisance-based land use conflicts along the following lines: Land use conflicts adjudicated in a nuisance setting present a classic case of legal intervention to modify externalities. Let us assume a developing residential area; a factory now seeks to locate in that area. If that location is the best location possible for that industry, then we can consider the location optimal if the gains to society from that location are greater than the costs that location imposes on existing uses. Unfortunately, the private market has no way to force the intruding use to compensate those already in the neighborhood for negative externalities which its location imposes.

Nuisance law provides a method for imposing a duty to compensate on the intruding use. It does this either by awarding damages, or by granting equitable relief that will force the intruder to make improvements minimizing the effect on surrounding properties. If the harm cannot be minimized through improvements, the intruder will be compelled to relocate. The nuisance remedy may not always work well, however: (1) It ignores the fact that a land use conflict is two-sided, and arises as much from the fact that existing uses may be harm-sensitive as from the fact that the intruder may be harm-productive; (2) the judicial context of the nuisance lawsuit is not conducive to a full consideration of aggregate social and economic costs and benefits; (3) to assume that existing uses are entitled to preempt any given spatial location improperly ratifies private land use decisions; (4) relocation of the existing use may be less costly and impose less economic dislocation than relocation of the intruding use; and (5) the intruder may bring positive as well as negative externalities. Thus a new factory may attract other related and economically desirable uses to the area. In view of these considerations, what alternative decision model would you construct for nuisance litigation? See D. Mandelker, The Zoning Dilemma, ch. 2 (1971); Note, *An Economic Analysis of Land Use Conflicts*, 21 Stan. L. Rev. 293 (1969).

B. THE TAKINGS ISSUE

Among the inherent powers of sovereignty recognized since ancient common law times is the power of "eminent domain," the power to take private property for public use, a power possessed by federal and state governments. In addition, the states possess a general power to regulate, called "the police power," to protect "the public health, safety, morals, or general welfare," on which the power to regulate land use and development is based. The federal government possesses no general police power, but through the grant of enumerated powers in U.S. Const. Art. I, § 8, it also possesses a large power to regulate in ways that affect land use and development. Exercise of the powers delegated to the federal government is limited by the Fifth Amendment: "No person shall be deprived of life, liberty, or property, without due process of law; nor shall private property be taken for public use without just compensation." The exercise of the powers reserved to the states is limited by state constitutional provisions and by the Fourteenth Amendment to the United States Constitution, which provides, *inter alia*, "No state shall . . . deprive any person of life, liberty, or property, without due process of law; nor deny to any person within its jurisdiction the equal protection of the laws."

These constitutional provisions require the federal government to pay "just compensation" when private property is taken for public use. The constitutions of all but three states expressly prohibit the taking of private property for public use without compensation, and in these three states, the constitutions have been judicially interpreted to require compensation. Moreover, the United States Supreme Court has held that the Due Process Clause of the Fourteenth Amendment makes the Compensation Clause of the Fifth Amendment applicable to the states.

Chicago, B. & Q.R.R. v. Chicago, 166 U.S. 226 (1897).

[1.] Eminent Domain

Governments traditionally use the eminent domain power to acquire private property on which they build highways, bridges and public buildings. For these activities, the "public use" part of the Fifth Amendment limitation does not cause any interpretative problems. With the advent of urban renewal legislation that authorized local governments to acquire "blighted" or "slum" property by eminent domain, clear it, and sell it at a discount to private developers carrying out redevelopment plans, the constitutional issues became more complex. In *Berman v. Parker*, 348 U.S. 26 (1954), the Supreme Court upheld the use of eminent domain to effect redevelopment in the District of Columbia. The case involved the then-new federal urban renewal program, through which municipalities received federal assistance to acquire property in blighted areas, clear the land and make it ready for redevelopment by installing new infrastructure (streets, water and sewer lines, etc.) and resell the land at below-market prices to private developers who agree to redevelop the property in accordance with locally-adopted urban renewal plans. The program was challenged on two main grounds; 1) the particular parcel being taken was not itself blighted, and 2) the land taken ultimately was going to be transferred to another private entity. In upholding the use of eminent domain, the Court equated the constitutional requirement of "public use" with legislative determinations of "public purpose." The fact that property acquired by eminent domain might be transferred to other private persons did not automatically mean the taking was not for a "public use." "The definition [of public use] is essentially the product of legislative determinations addressed to the purposes of government. . . . [S]ubject to specific constitutional limitations, when the legislature has spoken, the public interest has been declared in terms well-nigh conclusive." *Id.* at 31–32. An area-wide definition of blight, rather than a parcel-by-parcel approach, was within the legislative prerogative. "Property may . . . be taken for this redevelopment which, standing by itself, is innocuous and unoffending. . . . [C]ommunity redevelopment programs need not, by force of the Constitution, be on a piecemeal basis — lot by lot, building by building." *Id.* at 35.

Thirty years later, the Court returned to the "public use" question, upholding a Hawaii statute authorizing the Hawaii Housing Authority to acquire title from residential lessors and convey it to residential lessees in order to reduce the concentration of land ownership in Hawaii. *Hawaii Housing Auth. v. Midkiff*, 467 U.S. 229 (1984). The statute in question was designed to open up a restricted residential land market in which most of the land devoted to residential uses in Hawaii was held by a small number of large land owners, who leased the land under 99-year ground leases. After Hawaii achieved statehood in 1950, pressures built in the land market. Because of the high demand, land owners began refusing to renew expiring ground leases, or imposing significant increases in ground rental as a condition for renewal. In response, the Hawaii legislature authorized the use of eminent domain to compel transfer of the land owners' reversionary interests to residential renters who wished to acquire fee simple title to the land on which their houses stood. Justice O'Connor, writing for the majority, quoted *Berman* extensively and concluded that "where the exercise of the eminent domain power is rationally related to a conceivable public purpose, the Court has never held a compensated taking to be proscribed by the Public Use Clause. . . . [I]t is only the taking's purpose, and not its mechanics, that must pass scrutiny under the Public Use Clause." *Id.* at 244.

Twenty-three years after *Midkiff*, the Court again visited the "public use" question in a case that ignited a firestorm of controversy, one of three takings cases decided in 2005.

KELO v. CITY OF NEW LONDON

545 U.S. 469 (2005)

JUSTICE STEVENS delivered the opinion of the Court.

In 2000, the city of New London approved a development plan that, in the words of the Supreme Court of Connecticut, was "projected to create in excess of 1,000 jobs, to increase tax and other revenues, and to revitalize an economically distressed city, including its downtown and waterfront areas." 268 Conn. 1, 5, 843 A.2d 500, 507 (2004). [The development plan also was approved by several state agencies. — Eds.] In assembling the land needed for this project, the city's development agent has purchased property from willing sellers and proposes to use the power of eminent domain to acquire the remainder of the property from unwilling owners in exchange for just compensation. [Owners unwilling to sell, including several long-time residents, sued to block the use of eminent domain to acquire their property. From an adverse decision by the Supreme Court of Connecticut, the homeowners appealed to the U.S. Supreme Court. — Eds.] The question presented is whether the city's proposed disposition of this property qualifies as a "public use" within the meaning of the Takings Clause of the Fifth Amendment to the Constitution.

III

Two polar propositions are perfectly clear. On the one hand, it has long been accepted that the sovereign may not take the property of *A* for the sole purpose of transferring it to another private party *B*, even though *A* is paid just compensation. On the other hand, it is equally clear that a State may transfer property from one private party to another if future "use by the public" is the purpose of the taking; the condemnation of land for a railroad with common-carrier duties is a familiar example. Neither of these propositions, however, determines the disposition of this case.

As for the first proposition, the City would no doubt be forbidden from taking petitioners' land for the purpose of conferring a private benefit on a particular private party. . . . Nor would the City be allowed to take property under the mere pretext of a public purpose, when its actual purpose was to bestow a private benefit. The takings before us, however, would be executed pursuant to a "carefully considered" development plan. 268 Conn., at 54, 843 A. 2d, at 536. The trial judge and all the members of the Supreme Court of Connecticut agreed that there was no evidence of an illegitimate purpose in this case. Therefore, as was true of the statute challenged in *Midkiff*, the City's development plan was not adopted "to benefit a particular class of identifiable individuals."

On the other hand, this is not a case in which the City is planning to open the condemned land — at least not in its entirety — to use by the general public. Nor will the private lessees of the land in any sense be required to operate like common carriers, making their services available to all comers. But although such a projected use would be sufficient to satisfy the public use requirement, this "Court long ago rejected any literal requirement that condemned property be put into use for the general public." [*Midkiff*, 467 U.S. at 244.] Indeed, while many state courts in the mid-19th century endorsed "use by the public" as the proper definition of public use, that narrow view steadily eroded over time. Not only was the "use by the public" test difficult to administer (*e.g.*, what proportion of the public need have access to the property? at what price?), but it proved to be impractical given the diverse and always evolving needs of society. Accordingly, when this Court began applying the Fifth Amendment to the States at the close of the 19th century, it embraced the broader and more natural interpretation of public use as "public purpose." . . . Thus, in a case upholding a mining company's use of an aerial bucket line to transport ore over property it did not own, Justice Holmes' opinion for the Court stressed "the inadequacy of use by the general public as a universal test." *Strickley v. Highland Boy Gold Mining Co.*, 200 U.S. 527, 531 (1906). We have repeatedly and consistently rejected that narrow test ever since.

The disposition of this case therefore turns on the question whether the City's development plan serves a "public purpose." Without exception, our cases have defined that concept broadly, reflecting our longstanding policy of deference to legislative judgments in this field. . . . [Justice Stevens summarized modern precedents, including *Berman* and *Hawaii Housing*. — Eds.]

Viewed as a whole, our jurisprudence has recognized that the needs of society have varied between different parts of the Nation, just as they have evolved over time in response to changed circumstances. Our earliest cases in particular embodied a strong theme of federalism, emphasizing the "great respect" that we owe to state legislatures and state courts in discerning local public needs. *See Hairston v. Danville & Western R. Co.*, 208 U.S. 598, 606–607 (1908) (noting that these needs were likely to vary depending on a State's "resources, the capacity of the soil, the relative importance of industries to the general public welfare, and the long-established methods and habits of the people"). For more than a century, our public use jurisprudence has wisely eschewed rigid formulas and intrusive scrutiny in favor of affording legislatures broad latitude in determining what public needs justify the use of the takings power.

IV

Those who govern the City were not confronted with the need to remove blight in the Fort Trumbull area, but their determination that the area was sufficiently distressed to justify a program of economic rejuvenation is entitled to our deference. The City has carefully formulated an economic development plan that it believes will provide appreciable benefits to the community, including — but by no means limited to — new jobs and increased tax revenue. As with other exercises in urban planning and development, the City is endeavoring to coordinate a variety of commercial, residential, and recreational uses of land, with the hope that they will form a whole greater than the sum of its parts. To effectuate this plan, the City has invoked a state statute that specifically authorizes the use of eminent domain to promote economic development. Given the comprehensive character of the plan, the thorough deliberation that preceded its adoption, and the limited scope of our review, it is appropriate for us, as it was in *Berman*, to resolve the challenges of the individual owners, not on a piecemeal basis, but rather in light of the entire plan. Because that plan unquestionably serves a public purpose, the takings challenged here satisfy the public use requirement of the Fifth Amendment.

To avoid this result, petitioners urge us to adopt a new bright-line rule that economic development does not qualify as a public use. Putting aside the unpersuasive suggestion that the City's plan will provide only purely economic benefits, neither precedent nor logic supports petitioners' proposal. Promoting economic development is a traditional and long accepted function of government. There is, moreover, no principled way of distinguishing economic development from the other public purposes that we have recognized. In our cases upholding takings that facilitated agriculture and mining, for example, we emphasized the importance of those industries to the welfare of the States in question, . . . ; in *Berman*, we endorsed the purpose of transforming a blighted area into a "well-balanced" community through redevelopment, 348 U.S., at 33;[13] in *Midkiff*, we upheld the interest in breaking up a land oligopoly that "created artificial deterrents to the normal functioning of the State's residential land market," 467 U.S., at 242. . . . It would be incongruous to hold that the City's interest in the economic benefits to be derived from the development of the Fort Trumbull area has less of a public character than any of those other interests. Clearly, there is no basis for exempting economic development from our traditionally broad understanding of public purpose.

Petitioners contend that using eminent domain for economic development impermissibly blurs the boundary between public and private takings. Again, our cases foreclose this objection. Quite simply, the government's pursuit of a public purpose will often benefit individual private parties. For example, in *Midkiff*, the forced transfer of property conferred a direct and significant benefit on those lessees who were previously unable to purchase their homes. . . . The owner of the department store in *Berman* objected to "taking from one businessman for the benefit of another businessman," 348 U.S., at 33, referring to the fact that under the redevelopment plan land would be leased or sold to private developers for redevelopment. Our rejection of that contention has particular relevance to the instant case: "The public end may be as well or better served through an agency of private enterprise than through a department of government — or so the Congress might conclude. We cannot say that public ownership is the sole method of promoting the public purposes of community redevelopment projects." *Id.*, at 34.

It is further argued that without a bright-line rule nothing would stop a city from transferring citizen *A*'s property to citizen *B* for the sole reason that citizen *B* will put the property to a more productive use and thus pay more taxes. Such a one-to-one transfer of property, executed outside the confines of an integrated development plan, is not presented in this case. While such an unusual exercise of government power would certainly raise a suspicion that a private purpose was afoot, the hypothetical cases posited by petitioners can be confronted if and when they arise. They do not warrant the crafting of an artificial restriction on the concept of public use.

Alternatively, petitioners maintain that for takings of this kind we should require a "reasonable certainty" that the expected public benefits will actually accrue. Such a rule, however, would represent an even greater departure from our precedent. "When the legislature's purpose is legitimate and its means are not irrational, our cases make clear that

---

[13] It is a misreading of *Berman* to suggest that the only public use upheld in that case was the initial removal of blight. *See* Reply Brief for Petitioners 8. The public use described in *Berman* extended beyond that to encompass the purpose of developing that area to create conditions that would prevent a reversion to blight in the future. *See* 348 U.S., at 34–35 ("It was not enough, [the experts] believed, to remove existing buildings that were insanitary or unsightly. It was important to redesign the whole area so as to eliminate the conditions that cause slums . . . . The entire area needed redesigning so that a balanced, integrated plan could be developed for the region, including not only new homes, but also schools, churches, parks, streets, and shopping centers. In this way it was hoped that the cycle of decay of the area could be controlled and the birth of future slums prevented"). Had the public use in *Berman* been defined more narrowly, it would have been difficult to justify the taking of the plaintiff's nonblighted department store.

empirical debates over the wisdom of takings — no less than debates over the wisdom of other kinds of socioeconomic legislation — are not to be carried out in the federal courts." *Midkiff*, 467 U.S., at 242. Indeed, earlier this Term we explained why similar practical concerns (among others) undermined the use of the "substantially advances" formula in our regulatory takings doctrine. *See Lingle v. Chevron U.S.A. Inc.*, 544 U.S. 528, 544 (2005) (noting that this formula "would empower — and might often require — courts to substitute their predictive judgments for those of elected legislatures and expert agencies"). The disadvantages of a heightened form of review are especially pronounced in this type of case. Orderly implementation of a comprehensive redevelopment plan obviously requires that the legal rights of all interested parties be established before new construction can be commenced. A constitutional rule that required postponement of the judicial approval of every condemnation until the likelihood of success of the plan had been assured would unquestionably impose a significant impediment to the successful consummation of many such plans.

Just as we decline to second-guess the City's considered judgments about the efficacy of its development plan, we also decline to second-guess the City's determinations as to what lands it needs to acquire in order to effectuate the project. "It is not for the courts to oversee the choice of the boundary line nor to sit in review on the size of a particular project area. Once the question of the public purpose has been decided, the amount and character of land to be taken for the project and the need for a particular tract to complete the integrated plan rests in the discretion of the legislative branch." *Berman*, 348 U.S., at 35–36.

In affirming the City's authority to take petitioners' properties, we do not minimize the hardship that condemnations may entail, notwithstanding the payment of just compensation. We emphasize that nothing in our opinion precludes any State from placing further restrictions on its exercise of the takings power. Indeed, many States already impose "public use" requirements that are stricter than the federal baseline. Some of these requirements have been established as a matter of state constitutional law, while others are expressed in state eminent domain statutes that carefully limit the grounds upon which takings may be exercised. As the submissions of the parties and their *amici* make clear, the necessity and wisdom of using eminent domain to promote economic development are certainly matters of legitimate public debate. This Court's authority, however, extends only to determining whether the City's proposed condemnations are for a "public use" within the meaning of the Fifth Amendment to the Federal Constitution. Because over a century of our case law interpreting that provision dictates an affirmative answer to that question, we may not grant petitioners the relief that they seek.

The judgment of the Supreme Court of Connecticut is affirmed.

It is so ordered.

Justice Kennedy, concurring.

[Justice Kennedy's concurring opinion pointed out that "[t]here may be private transfers in which the risk of undetected impermissible favoritism of private parties is so acute that a presumption (rebuttable or otherwise) of invalidity is warranted," but this was not such a case. — Eds.]

Justice O'Connor, with whom The Chief Justice, Justice Scalia, and Justice Thomas join, dissenting.

[Justice O'Connor, the author of the *Midkiff* opinion, filed a strong dissent for the four-person minority in which she asserted that the majority had "wash[ed] out any distinction between private and public use of property." She distinguished *Berman* and *Midkiff* because in both, "the extraordinary, precondemnation use of the targeted property inflicted affirmative harm on society," whereas no one claimed that the "well maintained homes [of the petitioners were] the source of any social harm." She dismissed Justice Stevens' claim that the Court "does not sanction the bare transfer from A to B for B's benefit," arguing that "private benefit and incidental public benefit are, by definition, merged and mutually reinforcing" in economic development projects. As a result, "[t]he specter of condemnation hands over all property. Nothing is to prevent the State from replacing any Motel 6 with a Ritz-Carlton, any home with a shopping mall, or any farm with a factory." — Eds.]

[Justice Thomas' dissent is omitted. — Eds.]

NOTES AND QUESTIONS

1. *Economic development as a public purpose.* By its very nature, economic development contemplates activity by the private sector. How then can economic development justify the use of eminent domain? Why not adopt a bright line standard that economic development alone is not sufficient to meet the Fifth Amendment standard? What was it about the New London approach that persuaded the Court majority that the constitutional standard was met — the fact that it was based on a legislatively-approved development plan? That use of eminent domain in implementing such a plan was specifically authorized by a state statute? That the state had approved the plan and was actively participating in the redevelopment effort? That the plan, if successful, would generate substantial additional city tax revenues as well as more than 1000 new jobs? Or was it simply that the Court majority believed that it should not second guess the city's legislative leaders?

2. *Berman and Midkiff as precedent.* Both Justice Stevens and Justice O'Connor drew heavily on *Berman* and *Midkiff* in their respective opinions. What lessons did each Justice draw from those cases? Which Justice was more persuasive? Condemnation for redevelopment often is necessary to deal with holdouts. See the classic story on private redevelopment in New York, Hellman, *How They Assembled the Most Expensive Block in New York's History*, New York Magazine, Feb. 25, 1974, at 31. For an argument that insufficient attention has been paid to the facts and the historical context of *Berman*, see Lavine, *Urban Renewal and the Story of* Berman v. Parker, 42 Urb. Law. 423 (2010). The author maintains that "the Supreme Court's extreme deference allowed urban renewal projects to go forward across the country with an astonishing lack of attention to the welfare of the people that the programs were supposed to benefit." *Id.* at 425.

3. *An extraordinary public response.* The *Kelo* decision triggered considerable controversy. In a review of a book examining the *Kelo* decision, Eminent Domain Use and Abuse: *Kelo* in Context, (D. Merriam & M. Massaron, eds. 2006), Henry Underhill, Executive Director and General Counsel, International Municipal Lawyers Association, commented that "[r]eaction to [the] *Kelo* case has been enormous, swift, and seismic from the halls of the U.S. Congress to virtually every state legislative body in the nation." ABA State & Local Govt. Book Announcements, www.abanet.org/abastore/productpage/5330090. See also Sandefur, *The "Backlash" So Far: Will Americans Get Meaningful Eminent Domain Reform?*, 2006 Mich. St. L. Rev. 709 (reviewing the public and legislative responses to *Kelo*); Kanner, *Kelo v. New London: Bad Law, Bad Policy, and Bad Judgment*, 38 Urb. Law. 201 (2006); Jacobs, *Social Conflict over Property Rights*, Land Lines (Lincoln Inst. of Land Policy, 2007), at 14.

President Bush issued an Executive Order "limiting the taking of private property by the Federal Government to situations in which the taking is . . . for the purpose of benefiting the general public and not merely for the purpose of advancing the economic interests of private parties . . . ." President George W. Bush, Executive Order: Protecting the Property Rights of the American People, 71 Fed. Reg. 36973 (2006).

Why should a case that arguably applied over 100 years of Supreme Court precedent trigger such a response? Commentators suggest two basic reasons: 1) the fact that the properties being taken by eminent domain for economic development purposes were private homes occupied by elderly persons, apparently the first time the Supreme Court had confronted that factual context, Echeverria, *Lingle, Etc.: The U.S. Supreme Court's 2005 Takings Trilogy*, 35 E.L.R. 10577, 10586 (2005), and 2) the Court's failure "to address directly citizens' expectations about the extent to which the Constitution should provide special or absolute protection for property rights" in favor of a "focus on precedent." Baron, *Winding Toward the Heart of the Takings Muddle: Kelo, Lingle, and Public Discourse About Private Property*, 34 Ford. Urb. L.J. 613, 621 (2007).

Lavine, *supra*, argues that *Kelo*, similar to *Berman*, "contains very little policy guidance." Concurring Justice Kennedy suggests the importance of a "carefully developed plan," but he "does not explain what policies economic development plans should advance or how those plans should assure that their goals are fulfilled. Redevelopment under *Berman v. Parker* proceeded under the aegis of a redevelopment plan, yet it failed in many ways. A similar legacy has, and will likely continue, to follow *Kelo*." 42 Urb. Law. at 474–475 (noting the controversy surrounding the Atlantic Yards redevelopment project in Brooklyn, discussed in Lavine & Oder, *Urban Redevelopment Policy, Judicial Deference to Unaccountable Agencies, and Reality in Brooklyn's Atlantic Yards Project*, 42 Urb. Law. 287 (2010)). For an argument that the *Kelo* decision really is an example of judicial restraint, see Merrill, *The Kelo Decision: Investigating Takings of Homes and Other Private Property: Hearing Before the Senate Committee on the Judiciary*, 109th Cong. 15 (2005); *accord*, Echeverria, *From a "Darkling Plain" to What?: The Regulatory Takings Issue in U.S. Law and Policy*, 30 Vermont L. Rev. 969, 979 (2006). See also Christopher Serkin & Nelson Tebbe, *Condemning Religion: RLUIPA and the Politics of Eminent Domain*, 85 Notre Dame L. Rev. 1 (2009) (arguing that the Religious Land Use and Institutionalized Persons Act (RLUIPA), discussed *infra*, should not be viewed as giving religious institutions any extraordinary ability to resist condemnation),

In a comprehensive analysis, Professor George Lefcoe groups economic development projects likely to seek the use of eminent domain into three types: (1) "civic enhancement projects" that "generate broad public benefits through a transformation in the appearance and utility of the reused land"; (2) projects that provide public infrastructure to achieve planning goals, such as higher density "smart growth"; and (3) projects whose primary goal is "tax enhancing," such as ones designed to capture additional sales tax revenue from development of a new retail center. He believes the first two types can be justified under public use/public purpose standards, but has great difficulty in finding a public use in the third type. Lefcoe, *Curbing Opportunistic TIF-Driven Economic Development: Foregoing Ineffectual Blight Tests; Empowering Property Owners and School Districts*, 83 Tulane L. Rev. 1, 6-23 (2008).

4. *State legislative responses.* In addition to statutory approaches to takings problems prior to *Kelo* discussed *infra*, within four years after the *Kelo* decision, all but seven states (Arkansas, Hawaii, Mississippi, Massachusetts, New Jersey, New York and Oklahoma) had responded with legislation, legislation-sponsored referenda or citizen-sponsored initiatives.

The National Conference of State Legislatures (NCSL) grouped the legislation into five categories 1) restrictions on or prohibition of eminent domain's use for projects designed to foster economic development or increase tax revenue by transferring private property to another private entity; 2) definitions of the term "public use"; 3) more restrictive definitions of "blighted areas"; 4) strengthened procedural protections such as public notice and hearing requirements, along with negotiation criteria and formal approval requirements, and 5) imposition of moratoria on the use of eminent domain while task forces study the issue and make recommendations to the legislature. Most feature a combination of some or all of these categories. National Conference of State Legislatures, Issues and Research, Environment and Natural Resources, Eminent Domain, available at http://www.ncsl.org/IssuesResearch/EnvironmentandNaturalResources/EminentDomainpage/tabid/13252/Default.aspx (last visited July 6, 2010). See also APA, Eminent Domain Legislation across America (2006), available at http//myapa.planning.org/legislation/eminentdomain/; Castle Coalition, Eminent Domain Report Card: Tracking Eminent Domain Reform Legislation Since Kelo, available at castlecoalition.org; Echeverria & Hansen-Young, *The Track record on Takings Legislation: Lessons from Democracy's Laboratories*, 28 Stan. Envtl. L.J. 439 (2009).

Professor Ilya Somin of George Mason University School of Law, writing from the property owner perspective that economic development, or person-to-person, condemnations should be stopped, analyzes the post-*Kelo* enactments as "effective" or "ineffective." Statutes are said to be effective if "they provide property owners with at least some significant protection against economic-development condemnations beyond that available under preexisting law"; while statutes are thought to be ineffective "if they forbid economic-development condemnations but essentially allow them to continue under another name," such as through a loose definition of "blight." By her standards, nineteen states have enacted effective reforms either through state legislation, citizen-initiated referenda or legislature-initiated referenda, while twenty three states have enacted reforms that are ineffective, one by legislature-initiated referendum and the rest by state legislation. The major loopholes in the ineffective statutes, according to Professor Somin, are loose definitions of "blight" that include areas that contain "obstacles to 'sound growth' or conditions that constitute an 'economic or social liability.'" She also is critical of popular "blight" definition phrases such as "a menace to the public health, safety, morals, or welfare . . . because almost any condition that impedes economic development could be considered a 'menace to the public . . . welfare.'" Somin, *The Limits of Backlash: Assessing the Political Response to* Kelo, 93 Minn. L. Rev. 2100, 2102, 2114–2116, 2122–2124 (2009). For a criticism of Louisiana's restrictive constitutional amendment adopted in the wake of *Kelo* and Hurricane Katrina, see Costonis, *New Orleans, Katrina and Kelo: American Cities in the Post-Kelo Era*, 83 Tul. L. Rev. 395 (2008), summarized in Costonis, *Narrative as Lawmakng: The Anti-*Kelo *Story*, 62 Planning & Envtl. L., Jan. 2010, at 3, 10 (expressing concern that prohibiting transfer of expropriated property to private entities "vetoes the public-private partnership by cutting out the private partner . . . [despite the fact that a public redevelopment agency] needs the private sector as a partner in the recovery effort").

What effect might a post-*Kelo* restrictive state statute have on a federal court's review of the exercise of eminent domain in support of a redevelopment project? In *Whittaker v. County of Lawrence*, 674 F. Supp. 2d 668 (W.D. Pa. 2009), the Federal District Court declined to apply a restrictive Pennsylvania statutory definition of blight in a Fifth Amendment challenge to the use of eminent domain to support a high technology business park development. The challenge was brought under § 1983 of the Federal Civil Rights Act. In refusing to apply the state statutory restrictions on the use of eminent domain, the court stated: "[a]s far as the United

States Constitution is concerned, a 'public use' in Connecticut is a 'public use' in Pennsylvania. The Plaintiffs attempt to convert state statutory standards into federal constitutional requirements, '[b]ut constitutional law does not work that way.'" *Id.* at 689–690. Does this suggest that federal courts may not be the best venue for challenging the use of eminent domain in support of economic development projects? Section 1983 is discussed *infra.*

5. *State judicial responses.* State courts have felt free to reject the *Kelo* rationale in applying state constitutional provisions. While the court in *Kelo* stressed that deference must be given the legislative declaration of public purpose, the legislative discretion is not absolute. The Supreme Court of Hawaii, applying Justice Stevens' warning that "the City would [not] be allowed to take property under the mere pretext of a public purpose, when its actual purpose was to bestow a private benefit," *Kelo*, 545 U.S. at 477, remanded a challenge to condemnation of a condominium development for construction of a public highway bypass that was to be built by a private developer for a determination whether the stated public purpose was a pretext. *County of Hawaii v. C&J Coupe Family Limited Partnership*, 198 P.3d 615, 620 (Hawaii 2008) ("[A]lthough our courts afford substantial deference to the government's asserted public purpose for a taking in condemnation proceeding, where there is evidence that the asserted purpose is pretextual, courts should consider a landowner's defense of pretext").

The Supreme Court of New Jersey concluded that the state constitutional provision authorizing the use of eminent domain to acquire property in "blighted areas" did not include the power to take wetlands and waterfront property that was "not fully productive." Community redevelopment may be an important state goal, the court acknowledged, but eminent domain may not be employed to implement such redevelopment unless the property in question meets the constitutional concept of blight, which the court described as "deterioration or stagnation that negatively affects surrounding properties." The statutory criterion the court said was applied incorrectly was directed toward problems of title, diverse ownership and similar conditions preventing normal market development, the court noted. *Gallenthin Realty Development, Inc. v. Borough of Paulsboro*, 924 A.2d 447, 459–63 (N.J. 2007). In two cases that began before the *Gallenthin* decision but in which the courts applied the *Gallenthin* conditions for meeting the state constitutional standard of "blight" as "pipeline precedent," one city won and one city lost. A New Jersey court in an unpublished opinion reversed the trial court and held that a city's "designation of the study area as in need of redevelopment does not satisfy the heightened standard" of *Gallenthin.* Cottage Emporium, Inc. v. City of Long Branch, 2010 N.J. Super. Unpub. LEXIS 835 (N.J. App. 2010). In another unpublished decision, *Suburban Jewelers v. City of Plainfield*, 2010 N.J. Super. Unpub. LEXIS 992 (N.J. App. 2010), the court held that the city had correctly applied the statutory criteria for meeting the constitutional standard of "blight" in determining that several small parcels in the central business district containing deteriorated buildings over 100 years old were "in need of redevelopment" and thus blighted. See also *Mayor and City Council of Baltimore City v. Valsamaki*, 916 A.2d 324, 344 (Md. 2007) (general goal of "business expansion" does not meet public use standard for a "quick-take" (expedited) condemnation).

In a similar vein, the Supreme Court of Ohio accepted the analyses of the dissenters in *Kelo* and the Supreme Court of Michigan in *Wayne Cty. v. Hathcock*, 684 N.W.2d 765 (2004), as "better models for interpreting" the Ohio Constitution and held that "an economic or financial benefit alone is insufficient to satisfy the public-use requirement" of the Ohio Constitution. *City of Norwood v. Horney*, 853 N.E.2d 1115 (Ohio 2006). In a lengthy opinion that contained an extended review of the conceptual underpinnings of eminent domain law, the Ohio Court concluded that the modern public-private partnership economic development strategy carries with it the "danger . . . that the state's decision to take may be influenced by the financial gains that would flow to it or to the private entity because of the taking." Thus, "both common sense and the law command independent judicial review of the taking." *Id.* at 1140.

In a major blow to local government flexibility, the court also held that local governments in Ohio could not base takings solely on the fact that property is in a "deteriorating area," characterized by the Norwood Code (modeled on Ohio statutory law) as an area with incompatible land uses, nonconforming uses, faulty street arrangement, diversity of ownership and the like, because the term "describes almost any city" and thus was too vague to give appropriate notice to landowners of the possibility that their land could be subject to eminent domain proceedings. *Id.* at 1144. See also *Board of County Commissioners of Muskogee County v. Lowery*, 136 P.3d 639, 652 (Okla. 2006) (rejecting use of eminent domain to acquire right-of-way easements for a proposed private electric generation plant designed to foster economic development).

In *Hathcock*, the Supreme Court of Michigan invalidated the use of eminent domain by Wayne County to acquire land for a privately-owned business and technology park adjacent the Detroit metropolitan airport. Overruling *Poletown Neighborhood Council v. City of Detroit*, 304 N.W.2d 455 (Mich. 1981), an earlier case that upheld an urban renewal project, the court held that acquisition of private property by eminent domain and subsequent transfer to a private entity would satisfy the "public use" requirement only in one of three situations: "(1) where 'public necessity of the extreme sort' requires collective action [highways, railroads, sewer lines]; (2) where the property remains subject to public oversight after transfer to a private entity [petroleum pipeline regulated by state Public Service Commission]; and (3) where the property is selected because of 'facts of independent public significance' [health and safety] rather than the interests of the private entity to which the property is eventually transferred." *Id.* at 783. A desire to create jobs and improve the local economy wasn't enough, the court held. For an argument that the Michigan and Ohio decisions, and subsequent legislative responses to those decisions limiting the use of eminent domain in economic development settings, represent examples of the "greater cooperation between the legislative and judicial branches [that is necessary] to develop and enforce" protections against "the excesses of economic development takings . . . [and to] provide sufficient protection of residents displaced by condemnation," see Lyons, *Public Use, Public Choice, and the Urban Growth Machine: Competing Political Economies of Takings Law*, 42 U. Mich. J. L. Reform 265, 310 (2009).

But in *Matter of Kaur v. New York State Urban Development Corporation*, 15 N.Y.3d 235, 907 N.Y.S.2d 122, 933 N.E.2d 721 (2010), the New York Court of Appeals concluded that the use of eminent domain to acquire property for the development of a new Columbia University campus "was supported by a sufficient public use, benefit or purpose . . . [and] the Empire State Development Corporation's ('ESDC') findings of blight and determination that the condemnation of petitioners' property qualified as a 'land use improvement project' were rationally based and entitled to deference. . . . Thus, given our precedent, the de novo review of the record undertaken by the plurality of the Appellate Division was improper." The precedent the court applied, *Matter of Goldstein v New York State Urban Dev. Corp.*, 921 N.E.2d 164 (N.Y. 2009), upheld an economic development project including a new arena for the New Jersey Nets professional basketball team, new subway infrastructure and new commercial and residential towers as meeting the eminent domain standard of public use:

> Whether a matter should be the subject of a public undertaking — whether its pursuit will serve a public purpose or use — is ordinarily the province of the Legislature, not the Judiciary, and the actual specification of the uses identified by the Legislature as public has been largely left to quasi-legislative administrative agencies. It is only where there is no room for reasonable difference of opinion as to whether an area is blighted, that judges may substitute their views as to the adequacy with which the public purpose of blight removal has been made out for that of the legislatively designated agencies. [*Id.* at 172.]

The same court also upheld the acquisition of farmland by eminent domain to implement a farmland preservation policy sanctioned by the state legislature and included in the town's master plan. *Aspen Creek Estates, Ltd. v. Town of Brookhaven*, 904 N.E.2d 816 (N.Y. 2009).

6. *Kelo is not a blank check.* Note the importance of the comprehensive planning process and the statutory authorization in *Kelo.* State courts applying *Kelo* are not giving local governments carte blanche. In *Mayor and City Council of Baltimore City v. Valsamaki*, 916 A.2d 324 (Md. 2007), the Maryland Court of Appeals (highest court) held that a city could not condemn private property for economic development purposes without a definite plan for the land's use. A general goal of "business expansion" was insufficient. And in *Centene Plaza Redevelopment Corp. v. Mint Properties*, 225 S.W.3d 431 (Mo. 2007), the Supreme Court of Missouri held that a statutory definition of blight that required a showing of both economic and social liabilities as a precondition for the exercise of eminent domain could not be satisfied by focusing only on economic factors.

7. *Alternatives to the use of eminent domain.* Frank Schnidman, Senior Fellow at the Center for Urban and Environmental Solutions, Florida Atlantic University, argued in an *amicus curiae* brief filed in *Kelo* on behalf of John Norquist, President of the Congress for the New Urbanism, available at cues-fau.org/cra/ that many effective land assembly techniques exist that do not require eminent domain, but that modern developers and elected officials are too interested in "fast-tracking" the development process and showing results to engage in a more nuanced land assembly process. Schnidman, *Alternatives to Eminent Domain*, Planning & Envtl. L., Sept. 2005, at 14. The Lincoln Institute of Land Policy has published a book, Hong & Needham, Analyzing Land Readjustment (2007), suggesting a new approach to land assemblage in which property owners whose land is being sought are given a stake in the development through the ability to approve or disapprove use of their property and the opportunity to contribute their land to the development as a form of capital investment. What do you think of that idea?

8. *Kelo aftermath.* Suzette Kelo continued to fight the decision until finally agreeing to a settlement one year later that allowed her to stay in her waterfront house an additional year while a new site was selected to which her house would be moved. But five years after the decision was handed down, the redevelopment site remained vacant; Susette Kelo's house had been moved to a different site and refurbished by a preservationist who bought it from the city's development agent for one dollar; Mrs. Kelo had moved across the Thames River, and the main beneficiary of the redevelopment plan, Pfizer Inc. had announced plans to abandon its plant in New London. McGeehan, *Pfizer to Leave City That Won Land-Use Case*, N.Y. Times, Nov. 13, 2009, at p. A1. The story behind the *Kelo* litigation is told in Benedict, Little Pink House (2009).

9. *Eminent domain history.* For a brief history of the law of eminent domain, see Calandrillo, *Eminent Domain Economics: Should "Just Compensation" Be Abolished and*

Would "Takings Insurance" Work Instead? 64 Ohio St. L.J. 451, 460–88 (2003). The classic treatment is P. Nichols, The Law of Eminent Domain (3d ed., J. Sackman rev. ed. 1979).

For examinations of eminent domain from the perspective of the *Kelo* case, see Eminent Domain Use and Abuse: Kelo in Context *supra*; Zeiner, *Eminent Domain Wolves in Sheep's Clothing: Private Benefit Masquerading as Classic Public Use*, 28 Va. Envtl. L.J. 1 (2010); Dana, *Exclusionary Eminent Domain*, 17 Sup. Ct. Econ. Rev. 7 (2009); Ely, *Post-*Kelo *Reform: Is the Glass Half Full or Half Empty?*, 17 Sup. Ct. Econ. Rev. 127 (2009); Lyons, *Public Use, Public Choice, and the Urban Growth Machine: Competing Political Economies of Takings Law*, 42 U. Mich. J.L. Reform 265 (2009); Morriss, *Symbol or Substance? An Empirical Assessment of State Responses to Kelo*, 17 Sup. Ct. Econ. Rev. 237 (2009); Morrison, *Protecting Private Property: An Analysis of Georgia's Response to Kelo v. City of New London*, 2 J. Marshall L.J. 51 (2009); Hoting, *The Kelo Revolution*, 86 U. Det. Mercy L. Rev. 65 (2009); Lopez, *Revisiting Kelo and Eminent Domain's "Summer of Scrutiny,"* 59 Ala. L. Rev. 561 (2008); Taub, *Post-*Kelo *State Constitutional and Legislative Reforms*, ALI-ABA 23rd Annual Land Use Inst. (2007); Hudson, Note, *Eminent Domain Due Process*, 119 Yale L.J. 1280 (2010); Hafetz, *Ferriting Out Favoritism: Bringing Claims After Kelo*, 77 Fordham L. Rev. 3095 (2009); Han, Note, *From New London to Norwood: A Year in the Life of Eminent Domain*, 57 Duke L.J. 1449 (2008); Kennelly, Note, *Florida's Eminent Domain Overhaul: Creating More Problems Than It Solved*, 60 Fla. L. Rev. 471 (2008).

[2.] Regulatory Takings

Governments can regulate the use of property by exercising their "police power." This is an inherent power of government that is limited by the Due Process Clauses of the Fifth and Fourteenth Amendments. When state or local regulatory legislation is found not to be a proper exercise of the police power, it can be enjoined as a deprivation of liberty or property, or both, without due process of law, discussed *infra*. While there is no express constitutional requirement to pay compensation for the exercise of the police power, the Supreme Court has concluded that under some circumstances, a regulation can affect land so significantly that it is the functional equivalent of a taking of property for which compensation must be paid — a "regulatory taking," to use the current terminology.

This simplistic summary of the constitutional framework will be elaborated in complex detail in the materials that follow. Most commentators (to say nothing of novice students of land use law) have concluded that the cases are far from internally consistent, and that the Supreme Court has from time to time steered an erratic course. However, by keeping in sight these guideposts — police power regulation versus takings, substantive due process versus compensation (and occasionally equal protection) — you should be able eventually to frame your own conclusions about what the law is and what it ought to be.

Judicial takings? Takings controversies are triggered by actions of the executive or legislative branches of government. But can a judicial decision upholding a state statute and in the process construing state common law amount to an unconstitutional "judicial taking"? In *Stop the Beach Renourishment, Inc v. Florida Department of Environmental Protection*, 130 S. Ct. 2592 (2010), the U.S. Supreme Court concluded that the Florida Supreme Court had not taken private property when it upheld a state statute, the Florida Beach and Shore Preservation Act, Fla. Stat. § 161.011–61.45 (2007), which established a beach renourishment program in which sand from offshore sites owned by the state was deposited on seriously eroded beaches. The renourishment program proposed to add about 75 feet of dry sand seaward of the mean high-water line. Property owners contended that this would eliminate two of their "littoral rights: (1) the right to receive accretions [gradual additions of sand and sediment to waterfront land] to their property; and (2) the right to have the contact of their property with the water remain intact." 130 S. Ct. at 2610.

Under Florida property law, "the State as owner of the submerged land adjacent to littoral property has the right to fill that land, so long as it does not interfere with the rights of the public and the rights of littoral landowners. . . . [I]f an avulsion [a sudden addition or loss of land caused by action of water] exposes land that had previously been submerged, that land belongs to the State even if it interrupts the littoral owner's contact with the water. . . . The issue here is whether there is an exception to this rule when the State is the cause of the avulsion. Prior law suggests there is not." 130 S. Ct. at 2611.

All eight participating Justices concurred in the decision, but four agreed that a compensable judicial taking could occur. "[T]he particular state *actor* is irrelevant. If a legislature *or a court* declares that what was once an established right of private property no longer exists, it has taken that property, no less than if the State had physically appropriated or destroyed its value by regulation." 130 S. Ct. at 2602 (Scalia, J.) (emphasis in original). Four believed that the question did not need to be decided to resolve the case. 130 S. Ct. at 2618-2619. Justice Stevens, a Florida beachfront landowner, did not participate in the case.

For an argument that there are numerous reasons for treating courts differently, including (1) the judiciary is not vested with the eminent domain power; (2) the rationale that takings liability serves to constrain majoritarian political impulses generally does not apply to the judicial branch; (3) the judicial takings concept would undermine the relationship between the federal and state court systems; (4) the state courts' institutional structure provides a relatively strong assurance of fidelity to federal constitutional values; and (5) court rulings on property law issues tend to apply broadly across the community rather than single out particular individuals to bear special burdens, see Echeverria, *Stop the Beach Renourishment: Why the Judiciary is Different*, Vermont Law School Legal Studies Research Paper Series Research Paper Number 10-45 (August 2, 2010), available at: :http://papers.ssrn.com/sol3/papers.cfm?abstract_id=1652351.

[a.] The Early Supreme Court Cases

Both the compensation and due process issues were resolved squarely in *Mugler v. Kansas*, 123 U.S. 623 (1887), an important early case interpreting the Fourteenth Amendment. Upholding a Kansas statute prohibiting the manufacture of intoxicating liquors, the Supreme Court concluded that the Fourteenth Amendment did not abrogate the police powers of the states. It concluded "that all property in this country is held under the implied obligation that the owner's use of it shall not be injurious to the community." *Id.* at 669. However, the Amendment also imposed on all courts a duty to strike down legislative acts purportedly enacted pursuant to the police power of a state when such acts have "no real or substantial relation" to the proper objects of the police power — protection of "the public health, the public morals, or the public safety." *Id.* at 662.

A few years after *Mugler*, in *Lawton v. Steele*, 152 U.S. 133 (1894), the Supreme Court, in upholding a New York statute authorizing seizure and destruction of illegal fishing nets without payment of compensation to their owners, confirmed the "no compensation" principle of *Mugler* and laid down the classic test for substantive due process: a purported exercise of the police power does not violate the Fourteenth Amendment's Due Process Clause if it appears, "first that the interests of the public . . . require such interference; second, that the means are reasonably necessary for the accomplishment of the purpose, and not unduly oppressive on individuals." *Id.* at 137. This has long been considered the classic statement of the requirements of substantive due process. But *Lawton* did not indicate the relative weight to be attached to each of the designated factors.

Twenty one years later, in *Hadacheck v. Sebastian*, 239 U.S. 394 (1915), the Court extended the basic police power due process test to a land use case in sustaining an ordinance prohibiting operation of brick factories within defined residential areas in the City of Los Angeles. The Court upheld the ordinance as a valid exercise of the police power. In so doing, it applied the first two prongs of *Lawton*: a public interest requiring intervention and means "reasonably necessary" to accomplish the purpose, but ignored the third prong, that the regulation "not [be] unduly oppressive on individuals." The landowner had alleged that the regulation reduced the value of deposits of clay in his land from $800,000 to $60,000 by its prohibition of brick-making on site.

The case has been called the first Supreme Court *land use* case, in that the Court permitted a local government to control competing, reasonable use of land by regulation closely modeled on common law nuisance but free of its more restrictive features. In so doing, the Court accorded a presumption of validity to the exercise of the police power, what it called "the imperative necessity" that "precludes any limitation upon it when not exerted arbitrarily." The Court also disposed of an equal protection claim in an approach that later became characterized as rational basis review.

Takings doctrine may have influenced the Court's thinking in its analysis of the economic burden on Hadacheck: the traditional rule in formal eminent domain cases (recall the "regulatory takings" analog to eminent domain) is that just compensation does not include payment for consequential business losses, even if the business is completely destroyed, because the business on the land is distinct from the value of the land itself. Although *Hadacheck* precedes the development of a "regulatory takings" theory by the Court, its analysis of Hadacheck's losses plays a major role in later takings cases. See also Michelman, *Property and Fairness: Comments on the Ethical Foundations of "Just Compensation" Law*, 80 Harv. L. Rev. 1165, 1198, 1237, 1242–44 (1967). The next case famously began the evolution of the "regulatory takings" doctrine:

PENNSYLVANIA COAL CO. v. MAHON

260 U.S. 393 (1922)

JUSTICE HOLMES delivered the opinion of the Court:

This is a bill in equity brought by the defendants in error to prevent the Pennsylvania Coal Company from mining under their property in such way as to remove the supports and cause a subsidence of the surface and of their house. The bill sets out a deed executed by the Coal Company in 1878, under which the plaintiffs claim. The deed conveys the surface, but in express terms reserves the right to remove all the coal under the same, and the grantee takes the premises with the risk, and waives all claim for damages that may arise from mining out the coal. But the plaintiffs say that whatever may have been the Coal Company's rights, they were taken away by an Act of Pennsylvania, approved May 27, 1921, P.L. 1198, commonly known there as the Kohler Act. The Court of Common Pleas found that if not restrained the defendant would cause the damage to prevent which the bill was brought, but denied an injunction, holding that the statute if applied to this case would be unconstitutional. On appeal the Supreme Court of the State agreed that the defendant had contract and property rights protected by the Constitution of the United States, but held that the statute was a legitimate exercise of the police power and directed a decree for the plaintiffs. A writ of error was granted bringing the case to this Court.

The statute forbids the mining of anthracite coal in such way as to cause the subsidence of, among other things, any structure used as a human habitation, with certain exceptions, including among them land where the surface is owned by the owner of the underlying coal and is distant more than one hundred and fifty feet from any improved property belonging to any other person. As applied to this case the statute is admitted to destroy previously existing rights of property and contract. The question is whether the police power can be stretched so far.

Government hardly could go on if to some extent values incident to property could not be diminished without paying for every such change in the general law. As long recognized, some values are enjoyed under an implied limitation and must yield to the police power. But obviously the implied limitation must have its limits, or the contract and due process clauses are gone. One fact for consideration in determining such limits is the extent of the diminution. When it reaches a certain magnitude, in most if not in all cases there must be an exercise of eminent domain and compensation to sustain the act. So the question depends upon the particular facts. The greatest weight is given to the judgment of the legislature, but it always is open to interested parties to contend that the legislature has gone beyond its constitutional power.

This is the case of a single private house. No doubt there is a public interest even in this, as there is in every purchase and sale and in all that happens within the commonwealth. Some existing rights may be modified even in such a case. But usually in ordinary private affairs the public interest does not warrant much of this kind of interference. A source of damage to such a house is not a public nuisance even if similar damage is inflicted on others in different places. The damage is not common or public. The extent of the public interest is shown by the statute to be limited, since the statute ordinarily does not apply to land when the surface is owned by the owner of the coal. Furthermore, it is not justified as a protection of personal safety. That could be provided for by notice. Indeed the very foundation of this bill is that the defendant gave timely notice of its intent to mine under the house. On the other hand the extent of the taking is great. It purports to abolish what is recognized in Pennsylvania as an estate in land — a very valuable estate — and what is declared by the Court below to be a contract hitherto binding the plaintiffs. If we were called upon to deal with the plaintiffs' position alone, we should think it clear that the statute does not disclose a public interest sufficient to warrant so extensive a destruction of the defendant's constitutionally protected rights.

But the case has been treated as one in which the general validity of the act should be discussed. The Attorney General of the State, the City of Scranton, and the representatives of other extensive interests were allowed to take part in the argument below and have submitted their contentions here. It seems, therefore, to be our duty to go farther in the statement of our opinion, in order that it may be known at once, and that further suits should not be brought in vain.

It is our opinion that the act cannot be sustained as an exercise of the police power, so far as it affects the mining of coal under streets or cities in places where the right to mine such coal has been reserved. As said in a Pennsylvania case, "For practical purposes, the right to coal consists in the right to mine it." *Commonwealth v. Clearview Coal Co.*, 256 Pa. St. 328, 331. What makes the right to mine coal valuable is that it can be exercised with profit. To make it commercially impracticable to mine certain coal has very nearly the same effect for constitutional purposes as appropriating or destroying it. This we think that we are warranted in assuming that the statute does.

It is true that in *Plymouth Coal Co. v. Pennsylvania*, 232 U.S. 531, it was held competent for the legislature to require a pillar of coal to be left along the line of adjoining property, that, with the pillar on the other side of the line, would be a barrier sufficient for the safety of the employees of either mine in case the other should be abandoned and allowed to fill with water. But that was a requirement for the safety of employees invited into the mine, and secured an average reciprocity of advantage that has been recognized as a justification of various laws.

The rights of the public in a street purchased or laid out by eminent domain are those that it has paid for. If in any case its representatives have been so short sighted as to acquire only surface rights without the right of support, we see no more authority for supplying the latter without compensation than there was for taking the right of way in the first place and refusing to pay for it because the public wanted it very much. The protection of private property in the Fifth Amendment presupposes that it is wanted for public use, but provides that it shall not be taken for such use without compensation. A similar assumption is made in the decisions upon the Fourteenth Amendment. When this seemingly absolute protection is found to be qualified by the police power, the natural tendency of human nature is to extend the qualification more and more until at last private property disappears. But that cannot be accomplished in this way under the Constitution of the United States.

The general rule at least is, that while property may be regulated to a certain extent, if regulation goes too far it will be recognized as a taking. It may be doubted how far exceptional cases, like the blowing up of a house to stop a conflagration, go — and if they go beyond the general rule, whether they do not stand as much upon tradition as upon principle. In general it is not plain that a man's misfortunes or necessities will justify his shifting the damages to his neighbor's shoulders. We are in danger of forgetting that a strong public desire to improve the public condition is not enough to warrant achieving the desire by a shorter cut than the constitutional way of paying for the change. As we already have said, this is a question of degree — and therefore cannot be disposed of by general propositions. But we regard this as going beyond any of the cases decided by this Court. The late decisions upon laws dealing with the congestion of Washington and New York, caused by the war, dealt with laws intended to meet a temporary emergency and providing for compensation determined to be reasonable by an impartial board. They went to the verge of the law but fell far short of the present act. *Block v. Hirsh*, 256 U.S. 135; *Marcus Brown Holding Co. v. Feldman*, 256 U.S. 170; *Levy Leasing Co. v. Siegel*, 258 U.S. 242.

We assume, of course, that the statute was passed upon the conviction that an exigency existed that would warrant it, and we assume that an exigency exists that would warrant the exercise of eminent domain. But the question at bottom is upon whom the loss of the changes desired should fall. So far as private persons or communities have seen fit to take the risk of acquiring only surface rights, we cannot see that the fact that their risk has become a danger warrants the giving to them greater rights than they bought.

Decree reversed.

JUSTICE BRANDEIS, dissenting. . . . [Most of Justice Brandeis' dissent is omitted. He would have upheld the statute as a restriction on a noxious use. The following paragraphs contain his views on the "whole parcel" issue and the relevance of "reciprocity of advantage" to taking questions:]

It is said that one fact for consideration in determining whether the limits of the police power have been exceeded is the extent of the resulting diminution in value; and that here the restriction destroys existing rights of property and contract. But values are relative. If we are to consider the value of the coal kept in place by the restriction, we should compare it with the value of all other parts of the land. That is, with the value not of the coal alone, but with the value of the whole property. The rights of an owner as against the public are not increased by dividing the interests in his property into surface and subsoil. The sum of the rights in the parts can not be greater than the rights in the whole. The estate of an owner in land is grandiloquently described as extending *ab orco usque ad coelum*. But I suppose no one would contend that by selling his interest above one hundred feet from the surface he could prevent the State from limiting, by the police power, the height of structures in a city. And why should a sale of underground rights bar the State's power? For aught that appears the value of the coal kept in place by the restriction may be negligible as compared with the value of the whole property, or even as compared with that part of it which is represented by the coal remaining in place and which may be extracted despite the statute. . . .

A prohibition of mining which causes subsidence of such structures and facilities is obviously enacted for a public purpose; and it seems, likewise, clear that mere notice of intention to mine would not in this connection secure the public safety. Yet it is said that these provisions of the act cannot be sustained as an exercise of the police power where the right to mine such coal has been reserved. The conclusion seems to rest upon the assumption that in order to justify such exercise of the police power there must be "an average reciprocity of advantage" as between the owner of the property restricted and the rest of the community; and that here such reciprocity is absent. Reciprocity of advantage is an important consideration, and may even be an essential, where the State's power is exercised for the purpose of conferring benefits upon the property of a neighborhood, as in drainage projects, or upon adjoining owners, as by party wall provisions. But where the police power is exercised, not to confer benefits upon property owners, but to protect the public from detriment and danger, there is, in my opinion, no room for considering reciprocity of advantage. There was no reciprocal advantage to the owner prohibited from using [his brickyard in the *Hadacheck* case and similar uses in similar cases where use prohibitions were upheld] unless it be the advantage of living and doing business in a civilized community. That reciprocal advantage is given by the act to the coal operators.

NOTES AND QUESTIONS

1. *What Pennsylvania Coal did.* Given the *Mugler* line of cases, culminating in *Hadacheck*, how does Justice Holmes justify his holding that the Pennsylvania statute in the principal case should be "recognized as a taking" that could not be sustained unless compensation were paid to the coal mine owners? Do you understand Holmes to hold that protection of a large number of human habitations, factories, mercantile establishments, public buildings, streets and roads, bridges, and public service facilities of municipal corporations and private corporations was not a significant "public purpose"? Or that destruction of such properties by causing subsidence of the surface of the land was not a "noxious" use of the area below the surface? Or that prohibition of mining so as to cause subsidence was not a "reasonable means" of protecting the public safety, wealth, and property? What is the significance of the court's pointing out that "[t]his is the case of a single private house"? If that is so, is the Court's subsequent consideration of "the general validity of the act" only dictum?

2. *The property interest taken.* If Holmes was correct in holding that the Pennsylvania statute in the principal case amounted to a de facto "taking" of private property for public use, what kind of a "property interest" was "taken"? At oral argument, counsel for the Pennsylvania Coal Company identified three distinct estates in mining property: surface, subsurface, and a distinctive Pennsylvanian "right to have the surface supported by the subjacent strata." 260 U.S. at 395. The statute certainly "deprived" the coal companies of what might be called the "privilege" to destroy this support "estate," but Pennsylvania clearly did not "acquire" it. How, therefore, could the statute be deemed to effect a "taking" of private property for public use? Why should the deprivation of the privilege in question be "recognized as a taking" simply because the resulting economic loss to the coal companies would be substantial? Recall the language in *Hadacheck* indicating that substantial economic loss is irrelevant when the police power is exerted non-arbitrarily against property owners. Review the facts in *Pennsylvania Coal.* Might the case have been decided differently if the coal company had acquired its interest in the property *after* the Kohler Act came into force, even if the economic consequences were the same?

3. *The denominator problem.* Even if we accept the Holmes thesis that "while property may be regulated to a certain extent, if regulation goes too far it will be recognized as a taking," on what basis did Holmes find that the regulation went "too far" in *Mahon*? Was Brandeis not right in arguing that "[i]f we are to consider the value of the coal kept in place by the restriction, we should compare it with the value of all other parts of the [coal company's] land"? In ignoring this point, did Holmes implicitly hold that requiring "pillars" of coal to be kept in place to support the surface was ipso facto a "taking," without regard to the relative value of the "pillars" and "all other parts of the land"? This problem has come to be known as the "denominator" problem and has an important place in modern takings law.

4. *Financial loss.* In *Mahon*, Holmes said that "[t]o make it commercially impracticable to mine certain coal [i.e., the 'pillars' required for surface support] has very nearly the same effect for constitutional purposes as appropriating or destroying it." This statement was based on the fact the cost of providing artificial support in lieu of the "pillars" of coal would exceed the value of the "pillars." See the coal company's argument, 260 U.S. at 395. Is Holmes' statement consistent with the Court's conclusion in *Hadacheck v. Sebastian* that there was no "taking" despite the fact that transportation of Hadacheck's brick clay to some other locality for manufacturing would be impractical "from a financial standpoint," since the Los Angeles ordinance only prohibited the manufacture of bricks and not the removal of the clay? *Keystone Bituminous Coal Ass'n v. De Benedictis*, 480 U.S. 470 (1987), which is discussed *infra*, sustained a Pennsylvania statute very similar to the Kohler Act and distinguished *Pennsylvania Coal.*

5. *Pennsylvania Coal as history.* Friedman, *A Search for Seizure: Pennsylvania Coal Co. v. Mahon in Context*, 4 L. & Hist. Rev. 1 (1986), provides background. Noting that the Mahons (or their predecessors) had sold the "support estate" and that "[n]o doubt, these risks looked small at the time," he points out that by 1922

> the times . . . had changed radically. . . . The surface now supported a large population; nine counties, with about 1,000,000 people. . . . Moreover, "pillar robbing"

had become a serious problem, partly, it was said, because courts had upheld the clauses which waived rights to damages for subsidence. Whole chunks of Scranton were on the verge of collapse. [*Id.* at 2.]

Friedman also notes that a companion Pennsylvania law, the Fowler Act, ignored by both Holmes and Brandeis, provided for an optional fund to compensate victims, supported by

> "a tax or, if you will, a kind of private eminent domain. The companies would pay for what they took; the original contracts were in a sense renegotiated. . . . If the state had taxed the public generally, rather than solely the companies, there is little question the scheme would have worked. The companies wanted their cake and eat it too. Pennsylvania Coal Co. refused to pay the Fowler tax [which was optional]; this brought it under the tough terms of the Kohler Act — the iron fist designed to force companies to accept . . . the Fowler Act."

6. *Sources.* For some recent scholarship on *Pennsylvania Coal*, see Claeys, *Takings, Regulations, and Natural Property Rights*, 88 Cornell L. Rev. 1549, 1618-26 (2003) (arguing that Justice Holmes combined natural-right legal principles emphasizing free control and action over property with utilitarian focus on value in a way that "was bound to confuse federal regulatory takings law no matter how it developed"); Treanor, *Jam for Justice Holmes: Reassessing the Significance of Mahon*, 86 Geo. L.J. 813 (1998); Brauneis, *The Foundation of Our "Regulatory Takings" Jurisprudence: The Myth and Meaning of Justice Holmes's Opinion in Pennsylvania Coal Company v. Mahon*, 106 Yale L.J. 613 (1996) (arguing that *Pennsylvania Coal* was not a takings case); Rose, *Mahon Reconstructed: Why the Takings Issue is Still a Muddle*, 57 S. Cal. L. Rev. 561 (1984) (questioning decision).

Four years after *Pennsylvania Coal*, the Supreme Court considered the constitutionality of a modern comprehensive zoning ordinance for the first time in *Euclid v. Ambler Realty*. The decision is the leading case on the constitutionality of zoning. The District Court had held the Euclid ordinance unconstitutional, approaching the question from a different perspective than that later taken by the Supreme Court. Faced with the prospect that the nascent movement to plan and control land uses would be snuffed out by the high Court, the proponents of zoning rallied with *amicus* support. To give you the flavor of the fight, we first set out the facts of the *Euclid* case, taken verbatim from the Supreme Court opinion, followed by excerpts from the District Court opinion and finally the legal analysis of the Supreme Court. The *amicus* brief is described in the notes following. As you read, note how the doctrinal themes of earlier cases are used (or ignored).

VILLAGE OF EUCLID v. AMBLER REALTY CO.

272 U.S. 365 (1926)

[Justice Sutherland stated the facts as follows:] The Village of Euclid is an Ohio municipal corporation. It adjoins and practically is a suburb of the City of Cleveland. Its estimated population is between 5,000 and 10,000, and its area from twelve to fourteen square miles, the greater part of which is farm lands or unimproved acreage. It lies, roughly, in the form of a parallelogram measuring approximately three and one-half miles each way. East and west it is traversed by three principal highways: Euclid Avenue, through the southerly border, St. Clair Avenue, through the central portion, and Lake Shore Boulevard, through the northerly border in close proximity to the shore of Lake Erie. The Nickel Plate railroad lies from 1,500 to 1,800 feet north of Euclid Avenue, and the Lake Shore railroad 1,600 feet farther to the north. The three highways and the two railroads are substantially parallel.

Appellee is the owner of a tract of land containing 68 acres, situated in the westerly end of the village, abutting on Euclid Avenue to the south and the Nickel Plate railroad to the north. Adjoining this tract, both on the east and on the west, there have been laid out restricted residential plats upon which residences have been erected.

On November 13, 1922, an ordinance was adopted by the Village Council, establishing a comprehensive zoning plan for regulating and restricting the location of trades, industries, apartment houses, two-family houses, single family houses, etc., the lot area to be built upon, the size and height of buildings, etc.

The entire area of the village is divided by the ordinance into six classes of use districts, denominated U-1 to U-6, inclusive; three classes of height districts, denominated H-1 to H-3, inclusive; and four classes of area districts, denominated A-1 to A-4, inclusive. The use districts are classified in respect of the buildings which may be erected within their respective limits, as follows: U-1 is restricted to single family dwellings, public parks, water towers and reservoirs, suburban and interurban electric railway passenger stations and rights of way, and farming, non-commercial greenhouse nurseries and truck gardening; U-2 is extended to include two-family dwellings; U-3 is further extended to include apartment houses, hotels, churches, schools, public libraries, museums, private clubs, community center buildings, hospitals, sanitariums, public playgrounds and recreation buildings, and a city hall and courthouse; U-4 is further extended to include banks, offices, studios, telephone exchanges, fire and police stations, restaurants, theaters and moving picture shows, retail stores and shops, sales offices, sample rooms, wholesale stores for hardware, drugs and groceries, stations for gasoline and oil (not exceeding 1,000 gallons storage) and for ice delivery, skating rinks and dance halls, electric substations, job and newspaper printing, public garages for motor vehicles, stables and wagon sheds (not exceeding five horses, wagons or motor trucks) and distributing stations for central store and commercial enterprises; U-5 is further extended to include billboards and advertising signs (if permitted), warehouses, ice and ice cream manufacturing and cold storage plants, bottling works, milk bottling and central distribution stations, laundries, carpet cleaning, dry cleaning and dyeing establishments, blacksmith, horseshoing, wagon and motor vehicle repair shops, freight stations, street car barns, stables and wagon sheds (for more than five horses, wagons or motor trucks), and wholesale produce markets and salesrooms; U-6 is further extended to include plants for sewage disposal and for producing gas, garbage and refuse incineration, scrap iron, junk, scrap paper and rag storage, aviation fields, cemeteries, crematories, penal and correctional institutions, insane and feeble minded institutions, storage of oil and gasoline (not to exceed 25,000 gallons), and manufacturing and industrial operations of any kind other than, and any public utility not included in, a class U-1, U-2, U-3, U-4 or U-5 use. There is a seventh class of uses which is prohibited altogether.

Class U-1 is the only district in which buildings are restricted to those enumerated. In the other classes the uses are cumulative; that is to say, uses in class U-2 include those enumerated in the preceding class, U-1; class U-3 includes uses enumerated in the preceding classes, U-2 and U-1; and so on. In addition to the enumerated uses, the ordinance provides for accessory uses, that is, for uses customarily incident to the principal use, such as private garages. Many regulations are provided in respect of such accessory uses.

The height districts are classified as follows: In class H-1, buildings are limited to a height of two and one-half stories or thirty-five feet; in class H-2, to four stories or fifty feet; in class H-3, to eighty feet. To all of these, certain exceptions are made, as in the case of church spires, water tanks, etc.

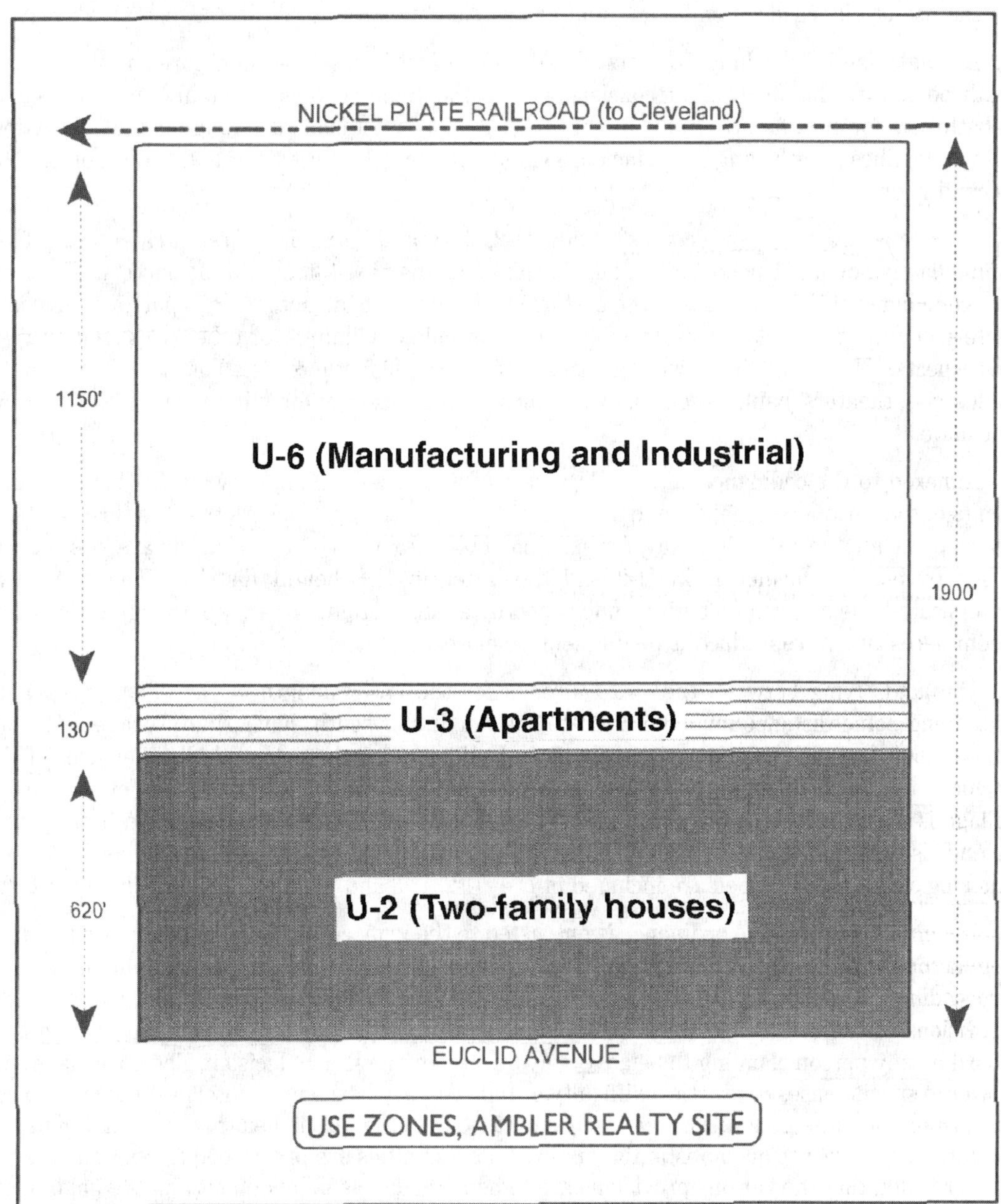

USE ZONES, AMBLER REALTY SITE

The classification of area districts is: In A-1 districts, dwellings or apartment houses to accommodate more than one family must have at least 5,000 square feet for interior lots and at least 4,000 square feet for corner lots; in A-2 districts, the area must be at least 2,500 square feet for interior lots, and 2,000 square feet for corner lots; in A-3 districts, the limits are 1,250 and 1,000 square feet, respectively; in A-4 districts, the limits are 900 and 700 square feet, respectively. The ordinance contains, in great variety and detail, provisions in respect of width of lots, front, side and rear yards, and other matters, including restrictions and regulations as to the use of billboards, sign boards and advertising signs.

A single family dwelling consists of a basement and not less than three rooms and a bathroom. A two-family dwelling consists of a basement and not less than four living rooms and a bathroom for each family; and is further described as a detached dwelling for the occupation of two families, one having its principal living rooms on the first floor and the other on the second floor.

Appellee's tract of land comes under U-2, U-3 and U-6. The first strip of 620 feet immediately north of Euclid Avenue falls in class U-2, the next 130 feet to the north, in U-3, and the remainder in U-6. The uses of the first 620 feet, therefore, do not include apartment houses, hotels, churches, schools, or other public and semi-public buildings, or other uses enumerated in respect of U-3 to U-6, inclusive. The uses of the next 130 feet include all of these, but exclude industries, theaters, banks, shops, and the various other uses set forth in respect of U-4 to U-6, inclusive.[*]

Annexed to the ordinance, and made a part of it, is a zone map, showing the location and limits of the various use, height and area districts, from which it appears that the three classes overlap one another; that is to say, for example, both U-5 and U-6 use districts are in A-4 area districts, but the former is in H-2 and the latter in H-3 height districts. The plan is a complicated one and can be better understood by an inspection of the map, though it does not seem necessary to reproduce it for present purposes.

The lands lying between the two railroads for the entire length of the village area and extending some distance on either side to the north and south, having an average width of about 1,600 feet, are left open, with slight exceptions, for industrial and all other uses. This includes the larger part of appellee's tract. Approximately one-sixth of the area of the entire village is included in U-5 and U-6 use districts. That part of the village lying south of Euclid Avenue is principally in U-1 districts. The lands lying north of Euclid Avenue and bordering on the long strip just described are included in U-1, U-2, U-3 and U-4 districts, principally in U-2.

The enforcement of the ordinance is entrusted to the inspector of buildings, under rules and regulations of the board of zoning appeals. Meetings of the board are public, and minutes of its proceedings are kept. It is authorized to adopt rules and regulations to carry into effect provisions of the ordinance. Decisions of the inspector of buildings may be appealed to the board by any person claiming to be adversely affected by any such decision. The board is given power in specific cases of practical difficulty or unnecessary hardship to interpret the ordinance in harmony with its general purpose and intent, so that the public health, safety and general welfare may be secure and substantial justice done. Penalties are prescribed for violations, and it is provided that the various provisions are to be regarded as independent and the holding of any provision to be unconstitutional, void or ineffective shall not affect any of the others.

---

[*] The court below seemed to think that the frontage of this property on Euclid Avenue to a depth of 150 feet came under U-1 district and was available only for single family dwellings. An examination of the ordinance and subsequent amendments, and a comparison of their terms with the maps, shows very clearly, however, that this view was incorrect. Appellee's brief correctly interpreted the ordinance: "The northerly 500 feet thereof immediately adjacent to the right of way of the New York, Chicago & St. Louis Railroad Company under the original ordinance was classed as U-6 territory and the rest thereof as U-2 territory. By amendments to the ordinance a strip 630 [620] feet wide north of Euclid Avenue is classed as U-2 territory, a strip 130 feet wide next north as U-3 territory and the rest of the parcel to the Nickel Plate right of way as U-6 territory."

AMBLER REALTY CO. v. VILLAGE OF EUCLID

297 F. 307, 313–16 (N.D. Ohio 1924)

Westenhaver, J. The argument supporting this ordinance proceeds . . . both on a mistaken view of what is property and of what is police power. Property, generally speaking, defendant's counsel concedes, is protected against a taking without compensation, by the guaranties of the Ohio and United States Constitutions. But their view seems to be that so long as the owner remains clothed with the legal title thereto and is not ousted from the physical possession thereof, his property is not taken, no matter to what extent his right to use is invaded or destroyed or its present or prospective value is depreciated. This is an erroneous view. The right to property, as used in the Constitution, has no such limited meaning. As has often been said in substance by the Supreme Court: "There can be no conception of property aside from its control and use, and upon its use depends its value." . . .

In defendants' view, the only difference between the police power and eminent domain is that the taking under the former may be done without compensation and under the latter a taking must be paid for. It seems to be the further view that whether one power or the other is exercised depends wholly on what the legislative department may see fit to recite on that subject. Such, however, is not the law. If police power meant what is claimed, all private property is now held subject to temporary and passing phases of public opinion, dominant for a day, in legislative or municipal assemblies. . . . Obviously, police power is not susceptible of exact definition. . . . And yet there is a wide difference between the power of eminent domain and the police power; and it is not true that the public welfare is a justification for the taking of private property for the general good. . . .

Nor can the ordinances here be sustained by invoking the average reciprocity of advantage rule. . . . It is a futile suggestion that plaintiff's present and obvious loss from being deprived of the normal and legitimate use of its property would be compensated indirectly by benefits accruing to that land from the restrictions imposed by the ordinance on other land. It is equally futile to suppose that other property in the village will reap the benefit of the damage to plaintiff's property and that of others similarly situated. The only reasonable probability is that the property values taken from plaintiff and other owners similarly situated will simply disappear, or at best be transferred to other unrestricted sections of the Cleveland industrial area, or at the worst, to some other and far distant industrial area. So far as plaintiff is concerned, it is a pure loss. In the average reciprocity of advantage there is a measureless difference between adjoining property owners as regards a party wall or a boundary pillar, and the owners of property restricted as in this case. In the former there may be some reciprocity of advantage, even though unequal in individual cases. In the present case, the property values are either dissipated or transferred to unknown and more or less distant owners.

The plain truth is that the true object of the ordinance is to place all of the property in an undeveloped area of 16 square miles in a straitjacket. The purpose to be accomplished is really to regulate the mode of living of persons who may hereafter inhabit it. In the last analysis, the result to be accomplished is to classify the population and segregate them according to their income or situation in life. . . .

VILLAGE OF EUCLID v. AMBLER REALTY CO.

272 U.S. 365 (1926)

JUSTICE SUTHERLAND delivered the opinion of the Court:

The ordinance is assailed on the grounds that it is in derogation of § 1 of the Fourteenth Amendment to the Federal Constitution in that it deprives appellee of liberty and property without due process of law and denies it the equal protection of the law, and that it offends against certain provisions of the Constitution of the State of Ohio. The prayer of the bill is for an injunction restraining the enforcement of the ordinance and all attempts to impose or maintain as to appellee's property any of the restrictions, limitations or conditions. The court below held the ordinance to be unconstitutional and void, and enjoined its enforcement. 297 F. 307.

Before proceeding to a consideration of the case, it is necessary to determine the scope of the inquiry. The bill alleges that the tract of land in question is vacant and has been held for years for the purpose of selling and developing it for industrial uses, for which it is especially adapted, being immediately in the path of progressive industrial development; that for such uses it has a market value of about $10,000 per acre, but if the use be limited to residential purposes the market value is not in excess of $2,500 per acre; that the first 200 feet of the parcel back from Euclid Avenue, if unrestricted in respect of use, has a value of $150 per front foot, but if limited to residential uses, and ordinary mercantile business be excluded therefrom, its value is not in excess of $50 per front foot.

It is specifically averred that the ordinance attempts to restrict and control the lawful uses of appellee's land so as to confiscate and destroy a great part of its value; that it is being enforced in accordance with its terms; that prospective buyers of land for industrial, commercial and residential uses in the metropolitan district of Cleveland are deterred from buying any part of this land because of the existence of the ordinance and the necessity thereby entailed of conducting burdensome and expensive litigation in order to vindicate the right to use the land for lawful and legitimate purposes; that the ordinance constitutes a cloud upon the land, reduces and destroys its value, and has the effect of diverting the normal industrial, commercial and residential development thereof to other and less favorable locations.

The record goes no farther than to show, as the lower court found, that the normal, and reasonably to be expected, use and development of that part of appellee's land adjoining Euclid Avenue is for general trade and commercial purposes, particularly retail stores and like establishments, and that the normal, and reasonably to be expected, use and development of the residue of the land is for industrial and trade purposes. Whatever injury is inflicted by the mere existence and threatened enforcement of the ordinance is due to restrictions in respect of these and similar uses; to which perhaps should be added — if not included in the foregoing — restrictions in respect of apartment houses. Specifically, there is nothing in the record to suggest that any damage results from the presence in the ordinance of those restrictions relating to churches, schools, libraries and other public and semi-public buildings. It is neither alleged nor proved that there is, or may be, a demand for any part of appellee's land for any of the last named uses; and we cannot assume the existence of facts which would justify an injunction upon this record in respect of this class of restrictions.

For present purposes the provisions of the ordinance in respect of these uses may, therefore, be put aside as unnecessary to be considered. It is also unnecessary to consider the effect of the restrictions in respect of U-1 districts, since none of appellee's land falls within that class.

We proceed, then, to a consideration of those provisions of the ordinance to which the case as it is made relates, first disposing of a preliminary matter.

A motion was made in the court below to dismiss the bill on the ground that, because complainant [appellee] had made no effort to obtain a building permit or apply to the zoning board of appeals for relief as it might have done under the terms of the ordinance, the suit was premature. The motion was properly overruled. The effect of the allegations of the bill is that the ordinance of its own force operates greatly to reduce the value of appellee's lands and destroy their marketability for industrial, commercial and residential uses; and the attack is directed, not against any specific provision or provisions, but against the ordinance as an entirety. Assuming the premises, the existence and maintenance of the ordinance, in effect, constitutes a present invasion of appellee's property rights and a threat to continue it. Under these circumstances, the equitable jurisdiction is clear.

It is not necessary to set forth the provisions of the Ohio Constitution which are thought to be infringed. The question is the same under both Constitutions, namely, as stated by appellee: Is the ordinance invalid in that it violates the constitutional protection "to the right of property in the appellee by attempted regulations under the guise of the police power, which are unreasonable and confiscatory?"

Building zone laws are of modern origin. They began in this country about twenty-five years ago. Until recent years, urban life was comparatively simple; but with the great increase and concentration of population, problems have developed, and constantly are developing, which require, and will continue to require, additional restrictions in respect of the use and occupation of private lands in urban communities. Regulations, the wisdom, necessity and validity of which, as applied to existing conditions, are so apparent that they are now uniformly sustained, a century ago, or even half a century ago, probably would have been rejected as arbitrary and oppressive. Such regulations are sustained, under the complex conditions of our day, for reasons analogous to those which justify traffic regulations, which, before the advent of automobiles and rapid transit street railways, would have been condemned as fatally arbitrary and unreasonable. And in this there is no inconsistency, for while the meaning of constitutional guaranties never varies, the scope of their application must expand or contract to meet the new and different conditions which are constantly coming within the field of their operation. In a changing world, it is impossible that it should be otherwise. But although a degree of elasticity is thus imparted, not to the *meaning*, but to the *application* of constitutional principles, statutes and ordinances, which, after giving due weight to the new conditions, are found clearly not to conform to the Constitution, of course, must fall.

The ordinance now under review, and all similar laws and regulations, must find their justification in some aspect of the police power, asserted for the public welfare. The line which in this field separates the legitimate from the illegitimate assumption of power is not capable of precise delimitation. It varies with circumstances and conditions. A regulatory zoning ordinance, which would be clearly valid as applied to the great cities, might be clearly invalid as applied to rural communities. In solving doubts, the maxim *sic utere tuo ut alienum non laedas*, which lies at the foundation of so much of the common law of nuisances, ordinarily will furnish a fairly helpful clew. And the law of nuisances, likewise, may be consulted, not for the purpose of controlling, but for the helpful aid of its analogies in the process of ascertaining the scope of, the power. Thus the question whether the power exists to forbid the erection of a building of a particular kind or for a particular use, like the question whether a particular thing is a nuisance, is to be determined, not by an abstract consideration of the building or of the thing considered apart, but by considering it in connection with the circumstances and the locality. A nuisance may be merely a right thing in the wrong place, — like a pig in the parlor instead of the barnyard. If the validity of the legislative classification for zoning purposes be fairly debatable, the legislative judgment must be allowed to control.

There is no serious difference of opinion in respect of the validity of laws and regulations fixing the height of buildings within reasonable limits, the character of materials and methods of construction, and the adjoining area which must be left open, in order to minimize the danger of fire or collapse, the evils of over-crowding, and the like, and excluding from residential sections offensive trades, industries and structures likely to create nuisances.

Here, however, the exclusion is in general terms of all industrial establishments, and it may thereby happen that not only offensive or dangerous industries will be excluded, but those which are neither offensive nor dangerous will share the same fate. But this is no more than happens in respect of many practice-forbidding laws which this Court has upheld although drawn in general terms so as to include individual cases that may turn out to be innocuous in themselves. The inclusion of a reasonable margin to insure effective enforcement, will not put upon a law, otherwise valid, the stamp of invalidity. Such laws may also find their justification in the fact that, in some fields, the bad fades into the good by such insensible degrees that the two are not capable of being readily distinguished and separated in terms of legislation. In the light of these considerations, we are not prepared to say that the end in view was not sufficient to justify the general rule of the ordinance, although some industries of an innocent character might fall within the proscribed class. It can not be said that the ordinance in this respect "passes the bounds of reason and assumes the character of a merely arbitrary fiat." *Purity Extract Co. v. Lynch*, 226 U.S. 192. Moreover, the restrictive provisions of the ordinance in this particular may be sustained upon the principles applicable to the broader exclusion from residential districts of all business and trade structures, presently to be discussed.

It is said that the Village of Euclid is a mere suburb of the City of Cleveland; that the industrial development of that city has now reached and in some degree extended into the village and, in the obvious course of things, will soon absorb the entire area for industrial enterprises; that the effect of the ordinance is to divert this natural development elsewhere with the consequent loss of increased values to the owners of the lands within the village borders. But the village, though physically a suburb of Cleveland, is politically a separate municipality, with powers of its own and authority to govern itself as it sees fit within the limits of the organic law of its creation and the State and Federal Constitutions. Its governing authorities, presumably representing a majority of its inhabitants and voicing their will, have determined, not that industrial development shall cease at its boundaries, but that the course of such development shall proceed within definitely fixed lines. If it be a proper exercise of the police power to relegate industrial establishments to localities separated from residential sections, it is not easy to find a sufficient reason for denying the power because the effect of its exercise is to divert an industrial flow from the course which it would follow, to the injury of the residential public if left alone, to another course where such injury will be obviated. It is not meant by this, however, to exclude the possibility of cases where the general public interest would so far outweigh the interest of the municipality that the municipality would not be allowed to stand in the way.

We find no difficulty in sustaining restrictions of the kind thus far reviewed. The serious question in the case arises over the provisions of the ordinance excluding from residential districts, apartment houses, business houses, retail stores and shops, and other like establishments. This question involves the validity of what is really the crux of the more recent zoning legislation, namely, the creation and maintenance of residential districts, from which business and trade of every sort, including hotels and apartment houses, are excluded. Upon that question this Court has not thus far spoken. The decisions of the state courts are numerous and conflicting; but those which broadly sustain the power greatly outnumber those which deny altogether or narrowly limit it; and it is very apparent that there is a constantly increasing tendency in the direction of the broader view. . . .

As evidence of the decided trend toward the broader view, it is significant that in some instances the state courts in later decisions have reversed their former decisions holding the other way. . . .

The decisions enumerated in the first group cited above agree that the exclusion of buildings devoted to business, trade, etc., from residential districts, bears a rational relation to the health and safety of the community. Some of the grounds for this conclusion are — promotion of the health and security from injury of children and others by separating dwelling houses from territory devoted to trade and industry; suppression and prevention of disorder; facilitating the extinguishment of fires, and the enforcement of street traffic regulations and other general welfare ordinances; aiding the health and safety of the community by excluding from residential areas the confusion and danger of fire, contagion and disorder which in greater or less degree attach to the location of stores, shops and factories. Another ground is that the construction and repair of streets may be rendered easier and less expensive by confining the greater part of the heavy traffic to the streets where business is carried on. . . .

The matter of zoning has received much attention at the hands of commissions and experts, and the results of their investigations have been set forth in comprehensive reports. These reports, which bear every evidence of painstaking consideration, concur in the view that the segregation of residential, business, and industrial buildings will make it easier to provide fire apparatus suitable for the character and intensity of the development in each section; that it will increase the safety and security of home life; greatly tend to prevent street accidents, especially to children, by reducing the traffic and resulting confusion in residential sections; decrease noise and other conditions which produce or intensify nervous disorders; preserve a more favorable environment in which to rear children, etc. With particular reference to apartment houses, it is pointed out that the development of detached house sections is greatly retarded by the coming of apartment houses, which has sometimes resulted in destroying the entire section for private house purposes; that in such sections very often the apartment house is a mere parasite, constructed in order to take advantage of the open spaces and attractive surroundings created by the residential character of the district. Moreover, the coming of one apartment house is followed by others, interfering by their height and bulk with the free circulation of air and monopolizing the rays of the sun which otherwise would fall upon the smaller homes, and bringing, as their necessary accompaniments, the disturbing noises incident to increased traffic and business, and the occupation, by means of moving and parked automobiles, of larger portions of the streets, thus detracting from their safety and depriving children of the privilege of quiet and open spaces for play, enjoyed by those in more favored localities, — until, finally, the residential character of the neighborhood and its desirability as a place of detached residences are utterly destroyed. Under these circumstances, apartment houses, which in a different environment would be not only entirely unobjectionable but highly desirable, come very near to being nuisances.

If these reasons, thus summarized, do not demonstrate the wisdom or sound policy in all respects of those restrictions which we have indicated as pertinent to the inquiry, at least, the reasons are sufficiently cogent to preclude us from saying, as it must be said before the ordinance can be declared unconstitutional, that such provisions are clearly arbitrary and unreasonable, having no substantial relation to the public health, safety, morals, or general welfare.

It is true that when, if ever, the provisions set forth in the ordinance in tedious and minute detail, come to be concretely applied to particular premises, including those of the appellee, or to particular conditions, or to be considered in connection with specific complaints, some of them, or even many of them, may be found to be clearly arbitrary and unreasonable. But where the equitable remedy of injunction is sought, as it is here, not upon the ground of a present infringement or denial of a specific right, or of a particular injury in process of actual execution, but upon the broad ground that the mere existence and threatened enforcement of the ordinance, by materially and adversely affecting values and curtailing the opportunities of the market, constitute a present and irreparable injury, the court will not scrutinize its provisions, sentence by sentence, to ascertain by a process of piecemeal dissection whether there may be, here and there, provisions of a minor character, or relating to matters of administration, or not shown to contribute to the injury complained of, which, if attacked separately, might not withstand the test of constitutionality. In respect of such provisions, of which specific complaint is not made, it cannot be said that the land owner has suffered or is threatened with an injury which entitles him to challenge their constitutionality. . . .

. . . What would be the effect of a restraint imposed by one or more of the innumerable provisions of the ordinance, considered apart, upon the value or marketability of the lands is neither disclosed by the bill nor by the evidence, and we are afforded no basis, apart from mere speculation, upon which to rest a conclusion that it or they would have any appreciable effect upon those matters. Under these circumstances, therefore, it is enough for us to determine, as we do, that the ordinance in its general scope and dominant features, so far as its provisions are here involved, is a valid exercise of authority, leaving other provisions to be dealt with as cases arise directly involving them.

And this is in accordance with the traditional policy of this Court. In the realm of constitutional law, especially, this Court has perceived the embarrassment which is likely to result from an attempt to formulate rules or decide questions beyond the necessities of the immediate issue. It has preferred to follow the method of a gradual approach to the general by a systematically guarded application and extension of constitutional principles to particular cases as they arise, rather than by out of hand attempts to establish general rules to which future cases must be fitted. This process applies with peculiar force to the solution of questions arising under the due process clause of the Constitution as applied to the exercise of the flexible powers of police, with which we are here concerned.

Decree reversed.

JUSTICE VAN DEVANTER, JUSTICE MCREYNOLDS, and JUSTICE BUTLER, dissent.

NOTES AND QUESTIONS

1. *A change of heart.* "Justice Sutherland . . . was writing an opinion for the majority in *Village of Euclid v. Ambler Realty Co.*, holding the zoning ordinance unconstitutional, when talks with his dissenting brethren (principally Stone, I believe) shook his convictions and led him to request a re-argument, after which he changed his mind and the ordinance was upheld." McCormack, *A Law Clerk's Recollections*, 46 Colum. L. Rev. 710, 712 (1946). In view of the district court's opinion, the powerful argument of Newton D. Baker, a highly capable attorney, on behalf of Ambler Realty, and the decision in favor of the Euclid ordinance after the rehearing, the Court's opinion by the conservative Justice Sutherland was rather surprising. The three dissenting Justices did not write an opinion.

2. *Euclid as a "test case."* One of the factors strongly influencing the Court toward a favorable decision on the broad issue of constitutionality of zoning was undoubtedly the brief filed by Alfred Bettman as counsel for several *amici curiae*, including the National Conference on City Planning, the Ohio State Conference on City Planning, the National Housing Association, and the Massachusetts Federation of Town Planning Boards. Brief on Behalf of the National Conference on City Planning et al., *Amici Curiae, Village of Euclid v. Ambler Realty Co.*, 272 U.S. 365 (1926) (No. 665, *reprinted in* 24 Landmark Briefs and Arguments of the Supreme Court of the United States: Constitutional Law 757 (P. Kurland & G. Casper eds., 1975)). Alfred Bettman was a leading national land use attorney in the years between the two world wars. His views on the *Euclid* case after the decision of the federal district court were expressed in the following letter:

> Regarding the Euclid Village zoning decision, the case was unfortunate. . . . The City made no scientific survey, and in an effort to keep the village entirely residential, the local authorities zoned all as residential and business, except a very narrow piece along the railroads, too narrow for a practical industrial development. It was a piece of arbitrary zoning and on the facts not justifiable. . . . Everybody advised against an appeal [from the District Court decision], because on appeal the decision is sure to be affirmed, even though the upper court disagrees with the opinion. [Letter from A. Bettman to D.J. Underwood, City Attorney, Tulsa, Oklahoma, Sept. 29, 1924, letter shown to one of the editors by Mr. Underwood's grandson, a planning student at the time.]

The views thus expressed by Bettman in 1924 no doubt account for his decision to ask the Supreme Court, on rehearing the *Euclid* case, to decide only "the constitutionality of comprehensive zoning" *in principle*, and not to consider "the reasonableness or arbitrariness of that detail of the ordinance which . . . placed appellee's land in a residential rather than an industrial zone." For an extensive discussion of the motivations for single family residential zoning in the years before *Euclid*, see Lees, *Preserving Property Values? Preserving Proper Homes? Preserving Privilege?: The Pre-Euclid Debate over Zoning for Exclusively Private Residential Areas, 1916-1926*, 56 U. Pitt. L. Rev. 367 (1994). She finds the expected concerns about preserving residential quality as well as discriminatory motives. For an argument that conflicts over race relations during the 1920s influenced both District Court Judge Westenhaver, in invalidating zoning as a violation of private contractual rights, and Justice Sutherland, in approving zoning as a reasonable exercise of the police power, see Chused, *Euclid's Historical Imagery*, 51 Case W. Res. L. Rev. 597 (2001).

3. *A critique of Euclid.* For all its celebrity, *Euclid* is not without its critics. Professor Tarlock uses the Bettman brief as his starting point.

Tarlock, Euclid Revisited, Land Use Law & Zoning Digest, Vol. 34, No. 1, at 4, 6-8 (1982)[*]

The Taking Issue

. . . Bettman's argument rested on a factual assumption that was unwarranted and proceeded to a theory that would read the taking clause out of the Constitution. Ambler Realty Co.'s claim that the value of its property had been taken was called "speculative" and thus not entitled to compensation because "one may not speculate upon a community's not exercising its constitutional police power and then claim a property right in the community's non-action. In truth the old value for which protection is claimed may have been produced, in whole or in part, by the very evil against which the legislation is directed."

Bettman quickly went on to point out what the court held two years later in *Nectow v. City of Cambridge*: the fact that a specific line drawing may be unconstitutional does not impair the validity of the plan as a whole.

Then, to bolster the basic argument that the Court should focus on comprehensive zoning in the abstract, Bettman distinguished Ambler's best case, *Pennsylvania Coal v. Mahon*, first on the technical ground that zoning was an exercise of the police power and not the power of eminent domain, and, second, that the property rights asserted by Ambler Realty Co., unlike the property rights created by deed in *Pennsylvania Coal*, were "simply those which inhere generally in all owners of land: and it is axiomatic that all property is held subject to the general right of the public to regulate its use for the protection of public health, safety, convenience, welfare."

Average Reciprocity of Advantage

These arguments that the ordinance was not a taking are essentially negative, but at two points in the brief Bettman advanced a powerful affirmative abstract argument in favor of the ordinance. The strongest general justification for zoning is that it is a publicly imposed restrictive covenant scheme; thus, restrictions on one lot can be justified by the average reciprocity of advantage that the complaining lot receives from similar restrictions imposed on adjoining lots. . . . Bettman argued that a comprehensive ordinance was constitutional because "each piece of property pays, in the shape of reasonable regulation of its use, for the protection which the plan gives to all property lying within its boundaries." Later in the brief, he asserted that a comprehensive zoning ordinance "gives to each piece of property its share of the general health, order, convenience, and security which the whole plan brings to the community."

Public Nuisance Analogy

The core of [Bettman's] argument is found in a paragraph [from his brief]:

> The law of nuisance operates by way of prevention as well as by suppression. The zoning ordinance, by segregating the industrial districts from the residential districts, aims to produce, by a process of prevention applied over the whole territory of the city

[*] Reprinted by permission.

> throughout an extensive period of time, the segregation of the noises and odors and turmoils necessarily incident to the operation of industry from those sections of the city in which the homes of the people are or may be appropriately located. The mode of regulation may be new; but the purpose and the fundamental justification are the same. . . .

[Bettman anticipated an argument that], if the purpose of zoning is to segregate nuisance-like activities, [shouldn't an owner have the opportunity] to prove that his use would not in fact be a nuisance? Bettman answered this objection by denying that a zoning ordinance was "restricted to or identical with nuisance regulation." He argued that nuisance law had become so confused that it was impossible to advise a client about the fate of a proposed use, and thus it was proper to make use segregations in advance of construction based on the probable nuisance like characteristics of a proposed use.

Market Allocation

[Bettman's final argument was] . . . that (1) zoning is necessary to correct a market failure that prevents the market from achieving an efficient allocation of land uses; (2) it is quite possible for cities to predict the course of the market and to draw a zoning map that will be filled in efficiently over time; and (3) therefore, a comprehensive zoning ordinance is entitled to the full presumption of constitutionality.

The end result was to be a tidy zoning map with everything in its proper place. "[T]he zone plan is one consistent whole, with parts adjusted to each other, carefully worked out on the basis of actual facts and tendencies, including actual economic factors, so as to secure development of all the territory within the city in such a way as to promote the public health, safety, convenience, order, and general welfare." . . .

Justice Sutherland's Response

Bettman's analysis of nuisance law seems to have been directly incorporated in three places in Justice Sutherland's opinion. . . . "In solving doubts [Sutherland says], the maxim *sic utere tuo ut alienum non laedes*, which lies at the foundation of so much of the common law of nuisances, ordinarily will furnish a fairly helpful clew." This is simply another way of stating that in nuisance law everything depends on the context of the dispute.

Bettman's "margin of safety" argument . . . impressed Sutherland. After advancing the nuisance analogy as a justification for zoning, Justice Sutherland quickly concluded that zoning ordinances need be no more over-inclusive than other types of regulation that had been held constitutional. Thus, the risk that inoffensive uses would be kept out of an area was not a sufficient reason to invalidate a comprehensive ordinance.

The hardest problem for Justice Sutherland was the constitutionality of segregating one type of residential use from another, but he resolved it in favor of zoning by characterizing apartment houses as parasites robbing single-family neighborhoods of value.

Conclusion

. . . On the basis of published accounts of the circumstances that led to the case, as well as the evidence presented at trial and the famous Bettman *amicus* brief that influenced the court on rehearing, the case at best validates a limited and flawed vision of zoning. Thus *Euclid* is not a sufficient basis for much contemporary zoning. The most difficult issues in zoning were glossed over or ignored by most parties to the litigation, and they continue to plague the courts. There is nothing very surprising in this conclusion. Most land use scholars have known it for years.

NOTES AND QUESTIONS

1. *Repositioning Euclid as a facial challenge.* It is quite clear that Justice Sutherland decided only "the constitutionality of comprehensive zoning" and not "the reasonableness or arbitrariness of that detail of the ordinance which . . . placed appellee's land in a residential rather than an industrial zone," as Bettman urged in the part of his brief quoted above. Thus the Court was able to avoid any serious consideration of the appellee's contention that the Euclid zoning ordinance reduced the value of its land so greatly as to result in a "taking" without compensation, in violation of the Fourteenth Amendment's Due Process Clause.

2. *Zoning "as applied."* Had the case been decided "as applied," it is more likely that Ambler Realty would have won. (On what theory: takings; substantive due process; equal protection?) Had Ambler Realty won, would the inevitable result have been to cast constitutional doubt on *all* zoning schemes? Conversely, because the Village of Euclid won, did that imply that *all* zoning was constitutional? Two years later, in *Nectow v. City of Cambridge*, 277 U.S. 183 (1928), the Court took an "as applied" case and held against the city. *Nectow* is discussed further in Ch. 3, *infra*.

3. *Euclid and Pennsylvania Coal.* Lacking confidence in the professional quality of Euclid's ordinance, it is understandable why Bettman was so anxious to have it facially reviewed. Even so, why did the court completely ignore *Pennsylvania Coal Co. v. Mahon*, decided only four years earlier? Under the holding in *Pennsylvania Coal*, wouldn't Ambler Realty's allegations about the diminution in value as a result of the *adoption* of the ordinance, if supported by evidence, tend strongly to show that the zoning regulations "went too far" and amounted to a *de facto* "taking"? Does the court's failure to even cite *Pennsylvania Coal* imply that a comprehensive zoning ordinance can never amount to a regulatory taking? This question informs much of the modern constitutional law of land use controls.

4. *Average reciprocity of advantage.* Note that Justice Sutherland's opinion does not refer to, much less rely on, the "average reciprocity of advantage" argument included in the Bettman brief. Justices Holmes and Brandeis each discussed this concept in *Pennsylvania Coal*, but Bettman cites neither. Holmes used the concept narrowly; Brandeis, whose dissenting position would have been supported by the broad concept that Bettman stated, apparently thought that such a broad use of "average reciprocity" was untenable, as did Judge Westenhaver in the *Euclid* trial opinion. Justice Sutherland no doubt agreed with Justice Brandeis and Judge Westenhaver. But consider Professor Michelman's point:

> [W]e might choose to view majoritarian collective action not as a succession of unrelated particular measures, each having an independently calculable distributional impact, but — more faithfully to the facts of political life — as an ongoing process of accommodation leaving in its wake a deposit of varied distributional impacts which significantly offset each other. [Michelman, *Property and Fairness: Comments on the Ethical Foundations of "Just Compensation" Law*, 80 Harv. L. Rev. 1165, 1177 (1967).]

Does Michelman embrace Bettman's argument? If (for sake of argument) Holmes' narrow use is correct and Bettman's broad use is untenable, where is the dividing line? Would the average reciprocity of advantage concept be applicable, for instance, within a built-up urban residential area "zoned" exclusively for residential use?

5. *Understanding Euclid.* As Professor Tarlock notes, *Euclid* was a poor vehicle for setting the 20th century course of American land use law. Consider the following factors: (1) the case arose in a middle-class suburban community, and the Court did not review the policy basis for that community's zoning ordinance; (2) while much of Euclid was not built up at the time of this decision, the case projects an image of the community that assumes a closely developed suburb at fairly high densities; (3) judicial notice was taken of techniques of apartment building, now outmoded, that provided an important factual backdrop for the opinion; (4) what worried the Court most was the separation of incompatible uses; and (5) an implied hierarchy of land use categories was erected that placed single-family residential at the top of the pyramid. But the Court completely failed to notice that if, e.g., single-family dwellings were built at the same density as apartments, the parking problems would be the same; and that, if apartments were built at the same height as single-family dwellings, the light and air problems would disappear. By ignoring the possibilities for accommodation between "uses" that more sophisticated site and density controls might have provided, the Supreme Court in the *Euclid* case ratified a control technique based on the separation of mutually incompatible land uses, and thus the exclusion of the less desirable "intruding" uses from what might be called "harm-sensitive" land. The "zoning" technique of land use regulation is treated in detail in Chapters 3–6, *infra.*

At one point in his opinion, Justice Sutherland uses the metaphor of "mere parasite" to characterize apartment buildings, concluding that in close proximity to single family houses they "come very near to being nuisances." 272 U.S. at 394. Can an inanimate object be a parasite? Or, would the parasites be the persons living in the apartments? On the other hand, District Judge Westenhaver, who invalidated the Euclid ordinance, concluded that the purpose of zoning "is really to regulate the mode of living of persons who may hereafter inhabit [the land]." 297 Fed. at 316. Who was more perceptive? Exclusionary zoning problems are discussed in Chapter 5, *infra.*

6. *Sources.* For additional discussion of the *Euclid* decision and arguments to the Court, see the collection of essays in Zoning and the American Dream (C. Haar & J. Kayden eds., 1989), especially Brooks, *The Office File Box — Emanations from the Battlefield,* at 3; S. Toll, Zoned American (1969). Knack, *Return to Euclid,* Planning, Vol. 62, No. 11 at 4 (1996), sketches the post-decision planning history of Euclid (bleak), with useful photographs. For an argument that *Euclid,* as "the case most closely identified with the denial of a constitutional right to speculative value," represents "an example of Progressive Jurisprudence . . . that views with great skepticism bold assertions of abstract rights," see Haar & Wolf, *Euclid Lives: The Survival of Progressive Jurisprudence,* 115 Harv. L. Rev. 2158 (2002). For a contrary view and a rejoinder, see Claeys, *Euclid Lives? The Uneasy Legacy of Progressivism in Zoning,* 73 Fordham L. Rev. 731 (2004); Haar & Wolf, *Yes, Thankfully, Euclid Lives,* 73 Fordham L. Rev. 771 (2004). See also Korngold, *The Emergence of Private Land Use Controls in Large-Scale Subdivisions: The Companion Story to Village of Euclid v. Ambler Realty Co.,* 51 Case W. Res. L. Rev. 617, 617 (2001) (*Euclid* "has had a profound effect on American life and jurisprudence"); Hylton, *Prelude to Euclid: The United States Supreme Court and the Constitutionality of Land Use Regulation, 1900-1920,* 3 Wash. U. J. L. & Pol'y 1, 2 (2000) (finding a "strong pro-regulation backdrop").

[b.] The Balancing Test

The next major Supreme Court case on the taking issue did not come until the late 1970s, and it was a highly charged case arising out of an attempt to construct what many considered an ugly skyscraper on the roof of Grand Central Station in New York City, a national icon. Justice Brennan's opinion for the majority follows:

PENN CENTRAL TRANSPORTATION CO. v. CITY OF NEW YORK

438 U.S. 104 (1978)

[The following statement of facts is taken from the official Syllabus.] Under New York City's Landmarks Preservation Law (Landmarks Law), which was enacted to protect historic landmarks and neighborhoods from precipitate decisions to destroy or fundamentally alter their character, the Landmarks Preservation Commission (Commission) may designate a building to be a "landmark" on a particular "landmark site" or may designate an area to be a "historic district." The Board of Estimate may thereafter modify or disapprove the designation, and the owner may seek judicial review of the final designation decision. The owner of the designated landmark must keep the building's exterior "in good repair" and before exterior alterations are made must secure Commission approval.

Under two ordinances owners of landmark sites may transfer development rights from a landmark parcel to proximate lots. Under the Landmarks Law, the Grand Central Terminal (Terminal), which is owned by the Penn Central Transportation Co. and its affiliates (Penn Central), was designated a "landmark" and the block it occupies a "landmark site." Appellant Penn Central, though opposing the designation before the Commission, did not seek judicial review of the final designation decision. Thereafter appellant Penn Central entered into a lease with appellant UGP, whereby UGP was to construct a multistory office building over the Terminal. (UGP agreed to pay Penn Central $1 million annually during construction and a minimum of $3 million annually thereafter.) After the Commission had rejected appellants' plans for the building as destructive of the Terminal's historic and aesthetic features, with no judicial review thereafter being sought, appellants brought suit in state court claiming that the application of the Landmarks Law had "taken" their property without just compensation in violation of the Fifth and Fourteenth Amendments and arbitrarily deprived them of their property without due process of law in violation of the Fourteenth Amendment. The trial court's grant of relief was reversed on appeal . . . .

JUSTICE BRENNAN delivered the opinion of the Court:

I

[Justice Brennan noted that Grand Central station, erected in 1913, was "a magnificent example of the French beaux-art style." It faces 42nd Street at its intersection with Park Avenue. "Although a 20-story office tower, to have been located above the Terminal, was part of the original design, the planned tower was never constructed." The Terminal was one of many buildings owned by Penn Central in the area, including a number of hotels and office buildings.

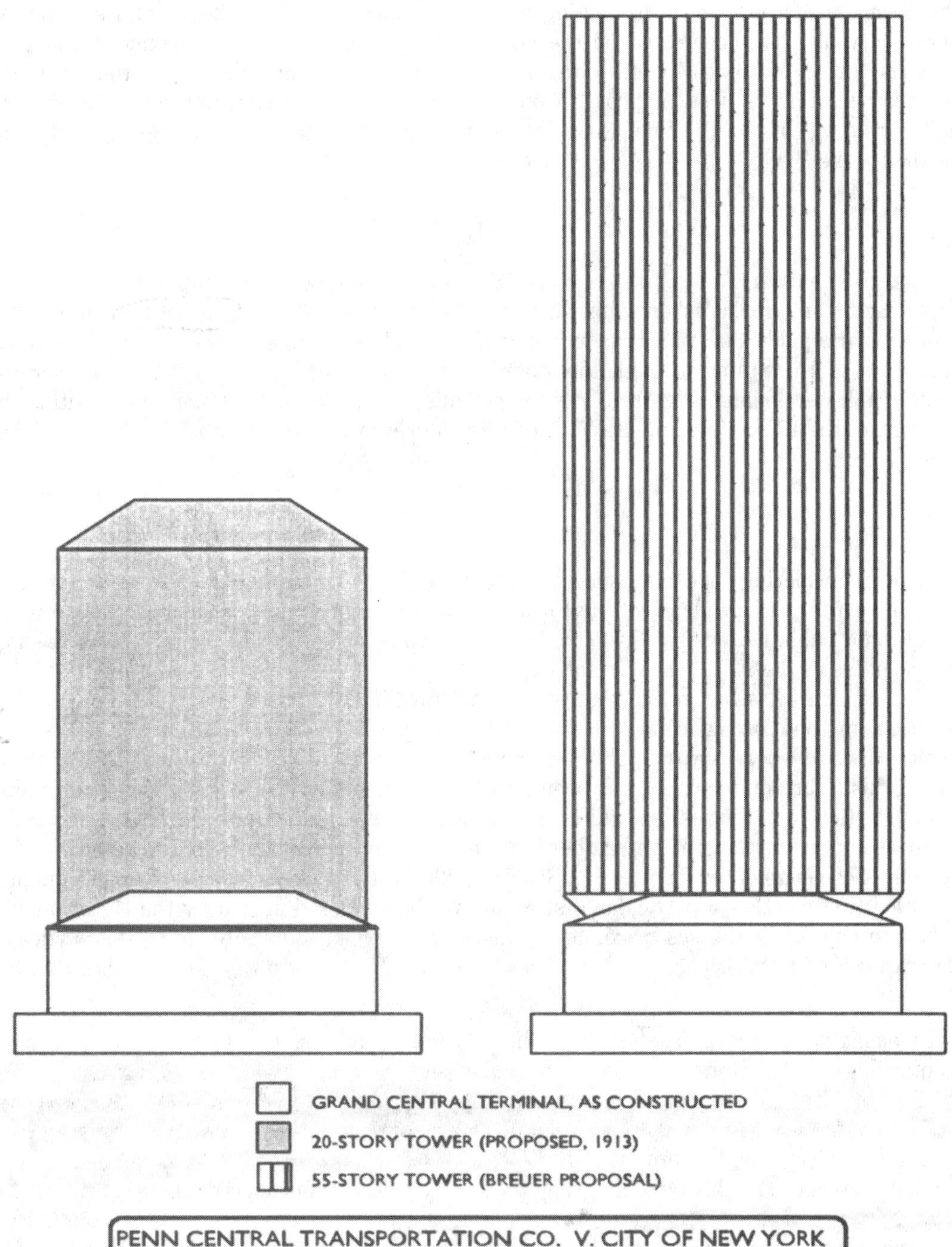

[Penn Central presented two proposals] "The first, Breuer I, provided for the construction of a 55-story office building, to be cantilevered above the existing facade and to rest on the roof of the Terminal. The second, Breuer II Revised, called for tearing down a portion of the Terminal that included the 42d Street facade, stripping off some of the remaining features of the Terminal's facade, and constructing a 53-story office building." The Commission denied both proposals. It concentrated on the view of the building from Park Avenue. Although a high-rise office building 375 feet away to the north had already destroyed this view, the commission found "majestic approach from the south to be still unique in the city." A 55-story building on top of the Terminal would be far more detrimental and "nothing more than an aesthetic joke."]

II

The issues presented by appellants are (1) whether the restrictions imposed by New York City's law upon appellants' exploitation of the Terminal site effect a "taking" of appellants' property for a public use within the meaning of the Fifth Amendment, which of course is made applicable to the States through the Fourteenth Amendment, and, (2) if so, whether the transferable development rights afforded appellants constitute "just compensation" within the meaning of the Fifth Amendment. We need only address the question whether a "taking" has occurred.[25]

A

Before considering appellants' specific contentions, it will be useful to review the factors that have shaped the jurisprudence of the Fifth Amendment injunction "nor shall private property be taken for public use, without just compensation." The question of what constitutes a "taking" for purposes of the Fifth Amendment has proved to be a problem of considerable difficulty. While this Court has recognized that the "Fifth Amendment's guarantee [is] designed to bar Government from forcing some people alone to bear public burdens which, in all fairness and justice, should be borne by the public as a whole," *Armstrong v. United States*, 364 U.S. 40, 49 (1960), this Court, quite simply, has been unable to develop any "set formula" for determining when "justice and fairness" require that economic injuries caused by public action be compensated by the Government, rather than remain disproportionately concentrated on a few persons. *See Goldblatt v. Hempstead*, 369 U.S. 590, 594 (1962). Indeed, we have frequently observed that whether a particular restriction will be rendered invalid by the Government's failure to pay for any losses proximately caused by it depends largely "upon the particular circumstances [in that] case." *United States v. Central Eureka Mining Co.*, 357 U.S. 155, 168 (1958).

In engaging in these essentially ad hoc, factual inquiries, the Court's decisions have identified several factors that have particular significance. The economic impact of the regulation on the claimant and, particularly, the extent to which the regulation has interfered with distinct investment backed expectations are of course relevant considerations. See *Goldblatt v. Hempstead, supra*, at 594. So too is the character of the governmental action. A "taking" may more readily be found when the interference with property can be characterized as a physical invasion by Government, *see, e.g., Causby v. United States*, 328 U.S. 256 (1946), than when interference arises from some public program adjusting the benefits and burdens of economic life to promote the common good.

"Government could hardly go on if to some extent values incident to property could not be

[25] As is implicit in our opinion, we do not embrace the proposition that a "taking" can never occur unless Government has transferred physical control over a portion of a parcel.

diminished without paying for every such change in the general law," *Pennsylvania Coal Co. v. Mahon*, 260 U.S. 393, 413 (1922), and this Court has accordingly recognized, in a wide variety of contexts, that Government may execute laws or programs that adversely affect recognized economic values. Exercises of the taxing power are one obvious example. A second are the decisions in which this Court has dismissed "taking" challenges on the ground that, while the challenged Government action caused economic harm, it did not interfere with interests that were sufficiently bound up with the reasonable expectations of the claimant to constitute "property" for Fifth Amendment purposes. *See, e.g., United States v. Willow River Power Co.*, 324 U.S. 499 (1945) (interest in high water level of river for run off for tail waters to maintain power head is not property); *United States v. Chandler-Dunbar Water Power Co.*, 229 U.S. 53 (1913) (no property interest can exist in navigable waters); *see also* Sax, *Takings and the Police Power*, 74 Yale L.J. 36, 61-62 (1963).

More importantly for the present case, in instances in which a state tribunal reasonably concluded that "the health, safety, morals or general welfare" would be promoted by prohibiting particular contemplated uses of land, this Court has upheld land use regulations that destroyed or adversely affected recognized real property interests. Zoning laws are of course the classic example, *see Euclid v. Ambler Realty Co.*, 272 U.S. 365 (1926) (prohibition of industrial use); *Gorieb v. Fox*, 274 U.S. 603, 608 (1927) (requirement that portions of parcels be left unbuilt); *Welch v. Swasey*, 214 U.S. 91 (1909) (height restriction), which have been viewed as permissible governmental action even when prohibiting the most beneficial use of the property.

Zoning laws generally do not affect existing uses of real property, but taking challenges have also been held to be without merit in a wide variety of situations when the challenged governmental actions prohibited a beneficial use to which individual parcels had previously been devoted and thus caused substantial individualized harm. *Miller v. Schoene*, 276 U.S. 272 (1928), is illustrative. In that case, a state entomologist, acting pursuant to a state statute, ordered the claimants to cut down a large number of ornamental red cedar trees because they produced cedar rust fatal to apple trees cultivated nearby. Although the statute provided for recovery of any expense incurred in removing the cedars, and permitted claimants to use the felled trees, it did not provide compensation for the value of the standing trees or for the resulting decrease in market value of the properties as a whole. A unanimous Court held that this latter omission did not render the statute invalid. The Court held that the State might properly make "a choice between the preservation of one class of property and that of the other" and since the apple industry was important in the State involved, concluded that the State had not exceeded "its constitutional powers by deciding upon the destruction of one class of property [without compensation] in order to save another, which, in the judgment of the legislature, is of greater value to the public." *Id.*, at 279.

Again, *Hadacheck v. Sebastian*, 239 U.S. 394 (1915), upheld a law prohibiting the claimant from continuing his otherwise lawful business of operating a brickyard in a particular physical community on the ground that the legislature had reasonably concluded that the presence of the brickyard was inconsistent with neighboring uses. *See also United States v. Central Eureka Mining Co., supra* (government order closing gold mines so that skilled miners would be available for other mining work held not a taking); *Atchison, T. & S.F.R. Co. v. Public Utilities Comm.*, 346 U.S. 346 (1953) (railroad may be required to pay cost of constructing railroad grade crossing); *Walls v. Midland Carbon Co.*, 254 U.S. 300 (1920) (law prohibiting manufacture of carbon black upheld); *Reinman v. Little Rock*, 237 U.S. 171 (1915) (law prohibiting livery stable upheld); *Mugler v. Kansas*, 123 U.S. 623 (1887) (law prohibiting liquor business upheld).

Goldblatt v. Hempstead, supra, is a recent example. There, a 1958 city safety ordinance banned any excavations below the water table and effectively prohibited the claimant from continuing a sand and gravel mining business that had been operated on the particular parcel since 1927. The Court upheld the ordinance against a "taking" challenge, although the ordinance prohibited the present and presumably most beneficial use of the property and had, like the regulations in *Miller* and *Hadacheck*, impacted severely on a particular owner. The Court assumed that the ordinance did not prevent the owner's reasonable use of the property since the owner made no showing of an adverse effect on the value of the land. Because the restriction served a substantial public purpose, the Court thus held no taking had occurred. It is of course implicit in *Goldblatt* that a use restriction on real property may constitute a "taking" if not reasonably necessary to the effectuation of a substantial public purpose, *see Nectow v. Cambridge*, [277 U.S. 183 (1928)]; *cf. Moore v. City of East Cleveland*, 431 U.S. 494, 513–514 (1977) (Stevens, J., concurring), or perhaps if it has an unduly harsh impact upon the owner's use of the property.

Pennsylvania Coal Co. v. Mahon, 260 U.S. 393 (1922), is the leading case for the proposition that a state statute that substantially furthers important public policies may so frustrate distinct investment-backed expectations as to amount to a "taking." There the claimant had sold the surface rights to particular parcels of property, but expressly reserved the right to remove the coal thereunder. A Pennsylvania statute, enacted after the transactions, forbade any mining of coal that caused the subsidence of any house, unless the house was the property of the owner of the underlying coal and was more than 150 feet from the improved property of another. Because the statute made it commercially impracticable to mine the coal, *id.*, at 414, and thus had nearly the same effect as the complete destruction of rights claimant had purchased from the owners of the surface land, *see id.*, at 414–415, the Court held that the statute was invalid as effecting a "taking" without just compensation. *See also Armstrong v. United States, supra.* (Government's complete destruction of a materialman's lien in certain property held a "taking"); *Hudson Water Co. v. McCarter*, 209 U.S. 349, 355 (1908) (if height restriction makes property wholly useless "the right of property prevails over the public interest" and compensation is required). *See generally* Michelman, *Property, Utility, and Fairness: Comments on the Ethical Foundations of "Just Compensation" Law*, 80 Harv. L. Rev. 1165, 1229–1234 (1967).

Finally, Government actions that may be characterized as acquisitions of resources to permit or facilitate uniquely public functions have often been held to constitute "takings." *Causby v. United States, supra*, is illustrative. In holding that direct overflights above the claimant's land, that destroyed the present use of the land as a chicken farm, constituted a "taking," *Causby* emphasized that Government had not "merely destroyed property [but was] using a part of it for the flight of its planes." *Id.*, at 262–263, n. 7. *See also Griggs v. Allegheny County*, 369 U.S. 84 (1962) (overflights held a taking); *Portsmouth Co. v. United States*, 260 U.S. 327 (1922) (United States' military installations repeated firing of guns over claimant's land is a taking); *United States v. Cress*, 243 U.S. 316 (1917) (repeated floodings of land caused by water project is taking); *but see YMCA v. United States*, 395 U.S. 85 (1969) (damage caused to building when federal officers who were seeking to protect building were attacked by rioters held not a taking). *See generally* Michelman, 80 Harv. L. Rev. 1165, 1226–1229 (1967); Sax, 74 Yale L.J. 36 (1963).

B

In contending that the New York City law has "taken" their property in violation of the Fifth and Fourteenth Amendments, appellants make a series of arguments, which, while tailored to the facts of this case, essentially urge that any substantial restriction imposed pursuant to a landmark law must be accompanied by just compensation if it is to be constitutional. Before considering these, we emphasize what is not in dispute. Because this Court has recognized, in a number of settings, that States and cities may enact land use restrictions or controls to enhance the quality of life by preserving the character and desirable aesthetic features of a city, *see New Orleans v. Dukes*, 427 U.S. 297 (1976); *Young v. American Mini Theatres, Inc.*, 427 U.S. 50 (1976); *Village of Belle Terre v. Boraas*, 416 U.S. 1, 9-10 (1974); *Berman v. Parker*, 348 U.S. 26, 33 (1954); *Welch v. Swasey, supra*, at 108, appellants do not contest that New York City's objective of preserving structures and areas with special historic, architectural, or cultural significance is an entirely permissible governmental goal. They also do not dispute that the restrictions imposed on its parcel are appropriate means of securing the purposes of the New York City law. Finally, appellants do not challenge any of the specific factual premises of the decision below. They accept for present purposes both that the parcel of land occupied by Grand Central Terminal must, in its present state, be regarded as capable of earning a reasonable return, and that the transferable development rights afforded appellants by virtue of the Terminal's designation as a landmark are valuable, even if not as valuable as the rights to construct above the Terminal. In appellants' view none of these factors derogate from their claim that New York City's law has effected a "taking."

They first observe that the air space above the Terminal is a valuable property interest, citing *United States v. Causby, supra.* They urge that the Landmark Law has deprived them of any gainful use of their "air rights" above the Terminal and that, irrespective of the value of the remainder of their parcel, the city has "taken" their right to this superadjacent air space, thus entitling them to "just compensation" measured by the fair market value of these air rights.

Apart from our own disagreement with appellants' characterization of the effect of the New York law, *see infra*, the submission that appellants may establish a "taking" simply by showing that they have been denied the ability to exploit a property interest that they heretofore had believed was available for development is quite simply untenable. Were this the rule, this Court would have erred not only in upholding laws restricting the development of air rights, *see Welch v. Swasey, supra*, but also in approving those prohibiting both the subjacent, *see Goldblatt v. Hempstead, supra*, and the lateral development, *see Gorieb v. Fox, supra*, of particular parcels.[27]

"Taking" jurisprudence does not divide a single parcel into discrete segments and attempt to determine whether rights in a particular segment have been entirely abrogated. In deciding whether a particular governmental action has effected a taking, this Court focuses rather both on the character of the action and on the nature and extent of the interference with rights in the parcel as a whole, here, the city tax block designated as the "landmark site."

[27] These cases dispose of any contention that might be based on *Pennsylvania Coal Co. v. Mahon supra*, that full use of air rights is so bound up with the investment backed expectations of appellants that Governmental deprivation of these rights invariably — *i.e.*, irrespective of the impact of the restriction on the value of the parcel as a whole — constitutes a "taking." Similarly, *Welch*, *Goldblatt*, and *Gorieb* illustrate the fallacy of appellants' related contention that a "taking" must be found to have occurred whenever the land use restriction may be characterized as imposing a "servitude" on the claimant's parcel.

Secondly, appellants, focusing on the character and impact of the New York City law, argue that it effects a "taking" because its operation has significantly diminished the value of the Terminal site. Appellants concede that the decisions sustaining other land use regulations, which, like the New York law, are reasonably related to the promotion of the general welfare, uniformly reject the proposition that diminution in property value, standing alone, can establish a taking, *see Euclid v. Ambler Realty Co., supra* (75% diminution in value caused by zoning law); *Hadacheck v. Sebastian, supra* (87 1/2 % diminution in value), and that the taking issue in these contexts is resolved by focusing on the uses the regulations permit. *See also Goldblatt v. Hempstead, supra.* Appellants, moreover, also do not dispute that a showing of diminution in property value would not establish a taking if the restriction had been imposed as a result of historic district legislation, *see generally Maher v. City of New Orleans*, 516 F.2d 1051 (5th Cir. 1975), but appellants argue that New York City's regulation of individual landmarks is fundamentally different from zoning or from historic district legislation because the controls imposed by New York City's law apply only to individuals who own selected properties.

Stated baldly, appellants' position appears to be that the only means of ensuring that selected owners are not singled out to endure financial hardship for no reason is to hold that any restriction imposed on individual landmarks pursuant to the New York scheme is a "taking" requiring the payment of "just compensation." Agreement with this argument would of course invalidate not just New York City's law, but all comparable landmark legislation in the Nation. We find no merit in it.

It is true, as appellants emphasize, that both historic district legislation and zoning laws regulate all properties within given physical communities whereas landmark laws apply only to selected parcels. But, contrary to appellants' suggestions, landmark laws are not like discriminatory, or "reverse spot," zoning: that is, a land use decision which arbitrarily singles out a particular parcel for different, less favorable treatment than the neighboring ones. In contrast to discriminatory zoning, which is the antithesis of land use control as part of some comprehensive plan, the New York City law embodies a comprehensive plan to preserve structures of historic or aesthetic interest wherever they might be found in the city,[28] and as noted, over 400 landmarks and 31 historic districts have been designated pursuant to this plan.

Equally without merit is the related argument that the decision to designate a structure as a landmark "is inevitably arbitrary or at least subjective because it basically is a matter of taste," Reply Brief of Appellant 22, thus unavoidably singling out individual landowners for disparate and unfair treatment. The argument has a particularly hollow ring in this case. For appellants not only did not seek judicial review of either the designation or of the denials of the certificates of appropriateness and of no exterior effect, but do not even now suggest that the Commission's decisions concerning the Terminal were in any sense arbitrary or unprincipled. But, in any event, a landmark owner has a right to judicial review of any Commission decision, and, quite simply, there is no basis whatsoever for a conclusion that courts will have any greater difficulty identifying arbitrary or discriminatory action in the context of landmark regulation

---

[28] Although the New York Court of Appeals contrasted the New York City Landmark Law with both zoning and historic district legislation and stated at one point that landmark laws do not "further a general community plan," 42 N.Y.2d at 330, it also emphasized that the implementation of the objectives of the landmark law constitutes an "acceptable reason to single out one particular parcel for different and less favorable treatment." *Ibid.* Therefore, we do not understand the New York Court of Appeals to disagree with our characterization of the Act.

than in the context of classic zoning or indeed in any other context.[29]

Next, appellants observe that New York City's law differs from zoning laws and historic district ordinances in that the Landmark Law does not impose identical or similar restrictions on all structures located in particular physical communities. It follows, they argue, that New York City's law is inherently incapable of producing the fair and equitable distribution of benefits and burdens of governmental action which is characteristic of zoning laws and historic district legislation and which they maintain is a constitutional requirement if "just compensation" is not to be afforded. It is of course true that the Landmark Law has a more severe impact on some landowners than on others, but that in itself does not mean that the law effects a "taking." Legislation designed to promote the general welfare commonly burdens some more than others. The owners of the brickyard in *Hadacheck*, of the cedar trees in *Miller v. Schoene*, and of the gravel and sand mine in *Goldblatt v. Hempstead*, were uniquely burdened by the legislation sustained in those cases.[30]

Similarly, zoning laws often impact more severely on some property owners than others but have not been held to be invalid on that account. For example, the property owner in *Euclid* who wished to use his property for industrial purposes was affected far more severely by the ordinance than his neighbors who wished to use their land for residences.

In any event, appellants' repeated suggestions that they are solely burdened and unbenefited is factually inaccurate. This contention overlooks the fact that the New York City law applies to vast numbers of structures in the city in addition to the Terminal — all the structures contained in the 31 historic districts and over 400 individual landmarks, many of which are close to the Terminal.[31]

Unless we are to reject the judgment of the New York City Council that the preservation of landmarks benefits all New York citizens and all structures, both economically and by improving the quality of life in the city as a whole — which we are unwilling to do — we cannot conclude that the owners of the Terminal have in no sense been benefited by the Landmark Law. Doubtless appellants believe they are more burdened than benefited by the law, but that

---

[29] When a property owner challenges the application of a zoning ordinance to his property, the judicial inquiry focuses upon whether the challenged restriction can reasonably be deemed to promote the objectives of the community land use plan, and will include consideration of the treatment of similar parcels. *See generally Nectow v. Cambridge, supra.* When a property owner challenges a landmark designation or restriction as arbitrary or discriminatory, a similar inquiry presumably will occur.

[30] Appellants attempt to distinguish these cases on the ground that, in each, Government was prohibiting a "noxious" use of land and that in the present case, in contrast, appellants' proposed construction above the Terminal would be beneficial. We observe that the uses in issue in *Hadacheck, Miller*, and *Goldblatt* were perfectly lawful in themselves. They involved no "blameworthiness, . . . moral wrongdoing, or conscious act of dangerous risk-taking which induce[d society] to shift the cost to a particular individual." Sax, 74 Yale L.J. 36, 50 (1964). These cases are better understood as resting not on any supposed "noxious" quality of the prohibited uses but rather on the ground that the restrictions were reasonably related to the implementation of a policy — not unlike historic preservation — expected to produce a widespread public benefit and applicable to all similarly situated property.

Nor, correlatively, can it be asserted that the destruction or fundamental alteration of a historic landmark is not harmful. The suggestion that the beneficial quality of appellants' proposed construction is established by the fact that construction would have been consistent with applicable zoning laws ignores the development in sensibilities and ideals reflected in landmark legislation like New York City's.

[31] There are some 53 designated landmarks and three historic districts or scenic landmarks in Manhattan between 14th and 59th Streets. *See* Landmarks Preservation Commission, Landmarks and Historic Districts (1977).

must have been true too of the property owners in *Miller, Hadacheck, Euclid*, and *Goldblatt*.[32]

Appellants' final broad-based attack would have us treat the law as an instance, like that in *United States v. Causby, supra,* in which Government, acting in an enterprise capacity, has appropriated part of their property for some strictly governmental purpose. Apart from the fact that *Causby* was a case of invasion of airspace that destroyed the use of the farm beneath and this New York City law has in no wise impaired the present use of the Terminal, the Landmark Law neither exploits appellants' parcel for city purposes nor facilitates nor arises from any entrepreneurial operations of the city. The situation is not remotely like that in *Causby* when the airspace above the Terminal was in the flight pattern for military aircraft. The Landmarks Law's effect is simply to prohibit appellants or anyone else from occupying portions of the airspace above the Terminal, while permitting appellants to use the remainder of the parcel in a gainful fashion. This is no more an appropriation of property by Government for its own uses than is a zoning law prohibiting, for "aesthetic" reasons, two or more adult theaters within a specified area, *see Young v. American Mini Theatres, Inc., supra*, or a safety regulation prohibiting excavations below a certain level. *See Goldblatt v. City of Hempstead, supra.*

C

Rejection of appellants' broad arguments is not however the end of our inquiry, for all we thus far have established is that the New York law is not rendered invalid by its failure to provide "just compensation" whenever a landmark owner is restricted in the exploitation of property interests, such as air rights, to a greater extent than provided for under applicable zoning laws. We now must consider whether the interference with appellants' property is of such a magnitude that "there must be an exercise of eminent domain and compensation to sustain [it]." *Pennsylvania Coal Co. v. Mahon*, 260 U.S., at 413. That inquiry may be narrowed to the question of the severity of the impact of the law on appellants' parcel, and its resolution in turn requires a careful assessment of the impact of the regulation on the Terminal site.

Unlike the governmental acts in *Goldblatt, Miller, Causby, Griggs*, and *Hadacheck*, the New York City law does not interfere in any way with the present uses of the Terminal. Its designation as a landmark not only permits but contemplates that appellants may continue to use the property precisely as it has for the past 65 years: as a railroad terminal containing office space and concessions. So the law does not interfere with what must be regarded as Penn Central's primary expectation concerning the use of the parcel. More importantly, on this record, we must regard the New York City law as permitting Penn Central not only to profit from the Terminal but to obtain a "reasonable return" on its investment.

Appellants, moreover, exaggerate the effect of the Act on its ability to make use of the air rights above the Terminal in two respects.[33]

First, it simply cannot be maintained, on this record, that appellants have been prohibited from occupying *any* portion of the airspace above the Terminal. While the Commission's

---

[32] It is of course true that the fact the duties imposed by zoning and historic district legislation apply throughout particular physical communities provides assurances against arbitrariness, but the applicability of the landmarks law to large numbers of parcels in the city, in our view, provides comparable, if not identical, assurances.

[33] Appellants of course argue at length that the transferable development rights, while valuable, do not constitute "just compensation."

actions in denying applications to construct an office building in excess of 50 stories above the Terminal may indicate that it will refuse to issue a certificate of appropriateness for any comparably sized structure, nothing the Commission has said or done suggests an intention to prohibit *any* construction above the Terminal. The Commission's report emphasized that whether any construction would be allowed depended upon whether the proposed addition "would harmonize in scale, material, and character with [the Terminal]." Since appellants have not sought approval for the construction of a smaller structure, we do not know that appellants will be denied any use of any portion of the airspace above the Terminal.(34)

Second, to the extent appellants have been denied the right to build above the Terminal, it is not literally accurate to say that they have been denied *all* use of even those pre-existing air rights. Their ability to use these rights has not been abrogated; they are made transferable to at least eight parcels in the vicinity of the Terminal, one or two of which have been found suitable for the construction of new office buildings. Although appellants and others have argued that New York City's transferable development rights program is far from ideal, the New York courts here supportably found that, at least in the case of the Terminal, the rights afforded are valuable. While these rights may well not have constituted "just compensation" if a "taking" had occurred, the rights nevertheless undoubtedly mitigate whatever financial burdens the law has imposed on appellants and, for that reason, are to be taken into account in considering the impact of regulation. *Cf. Goldblatt v. Hempstead, supra*, at 594 n.3.

On this record we conclude that the application of New York City's Landmark Preservation Law has not effected a "taking" of appellants' property. The restrictions imposed are substantially related to the promotion of the general welfare and not only permit reasonable beneficial use of the landmark site but afford appellants opportunities further to enhance not only the Terminal site proper but also other properties.(36)

Affirmed.

JUSTICE REHNQUIST, with whom THE CHIEF JUSTICE and JUSTICE STEVENS join, dissenting. . . .

[The following excerpts from then-Justice Rehnquist's opinion explain his view on the nuisance basis for taking law and the role of average reciprocity of advantage:]

1

As early as 1887, the Court recognized that the government can prevent a property owner from using his property to injure others without having to compensate the owner for the value of the forbidden use. . . . [Citing and quoting from *Mugler v. Kansas*, 123 U.S. 623, 668–69 (1887). — Eds.]

Appellees are not prohibiting a nuisance. The record is clear that the proposed addition to the Grand Central Terminal would be in full compliance with zoning, height limitations, and other health and safety requirements. Instead, appellees are seeking to preserve what they believe to be an outstanding example of Beaux Arts architecture. Penn Central is prevented

(34) Counsel for appellants admitted at oral argument that the Commission has not suggested that it would not, for example, approve a 20-story office tower along the lines of that which was part of the original plan for the Terminal.

(36) We emphasize that our holding today is on the present record which in turn is based on Penn Central's present ability to use the Terminal for its intended purposes and in a gainful fashion. The city conceded at oral argument that if appellants can demonstrate at some point in the future that circumstances have changed such that the Terminal ceases to be, in the city's counsel's words, "economically viable," appellants may obtain relief.

from further developing its property basically because it did *too good* of a job in designing and building it. The city of New York, because of its unadorned admiration for the design, has decided that the owners of the building must preserve it unchanged for the benefit of sightseeing New Yorkers and tourists.

Unlike in the case of land use regulations, appellees are not prohibiting Penn Central from using its property in a narrow sense. Instead, appellees have placed an affirmative duty on Penn Central to maintain the Terminal in its present state of "good repair." Appellants are not free to use their property as they see fit within broad outer boundaries but must strictly adhere to their past use except where appellees conclude that alternative uses would not detract from the Landmark. While Penn Central may continue to use the Terminal as it is presently designed, appellees otherwise "exercise complete dominion and control over the surface of the land," *United States v. Causby*, 328 U.S. 256, 262 (1946), and must compensate the owner for his loss. . . .

2

Even where the government prohibits a noninjurious use, the Court has ruled that a taking does not take place if the prohibition applies over a broad cross section of land and thereby "secure[s] an average reciprocity of advantage." *Pennsylvania Coal Co. v. Mahon*, 260 U.S. 393, 415 (1922). While zoning at times reduces *individual* property values, the burden is shared relatively evenly and it is reasonable to conclude that on the whole an individual who is harmed by one aspect of the zoning will be benefited by another.

Here, however, a multimillion dollar loss has been imposed on appellants; it is uniquely felt and is not offset by any benefits flowing from the preservation of some 500 other "Landmarks" in New York. Appellees have imposed a substantial cost on less than one-tenth of one percent of the buildings in New York for the general benefit of all its people. It is exactly this imposition of general costs on a few individuals at which the "taking" protection is directed. . . .

NOTES AND QUESTIONS

1. *Penn Central* is a critical case in takings jurisprudence. For the first time, the Court attempted to integrate its "essentially ad hoc, factual inquiries" by providing a comprehensive three-factor balancing test. But does Justice Brennan then apply his own test? Penn Central lost a valuable business opportunity under a law that postdated its acquisition of the Terminal, facts which fit comfortably with two of the three factors in his test ("physical invasion" was not an issue). Shouldn't the case have come out the other way? Is *Hadacheck v. Sebastian* still good law? Is economic impact, the three-factor test notwithstanding, still the only test that really matters? And if so, what about *Pennsylvania Coal*?

2. *Nuisance.* What has happened to the nuisance rationale for land use regulation so explicitly endorsed in *Euclid*? Reread footnote 30 in the majority opinion. Justice Brennan's apparent rejection of the harm-benefit rule was confirmed in the Court's *Lucas* decision, reproduced *infra*.

3. *Average reciprocity of advantage.* The railroad argued that the landmark law "is inherently incapable of producing the fair and equitable distribution of benefits and burdens of governmental action," to which Justice Brennan replied that the landmark owners benefit as "citizens" of New York. Has Alfred Bettman's theory finally been adopted by the Court?

Arguably, Brennan's approach, if pushed far enough, could read the Takings Clause out of the constitution. See Mandelker, *Waiving the Taking Clause: Conflicting Signals from the Supreme Court, in* 1994 Proceedings of the Institute on Planning, Zoning, and Eminent Domain (1995). The "average reciprocity" maxim was applied in the *Agins* case, discussed *infra*, but then appeared to lose importance as the Court fashioned new and more restrictive takings theories. See generally Oswald, *The Role of the "Harm/Benefit" and "Average Reciprocity of Advantage" Rules in a Comprehensive Takings Analysis*, 50 Vand. L. Rev. 1449 (1997). But it reappeared in the *Lake Tahoe* case, reproduced *infra*. See Wade & Bunting, *Average Reciprocity of Advantage: "Magic Words" or Economic Realty — Lessons from Palazzolo*, 39 Urb. L. 319 (2007).

4. *Investment-backed expectations. Penn Central* is the first Supreme Court opinion to embrace this concept, which seemed to introduce a tilt in takings law that favors landowners. Can you see why? Justice Brennan never really defines the term, however, except to note where it would not apply. An example is his statement that a landowner does not have an investment-backed expectation in the "ability to exploit" a property interest he believed was available for development. Another is his statement that "unilateral" expectations are not protected. This takings factor remains unclear more than a quarter-century after *Penn Central*, although courts have applied it to uphold takings claims when a landowner had a vested property right. See *Pace Resources, Inc. v. Shrewsbury Township*, 808 F.2d 1023 (3d Cir. 1987). They also apply it to uphold takings claims to protect a landowner's expectations at the time she purchased the land. See *Gil v. Inland Wetlands & Watercourses Agency*, 593 A.2d 1368, 1372 (Conn. 1991) (accepting "fact-bound determination" that landowner had reasonable investment-backed expectations that he could build on lot). For a review of the investment-backed expectations factor after *Palazzolo* and *Tahoe-Sierra*, reproduced *infra*, see Stein, *Takings in the 21st Century: Reasonable Investment-Backed Expectations after Palazzolo and Tahoe-Sierra*, 69 Tenn. L. Rev. 891 (2002). Recent cases applying this Takings Clause factor are discussed *infra*.

5. *Notice.* One of the important contributions of the investment-backed expectations takings factor to takings law is the notice rule. Should a landowner lose her investment-backed expectations if a restrictive land use regulation is adopted before or after she purchases her property? Wouldn't this approach read the Takings Clause out of the constitution? In *Ruckelshaus v. Monsanto Co.*, 467 U.S. 986 (1984), the Court said yes in a non-land use context. It held that a statute giving notice that disclosure of trade secrets would be required when applying to register a pesticide was not a taking. The Court went even further and held that the "force" of the investment-backed expectations factor partly defeated the takings claim, suggesting that proof of expectations is a necessary condition to a takings suit. Lower federal courts applied the notice rule to reject takings claims when property owners purchased land that was subject to wetlands and similar regulation that restricted the use of their property, see, e.g., *Claridge v. New Hampshire Wetlands Bd.*, 485 A.2d 287 (1984), but the *Nollan* case, reproduced *infra*, and especially footnote 2, cast doubt on these holdings. In the *Lucas* case, also reproduced *infra*, Justice Kennedy referred to the investment-backed expectations factor as circular. Is he right?

In *Palazzolo v. Rhode Island*, 533 U.S. 606, 626–30 (2001), the Court rejected the idea that the purchase of a property after the enactment of a regulation was a per se loss of investment-backed expectations that prevented a court from finding that the regulation amounted to a taking. Anthony Palazzolo, a lifelong resident of Westerly, Rhode Island, acquired three underdeveloped parcels in 1959, holding them through a corporation, and made several unsuccessful attempts to develop them in the 1960s. Coastal regulations were enacted by the state of Rhode Island in 1971 and in 1978 title passed from the corporation to Palazzolo when the corporation's charter was revoked for failure to pay corporate income taxes. Several unsuccessful attempts to obtain development permission from the coastal regulatory agency during the 1980s led to an inverse condemnation action. In reversing a Supreme Court of Rhode Island decision in favor of the state, the Court stated: "A challenge to the application of a land-use regulation . . . does not mature until ripeness requirements have been satisfied [discussed *infra*]. . . . It would be illogical, and unfair, to bar a regulatory takings claim because of the post-enactment transfer of ownership where the steps necessary to make the claim ripe were not taken, or could not have been taken, by a previous owner." *Id.* at 628, applying *Nolan* and distinguishing *Lucas* (reproduced *infra*).

Justice O'Connor's concurring opinion, which really was the majority opinion when you count the number of Justices agreeing with her, leaves some room for the notice rule. She emphasized that in a *Penn Central* analysis, the reasonableness of investment-backed expectations remains important. The reasonableness of those expectations is shaped in part by "the regulatory regime in place at the time the claimant acquires the property at issue," she stated. *Id.* at 633. For a case applying the notice rule to defeat a takings claim when the landowner purchased after the regulation was adopted, see *Zanghi v. Board of Appeals of Bedford*, 807 N.E.2d 221 (Mass. App. 2004).

Following remand from the Rhode Island Supreme Court for additional analysis of the question whether Anthony Palazzolo had reasonable investment backed expectations entitling him to compensation for a regulatory taking, a Rhode Island Superior Court justice took eleven days of additional testimony to augment the trial record. In a lengthy but unreported opinion, the justice applied public and private nuisance law, the public trust doctrine and the *Penn Central* test and concluded that no taking had occurred. "[U]nder the unique case-specific facts presented here, the economic impact of the regulations complained of do not adversely affect Plaintiff." *Palazzolo v. State of Rhode Island*, 2005 R.I. Super. LEXIS (unreported). The decision was not appealed.

For an argument that a takings claim "is a distinct and recognizable form of property that exists independent of the property owner," and thus should not be subject to a *per se* notice rule, see Brown, *Taking the Takings Claim: A Policy and Economic Analysis of the Survival of Takings Claims After Property Transfers*, 36 Conn. L. Rev. 7 (2003). Professor Brown is critical, though, of the *Palazzolo* Court for its "failure . . . to articulate a clear rule on how lower courts should constitutionally consider the notice rule." *Id.* at 73. For a comprehensive review of the notice rule, see Eagle, *The Regulatory Takings Notice Rule*, 24 U. Haw. L. Rev. 533 (2002).

6. *Whole parcel rule.* Justice Brennan stated in *Penn Central* that "[t]aking jurisprudence does not divide a single parcel into discrete segments and attempt to determine whether rights in a particular segment have been entirely abrogated," but "focuses rather both on the character of the action and on the nature and extent of the interference with rights in the parcel as a whole." Is this statement consistent with the majority opinion in *Mahon*? Would it be accurate to say that the majority opinion in *Penn Central* adopts, in general, the views stated by Justice Brandeis in *Mahon*, and that the dissent in *Penn Central* adopts the views stated by Justice Holmes in *Mahon*? The whole parcel rule, sometimes called the denominator rule, has become important in takings law, and is discussed in more detail *infra*.

7. *Character of the government action.* What value does the "character of the government action" factor bring to a takings analysis? Logically, it would be a useful way to distinguish physical occupation cases, but that is no longer meaningful because the Court subsequently held that physical occupation is a *per se* taking. See the Note on Physical Occupation, *infra.* Might it have to do with the "fairness" of a regulatory provision, something Justice Stevens discusses in depth in the *Tahoe-Sierra* case reproduced *infra*? Would an analysis that "focuses not only on the intended benefits of the government action, but also on whether the burdens the action imposed were borne disproportionately by relatively few property owners" give meaning to the "character" factor without risking judicial intrusion into legislative and executive prerogatives? *CCA Associates v. United States*, 75 Fed. Cl. 170, 188 (Fed. Cl. 2007), *discussed in* Radford, *Instead of a Doctrine: Penn Central as the Supreme Court's Retreat from the Rule of Law*, Program for Judicial Awareness, Working Paper 07-001, at 10–11 (Pacific Legal Foundation 2007), available at ssrn.com.

8. *Cross references.* We will look at "zoning laws" in detail in Ch. 3 and take a closer look at "historic district" and "landmark preservation" ordinances in Ch. 8. The transfer of development rights technique is considered in Chs. 7 and 8.

A NOTE ON THE *KEYSTONE* CASE

The decision. Keystone Bituminous Coal Ass'n v. De Benedictis, 480 U.S. 470 (1987), which involved a modern version of the coal mining subsidence law struck down in *Pennsylvania Coal*, was a replay of that landmark case. The act prohibited mining that causes subsidence below three categories of structures and as interpreted by the state required that 50 percent of the coal beneath these structures remain in place to provide surface support. The Court upheld the act.

The Court cited the two-part *Agins* test as a basis for distinguishing *Pennsylvania Coal.* Unlike the earlier statute, the act under review prevented "a significant threat to the public welfare." In addition it did not make it "impossible for petitioners to profitably engage in their business" and there had been no "undue interference with their investment-backed expectations."

On the first point, the Court found that "important public interests are served by enforcing a policy that is designed to minimize subsidence in certain areas." It added that its "hesitance to find a taking when the state merely restrains uses of property that are tantamount to public nuisances is consistent with the notion of 'reciprocity of advantage' that Justice Holmes referred to in *Pennsylvania Coal.*" It then cited *Mugler v. Kansas* for the proposition that "all property in this country is held under the implied obligation that the owner's use of it shall not be injurious to the community."

On the second point, the Court turned to a discussion of "diminution in value and investment-backed expectations." It held that the plaintiffs here, unlike the plaintiff in *Pennsylvania Coal*, had not shown that the act made coal mining commercially impracticable. The Court applied the whole parcel rule to hold that the plaintiffs could not segment the coal that had to be left in place, so that they could claim that a taking of this segment of their property had occurred. The Court also rejected an argument that a taking occurred because the plaintiffs' support estate had been taken, noting that "in *Penn Central*, the Court rejected the argument that the 'air rights' above the terminal constituted a separate segment of property for Takings Clause purposes."

Keystone was one of three takings cases decided in 1987 that came to be known as the "1987 Trilogy," and it was the only one won by government. (The others are *Nollan* and *First English*, reproduced *infra.*) All were decided by 5-4 majorities. Whether a majority of the present Court would accept all of the broad holdings in the *Keystone* decision is not clear. The nuisance basis for the decision has also limited its value as a takings precedent.

A NOTE ON PHYSICAL OCCUPATION AS A PER SE TAKING

In *Penn Central*, Justice Brennan said "A 'taking' may more readily be found when the interference with property can be characterized as a physical invasion by Government . . . than when interference arises from some public program adjusting the benefits and burdens of economic life to promote the common good," citing *Causby v. United States*, 328 U.S. 256 (1946). In *Causby* the Court held that repeated and long-continued overflights by military aircraft that destroyed the existing use of plaintiffs' land as a chicken farm amounted to a de facto "taking."

Loretto. In *Loretto v. Teleprompter Manhattan CATV Corp.*, 458 U.S. 419 (1982), the Court held that a New York statute requiring landlords to allow CATV carriers to run cables across and attach the cables to apartment buildings effected a "per se taking" because it resulted in a "permanent physical occupation" of less than one-eighth of a cubic foot of space on plaintiff's apartment building. In an opinion by Justice Marshall, the Court said that "our cases uniformly have found a taking to the extent of the occupation, without regard to whether the action achieves an important public benefit or has only minimal economic impact on the owner." Marshall explained that "[s]uch an appropriation is perhaps the most serious form of invasion of an owner's property interests" because "the government does not simply take a single 'strand' from the 'bundle' of property rights" but "chops through the bundle, taking a slice of every strand," and also because it triggers the property owner's "historically rooted expectation of compensation." In a footnote, Justice Marshall also said that "[t]he permanence and absolute exclusivity of a physical occupation distinguish it from temporary limitations on the right to exclude. Not every physical *invasion* is a taking. . . . [S]uch temporary limitations are subject to a more complex balancing process to determine whether they are a taking. The rationale is evident: they do not absolutely dispossess the owner of his rights to use, and exclude others from his property."

Justice Blackmun (joined by Justices Brennan and White) dissented in *Loretto.* They argued that (1) "the Court . . . acknowledges its historical disavowal of set formulas [for 'takings'] in almost the same breath as it constructs a rigid per se takings rule"; (2) the Court's "talismanic distinction between a continuous 'occupation' and a transient 'invasion' had 'no basis in either economic logic or Takings Clause precedent' "; and (3) "history teaches that takings claims are properly evaluated under a multi-factor balancing test." Under such a "balancing test," the dissenters said, the interference with Mrs. Loretto's use of her apartment building was not "so severe as to constitute a compensable taking in light of the alternative uses of the property." They also noted that Mrs. Loretto "freely admitted that she would have no other use for the cable-occupied space were Teleprompter's equipment not on her building" and that she conceded "not only that owners of other apartment buildings thought that the cable's presence had enhanced the market value of their buildings, . . . but also that her own tenants would have been upset if the cable connections were removed."

In *Property, Utility, and Fairness: Comments on the Ethical Foundations of "Just Compensation" Law*, 80 Harv. L. Rev. 1165 (1967), which is cited in the majority opinion in

Loretto, Professor Michelman criticizes the "per se taking" rule. He argues that the rule requires compensation "although the invasion is . . . trifling from the owner's point of view" and "the actual harm to . . . [him] is indistinguishable from the noncompensable harm to him which results from activity on the part of the government identical in every respect save that it apparently does not invade 'his' sector of space," and because it makes an arbitrary distinction between "governmental encroachments which take the different forms of affirmative occupancy and negative restraint." *Id.* at 1185–87. Michelman finally concludes that the "per se taking" rule can be justified only "if we are to take a utilitarian rather than an absolute view of fairness." He dismisses the common utilitarian argument that the "per se taking" rule can be justified as isolating situations where the cost of settling property owners' claims for compensation will not be prohibitively high as "rather weak," but suggests, as a possible justification, that the "per se taking" rule allows courts to assuage "the psychological shock, the emotional protest, the symbolic threat to all property and security" arising in cases where "government is an unabashed invader." *Id.* at 1227–28. Reconsider these arguments after you have studied the extension of the per se taking rule in the *Lucas* case, which is reproduced *infra*.

Yee. The Court limited its holding in *Loretto* in *Yee v. City of Escondido*, 503 U.S. 519 (1992). Plaintiffs were mobile home park owners who rented pads of land to owners of mobile homes. Under state law, a park owner may not require the removal of a mobile home when it is sold or disapprove a purchaser who is able to pay rent. A city ordinance rolled back rents to an earlier level and prohibited rent increases without city approval. The Court held that a taking by physical occupation had not occurred, and that a claim of regulatory taking was not properly before the Court.

The Court rejected an argument that the rent control ordinance authorized a physical taking because, together with the state law's restrictions, it increased the value of a mobile home by giving the owner the right to occupy the pad indefinitely at a sub-market rent. A physical taking occurs only when a law requires an owner to submit to a physical occupation of his land, and here the mobile home park owners voluntarily rented their land to mobile home owners and were not required to do so either by state or local law. These laws merely regulated the landlord-tenant relationship, and a transfer of wealth to mobile home owners does not convert regulation into a physical taking.

Yee seems to limit the physical occupation per se category of takings to actual physical occupation. What was the argument in *Yee* that a physical taking had occurred? That there was a "physical" taking of the intangible possessory interest in property? See *Hall v. City of Santa Barbara*, 833 F.2d 1270 (9th Cir. 1987), where Judge Kozinski had adopted a similar argument in a case challenging a rent control ordinance requiring landlords in mobile home parks to grant their tenants an indefinite tenancy. *Yee* is a rejection of this decision by a well-known conservative judge.

In *Brown v. Legal Foundation of Washington*, 538 U.S. 216 (2003), the Supreme Court, although denying a takings objection to a state's use of interest from trust accounts lawyers keep of funds clients deposit for litigation expenses ("IOLTA" funds), noted that "[a] law that requires . . . funds to be transferred to a different owner for a legitimate public use . . . could be a *per se* taking requiring the payment of 'just compensation.'" *Id.* at 240 (emphasis in original). Does this mean that denial of a logging permit because of concern over the habitat of the spotted owl, protected by federal law as an "endangered species," is a physical taking — denial of the power to exclude spotted owls? The Federal Circuit said no in *Seiber v. United*

States, 364 F.3d 1356, 1366–67 (Fed. Cir. 2004) ("governmental protection of owls . . . is not comparable to a government authorization to third parties to utilize property"). In *Tennessee Scrap Recyclers Ass'n v. Bredesen*, 556 F.3d 442 (6th Cir. 2009), the Sixth Circuit Court of Appeals refused to enjoin enforcement of a city ordinance requiring scrap metal dealers to "tag and hold" the scrap metal they acquire for a period of ten days. The ordinance also requires "that the tagged scrap metal be open to inspection 'by anyone desiring to investigate.' " Citing *Loretto*, the Court found "the holding period does not constitute a 'direct governmental appropriation or physical invasion' of the scrap dealers' property. . . . Rather, the holding period limits the scrap dealers' *use* of their scrap metal (and derivatively, wherever they choose to keep it) for a period of ten days. Regulations of a party's use of its property are not physical takings." 556 F.3d at 453.

But the Supreme Court of Nevada concluded that a Clark County (Las Vegas) height restriction ordinance near its airport had the effect of permitting aircraft "to make a permanent, physical invasion" of private property and thus amounted to a "*Loretto*-type regulatory *per se* taking." In upholding a $6.5 million takings award, the court held that the ordinance was not a mere height restriction to be evaluated under traditional police power analysis, but amounted to a taking because it "facilitate[d] flights through private property." *McCarran Int'l Airport v. Sisolak*, 137 P.3d 1110 (Nev. 2006). See also *Banks v. United States*, 69 Fed. Cl. 206 (2006) (shoreline landowner had physical takings claim because of shoreline erosion allegedly caused by Corps of Engineers-constructed jetties on Lake Michigan); *McNamara v. City of Richmond*, 838 N.E.2d 640 (Ohio 2005) (loss of and/or damage to groundwater under privately-owned land caused by city's drilling of wells can support a compensable takings claim); *Maunalua Bay Beach Ohana 28 v. State*, 222 P.3d 441, 462 (Haw. App 2009) (state statute preventing oceanfront landowners from registering or recording title to existing accretions of land after the effective date of the statute "effectuated a taking of such accretions").

A NOTE ON "FACIAL" AND "AS-APPLIED" TAKINGS CHALLENGES

Practitioners and their landowner clients face a crucial strategic decision when deciding to challenge a land use regulation as a "taking": should the regulation be attacked "on its face" — the mere fact the regulation was enacted constitutes a taking — or should it be attacked because the impact of its application to the landowner's property constitutes a taking? As illustrated by *Euclid*, *Penn Central* and *Keystone*, landowners are likely to favor facial challenges over as-applied challenges because of the substantial savings in time and money that can be realized with a facial challenge. "[A]n assessment of the actual impact that the Act has on petitioners' operations 'will involve complex and voluminous proofs.' " *Keystone*, 480 U.S. at 493. But, also as illustrated by those cases, it is extremely difficult for a landowner to be successful in a facial challenge. Evidence of the impact of the regulation will not have been presented because a development proposal will not have been rejected nor will a permit have been denied.

Penn Central's "ad hoc, factual inquir[y]" standard, 438 U.S. at 124, requiring a three-factor analysis tilts the scales heavily toward an as-applied approach. The economic impact and investment-backed expectations factors certainly suggest an evidentiary presentation requirement. But does this mean that a facial challenge would not be "a viable legal claim" under *Penn Central*? In a challenge to a city's mobile-home rent control ordinance by mobile home park owners, the Ninth Circuit faced that question. *Guggenheim v. City of Goleta*, 582

F.3d 996 (9th Cir. 2009). "The Park Owner's facial *Penn Central* claim requires us to address this apparent paradox: we must confront the question of whether a facial challenge under *Penn Central* is actually a viable legal claim; and if we determine that it is, we must then consider what evidence the Park Owners may present to prove their claim." *Id.* at 1014. In concluding that a facial challenge is a viable legal claim under *Penn Central*, the court stressed the logic supporting its decision, "[i]t would seem incongruous . . . if only the disfavored exceptions to *Penn Central* [*i.e., Loretto, supra*, and *Lucas, infra*] could be brought as facial challenges, where a claim under the general rule of *Penn Central* could not," as well as Supreme Court precedent, "*Keystone* . . . demonstrate[s] that a facial challenge under *Penn Central* may be difficult, but the mere fact that *Penn Central* requires an ad-hoc multi-factor balancing test does not bar a facial challenge." *Id.* at 1016.

After concluding that a facial challenge under *Penn Central* was viable, the court then considered the kinds of evidence that could be considered.

> The proper inquiry in a facial challenge is not whether the property owners can demonstrate that property has been taken without providing evidence beyond the text of the regulation; the inquiry is whether the "mere enactment" of the regulation constitutes a taking. . . . Thus, in a takings claim, we must look not only at what the statute says, but also at what its mere enactment does. . . . At a minimum, we must look to the general economic principles that allow us to interpret the statute's effect, so that we may understand the regulation's general scope and dominant features. . . . In addition, there must be a way to understand the economic impact on the complaining property owner. A property owner who is not permitted at least to present evidence that proves that he has actually suffered the kind of economic harm of which he complains would be precluded from even proving his own standing to bring the claim — the property owner must be permitted to adduce evidence that he has suffered the injury for which he seeks redress. . . . Thus, even in a facial challenge, the court may consider evidence related to the individual property owner that illustrates the economic impact that the mere enactment of the statute had on that owner and proves that the owner has suffered the injury of which he complains. . . .
>
> We need not, however, determine the exact boundaries between permissible and impermissible kinds of evidence to support a facial challenge. The City has defended the district court's use of core findings from each party's [expert witness] report. Therefore, we will confine ourselves to review of these same core findings in our review of the Park Owners' facial *Penn Central* challenge. We will provide additional figures from the Quigley Report only for purposes of demonstrating that the Park Owners have suffered the actual economic injury of which they complain and illustrating in concrete terms the economic impact that the "mere enactment" of the [rent control ordinance] had in Goleta. In addition, we may consider the district court's undisputed factual findings about property values in the City of Goleta, as these values affect the entire City, and thus everyone subject to the City's [ordinance], and are not specific to the [ordinance]'s application to the Park Owners. With these limitations in mind, we consider the three factors of the *Penn Central* analysis. [*Id.* at 1016–1018.]

Applying the three factors, the court found a taking. The enactment of the rent control ordinance "caused a significant economic loss for the Park Owners" (*economic impact*); a regulatory takings claim was not forfeited "simply because the property changed hands after the regulations went into effect" (*investment-backed expectations* — applying *Palazzolo*, *infra*), and "[t]he City has singled out the Park Owners and imposed solely on them a burden to support affordable housing" (*character of the government action*). *Id.* at 1023, 1025, 1029. Weighing them together, the court concluded that the mobile-home rent control ordinace "goes too far." *Id.* at 1030.

The rule that a physical occupation of land is a per se taking had an important influence on the Supreme Court's next takings decision, where it considered a case involving a somewhat different kind of land use regulation — an exaction.

NOLLAN v. CALIFORNIA COASTAL COMMISSION

483 U.S. 825 (1987)

JUSTICE SCALIA delivered the opinion of the Court:

James and Marilyn Nollan appealed from a decision of the California Court of Appeal ruling that the California Coastal Commission could condition its grant of permission to rebuild their house on their transfer to the public of an easement across their beachfront property. 223 Cal. Rptr. 28 (1986). The California Court rejected their claim that imposition of that condition violates the Takings Clause of the Fifth Amendment, as incorporated against the States by the Fourteenth Amendment. *Ibid.* We noted probable jurisdiction.

I

The Nollans own a beachfront lot in Ventura County, California. A quarter-mile north of their property is Faria County Park, an oceanside public park with a public beach and recreation area. Another public beach area, known locally as "the Cove," lies 1,800 feet south of their lot. A concrete seawall approximately eight feet high separates the beach portion of the Nollans' property from the rest of the lot. The historic mean high tide line determines the lot's oceanside boundary.

The Nollans originally leased their property with an option to buy. The building on the lot was a small bungalow, totaling 504 square feet, which for a time they rented to summer vacationers. After years of rental use, however, the building had fallen into disrepair, and could no longer be rented out.

The Nollans' option to purchase was conditioned on their promise to demolish the bungalow and replace it. In order to do so, under California Public Resources Code §§ 30106, 30212, and 30600, they were required to obtain a coastal development permit from the California Coastal Commission. On February 25, 1982, they submitted a permit application to the Commission in which they proposed to demolish the existing structure and replace it with a three-bedroom house in keeping with the rest of the neighborhood.

The Nollans were informed that their application had been placed on the administrative calendar, and that the Commission staff had recommended that the permit be granted subject to the condition that they allow the public an easement to pass across a portion of their property bounded by the mean high tide line on one side, and their seawall on the other side. This would make it easier for the public to get to Faria County Park and the Cove. The Nollans protested imposition of the condition, but the Commission overruled their objections and granted the permit subject to their recordation of a deed restriction granting the easement.

On June 3, 1982, the Nollans filed a petition for writ of administrative mandamus asking the Ventura County Superior Court to invalidate the access condition. They argued that the condition could not be imposed absent evidence that their proposed development would have a direct adverse impact on public access to the beach. The court agreed, and remanded the case to the Commission for a full evidentiary hearing on that issue.

On remand, the Commission held a public hearing, after which it made further factual findings and reaffirmed its imposition of the condition. It found that the new house would increase blockage of the view of the ocean, thus contributing to the development of "a 'wall' of residential structures" that would prevent the public "psychologically . . . from realizing a stretch of coastline exists nearby that they have every right to visit." The new house would also increase private use of the shorefront. These effects of construction of the house, along with other area development, would cumulatively "burden the public's ability to traverse to and along the shorefront." Therefore the Commission could properly require the Nollans to offset that burden by providing additional lateral access to the public beaches in the form of an easement across their property. The Commission also noted that it had similarly conditioned 43 out of 60 coastal development permits along the same tract of land, and that of the 17 not so conditioned, 14 had been approved when the Commission did not have administrative regulations in place allowing imposition of the condition, and the remaining 3 had not involved shorefront property.

The Nollans filed a supplemental petition for a writ of administrative mandamus with the Superior Court, in which they argued that imposition of the access condition violated the Takings Clause of the Fifth Amendment, as incorporated against the States by the Fourteenth Amendment. The Superior Court ruled in their favor on statutory grounds . . . . [The court found that the Commission could impose access conditions on development permits for replacement homes only where the proposed development would have an adverse impact on public access to the sea, and that this requirement was not met.]

The Commission appealed to the California Court of Appeal. While that appeal was pending, the Nollans satisfied the condition on their option to purchase by tearing down the bungalow and building a new house, and bought the property. They did not notify the Commission that they were taking that action.

The Court of Appeal reversed the Superior Court. 223 Cal. Rptr. 28 (1986). It disagreed with the Superior Court's interpretation of the Coastal Act . . . . It also ruled that that requirement did not violate the Constitution under the reasoning of an earlier case of the Court of Appeal, *Grupe v. California Coastal Comm'n*, 212 Cal. Rptr. 578 (Cal. App. 1985). In that case, the court had found that so long as a project contributed to the need for public access, even if the project standing alone had not created the need for access, and even if there was only an indirect relationship between the access exacted and the need to which the project contributed, imposition of an access condition on a development permit was sufficiently related to burdens created by the project to be constitutional. The Court of Appeal ruled that the record established that that was the situation with respect to the Nollans' house. It ruled that the Nollans' taking claim also failed because, although the condition diminished the value of the Nollans' lot, it did not deprive them of all reasonable use of their property. Since, in the Court of Appeal's view, there was no statutory or constitutional obstacle to imposition of the access condition, the Superior Court erred in granting the writ of mandamus. The Nollans appealed to this Court, raising only the constitutional question.

II

Had California simply required the Nollans to make an easement across their beachfront available to the public on a permanent basis in order to increase public access to the beach, rather than conditioning their permit to rebuild their house on their agreeing to do so, we have no doubt there would have been a taking. To say that the appropriation of a public easement across a landowner's premises does not constitute the taking of a property interest but rather (as Justice Brennan contends) "a mere restriction on its use," is to use words in a manner that deprives them of all their ordinary meaning. Indeed, one of the principal uses of the eminent domain power is to assure that the government be able to require conveyance of just such interests, so long as it pays for them. Perhaps because the point is so obvious, we have never been confronted with a controversy that required us to rule upon it, but our cases' analysis of the effect of other governmental action leads to the same conclusion. We have repeatedly held that, as to property reserved by its owner for private use, "the right to exclude [others is] one of the most essential sticks in the bundle of rights that are commonly characterized as 'property.'" *Loretto v. Teleprompter Manhattan CATV Corp.*, 458 U.S. 419, 433 (1982), quoting *Kaiser Aetna v. United States*, 444 U.S. 164, 176 (1979). In *Loretto* we observed that where governmental action results in "[a] permanent physical occupation" of the property, by the government itself or by others, *see* 458 U.S., at 432–433, n.9, "our cases uniformly have found a taking to the extent of the occupation, without regard to whether the action achieves an important public benefit or has only minimal economic impact on the owner," *id.*, at 434–435. We think a "permanent physical occupation" has occurred, for purposes of that rule, where individuals are given a permanent and continuous right to pass to and fro, so that the real property may continuously be traversed, even though no particular individual is permitted to station himself permanently upon the premises.(1)

Justice Brennan argues that while this might ordinarily be the case, the California Constitution's prohibition on any individual's "exclu[ding] the right of way to [any navigable] water whenever it is required for any public purpose," Article X, § 4, produces a different result here. . . . [The discussion of this issue is omitted.]

Given, then, that requiring uncompensated conveyance of the easement outright would violate the Fourteenth Amendment, the question becomes whether requiring it to be conveyed as a condition for issuing a land use permit alters the outcome. We have long recognized that land use regulation does not effect a taking if it "substantially advance[s] legitimate state interests" and does not "den[y] an owner economically viable use of his land," *Agins v. Tiburon*, 447 U.S. 255, 260 (1980). . . . Our cases have not elaborated on the standards for determining what constitutes a "legitimate state interest" or what type of connection between the regulation and the state interest satisfies the requirement that the former "substantially advance" the latter.

They have made clear, however, that a broad range of governmental purposes and

(1) The holding of *Prune Yard Shopping Center v. Robins*, 447 U.S. 74 (1980), is not inconsistent with this analysis, since there the owner had already opened his property to the general public, and in addition permanent access was not required. The analysis of *Kaiser Aetna v. United States*, 444 U.S. 164 (1979), is not inconsistent because it was affected by traditional doctrines regarding navigational servitudes. Of course neither of those cases involved, as this case does, a classic right-of-way easement.

regulations satisfies these requirements. *See Agins v. Tiburon* (scenic zoning); *Penn Central Transportation Co. v. New York City* (landmark preservation); *Euclid v. Ambler Realty Co.* (residential zoning); Laitos and Westfall, *Government Interference with Private Interests in Public Resources*, 11 Harv. Envtl. L. Rev. 1, 66 (1987). The Commission argues that among these permissible purposes are protecting the public's ability to see the beach, assisting the public in overcoming the "psychological barrier" to using the beach created by a developed shorefront, and preventing congestion on the public beaches. We assume, without deciding, that this is so — in which case the Commission unquestionably would be able to deny the Nollans their permit outright if their new house (alone, or by reason of the cumulative impact produced in conjunction with other construction) would substantially impede these purposes, unless the denial would interfere so drastically with the Nollans' use of their property as to constitute a taking. *See Penn Central Transportation Co. v. New York City, supra.*

The Commission argues that a permit condition that serves the same legitimate police-power purpose as a refusal to issue the permit should not be found to be a taking if the refusal to issue the permit would not constitute a taking. We agree. Thus, if the Commission attached to the permit some condition that would have protected the public's ability to see the beach notwithstanding construction of a new house — for example, a height limitation, a width restriction, or a ban on fences — so long as the Commission could have exercised its police power (as we have assumed it could) to forbid construction of the house altogether, imposition of the condition would also be constitutional. Moreover (and here we come closer to the facts of the present case), the condition would be constitutional even if it consisted of the requirement that the Nollans provide a viewing spot on their property for passersby with whose sighting of the ocean their new house would interfere. Although such a requirement, constituting a permanent grant of continuous access to the property, would have to be considered a taking if it were not attached to a development permit, the Commission's assumed power to forbid construction of the house in order to protect the public's view of the beach must surely include the power to condition construction upon some concession by the owner, even a concession of property rights, that serves the same end. If a prohibition designed to accomplish that purpose would be a legitimate exercise of the police power rather than a taking, it would be strange to conclude that providing the owner an alternative to that prohibition which accomplishes the same purpose is not.

The evident constitutional propriety disappears, however, if the condition substituted for the prohibition utterly fails to further the end advanced as the justification for the prohibition. When that essential nexus is eliminated, the situation becomes the same as if California law forbade shouting fire in a crowded theater, but granted dispensations to those willing to contribute $100 to the state treasury. While a ban on shouting fire can be a core exercise of the State's police power to protect the public safety, and can thus meet even our stringent standards for regulation of speech, adding the unrelated condition alters the purpose to one which, while it may be legitimate, is inadequate to sustain the ban. Therefore, even though, in a sense, requiring a $100 tax contribution in order to shout fire is a lesser restriction on speech than an outright ban, it would not pass constitutional muster. Similarly here, the lack of nexus between the condition and the original purpose of the building restriction converts that purpose to something other than what it was. The purpose then becomes, quite simply, the obtaining of an easement to serve some valid governmental purpose, but without payment of compensation. Whatever may be the outer limits of "legitimate state interests" in the takings and land use context, this is not one of them. In short, unless the permit condition serves the same governmental purpose as the development ban, the building restriction is not a valid

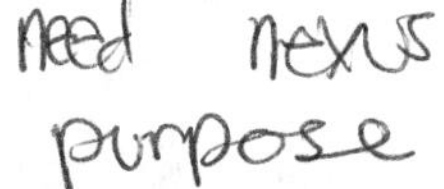

regulation of land use but "an out-and-out plan of extortion." *J.E.D. Associates, Inc. v. Atkinson*, 432 A.2d 12, 14-15 (N.H. 1981). *See also Loretto v. Teleprompter Manhattan CATV Corp.*, 458 U.S., at 439, n.17.

III

The Commission claims that it concedes as much, and that we may sustain the condition at issue here by finding that it is reasonably related to the public need or burden that the Nollans' new house creates or to which it contributes. We can accept, for purposes of discussion, the Commission's proposed test as to how close a "fit" between the condition and the burden is required, because we find that this case does not meet even the most untailored standards. The Commission's principal contention to the contrary essentially turns on a play on the word "access." The Nollans' new house, the Commission found, will interfere with "visual access" to the beach. That in turn (along with other shorefront development) will interfere with the desire of people who drive past the Nollans' house to use the beach, thus creating a "psychological barrier" to "access." The Nollans' new house will also, by process not altogether clear from the Commission's opinion but presumably potent enough to more than offset the effects of the psychological barrier, increase the use of the public beaches, thus creating the need for more "access." These burdens on "access" would be alleviated by a requirement that the Nollans provide "lateral access" to the beach.

Rewriting the argument to eliminate the play on words makes clear that there is nothing to it. It is quite impossible to understand how a requirement that people already on the public beaches be able to walk across the Nollans' property reduces any obstacles to viewing the beach created by the new house. It is also impossible to understand how it lowers any "psychological barrier" to using the public beaches, or how it helps to remedy any additional congestion on them caused by construction of the Nollans' new house. We therefore find that the Commission's imposition of the permit condition cannot be treated as an exercise of its land use power for any of these purposes. Our conclusion on this point is consistent with the approach taken by every other court that has considered the question, with the exception of the California state courts. [At this point, the Court cited a number of state and federal court cases that both upheld and struck down subdivision exactions.]

. . . We view the Fifth Amendment's Property Clause to be more than a pleading requirement, and compliance with it to be more than an exercise in cleverness and imagination. As indicated earlier, our cases describe the condition for abridgement of property rights through the police power as a "substantial advanc[ing]" of a legitimate State interest. We are inclined to be particularly careful about the adjective where the actual conveyance of property is made a condition to the lifting of a land use restriction, since in that context there is a heightened risk that the purpose is avoidance of the compensation requirement, rather than the stated police power objective. . . .

[The dissenting opinions of Justice Brennan, with whom Justice Marshall joined, Justice Blackmun and Justice Stevens are omitted.]

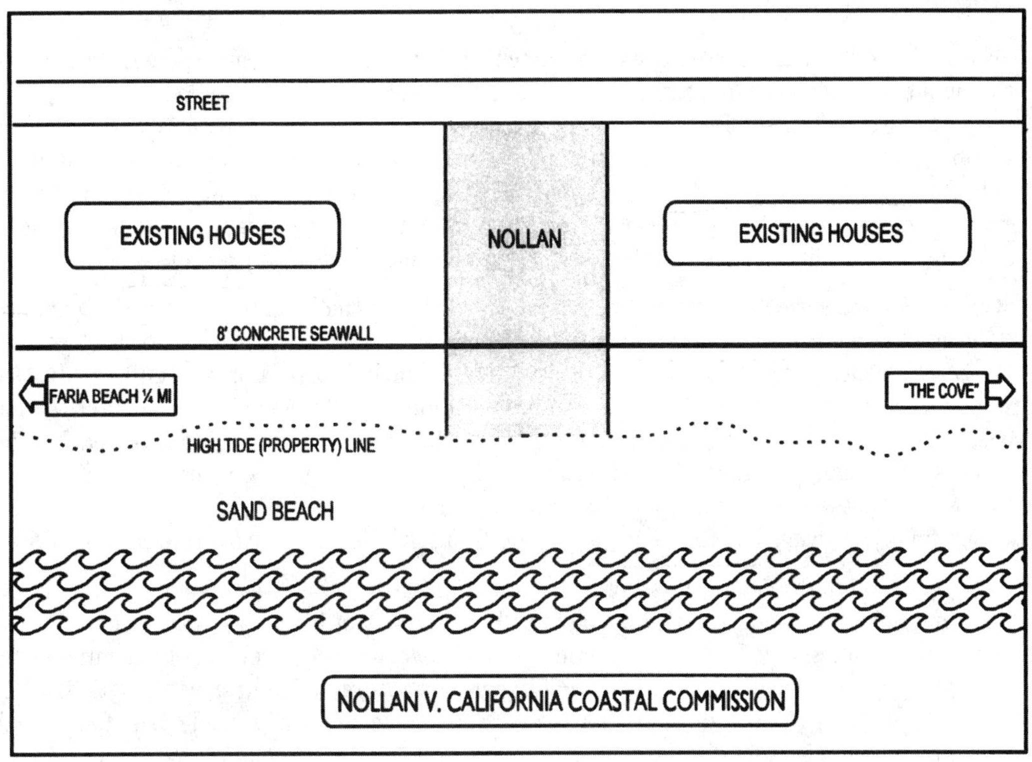

NOTES AND QUESTIONS

1. *A new class of "takings"? Nollan* is a very different type of takings case, if indeed it is properly a takings case at all. The Court quoted the two-part *Agins* test, but the Court disavowed this test in the *Lingle* case, reproduced *infra.* So what, then, is the basis for the *Nollan* case? A reading of *Lingle* may answer this question. In *Lingle*, the Court distinguished *Nollan*'s "substantially advances" language as addressing "dedications of property so onerous that, outside the exactions context, they would be deemed *per se* physical takings," but held the case did not turn on an application of the "substantially advance" test. Exactions are discussed in Chapter 7 *infra.*

2. *The nexus test.* Although the *Nollan* opinion doesn't make it clear, the Court was influenced by a nexus test applied in state court cases to determine the validity of "subdivision exactions" imposed on subdivision developers by local governments in order to provide a variety of public facilities such as paved streets, water and sanitary sewer mains, storm drainage, and land for new parks, playgrounds, and school sites. In an omitted part of the opinion, the Court cited many state court cases dealing with challenges to such "subdivision exactions" on constitutional grounds. Some of these cases decide the constitutional validity of such "subdivision exactions" by inquiring whether there is a "rational relationship" (or "nexus") between the exactions and the need for new public facilities generated by the proposed subdivision development. Some of the cases, however, also apply a second test and sustain exactions only if the value of the property (or cash in lieu of property) exacted from the developer is roughly proportional to the benefit conferred on the developer by the provision of new facilities.

The nexus test in the state cases was much easier to satisfy because it was applied to residential subdivisions that created the need for the public facility demanded as an exaction. The special circumstances of *Nollan* made the nexus test more difficult to apply because there is no obvious linkage between construction of a residential dwelling and access to an adjacent beach. In *Dolan v. City of Tigard*, reproduced in Chapter 7, where the subject of exactions is pursued in more detail, the Court considered the related topic of showing that the facility need created by the subdivision justifies the exaction, assuming a nexus is present.

3. *Heightened scrutiny.* Justice Brennan disagreed with the heightened scrutiny standard the Court adopted. He argued that "the Court imposed a standard of precision for the exercise of the State's police power that has been discredited for the better part of this century." Justice Brennan thought that the deferential "minimal rationality" standard of "substantive due process" review was appropriate, rather than the "heightened scrutiny" suggested by the phrase "substantially advance[s] legitimate state interests." Heightened scrutiny is linked to the question whether inquiry into legitimacy of purpose is proper under the Takings Clause, a question finally answered in the negative by the Court in the *Lingle* case reproduced *infra.*

4. *Physical occupation.* The second test mentioned by the *Nollan* Court, whether the regulation denies the landowner "an economically viable use of his land," is the second *Agins* prong. This inquiry should be irrelevant under *Loretto* because the government has imposed "a permanent physical occupation on an unwilling owner." *Loretto* found a per se "taking" of property even though the landowner clearly retained "an economically viable use of his land." Hence it is difficult to understand the *Nollan* Court's statement, *arguendo*, that the California Coastal Commission could constitutionally have required "that the Nollans provide a viewing spot on their property for passersby with whose sighting of the ocean their new house would interfere."

Is it a sufficient answer to say that, although a viewing spot would be a taking if not attached to a permit because it is a permanent grant of access, it is constitutional if attached to a permit because the Commission could prohibit construction of the house to protect the public's view of the beach? If the Coastal Commission had only imposed a restriction on the Nollan's use of their land, it might be constitutionally justified because the Nollans would retain "an economically viable use" of their land; but as we have seen, that is not the test where government imposes "a permanent physical occupation on an unwilling owner."

5. *Average reciprocity of advantage.* Justice Brennan invoked the average reciprocity of advantage principle in his dissent:

> Appellants [the Nollans] have been allowed to replace a one-story 521-square foot beach home with a two-story, 1674-square foot residence and an attached two-car garage, resulting in development covering 2,464 square feet of the lot. Such development obviously significantly increases the value of appellants' property; appellants make no contention that this increase is offset by any diminution in value resulting from the deed restriction, much less that the restriction made the property less valuable than it would have been without the new construction.

Justice Brennan also noted the Nollans gained a new benefit because the deed restrictions on other property in the area allowed them to walk along the beach outside the "confines" of their own property. "Thus, appellants benefit both as private landowners and as members of the public from the fact that new development permit requests are conditioned on preservation of public access."

Is this argument a fair statement of the average reciprocity rule from *Penn Central*? Is it consistent with Justice Rehnquist's reformulation of this rule in his *Penn Central* dissent?

6. *Investment-backed expectations.* What do you think of Justice Brennan's argument that because "appellants were clearly on notice when requesting a new development permit that a condition of approval would be a provision ensuring public lateral access to the shore . . . they surely could have had no expectation that they could obtain approval of their new development and exercise any right of exclusion afterward"? The majority rejected this argument in footnote 2 (not reproduced here). Does this constitute the death-knell of the "investment-backed expectations" test first set out in *Penn Central* and applied in *Keystone Bituminous*, insofar as that test might have been deemed applicable to cases where ownership of land was acquired with notice of governmental intent to impose an "exaction" at some future time? See *Palazzolo*, discussed *supra*. Reconsider this question after *Tahoe-Sierra*, reproduced *infra*. The investment-backed expectations takings factor has become important as an exception to the per se taking rule adopted in the *Lucas* case, which is reproduced *infra*, and is considered in a Note following that case.

7. *Sources.* For discussion of *Nollan*, see Kayden, *Judges as Planners: Limited or General Partners?*, *in* Zoning and the American Dream 223 (C. Haar & J. Kayden eds., 1989); Note, *Municipal Development Exactions, The Rational Nexus Test, and the Federal Constitution*, 102 Harv. L. Rev. 992 (1989); Note, *Taking a Step Back: A Reconsideration of the Takings Test of Nollan v. California Coastal Commission*, 102 Harv. L. Rev. 449 (1988). For an article finding that federal and state courts have interpreted *Nollan* in similar ways, see Gerry, *Parity Revisited: An Empirical Comparison of State and Lower Federal Court Interpretations of Nollan v. California Coastal Commission*, 23 Harv. J.L. & Pub. Pol'y 233 (1999).

[3.] *First English:* The Inverse Condemnation Remedy

The case which follows is the third of the 1987 "trilogy" of important takings cases, *Keystone* and *Nollan* being the others:

FIRST ENGLISH EVANGELICAL LUTHERAN CHURCH OF GLENDALE v. COUNTY OF LOS ANGELES

482 U.S. 304 (1987)

Chief Justice Rehnquist delivered the opinion of the Court:

In this case the California Court of Appeal held that a landowner who claims that his property has been "taken" by a land-use regulation may not recover damages for the time before it is finally determined that the regulation constitutes a "taking" of his property. We disagree, and conclude that in these circumstances the Fifth and Fourteenth Amendments to the United States Constitution would require compensation for that period.

In 1957, appellant First English Evangelical Lutheran Church purchased a 21-acre parcel of land in a canyon along the banks of the Middle Fork of Mill Creek in the Angeles National Forest. The Middle Fork is the natural drainage channel for a watershed area owned by the National Forest Service. Twelve of the acres owned by the church are flat land, and contained a dining hall, two bunkhouses, a caretaker's lodge, an outdoor chapel, and a footbridge across the creek. The church operated on the site a campground, known as "Lutherglen," as a retreat center and a recreational area for handicapped children.

In July 1977, a forest fire denuded the hills upstream from Lutherglen, destroying approximately 3,860 acres of the watershed area and creating a serious flood hazard. Such flooding occurred on February 9 and 10, 1978, when a storm dropped 11 inches of rain in the watershed. The runoff from the storm overflowed the banks of the Mill Creek, flooding Lutherglen and destroying its buildings.

In response to the flooding of the canyon, appellee County of Los Angeles adopted Interim Ordinance No. 11,855 in January 1979. The ordinance provided that "[a] person shall not construct, reconstruct, place or enlarge any building or structure, any portion of which is, or will be, located within the outer boundary lines of the interim flood protection area located in Mill Creek Canyon. . . ." The ordinance was effective immediately because the county determined that it was "required for the immediate preservation of the public health and safety. . . ." The interim flood protection area described by the ordinance included the flat areas on either side of Mill Creek on which Lutherglen had stood.

The church filed a complaint in the Superior Court of California a little more than a month after the ordinance was adopted. As subsequently amended, the complaint alleged two claims against the county and the Los Angeles County Flood Control District. The first alleged that the defendants were liable under Cal. Gov't Code Ann. § 835 (1980)[1] for dangerous conditions on their upstream properties that contributed to the flooding of Lutherglen. As a part of this claim, appellant also alleged that "Ordinance No. 11,855 denies [appellant] all use of Lutherglen." The second claim sought to recover from the Flood District in inverse condemnation and in tort for engaging in cloud seeding during the storm that flooded Lutherglen. Appellant sought damages under each count for loss of use of Lutherglen. The defendants moved to strike the portions of the complaint alleging that the county's ordinance denied all use of Lutherglen, on the view that the California Supreme Court's decision in *Agins v. Tiburon*, 598 P.2d 25 (Cal. 1979), *aff'd on other grounds*, 447 U.S. 255 (1980), rendered the allegation "entirely immaterial and irrelevant, [with] no bearing upon any conceivable cause of action herein." *See* Cal. Civ. Proc. Code Ann. § 436 (Supp. 1987) ("The court may . . . strike out any irrelevant, false, or improper matter inserted in any pleading").

In *Agins v. Tiburon, supra*, the Supreme Court of California decided that a landowner may not maintain an inverse condemnation suit in the courts of that State based upon a "regulatory" taking. In the court's view, maintenance of such a suit would allow a landowner to force the legislature to exercise its power of eminent domain. Under this decision, then, compensation is not required until the challenged regulation or ordinance has been held excessive in an action for declaratory relief or a writ of mandamus and the government has nevertheless decided to continue the regulation in effect. Based on this decision, the trial court in the present case granted the motion to strike the allegation that the church had been denied all use of Lutherglen. It explained that "a careful re-reading of the *Agins* case persuades the Court that when an ordinance, even a non-zoning ordinance, deprives a person of the total use of his lands, his challenge to the ordinance is by way of declaratory relief or possibly mandamus." Because the appellant alleged a regulatory taking and sought only

---

[1] Section 835 of the California Government Code establishes conditions under which a public entity may be liable "for injury caused by a dangerous condition of its property. . . ."

damages, the allegation that the ordinance denied all use of Lutherglen was deemed irrelevant.[2]

On appeal, the California Court of Appeal read the complaint as one seeking "damages for the uncompensated taking of all use of Lutherglen by County Ordinance No. 11,855. . . ." It too relied on the California Supreme Court's decision in *Agins* in rejecting the cause of action, declining appellant's invitation to reevaluate *Agins* in light of this Court's opinions in *San Diego Gas & Electric Co. v. San Diego*, 450 U.S. 621 (1981). The court found itself obligated to follow *Agins* "because the United States Supreme Court has not yet ruled on the question of whether a state may constitutionally limit the remedy for a taking to nonmonetary relief. . . ." It accordingly affirmed the trial court's decision to strike the allegations concerning appellee's ordinance.[3]

The Supreme Court of California denied review.

This appeal followed, and we noted probable jurisdiction. Appellant asks us to hold that the Supreme Court of California erred in *Agins v. Tiburon* in determining that the Fifth Amendment, as made applicable to the States through the Fourteenth Amendment, does not require compensation as a remedy for "temporary" regulatory takings — those regulatory takings which are ultimately invalidated by the courts. Four times this decade, we have considered similar claims and have found ourselves for one reason or another unable to consider the merits of the *Agins* rule. For the reasons explained below, however, we find the constitutional claim properly presented in this case, and hold that on these facts the California courts have decided the compensation question inconsistently with the requirements of the Fifth Amendment.

I

Concerns with finality left us unable to reach the remedial question in the earlier cases where we have been asked to consider the rule of *Agins*. In each of these cases, we concluded either that regulations considered to be in issue by the state court did not effect a taking, or that the factual disputes yet to be resolved by state authorities might still lead to the

---

[2] The trial court also granted defendants' motion for judgment on the pleadings on the second cause of action, based on cloud seeding. It limited trial on the first cause of action for damages under Cal. Gov't Code Ann. § 835 (1980), rejecting the inverse condemnation claim. At the close of plaintiff's evidence, the trial court granted a nonsuit on behalf of defendants, dismissing the entire complaint.

[3] The California Court of Appeal also affirmed the lower court's orders limiting the issues for trial on the first cause of action, granting a nonsuit on the issues that proceeded to trial, and dismissing the second cause of action — based on cloud seeding — to the extent it was founded on a theory of strict liability in tort. The court reversed the trial court's ruling that the second cause of action could not be maintained against the Flood Control District under the theory of inverse condemnation. The case was remanded for further proceedings on this claim. These circumstances alone, apart from the more particular issues presented in takings cases and discussed in the text, require us to consider whether the pending resolution of further liability questions deprives us of jurisdiction because we are not presented with a "final judgmen[t] or decre[e]" within the meaning of 28 U.S.C. § 1257. We think that this case is fairly characterized as one "in which the federal issue, finally decided by the highest court in the State [in which a decision could be had], will survive regardless of the outcome of future state-court proceedings." *Cox Broadcasting Corp. v. Cohn*, 420 U.S. 469, 480 (1975).

As we explain *infra*, the California Court of Appeal rejected appellant's federal claim that it was entitled to just compensation from the county for the taking of its property; this distinct issue of federal law will survive and require decision no matter how further proceedings resolve the issues concerning the liability of the flood control district for its cloud seeding operation.

conclusion that no taking had occurred. Consideration of the remedial question in those circumstances, we concluded, would be premature.

The posture of the present case is quite different. Appellant's complaint alleged that "Ordinance No. 11,855 denies [it] all use of Lutherglen," and sought damages for this deprivation. In affirming the decision to strike this allegation, the Court of Appeal assumed that the complaint sought "damages for the uncompensated *taking* of all use of Lutherglen by County Ordinance No. 11,855." (emphasis added). It relied on the California Supreme Court's *Agins* decision for the conclusion that "the remedy for a *taking* [is limited] to nonmonetary relief. . . ." (emphasis added). The disposition of the case on these grounds isolates the remedial question for our consideration. The rejection of appellant's allegations did not rest on the view that they were false. Nor did the court rely on the theory that regulatory measures such as Ordinance No. 11,855 may never constitute a taking in the constitutional sense. Instead, the claims were deemed irrelevant solely because of the California Supreme Court's decision in *Agins* that damages are unavailable to redress a "temporary" regulatory taking. The California Court of Appeal has thus held that regardless of the correctness of appellants' claim that the challenged ordinance denies it "all use of Lutherglen" appellant may not recover damages until the ordinance is finally declared unconstitutional, and then only for any period after that declaration for which the county seeks to enforce it. The constitutional question pretermitted in our earlier cases is therefore squarely presented here.(6)

We reject appellee's suggestion that, regardless of the state court's treatment of the question, we must independently evaluate the adequacy of the complaint and resolve the takings claim on the merits before we can reach the remedial question. However "cryptic" — to use appellee's description — the allegations with respect to the taking were, the California courts deemed them sufficient to present the issue. We accordingly have no occasion to decide whether the ordinance at issue actually denied appellant all use of its property(7) or whether the county might avoid the conclusion that a compensable taking had occurred by establishing that the denial of all use was insulated as a part of the State's authority to enact safety regulations. These questions, of course, remain open for decision on the remand we direct today. We now turn to the question of whether the Just Compensation Clause requires the government to pay for "temporary" regulatory takings.

II

Consideration of the compensation question must begin with direct reference to the language of the Fifth Amendment, which provides in relevant part that "private property

(6) Our cases have also required that one seeking compensation must "seek compensation through the procedures the State has provided for doing so" before the claim is ripe for review. *Williamson County Regional Planning Comm'n v. Hamilton Bank*, 473 U.S. 172, 194 (1985). It is clear that appellant met this requirement. Having assumed that a taking occurred, the California court's dismissal of the action establishes that "the inverse condemnation procedure is unavailable. . . ." *Id.*, at 197. The compensation claim is accordingly ripe for our consideration.

(7) Because the issue was not raised in the complaint or considered relevant by the California courts in their assumption that a taking had occurred, we also do not consider the effect of the county's permanent ordinance on the conclusions of the courts below. That ordinance, adopted in 1981 . . . , provides that "[a] person shall not use, erect, construct, move onto, or . . . alter, modify, enlarge or reconstruct any building or structure within the boundaries of a flood protection district except . . . [a]ccessory buildings and structures that will not substantially impede the flow of water, including sewer, gas, electrical, and water systems, approved by the county engineer . . . [a]utomobile parking facilities incidental to a lawfully established use . . . [and] [f]lood-control structures approved by the chief engineer of the Los Angeles County Flood Control District." County Code § 22.44.220.

[shall not] be taken for public use, without just compensation." As its language indicates, and as the Court has frequently noted, this provision does not prohibit the taking of private property, but instead places a condition on the exercise of the power. This basic understanding of the Amendment makes clear that it is designed not to limit the governmental interference with property rights per se, but rather to secure compensation in the event of otherwise proper interference amounting to a taking. Thus, government action that works a taking of property rights necessarily implicates the "constitutional obligation to pay just compensation." *Armstrong v. United States*, 364 U.S. 40, 49 (1960).

We have recognized that a landowner is entitled to bring an action in inverse condemnation as a result of " 'the self-executing character of the constitutional provision with respect to compensation. . . .' " *United States v. Clarke*, 445 U.S. 253, 257 (1980), quoting 6 P. Nichols, Eminent Domain § 25.41 (3d rev. ed. 1972). As noted in Justice Brennan's dissent in *San Diego Gas & Electric Co.*, 450 U.S., at 654–655, it has been established at least since *Jacobs v. United States*, 290 U.S. 13 (1933), that claims for just compensation are grounded in the Constitution itself:

> "The suits were based on the right to recover just compensation for property taken by the United States for public use in the exercise of its power of eminent domain. *That right was guaranteed by the Constitution.* The fact that condemnation proceedings were not instituted and that the right was asserted in suits by the owners did not change the essential nature of the claim. The form of the remedy did not qualify the right. It rested upon the Fifth Amendment. Statutory recognition was not necessary. A promise to pay was not necessary. Such a promise was implied because of the duty imposed by the Amendment. *The suits were thus founded upon the Constitution of the United States.*" *Id.*, at 16. (Emphasis added.)

Jacobs, moreover, does not stand alone, for the Court has frequently repeated the view that, in the event of a taking, the compensation remedy is required by the Constitution. *See, e.g., Kirby Forest Industries, Inc. v. United States*, 467 U.S. 1, 5 (1984). [Other citations omitted.][9]

It has also been established doctrine at least since Justice Holmes' opinion for the Court in *Pennsylvania Coal Co. v. Mahon*, 260 U.S. 393 (1922), that "[t]he general rule at least is, that while property may be regulated to a certain extent, if regulation goes too far it will be recognized as a taking." *Id.*, at 415. While the typical taking occurs when the government acts to condemn property in the exercise of its power of eminent domain, the entire doctrine of inverse condemnation is predicated on the proposition that a taking may occur without such formal proceedings. In *Pumpelly v. Green Bay Co.*, 13 Wall. 166, 177–178 (1872), construing a provision in the Wisconsin Constitution identical to the Just Compensation Clause, this Court said:

> "It would be a very curious and unsatisfactory result if . . . it shall be held that if the government refrains from the absolute conversion of real property to the uses of the

[9] The Solicitor General urges that the prohibitory nature of the Fifth Amendment, combined with principles of sovereign immunity, establishes that the Amendment itself is only a limitation on the power of the Government to act, not a remedial provision. The cases cited in the text, we think, refute the argument of the United States that "the Constitution does not, of its own force, furnish a basis for a court to award money damages against the government." Though arising in various factual and jurisdictional settings, these cases make clear that it is the Constitution that dictates the remedy for interference with property rights amounting to a taking. *See San Diego Gas & Electric Co. v. San Diego*, 450 U.S. 621, 655, n. 21 (1981) (Brennan, J., dissenting), *quoting United States v. Dickinson*, 331 U.S. 745, 748 (1947).

public it can destroy its value entirely, can inflict irreparable and permanent injury to any extent, can, in effect, subject it to total destruction without making any compensation, because, in the narrowest sense of that word, it is not *taken* for the public use."

Later cases have unhesitatingly applied this principle. *See, e.g., Kaiser Aetna v. United States*, 444 U.S. 164 (1979). [Other citations omitted.]

While the Supreme Court of California may not have actually disavowed this general rule in *Agins*, we believe that it has truncated the rule by disallowing damages that occurred prior to the ultimate invalidation of the challenged regulation. The Supreme Court of California justified its conclusion at length in the *Agins* opinion, concluding that:

> "In combination, the need for preserving a degree of freedom in the land-use planning function, and the inhibiting financial force which inheres in the inverse condemnation remedy, persuade us that on balance mandamus or declaratory relief rather than inverse condemnation is the appropriate relief under the circumstances." *Agins v. Tiburon*, 598 P.2d, at 31.

We, of course, are not unmindful of these considerations, but they must be evaluated in the light of the command of the Just Compensation Clause of the Fifth Amendment. The Court has recognized in more than one case that the government may elect to abandon its intrusion or discontinue regulations. *See, e.g., Kirby Forest Industries, Inc. v. United States*, 467 U.S. 1 (1984); *United States v. Dow*, 357 U.S. 17, 26 (1958). Similarly, a governmental body may acquiesce in a judicial declaration that one of its ordinances has affected an unconstitutional taking of property; the landowner has no right under the Just Compensation Clause to insist that a "temporary" taking be deemed a permanent taking. But we have not resolved whether abandonment by the government requires payment of compensation for the period of time during which regulations deny a landowner all use of his land.

In considering this question, we find substantial guidance in cases where the government has only temporarily exercised its right to use private property. In *United States v. Dow, supra*, at 26, though rejecting a claim that the Government may not abandon condemnation proceedings, the Court observed that abandonment "results in an alteration in the property interest taken — from [one of] full ownership to one of temporary use and occupation. . . . In such cases compensation would be measured by the principles normally governing the taking of a right to use property temporarily. *See Kimball Laundry Co. v. United States*, 338 U.S. 1 [1949]; *United States v. Petty Motor Co.*, 327 U.S. 372 [1946]; *United States v. General Motors Corp.*, 323 U.S. 373 [1945]." Each of the cases cited by the *Dow* Court involved appropriation of private property by the United States for use during World War II. Though the takings were in fact "temporary," there was no question that compensation would be required for the Government's interference with the use of the property; the Court was concerned in each case with determining the proper measure of the monetary relief to which the property holders were entitled.

These cases reflect the fact that "temporary" takings which, as here, deny a landowner all use of his property, are not different in kind from permanent takings, for which the Constitution clearly requires compensation. *Cf. San Diego Gas & Electric Co.*, 450 U.S., at 657 (Brennan, J., dissenting) ("Nothing in the Just Compensation Clause suggests that 'takings' must be permanent and irrevocable"). It is axiomatic that the Fifth Amendment's just compensation provision is "designed to bar Government from forcing some people alone to bear public burdens which, in all fairness and justice, should be borne by the public as a whole." *Armstrong v. United States*, 364 U.S., at 49. In the present case, the interim ordinance was adopted by the county of Los Angeles in January 1979, and became effective immediately. Appellant filed suit within a month after the effective date of the ordinance and yet when the Supreme Court of California denied a hearing in the case on October 17, 1985, the merits of appellant's claim had yet to be determined. The United States has been required to pay compensation for leasehold interests of shorter duration than this. The value of a leasehold interest in property for a period of years may be substantial, and the burden on the property owner in extinguishing such an interest for a period of years may be great indeed. *See, e.g., United States v. General Motors, supra.* Where this burden results from governmental action that amounted to a taking, the Just Compensation Clause of the Fifth Amendment requires that the government pay the landowner for the value of the use of the land during this period. *Cf. United States v. Causby*, 328 U.S., at 261 ("It is the owner's loss, not the taker's gain, which is the measure of the value of the property taken"). Invalidation of the ordinance or its successor ordinance after this period of time, though converting the taking into a "temporary" one, is not a sufficient remedy to meet the demands of the Just Compensation Clause.

Appellee argues that requiring compensation for denial of all use of land prior to invalidation is inconsistent with this Court's decisions in *Danforth v. United States*, 308 U.S. 271 (1939), and *Agins v. Tiburon*, 447 U.S. 255 (1980). In *Danforth*, the landowner contended that the "taking" of his property had occurred prior to the institution of condemnation proceedings, by reason of the enactment of the Flood Control Act itself. He claimed that the passage of that Act had diminished the value of his property because the plan embodied in the Act required condemnation of a flowage easement across his property. The Court held that in the context of condemnation proceedings a taking does not occur until compensation is determined and paid, and went on to say that "[a] reduction or increase in the value of property may occur by reason of legislation for or the beginning or completion of a project," but "[s]uch changes in value are incidents of ownership. They cannot be considered as a 'taking' in the constitutional sense." *Danforth, supra*, at 285. *Agins* likewise rejected a claim that the city's preliminary activities constituted a taking, saying that "[m]ere fluctuations in value during the process of governmental decisionmaking, absent extraordinary delay, are 'incidents of ownership.' " *See* 447 U.S., at 263, n. 9.

But these cases merely stand for the unexceptional proposition that the valuation of property which has been taken must be calculated as of the time of the taking, and that depreciation in value of the property by reason of preliminary activity is not chargeable to the government. Thus, in *Agins*, we concluded that the preliminary activity did not work a taking. It would require a considerable extension of these decisions to say that no compensable regulatory taking may occur until a challenged ordinance has ultimately been held invalid.[10]

Nothing we say today is intended to abrogate the principle that the decision to exercise the

---

[10] *Williamson County Regional Planning Comm'n*, is not to the contrary. There, we noted that "no constitutional violation occurs until just compensation has been denied." 473 U.S., at 194, n. 13. This statement, however, was addressed to the issue of whether the constitutional claim was ripe for review and did not establish that compensation is unavailable for government activity occurring before compensation is actually denied. Though, as a matter of law, an illegitimate taking might not occur until the government refuses to pay, the interference that effects a taking might begin much earlier, and compensation is measured from that time. *See Kirby Forest Industries, Inc. v. United States*, 467 U.S. 1, 5 (1984) (where Government physically occupies land without condemnation proceedings, "the owner has a right to bring an 'inverse condemnation' suit to recover the value of the land on the date of the intrusion by the Government").

power of eminent domain is a legislative function, " 'for Congress and Congress alone to determine.' " *Hawaii Housing Authority v. Midkiff*, 467 U.S. 229, 240 (1984), quoting *Berman v. Parker*, 348 U.S. 26, 33 (1954). Once a court determines that a taking has occurred, the government retains the whole range of options already available — amendment of the regulation, withdrawal of the invalidated regulation, or exercise of eminent domain. Thus we do not, as the Solicitor General suggests, "permit a court, at the behest of a private person, to require the . . . Government to exercise the power of eminent domain. . . ." Brief for United States as *Amicus Curiae* 22. We merely hold that where the government's activities have already worked a taking of all use of property, no subsequent action by the government can relieve it of the duty to provide compensation for the period during which the taking was effective.

We also point out that the allegation of the complaint which we treat as true for purposes of our decision was that the ordinance in question denied appellant all use of its property. We limit our holding to the facts presented, and of course do not deal with the quite different questions that would arise in the case of normal delays in obtaining building permits, changes in zoning ordinances, variances, and the like which are not before us. We realize that even our present holding will undoubtedly lessen to some extent the freedom and flexibility of land-use planners and governing bodies of municipal corporations when enacting land-use regulations. But such consequences necessarily flow from any decision upholding a claim of constitutional right; many of the provisions of the Constitution are designed to limit the flexibility and freedom of governmental authorities and the Just Compensation Clause of the Fifth Amendment is one of them. As Justice Holmes aptly noted more than 50 years ago, "a strong public desire to improve the public condition is not enough to warrant achieving the desire by a shorter cut than the constitutional way of paying for the change." *Pennsylvania Coal Co. v. Mahon*, 260 U.S., at 416.

Here we must assume that the Los Angeles County ordinances have denied appellant all use of its property for a considerable period of years, and we hold that invalidation of the ordinance without payment of fair value for the use of the property during this period of time would be a constitutionally insufficient remedy. The judgment of the California Court of Appeals is therefore reversed, and the case is remanded for further proceedings not inconsistent with this opinion.

It is so ordered.

JUSTICE STEVENS, with whom JUSTICE BLACKMUN and JUSTICE O'CONNOR join as to Parts I and III, dissenting. [Most of Justice Stevens' dissent is omitted, but his comments on the notion that a normal delay in decision making is not a taking are of interest:]

The Court's reasoning also suffers from severe internal inconsistency. Although it purports to put to one side "normal delays in obtaining building permits, changes in zoning ordinances, variances and the like," the Court does not explain why there is a constitutional distinction between a total denial of all use of property during such "normal delays" and an equally total denial for the same length of time in order to determine whether a regulation has "gone too far" to be sustained unless the Government is prepared to condemn the property. Precisely the same interference with a real estate developer's plans may be occasioned by protracted proceedings which terminate with a zoning board's decision that the public interest would be served by modification of its regulation and equally protracted litigation which ends with a judicial determination that the existing zoning restraint has "gone too far," and that the board must therefore grant the developer a variance. The Court's analysis takes no cognizance of these realities. Instead, it appears to erect an artificial distinction between "normal delays" and the delays involved in obtaining a court declaration that the regulation constitutes a taking.

NOTES AND QUESTIONS

1. *All use?* Note Chief Justice Rehnquist's statement in *First English* that he "treated as true" the allegations in the complaint that the ordinance denied "all use" of the property and that he limited the holding to "the facts presented." Does this statement mean that compensation for a temporary taking is available only in this circumstance? Assume an owner's land is zoned single-family, that he wants to build a multifamily development, and that he successfully brings an action in federal court claiming the single family zoning is a taking. Is he entitled to compensation for a temporary taking under *First English*?

Some cases hold not, a result which if generally applied would seriously limit compensation in land use cases. *E.g., Cobb County v. McColister*, 413 S.E.2d 441 (Ga. 1992); *Lake Forest Chateau v. City of Lake Forest*, 549 N.E.2d 336 (Ill. 1990); *Staubes v. City of Folly Beach*, 500 S.E.2d 160 (S.C. 1998). *But see Cannone v. Noey*, 867 P.2d 797 (Alaska 1994) (contra); *Whitehead Oil Co. v. City of Lincoln (III)*, 515 N.W.2d 401 (Neb. 1994).

2. *The property interest taken.* Is an award of monetary compensation necessarily required by the Fifth and Fourteenth Amendments once a state court determines that a "*temporary* regulatory taking" has occurred? If so, will it not be necessary to define the property interest "taken"? *Florida Rock Indus., Inc. v. United States*, 45 Fed. Cl. 21, 43 n. 13 (1999), held that "[i]f it is necessary to name the government's interest post taking, the court would suggest the government now owns a negative easement." How easy is this to accomplish? The court did not actually suggest that an easement be conveyed to the government. What if the property owner, after he receives compensation, applies again for permission? Does payment of compensation preclude this?

How should the duration of the "negative easement" be determined? In *Hernandez v. City of Lafayette*, 643 F.2d 1188 (5th Cir. 1981), the court stated that the "regulatory taking" should not be deemed to begin (1) until the time when, "due to changing circumstances," a previously valid "general zoning ordinance" becomes so restrictive as to deny a landowner any "economically viable use of his land," or (2) until expiration of a reasonable time after a landowner questions the validity of a new zoning classification that denies him any "economically viable use of his land." The second alternative is designed to give the local governing body "a realistic time within which to review its zoning legislation vis-a-vis the particular property and to correct the inequity." Under *First English*, the "*temporary* regulatory taking" period should end either when, prior to a judicial declaration of unconstitutionality, the offending regulation is repealed (or, presumably, amended so as to make it clearly constitutional), or when the court holds the regulation to be unconstitutional.

3. *The measure of compensation. First English* is a remedies case; the Court made this clear in *Tahoe-Sierra Preservation Council, Inc. v. Tahoe Regional Planning Agency*, 535 U.S. 302, decided in 2002 and discussed *infra*. As such, *First English* provides no guidance on the question of which measure of compensation courts should employ in inverse condemnation cases. Since *First English* was decided, courts have struggled with the measure of compensation. The inquiry into the appropriate measure of compensation is inherently reflective of the extent of the constitutional protections that will be afforded to private property rights. *See*

Serkin, *The Meaning of Value: Assessing Just Compensation for Regulatory Takings*, 99 Nw. U.L. Rev. 677 (2005).

The measure of compensation for temporary regulatory takings is different from the measure of compensation for permanent takings. In the latter case, loss in market value of the property generally is the criterion. *Mills v. Iowa Dept. of Transp.*, 462 N.W.2d 300 (Iowa App. 1990). In *A.A. Profiles, Inc. v. City of Fort Lauderdale*, 253 F.3d 576 (11th Cir. 2001), for example, a downzoning that blocked construction of a wood-chipping facility after neighbors objected was held to be a permanent taking because the owner then lost the property in foreclosure proceedings. Using the standard "what has the owner lost?" approach of eminent domain proceedings, the court "applied a modified market value test" that "subtract[s] the market value of the property as encumbered by the regulation from the market value of the property without the offending regulation in place." *Id.* at 584. Market value is usually determined through an examination of sales of comparable property. *Florida Rock Indus., Inc. v. United States, supra*, used this measure of damages and awarded compensation when a denial of a permit for mining in a wetlands deprived the landowner of 73.1% of the value of its property. The market value approach may be best suited for permanent takings cases that involve downzoning. The owner's property initially has fewer restrictions and a higher value and, as a result of newly imposed restrictions, the property's value declines. The measure of the owner's loss is the difference between the pre- and post-regulation values. But matters are not always this simple, as is discussed below.

Courts are more likely to consider factors other than loss in market value when the regulatory taking is temporary. See *Bass Enterprises Production Co. v. United* States, 48 Fed. Cl. 621 (2001) (*Bass IV*). There are some basic approaches to measuring compensation that courts have tended to use in these cases which include: (1) rental return or lost rents, (2) option price, (3) interest on lost profits, and (4) before and after valuation. 8 Rohan & Reskin, Nichols on Eminent Domain § G14E/09[5] (3d ed. 2008).

The measure of compensation under the rental return approach is the rent the parties supposedly would have negotiated for the period of the temporary taking. In *Yuba Natural Resources, Inc. v. United* States, 904 F.2d 1577 (Fed. Cir. 1990), the court awarded the plaintiff $580,555.40 plus interest in damages after finding that the United States government had temporarily taken the plaintiff's mineral rights over a six year period. The court calculated the damages based upon "the minimum amount in rent and royalties that Yuba would have received under the joint venture agreement." The plaintiff entered into the joint venture agreement with another company prior to the taking and the agreement covered the period of the taking. *Id.* at 1580. But see *SDDS, Inc. v. State*, 650 N.W.2d 1 (S.D. 2002) (rejecting rental return approach as too speculative and using interest on cash flow as alternative).

Under the option approach, the measure of compensation is the value of an option to purchase the property during the period of the temporary taking. *Lomarch Corp. v. Mayor of Englewood*, 237 A.2d 881 (N.J. 1968) (designation of owner's property for use as a public park with one year to enter a purchase contract or institute condemnation proceedings held to be a taking and stating that fair compensation is the value of the option).

The traditional rule on takings compensation is that lost profits are not compensable because they are too speculative and because they are personal to the property owner. Only a few courts have awarded interest on lost profits, but more have held that compensation based upon speculative future profits is inappropriate. But see *Prince George's County v. Blumberg*, 407 A.2d 1151 (Md. App. 1979) (recognizing the potential for awarding lost profits).

4. *Return on equity test.* According to the before and after valuation approach, the measure of compensation is equal to the lost return on equity in the future project. In *Wheeler v. City of Pleasant Grove*, 833 F.2d 267 (11th Cir. 1987) *(Wheeler III)*, the court held that compensation for a temporary regulatory taking occasioned by a downzoning should be based on the property's potential for producing income or profit, measured by "the market rate return computed over the period of the temporary taking on the difference between the property's fair market value without the regulatory restriction and its fair market value with the restriction." *Id.* at 271.

The Court of Appeals affirmed this holding in a later appeal after the district court refused to award compensation on remand. *Wheeler v. City of Pleasant Grove*, 896 F.2d 1347 (11th Cir. 1990) *(Wheeler IV)*. It awarded compensation at the market rate of return for the temporary taking period on plaintiffs' equity in the project. Instead of looking at the market value of the land as of the date of the taking, the court used the "undisputed appraised fair market value of $2.3 million" which was the court's assessment of the value of the proposed, but unbuilt apartment complex. *Id.* at 1351. Based upon expert testimony, the court concluded that the loan-to-value ratio was seventy-five percent, leaving the plaintiffs with a twenty-five percent equity interest or $575,000. As a result of the regulatory restrictions, the difference in the fair market value that was lost was $525,000. Next, the court applied a 9.77 percent market rate of return for the fourteen month period of the temporary taking, and concluded that the measure of compensation was $59,841.23 plus interest starting from the date of the entry of the injunction.

The court refused to award compensation for lost profits or increased development costs, but held that compensation was payable even though the property increased in value during the time the ordinance was in force. Does this make sense? *Wheeler* did not consider the uncertainty that the project might not have been built. Is this correct?

Some courts and commentators have criticized *Wheeler IV* as being fundamentally flawed because it uses proposed but nonexistent projects as the basis for its calculation of market value and because it was not certain that the project in *Wheeler* would actually be built after the downzoning was invalidated. This seems like awarding speculative or incidental damages, including lost profits, which generally are not compensable. *Corn v. City of Lauderdale Lakes*, 771 F. Supp. 1557 (S.D. Fla. 1991). Another criticism of *Wheeler IV* is its focus on the plaintiffs' equity rather than on the market value of the property. Equity positions can and do vary depending upon the nature of the real estate investment. See also *A.A. Profiles, supra* (*Wheeler III*) compensation framework appropriate only in temporary takings cases). *Nemmers v. City of Dubuque (II)*, 764 F.2d 502 (8th Cir. 1985) (compensation for downzoning based on difference in value as light industrial and value as residential, stating that for a temporary taking, market value should be determined *as of the date of the taking*).

5. *Delay as a taking.* What about the "different questions" Chief Justice Rehnquist raises concerning "normal delays" in obtaining zoning changes and the like? Do you agree with Justice Stevens' criticism of this distinction? Most courts have applied this dictum to hold that even prolonged decision-making by government agencies on land use applications is not a taking during the decision-making period. *Bass Enterprises Production Co. v. United States*, 381 F.3d 1360 (Fed. Cir. 2004) (45-month delay in permit approval for oil and gas drilling on land condemned by the federal government was not a temporary taking). The key issue is whether the delay was reasonable or extraordinary, *Tabb Lakes v. United States*, 10 F.3d 796 (D.C. Cir. 1993), but most courts are willing to assume that local officials are carrying out their

duties in good faith. *Byrd v. City of Hartsville*, 620 S.E.2d 76 (S.C. 2005) (11-month delay on rezoning petition was reasonable); *Loewenstein v. City of Lafayette*, 127 Cal. Rptr. 2d 79 (Cal. App. 2002) (2-year delay on lot line adjustment application held reasonable). But see *DeSai v. Board of Adjustment*, 824 A.2d 166, 171–73 (N.J. App. Div. 2003) (approving award of damages for arbitrary delay).

A somewhat different problem arises if a municipality improperly denies a rezoning, variance or some other approval for the use of land, the landowner appeals and the court holds the denial was invalid but was not a taking. Most courts do not find a temporary taking occurred during the time the case was litigated. *Torromeo v. Town of Fremont*, 813 A.2d 389 (N.H. 2002) (delay damages not available for application of growth control ordinance invalidated because of a procedural error — failure to adopt statutorily required capital improvements plan prior to enacting growth control ordinance); *Landgate, Inc. v. California Coastal Comm'n*, 953 P.2d 1188 (Cal. 1998). *Eberle v. Dane County Bd. of Adjustment*, 595 N.W.2d 730 (Wis. 1999), held the other way in a case in which the court found the board had improperly denied access to two residential lots. It held that a "complete lack of access" was a denial of all or substantially all practicable uses during the time the case was litigated. The dissent argued the landowner's eventual receipt of a permit after the court reversed the board's decision made the case one of temporary delay and not a temporary taking. *SDDS, Inc. v. State*, noted *supra*, held that a 43-month delay in receipt of a previously-approved permit to operate a landfill because of an initiative blocking the permit that was later overturned was a temporary taking of the right to operate the landfill. Whether a moratorium on the use of property is a noncompensable normal delay is considered in Chapter 6, *infra*.

6. *Subsequent proceedings in First English.* On remand from the Supreme Court, the California Court of Appeal, without returning *First English* to the trial court for a hearing and a determination whether the facts established at the hearing effected a de facto taking, made its own determination that the complaint failed to state a cause of action, because the interim ordinance substantially advanced a legitimate state purpose and did not deny plaintiff all use of its property. 258 Cal. Rptr. 893 (1989). Moratoria of this kind are considered in *Tahoe-Sierra*, reproduced *infra*.

7. *Sources.* For discussion of *First English*, see Cooperstein, *Sensing Leave for One's Takings: Interim Damages and Land Use Regulation*, 7 Stan. Envtl. L.J. 49 (1987-88); White & Barkhordari, *The First English Evangelical Lutheran Church Case: What Did It Actually Decide?*, 7 UCLA J. Envtl. L. & Pol'y 155 (1988) (co-author argued case in Supreme Court).

[4.] The *Lucas* Case: A Per Se Takings Rule

LUCAS v. SOUTH CAROLINA COASTAL COUNCIL
505 U.S. 1003 (1992)

JUSTICE SCALIA delivered the opinion of the Court:

In 1986, petitioner David H. Lucas paid $975,000 for two residential lots on the Isle of Palms in Charleston County, South Carolina, on which he intended to build single-family homes. In 1988, however, the South Carolina Legislature enacted the Beachfront Management Act, S.C. Code § 48-39-250 *et seq.* (Supp. 1990) (Act), which had the direct effect of barring petitioner from erecting any permanent habitable structures on his two parcels. *See* § 48-39-

290(A). A state trial court found that this prohibition rendered Lucas's parcels "valueless." This case requires us to decide whether the Act's dramatic effect on the economic value of Lucas's lots accomplished a taking of private property under the Fifth and Fourteenth Amendments requiring the payment of "just compensation." U.S. Const., Amdt. 5.

I

A

South Carolina's expressed interest in intensively managing development activities in the so-called "coastal zone" dates from 1977 when, in the aftermath of Congress's passage of the federal Coastal Zone Management Act of 1972, 16 U.S.C. § 1451 *et seq.*, the legislature enacted a Coastal Zone Management Act of its own. *See* S.C. Code § 48-39-10 *et seq.* (1987). In its original form, the South Carolina Act required owners of coastal zone land that qualified as a "critical area" (defined in the legislation to include beaches and immediately adjacent sand dunes, § 48-39-10(J)) to obtain a permit from the newly created South Carolina Coastal Council (respondent here) prior to committing the land to a "use other than the use the critical area was devoted to on [September 28, 1977]." § 48-39-130(A).

In the late 1970s, Lucas and others began extensive residential development of the Isle of Palms, a barrier island situated eastward of the City of Charleston. Toward the close of the development cycle for one residential subdivision known as "Beachwood East," Lucas in 1986 purchased the two lots at issue in this litigation for his own account. No portion of the lots, which were located approximately 300 feet from the beach, qualified as a "critical area" under the 1977 Act; accordingly, at the time Lucas acquired these parcels, he was not legally obliged to obtain a permit from the Council in advance of any development activity. His intention with respect to the lots was to do what the owners of the immediately adjacent parcels had already done: erect single-family residences. He commissioned architectural drawings for this purpose.

The Beachfront Management Act brought Lucas's plans to an abrupt end. Under that 1988 legislation, the Council was directed to establish a "baseline" connecting the landward-most "points of erosion . . . during the past forty years" in the region of the Isle of Palms that includes Lucas's lots. § 48-39-280(A)(2) (Supp.1988).[1]

In action not challenged here, the Council fixed this baseline landward of Lucas's parcels. That was significant, for under the Act construction of occupiable improvements[2] was flatly prohibited seaward of a line drawn 20 feet landward of, and parallel to, the baseline, § 48-39-290(A) (Supp.1988). The Act provided no exceptions.

---

[1] This specialized historical method of determining the baseline applied because the Beachwood East subdivision is located adjacent to a so-called "inlet erosion zone" (defined in the Act to mean "a segment of shoreline along or adjacent to tidal inlets which is influenced directly by the inlet and its associated shoals," S.C. Code § 48-39-270(7) (Supp.1988)) that is "not stabilized by jetties, terminal groins, or other structures," § 48-39-280(A)(2). For areas other than these unstabilized inlet erosion zones, the statute directs that the baseline be established "along the crest of the primary oceanfront sand dune." § 48-39-280(A)(1).

[2] The Act did allow the construction of certain nonhabitable improvements, e.g., "wooden walkways no larger in width than six feet," and "small wooden decks no larger than one hundred forty-four square feet." §§ 48-39-290(A)(1) and (2) (Supp.1988).

B

Lucas promptly filed suit in the South Carolina Court of Common Pleas, contending that the Beachfront Management Act's construction bar effected a taking of his property without just compensation. . . . The court concluded that Lucas's properties had been "taken" by operation of the Act, and it ordered respondent to pay "just compensation" in the amount of $1,232,387.50.

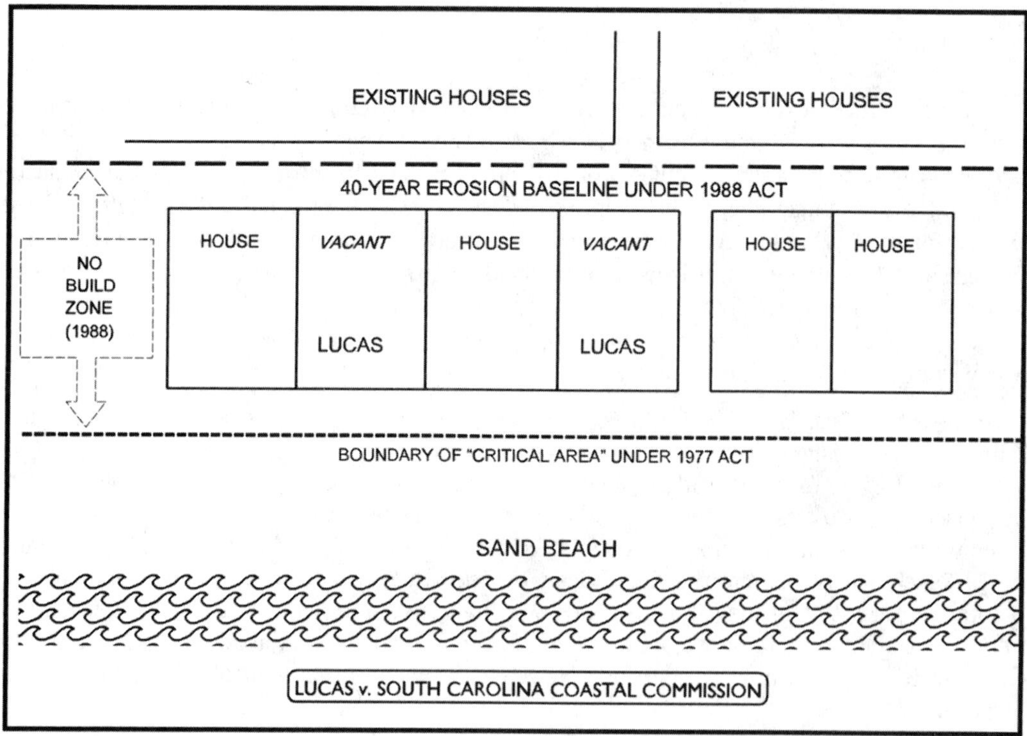

The Supreme Court of South Carolina reversed. It found dispositive what it described as Lucas's concession "that the Beachfront Management Act [was] properly and validly designed to preserve . . . South Carolina's beaches." 404 S.E.2d 895, 896 (1991). Failing an attack on the validity of the statute as such, the court believed itself bound to accept the "uncontested . . . findings" of the South Carolina legislature that new construction in the coastal zone — such as petitioner intended — threatened this public resource. *Id.*, at 898. The Court ruled that when a regulation respecting the use of property is designed "to prevent serious public harm," *id.*, at 899, (citing, *inter alia*, *Mugler v. Kansas*, 123 U.S. 623 (1887)), no compensation is owing under the Takings Clause regardless of the regulation's effect on the property's value. . . .

We granted certiorari.

II

As a threshold matter, we must briefly address the Council's suggestion that this case is inappropriate for plenary review. After briefing and argument before the South Carolina Supreme Court, but prior to issuance of that court's opinion, the Beachfront Management Act was amended to authorize the Council, in certain circumstances, to issue "special permits" for the construction or reconstruction of habitable structures seaward of the baseline. *See* S.C. Code § 48-39-290(D)(1) (Supp.1991). According to the Council, this amendment renders Lucas's claim of a permanent deprivation unripe, as Lucas may yet be able to secure permission to build on his property. . . . [The Council cited Supreme Court decisions that hold a taking case is not ripe unless the landowner has obtained a final decision, citing *Williamson County Regional Planning Comm'n of Johnson City v. Hamilton Bank*, 473 U.S. 172, 190 (1985), reproduced *infra*.]

We think these considerations would preclude review had the South Carolina Supreme Court rested its judgment on ripeness grounds, as it was (essentially) invited to do by the Council, *see* Brief for Respondent 9, n.3. The South Carolina Supreme Court shrugged off the possibility of further administrative and trial proceedings, however, preferring to dispose of Lucas's takings claim on the merits. This unusual disposition does not preclude Lucas from applying for a permit under the 1990 amendment for *future* construction, and challenging, on takings grounds, any denial. But it does preclude, both practically and legally, any takings claim with respect to Lucas's *past* deprivation, *i.e.*, for his having been denied construction rights during the period before the 1990 amendment. . . . [The Court held that Lucas had no need to pursue a temporary taking claim at trial because "as the Act then read, the taking was unconditional and permanent."]

III

A . . .

[The Court discussed *Pennsylvania Coal Co. v. Mahon* and continued:] Nevertheless, our decision in *Mahon* offered little insight into when, and under what circumstances, a given regulation would be seen as going "too far" for purposes of the Fifth Amendment. In 70-odd years of succeeding "regulatory takings" jurisprudence, we have generally eschewed any " 'set formula' " for determining how far is too far, preferring to "engag[e] in . . . essentially ad hoc, factual inquiries," *Penn Central Transportation Co. v. New York City*, 438 U.S. 104, 124 (1978) (quoting *Goldblatt v. Hempstead*, 369 U.S. 590, 594 (1962)). *See* Epstein, *Takings: Descent and Resurrection*, 1987 Sup. Ct. Rev. 1, 4. We have, however, described at least two discrete categories of regulatory action as compensable without case-specific inquiry into the public interest advanced in support of the restraint. The first encompasses regulations that compel the property owner to suffer a physical "invasion" of his property. In general (at least with regard to permanent invasions), no matter how minute the intrusion, and no matter how weighty the public purpose behind it, we have required compensation. For example, in *Loretto v. Teleprompter Manhattan CATV Corp.*, 458 U.S. 419 (1982), we determined that New York's law requiring landlords to allow television cable companies to emplace cable facilities in their apartment buildings constituted a taking, *id.*, at 435-440, even though the facilities occupied at most only 12 cubic feet of the landlords' property, *see id.*, at 438, n. 16. *See also United States v. Causby*, 328 U.S. 256, 265, and n. 10 (1946) (physical invasions of airspace); *cf. Kaiser Aetna v. United States*, 444 U.S. 164 (1979) (imposition of navigational servitude upon private marina).

The second situation in which we have found categorical treatment appropriate is where regulation denies all economically beneficial or productive use of land. *See Agins*, 447 U.S., at 260. As we have said on numerous occasions, the Fifth Amendment is violated when land-use regulation "does not substantially advance legitimate state interests *or denies an owner economically viable use of his land.*" *Agins, supra,* at 260 (citations omitted) (emphasis added).[7]

[The Court has now repudiated the substantially advance test. — Eds.]

We think, in short, that there are good reasons for our frequently expressed belief that when the owner of real property has been called upon to sacrifice *all* economically beneficial uses in the name of the common good, that is, to leave his property economically idle, he has suffered a taking.

B

The trial court found Lucas's two beachfront lots to have been rendered valueless by respondent's enforcement of the coastal-zone construction ban. Under Lucas's theory of the case, which rested upon our "no economically viable use" statements, that finding entitled him to compensation. Lucas believed it unnecessary to take issue with either the purposes behind the Beachfront Management Act, or the means chosen by the South Carolina Legislature to effectuate those purposes. The South Carolina Supreme Court, however, thought otherwise. In its view, the Beachfront Management Act was no ordinary enactment, but involved an exercise of South Carolina's "police powers" to mitigate the harm to the public interest that petitioner's use of his land might occasion. 404 S.E.2d, at 899. By neglecting to dispute the findings enumerated in the Act or otherwise to challenge the legislature's purposes, petitioner "conceded that the beach/dune area of South Carolina's shores is an extremely valuable public resource; that the erection of new construction, *inter alia*, contributes to the erosion and destruction of this public resource; and that discouraging new construction in close proximity to the beach/dune area is necessary to prevent a great public harm." 404 S.E.2d, at 898. In the court's view, these concessions brought petitioner's challenge within a long line of this Court's cases sustaining against Due Process and Takings Clause challenges the State's use of its "police powers" to enjoin a property owner from activities akin to public nuisances. . . .

It is correct that many of our prior opinions have suggested that "harmful or noxious uses"

---

(7) Regrettably, the rhetorical force of our "deprivation of all economically feasible use" rule is greater than its precision, since the rule does not make clear the "property interest" against which the loss of value is to be measured. When, for example, a regulation requires a developer to leave 90% of a rural tract in its natural state, it is unclear whether we would analyze the situation as one in which the owner has been deprived of all economically beneficial use of the burdened portion of the tract, or as one in which the owner has suffered a mere diminution in value of the tract as a whole. (For an extreme — and, we think, unsupportable — view of the relevant calculus, *see Penn Central Transportation Co. v. New York City*, 42 N.Y.2d 324, 333-334, 397 N.Y.S.2d 914, 366 N.E.2d 1271, 1276-1277 (1977), *aff'd*, 438 U.S. 104 (1978), where the state court examined the diminution in a particular parcel's value produced by a municipal ordinance in light of total value of the takings claimant's other holdings in the vicinity.) Unsurprisingly, this uncertainty regarding the composition of the denominator in our "deprivation" fraction has produced inconsistent pronouncements by the Court. *Compare Pennsylvania Coal Co. v. Mahon*, 260 U.S. 393, 414 (1922) (law restricting subsurface extraction of coal held to effect a taking), *with Keystone Bituminous Coal Assn. v. DeBenedictis*, 480 U.S. 470, 497–502 (1987) (nearly identical law held not to effect a taking); *see also id.*, at 515–520 (Rehnquist, C.J., dissenting); Rose, *Mahon Reconstructed: Why the Takings Issue is Still a Muddle*, 57 S. Cal. L. Rev. 561, 566–569 (1984). The answer to this difficult question may lie in how the owner's reasonable expectations have been shaped by the State's law of property — i.e., whether and to what degree the State's law has accorded legal recognition and protection to the particular interest in land with respect to which the takings claimant alleges a diminution in (or elimination of) value. In any event, we avoid this difficulty in the present case, since the "interest in land" that Lucas has pleaded (a fee simple interest) is an estate with a rich tradition of protection at common law, and since the South Carolina Court of Common Pleas found that the Beachfront Management Act left each of Lucas's beachfront lots without economic value.

of property may be proscribed by government regulation without the requirement of compensation. For a number of reasons, however, we think the South Carolina Supreme Court was too quick to conclude that that principle decides the present case. The "harmful or noxious uses" principle was the Court's early attempt to describe in theoretical terms why government may, consistent with the Takings Clause, affect property values by regulation without incurring an obligation to compensate — a reality we nowadays acknowledge explicitly with respect to the full scope of the State's police power. . . .

The transition from our early focus on control of "noxious" uses to our contemporary understanding of the broad realm within which government may regulate without compensation was an easy one, since the distinction between "harm-preventing" and "benefit-conferring" regulation is often in the eye of the beholder. It is quite possible, for example, to describe in *either* fashion the ecological, economic, and aesthetic concerns that inspired the South Carolina legislature in the present case. One could say that imposing a servitude on Lucas's land is necessary in order to prevent his use of it from "harming" South Carolina's ecological resources; or, instead, in order to achieve the "benefits" of an ecological preserve.

Where the State seeks to sustain regulation that deprives land of all economically beneficial use, we think it may resist compensation only if the logically antecedent inquiry into the nature of the owner's estate shows that the proscribed use interests were not part of his title to begin with. This accords, we think, with our "takings" jurisprudence, which has traditionally been guided by the understandings of our citizens regarding the content of, and the State's power over, the "bundle of rights" that they acquire when they obtain title to property. It seems to us that the property owner necessarily expects the uses of his property to be restricted, from time to time, by various measures newly enacted by the State in legitimate exercise of its police powers; "[a]s long recognized, some values are enjoyed under an implied limitation and must yield to the police power." *Pennsylvania Coal Co. v. Mahon*, 260 U.S., at 413. And in the case of personal property, by reason of the State's traditionally high degree of control over commercial dealings, he ought to be aware of the possibility that new regulation might even render his property economically worthless (at least if the property's only economically productive use is sale or manufacture for sale), *see Andrus v. Allard*, 444 U.S. 51, 66–67 (1979) (prohibition on sale of eagle feathers). In the case of land, however, we think the notion pressed by the Council that title is somehow held subject to the "implied limitation" that the State may subsequently eliminate all economically valuable use is inconsistent with the historical compact recorded in the Takings Clause that has become part of our constitutional culture.

Where "permanent physical occupation" of land is concerned, we have refused to allow the government to decree it anew (without compensation), no matter how weighty the asserted "public interests" involved, *Loretto v. Teleprompter Manhattan CATV Corp.*, 458 U.S., at 426 — though we assuredly *would* permit the government to assert a permanent easement that was a pre-existing limitation upon the landowner's title. *Compare Scranton v. Wheeler*, 179 U.S. 141, 163 (1900) (interests of "riparian owner in the submerged lands . . . bordering on a public navigable water" held subject to Government's navigational servitude), *with Kaiser Aetna v. United States*, 444 U.S., at 178-180 (imposition of navigational servitude on marina created and rendered navigable at private expense held to constitute a taking). We believe similar treatment must be accorded confiscatory regulations, *i.e.*, regulations that prohibit all economically beneficial use of land: Any limitation so severe cannot be newly legislated or decreed (without compensation), but must inhere in the title itself, in the restrictions that background principles of the State's law of property and nuisance already place upon land ownership. A law or decree with such an effect must, in other words, do no more than duplicate the result that could have been achieved in the courts — by adjacent landowners (or other uniquely affected persons) under the State's law of private nuisance, or by the State under its complementary power to abate nuisances that affect the public generally, or otherwise.[16]

On this analysis, the owner of a lake bed, for example, would not be entitled to compensation when he is denied the requisite permit to engage in a landfilling operation that would have the effect of flooding others' land. Nor the corporate owner of a nuclear generating plant, when it is directed to remove all improvements from its land upon discovery that the plant sits astride an earthquake fault. Such regulatory action may well have the effect of eliminating the land's only economically productive use, but it does not proscribe a productive use that was previously permissible under relevant property and nuisance principles. The use of these properties for what are now expressly prohibited purposes was *always* unlawful, and (subject to other constitutional limitations) it was open to the State at any point to make the implication of those background principles of nuisance and property law explicit. *See* Michelman, *Property, Utility, and Fairness, Comments on the Ethical Foundations of "Just Compensation" Law*, 80 Harv. L. Rev. 1165, 1239-1241 (1967). In light of our traditional resort to "existing rules or understandings that stem from an independent source such as state law" to define the range of interests that qualify for protection as "property" under the Fifth (and Fourteenth) Amendments, *Board of Regents of State Colleges v. Roth*, 408 U.S. 564, 577 (1972), this recognition that the Takings Clause does not require compensation when an owner is barred from putting land to a use that is proscribed by those "existing rules or understandings" is surely unexceptional. When, however, a regulation that declares "off-limits" all economically productive or beneficial uses of land goes beyond what the relevant background principles would dictate, compensation must be paid to sustain it.

The "total taking" inquiry we require today will ordinarily entail (as the application of state nuisance law ordinarily entails) analysis of, among other things, the degree of harm to public lands and resources, or adjacent private property, posed by the claimant's proposed activities, *see, e.g.*, Restatement (Second) of Torts §§ 826, 827, the social value of the claimant's activities and their suitability to the locality in question, *see, e.g., id.*, §§ 828(a) and (b), 831, and the relative ease with which the alleged harm can be avoided through measures taken by the claimant and the government (or adjacent private landowners) alike, *see, e.g., id.*, §§ 827(e), 828(c), 830. The fact that a particular use has long been engaged in by similarly situated owners ordinarily imports a lack of any common-law prohibition (though changed circumstances or new knowledge may make what was previously permissible no longer so, *see* Restatement (Second) of Torts, *supra*, § 827, comment *g*). So also does the fact that other landowners, similarly situated, are permitted to continue the use denied to the claimant.

It seems unlikely that common-law principles would have prevented the erection of any habitable or productive improvements on petitioner's land; they rarely support prohibition of the "essential use" of land, *Curtin v. Benson*, 222 U.S. 78, 86 (1911). The question, however, is one of state law to be dealt with on remand. We emphasize that to win its case South Carolina must do more than proffer the legislature's declaration that the uses Lucas desires are inconsistent with the public interest, or the conclusory assertion that they violate a common-law maxim such as *sic utere tuo ut alienum non laedas*. As we have said, a "State, by *ipse dixit*,

---

[16] The principal "otherwise" that we have in mind is litigation absolving the State (or private parties) of liability for the destruction of "real and personal property, in cases of actual necessity, to prevent the spreading of a fire" or to forestall other grave threats to the lives and property of others. *Bowditch v. Boston*, 101 U.S. 16, 18–19 (1880); *see United States v. Pacific Railroad*, 120 U.S. 227, 238–239 (1887).

may not transform private property into public property without compensation . . . ." *Webb's Fabulous Pharmacies, Inc. v. Beckwith*, 449 U.S. 155, 164 (1980). Instead, as it would be required to do if it sought to restrain Lucas in a common-law action for public nuisance, South Carolina must identify background principles of nuisance and property law that prohibit the uses he now intends in the circumstances in which the property is presently found. Only on this showing can the State fairly claim that, in proscribing all such beneficial uses, the Beachfront Management Act is taking nothing.[18]

. . . .

The judgment is reversed and the cause remanded for proceedings not inconsistent with this opinion. *So ordered.*

NOTES AND QUESTIONS

1. *The several Lucas opinions.* Chief Justice Rehnquist and Justices O'Connor, Thomas, and White joined in Justice Scalia's opinion. Justice Kennedy concurred in the Court's disposition of the case but not in its opinion, and filed a separate opinion in which he adopted a much broader concept of the police power than did the Court. Justice Souter filed a "statement" rejecting both the decision and the reasoning of the Court because he believed the record was so uncertain "that there is little utility in attempting to deal with this case on the merits."

Justices Blackmun and Stevens dissented and filed separate opinions in which they rejected the Court's new "categorical rule" that a regulation depriving land of all "beneficial" or "viable" use effects a compensable "taking" under the Fifth Amendment as made applicable to the States by the Fourteenth Amendment's Due Process Clause. The majority opinion discusses some of the arguments in Justice Blackmun's dissent.

Justice Blackmun also criticized the Court for launching "a missile to kill a mouse," noting that Justice Scalia had conceded that the situation assumed to exist in *Lucas* "never has arisen in any of our prior cases" and would arise, in the future, "relatively rarely" or only in "extraordinary circumstances" — a concession apparently based on the belief that land use regulations rarely prohibit *all* economic uses of land.

2. *Disposition of Lucas on remand to the South Carolina Supreme Court.* On remand, the South Carolina Supreme Court reversed its original judgment for the Coastal Commission, holding: (1) that the Council did not have a basis under the common law to prohibit Lucas from building a habitable structure on his property, and (2) that the landowner "suffered a temporary taking deserving of compensation commencing with the enactment of the 1988 Act and continuing through" the date of the court's order remanding the case to the trial court for "determination of the actual damages Lucas has sustained as a result of his being temporarily deprived of the use of his property." 424 S.E.2d 484, 486 (1992). The court chose the date of its order (1992) as the ending date of the temporary taking instead of the date the Beachfront

---

[18] Justice Blackmun decries our reliance on background nuisance principles at least in part because he believes those principles to be as manipulable as we find the "harm prevention"/"benefit conferral" dichotomy. There is no doubt some leeway in a court's interpretation of what existing state law permits — but not remotely as much, we think, as in a legislative crafting of the reasons for its confiscatory regulation. We stress that an affirmative decree eliminating all economically beneficial uses may be defended only if an objectively reasonable application of relevant precedents would exclude those beneficial uses in the circumstances in which the land is presently found.

Management Act was amended to authorize the issuance of special permits for construction (1990). Why did the court not use the earlier date? *First English, supra.* The South Carolina Supreme Court stated two reasons: (1) Lucas was not permitted to assert his temporary takings claim until the South Carolina Supreme Court's earlier decision had been reversed by the United States Supreme Court and (2) Lucas could not take any action until the South Carolina Supreme Court had made its decision upon remand. The South Carolina Supreme Court expressly refused to "dictate any specific method of calculating the damages for the temporary nonacquisitory taking." *Id.* The state later settled with Lucas, acquired the property for approximately $1.5 million, and resold it for development. Dick & Chandler, *Shifting Sands: The Implementation of Lucas on the Evolution of Takings Law and South Carolina's Application of the Lucas Rule*, 37 Real Prop., Prob. & T.J. 637, 696 (2003). In 2009, the Lucas property, complete with a home built in 1996, sold for $2.59 million.

3. *What constitutes deprivation of "all economic use"?* What does it mean to deprive the owner of all "economically viable" or "economically beneficial or productive" use of the land? Note that the *Lucas* Court rejected the argument that Mr. Lucas' lot, even subject to the prohibition against building a permanent structure, still had some economic value for recreational uses such as camping, swimming, and picnicking. See Justice Blackmun's dissent in *Lucas*, citing state court decisions recognizing economic value in such cases. This issue is revisited in *Tahoe-Sierra*, reproduced *infra.*

Justice Blackmun said that the compensation requirement established in *Lucas* will apply "relatively rarely" or only in "extraordinary circumstances." This statement is almost certainly correct if we consider only ordinary land use regulations adopted by local governments, such as zoning and subdivision regulations. The ordinance will always allow some use and the issue is whether a more intensive use is required. For this reason, cases since *Lucas* have uniformly refused to find a *per se* taking when the regulation allowed some use of the property. See, e.g., *Cooley v. United States*, 324 F.3d 1297 (Fed. Cir. 2003) (denial of wetlands fill permit that destroyed 98.8% of property's value not a categorical taking); *Gove v. Zoning Bd. of Chatham*, 831 N.E.2d 865 (Mass. 2005) (residential development prohibition on coastal lot that caused 88.5% diminution in value neither a categorical nor a *Penn Central* taking); *Sheffield Dev. Co. v. City of Glenn Heights*, 140 S.W.3d 660, 667 (Tex. 2004) (50% diminution in value was "severe" but not a compensable taking because "the property was still worth four times what it cost, despite the rezoning"). But see *Friedenburg v. New York State Dep't of Envtl. Conservation*, 767 N.Y.S.2d 451 (App. Div. 2003) (wetlands regulation depriving land owner of 95% of value, while not a categorical taking, was a compensable taking under the *Penn Central* balancing test). One must remain mindful of the Court's admonition in *Palazzolo, supra*: "Assuming a taking is otherwise established, a State may not evade the duty to compensate on the premise that the landowner is left with a token interest." 533 U.S. 606, 613 (2001).

4. *First English, Lucas and public nuisance: Can temporary takings constitute a Lucas taking?* Can a prospectively temporary regulation that deprives a person of all use of his property for a proscribed period of time qualify for categorical takings treatment under the rationale of *Lucas*? The court in *Keshbro, Inc. v. City of Miami*, 801 So. 2d 864 (Fla. 2001), held that the city's complete closure of a motel for six months and of an apartment complex for one year pursuant to a public nuisance abatement statute deprived the owners of all beneficial use of their property and that the takings analysis established in *Lucas* should be applied. See *First English, supra*, in which the Court states that " 'temporary' takings which . . . deny a landowner all use of his property, are not different in kind from permanent takings. . . ." The

Florida Supreme Court said it was unable to justify precluding prospectively temporary regulations from *Lucas* categorical treatment.

Moreover, it distinguished land use regulations from nuisance abatement statutes stating: "the courts refusing to extend *First English* beyond its remedial genesis to prospectively temporary regulations have done so in the land use and planning arena, where an entirely different set of considerations are implicated from those in the context of nuisance abatement where a landowner is being deprived of a property's dedicated use." *Keshbro, supra* at 874. The Florida Supreme Court applied *Lucas'* nuisance exception and after doing so, found no compensation was due to the motel owner but that the closing of the apartment was a compensable taking. See also *City of Seattle v. McCoy*, 4 P.3d 159 (Wash. Ct. App. 2000), and *State ex rel. Pizza v. Rezcallah*, 702 N.E.2d 81 (Ohio 1998), both of which held one year closures of property pursuant to nuisance abatement statutes were denials of all economically viable uses under *Lucas*. Temporary takings are subject to the same categorical treatment as permanent takings where the regulation denies all use of the property. Is this consistent with the "parcel as a whole rule" discussed below? Is it consistent with *Tahoe-Sierra, infra*?

5. *Sources.* For discussion of *Lucas*, see Want, *The Lucas Case: The Trial Court Strategy and the Case's Effect on the Property Rights Movement*, 27 Stan. Envtl. L.J. 271 (2008); Burling, *Can the Existence of Value in Property Avert a Regulatory Taking When Economically Beneficial Use Has Been Destroyed*, in Taking Sides on Takings Issues 451 (T. Roberts ed., 2002); Huffman, *Background Principles and the Rule of Law: Fifteen Years After Lucas*, 35 Ecology L.Q. 1 (2008); Meltz, *Takings Law Today: A Primer for the Perplexed*, 34 Ecology L.Q. 307 (2007); Dick & Chandler, *Shifting Sands: The Implementation of Lucas on the Evolution of Takings Law and South Carolina's Application of the Lucas Rule*, 37 Real Prop. Prob. & T.J. 637, 699 (2003); Callies & Breemer, *Selected Legal and Policy Trends in Takings Law: Background Principles, Custom and Public Trust "Exceptions" and the (Mis)Use of Investment-Backed Expectations*, 36 Val. U. L. Rev. 339 (2002); Epstein, *Lucas v. South Carolina Coastal Council: A Tangled Web of Expectations*, 45 Stan. L. Rev. 1369 (1993); Lazarus, *Putting the Correct "Spin" on Lucas*, 45 Stan. L. Rev. 1411 (1993); Mandelker, *Of Mice and Missiles: A True Account of Lucas v. South Carolina Coastal Council*, 8 J. Land Use & Envtl. L. 285 (1993); Sax, *Property Rights and the Economy of Nature: Understanding Lucas v. South Carolina Coastal Council*, 45 Stan. L. Rev. 1433 (1993); Washburn, *Land Use Control, the Individual, and Society: Lucas v. South Carolina Coastal Council*, 52 Md. L. Rev. 162 (1993).

A NOTE ON HOW THE COURTS HAVE DRAWN THE TEETH OF THE *LUCAS* DECISION

What Lucas seemed to mean. The *Lucas* per se rule cast a shadow over land use regulation. It especially threatened environmental land use regulations where total prohibitions on development are necessary. An example is a regulation that prohibits all development in a flood plain. This has not occurred, however, as lower courts have emphasized the exceptions to *Lucas* and have found no takings in cases where *Lucas* might have suggested otherwise. This Note discusses federal and state cases that have interpreted *Lucas* narrowly. The Supreme Court's *Tahoe-Sierra* decision, reproduced *infra*, also narrows the *Lucas* holding.

Parcel as a whole: Segmentation or the denominator rule. — Following the *Lucas* decision, courts struggled to determine when regulations constituted a total deprivation of all economically viable use of land. The regulatory takings analysis must begin with identifying the denominator of the " 'deprivation' fraction," which is the relevant property interest against which the landowner's loss is to be measured. *Lucas, supra.* (The numerator of course is the value of the rights impacted by the regulation, e.g., the property interest lost as a result of the regulation.) To determine the denominator, courts have had to decide whether to consider the impact of the regulation on the parcel as a whole or whether to segment the parcel. Recall that the United States Supreme Court first adopted the parcel as a whole rule in *Penn Central, supra*, which considered vertical segmentation. Later, the Court applied the parcel as a whole rule in *Tahoe-Sierra, infra*, which discusses temporal segmentation (development moratoria). *Lucas*, in footnote 7, addresses the more typical instance of horizontal segmentation.

The parcel as a whole rule has significantly impacted the development of takings jurisprudence. As the denominator increases in size relative to the numerator, the perceived harm to the value of the property impacted by the regulation decreases. Thus, application of the parcel as a whole rule decreases the likelihood that a court will find that a regulatory taking has occurred while segmentation, which reduces the size of the denominator, increases the likelihood that a court will find that a regulatory taking has occurred.

This problem is especially critical in wetland cases, where all development may be prohibited to preserve wetlands. In many of these cases, the parcel includes areas that are not wetlands, on which there is no restriction on development. The owner of the wetland may claim a "conceptual severance," arguing that the wetlands portion should be severed from the rest for takings analysis, and that a per se taking has occurred because no development of the wetlands is permitted. Considering the parcel as a whole avoids the *Lucas* per se takings rule whenever, as is usually the case, the court finds an economically viable use is available on the portion outside the wetlands area. Most of the cases have taken this position. What are the issues here? Consider the suggestion in footnote 7 of *Lucas*, that an "owner's reasonable expectations" as shaped by state property law should be determinative. Is it circular if expectations determine the property interest and also help decide the takings claim? For discussion, see Lisker, *Regulatory Takings and the Denominator Problem*, 27 Rutgers L.J. 663 (1996); Mandelker, *New Property Rights Under the Taking Clause*, 81 Marq. L. Rev. 9 (1997); Merriam, *Rules for the Relevant Parcel*, 25 U. Haw. L. Rev. 353 (2003); Note, *Conceptual Severance and Takings in the Federal Circuit*, 85 Cornell L. Rev. 586 (2000).

The Supreme Court in *Palazzolo, supra*, refused to review "the difficult, persisting question of what is the proper denominator in the takings fraction," which was raised for the first time in petitioner's brief to the Court. 533 U.S. at 631. Treating the entire tract, including a wetlands portion and an upland portion, as the denominator, the Court concluded that wetlands regulations which permitted a landowner to build a substantial residence on the upland portion precluded a categorical taking. The case was remanded for a *Penn Central* analysis. The Court returned to this issue in *Tahoe-Sierra*, reproduced *infra*.

State courts have taken a rather ad hoc approach to the denominator problem "to dilute the harsh [parcel as a whole] rule." Comment, *A Victory for Property Rights: How State Courts Have Interpreted and Applied the Decision from Tahoe-Sierra Preservation Council, Inc. v. Tahoe Regional Planning Agency*, 36 U. Tol. L. Rev. 405, 415–16 (2005). For instance, in an interesting mining case, the Supreme Court of Ohio in *State ex rel. R.T.G., Inc. v. State of Ohio*, 780 N.E.2d 998 (Ohio 2002), rejected the parcel as a whole approach in a suit brought pursuant to the Takings Clause of the Ohio Constitution and held that coal rights were a separate property estate under Ohio law. As such, they were severable and should be treated as a "separate property interest if the property owner's intent was to purchase the property solely for the purpose of mining coal." *Id.* at 1008. Five years later, the Supreme Court of Ohio clarified its holding in *R.T.G.*, stating: "A mineral estate may be considered the relevant parcel for a compensable regulatory taking if the mineral estate was purchased separately from the other interests in the real property. Otherwise, the property should be considered as a whole when a regulatory takings claim is made." *State ex rel. Shelly Materials, Inc. v. Clark County Bd. of Commissioners*, 875 N.E.2d 59, 67 (Ohio 2007).

Suppose a landowner acquires two contiguous lots at the same time. On one lot sits a house, while wetlands occupy the other lot. Each lot has a separate address and is assessed separately for property tax purposes. Several months after the acquisition, the jurisdictional municipality enacts a wetlands ordinance, following which the municipality denies the owner a building permit. Has a compensable taking occurred? The Supreme Judicial Court of Massachusetts, in *Giovanella v. Conservation Comm'n of Ashland*, 857 N.E.2d 451 (Mass. 2006), rejected such a claim. Drawing on applicable precedents, the court concluded that common ownership of contiguous lots establishes a rebuttable presumption that the lots should be considered as one parcel when evaluating the economic effect of a governmental regulation. While either side can rebut the presumption by appropriate evidence that the lots should be treated separately, separate addresses and/or separate tax treatment carry "little weight" and the lack of a common development plan for the two lots, by itself, is not enough to overcome the presumption, the court concluded. Applying *Penn Central*, the court held that a 29 percent reduction in property value was insufficient for a takings finding, nor did the subsequently-enacted wetlands ordinance interfere with reasonable investment-backed expectations because the owner had failed to show any investment that relied on expectations that the second lot was buildable. *Id.* at 461–62. For discussion of *Palazzolo*, see *Symposium: Property Rights After Palazzolo*, 24 U. Haw. L. Rev. 441–657 (2002); Holloway & Guy, *Palazzolo's Impact on Determining the Extent of Interference with Investment-Backed Expectations*, 32 Real Est. L.J. 19 (2003); Burling, *Private Property Rights and the Environment After Palazzolo*, 30 B.C. Envtl. Aff. L. Rev. 1 (2002); Blumm, *Palazzolo and the Decline of Justice Scalia's Categorical Takings Doctrine*, 30 B.C. Envtl. Aff. L. Rev. 137 (2002). See also the discussion of wetlands regulation in Chapter 4.

The same problem can arise under a zoning ordinance when the property is in more than one zone. When the property is under single ownership, the courts tend to treat the entire property as the whole parcel, even though different parts of the property are zoned differently. *Quirk v. Town of New Boston*, 663 A.2d 1328 (N.H. 1995) (part of property zoned as buffer); *Zealy v. City of Waukesha*, 548 N.W.2d 528 (Wis. 1996) (two zones on property); *Zanghi v. Board of Appeals of Bedford*, 807 N.E.2d 221, 226 (Mass. App. 2004) (lot can be used for cluster development with contiguous lots). *Contra Twain Harte Assocs. v. County of Tuolumne*, 265 Cal. Rptr. 737 (Cal. App. 1990) (two zones on property).

A flexible approach adopted by the Court of Federal Claims also has influenced the cases. Although the factors given consideration vary, the underlying principle is one of fairness. *Ciampitti v. United States*, 22 Cl. Ct. 310 (1991) (single parcel when lots treated as such for purpose of purchase and financing). The court held it would consider factors such as the degree of contiguity, dates of acquisition, the extent to which the parcel was treated as a single parcel, and the extent to which the regulated lands enhance the value of the remaining lands. The court added that "no doubt many others would enter into the calculus." See also *Walcek v. United States*, 49 Fed. Cl. 248 (2001) (quoting *Ciampitti*, "identify the parcel as realistically as possible"); *Brace v. United States*, 48 Fed. Cl. 272 (2000) (applying *Ciampitti* factors but distinguishing facts); *Tabb Lakes, Ltd. v. United States*, 10 F.3d 796 (Fed. Cir. 1993). For a three-part segmentation problem, see *Palm Beach Isles Assocs. v. United States*, 208 F.3d 1374 (Fed. Cir. 2000) (lake- and ocean-front parcels purchased together but divided by highway are separate despite profitable sale of ocean parcel; lake-front parcel, partially wetlands and partially submerged land, treated as one).

Is it possible to identify general principles for resolution of the denominator problem, e.g., the original tract purchased by the landowner, or the contiguous tract owned by the landowner at the time the regulation was enacted? Or is a multi-factor test emphasizing fairness more appropriate?

Background principles that inhere in the title as exceptions to the categorical rule. Perhaps the most puzzling part of Justice Scalia's *Lucas* opinion is his exception for restrictions that "inhere in the title itself." What are we to make of this? Scalia included two kinds of "background principles" — the state's "law of property" and its "law of nuisance." The first clearly includes the second, but it is much broader in scope; it would include, e.g., the common law of trespass, support, and riparian rights, as well as nuisance. Does Justice Scalia's reference, in his discussion of the "nuisance exception," to restrictions that "inhere in the title" apparently "freeze" the scope of the "nuisance exception" to that defined by the state's law of nuisance at the time when a landowner acquires title to his property?

When *Lucas* was decided, it was generally thought that the background principles exception to the per se takings rule was limited to common law principles, primarily nuisance. Several cases later held the exception included other common law principles as well as statutes and local regulations in effect when a landowner purchased the property. See, e.g., *Kim v. City of New York*, 681 N.E.2d 312 (N.Y. 1997) (city charter provision in effect prior to acquisition held a background principle precluding landowner's taking claim). In *Palazzolo*, the Court rejected the notion that the *Lucas* background principles exception includes all regulations that happen to be enacted prior to acquisition of title by the person challenging the regulation. Influenced in part by the impact the Court's ripeness rules, discussed *infra*, can have on a regulatory takings claim, the Court held that "objective factors, such as the nature of the land use proscribed," rather than the transfer of title must determine "whether an existing, general law can limit all economic use of property." 533 U.S. 606, 630. See also *Esplanade Properties, LLC v. City of Seattle*, 307 F.3d 978 (9th Cir. 2002) (public trust doctrine reserving to the state ownership of the beds and shores of navigable waters is a background principle of state law precluding a takings claim); *McQueen v. South Carolina Coastal Council*, 580 S.E.2d 116 (S.C. 2003) (public trust doctrine); *Hunziker v. State*, 519 N.W.2d 367 (Iowa 1994) (statute requiring buffer around Indian burial ground is a background principle). For discussion, see Burling, *The Latest Take on Background Principles and the States' Law of Property After Lucas and Palazzolo*, 24 U. Haw. L. Rev. 497 (2002); Eagle, *The 1997 Regulatory Takings Quartet: Retreating from the "Rule of Law,"* 42 N.Y.L. Sch. L. Rev. 345, 367–70 (1998); Note, *The Lucas Exception: Inclusion, Exclusion, and a Statute of Limitation*, 68 Geo. Wash. L. Rev. 134 (1999).

In any event, does the takings inquiry end if a restrictive land use regulation is a background principle? See *Palm Beach Isles Assocs.*, *supra* ("background" navigation servitude may not apply if government bases denial of permit on environmental concerns instead).

The background principles defense and the public trust doctrine. The *Lucas* Court's statement that government could defeat a regulatory takings challenge if it could prove that a regulatory limitation inhered in a state's background principles of property law created a renewed interest in the public trust doctrine. Many scholars and lawyers viewed the doctrine as a viable defense to "'preservation takings.'" Hudson, *The Public and Wildlife Trust Doctrines and the Untold Story of the Lucas Remand*, 34 Colum. J. Envtl. L. 99, 100 (2009). The public trust doctrine's origins are in Roman law and it traces its American roots back to *Illinois Central Railroad Co. v. Illinois*, 146 U.S. 387 (1892), in which the Supreme Court held that the state of Illinois held its navigable waters and submerged lands under them in trust for the public's use. Consequently, the Court ruled that the state's grant of a portion of the bed of Lake Michigan to a private railroad was void. Post-*Lucas*, courts have eagerly considered the scope of the background principles exception, and have "employ[ed] the public trust doctrine to defeat takings claims dealing with coastal areas[,] . . . other submerged lands . . ." and non-tidal lands. Blumm & Ritchie, *Lucas's Unlikely Legacy: The Rise of Background Principles as Categorical Takings Defenses*, 29 Harv. Envtl. L. Rev. 321, 342 (2005). The essence of a public trust doctrine-based takings defense is that so long as "there is no pre-existing right arising from a landowner's title to property that allows the landowner to use, allocate or destroy trust resources, then no takings of private property can occur." Hudson, *The Public and Wildlife Trust Doctrines and the Untold Story of the Lucas Remand, supra*; Babcock, *Should Lucas v. South Carolina Coastal Council Protect Where the Wild Things Are? Of Beavers, Bob-O-Links, and Other Things that Go Bump in the Night*, 85 Iowa L. Rev. 849 (2000); *see also McQueen, supra* (no taking where public trust doctrine forbade backfilling or locating bulkheads on public trust lands); *Esplanade, supra*; *R.W. Docks & Slips v. Wisconsin*, 628 N.W.2d 781 (Wis. 2001) (landowner's riparian rights are subordinate to the public trust doctrine).

Investment-backed expectations: What is the continuing significance of the notice rule? Recall that in applying the investment-backed expectations factor, the United States Supreme Court in *Palazzolo* applied the notice rule it had adopted to decide whether a landowner had investment-backed expectations, and squarely held that persons who acquired land subject to a land use restriction are not precluded from a takings claim because they have notice of the restriction. Earlier, the Rhode Island Supreme Court concluded that because Palazzolo had notice of the wetlands regulation which existed before Palazzolo acquired his title, Palazzolo lacked a reasonable investment-backed expectation and therefore had no viable takings claim under *Penn Central*. The United States Supreme Court reversed the Rhode Island Supreme Court and stated: "If investment-backed expectations are given exclusive significance in the *Penn Central* analysis and existing regulations dictate the reasonableness of those expectations in every instance, then the State wields far too much power to redefine property rights upon passage of title." *Palazzolo, supra;* see, e.g., *Guggenheim v. City of Goleta*, 582 F.3d 996 (9th Cir. 2009) (taking found in facial *Penn Central* challenge of rent control ordinance applied to mobile home park even though park owners made return on investment; court also applied the notice rule and found park owners could still prevail even though the property was subject to rent control regulation at the time of park owners' acquisition). In her concurring opinion, in *Palazzolo*, Justice O'Connor left room for application of the notice rule as an important factor in determining the reasonableness of investment-backed expectations in a *Penn Central* analysis. 533 U.S. 606, 633. For discussion of *Palazzolo*'s notice rule, see Brown, *Taking the Takings Claim: A Policy and Economic Analysis of the Survival of Takings Claims After Property Transfers, supra*; Shelby, *Taking Public Interests in Private Property Seriously: How the Supreme Court Short-Changes Public Property Rights in Regulatory Takings Cases*, 24 J. Land Use & Envtl. Law 45 (2008); Breemer & Radford, *The (Less?) Murky Doctrine of Investment-Backed Expectations After Palazzolo, and the Lower*

Courts' Disturbing Insistence on Wallowing in the Pre-Palazzolo Muck, 34 Sw. U. L. Rev. 351 (2005).

Cases in the Court of Federal Claims and its appellate Federal Circuit, which hear takings cases arising out of the wetlands permit program of the Clean Water Act, illustrate how the notice rule has been applied. In *Good v. United States*, 189 F.3d 1355 (Fed. Cir. 1999), the statute under which the permit was denied was enacted after the property was purchased. The court held that the landowner should have been aware that increasing concern for environmental protection (a "regulatory climate") affected his property when he bought it, and that regulations could ultimately prevent him from building. Under this approach, time of purchase remains the relevant point of inquiry, but the owner is held to have *present* notice of *prospective* regulations. The court also held that the investment-backed expectations takings factor was relevant even in per se, total destruction of value claims under *Lucas*, and that the failure to show expectations defeated the takings claim. A Federal Court of Claims judge reached a contrary conclusion soon after in *Florida Rock Indus. v. United States*, 45 Fed. Cl. 21 (1999), holding that a federal law enacted after purchase did not destroy investment-backed expectations. In *Palm Beach Isles Assocs. v. United States*, 231 F.3d 1354 (Fed. Cir. 2000), the court attempted to resolve these conflicting views on whether reasonable investment-backed expectations are relevant in a categorical takings challenge. Focusing on *Lucas*, the court concluded that they are not. *Id.* at 1364. Does *Palazzolo* resolve the question? Recall that Justice O'Connor's concurrence focuses on "a proper *Penn Central* analysis." 533 U.S. at 633. In a footnote to his 2002 *Tahoe-Sierra* opinion applying *Penn Central*, reproduced *infra*, Justice Stevens noted that persons purchasing land after adoption of a 1972 regional planning compact "did so amidst a heavily regulated zoning scheme." 535 U.S. at 313, n.5. Can you see a difference between the "background principles" rule and the investment-backed expectations test? The plurality in *Palazzolo* suggested that these two principles might be convergent.

Mandelker, *Investment-Backed Expectations in Taking Law*, 27 Urb. Law. 215, 236 (1995), surveys a variety of approaches to the investment-backed expectations test and suggests a middle-ground approach based on a regulatory risk theory: "If a landowner knows at the time she enters a land market that she is or might be covered by a regulatory program in which government can deny permission to develop her land, it is only fair she should assume the regulatory risk this program creates. . . ." Despite the pervasive murkiness of the doctrine, courts continue to rely upon it in deciding takings cases. See Radford & Breemer, *Great Expectations: Will Palazzolo v. Rhode Island Clarify the Murky Doctrine of Investment-Backed Expectations in Regulatory Takings Law?*, 9 N.Y.U. Envtl. L.J. 449 (2001); Washburn, *"Reasonable Investment-Backed Expectations" as a Factor in Defining Property Interest*, 49 Wash. U. J. Urb. & Contemp. L. 63 (1996). On the wetlands cases, see Meltz, *Wetlands Regulation and the Law of Regulatory Takings*, 30 Envtl. L. Rep. 10468 (2000).

Nuisance. Although Justice Scalia rejected the "balancing" approach adopted where land use regulations deprive the owner of some, but not all, "economically productive uses" of his land, by creating the "nuisance exception," he indirectly reintroduced "balancing" as a basis for decision in cases like *Lucas*. This is because common-law adjudication of "nuisance" cases has always involved, as a primary element, the "balancing" of the "gravity of the harm" suffered by the plaintiff against the "utility of the conduct" of the defendant. See Rest. Torts 2d §§ 826, 827, 828. The courts have taken Justice Scalia's exception further than he may have intended.

The nuisance exception to the *Lucas* per se takings rule has had limited application. Justice Scalia's example of damage caused by flooding suggests that this exception might be limited to cases of actual physical invasion. See *Rith Energy, Inc. v. United States*, 44 Fed. Cl. 108 (1999) (relying on state law to hold that mining plan that had high probability of acid mine drainage into water aquifer was a nuisance); *Neifert v. Department of the Environment*, 910 A.2d 1100 (Md. 2006) (regulation prohibiting the leaking of untreated sewage into drinking water held to be a nuisance-prevention measure rather than a taking). But the nuisance exception rarely has been applied. *State ex rel. R.T.G. v. Ohio*, 753 N.E.2d 869, 881–84 (Ohio App. 2001) (mining coal under state-issued permit is neither an absolute nor a qualified public nuisance). In most cases in which a state court would hold that a land use is a nuisance, a zoning ordinance prohibiting that use would allow other viable uses and most likely would escape the per se takings rule. *Vulcan Materials Co. v. City of Tehuacana*, 369 F.3d 882 (5th Cir. 2004) (concluding that Texas Supreme Court would limit relevant parcel to land within the city limits, ban on quarrying on 48 of claimant's 298-acre parcel would be a taking unless quarrying is held to be a nuisance); *John R. Sand & Gravel Co. v. United States*, 60 Fed. Cl. 230 (2004) (background principles of Michigan's nuisance and property law can provide defense to takings claim for refusal to permit mining within the vicinity of landfill remediation activity).

Despite the relatively limited use of the nuisance exception, students should be aware that moratoria may be a taking under *Lucas* if the public nuisance, rather than the zoning power, is used. For example, in *Keshbro, Inc. v. City of Miami*, 801 So. 2d 864 (Fla. 2001), the court held that the city's complete closure of a motel for six months and of an apartment complex for one year pursuant to a public nuisance abatement statute deprived the owners of all beneficial use of their property, and that the takings analysis established in *Lucas* should be applied. The court applied a two step process. First, the court held that *Lucas* applied to prospectively temporary moratoria challenged under nuisance law as opposed to land use law. The court distinguished land use cases from nuisance cases, stating: "Moreover, the courts refusing to extend *First English* beyond its remedial genesis to prospectively temporary regulations have done so in the land use and planning arena, where an entirely different set of considerations are implicated from those in the context of nuisance abatement where a landowner is being deprived of a property's dedicated use." *Id.* at 874. Second, the court considered whether the *Lucas* nuisance exception applied to the closure orders, which prohibited all uses, both legal and illegal, during the prescribed period. The court held that the nuisance exception only applied to the motel and not to the apartment complex. According to the court, drug and prostitution use had become inextricably intertwined with, "part and parcel of the operation" of the motel; thus, it was reasonable for the city to enjoin all use of the motel. *Id.* In contrast, the drug activity at the apartment complex had not become an inseparable part of the apartment's operation. The court stated that pursuant to *Lucas*, its "inquiry must . . . focus on whether the closure orders mirror the relief which 'could have been achieved in the courts . . . under the State's law of private nuisance or by the State under its complementary power to abate nuisances that affect the public generally . . . .' " *Id.* at 876. Is this consistent with the "parcel as a whole rule" discussed above? See accord *City of Seattle v. McCoy*, 4 P.3d 159 (Wash. App. 2000).

Impact of Public Subsidies for Development. Should the fact that the National Flood Insurance Program, 42 U.S.C. §§ 4011–4029, and the South Carolina Wind & Hail Underwriting Association, provided subsidized flood, wind and hail damage insurance to beachfront property owners in South Carolina be factored into the takings equation? If so, how? See Beach & Connolly, *A Retrospective on Lucas v. South Carolina Coastal Council: Public Policy Implications for the 21st Century*, 12 Southeastern Envtl. L.J. 1 (2003) (arguing for reform of flood insurance program). Should the fact that private insurance is not available because of a high risk of storms and floods be a limitation that " 'inhere[s] in the title [of the property] itself' "? *Id.* at 20 (quoting Nolan, *Private Property Investment, Lucas and the Fairness Doctrine,* 10 Pace Envtl. L. Rev. 43, 57 (1992)). *See generally* Runge, Duclos, Adams, Goodwin, Martin & Squires, *Government Actions Affecting Land and Property Values: An Empirical Review of Takings and Givings* (Lincoln Institute of Land Policy 1996) (arguing that regulatory takings analysis should include non-regulatory government actions that benefit private property owners). Flood insurance is discussed in Chapter 4.

[5.] *Penn Central* Vindicated

TAHOE-SIERRA PRESERVATION COUNCIL, INC. v. TAHOE REGIONAL PLANNING AGENCY, INC.

535 U.S. 302 (2002)

JUSTICE STEVENS delivered the opinion of the Court.

The question presented is whether a moratorium on development imposed during the process of devising a comprehensive land-use plan constitutes a *per se* taking of property requiring compensation under the Takings Clause of the United States Constitution. This case actually involves two moratoria ordered by respondent Tahoe Regional Planning Agency (TRPA) to maintain the status quo while studying the impact of development on Lake Tahoe and designing a strategy for environmentally sound growth. The first, Ordinance 81-5, was effective from August 24, 1981, until August 26, 1983, whereas the second more restrictive Resolution 83-21 was in effect from August 27, 1983, until April 25, 1984. As a result of these two directives, virtually all development on a substantial portion of the property subject to TRPA's jurisdiction was prohibited for a period of 32 months. Although the question we decide relates only to that 32-month period, a brief description of the events leading up to the moratoria and a comment on the two permanent plans that TRPA adopted thereafter will clarify the narrow scope of our holding.

I

The relevant facts are undisputed. The Court of Appeals, while reversing the District Court on a question of law, accepted all of its findings of fact, and no party challenges those findings. All agree that Lake Tahoe is "uniquely beautiful," 34 F. Supp. 2d 1226, 1230 (Nev. 1999), that President Clinton was right to call it a " 'national treasure that must be protected and preserved,' " *ibid.* and that Mark Twain aptly described the clarity of its waters as " 'not *merely* transparent, but dazzlingly, brilliantly so,' " *ibid.* (emphasis added) (quoting M. Twain, Roughing It 174–175 (1872)).

Lake Tahoe's exceptional clarity is attributed to the absence of algae that obscures the waters of most other lakes. Historically, the lack of nitrogen and phosphorous, which nourish the growth of algae, has ensured the transparency of its waters. Unfortunately, the lake's pristine state has deteriorated rapidly over the past 40 years; increased land development in the Lake Tahoe Basin (Basin) has threatened the " 'noble sheet of blue water' " beloved by

Twain and countless others. 34 F. Supp. 2d at 1230. As the District Court found, "dramatic decreases in clarity first began to be noted in the 1950's/early 1960's, shortly after development at the lake began in earnest." *Id.* at 1231. The lake's unsurpassed beauty, it seems, is the wellspring of its undoing. . . .

In the 1960's, when the problems associated with the burgeoning development began to receive significant attention, jurisdiction over the Basin, which occupies 501 square miles, was shared by the States of California and Nevada, five counties, several municipalities, and the Forest Service of the Federal Government. In 1968, the legislatures of the two States adopted the Tahoe Regional Planning Compact. The compact set goals for the protection and preservation of the lake and created TRPA as the agency assigned "to coordinate and regulate development in the Basin and to conserve its natural resources." *Lake Country Estates, Inc. v. Tahoe Regional Planning Agency*, 440 U.S. 391 (1979). . . .

[In 1980, extensive amendments to the Tahoe Regional Planning Compact (Compact) directed TRPA to adopt regional standards for air and water quality, soil conservation, vegetation preservation and noise, along with a regional plan within an 18-month period. When it had difficulty meeting the Compact deadlines, it adopted two moratoria on development which were in effect until the adoption of a regional plan in 1984. — Eds.]

II

Approximately two months after the adoption of the 1984 Plan, petitioners filed parallel actions against TRPA and other defendants in federal courts in Nevada and California that were ultimately consolidated for trial in the District of Nevada. The petitioners include the Tahoe Sierra Preservation Council, a nonprofit membership corporation representing about 2,000 owners of both improved and unimproved parcels of real estate in the Lake Tahoe Basin, and a class of some 400 individual owners of vacant lots located either on SEZ lands or in other parts of districts 1, 2, or 3. Those individuals purchased their properties prior to the effective date of the 1980 Compact, primarily for the purpose of constructing "at a time of their choosing" a single-family home "to serve as a permanent, retirement or vacation residence." When they made those purchases, they did so with the understanding that such construction was authorized provided that "they complied with all reasonable requirements for building." *Ibid.*

Petitioners' complaints gave rise to protracted litigation that has produced four opinions by the Court of Appeals for the Ninth Circuit and several published District Court opinions. For present purposes, however, we need only describe those courts' disposition of the claim that three actions taken by TRPA — Ordinance 81-5, Resolution 83-21, and the 1984 regional plan — constituted takings of petitioners' property without just compensation. . . . Thus, we limit our discussion to the lower courts' disposition of the claims based on the 2-year moratorium (Ordinance 81-5) and the ensuing 8-month moratorium (Resolution 83-21). . . .

[The District Court held that the regulation passed the "substantial advancement of a legitimate state interest" test of *Agins*, now repudiated by the Court, and that it did not effect a "partial taking" under *Penn Central*. However, the court concluded that petitioners had been temporarily deprived of "all economically viable use of their land" and ordered TRPA to pay damages for the time the moratoria were in effect. — Eds.]

Both parties appealed. TRPA successfully challenged the District Court's takings determination, and petitioners unsuccessfully challenged the dismissal of their claims based on the 1984 and 1987 plans. Petitioners did not, however, challenge the District Court's findings or conclusions concerning its application of *Penn Central.* With respect to the two moratoria, the Ninth Circuit noted that petitioners had expressly disavowed an argument "that the regulations constitute a taking under the ad hoc balancing approach described in *Penn Central*" and that they did not "dispute that the restrictions imposed on their properties are appropriate means of securing the purpose set forth in the Compact." Accordingly, the only question before the court was "whether the rule set forth in *Lucas* applies — that is, whether a categorical taking occurred because Ordinance 81-5 and Resolution 83-21 denied the plaintiffs' 'all economically beneficial or productive use of land.'" Moreover, because petitioners brought only a facial challenge, the narrow inquiry before the Court of Appeals was whether the mere enactment of the regulations constituted a taking.

[The Court of Appeals disagreed with the District Court, concluding that no categorical taking had occurred because the moratoria had only a temporary impact on petitioners' fee interest in the property. — Eds.]

III

Petitioners make only a facial attack on Ordinance 81-5 and Resolution 83-21. They contend that the mere enactment of a temporary regulation that, while in effect, denies a property owner all viable economic use of her property gives rise to an unqualified constitutional obligation to compensate her for the value of its use during that period. Hence, they "face an uphill battle," *Keystone Bituminous Coal Ass'n v. DeBenedictis*, that is made especially steep by their desire for a categorical rule requiring compensation whenever the government imposes such a moratorium on development. Under their proposed rule, there is no need to evaluate the landowners' investment-backed expectations, the actual impact of the regulation on any individual, the importance of the public interest served by the regulation, or the reasons for imposing the temporary restriction. For petitioners, it is enough that a regulation imposes a temporary deprivation — no matter how brief — of all economically viable use to trigger a *per se* rule that a taking has occurred. Petitioners assert that our opinions in *First English* and *Lucas* have already endorsed their view, and that it is a logical application of the principle that the Takings Clause was "designed to bar Government from forcing some people alone to bear burdens which, in all fairness and justice, should be borne by the public as a whole." *Armstrong v. United States*, 364 U.S. 40, 49 (1960).

We shall first explain why our cases do not support their proposed categorical rule — indeed, fairly read, they implicitly reject it. Next, we shall explain why the *Armstrong* principle requires rejection of that rule as well as the less extreme position advanced by petitioners at oral argument. In our view the answer to the abstract question whether a temporary moratorium effects a taking is neither "yes, always" nor "no, never"; the answer depends upon the particular circumstances of the case. Resisting "the temptation to adopt what amount to *per se* rules in either direction," *Palazzolo v. Rhode Island* (O'Connor, J., concurring), we conclude that the circumstances in this case are best analyzed within the *Penn Central* framework.

IV

The text of the Fifth Amendment itself provides a basis for drawing a distinction between physical takings and regulatory takings. Its plain language requires the payment of compensation whenever the government acquires private property for a public purpose, whether the acquisition is the result of a condemnation proceeding or a physical appropriation. But the Constitution contains no comparable reference to regulations that prohibit a property owner from making certain uses of her private property. Our jurisprudence involving condemnations and physical takings is as old as the Republic and, for the most part, involves the straightforward application of *per se* rules. Our regulatory takings jurisprudence, in contrast, is of more recent vintage and is characterized by "essentially ad hoc, factual inquiries," *Penn Central*, 438 U.S. at 124, designed to allow "careful examination and weighing of all the relevant circumstances." *Palazzolo*, 533 U.S. at 636 (O'Connor, J., concurring).

When the government physically takes possession of an interest in property for some public purpose, it has a categorical duty to compensate the former owner, regardless of whether the interest that is taken constitutes an entire parcel or merely a part thereof. . . . But a government regulation that merely prohibits landlords from evicting tenants unwilling to pay a higher rent, *Block v. Hirsh*, 256 U.S. 135 (1921); that bans certain private uses of a portion of an owner's property [citing *Euclid* and *Keystone*]; or that forbids the private use of certain airspace [citing *Penn Central*], does not constitute a categorical taking. . . .

This longstanding distinction between acquisitions of property for public use, on the one hand, and regulations prohibiting private uses, on the other, makes it inappropriate to treat cases involving physical takings as controlling precedents for the evaluation of a claim that there has been a "regulatory taking," and vice versa. For the same reason that we do not ask whether a physical appropriation advances a substantial government interest or whether it deprives the owner of all economically valuable use, we do not apply our precedent from the physical takings context to regulatory takings claims. Land-use regulations are ubiquitous and most of them impact property values in some tangential way — often in completely unanticipated ways. Treating them all as *per se* takings would transform government regulation into a luxury few governments could afford. By contrast, physical appropriations are relatively rare, easily identified, and usually represent a greater affront to individual property rights.

[The Court's review of its takings cases is omitted. — Eds.]

The Chief Justice stretches *Lucas*' "equivalence" language too far. For even regulation that constitutes only a minor infringement on property may, from the landowner's perspective, be the functional equivalent of an appropriation. *Lucas* carved out a narrow exception to the rules governing regulatory takings for the "extraordinary circumstance" of a permanent deprivation of all beneficial use. The exception was only partially justified based on the "equivalence" theory cited by his dissent. It was also justified on the theory that, in the "relatively rare situations where the government has deprived a landowner of all economically beneficial uses," it is less realistic to assume that the regulation will secure an "average reciprocity of advantage," or that government could not go on if required to pay for every such restriction. 505 U.S. at 1017–1018. But as we explain, . . . these assumptions hold true in the context of a moratorium.

While the foregoing cases considered whether particular regulations had "gone too far" and were therefore invalid, none of them addressed the separate remedial question of how compensation is measured once a regulatory taking is established. In his dissenting opinion in *San Diego Gas & Elec. Co. v. San Diego*, 450 U.S. 621, 636 (1981), Justice Brennan identified that question and explained how he would answer it:

"The constitutional rule I propose requires that, once a court finds that a police power regulation has effected a 'taking,' the government entity must pay just compensation for the period commencing on the date the regulation first effected the 'taking,' and ending on the date the government entity chooses to rescind or otherwise amend the regulation." *Id.* at 658.

Justice Brennan's proposed rule was subsequently endorsed by the Court in *First English*, 482 U.S. at 315, 318, 321. *First English* was certainly a significant decision, and nothing that we say today qualifies its holding. Nonetheless, it is important to recognize that we did not address in that case the quite different and logically prior question whether the temporary regulation at issue had in fact constituted a taking.

In *First English* the Court unambiguously and repeatedly characterized the issue to be decided as a "compensation question" or a "remedial question." *Id.* at 311 ("The disposition of the case on these grounds isolates the remedial question for our consideration"); *see also id.* at 313, 318. And the Court's statement of its holding was equally unambiguous: "We merely hold that where the government's activities *have already worked a taking* of all use of property, no subsequent action by the government can relieve it of the duty to provide compensation for the period during which the taking was effective." *Id.* at 321 (emphasis added). In fact, *First English* expressly disavowed any ruling on the merits of the takings issue because the California courts had decided the remedial question on the assumption that a taking had been alleged. *Id.* at 312–313 ("We reject appellee's suggestion that . . . we must independently evaluate the adequacy of the complaint and resolve the takings claim on the merits before we can reach the remedial question"). After our remand, the California courts concluded that there had not been a taking, *First English Evangelical Church of Glendale v. County of Los Angeles*, 258 Cal. Rptr. 893 (1989), and we declined review of that decision, 493 U.S. 1056 (1990).

To the extent that the Court in *First English* referenced the antecedent takings question, we identified two reasons why a regulation temporarily denying an owner all use of her property might not constitute a taking. First, we recognized that "the county might avoid the conclusion that a compensable taking had occurred by establishing that the denial of all use was insulated as a part of the State's authority to enact safety regulations." 482 U.S. at 313. Second, we limited our holding "to the facts presented" and recognized "the quite different questions that would arise in the case of normal delays in obtaining building permits, changes in zoning ordinances, variances, and the like which [were] not before us." *Id.* at 321. Thus, our decision in *First English* surely did not approve, and implicitly rejected, the categorical submission that petitioners are now advocating.

Similarly, our decision in *Lucas* is not dispositive of the question presented. Although *Lucas* endorsed and applied a categorical rule, it was not the one that petitioners propose. Lucas purchased two residential lots in 1988 for $975,000. These lots were rendered "valueless" by a statute enacted two years later. The trial court found that a taking had occurred and ordered compensation of $1,232,387.50, representing the value of the fee simple estate, plus interest. As the statute read at the time of the trial, it effected a taking that "was unconditional and permanent." 505 U.S. at 1012. While the State's appeal was pending, the statute was amended to authorize exceptions that might have allowed Lucas to obtain a building permit. Despite the fact that the amendment gave the State Supreme Court the opportunity to dispose of the appeal on ripeness grounds, it resolved the merits of the permanent takings claim and reversed. Since "Lucas had no reason to proceed on a 'temporary taking' theory at trial," we decided the case on the permanent taking theory that both the trial court and the State Supreme Court had addressed. *Ibid.*

The categorical rule that we applied in *Lucas* states that compensation is required when a regulation deprives an owner of "*all* economically beneficial uses" of his land. *Id.* at 1019. Under that rule, a statute that "wholly eliminated the value" of Lucas' fee simple title clearly qualified as a taking. But our holding was limited to "the extraordinary circumstance when *no* productive or economically beneficial use of land is permitted." *Id.* at 1017. The emphasis on the word "no" in the text of the opinion was, in effect, reiterated in a footnote explaining that the categorical rule would not apply if the diminution in value were 95% instead of 100%. *Id.* at 1019, n. 8. Anything less than a "complete elimination of value," or a "total loss," the Court acknowledged, would require the kind of analysis applied in *Penn Central. Lucas*, 505 U.S. at 1019-1020, n. 8.

Certainly, our holding that the permanent "obliteration of the value" of a fee simple estate constitutes a categorical taking does not answer the question whether a regulation prohibiting any economic use of land for a 32-month period has the same legal effect. Petitioners seek to bring this case under the rule announced in *Lucas* by arguing that we can effectively sever a 32-month segment from the remainder of each landowner's fee simple estate, and then ask whether that segment has been taken in its entirety by the moratoria. Of course, defining the property interest taken in terms of the very regulation being challenged is circular. With property so divided, every delay would become a total ban; the moratorium and the normal permit process alike would constitute categorical takings. Petitioners' "conceptual severance" argument is unavailing because it ignores *Penn Central*'s admonition that in regulatory takings cases we must focus on "the parcel as a whole." 438 U.S. at 130–131. We have consistently rejected such an approach to the "denominator" question. *See Keystone*, 480 U.S. at 497. *See also, Concrete Pipe & Products of Cal., Inc. v. Construction Laborers Pension Trust for Southern Cal.*, 508 U.S. 602 (1993) ("To the extent that any portion of property is taken, that portion is always taken in its entirety; the relevant question, however, is whether the property taken is all, or only a portion of, the parcel in question"). Thus, the District Court erred when it disaggregated petitioners' property into temporal segments corresponding to the regulations at issue and then analyzed whether petitioners were deprived of all economically viable use during each period. The starting point for the court's analysis should have been to ask whether there was a total taking of the entire parcel; if not, then *Penn Central* was the proper framework.

An interest in real property is defined by the metes and bounds that describe its geographic dimensions and the term of years that describes the temporal aspect of the owner's interest. *See Restatement of Property* §§ 7-9 (1936). Both dimensions must be considered if the interest is to be viewed in its entirety. Hence, a permanent deprivation of the owner's use of the entire area is a taking of "the parcel as a whole," whereas a temporary restriction that merely causes a diminution in value is not. Logically, a fee simple estate cannot be rendered valueless by a temporary prohibition on economic use, because the property will recover value as soon as the prohibition is lifted. . . .

Neither *Lucas*, nor *First English*, nor any of our other regulatory takings cases compels us to accept petitioners' categorical submission. In fact, these cases make clear that the categorical rule in *Lucas* was carved out for the "extraordinary case" in which a regulation permanently deprives property of all value; the default rule remains that, in the regulatory taking context, we require a more fact specific inquiry. Nevertheless, we will consider whether the interest in protecting individual property owners from bearing public burdens "which, in all fairness and justice, should be borne by the public as a whole," *Armstrong v. United States*, 364 U.S. at 49, justifies creating a new rule for these circumstances.

V

Considerations of "fairness and justice" arguably could support the conclusion that TRPA's moratoria were takings of petitioners' property based on any of seven different theories. First, even though we have not previously done so, we might now announce a categorical rule that, in the interest of fairness and justice, compensation is required whenever government temporarily deprives an owner of all economically viable use of her property. Second, we could craft a narrower rule that would cover all temporary land-use restrictions except those "normal delays in obtaining building permits, changes in zoning ordinances, variances, and the like" which were put to one side in our opinion in *First English*, 482 U.S. at 321. Third, we could adopt a rule like the one suggested by an *amicus* supporting petitioners that would "allow a short fixed period for deliberations to take place without compensation — say maximum one year — after which the just compensation requirements" would "kick in." Fourth, with the benefit of hindsight, we might characterize the successive actions of TRPA as a "series of rolling moratoria" that were the functional equivalent of a permanent taking. Fifth, were it not for the findings of the District Court that TRPA acted diligently and in good faith, we might have concluded that the agency was stalling in order to avoid promulgating the environmental threshold carrying capacities and regional plan mandated by the 1980 Compact. *Cf. Monterey v. Del Monte Dunes at Monterey, Ltd.* Sixth, apart from the District Court's finding that TRPA's actions represented a proportional response to a serious risk of harm to the lake, petitioners might have argued that the moratoria did not substantially advance a legitimate state interest, *see Agins* and *Monterey*. Finally, if petitioners had challenged the application of the moratoria to their individual parcels, instead of making a facial challenge, some of them might have prevailed under a *Penn Central* analysis.

As the case comes to us, however, none of the last four theories is available. [The Court noted that the case was not tried on the "rolling moratoria" theory. The District Court's "unchallenged findings of fact" precluded bad faith or insubstantial state interest theories. Petitioners "expressly disavowed" a *Penn Central* analysis, and failed to appeal the District Court's conclusion that the evidence would not support recovery under that analysis. — Eds.] Nonetheless, each of the three *per se* theories is fairly encompassed within the question that we decided to answer.

With respect to these theories, the ultimate constitutional question is whether the concepts of "fairness and justice" that underlie the Takings Clause will be better served by one of these categorical rules or by a *Penn Central* inquiry into all of the relevant circumstances in particular cases. From that perspective, the extreme categorical rule that any deprivation of all economic use, no matter how brief, constitutes a compensable taking surely cannot be sustained. Petitioners' broad submission would apply to numerous "normal delays in obtaining building permits, changes in zoning ordinances, variances, and the like," 482 U.S. at 321, as well as to orders temporarily prohibiting access to crime scenes, businesses that violate health codes, fire-damaged buildings, or other areas that we cannot now foresee. Such a rule would undoubtedly require changes in numerous practices that have long been considered permissible exercises of the police power. As Justice Holmes warned in *Mahon*, "government hardly could go on if to some extent values incident to property could not be diminished without paying for every such change in the general law." 260 U.S. at 413. A rule that required compensation for every delay in the use of property would render routine government processes prohibitively expensive or encourage hasty decisionmaking. Such an important change in the law should be the product of legislative rulemaking rather than adjudication.

More importantly, for reasons set out at some length by Justice O'Connor in her concurring opinion in *Palazzolo v. Rhode Island*, 533 U.S. at 636 (2001), we are persuaded that the better approach to claims that a regulation has effected a temporary taking "requires careful examination and weighing of all the relevant circumstances." In that opinion, Justice O'Connor specifically considered the role that the "temporal relationship between regulatory enactment and title acquisition" should play in the analysis of a takings claim. *Id.* at 632. . . . [Her comments on this issue are discussed *supra.* — Eds.]

In rejecting petitioners' *per se* rule, we do not hold that the temporary nature of a land-use restriction precludes finding that it effects a taking; we simply recognize that it should not be given exclusive significance one way or the other.

A narrower rule that excluded the normal delays associated with processing permits, or that covered only delays of more than a year, would certainly have a less severe impact on prevailing practices, but it would still impose serious financial constraints on the planning process. . . .

The interest in facilitating informed decisionmaking by regulatory agencies counsels against adopting a *per se* rule that would impose such severe costs on their deliberations. Otherwise, the financial constraints of compensating property owners during a moratorium may force officials to rush through the planning process or to abandon the practice altogether. To the extent that communities are forced to abandon using moratoria, landowners will have incentives to develop their property quickly before a comprehensive plan can be enacted, thereby fostering inefficient and ill-conceived growth. . . .

We would create a perverse system of incentives were we to hold that landowners must wait for a taking claim to ripen so that planners can make well-reasoned decisions while, at the same time, holding that those planners must compensate landowners for the delay.

Indeed, the interest in protecting the decisional process is even stronger when an agency is developing a regional plan than when it is considering a permit for a single parcel. In the proceedings involving the Lake Tahoe Basin, for example, the moratoria enabled TRPA to obtain the benefit of comments and criticisms from interested parties, such as the petitioners, during its deliberations. Since a categorical rule tied to the length of deliberations would likely create added pressure on decisionmakers to reach a quick resolution of land-use questions, it would only serve to disadvantage those landowners and interest groups who are not as organized or familiar with the planning process. Moreover, with a temporary ban on development there is a lesser risk that individual landowners will be "singled out" to bear a special burden that should be shared by the public as a whole. *Nollan v. California Coastal Comm'n*, 483 U.S. 825, 835. At least with a moratorium there is a clear "reciprocity of advantage," *Mahon*, 260 U.S. at 415, because it protects the interests of all affected landowners against immediate construction that might be inconsistent with the provisions of the plan that is ultimately adopted. "While each of us is burdened somewhat by such restrictions, we, in turn, benefit greatly from the restrictions that are placed on others." *Keystone*, 480 U.S. at 491. In fact, there is reason to believe property values often will continue to increase despite a moratorium. *See, e.g., Growth Properties, Inc. v. Klingbeil Holding Co.*, 419 F. Supp. 212, 218 (Md. 1976) (noting that land values could be expected to increase 20% during a 5-year moratorium on development). *Cf. Forest Properties, Inc. v. United States*, 177 F.3d 1360, 1367 (Fed. Cir. 1999) (record showed that market value of the entire parcel increased despite denial of permit to fill and develop lake-bottom property). Such an increase makes sense in this context because property values throughout the Basin can be expected to reflect the added assurance that Lake Tahoe will remain in its pristine state. Since in some cases a 1-year moratorium may not impose a burden at all, we should not adopt a rule that assumes moratoria always force individuals to bear a special burden that should be shared by the public as a whole.

It may well be true that any moratorium that lasts for more than one year should be viewed with special skepticism. But given the fact that the District Court found that the 32 months required by TRPA to formulate the 1984 Regional Plan was not unreasonable, we could not possibly conclude that every delay of over one year is constitutionally unacceptable. Formulating a general rule of this kind is a suitable task for state legislatures. In our view, the duration of the restriction is one of the important factors that a court must consider in the appraisal of a regulatory takings claim, but with respect to that factor as with respect to other factors, the "temptation to adopt what amount to *per se* rules in either direction must be resisted." *Palazzolo*, 533 U.S. at 636 (O'Connor, J., concurring). There may be moratoria that last longer than one year which interfere with reasonable investment-backed expectations, but as the District Court's opinion illustrates, petitioners' proposed rule is simply "too blunt an instrument," for identifying those cases. *Id.* at 628. We conclude, therefore, that the interest in "fairness and justice" will be best served by relying on the familiar *Penn Central* approach when deciding cases like this, rather than by attempting to craft a new categorical rule.

Accordingly, the judgment of the Court of Appeals is affirmed.

It is so ordered.

CHIEF JUSTICE REHNQUIST, with whom JUSTICE SCALIA and JUSTICE THOMAS join, dissenting.

[Chief Justice Rehnquist argued that the *Lucas* rule should be applied. The moratoria prevented petitioners from using their land productively for six years. Such moratoria are not "longstanding, implied limitations of state property law," and thus not within the exception to the *Lucas* rule. — Eds.]

NOTES AND QUESTIONS

1. *After Tahoe-Sierra, what is First English's significance?* Justice Stevens, who dissented in *First English*, wrote the majority opinion in *Tahoe-Sierra*. In his *First English* dissent, *supra*, Justice Stevens argued that the majority had "erect[ed] an artificial distinction between 'normal delays' [which implicitly would not constitute regulatory takings] and the delays involved in obtaining a court declaration that the regulation constitutes a taking." According to Justice Stevens, the determination of whether there has been a temporary taking should not be based upon the reason for the government's temporary interference with private property rights. Fifteen years later, writing for the majority in *Tahoe-Sierra*, *supra*, Justice Stevens rejected "the extreme categorical rule that any deprivation of all economic use, no matter how brief, constitutes a compensable taking . . . ." In so doing, the Court rejected *Lucas* and endorsed the *Penn Central* framework in the case of temporary development moratoria and protected development moratoria as valuable land use tools for state and local governments. Is this consistent with the Court's ruling in *First English*, *supra* (" 'temporary' takings which as here, deny a landowner all use of his property, are not different in kind from permanent takings")?

What is the continuing impact of *First English* after the decision in *Tahoe-Sierra*? The Court in *Tahoe-Sierra* stated that *First English* "was certainly a significant decision, and nothing that [the Court said] . . . qualifie[d] its holding." But, does *First English* remain "intact" following *Tahoe-Sierra*? What explains the seemingly incongruous positions taken in the two cases? See Berger, *Tahoe Sierra: Much Ado About — What?*, 25 Haw. L. Rev. 295, 321–22 (2003). Michael Berger, who was counsel of record in *Tahoe-Sierra* has stated the following about the impact of *Tahoe-Sierra* on *First English*: "The context of *First English* is important to understand its holding. . . . Unless one reads the two opinions with blinders on, it is not possible to lay *First English* and *Tahoe-Sierra* side by side and find a comfortable match. They don't mesh. Except that the highest court in the land has said that — as a matter of law — they do." *Id.* at 322.

2. *Vindication for Penn Central?* While the 6-3 split in *Tahoe-Sierra* indicates that the Court remains divided on the proper approach to the difficult problem of determining when a land use regulation crosses the line and becomes a compensable taking, *Penn Central* gained new life. Justice Stevens' strong endorsement of *Penn Central*'s multiple factor analytical approach, his refusal to apply the categorical approach of possessory takings law to governmental regulations that do not amount to physical appropriations, and his endorsement of the "parcel as a whole" approach first articulated by Justice Brandeis in his *Pennsylvania Coal* dissent and applied by Justice Brennan in *Penn Central* all served to reinforce the ad hoc approach advocated by the majority in *Penn Central*. See, e.g., Claeys, *Takings, Regulations, and Natural Property Rights*, 88 Cornell L. Rev. 1549, 1660 (2003) ("*Tahoe-Sierra* confirms *Penn Central*'s status as the dominant case in regulatory takings law and relegates *Lucas* to the status of a narrow exception"); Gold, *The Diminishing Equivalence between Regulatory Takings and Physical Takings*, 107 Dick. L. Rev. 571, 576 (2003) ("*Tahoe-Sierra* . . . is one of the Court's strongest endorsements yet of ad hoc jurisprudence"); Kayden, *Celebrating Penn Central*, Planning, June 2003, at 20, 23 ("*Tahoe-Sierra* is an unapologetic, unabashed champion of *Penn Central*'s ad hoc, no-set-formula, factual decision-making approach").

3. *Applying the Penn Central test.* While the Supreme Court may have restored the *Penn Central* three-factor test to prominence, has it made takings cases any easier to resolve? See Echeverria, *A Turning of the Tide: The Tahoe-Sierra Regulatory Takings Decision*, 32 Envtl. L. Rep. 11235, 11235 (2002) (*Tahoe-Sierra* "provides little guidance on what the *Penn Central* test actually is or how it should be applied"). Disagreements continue to surface regarding the parcel-as-a-whole rule. *See supra* (denominator rule and segmentation discussion following *Lucas* case); compare *Apollo Fuels, Inc. v. United States*, 54 Fed. Cl. 717 (Fed. Cl. 2002), and *Machipongo Land & Coal Co. v. Pennsylvania*, 799 A.2d 751 (Pa. 2002) (parcel-as-a-whole rule applied to mining restrictions taking claim), *with R.T.G., Inc. v. State of Ohio*, 780 N.E.2d 998 (Ohio 2002) (segmenting mining rights from surface land), limited to its facts by *State ex rel. Shelly Materials, Inc. v. Clark Cnty. Bd. of Commrs.*, 875 N.E.2d 59 (Ohio 2007). See Dowling, *Wandering Far from Tahoe: Reflections on the Relevant Parcel Definition and Nuisance Defense in R.T.G., Inc. v. State of Ohio*, Land Use L. & Zoning Dig. May, 2003 at 5. See also *Vulcan Materials Co. v. City of Tehuacana*, *supra* (parcel-as-a-whole rule limited to that portion (about 20%) of parcel within city limits of the regulating municipality).

Courts continue to be unimpressed with arguments that claimants lost substantial value from heavy-handed land use regulations. *Cane Tennessee, Inc. v. United States*, 57 Fed. Cl. 115, 129 (Fed. Cl. 2003) ("The character of the government action could, in conjunction with other factors, support a taking, but this single factor does not support a taking in the absence of reasonable investment-backed expectations and where the economic diminution does not reach a level that has been associated with a finding of a taking"); *Sheffield Dev. Co. v. City of Glenn Heights*, 140 S.W.3d 660, 677–79 (Tex. 2004) (while rezoning "significantly interfered" with landowner's reasonable, investment backed expectations, investment was "minimal" and "speculative" and, "on balance" did not rise to a taking). In *Zanghi v. Board of Appeals, supra*, a Massachusetts court applied the *Penn Central* test to reject an as-applied challenge to a regulation that prevented the landowner from building on one lot in a subdivision because it was partially in a flood plain. While the regulation had been added several years after the property was purchased, the court found insufficient interference with reasonable investment-backed expectations because the lot could be used as part of a cluster subdivision (discussed in Chapter 7, *infra*) and the landowner could have built on the lot during the years he owned it prior to enactment of the regulation. The court applied *Leonard v. Town of Brimfield*, 666 N.E.2d 1300, 1303 (Mass. 1996) (another flood plain case), for the point that economic impact must be "severe." Flood plain regulation is discussed in the environmental land use regulation section of Chapter 4, *infra*.

4. *Burden sharing.* Significant by its absence from Justice Brennan's three-factor analysis in *Penn Central* is a point that the Court has long made clear, namely that the Takings Clause "is designed to bar Government from forcing some people alone to bear burdens which, in all fairness and justice should be borne by the populace as a whole." *Armstrong v. United States*, 364 U.S. 40, 49 (1960). This rule formed the core of Justice Rehnquist's dissent in *Penn Central* and was highlighted in Justice O'Connor's *Palazzolo* concurrence and Justice Stevens in *Tahoe-Sierra*, who concluded that "the interest in 'fairness and justice' will be best served by relying on the familiar *Penn Central* approach when deciding cases like this, rather than by attempting to craft a new categorical rule." 535 U.S. 302, 342. Is this an equal protection argument by another name? Another one of the "factors"? How does this approach relate to the "average reciprocity" theory? The Equal Protection Clause of the Fourteenth Amendment is considered *infra*.

5. *Revision of the Lucas test.* Has *Tahoe-Sierra* "subtly revised" the *Lucas* test? (Gold, *supra*, at 576.) Recall that *Lucas* stated a categorical rule of compensation when a regulation denies the owner "all economically beneficial use of land." 505 U.S. at 1019. In concluding that the lower court erred in applying *Lucas* to "temporal segments" of petitioners' land corresponding to the duration of the moratoria, Justice Stevens stated that "a fee simple estate cannot be rendered valueless by a temporary prohibition on economic use, because the property will recover value as soon as the prohibition is lifted." 535 U.S. at 332. Does this mean that the *per se* takings rule of *Lucas* is not applicable to temporary regulations? "[T]he categorical rule in *Lucas* was carved out for the 'extraordinary case' in which a regulation permanently deprives property of all value." *Id.* Does it also mean that the *Lucas* test applies only to fee simple estates and not to other property rights such as mining rights and leasehold interests? Both Gold and Echeverria, *supra*, see that as a distinct possibility.

6. *The use vs. value dichotomy.* Are "use" and "value" the same concept? Doesn't land have "value" even if it cannot be "used"? Can land ever be "worthless"? Is "value" simply evidence of "uses" to which land can be put? Cf. Gold, *supra*, at 598 ("Value consistently has played a role in calculations of what is fair, but has not generally been equated with what has been taken"). For an argument that the discussion of "value" in *Tahoe-Sierra* is "non binding dicta," see Breemer, *Of Nominal Value: The Impact of Tahoe-Sierra on Lucas and the Fundamental Right to Use Private Property*, 33 Envtl. L. Rep. 10331, 10334–10337 (2003). See also Wright & Laughner, *Shaken, Not Stirred: Has Tahoe-Sierra Settled or Muddled the Regulatory Takings Water?*, 32 Envtl. L. Rep. 11177, 11187–89 (2002) (criticizing *Tahoe-Sierra* for "fail[ing] to adequately reject value as the critical indicator of property" for takings analysis and thus encouraging segmentation by landowners). Short commentaries by two attorneys involved in *Tahoe-Sierra* are Kendall, *The Use/Value Debate and Tahoe* and Burling, *Use Versus Value in the Wake of Tahoe-Sierra, in* Taking Sides on Takings Issues: The Impact of Tahoe-Sierra 95 & 99 (T. Roberts ed., 2003).

7. *Is the Court's distinction between physical and regulatory takings meaningful?* Citing the "longstanding distinction between acquisitions of property for public use, on the one hand, and regulations prohibiting private uses, on the other," the Court makes the case for analyzing the two types of takings claims differently. *Tahoe-Sierra, supra.* Does this analytical distinction between regulatory and physical takings make sense? Peterson, in her article, *The False Dichotomy between Physical and Regulatory Takings Analysis: A Critique of Tahoe-Sierra's Distinction between Physical and Regulatory Takings*, 34 Ecology L.Q. 381 (2007), argues that physical and regulatory takings claims should be analyzed under the same principles since the critical issue in any takings case is whether, in fairness, compensation should be paid. *Id.* at 392. Peterson noted that just three years after deciding *Tahoe-Sierra*, "the Court . . . stressed the functional equivalence of different types of takings in *Lingle v. Chevron U.S.A., Inc.* Returning to the basic analogies that underlay its takings decisions, the Court emphasized the similarity of takings that occur through a formal exercise of the power of eminent domain, through physical action, and through regulation." *Id.* at 416; *see also Lingle, infra.*

8. *Can local land use regulators avoid takings problems?* In *Tahoe-Sierra* and in its predecessor, *First English*, the Court considers the impact of its holdings on the planning process. Justice Stevens rejects a per se takings rule in *Tahoe-Sierra* in favor of facilitating comprehensive planning and reducing incentives for landowners to prematurely "develop their property . . . thereby fostering inefficient and ill-conceived growth. . . ." *Tahoe-Sierra, supra.* In *First English, supra*, Justice Rehnquist acknowledges that the Court's decision (that temporary development moratoria could constitute temporary regulatory takings) "will undoubtedly lessen to some extent the freedom and flexibility of land-use planners and governing bodies of municipal corporations when enacting land-use regulations." Are these two decisions discordant, from a planning perspective? Do they strike the proper balance?

Local government officials and the land use planning community justifiably may be pleased with *Tahoe-Sierra's* planning-friendly rhetoric. See, e.g., Kayden, *Tahoe-Sierra Preservation Council v. Tahoe Regional Planning Agency: About More than Moratoria*, Land Use L. & Zoning Dig., October, 2002, at 3, 5 ("The opinion shows a genuine appreciation for, and sophisticated understanding of, land-use planning and planners"). But note Justice Stevens' lengthy review of "fairness and justice" concerns. 535 U.S. at 333–42. Is this also a reminder that local governments have a serious responsibility to review their regulatory decision-making processes and to make sure that land use regulations not only foster articulated public goals but also permit private landowners to use their property in some reasonable economic manner? "[T]he temptation to adopt what amount to *per se* rules in either direction must be resisted." *Id.* at 342, *quoting Palazzolo*, 533 U.S. at 636 (O'Connor, J., concurring).

Practitioners consistently have argued that local governments can avoid takings claims by considering the interests of private land owners, as well as the public, when drafting and implementing land use regulations. Dwight Merriam argues that "improvements in how government regulates can greatly diminish the damage to private property and the potential for takings." Merriam, *Reengineering Regulation to Avoid Takings*, 33 Urb. Law. 1, 2 (2001) (reviewing regulatory techniques). In *Sheffield Dev. Co., supra*, the Supreme Court of Texas, in applying *Penn Central* and finding no taking from a rezoning, was highly critical of the city's actions. "The evidence is quite strong that the City attempted to take unfair advantage of Sheffield." 140 S.W.3d at 678. As you study the principal land use regulatory techniques, examine them for takings problems and how those problems might be avoided. See also Mandelker, *Model Legislation for Land Use Decisions*, 35 Urb. Law 635, 652–56 (2003), discussing a Remedial Measure proposed for inclusion in the APA's Growing Smart Legislative Guidebook that included authorization for density and intensity increases as a mechanism for resolving potential takings disputes. The proposal drew heavily on an article by Maryland land use attorney John J. Delaney, *Avoiding Regulatory Wipe-Outs: Proposed Model Legislation for a Local Mechanism*, Land Use L. & Zoning Dig., July, 1998 at 3. It generated considerable discussion but was omitted from the final draft, in part because of concern over standards for approval, in favor of a mediation provision. Mediation of land use disputes is discussed in Chapter 7.

9. For additional discussion of *Tahoe-Sierra*, see Siegel & Meltz, *Temporary Takings: Settled Principles and Unresolved Questions*, 11 Vt. J. Evntl. L. 479 (2010); Taking Sides on Takings Issues: The Impact of Tahoe Sierra (T. Roberts ed., 2003); Commentaries, Land Use L. & Zoning Dig., June, 2002 at 3; Kahn, *Lake Tahoe Clarity and Takings Jurisprudence: The Supreme Court Advances Land Use Planning in Tahoe-Sierra*, 26 Environs Envtl. L. & Pol'y J. 33 (2002); Stein, *Takings in the 21st Century: Reasonable Investment-Backed Expectations After Palazzolo and Tahoe-Sierra*, 69 Tenn. L. Rev. 891 (2002); Comment, *The Metaphysics of Property: Looking Beneath the Surface of Regulatory Takings Law After Tahoe-Sierra Preservation Council v. Tahoe Regional Planning Agency*, 48 Saint Louis U. L.J. 703 (2004); Note, *Regulatory Takings: Correcting the Supreme Court's Wrong Turn in Tahoe Regional Planning Agency*, 17 B.Y.U. J. Pub. L. 391 (2003).

[6.] Removal of the "Substantially Advances" Test From Takings Jurisprudence

For twenty-five years, a takings test established by the Supreme Court in *Agins v. City of Tiburon*, 447 U.S. 255 (1980), included a requirement that government regulations "substantially advance legitimate state interests." As noted previously in this chapter, the Court relied on this test to invalidate land use exactions and occasionally referred to it when deciding other takings questions. *Agins* also raised the question whether the failure of a land use regulation to meet that test, standing alone, would support a takings claim in federal court. Justice Stevens raised just such a possibility in *Tahoe-Sierra* with his discussion of "fairness and justice" considerations as a basis for finding that moratoria could become compensable takings. The following case addresses that question.

LINGLE v. CHEVRON U.S.A. INC.

544 U.S. 528 (2005)

JUSTICE O'CONNOR delivered the opinion of the Court.

On occasion, a would-be doctrinal rule or test finds its way into our case law through simple repetition of a phrase — however fortuitously coined. A quarter century ago, in *Agins v. City of Tiburon*, 447 U.S. 255 (1980), the Court declared that government regulation of private property "effects a taking if [such regulation] does not substantially advance legitimate state interests . . . ." 447 U.S., at 260. Through reiteration in a half dozen or so decisions since *Agins*, this language has been ensconced in our Fifth Amendment takings jurisprudence. *See Monterey v. Del Monte Dunes at Monterey, Ltd.*, 526 U.S. 687, 704 (1999) (citing cases).

In the case before us, the lower courts applied *Agins*' "substantially advances" formula to strike down a Hawaii statute that limits the rent that oil companies may charge to dealers who lease service stations owned by the companies. The lower courts held that the rent cap effects an uncompensated taking of private property in violation of the Fifth and Fourteenth Amendments because it does not substantially advance Hawaii's asserted interest in controlling retail gasoline prices. This case requires us to decide whether the "substantially advances" formula announced in *Agins* is an appropriate test for determining whether a regulation effects a Fifth Amendment taking. We conclude that it is not.

I

[The statute in question, Act 257, was enacted in 1957, apparently in response to concerns about retail gasoline prices in a concentrated market. At the time of the lawsuit, retail gasoline was sold from about 300 different service stations, about half of which were leased from oil companies by independent lessee-dealers, with the remainder split between "open" dealers and oil-company owned and operated stations. The plaintiff in the case, Chevron, sold most of its products through 64 independent lessee-dealer stations, who agreed to pay as rent a percentage of the dealers' margin on retail sales of gasoline and other products. Chevron unilaterally set the wholesale price of its product and required leaseholders to enter into a supply contract agreeing to purchase whatever is necessary to satisfy demand for Chevron's product at the station. The statute in question prohibited oil companies from converting existing lessee-dealer stations to company-operated stations and from locating new company-operated stations near existing dealer-operated stations. The statute also limited the amount of rent oil companies could charge a lessee-dealer to 15 percent of gross profits from gasoline sales and 15 percent of gross profits from sales of other products. Chevron's suit alleged that the rent-cap provision amounted to a facial taking of Chevron's property in violation of the Fifth and Fourteenth Amendments. — Eds.]

To facilitate resolution of summary judgment motions filed by both parties, the parties jointly stipulated to certain relevant facts. They agreed that Act 257 reduces by about $207,000 per year the aggregate rent that Chevron would otherwise charge on 11 of its 64 lessee-dealer stations. On the other hand, the statute allows Chevron to collect more rent than it would otherwise charge at its remaining 53 lessee-dealer stations, such that Chevron could increase its overall rental income from all 64 stations by nearly $1.1 million per year. The parties further stipulated that, over the past 20 years, Chevron has not fully recovered the costs of maintaining lessee-dealer stations in any State through rent alone. Rather, the company recoups its expenses through a combination of rent and product sales. Finally, the joint stipulation states that Chevron has earned in the past, and anticipates that it will continue to earn under Act 257, a return on its investment in lessee-dealer stations in Hawaii that satisfies any constitutional standard. . . .

[Both the District Court and the Ninth Circuit found for Chevron on the basis that "Act 257 fails to substantially advance a legitimate state interest, and as such, effects an unconstitutional taking in violation of the Fifth and Fourteenth Amendments." — Eds.]

A

The Takings Clause of the Fifth Amendment, made applicable to the States through the Fourteenth, *see Chicago, B. & Q. R. Co. v. Chicago*, 166 U.S. 226 (1897), provides that private property shall not "be taken for public use, without just compensation." As its text makes plain, the Takings Clause "does not prohibit the taking of private property, but instead places a condition on the exercise of that power." *First English Evangelical Lutheran Church of Glendale v. County of Los Angeles*, 482 U.S. 304, 314 (1987). In other words, it "is designed not to limit the governmental interference with property rights *per se*, but rather to secure *compensation* in the event of otherwise proper interference amounting to a taking." 482 U.S., at 315 (emphasis in original). While scholars have offered various justifications for this regime, we have emphasized its role in "barring Government from forcing some people alone to bear public burdens which, in all fairness and justice, should be borne by the public as a whole." *Armstrong v. United States*, 364 U.S. 40, 49 (1960). . . .

The paradigmatic taking requiring just compensation is a direct government appropriation or physical invasion of private property. . . . Indeed, until the Court's watershed decision in *Pennsylvania Coal Co. v. Mahon*, 260 U.S. 393 (1922), "it was generally thought that the Takings Clause reached *only* a 'direct appropriation' of property, or the functional equivalent of a 'practical ouster of [the owner's] possession.'" *Lucas v. South Carolina Coastal Council*, 505 U.S. 1003, 1014 (1992) (citations omitted and emphasis added; brackets in original). . . .

Beginning with *Mahon*, however, the Court recognized that government regulation of private property may, in some instances, be so onerous that its effect is tantamount to a direct appropriation or ouster — and that such "regulatory takings" may be compensable under the Fifth Amendment. In Justice Holmes' storied but cryptic formulation, "while property may be regulated to a certain extent, if regulation goes too far it will be recognized as a taking." 260 U.S. at 415. The rub, of course, has been — and remains — how to discern how far is "too far." In answering that question, we must remain cognizant that "government regulation — by definition — involves the adjustment of rights for the public good," *Andrus v. Allard*, 444 U.S. 51, 65 (1979), and that "Government hardly could go on if to some extent values incident to property could not be diminished without paying for every such change in the general law," *Mahon, supra*, 260 U.S., at 413.

Our precedents stake out two categories of regulatory action that generally will be deemed *per se* takings for *Fifth Amendment* purposes. . . . [The court summarized *Loretto* and *Lucas*. — Eds.]

Outside these two relatively narrow categories (and the special context of land-use exactions discussed below, . . .), regulatory takings challenges are governed by the standards set forth in *Penn Central Transp. Co. v. New York City*, 438 U.S. 104 (1078). . . . The *Penn Central* factors — though each has given rise to vexing subsidiary questions — have served as the principal guidelines for resolving regulatory takings claims that do not fall within the physical takings or *Lucas* rules. . . .

Although our regulatory takings jurisprudence cannot be characterized as unified, these three inquiries (reflected in *Loretto*, *Lucas*, and *Penn Central*) share a common touchstone. Each aims to identify regulatory actions that are functionally equivalent to the classic taking in which government directly appropriates private property or ousts the owner from his domain. Accordingly, each of these tests focuses directly upon the severity of the burden that government imposes upon private property rights. The Court has held that physical takings require compensation because of the unique burden they impose: A permanent physical invasion, however minimal the economic cost it entails, eviscerates the owner's right to exclude others from entering and using her property — perhaps the most fundamental of all property interests. . . . In the *Lucas* context, of course, the complete elimination of a property's value is the determinative factor. . . . And the *Penn Central* inquiry turns in large part, albeit not exclusively, upon the magnitude of a regulation's economic impact and the degree to which it interferes with legitimate property interests.

B

In *Agins v. City of Tiburon*, a case involving a facial takings challenge to certain municipal zoning ordinances, the Court declared that "the application of a general zoning law to particular property effects a taking if the ordinance does not substantially advance legitimate state interests, . . . or denies an owner economically viable use of his land . . . ." 447 U.S., at 260. Because this statement is phrased in the disjunctive, *Agins*' "substantially advances" language has been read to announce a stand-alone regulatory takings test that is wholly independent of *Penn Central* or any other test. Indeed, the lower courts in this case struck down Hawaii's rent control statute as an "unconstitutional regulatory taking," 198 F. Supp. 2d, at 1193, based solely upon a finding that it does not substantially advance the State's asserted interest in controlling retail gasoline prices. Although a number of our takings precedents have recited the "substantially advances" formula minted in *Agins*, this is our first opportunity to consider its validity as a freestanding takings test. We conclude that this formula prescribes an inquiry in the nature of a due process, not a takings, test, and that it has no proper place in our takings jurisprudence.

There is no question that the "substantially advances" formula was derived from due process, not takings, precedents. In support of this new language, *Agins* cited *Nectow v. Cambridge*, 277 U.S. 183, a 1928 case in which the plaintiff claimed that a city zoning ordinance "deprived him of his property without due process of law in contravention of the Fourteenth Amendment," 277 U.S., at 185. *Agins* then went on to discuss *Village of Euclid v. Ambler Realty Co.*, 272 U.S. 365 (1926), a historic decision holding that a municipal zoning ordinance would survive a substantive due process challenge so long as it was not "clearly arbitrary and unreasonable, having no *substantial relation to the public health, safety, morals, or general welfare*." 272 U.S., at 395 (emphasis added). . . .

[Justice O'Connor defended what she described as the *Agins* Court's reliance on due process precedents from *Euclid* and *Nectow*, *supra*, noting that *Agins* was the Court's first zoning case "in many decades," that some "commingling of due process and takings inquiries" appeared in dicta in *Penn Central*, and that the Court "had yet to clarify" the proper constitutional clause to apply in regulatory takings claims. — Eds.]

Although *Agins*' reliance on due process precedents is understandable, the language the Court selected was regrettably imprecise. The "substantially advances" formula suggests a means-ends test: It asks, in essence, whether a regulation of private property is *effective* in achieving some legitimate public purpose. An inquiry of this nature has some logic in the context of a due process challenge, for a regulation that fails to serve any legitimate governmental objective may be so arbitrary or irrational that it runs afoul of the Due Process Clause. *See, e.g.*, *County of Sacramento v. Lewis*, 523 U.S. 833, 846 (1998) (stating that the *Due Process Clause* is intended, in part, to protect the individual against "the exercise of power without any reasonable justification in the service of a legitimate governmental objective"). But such a test is not a valid method of discerning whether private property has been "taken" for purposes of the Fifth Amendment.

In stark contrast to the three regulatory takings tests discussed above, the "substantially advances" inquiry reveals nothing about the *magnitude or character of the burden* a particular regulation imposes upon private property rights. Nor does it provide any information about how any regulatory burden is *distributed* among property owners. In consequence, this test does not help to identify those regulations whose effects are functionally comparable to government appropriation or invasion of private property; it is tethered neither to the text of the Takings Clause nor to the basic justification for allowing regulatory actions to be challenged under the Clause.

. . . A test that tells us nothing about the actual burden imposed on property rights, or how that burden is allocated cannot tell us when justice might require that the burden be spread among taxpayers through the payment of compensation. The owner of a property subject to a regulation that *effectively* serves a legitimate state interest may be just as singled out and just as burdened as the owner of a property subject to an *ineffective* regulation. It would make little sense to say that the second owner has suffered a taking while the first has not. Likewise, an ineffective regulation may not significantly burden property rights at all, and it may distribute any burden broadly and evenly among property owners. The notion that such a regulation nevertheless "takes" private property for public use merely by virtue of its ineffectiveness or foolishness is untenable.

Instead of addressing a challenged regulation's effect on private property, the "substantially advances" inquiry probes the regulation's underlying validity. But such an inquiry is logically prior to and distinct from the question whether a regulation effects a taking, for the Takings Clause presupposes that the government has acted in pursuit of a valid public purpose. The Clause expressly requires compensation where government takes private property "*for public use.*" It does not bar government from interfering with property rights, but rather requires compensation "in the event of *otherwise proper interference* amounting to a taking." *First English Evangelical Lutheran Church*, 482 U.S., at 315 (emphasis added). Conversely, if a government action is found to be impermissible — for instance because it fails to meet the "public use" requirement or is so arbitrary as to violate due process — that is the end of the inquiry. No amount of compensation can authorize such action.

Chevron's challenge to the Hawaii statute in this case illustrates the flaws in the "substantially advances" theory. To begin with, it is unclear how significantly Hawaii's rent cap actually burdens Chevron's property rights. The parties stipulated below that the cap would reduce Chevron's aggregate rental income on 11 of its 64 lessee-dealer stations by about $207,000 per year, but that Chevron nevertheless expects to receive a return on its investment in these stations that satisfies any constitutional standard. Moreover, Chevron asserted below, and the District Court found, that Chevron would recoup any reductions in its rental income by raising wholesale gasoline prices. In short, Chevron has not clearly argued — let alone established — that it has been singled out to bear any particularly severe regulatory burden. Rather, the gravamen of Chevron's claim is simply that Hawaii's rent cap will not actually serve the State's legitimate interest in protecting consumers against high gasoline prices. Whatever the merits of that claim, it does not sound under the Takings Clause. Chevron plainly does not seek compensation for a taking of its property for a legitimate public use, but rather an injunction against the enforcement of a regulation that it alleges to be fundamentally arbitrary and irrational. . . .

[To illustrate what it called "the flaws in the 'substantially advances' theory," the Court reviewed the substance of Chevron's challenge to the Hawaii statute and concluded that Chevron actually was seeking an injunction against what it perceived to be an arbitrary regulation rather than compensation for a taking of its property. — Eds.]

Finally, the "substantially advances" formula is not only *doctrinally* untenable as a takings test — its application as such would also present serious practical difficulties. The *Agins* formula can be read to demand heightened means-ends review of virtually any regulation of private property. If so interpreted, it would require courts to scrutinize the efficacy of a vast array of state and federal regulations — a task for which courts are not well suited. Moreover, it would empower — and might often require — courts to substitute their predictive judgments for those of elected legislatures and expert agencies.

. . . The reasons for deference to legislative judgments about the need for, and likely effectiveness of, regulatory actions are by now well established, and we think they are no less applicable here. . . .

III

We emphasize that our holding today — that the "substantially advances" formula is not a valid takings test — does not require us to disturb any of our prior holdings. To be sure, we applied a "substantially advances" inquiry in *Agins* itself, *see* 447 U.S., at 261–262 (finding that the challenged zoning ordinances "substantially advanced legitimate governmental goals"), and arguably also in *Keystone Bituminous Coal Assn. v. DeBenedictis*, 480 U.S. 470, 485–492 (1987) (quoting " 'substantially advance[s]' " language and then finding that the challenged statute was intended to further a substantial public interest). But in no case have we found a compensable taking based on such an inquiry. Indeed, in most of the cases reciting the "substantially advances" formula, the Court has merely assumed its validity when referring to it in dicta. . . .

It might be argued that this formula played a role in our decisions in *Nollan v. California Coastal Comm'n*, U.S. 483 825 (1987), and *Dolan v. City of Tigard*, 512 U.S. 374 (1994) [reproduced in Chapter 7 — Eds.]. *See* Brief for Respondent 21–23. But while the Court drew upon the language of *Agins* in these cases, it did not apply the "substantially advances" test that is the subject of today's decision. Both *Nollan* and *Dolan* involved Fifth Amendment takings challenges to adjudicative land-use exactions — specifically, government demands that a landowner dedicate an easement allowing public access to her property as a condition of obtaining a development permit. . . .

. . . The question was whether the government could, without paying the compensation that would otherwise be required upon effecting such a taking, demand the easement as a condition for granting a development permit the government was entitled to deny. The Court in *Nolan* answered in the affirmative, provided that the exaction would substantially advance the same government interest that would furnish a valid ground for denial of the permit. 483 U.S., at 834–837. The Court further refined this requirement in *Dolan*, holding that an adjudicative exaction requiring dedication of private property must also be " 'roughly proportional' . . . both in nature and extent to the impact of the proposed development." 512 U.S., at 391.

Although *Nollan* and *Dolan* quoted *Agins'* language, the rule those decisions established is entirely distinct from the "substantially advances" test we address today. Whereas the "substantially advances" inquiry before us now is unconcerned with the degree or type of burden a regulation places upon property, *Nollan* and *Dolan* both involved dedications of property so onerous that, outside the exactions context, they would be deemed *per se* physical takings. In neither case did the Court question whether the exaction would substantially advance *some* legitimate state interest. Rather, the issue was whether the exactions substantially advanced the *same* interests that land-use authorities asserted would allow them to deny the permit altogether. As the Court explained in *Dolan*, these cases involve a special application of the "doctrine of 'unconstitutional conditions,'" which provides that "the government may not require a person to give up a constitutional right — here the right to receive just compensation when property is taken for a public use — in exchange for a discretionary benefit conferred by the government where the benefit has little or no relationship to the property." 512 U.S., at 385. That is worlds apart from a rule that says a regulation affecting property constitutes a taking on its face solely because it does not substantially advance a legitimate government interest. In short, *Nollan* and *Dolan* cannot be characterized as applying the "substantially advances" test we address today, and our decision should not be read to disturb these precedents.

. . . .

Twenty-five years ago, the Court posited that a regulation of private property "effects a taking if [it] does not substantially advance [a] legitimate state interest." *Agins, supra*, 477 U.S., at 260. The lower courts in this case took that statement to its logical conclusion, and in so doing, revealed its imprecision. Today we correct course. We hold that the "substantially advances" formula is not a valid takings test, and indeed conclude that it has no proper place in our takings jurisprudence. In so doing, we reaffirm that a plaintiff seeking to challenge a government regulation as an uncompensated taking of private property may proceed under one of the other theories discussed above — by alleging a "physical" taking, a *Lucas*-type "total regulatory taking," a *Penn Central* taking, or a land-use exaction violating the standards set forth in *Nollan* and *Dolan*. Because Chevron argued only a "substantially advances" theory in support of its takings claim, it was not entitled to summary judgment on that claim. Accordingly, we reverse the judgment of the Ninth Circuit and remand the case for further proceedings consistent with this opinion.

It is so ordered.

JUSTICE KENNEDY, concurring. [Omitted.]

NOTES AND QUESTIONS

1. *What does Lingle mean?* Justice Kennedy in his concurrence noted that the *Lingle* decision "does not foreclose the possibility that a regulation might be so arbitrary and irrational as to violate due process." What types of regulations might be in that category? Due process issues are considered *infra*.

2. What is the significance of the Court's conclusion that the "substantially advances" test does not belong in takings analysis? Does the test address the remedy question? The level of scrutiny courts give to legislative decisions? See Byrne, *Due Process Land Use Claims After Lingle*, 34 Ecology L.Q. 471, 480 (2007) ("*Lingle* emphatically rejected any heightened scrutiny for property regulation.").

3. Following the *Lingle* decision, a number of state courts moved to eliminate consideration of the "substantially advances" test from their takings jurisprudence. *St. Johns River Water Mgmt. Dist. v. Koontz*, 5 So. 3d 8, 20 (Fla. App. 2009) ("The position that a regulatory taking can occur under a land-use exaction theory in circumstances where the permit is denied and no property interest is actually conveyed may have made some sense in the *pre-Lingle* world; however, now that *Lingle* has clarified the proper focus of regulatory takings analysis, the position that a 'taking' has occurred solely because the State made an offer that was rejected is untenable."); *Biddle v. BAA Indianapolis, LLC*, 860 N.E.2d 570, 578, n.17 (2007) ("To the extent our prior decisions have relied on the *Agins* formulation, they are overruled."); *City of Coeur D'Alene v. Simpson*, 136 P.3d 310 (Idaho 2006) (discussing *Lingle* and emphasizing the difference between takings and due process issues). A California appellate court, however, raised the possibility that the "substantially advances" test might survive under a state constitutional provision that includes "damage" to property within its "takings" provision. *Herzberg v. County of Plumas*, 34 Cal. Rptr. 3d 588, 597–98 (Cal. App. 2005).

4. *Application of the Penn Central factors after Lingle.* The Court of Federal Claims applied *Penn Central* to find a taking in one case and reject a taking in another. In *CCA Associates v. United States*, 75 Fed. Cl. 170 (2007), the court adopted a return on equity approach, rather than property value differential, to measure regulatory impact and concluded that a federal statute restricting mortgage prepayment options by owners of federally subsidized housing developments amounted to a compensable taking. *CCA Associates* was appealed and the Federal Circuit court "vacated the disposition of the takings analysis . . . and remanded the case for further proceedings." *CCA Associates v. United States*, 91 Fed. Cl. 580, 598, 618–19 (2010) (economic impact of 18 percent was sufficient to find a taking and stating that 'an 18% economic loss concentrated over approximately five years constitutes a 'serious financial loss' "). But in *Brace v. United States*, 72 Fed. Cl. 337 (2006), the court refused to find a taking arising from wetlands regulations that caused a farmer approximately a 14 percent loss in value, about $55,000. While the farmer did suffer economic loss, the court concluded that the wetlands regulations served a legitimate public purpose and the farmer failed to establish legitimate investment-backed expectations. In *Wensmann Realty, Inc. v. City of Eagan*, 734 N.W.2d 623 (Minn. 2007), the Supreme Court of Minnesota applied the *Penn Central* framework and held that refusal to amend a comprehensive plan to permit residential development to replace a privately-owned public golf course would be a compensable taking if, on remand, the evidence establishes that such action leaves the owner with no reasonable use of the property. In applying the factors, the court concluded that insufficient evidence was presented to determine whether retaining the golf course was a reasonable, economically viable use of the property. The investment-backed expectations factor favored the city because the land owner had no expectations of any use other than as a golf course when the property was acquired and had made no additional investments based on an expectation that residential development might later be approved. The character of the government action factor favored the land owner because the city's decision affected only one land owner. Thus the economic impact factor became critical. "[In] balancing the *Penn Central* factors . . . we conclude that the determinative factor in this case is whether the denial of the comprehensive plan amendment leaves the property owner with any reasonable use of the property." *Id.* at 641.

5. For additional discussion of *Lingle*, see Merrill, *Why Lingle is Half Right*, 11 Vt. J. Envtl. L. 421, 421 (2010) (arguing that the Court was incorrect when it stated that the " 'substantially advances' inquiry has 'no proper place' in takings jurisprudence" and discussing instances in which the test might have some probative value); Siegel, *Exactions After Lingle:*

How Basing Nollan and Dolan on the Unconstitutional Conditions Doctrine Limits Their Scope, 28 Stan. Envtl. L.J. 577 (2009); Burling & Owen, *The Implications of Lingle on Inclusionary Zoning and Other Legislative and Monetary Exactions*, 28 Stan. Envtl. L.J. 397 (2009); Baron, *Winding Toward the Heart of the Takings Muddle: Kelo, Lingle, and Public Discourse About Private Property, supra*, 34 Fordham Urb. L.J. at 634–52 (arguing that *Lingle* "returned takings law to its central question, that of the distribution of the burdens of regulatory intervention"); Singer, *The Ownership Society and Takings of Property: Castles, Investments, and Just Obligations*, 30 Harv. Envtl. L. Rev. 309, 328–38 (2006) (arguing that *Lingle* is premised on a "citizenship model" of property ownership that requires consideration of the impact of property use on others, rather than models that emphasize an owner's power to exclude or that view property solely as an economic investment); Dreher, *Lingle's Legacy: Untangling Substantive Due Process from Takings Doctrine*, 30 Harv. Envtl. L. Rev 371 (2006); Note, *Taking the Courts: A Brief History of Takings Jurisprudence and the Relationship Between State, Federal, and the United States Supreme Courts*, 35 Hastings Const. L.Q. 897 (2008).

[7.] Federal Takings Executive Orders and Federal and State Takings Legislation

An active property rights movement that seeks greater protection for landowners under the Takings Clause has so far produced Presidential Executive Orders and a growing number of state takings laws. Commentators and scholars suggest that the Executive Orders lean toward a property rights advocacy position.

Takings Executive Orders. President Reagan issued an Executive Order in 1988 that adopted principles and criteria for federal regulatory programs that cause taking problems, such as the wetlands permit program of the Clean Water Act. Executive Order 12,630, 53 Fed. Reg. 8859 (Mar. 15, 1988). The Order says that it is codifying the Supreme Court's 1987 Trilogy of takings cases. For example, the Order states that a taking may occur if a regulation "substantially affects" the value of property "and even if the action constituting a taking is temporary in nature." The Order also contains a requirement that a government agency should adopt the least restrictive alternative in its regulatory programs when regulations are imposed for public health and safety purposes. Is there any support for this requirement in the Supreme Court cases? Most experts agree that there is no clear support for the least restrictive alternative in federal case law, though it is sometimes used as a makeweight to establish the substantiality of regulatory effects. Despite considerable congressional activity in the mid-1990s, no federal freestanding property rights legislation was enacted.

The Order requires federal agencies to prepare a Takings Implications Assessment (TIA) that evaluates the takings impacts of their actions. In the summer of 1988, the Attorney General issued Guidelines that further explain and implement the Executive Order. Attorney General's Guidelines for the Evaluation of Risk and Avoidance of Unanticipated Takings (1988). For discussion of the Order, see McElfish, *The Takings Executive Order: Constitutional Jurisprudence or Political Philosophy?*, 18 Envtl. L. Rep. 10474 (1988); Pollot, *The Effect of the Federal Takings Executive Order*, Land Use L. & Zoning Dig., May 1989, at 3.

In an analysis of the implementation of the Executive Order by the Justice Department and four agencies most directly affected — the Department of Agriculture, the Army Corps of Engineers, the Environmental Protection Agency (EPA) and the Department of the Interior

— the General Accounting Office (GAO) noted that annual reports of just compensation awards have not been required since 1994 because of the "relatively small" number and dollar amounts. During fiscal years 2000 through 2002, forty-four regulatory takings cases were brought against the four agencies. Two resulted in court awards totaling $4.2 million and twelve others were settled for a total of $32.3 million. Only three cases involved wetlands, with the other eleven dealing with mining claims or access to public lands. GAO, Regulatory Takings: Implementation of Executive Order on Government Actions Affecting Private Property Use 15, 20–21 (2003).

A second takings Executive Order was signed by President George W. Bush on June 23, 2006, the one-year anniversary of the *Kelo* decision, discussed *supra.* Executive Order 13,406, Protecting the Property Rights of the American People, 71 Fed. Reg. 36973. This Executive Order expressed a policy of restricting the use of eminent domain by the federal government to situations "benefiting the general public and not merely for the purpose of advancing the economic interest of private parties . . . ." The Executive Order instructs the Attorney General to "issue [implementing] instructions . . . and monitor [federal government] takings . . . for compliance . . . in a manner consistent" with the 1988 Executive Order. President Bush strongly supported private property rights. He signed Executive Order 13,406 intending that it would establish a record that the federal government stood in opposition to the use of eminent domain for the mere purpose of economic development. See Kaufman, *Community Efforts to Attract and Retain Corporations: Legal and Policy Implications of State and Local Tax Incentives and Eminent Domain: Regional Economies and the Constitutional Imperative of Eminent Domain*, 58 Case W. Res. L. Rev. 1199 (2008).

State takings legislation and federal takings policy, the 1988 Federal Executive Order. Over half the states now have takings laws. There are essentially two types or models of takings statutes: (1) assessment statutes and (2) compensation statutes. Oswald, *Property Rights Legislation and the Police Power*, 37 Am. Bus. L.J. 527, 540 (2000); *see also*, Martinez, *Statutes Enacting Takings Law: Flying in the Face of Uncertainty*, 26 Urb. Law. 327, 337 (1994) (breaking compensation statutes into three categories, extreme substantive statutes, moderate substantive statutes and hybrid statutes).

Assessment Statutes: Assessment statues reflect Executive Order 12,630 and require the production of TIAs, *supra*. The majority of state takings laws are modeled on the 1988 federal Executive Order. They require state agencies to do extensive takings reviews of proposed laws and regulations, or require the state attorney general to establish a process to evaluate the takings implications of proposed regulations. E.g., Ariz. Rev. Stat. Ann. §§ 41-1311 to -1313; Idaho Code §§ 67-8001 to 67-8004; Ind. Code Ann. § 4-22-2-32; Utah Code Ann. §§ 63L-3-101 to 63L-3-202 and 63L-4-101 to 63L-4-301; W. Va. Code §§ 22-1A-1 to 22-1A-6. In some states these laws include local governments. These laws do not have a substantive effect. For example:

• The Utah law requires each state agency to prepare an assessment of the takings implications of government action. Utah Code Ann. §§ 63L-3-202 (stating that the assessment should provide "an analysis of . . . the likelihood that the action may result in a constitutional taking . . . alternatives to the proposed action . . . [and] an estimate of financial cost to the state").

• West Virginia requires the Division of Environmental Protection to prepare an assessment whenever "any action within its statutory authority . . . is reasonably likely to deprive a private real property owner of his . . . property in fee simple or to deprive an owner of all productive use of his . . . private real property." W. Va. Code § 22-1A-3.

A handful of states have laws that have a substantive effect. These states' laws go beyond takings impact analysis and require compensation for takings.

Compensation Statutes: Compensation statutes deem a taking to have occurred if a regulation results in a reduction in the fair market value of the property below a designated percent or threshold. Some statutes establish categorical definitions for takings (e.g., Texas, Mississippi and Louisiana, discussed below) and some do not (e.g. Florida, also discussed below). "Under [certain compensation statutes], the initial — and only — question would be whether the relevant property was diminished in value [by more than the relevant percentage]. Of course, quite a lot would turn on the threshold definition of the relevant property right. Is the relevant property right the right to exclude? The right to use? The right to develop under existing zoning?" Martinez, *supra* at 337; *see also*, Oswald, *supra* (discussing compensation statutes and the phenomenon of property rights legislation). Examples of states following this type of compensation statute include the following:

• The Texas law requires compensation when governmental action reduces the value of real property by twenty-five percent or more. Tex. Gov't Code Ann. § 2007.002(5)(B).

• Mississippi defines a taking of forest or agricultural property as a regulation that "reduce[s] the fair market value of forest or agricultural land . . . or personal property rights associated with conducting forestry or agricultural activities on [such] . . . land by more than forty percent" of the land's value before the regulation. Miss. Code Ann. § 49-33-7 and § 49-33-3.

• Louisiana law defines a taking of private agricultural property as government action that reduces the value of the property by twenty percent or more. La. Rev. Stat. § 3:3610.

Some compensation statutes, while providing greater protection of private property rights than do existing federal and state takings cases, do not "establish categorical definitions of takings . . . [by setting] out rote numerical criteria as determinative of takings." Martinez, *supra* at 337. For example:

• Florida's Bert J. Harris, Jr., Private Property Rights Protection Act, adopted in 1995, is one of the broadest and most successful state measures, at least according to property rights advocates. Echeverria & Hansen-Young, *The Track Record on Takings Legislation: Lessons from Democracy's Laboratories*, 28 Stan. Envtl. L.J. 439 (2009). The Bert Harris Act requires compensation when a regulation places an "inordinate burden" on property that doesn't amount to a constitutional taking. § 70.001(1). An inordinate burden exists if a property owner is unable to attain the reasonable investment-backed expectations to an existing or vested use of the property or, in the alternative, if the owner must permanently bear "a disproportionate share of a burden imposed for the good of the public, which in fairness should be borne by the public at large." Fla. Stat. Ann. § 70.001(3)(e); Fla. Stat. Ann. § 70.001(3)(b) (defining existing use); *Royal World Metro. Inc. v. City of Miami Beach*, 863 So. 2d 320 (Fla. App. 2003) (statute preserves sovereign immunity benefits but does not bar private property rights claim). The Bert Harris Act applies to as-applied challenges and not to facial challenges to regulations. *M&H Profit, Inc. v. City of Panama City*, 28 So. 3d 71 (Fla. App. 2009); Fla. Stat. Ann. § 70.001(1). Claims must be filed within one year after the law or regulation at issue is first applied to the claimant's property. Fla. Stat. Ann. § 70.001(11). Unlike Oregon's Measure 37, discussed below, it is completely prospective and only applies to land use restrictions adopted after May 11, 1995. Echeverria & Hansen-Young, *supra*. The

Florida statute requires a mandatory negotiation process for six months before a takings claim can be brought into court.

The cases have begun to interpret how the law should be applied. In *City of Jacksonville v. Coffield*, 18 So. 3d 589 (Fla. App. 2009), the developer entered into a contract to purchase land for the purpose of developing it into eight residential lots. Prior to acquiring the property, the developer learned that a neighboring homeowners' association had filed an application with the city to close and abandon, as a public road, the only roadway providing public access to his property. Without this access, only two residences could be built. Notwithstanding this information, the developer acquired the property and proceeded with his development plans based upon the mistaken belief that the city would not approve the application. After the city approved the application, the developer sued the city "alleging damages in the amount of $2,212,000 as a result of [its] inability to proceed with the proposed development, which the [developer] attributed to the closure of . . . the [roadway] as a public road." *Id.* at 593. The court held that the developer's expectation of subdividing property into eight lots "was not objectively reasonable" once he learned of the filing of an application seeking to close, abandon and make private the only road providing access to his proposed lots and the developer failed to prove that equitable estoppel should be applied against the City to establish a vested right to his intended use. *Id.* at 599. In *Palm Beach Polo, Inc. v. Village of Wellington*, 918 So. 2d 988 (Fla. App. 2006), the plaintiff alleged that the Bert Harris Act was violated when Big Blue Reserve, a preserve area, was designated as a " 'conservation area' " in the defendant's comprehensive plan. *Id.* at 995. The court ruled against the plaintiff stating that there was no reasonable investment-backed expectation to develop land that had been designated as a natural reserve since 1972, and where "extraordinary efforts were made to preserve [an] important pristine forest." *Id.* According to the court, the designation did not change anything regarding the development potential of the property. *Id.* The agreement with the plaintiff's "predecessor-in-title contemplated the preservation of Big Blue and made specific provisions therefore, and because the developmental densities were transferred from the area in exchange for higher densities elsewhere" the court concluded there was no taking under the Bert Harris Act. *Id.* at 990. How do these cases compare with the application of the investment-backed takings factor under the federal Constitution? See also *Citrus Co. v. Halls River Dev.*, 8 So. 3d 413, 422 (Fla. App. 2009) (stating that any adverse impact suffered by the developer was caused by the reclassification of the property under the county's comprehensive plan which occurred well prior to the developer's acquisition of the property; thus the developer never had "a lawful right to the proposed use for a multifamily dwelling, the County Staff's misadvice notwithstanding"); *Holmes v. Marion County*, 960 So. 2d 828 (Fla. App. 2007) (stating that a time-limited permit cannot create a reasonable investment-backed expectation that the plaintiffs would receive renewals indefinitely and also holding that the denial of the permit extension was not an inordinate burden on plaintiffs' property).

How would you apply this law to a denial of a permit for development in a wetlands?

Arizona's response to Kelo: Proposition 207. Another example of a state compensation statute that avoids categorical takings definitions is Arizona's Proposition 207. In response to the 2005 *Kelo* decision, *supra*, voters in Arizona in the November 2006 elections approved Proposition 207, The Private Property Rights Protection Act, Ariz. Rev. Stat. Ann. §§ 12-1131 *et seq* by a margin of 65% to 35%. Proposition 207 requires that a private property owner receive just compensation or, in the alternative, a waiver of land use restrictions if, after the property is transferred to the owner, the state or a political subdivision enacts or applies any land use law that reduces the owner's right to divide, sell, possess or use his private property and the action reduces the property's fair market value. Ariz. Rev. Stat. Ann. § 12-1134. The legislation, proposed by initiative petition, also limits the exercise of eminent domain to situations involving a public use, defined to include 1) "possession, occupation, and enjoyment of the land by the general public, or by public agencies," 2) use by utilities, 3) elimination of "a direct threat to public health or safety caused by the property in its current condition," and 4) "acquisition of abandoned property." Ariz. Rev. Stat. Ann. § 12-1136(5)(a). The "public benefits of economic development, including an increase in tax base, tax revenues, employment or general economic health," are specifically excluded from the definition of public use. Ariz. Rev. Stat. Ann. § 12-1136(5)(b); Kusy & Stephenson, *Arizona has the Distinction of Being the Only State to Pass a Regulatory Takings Ballot Initiative in November 2006*, Planning & Envtl. L., Jan. 2007, at 3. A closely watched California initiative, Proposition 90, that would have added a narrow definition of "public use" to the California Constitution, was defeated by the voters. MacVey & Martinez, *California's Proposition 90: The Kelo-Plus Strategy Fails*, Kusy & Stephenson, *supra*, at 8.

Arizona's legislation articulates a very broad standard — diminished fair market value due to a land use law. How does a property owner demonstrate diminished fair market value? Is appraisal testimony the best source of evidence? What qualifies as a "land use law"? See Ariz. Rev. Stat. Ann. § 12-1134(B). There has not been much litigation surrounding Proposition 207, to date, less than a handful of cases, and so these questions have not received a judicial answer. Thus far, property owners and government authorities have been working together, on a very practical level, to avoid harsh economic impacts from downzoning. It could be that part of the explanation for this result is that, unlike in other parts of the country, many of Arizona's property rights activists are not big developers; rather, they are mostly "average" individuals who are perhaps less willing to pursue costly and time-consuming litigation when the outcome is so uncertain.

Proposition 207 does not apply retroactively, unlike Oregon's Measure 37 which had retroactive effects; land use laws that were enacted before the effective date of Proposition 207 are exempt from claims for diminution in property value under the law. Ariz. Rev. Stat. Ann. § 12-1134(B)(7); Echeverria & Hansen-Young, *supra*. Also, claims based upon indirect regulatory impacts are excluded from coverage. Thus, a property owner located adjacent to property that has been directly impacted by a land use regulation is not eligible to file a Proposition 207 claim. Ariz. Rev. Stat. Ann. § 12-1136(B)(6); Stephenson & Lane, *Arizona's Regulatory Takings Measure: Proposition 207*, Planning & Envtl. L., Nov. 2008, 12,14. As mentioned earlier, few Proposition 207 claims have been filed to date especially in comparison to the thousands of Oregon's Measure 37 and 49 claims (discussed below). See, e.g., *Goodman v. City of Tucson*, C-20081560 (Ariz. Sup. Ct. 2009) (holding that developer's case was not rendered moot by striking down of anti-demolition ordinance as an unreasonable exercise of the city's police power where the ordinance had affected the developer's property for more than one year).

Arizona's legislation is that state's version of Oregon's Measures 37 and 49. Stephenson & Lane, *supra*, at 12. Measure 37 is a citizen initiative approved in 2004 that seriously readjusted private property rights in Oregon. It was subsequently amended in 2007 by Measure 49 which "radically overhaul[ed] Measure 37." Potapov, *Making Regulatory Takings Reform Work: The Lessons of Oregon's Measure 37*, 39 Envtl. L. Rptr. 10516 (2009). Oregon's initiatives are discussed below.

Note on Takings Legislation in the Oregon State Land Use Program.

In 2004, Oregon voters, by a vote of 61% to 39%, adopted a statute by initiative that required either compensation or a waiver of restrictions for land use regulations that decreased fair market value of property. The initiative, popularly known as Measure 37, had a dramatic effect on Oregon land use programs. "Measure 37 established a broad policy of either payment of 'just compensation' to landowners whose real property values were reduced as a result of land-use regulations, or, alternatively, a waiver of many regulations in place when the current owner acquired the real property in question." Sullivan & Bragar, *The Augean Stables: Measure 49 and the Herculean Task of Correcting an Improvident Initiative Measure in Oregon*, 46 Willamette L.R. 577, 578 (2010). It is safe to say that Measure 37 was a significant departure from established takings principles; "no other state had such a generous compensation provision." Potapov, *Making Regulatory Takings Reform Work: The Lessons of Oregon's Measure 37*, 39 Envtl. L.R. 10516 (2009). Just recently, the Ninth Circuit Court of Appeals held that Measure 37 waivers were not contracts, as the appellees argued, that required the payment of compensation if abrogated. *Citizens for Constitutional Fairness v. Jackson Co.*, 2010 U.S. App. LEXIS 14922 (9th Cir. 2010). This is one of the last Measure 37 cases on appeal and the result seems to be a good one for the Oregon planning system. The Oregon land use program is considered further in Chapter 8 *infra*.

A database assembled by Portland State University shows claims on more than 790,000 acres as of December 2007, available at pdx.edu/ims/m37database.html. See also Sullivan & Bragar, *supra* at 589 (stating that as of December 2007, more than 6,850 claims for payment or waiver had been filed against the government); Potapov, *supra* at 10517 (stating that the nearly 7,000 claims represented $19.8 billion in total compensation requested). In almost all cases, the local government waived the regulation rather than pay compensation. Ninety percent of all claims are outside and within five miles of Urban Growth Boundaries (a mapped line that has been officially adopted to mark the separation of urban areas from surrounding open lands "green belts" such as parks, watersheds and farms, for the purpose of combating sprawl and discouraging speculation at the suburban/urban boundary). Most have been for subdivisions on farm and forest land. One problem with approved claims is that they were ruled nontransferable by the attorney general. The Oregon Supreme Court upheld the initiative as constitutional. *MacPherson v. Department of Admin. Servs.*, 130 P.3d 308 (Or. 2006).

Opposition to Measure 37 rose quickly. Critics argued the right to compensation under Measure 37 is unjustified because it assumes loss in property value where none may have occurred. They argue that amenity and scarcity effects may actually increase the value of land subject to regulation. Amenity effects can occur because the value of a property may reflect the quality of surrounding land uses. Exclusive farm use zoning, for example, may have positive effects on farm values. Scarcity effects occur when land use regulation changes the supply of land that is allowed in a particular location. Jaeger & Plantinga, *How Have Land-Use Regulations Affected Property Values in Oregon?* (Oregon State University Extension Serv., 2007). See also Echeverria, *Property Values and Oregon Measure 37: Exposing the False Premise of Regulation's Harm to Landowners* (Georgetown Envtl. L. & Pol'y Inst., 2007), available at www.law.georgetown.edu/gelpi/GELPIMeasure37Report.pdf; Jaeger, *The Effects of Land Use Regulations on Property Values*, 36 Envtl. L. 105 (2006). Many Oregonians perceived Measure 37 as jeopardizing Oregon's landscape for the undue benefit of timber and other big money interests. Others were concerned that the state would be bankrupt if the government paid all of the Measure 37 claims.

In June 2007, the legislature referred Measure 49 to the voters for approval and it passed with 62% of Oregonians voting in favor of Measure 49. "Measure 49 modifies Measure 37 'by narrowing the circumstances that trigger its remedies and limiting the scope of those remedies.' " *Pete's Mountain Homeowners Assoc. v. Clackamas County*, 204 P.3d 802, 806 (Or. App. 2009). For example:

- Commercial and industrial claims are prohibited under Measure 49; only residential claims are allowed. Measure 49, Section 5.
- Measure 49 claims are expressly transferable. Measure 49, Section 11(7) (stating that "authorization to partition or subdivide the property, or to establish dwellings on the property . . . runs with the property and may be either transferred with the property or encumbered by another person without affecting the authorization").
- Measure 49 provides additional protections for high-value farmland and forestland and for ground water restricted areas. Development on these lands is restricted to three dwellings. Other types of land are eligible for as many as ten dwellings. Measure 49, Section 7. Impacts on farmlands and forestlands are also minimized by limiting home sites to two acres on these lands, requiring clustering and by enacting a "human health and safety" exception for statutes and regulations restricting farm and forest practices. ORS § 195.305(3)(b).
- An "express lane" is set up for claims to develop up to three homes if there was a right to develop when the property was acquired. For claims to develop up to ten homes, there must also be a showing of loss of value that justifies the number of new homes permitted. Measure 49, Section 6. Rights to develop are transferable under either option.

Note, Measure 49 can be found at ORS 195.300 *et seq.* However many of the provisions are adopted as temporary provisions and listed by section number, as the citations above show.

To achieve its purpose of modifying Measure 37 so as to protect Oregon's farm, forest and water resources while ensuring that private property owners receive just compensation for unfair burdens, "Measure 49 provides that, with one exception that applies to common-law 'vested rights,' all Measure 37 claims must be refiled under the new law. . . ." *Pete's Mountain Homeowners Assoc., supra* at 806; *Corey v. DLCD*, 184 P.3d 1109, 1113 (2008) (stating that Measure 49 extinguishes and replaces "*all* Measure 37 claims, successful or not, and regardless of where they are in the Measure 37 process" but subject to the vested rights exception); Measure 49, Section 5(1)-(3). The Oregon Supreme Court has held that the common law vested rights exception refers to legal precedents that are applied broadly and that describe the rights of property owners upon the enactment of land use laws that make it unlawful to continue with a project that is already underway and that is partially completed. *Corey, supra* at 1113; see also *Cyrus v. Board of County Commissioners of Deschutes County*, 202 P.3d 274 (2009) (discussing vested rights exception).

In response to Measure 37 and continuing concerns that there had been no systematic review of the current Oregon land use system since its inception in 1973, the 2005 Oregon legislature authorized the creation of a task force to review that system and make recommendations for changes to the 2009 legislature. Unfortunately, the composition of the task force was subject to veto by the presiding officers of the legislature (who were of different political parties) and the governor and was delayed by political wrangling, with the result that none of the "usual suspects" who were familiar with the system and presented the best opportunity to effect change, were appointed. The task force results were relatively bland, but included a recommendation for a "policy neutral" audit of existing legislation. In the end, little of import was enacted by the legislature — even the audit recommendation failed — so the system continues to lack a comprehensive review, encouraging ad hoc "fixes" to particular issues, such as Measures 37 and 49.

The future of Measure 49 is still undetermined and Measure 49 litigation is ongoing. Many opine that Measure 49 will be judged as a success and as a welcomed correction of Measure 37's harshness. As the statutory timeline runs for Measure 49 claimants seeking relief based on a Measure 37 waiver, the Oregon Department of Land Conservation Development (DLCD) has compiled preliminary statistics for approximately 80% of the claims it has processed. Carmel Bender-Charland, the DLCD Measure 49 Ombudsman, provided the following statistics. 4,660 total claims have been processed under the original Measure 49 process. The total acreage affected by Measure 49 claims is approximated 239,099 acres affecting 4,954 parcels. DLCD has issued approvals for approximately 80% of Measure 49 claims received and approved 7,297 dwellings. These numbers show a marked reduction in the 750,000 acres that would have been affected under Measure 37. Complete analysis will await further statistics from DLCD and the outcome of the vested rights debate for some Measure 37 claims.

Critics complain that the compensation laws base a taking solely on economic loss and do not permit consideration of governmental interests. In this sense, they resemble the *Lucas* per se takings rule, although the Texas law goes further. How would you revise these laws to remedy this problem? State legislation addressing the use of eminent domain, post-*Kelo*, is discussed earlier in this chapter in Section B.

For discussion of these laws. See Echeverria & Hansen-Young, *The Track Record on Takings Legislation: Lessons from Democracy's Laboratories*, 28 Stan. Envtl. L.J. 439 (2009); Berger, *What Owners Want and Governments Do — Evidence from the Oregon Experiment*, 78 Fordham L. Rev. 1281 (2009); Hirokawa, *Property Pieces in Compensation Statutes: Law's Eulogy for Oregon's Measure 37*, 38 Envtl. L. 1111 (2008); Carter, *Oregon's Experience with Property Rights Compensation Statutes*, 17 Southeastern Envtl. L.J. 137 (2008); Liberty, *Give and Take Over Measure 37: Could Metro Reconcile Compensation for Reductions in Value with A Regional Plan for Compact Urban Growth and Preserving Farmland?*, 36 Envtl. L. 187 (2006); MacLaren, *Oregon at a Crossroads: Where Do We Go From Here?*, 36 Envtl. L. 53 (2006); Sullivan, *Year Zero: The Aftermath of Measure 37*, 36 Envtl. L. 131 (2006); Note, *Gone Too Far: Oregon's Measure 37 and the Perils of Over-Regulating Land*, 23 Yale L. & Pol'y Rev. 587 (2005); Oswald, *Property Rights Legislation and the Police Power*, 37 Am. Bus. L.J. 527 (2000); Coursen, *Property Rights Legislation: A Survey of Federal and State Assessment and Compensation Measures*, 26 Envtl. L. Rep. 10,239 (1996); Juergensmeyer, *Florida's Private Property Protection Act: Does It Inordinately Burden the Public Interest?*, 48 U. Fla. L. Rev. 695 (1996). For discussion of the property rights movement, see H.M. Jacobs, State Property Rights Laws: The Impacts of Those Laws on My Land (1999). See also Private Property in the 21st Century: The Future of an American Ideal (H.M. Jacobs ed., 2004). For a good website providing information on Measure 49, see www.oregon.gov/LCD/MEASURE49/index.shtml. For an interesting article discussing criticisms of the Measure 49 "express lane" provision and other Measure 49 processes, see Mortenson, *Measure 49 Housing Boom is a Bust*, The Oregonian, Sept. 1, 2010.

Federal takings legislation. Federal takings legislation based on the 1988 Executive Order was considered but rejected by Congress. See, e.g., The Omnibus Property Rights Act of 1995,

S. 605, S. Rep. No. 104-239 (1996). For the history of this legislation, see Sax, *Takings Legislation: Where It Stands and What Is Next*, 23 Ecology L.Q. 509 (1996). See also C.F. Runge, The Congressional Budget Office's "Regulatory Takings and Proposals for Change": One-Sided and Uninformed (1999).

A NOTE ON THE TAKINGS CLAUSE LITERATURE

The literature on the Takings Clause is voluminous. Useful books include Eminent Domain Use and Abuse: Kelo in Context (D. Merriam & M. Ross eds., 2006); Taking Sides on the Takings Issues (T. Roberts ed., 2002); S. Eagle, Regulatory Takings (2d ed. 2001); D. Kendall, T. Dowling & A. Schwartz, Takings Litigation Handbook (2000); R. Meltz, D. Merriam & R. Frank, The Takings Issue (1999). For a state legislative proposal to authorize local governments to choose a particular level of property protection by restricting or liberalizing the use of eminent domain, see Serkin, *Local Property Law: Adjusting the Scale of Property Protection*, 107 Colum. L. Rev. 883 (2007). For an argument that the debate over eminent domain should be reframed to focus on the nature of the proposed new development, with eminent domain available "when the anticipated new development would have features likely to contribute to reductions in the concentration of poverty," see Dana, *Reframing Eminent Domain: Unsupported Advocacy, Ambiguous Economics, and the Case for a New Public Use Test*, 32 Vermont L. Rev. 129 (2007). Other articles include Lopez, *Weighing and Reweighing Eminent Domain's Political Philosophies Post-Kelo*, 41 Wake Forest L. Rev. 237 (2006); Feffer, *Show Down in Center City: Staging Redevelopment and Citizenship in Bicentennial Philadelphia 1974-1977*, 30 J. of Urban Hist. 791 (2004); Pritchett, *The "Public Menace" of Blight: Urban Renewal and the Private Uses of Eminent Domain*, 21 Yale L. & Pol'y Rev. 1 (2003); Note, *Lessons from Oregon: Arizona's Approach to Land Use Regulation*, 41 Ariz. St. L.J. 505 (2009). References to the periodical literature can be found in the articles cited in this section and in D. Mandelker, Land Use Law 2-64 to 2-70 (5th ed. 2003 & annual supplements).

C. SUBSTANTIVE DUE PROCESS LIMITATIONS UNDER THE FEDERAL CONSTITUTION

A land use regulation, or the way in which it is applied, can raise substantive due process or equal protection problems, often in cases in which the landowner cannot make a takings claim. Consider the following:

> A developer applies to the planning commission for site plan review and approval for a multifamily residential development in an area zoned for this use at the proposed density. Site plan review is a procedure in which the local planning commission decides whether the development meets standards for site access, landscaping and other site requirements. The ordinance contains a number of these requirements. For example, the ordinance specifies how much of the site must be landscaped and what kind of landscaping must be provided. The application meets all these requirements, but the planning commission told the landowner it will not approve the application unless she reduces the density in her development by twenty percent. This is the first time the commission has made this demand, and there is no requirement in the site plan ordinance that authorizes a reduction in the density of a development. At the planning commission meeting, the chair stated that "there is too much development in this area. We have to hold it down."

The developer can appeal the commission's decision or can bring an action to compel approval of the site plan in state court. She can also consider a constitutional claim in federal court under the federal Constitution. She does not have a takings claim, because the property can still be put to an economically viable use. She has a facial substantive due process claim if she claims landscaping is an aesthetic requirement that is not constitutionally permitted. She has an as-applied substantive due process claim if she can establish the density reduction demand is not legitimately related to site plan review. She also has an equal protection claim if the commission has not made similar demands on other developments. The next case considers these problems, and the case that follows considers equal protection issues. Both cases discuss these issues as they arise under federal constitutional law, which contains quite different requirements than the state courts apply under state constitutional law. Chapter 6 considers procedural due process issues.

GEORGE WASHINGTON UNIVERSITY v. DISTRICT OF COLUMBIA

318 F.3d 203 (D.C. Cir. 2003)

WILLIAMS, SENIOR CIRCUIT JUDGE: This case is the most recent stage of a long-running land-use dispute between George Washington University ("GW" or "the university") and the District of Columbia's Board of Zoning Adjustment (the "Board" or the "BZA"). GW's campus is bounded on the west and north by the District's Foggy Bottom and West End neighborhoods (here referred to collectively as "Foggy Bottom"), and the BZA has been concerned about protecting their residential character and "stability." In an order approving the university's long-term campus improvement plan (the "BZA Order" or the "Order") the BZA imposed conditions aimed at limiting, and even rolling back, encroachment into Foggy Bottom by the university — or, more precisely, its students. The district court upheld some of the conditions, but also found some to be unconstitutional denials of substantive due process. Both sides appealed; we find no constitutional violation.

The District's zoning scheme for universities, promulgated by the Zoning Commission pursuant to the authority granted by D.C. Code § 6-641 and codified at 11 District of Columbia Municipal Regulations ("DCMR") §§ 210, 302.2 & 507, permits university use as a matter of right in areas zoned for high-density commercial use. For land zoned residential or "special purpose," it permits university use as a special exception. GW's land evidently includes high-density commercial, special purpose, and residential portions. In the areas where university use is by special exception, the owner must secure permission for specific university projects in a two-stage application process. In the first stage, the university submits a "campus plan" that describes its general intentions for new land use over a substantial period (GW's preceding plan was for 15 years). On approval by the Board — an approval that can be subject to a set of conditions designed to minimize the impact of the proposed development — the campus plan "establishes distinct limitations within which all future construction must occur." *Levy v. District of Columbia Bd. of Zoning Adjustment*, 570 A.2d 739, 748 (D.C. App. 1990). In the second stage, the BZA reviews individual projects that the university proposes to undertake, evaluating them both for consistency with the campus plan and the zoning regulations.

In both stages, the BZA has substantial, but not unbounded, discretion to reject or approve the university's application. It is instructed to make sure that any university use is located so that it is "not likely to become objectionable to neighboring property because of noise, traffic, number of students or other objectionable conditions." 11 DCMR § 210.2. When reviewing a special exception application for a university, the BZA is also to consider the policies of the so-called "District Elements of the [Comprehensive] Plan," *id.* § 210.7, a planning document setting out development policies for the District, 10 DCMR § 112.6(b). If the application meets these criteria — that is to say, the proposed use is consistent with the Comprehensive Plan and is not likely to become objectionable to users of neighboring property — the Board "ordinarily must grant [the] application." *Stewart v. District of Columbia Bd. of Zoning Adjustment*, 305 A.2d 516, 518 (D.C. App. 1973). [This is a typical special use procedure, which is covered in Chapter 5. The important point here is to understand that the Board has the power to review the university's housing plan and set conditions. Foggy Bottom is an important historic neighborhood. — Eds.]

In late 1999 the university submitted a campus plan for the years 2000-10, reflecting its intentions to expand. Although BZA's concern over the university's effects on Foggy Bottom had been expressed in review of its 1985 plan, the sharp expansion of its enrollment in the 1990s made the issue more acute. Relying in part on submissions of the District's Office of Planning, the BZA found that the university's past acquisition of buildings in Foggy Bottom (and their subsequent conversion into dormitories or student apartments), as well as undergraduates' informal off-campus housing, threatened the "livability and residential character" of the Foggy Bottom neighborhood. As a result, it conditioned its approval of the 2000 Campus Plan on a series of measures designed to limit the presence of undergraduates; these measures included provisions requiring the university to house its freshmen and sophomores on campus and to provide on-campus housing for at least 70% of its students, and imposing an enrollment cap tied to the university's supply of on-campus housing. . . .

[After litigation in federal and state court, the BZA] eliminated the enrollment cap but required the university to provide housing on campus or outside of Foggy Bottom for 70% of its approximately 8000 undergraduates, plus one on campus or non-Foggy Bottom bed for every full-time undergraduate student over 8000. The new Order issued on January 23, 2002, and GW promptly renewed its [federal district] court challenge. The district court found that several conditions of the BZA Order, including the new housing requirements, violated the university's right to substantive due process, but rejected its claims that the zoning regulations were facially unconstitutional and that the District's actions infringed on its First Amendment rights. *George Washington University v. District of Columbia*, Civil Action No. 01-0895 (D.D.C. Apr. 12, 2002). Both sides appealed. We reverse in part, finding no constitutional infirmities.

The university's primary challenges sound in substantive due process. Although that doctrine normally imposes only very slight burdens on the government to justify its actions, it imposes none at all in the absence of a liberty or property interest.

In the land-use context courts have taken (at least) two different approaches for determining the existence of a property interest for substantive due process purposes. In *DeBlasio v. Zoning Bd. of Adjustment*, 53 F.3d 592, 601 (3d Cir. 1995), the Third Circuit held that an ownership interest in the land qualifies. Other circuits, including the Second, Fourth, Eighth, Tenth and Eleventh Circuits, have focused on the structure of the land-use regulatory process, pursuing a "new property" inquiry, *cf.* Charles Reich, *The New Property*, 73 Yale L.J. 733 (1964), and looking to the degree of discretion to be exercised by state officials in granting or withholding the relevant permission. [Citing, e.g., *RRI Realty Corp. v. Village of Southampton*, 870 F.2d 911, 917 (2d Cir. 1989), a leading case.] GW urges us to adopt the Third Circuit's approach but also contends that it has a "new property." Because we agree on the latter point, we need not decide whether the Third Circuit's approach is sound or exactly how it would apply.

The majority approach may seem at odds with ordinary language, in which we would say, for example, that a particular piece of land in Washington is "the property" of GW. But an all-encompassing land use regulatory system may have either replaced that "property" with a "new property" (or with several, one for each authorized class of use), or conceivably have replaced it with less than a new property (thereby, one would suppose, effecting a taking).

Within the majority there is considerable variety in the courts' formulae for how severely official discretion must be constrained to establish a new property. The Second Circuit apparently will not find one if the authority has any discretion to deny approval of the proposed land use. *See Natale v. Town of Ridgefield*, 170 F.3d 258, 263 (2d Cir. 1999). The Eighth Circuit, in contrast, inquires whether the "statute or regulation places substantial limits on the government's exercise of its licensing discretion," *Bituminous Materials v. Rice County*, 126 F.3d 1068, 1070 (8th Cir. 1997), finding a property interest if the agency is so constrained. In our view, the Eighth Circuit's analysis is more in line with analogous Supreme Court precedent and the precedent of this circuit. *See, e.g., Kentucky Dep't of Corrections v. Thompson*, 490 U.S. 454 (1989) (finding discretion to be constrained by "substantive predicates," such as an instruction that prison visitation may be denied when "the visitor's presence . . . would constitute a clear and probable danger"); *Olim v. Wakinekona*, 461 U.S. 238, 249 (1983) (inquiring as to whether there exist "substantive limitations on official discretion").

In practice, the fact patterns of new property cases in the land use arena seem to divide into two sets, one set involving virtually unlimited discretion, the other rather absolute entitlement. In *Bituminous Materials*, for instance, the regulation in question specified that the agency "may" grant the permit, without setting out any substantive standards to follow. Similar substanceless directives form the basis for the regulations at issue in *Gardner v. Baltimore*, 969 F.2d [63] at 70 [4th Cir. 1992] (noting that the regulations were "silent as to the substantive criteria used by the Commission to evaluate the sufficiency of those plans"). [The court cited other cases where there was no new property interest because "the board's discretion was limited only by a general 'reasonableness' requirement, not a substantive standard," and where a certificate "*may* be issued for a portion of or portions of a building which may be safely occupied" but with no mandate for issuance even then. Courts found a property interest "when the highway superintendent was to issue a permit for street excavation to a public utility so long as its application stated 'the nature, location, extent and purpose' of the excavation, and gave adequate undertakings that it would restore the street to its original condition," and when a permit "must issue upon 'presentation of an application and plans showing a use expressly permitted under the then-current zoning ordinance.' "]

The university's expectations for a "special exception" fall between these poles, but we think closer to establishing, as *Bituminous Materials* said, "substantial limits on the government's exercise of its licensing discretion." Here, for a residential or special purpose parcel, university use "shall be permitted as a special exception" if the criteria for the exception are met. 11 DCMR § 210.1. Moreover, the District of Columbia courts have interpreted this provision to mean what it says — namely, that special exceptions must be issued as a matter of right if the qualifying criteria are met. "The Board's discretion . . . is limited to a determination whether the exception sought meets the requirements of the regulation. . . . [If so,] the Board ordinarily must grant [the] application." *Stewart v. District of Columbia Bd. of Zoning Adjustment*, 305 A.2d 516, 518 (D.C. App. 1973).

Of course, some of these qualifying criteria are by no means self-defining. In particular, 11 DCMR § 210.2 says that university use shall be located so that it is "not likely to become objectionable to neighboring property." But combining this provision with 11 DCMR § 210.1 (see above), it seems inescapable that the BZA can deny the university a special exception only by an explicit finding that the proposed use is likely to become "objectionable" — a term that we think clearly places "substantive limitations on official discretion." Although 11 DCMR § 210.2 speaks of uses "objectionable to neighboring property because of noise, traffic, number of students or other objectionable conditions," plainly the final wrap-up clause does not invite the BZA members to apply their own personal tastes; they must rest the "objections" either on the criteria specified in § 210.2 or otherwise made relevant by the Code, regulations, the Comprehensive Plan or other pertinent legal provisions.

In addition, the BZA's conduct and procedures indicate that it interprets the regulations as imposing substantive limits on its discretion. For instance, its Order of March 29, 2001 started with a series of detailed "findings of fact" establishing for the record the objective conditions created by the university's property use. It states that it is "authorized to grant a special exception where, in the judgment of the Board *based on a showing of substantial evidence*, the special exception . . . will not tend to affect adversely the use of neighboring property." (emphasis added). Although of course a local law mandate of minimum procedures cannot generate an entitlement, the District's provision of fairly formal procedures supports our reading of the regulations as imposing "substantial limits on the [Board's] exercise of its licensing discretion." *Bituminous Materials*, 126 F.3d at 1070.

Once a property interest is found, however, the doctrine of substantive due process constrains only egregious government misconduct. We have described the doctrine as preventing only "grave unfairness," *Silverman v. Barry*, 845 F.2d 1072, 1080 (D.C. Cir. 1988), and identified two ways in which such unfairness might be shown: "Only [1] a substantial infringement of state law prompted by personal or group animus, or [2] a deliberate flouting of the law that trammels significant personal or property rights, qualifies for relief under § 1983." *Id. See also Coniston Corp. v. Village of Hoffman Estates*, 844 F.2d 461, 465–67 (7th Cir. 1988) (noting the "uncanalized discretion" inherent in substantive due process review and thus, given the otherwise resulting federal judicial intrusions on state and legislative authority, the need to limit its role to extreme cases).

In attacking the conditions, the university makes a stab at the "group animus" angle suggested in *Silverman*, saying that the BZA Order reflects the hostility of the Foggy Bottom residents to students. As Foggy Bottom is a residential area, and apartments occupied by students are indisputably a residential use, it seems inescapable that the District is drawing a distinction based on student status. But just what sort of "group animus" the *Silverman* court had in mind is unclear. An equal protection violation would of course be independently unlawful, and the university does not make a serious analytical case for the proposition that students should be viewed as a "suspect class" for equal protection purposes. On the other hand, creation of a sort of shadow equal protection doctrine in the name of "substantive due process" seems just the sort of error against which we and others have cautioned.

In any event, even assuming the legitimacy of any such shadow doctrine, the university offers us neither a "Brandeis brief" nor any other basis for even doubting the implicit basis for the Board's distinction of students from others — namely, that on average they pose a risk of behavior different from that generally preferred by non-student residents and legally relevant. Instead GW invokes District law to show the impropriety of such a distinction, pointing to provisions such as D.C. Code § 2-1402.21, which bars discrimination "based on . . . matriculation" for certain types of real estate transactions, and *id.* § 2-1401.01, saying that it "is the intent of the Council of the District of Columbia . . . to secure an end in the District of Columbia to discrimination . . . by reason of . . . matriculation." It also notes the District of Columbia Court of Appeals' observation that "a university — even a law school — is not to be presumed, for the purposes of the Zoning Regulations, to be the land use equivalent of the bubonic plague." *Glenbrook Rd. Ass'n v. District of Columbia Bd. of Zoning Adjustment*, 605 A.2d 22, 32 (D.C. App. 1992). But even if GW reads District law correctly, a breach of local law does not of itself violate substantive due process. Accordingly, we think the university falls short in its effort to show a deprivation of substantive due process by reference to "group animus."

Perhaps implicitly pointing to a "deliberate flouting of the law that trammels significant . . . property rights," GW also complains of what the District now calls the "transitional housing plan," Conditions 9(a)-(c) of the Order, which the district court found unconstitutional. These require the university to provide its undergraduates, no later than August 31, 2002, with a total of approximately 5600 beds (corresponding to 70% of the approximately 8000 undergraduates) located either on campus or off campus but outside the Foggy Bottom area. After August 31, 2006, the 5600 beds must be located entirely on campus. The parties agree that this requirement will force the university to acquire temporary accommodations for about 1400 students in off-campus, non-Foggy Bottom locations — accommodations that might be not only expensive (though the university has offered no data on just how large an expense) but less desirable for students than the university housing already available to students off-campus in Foggy Bottom.

GW spins these conditions as generating a completely irrational expense. It says that they in effect render "duplicative" the university's current off-campus student housing in Foggy Bottom, which is (concededly) in full conformity to the residential zoning there. But in reality nothing in the transitional housing plan forces the university to give up its off-campus Foggy Bottom dorms or prevents it from continuing to house students there. If it chooses, it can continue supplying that housing *in addition* to the 5600 beds required by Conditions 9(a)-(c). If it chose that option, it would be providing housing to approximately 85% of its undergraduate students, a percentage that is hardly extraordinary for modern urban American universities; Harvard University, for instance, houses 98% of its undergraduates on campus, and Columbia University about 90%. Of course, the university might choose instead to sell its off-campus Foggy Bottom properties or convert them to another use. But the fact that it might do so doesn't render the District's regulation an improper encroachment on its by-right use of those properties.

Nor is there any irrationality in the District's policy. Given the District's concern that an excess of students in the Foggy Bottom area is negatively affecting the character of the neighborhood, it cannot be irrational for the District to adopt rules likely to limit or reduce the number of students in the area. That seems to be the effect of the BZA Order: it guarantees that, of the approximately 8000 undergraduates, at least 5600 (70%) of them will be provided housing on-campus or outside of Foggy Bottom; and since about 1250 students are commuters, married, disabled or for some other reason are not considered by GW to be "well suited for dormitory life," this leaves only about 1150 traditional undergraduates living off-campus in Foggy Bottom, whether their residence was in the university properties or in private apartments. Obviously the university's alternative proposal — to count the off-campus

Foggy Bottom properties towards the 70% requirement — would not as effectively limit the student presence in Foggy Bottom. . . .

The university also argues that the District's zoning regulations are facially unconstitutional under the equal protection element of Fifth Amendment due process because their requirement of two stages of approval imposes burdens on university landowners not imposed on similarly situated non-university actors. But GW acknowledges that universities do not constitute a protected class and so the legislation need only "classify the persons it affects in a manner rationally related to legitimate governmental objectives." *Schweiker v. Wilson*, 450 U.S. 221 (1981). As universities are larger, make more intensive use of their land, and have greater spillover effects on neighboring communities than most other landowners, however, the District's legislative classifications meet this criterion.

Accordingly, the decision of the district court is reversed in so far as it found constitutional violations in the BZA Order and is otherwise affirmed.

So ordered.

[Judge Henderson concurred, believing the majority had improperly recognized a constitutionally protected property interest, and that "the majority chooses not to embrace firmly, as I would, the substantial authority that employs the claim to entitlement approach." She noted that under the majority approach "a landowner has a protected property interest in a favorable land-use decision only if a 'statute or regulation places substantial limits on the government's exercise of its [land-use] discretion,' " citing *Bituminous Materials.* She stated that "[t]hose courts follow the U.S. Supreme Court's guidance found in *Board of Regents v. Roth*, 408 U.S. 564, 569–70 (1972) ('To have a property interest in a benefit, a person clearly must have more than an abstract need or desire for it. He must have more than a unilateral expectation of it. He must, instead, have a legitimate claim of entitlement to it.')." Applying these standards, she would not find an entitlement. She found that the "crucial criterion" was whether the proposed use was "objectionable," and that this criterion "requires the BZA to use its judgment in considering numerous factors."]

NOTES AND QUESTIONS

1. *Substantive due process.* The substantive Due Process Clause requires land use and other government regulations to serve a legitimate governmental purpose. As noted earlier, there is a clear overlap here with a similar requirement the Supreme Court has included as part of its Takings Clause doctrine, though the courts apply this requirement differently under the substantive Due Process Clause. As all students of constitutional law also know, substantive due process has been in disrepute since the so-called Lochner Era, named after a Supreme Court decision decided early in the last century. At that time, the Supreme Court used substantive due process to strike down socially progressive legislation. See *Lochner v. New York*, 198 U.S. 45 (1905).

Despite the shadow of *Lochner*, the courts have revived substantive due process in areas such as family law and the award of punitive damages in tort cases. Substantive due process issues are often present in land use regulation. The *Euclid* case, reproduced *supra*, which upheld the constitutionality of zoning, is an important example. Another example are cases that consider exclusionary and aesthetic zoning and other regulations that raise legitimacy of purpose issues. These cases are facial attacks on a regulation. The *Belle Terre* case, reproduced *infra* in Chapter 3, is a facial substantive due process case in which the Supreme Court upheld a zoning ordinance limiting the number of unrelated persons who could live together as a family. Facial substantive due process challenges to land use regulations are "the most difficult challenge[s] to mount successfully, since the challenger must establish that no set of circumstances exists under which the [law] would be valid." *Guggenheim v. City of Goleta*, 582 F.3d 996, 1032 (9th Cir. 2009), quoting *United States v. Salerno*, 481 U.S. 739, 745 (1987), in rejecting facial substantive due process and equal protection challenges to the city's rent control ordinance, but holding that the ordinance was a "classis" taking for which compensation was required. In March 2010, the Ninth Circuit agreed to hear the *Guggenheim* en banc. 598 F.3d 1061 (March 12, 2010).

The *George Washington* case was an as-applied substantive due process attack on a zoning ordinance that adopted special regulations for another type of "family" — students who attend a university. This type of case, as the decision notes, raises more difficult questions because of the entitlement barrier to litigation. It also raises the important means-end distinction in constitutional law: the distinction between the purpose of the regulation and the means used to carry out that purpose. Both must meet substantive due process (and equal protection) tests for validity.

2. *The Graham v. Connor problem.* The reluctance of the federal courts to accept substantive due process claims has led some circuits to refuse substantive due process claims when the claim would also lie under the Takings Clause, even though a taking might not be present. For example, in *Macri v. King County*, 126 F.3d 1125 (9th Cir. 1997), the plaintiff brought a substantive due process claim that denial of a subdivision approval did not have a legitimate governmental purpose. The court dismissed the claim and reaffirmed the rule in its circuit that "when an explicit textual provision of the Constitution protects against the challenged government action, the claim must be analyzed under that specific provision alone and not under the more general guarantee of substantive due process." Here, where plaintiff also claimed the subdivision refusal denied all beneficial use of the land, the claim could be brought under the more specific protections of the Takings Clause. Substantive due process, the court noted, "must be expanded only with the greatest care," and limited to liberties deeply rooted in the nation's history and traditions. The Ninth Circuit cases rely on *Graham v. Connor*, 490 U.S. 386 (1989), where the Court refused to allow a substantive due process claim under facts raising a Fourth Amendment violation. Some other circuits have followed the Ninth Circuit lead.

One commentator believes this "one-shot only" rule of constitutional interpretation has no defensible basis. Massaro, *Reviving Hugo Black? The Court's "Jot-for-Jot" Account of Substantive Due Process*, 73 N.Y.U. L. Rev. 1086 (1998). If this rule continues to spread, most land use cases will have to be brought as takings claims where difficult ripeness rules, discussed *infra*, apply. Does *Lingle* help resolve the *Graham v. Connor* block by eliminating the *Agins* "substantially advances" test from takings analysis, or does a due process claim remain blocked if a takings claim could be brought on other grounds? "[T]he 'substantially advances' inquiry probes the regulation's underlying validity. But such an inquiry is logically prior to and distinct from the question whether a regulation effects a taking." 544 U.S. at 543.

3. Impact of *Lingle*. As Justice Kennedy emphasized in his concurring opinion, *Lingle* eliminated substantive due process from the Takings Clause but preserved it as an independent cause of action. He emphasized, however, that success in a substantive due process case would be rare. 544 U.S. at 548–49. See *Gove v. Zoning Bd. of Chatham*, 831 N.E.2d 865, 871 (Mass. 2005) ("In practical effect, *Lingle* renders a zoning ordinance valid under the United States

Constitution unless its application bears no 'reasonable relation to the State's legitimate purpose' "). The Ninth Circuit Court of Appeals has held in several recent cases that the Takings Clause does not preempt a substantive due process claim. *North Pacifica LLC v. City of Pacifica*, 526 F.3d 478, 484–85 (9th Cir. 2008); *Action Apartment Ass'n, Inc. v. Santa Monica Rent Control Bd.*, 509 F.3d 1020, 1025 (9th Cir. 2007); *Crown Point Dev., Inc. v. City of Sun Valley*, 506 F.3d 851, 856 (9th Cir. 2007). In *Crown Point*, the court noted that the Supreme Court, in *Lingle*, *supra*, "pull[ed] the rug out from under our rationale for totally precluding substantive due process claims based on arbitrary or unreasonable conduct." 506 F.3d at 855. The court was alluding to its earlier refusal to entertain substantive due process claims when the claims would also lie under the Takings Clause, even though a taking might not be present.

4. *The entitlement rule.* A major obstacle in as-applied substantive due process cases is the rule, adopted in almost all circuits, that a plaintiff cannot sue in substantive due process unless he has an entitlement to a land use approval. The constitutional origins of this rule are complex. It is part of Supreme Court doctrine, as explained in the *Roth* case quoted in the concurring opinion, that a mere expectation is not enough for a due process claim. The plaintiff must have an entitlement, and whether an entitlement exists is defined by state law or local ordinance. (Recall the holding in *Lucas* on the property definition issue.) This means, as in the principal case, that the local zoning ordinance can define the "entitlement" the plaintiff has and keep him out of court by reserving discretion to approve or reject to the local government. See Mandelker, *Entitlement to Substantive Due Process: Old versus New Property in Land Use Regulation*, 3 Wash. U. J.L. & Pol'y 61 (2000). An entitlement exists only if the municipality has a mandatory duty to issue the approval, such as a building permit. See *Cine SK8, Inc. v. Town of Henrietta*, 507 F.3d 778, 784–785 (2d Cir. 2007) (sufficient evidence of valid special use permit to counter summary judgment motion).

Notice how the principal case avoided the entitlement trap by holding that the review standards were objective. Do you agree with the concurring opinion's criticism of this holding? How would you revise the ordinance to confer enough discretion so that the plaintiff would not have an entitlement? What is the impact of the entitlement rule in defining the scope of discretion in local decision making on land use applications, an issue discussed in Chapter 5? If stringently applied, the entitlement rule will keep most as-applied substantive due process cases out of court. For a review of the cases, see Blaesser, *Substantive Due Process Protection at the Outer Margins of Municipal Behavior*, 3 Wash. U. J.L. & Pol'y 583 (2000).

5. *Standard of judicial review.* The Supreme Court considered this question in *City of Cuyahoga Falls v. Buckeye Community Hope Foundation*, 538 U.S. 188 (2003). It held the city engineer's refusal to issue building permits while a referendum was pending on a site plan ordinance authorizing the construction of low-income housing did not violate substantive due process:

> We need not decide whether respondents possessed a property interest in the building permits, because the city engineer's refusal to issue the permits while the petition was pending in no sense constituted egregious or arbitrary government conduct. *See County of Sacramento v. Lewis*, 523 U.S. 833 (1998) (noting that in our evaluations of "abusive executive action," we have held that "only the most egregious official conduct can be said to be 'arbitrary in the constitutional sense' "). [538 U.S. at 198.]

This is a difficult standard to meet. See *Thunderbird Mobile Club, LLC v. City of Wilsonville*, 228 P.3d 650, 663–664 (Ore. App. 2010), citing *Buckeye* and concluding that ordinances regulating the conversion of mobile home parks to other uses "in no sense are arbitrary or irrational so as to violate substantive due process." Likewise, the *George Washington* court held that substantive due process only protects against "egregious government misconduct" or "grave unfairness." The test for substantive due process has also been stated as a "shocks the conscience" test. The *Lewis* case held "the substantive component of the Due Process Clause is violated by executive action only when it 'can properly be characterized as arbitrary, or conscience shocking, in a constitutional sense.' " 538 U.S. at 847. See *Mongeau v. City of Marlborough*, 492 F.3d 14 (1st Cir. 2007), where the First Circuit held that the proper standard for evaluating substantive due process claims is whether the action complained of "shocks the conscience" rather than whether it is "arbitrary and capricious." Applying the standard, the court affirmed a rejection of a claim that a building commissioner's persistent opposition to issuance of a building permit, even though the zoning board of appeals had granted a variance, amounted to a substantive due process violation.

Some federal courts had found a due process violation when municipalities withheld a building permit or other approval for political or other improper reasons. The Second Circuit, in *Cine SK8, Inc. v. Town of Henrietta, supra*, held that allegations of racial animus by town officials, as well as allegations of fundamental procedural irregularities such as amending a special permit without authorization to do so, were sufficient to state a substantive due process claim. The principal case also refers to personal or group animus, or deliberate flouting of the law that violates constitutional rights, as examples of due process violations. Recent Supreme Court cases put these decisions in doubt. See the discussion in *United Artists Theatre Circuit, Inc. v. Township of Warrington*, 316 F.3d 392 (3d Cir. 2003). There may be an equal protection violation in this kind of case. See the *Olech* case, reproduced next.

In the principal case, the reason for the ordinance, not the conduct of an official, was at issue. Do you agree with the reasons for upholding the ordinance in the principal case? Are college students "parasites" like the apartments restricted from residential areas in the *Euclid* case?

6. *Proving a violation.* Review the problem at the beginning of this section. Does the landowner have an entitlement that provides a basis for a substantive due process claim? Would she succeed? In *Shanks v. Dressel*, 540 F.3d 1082 (9th Cir. 2008), the court held that the City of Spokane had no constitutional duty to protect residents of a historic district from an improvident decision to grant a building permit, thus a substantive due process claim, although not preempted, failed.

7. *Do state courts have a special due process role in land use cases?* Justice Kennedy's reminder in his *Lingle* concurrence that regulations "might be so arbitrary or irrational as to violate due process," coupled with the continued reluctance of federal courts to entertain substantive due process claims, suggests that state courts may have a significant due process role to play. Suits on what amount to substantive due process claims under state constitutions may be handled differently from suits under the federal Constitution. State courts often apply an "arbitrary and capricious" standard in the review of land use regulations and their implementation, which is the equivalent of substantive due process review. In many state zoning cases, however, it often is difficult to determine whether courts are reviewing under Taking Clause or substantive due process limitations.

For an argument that state courts have an important due process role in "subjecting to heightened scrutiny those local land use decisions most likely to be distorted by unequal participation in the political process," see Byrne, *Due Process Land Use Claims after Lingle*, 34 Ecology L.Q. 471 (2007) (suggesting, for example, cases raising "spot zoning," excessive external effects, regional costs and benefits, or exclusionary zoning, all discussed *infra*, as examples). Rosalie Berger Levinson, in *Reining in Abuses of Executive Power Through Substantive Due Process*, 60 Fla. L. Rev. 519 (2008), argues that "substantive due process should be recognized as a meaningful limitation on arbitrary abuses of executive power and that victims of such abuse should not be relegated to the vagaries and increasing hurdles imposed by state tort law." Professor Levinson also "suggests ways for attorneys litigating on behalf of government employees, arrestees and detainees, students, and landowners to invoke substantive due process as a meaningful restraint against misuse of executive power." 60 Fla. L. Rev. at 520. See also Comment, *Property Rights: Substantive Due Process and the "Shocks the Conscience" Standard*, 31 U. Haw. L. Rev. 577 (2009) (discussing different standards of review the circuits employ for substantive due process claims and advocating a uniform "arbitrary and capricious" standard); Note, *Realizing Judicial Substantive Due Process in Land Use Claims: The Role of Land Use Statutory Schemes*, 36 Ecology L.Q. 381 (2009) (arguing that *Lingle* has had a marginal effect on lower federal courts with respect to substantive due process claims and advocating state statutory reforms such as mandatory comprehensive planning as possible antidotes to continued judicial resistance to substantive due process claims).

D. EQUAL PROTECTION LIMITATIONS UNDER THE FEDERAL CONSTITUTION

Standards of Judicial Review. Equal protection requires fairness in the application of government regulation. It, too, has a facial and as-applied dimension, but the limitations that many courts place on substantive due process do not apply to equal protection cases. The Due Process Clause applies to "property," which is why the courts can insist on entitlements, or conclude that the Takings Clause is the appropriate remedy. The Equal Protection Clause, by contrast, applies to persons.

Federal courts apply (with some fuzziness at the margins) a three-tiered standard of judicial review in equal protection cases. Strict scrutiny equal protection review applies to suspect classifications and when a fundamental constitutional interest is involved. Racial discrimination is an example of a suspect classification in land use regulation. Free speech is a fundamental interest that can be affected by some land use regulation, such as sign regulations. In either case, the regulation must be justified by a compelling governmental interest, which courts seldom find.

Next, there is a level of intermediate scrutiny the Supreme Court applies to discrimination based on certain characteristics, such as gender. This standard of review lies between strict scrutiny and rational relationship review. The Supreme Court considered whether this level of review applies to land use regulation in the *Cleburne* case, reproduced *infra* in Chapter 3, where a municipality denied a special exception for a group home for the mentally disabled.

Finally, the bulk of land use regulation falls under rational relationship review because it affects only economic interests in land. This standard of review is quite relaxed. It requires government only to show some "rational basis" for its regulation, aided by applying a presumption of constitutionality. The *George Washington* case adopted this test by holding the university was not a "protected class" entitled to more rigorous judicial review. Land use cases triggering more rigorous judicial review in racial discrimination and free speech cases are included later in this book.

Selective enforcement in equal protection cases. There is a group of equal protection cases that apply different rules when a government selectively enforces a government regulation, such as a land use regulation. The Supreme Court considered this problem in the following case:

VILLAGE OF WILLOWBROOK v. OLECH
528 U.S. 562 (2000)

PER CURIAM.

Grace Olech and her late husband Thaddeus asked petitioner Village of Willowbrook to connect their property to the municipal water supply. The Village at first conditioned the connection on the Olechs granting the Village a 33-foot easement. The Olechs objected, claiming that the Village only required a 15-foot easement from other property owners seeking access to the water supply. After a 3-month delay, the Village relented and agreed to provide water service with only a 15-foot easement.

Olech sued the Village claiming that the Village's demand of an additional 18-foot easement violated the Equal Protection Clause of the Fourteenth Amendment. Olech asserted that the 33-foot easement demand was "irrational and wholly arbitrary"; that the Village's demand was actually motivated by ill will resulting from the Olechs' previous filing of an unrelated, successful lawsuit against the Village; and that the Village acted either with the intent to deprive Olech of her rights or in reckless disregard of her rights.

The District Court dismissed the lawsuit pursuant to Federal Rule of Civil Procedure 12(b)(6) for failure to state a cognizable claim under the Equal Protection Clause. Relying on Circuit precedent, the Court of Appeals for the Seventh Circuit reversed, holding that a plaintiff can allege an equal protection violation by asserting that state action was motivated solely by a " 'spiteful effort to "get" him for reasons wholly unrelated to any legitimate state objective.' " 160 F.3d 386, 387 (7th Cir. 1998) (quoting *Esmail v. Macrane*, 53 F.3d 176, 180 (7th Cir. 1995)). It determined that Olech's complaint sufficiently alleged such a claim. We granted certiorari to determine whether the Equal Protection Clause gives rise to a cause of action on behalf of a "class of one" where the plaintiff did not allege membership in a class or group.[*]

Our cases have recognized successful equal protection claims brought by a "class of one," where the plaintiff alleges that she has been intentionally treated differently from others similarly situated and that there is no rational basis for the difference in treatment. *See Sioux City Bridge Co. v. Dakota County*, 260 U.S. 441 (1923); *Allegheny Pittsburgh Coal Co. v. Commission of Webster Cty.*, 488 U.S. 336 (1989). In so doing, we have explained that " 'the purpose of the equal protection clause of the Fourteenth Amendment is to secure every person within the State's jurisdiction against intentional and arbitrary discrimination, whether occasioned by express terms of a statute or by its improper execution through duly

[*] We note that the complaint in this case could be read to allege a class of five. In addition to Grace and Thaddeus Olech, their neighbors Rodney and Phyllis Zimmer and Howard Brinkman requested to be connected to the municipal water supply, and the Village initially demanded the 33-foot easement from all of them. The Zimmers and Mr. Brinkman were also involved in the previous, successful lawsuit against the Village, which allegedly created the ill will motivating the excessive easement demand. Whether the complaint alleges a class of one or of five is of no consequence because we conclude that the number of individuals in a class is immaterial for equal protection analysis.

constituted agents.' " *Sioux City Bridge Co., supra*, at 445 (quoting *Sunday Lake Iron Co. v. Township of Wakefield*, 247 U.S. 350 (1918)).

That reasoning is applicable to this case. Olech's complaint can fairly be construed as alleging that the Village intentionally demanded a 33-foot easement as a condition of connecting her property to the municipal water supply where the Village required only a 15-foot easement from other similarly situated property owners. *See Conley v. Gibson*, 355 U.S. 41, 45–46 (1957). The complaint also alleged that the Village's demand was "irrational and wholly arbitrary" and that the Village ultimately connected her property after receiving a clearly adequate 15-foot easement. These allegations, quite apart from the Village's subjective motivation, are sufficient to state a claim for relief under traditional equal protection analysis. We therefore affirm the judgment of the Court of Appeals, but do not reach the alternative theory of "subjective ill will" relied on by that court.

It is so ordered.

JUSTICE BREYER, concurring in the result.

The Solicitor General and the village of Willowbrook have expressed concern lest we interpret the Equal Protection Clause in this case in a way that would transform many ordinary violations of city or state law into violations of the Constitution. It might be thought that a rule that looks only to an intentional difference in treatment and a lack of a rational basis for that different treatment would work such a transformation. Zoning decisions, for example, will often, perhaps almost always, treat one landowner differently from another, and one might claim that, when a city's zoning authority takes an action that fails to conform to a city zoning regulation, it lacks a "rational basis" for its action (at least if the regulation in question is reasonably clear).

This case, however, does not directly raise the question whether the simple and common instance of a faulty zoning decision would violate the Equal Protection Clause. That is because the Court of Appeals found that in this case respondent had alleged an extra factor as well — a factor that the Court of Appeals called "vindictive action," "illegitimate animus," or "ill will." And, in that respect, the court said this case resembled *Esmail v. Macrane*, 53 F.3d 176 (7th Cir. 1995), because the *Esmail* plaintiff had alleged that the municipality's differential treatment "was the result not of prosecutorial discretion honestly (even if ineptly — even if arbitrarily) exercised but of an illegitimate desire to 'get' him."

In my view, the presence of that added factor in this case is sufficient to minimize any concern about transforming run-of-the-mill zoning cases into cases of constitutional right. For this reason, along with the others mentioned by the Court, I concur in the result.

NOTES AND QUESTIONS

1. *What Olech means. Olech* does not fit neatly into the existing categories of equal protection review, and opens up a new category of cases based on the selective enforcement of a land use ordinance. The plaintiff could also have made a takings claim based on the exaction but did not do so, probably because Supreme Court doctrine requires plaintiffs to sue in state court first, as noted *infra* in the discussion of ripeness. By deciding the case, the Court may have indicated it will not apply ripeness rules to equal protection cases, as some lower courts do.

The decision is also puzzling because, in holding that intent and arbitrariness are sufficient, the Court went farther than the petitioner requested. This holding concerned Justice Breyer, as his concurring opinion indicates. The other Justices "did not reach" the subjective ill will theory. Might they eventually have to conclude, at least in "ordinary" zoning cases, that erroneous decisions are not arbitrary without vindictiveness or its equivalent? The *Conley* case cited by the majority may be of interest here. There, the Court found a union guilty of racial discrimination for failing to represent minority employees who had been discharged before the national labor relations agency, and held the union could not make "irrelevant and invidious" distinctions.

Though not cited by the court, *Snowden v. Hughes*, 321 U.S. 1 (1944), is also relevant. A candidate for office claimed the election board willfully, maliciously, and arbitrarily failed to file a correct certificate showing he was one of the nominees selected in a primary election. The Court did not find an equal protection violation and held "[t]he unlawful administration by state officers of a state statute fair on its face, resulting in its unequal application to those who are entitled to be treated alike, is not a denial of equal protection unless there is shown to be present in it an element of intentional or purposeful discrimination." The Supreme Court also requires a showing of intentional discrimination in racial discrimination cases. *Washington v. Davis*, 426 U.S. 229 (1976).

2. *Applying Olech.* The Supreme Court, in *Engquist v. Oregon Dep't of Agric.*, 553 U.S. 591 (2008), held that the class-of-one theory of equal protection recognized in *Olech* could not be applied to state actions, such as employment decisions, in which officials are called on to make discretionary decisions "based on a vast array of subjective, individualized assessments." 553 U.S. at 602. In so doing, the Court limited *Olech* to situations in which a "clear standard" existed "against which departures, even for a single plaintiff, could be readily assessed." *Id.* at 603.

In *Srail v. Village of Lisle*, 588 F.3d 940 (7th Cir. 2009), the court refused to apply the class-of-one theory, on behalf of members of a certified class of subdivision residents, to the Village's decision not to extend its water system to those residents, even though the court acknowledged that *Olech* did not necessarily preclude such treatment, Applying *Engquist*'s "vast array of subjective, individualized assessments" standard, the court concluded that decisions by the Village to extend its water system to some communities but not others met that standard. "Even though Lisle's decisions affect the communities at-large, the decision to extend water services is inherently individualized because, in essence, it involves the decision to extend water to particular residences," the court reasoned. *Id.* at 945.

A federal district court in New York made the following comments in considering a case in which a property owner was subjected to a search warrant and police raid because of alleged building or zoning code violations:

> *Engquist*'s discussion of [*Olech*] appears to define "discretionary" decisions, for the purpose of barring "class of one" claims, as those that involve discretion that is actually exercised on a *day-by-day* basis, rather than decisions that are theoretically discretionary but — as a practical matter — actually depend on *de facto* standards. . . . [H]ere the issue is not whether Southampton lacked the theoretical discretionary power to enforce its zoning code through search warrants and police raids. It's the fact, . . . that it had *never* exercised that power *except* against Mr. Alfaro, placing Mr. Alfaro in a class all by himself amongst zoning code violators. So, viewing the facts in the light most favorable to Mr. Alfaro, Southampton — much like the Village of

> Willowbrook - had a de facto "clear standard" on how to handle zoning violations — which avoided the use of search warrants and police raids — and violated that standard by peculiarly targeting Mr. Alfaro. And thus, for purposes of this [summary judgment] motion, the Court holds that — even if class of one claims cannot challenge discretionary decisions — Southampton's actions here were not "discretionary" enough to bar Mr. Alfaro's claim. [*Alfaro v.Labrador*, 2009 U.S. Dist. LEXIS 72532, (31–33).]

Do *Engquist* and cases applying it clarify *Olech*?

Courts have divided in deciding what test the Court adopted to decide whether a plaintiff has successfully asserted an *Olech* claim. The Seventh Circuit Court of Appeals, in *Flying J, Inc. v. City of New Haven*, 549 F.3d 538, 547 (7th Cir. 2008), elaborated on the standards for successfully pleading a class-of-one case. "Allegations of animus," while sufficient to establish that an equal protection claim may be ripe, "do not overcome the presumption of rationality and the court evaluates those allegations once a plaintiff has pled facts that show the irrationality of the government action in question. This standard reflects the fairly intuitive idea that a given action can have a rational basis and be a perfectly logical action for a government entity to take even if there are facts casting it as one taken out of animosity. It is only when courts can hypothesize no rational basis for the action that allegations of animus come into play," the court stressed.

Conflicting enforcement orders under the Massachusetts Wetland Protections Act directed to the developer of a condominium project but not to purchasers of completed units and which caused the developer's lenders to cut off funding stated a class-of-one equal protection claim, the First Circuit Court of Appeals held in *SBT Holdings, LLC v. Town of Westminster*, 547 F.3d 28 (1st Cir. 2008). The requisite showings that plaintiff was treated differently from similarly-situated persons and that defendants' actions were motivated by malice or bad faith were established by allegations that the enforcement orders in question were not being enforced against purchasers of completed units even though the purchasers were subject to the enforcement orders because violations of environmental regulations run with the land, and by derogatory emails sent by the chair of the state commission seeking enforcement. Other cases recognizing *Olech* claims include *Carpinteria Valley Farms, Ltd. v. County of Santa Barbara*, 344 F.3d 822 (9th Cir. 2003); *Gavlak v. Town of Somers*, 267 F. Supp. 2d 214 (D. Conn. 2003) (based on intent to drive plaintiff out of business).

For cases rejecting *Olech* claims, see *Ruston v. Town of Skaneateles*, 610 F.3d 55, 59 (2d Cir. 2010) ("complaint fails to allege facts that 'plausibly suggest an entitlement to relief' "); *Reget v. City of La Crosse*, 595 F.3d 691, 695 (7th Cir. 2010) ("To be similarly situated for purposes of a class-of-one equal protection claim, the persons alleged to have been treated more favorably must be identical or directly comparable to the plaintiff in all material aspects"); *Cordi-Allen v. Conlon*, 494 F.3d 245, 255 (1st Cir. 2007) (*Olech* "is not a vehicle for federalizing run-of-the-mine zoning, environmental, and licensing decisions"); *Barstad v. Murrary County*, 420 F.3d 880 (8th Cir. 2005) (*Olech* claim rejected in denial of development and conditional use permits); *Indiana Land Co., LLC v. City of Greenwood*, 378 F.3d 705 (7th Cir. 2004) (two-thirds majority vote not a violation applying animus rule); *New Castle County v. Wilmington Hospitality, LLC*, 963 A.2d 738 (Del. 2008) (former owners who failed to appeal denial of variances not treated unfairly when city granted variances to new owners); *Las Lomas Land Co., LLC v. City of Los Angeles*, 99 Cal. Rptr. 3d 503, 522 (Cal. App. 2009) (proposed project presenting complex urban planning and land use issues which "would involve numerous public policy considerations and the exercise of discretion . . . is the antithesis of the simple issue presented in *Olech*).

An important factor in the *Olech* case may be that the case was decided on a motion to dismiss. This means the case tells landowners how to plead a cause of action that is motion-proof, and allows courts to control their docket by deciding which cases go to trial. Success in litigation on either side is not necessarily guaranteed. *Olech* also raises some interesting questions of constitutional choice in as-applied land use cases. Assume a landowner has a parcel of land zoned for single family use. She applies for a rezoning to multi-family use and claims the city approved a similar rezoning on a parcel a block away the previous week. What constitutional clause applies?

3. *The "run-of-the-mill" zoning dispute.* A number of courts refuse to find an equal protection or due process violation in "run-of-the-mill" zoning disputes when a municipality rejects a land use application for incorrect or discriminatory reasons. This could include the example at the beginning of this section. First Circuit cases have held that this kind of dispute is not actionable under § 1983 of the federal Civil Rights Act, which is discussed in the next section. *Creative Env'ts, Inc. v. Estabrook*, 680 F.2d 822 (1st Cir. 1982), is a leading case. Plaintiff claimed a municipality violated due process when it rejected its subdivision application for erroneous reasons and by misapplying state law and local regulations. The court disagreed and held that "such a theory" would destroy "any hope of maintaining a meaningful separation between federal and state. . . . Virtually every alleged legal or procedural error of a local planning authority or zoning board of appeal could be brought to a federal court on the theory that the erroneous application of state law amounted to a taking of property without due process." *Id.* at 831. The court said, however, that it would hold differently in cases of "egregious" behavior, or where there was a "gross abuse of power, invidious discrimination, or fundamentally unfair procedures," an exception that seems to state the usual standard for judicial review in these cases.

Several other circuits have followed this holding. See *Sameric Corp. v. City of Philadelphia*, 142 F.3d 582 (3d Cir. 1998). But see *Littlefield v. City of Afton*, 785 F.2d 596 (8th Cir. 1985). How does *Olech* affect these cases?

4. *Sources.* For additional discussion of selective enforcement cases after *Olech*, see Araiza, *Constitutional Rules and Institutional Roles: The Fate of the Equal Protection Class of One and What It Means for Congressional Power to Enforce Constitutional Rights*, 62 SMU L. Rev. 27 (2009); Farrell, *The Equal Protection Class of One Claim:* Olech, Engquist, *and the Supreme Court's Misadventure*, 61 S.C. L. Rev. 107 (2009); Cheval, *By the Way — The Equal Protection Clause Has Always Protected a "Class-of-One": An Examination of Village of Willowbrook v. Olech*, 104 W. Va. L. Rev. 593 (2002). For an argument that "class-of-one claims must include allegations of animus or ill will in order to proceed, . . . [and] that class-of-one claims lacking such allegations, such as claims simply alleging irrational, if 'innocent,' government action, should be relegated to the Due Process Clause for review under standards developed to ensure that government action satisfies some minimal level of substantive reasonableness," see Araiza, *Irrationality and Animus in Class-of-One Equal Protection Cases*, 34 Ecology L.Q. 493, 495 (2007).

E. FEDERAL REMEDIES FOR CONSTITUTIONAL VIOLATIONS

Bringing a land use action in federal court presents a set of problems very different from bringing a land use action in state court. Federal courts have jurisdiction over claims arising under the federal Constitution, but plaintiffs must have a remedy that can take them into federal court. Plaintiffs who wish to bring constitutional claims against municipalities in land use cases must sue under § 1983 of the Civil Rights Act, a Reconstruction Era statute first enacted in 1871. A § 1983 action is the only way to bring an equal protection or due process claim, a claim under the First Amendment, or under a federal statute. A plaintiff may bring an inverse condemnation action claiming a land use regulation is a taking directly under the Constitution as held by the *First English* case, reproduced *supra*, but these actions are also usually brought under § 1983 so the plaintiff can claim an award of attorney's fees if successful.

A federal court may decline jurisdiction even if a plaintiff has a remedy to sue for a constitutional violation. The ripeness doctrine limits federal court jurisdiction over as-applied takings claims and over other constitutional claims to some extent, while the abstention doctrines allow federal courts to abstain when they believe federal jurisdiction is inappropriate.

[1.] Relief Under Section 1983 of the Federal Civil Rights Act

Section 1983 provides:

> Every person who, under color of any statute, ordinance, custom or usage, of any State or Territory, subjects, or causes to be subjected, any citizen of the United States or other person within the jurisdiction thereof to the deprivation of any rights, privileges, or immunities secured by the Constitution and laws, shall be liable to the party injured in an action at law or suit in equity, or other proper proceeding for redress.

Section 1983 remedies against municipalities were barred for decades by a Supreme Court decision holding that municipalities were not "persons" under the act, but the Court reversed this ruling in *Monell v. Department of Social Servs.*, 436 U.S. 658 (1978). Since then, there has been a substantial increase in land use litigation in federal courts. The availability of § 1983 as the basis for a federal action requires land use lawyers to make an important and often critical choice between bringing a federal or state court action.

The world of § 1983 jurisprudence is a labyrinth that requires extensive study. The following sections raise some of the more important issues as they apply to land use litigation. As you study these materials, keep in mind the interplay between the rules that govern liability and immunity. A land use official may be immune from liability, for example, in a case in which the municipality is not responsible for the official's actions. In that situation, a § 1983 action is not possible.

[a.] The Scope of Section 1983

Section 1983 creates a cause of action for any person whose federal constitutional or statutory rights are violated, "under color of" state law, by any other "person." The "color of law" requirement is usually not troublesome in § 1983 land use actions, since most of these actions arise out of the conduct of state or local land use agencies or officials. The "persons" who may be liable under § 1983 include natural persons, citizens' groups, corporations and other business entities, and — under *Monell* — local government units. States, however, are not "persons" and therefore are not subject to liability under § 1983. *Quern v. Jordan*, 440 U.S. 332 (1980).

[b.] Custom and Policy

An important issue in § 1983 litigation is when a municipality will be held liable. The statute attaches liability when an action is taken "under color of ordinance, custom or usage." This language means a municipality is liable when a zoning or other ordinance is claimed to violate constitutional rights, but more difficult problems can arise in other types of cases.

Monell refused to adopt the respondeat superior theory of municipal liability under § 1983. This holding means a municipality is not liable just because one of its agencies or officials has committed an action that could be unconstitutional. Instead, the Court interpreted the "custom and usage" requirement in the statute to mean that local governments are liable only for actions that are "official policy" or "visited pursuant to governmental custom," but did not fully explain these terms. The "custom and policy" question is not a problem in many land use cases because a formal action by the city council or a zoning board often triggers the litigation. *Discovery House, Inc. v. Consolidated City of Indianapolis*, 43 F. Supp. 2d 997 (N.D. Ind. 1999) (zoning board). Actions by individual officers or employees may constitute a municipal custom or policy only if the officer has decisionmaking authority. See *Zahra v. Town of Southold*, 48 F.3d 674 (2d Cir. 1995) (no proof of municipal policy on enforcement).

The Supreme Court has not decided a land use case that raised a "custom and policy" question but has considered this issue in other cases. In the first case, *Pembaur v. City of Cincinnati*, 475 U.S. 469 (1986), the Court held that "municipal liability may be imposed for a single decision by municipal policymakers under appropriate circumstances," though only a plurality of the Justices agreed on a standard for imposing liability. The plurality said that

> municipal liability under § 1983 attaches where — and only where — a deliberate choice to follow a course of action is made from among various alternatives by the official or officials responsible for establishing a final policy with respect to the subject matter in question. [*Id.* at 482.]

The Court considered this question again in *City of St. Louis v. Praprotnik*, 485 U.S. 112 (1988), an employee discharge case that was another plurality decision. It confirmed a statement in *Pembaur* that the identification of policymaking officials was a matter of state law. An excessive force case, *Board of County Comm'rs v. Brown*, 520 U.S. 397 (1997), summarized the rules adopted in these two cases in a majority decision. It held an action taken or directed by a municipality or authorized decisionmaker violates federal law if "the municipal action was the moving force behind the injury of which the plaintiff complains." These cases mean that municipalities must be careful to articulate policies that govern actions by land use officials and must monitor their actions. See *Rasche v. Village of Beecher*, 336 F.3d 588 (7th Cir. 2003) (zoning enforcement office and president of village board held not to have final authority).

[c.] Procedural Due Process Actions

A set of complicated rules the Supreme Court has adopted for procedural due process actions under § 1983 create additional barriers. These rules hold a violation of procedural due process cannot be litigated in federal court if state procedures are available to correct the violation after it has occurred. See *Zinermon v. Burch*, 494 U.S. 113 (1990); *Parratt v. Taylor*, 451 U.S. 527 (1981). To decide whether a procedural due process violation has occurred, courts must apply a balancing test that identifies the risk of not providing procedural safeguards before decisions are made, and then evaluates the effectiveness of predeprivation safeguards in relationship to that risk. The revocation of a building permit is an example in a land use setting. *Lanmar Corp. v. Rendine*, 811 F. Supp. 47 (D.R.I. 1993), held a hearing had to be provided in such cases before a permit could be revoked.

[d.] State Tort Liability Analogy

The Supreme Court held in *Monroe v. Pape*, 365 U.S. 167, 187 (1961), that courts should interpret § 1983 against a "background of tort liability." This holding requires a § 1983 plaintiff to show that the "deprivation" complained of was "caused" by official action. The "causation" requirement is usually not a problem in land use cases because legislative or administrative action is ordinarily responsible for the "deprivation," although "causation" problems may occasionally arise. See *Bateson v. Geisse*, 857 F.2d 1300 (9th Cir. 1988) (wrongful withholding of building permit was moving force behind damage to plaintiff).

In *Loosli v. City of Salem*, 193 P.3d 623 (2008), the Supreme Court of Oregon held that the city incurred no liability in tort for the economic loss occasioned by an associate city planner's mistaken certification that the plaintiffs' business complied with the city's land use ordinance. The court applied section 552 of the Restatement of Torts and concluded that, because the land use law compliance certification was for the protection of the public and not to benefit the plaintiffs specifically, the city was not liable for purely economic loss.

[e.] Immunity from Section 1983 Liability

Municipal immunity. After the Supreme Court's decision in *Monell*, it was generally expected that municipalities would enjoy complete immunity from § 1983 liability if the governmental officials responsible for depriving a plaintiff of his or her federal rights acted in good faith. But the Court refused, in *Owen v. City of Independence*, 445 U.S. 622 (1980), to recognize any official immunity in such a case. Moreover, the Court refused to recognize any distinction, with respect to § 1983 liability, between either the "governmental" and "proprietary" functions or the "discretionary" and "ministerial functions" of municipalities. But *Owen* did not hold that municipalities are absolutely liable for violations of federal rights; Constitution-violating municipal conduct is still required. "Municipalities" in their corporate sense are responsible for the actions of their constituent bodies, such as a legislature or a planning board.

Individual immunity. Individuals employed by, or acting on behalf of, the corporate municipal body often will not be financially attractive defendants, but that is not always the case and it is common for municipalities to reimburse officials and employees for liability incurred from actions that are not intentional. The question is whether they enjoy an absolute or qualified immunity from liability in § 1983 actions.

Legislative immunity. The Supreme Court held that local legislators are entitled to absolute immunity in § 1983 cases in *Bogan v. Scott-Harris*, 523 U.S. 44 (1998), in which a city council adopted a budget that eliminated a temporary employee. The Court held it was the "pervasive view" at common law, at the time § 1983 was adopted, that local legislators were absolutely immune from liability. Judicial interference, distorted by the fear of personal liability, should not be allowed to inhibit the exercise of legislative discretion. At the local level, the Court noted, the time and energy necessary to defend against a lawsuit were of particular concern because part-time legislators are common. In addition, deterrents to legislative abuse are greater at the local level because municipalities are liable for constitutional violations, and there is the electoral check on governmental abuse.

The Court then held whether an act is legislative turns, not on the motive of the legislators, but on whether the act was "formally legislative" and within the "traditional sphere of legislative activity." In this case, the act was legislative because it was a "discretionary, policymaking decision" that could well have prospective effect. If this test is not met, the legislative body is not exercising a legislative function, and immunity is not available. See *Kaahumanu v. Maui County*, 315 F.3d 1215 (9th Cir. 2003), holding the denial of a use permit by a legislative body was not a legislative act because it was ad hoc decisionmaking that affected only a few individuals. See also Chapter 6, which deals with the question of whether a legislative body exercises a legislative or "quasi-judicial" function when it rezones a tract of land.

Land use agencies and officials. Judges are absolutely immune from § 1983 liability, and the Court has held that adjudication by agencies is "functionally comparable" to adjudication by judges and should enjoy the same absolute immunity judges enjoy. *Butz v. Economou*, 438 U.S. 478 (1978). Land use agencies and officials also enjoy an absolute immunity if they exercise adjudicatory functions. See *Bass v. Attardi*, 868 F.2d 45 (3d Cir. 1989) (duties of planning board integrally related to judicial process).

Qualified immunity. Planning and zoning officials enjoy a qualified good faith immunity if they do not have absolute immunity. The land use cases apply a good faith immunity rule developed in several Supreme Court cases not involving land use. *Scheuer v. Rhodes*, 416 U.S. 232 (1974); *Harlow v. Fitzgerald*, 457 U.S. 800 (1982); *Davis v. Scherer*, 468 U.S. 183 (1984); *Anderson v. Creighton*, 483 U.S. 635 (1987), noted, *The Supreme Court: 1986 Term: Leading Cases*, 101 Harv. L. Rev. 101, 220 (1987).

In *Davis*, the Court held that good faith immunity is defeated only if the public official has violated a clearly established federal right. *Anderson, supra*, held that whether the defendant acted reasonably is determined by the "contours" of a constitutional right, and these contours must be sufficiently clear so that "a reasonable official would understand that what he is doing violates that right." The Court added that the action in question need not have been held unlawful, but that "in light of preexisting law the unlawfulness must be apparent." *Hope v. Pelzer*, 536 U.S. 730 (2002), also held that a right can be clearly established even though the facts of the case establishing the right are not fundamentally or similarly familiar.

Review the *George Washington* case and the takings cases reproduced *supra* and decide to what extent these cases have "clearly" established constitutional rights that should put officials on notice in land use cases. Compare *Natale v. Town of Ridgefield*, 927 F.2d 101 (2d Cir. 1991) (official could reasonably believe that plaintiff's "grandparented" status under zoning ordinance was in doubt), with *R.S.S.W., Inc. v. City of Keego Harbor*, 18 F. Supp. 2d 738 (E.D. Mich. 1998) (city violated clearly established right to operate a business). An interesting question is whether a constitutional right can be clearly established by a case in another circuit. The cases are divided. See *Marks v. City of Chesapeake*, 883 F.2d 308 (4th Cir. 1989) (holding no).

[f.] Damages and Attorney's Fees

In appropriate cases, declaratory and injunctive relief, damages, and attorney's fees may be awarded in § 1983 actions. Recovery of damages must be sought under § 1983 for due process and equal protection violations; it is not clear whether § 1983 may be used in temporary takings cases, though these cases are regularly sued as § 1983 actions.

The rule for damages in § 1983 cases is different from the measure of compensation in a takings cases. The common law of torts provides an analogy for damages in § 1983 cases, but courts must adapt tort law carefully when a constitutional right does not have a tort analogy. *Memphis Community School Dist. v. Stachura*, 477 U.S. 299 (1986). The Court added that damages in § 1983 cases are awarded for actual losses caused by a defendant's breach of duty. This rule is the same as the rule in some state courts that awards compensation only for actual losses in temporary takings cases. Punitive damages are not available against local governments. *City of Newport v. Fact Concerts, Inc.*, 453 U.S. 247 (1981). Courts may award punitive damages against local officials, but the facts have not usually justified an award of punitive damages in land use cases. See *Johansen v. City of Bartlesville*, 862 F.2d 1423 (10th Cir. 1988).

What should the measure of damages in a land use case be? Assume your client was denied zoning approval for a residential project. You sued for her in federal court under § 1983, and the court held the zoning denial violated substantive due process and equal protection. What do you think of the following formula for awarding damages?

> $[(a\,X + b\,Y) - Y]\,R\,t + ac$ = damages, where a is the probability of approval, b is the probability of disapproval, X is the value of the land with approval, Y is the value of the land without approval, $(a\,X + b\,Y)$ is the weighted probability of approval, R is the rate of interest, t is the duration of the delay after denial, and c is the increased cost of development resulting from the delay.

Probabilities of approval and disapproval are in the equation because the decision invalidating the denial does just that: it does not guarantee an approval, and it is possible the municipality could deny approval later in a way that would withstand a court challenge. Try this formula out on a number of hypotheticals. For the case approving this formula, see *Herrington v. County of Sonoma*, 790 F. Supp. 909 (N.D. Cal. 1991), *aff'd*, 12 F.3d 901 (9th Cir. 1993). See also *Manta Mgmt. Corp. v. City of San Bernadino*, 44 Cal. Rptr. 3d 35 (Cal. App. 2006), remanded, 181 P.3d 159 (Cal. 2008) (upholding $1.4 million jury award for seeking to enforce unconstitutional adult use restrictions through preliminary injunction).

The plaintiff in a § 1983 action can recover attorney's fees by virtue of Civil Rights Attorney's Fees Award Act of 1976, 42 U.S.C. § 1988. Attorney's fees may be substantial, and the possibility of a fee recovery may be more important than the risk of losing a suit in a § 1983 action. Courts award attorney's fees to prevailing parties. *Hensley v. Eckerhart*, 461 U.S. 424 (1983), held that plaintiffs can recover attorney's fees as a prevailing party if they "succeed on a significant issue in litigation which achieves some of the benefits" the plaintiffs sought in bringing suit. See also *Maher v. Gagne*, 448 U.S. 122 (1980) (can recover fees even if favorable settlement obtained).

What if a municipality denies an applicant a special use permit, the applicant sues under § 1983, and before the case comes to trial, the municipality grants the permit? Lower court cases had held the plaintiff was entitled to attorney's fees if the litigation was a "material factor" or played a "catalytic role" in the municipality's decision. The Supreme Court rejected this "catalyst" theory in *Buckhannon Bd. & Care Home, Inc. v. West Virginia Dep't of Health*

& Human Resources, 532 U.S. 598 (2001), a decision that reduces the likelihood that plaintiffs can obtain attorney's fees in § 1983 cases. What problems of litigation strategy does this case create?

2. For discussion of § 1983, see Sword and Shield: A Practical Guide to Section 1983 Litigation (M. Ross & E. Voss eds., 3d ed. 2006); S. Nahmod, Civil Rights and Civil Liberties Litigation: A Guide to § 1983 (4th ed. 1997 & 2006 Update); M. Schwartz & J. Kirlin, Section 1983 Litigation: Claims, Defenses and Remedies (3d ed. 1997); Blum, *The Qualified Immunity Defense: What's "Clearly Established" and What's Not*, 24 Touro L. Rev. 501 (2008); Brown, *The Rise and Fall of Qualified Immunity: From* Hope *to* Harris, 9 Nev. L.J. 185 (2008); Chemerinsky, *Absolute Immunity: General Principles and Recent Developments*, 24 Touro L. Rev. 473 (2008)

PROBLEM

Your client is a developer who plans to build a convenience store on a major highway in a developing area of a county. The county ordinance requires submission of a site plan, which your client submitted, and which the county council then reviewed under the zoning ordinance. This ordinance contains a number of criteria for site plan approval, all of which require a considerable exercise of judgment by the council. The ordinance requires "adequate" site landscaping, for example. The council, following its rules, did not hold a hearing on the site plan but considered the plan in executive session. Your client was not present. The council denied approval of the plan and notified your client of its decision.

Similar stores are located in this area, and your client claims the council denied the plan because of a dispute he had earlier with one of the council members concerning an approval it gave to a competitive store. Your client also claims his project meets all the criteria of the site plan review ordinance, and that the council should have given its approval. Would you advise suing the city under § 1983? The city council members? What defenses might the council members raise? Assuming the council members do not have an absolute immunity, can you think of any cases that established a "clear" constitutional right sufficient to deny them a good faith immunity defense?

[2.] Barriers to Judicial Relief: Ripeness

Ripeness is a judicial doctrine that determines when a case is ready for adjudication in federal court. Ripeness is jurisdictional: a federal court does not have jurisdiction of a case that is not ripe. The Supreme Court adopted ripeness rules for land use cases during a time when landowners were pressing the court to decide whether the federal Constitution requires compensation for land use takings. In several of these cases, the Court held the takings claim was not ripe to avoid deciding this question. In so doing, the Court set up barriers to suits on takings claims in federal court that have substantially closed the federal courthouse door. Many federal courts also apply the ripeness rules to due process and equal protection claims.

There are several prongs to the land use ripeness rules: a landowner must make at least one meaningful application for approval of her development and must reapply if the application is rejected; the local land use agency must make a final decision on the application; the landowner must apply for a variance or other available administrative relief from an adverse decision; and the landowner must sue in state court for compensation if a state compensation remedy is available. This last requirement is decisive, because the federal courts have held that practically all states have the required compensation remedy.

The Supreme Court adopted the ripeness rules in the following decision:

WILLIAMSON COUNTY REGIONAL PLANNING COMMISSION v. HAMILTON BANK OF JOHNSON CITY

473 U.S. 172 (1985)

JUSTICE BLACKMUM delivered the opinion of the Court.

Respondent, the owner of a tract of land it was developing as a residential subdivision, sued petitioners, the Williamson County (Tennessee) Regional Planning Commission and its members and staff, in United States District Court, alleging that petitioners' application of various zoning laws and regulations to respondent's property amounted to a "taking" of that property. At trial, the jury agreed and awarded respondent $350,000 as just compensation for the "taking." . . . Petitioners and their *amici* urge this Court to overturn the jury's award on the ground that a temporary regulatory interference with an investor's profit expectation does not constitute a "taking" within the meaning of the Just Compensation Clause of the Fifth Amendment, or, alternatively, on the ground that even if such interference does constitute a taking, the Just Compensation Clause does not require money damages as recompense. Before we reach those contentions, we examine the procedural posture of respondent's claim.

I

A . . .

[Under Tennessee law, the legislative body is responsible for zoning, while the planning commission is responsible for regulations governing the subdivision of land and must approve a plat for a subdivision before it can be recorded.] [I]n 1973 [the county] adopted a zoning ordinance that allowed "cluster" development of residential areas. Under "cluster" zoning, "both the size and the width of individual residential lots in . . . [a] development may be reduced, provided . . . that the overall density of the entire tract remains constant — provided, that is, that an area equivalent to the total of the areas thus 'saved' from each individual lot is pooled and retained as common open space." 2 N. Williams, American Land Planning Law § 47.01, pp. 212–213 (1974).

Cluster zoning thus allows housing units to be grouped, or "clustered" together, rather than being evenly spaced on uniform lots. . . .

[R]espondent's predecessor-in-interest (developer) in 1973 submitted a preliminary plat for the cluster development of its tract, the Temple Hills Country Club Estates (Temple Hills), to the Williamson County Regional Planning Commission for approval. At that time, the county's zoning ordinance and the Commission's subdivision regulations required developers to seek review and approval of subdivision plats in two steps. The developer first was to submit for approval a preliminary plat, or "initial sketch plan," indicating, among other things, the boundaries and acreage of the site, the number of dwelling units and their basic design, the location of existing and proposed roads, structures, lots, utility layouts, and open space, and the contour of the land. Once approved, the preliminary plat served as a basis for the preparation of a final plat. Under the Commission's regulations, however, approval of a preliminary plat "will not constitute acceptance of the final plat." Approval of a preliminary plat lapsed if a final plat was not submitted within one year of the date of the approval, unless the Commission granted an extension of time, or unless the approval of the preliminary plat was renewed. The final plat, which is the official authenticated document that is recorded, was required to conform substantially to the preliminary plat, and, in addition, to include such details as the lines of all streets, lots, boundaries, and building setbacks. . . .

[The Commission approved the developer's preliminary plat on May 3, 1973. It included 676 acres with 260 acres in open space, primarily as a golf course. A plat notation showed 736 "allowable units for total development, lot lines were drawn for 469 units, and the area for the remaining 276 units was left blank with the notation 'this parcel not to be developed until approved by the planning commission.' " When the plat was approved, the developer conveyed a permanent open space easement for the golf course, and spent approximately three million dollars for the golf course and $500,000 installing sewer and water facilities.] Before housing construction was to begin on a particular section, a final plat of that section was submitted for approval. Several sections, containing a total of 212 units, were given final approval by 1979. The preliminary plat, as well, was reapproved four times during that period.

[In 1977, the county changed its zoning ordinance to the disadvantage of the developer, including a decrease in residential density, and in 1979 it decided that the new ordinance would apply to plats submitted for renewal in Temple Hills.] The Commission then renewed the Temple Hills plat under the ordinances and regulations in effect at that time.

In January 1980, the Commission asked the developer to submit a revised preliminary plat before it sought final approval for the remaining sections of the subdivision. . . . [It found surveying errors, some of the land had been condemned by the state] and the areas marked "reserved for future development" had never been platted. A special committee (Temple Hills Committee) was appointed to work with the developer on the revision of the preliminary plat.

The developer submitted a revised preliminary plat for approval in October 1980. Upon review, the Commission's staff and the Temple Hills Committee noted several problems with the revised plat. First, the allowable density under the zoning ordinance and subdivision regulations then in effect was 548 units, rather than the 736 units claimed under the preliminary plat approved in 1973. The difference reflected a decrease in 18.5 acres for the parkway, a decrease of 66 acres for the 10% deduction for roads, and an exclusion of 44 acres for 50% of the land lying on slopes exceeding a 25% grade. Second, two cul-de-sac roads that had become necessary because of the land taken for the parkway exceeded the maximum length allowed for such roads under the subdivision regulations in effect in both 1980 and 1973. Third, approximately 2,000 feet of road would have grades in excess of the maximum allowed by county road regulations. Fourth, the preliminary plat placed units on land that had grades in excess of 25% and thus was considered undevelopable under the zoning ordinance and subdivision regulations. Fifth, the developer had not fulfilled its obligations regarding the construction and maintenance of the main access road. Sixth, there were inadequate fire protection services for the area, as well as inadequate open space for children's recreational activities. Finally, the lots proposed in the preliminary plat had a road frontage that was below the minimum required by the subdivision regulations in effect in 1980. . . .

[The Commission disapproved the plat because it did not comply with density requirements and because required acreage deductions had not been made. The developer appealed to the County Board of Zoning Appeals for an interpretation of the cluster zoning ordinance as it applied to its subdivision. On November 11, 1980, it held the Commission should apply the zoning and subdivision regulations in effect in 1973 in evaluating the density, and required lots with excessive grades to be measured more favorably to the developer.]

On November 26, [1980] respondent, Hamilton Bank of Johnson City, acquired through foreclosure the property in the Temple Hills subdivision that had not yet been developed, a total of 257.65 acres. This included many of the parcels that had been left blank in the preliminary plat approved in 1973. In June 1981, respondent submitted two preliminary plats to the Commission — the plat that had been approved in 1973 and subsequently reapproved several times, and a plat indicating respondent's plans for the undeveloped areas, which was similar to the plat submitted by the developer in 1980. The new plat proposed the development of 688 units; the reduction from 736 units represented respondent's concession that 18.5 acres should be removed from the acreage because that land had been taken for the parkway.

On June 18, the Commission disapproved the plat for eight reasons, including the density and grade problems cited in the October 1980 denial, as well as the objections the Temple Hills Committee had raised in 1980 to the length of two cul-de-sacs, the grade of various roads, the lack of fire protection, the disrepair of the main-access road, and the minimum frontage. . . . The Commission declined to follow the decision of the Board of Zoning Appeals that the plat should be evaluated by the 1973 zoning ordinance and subdivision regulations, stating that the Board lacked jurisdiction to hear appeals from the Commission.

B

Respondent then filed this suit in the United States District Court for the Middle District of Tennessee, pursuant to 42 U.S.C. § 1983, alleging that the Commission had taken its property without just compensation and asserting that the Commission should be estopped under state law from denying approval of the project. Respondent's expert witnesses testified that the design that would meet each of the Commission's eight objections would allow respondent to build only 67 units, 409 fewer than respondent claims it is entitled to build, and that the development of only 67 sites would result in a net loss of over $1 million. Petitioners' expert witness, on the other hand, testified that the Commission's eight objections could be overcome by a design that would allow development of approximately 300 units. . . .

[The jury awarded the developer $350,000 in damages for a taking, but the court granted judgment notwithstanding the verdict because it believed a temporary deprivation of economic benefit was not a taking. The court of appeal reversed, and the Court granted certiorari to determine whether compensation was payable for a temporary taking, but decided the case was premature. While the developer's appeal was pending in the Court of Appeals, the parties reached an agreement under which the Commission granted a variance from its cul-de-sac and road-grade regulations and approved the development of 476 units. The developer agreed, among other promises, to rebuild existing roads and build all new roads in compliance with current regulations.]

III

. . . Because respondent has not yet obtained a final decision regarding the application of the zoning ordinance and subdivision regulations to its property, nor utilized the procedures Tennessee provides for obtaining just compensation, respondent's [takings] claim is not ripe.

A

As the Court has made clear in several recent decisions, a claim that the application of government regulations effects a taking of a property interest is not ripe until the government entity charged with implementing the regulations has reached a final decision regarding the application of the regulations to the property at issue. In *Hodel v. Virginia Surface Mining & Reclamation Ass'n, Inc.*, 452 U.S. 264 (1981), for example, the Court rejected a claim that the Surface Mining Control and Reclamation Act of 1977, 30 U.S.C. § 1201 et seq., effected a taking because:

> "There is no indication in the record that appellees have availed themselves of the opportunities provided by the Act to obtain administrative relief by requesting either a variance from the approximate-original-contour requirement of § 515(d) or a waiver from the surface mining restrictions in § 522(e). If [the property owners] were to seek administrative relief under these procedures, a mutually acceptable solution might well be reached with regard to individual properties, thereby obviating any need to address the constitutional questions. The potential for such administrative solutions confirms the conclusion that the taking issue decided by the District Court simply is not ripe for judicial resolution." 452 U.S., at 297 (footnote omitted).

Similarly, in *Agins v. Tiburon*, 447 U.S. 255 (1980), the Court held that a challenge to the application of a zoning ordinance was not ripe because the property owners had not yet submitted a plan for development of their property. . . .

Respondent argues that it "did everything possible to resolve the conflict with the commission," and that the Commission's denial of approval for respondent's plat was equivalent to a denial of variances. . . . [The Court found the developer had never applied for a variance.] Thus, in the face of respondent's refusal to follow the procedures for requesting a variance, and its refusal to provide specific information about the variances it would require, respondent hardly can maintain that the Commission's disapproval of the preliminary plat was equivalent to a final decision that no variances would be granted.

As in *Hodel*, *Agins*, and *Penn Central* [the Court's discussion of *Penn Central* is omitted], then, respondent has not yet obtained a final decision regarding how it will be allowed to develop its property. Our reluctance to examine taking claims until such a final decision has been made is compelled by the very nature of the inquiry required by the Just Compensation Clause. Although "[the] question of what constitutes a 'taking' for purposes of the Fifth Amendment has proved to be a problem of considerable difficulty," *Penn Central Transp. Co. v. New York City*, 438 U.S., at 123, this Court consistently has indicated that among the factors of particular significance in the inquiry are the economic impact of the challenged action and the extent to which it interferes with reasonable investment-backed expectations. *Id.*, at 124. Those factors simply cannot be evaluated until the administrative agency has arrived at a final, definitive position regarding how it will apply the regulations at issue to the particular land in question.

Here, for example, the jury's verdict indicates only that it found that respondent would be denied the economically feasible use of its property if it were forced to develop the subdivision in a manner that would meet each of the Commission's eight objections. It is not clear whether the jury would have found that the respondent had been denied all reasonable beneficial use of the property had any of the eight objections been met through the grant of a variance. Indeed, the expert witness who testified regarding the economic impact of the Commission's actions did not itemize the effect of each of the eight objections, so the jury would have been unable to discern how a grant of a variance from any one of the regulations at issue would have affected the profitability of the development. Accordingly, until the Commission determines that no variances will be granted, it is impossible for the jury to find, on this record, whether respondent "will be unable to derive economic benefit" from the land.

Respondent asserts that it should not be required to seek variances from the regulations because its suit is predicated upon 42 U.S.C. § 1983, and there is no requirement that a plaintiff exhaust administrative remedies before bringing a § 1983 action. *Patsy v. Florida Board of Regents*, 457 U.S. 496 (1982). The question whether administrative remedies must be exhausted is conceptually distinct, however, from the question whether an administrative action must be final before it is judicially reviewable. While the policies underlying the two concepts often overlap, the finality requirement is concerned with whether the initial decisionmaker has arrived at a definitive position on the issue that inflicts an actual, concrete injury; the exhaustion requirement generally refers to administrative and judicial procedures by which an injured party may seek review of an adverse decision and obtain a remedy if the decision is found to be unlawful or otherwise inappropriate. *Patsy* concerned the latter, not the former.

The difference is best illustrated by comparing the procedure for seeking a variance with the procedures that, under *Patsy*, respondent would not be required to exhaust. While it appears that the State provides procedures by which an aggrieved property owner may seek a declaratory judgment regarding the validity of zoning and planning actions taken by county authorities [case and statutory citation omitted], respondent would not be required to resort to those procedures before bringing its § 1983 action, because those procedures clearly are remedial. Similarly, respondent would not be required to appeal the Commission's rejection of the preliminary plat to the Board of Zoning Appeals, because the Board was empowered, at most, to review that rejection, not to participate in the Commission's decisionmaking.

Resort to those procedures would result in a judgment whether the Commission's actions violated any of respondent's rights. In contrast, resort to the procedure for obtaining variances would result in a conclusive determination by the Commission whether it would allow respondent to develop the subdivision in the manner respondent proposed. The Commission's refusal to approve the preliminary plat does not determine that issue; it prevents respondent from developing its subdivision without obtaining the necessary variances, but leaves open the possibility that respondent may develop the subdivision according to its plat after obtaining the variances. In short, the Commission's denial of approval does not conclusively determine whether respondent will be denied all reasonable beneficial use of its property, and therefore is not a final, reviewable decision.

B

A second reason the taking claim is not yet ripe is that respondent did not seek compensation through the procedures the State has provided for doing so. The Fifth Amendment does not proscribe the taking of property; it proscribes taking without just compensation. Nor does the Fifth Amendment require that just compensation be paid in advance of, or contemporaneously with, the taking; all that is required is that a " 'reasonable, certain and adequate provision for obtaining compensation' " exist at the time of the taking. *Regional Rail Reorganization Act Cases*, 419 U.S. 102, 124–125 (1974) (quoting *Cherokee Nation v. Southern Kansas R. Co.*, 135 U.S. 641, 659 (1890)). If the government has provided

an adequate process for obtaining compensation, and if resort to that process "[yields] just

compensation," then the property owner "has no claim against the Government" for a taking. Thus, we have held that taking claims against the Federal Government are premature until the property owner has availed itself of the process provided by the Tucker Act, 28 U.S.C. § 1491. [*Ruckelshaus v.*] *Monsanto* [*Co.*], 467 U.S. [986] at 1016–1020 [1984]. Similarly, if a State provides an adequate procedure for seeking just compensation, the property owner cannot claim a violation of the Just Compensation Clause until it has used the procedure and been denied just compensation.

The recognition that a property owner has not suffered a violation of the Just Compensation Clause until the owner has unsuccessfully attempted to obtain just compensation through the procedures provided by the State for obtaining such compensation is analogous to the Court's holding in *Parratt v. Taylor*, 451 U.S. 527 (1981). There, the Court ruled that a person deprived of property through a random and unauthorized act by a state employee does not state a claim under the Due Process Clause merely by alleging the deprivation of property. In such a situation, the Constitution does not require predeprivation process because it would be impossible or impracticable to provide a meaningful hearing before the deprivation. Instead, the Constitution is satisfied by the provision of meaningful postdeprivation process. Thus, the State's action is not "complete" in the sense of causing a constitutional injury "unless or until the state fails to provide an adequate postdeprivation remedy for the property loss." *Hudson v. Palmer*, 468 U.S. 517, 532, n. 12 (1984). Likewise, because the Constitution does not require pretaking compensation, and is instead satisfied by a reasonable and adequate provision for obtaining compensation after the taking, the State's action here is not "complete" until the State fails to provide adequate compensation for the taking.

Under Tennessee law, a property owner may bring an inverse condemnation action to obtain just compensation for an alleged taking of property under certain circumstances. Tenn. Code Ann. § 29-16-123 (1980). The statutory scheme for eminent domain proceedings outlines the procedures by which government entities must exercise the right of eminent domain. §§ 29-16-101 to 29-16-121. The State is prohibited from "[entering] upon [condemned] land" until these procedures have been utilized and compensation has been paid the owner, § 29-16-122, but if a government entity does take possession of the land without following the required procedures, "the owner of such land may petition for a jury of inquest, in which case the same proceedings may be had, as near as may be, as hereinbefore provided; or he may sue for damages in the ordinary way . . . ." § 29-16-123.

The Tennessee state courts have interpreted § 29-16-123 to allow recovery through inverse condemnation where the "taking" is effected by restrictive zoning laws or development regulations. *See Davis v. Metropolitan Govt. of Nashville*, 620 S.W.2d 532, 533–534 (Tenn. App. 1981); *Speight v. Lockhart*, 524 S.W.2d 249 (Tenn. App. 1975). Respondent has not shown that the inverse condemnation procedure is unavailable or inadequate, and until it has utilized that procedure, its taking claim is premature. . . .

V

In sum, respondent's claim is premature, whether it is analyzed as a deprivation of property without due process under the Fourteenth Amendment, or as a taking under the Just Compensation Clause of the Fifth Amendment. We therefore reverse the judgment of the Court of Appeals and remand the case for further proceedings consistent with this opinion.

It is so ordered.

NOTES AND QUESTIONS

1. *The reapplication rule. MacDonald, Sommer & Frates v. Yolo County*, 477 U.S. 340 (1986), made federal litigation even more difficult by adding a requirement that a second application is necessary after a first application is rejected. The county rejected a subdivision map submitted by plaintiff proposing subdivision of its land into single-family and multi-family residential lots. Plaintiff filed suit in state court and appealed to the Supreme Court after a state appellate court affirmed the dismissal of its complaint. The Supreme Court again held the case was not ripe:

> [The landowner] has submitted one subdivision proposal and has received the Board's response thereto. Nevertheless, [the landowner] still has yet to receive the Board's "final, definitive position regarding how it will apply the regulations at issue to the particular land in question." . . . [T]he holding of both courts below leave open the possibility that some development will be permitted. [*Id.* at 351–52, quoting *Williamson County.*]

2. *More on the final decision requirement.* The Court found a decision final in *Palazzolo*, discussed *supra.* It held the plaintiff had obtained a final decision when the state agency denied two applications to develop in wetlands. It concluded that no doubt remained concerning the extent of development the agency would allow due to a failure to explore other uses for the property that would involve filling substantially less wetlands. It was also clear that a special exception would not have been available. The fact-specific holding in the case may limit its value in establishing finality in other cases, however.

State law does not control the final decision requirement in federal court. A decision may be final under state law, but not final enough for federal jurisdiction. A formal denial is not necessary, however. It is enough if the agency's decision is the functional equivalent of a denial. In *A.A. Profiles, Inc. v. City of Ft. Lauderdale*, 850 F.2d 1483 (11th Cir. 1988), the court held there was a final decision when the city stopped a project by suspending project approval and then downzoning the property.

The federal courts have followed Supreme Court dicta that the submission of "grandiose" plans is not enough. A developer in Hawaii, for example, was required to scale down plans for a beach hotel. *Kaiser Dev. Co. v. City & County of Honolulu*, 649 F. Supp. 926 (D. Haw. 1986), *aff'd*, 898 F.2d 112 (9th Cir. 1990). Must a developer seek to compromise with a city? *Landmark Land Co. v. Buchanan*, 874 F.2d 717 (10th Cir. 1989) (yes, unless this would result in excessive delay).

The Supreme Court has held that the final decision rules do not apply to facial takings claims. E.g., *Lucas v. South Carolina Coastal Council*, 505 U.S. 1003, 1014 n.4 ("Facial challenges are ripe when the act is passed; applied challenges require a final decision on the act's application to the properly in question."). What do you suppose the reason is for making this exception? The Court in *Lucas* emphasized that the *Williamson County* requirements were prudential, rather than constitutional, thus allowing courts a degree of flexibility in applying them. For example, in *Guggenheim v. City of Goleta*, 582 F.3d 996 (9th Cir. 2009), the court emphasized the prudential nature of *Williamson County* in concluding that the court was not required to raise the ripeness issue *sua sponte* and that the city had "forfeited the claim that this case was not ripe for review by failing to raise it." *Id.* at 1009.

3. *Variances and administrative relief. Williamson County* required landowners to seek administrative relief through a variance in order to comply with the ripeness rules. As will be

seen in Chapter 6, state courts have long imposed an identical requirement as part of the rule that plaintiffs must exhaust administrative remedies before suing in court. Yet *Williamson County* distinguished the ripeness requirement from exhaustion of remedies, which is not required under § 1983. Does this distinction make sense? A landowner need not apply for a variance if it is not available. *Schulz v. Milne*, 849 F. Supp. 708 (N.D. Cal. 1994). Should he have to appeal a denial of a variance to a court if it is denied? The courts are divided. See *Bannum, Inc. v. City of Ft. Lauderdale*, 996 F. Supp. 1230 (S.D. Fla. 1997) (holding no). What about a map amendment to the zoning ordinance or a comprehensive plan? There is some confusion in the courts on this point, and you should reconsider this issue after you study zoning amendments in Chapter 6. See *Tahoe-Sierra Preservation Council v. Tahoe Regional Plan. Agency (II)*, 938 F.2d 153 (9th Cir. 1991) (need not apply for amendment to comprehensive plan).

4. *The futility rule.* In *Yolo County*, the Supreme Court indicated that repeated "futile" applications need not be made. Some lower federal courts have followed this suggestion. For example, what if a developer's proposal for five dwelling units on 60 acres complies with the zoning ordinance, but is rejected because environmental problems make it inconsistent with the comprehensive plan? The property is then downzoned to require 40 acres for each dwelling unit in order to comply with the plan's environmental policies. The court held that reapplication would be futile in *Hoehne v. County of San Benito*, 870 F.2d 529 (9th Cir. 1989). Why didn't the court require reapplication under the new zoning ordinance for one dwelling unit? There is a similar futility exception to the state court requirement that plaintiffs must exhaust administrative remedies before bringing suit. The federal courts are not yet clear on how the futility rule should be applied. A First Circuit rent control case provided one statement of what is required. There must be special circumstances indicating a permit application is not a "viable option," or that the local authority has "dug in its heels" and made it abundantly clear that the permit will not be granted. *Gilbert v. City of Cambridge*, 932 F.2d 51 (1st Cir. 1991). In *Holt v. Town of Stonington*, 2010 U.S. Dist. LEXIS 62964 * 15 (D. Conn. 2010), the federal District Court for the District of Connecticut refused to accept a futility rule argument because plaintiff's "failure to allege even one application for a variance is sufficient, as a matter of law, to prevent her from relying on the futility exception."

The reapplication and futility rules are interconnected. See *Southview Assoc., Ltd. v. Bongartz*, 980 F.2d 84 (2d Cir. 1992), requiring reapplication when the municipality did not indicate that the landowner's development was effectively barred. How does a landowner know which to choose?

5. *The state compensation remedy. Williamson County* held that plaintiffs must seek compensation in state court if a state remedy is available before suing in federal court. Lower federal courts have seized on this requirement to bar land use claims by finding that a state compensation remedy is available. *Dahlen v. Shelter House*, 598 F.3d 1007 (8th Cir. 2010) (proposed homeless shelter meets public purpose standard, so adjacent mobile home park owner must seek compensation in state court before federal takings claim is ripe); *Muscarello v. Ogle County Bd. of Comm'rs*, 610 F.3d 416 (7th Cir. 2010) (no basis for excusing plaintiffs from exhaustion requirement in challenge to permit granted for wind farm on adjacent property). Some hold a plaintiff must seek compensation in state court even if the availability of this remedy is not clear, until the state court holds the remedy is not available. *Deniz v. Municipality of Guaynabo*, 285 F.3d 142 (1st Cir. 2002). Is this a correct interpretation of *Williamson County*?

The state compensation remedy requirement became even more complex after the Supreme Court decided in *First English*, reproduced *supra*, that a direct remedy under the federal Constitution is available to seek compensation in land use cases. The federal Constitution is enforceable in state courts. Should a federal court hold a claim can never be ripe because a plaintiff can always sue for compensation on the federal Constitution in state court? Some courts have taken this position, but a Ninth Circuit case held to the contrary, reasoning that otherwise plaintiffs could never bring takings claims in federal court. *Dodd v. Hood River County*, 59 F.3d 852 (9th Cir. 1995).

6. *The standing requirement.* As discussed in Chapter 3 *infra*, the standing requirement can be difficult for third parties who wish to challenge land use regulatory decisions. Two Ohio appellate courts emphasized this point in denying standing to landowners seeking to bring takings challenge, against rezoning decisions in neighboring municipalities. In *Clifton v. Village of Blanchester*, 2010 Ohio App. LEXIS 1903 **13 (Ohio App. 2010), the court concluded that a non-resident landowner did not have standing to challenge on takings grounds a rezoning to allow more intensive development of adjacent property located totally within the village because the decision "did not hinder Clifton's use of his own property in any way. . . . [and the municipality's powers] do not include the power of eminent domain beyond the geographical limits of the municipality." Calling the issue one of first impression, the court reviewed cases granting third party standing and found them unpersuasive. Accord, *Moore v. Middletown*, 2010 Ohio App. LEXIS 2464 (Ohio App. 2010).

7. *Returning to federal court.* The Supreme Court has now held that a plaintiff who sues in state court to ripen her federal takings claim may not return to federal court. *San Remo Hotel, L.P. v. City & County of San Francisco*, 545 U.S. 323 (2005). Plaintiffs attempted to reserve their federal takings claim when returning to state court after the federal district court abstained. Because they broadened their state action to address the federal claims they had reserved, they were barred by 28 U.S.C. § 1738, the full faith and credit statute, from returning to federal court. No exception to that bar could be created without congressional action. The late Chief Justice Rehquist suggested, in a concurring opinion, that the ripeness rule adopted in *Williamson County* that requires a state suit for compensation to ripen a federal takings claim, was incorrect and should be repudiated.

The situation is different, however, if a municipality wants to remove a case to federal court. In *City of Chicago v. International College of Surgeons*, 522 U.S. 156 (1997), a plaintiff sued a city in state court to challenge an administrative determination refusing a demolition permit for historically designated property and raised federal takings and other constitutional claims along with state law claims. The Court held the city could remove the case to federal court rather than try it in state court. It is not clear whether the Court simply found federal question jurisdiction adequate for removal, or whether it held a municipality can remove an unripe takings claim to federal court if it is sued in state court. Landowners claim the decision unfairly favors local government. See *Kottschade v. City of Rochester*, 319 F.3d 1038 (8th Cir. 2003) (*International College* does not overrule *Williamson County*). The Federal District Court for Utah, applying language from *San Remo Hotel*,, held that the court could entertain alternate federal claims, as well as state claims, because the defendant had removed the case to federal court. The court found "no basis for dismissing the federal claims on the grounds of ripeness or finality." *Merrill v. Summit County*, 2009 U.S. Dist. LEXIS 16056 (D. Utah 2009).

8. *Equal protection and due process claims.* There is language in *Yolo County* indicating that the ripeness rules apply to substantive due process and equal protection claims, and a number of federal courts have taken that position. See, e.g., *Muscarello v. Ogle County Bd. of Com'rs, supra; Sameric Corp. v. City of Philadelphia*, 142 F.3d 582 (3d Cir. 1998). A Ninth Circuit panel initially held the ripeness rules do not apply to these claims because they do not require factual inquiries into the economic loss imposed by land use regulations. It then amended its opinion and held the ripeness rules applied. *Herrington v. Sonoma County*, 834 F.2d 1488 (9th Cir. 1987), *amended*, 857 F.2d 567 (9th Cir. 1988). A procedural due process claim that is part of a takings claim is subject to the ripeness rules. *Braun v. Ann Arbor Charter Twp.*, 519 F.3d 564 (6th Cir.), *cert. denied*, 129 S. Ct. 628 (2008).

Other circuits have held that some or all of the ripeness rules do not apply. Construing the ripeness rules of *Williamson County* "broadly," the Seventh Circuit Court of Appeals held that a "bona fide equal protection claim," such as an allegation of ill will or malice by zoning officials toward the plaintiff, is not subject to the *Williamson County* ripeness rules. *Flying J, Inc. v. City of New Haven*, 549 F.3d 538 (7th Cir. 2008). In *McKenzie v. Whitehall*, 112 F.3d 313 (8th Cir. 1997), the court held that only the final decision rule applies, not the rule that suit must be brought in state court first when there is a state compensation remedy. This view at least allows a landowner into federal court to make a finality claim, which may be less stringently applied in equal protection and due process cases. E.g., *Bannum, Inc. v. City of Louisville*, 958 F.2d 1354 (6th Cir. 1992) (proceedings must have reached some sort of "impasse," and position of the parties must be defined). Other cases have held the ripeness rules do not apply to facial due process and equal protection claims. *Smithfield Concerned Citizens for Fair Zoning v. Town of Smithfield*, 907 F.2d 239 (1st Cir. 1990). See Note, *Determining Ripeness of Substantive Due Process Claims Brought by Landowners Against Local Governments*, 95 Mich. L. Rev. 492 (1996).

9. *Criticism of Williamson County.* For an example of the "sisyphean task" *Williamson County* "has created for plaintiffs who seek to have their federal takings claims adjudicated in federal court," see *Los Altos El Granada Investors v. City of Capitola*, 583 F.3d 674, 678 (9th Cir. 2009) ("After a full complement of administrative appeals, three California Superior Court decisions, a California Court of Appeal decision, three federal district court decisions, and one prior federal appellate decision," a federal district court held that plaintiff's efforts at exhaustion had created a bar to subsequent federal action. The Ninth Circuit reversed.). For a strong criticism of the *Williamson County* rule, see *Del-Prairie Stock Farm, Inc. v. County of Walworth*, 572 F. Supp. 2d 1031 (E.D. Wis. 2008).

> The requirement that a federal takings plaintiff must first litigate its claim in state court has led to a number of serious problems. First, it prevents most plaintiffs from ever litigating their claims in federal court. Title 28 U.S.C. § 1738 requires that federal courts give "full faith and credit" to state court judgments. Thus, issue preclusion bars federal court relitigation of any issue decided in a state court, and claim preclusion bars relitigation of any issue that could have been raised. These doctrines are important in connection with federal takings claims because almost every state has a compensation provision similar to the federal provision. . . . Thus, a takings plaintiff trying to get into federal court faces a "true 'Catch 22' conundrum"; it cannot bring its claim in federal court without litigating in state court, but once it litigates in state court, its federal claim is precluded. . . .
>
> A further problem is that the *Williamson County* Court appears to have mischaracterized the state litigation requirement as a ripeness rule when, in actuality, it strips federal courts of jurisdiction over federal takings claims. . . . [T]he purpose of the

> ripeness doctrine is to ensure that a federal court does not hear a case unless the case involves a concrete injury, and the state litigation requirement does not serve that purpose. . . . This is so because a concrete takings injury can occur without state litigation. . . . A property owner can suffer a concrete injury — as the plaintiff in the present case allegedly did — whether or not a legal right was violated. [572 F. Supp. 2d at 1032-1033.]

Rather than dismissing the case for lack of subject matter jurisdiction, which the court thought would be unfair, the court remanded the case to the state court.

10. *A statutory remedy?* The ripeness rules have effectively kept as-applied takings cases out of the federal courts. Concern about this outcome led to congressional legislation, first introduced in 1998, that would have modified the final decision rule and repealed the requirement that suit be brought first in state court when a state compensation remedy is available. The bill passed the House but could not command a cloture vote to stop a filibuster in the Senate. The constitutionality of the compensation repeal provision has been questioned. Kidalov & Seamon, *The Missing Pieces of the Debate Over Federal Property Rights Legislation*, 27 Hastings Const. L.Q. 1 (1999). For discussion, see *Testimony of Daniel R. Mandelker on H.R. 1534 Before the House Judiciary Committee*, 31 Urb. Law. 323 (1999).

The federal ripeness rules suggest the need for state legislation especially, as Chapter 6 will note, since state courts are applying these rules in state cases. Model state land use legislation proposed by the American Planning Association makes a decision final for purposes of review in state court if "(a) an application for a development permit is complete or deemed complete . . . ; and (b) the local government has approved the application, has approved the application with conditions, or has denied the application; or (c) the application is deemed approved" because the local government did not make a decision within required time limits. American Planning Association, Growing Smart Legislative Guidebook: Model Statutes for Planning and Management of Change § 10-603(2) (S. Meck ed., 2002). Paragraph (c) is optional. Under Florida law, the local government must issue a ripeness decision if a landowner requests compensation for an action by government that "inordinately burdens" a property right, an action that is less than a taking. Fla. Stat. Ann. § 70.001(5)(a).

The model law includes detailed provisions on the completeness requirement. *Id.* § 10-203. Some states have this requirement. Wash. Rev. Code § 36.70B.070.

11. *Sources.* For additional discussion of ripeness problems, see Breemer, *Ripeness Madness: The Expansion of* Williamson County's *Baseless "State Procedures" Takings Ripeness Requirements to Non-Takings Claims*, 41 Urb. Law. 615 (2009); Keller, *Judicial Jurisdiction Stripping Masquerading as Ripeness: Eliminating the Williamson County State Litigation Requirement for RegulatoryTakings Claims*, 85 Tex. L. Rev. 199 (2006); Berger & Kanner, *Shell Game! You Can't Get There from Here: Supreme Court Ripeness Jurisprudence in Takings Cases at Long Last Reaches the Self-Parody Stage*, 36 Urb. Law. 671 (2004); Breemer, *Overcoming Williamson County's Troubling State Procedures Rule: How the England Reservation Issue Preclusion Exceptions, and the Inadequacy Exception Open the Federal Courthouse Door to Ripe Takings Claims*, 18 J. Land Use & Envtl. L. 209 (2003); Roberts, *Procedural Implications of Williamson/First English in Regulatory Takings Legislation: Reservations, Removal, Diversity, Supplemental Jurisdiction, Rooker-Feldman, and Res Judicata*, 31 Envt. L. Rep. 10350 (2001); Berger, *Supreme Bait & Switch: The Ripeness Ruse in Regulatory Takings*, 3 Wash. U. J. L. & Pol'y 99 (2000); Delaney & Desisiderio, *Who*

Will Clean Up the Ripeness Mess? A Call for Reform so Takings Plaintiffs Can Enter the Federal Courthouse, 31 Urb. Law. 195 (1999).

[3.] Barriers to Judicial Relief: Abstention

Abstention is another doctrine that limits federal court jurisdiction in land use and other cases brought to federal court. The principal theme of the abstention doctrine is that state courts should be allowed to decide cases when there are strong reasons for allowing litigation to be tried in a state, rather than a federal, court. Abstention is optional with the federal judge, who may abstain based on abstention doctrines that originated in three United States Supreme Court cases — *Railroad Comm'n v. Pullman Co.*, 312 U.S. 496 (1941), *Burford v. Sun Oil Co.*, 319 U.S. 315 (1943), and *Younger v. Harris*, 401 U.S. 37 (1971). Though the Supreme Court has often stated that abstention is the exception rather than the rule, federal courts often abstain in land use cases. A plaintiff may return to federal court after presenting its case in state court if she has preserved the federal claim. *England v. Louisiana State Bd. of Medical Examiners*, 375 U.S. 411 (1964).

Pullman abstention. In *Pullman*, the Supreme Court held that federal courts should abstain from exercising their jurisdiction when resolution of a difficult and unsettled question of state law would make a decision on a federal constitutional issue unnecessary. This would especially be the case if the unsettled state law question "touches a sensitive area of social policy upon which the federal courts ought not to enter unless no alternative to its adjudication is open." 312 U.S. at 498.

In *Hawaii Hous. Auth. v. Midkiff*, 467 U.S. 229 (1984), the Court made it clear that a state or local law must be "fairly subject" to an interpretation that would make a decision of federal constitutional questions unnecessary, and must be uncertain and obviously susceptible of a limiting construction, before the abstention doctrine may be applied. See also *Quackenbush v. Allstate Ins. Co.*, 517 U.S. 706 (1996) (federal question might be obviated if state court can interpret ambiguous state law).

The federal courts have applied the *Pullman* abstention doctrine when state law was unsettled. This is especially true in the Ninth Circuit, which has consistently held that land use planning is a sensitive area of social policy under the *Younger* test. *San Remo Hotel v. City & County of San Francisco*, 145 F.3d 1095 (9th Cir. 1998) (definition of residential hotel); *Kollsman v. City of Los Angeles*, 737 F.2d 830 (9th Cir. 1985) (answer to question whether plaintiff's subdivision should be deemed "approved" depended on interlocking state statutes whose interpretation was unsettled). See contra, e.g., *Currier Builders, Inc. v. Town of York*, 146 F. Supp. 2d 71 (D. Me. 2001) (statutory definition of moratorium). Courts are less likely to apply *Pullman* abstention when First Amendment issues are raised in land use cases. *Cinema Arts, Inc. v. Clark County*, 722 F.2d 579 (9th Cir. 1983).

"Mirror image" constitutional problems frequently arise when a defendant asks a federal court to abstain so that a state court can interpret a state constitutional provision that closely parallels a federal constitutional provision — e.g., a state constitutional "taking" clause that closely parallels the Fifth and Fourteenth Amendment "taking" clauses. The Supreme Court held in *Midkiff, supra*, that abstention is inappropriate in such a case.

Burford abstention. In *Burford*, the Supreme Court approved abstention in a case challenging a state regulatory program, and held a court should abstain where federal court action would disrupt "state efforts to establish a coherent policy with respect to a matter of substantial state concern." Federal courts almost universally refuse to apply *Burford* abstention in land use cases because land use regulation is a local function.

Younger abstention. Younger held that federal courts should abstain from enjoining pending criminal court proceedings if the criminal defendant can make an adequate federal defense in the state court proceedings, and if abstention does not cause irreparable injury to the criminal defendant. *Younger* abstention does not often apply in land use cases because criminal prosecution in such cases is uncommon, but examples can be found. See, e.g., *Night Clubs v. City of Fort Smith*, 163 F.3d 475 (8th Cir. 1998) (prosecution of adult uses).

The extension of the *Younger* abstention doctrine to pending state civil proceedings that implicate important state interests, see *Middlesex County Ethics Comm'n v. Garden State Bar Ass'n*, 457 U.S. 423 (1982), and to state administrative proceedings, see *Ohio Civil Rights Comm'n v. Dayton Christian Schools, Inc.*, 477 U.S. 619 (1986), has more potential impact on land use cases. For *Younger* abstention purposes, proceedings by local zoning administrative agencies would seem to qualify as state administrative proceedings.

Sources. For additional discussion of abstention, see Blaesser, *Closing the Federal Courthouse Door on Property Owners: The Ripeness and Abstention Doctrines in Section 1983 Land Use Cases*, 2 Hofstra Prop. L.J. 73 (1989). See also Rehnquist, *Taking Comity Seriously: How to Neutralize the Abstention Doctrine*, 46 Stan. L. Rev. 1049 (1994); Staver, *The Abstention Doctrines: Balancing Comity with Federal Court Intervention*, 28 Seton Hall L. Rev. 1102 (1998).

PROBLEM

A client has told you he has a 500-acre tract of land on the edge of an urbanizing area in your county that he wishes to develop as a residential subdivision. He submitted a plan to the county at a density of eight units to the acre. The county rejected the plan because it exceeded the density of six units to the acre allowed by the zoning ordinance, and because the comprehensive plan designated this area as a no-growth area where development is be delayed until necessary public facilities were available. The county suggested the developer submit a new plan containing affordable housing units, which would entitle him to a density bonus under a state statute and the county ordinance.

The developer does not know whether to proceed with the new submission, which would be costly, or sue in federal court. He is dubious about the county's interest in amending the plan and increasing the zoning density, even if he provides affordable housing, as several county council members are on record as opposing such changes in the area. Moreover, the state court decisions on the state density bonus statute do not clearly indicate density bonuses are available in no-growth areas designated on county plans. What should you advise?

Chapter 3

CONTROL OF LAND USE BY ZONING

A. THE HISTORY AND STRUCTURE OF THE ZONING SYSTEM

[1.] Some History

The origins of modern zoning. The most important form of land use control in developed and developing areas — urban and suburban communities as well as rural areas experiencing development pressure — has been zoning. Edward M. Bassett, the "father of zoning," defined zoning as "the division of land into districts having different regulations." E. Bassett, Zoning 9 (1940). Early examples of zoning may be found in Boston and Los Angeles. But New York City was the first American municipality to adopt a comprehensive zoning ordinance of the modern type. The New York City Building Zone Resolution of 1916, authorized by a 1914 special act of the New York legislature, was based on three years of painstaking research and investigation by a committee of which Bassett was a member.[(1)]

The Building Zone Resolution of 1916 created a complete and comprehensive system of building and land use control for all the five boroughs of New York City. It established three separate classes of districts to regulate, respectively, the use of land and buildings, the height of buildings, and the percentage of a lot that could be occupied by buildings, with a separate set of maps for each class. There were three "use" districts: residential, business, and unrestricted. In the residence districts, business and industry of all types were prohibited. In business districts, specified businesses and industries — mainly nuisance-creating manufacturing businesses such as boiler making, ammonia manufacturing, and paint manufacturing — were prohibited, and all other uses were permitted. In unrestricted districts, all kinds of residential, business, and industrial uses were permitted.

The New York City Building Zone Resolution of 1916 did not apply retroactively to existing, lawfully established uses of land or buildings. As one early commentator stated, "[i]t did not attempt to cure past and existing evils by ordering the demolition of particular types of buildings or removal of certain types of businesses to other areas. But it did prescribe a rational plan for future building in the city." J. McGoldrick, S. Graubard & R. Horowitz, Building Regulation in New York City 93 (1944). (For a more detailed discussion of the

---

(1) The Massachusetts legislature enacted height regulations for the entire city of Boston in 1904–05. These restrictions embodied the "zoning" principle, since there were different maximum heights in different districts. The Boston height restrictions were sustained against constitutional attack in *Welch v. Swasey*, 214 U.S. 91 (1909). In 1909, Los Angeles adopted an ordinance dividing the city into industrial and residential districts. The exclusion of laundries from a residential district was upheld by the California court in *Ex parte Quong Wo*, 118 P. 714 (Cal. 1911). In 1910, Los Angles adopted an ordinance excluding brick factories from one or two of the industrial districts. The 1910 ordinance was sustained against constitutional attack in *Hadacheck v. Sebastian*, [239 U.S. 394 (1915)].

background and drafting of the New York City Building Zone Resolution of 1916, see S. Toll, Zoned America 78-187 (1969)).

Zoning in the Supreme Court. Zoning spread rapidly after the New York court in 1920 upheld the New York City Building Zone Resolution against constitutional attack. *Lincoln Trust Co. v. Williams Bldg. Corp.*, 128 N.E. 209 (N.Y. 1920). In 1922, it was reported that some twenty state zoning enabling acts and fifty municipal zoning ordinances were in force or under consideration. Some municipalities proceeded to adopt zoning ordinances without waiting for enabling legislation, but it was generally believed, and occasionally held, that the broad grant of police power by state legislatures to local units of government, even under home rule constitutional provisions, was insufficient to empower local governments to regulate land use by means of zoning. Hence, where interest in zoning was greatest, the states generally enacted new enabling legislation.

By 1926, all but five of the then forty-eight states had adopted zoning enabling acts; some 420 municipalities with a total population of more than 27,000,000 had adopted zoning ordinances; and hundreds of other municipalities were engaged in preparing zoning ordinances. But judicial acceptance of zoning was far from unanimous in 1926. The highest courts of California, Illinois, Kansas, Louisiana, Massachusetts, Minnesota, New York, Ohio, Oregon, and Wisconsin handed down decisions favorable to the constitutionality of zoning. Adverse decisions came from the highest courts of Delaware, Georgia, Maryland, Missouri, and New Jersey. The future of zoning as a governmental control of private land use was not assured until the Supreme Court, in *Village of Euclid v. Ambler Realty Co.*, reprinted in Chapter 2 as a principal case, held that the new zoning technique, in its general aspects, does not violate the Fourteenth Amendment's Due Process Clause. Although state courts were still free, after *Euclid*, to find that zoning violated *state* constitutional provisions, judicial attention shifted from the concept of zoning to the details of its implementation. (To remove all doubts, some states amended their constitutions to explicitly authorize zoning. See, e.g., N.J. Const. Art. IV, § 6, ¶ 2, initially adopted in 1927.) Michael Allan Wolf adeptly tells the story of *Euclid* in The Zoning of America (2008), detailing the social, political and historical setting and explaining the modern implications of *Euclid* and why it has stood the test of time.

The shift to state law. Two years after the *Euclid* decision, the U.S. Supreme Court signaled that it might be embarking on a course foreshadowed by *Euclid*, namely, close supervision of the exercise of the zoning power "concretely applied to particular premises." In *Nectow v. City of Cambridge*, 277 U.S. 183 (1928), discussed later in this chapter, the Court struck down on substantive due process grounds a residential-use classification as applied to a "split lot" that was partially in the residential zone and partially in an industrial zone. However, after 1928, the Supreme Court consistently refused to review any cases raising legal issues in the planning and zoning field. Having established the basic constitutionality of zoning, the Supreme Court, for nearly four decades, left it to the state courts to apply the constitutional test of reasonableness and the constitutional "taking" test to individual cases in which the exercise of the zoning power was challenged, "as concretely applied to particular premises." Thus, the "American law of zoning" was largely (though not entirely) developed by the decisions of the state courts, with decided differences in legal doctrine and judicial approach in different jurisdictions. For an essay on the persistence of localism, see W. Fischel, *The Evolution of Zoning since the 1980's*, draft of September 2010, available at http://ssrn.com/abstract=1686009.

The Supreme Court tentatively returned to conventional zoning issues in *Goldblatt v. Town of Hempstead*, 369 U.S. 590 (1962), where it sustained what was essentially a zoning ordinance enacted under the town's general police power, prohibiting the mining of sand and gravel to a depth below the water table and requiring the backfilling of any existing excavation below that level. The Court indicated even more interest in land use issues with a 1974 decision on family zoning. Its decision in *Penn Central* in 1978, establishing bedrock principles of takings law arising out of local regulation, was followed less than a decade later with the 1987 trilogy of taking decisions, revitalizing regulatory takings doctrine as a source of land use law. In the years since, it has continued to decide cases with land use implications, including free speech decisions on sign ordinances and "adult" uses. The resulting interplay between state and Supreme Court zoning law is critically important. Since the federal Constitution is directly enforceable in state courts, however, state courts are bound to apply federal law in areas such as takings and free speech. For a proficient overview of the history of zoning and a keen analysis of the assumptions underlying America's zoning ordinances and the efficacy of zoning, see D. Elliott, A Better Way to Zone (2008) (providing ten key principles for simpler, fairer, more effective and more workable zoning laws).

[2.] Zoning Enabling Legislation

It is only a slight exaggeration to say (as many have) that local governments exist for two purposes: to operate public schools and to control the use of land. It thus becomes important to understand how state and local law — constitutional and statutory — shapes the exercise of zoning power at the local level. Indeed, a thorough study of state and local government law, a task well beyond the scope of this book, is essential for anyone contemplating practice in the field of land use controls. A brief introduction is in order, however.

Background: Delegation and Home Rule. In the United States, local governments ("municipal corporations") possess no inherent right of self government. They exist as creatures of the state, created for the purpose of carrying out tasks at the local level that are assigned to them by the state legislature. When this is done, the state is said to have "delegated" authority to the municipality to act on a certain subject. Because the municipality has no inherent legislative power of its own, when disputes arise about the scope of local regulation, it often becomes important to determine whether the legislature has "delegated" a given power to the municipality. If municipalities act outside their delegated authority, such actions are void from the outset and to no legal effect. In virtually all states, the legislature is required to act with respect to municipalities by "general laws" whenever possible, a reform which limits the possibility of specific meddling in the affairs of individual municipalities.

In addition, about half the states have constitutional provisions for "home rule," which allows individual municipalities to handle local matters without a specific delegation of authority from the state legislature. The highest courts in some states have held that their home rule powers authorize the adoption of zoning ordinances, but all states have passed enabling legislation expressly authorizing zoning. It might seem that enabling legislation is unnecessary in "home rule" states, but many courts have found that enabling legislation is still required. Home rule power is granted to municipalities only to the extent that "local" matters are affected, and most states have concluded that zoning is of such statewide concern that the state legislature may continue to control the subject.

As one might suspect, delegating power to local governments, particularly in the form of "general laws" covering a myriad of different situations, provides many opportunities for interpretation of the scope of the grant. "Dillon's Rule," named after a prominent 19th century treatise writer (and judge), is that grants should be narrowly construed. Many states have reversed Dillon's Rule by statute, judicial interpretation, or specific constitutional command (for the latter, see N.J. Const. Art. IV, § 7, ¶ 11). Broad delegations broadly interpreted are now the rule, but it is important to recognize that the underlying doctrinal structure remains. Courts can sometimes rein in an abuse of delegated power at the local level by holding that it violates an ambiguous provision of the zoning enabling act. They can also focus political attention on an issue by refusing to construe a power as within the grant, meaning that the legislature will have to amend the law (with attendant political debate) if it wants a given result. You should be alert to these and other uses of delegation doctrine as you proceed.

The Standard Zoning Enabling Act. All fifty states have zoning enabling legislation for municipalities, and many have zoning enabling legislation for counties. Most of the enabling legislation originally adopted prior to 1924 was based on the New York general city enabling act of 1917. In 1924, however, the U.S. Department of Commerce formally published a Standard Zoning Enabling Act (SSZEA); an earlier, mimeographed version had been circulated in 1923, and the 1924 Act was republished in 1926. This model act was, in fact, a draft "general law" offered to state legislatures for their consideration in enacting legislation to delegate the power to zone to municipalities. In the years after 1926, using the SSZEA as a guide, most states adopted the model act. The Standard Act was itself based on the New York general city enabling act, but departed substantially in some respects from the New York model. Although many current zoning enabling acts embody even more substantial changes from the Standard Act, most state legislation still retains the form and substance of the Standard Act. It therefore is useful to become familiar with the principal provisions of the SSZEA, which are reprinted here. It is available in full in the Statutes section of the casebook web site, www.law.wustl.edu./landuselaw.

A STANDARD STATE ZONING ENABLING ACT[2]

Section 1. *Grant of Power.* For the purpose of promoting health, safety, morals, or the general welfare of the community, the legislative body of cities and incorporated villages is hereby empowered to regulate and restrict the height, number of stories, and size of buildings and other structures, the percentage of lot that may be occupied, the size of yards, courts, and other open spaces, the density of population, and the location and use of buildings, structures, and land for trade, industry, residence, or other purposes.

Sec. 2. *Districts.* For any or all of said purposes the local legislative body may divide the municipality into districts of such number, shape, and area as may be deemed best suited to carry out the purposes of this act; and within such districts it may regulate and restrict the erection, construction, reconstruction, alteration, repair, or use of buildings, structures, or land. All such regulations shall be uniform for each class or kind of building throughout each district, but the regulations in one district may differ from those in other districts.

Sec. 3. *Purposes in View.* Such regulations shall be made in accordance with a comprehensive plan and designed to lessen congestion in the streets; to secure safety from fire, panic, and other dangers; to promote health and the general welfare; to provide adequate

[2] The drafter's footnotes have been omitted. The Standard State Zoning Enabling Act is no longer in print in its original form as a publication of the U.S. Department of Commerce, but it is reprinted in full, with the drafter's footnotes as appendix A, in American Law Institute, A Model Land Development Code, Tentative Draft No. 1, at p. 210 (1968).

light and air; to prevent the overcrowding of land; to avoid undue concentration of population; to facilitate the adequate provision of transportation, water, sewerage, schools, parks, and other public requirements. Such regulations shall be made with reasonable consideration, among other things, to the character of the district and its peculiar suitability for particular uses, and with a view to conserving the value of buildings and encouraging the most appropriate use of land throughout such municipality.

[Sections 4 and 5 dealt with procedures for adopting and changing a zoning ordinance. A "change" is now called an amendment. No standards are provided for amendments. Three-fourths of the members of the legislative body must vote for an amendment if 20% of the owners of the lots included in an amendment or 20% of the owners of adjacent lots protest. Section 6 provided for the establishment of a Zoning Commission, an anachronism that today is almost always replaced by a Planning Commission or Planning Board. — Eds.]

Sec. 7. *Board of Adjustment.* Such local legislative body may provide for the appointment of a board of adjustment, and in the regulations and restrictions adopted pursuant to the authority of this act may provide that the said board of adjustment may, in appropriate cases and subject to appropriate conditions and safeguards, make special exceptions to the terms of the ordinance in harmony with its general purpose and intent and in accordance with general or specific rules therein contained. [Procedures are specified. — Eds.]

The board of adjustment shall have the following powers:

1. To hear and decide appeals where it is alleged there is error in any order, requirement, decision, or determination made by an administrative official in the enforcement of this act or of any ordinance adopted pursuant thereto.

2. To hear and decide special exceptions to the terms of the ordinance upon which such board is required to pass under such ordinance.

3. To authorize upon appeal in specific cases such variance from the terms of the ordinance as will not be contrary to the public interest, where, owing to special conditions, a literal enforcement of the provisions of the ordinance will result in unnecessary hardship, and so that the spirit of the ordinance shall be observed and substantial justice done.

[The remainder of Section 7 specified voting procedures and a method of appeal, Section 8 provided for enforcement and remedies, and Section 9 provided for conflicts between this and other regulations. The statutory provisions for the judicial review of board decisions are reproduced *infra*, in Section B.3. — Eds.]

NOTES AND QUESTIONS

1. *Zoning powers.* Read the first two sections of the act carefully. What is the "zoning" power that these sections confer? What is the power to adopt "districts"? Do you read § 1 of the Standard Act as requiring the local legislative body to divide the municipality into two or more districts? Would a "bedroom suburb" be required to zone at least some land for non-residential uses? See *Village of Belle Terre v. Boraas, infra.*

2. *The comprehensive plan.* What is the "comprehensive plan" mentioned in § 3 of the SSZEA? Can "comprehensive plan" be deemed to refer to the "master plan" authorized by § 6 of the Standard City Planning Enabling Act reproduced in Ch. 1, *supra*? If not, what does the term "comprehensive plan" mean? Must it be a document prepared by the municipal planning commission and adopted by the planning commission or the local governing body? See Ch. 5, sec. G, *infra.*

3. *Amendments and administrative relief.* Sections 5 and 7 contain the provisions for amendments and administrative relief. What do these sections indicate about these methods for change and the regulations contained in zoning district regulations? Section 7, including the parts omitted, is longer than all the rest of the SSZEA put together. Do the drafters imply that "special exceptions" and "variances" are where the real work of zoning is done? Read on.

4. *The politics of the SSZEA.* Although the concept of zoning was born and first implemented in major cities like New York, and it is now practiced widely in all types of communities, even relatively rural ones, undoubtedly its greatest influence has been in America's suburbs. Professor Stahl argues that this was intentional, that the SSZEA was promulgated to empower nascent suburbs as an individualistic counterweight to the influence of center cities, and that the U.S. Supreme Court in *Euclid* well understood that this was its purpose. See Stahl, *The Suburb as a Legal Concept: The Problem of Organization and the Fate of Municipalities in American Law*, 29 Cardozo L. Rev. 1193-1272 (2008).

A NOTE ON CONTEMPORARY APPROACHES TO ZONING ENABLING LEGISLATION

Model Codes. The extraordinary pace and scope of land development after World War II severely tested the SSZEA's simple framework for regulation, leading to several efforts to devise new "models" that might serve local governments better during the second half of the century. These studies are summarized in the American Planning Association's Growing Smart Legislative Guidebook: Model Statutes for Planning and Management of Change, pp. 8-4 through 8-18 (S. Meck ed., 2002), www.planning.org/growingsmart. The most elaborate of these efforts was the American Law Institute's *A Model Land Development Code,* often referred to as the *ALI Code,* published in 1976. More recently, the American Planning Association itself has undertaken a massive study of land development legislation and has now published its own set of "models" in the above-cited *Legislative Guidebook.* The APA does not recommend a single, comprehensive "model code," intended to be adopted *in toto.* Rather, for many issues, it presents a menu of options, from which legislatures can pick and choose to meet their particular needs.

Both the ALI and APA models address the enormous changes that have occurred in land regulation since the 1920s. As one modern legislative finding put it in the preamble to a new enabling act, "The zoning enabling statutes [being repealed] were largely enacted in 1921[.] The character of land development and public and private services have changed substantially in the intervening years [and] it is necessary to provide for innovative land development practices to enable cities and towns to adequately regulate the use of land and employ modern land development practices . . . ." R.I. Stat. Ann. § 45-24-29(a)(2)(i-iii). By its terms, the SSZEA only authorized the adoption of zoning ordinances. "Innovative" regulatory practices, unknown or relatively unimportant in 1920, but later regarded as basic to the land regulation process, such as historic preservation and site plan review, either were added piecemeal by subsequent legislation or were "interpreted into" the SSZEA model by the courts. Neither approach is a satisfactory alternative to a comprehensive statute. Piecemeal legislation leads to gaps, overlaps, lack of clarity, and inconsistencies as various interested parties tug and haul at the legislative process. The alternative of judicial interpretation is almost always uncertain in its result and often transitory, because the legislature can always step in with a different approach, and it is at worst perceived as judicial usurpation of legislative prerogatives.

Reflecting the sophistication and complexity of the land regulation process as it had evolved over the 20th century, first the ALI model and more recently the APA proposal sought to reach the full scope of modern local planning and regulation in a single enabling act. The ALI emphasized the relationship between subdivision regulation and zoning; the current APA "Growing Smart" model proposes that a wide range of regulatory techniques be authorized in a single, internally consistent statute. In addition to zoning and subdivision regulations, the APA model statute includes seventeen other categories of regulations, dealing with: planned unit developments, site plan review, "improvements and exactions," development impact fees, concurrency or adequacy of public facilities, transfer of development rights, "corridor maps," historic preservation or design review, "trip reduction and transportation management," critical and sensitive natural areas, floodplains, stormwater and erosion, "mitigation banking," affordable housing, infill and "brownfields" redevelopment, and development agreements. Most of these techniques will be canvassed in the pages that follow.

A modern enabling act. Zoning remains the backbone of the land regulation regime, however, and it is now rare to find a zoning enabling act as simple as the original SSZEA. Here are excerpts from Rhode Island's revised zoning enabling act, implemented in the early 1990s:

GENERAL LAWS OF RHODE ISLAND TITLE 45

§ 45-24-30 General purposes of zoning ordinances.

Zoning regulations shall be developed and maintained in accordance with a comprehensive plan prepared, adopted, and as may be amended, in accordance with . . . this title and shall be designed to address the following purposes . . . :

(1) Promoting the public health, safety and general welfare.

(2) Providing for a range of uses and intensities of use appropriate to the character of the city or town and reflecting current and expected future needs.

(3) Providing for orderly growth and development . . .
[13 additional listed purposes follow.]

§ 45-24-33 Standard provisions.

(a) A zoning ordinance addresses each of the purposes stated in § 45-24-30 and addresses the following general provisions . . . [There are 23 provisions. Here are some of the most important:]

(1) Permitting, prohibiting, limiting, and restricting the development of land and structures in zoning districts, and regulating those land [sic] and structures according to their type, and the nature and extent of their use;

(2) Regulating the nature and extent of the use of land for residential, commercial, industrial, institutional, recreational, agricultural, open space, or other use or combination of uses, as the need for land for those purposes is determined by the city or town's comprehensive plan;

(3) Permitting, prohibiting, limiting, and restricting buildings, structures, land uses, and

other development by performance standards, or other requirements, related to air and water and groundwater quality, noise and glare, energy consumption, soil erosion and sedimentation, and/or the availability and capacity of existing and planned public or private services;

(4) Regulating within each district and designating requirements for:

(i) The height, number of stories, and size of buildings;

(ii) The dimensions, size, lot coverage, floor area ratios, and layout of lots or development areas;

(iii) The density and intensity of use;

(iv) Access to air and light, views, and solar access;

(v) Open space, yards, courts, and buffers;

(vi) Parking areas, road design, and, where appropriate, pedestrian, bicycle, and other circulator systems;

(vii) Landscaping, fencing, and lighting;

(viii) Appropriate drainage requirements and methods to manage stormwater runoff;

(ix) Public access to waterbodies, rivers, and streams; and

(x) Other requirements in connection with any use of land or structure; . . .

(8) Providing for adequate, safe, and efficient transportation systems; and avoiding congestion by relating types and levels of development to the capacity of the circulation system, and maintaining a safe level of service of the system; . . . [This provision authorizes adequate public facilities ordinances, which are discussed in Chapter 8.]

(19) Providing standards and requirements for the regulation, review, and approval of any proposed development in connection with those uses of land, buildings, or structures specifically designated as subject to development plan review in a zoning ordinance; . . . [This provision authorizes site plan review, which is discussed in Chapter 6.]

[Provisions are also required for regulating development in floodplains, hazardous and historic areas; promoting energy conservation; protecting drinking water; and the application of state and federal fair housing acts. The statute also authorizes "special provisions," including incentive zoning provisions, which are discussed in this chapter, *infra*.]

NOTES AND QUESTIONS

1. *Comparisons.* Both the Rhode Island statute and the APA model act authorize many land use control techniques that were unknown when the SSZEA was promulgated in 1923. Look back at the SSZEA and identify the differences. Does the Standard Act authorize by implication the measures that are explicitly covered by the modern legislation? Are there differences between the Rhode Island statute and the APA model that makes one preferable to the other?

2. *The comprehensive plan.* As discussed in Chapter 1, a very important provision in this modern statute is that the zoning ordinance must be consistent with an *adopted* comprehensive plan. This is a departure from the much more permissive way the Standard Act's "in accordance with a comprehensive plan" language had generally been interpreted. Most states still do not specifically require consistency with the plan in their zoning legislation because most are still based on the Standard Act. This requirement will be considered in some detail later in this casebook.

3. *The role of a general welfare clause.* With its extensive list of specific purposes, why does the Rhode Island statute carry forward from the SSZEA the catch-all purpose to "promot[e] the public health, safety and general welfare." (Note that, as is typical of many modern versions of this clause, promotion of the "morals" of the community has been dropped from the SSZEA text by Rhode Island.) Does this "general welfare clause" add anything that is legally relevant? The APA model act offers drafters two choices: a stripped down version that states only two purposes, implementing the local comprehensive plan and promoting "the public health, safety, environment, morals and general welfare"; and a more detailed version that in addition to invoking the comprehensive plan, includes a long list of purposes similar to Rhode Island's. §§ 8-102, 2-102. Note the atypical insertion of an environmental purpose into the APA's stripped down alternative.

[3.] The Zoning Ordinance

Whatever else their land use enabling acts may contain, all states delegate to local governments the power to enact and enforce *zoning* regulations, the type of regulation upheld by the U.S. Supreme Court in the *Euclid* case, Chapter 2, *supra*. As you read on, consider how and why zoning came to be the predominant regulatory technique over the course of the 20th century, and whether this is a good idea or a bad one.

Section 2 of the Standard State Zoning Enabling Act, and a similar provision in each of the state zoning enabling acts now in force, authorizes but does not require the local governing body to divide the municipality or other unit of local government "into districts of such number, shape, and area as may be deemed best suited to carry out the purposes of" the act. For better or for worse, districting has become the core feature of the modern zoning ordinance, and most legal and policy issues about zoning originate in the choices local officials make in drawing district lines on maps and crafting the language of regulations. As previously indicated, the New York City Zoning Resolution of 1916 divided New York City into three classes of districts designed to regulate, respectively, the use of land and buildings, the height of buildings, and the percentage of a lot that could be occupied by buildings, with a separate set of maps for each class. Residential, business, and unrestricted were the only three use districts. The Euclid, Ohio zoning ordinance sustained in the *Euclid* case, by contrast, provided for six use districts, three height districts, and four area districts, although Euclid was only a small suburban village. Regulations other than those relating to the permitted uses of land and buildings within a district are generally termed "bulk and density" regulations. As we shall see, the distinction between "use" regulations and "bulk" regulations can be legally important, such as when a variance is requested. This problem is taken up in Chapter 6.

As already noted, the typical zoning ordinance of today is much more complex than the relatively simple structure of cumulative classes of regulations for "use," "height," and "land coverage" considered by the *Euclid* court in 1926. Today, there are vast differences between the zoning ordinances adopted in different municipalities and counties and no single example can suffice; you will catch the flavor of the variety as you read the cases that follow.

Don Elliott, in his book A Better Way to Zone (2008), points out that the so-called Euclidean form of zoning, named after the landmark *Euclid* case, is both very durable and clearly flawed. He notes that Euclidean zoning systems today are "actually hybrids that draw on the major innovations of the past ninety years." *Id.* at 129. Innovations such as performance zoning, design and form-based controls, and the approval of new development as planned unit developments have led to many changes in the zoning system. There are others, including historic district and historic landmark regulations and a wide variety of environmental land use regulations. These regulations are often adopted as overlay districts or add-on regulations that supplement but do not replace the traditional Euclidean system of zoning by districts. All of these innovations are discussed later in this book, and have substantially transformed the core concepts of zoning, which rests on the Euclidean zoning district concept. The materials that immediately follow set forth the elements of the traditional Euclidean system.

NOTES AND QUESTIONS

1. *Zoning districts.* The zoning district is the building block of Euclidean zoning. The following chart illustrates a typical zoning format found in many cities, though some have even more zoning districts. Note that the different residential zoning districts are distinguished by density.

A Standard Zoning Format

SR-1, Single-Family Large Lot	One-Acre Lots
SR-2, Single-Family Medium	Half-Acre Lots
SR-3, Single-Family Standard	6,000 Sq. Ft. Lot Minimum
MR-1, Multifamily Low Density	18-26 Units/Acre
MR-2, Multifamily Medium Density	24-29 Units/Acre
MR-3, Multifamily High Density	37-44 Units/Acre
GO, General Office	Offices and Limited Uses Serving Community and City-Wide Needs
NC, Neighborhood Commercial	Neighborhood Retail and Office Facilities
GC, General Community	Commercial Shopping Centers Providing Sub-Regional and Regional Retail and Office Facilities
SC, Service Commercial	Commercial Service Facilities in Central Business Area CBD, Central Business District Office and Commercial Facilities in Central Business Area
LM, Limited Industrial	Light Manufacturing
HM, Heavy Industrial	Heavy Manufacturing
PA, Public Activity	Public Facilities such as Schools, Hospitals and Cemeteries

[Adapted from D. Mandelker, Land Use Law 5-3, 5-4 (5th ed. 2003).]

At the other end of the scale, consider the New York City zoning ordinance, which was comprehensively revised in 2006. It is 3,343 pages (not a typo, it is 3,343 pages long) as of 2010 with all sections and appendices and can be viewed at http://www.nyc.gov/html/dcp/html/zone/

allarticles.pdf. See Dunlap, *New Book Breaks the Code (That's the Zoning Code)*, N.Y. Times, Mar. 19, 2006, at p.31.

2. *The zoning map.* The map that follows is a part of a zoning map from a small suburban community in the St. Louis, Missouri, metropolitan area, and accompanies a zoning ordinance which employs a simplified adaptation of the zoning format reproduced above. The SR (Single-Family Residential) District on the map is the equivalent of the SR-3 District in the zoning format. The MR (Multifamily Residential), NC (Neighborhood Commercial) and GC (General Community Commercial) Districts on the zoning map are the equivalent of the MR-3, NC and GC Districts in the zoning format. What does this tell you about the character of this community?

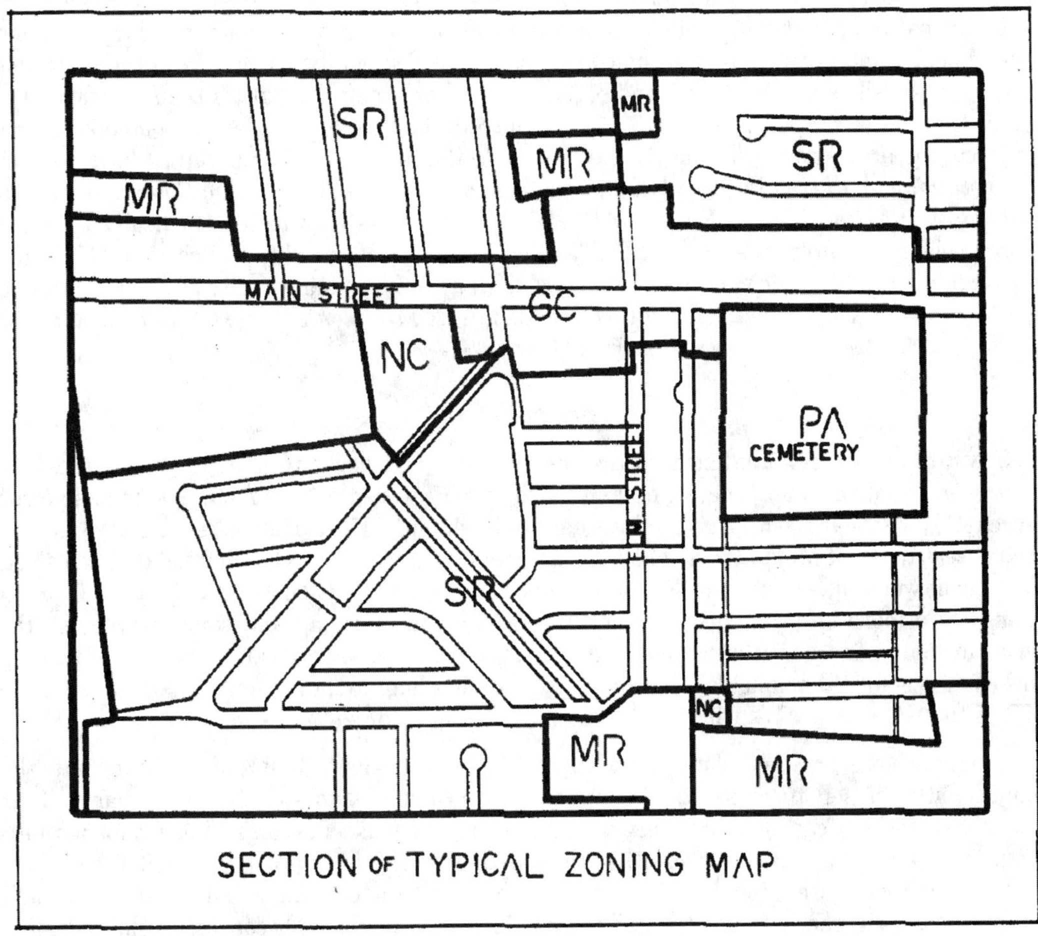

SECTION OF TYPICAL ZONING MAP

Note the large number of zoning districts in a relatively small geographic area. There usually are two reasons for this. First, most zoning plans, most of the time, try to follow established existing uses, unless a conscious planning decision has been made to encourage a use change in the district. Second, the Standard Zoning Act requires that uses be uniform within districts. This makes it difficult to adopt a single district for an area where land uses are mixed, such as in the illustration above. Even before you begin reading the cases in this chapter, consider what legal problems this map might present. Does this approach to land use control complicate zoning administration? Is it consistent with the "market failure" theory of land use controls to use the zoning map to "freeze" privately determined land uses?

3. *Zoning administration.* Zoning codes such as the simplified one reproduced here are intended to be administered by a combination of paid professional employees of the municipality and volunteer members of the community who sit on planning and zoning boards. A large city will usually have a commensurately large professional staff because of the volume of applications to be processed, whereas the numerous small suburban and rural places that regulate land use may have but a single full-time employee (if that), placing substantial reliance on board members, land use "amateurs," to actually make the system work. This is particularly so because the traditional structure of Euclidean zoning, pioneered by the SSZEA and carried forward in various ways by modern enabling acts, requires planning boards and boards of adjustments to make detailed, site-specific decisions about variances, conditional uses, zoning amendments and a host of related matters, many of which will be canvassed in the materials to follow, as well as in Chapters 5 and 6. As you read on, keep this "grass roots" structure in mind. Does it work well or poorly? Does it introduce a desirable element of populism or undercut the professionalism that planners bring to the table? See Salkin, *States Beginning to Recognize that Training Is Essential for Members of Planning and Zoning Boards and Local Legislative Bodies*, 35 Real Estate L.J. (2006). Oregon has a website specifically to assist citizen planners. http://www.oregon.gov/LCD/citizeninvolvement.shtml. See also Michigan Citizen Planner at http://citizenplanner.msu.edu. Mandatory training is discussed in Comment, *A Proposal to Implement Mandatory Training Requirements for Home Rule Zoning Officials*, 2008 Mich. St. L. Rev. 879 (Fall 2008).

PROBLEM

It will help in understanding how the zoning ordinance works to imagine a case in which your client wants a zoning change on a lot in the area covered by this map. Assume she owns a vacant 6,000-square-foot lot in the Multifamily Residential (MR) District on the west side of Elm Street north of Main Street. The lot is adjacent to the General Commercial (GC) District. Your client would like to use this lot for a use permitted in the GC District. This type of zoning change to a more intensive use is typically known as an upzoning, but some people use the terms upzoning and downzoning in exactly the opposite way, so take care. One way of making this change is for the municipality to amend the zoning map to move your client's lot from the MR to the GC district. We will consider zoning map amendments in Chapter 6.

Assume, however, that your client applied for a zoning map amendment, but the municipality refused to make it. One option at this point is to sue the municipality. It is unlikely your client can claim a taking of her property, because she can still use it for a multi-family use. However, she can claim that the existing zoning is arbitrary. Consider how your client can get this case into court, how she can show that the existing zoning is arbitrary, and what remedy she can get if she wins her case. These issues are all considered later in this chapter.

B. ZONING LITIGATION IN STATE COURTS

Most zoning litigation is brought in state courts, and issues of standing and the scope of review shape the process and outcomes. Not just anyone can sue in a zoning case. Special standing rules that apply only to zoning cases determine who can bring such appeals. Exhaustion of remedies is another procedural doctrine that affects zoning litigation. Zoning ordinances provide a number of opportunities for discretionary administrative and legislative decision making on land use proposals. The courts hold that litigants must exhaust these remedies before bringing suit.

To get into court with a zoning appeal, the complainant must either have the right to do so by express statutory authority or demonstrate a direct interest or injury, such as being the applicant or owning property abutting which is adversely affected. The only statutory appeal provided by the Standard State Zoning Enabling Act is an appeal by writ of certiorari from decisions by a board of adjustment, but state enabling statutes have been extensively amended to create and limit the right to appeal. States also have extensive common law precedent interpreting the statutory provisions and also establishing impendent rights to sue.

Although these procedural rules are complex, and vary substantially from state to state, this problem is not usually as serious as it might appear at first glance because of the widespread availability of conventional injunction actions to litigate zoning claims, but some problems still arise. One is that judicial relief may be limited if the appeal is challenging a local legislative decision because of the separation of powers doctrine under which the judiciary may not substitute its judgment for that of the legislature, which can include a local zoning authority acting under state enabling authority in making a map change or amending an ordinance.

PROBLEM

The Willow Hill Neighborhood Association, a group representing a subdivision of attractive single-family homes, is upset by a decision of the city council rezoning land on one edge and across the street from the subdivision for a multifamily residential development. The land previously was zoned for single-family development on three-acre lots. The homes in the Willow Creek subdivision are on half-acre lots. They wish to bring a lawsuit claiming the rezoning is invalid. Can they bring suit? What kind of action should they bring? If they win, what kind of relief can they get from the court? Will it solve all their problems with this tract of land? What if the would-be plaintiff is the owner of a home approximately one-half mile from the multifamily development. Would she have standing to sue to challenge the rezoning for the development?

[1.] Standing

A landowner normally has standing to challenge a zoning restriction on his own property, but standing can be a serious problem when a third party brings suit to challenge the approval of a development project on someone else's property. Third-party standing is critical in these cases. If third-party litigation is not allowed, the zoning approval will go unchallenged. Third-party standing law in state courts differs from third-party-standing law in federal courts. Standing in federal courts is governed by the "case and controversy" requirement of the federal Constitution, and by "prudential" standing rules adopted by the Supreme Court that also limit standing to sue. State constitutions do not usually have constitutional "case and controversy" limitations on state-court jurisdiction. State courts prudentially limit standing to sue by limiting their jurisdiction to justiciable controversies.

Third-party standing in state courts can also be controlled by statute. In most states, the controlling provision for appeals from decisions by the board of adjustment is § 7 of the Standard Zoning Act, which provides for appeals by "persons aggrieved." Some states apply this requirement to all judicial appeals, or may require a showing of "special damage" or "adverse effect." *Palmer v. St. Louis County*, 591 S.W.2d 39 (Mo. App. 1980). These rules assure the court that the controversy is justiciable. They reflect the nuisance basis of zoning law, which allows courts to uphold zoning as a means for separating incompatible uses to prevent injury to adjacent property. Third party standing law reflects this rationale, because it turns on how close the complaining third party is to the property for which the zoning is being litigated, and on whether the third party suffered enough damage from the zoning action that is challenged to justify standing to challenge it. How the standing rules are applied to standing claims by neighboring property owners is indicated in the following case:

CENTER BAY GARDENS, LLC v. CITY OF TEMPE CITY COUNCIL

214 Ariz. App. 353, 153 P.3d 374 (Ariz. App. 2007), rev. denied, 2007 Ariz. LEXIS 84 (Ariz. 2007)

BARKER, JUDGE:

We address in this opinion the issue of standing as applied to those seeking to challenge zoning variances granted by a city council to an adjacent property owner. For the reasons that follow, we reverse the trial court's decision finding a lack of standing in this case. I.

Plaintiffs-Appellants Center Bay Gardens, L.L.C., Wood River University Square, L.L.C., and University Pointe Limited Partnership, (collectively "Center Bay") each own one of three apartment complexes on East Lemon Street in Tempe. The apartment complex that is the subject of the proposed development is also on Lemon Street, directly across the street from Center Bay's apartment complexes. The development proposal for the subject property is for a mixed-use development that would include four stories of housing above three levels of parking, two of which would be underground. Some retail space would be built at street level. A mobile home park currently sits on the subject site.

In April 2003, Meyer Residential, L.L.C. submitted three applications to the City of Tempe regarding the property. One, designated ZON-2003-09, sought to change the zoning on the property from R-4 (multi-family residential) to MG (multi-use general district). A second application, GEP 2003.46, was for a general plan amendment, and the third, SPD 2003.35, sought a preliminary and final planned area development with seven zoning variances and a use permit. On July 8, 2003, Tempe's Planning and Zoning Commission held public hearings on the three applications. Representatives of Center Bay expressed their opposition and concerns both at the hearing and in an earlier letter forwarded to the Commission. The Commission unanimously recommended approval of all three applications to Tempe's City Council.

The Tempe City Council held a hearing on July 17, 2003, on the general plan amendment and a second hearing on August 14, 2003, on all three applications. Representatives of Center Bay appeared at the hearings and voiced opposition to the applications. Center Bay also submitted letters to the City Council outlining its objections. On August 14, 2003, the Tempe City Council unanimously approved all three applications.

On September 4, 2003, Center Bay filed a special action complaint against the City of Tempe Board of Adjustment, the City of Tempe, and Meyer Residential. Count one of the complaint asserted that the granting of the variances was arbitrary, capricious, and an abuse of discretion. Counts two and three sought declaratory judgments that the City Council had failed to make findings required by law before granting the variances and acted in excess of its authority. Count four sought a declaratory judgment that the zoning change from R-4 to MG constituted illegal spot zoning. Count five sought a declaratory judgment that Tempe's existing general plan was null and void because it had not been ratified by public vote and that therefore the general plan amendment approved by the City Council was also null and void.

In November 2003, University Mobile Home Park, L.L.C. ("UMHP") moved to intervene in the action, explaining that it owned the subject property and that the original defendant, Meyer Residential, L.L.C., had failed to fulfill its purchase obligations and no longer had any interest in the property. Intervention was granted. In June 2004, UMHP moved to dismiss counts four and five, asserting that Center Bay lacked standing to challenge the City of Tempe's zoning change and general plan amendment. UMHP did not challenge standing as to counts one through three, dealing with the variances. UMHP argued that, to have standing, Center Bay was required to demonstrate a particularized injury beyond general economic or aesthetic losses and greater than any injury suffered by the community. UMHP argued that Center Bay had not articulated any particularized harm it would suffer separate from the effects on the community and that therefore Center Bay lacked standing to challenge the Council's decision. Center Bay asserted that, because of the proximity of its property to the development, it would be particularly affected by the development. Center Bay acknowledged that its objection to the development was economically motivated but also argued that it would suffer special damage because of the increase in the number of dwelling units per acre, the lack of setbacks and landscaping, the height of the proposed structure, and the apparent intent to change the character of the neighborhood through development like the proposed project.

The trial court granted UMHP's motion to dismiss. It found that Center Bay had no standing on the specified counts because it did not claim a particular injury other than general economic or aesthetic losses. The trial court entered judgment dismissing counts four and five on August 26, 2004. Center Bay appealed the court's ruling. This court affirmed. *Center Bay Gardens, L.L.C. v. City of Tempe City Council*, 1 CA-CV 04-0699 (Ariz. App. Aug. 16, 2005) (mem. decision) ("Memorandum Decision").

On March 30, 2004, while the first action was proceeding, UMHP submitted to the Tempe City Council another application, designated SPD 2004.29, for a preliminary and final planned area development with five variances for the same property with a new developer, JPI Apartment Development, L.P. The proposed project was essentially the same as the first. The requested variances were five of the seven sought in the first application. . . . [The planning commission and council again approved the application, and Center Bay addressed the commission and voiced concerns raised about the first project — the increase in density, the increase in building mass, and the lack of landscaping and setbacks. The city again argued that Center Bay lacked standing.]

Center Bay argued that its amended special action complaint adequately pleaded special damages sufficient to establish standing to maintain the challenge. Specifically, Center Bay relied on its allegations that it would be specially damaged because it owned property adjacent to the proposed project and the value of its property and the quiet use and enjoyment of the property would be compromised if the project were constructed. Center Bay based this claim on the lack of setbacks for the proposed structure, the building mass and height, the lack of landscaping, and the density of the project. Center Bay also alleged that its property would be at an economic disadvantage because it did not enjoy the same land use entitlements granted to the project, and that because its property would directly front the project its apartment units would be less desirable because of the lack of setbacks and landscaping. [The trial court consolidated the cases, dismissed them because the claimed damages were not specific and could be categorized as generalized economic or aesthetic effects for which standing was not appropriate, and Center Bay appealed. The appellate court dismissed the city's "law of the case" argument.]

IV.

Turning to standing, one of Center Bay's alternative requests is that this court adopt the view of several other states that an adjacent property owner has standing to challenge a zoning decision without showing special harm.[5]

This court has previously stated that "[a]n adjacent property owner who suffers no special damage from the granting of a variance cannot seek judicial review of an administrative decision to grant a variance." *Perper v. Pima County*, 600 P.2d 52, 54 (Ariz. App. 1979). Based on current Arizona case law, we find that Center Bay's allegations are sufficient to show the specialized harm necessary to provide standing. Thus, we need not address whether proximity alone creates standing or a presumption of standing.

A.

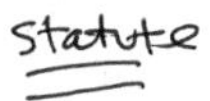

In Arizona, a person "aggrieved" by a zoning decision of a legislative body or board may appeal that decision by special action to the superior court. A.R.S. § 9-462.06(K) (1996).[7] To

---

[5] For example, the Massachusetts Supreme Court has stated the rule that "[a]butters entitled to notice of zoning board of appeals hearings enjoy a rebuttable presumption they are 'persons aggrieved.' " *Marashlian v. Zoning Bd. of Appeals of Newburyport*, 660 N.E.2d 369, 372 (Mass. 1996). Maine has stated the following: "While we have not as yet declared that any abutting owner has a potential for injury sufficient to confer standing, we have on many occasions found such a relationship sufficient in combination with an additional allegation of injury." *Anderson v. Swanson*, 534 A.2d 1286, 1288 (Me. 1987). In Vermont, the issue is resolved by a statute which allows any property owner "in the immediate neighborhood" to challenge a zoning decision if the decision would not be in accordance with "the policies, purposes or terms of the plan of that municipality." *Kalakowski v. John A. Russell Corp.*, 401 A.2d 906, 908 (Vt. 1979). Courts in Illinois appear to follow a rule that allows any adjoining landowner to challenge a zoning decision. *See Truchon v. City of Streator*, 26 Ill. Dec. 625, 388 N.E.2d 249, 251–252 (Ill. App. 1979); *Anundson v. City of Chicago*, 256 N.E.2d 1, 3–4 (Ill. 1970); *Bredberg v. City of Wheaton*, 182 N.E.2d 742, 747–48 (Ill. 1962). Illinois justifies the rule on the grounds that adjoining landowners are more affected than the general public and that the "municipality, concerned primarily with the maintaining of the municipality-wide zoning pattern, might inadvertently compromise or neglect the rights of adjoining landowners in such a lawsuit." *Anundson*, 256 N.E.2d at 3. Hawaii has held that an adjoining landowner has a "legal interest worthy of judicial recognition should he seek redress . . . to preserve the continued enjoyment of his realty by protecting it from threatening neighborhood change." *East Diamond Head Ass'n v. Zoning Bd. of Appeals of City and County of Honolulu*, 479 P.2d 796, 798 (Haw. 1971) (citing *Dalton v. City and County of Honolulu*, 462 P.2d 199, 202 (Haw. 1969) (finding that living across the street from proposed high rise buildings that would restrict the scenic view, limit the sense of space, and increase density, was sufficient for standing). Maryland adopts yet another approach: "An adjoining, confronting or nearby property owner is deemed, prima facie, to be specially damaged and, therefore, a person aggrieved. The person challenging the fact of aggrievement has the burden of denying such damage in his answer to the petition for appeal and of coming forward with evidence to establish that the petitioner is not, in fact, aggrieved." *Bryniarski v. Montgomery County Bd. of Appeals*, 230 A.2d 289, 294 (Md. 1967). A landowner whose property is farther away must show special damages. *Id. at* 295.

Thus, among the states that take different approaches than Arizona, no uniform rule emerges automatically granting standing to adjacent property owners. *See* 4 Ziegler, Rathkopf's The Law of Zoning and Planning § 63:18 (4th ed. 2005) (documenting various approaches among the states).

[7] Arizona Revised Statutes § 9-462.06(K) states: "A person aggrieved by a decision of the legislative body or board

have standing to bring such an action, however, a plaintiff must allege "particularized harm" resulting from the decision. The plaintiff must have suffered an "injury in fact, economic or otherwise." The damage alleged must be peculiar to the plaintiff or at least more substantial than that suffered by the community at large. General economic losses or general concerns regarding aesthetics in the area without a particularized palpable injury to the plaintiff are typically not sufficient to confer standing. Finally, although proximity is a factor in determining whether a plaintiff has standing, the plaintiff must still demonstrate special damages or particularized harm. [Citing cases]

Center Bay argues that it alleged specific harm peculiar to itself and different from that of the general public. We agree. Among other things that Center Bay alleged were that the "zero setbacks, building mass and height, minimal and non-existent landscaping, and density" of the proposed project created a particularized injury. With respect to density, Center Bay argued in hearings for the first proposed project that it was inappropriate to have "an increase from 24 dwelling units per acre to 63 dwelling units per acre, dwelling units that are all four bedrooms." This is almost a threefold increase. As to the lack of setbacks and building mass, Center Bay alleged that aesthetically their property would be less pleasing because of the obstruction of view and having a five-story structure (as contrasted with a three-story structure), with no landscaping setback, immediately across the street from them.

In *Blanchard* [*v. Show Low Planning & Zoning Comm'n*, 993 P.2d 1078 (Ariz. App. 1999)] the plaintiffs lived and had a business within 750 feet of property that had been rezoned to permit construction of a Wal-Mart Supercenter. The plaintiffs alleged that the use of their property would be adversely affected because of the greatly increased traffic, the noise and pollution from cars, a possible increase in crime, and the lights that would be illuminated in the Wal-Mart parking lot. The court found that close proximity made it sufficiently likely that the damages alleged might affect their property, giving them standing.

In contrast, a second plaintiff in *Blanchard* owned property approximately 1,875 feet away from the proposed construction site. This plaintiff only made "general allegations of harm" and relied on evidence of "general harm to the area around the parcel in the form of increased traffic and noise." The court held that such a showing was insufficient to find standing.

Turning to our decision in *Buckelew* [*v. Town of Parker*, 937 P.2d 368 (Ariz. App. 1996)], in that case the plaintiff asserted that adjoining property that had been used as a recreational vehicle park for temporary residents was being used as a mobile home park for permanent residents in violation of the zoning ordinance. After the board of adjustment denied the plaintiff's request for relief, the plaintiff brought a special action in superior court. The superior court found that the plaintiff lacked standing. This court rejected the plaintiff's argument that the court could take judicial notice of special damages based on the proximity of the plaintiff's property to the subject property. This court nevertheless found that the plaintiff had standing based on his allegations that his property shared a boundary with the subject property and was damaged by noise coming from the trailer park, littering and threats of violence by the tenants, fire and health hazards including raw sewage, increased criminal activity, and the destruction of his personal property by children living in the park.

In both *Blanchard* and *Buckelew*, we found standing when the plaintiffs alleged specific claims of damage to their use and enjoyment of their property. Close proximity was a factor in

. . . may . . . file a complaint for special action in the superior court . . . ." We do not consider the "aggrieved person" standard to create a substantially different test than that set forth in [earlier Arizona cases].

each because the nature of the property uses made the harms greater to plaintiffs located close to the property. For example, the court in *Blanchard* found that "proximity makes it sufficiently likely that traffic, litter, drainage, and noise from the project will significantly affect" the closer property, but not the property located further away. 993 P.2d at 1082. *See also Armory Park Neighborhood Ass'n v. Episcopal Cmty. Servs. in Ariz.*, 712 P.2d 914, 918 (Ariz. 1985) (finding standing for residents to seek damages and injunctive relief "because the acts allegedly committed by the patrons of the neighborhood center affected the residents' use and enjoyment of their real property, a damage special in nature and different in kind from that experienced by the residents of the city in general").

Viewing the facts and inferences in a light most favorable to Center Bay, as we must, this development project across the street from the presently existing apartment complex that comes close to tripling the existing density, doubling the existing mass, and dropping previously required landscape setoffs satisfies the standing requirement as set forth in *Blanchard* and *Buckelew*.

B.

We emphasize that the issue before us is standing. The issue is not whether on the *merits* it was arbitrary and capricious for Tempe to enact the variances; it is whether Center Bay can even bring the claim to *contend* that the Tempe City Council acted in an arbitrary and capricious fashion.

When resolving standing we look only to whether there have been sufficient allegations of particularized harm, not whether there is a likelihood of success on the merits. Thus, whether or not Center Bay has a strong case on the merits is not our concern.

C.

Appellees assert that because the damage can be characterized as being primarily economic in nature, "particularized harm" cannot be shown. We disagree. . . . [P]articularized *economic* harm may suffice for standing. Likewise, the statutory language permitting standing for a "person aggrieved," A.R.S. § 9-462.06(K), does not rule out economic damages as a basis for being aggrieved. Rather, the plain language of the statute would include it. Also, the language of the Zoning and Development Code of the City of Tempe requires the Board of Adjustment to find by sufficient evidence "[t]hat authorizing the *variance* will not be materially detrimental to persons residing or working in the vicinity, to adjacent property, [or] to the neighborhood." Tempe, Ariz., Zoning and Development Code § 6-309 (Jan. 5, 2006). "Materially detrimental" does not preclude consideration of the economic effects of proposed developments requiring variances.

D.

We recognize that Center Bay's allegations of particularized harm can also be cast in a setting of an objection to increased competition from a neighboring project. Some states have found potential harm from economic competition as insufficient to confer standing. [This issue is discussed in Section D.3.b., *infra*.]

Arizona case law reflects a long-standing policy to promote competition that we do not seek to inhibit. This policy may be considered below in a decision on the merits. The issue before us, however, is not whether there will be increased or decreased competition, but whether Center Bay has made allegations of "particularized harm" sufficient to confer standing. As stated above, Center Bay has met this test.

V.

Center Bay has alleged facts sufficient to confer standing. The decision of the superior court is therefore reversed and this matter is remanded for proceedings consistent with this opinion.

NOTES AND QUESTIONS

1. *The legal basis for standing.* Do you understand what a third party plaintiff must show damage different from what is suffered by the general public? Why is a showing of "peculiar injury" similar to the harm that must be shown to succeed in a private nuisance suit? The harm is not physical, but in *Center Bay*, the court agreed that "zero setbacks, building mass and height, minimal and non-existent landscaping, and density" were enough to show peculiar injury. How does this harm differ from the harm found to provide standing in the *Blanchard* and *Buckelew* cases, discussed in the *Center Bay* decision? See *Hoke v. Moyer*, 865 P.2d 624 (Wyo. 1993) ("Doubling the density of adjacent property raises a number of perceptible harms for a property owner which are different than the harm to the general public, such as increased traffic and congestion.").

Some courts apply a presumption that neighbors have standing, or take a lenient view toward their standing claims, as noted in the cases cited in footnote 5 of the principal decision. See *Evans v. Teton County*, 139 Idaho 71 (Idaho 2003) (stating that proximity is an important factor); *Mangum v. Raleigh Bd. of Adjustment*, 669 S.E.2d 279 (N.C. 2008) (increased traffic, increased water runoff, parking, and safety concerns and secondary adverse effects on petitioners' businesses held sufficient special damages to confer standing to challenge special use permit for adult use); *Davenport v. Planning Board of Dennis*, 76 Mass. App. Ct. 221 (2010) (abutter presumed to have standing). Cases giving weight to proximity would seem to reflect the nuisance basis of standing. Why?

Many courts impose a "zone of interest" requirement, and will confer standing only if the plaintiff is within the same zone of interest as that protected by the ordinance. *Matter of Legacy at Fairways, LLC v. McAdoo*, 76 A.D.3d 786 (N.Y. App. Div. 2010). Protection of competition from another land use is not usually within the zone of interest. *ATC South, Inc. v. Charleston County*, 669 S.E.2d 337 (S.C. 2008). Contra *DePetro v. Township of Wayne Planning Bd.*, 842 A.2d 266 (N.J. App. Div. 2004) (where plaintiff challenged authority to approve competitor's site plan). How did the court in *Center Bay* dodge this issue?

Rules for granting standing to third parties differ. Some courts apply a multi-factor balancing test to determine standing. See *Reynolds v. Dittmer*, 312 N.W.2d 75 (Iowa 1981) (proximity, character of neighborhood, type of zoning change, right to notice). Other courts follow liberalized standing rules adopted by the U.S. Supreme Court in environmental cases. See the cases discussed in Note 4, *infra*. If the appeal is from an administrative proceeding, a court may grant standing only to a party who participates in the proceedings below. *Bryniarski v. Montgomery County Bd. of Appeals*, 230 A.2d 289 (Md. 1967).

2. *The proximity factor.* The success of third party standing claims diminishes with distance. *Perper v. Pima County*, discussed in the principal case, is typical. The plaintiff alleged "general economic damage to the whole area," and the court denied standing because it found only "general economic and aesthetic losses." Increased traffic was also alleged, and many courts will not base standing on an increase in traffic from the challenged project, viewing it as part of urban development. The cases are reviewed in *Sanitary & Improvement Dist. No. 347 v. City of Omaha*, 589 N.W.2d 160 (Neb. App. 1999). Distance from the site is often a factor in denying standing. *Nickerson v. Zoning Bd. of Appeals*, 761 N.E.2d 544 (Mass. App. 2002) (plaintiff one mile from site); *Cable v. Union County Bd. of County Comm'rs*, 769 N.W.2d 817 (S.D. 2009) (denying standing to plaintiffs living within one mile from proposed refinery); *Diamond v. Nestor*, 2010 N.Y. Misc. LEXIS 5140 (Supreme Court of New York County, 2010) ("It is well established, however, that a 'property holder in nearby proximity to premises that are the subject of a zoning determination may have standing to seek judicial review without pleading and proving special damage, because adverse effect or aggrievement can be inferred from the proximity' "). This is consistent with the nuisance cases, which link proximity to harm.

3. *Nonresident landowners.* What about residents of one municipality who own land contiguous with or near land affected by a zoning change in another municipality? Should municipal boundaries make a difference? Almost all courts think not. *Scott v. City of Indian Wells*, 492 P.2d 1137 (Cal. 1972), is a leading case. The court held that denying standing would " 'make a fetish out of invisible boundary lines and mockery of the principles of zoning.' " *Id.* at 1140 (quoting another case). Contra *Clifton v. Village of Blanchester*, 2010 Ohio 2309, 2010 Ohio App. LEXIS 1903 (Ohio App. 2010) (reviewing cases).

4. *Citizens, organizations and taxpayers.* Some courts, recognizing the economic difficulties faced by landowners who want to challenge zoning decisions, have granted standing to neighborhood associations to bring these cases. *Douglaston Civic Ass'n v. Galvin*, 324 N.E.2d 317 (N.Y. 1974), is an early leading case. The court, recognizing that "the neighboring property owners rarely fight as hard for zoning protection as the developer or speculator does for relaxation of zoning restrictions," held that "[b]y granting the neighborhood and civic associations standing . . . , the expense can be spread out over a number of property owners putting them on an economic parity with the developer." The court adopted a set of factors to determine whether an organization should have standing, including the ability of the organization to take an adversary position and the extent to which it represented neighborhood interests. For more recent cases in accord with this approach, see *Tri-County Concerned Citizens, Inc. v. Board of County Comm'rs*, 95 P.3d 1012 (Kan. App. 2004); *Alliance for Metropolitan Stability v. Metropolitan Council*, 671 N.W.2d 905 (Minn. App. 2003).

The U.S. Supreme Court has granted standing to organizations, but only where actual injury to the organization or its members is alleged. Compare *United States v. SCRAP*, 412 U.S. 669 (1973) (injury to members alleged; standing granted), with *Sierra Club v. Morton*, 405 U.S. 727 (1972) (injury to public interest alleged; no standing). *Warth v. Seldin*, discussed *infra* Ch. 5, sec. B.2., recognized the principle of organizational standing in an exclusionary zoning case, but applied the rules stringently and denied standing to all of the organizational plaintiffs. See *Metropolitan Builders Ass'n v. Village of Germantown*, 698 N.W.2d 301 (Wis. App. 2005), applying the federal rules and granting standing.

Citizens and organizations may also attempt to bring litigation that makes a facial challenge to a zoning ordinance, or that challenges a failure to act. They have difficulty getting standing in these cases. For example, in *Concerned Citizens for the Pres. of Watertown, Inc. v. Planning*

& Zoning Comm'n, 984 A.2d 72 (Conn. App. 2009), the organization filed a petition to amend the zoning ordinance to limit the construction of "big box" retail development. The court held the organization did not have standing to challenge a rejection of the petition. It said, inter alia, that the organization was not "classically aggrieved" because the proposed amendments were not site-specific and applied townwide. Neither had it been shown that any members of the organization owned property in the town. The organization was not affected by the rejection any differently than any other property owner in the town. See also *Andross v. Town of W. Hartford*, 939 A.2d 1146 (Conn. 2008) (no standing to challenge refusal to enforce zoning ordinance); *Matter of Brunswick Smart Growth, Inc. v. Town of Brunswick*, 2010 N.Y. App. Div. LEXIS 3745 (App. Div. 2010) (no standing to challenge procedures for approving development projects); *Robin's Trace Homeowners' Association v. City of Green Planning and Zoning Commission*, 2010 Ohio 1168, 2010 Ohio App. LEXIS 974 (Ohio App. 2010) (merely being an abutter not sufficient for association standing).

The Standard Act authorizes appeals by "any taxpayer," but only a minority of states have enacted this provision. In the absence of a statutory provision, most states deny standing to taxpayers or citizens who do not own property affected by the zoning action.

5. *Local governments and their agencies.* The courts are divided on whether a board of zoning appeals or similar body has standing to appeal a reversal of its decision, some courts taking the view that this is not a board function. 13 A.L.R.4th 1130 (1982). However, most hold that a governing body, in order to protect the integrity of its zoning ordinance, has standing to challenge a decision to grant a variance. *Board of Supervisors v. Board of Zoning Appeals*, 268 Va. 441 (Va. 2004) (reviewing cases). Contra *Coldsprings Twp. v. Kalkaska County Zoning Bd. of Appeals*, 755 N.W.2d 553 (Mich. App. 2008) (political subdivision has only derivative powers and cannot sue as *parens patriae* but must show concrete interest).

6. *Model legislation.* The American Planning Association's proposed model planning legislation grants standing to "aggrieved" parties and defines "aggrieved" as follows:"

> "Aggrieved" means that a land-use decision has caused, or is expected to cause, [special] harm or injury to a person, neighborhood planning council, neighborhood or community organization, or governmental unit, [distinct from any harm or injury caused to the public generally]; and that the asserted interests of the person, council, organization, or unit are among those the local government is required to consider when it makes the land-use decision. [American Planning Association, Growing Smart Legislative Guidebook: Model Statutes for Planning and Management of Change § 10-101 (S. Meck ed., 2002).]

The bracketed language is optional. What does it add? What standing issues does this statute address? A separate provision gives abutting and confronting property owners standing as of right. *Id.* § 10-607(3). Remember, the legislature cannot override prudential standing rules established by judicial decisions.

7. *Sources.* Standing questions in zoning litigation have not received as much attention in the literature as they deserve. For two helpful early articles, see Ayer, *The Primitive Law of Standing in Land Use Disputes: Some Notes From a Dark Continent*, 55 Iowa L. Rev. 344 (1969); Note, *The "Aggrieved Person" Requirement in Zoning*, 8 Wm. & Mary L. Rev. 294 (1967). See generally Magill, *Standing for the Public: A Lost History*, University of Virginia Law School Public Law and Legal Theory Working Paper Series Year 2009 Paper 119, http://papers.ssrn.com.

[2.] Exhaustion of Remedies

The widely applied rule that a plaintiff may not sue to challenge the legality of a statute or ordinance unless she has exhausted her administrative remedies applies to zoning litigation. The exhaustion of remedies doctrine is distinguishable from the ripeness doctrine, which is similar and is discussed in Chapter 2. The following case shows how the exhaustion rule applies in zoning litigation:

BEN LOMOND, INC. v. MUNICIPALITY OF ANCHORAGE

761 P.2d 119 (Alaska 1988)

COMPTON, JUSTICE:

The case arises from the revocation of building permits for the renovation of the S & S Apartments in Anchorage. The building's owner, Ben Lomond, Inc. (Ben Lomond), chose not to appeal the revocation or seek a variance. Ben Lomond claims that the Municipality unconstitutionally revoked its permits and, therefore, is liable in damages to Ben Lomond. The trial court denied Ben Lomond compensation reasoning that the Municipality of Anchorage (Municipality) was immune from an action for damages. We affirm the judgment on different grounds.

I. *Factual and Procedural Background*

The S & S Apartments are a group of eight wooden, two-story buildings constructed in 1952. The buildings have had several owners. In 1977 Glen Cassity of New Alaska Development Corporation purchased the property from the Alaska Housing Corporation. In 1983 the United States Department of Housing and Urban Development (HUD), which insured the mortgage on the apartments, determined that the buildings had been vacant for over four years and the property was "in very poor, abandoned and condemned condition." . . .

[Ben Lomond purchased Cassity's interest in the apartments on March 14, 1983. It took possession of the property sometime before May 3, 1983 and started to strip the buildings down to bare framing. The United States then foreclosed on Cassity's interest and Ben Lomond was the successful bidder at the foreclosure sale. It tendered $218,000 to HUD as a 10% down payment with the remaining 90% due August 26, 1983.]

On May 13, 1983 Ben Lomond applied for the first time to the Municipality for building and demolition permits. The permits indicated Ben Lomond intended to demolish the interior of and then renovate building #4. Shortly thereafter Ben Lomond's architect prepared a report for the entire project showing that the apartment complex then contained 224 units and that when all the buildings were renovated there would be a total of 280 apartment units. The record does not indicate when the city received a copy of that report.

On June 8, 1983, Ben Lomond applied to the city for building permits to renovate the other seven buildings. Taken together the applications show an intent to renovate 264 apartment units. However, as required by the building code, Thompson [president of Ben Lomond] submitted architectural plans with the applications; those plans showed a total of 280 proposed units. At that time the site was zoned R-3, which allowed only 234 units.

On June 28, 1983 the Municipality's building official, John Bishop, met with Thompson to discuss the size of the apartment complex's parking lot. The number of parking spaces shown on the plans for 280 units did not meet the parking requirements of Anchorage Municipal Code (AMC) Title 21. However, Bishop thought Ben Lomond had grandfather rights to maintain a parking deficiency. After consulting a city attorney, Bishop decided to issue the permits. When Bishop issued the permits he was unaware the R-3 zoning limited the number of units to 234. . . .

Sometime during late July or early August, the Municipality's executive manager for public services Chip Dennerlein received numerous complaints from persons in the Fairview community regarding Ben Lomond's proposed project. Dennerlein then had several conferences with various city officials to review the validity of the complaints. Dennerlein concluded that the zoning designation allowed only 234 units and that Ben Lomond could not be allowed to build 280 units. See AMC 21.40.050(f). Consequently, Bishop notified Ben Lomond that the building permits for the project were revoked. In a letter dated August 19, 1983 Bishop explained that the project did not enjoy non-conforming use status, see AMC 21.55.030(c), and that it therefore had to meet the current zoning code. Bishop wrote:

> Based on the current R-3 zoning and the size of property, a maximum of 234 dwelling units may be permitted. For that number of dwelling units, you would need to provide 351 parking spaces.

The letter indicated new permits would be issued if Ben Lomond submitted a revised site plan that complied with the code.

After sending the August 19 letter, Dennerlein met with Thompson regarding possible options for Ben Lomond. Over the course of several meetings they discussed the following options: Ben Lomond could (1) appeal the Municipality's action denying the 280 unit project to the Zoning Board of Examiners and Appeals (Zoning Board); (2) apply to the Zoning Board for a variance from the 234 unit limit; or (3) build the project with 234 units. Thompson responded that he did not wish to pursue any remedies before the Zoning Board that would involve a public hearing. Accordingly Ben Lomond did not appeal the revocation of the permits.

In light of the August 19 letter Ben Lomond did not tender the remainder of the sale price by August 26, 1983 and thereby forfeited its right to purchase the S & S Apartments from HUD. On September 30, 1983 the United States Marshall conducted a second foreclosure sale. Ben Lomond did not bid at the second sale and HUD obtained title to the property. In February 1984 Ben Lomond filed suit against the Municipality requesting over $3 million in damages resulting from the permit revocations. In March 1984, the Municipality purchased the property from HUD.

Almost a year later Ben Lomond learned through the newspaper that the Municipality planned to demolish the buildings. Ben Lomond moved for, but was denied, a temporary restraining order to halt the demolition. The Municipality demolished the buildings and built a park.

Ben Lomond then moved for a summary judgment on the issue that it was deprived of property without due process. The Municipality also moved for partial summary judgment to dismiss all causes of action for damages arguing that it was immune under AS 09.65.070. The superior court granted the Municipality's motion for summary judgment. The parties stipulated to an entry of final judgment. Ben Lomond appeals.

II. Discussion

This case was decided upon cross-motions for summary judgment. The moving party must show that there is no genuine issue as to any material fact and that the moving party is entitled to judgment as a matter of law. All factual matters are to be resolved in favor of the non-moving party.

The parties to this appeal raise two major issues. First, whether the permits were unconstitutionally revoked and second, whether the Municipality was immune from suit for such actions. We need not reach these issues because we decide the case on other grounds. We believe the trial court improperly reached the merits in this case because Ben Lomond failed to exhaust its administrative remedies.

"The doctrine of exhaustion of administrative remedies is an expression of administrative autonomy and a rule of sound judicial administration." *State Dep't of Labor v. University of Alaska*, 664 P.2d 575, 581 (Alaska 1983) (citing B. Schwartz, Administrative Law § 172, at 498 (1976)). Whether a court will require exhaustion of remedies turns on an assessment of the benefits obtained through affording an agency an opportunity to review the particular action in dispute. In particular we have observed that "[t]he basic purpose of the exhaustion doctrine is to allow an administrative agency to perform functions within its special competence — to make a factual record, to apply its expertise, and to correct its own errors so as to moot judicial controversies." *Van Hyning v. University of Alaska*, 621 P.2d 1354, 1355–56 (Alaska 1981) (quoting *Parisi v. Davidson*, 405 U.S. 34, 37 (1972), *cert. denied*, 454 U.S. 958 (1981)).

We have not articulated a principle governing when a regulatory scheme's constitutionality may be challenged without exhausting administrative remedies. According to Professor Davis, exhaustion, generally, is not required when the constitutionality of the statute is the only issue raised in a case. See 4 K. Davis, Administrative Law Treatise § 26:6 (2d ed. 1983). Davis concludes that exhaustion may be required when non-constitutional issues are present or when a factual context is needed for deciding the constitutional issue. *Id.* We believe that requiring exhaustion is particularly appropriate where a complainant raises both constitutional and non-constitutional issues. This is because successful pursuit of a claim through the administrative process could obviate the need for judicial review of the constitutional issues. We further believe that it is axiomatic to our system of justice that we have a factual context within which to review a case. Applying these principles to the instant case we conclude that the benefits that could have been obtained from allowing the agency to review this case justify application of the exhaustion doctrine.

When the Municipality revoked Ben Lomond's permits, Ben Lomond could have promptly appealed the revocation to the Zoning Board of Examiners and Appeals. AMC 21.30.110. At that time Ben Lomond could have presented its interpretation of various Building and Zoning Code provisions as applied to the apartment site. In addition, Ben Lomond could have argued to the Zoning Board that the Municipality was estopped to revoke the permits. By failing to take even the first step in the administrative appeal process Ben Lomond deprived the Municipality of the opportunity to make a factual record and correct its own errors.

The record indicates that the Municipality erroneously issued Ben Lomond's building permits for 264 apartments. The record also indicates that if given the opportunity the Zoning Board could have corrected the Municipality's error and directed that building permits be issued for 234 units. Alternatively, the Zoning Board could have accepted Ben Lomond's estoppel argument and reinstated the permit for 280 units. As another alternative, the Zoning

Board could have determined it was appropriate to issue building permits for any number of units between 234 and 280. Had Ben Lomond pursued and obtained relief from the Zoning Board we might not now be faced with a constitutional challenge to the Building and Zoning Codes. For the foregoing reasons we hold that Ben Lomond has waived its right to pursue its claim because it failed to exhaust its administrative remedies.

NOTES AND QUESTIONS

1. *When exhaustion is required.* The principal case explains when exhaustion is required. It is required in as-applied cases, where a decision by an administrative body can provide the landowner a remedy and thus avoid litigation. It also helps determine the measure of damages when there is liability by establishing how much development and use the government will approve. It is not required when a plaintiff makes a facial attack on an ordinance or statute, as that only raises questions of law. This rule comes from the *Euclid* case, reproduced in Chapter 2, where the Court allowed a facial attack on the textual provisions of a zoning ordinance excluding multifamily dwellings from a two-family residential district. Do you see the reason for this exception? See *Poe v. City of Baltimore*, 216 A.2d 707 (Md. 1966) (exhaustion required only in as-applied takings cases). What was the basis for plaintiff's claim in the principal case? Was it constitutional or was it based on an interpretation of the zoning ordinance? Does it make a difference? What was the disagreement between the plaintiff and the city over the zoning ordinance? Why did the city revoke the building permit?

The exhaustion rule requires the plaintiff to go before an administrative board to make his constitutional claim. Is this practicable? Does the board have jurisdiction to hear the constitutional claim? Consult § 7 of the Standard Act, in sec. A of this chapter, *supra*, on this point. What kind of a record do you think a plaintiff could make on the constitutional claim before the board? The courts are divided on whether they can consider the constitutionality of a zoning ordinance when a variance is appealed. See *City of Cherokee v. Tatro*, 636 P.2d 337 (Okla. 1981) (may consider if facially unconstitutional). Often, a variance request is coupled with an appeal of an enforcement decision and the subsequent court action will consider the constitutionality of the ordinance. See, e.g., *Allamakee County v. Schaumberg Living Trust*, 2010 Iowa App. LEXIS 163, No. 9-650/09-0082 (Court of Appeals of Iowa 2010).

2. *Administrative remedies.* It is clear that administrative remedies provided by a zoning or other land use ordinance, or by statute, must be exhausted. See *Prince George's County v. Ray's Used Cars*, 922 A.2d 495, 504 (Md. 2007) (fully adequate administrative adjudicatory remedies could have been pursued by plaintiff used car dealers). Exhaustion is not required when administrative remedies are inadequate. See *Smoke v. City of Seattle*, 937 P.2d 186 (Wash. 1997), reviewing the cases on adequacy and holding that an interpretation of the zoning ordinance could not reverse a permit denial, and *Caltabiano v. L&L Real Estate Holdings II, LLC*, 998 A.2d 1256 (Conn. App. 2010). See also *Berlin Batting Cages, Inc. v. Planning & Zoning Comm'n*, 821 A.2d 269 (Conn. App. 2003) (no right to appeal decision of commission). A judicial appeal from an administrative decision is required.

3. *The futility rule.* An important exception to the exhaustion doctrine is the futility rule: A plaintiff need not exhaust an administrative remedy when to do so would be futile. The rule applies when the agency does not have the authority to grant the requested relief. See *Sinclair Pipe Line Co. v. Village of Richton Park*, 167 N.E.2d 406 (Ill. 1960) (need not apply for variance because no authority to grant for change in use), *Hendee v. Putnam Township*, 786 N.W.2d 521

(Mich. 2010) (must make "at least one unsuccessful meaningful application" before claiming futility).

The futility rule also applies when it is clear that administrative relief will not be granted. *League of Women Voters of Appleton, Inc. v. Outagamie County*, 334 N.W.2d 887 (Wis. 1983), illustrates this application of the futility rule. The League appealed the issuance of a use permit for a shopping mall. The court held no exhaustion was required:

> [A]ssuming that the plaintiffs had a right to appeal to the board of adjustment, such an appeal would have been futile. The attorney for the county and the board of adjustment had made very clear, on the record of this case, his clients' position that no appeal to the board of adjustment would be entertained. [*Id.* at 890.]

How much opposition must a plaintiff show before he can invoke the futility rule? What if he claims that relief probably will not be granted, but there is no history as in the *League of Women Voters* case indicating relief will be denied? A court may apply a presumption that a zoning agency is not biased, and hold that a plaintiff must demonstrate actual rather than potential bias. See *O & G Indus. v. Planning & Zoning Comm'n*, 655 A.2d 1121 (Conn. 1995) (bias not found).

4. *Amendments.* Does the exhaustion doctrine require a plaintiff to apply for a zoning amendment that would allow his project? The answer to this question usually turns on whether the amendment is a legislative or quasi-judicial act. See Ch. 6, sec. E.3., *infra.* Exhaustion usually is required only when the amendment is considered quasi-judicial, which is the characterization the courts give to it in several states. See *Fifth Ave. Corp. v. Washington County*, 581 P.2d 50 (Or. 1978). Can you see why this is so?

5. *The ripeness alternative.* Recall that the ripeness rule adopted by the federal courts, and discussed in Ch. 2, requires plaintiffs to obtain a final decision from local agencies before bringing a takings claim in federal court. Is this rule the equivalent of the exhaustion of remedies rule? The Supreme Court thought not in *Hamilton Bank*, reproduced *supra* in Chapter 2, where the plaintiff claimed a taking based on a denial of a subdivision plat, and the subdivision ordinance contained variance provisions. The Court drew a distinction between finality ("whether the initial decision maker has arrived at a definitive position on the issue that inflicts an actual, concrete injury") and exhaustion ("administrative and judicial procedures by which an injured party may seek review of an adverse decision and obtain a remedy if the decision is found to be unlawful or otherwise inappropriate"). 473 U.S. at 192–93.

Can you see the difference? A number of states now apply the federal ripeness rules, rather than the exhaustion of remedies rule, to takings claims in state courts. See *Paragon Props. Co. v. City of Novi*, 550 N.W.2d 772 (Mich. 1996); *Beverly Bank v. Illinois Dep't of Transp.*, 579 N.E.2d 815 (Ill. 1991); *Ward v. Bennett*, 592 N.E.2d 787 (N.Y. 1992). This includes only the rule that a decision must be final, since the plaintiff is already in state court claiming compensation. See *Golf Club of Plantation, Inc. v. City of Plantation*, 847 So. 2d 1028 (Fla. App. 2003) (city made it clear beyond doubt that ban against converting golf course was absolute). Does it make sense to apply rules concerning the limited jurisdiction of federal courts to takings claims in state courts that do not have comparable jurisdictional limitations?

6. *A Problem.* Your client tells you he wants to build a filling station combined with a quick-service food store, but that the zoning ordinance won't let him do it. He wants to sue but has not applied for any kind of remedy under the zoning ordinance. What kind of questions should you ask him, and what should you look for in the zoning ordinance before deciding whether to sue?

7. *Model legislation.* The APA proposed model land use legislation codifies the exhaustion of remedies rule. Legislative Guidebook, *supra,* § 10-604. The model law also contains a ripeness requirement that recognizes state court application of the ripeness rules. A land use decision is final if a development permit application is complete and if the local government has approved it, with or without conditions; has denied it; or if the application is deemed approved because time limits for decision have expired. *Id.* § 10-603(2). The statute is more lenient than the federal decisional rules. Of course, a court need not accept a statutory codification of exhaustion or ripeness as binding.

8. *Sources.* For additional discussion of the exhaustion doctrine, see Note, *Exhaustion of Remedies in Zoning Cases*, 1964 Wash. U. L.Q. 368; Comment, *Exhausting Administrative and Legislative Remedies in Zoning Cases*, 48 Tul. L. Rev. 665 (1974); Kochan, *Ripe Standing Vines and the Jurisprudential Tasting of Matured Legal Wines — and Law & Bananas: Property and Public Choice in the Permitting Process*, 24 BYU J. Pub. L. 49 (2009) ("justiciability doctrines allow unilateral powers on the part of government officials to make things 'unfit' for review and insulated from scrutiny, which creates perverse incentives in the permitting process.").

[3.] Securing Judicial Review

The problem. Securing judicial review of zoning ordinances and decisions is complicated in several ways. First, civil procedure is usually an intricate body of law in each state, and jurisdictions vary widely in how litigation is structured, including the labels used to denominate actions. Thus, in this casebook, we can do no more than sketch the broadest outlines of the topic. You are encouraged to consult your own state's statutes and caselaw to acquire more specific insight into these matters.

Another complication is that some of the land use decisions a party might wish to challenge will be characterized as "legislative" decisions, and others will be characterized as "administrative" (or, sometimes, "quasi-judicial"). Adoption of a revised zoning ordinance, downzoning (or upzoning) a belt of farmland at the edge of the community, is an example of the first type of action; denying (or granting) a variance for a specific parcel of land in a suburban residential neighborhood is an example of the second. This problem is further complicated because legislative bodies may sometimes act administratively, and bodies that nominally have only advisory functions, planning commissions under the Standard Zoning Act, for example, may in fact have decision making duties assigned to them as well. The authority to issue special-use permits illustrates both points, this duty sometimes being lodged in the legislative body that also adopts the underlying ordinance, and sometimes in bodies such as the planning commission.

Certiorari. The Standard Zoning Act on which most states have modeled their zoning legislation provides little guidance on the availability of judicial review. Section 7 of the Act provides that persons "aggrieved" by a decision of the board of adjustment may obtain review by way of a writ of certiorari, the standard remedy available to review administrative agency decisions. Most states have adopted this Standard Act provision. For a typical case applying the arbitrary and capricious standard of judicial review to uphold the denial of an application for a planned unit development, see *Lakeland Commons, L.P. v. Town of Lakeland*, 2010 Tenn.

App. LEXIS 359 (Tenn. App. 2010).

Certiorari is available only for the review of administrative or quasi-judicial decisions. *State ex rel. Moore & Assocs. v. West*, 246 S.W.3d 569 (Tenn. App. 2005). Review by way of certiorari of these decisions is on the record made before the board, though § 7 allows a court to take additional evidence if "testimony is necessary for the proper disposition of the matter." See *Bontrager Auto Serv. v. Iowa City Bd. of Adjustment*, 748 N.W.2d 483 (Iowa 2008) (can take additional evidence only on issues not in the record); *Bentley v. Chastain*, 249 S.E.2d 38 (Ga. 1978) (de novo trial unconstitutional). Certiorari is thus the typical method for reviewing zoning board decisions on variances and conditional uses.

But the Standard Zoning Act says nothing about decisions of other bodies, nor does it address the administrative/legislative distinction. The following case provides one answer:

COPPLE v. CITY OF LINCOLN

210 Neb. 504, 315 N.W.2d 628 (1982)

CLINTON, JUSTICE:

This action originates by a "petition on appeal" filed in the District Court for Lancaster County by the plaintiff Copple against the City of Lincoln, its mayor, the members of its city council, and Old Cheney Road, Inc. The plaintiff's petition alleges the action is an appeal under the provisions of Neb. Rev. Stat. § 15-1202 from an amendment to a zoning ordinance of the City. It further alleges, among other things, that on May 9, 1977, the council approved ordinance No. 11976 which changed the zoning classification of a tract of land in the southwest quarter of Section 9, Township 9 North, Range 7 East, Lancaster County, from "G-Local Business District Zoning and A-1 Single Family Dwelling District Zoning to J-1 Planned Regional Commercial District Zoning." The plaintiff alleges he is a citizen, resident, and taxpayer of Lincoln and Lancaster County, and he is owner of a tract of land described as the northeast quarter of Section 18, Township 9 North, Range 7 East of the 6th P. M., Lancaster County, Nebraska. He further alleges the zone change "will have a detrimental affect [sic] on plaintiff and his real property, in that plaintiff wishes to build a regional shopping center in close proximity to the area here involved, specifically at 40th Street and Old Cheney Road and currently has pending applications for said regional shopping center and a lawsuit to determine plaintiff's right to build said regional shopping center. The decision of the City Council herein would cause undue hardship on the plaintiff if in fact a shopping center is allowed to be built on the rezoned tract in said close proximity to plaintiff's proposed shopping center site."

The petition further alleges the city council of the City of Lincoln acted arbitrarily and capriciously in enacting the amendment to the zoning ordinance and sets forth various reasons for the conclusion.

The District Court, after a hearing on the merits of the plaintiff's petition, found that the plaintiff was not a person aggrieved within the meaning of Neb. Rev. Stat. § 15-1201; that he did not have standing to sue; and that even if he had legal standing, he had failed to prove he suffered some special injury peculiar to himself as required by law to have standing to appeal the action of the council. It further found: "That if it should be determined that the plaintiff possesses legal standing to appeal this action, the plaintiff still has the burden of proving that the action of the defendant, City of Lincoln, was arbitrary, unreasonable, and without substantial relation to the public safety, health, morals, or the general welfare." The court then made findings indicating a lack of merit in each of the plaintiff's specific claims of invalidity of the ordinance. It ordered the plaintiff's appeal dismissed.

We affirm on two alternative grounds. The first ground is that the enactment of a zoning ordinance by a municipal governing body is an exercise of legislative authority from which no direct appeal lies. An appeal or error proceeding does not lie from a purely legislative act by a public body to which legislative authority has been delegated. The only remedy in such cases is by collateral attack, that is, by injunction or other suitable actions. . . .

Section 15-1201 provides: "Any person or persons, jointly or severally aggrieved by any final administrative or judicial order or decision of the board of zoning appeals, the board of equalization, the city council, or any officer or department or board of a city of the primary class, shall, except as provided for claims in sections 15-840 to 15-842.01, appeal from such order or decision to the district court in the manner herein prescribed." The above statute applies only where the bodies mentioned act judicially or quasi-judicially. Any other construction would render the statute unconstitutional. The Legislature may not delegate legislative power to the courts. A delegation of legislative power to the courts is violative of article II, § 1, of the Constitution of Nebraska.

The alternative ground of our decision is that the plaintiff has not shown that he is an "aggrieved" person within the meaning of § 15-1201. In order to have standing as an aggrieved person for the purpose of attacking a change of zone, the plaintiff must demonstrate that he suffers a special injury different in kind from that suffered by the general public. The possibility that zone changes may afford competition for businesses which the plaintiff hopes will be established on his property if it is rezoned is not sufficient to give standing. An increase in business competition is not sufficient to confer standing to challenge a change of zone.

Affirmed.

NOTES AND QUESTIONS

1. *Understanding* Copple. The Nebraska statute authorized appeals from decisions by the city council, but the court held an injunction must be brought instead. Do you see why? The use of injunctions in land use litigation is considered below. Certiorari is available if the court holds the council acted quasi-judicially, *Snyder v. City of Lakewood*, 542 P.2d 371 (Colo. 1975), but not if it acts legislatively, *Leavitt v. Jefferson County*, 875 P.2d 681 (Wash. App. 1994) (adoption of countywide development code). See also *Burns Holdings, LLC v. Madison County Bd.*, 214 P.3d 646 (Idaho 2009) (denial of rezoning not appealable under statutory appeal provision). Note the holding in *Copple* on the standing question.

2. *The judicial review problem.* The following commentary explains the judicial review problem in land use cases:

> The structure for the review of land use decisions is chaotic. The *Standard State Enabling Act*, which state laws followed, contains limited provisions for the judicial review of zoning decisions. Courts have had to find additional methods of judicial review for actions not reviewable under the statutory procedures. These procedures are incomplete and unclear, standing to sue requirements can limit opportunities for judicial review, and remedial relief available is inadequate. Important land-use disputes often cannot get to court. [Legislative Guidebook, p. 10-60.]

The APA model legislation attempts to deal with this problem by providing a comprehensive judicial review procedure for quasi-judicial decisions taken on development permit applications. Legislative Guidebook, §§ 10-601 to 10-618. It is based on the Washington Land Use Petition Act, Wash. Rev. Code §§ 36.70C.005 et seq., which is the most comprehensive state statute providing for the judicial review of land use decisions.

[4.] Remedies in Land Use Cases

[a.] Forms of Remedy

Choosing the right remedy in a zoning case can be critical, as the *Copple* case showed. This note surveys the injunction and other forms of remedies in land use cases.

Injunctions. An injunction is the standard remedy to challenge zoning actions by the governing body in states where the zoning process is legislative. An injunction lies because an alternate legal remedy is not available. Appeal and certiorari are not available, for example, to review zoning actions by the governing body if these actions are legislative. The injunction is a negative, not an affirmative, remedy. The landowner argues a zoning restriction as applied to her property is unconstitutional or arbitrary, and that its enforcement by the municipality should be enjoined. Most states require a plaintiff to post a bond before obtaining an injunction. A court will grant an injunction only to enjoy an illegal action. Zoning ordinances claimed to be a taking of property, or to violate a statutory provision, are an example of illegal actions subject to injunction.

The Standard Act, § 8, authorizes municipalities to bring "any appropriate action or proceedings" to prevent a violation of the Act or a zoning ordinance, and this authority includes enforcement injunctions brought by local governments. The courts do not require an irreparable injury as the basis for an enforcement injunction. See *Culbertson v. Board of County Comm'rs*, 44 P.3d 652 (Utah 2002). Neither do the courts apply the rule that an injunction is not available to enjoin the violation of a crime. This exception is necessary because the Standard Act makes the violation of a zoning ordinance a misdemeanor.

Declaratory judgment. Plaintiffs in zoning cases may seek a declaratory judgment, which is authorized under the Uniform Declaratory Judgment Act adopted in most states. The declaratory judgment is a helpful alternative to an injunction because it authorizes the court to make a declaration of rights, even though the plaintiff has not suffered actual harm. In many zoning actions, the plaintiff asks for both an injunction and a declaratory judgment. Relief through declaratory judgment is limited, however, because courts usually insist that a justiciable controversy exist. They may not provide declaratory relief if the plaintiff has not been adversely affected by the zoning ordinance, though they may apply this requirement liberally.

Anderson House, LLC v. Mayor of Rockville, 939 A.2d 116 (Md. 2008), is a typical example of the use of a declaratory judgment action to challenge a zoning ordinance. The court first considered whether a statutory judicial appeal existed. Concluding that it did not, the court considered whether the ordinance violated the statutory uniformity requirement for zoning ordinances, an example of the use of a declaratory judgment to decide whether a local government had violated its statutory powers. See also *ML Plainsboro Ltd. Pshp. v. Township of Plainsboro*, 719 A.2d 1285 (N.J. App. Div. 1998) (interpretation of zoning ordinance to clarify zoning requirements that might impede sale or use of a property); *County v. Southland Corp.*,

297 S.E.2d 718 (Va. 1982) (validity of conditional use procedure), *reproduced infra*, Chapter 6; *County Comm'rs v. Days Cove Reclamation Co.*, 713 A.2d 351 (Md. App. 1998) (imminent adoption of comprehensive plan excluding plaintiff's use).

Mandamus. Mandamus is an extraordinary remedy that can sometimes be useful in zoning litigation. It lies to compel a public official or agency to do a ministerial act, if the plaintiff has shown a clear legal right to have the duty performed because she has complied with all the requirements for the exercise of that duty. Rights to a building permit or administrative relief are examples. *Furlong Cos. v. City of Kansas City*, 189 S.W.3d 157 (Mo. 2006) (conditions for approval of subdivision met); *Clark v. City of Shreveport*, 655 So. 2d 617 (La. App. 1995) (issuance of variance). Compare *1350 Lake Shore Assocs. v. Randall*, 928 N.E.2d 181 (Ill. App. 2010) (rejecting vested rights claim as basis for writ of mandamus for a building certificate).

Mandamus does not lie to compel the performance of a discretionary act, though a court will allow a writ of mandamus to compel an official to make a discretionary decision or to set aside an exercise of discretion when it is arbitrary. See *Trojnacki v. Board of Supervisors*, 842 A.2d 503 (Pa. Commw. 2004) (approval of subdivision held discretionary). Neither may a court issue a writ of mandamus when a statutory appeal is available, such as an appeal from a decision of a board of adjustment. The rule that mandamus will not issue to compel the exercise of discretionary authority limits its availability because much zoning administration is discretionary. Applications for a rezoning, a variance or a special exception all require the exercise of discretion. These zoning actions are discussed in Chapter 6.

For general discussion of the judicial remedies available against local government, see D. Mandelker, D. Netsch, P. Salsich, J. Wegner & J. Griffith, State and Local Government in a Federal System, ch. 12 (7th ed. 2010); O. Reynolds, Handbook of Local Government Law, ch. 31 (3d ed. 2009).

[b.] Specific Relief

The problem. A plaintiff who succeeds in land use litigation needs a remedy that will give her specific relief that will allow her to proceed with the project she has proposed. For example, if she takes an appeal from a decision by the board of zoning adjustment on the denial of a variance, a court may grant specific relief awarding the remedy if it believes the appellant has sufficiently proved facts that support this relief. Otherwise, it will remand.

More difficult problems arise when a plaintiff who has proposed a specific development project brings an injunction to enjoin the enforcement of a zoning ordinance that prohibits the project. The focus of the litigation is on the zoning ordinance, not the development proposed, as *Jaylin Investments, Inc. v. Village of Moreland Hills*, 839 N.E.2d 903 (Ohio 2006), explains. The plaintiff's subdivision was denied approval, in part because its one-acre lot size violated the minimum lot size requirement. The landowner brought a declaratory judgment action to require the village to approve the development. The court described the focal point of the litigation as follows:

> In a constitutional analysis, the object of scrutiny is the legislative action. The zoning ordinance is the focal point of the analysis, not the property owner's proposed use, and the analysis begins with a presumption that the ordinance is constitutional. The analysis focuses on the legislative judgment underlying the enactment, as it is applied to the particular property, not the municipality's failure to approve what the owner suggests may be a better use of the property. If application of the zoning ordinance

> prevents an owner from using the property in a particular way, the proposed use is relevant but only as one factor to be considered in analyzing the zoning ordinance's application to the particular property at issue. [*Id.* at 908.]

This is the traditional view, and it presents a difficult problem for landowners. A court decision striking down a zoning restriction is not a holding that the plaintiff's proposed development is acceptable. If the court had struck down the minimum lot size requirement in *Jaylin*, for instance, the village could have responded by reducing the lot size somewhat, but still not enough to allow the Jaylin development. What incentive does Jaylin have to bring its lawsuit in the first instance if it does not result in its development being approved? (As will be explored later in this Chapter, courts often give very substantial deference to choices made by municipalities when acting "legislatively," such as by rezoning.) To overcome this problem, plaintiffs can ask for specific relief that will require an amendment to the ordinance so that their development can proceed, but they have not usually been successful in making this claim.

This type of relief is not usually available because the usual relief in this type of case is a preliminary injunction that enjoins the municipality from enforcing the zoning ordinance against the plaintiff. Most courts will not affirmatively order the municipality to rezone to allow the development the plaintiff has proposed to proceed. (Requests for a declaratory judgment do not encompass specific relief for similar reasons.) The rationale for not giving specific affirmative relief was explained in *City of Conway v. Housing Auth.*, 584 S.W.2d 10 (Ark. 1979):

> [I]t follows that the power of the court to review the action of the municipalities is limited to determining whether or not such action was arbitrary, capricious, or wholly inequitable. The judiciary has no right or authority to substitute its judgment for that of the legislative branch of government. . . . Courts are not super zoning commissions and have no authority to classify property according to zones. [*Id.* at 13.]

The following case takes a contrary view:

CITY OF RICHMOND v. RANDALL

215 Va. 506, 211 S.E.2d 56 (1975)

POFF, JUSTICE:

Dr. Russell E. Randall, Jr., and J.W. Keith (landowners) filed a motion for declaratory judgment against City of Richmond (City) asking the chancellor to declare that "(1) the R-2 (single family residence on minimum 12,500 square foot lot) zoning classification as it applies to their 3.24 acres of vacant land . . . is invalid; (2) the refusal . . . to grant their Special Use request . . . is unreasonable, arbitrary and capricious; and (3) the Court order the City Council to issue the Special Use permit. . . ." By letter opinion dated October 12, 1973, and final decree entered November 9, 1973, the chancellor made extensive findings of fact and ruled, *inter alia*, that the "existing ordinance . . . in its application to Plaintiffs' property is unreasonable and confiscatory and therefore unconstitutional"; that since "the unchallenged *evidence* before Council established that Council's action [denying the special use permit] would result in completely depriving the plaintiffs of the beneficial use of their property by precluding all practical uses, Council's action was unreasonable, confiscatory and arbitrary" and "bears no substantial relationship . . . [to] the public health, safety, morals or general welfare"; and that "Council of the City of Richmond within thirty (30) days from the entry of this Decree shall either adopt Ordinance 73-112 [granting the special use permit] or rezone the land to a zoning category which will permit construction of the proposed building" . . . .

[The plaintiffs, who planned to build a three-story building for medical and general office purposes, requested a change from R-2 residential zoning to RO-1, a Residential-Office District. They also requested a special use permit. The city council rejected the special use permit. At the trial court level, the chancellor held that the R-2 zoning was unreasonable as applied to plaintiffs' property. He also held that the special use permit was improperly rejected.]

Having made these two adjudications of invalidity, the chancellor proceeded to determine what definitive relief would be appropriate. It was apparent that entry of a simple adjudicatory decree granting no definitive relief would work a legal absurdity; the governing body might be left with an island of unzoned land, and the landowners might be left free to put their land to any use, short of a nuisance, they saw fit. Left in that posture, the governing body would be constrained to act hurriedly to zone the unzoned island to a new category. In the rush, and absent definitive guidelines from the court, it might select a category that did not allow the one use shown by the record to be reasonable. In such case, new litigation would ensue. If the new court decree declared the new category unreasonable but again granted no definitive relief, the process of re-zoning and re-litigation could continue *ad infinitum.* The law eschews multiplicity of litigation. When the property rights of an individual and the interests of the community collide, the conflict must be resolved. To expedite a full and final resolution, a court confronted with the conflict must have the power not only to adjudicate the dispute but also to order action not inconsistent with its adjudication.

In the exercise of its power to order such action, a court may not usurp the legislative prerogative. "Zoning is properly a legislative function" and "this court will not substitute its judgment for that of the Board. . . ." But when the evidence shows that the existing zoning ordinance is invalid and the requested use reasonable, and when, as here, the legislative body produces no evidence that an alternative reasonable use exists, then no legislative options exist and a court decree enjoining the legislative body from taking any action which would disallow the one use shown to be reasonable is not judicial usurpation of the legislative prerogative.[3]

This Court has no power to re-zone land to any classification or to order a legislative body to do so. *See Board of Supervisors v. Allman,* [Va.], 211 S.E.2d 48 (1975), this day decided. It follows that trial courts have no such power.

Nor does this Court or any court have power, even when it finds the existing zoning ordinance invalid and a requested use reasonable, to order approval of a special use permit, where, as here, a legislative body is vested by law with jurisdiction over such permits, including legislative discretion to amend the permit ordinance and impose conditions upon the use requested.[4]

---

[3] Courts in Illinois have held that a court has power to grant a requested use after it has found the existing zoning ordinance void and the requested use reasonable. *See Sinclair Pipe Line Co. v. Village of Richton Park,* 167 N.E.2d 406, 411 (Ill. 1960). We believe these holdings, which compel affirmative action by legislative bodies, go too far. The injunction is a more traditional remedy and one less offensive to the concept of separation of powers. Concerning use of an injunction as definitive relief in resolving land use disputes, see *City of Miami Beach v. Weiss,* 217 So. 2d 836, 837 (Fla. 1969).

[4] City's charter § 17.11(b) (Acts 1960, c. 7, pp. 12, 13; Acts 1968, c. 644, pp. 972, 980) vests Council with jurisdiction over special use permits and provides in part that "the council may impose such conditions upon the use of the land, buildings and structures as will, in its opinion, protect the community and area involved and the public from adverse

The power to amend is part of the legislative prerogative.

Here, the chancellor ordered City Council to either enact a new zoning classification for the property which would allow construction of "the proposed building" or to enact Ordinance 73-112, the specific permit ordinance proposed. The order restricts Council to two alternatives. As to the first, the order transgresses the legislative prerogative. As to the second, by foreclosing Council's right under its charter to amend the permit ordinance and impose conditions upon the requested use, the order infringes legislative discretion. For these reasons, the decree must be reversed in part.

As to the chancellor's two adjudications of invalidity, we affirm the decree. As to the chancellor's directions to City Council, we reverse the decree and remand the cause with instructions to modify the decree. The new decree will suspend the adjudications of invalidity for a prescribed period of time and remand the cause to City Council for further legislative action. Since City made no showing of an alternative reasonable use, the new decree will enjoin Council during that period from taking any action which would disallow the one use shown by the record to be reasonable, subject to Council's right under its charter to amend a permit ordinance and impose reasonable conditions not inconsistent with such use. The new decree will further provide that if Council fails to comply within the time prescribed, the adjudications of invalidity will become operative and the injunction will become permanent, provided that landowners shall not put their property to any use other than the use shown by the record to be reasonable.

Affirmed in part, reversed in part and remanded.

NOTES AND QUESTIONS

1. *Understanding* Randall. *Sinclair Pipe Line*, which is cited in footnote 3 of the principal case, suggests the rationale for specific relief. The trial court granted the plaintiff a "variation" from the applicable zoning restriction and ordered the issuance of all permits. The supreme court affirmed. It held it was "appropriate" to frame the decree with reference to the record and the evidence developed at trial. This type of relief "did not go beyond the realm of adjudication" but was simply a form of specific relief comparable to the relief available in mandamus and administrative review actions. Accord *Schwartz v. City of Flint*, 395 N.W.2d 678 (Mich. 1986).

Justice Poff in *Randall*, though appreciating the need for specific relief, rejected *Sinclair Pipe*. But notice how the decree limits the city's ability to reject the development. The adjudication of invalidity is suspended for a period of time for further legislative action, and the city during that time cannot disallow the use shown to be reasonable by the record. The injunction is permanent if the city does not comply, but "the landowners shall not put their property to any other use other than the use shown by the record to be reasonable." If the injunction becomes permanent, can the landowners proceed with their project? In view of *Randall*, what should you be prepared to prove at trial in a similar case in order to get a similar remedy? For the interplay of nonconforming uses with the remedy of an injunction for a certain intensity of use, see *Thieman v. Cedar Valley Feeding Company, Inc.*, 789 N.W.2d 714 (2010).

---

effects and detriments that may result therefrom." Like other legislative zoning actions, conditions imposed by such amendments must meet the test of reasonableness.

2. *Alternatives to specific relief.* Some courts have approved other alternatives that provide some form of specific affirmative relief in zoning actions:

(a) A court will occasionally invalidate the current zoning and leave the land unzoned. See *State ex rel. Nagawicka Island Corp. v. City of Delafield*, 343 N.W.2d 816 (Wis. App. 1983) (use subject only to Building Code requirements); *City of Cherokee v. Tatro*, 636 P.2d 337 (Okla. 1981). Generally, however, the courts are agreed that leaving the land unzoned is an unacceptable remedy, though they may invalidate the zoning regulations as applied to the plaintiff's land, and threaten to leave it unregulated unless the municipality rezones within a specified period of time. See *City of Atlanta v. McLennan*, 226 S.E.2d 732 (Ga. 1976). How did the court in the principal case address this possibility?

(b) If the municipality downzones the plaintiff's land to a more restrictive use, a court may invalidate the downzoning and may then order the reinstatement of the prior zoning classification. *H. Dev. Corp. v. City of Yonkers*, 407 N.Y.S.2d 573 (App. Div. 1978).

3. *Specific relief in appeals from quasi-judicial decisions.* The specific relief issue is also important in appeals of quasi-judicial decisions, such as appeals from a denial of a variance by the board of adjustment. The Standard Act, § 7, provides that "[t]he court may reverse or affirm, wholly or partly, or may modify the decision brought up for review." A remand is appropriate when the right to judicial relief has not been clearly shown. See *Bogue v. Zoning Bd. of Appeals*, 345 A.2d 9 (Conn. 1975). Compare *Gary Bd. of Zoning Appeals v. Eldridge*, 774 N.E.2d 579 (Ind. Ct. App. 2002) (remand is proper remedy in absence of factual findings), with *Mohican Valley Concrete Corp. v. Zoning Bd. of Appeals*, 815 A.2d 145 (Conn. App. 2003) (court should search record for evidence to support board and not remand if board did not state reasons for decision).

In the absence of specific relief, the appellant will have to return to the board that turned her down in the first place. A remand can be avoided if the statute requires the board to make findings of fact on all of the issues litigated in the board proceeding. In the proposed APA model legislation, a court "may grant such relief as it considers appropriate" if it reverses a decision based on a record developed at a public hearing on a development application, or if it reverses a decision made after an appeal on a record hearing. Legislative Guidebook, *supra*, § 10-618. See *Kiely Constr. L.L.C. v. City of Red Lodge*, 57 P.3d 836 (Mont. 2002) (upholding a court ordering of approval of subdivision under statute authorizing appeals and not containing language on what relief is available); *Keebler v. Zoning Board of Adjustment of City of Pittsburgh*, 998 A.2d 670 (Pa. Commw. Ct. 2010) ("remedy is a remand to afford them [objectors] an opportunity to present evidence in opposition to the use variance").

4. For additional discussion of judicial relief in zoning cases, see Krasnowiecki, *Zoning Litigation — How to Win Without Really Losing*, 1976 Inst. on Plan. Zoning & Eminent Domain 1 (1976); Note, *The Rezoning Dilemma: What May a Court do With an Invalid Zoning Classification?*, 25 S.D. L. Rev. 116 (1980); Note, *Beyond Invalidation: The Judicial Power to Zone*, 9 Urb. L. Ann. 159 (1975).

PROBLEM

Premier Foods would like to open a Mexican-style restaurant, but the lot it owns is zoned Neighborhood Limited Commercial, and restaurants are not allowed in this zoning district. They applied for but were denied a rezoning to a district in which their restaurant would be allowed. What kind of action should you bring to challenge the existing zoning district? If you succeed, what kind of relief do you think you can get?

Now assume the board of adjustment has granted Premier Foods a hardship variance for the restaurant, but with a condition that the restaurant be open only from 8:00 a.m. until 10:00 p.m. Premier is unhappy with the decision and wants to appeal it, claiming the condition is illegal. If it succeeds, what relief can the court give?

Your client's restaurant is opposed by the owner of a competitive restaurant one block away who is located in a zoning district in which restaurants are allowed. Does it have standing to challenge the variance? What about a single family homeowner across the street from the restaurant? One block away? A half-mile away?

C. JUDICIAL REVIEW OF ZONING DISPUTES

A PRELIMINARY NOTE ON JUDICIAL REVIEW

After surmounting the sometimes formidable procedural hurdles necessary to get a land use dispute into state court, as explored in the prior section, the land use plaintiff then faces another potentially daunting challenge — satisfying a judicially-fashioned standard of review that, taken at face value, is weighted heavily in favor of deference towards the government. Appearances can be deceiving, however, and state courts have also fashioned a number of countervailing rules that permit considerable judicial oversight of zoning decisions. This Note offers some preliminary ideas about judicial review, to help you evaluate these cases.

As we have seen in Chapter 2, federal courts are quite reluctant to be drawn into "garden variety" zoning disputes, and have fashioned a variety of procedural and substantive rules to avoid doing so. State courts sometimes exhibit the same tendencies, particularly where there does not appear to be a larger issue of principle or policy involved. Recall the justifications identified in Chapter 1 for regulatory interference with private land use decision making. Is there a consistent rationale either for judicial activism or judicial deference in these small-scale, fact-intensive disputes? Noting the recitation of "familiar due process and equal protection" arguments, one state Supreme Court reasoned this way when confronted with a petition to hear an appeal "as of right" because a constitutional issue was presented:

> While [the issues] have loose constitutional connotations, the fundamental question here resolves itself into a matter of application of statutory standards to a particular factual situation under long established principles. At this relatively advanced stage of the law of land use regulation, it will be the rare case concerned with the validity of use classification which will present an issue of sufficient constitutional involvement for purposes of [an appeal as of right]. . . . [*Tidewater Oil Co. v. Mayor & Council*, 209 A.2d 105, 108 (N.J. 1965).]

The *Tidewater* court was concerned with appellate review, and of course it had the discretionary power to take cases to resolve conflicting decisions when a recurring fact pattern appears. State *trial* courts, by contrast, must hear most if not all of the cases presented to them, big and small, important and unimportant. Like their federal and appellate counterparts, however, they, too, understand the unsettling effect that judicial review can have on the process of democratic self-government, a concern that frequently counsels deference to legislative decision making. This concern is particularly heightened in review of zoning cases because zoning, virtually by definition, requires line drawing between areas where different uses are permitted, and line drawing, as all lawyers and judges know, is inherently arbitrary at the margins of policy. State courts, in other words, are normally disinclined to substitute their judgment for local legislatures, just as judges are normally disinclined to substitute their judgment for a jury verdict with which they disagree, because reasonable people can differ and one result is not demonstrably superior to the other.

This might suggest that judicial intervention and oversight can be justified only when, as one federal Court of Appeals put it, the decision is "egregious" or a "gross abuse of power." *Creative Environments, Inc. v. Estabrook*, 680 F.2d 822 (1st Cir. 1982). Indeed, applying this standard, the federal courts have largely avoided becoming a forum for hearing zoning disputes and, if the New Jersey Supreme Court's language in *Tidewater Oil*, quoted above, is to be believed, so too might state courts play a minimal role. The actual posture of state courts with respect to review of zoning decisions is considerably more complex than this, however. State courts, at both the trial and appellate levels, generally interpret their oversight role more freely than do the federal courts, and they do so with particular vigor when land use controversies are brought to them.

There are many possible explanations for this. Arguably, a more expansive state judicial role is an inevitable consequence of the federal courts' withdrawal from the scene, if principles of fairness and justice are to be served. Moreover, state land use decisions seldom if ever have direct application beyond the state of decision, and so state judges don't have to worry about federalism, i.e. about imposing their own singular solution on 49 other states whose circumstances vary widely. Federal judges, by contrast, are understandably hesitant to fashion a result, particularly in a fact sensitive context, that must equally serve the needs of New York, New Mexico and North Dakota. In addition, as has already been discussed, local zoning decisions are typically made pursuant to a delegation of power from the state, and the state enabling statute often can be construed to find a standard that municipalities must follow; state courts generally are more comfortable than federal courts in freely construing the state's own legislation. Finally, and further related to the decentralized decision making that follows from the system of delegated power, state courts often seem particularly sensitive to the potential misuse of that decentralized power, particularly by small units of governments responsive to stable political majorities (suburban homeowners, for instance).

As a result of considerations such as those just sketched, the standard of review that state courts apply to land use controversies, and the rigor (or lack thereof) with which that standard is applied in individual cases, becomes a critical variant in many litigated cases. The case that follows is a typical state court case in which the majority applies a deferential judicial review to a challenge to a zoning classification. The key to understanding the case is being able to identify the various standards of review articulated and applied by the majority and dissenting opinions. Consider how the different judicial approaches (or nuances) play a kind of "gate keeping" function, adjusting the role that the court will play. Notice also how a litigant can attempt to change the court's approach by invoking some independent constitutional ground (such as the Takings Clause) with a different standard of review. This case also shows the way a typical zoning system actually works in practice, an overview that may be helpful as you begin your exploration of this topic.

KRAUSE v. CITY OF ROYAL OAK

11 Mich. App. 183, 160 N.W.2d 769 (1968)

BURNS, JUDGE:

The city of Royal Oak appeals from a judgment restraining it from enforcing a zoning ordinance which places plaintiffs' property in a one-family residential use classification. The judgment permits plaintiffs to use their land for multiple-family residential purposes.

Plaintiffs' property is located in the city of Royal Oak and consists of approximately 3.5 acres of land, which, for purposes of this opinion, can be described in terms of a geometrically imperfect right triangle. . . . [The Court describes the site as shown in the accompanying plan. — Eds.] The territory bounded by the railroad, Starr road and Benjamin avenue has been zoned for one-family residential use since 1957. Other than one nonconforming 3-family multiple dwelling, which was erected prior to 1957 when multiple dwellings were permissible, the east side of Benjamin avenue and the first 2 lots on the north side of Starr avenue, east of Benjamin, are developed with single-family residences. Located upon the subject property itself are 2 comparatively old one-family homes which, all parties agree, will be removed for purposes of replatting, regardless of the course of future development. . . .

Since 1961, owners of part of the subject property have made unsuccessful applications for a zoning change, but it was not until 1966 that plaintiffs commenced this action to enjoin the defendant from enforcing the zoning ordinance as it affects their land. The trial judge listened to the proofs, viewed the premises, and held that the one-family zoning classification was void because it constituted an unreasonable and arbitrary exercise of the police power of the city of Royal Oak and was confiscatory in that it deprived plaintiffs of their property without due process of law.

Our review of this judgment is guided by certain elementary principles. . . .

The propositions that an "ordinance is presumed valid" and that it is plaintiff's burden to overcome that presumption "by clear and satisfactory proof" are of critical importance in this case. . . .

To place this case in its proper perspective, we should note that plaintiff did not claim that any depreciation in property value resulted from the adoption of the zoning ordinance imposing the restriction to which the property was not previously subject. Rather, it appears that the essence of plaintiffs' objection is that their land should be freed of the restriction imposed by the ordinance of 1957 to the end that they might have the benefit of appreciated value. Although one witness, a home builder testifying on behalf of plaintiffs, stated the land was unsuited for single-residential use, another one of the plaintiffs' witnesses, an appraiser who was more familiar with property values, testified that the land was not without value as zoned but that it would be more valuable for multiple-family use. Defendant conceded that such was the case but disputed the ratio of difference in valuations as computed by plaintiffs' witnesses.

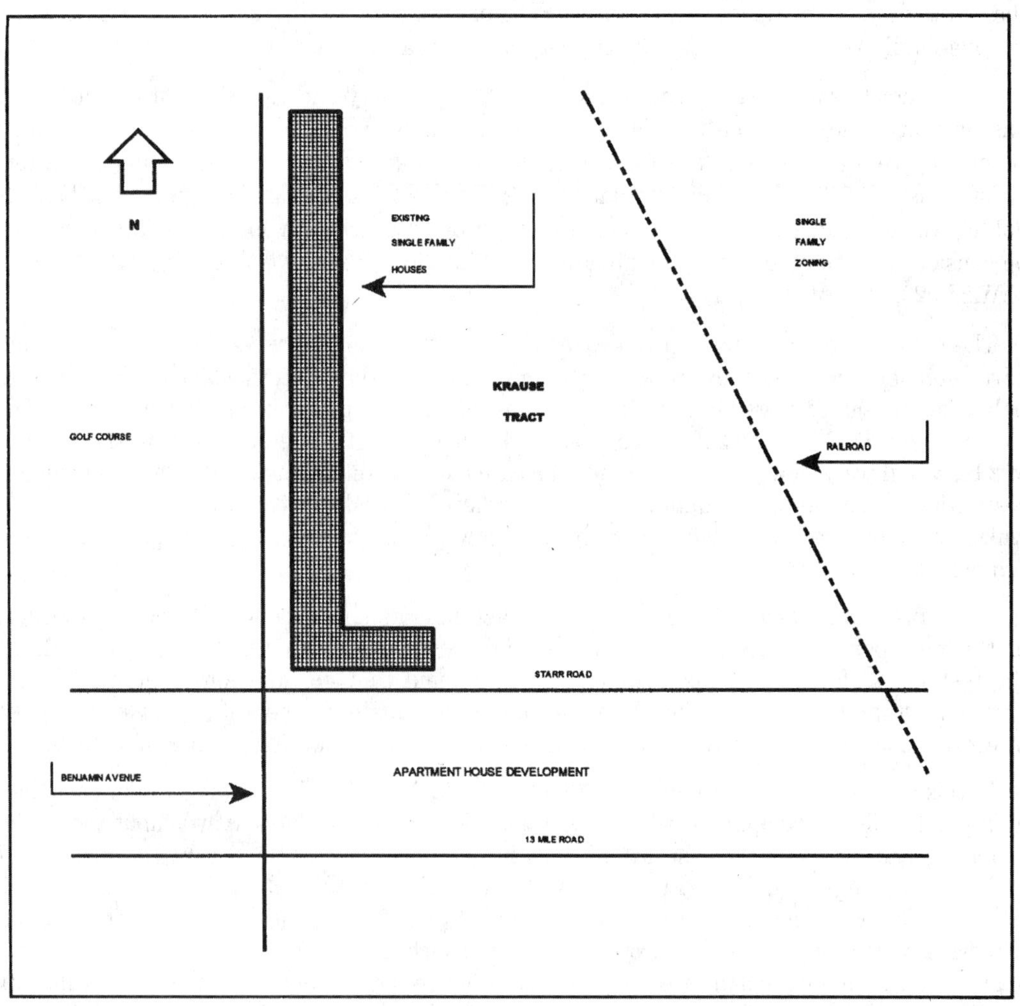

Krause v. City of Royal Oak, Michigan, 1968

According to the plaintiffs' witnesses, the marketability of the property for one-family residences was impaired by the presence of the railroad. The proximity of the tracks to the lots made it impossible to obtain Federal Housing Administration financing, thereby eliminating a good percentage of prospective buyers who could not secure Veterans Administration or conventional loans. In addition, plaintiffs' witnesses pointed out the undesirability of constructing one-family residences next to a railroad because of the vibration, noise, possible danger to children, and the smell. Yet, by plaintiffs' proposal to build multiple dwellings (40 one-bed units and 40 two-bed units) they would invite many more persons (than the 14 one-family houses would accommodate) to share in this feigned misery. The alleged adverse effect the railroad may have on marketability of single-family homes is at best dubious because of plaintiffs' own appraiser's acknowledgment upon cross-examination that a number of single-family homes in Royal Oak lie adjacent to the railroad although these areas located next to the tracks have been the last to develop for residential purposes. The proximity of a railroad does not render zoning for one-family residential purposes arbitrary and unreasonable.

This is not to say, however, that the value of the property and the effect, if any, a railroad has on that value, plays no role in our deliberations. The Supreme Court of Michigan has repeatedly recognized that "the mere fact that land may have a greater selling value for a possible use of different character than that for which it is zoned is not a sufficient basis for holding the ordinance invalid, as applied to such property, although, of course, it is a matter to be considered with other elements affecting the situation." *Paka Corp. v. City of Jackson*, 110 N.W.2d 620, 623 (Mich. 1961).

The disparity of valuations in the cases cited by the plaintiffs wherein zoning ordinances have been held for naught are invariably accompanied by other factors which clearly affect the public health, safety or general welfare of the people. For instance, in *Smith v. Village of Wood Creek Farms*, [123 N.W.2d 210 (Mich. 1963)], the disparity of value of 3 lots and the presence of 2 busy highways and nearby commercial locations were sufficient to invalidate an ordinance restricting those lots to residential purposes, whereas the disparity of value of a fourth lot, which was bordered on but one side by a highway, was insufficient to negate the zoning ordinance.

In the present case the difference in value is accompanied by no convincing evidence bearing on the improper use of the police power. The most positive evidence tendered by plaintiffs was the testimony of the city's planning director who said that no question of public health is involved. Other than this, plaintiffs' proofs fail to adequately cope with most of the public interest considerations which we must assume prompted the adoption of the zoning ordinance.

In this respect, however, there was some testimony introduced regarding the impact that a multiple dwelling development would have upon the people whose backyards abut the subject property. During plaintiffs' case in chief, plaintiffs' appraiser testified that the presence of multiple dwellings would have no adverse effect on the immediate neighborhood, but the adverse effect to which he referred was in terms of price not people. Plaintiffs' home building witness also testified as to this problem, but his concept of adverse effect was his personal opinion of whether or not he would purchase a house completely surrounded with multiple dwellings. Both of plaintiffs' witnesses who spoke on this issue approached the problem as one of basic economics. Contrary to this dollars and cents approach, we have the defendant's planning director's testimony which probably explains a portion of the rationale for having the subject property zoned as it is. . . .

A: *[City planning director]* . . . [I]n this specific area the public involved would be the public that would be in the triangle for the immediate vicinity of the lots in question. This would be from 13 Mile road on the south, Benjamin on the west, and essentially the Grand Trunk on the easterly boundary. They would be the immediate public involved. The area is predominantly single-family north of Starr road and these people would be forced to experience the increased confusion and congestion, noise, *et cetera* that would accompany a development other than single-family, a development that would allow a drastic increase in the total number of people that would live in the three acres more or less in question. The single-family zoning in the area would promote a 13-family development, at least 13 families, would generate at best 26 cars so there would not be a traffic problem coming into or off of Benjamin from Starr road. Also the nature of the residential amenities that accrue to other residential properties from single-family developments would tend to go along with the type of development that is already north of Starr road. Also, we feel that this type of zoning does allow for the natural growth of single-family development with the schools and the other residential amenities [which] are in the area. . . .

Q: *[Counsel for defendant]* Mr. Bowman, as a professional in the field of planning and zoning, what is your opinion as to the comparative desirability of having multiple-family residences back up to single-family residences, compared to facing multiple-family to single-family with a street in between, sir?

A: Well, it's my opinion, based upon the experiences we have had in the recent past, over the past 2 or 3 years, with the rapid development of apartments in Royal Oak and in our surrounding communities, that due to the general demand of the occupants of apartments for parking, for the use of a swimming pool, other recreational facilities, the high density of people living in these developments, that it is far better to face the apartment development across a street which is 50 or 60 feet in width to the single-family development rather than having it abut to the rear yards where all of the service parking and all of the congestion takes place; that we have found that we have more and more of our abutting property owners object where it is a rear yard situation rather than a face to face situation.

We think it is fair to conclude, therefore, that the municipal authority enacting this ordinance was trying to avoid the situation described in *Euclid v. Ambler Realty Company.* [Here the court quoted the paragraph in the *Euclid* case which held, in effect, that apartment development was parasitical in single-family residential areas. — Eds.]

Not to be overlooked is plaintiffs' evidence which, we surmise, was directed to the claim that the city's zoning practice in this instance was arbitrary and capricious. In 1964 a triangular-shaped parcel of property, which is also situated next to the Grand Trunk Western railroad and directly northwest of the subject property, was rezoned from one-family to multiple-family residential. We gather from the city planning director's testimony, however, that there were no existing one-family houses on the rezoned land and there are on the subject property. Furthermore, it is important to note that the area catercorner from this parcel is zoned for heavy industry purposes and that it is bordered predominantly with multiple-family or non-residential zoning classifications. The 1964 rezoning was completely reasonable in our opinion and bears no relation to the alleged unreasonable characterization of plaintiffs' property.

Plaintiffs' case, amounting to substantially nothing more than a partial deprivation of the best economic use of their property, does not persuade us to subvert the interests of the public as expressed by the legislative body which enacted the zoning ordinance in question. The evidence introduced by plaintiffs is alarmingly insufficient to rebut the ordinance's presumption of validity. At best, plaintiffs' evidence presents nothing more than a debatable question.

Judgment vacated. No costs, a public question being involved.

LEVIN, PRESIDING JUDGE (dissenting):

. . . .

Concluding that at best plaintiffs' evidence presented nothing more than a "debatable question" on the rationality of present zoning, the majority reverses the trial judge. However, even if zoning is entirely reasonable in the sense it bears a substantial relationship to public health, morals, safety, or general welfare, it may nonetheless be unreasonable in its application to particular property if that property cannot reasonably be used as zoned. Zoning which prevents any reasonable use of property is confiscatory and, for that reason, invalid.

While the trial judge and we must find for the municipality if we find there is a debatable question concerning the rationality of the zoning, i.e., zoning is not irrational if, on the evidence presented, its rationality remains debatable, a "debatable question" rule has not been established where the question presented is whether the zoning is unreasonable because it is confiscatory. Whether zoning is confiscatory is more a question of fact than of judgment. That fact may be proved like any other fact. It is not necessary for one claiming confiscation to prove it beyond dispute.

The evidence presented here concerning the confiscation issue was in conflict. The trial judge correctly went about resolving that factual dispute in the same manner he would approach decision of any disputed factual issue in a case tried to him. Merely because all reasonable men would not necessarily have reached the same decision did not oblige the trial judge to decide the issue of confiscation for the municipality. . . .

On the entire evidence I am not left with the *definite and firm conviction* that a mistake was committed by the trial judge. The trial judge stated that the plaintiffs' house builder witness "made the greatest impression on the court. A home builder with considerable experience in Royal Oak, he testified that plaintiff's land was totally unsuited to single residence development and that at least to him the land had no value for that purpose. Based on his own experience he said that lots adjacent to the unsightly and noisy railroad tracks were not readily salable for single residence purposes. He has owned 2 comparable lots for some time and has been unable to dispose of them. Furthermore, again based on his own experience, he said that adequate home financing could not be obtained on land adjacent to railroad tracks."

The trial judge thereby indicated he chose to adopt the testimony offered in behalf of the plaintiffs in preference to testimony offered in behalf of the defendant.

There is no reason to reject the trial judge's evaluation of the conflicting testimony. The testimony of plaintiffs' house builder witness so adopted by the trial judge was not incredible. It was supported by the testimony of plaintiffs' appraisal witness who, while he valued the property at $11,500, stated that a prudent developer would not buy it. I interpret that to mean a speculator could be found to buy the property, but not a developer. The question before the trial judge and us, on the issue of confiscation, is whether the property can reasonably be *used* as zoned, not whether it has an exchange value. That a buyer could be found for it, that it has a buying and selling value, does not establish that anyone could be found who would develop and use the property.

Passage of time and accompanying changes in controlling facts, a change in zoning itself, might make the property more valuable and justify a speculator's investment. And then again the property might become worth less. The judicial inquiry is not concerned with the speculative possibilities of the property, but rather seeks to determine whether it can now be reasonably *used* as now zoned. . . .

On the record before him, the trial judge was entirely justified in concluding it would be so difficult to find a land developer or house builder willing to speculate in the improvement of this land in preference to land which does not have the location disadvantages which this land has, that this land was not suitable for *development* with single-family residences, and that, accordingly, present zoning was confiscatory. Such finding not being clearly erroneous, I would affirm on that issue.

NOTES AND QUESTIONS

1. *The problem.* The *Krause* case is illustrative of hundreds, if not thousands, of ordinary zoning disputes. In this paradigm, the municipality has placed the plaintiff's property in one use zone (usually a zone that permits a relatively low-intensity use, such as single family residences) and plaintiff contends that a different use category (usually a higher-intensity use, such as apartments) is appropriate. Does the majority agree with the City of Royal Oak that single family zoning is the "best" use of Krause's land? Or does the court simply defer to the city's choice, whatever it may be? Are there any circumstances under which the dissenting judge would agree that the single-family zoning was valid? How do standard of review rules influence the approaches of the majority and dissenting opinions? Why, considering the uses in the surrounding area, do you suppose the city refused this rezoning?

2. *Arbitrary or reasonable?* One way to test the majority's approach is to ask how it would have decided the case if the facts were flipped — if Royal Oak had rezoned the Krause land for apartments, and the owners of the adjoining single-family homes had challenged that decision. Rezoning issues are discussed in Chapter 6. The majority opinion points in two different directions:

a. *The hierarchy of uses.* In *Krause*, the majority seems to assume the incompatibility of single-family residential and multiple family dwelling zoning classifications, and its rhetoric implies that the former need to be protected against the latter. Recall the "parasite" characterization of apartments in the *Euclid* opinion, in which the Court sustained the exclusion of apartments from the one- and two-family districts. But isn't this, at very least, a "debatable question"? As pointed out in a Note following the *Euclid* case reprinted *supra*, this part of the *Euclid* opinion is based upon an unwarranted assumption that apartments must always be built at high density and have those noxious attributes so graphically described by Justice Sutherland. Modern "garden" apartments are often built at relatively low densities, with ample open space around the buildings, and are therefore not really incompatible with nearby "single-family residential" zoning. Compare *Allred v. City of Raleigh*, 173 S.E.2d 533, 538 (N.C. App. 1970), *rev'd on other grounds*, 178 S.E.2d 432 (N.C. 1971) ("Many modern and luxurious apartment buildings tend to complement the area where they are located.").

b. *An economic hierarchy?* The majority takes a more evenhanded approach by criticizing the plaintiff's argument that apartments are better suited than single family homes to the "vibration, noise, danger and smell" of the land adjacent to the railroad tracks. Why is it more acceptable, Judge Burns asks, to subject 80 apartment-dwelling families to the railroad than 14 families in freestanding houses? Why indeed? — a question that can be asked of the many zoning plans that use multiple dwelling zones this way to buffer a single family zone from a less desirable nearby use. Despite the majority's insistence that plaintiff asserts a "feigned misery," suppose the judges were persuaded that the "misery" was real. Do either of the opinions in *Krause* provide an argument for invalidating *any* residential zoning on the site, or is this an instance in which the court must give deference to the city's choice of one or the other of the residential uses? (As an aside, you might also want to consider whether there is a market-based justification for using high density zones as buffers, in that the increased density may offset the lower value of each undesirable unit. Or should such an amoral approach be beneath the dignity of the law?)

3. *Confiscatory?* What do the majority and the dissenting opinions mean by "confiscatory" with respect to a zoning classification? Is it fair to assume that they mean "amounting to a taking of private property without compensation"? If so, do you agree with Judge Levin in dissent that "whether zoning is confiscatory is more a question of fact than of judgment" and that the "debatable question" test is not applicable "where the question presented is whether the zoning is unreasonable because it is confiscatory"? Would it be accurate to conclude that the majority implicitly applies a "balancing" test when zoning is claimed to be "confiscatory," while Judge Levin's test is simply whether the economic impact of the landowner or developer is too severe, regardless of the "reasonableness" of the zoning when the economic impact is not considered? Can you tell, by the way, whether they are applying federal or state taking rules? Why does Judge Levin defer to the trial court's conclusion about this, rather than making his own? What would it take to convince him that the city's single-family zoning was not "confiscatory"?

For other examples of overcoming the presumption of validity see, e.g., *Bartlett v. City of Chicago*, 204 N.E.2d 780 (Ill. App. 1965) (court invalidated single-family residential zoning on tract virtually surrounded by high-rise apartments); *Clarke v. Board of County Comm'rs*, 778 N.E.2d 1116 (Ohio App. 2002) (residential zoning invalid in rural area with substantial mineral extraction and heavy industrial uses); *Reuschenberg v. Town of Huntington*, 532 N.Y.S.2d 148 (App. Div. 1988) (residential zoning next to heavy industrial uses inconsistent with comprehensive plan and therefore discriminatory; no need to also show that it is confiscatory); *Palmer Trinity Sch., Inc. v. Village of Palmetto Bay*, 31 So. 3d 260 (Fla. 3d D.C.A. 2010) ("reverse spot zoning" confiscatory). Cases to the contrary are legion. See, e.g., *Buskey v. Hanover*, 577 A.2d 406 (N.H. 1990) (refusal to rezone from low-rise apartment use to commercial in bustling college town upheld); *Miller v. Board of County Comm'rs*, 2008 Ohio App. LEXIS 1807 (Ohio App. May 5, 2008); *M.C. Props., Inc. v. City of Chattanooga*, 994 S.W.2d 132 (Tenn. App. 1999) (residential zoning justified by need to stop outward expansion of commercial district); *Thomas v. Panola County*, 45 So. 3d 1173 (Miss. 2010) (zoning decisions not set aside unless "arbitrary, capricious, discriminatory, or is illegal, or without substantial evidentiary basis").

4. *Post-Lucas.* If *Krause* had been decided after *Lucas*, would this decision be relevant to any issue in *Krause*? It seems clear that a court after *Lucas* would hold the residential zoning unconstitutional if it equated the trial court's finding that the zoning was confiscatory with a finding that it denied all economically viable use of the property. This seems to be the teaching of similar cases decided post-*Lucas*, but only two or three cases have applied *Lucas* to invalidate a zoning restriction. For the usual view, see *Tim Thompson, Inc. v. Village of Hinsdale*, 617 N.E.2d 1227 (Ill. App. 1993) (upholding downzoning because landowner could build at lower density). How does the court's approach to the issues in *Krause* compare with the "default" takings test in *Penn Central* now adopted by the Supreme Court? Many states, despite the ascendance of *Penn Central*, continue to apply an "arbitrary and capricious" test to zoning restrictions. See *Gerchen v. City of Ladue*, 784 S.W.2d 232 (Mo. App. 1989) (residential zoning upheld; presumption of validity).

A NOTE ON FACIAL AND AS-APPLIED CHALLENGES: *NECTOW v. CITY OF CAMBRIDGE*

An additional consideration that both litigants and judges take into account when planning (or deciding) zoning cases is whether to deal with the regulation "on its face" or "as applied."

Generally, "[a] facial challenge to the constitutional validity of a statute or ordinance considers only the text of the measure itself, not its application to the particular circumstances of an individual." On the other hand, "[a]n as applied challenge may seek . . . relief from a specific application of a facially valid statute or ordinance to an individual or class of individuals who are under allegedly impermissible present restraint or disability as a result of the manner or circumstances in which the statute or ordinance has been applied . . . ." *Santa Monica Beach, Ltd. v. Superior Court*, 19 Cal. 4th 952, 961 (1999).

When a court holds that an ordinance provision is facially invalid, the regulation is effectively wiped off the books and cannot be enforced by the municipality against any land user. Facial attacks can be attractive to a plaintiff who is (consciously or otherwise) the stand-in for an entire class of land users who are affected by the regulation, because a successful lawsuit will resolve the issue for all at one time. On the other hand, for a facial attack to be successful, the court must be persuaded that there are, as a practical matter, no circumstances at all under which the ordinance could be validly applied. It may be easier by far to show that the regulation is arbitrary (or otherwise invalid) in its application to a specific site than to show that this will *always* be the case. Moreover, as the ancient common law maxim has it, real property is, by its very nature, unique, and it follows that land use regulation, particularly zoning ordinances, will frequently touch and affect that uniqueness in unpredictable ways.

When the U.S. Supreme Court validated the concept of zoning in the *Euclid* case, it limited itself to considering the ordinance facially, which illustrates a converse strategic point from the defending municipality's perspective.

In *Nectow v. City of Cambridge*, 277 U.S. 183 (1928), the Court had before it a comprehensive zoning ordinance that, in its general scope, was conceded to be constitutional under the decision in *Euclid v. Ambler Realty Co.* Plaintiff Nectow attacked the ordinance, however, on the ground that, as specifically applied to him, it deprived him of his property without due process of law in contravention of the Fourteenth Amendment, because it did not promote "the health, safety, convenience and general welfare of the inhabitants of the part of the city affected." In *Nectow*, the Court accepted, as a basis for its decision, the findings of the master appointed by the Massachusetts court, as follows:

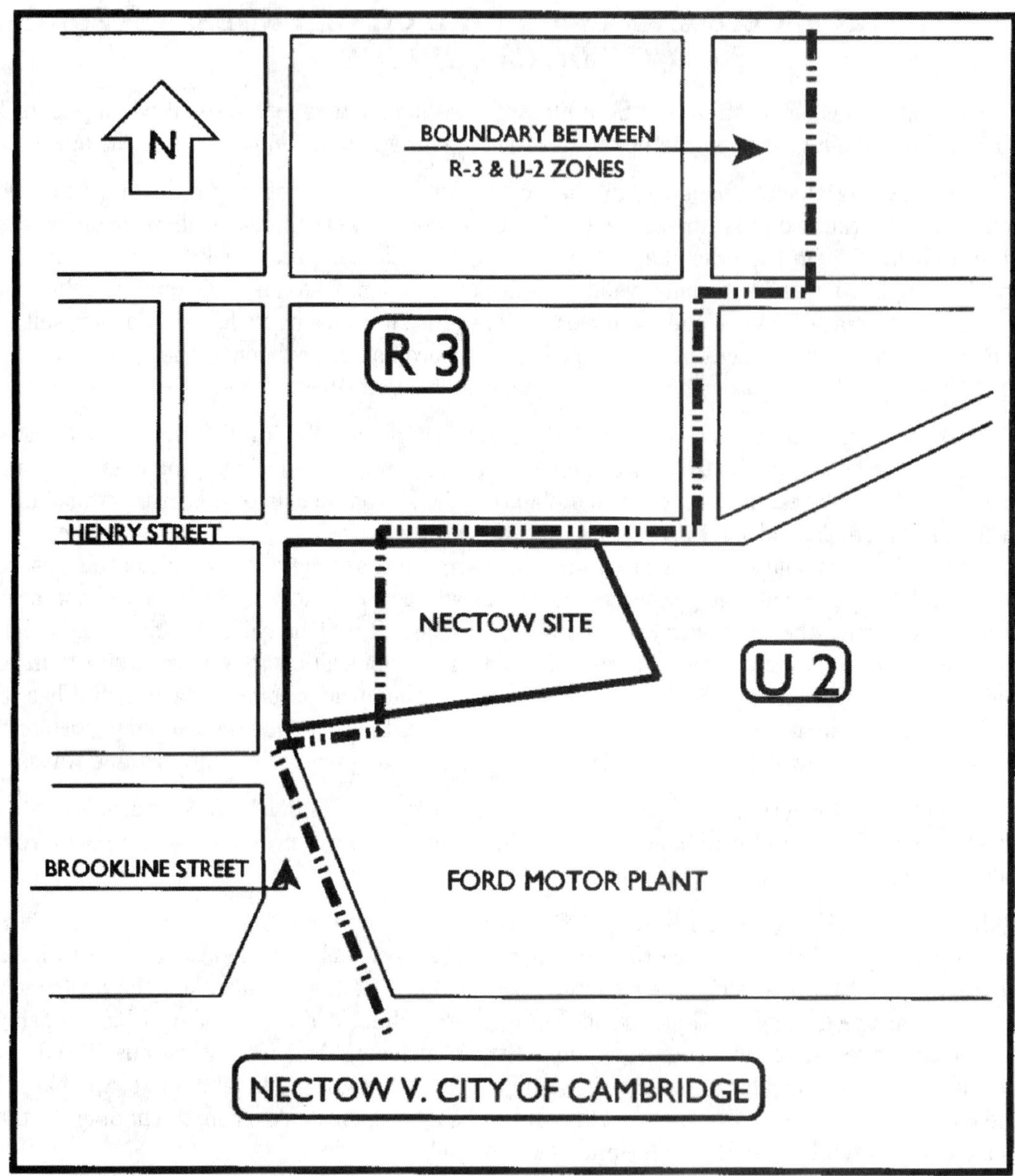

When the zoning ordinance was enacted, plaintiff in error was and still is the owner of a tract of land containing 140,000 square feet, of which the locus here in question is a part. The locus contains 29,000 square feet, with a frontage on Brookline street, lying west, of 304.75 feet, on Henry street, lying north, of 100 feet, on other land of the plaintiff in error, lying east, of 264 feet, and on land of the Ford Motor Company, lying southerly, of 75 feet. The territory lying east and south is unrestricted. The lands beyond Henry street to the north and beyond Brookline street to the west are within a residential district. The effect of the zoning is to separate from the west end of plaintiff in error's tract a strip 100 feet in width. The Ford Motor Company has a large

> auto assembling factory south of the locus; and a soap factory and the tracks of the Boston & Albany Railroad lie near. Opposite the locus, on Brookline street, and included in the same district, there are some residences; and opposite the locus, on Henry street, and in the same district, are other residences. The locus is now vacant, although it was once occupied by a mansion house. Before the passage of the ordinance in question, plaintiff in error had outstanding a contract for the sale of the greater part of his entire tract of land for the sum of $63,000. Because of the zoning restrictions the purchaser refused to comply with the contract. Under the ordinance, business and industry of all sorts are excluded from the locus, while the remainder of the tract is unrestricted. It further appears that provision has been made for widening Brookline street, the effect of which, if carried out, will be to reduce the depth of the locus to 65 feet. [*Id.* at 186–87.]

The Supreme Court held the residential-use classification of plaintiff's property to be invalid. In his opinion for the court, Justice Sutherland stated:

> Here, the express finding of the master, already quoted, confirmed by the court below, is that the health, safety, convenience and general welfare of the inhabitants of the part of the city affected will not be promoted by the disposition made by the ordinance of the locus in question. This finding of the master, after a hearing and an inspection of the entire area affected, supported, as we think it is, by other findings of fact, is determinative of the case. That the invasion of the property of plaintiff in error was serious and highly injurious is clearly established; and, since a necessary basis for the support of that invasion is wanting, the action of the zoning authorities comes within the ban of the Fourteenth Amendment and cannot be sustained. [277 U.S. at 188–89.]

Although the record in the *Nectow* case "made it pretty clear that because of the industrial and railroad purposes to which the immediately adjoining lands to the south and east have been devoted and for which they are zoned, the locus is of comparatively little value for the limited uses permitted by the ordinance," the Court did not hold that the zoning ordinance, as applied to the locus, amounted to a de facto taking. *Id.* at 187.

As-applied challenges come in all sizes and shapes. *Nectow* is illustrative, however, of a unique subcategory of as-applied cases, the "split lot" problem. Deliberately or accidentally over time, a site ends up partially in one zone and partially in another, as was the case with Nectow's land. (Recall that in both *Nectow* and *Krause*, the sites held outmoded structures that were to be demolished to permit a modern use.) Each use zone may be rational in itself, but arbitrary as applied to a site not large enough or otherwise configured so as to be unusable when divided. For a modern example of a "split lot" problem, see *Application of McDonald's Corp.*, 560 A.2d 362 (Vt. 1989) (irregularly shaped lot split between commercial and residential zones; use of residential zone for parking denied).

D. RECURRING ISSUES IN ZONING LAW

As we have seen, the legitimacy of separating residential from non-residential uses ("a pig in the parlor instead of the barnyard") was readily accepted by the Supreme Court in *Euclid v. Ambler Realty*, and it is now so well established as to have become axiomatic. *Euclid* also demonstrates, however, that the progression from the least intense residential use through the most intense industrial use possible is at least as much a continuum as it is a dichotomy. A large residential tower with hundreds of apartments, might well be regarded as more burdensome on adjoining uses than a modest group of neighborhood retail and service stores. One way to bridge the gap between these nominally distinct classes of regulations is to focus on the density and intensity of the permitted use, whether it is residential or non-residential. Sec. 1 below does so, followed by separate sections exploring issues relating to residential and non-residential uses, respectively. It will be useful to keep an open mind about the continuum of uses just described as you read on.

[1.] Density and Intensity of Use

A NOTE ON THE BUSINESS OF DEVELOPMENT

Land development is a business, and no matter what other motivations a developer may have (the desire of a non-profit developer to provide low-cost housing for poor people, for instance), in the end, the bottom line must work in dollars and cents terms. Regulation of land development is no less a business for municipalities, although they are generally loathe to express their interests this way. Development brings "profit" to municipalities in the form of new tax revenues and new economic activity, but it can also impose the cost of providing substantial new municipal services (bigger schools, better sewers, wider roads) to accommodate the growth in population or business activity. The separate interests of land developers and local governments often lead them in opposite directions as they contest what regulations will control the use of any particular site. Generally speaking, developers will prefer a more intense use, while municipalities will prefer a less intense use, each believing that this outcome will maximize gain and minimize costs. (This is only a broad generalization, however. For a case in which the developer insisted, successfully, on building fewer housing units because of market demand than the municipality wanted, see *Toll Brothers, Inc. v. Township of West Windsor*, 807 A.2d 193 (N.J. 2002).) In *Albuquerque Commons Partnership v. City Council of Albuquerque*, 212 P.3d 1122 (N.M. Ct. App. 2009), the planning objectives of mixed use, new urbanism and creation of an urban scale were insufficient to support mandating a *minimum* density when the developer wanted to do lower density "big box" retail, and it was held it had a vested right in the existing zoning.

One of the most important ways in which land users and land regulators work out their separate interests is by contesting the permitted *density* of use of a tract of land. The typical measure of density in residential development is the number of dwelling units permitted per acre of land, although the same result can be achieved by alternate measures as well. The same intensity of use is permitted, for instance, by a zoning ordinance that permits two dwelling units per acre (2 d.u./a.) and one that requires a minimum lot size of 20,000 sq. feet (a standard acre contains 40,000 sq. feet). Non-residential densities are normally controlled by a measure such as number of square feet of building allowed. Density calculations intersect with other regulations as well; the buildable density of a site that contains wetlands or steep slopes will be much lower than the nominal density allowed by the ordinance, unless the municipality permits an increase in the density on the remainder of the site. This process is sometimes spoken of in terms of *gross* and *net* densities.

The facts described by the Texas Supreme Court in *Sheffield Development Co., Inc. v. City of Glenn Heights*, 140 S.W.3d 660 (Tex. 2004), serve to illustrate the importance of density regulation. *Sheffield* was litigated as a regulatory takings claim, so the plaintiff had good reason to emphasize the magnitude of its loss due to the City's downzoning. Out of the public eye, however, both developers and municipalities are constantly calculating and recalculating their positions much as the parties do here. Consider these facts both from the developer's perspective and that of the City:

> The City of Glenn Heights is a growing suburban community (1990 pop. 4,564; 2000 pop. 8,050) south of Dallas astraddle the Dallas/Ellis County border. In 1986, the City zoned a 236-acre tract ["Stone Creek" — Eds.] as Planned Development District 10 (PD 10), allowing most of it to be developed for single-family residences on lots no smaller than 6,500 square feet, with a maximum density of 5.5 dwelling units per acre. . . .
>
> In 1995, the City adopted a comprehensive "Future Land Use Plan" which found that the City had an oversupply of high-density residential areas. The plan designated the neighborhood including Stone Creek primarily as a lower density residential area to contain four to five dwelling units per acre. Though PD 10 zoning allowed a maximum of 5.5 dwelling units per acre in the relevant area, the first phase of the development had been built with only 3.9 dwelling units per acre, the trial court found, and thus would comply with the new plan. In the summer of 1996, Sheffield Development Co. contracted to purchase the undeveloped part of Stone Creek including certain unbuilt lots in the first phase area, in all about 194 acres, for $600 an acre. The price was below market because the owner, a firm headquartered in England, was anxious to liquidate its real estate portfolio in the United States. [Thereafter,] the City's consultant recommended that PD 10 be rezoned to require lots no smaller than 12,000 square feet, thereby permitting construction of about half the number of houses permitted by PD 10.
>
> In both the bench trial and the subsequent jury trial, the parties offered evidence of the value of Sheffield's property before and after the rezoning. Witnesses for Sheffield testified that the property was worth $12,000-$14,000/acre before the rezoning and $600/acre afterward, a reduction of 95% or more. The City's appraiser testified that the property was worth only $4,000/acre before the rezoning and $2,500/acre afterward, a reduction of 37.5%. The jury found that the property was worth $970,000 ($5,000/acre) before rezoning and $485,000 ($2,500/acre) afterward, a reduction of 50%. In accordance with its findings and the jury's verdict, the trial court rendered judgment awarding Sheffield $485,000.

[a.] Density Restrictions: Large Lot Zoning

One of the most important trends in residential development has been the decline in residential densities in the last half-century. All metropolitan areas show a sloping density gradient, with the highest densities at the core and the lowest at the suburban fringe. The next case considers the constitutional issues raised by large lot zoning, which is a major land use strategy for achieving low densities in suburban areas:

JOHNSON v. TOWN OF EDGARTOWN

425 Mass. 117, 680 N.E.2d 37 (1997)

WILKINS, C.J. This case concerns a challenge to a three-acre minimum area requirement for residential lots in the RA-120 Residential/Agricultural zoning district (RA-120 district) in Edgartown on the island of Martha's Vineyard. The plaintiff landowners, trustees of the Herring Creek Farm Trust, whom we shall refer to as the trust, sought a declaratory judgment, pursuant to G.L. c. 240, § 14A, that the three-acre requirement is arbitrary and unreasonable because it does not advance any valid zoning objective.

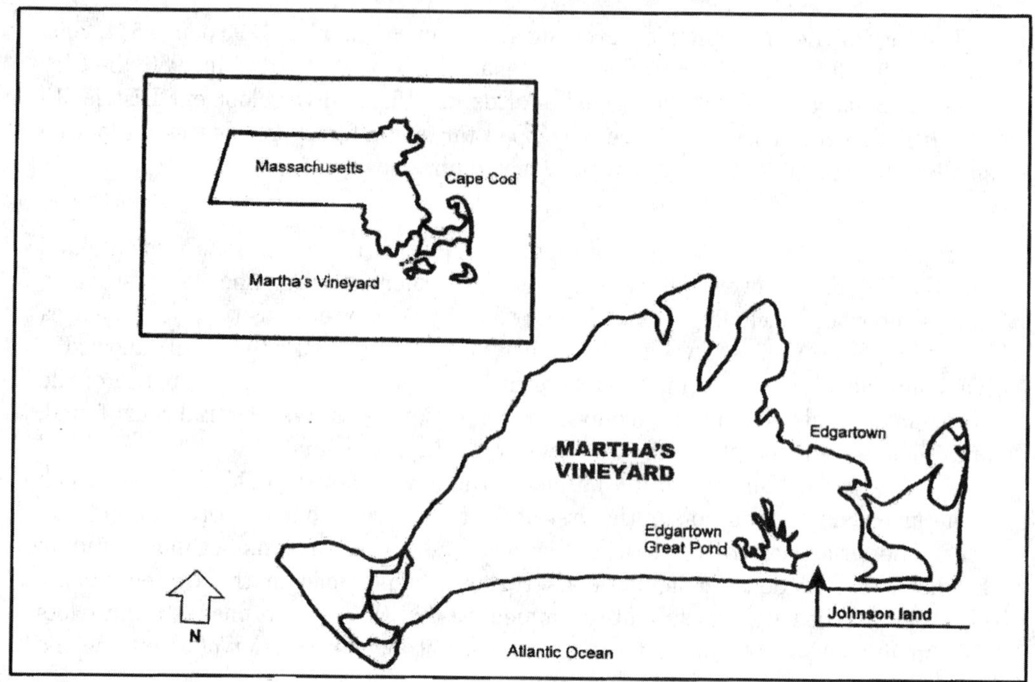

A judge of the Land Court entered a judgment that the challenged by-law serves a permissible public purpose and does not violate any constitutional or statutory provision. We granted direct appellate review of the trust's appeal. Before us, the trust asserts that the challenged by-law bears no substantial relation to any legitimate public interest. We affirm the judgment of the Land Court.

We summarize relevant parts of the judge's decision. Edgartown adopted a revised zoning by-law in 1973, establishing zoning districts with minimum lot requirements then ranging from 5,000 square feet to three acres. The RA-120 district boundaries are consistent with a plan prepared by the engineering firm of Metcalf & Eddy designating certain areas as "open space" due to the "fragile" nature of the environment. Now, about one-half the town (8,736 of 17,181 acres) is zoned for three-acre lots; about 4,900 acres are zoned for one-half acre or one acre lots; and about 3,200 acres are zoned for one and one-half acre lots.[4] During the early 1970s, other Martha's Vineyard towns (Tisbury, West Tisbury, and Chilmark on their south shores) as well as Nantucket adopted three-acre zoning for portions of their towns.

The trust owns 215 acres in the RA-120 district abutting the Atlantic Ocean on the south and Edgartown Great Pond on the west. A farm on the locus is devoted to horticultural uses and has received a special assessment and tax rate under G.L. c. 61A, § 4. Earlier in this decade, the trust submitted to the town's planning board a fifty-four lot subdivision plan for the locus, each lot having in excess of three acres and twenty-five acres dedicated to open space. That

---

(4) In 1990 a master plan indicated that there was a significant amount of vacant land in the one-half acre zone. There was evidence that Edgartown had more half-acre or smaller lots than any other town on the Vineyard.

plan was referred to the Martha's Vineyard Commission. *See* St. 1977, c. 831. On February 10, 1994, the commission voted to deny permission to grant the necessary development permits. [The court noted in a footnote that "the trust has appealed from the commission's decision. That appeal is not before us."]

The judge considered extensive expert testimony from both sides in relation to the permissible statutory objectives of zoning and concluded that there was a substantial relation between the by-law and the permissible objectives of zoning. He stated that the by-law "facilitates the provision of open space, conserves the value of land, promotes the conservation of natural resources, prevents blight and pollution of the environment, and preserves the Island's unique natural, ecological and other values." The judge credited the testimony of the town's expert, a marine ecologist specializing in coastal areas, to conclude that the effect of nitrate loading on drinking water and on Edgartown Great Pond justified three-acre zoning in the RA-120 district to protect the public health, water, water supply, and water resources. He also concluded that the three-acre requirement allowed a reasonable margin to provide for future problems. The judge identified an independent justification in the "unique ecological integrity of the area including coastal waters, embayments, plant and animal life."

The judge considered the trust's claim that the area requirement of the RA-120 district excluded certain people from the town. He said: "Edgartown is located on a relatively small island with limited accessibility and with inherent resulting economic issues including those of supply and demand. In addition, it is apparent that the setting, topography, weather and natural resources make the entire island highly desirable as a vacation and retirement area. One would reasonably expect such factors to exert an increasingly upward pressure on the price of real estate. Zoning most likely makes some contribution to such pressures, but there is herein a lack of credible evidence as to how and to what extent if any, zoning factors contribute to the availability (or unavailability) of real estate, and more importantly, whether or not the determinative factor of the equation is large lot zoning. I note further the lack of evidence of any person being denied housing because of, or largely because of, such zoning constraints."

We turn first to general principles that guide our decision. In a sense, insular thinking is appropriate here. The values that the town seeks to protect are not simply local ones. The Legislature has recognized "a regional and statewide interest in preserving and enhancing" Martha's Vineyard's "unique natural, historical, ecological, scientific, cultural, and other values," values that may be irreversibly damaged by inappropriate uses of land. St. 1977, c. 831, § 1. In a challenge to an Edgartown zoning by-law, the Legislature's expression of public interest in the preservation of the qualities of Martha's Vineyard is a relevant factor. *See Sturges v. Chilmark*, 402 N.E.2d 1346 (Mass. 1980). The Legislature's proclamation also blunts any claim that, in purporting to act to protect its environment, Edgartown is doing so only in support of its parochial interests.

The fact that Edgartown is on an island is important in another respect. Edgartown is not a rural or suburban municipality lying in the path of suburban growth. The trust's claim that large lot zoning is exclusionary, and thus particularly suspect, lacks the force it might have in many other situations. The trust did not establish, nor indeed did it seek to prove by direct evidence, that people were excluded from settling in Edgartown because of three-acre zoning in approximately half the town. In discussing a challenge to a zoning provision of another Martha's Vineyard town, we said that "in a rural, as opposed to a suburban, setting, where no showing has been made of regional demand for primary housing, the public interest in preserving the environment and protecting a way of life may outweigh whatever undesirable economic and social consequences inhere in partly 'closing the doors' to affluent outsiders primarily seeking vacation homes" (citation omitted). *Sturges v. Chilmark, supra* at 255. We reject any suggestion that Edgartown's three-acre zoning is presumptively exclusionary and that, therefore, the town should have the burden of proving the reasonableness of the zoning regulation.

Apart from its argument that the burden falls on a municipality to justify its large lot zoning because it is exclusionary, the trust argues, in any event, that the traditional, heavy burden on one challenging the constitutionality of a zoning law should not be imposed in a challenge to large lot zoning. We do not agree. The general rule is that a zoning by-law whose reasonableness is fairly debatable will be sustained. On occasion the court has adopted the criminal law concept of proof "beyond reasonable doubt" to describe the burden that is placed on one challenging the validity of a zoning provision. The characterization of a challenger's burden as one of proof beyond reasonable doubt may not be instructive. A better characterization is that the challenger must prove by a preponderance of the evidence that the zoning regulation is arbitrary and unreasonable, or substantially unrelated to the public health, safety, morals, or general welfare.

As residential lot size requirements increase, it becomes more difficult to justify the requirements. *See Aronson v.* [*Town of*] *Sharon*, [195 N.E.2d 341 (Mass. 1964)] (in such situations, "the law of diminishing returns will set in at some point"). In *Simon v.* [*Town of*] *Needham*, [42 N.E.2d 516 (Mass. 1942)], although skeptical of the town's position, this court rejected a challenge to a zoning requirement of one acre for each house lot, concluding that the town could fairly decide that such a requirement would enhance the public interest. The case appears to have been decided on the classical standard of what the town's legislative body could rationally have concluded. The court intimated that the result would have been different if a landowner had proved that the one-acre requirement created "a barrier against the influx of thrifty and respectable citizens who desire to live there and who are able and willing to erect homes upon lots upon which fair and reasonable restrictions have been imposed."

Twenty-two years later, in *Aronson v.* [*Town of*] *Sharon*, this court held invalid a town zoning by-law requiring house lots of 100,000 square feet. The court decided that the zoning provision exceeded the town's statutory authority and suggested that the operation of the by-law was confiscatory. The town sought to justify the large lot requirement on the ground that it would encourage the retention of land in its natural state for the benefit of the community. The court concluded that the permissible and judicially assumed advantages that justified one-acre zoning in *Simon v.* [*Town of*] *Needham*, would not justify 100,000 square foot house lots.

Although an objecting landowner has the burden of proving that large lot zoning is unjustified, the *Aronson* opinion indicates that a municipality's reliance on generalities concerning the public benefit of large lot zoning will not carry the day. In such a case, the municipality has the burden of coming forward with something tangible to justify its action. Thus, in 1975, in deciding a challenge to two-acre zoning in a portion of Sherborn, the Appeals Court stated that the record must show that there is a reasonable basis for concluding "that there are special needs that are met by two-acre zoning." *Wilson v.* [*Town of*] *Sherborn*, 326 N.E.2d 922 (Mass. App. 1975). The town successfully justified its two-acre zoning as an appropriate health protection measure based on an established and reasonable relationship between two-acre zoning and sewage and water conditions in the two-acre zone.

We are now in a position to move from general considerations to the specifics of the record in this case to see whether the judge was warranted in finding that the evidence justified his conclusion that the three-acre zoning requirement served a permissible public purpose authorized by The Zoning Act. Not every beneficial effect of the three-acre zoning requirement in the RA-120 district that the judge noted would, standing alone, justify the restriction. Neither the provision of open space nor the protection of plant and animal life, for example, would singly justify large lot zoning. That benefits of this character incidentally may flow from large lot zoning does not, however, detract from those justifications that do support large lot zoning. We, therefore, need not dwell on the trust's persuasive argument that the record does not support any claim that three-acre zoning in the RA-120 district is partially justified by a need to preserve animal and plant life. We turn, therefore, to other reasons advanced by the town in support of the area requirements of the RA-120 district.

The parties substantially agree that a lot of two acres in the RA-120 district would be sufficient to provide a safe on-site source of water on a lot having its own septic system. We need not decide whether there is any justification for adding an acre as a margin of safety for on-site drinking water, a concept whose reasonableness was not explained in the record. Nor need we reach the trust's doubtful argument that the State's requirements for septic systems somehow make inappropriate zoning requirements founded on considerations of safe drinking water and pollution from sewage. We need not decide these points because there is an independent ground for concluding that the town has come forward with sufficient proof of a reasonable basis for the need of three-acre zoning in the RA-120 district.

The town produced evidence, credited by the judge, that house lots of three acres or more were required in order to protect the ecology of Edgartown Great Pond. The pond, which consists of 890 acres, is a coastal and marine water formed in the sandy soil of the outwash plain of the melting glacier that created Martha's Vineyard. The pond, which the town opens to the ocean periodically and which opens naturally as well from time to time, is brackish (its water being between saline and fresh). It is vulnerable to nutrient pollution from excess nitrogen which would encourage plant growth that periodically deprives the water of oxygen. This anoxia kills shellfish and other organisms on the bottom of the pond and kills finfish. Without oxygen, sulfates in the water will produce hydrogen sulfide gas, "a sewer gas smell." The pond is on the brink of, and sometimes crosses the line of, becoming unhealthy.

The town's evidence concerning the need to protect the ecology of Edgartown Great Pond, evidence of the need for pollution control that the judge accepted, was sufficient to meet its burden of going forward with a demonstration of why three-acre zoning in the RA-120 district is rational and related to the public welfare. The town's expert testified that the nitrogen carrying capacity of the pond was five grams per square meter each year and that the appropriate average minimum lot size in the RA-120 district, to limit properly the nitrogen entering the pond, was three to three and one-half acres.[7] An expert presented by the trust had testified before the Martha's Vineyard Commission that his nutrient loading study validated "the density allowed by current zoning of one unit at three acres."

The judge's ruling is bolstered by the need to protect the amenities and character of a rural resort, such as the Vineyard, in order to assist its economic stability, including its shellfish industry and tourism. As one of the trust's experts testified, the quality of the Vineyard's

---

[7] He assumed that the town would operate its wastewater plant so as to produce effluent only within permitted limits. In his calculation he also excluded as a source of nitrates in the pond's watershed land that is protected from development.

landscape is important to the quality of life and the promotion of tourism. As we noted earlier, there are regional and Statewide interests in the preservation of the unique quality of Martha's Vineyard. Those interests justify the making of conservative assumptions about the consequences of land uses, even if standing alone protection of those interests might not support the imposition of three-acre zoning.

The trust makes much of the fact that part of its land is not within the watershed of Edgartown Great Pond. The burden was on the trust to prove that the zoning restriction was unlawful, and not on the town to prove its validity. The trust's land not within the watershed of the great pond is generally in the watershed of another coastal pond, and the trust did not prove that the circumstances of any other watershed were significantly different from the conditions in the watershed of Edgartown Great Pond.

This opinion should not be read as an endorsement of three-acre zoning. We have upheld the challenged zoning provision because of the special circumstances of this case, particularly the proximity of the restricted land to a coastal great pond. We are confident in the special circumstances of this case that the three-acre zoning provision has not been shown to be arbitrary and unreasonable or substantially unrelated to the public health, safety, and general welfare.

NOTES AND QUESTIONS

1. *Is Martha's Vineyard unique?* The special quality of Martha's Vineyard helped the court find that large-lot zoning protected its character and amenities, but the same issues arise in large lot zoning for mainland suburbs. For example, in the *Simon* case the court said:

> The advantages enjoyed by those living in one-family dwellings located upon an acre lot might be thought to exceed those possessed by persons living upon a lot of ten thousand square feet. More freedom from noise and traffic might result. The danger from fire from outside sources might be reduced. A better opportunity for rest and relaxation might be afforded. Greater facilities for children to play on the premises and not in the streets would be available. There may perhaps be more inducement for one to attempt something in the way of the cultivation of flowers, shrubs and vegetables. [42 N.E.2d at 562–63.]

The justifications used in *Simon* can be found in many cases upholding large-lot zoning. However, the question is whether oversized lots are needed to obtain these objectives, and why the separation of residential from nonresidential uses isn't enough to achieve these objectives. Notice that the *Johnson* court rejected the provision of open space and the protection of plant and animal life as justifications for the large lot zoning.

2. The *Aronson* case, discussed in the principal opinion, indicated there are limits on how far these justifications will carry, at least in Massachusetts. The large-lot requirement in that case was about 2.3 acres. The court also said:

> While initially an increase in lot size might have the effects there noted, the law of diminishing returns will set in at some point. As applied to the petitioners' property, the attainment of such advantages does not reasonably require lots of 100,000 square feet. Nor would they be attained by keeping the rural district undeveloped, even though this might contribute to the welfare of each inhabitant. Granting the value of

> recreational areas to the community as a whole, the burden of providing them should not be borne by the individual property owner unless he is compensated. [195 N.E.2d at 345.]

Does the *Johnson* case discredit the "diminishing returns" holding?

3. *Justifying large-lot zoning.* There appear to be two major justifications for the large lot zoning in *Johnson*: environmental problems and the need to preserve the character of the island. Are these acceptable justifications?

a. *Environmental protection.* The environmental issue raises what can be called the "upland" problem. The trust's land apparently presented no environmental problems, but its development could endanger the nearby pond. Why not provide public sewerage or enforce sanitary regulations? If the trust land had been a wetlands, development could have been prevented entirely. See Chapter 4 *infra*. Notice, however, that the court did not decide whether a margin of safety for on-site drinking water justified the large-lot zoning. It was doubtful about the argument that the state's septic system requirements made large lots unnecessary. But see the Pennsylvania cases, discussed in Note 8.

For other cases approving large-lot zoning on environmental grounds, see *Salamar Bldrs. Corp. v. Tuttle*, 275 N.E.2d 585 (N.Y. 1971) (two acres; protection of groundwater supply); *Bogert v. Washington Twp.*, 135 A.2d 1 (N.J. 1957) (one acre; protection against flooding and soil erosion); *Security Management Corp. v. Baltimore County*, 655 A.2d 1326 (Md. App. 1995) (orderly development of public services and the protection of natural resources); *Honeck v. County of Cook*, 146 N.E.2d 35 (Ill. 1957) (five acres; topography). Large lot zoning is also used as a regulatory technique in environmental regulation, such as regulations that protect groundwater. See Chapter 4.

b. *The "character of the community."* This justification comes in many different guises. See, as examples: *Mayhew v. Town of Sunnyvale*, 964 S.W.2d 922 (Tex. 1998) (upholding denial of high density planned development in low density rural community); *County Comm'rs v. Miles*, 228 A.2d 450 (Md. 1967) (five acres; preservation of specific historic sites and buildings in their historic settings); *Norbeck Village Joint Venture v. Montgomery County Council*, 254 A.2d 700 (Md. 1969) (two acres; preservation of community identity by providing "green belts" between communities).

4. *Exclusionary impacts?* The most striking and unusual features of the *Johnson* case are its skepticism about large-lot zoning and its concern about exclusionary impacts. This skepticism is justified by the baldness of some earlier decisions. In *Clary v. Borough of Eatontown*, 124 A.2d 54 (N.J. App. Div. 1956) (half-acre minimum), for instance, the court approved provision of some "high class" low-density residential areas, viewed as essential to the local economy, and prevention of the "blanketing" of the community with small, low-cost houses. See also *Flora Realty & Inv. Co. v. City of Ladue*, 246 S.W.2d 771 (Mo. 1954) (3 acres; protection of the value of houses previously constructed on large lots against the depreciation that would result "if sections here and there are developed with smaller lots"). Are the rationales of the *Clary* and *Flora Realty* cases actually the same? Recall that one of the boilerplate purposes of zoning has been, as § 3 of the Standard Zone Enabling Act (1924) expresses it, "conserving the value of buildings." In *Simon v. Needham*, however, the court indicated that large lot zoning could not be justified by fiscal reasons. For an unusual example of "small lot" zoning, see National Association of Home Builders, *Narrow Lots, Wide Appeal*, Land Development Magazine, Spring 2004 at 36–37 (describing a Portland, Oregon ordinance

that permits 15-foot-wide single family homes on 2500–square-foot lots as infill development to increase the supply of affordable housing).

Exclusionary zoning is explored in greater detail in Chapter 5. Suffice it here to note that studies (though dated) indicate that increasing lot size increases lot price, thus pricing out poorer households. See W. McEachern, *Large-Lot Zoning in Connecticut: Incentives and Effects*, U. Conn. Center for Real Est. & Urb. Econ. Studies (1979). A micro-economics argument to the contrary could be made, in that under large-lot zoning still only one dwelling may be built on the lot, so the price per square foot could decrease enough to offset the increase in lot size. This assumes, however, that the typical purchaser is in the market only for a dwelling, whereas the purchaser with sufficient means may value the lot size independently for what it advertises about his or her economic and social status. For better or worse, "conspicuous consumption" is one of our cultural norms; should (can?) land use law attempt to rein it in?

5. *Large lots and sound planning.* Even in an era when comprehensive planning was honored all too often in the breach, large-lot zoning was often justified on planning grounds. See, e.g., *Rockaway Estates v. Rockaway Twp.*, 119 A.2d 461 (N.J. App. Div. 1955) (regulation of the rate and pattern of suburban growth to assure orderly, efficient, and economical expansion of necessary public facilities); *Padover v. Farmington Twp.*, 132 N.W.2d 687 (Mich. 1965) (20,000 sq. ft., based on "neighborhoods of the optimum size" to "support an elementary school of an ideal size and . . . location"). As modern zoning enabling acts impose plan consistency requirements on zoning ordinances more and more, should large-lot zoning become more and more suspect? The APA Model Act recommends a balanced approach that authorizes (but does not require) specification of both minimum and maximum densities and intensities in the zoning ordinance. The APA explains: "This language takes into account the importance of density and intensity in establishing urban form. It is necessary if local governments are to incorporate urban growth areas into their planning system . . . ." *Id.* at 8-44, 8-45 (2002 ed.). For a case that upheld ten-acre zoning *because of* state-wide planning policies, see *Kirby v. Township of Bedminster*, 775 A.2d 209 (N.J. App. Div. 2000) (state-mapped low growth area; town had met affordable housing obligations).

6. *Standards of review.* A student article reviewing the early large-lot zoning cases concluded they had adopted an unspoken rule of reason leading to a "gentle" judicial treatment of large-lot zoning restrictions. Comment, *Large Lot Zoning*, 78 Yale L.J. 1418, 1436, 1437 (1969). To what extent does the principal case support this conclusion? The cases discussed in the Notes? See Note, *Judicial Acquiescence in Large Lot Zoning: Is It Time to Rethink the Trend?*, 16 Colum. J. Envtl. L. 183 (1991).

7. *Takings problems.* These are usually not serious in large-lot zoning cases. The landowner may develop her land for residential use, although at lower densities. *Security Management Corp., supra*, Note 3(a), easily dismissed a takings challenge post-*Lucas*.

8. *Held invalid.* The leading case invalidating large-lot zoning is *National Land & Inv. Co. v. Kohn*, 215 A.2d 597 (Pa. 1965). The court had upheld one-acre zoning pre-*National Land*, relying on the usual presumption of constitutionality and holding that the plaintiff had not introduced evidence sufficient to rebut the presumption. *Bilbar Constr. Co. v. Easttown Twp. Bd. of Adjustment*, 141 A.2d 851 (Pa. 1958). *National Land* involved a four-acre zoning restriction applied to thirty percent of a municipality that was in the path of development in the Philadelphia area. The court concluded that the reasons advanced for the four-acre zoning did not justify the loss in value it would impose on the property owner. The court rejected drainage

and sewer problems as a reason for the zoning, holding that the municipality could handle these problems through sanitary regulations. Neither was four-acre zoning a "necessary" or "reasonable" method to protect the community from pollution. The court rejected an argument that inadequate fire and road services justified the four-acre zoning. In an important dictum, it stated that zoning "may not be used . . . to avoid the increased responsibilities and economic burdens which time and natural growth inevitably bring." *Id.* at 612. Finally, the court rejected an argument that the four-acre zoning was necessary to preserve the "character" of the community by creating a green belt.

Later, in what amounted to a plurality opinion, the Pennsylvania court relied on *National Land* to invalidate two-acre and three-acre zoning. *In re Concord Twp. Appeal (Kit-Mar)*, 268 A.2d 765 (Pa. 1970). The court held that large-lot zoning of this size was invalid absent "extraordinary justification," and that the difference in size between a three-acre and one-acre lot was "irrelevant to the problem of sewage disposal." Recently, while rejecting the "extraordinary justification" standard of the *Concord* case, the court nonetheless struck down a complicated agricultural preservation zone that created an effective density of one unit per three acres on arbitrariness grounds. *C&M Developers, Inc. v. Bedminster Twp. Zoning Board*, 820 A.2d 143 (Pa. 2002). The subsequent history of large-lot zoning in Pennsylvania is best told as part of that state's efforts to deal more comprehensively with exclusionary zoning problems. See Chapter 4.

[b.] Site Development Requirements as a Form of Control

It is common for a modern zoning ordinance to regulate the physical arrangement of structures on the land, as well as the use to which those structures may be put. "Site plan" procedures will be explored in Chapter 5, but it is also important to note here that site development requirements can serve as an indirect but critical component of a municipality's approach to regulating the intensity of land use. At the extreme, site development controls may be invalidated as a form of exclusionary zoning. See Chapter 5, *infra*. We note here some bulk and intensity controls that are commonly included in zoning ordinances:

Yard and setback regulations. Zoning ordinances typically require front yards by requiring minimum setbacks from the street. They also usually include side and back yard setbacks. The constitutionality of these requirements was upheld in *Gorieb v. Fox*, 274 U.S. 603 (1927), an early case decided a year after the Court's *Euclid* decision upheld the constitutionality of zoning. The Court upheld street setbacks as a proper police power measure that would provide separation from street noise, improve the attractiveness of residential environments, and ensure the availability of light and air. As one court put it recently, the constitutionality of setbacks was decided "long ago." *In re Letourneau*, 726 A.2d 31 (Vt. 1998). See *Blair v. Department of Conservation and Recreation*, 932 N.E.2d 267 (Mass. 2010) (200-foot buffer setback not a taking).

Frontage requirements. Zoning ordinances also usually require that lots have a minimum street frontage. The reasons that led the Court in *Gorieb* to uphold setbacks also apply to frontage requirements. Courts may also uphold these requirements as a control on density. *Di Salle v. Giggal*, 261 P.2d 499 (Colo. 1953).

Height limitations. Maximum height limitations also limit building bulk. Another early U.S. Supreme Court case, *Welch v. Swasey*, 214 U.S. 91 (1909), upheld height limitations that were imposed under a state statute. The Court upheld the statute on traditional due process grounds, taking special note of the aesthetic basis for the height limitation.

FLOOR AREA RATIO (F.A.R.) CONCEPT

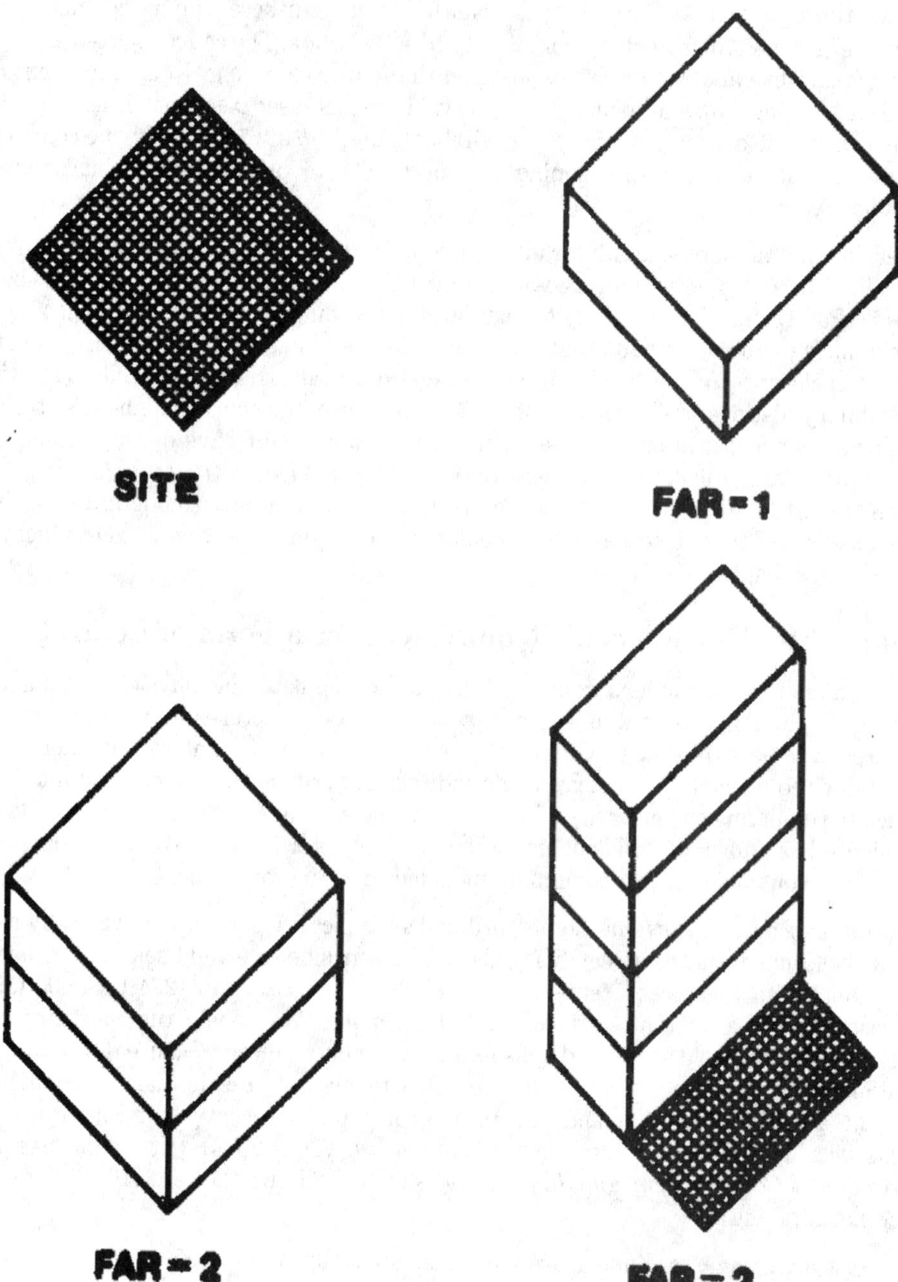

Site ratio. Some zoning ordinances also control density and building bulk by limiting the percentage of a lot that can be occupied by a building. This control is called a site ratio. In *La Salle Nat'l Bank v. City of Chicago*, 125 N.E.2d 609 (Ill. 1955), the court upheld a site ratio as applied to multi-family dwellings and applied the usual presumption of constitutionality. It found no evidence indicating that the site ratio was unreasonable. Alternatively, there is the open space ratio. *Cordes v. Board of Zoning Adjustments*, 31 So. 3d 504 (La. Ct. App. 2010).

Floor area ratio. Some communities, especially in downtown office and multi-family districts, regulate building bulk through a floor area ratio (FAR). The FAR specifies a ratio between the square footage allowable in a building and the square footage of the building lot. A FAR of 2:1, for example, allows two square feet of building for each square foot of the lot. The FAR encourages innovative building design because the developer may utilize the FAR any way it wishes subject to height and other limitations on the site, such as setbacks. Under a FAR of 2:1, for example, the developer could construct a four-story building on half the lot if a building height of four stories was permitted. No case has considered the validity of floor area ratios. But see *Broadway, Laguna, Vallejo Ass'n v. Board of Permit Appeals*, 427 P.2d 810 (Cal. 1967) (stressing the importance of the FAR as a zoning control). *KGF Development, LLC v. City of Ketchum*, 236 P.3d 1284 (Idaho 2010) (TDR used to increase FAR void because it violates uniformity requirement).

Minimum lot and building size requirements. In addition to lot sizes, see *Johnson v. Town of Edgartown, supra*, and Notes following, ordinances frequently specify minimum (but not maximum) building size. The classic case is *Lionshead Lake, Inc. v. Township of Wayne*, 89 A.2d 693 (N.J. 1952); but see *Builders Service Corp., Inc. v. Town of East Hampton*, 545 A.2d 530 (Conn. 1988) (1300-square-foot minimum not rationally related to any legitimate zoning purpose). As noted *supra*, the APA Model Act, § 8-201(2)(b), authorizes (but does not require) specification of both minimum and maximum "densities and intensities." These issues are discussed further in Chapter 6, *infra*. See *Paul T. Wilson v. County of McHenry*, 416 N.E.2d 426 (Ill. App. Ct. 1981) (160-acre lots upheld).

Off-street parking. The buildable area available on a lot also is limited by off-street parking requirements. The number of required parking spaces is based on the number of dwelling units in multifamily residential projects. For commercial, office, and industrial development, the required number of spaces may be based on square footage or on the type of use. One big-city planner has observed:

> Off-street parking standards have long been among the most challenging aspects of the drafting of zoning ordinances. The impacts of the choices made can influence the character of the community for many years, even decades, after the provisions take effect. [Wittenberg, *Parking Standards in the Zoning Code*, American Planning Ass'n, Planning Advisory Serv. Rep. No. 510/511 (2002); *id.*, Zoning News, Jan. 2003.]

In the only case directly addressing the issue, the court held off-street parking requirements constitutional. *Stroud v. City of Aspen*, 532 P.2d 720 (Colo. 1975) ("cannot believe" ordinance unconstitutional in "these days of environmental concerns"). For a critique of current regulatory approaches, see D. Shoup, The High Cost of Free Parking (Planner's Press, 2005). A review of the book, M. Lewyn & S. Crane, *Planners Gone Wild: The Overregulation of Parking*, Wm. Mitchell L. Rev., Vol. 33, 2007, is available at http://papers.ssrn.com.

Open space and landscaping requirements. Because parking areas are paved, communities that want to ensure that part of the lot is left in its natural state may also include a usable open space requirement. This requirement specifies a percentage of the lot that must be left in its natural condition. In addition, codes frequently specify landscaping requirements. See W. Martz, *Preparing a Landscape Ordinance*, American Planning Ass'n, Planning Advisory Serv. Rep. No. 431 (1990); R. Arendt, *Crossroads, Hamlet, Village, Town: Design Characteristics of Traditional Neighborhoods, Old and New*, *id.* No. 523/524 (revised edition 2004).

NOTES AND QUESTIONS

As-applied constitutional problems can still arise under site development standards:

1. *Setbacks.* In *Miller & Son Paving, Inc. v. Wrightstown Twp.*, 451 A.2d 1002 (Pa. 1982), a quarry owner claimed that setback regulations were a taking of property because they prevented it from quarrying over two million tons of stone that lay within the setback area. The court rejected this contention, noting that to adopt the owner's argument would make all setbacks per se unreasonable. The quarry owner had not met its burden of showing that the setback was "patently unreasonable" or that it did not serve the community's general welfare. Compare *Board of Supvrs. v. Rowe*, 216 S.E.2d 199 (Va. 1975) (invalidating setback eliminating twenty-nine percent of the buildable area of a lot). Can the cases be distinguished? See also *Giambrone v. City of Aurora*, 621 N.E.2d 475 (Ohio App. 1993) (setback held excessive); *Schmalz v. Buckingham Twp. Zoning Bd. of Adjustment*, 132 A.2d 233 (Pa. 1957) (reasons justifying setbacks in urban areas do not apply in rural areas).

2. *Frontage requirements.* The courts have considered "as applied" objections to frontage requirements. In *MacNeil v. Town of Avon*, 435 N.E.2d 1043 (Mass. 1982), a lot was ten feet short of a required 200-foot frontage. The court upheld the frontage requirement as applied to the lot, noting that the requirement would reduce the number of dwelling units and thus the amount and size of firefighting equipment needed to respond to fires. The requirement was valid even though the lot was only marginally short of the required frontage, the court noting that lines must be drawn somewhere in zoning ordinances. There was no taking of property because the lot could be put to uses allowed by the zoning ordinance. Contra under similar facts, *Metzger v. Town of Brentwood (II)*, 374 A.2d 954 (N.H. 1977). The court noted that "frontage requirements can be justified . . . [as] a method of determining lot size to prevent overcrowding," but that the lot size far exceeded the lot size implicitly contemplated by the frontage requirement. Neither was access by fire trucks and other vehicles restricted by the shorter frontage. Are the cases distinguishable?

3. *Height limitations.* Height limitations also are subject to "as applied" taking claims. In *Williams C. Haas & Co. v. City & County of San Francisco*, 605 F.2d 1117 (9th Cir. 1979), the city, in order to implement an urban design plan, downzoned the height limitation on a tract of land on which the owner had planned a high-rise building. The court rejected the taking claim, even though the owner argued that the downzoning imposed a $1.9 million loss on a $2 million investment in the property. The court also rejected a reverse spot zoning argument, holding that the downzoning was part of a comprehensive plan that affected all of the property owners in the area. For additional favorable height limitation cases, see *City of St. Paul v. Chicago, St. P., M. & O. Ry.*, 413 F.2d 762 (8th Cir. 1969) (applied to single property owner); *State v. Pacesetter Constr. Co.*, 571 P.2d 196 (Wash. 1977) (residential height limitation contained in shoreline management act). However, these cases were decided before the Supreme Court adopted a categorical per se takings rule in *Lucas.* How would *Lucas* affect these decisions? Height limitation cases frequently arise around airports. See *Lawrence County v. Miller*, 786 N.W.2d 360 (S.D. 2010) (possible takings claim for future height limitations).

4. *Teardowns.* The "teardown" phenomenon, which has drawn critical attention in recent years, vividly demonstrates market forces at work. Small houses are sold for the value of their site, usually in expensive, upscale communities where vacant land is scarce, to be demolished and replaced with new, usually much larger houses. These so-called "McMansions" are often out of scale with older structures in the neighborhood. Not all change is bad, of course, but particularly where issues of affordable housing or historic preservation are involved, there may be legitimate concerns. Review the site development techniques canvassed above. Could these be used to discourage teardowns by restricting the bulk and placement of replacement structures? (Note that the teardown/McMansion sequence is made possible by "as of right" development under site standards that are very permissive.) Can demolitions be restricted without running afoul of the takings rules discussed in Chapter 2? Regulation for purposes of aesthetic and historic preservation are explored in Chapter 9, *infra*. For an on-line resources guide, see www.nationaltrust.org/teardowns. The recession and growing interest in sustainability may have brought an end to the era of mansionization. R. Kaysen, *Builders Move Beyond McMansions in New Jersey*, N.Y. Times, October 5, 2010, http://www.nytimes.com/2010/10/06/realestate/06density.html. For a comprehensive ordinance regulating the bulk and scale of buildings to prevent McMansions, see www.cityoflakeforest.com/pdf/cd/bsord.pdf. The ordinance makes extensive use of graphics to clarify the intent and effect of the rules. One such illustration, showing how different rooflines affect the calculation of the permitted floor area, is reproduced here.

TEARDOWNS

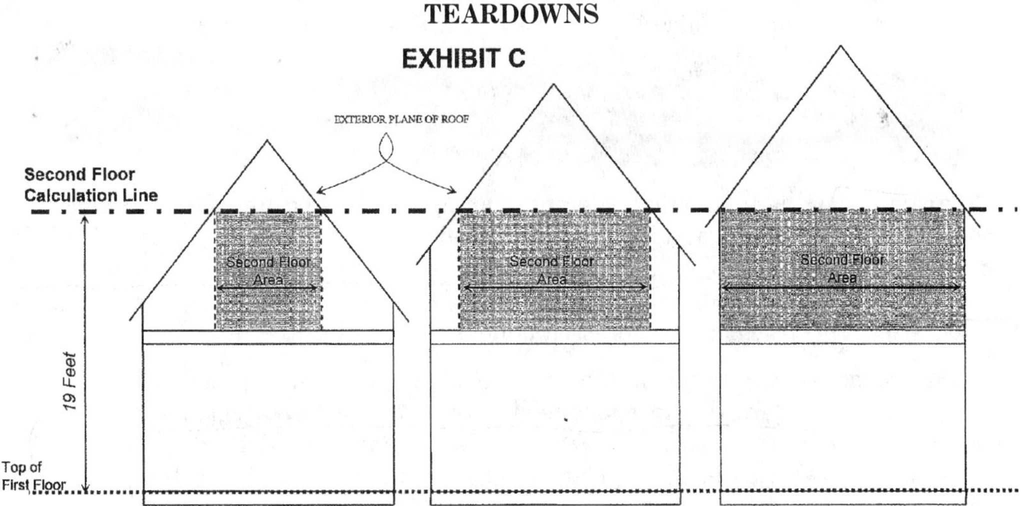

A NOTE ON OTHER APPROACHES TO REGULATING DENSITY AND INTENSITY OF USE

As the foregoing materials suggest, density issues are most often encountered in the context of residential subdivisions in developing areas. Related problems arise in urban settings as well, and also with respect to non-residential uses. Consider the following:

Urban areas and "downtowns." The Floor Area Ratio, or FAR, discussed earlier, is an important mechanism for regulating the density or intensity of use in large cities, such as New York or Houston. A simple amendment to a hypothetical zoning ordinance, to change the FAR from 4 to 5 (that is, from a building that is four times the size of the lot to one that is five times the size of the lot), achieves a 25% increase in the physical intensity of the use of the site.

Density can also be an important planning concern in smaller cities. In *Rectory Park, L.C. v. City of Delray Beach*, 208 F. Supp. 2d 1320 (S.D. Fla. 2002), the city sought to revive a dilapidated downtown by rezoning land for more intensive development. Landowners in an adjoining historic district objected to approval of a project under a conditional use ordinance that increased the density on a 2.38 acre site from 30 to 92 units per acre, and increased the building height from 48 to 60 feet to create a mixed-use residential and retail building with 219 residential units, at least 12,000 square feet of retail space and a large parking garage. The objectors focused on a provision in the ordinance that required "compatibil[ity] in terms of building mass and intensity of use with surrounding development," and argued that "none of the generally accepted measures that planners use to evaluate [compatibility] were applied in the City's analysis of the project." 208 F. Supp. 2d at 1328.

Summarizing its holding against the neighbors and in favor of the city, the District Court said:

> This case involves important issues regarding the deference to be afforded to a municipality in its effort to revitalize its downtown core through the use of a flexible mixed-use zoning policy. In this context, the deference is substantial. Federal courts are mindful that matters of land-use planning are primarily of local concern. The "routine application of zoning regulations . . . is distinctly a feature of local government." *Hill v. City of El Paso*, 437 F.2d 352, 357 (5th Cir. 1971). When a zoning regulation, such as the mixed-use policy in question here, contains clear and definite standards, it will not be declared impermissibly vague just because the decision-maker has flexibility in applying the standards. [208 F. Supp. 2d at 1334.]

Would a state court have taken so deferential an approach? Led by Oregon, an increasing number of state planning statutes have established a policy requiring more intensive land usage within "urban growth areas," in order to relieve development pressure on outlying areas where growth is discouraged. See, generally, APA Model Act, § 6-201.1, summarizing these statutes. Growth management is addressed in detail in Chapter 8, *infra*.

Non-residential uses. Although there is no shortage of site-specific litigation about commercial uses, it is relatively rare for the dispute to focus explicitly on density. Why might that be so? In *Marcus Associates, Inc. v. Town of Huntington*, 382 N.E.2d 1323 (N.Y. 1978), the owner of four undeveloped building plots challenged a zoning amendment that provided: "A building or premises shall be used for not more than 3 permitted uses and by not more than three occupants. Each separate use shall occupy no less than 20,000 square feet of building gross floor area." The Court said:

> [W]e reject plaintiff's argument that population density is a proper subject of zoning regulation in residential but not industrial areas. . . . [G]iven the proper circumstances, a town board is not without [delegated] regulatory power over industrial population density. . . . Legitimate governmental goals are those which in some way promote the public health, safety, morals, or general welfare. No extensive search is needed for discovery of such an objective here, where the express aim of the Huntington Town Board in enacting the challenged amendment was to preserve the established character of the area — certainly a permissible, if not salutary, goal. It matters not that the character of the area is industrial rather than residential, for surely that consideration alone does not dilute a municipality's right to conserve the desirable nature and economic value of an entire zone.
>
> Moreover, we conclude that there is a reasonable nexus between the town's objective and the zoning ordinance. Manifestly, the industrial district involved is predominantly single tenanted: 31 of 34 developed properties have one tenant, and two

others have two users each. It is precisely that character which defendant wishes to preserve, and it is difficult if not impossible to maintain that the amendment is not rationally designed to achieve this end.

It may be true, as plaintiff contends, that the Town of Huntington's zoning amendment has only an arguable impact upon population density and is not the best possible method for preserving the area's character. This is not our consideration, and we need only ascertain, as we have, that the challenged ordinance bears a rational relationship to a legitimate goal of government. There our inquiry must end. [382 N.E.2d at 1324–25.]

What do you suppose were the Town's actual reasons for adopting this ordinance provision? What does the Court mean when it speaks of preserving the "character" of the industrial zone? Commercial zoning is considered further in Sec. D.3, *infra*, where additional examples of regulating the intensity of commercial use can be found.

To meet housing needs and increase housing opportunities, some cities have encouraged higher density development by eliminating regulatory barriers. For example, Portland, Oregon's Living Smart Program promotes infill development on narrow lots by adopting skinny house design standards, waiving parking requirements for skinny houses, streamlining the permitting process with permit-ready skinny houses and reducing permit fees. Another example is Los Angeles' Adaptive Reuse Ordinance, which promotes the conversion of commercial buildings into housing and live-work spaces by exempting the projects from a site plan review, waiving density restrictions, grandfathering in nonconforming aspects and limiting parking requirements. For more information, see *Breakthroughs*, Regulatory Barriers Clearinghouse (Sept. 2007), www.huduser.org/rbc/newsletter/Volume6Iss5Print.html. For a recent case upholding a smart growth overlay zone allowing for higher density, mixed use, see *DiRico v. Town of Kingston*, 934 N.E.2d 208 (Mass. 2008).

[2.] Residential Districts

[a.] Separation of Single-Family and Multifamily Uses

Basis for single-family zoning. Although the New York City Zoning Resolution of 1916 did not do so, most municipal zoning ordinances, from the earliest days of zoning, provided for two or more residential use classifications, one of which was a "single-family residential use" classification. Indeed, the Euclid, Ohio zoning ordinance has such a single-family residential use classification. But the *Euclid* opinion did not expressly discuss the validity of such a classification; and the "nuisance prevention" rationale of *Euclid* with respect to segregation of apartments from other dwellings would not necessarily have justified the exclusion of two-family dwellings as well as apartment houses from a single-family residential use district. Since the 1920s, it seems generally to have been assumed that exclusive one-family residential districts are constitutionally permissible. *Euclid* purports to furnish a rationale for segregating residential buildings by building type. Lees, *Preserving Property Values? Preserving Proper Homes? Preserving Privilege?: The Pre-Euclid Debate over Zoning for Exclusively Private Residential Areas, 1916-1926*, 56 U. Pitt. L. Rev. 367 (1994), reviews the various justifications for exclusive residential zoning in the days before *Euclid.*

Arguments based upon "density" clearly are no longer always valid. Many modern "garden apartment" developments have comparatively modest densities and may have landscaping and other features that enhance the attractiveness of the project. Indeed, some of these developments arguably are more attractive than many older single-family residential areas where homes are built on small lots lined up along streets. Is the basis for single-family zoning really aesthetic?

Judicial review standards. Although the separation of single-family and multi-family uses, like other zoning restrictions, raises an "as applied" taking problem, state court handling of these cases is not always clear. Some courts do not explicitly consider the taking question, but examine zoning and existing development in the surrounding area to determine if the zoning restriction is "arbitrary and capricious," as the *Tim Jones* case indicates. This inquiry reflects the nuisance basis of zoning law and, as we have seen, can produce results that range from highly deferential, *Krause v. City of Royal Oak*, to highly skeptical, *Nectow v. City of Cambridge*. When the taking issue is considered, the majority of state courts follow the *Tahoe-Sierra/Penn Central* balancing approach, discussed *supra*, Chapter 2, and generally hold that a taking occurs only if the restriction does not allow any economically viable use of the land. The Supreme Court's *Lucas* case holds a per se taking occurs in this situation.

[b.] Single-Family Residential Use: The Non-Traditional "Family"

When a zoning ordinance creates a single-family residential use classification, it is necessary, of course, to define the meaning of the term "family" as used in the ordinance. Until the late 1960s, most zoning ordinances appear to have defined a family in pretty much the way it is defined in the Model Zoning Ordinance reprinted *supra:* "One or more persons occupying a single dwelling and using common cooking facilities, provided that no family shall contain more than five adult persons." The numerical limit on adult persons might vary substantially from one ordinance to another, but the "family" definitions commonly employed generally did not require that the persons comprising a family be related by blood, marriage, or adoption.

In a number of cases under the form of ordinance just described, state courts had to interpret such definitions of family in local zoning ordinances. Fraternities, sororities, and retirement homes for the elderly did not fare well when they claimed to be families for zoning purposes. State court decisions were more evenly divided, however, with respect to group homes for juvenile offenders or mentally retarded adults and residential drug treatment centers. And the state courts were generally favorable toward claims that religious groups living together in single-family residences were families for zoning purposes. See, e.g., *Carroll v. City of Miami Beach*, 198 So. 2d 643 (Fla. App. 1967) (group of novices living with a Mother Superior as a single housekeeping unit); *Missionaries of Our Lady of LaSallette v. Village of Whitefish Bay*, 66 N.W.2d 627 (Wis. 1954) (group of eight priests and lay brothers living together as a single housekeeping unit); *Laporte v. City of New Rochelle*, 152 N.Y.S.2d 916 (App. Div. 1956), *aff'd*, 141 N.E.2d 917 (N.Y. 1957) (proposed dormitory for sixty students in a Roman Catholic college would constitute a family within definition of family as "one or more persons occupying a dwelling unit as a single, non-profit housekeeping unit," and the dormitory would be a "single dwelling unit").

Beginning in the 1960s, however, many municipalities began to change the definition of a family in their zoning ordinances to exclude or limit the number of persons unrelated by blood, marriage or adoption who might constitute a family for zoning purposes. This was almost certainly motivated by the desire of local authorities to prevent establishment of "counter-culture" or "hippy" communes in single-family residential neighborhoods. As might be expected, such zoning ordinance restrictions on family composition led to court challenges on constitutional grounds. The first case to reach the Supreme Court of the United States is reprinted as the next principal case.

VILLAGE OF BELLE TERRE v. BORAAS

416 U.S. 1 (1974)

JUSTICE DOUGLAS delivered the opinion of the Court:

Belle Terre is a village on Long Island's north shore of about 220 homes inhabited by 700 people. Its total land area is less than one square mile. It has restricted land use to one-family dwellings excluding lodging houses, boarding houses, fraternity houses, or multiple dwelling houses. The word "Family" as used in the ordinance means, "One or more persons related by blood, adoption, or marriage, living and cooking together as a single housekeeping unit, exclusive of household servants. A number of persons but not exceeding two (2) living and cooking together as a single housekeeping unit though not related by blood, adoption, or marriage shall be deemed to constitute a family."

Appellees (Dickmans) are owners of a house in the village and leased it in December, 1971 for a term of 18 months to Michael Truman. Later Bruce Boraas became a colessee. Then Anne Parish moved into the house along with three others. These six are students at nearby State University at Stony Brook and none is related to the other by blood, adoption, or marriage. When the village served the Dickmans with an "Order to Remedy Violations" of the ordinance, the owners plus three tenants thereupon brought this action under 42 U.S.C. § 1983 for an injunction declaring the ordinance unconstitutional. The District Court held the ordinance constitutional and the Court of Appeals reversed, one judge dissenting. The case is here by appeal, 28 U.S.C. § 1254(2); and we noted probable jurisdiction.

This case brings to this Court a different phase of local zoning regulations than we have previously reviewed. [The court summarized the facts in *Euclid*.] . . .

The Court [in *Euclid*] sustained the zoning ordinance under the police power of the State, saying that the line "which in this field separates the legitimate from the illegitimate assumption of power is not capable of precise delimitation. It varies with circumstances and conditions." 272 U.S., at 387. And the Court added "A nuisance may be merely a right thing in the wrong place, like a pig in the parlor instead of the barnyard. If the validity of the legislative classification for zoning purposes be fairly debatable, the legislative judgment must be allowed to control." *Id.*, at 388. The Court listed as considerations bearing on the constitutionality of zoning ordinances the danger of fire or collapse of buildings, the evils of overcrowding people, and the possibility that "offensive trades, industries, and structures" might "create nuisance" to residential sections. *Ibid.* But even those historic police power problems need not loom large or actually be existent in a given case. For the exclusion of "all industrial establishments" does not mean that "only offensive or dangerous industries will be excluded." *Ibid.* That fact does not invalidate the ordinance; the Court held:

> "The inclusion of a reasonable margin to insure effective enforcement, will not put upon a law, otherwise valid, the stamp of invalidity. Such laws may also find their justification in the fact that, in some fields, the bad fades into the good by such insensible degrees that the two are not capable of being readily distinguished and separated in terms of legislation." *Id.*, 388–389.

The main thrust of the case in the mind of the Court was in the exclusion of industries and apartments and as respects that it commented on the desire to keep residential areas free of "disturbing noises"; "increased traffic"; the hazard of "moving and parked automobiles"; the "depriving children of the privilege of quiet and open spaces for play, enjoyed by those in more favored localities." *Id.*, at 394. The ordinance was sanctioned because the validity of the legislative classification was "fairly debatable" and therefore could not be said to be wholly arbitrary. *Id.*, at 388.

Our decision in *Berman v. Parker*, 348 U.S. 26, sustained a land use project in the District of Columbia against a land owner's claim that the taking violated the Due Process Clause and the Just Compensation Clause of the Fifth Amendment. The essence of the argument against the law was, while taking property for ridding an area of slums was permissible, taking it "merely to develop a better balanced, more attractive community" was not, 348 U.S., at 31. We refused to limit the concept of public welfare that may be enhanced by zoning regulations. We said:

> "Miserable and disreputable housing conditions may do more than spread disease and crime and immorality. They may also suffocate the spirit by reducing the people who live there to the status of cattle. They may indeed make living an almost unsufferable burden. They may also be an ugly sore, a blight on the community which robs it of charm, which makes it a place from which men turn. The misery of housing may despoil a community as an open sewer may ruin a river.
>
> "We do not sit to determine whether a particular housing project is or is not desirable. The concept of the public welfare is broad and inclusive. . . . The values it represents are spiritual as well as physical, aesthetic as well as monetary. It is within the power of the legislature to determine that the community should be beautiful as well as healthy, spacious as well as clean, well-balanced as well as carefully patrolled." *Id.*, 32–33.

If the ordinance segregated one area only for one race, it would immediately be suspect under the reasoning of *Buchanan v. Warley*, 245 U.S. 60, where the Court invalidated a city ordinance barring a Black from acquiring real property in a white residential area by reason of an 1866 Act of Congress, 42 U.S.C. § 1982 and an 1870 Act, 16 Stat. 144, both enforcing the Fourteenth Amendment. *Id.*, 78–82.

In *Seattle Title Trust Co. v. Roberge*, 278 U.S. 116, Seattle had a zoning ordinance that permitted a "philanthropic home for children or for old people" in a particular district "when the written consent shall have been obtained of the owners of two thirds of the property within four hundred (400) feet of the proposed building." *Id.*, at 118. The Court held that provision of the ordinance unconstitutional saying that the existing owners could "withhold consent for selfish reasons or arbitrarily and may subject the trustee [owner] to their will or caprice." *Id.*, at 122. Unlike the billboard cases (*Cusack Co. v. City of Chicago*, 242 U.S. 526), the Court concluded that the Seattle ordinance was invalid since the proposed home for the aged poor was not shown by its maintenance and construction "to work any injury, inconvenience or annoyance to the community, the district or any person." *Id.*, 278 U.S., at 122.

The present ordinance is challenged on several grounds: that it interferes with a person's right to travel; that it interferes with the right to migrate to and settle within a State; that it bars people who are uncongenial to the present residents; that the ordinance expresses the social preferences of the residents for groups that will be congenial to them; that social homogeneity is not a legitimate interest of government; that the restriction of those whom the neighbors do not like trenches on the newcomers' rights of privacy; that it is of no rightful concern to villagers whether the residents are married or unmarried; that the ordinance is antithetical to the Nation's experience, ideology and self-perception as an open, egalitarian, and integrated society.

We find none of these reasons in the record before us. It is not aimed at transients. *Cf. Shapiro v. Thompson*, 394 U.S. 618. It involves no procedural disparity inflicted on some but not on others such as was presented by *Griffin v. Illinois*, 351 U.S. 12. It involves no "fundamental" right guaranteed by the Constitution, such as voting, *Harper v. Virginia State Board*, 383 U.S. 663; the right of association, *NAACP v. Alabama ex rel. Patterson*, 357 U.S. 449; the right of access to the courts, *NAACP v. Button*, 371 U.S. 415; or any rights of privacy, *cf. Griswold v. Connecticut*, 381 U.S. 479; *Eisenstadt v. Baird*, 405 U.S. 438, 453–454. We deal with economic and social legislation where legislatures have historically drawn lines which we respect against the charge of violation of the Equal Protection Clause if the law be "reasonable, not arbitrary" (quoting *F. S. Royster Guano Co. v. Virginia*, 253 U.S. 412, 415) and bears "a rational relationship to a [permissible] state objective." *Reed v. Reed*, 404 U.S. 71, 76.

It is said, however, that if two unmarried people can constitute a "family," there is no reason why three or four may not. But every line drawn by a legislature leaves some out that might well have been included. That exercise of discretion, however, is a legislative not a judicial function.

It is said that the Belle Terre ordinance reeks with an animosity to unmarried couples who live together. There is no evidence to support it; and the provision of the ordinance bringing within the definition of a "family" two unmarried people belies the charge.

The ordinance places no ban on other forms of association, for a "family" may, so far as the ordinance is concerned, entertain whomever they like.

The regimes of boarding houses, fraternity houses, and the like present urban problems. More people occupy a given space; more cars rather continuously pass by; more cars are parked; noise travels with crowds.

A quiet place where yards are wide, people few, and motor vehicles restricted are legitimate guidelines in a land use project addressed to family needs. This goal is a permissible one within *Berman v. Parker, supra*. The police power is not confined to elimination of filth, stench, and unhealthy places. It is ample to lay out zones where family values, youth values, and the blessings of quiet seclusion, and clean air make the area a sanctuary for people.

The suggestion that the case may be moot need not detain us. A zoning ordinance usually has an impact on the value of the property which it regulates. But in spite of the fact that the precise impact of the ordinance sustained in *Euclid* on a given piece of property was not known, 272 U.S., at 397, the Court, considering the matter a controversy in the realm of city planning, sustained the ordinance. Here we are a step closer to the impact of the ordinance on the value of the lessor's property. He has not only lost six tenants and acquired only two in their place; it is obvious that the scale of rental values rides on what we decide today. When *Berman* reached us it was not certain whether an entire tract would be taken or only the buildings on it and a scenic easement. 348 U.S., at 36. But that did not make the case any the less a controversy in the constitutional sense. When Mr. Justice Holmes said for the Court in *Block v. Hirsh*, 256 U.S. 135, 155, "property rights may be cut down, and to that extent taken, without pay," he stated the issue here. As is true in most zoning cases, the precise impact on value may, at the threshold of litigation over validity, not yet be known.

Reversed.

JUSTICE BRENNAN, dissenting. [Justice Brennan found that no case or controversy existed. The tenants had moved out, and he would hold that the landlord does not have standing to assert the rights of his tenants.]

JUSTICE MARSHALL, dissenting. . . . In my view, the disputed classification burdens the students' fundamental rights of association and privacy guaranteed by the First and Fourteenth Amendments. Because the application of strict equal protection scrutiny is therefore required, I am at odds with my brethren's conclusion that the ordinance may be sustained on a showing that it bears a rational relationship to the accomplishment of legitimate governmental objectives. . . .

My disagreement with the Court today is based upon my view that the ordinance in this case unnecessarily burdens appellees' First Amendment freedom of association and their constitutionally guaranteed right to privacy. Our decisions establish that the First and Fourteenth Amendments protect the freedom to choose one's associates. Constitutional protection is extended not only to modes of association that are political in the usual sense, but also to those that pertain to the social and economic benefit of the members. The selection of one's living companions involves similar choices as to the emotional, social, or economic benefits to be derived from alternative living arrangements.

[The remainder of Justice Marshall's dissent is omitted. Justice Marshall concluded that the Belle Terre ordinance discriminated on the basis of "personal lifestyle choice as to household companions." It imposed "significantly greater restrictions" on "those who deviate from the community norm in their choice of living companions." He noted that this was not a case "where the Court is being asked to nullify a township's sincere efforts to maintain its residential character." He saw "no constitutional infirmity in a town limiting the density of use in residential areas by zoning regulations which do not discriminate on the basis of constitutionally suspect criteria." But this ordinance limited "the density of occupancy of only those homes occupied by unrelated persons." The means chosen to achieve legitimate zoning goals were both over-inclusive and under-inclusive.

[Justice Marshall noted that "[t]he village is justifiably concerned with density of population and the related problems of noise, traffic, and the like." He suggested the village could deal with these problems by limiting each household to a specified number of adults, without limiting the number of dependents; by adopting rent control; and by placing limits on the number of vehicles per household.]

NOTES

Belle Terre was the first zoning case to be reviewed by the United States Supreme Court since the late 1920s. The District Court had upheld Belle Terre's definition of "family" on the ground that the interest of conventional "families" in limiting residential areas to occupancy by their own kind was a "legally protectable affirmative interest," and thus was by itself a legitimate goal of zoning. The Second Circuit's majority explicitly repudiated that ground, stating:

> [W]e start by examination of the sole ground upon which it was upheld by the district court, namely the interest of the local community in the protection and maintenance

> of the prevailing traditional family pattern which consists of occupancy of one-family houses by families based on consanguinity or legal affinity. In our view such a goal fails to fall within the proper exercise of state police power. It can hardly be disputed — and the district court so found — that the ordinance has the purpose and effect of permitting existing inhabitants to compel all others who would take up residence in the community to conform to its prevailing ideas of life-style, thus insuring that the community will be structured socially on a fairly homogeneous basis. Such social preferences, however, while permissible in a private club, have no relevance to public health, safety or welfare.
>
> The effect of the Belle Terre ordinance would be to exclude from the community, without any rational basis, unmarried groups seeking to live together, whether they be three college students, three single nurses, three priests, or three single judges. Although local communities are given wide latitude in achieving legitimate zoning needs, they cannot under the mask of zoning ordinances impose social preferences of this character upon their fellow citizens. [476 F.2d 806, at 815.]

For an extended critique of *Belle Terre*, see 3 N. Williams, American Land Planning Law § 66.90 (Rev. ed. 1985). For a current view, see Note, *Altering "Family": Another Look at the Supreme Court's Narrow Protection of Families in Belle Terre*, 83 B.U. L. Rev. 875 (2003). *Belle Terre* is still frequently cited. See, e.g. *In the Matter of Bayram v. City of Binghamton*, 27 Misc. 3d 1032, 899 N.Y.S.2d 566, 2010 NY Slip Op 20116 (2010).

The Supreme Court's rhapsodic view of single-family zoning ("a quiet place where yards are wide [and] people few") soon came face to face with the grimmer reality that faces many households and individuals as they seek shelter. Later cases, without directly questioning the holding of *Belle Terre*, create alternate constitutional tools to challenge restrictive zoning. In addition, as a later Note will demonstrate, some state courts have explicitly repudiated *Belle Terre* and have followed a state constitutional path to a different outcome.

In *Moore v. City of East Cleveland*, 431 U.S. 494 (1977), the Supreme Court made it clear that the definition of family in a local zoning or housing ordinance may violate substantive due process even when it would satisfy the deferential, "minimum rationality" standard for judicial review employed in *Euclid* and *Belle Terre*. The East Cleveland ordinance had an unusually restrictive definition of family, limited to three generations consisting of a "head of household" and spouse, their parents, and their children. This definition excluded collateral blood relations and children of children, except for the following:

> [A] family may include not more than one dependent married or unmarried child of the nominal head of the household or of the spouse of the nominal head of the household and the spouse and dependent children of such dependent child. For the purpose of this subsection, a dependent person is one who has more than fifty percent of his total support furnished for him by the nominal head of the household and the spouse of the nominal head of the household.

By a five-to-four vote, the Supreme Court invalidated the East Cleveland ordinance's restrictive definition of family. But only Justices Brennan, Marshall, and Blackmun joined in the plurality opinion by Justice Powell who advanced the following rationale for invalidation:

> When a city undertakes such intrusive regulation of the family, neither *Belle Terre* nor *Euclid* governs; the usual judicial deference to the legislature is inappropriate. "This Court has long recognized that freedom of personal choice in matters of

marriage and family life is one of the liberties protected by the Due Process Clause of the Fourteenth Amendment." *Cleveland Board of Education v. LaFleur*, 414 U.S. 632, 639–640 (1974). A host of cases, tracing their lineage to *Meyer v. Nebraska*, 262 U.S. 390, 399–401 (1923), and *Pierce v. Society of Sisters*, 268 U.S. 510, 534–535 (1925), have consistently acknowledged a "private realm of family life which the state cannot enter." *Prince v. Massachusetts*, 321 U.S. 158, 166 (1944). Of course, the family is not beyond regulation. But when the government intrudes on choices concerning family living arrangements, this Court must examine carefully the importance of the governmental interests advanced and the extent to which they are served by the challenged regulation.

When thus examined, this ordinance cannot survive. The city seeks to justify it as a means of preventing overcrowding, minimizing traffic and parking congestion, and avoiding an undue financial burden on East Cleveland's school system. Although these are legitimate goals, the ordinance before us serves them marginally, at best. For example, the ordinance permits any family consisting only of husband, wife, and unmarried children to live together, even if the family contains a half-dozen licensed drivers, each with his or her own car. At the same time it forbids an adult brother and sister to share a household, even if both faithfully use public transportation. The ordinance would permit a grandmother to live with a single dependent son and children, even if his school-age children number a dozen, yet it forces Mrs. Moore to find another dwelling for her grandson John, simply because of the presence of his uncle and cousin in the same household. We need not labor the point. Section 1341.08 has but a tenuous relation to alleviation of the conditions mentioned by the city. . . . [*Id* at 499–500.]

The following case examines an exclusion issue that arose in the denial of a special permit for a group home for the mentally disabled:

CITY OF CLEBURNE v. CLEBURNE LIVING CENTER

473 U.S. 432 (1985)

Justice White delivered the opinion of the Court:

A Texas city denied a special use permit for the operation of a group home for the mentally retarded, acting pursuant to a municipal zoning ordinance requiring permits for such homes. The Court of Appeals for the Fifth Circuit held that mental retardation is a "quasi-suspect" classification and that the ordinance violated the Equal Protection Clause because it did not substantially further an important governmental purpose. We hold that a lesser standard of scrutiny is appropriate, but conclude that under that standard the ordinance is invalid as applied in this case.

I

In July 1980, respondent Jan Hannah purchased a building at 201 Featherston Street in the city of Cleburne, Texas, with the intention of leasing it to Cleburne Living Center, Inc. (CLC), for the operation of a group home for the mentally retarded. It was anticipated that the home would house 13 retarded men and women, who would be under the constant supervision of CLC staff members. The house had four bedrooms and two baths, with a half bath to be added. CLC planned to comply with all applicable state and federal regulations.

The city informed CLC that a special use permit would be required for the operation of a group home at the site, and CLC accordingly submitted a permit application. In response to a subsequent inquiry from CLC, the city explained that under the zoning regulations applicable to the site, a special use permit, renewable annually, was required for the construction of "[h]ospitals for the insane or feeble-minded, or alcoholic [sic] or drug addicts, or penal or correctional institutions." The city had determined that the proposed group home should be classified as a "hospital for the feebleminded." After holding a public hearing on CLC's application, the City Council voted 3 to 1 to deny a special use permit.[(4)]

CLC then filed suit in Federal District Court against the city and a number of its officials, alleging, inter alia, that the zoning ordinance was invalid on its face and as applied because it discriminated against the mentally retarded in violation of the equal protection rights of CLC and its potential residents. . . . [T]he District Court held the ordinance and its application constitutional. . . .

The Court of Appeals for the Fifth Circuit reversed, determining that mental retardation was a quasi-suspect classification and that it should assess the validity of the ordinance under intermediate-level scrutiny. . . .[(8)]

[Applying principles of equal protection law, the Court concluded that the mentally retarded were not a "quasi-suspect class" entitled to an intermediate standard of review, because of the diversity of the disabilities involved, the history of supportive care provided by federal and state governments, and the potential extension of any rule to other disabled classes. The Court then continued as follows:]

Our refusal to recognize the retarded as a quasi-suspect class does not leave them entirely unprotected from invidious discrimination. To withstand equal protection review, legislation that distinguishes between the mentally retarded and others must be rationally related to a legitimate governmental purpose. This standard, we believe, affords government the latitude necessary both to pursue policies designed to assist the retarded in realizing their full potential, and to freely and efficiently engage in activities that burden the retarded in what is essentially an incidental manner. The State may not rely on a classification whose relationship to an asserted goal is so attenuated as to render the distinction arbitrary or irrational. *See Zobel v. Williams*, 457 U.S. 55, 61–63 (1982); *United States Dept. of Agriculture v. Moreno*, 413 U.S. 528, 535 (1973). Furthermore, some objectives — such as "a bare . . . desire to harm a politically unpopular group," *id.*, at 534 — are not legitimate state interests. *See also Zobel, supra*, at 63. Beyond that, the mentally retarded, like others, have and retain their substantive constitutional rights in addition to the right to be treated equally by the law.

---

(4) The city's Planning and Zoning Commission had earlier held a hearing and voted to deny the permit.

(8) *Macon Ass'n for Retarded Citizens v. Macon-Bibb County Planning and Zoning Comm'n*, 314 S.E.2d 218 (Ga. 1984), *dism'd for want of a substantial federal question*, 469 U.S. 802 (1984), has no controlling effect on this case. *Macon Ass'n for Retarded Citizens* involved an ordinance that had the effect of excluding a group home for the retarded only because it restricted dwelling units to those occupied by a single family, defined as no more than four unrelated persons. In *Village of Belle Terre v. Boraas*, 416 U.S. 1 (1974), we upheld the constitutionality of a similar ordinance, and the Georgia Supreme Court in *Macon Ass'n* specifically held that the ordinance did not discriminate against the retarded. 314 S.E.2d, at 221.

IV

We turn to the issue of the validity of the zoning ordinance insofar as it requires a special use permit for homes for the mentally retarded.[14] We inquire first whether requiring a special use permit for the Featherston home in the circumstances here deprives respondents of the equal protection of the laws. If it does, there will be no occasion to decide whether the special use permit provision is facially invalid where the mentally retarded are involved, or to put it another way, whether the city may never insist on a special use permit for a home for the mentally retarded in an R-3 zone. This is the preferred course of adjudication since it enables courts to avoid making unnecessarily broad constitutional judgments.

The constitutional issue is clearly posed. The city does not require a special use permit in an R-3 zone for apartment houses, multiple dwellings, boarding and lodging houses, fraternity or sorority houses, dormitories, apartment hotels, hospitals, sanitariums, nursing homes for convalescents or the aged (other than for the insane or feebleminded or alcoholics or drug addicts), private clubs or fraternal orders, and other specified uses. It does, however, insist on a special permit for the Featherston home, and it does so, as the District Court found, because it would be a facility for the mentally retarded. May the city require the permit for this facility when other care and multiple-dwelling facilities are freely permitted?

It is true, as already pointed out, that the mentally retarded as a group are indeed different from others not sharing their misfortune, and in this respect they may be different from those who would occupy other facilities that would be permitted in an R-3 zone without a special permit. But this difference is largely irrelevant unless the Featherston home and those who would occupy it would threaten legitimate interests of the city in a way that other permitted uses such as boarding houses and hospitals would not. Because in our view the record does not reveal any rational basis for believing that the Featherston home would pose any special threat to the city's legitimate interests, we affirm the judgment below insofar as it holds the ordinance invalid as applied in this case.

The District Court found that the City Council's insistence on the permit rested on several factors. First, the Council was concerned with the negative attitude of the majority of property owners located within 200 feet of the Featherston facility, as well as with the fears of elderly residents of the neighborhood. But mere negative attitudes, or fear, unsubstantiated by factors which are properly cognizable in a zoning proceeding, are not permissible bases for treating a home for the mentally retarded differently from apartment houses, multiple dwellings, and the like. It is plain that the electorate as a whole, whether by referendum or otherwise, could not order city action violative of the Equal Protection Clause, *Lucas v. Forty-Fourth General Assembly of Colorado*, 377 U.S. 713, 736–737 (1964), and the city may not avoid the strictures of that Clause by deferring to the wishes or objections of some fraction of the body politic. "Private biases may be outside the reach of the law, but the law cannot, directly or indirectly, give them effect." *Palmore v. Sidoti*, 466 U.S. 429, 433 (1984).

Second, the Council had two objections to the location of the facility. It was concerned that the facility was across the street from a junior high school, and it feared that the students might harass the occupants of the Featherston home. But the school itself is attended by about 30 mentally retarded students, and denying a permit based on such vague, undifferentiated fears is again permitting some portion of the community to validate what

[14] It goes without saying that there is nothing before us with respect to the validity of requiring a special use permit for the other uses listed in the ordinance.

would otherwise be an equal protection violation. The other objection to the home's location was that it was located on "a five hundred year flood plain." This concern with the possibility of a flood, however, can hardly be based on a distinction between the Featherston home and, for example, nursing homes, homes for convalescents or the aged, or sanitariums or hospitals, any of which could be located on the Featherston site without obtaining a special use permit. The same may be said of another concern of the Council — doubts about the legal responsibility for actions which the mentally retarded might take. If there is no concern about legal responsibility with respect to other uses that would be permitted in the area, such as boarding and fraternity houses, it is difficult to believe that the groups of mildly or moderately mentally retarded individuals who would live at 201 Featherston would present any different or special hazard.

Fourth, the Council was concerned with the size of the home and the number of people that would occupy it. The District Court found, and the Court of Appeals repeated, that "[i]f the potential residents of the Featherston Street home were not mentally retarded, but the home was the same in all other respects, its use would be permitted under the city's zoning ordinance." 726 F.2d, at 200. Given this finding, there would be no restrictions on the number of people who could occupy this home as a boarding house, nursing home, family dwelling, fraternity house, or dormitory. The question is whether it is rational to treat the mentally retarded differently. It is true that they suffer disability not shared by others; but why this difference warrants a density regulation that others need not observe is not at all apparent. At least this record does not clarify how, in this connection, the characteristics of the intended occupants of the Featherston home rationally justify denying to those occupants what would be permitted to groups occupying the same site for different purposes. Those who would live in the Featherston home are the type of individuals who, with supporting staff, satisfy federal and state standards for group housing in the community; and there is no dispute that the home would meet the federal square-footage-per-resident requirement for facilities of this type. *See* 42 CFR § 442.447 (1984). In the words of the Court of Appeals, "[t]he City never justifies its apparent view that other people can live under such 'crowded' conditions when mentally retarded persons cannot." 726 F.2d, at 202.

In the courts below the city also urged that the ordinance is aimed at avoiding concentration of population and at lessening congestion of the streets. These concerns obviously fail to explain why apartment houses, fraternity and sorority houses, hospitals and the like, may freely locate in the area without a permit. So, too, the expressed worry about fire hazards, the serenity of the neighborhood, and the avoidance of danger to other residents fail rationally to justify singling out a home such as 201 Featherston for the special use permit, yet imposing no such restrictions on the many other uses freely permitted in the neighborhood.

The short of it is that requiring the permit in this case appears to us to rest on an irrational prejudice against the mentally retarded, including those who would occupy the Featherston facility and who would live under the closely supervised and highly regulated conditions expressly provided for by state and federal law.

The judgment of the Court of Appeals is affirmed insofar as it invalidates the zoning ordinance as applied to the Featherston home. The judgment is otherwise vacated.

It is so ordered.

[Most of the discussion in the concurring and dissenting opinions is omitted, but Justice

Marshall's arguments in his concurring and dissenting opinion are of interest:]

JUSTICE MARSHALL, with whom JUSTICE BRENNAN and JUSTICE BLACKMUN join, concurring in the judgment in part and dissenting in part:

The Court holds that all retarded individuals cannot be grouped together as the "feebleminded" and deemed presumptively unfit to live in a community. Underlying this holding is the principle that mental retardation per se cannot be a proxy for depriving retarded people of their rights and interests without regard to variations in individual ability. With this holding and principle I agree. The Equal Protection Clause requires attention to the capacities and needs of retarded people as individuals.

I cannot agree, however, with the way in which the Court reaches its result or with the narrow, as-applied remedy it provides for the city of Cleburne's equal protection violation. The Court holds the ordinance invalid on rational-basis grounds and disclaims that anything special, in the form of heightened scrutiny, is taking place. Yet Cleburne's ordinance surely would be valid under the traditional rational-basis test applicable to economic and commercial regulation. In my view, it is important to articulate, as the Court does not, the facts and principles that justify subjecting this zoning ordinance to the searching review — the heightened scrutiny — that actually leads to its invalidation. Moreover, in invalidating Cleburne's exclusion of the "feebleminded" only as applied to respondents, rather than on its face, the Court radically departs from our equal protection precedents. Because I dissent from this novel and truncated remedy, and because I cannot accept the Court's disclaimer that no "more exacting standard" than ordinary rational-basis review is being applied, I write separately. [The dissenting opinion argued that the Court should have invalidated the special permit requirement under "second-order" heightened scrutiny review.]

NOTES AND QUESTIONS

1. *Disadvantaged groups in the zoning process. Cleburne* is an important case because it again deals with the legal status of a politically unpopular group in the zoning process. You should compare the way in which the Court handled the denial of the special use permit with the way in which the Court rejected a facial attack on an ordinance limiting the number of persons who can live together in *Belle Terre.* Are the groups distinguishable?

2. *What was unconstitutional?* The majority makes it clear that it is undertaking an as-applied analysis of Cleburne's zoning ordinance:

> We inquire first whether requiring a special use permit for the Featherston home in the circumstances here deprives respondents of the equal protection of the laws. If it does, there will be no occasion to decide whether the special use permit provision is facially invalid where the mentally retarded are involved, or to put it another way, whether the city may never insist on a special use permit for a home for the mentally retarded in an R-3 zone.

But even within this as-applied context, is it the specific decision to deny CLC's permit that is invalid, or the broader decision to single out group homes for the mentally retarded for the special permit requirement? Wasn't the language of the permit requirement in *Cleburne* facially unconstitutional as the dissent suggested?

Does *Cleburne* require heightened scrutiny whenever state decision making reflects negative attitudes or fear about a disfavored group? In a non-land use case involving people with disabilities, Chief Justice Rehnquist sought to limit the scope of *Cleburne*:

> Although such biases may often accompany irrational (and therefore unconstitutional) discrimination, their presence alone does not a constitutional violation make. As we noted in *Cleburne*: "Mere negative attitudes, or fear, *unsubstantiated by factors which are properly cognizable in a zoning proceeding*, are not permissible bases for treating a home for the mentally retarded differently . . . ." *Id.* at 448 (emphasis added). This language, read in context, simply states the unremarkable and widely acknowledged tenet of this Court's equal protection jurisprudence that state action subject to rational-basis scrutiny does not violate the Fourteenth Amendment when it "rationally furthers the purpose identified by the State." [*Garrett v. Board of Trustees*, 531 U.S. 356, 367 (2001).]

3. *Post-Cleburne cases.* The cases have applied *Cleburne* to invalidate restrictions on group homes and permit denials. *New Directions Treatment Servs. v. City of Reading*, 490 F.3d 293 (3d Cir. 2007) (invalidating state statute prohibiting methadone clinic within certain distance of residential and other uses under Americans with Disabilities and Rehabilitation Acts and Equal Protection Clause); *Community Resources for Justice, Inc. v. City of Manchester*, 949 A.2d 681 (N.H. 2008) (denial of approval of halfway house violates New Hampshire equal protection tests).

The cases since *Cleburne* have divided on whether a municipality can constitutionally require a conditional use permit for a group home. See *Bannum, Inc. v. City of Louisville*, 958 F.2d 1354 (6th Cir. 1992) (invalidating requirement). In *Doe v. City of Butler*, 892 F.2d 315 (3d Cir. 1989), the court upheld a requirement for conditional uses for group homes in single-family residential districts, the denial of a permit for a group home for battered women, and a provision limiting occupancy in group homes to six persons. The court relied on *Belle Terre* to hold that the occupancy restriction was a reasonable density limitation in an R-2 (two-family) residential district. The court distinguished *Cleburne* because it said that the "vice" in that case was that group homes for the mentally retarded required a special use permit while other group homes did not. Is this a correct reading? The court in *Doe* then remanded the case to determine whether the occupancy limitation was reasonable in apartment building residential districts. *Open Homes Fellowship, Inc. v. Orange County*, 325 F. Supp. 2d 1349 (M.D. Fla. 2004), invalidated a permit denial as applied on facts similar to *Cleburne*. The Second Circuit cited *Cleburne* in rejecting the rational basis test in favor of the majority heightened scrutiny test in FHA claims where there is disparate impact. *HRRMG. v. County of Suffolk*, 687 F. Supp. 2d 237 (E.D.N.Y. 2010).

Macon Ass'n for Retarded Citizens v. Macon-Bibb County Planning & Zoning Comm'n, discussed in the principal case, is a state case rejecting a challenge to a zoning ordinance excluding group homes. The court explained that the group home exclusion was acceptable because it was produced by a zoning ordinance restricting dwelling units to families of no more than four unrelated persons. The Court noted it had upheld a similar ordinance in *Belle Terre* and that the ordinance in *Macon* did not discriminate against the retarded. *Macon* is of particular interest because it is cited and distinguished by the Court in footnote 8 of *Cleburne*. See also *Frazier v. City of Grand Ledge*, 135 F. Supp. 2d 845 (W.D. Mich. 2001) (zoning ordinance excluding foster care home did not violate equal protection).

The *Bannum* case, *supra*, is one of a series of decisions involving Bannum, Inc., a commercial operator of group homes for prisoners in the last stages of their sentence before release. In *Bannum, Inc. v. City of St. Charles*, 2 F.3d 267 (8th Cir. 1993), the court upheld a conditional use requirement, distinguishing *Cleburne* on the basis that "[i]t is not irrational for the City to believe that recidivism could be a problem with some persons served by half-way houses. This is a legitimate concern which can be addressed on a case-by-case basis through application for conditional permits." *Id.* at 272. Accord in distinguishing *Cleburne*, *Bannum, Inc. v. City of Fort Lauderdale*, 157 F.3d 819 (11th Cir. 1998), *cert. denied*, 120 S. Ct. 67 (1999). Would these cases have been decided any differently had *Cleburne* adopted an intermediate scrutiny standard?

4. *Irrational opposition.* State courts are quite capable of striking down a denial of a conditional use for a group home when the denial was based on opposition by neighbors unsupported by evidence, and they can do so without the help of *Cleburne*. See *Wilson County Youth Emergency Shelter, Inc. v. Wilson County*, 13 S.W.3d 338 (Tenn. App. 2000). The board denied the group home because of a vague reference to "location," a lack of fire protection and the number of people living in the home. Accord *Bannum, Inc. v. City of Columbia*, 516 S.E.2d 439 (S.C. 1999). Conditional uses are reviewed in Chapter 6, *infra*.

"GROUP HOMES ARE A REAL PROBLEM IN OUR COMMUNITY"

5. *Defining "family."* A number of state cases have interpreted the definition of "family" or "accessory use" in zoning ordinances to include group homes. They sometimes stress that a zoning ordinance may regulate only uses, not users, and that a regulation based on users would violate substantive due process. Some cases have adopted a "functional equivalence" rule as the basis for bringing group homes within the definition of "family." In *City of White Plains v. Ferraioli*, 313 N.E.2d 756 (N.Y. 1974), for example, the court distinguished *Belle Terre* and held that a foster home was a "relatively normal, stable, and permanent family unit." If a zoning ordinance adopted this definition, would it be constitutional under *Cleburne*? Consider the definition in *In the Matter of Bayram v. City of Binghamton*, 27 Misc. 3d 1032, 899 N.Y.S.2d 566, 2010 NY Slip Op 20116 (2010):

> A group of unrelated individuals living together and functioning together as a traditional family. In determining whether or not a group of unrelated individuals comprise [sic] a functional and factual family equivalent, a petition shall be presented before the Zoning Board of Appeals, who [sic] will consider, among other things, the following factors:

A.Whether the occupants share the entire dwelling unit or act as separate roomers.

B.Whether the household has stability akin to a permanent family structure. The criteria used to determine this test may include the following:

(1) Length of stay together among the occupants in the current dwelling unit or other dwelling units.

(2) The presence of minor, dependent children regularly residing in the household.

(3) The presence of one individual acting as head of household.

(4) Proof of sharing expenses for food, rent or ownership costs, utilities and other household expenses.

(5) Common ownership of furniture and appliances among the members of the household.

(6) Whether the household is a temporary living arrangement or a framework for transient living.

(7) Whether the composition of the household changes from year to year or within the year.

(8) Any other factor reasonably related to whether or not the group of persons is the functional equivalent of a family.

City of Binghamton Zoning Ordinance § 410-5.

Does this solve or create problems?

6. *Day care.* Caring for children is, of course, one of the prime attributes of family living. But what of a "temporary" family environment such as a day care provider, where children come during the day to learn or play in a home-like setting, and then go home? Zoning authorities are having to address this question more and more as employment outside the home becomes the norm for parents. Many states provide by statute that day care facilities (usually capped at a certain number of children) cannot be excluded from residential zones. See, e.g., *Rogers v. Town of Norfolk*, 734 N.E.2d 1143 (Mass. 2000) (town cannot deny permit on the basis of restrictive area and bulk requirements). But cf. *Martellini v. Little Angels Day Care, Inc.*, 847 A.2d 838 (R.I. 2004) (covenant limiting use to "single family private residence purposes" was not unenforceable as against public policy; Little Angels banished). See generally Pettygrove, *Child Care in Residential Zones: State Legislation and Local Options*, Zoning News, Dec., 2001. For the intersection of religious rights and day care, see *Shepherd Montessori v. Ann Arbor Charter*, 783 N.W.2d 695 (Mich. 2010).

7. *State and federal legislation.* All states now have legislation governing zoning for group homes and directing how group homes are handled in local zoning ordinances. The statutes vary in defining the protected groups that are covered by the statute. They also vary in indicating where group homes can locate. Some permit group homes in "all zones," while others limit them to single-family or multi-family districts. All the statutes have occupancy limits, some limit the number of staff, and some require supervision. Other statutes require the dispersal of group homes throughout residential areas, through spacing or other requirements, to avoid excessive concentration. For discussion, see Davis & Gaus, *Protecting Group Homes for the Non-Handicapped: Zoning in the Post-Edmonds Era*, 46 Kan. L. Rev. 777, 789–96 (1998). See, e.g., Ariz. Rev. Stat. Ann. §§ 36-581, 36-582; Kan. Stat. Ann. § 12-736. Are these statutes constitutional? The validity of spacing requirements under the federal Fair Housing Act is discussed in Chapter 5.

The federal Fair Housing Act, 42 U.S.C. §§ 3601 et seq., was amended in 1988 to prohibit discrimination against group homes for the mentally handicapped, including discrimination through zoning. The Fair Housing Act, where it applies, has generally eliminated the need to proceed directly under the Constitution, as in *Cleburne*. See, e.g., *Dr. Gertrude A. Barber Ctr., Inc. v. Peters Twp.*, 273 F. Supp. 2d 643, 652 (W.D. Pa. 2003) (group home for four mentally retarded adults cannot be rejected under ordinance's "family" definition). Other recent cases include: *Sanghvi v. City of Claremont*, 328 F.3d 532 (9th Cir. 2003) (city had reason to deny sewer service to proposed home); *Good Shepherd Manor Found'n v. City of Momence*, 323 F.3d 557 (7th Cir. 2003) (same; water service); *Community Housing Trust v. Department of Consumer and Reg. Aff.*, 257 F. Supp. 2d 208 (D.D.C. 2003) (Certificate of Occupancy requirement invalid); *Lewis v. Draper City*, 2010 U.S. Dist. LEXIS 100186 (D. Utah 2010) (violation of FHA; no reasonable accommodation).

Note however, that the Act's "handicap" basis limits its scope in comparison to *Cleburne*. This statute is discussed in Chapter 5. Do any provisions of the state statutes described above violate the federal Fair Housing Amendments Act of 1988, insofar as they cover the same classes of people?

8. *References.* As to the land use implications of *Cleburne*, see Jaffe, *Coping with Cleburne*, Land Use L. & Zoning Dig., Vol. 38, No. 2, at 5 (1986); Mandelker, *Group Homes: The Supreme Court Revives the Equal Protection Clause in Land Use Cases*, *in* 1986 Inst. on Plan. Zoning & Eminent Domain, ch. 3. The question of how disadvantaged groups should be treated in the zoning process is picked up again in Chapter 5, *infra.* See also R. Schwemm & S. Pratt, Disparate Impact Under the Fair Housing Act: A Proposed Approach (2010), http://papers.ssrn.com.

A NOTE ON FAMILY ZONING IN THE STATE COURTS

One might have expected that state courts would "fall into line" after the Supreme Court's decision in *Belle Terre* and sustain local zoning ordinances severely restricting the number of unrelated persons who might comprise a family for zoning purposes. Many have, but a few state courts have held that such restrictive definitions violate state constitutional guarantees of due process and/or privacy.

Following Belle Terre. Many states have followed *Belle Terre*. *State v. Champoux*, 555 N.W.2d 69 (Neb. App. 1996), applied a presumption of constitutionality to a restrictive family definition and found a legitimate purpose: "In enacting zoning ordinances to provide for the public health, safety, and general welfare, a municipality may consider the quality of living in its community and may attempt to promote values important to the community as a whole." 554. N.W.2d at 75-76. The Iowa Supreme Court followed *Belle Terre* and upheld an ordinance limiting single family dwellings to any number of related individuals or a maximum of three unrelated individuals as permissible under the state constitution. The court found that the government's interests of "promot[ing] a sense of community, sanctity of the family, quiet and peaceful neighborhoods, low population, limited congestion of motor vehicles and controlled transiency" were valid and rationally related to the ordinance. Finding the city's assertion that allowing large numbers of unrelated people to live together leads to greater noise and traffic and households that do not "take root" in the community to be credible, the court held it was rational for the city to believe the law would lead to quieter, safer and less dense family-oriented neighborhoods. *Ames Rental Prop. Ass'n v. City of Ames*, 736 N.W.2d 255 (Iowa 2007). See also *City of Brookings v. Winker*, 554 N.W.2d 827 (S.D. 1996) (city was college town with unavoidable population density problems).

Rejecting Belle Terre. Cases rejecting *Belle Terre* and holding that limitations on the size of unrelated families are invalid include *Kirsch v. Prince George's County*, 626 A.2d 372 (Md. 1993); *Charter Twp. of Delta v. Dinolfo*, 351 N.W.2d 831 (Mich. 1984); *Baer v. Town of Brookhaven*, 537 N.E.2d 619 (N.Y. 1989) — all holding that there was no rational relationship between the restrictive definition of family and the purported state interest in controlling population density and/or maintenance of property values. The leading case is *State v. Baker*, 405 A.2d 368 (N.J. 1979).

In *Baker*, the City of Plainfield prosecuted the owner of a large home shared by two families whose living arrangements, as the court described it, "arose out of the individuals' religious beliefs and resultant desire to go through life as 'brothers and sisters.'" The two families ate together, shared common areas and held communal prayer sessions. Each occupant contributed a fixed amount per week to defray household expenses. The city's ordinance prohibited occupancy by more than four persons not related by blood or marriage.

Noting that "[w]e, of course, remain free to interpret our constitution and statutes more stringently" than the federal Constitution, the New Jersey Supreme Court said:

> The courts of this and other states have often noted that the core concept underlying single family living is not biological or legal relationship but, rather, its character as a single housekeeping unit. As long as a group bears the "generic character of a family unit as a relatively permanent household," it should be equally as entitled to occupy a single family dwelling as its biologically related neighbors.
>
> Plainfield has a legitimate interest in preserving a "family" style of living in certain residential neighborhoods. Such a goal may be achieved, perhaps more sensibly, by the single-housekeeping unit requirement, as well as the exclusion of incompatible residential uses such as commercial residences, non-familial institutional uses, boarding homes and other such occupancies without infringing unnecessarily upon the freedom and privacy of unrelated individuals.
>
> In addition to preserving a "family" style of living, the municipality also defends its ordinance as necessary to prevent overcrowding and congestion. The instant regulation, however, is too tenuously related to these goals to justify its impingement upon the internal makeup of the housekeeping entity. The Plainfield Ordinance is both underinclusive and overinclusive. It is overinclusive because it prohibits single housekeeping units which may not, in fact, be overcrowded or cause congestion; it is underinclusive because it fails to prohibit certain housekeeping units — composed of related individuals — which do present such problems. Thus, for example, five unrelated retired gentlemen could not share a large eight bedroom estate situated upon five acres of land, whereas a large extended family including aunts, uncles and cousins, could share a small two bedroom apartment without violating this ordinance.
>
> An appropriate method to prevent overcrowding and congestion . . . [is by an ordinance of general application] limiting the number of occupants in reasonable relation to available sleeping and bathroom facilities or requiring a minimum amount of habitable floor area per occupant. [405 A.2d at 372–73.]

Does the *Baker* decision really reject the concept of a family or simply redefine it? What is the basis on which the court finds the definition of "family" unacceptable? Under the reasoning of *Baker*, could Plainfield have excluded the group home that was at issue in *Cleburne*? "In 2000, the most common type of household had neither a partner nor children (32 percent), followed by households with a partner and children (31 percent), households with a partner but without children (26 percent), and households with children but without a partner (12 percent)." Page 1 at http://www.census.gov/prod/2005pubs/censr-24.pdf. Will demographic shifts drive changes in local regulations and the common law?

Substantive due process and family occupancy. In another part of its decision, the Court in *Baker* says that the decision is based on "the requirement of due process" encompassed within Art. I, par. 1 of the New Jersey Constitution. Does this mean that the Plainfield zoning ordinance's definition of "family" failed to meet the usual substantive due process test of minimum rationality, just as Cleburne's ordinance failed the minimum rationality test of equal protection? Or is the court applying a stricter test — e.g., "strict scrutiny," or some middle-level test? The court added a statement that "the right of privacy is also included within the protection offered by" Art. I, par. 1, and that, "although this right is not absolute, it may be restricted only when necessary to promote a compelling government interest." Art. I, par. 1 of the New Jersey Constitution does not expressly mention either "due process" or "privacy."

Family occupancy and overcrowding. Does *Baker*'s disposition of the City's overcrowding argument mean that it would be constitutional to impose a requirement of a "minimum amount of habitable floor area per occupant" upon the number of persons who may compose a "family" for zoning purposes, regardless of whether the members of the "family" are, or are not, related by blood, marriage, or adoption? If such a restriction were imposed, would the court enforce the restriction in a case where the birth of additional children so enlarges a traditional biologically-based family as to render its continued occupation of a "single-family" house unlawful? Does *Moore v. East Cleveland* answer this question? See also *Borough of Glassboro v. Vallorosi*, 568 A.2d 888 (N.J. 1990), where the court held on the facts that ten unrelated male college students were a "family" under a zoning ordinance limiting the occupancy of dwellings in residential districts to families only. Minimum floor area per occupant should be of general application, reasonable and supported by evidence. *Ewing Citizens for Civil Rights, Inc. v. Township of Ewing*, 2010 N.J. Super. Unpub. LEXIS 647 (N.J. App. Div. 2010).

Families and privacy rights. In a case rather similar to the principal case on its facts, the California Supreme Court followed New Jersey in holding that a local zoning ordinance allowing only five persons unrelated by blood, marriage, or adoption to constitute a "family" for zoning purposes violated that state's constitution. *City of Santa Barbara v. Adamson*, 610 P.2d 436 (Cal. 1980). But the *Adamson* decision was explicitly premised on an amendment to the California Constitution that added "privacy" to the list of rights entitled to constitutional protection. In light of the way the concept of privacy entwines itself around the *Baker* and *Adamson* decisions, how is one to explain the way Justice Douglas dismisses privacy out of hand in *Belle Terre*, distinguishing such seminal federal privacy cases as *Griswold v. Connecticut* (which Justice Douglas wrote) and *Eisenstadt v. Baird* on the basis that zoning laws are mere "economic or social legislation," entitled to deferential review? The California Court of Appeal has extended *Adamson*'s privacy theory to hold unconstitutional an ordinance restricting accessory apartments. *CALHO v. City of Santa Monica*, 105 Cal. Rptr. 2d 802 (Cal. App. 2001). This issue is discussed in the Note, *infra*.

References. For discussion of the family definition problem in zoning, see Scott, *A Psycho-Social Analysis of the Concept of Family as Used in Zoning Laws*, 88 Dick. L. Rev. 368 (1984); Note, *Single-Family Zoning: Ramifications of State Court Rejection of Belle Terre on Use and Density Controls*, 32 Hastings L.J. 1687 (1981); Scott, *Restricting the Definitions of "Single Family,"* Land Use L. & Zoning Dig., Vol. 36, No. 10, at 7 (1984); Note, *Belle Terre and Single-Family Home Ordinances: Judicial Perceptions of Local Government and the Presumption of Validity*, 74 N.Y.U. L. Rev. 447 (1999); Merriam, *Ozzie and Harriet Don't Live Here Anymore: Time to Redefine Family*, Zoning Practice, Feb. 2007, at 2.; Note, *Five is a Crowd: A Constitutional Analysis of the Boston Zoning Amendment Prohibiting More Than Four College Students From Living Together*, 43 Suffolk U. L. Rev. 217 (2009).

A NOTE ON ALTERNATIVES TO SINGLE-FAMILY ZONING: THE ACCESSORY APARTMENT

Two leading land use commentators argued some time ago that single-family zoning is no longer defensible as a land use strategy. Babcock, *The Egregious Invalidity of the Exclusive Single-Family Zone*, Land Use L. & Zoning Dig., Vol 35, No. 7, at 4 (1983); Ziegler, *The Twilight of Single-Family Zoning*, 3 UCLA J. Envtl. L. & Pol'y 161 (1983). Both noted that single-family houses all across the nation are increasingly being converted into two-unit dwellings by internal subdivision to create an "accessory apartment," often for elderly parents. This kind of housing is even more important today, as the population ages and housing costs escalate.

Although accessory housing units can help with the affordable housing problem, popular (and some scholarly) concerns are often voiced about parking and traffic, about changing the character of residential neighborhoods by increased density, and about the impact of rental units amidst owner-occupied homes. See Weinberg & McGuire, *"Granny Flats" and Second Unit Housing: Who Speaks for the Neighborhood?*, 23 Zoning & Plan. L. Rep. 25 (2000). Where accessory housing is formally permitted, it is usually under the prod of state legislation. See, e.g., Vt. Stat. Ann. tit. 24, § 4412. Owners usually must occupy such housing, and ordinances usually restrict eligible tenants, lot and apartment size, exterior appearance, and parking. Ownership requirements may be problematic. *City of Wilmington v. Hill*, 657 S.E.2d 670 (N.C. App. 2008) held unconstitutional an ordinance requiring the owner of a garage apartment to live either in the apartment or in the primary residence. The court held that the municipality could regulate the use of the property, but it was unauthorized to regulate the manner of ownership of the property. Compare *Kasper v. Brookhaven*, 535 N.Y.S.2d 621 (App. Div. 1988), upholding an ordinance allowing residents who occupied their homes to secure permits for accessory rental apartments but denying permits to nonresidents.

Illegal accessory units can be a problem. Seattle, for example, assists property owners with legalizing accessory dwelling units, but also issues fines and penalties to owners who do not comply. See *Code Compliance: Illegal Dwelling Units*, Seattle Dep't of Plan. & Dev. (2009), *available at* www.seattle.gov/dpd/publications/cam/cam606.pdf. Many communities overlook illegal units unless there are complaints by neighbors because, despite fears to the contrary, they seldom cause significant noise or traffic problems.

California has been a leader in requiring local governments to accommodate accessory apartments. Cal. Govt. Code § 65852.2 authorizes local governments to adopt a special use permit system for accessory second residential units. The municipality either must affirmatively provide for accessory units or it *must* grant a variance for such units when certain standards specified by the legislature are met. *Id.* §§ (a)(1), (b)(1). Applications are to be considered "ministerially, without discretionary review or a hearing." *Id.* § (a)(3). Nominally, a municipality may totally prohibit such units, but only if it formally declares that its policy may "limit housing opportunities in the region" and makes findings about "specific adverse impacts on the public health, safety and welfare that would result from allowing second units." *Id.* § (c). The ordinance may designate areas of the city where these residences can be located, and may include parking, height, setback, lot coverage, architectural review, and maximum size standards. It may also provide that a second unit cannot exceed the allowable density for the lot upon which it is located, and that it is a residential use consistent with the existing general plan and zoning designation for the lot. The statute authorizes an owner occupancy requirement. For a description of the legislation and the story of one municipality's long running attempt to avoid approving accessory apartments, see *CALHO v. City of Santa Monica*, 105 Cal. Rptr. 2d 802 (Cal. App. 2001). See also *Sounhein v. City of San Dimas*, 55 Cal. Rptr. 2d 290 (Cal. App. 1996) (owner occupancy requirement runs with the land); *Kisil v. City of Sandusky*, 465 N.E.2d 848 (Ohio 1984) (reversing denial of lot area variance to allow conversion of single-family residence into two-family residence when much of surrounding area had been converted to such residences).

The APA Model Act takes a planning approach, recommending that the local comprehensive plan's Housing Element contain a provision for "modifying development regulations to permit accessory dwelling units." *Id.* § 2-207(6)(c)(3). A consistency requirement, if one exists in the state, would then insure that accessory apartments could be developed either as a permitted use or by special permits or variances.

For a discussion of zoning ordinance provisions for accessory apartments, see Cobb & Dvorak, Accessory Dwelling Units: Model State Act and Local Ordinance, (AARP, 2000), available at http://www.aarp.org/research/legis-polit/legislation/aresearch-import-163-D17158.html; P. Hare, Accessory Apartments: Using Surplus Space in Single-Family Houses (Am. Plan. Ass'n, Plan. Advisory Serv. Rep. No. 365, 1981); M. Gellen, Accessory Apartments in Single-Family Housing (1985); E. Stege, What Next For Accessory Dwellings? Getting From Bylaws To Buildings, MIT (2009), http://dspace.mit.edu/handle/1721.1/50124. For a more expansive critique, arguing in favor of "co-housing," see Note, *Altering "Family": Another Look at the Supreme Court's Narrow Protection of Families in Belle Terre*, 83 B.U. L. Rev. 875 (2003). Exclusionary zoning is discussed in Chapter 5, and zoning for the aged is discussed *infra* in this chapter.

[c.] Manufactured Housing

So-called mobile or manufactured housing is an important part of the affordable housing supply. Mobile homes are now more commonly referred to as manufactured housing, but the term "mobile home" is retained in this discussion because manufactured housing can also mean housing built in modular sections at a factory and assembled on-site. A mobile home is built in its entirety at the factory, shipped to its site and placed on a base. Mobile homes can make up as much as one-third of all housing starts nationally in any one year. They are more common in some sections of the country than others, such as the south, and are more common in rural areas.

Local resistance to mobile homes remains strong. Objections include health problems that can arise from a lack of proper facilities, the usual concerns about high density development, the association of mobile homes with low-income status, and lack of neighborhood stability because mobile home residents are transient. A number of these objections may not be valid, such as the transiency problem, and some can be solved, such as the facility problem. Claims that mobile homes do not last as long as conventionally built housing have been disproved by studies. A recent study found no greater rates of crime in mobile home communities. W. McCarty, *Trailers and Trouble? An Examination of Crime in Mobile Home Communities*, 12 Cityscape 127 (2010), www.ssrn.com.

An implicit objection may often be aesthetic. When people think about mobile homes they usually envision the narrow "single-wides," which can have a flat roof and unattractive corrugated metal siding. Today, only about 10% of all mobile home production is in this form. The "double-wide," a mobile home that consists of two single sections and can be as attractive as any conventionally built home, is more common. Two-story mobile homes are possible, and mobile home developments can be virtually identical in appearance to those with conventionally built housing. For a survey of issues, see Weill, *Manufactured Housing in North Carolina: Current Issues and Future Opportunities*, Carolina Planning, Vol. 28, No.2, at 3 (2003); Schwartz, *The Current State of Manufactured Housing*, Urban Land, Nov.-Dec. 2005, at 36. HUD's website at http://www.hud.gov/offices/hsg/rmra/mhs/mhshome.cfm and that of the Manufactured Housing Institute at www.manufacturedhousing.org offer more information.

Total exclusions. Municipalities may try to exclude mobile homes completely. An early New Jersey case upholding this tactic, *Vickers v. Township Comm.*, 181 A.2d 129 (N.J. 1963), was overruled in *Southern Burlington County NAACP v. Township of Mount Laurel, infra* Chapter 5, and more recent cases elsewhere have also held the total exclusion of mobile homes invalid or highly suspect. See, e.g., *Town of Glocester v. Olivo's Mobile Home Court, Inc.*, 300 A.2d 465 (R.I. 1973); *Town of Pompey v. Parker*, 377 N.E.2d 741 (N.Y. 1978) (challenged law does not exclude all mobile homes; validity of total exclusion reserved); *Oak Forest Mobile Home Park, Inc. v. City of Oak Forest*, 326 N.E.2d 473 (Ill. App. 1975). In *Yurczyk v. Yellowstone County*, 83 P.3d 266, 272 (Mont. 2004), the court held that an ordinance requiring "on-site construction" did not have "a substantial bearing on the public health, safety, morals, or general welfare of the community" and was invalid. In lower court decisions in Michigan, mobile home parks were determined to have been effectively excluded by township ordinance, reversed on ripeness rounds in *Hendee LLC v. Township*, 786 N.W.2d 521 (Mich. 2010).

The marketplace can also be used to exclude mobile home communities (recall the discussion in Chapter 1 of the relationship between regulation and market-based approaches to resolving land use disputes). Kilgannon, *Trailer-Park Sales Squeeze Out Residents*, The New York Times, April 18, 2007, p.B1, reports on the decline of mobile home parks on Long Island and in northern New Jersey as developers successfully buy out the owners of the land for shopping centers and other up-scale uses (residents typically own their units but must lease land from park owners). In a further twist, one New Jersey community, Lodi, failed in its attempt to use eminent domain to purchase a mobile home park for redevelopment as a more expensive age-restricted community. *LBK Assoc., LLC v. Borough of Lodi*, 2007 N.J. Super. Unpub. LEXIS 1792 (N.J. Super., App. Div., 2007) (unreported). There are also success stories, however. See Stromberg, *Mobile Home Parks Hold Their Own*, Planning, Feb. 2005, at 10 (Boulder, Colorado, conversion to community land trust).

Mobile home parks. When a local government does not totally exclude mobile homes, it often tries to minimize their supposed negative impact upon the community by requiring them to be located in "mobile home parks," which are often subject to a special licensing requirement. Most courts have upheld these ordinances. See, e.g., *Texas Manufactured Hous. Ass'n v. City of Nederland*, 101 F.3d 1095 (5th Cir. 1996); *People of Village of Cahokia v. Wright*, 311 N.E.2d 153 (Ill. 1974); *Town of Granby v. Landry*, 170 N.E.2d 364 (Mass. 1960); *State v. Larson*, 195 N.W.2d 180 (Minn. 1972); *City of Brookside Village v. Comeau*, 633 S.W.2d 790 (Tex. 1982). Will mobile home parks ever recover given the economy? See J. Hagerty & S. Ng, *Mobile-Home Makers Try To Stitch Together a Rebound*, Wall Street Journal, September 30, 2010. http://online.wsj.com/article/SB10001424052748704858304575497824280577124.html.

The leading case invalidating an ordinance limiting mobile homes to mobile home parks is *Robinson Twp. v. Knoll*, 302 N.W.2d 146 (Mich. 1981). The court noted that changes in mobile home construction made them as attractive as conventional single-family dwellings. Aesthetic objections to mobile homes were no longer justified, and the investment required for a modern mobile home precluded any objections based on transient occupancy. More appropriate regulations, such as local plumbing codes and a regulation requiring attachment to a solid foundation, could handle health and safety problems.

The Mississippi court reached the same conclusion in *Carpenter v. City of Petal*, 699 So. 2d 928 (Miss. 1997). It noted that most of the cases upholding such restrictions predated federal statutory requirements for mobile homes, discussed *infra*, and said:

> Prohibiting individual mobile home or even modular home sites in any area other than designated mobile home parks, however, bears no relationship to the goal of preserving surrounding residential property values. In the Rural Fringe District, where Carpenter's property is located, permitted land uses include agriculture, farming, forestry and livestock production; nurseries and truck gardens; public or commercial stables and kennels; poultry, livestock and small animal raising; single-family dwellings; two-family dwellings; and accessory uses including signs and incidental home occupations. [*Id.* at 933.]

The Court also quoted the Mississippi Manufactured Housing Association, whose *amicus* brief pointed out that

> [i]n the Rural Fringe District, Petal will allow commercial stables, dog runs, pig pens and chicken yards within 100 feet of a property line, but have [sic] refused to allow Mr. Carpenter to locate his manufactured home 550 feet from the street on a 100 by 200 foot tract in the middle of his 92 acres. [*Id.*]

Accord *Luczynski v. Temple*, 497 A.2d 211 (N.J. Ch. Div. 1985); contra, *King v. City of Bainbridge*, 577 S.E.2d 772 (Ga. 2003), overruling *Cannon v. Coweta County*, 389 S.E.2d 329 (Ga. 1990).

However, *Barre Mobile Home Park v. Town of Petersham*, 592 F. Supp. 633 (D. Mass. 1984), upheld an ordinance prohibiting a mobile home park anywhere in the community. This court said:

> The evidence justifies Petersham's prohibition of mobile home parks. It has a right to assure the orderly development of the entire community and avoid concentrations of populations such as mobile home parks unquestionably bring. The town could reasonably foresee a demand for additional municipal services which it is not prepared

> to provide. Its experience with its existing sewage and waste disposal systems alerted the town to the need to avoid concentrations of dwellings. Finally, no matter how improved mobile homes have become, they are out of character for the large, well-maintained colonial homes typical of Petersham. [*Id.* at 636.]

Go to a mobile home sales lot and try to decide which court is right.

Residential district exclusion. Sometimes zoning ordinances do not require mobile homes to be located in mobile home parks but exclude them from any of the traditional residential districts. This exclusion has generally been sustained. See, e.g., *Jensen's Inc. v. Town of Plainville*, 150 A.2d 297 (Conn. 1959); *McCollum v. City of Berea*, 53 S.W.3d 106 (Ky. 2001); *Morgan v. Town of West. Bloomfield*, 744 N.Y.S.2d 274 (App. Div. 2002) (upholding ordinance limiting percentage of units that can be located in parks); *Landon Holdings, Inc. v. Grattan Township*, 667 N.W.2d 93 (Mich. App. 2003). The exclusion of mobile homes from industrial and commercial districts and from rural and agricultural areas has also been sustained. See, e.g., *Camboni's, Inc. v. County of Du Page*, 187 N.E.2d 212 (Ill. 1962) (industrial zone). See also 42 A.L.R.3d 598 (1972). By state statute, Connecticut now requires double-wide mobile homes be treated the same as stick-built houses. Conn Gen Stat. § 8-2: "Such regulations shall not impose conditions and requirements on manufactured homes having as their narrowest dimension twenty-two feet or more and built in accordance with federal manufactured home construction and safety standards or on lots containing such manufactured homes which are substantially different from conditions and requirements imposed on single-family dwellings and lots containing single-family dwellings. Such regulations shall not impose conditions and requirements on developments to be occupied by manufactured homes having as their narrowest dimension twenty-two feet or more and built in accordance with federal manufactured home construction and safety standards which are substantially different from conditions and requirements imposed on multifamily dwellings, lots containing multifamily dwellings, cluster developments or planned unit developments."

What about an ordinance that permitted modular factory-built homes in residential districts that are assembled on-site, but prohibited mobile homes transported to sites on their own wheels? *Bourgeois v. Parish of St. Tammany*, 628 F. Supp. 159 (E.D. La. 1986), held such an ordinance violated equal protection because it had no aesthetic justification. Is this result compelled by *Cleburne*? (*Bourgeois* does not cite *Cleburne*.) The parish admitted the ordinance would permit a tar paper shack in a residential district if it was site-built.

Conditional uses. Another common way of regulating the location of mobile homes is to treat them as special exceptions or conditional uses that must be approved by the zoning board of adjustment (or appeals). Special exceptions or conditional uses in a zoning ordinance may, of course, be administered in such a way as to effect a practically complete exclusion of mobile homes from the community. For cases striking down vaguely drafted special exception or conditional use provisions such as those requiring proof of "necessity," see *Pioneer Trust & Sav. Bank v. County of McHenry*, 241 N.E.2d 454 (Ill. 1968) (necessity requirement invalid); *Lakewood Estates, Inc. v. Deerfield Twp. Zoning Bd. of Appeals*, 194 N.W.2d 511 (Mich. App. 1971) (vague standards invalid); *Walworth Leasing Corp. v. Sterni*, 316 N.Y.S.2d 851 (Sup. Ct. 1970). But see *Jensen's, Inc. v. City of Dover*, 547 A.2d 277 (N.H. 1988), where the court held that increased density justified a conditional use classification for mobile homes; the mobile home density would have been three times the density allowed by the "as of right" zoning classification. In *His Light Investments, Ltd v. County of San Bernardino*, 2010 Cal. App. Unpub. LEXIS 2716 (4th App. Dist., 2nd Div. 2010), the court upheld the trial court's rejection of an appeal by a mobile home park developer who was denied a conditional use permit because the "high-density" development would not be compatible with its "rural" surroundings.

Courts can, of course, reverse a denial of a conditional use if they believe it was improper. *Clark v. City of Asheboro*, 524 S.E.2d 46 (N.C. App. 1999).

Appearance codes. Another form of zoning that affects mobile homes is the appearance code. This type of code attempts to make mobile homes conform to conventional housing in appearance and size. For example, a Nebraska statute provides:

> (i) The home shall have no less than nine hundred square feet of floor area; (ii) The home shall have no less than an eighteen-foot exterior width; (iii) The roof shall be pitched with a minimum vertical rise of two and one-half inches for each twelve inches of horizontal run; (iv) The exterior material shall be of a color, material, and scale comparable with those existing in residential site-built, single-family construction; (v) The home shall have a nonreflective roof material which is or simulates asphalt or wood shingles, tile, or rock; and (vi) The home shall have wheels, axles, transporting lights, and removable towing apparatus removed. [Neb. Rev. Stat. § 14-402(2)(a).]

One of the purposes of a statute like this is to prevent the use of metal roofs and sides, which are not used on conventionally built housing. The roof pitch requirement is intended to prevent flat roofs, but once had the effect of precluding shipment of the mobile home if the roof pitch was so high that the mobile home truck could not get under bridges. This problem has apparently been solved by the manufacturers. Local ordinances may have similar requirements.

The courts have upheld these requirements, noting that "the County could have been pursuing the goal of 'aesthetic compatibility,' seeking to reduce friction between the appearance of site-built homes and manufactured homes by requiring manufactured homes to conform with standard characteristics of site-built homes, such as roof pitch and foundation. The goal of aesthetic compatibility is a legitimate government purpose." *Georgia Manufactured Hous. v. Spalding County*, 148 F.3d 1304 (11th Cir. 1998). Accord *CMH Mfg. v. Catawba County*, 994 F. Supp. 697 (W.D.N.C. 1998). What about the impact of these requirements on the cost of the mobile home? Aesthetic zoning is considered in Chapter 9. "Aesthetic compatibility" became the key to a mediated dispute over a subdivision with mobile homes in *James v. City of Russellville*, 2010 Ala. Civ. App. LEXIS 6 (Ala. Ct. Civ. App. 2010).

State legislation. There are many state statutes authorizing the licensing of mobile homes. The courts have generally not held that these statutes preempt local zoning control over mobile homes. E.g., *Adams v. Cowart*, 160 S.E.2d 805 (Ga. 1968). Some states have enacted statutes providing for state certification of mobile homes that meet state construction standards. These statutes preempt local regulation of local homes under building codes and, in some cases, under zoning ordinances. E.g., *Warren v. Municipal Officers*, 431 A.2d 624 (Me. 1981).

States have enacted statutes that prohibit discriminatory treatment of mobile homes in zoning ordinances. Some of this legislation deals with the mobile home exclusion problem by prohibiting exclusion "except upon the same terms and conditions as conventional housing is excluded." Vt. Stat. Ann. tit.24, § 4412(1)(B). See also Ark. Code Ann. §§ 14-54-1604, -1605 (regulating placement of manufactured housing); Idaho Code § 67-6509B. *In re Lunde*, 688 A.2d 1312 (Vt. 1997), held that the statute invalidated an ordinance that restricted mobile homes to mobile home parks. Accord *Bahl v. City of Asbury*, 656 N.W.2d 336 (Iowa 2002) ("equal treatment" statute). *Five C'S, Inc. v. County of Pasquotank*, 672 S.E.2d 737 (N.C. App.

2009), invalidated an ordinance requiring manufactured homes to be no more than 10 years old as contrary to state law. See Bredin, *Manufactured Housing Statutes*, Zoning News, June, 2000.

Federal legislation. Federal legislation requires mobile home manufacturers to comply with federal construction and safety standards. 43 U.S.C. § 5415. *City of Brookside Village v. Comeau*, 633 S.W.2d 790 (Tex. 1982), held that the federal legislation did not preempt local zoning. The *Nederland* case, *supra*, held it did not preempt a zoning ordinance limiting mobile homes to mobile home parks. But in *Scurlock v. City of Lynn Haven*, 858 F.2d 1521 (11th Cir. 1988), the court invalidated an ordinance provision that allowed mobile homes certified under federal law in residential districts only if they met additional safety requirements, because (1) the federal legislation preempted state law on this point and (2) the provision was also invalid under state law. Some states have enacted legislation that prohibits municipalities from adopting restrictive zoning applicable to manufactured housing certified under the federal legislation. E.g., Iowa Code Ann. § 414.28. The APA Model Act, § 8-201(4)(c)(1) recommends this approach. The *Spaulding* and *Catawba* cases, *supra*, held the federal statute did not preempt appearance codes. In *Lauderbaugh v. Hopewell Twp.*, 319 F.3d 568 (3d Cir. 2003), the court remanded for a determination whether ambiguous language in an ordinance restricting the location of manufactured homes was directed towards appearance or safety.

Sources. See W. Sanders, *Manufactured Housing: Regulation, Design Innovations, with Development Options*, American Planning Association, Planning Advisory Serv. Rep. No. 478 (1998); Jaffe, *Mobile Homes in Single-Family Neighborhoods*, Land Use L. & Zoning Dig., Vol. 35, No. 6, at 4 (1983); Kmiec, *Manufactured Home Siting: A Statutory and Judicial Overview*, 6 Zoning & Plan. L. Rep. 105, 113 (1983); Note, *Rescuing Manufactured Housing From the Perils of Municipal Zoning Laws*, 37 Wash. U. J. Urb. & Contemp. L. 189 (1990); C. Dawkins & C. Koebel, *Overcoming Barriers to Placing Manufactured Housing in Metropolitan Communities*, Journal of the American Planning Association (2009).

PROBLEM

You are the attorney for a suburban municipality on the edge of a metropolitan area of one million people. The municipality is about 15 miles square, is largely residential, and has a substantial amount of undeveloped land on its edges. Some of this consists of farms that are threatened by urban growth, and their owners have been talking to developers about selling their land for mobile home park subdivisions. All the homes in the parks would be double-wides situated on paved residential streets, and the subdivisions would meet all county requirements. Several owners of individual lots in these areas are considering the placement of mobile homes on their properties.

There presently are no regulations for mobile homes and mobile home parks in the zoning ordinance. There is no state statute, except the usual statute prohibiting the exclusion of a mobile home that meets federal standards. In light of these materials, what kind of an ordinance would you propose for mobile home development?

A NOTE ON ZONING AND THE ELDERLY

The over-65 age group is growing rapidly as a proportion of the total population. In 1900, only five percent of the population was over 65, but by 2050 it is estimated that 20 percent will be over 65. Edmonds & Merriam, *Zoning and the Elderly: Issues for the 21st Century*, Land

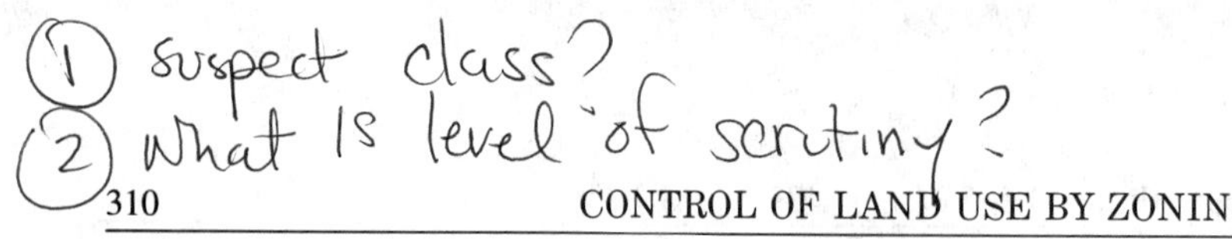

Use L. & Zoning Dig., Vol. 47, No. 3, at 3 (1995). That is 86.7 million people over 65 in 2050. http://usgovinfo.about.com/od/censusandstatistics/a/olderstats.htm. A number of zoning measures can provide for elderly housing needs, such as zoning ordinances that allow accessory apartments and shared housing. See the Note on the Future of Single-Family Residential Zoning, *supra.*

Shifting demographics and changing economic circumstances are making Elder Cottage Housing Opportunities (ECHO) an attractive housing option for seniors. ECHO housing units are small, temporary, manufactured homes that can be added to the property of single family homes usually owned by relatives. It is a cost effective way for seniors to live near family and maintain independence. For examples of ordinances allowing for ECHO housing, see Hamburg, Mich., Zoning Ordinance § 15.1 (2009); Lompoc, Cal., Municipal Code § 17.088.190 (2009).

Age-restrictive zoning. Age-restrictive zoning is another option. This type of zoning is intended to encourage the establishment of retirement communities designed especially for the elderly that can contain a variety of building types, living arrangements and supporting facilities. The legal question is whether a zoning ordinance may classify the elderly for special treatment by adopting an exclusive age-restricted zone.

One of the leading cases sustaining age-restrictive zoning is *Taxpayers Ass'n v. Weymouth Twp.*, 364 A.2d 1016 (N.J. 1976). On the issue of authority to adopt age-restrictive zoning regulations, the New Jersey court held that "the concept of the 'general welfare' in land use regulation is quite expansive, and encompasses the provision of housing for *all categories of people*, including the elderly"; and that age-restrictive zoning may advance the general welfare by "bringing about 'the greatest good of the greatest number.' " Moreover, the court concluded, "ordinances which regulate use by regulating identified users are not inherently objectionable" so long as they bear "a real and substantial relationship to the regulation of land within the community."

The court then continued with the most elaborate equal protection analysis in any zoning case dealing with age-restrictive regulations. Noting that housing has not been deemed a fundamental right under the Fourteenth Amendment — see *Lindsey v. Normet*, 405 U.S. 56 (1972) — the court moved on to the question whether the Weymouth zoning ordinance involved a suspect classification that would require strict scrutiny. The court concluded that age is not a suspect classification. The court then applied the traditional rational relationship test and held that the plaintiffs had failed to carry the burden of proving that the age-restrictive zoning regulations lacked a rational relationship to a legitimate state objective. Although it recognized that the choice of fifty-two as the minimum age for residency in the age-restrictive mobile park district might be debatable, the court characterized the choice of a minimum age as a legislative question "which ought not to be disturbed by the judiciary unless it exceeds the bounds of reasonable choice." Finally, the court analyzed the age-restrictive regulations under the New Jersey equal protection principle said to be embodied in the state constitution and concluded that these regulations would survive even close scrutiny because the legislative classification was "based upon real factual distinctions, and also [bore] a real and substantial relationship to the ends which the municipality [sought] to accomplish by that classification." Accord *Weymouth, Shepard v. Woodland Twp. Comm. & Planning Bd.*, 364 A.2d 1005 (N.J. 1976); *Maldini v. Ambro*, 330 N.E.2d 403 (N.Y. 1975). Is the New Jersey court's analysis sufficiently persuasive to withstand a challenge under *Cleburne*? Age-restrictive zoning may be challenged as having exclusionary effects. *Fair Housing in*

Huntington Committee v. Town of Huntington, 2010 U.S. Dist. LEXIS 68233 (E.D.N.Y. 2010).

Federal Fair Housing Act. In 1988, Congress added discrimination against "familial status" as another type of discrimination covered by the Fair Housing Act. 42 U.S.C. § 3602(k). Congress adopted this amendment to prohibit discrimination against families with children in the sale and rental of housing, but after intensive lobbying by developers and senior citizens' groups, Congress added an exemption for "housing for older persons," which includes housing projects specially designated by the Department of Housing and Urban Development for the elderly, and housing primarily occupied by persons over designated age limits or providing specific services for the elderly. 42 U.S.C. § 3607(b)(2). Do you see why, in the absence of this amendment, zoning such as that approved in *Weymouth* might violate the 1988 amendments? Although the exemption was intended to apply to private owners of elderly housing, not age-restricted zoning, it presumably preempts zoning that establishes a younger age cut-off than does the federal law. For additional discussion of the 1988 amendments, see Chapter 4, *infra*. See generally Weinstein, *The Challenge of Providing Adequate Housing for the Elderly . . . Along With Everyone Else*, 11 J.L. & Health 133 (1996-97).

PROBLEM

Your city council is concerned about recent case law on allowable uses in single-family districts and has asked you as city attorney for an opinion on the following proposed single-family zoning district ordinance: The ordinance defines a "single-family dwelling" as a "housekeeping unit" in which individuals share common living quarters, cooking and other facilities. The council also is considering a requirement that no more than four unrelated persons be allowed to live together, but is unsure about its constitutionality.

There is a separate provision for group homes. How would you draft the group home definition? Group homes with no more than six unrelated persons living together are allowed in single-family districts. Group homes with seven or more persons living together or that provide on-site medical treatment facilities are allowed in single-family districts only as conditional uses. Reconsider this problem when you study the group home provisions of the federal Fair Housing Act in Chapter 5.

A NOTE ON HOME OCCUPATIONS

Inherent in the modern classification of land uses into "residential" and "business" zones is the principle that what is permitted in one zone is prohibited in the other, and vice versa, *inclusio unius est exclusio alterius*. By sitting at the boundary line between regulation of residential uses, considered *supra*, and regulation of business and commercial uses, to which we turn in the section below, "home occupations" — living and working in the same structure — blur the traditional Euclidean framework.

Working at home (either full time or part time) has become increasingly common, but it often violates zoning ordinances written decades ago for the conventions of a different era. What explains this trend, which one commentator has described as "an explosion"? See Hansen, *Special Report: Homebased Zoning*, quoted in Salkin, *Zoning for Home Occupations: Modernizing Zoning Codes to Accommodate Growth in Home-Based Businesses*, 35 Real Estate L.J. 181 (2006). Globalization and attendant economic pressures have encouraged businesses to decentralize and outsource work that previously would have been done at a central office; computerization and other technological changes have made it possible to communicate from anywhere and to produce work product on a desktop that previously would have required back office support. Salkin, *supra*, at 182–83. Working from home also accommodates changing lifestyles, including the preference of many parents to combine careers and childcare. There are also traditional home occupations that have long existed, ranging from dentists in their offices to artists in their garrets to cookbook authors in their kitchens. Commentators increasingly point out that the traditional grudging attitude of zoning authorities toward home occupations (reflecting the place of single-family residences at the pinnacle of preferred land uses) is short-sighted: by eliminating long commutes to a central office, for instance, traffic congestion and air pollution are reduced, qualifying home occupations as a component of a modern "smart growth" strategy. See Meck, *Bringing Smart Growth to Your Community*, The Commissioner (American Planning Association, Summer 2000). Professor Garnett argues that overly-strict regulation of home occupations has particularly "counterproductive" consequences in the inner-city, where encouraging "grass roots" economic activity is often a more viable strategy than grandiose redevelopment schemes. Garnett, *Ordering (and Order in) the City*, 57 Stan. L. Rev. 1, 56–58 (2004) (describing Chicago's Englewood neighborhood).

Regulation of home occupations is almost always addressed in local zoning ordinances rather than in the state enabling act, derived from the broad delegation of power to classify land uses. Because of this, approaches to regulation vary widely and modernization of codes requires advocacy on a town-by-town basis. In her article on home occupations, *supra*, Professor Salkin reproduces a model law that could be adapted either for incorporation into a state enabling act, requiring municipalities to permit home occupations, or as a model ordinance to be adopted by individual municipalities. *Id.* at 198–200. The premise of the proposal is that home occupations should be recognized as an accessory use in any residential zone, without the need to obtain a use variance or other special land use approval, provided that the activity meets various performance criteria stated in the law. These could include, for instance, regulating the size (floor area) that can be devoted to the home occupation, the number of resident or non-resident employees, parking, traffic generation, signage, and the physical appearance of any structural modifications made to accommodate the home occupation. *Id.* at 189–194. Care should be taken to recognize the differences between home occupation, accessory use, and principal use. *Flava Works, Inc. v. City Of Miami*, 609 F. 3d 1233 (11th Cir. 2010).

[3.] Commercial and Industrial Uses

The conceptual basis for regulation of non-residential uses is the same as for residential zoning, but the different factual and policy settings create a distinct set of legal rules that have specific application to commercial and industrial sites. The first section below discusses some of the common zoning problems raised by industrial and commercial uses. The sections that follow discuss zoning problems raised by the use of zoning to control competition in land use and by application of the federal antitrust laws to anticompetitive zoning.

[a.] In the Zoning Ordinance

BP AMERICA, INC. v. COUNCIL OF THE CITY OF AVON
753 N.E.2d 947 (Ohio App. 2001)

CARR, JUDGE.

Appellant BP America, Inc. ("BP") has appealed a judgment of the Lorain County Court of Common Pleas that upheld the denial of BP's rezoning petition. This Court affirms.

I.

In 1992, the city of Avon adopted a Master Plan that set forth the city's official policy regarding its future growth and development, including land use. The city also established a zoning code, identifying land uses for commercial, industrial, and residential development.

Realizing dramatic growth in the city's population, in 1993, an ordinance was passed to preserve the city's central district, limiting development to residential and small retail and business establishments. This central district was designated as the French Creek District.

Section 1287.04 of the Codified Ordinances for the French Creek District prohibits any and all uses within the French Creek District that are prohibited within the zoned use in the District. The zoned use within the French Creek District consists solely of residential and general business development. Residential zoned parcels are categorized as R-1, R-2, and R-3, and general business districts are identified as C-2. Neither residential nor general business districts permit gasoline service stations. In fact, general business districts, C-2 districts, expressly prohibit such construction.

BP entered into a right to purchase three parcels of land located in the French Creek District, subject to the city's rezoning of the parcels. Two of the parcels are zoned as C-2 districts, and the other is zoned as an R-2 district. In 1998, BP filed an application to rezone each of the three parcels as C-4 "Motorists Service Districts," in connection with BP's plan to construct a gas station that would contain a car wash and an express convenience store, in addition to gasoline pumps and a canopy.

The city of Avon's Planning Commission reviewed BP's proposal, and by a majority vote, recommended that BP's rezoning request be granted. After both a public hearing and an open meeting on the matter, Avon City Council unanimously decided to deny BP's petition to rezone the parcels.

BP filed an administrative appeal pursuant to R.C. 2506, and a declaratory judgment action requesting a declaration that the current zoning ordinance as applied to BP's proposed use of the parcels is arbitrary, capricious, unreasonable, and unrelated to the public health, safety, welfare, and morals. The trial court consolidated the actions and held an evidentiary hearing, and heard oral arguments. The trial court declared that the ordinance was not unconstitutional as applied, and concluded that Avon's current zoning regulation is reasonable and bears a substantial relationship to the public health, safety, and general welfare. The court also determined that city council's decision to deny the rezoning was supported by a preponderance of substantial, reliable, and probative evidence.

BP has timely appealed and has asserted one assignment of error.

II.

THE LOWER COURT ERRED IN HOLDING THAT THE DECISION OF THE COUNCIL OF THE CITY OF AVON WAS NOT ARBITRARY, CAPRICIOUS, DISCRIMINATORY, UNCONSTITUTIONAL, UNREASONABLE OR ILLEGAL.

In its sole assignment of error, BP asserts that the common pleas court erred in finding the city's current zoning regulations constitutional and in upholding council's decision to deny BP's rezoning request. This Court disagrees. . . .

The decision of the Council of the City of Avon denying BP America Inc.'s rezoning plan is reasonable and bears a substantial relationship to the public health, safety and general welfare. The current zoning regulation is presumed constitutional and this court finds that it is constitutionally valid. Further, council's decision is supported by substantial, reliable and probative evidence. Therefore, the decision to deny Appellant's rezoning plan is affirmed. . . .

[The court held that it would address only the declaratory judgment action.]

In considering the evidence with respect to the declaratory judgment, this Court begins with the premise that all zoning ordinances are presumed constitutional. *Central Motors Corp. v. Pepper Pike*, 653 N.E.2d 639 (Ohio 1995). However, a zoning ordinance will be struck down if a party challenging the ordinance proves, beyond fair debate, that the ordinance is "arbitrary and unreasonable and without substantial relation to the public health, safety, morals, or general welfare of the community." *Goldberg Cos., Inc. v. Richmond Hts. City Council*, 690 N.E.2d 510 (Ohio 1998).

BP avers that the ordinances are unconstitutional because they fail to substantially advance a legitimate governmental interest. BP argues "that the overall constitutionality of the city's zoning ordinances as applied to BP's parcels constitutes an invalid prohibition of BP's specified uses." In support, BP asserts that the parcels, taken together, are perfectly suited for a C-4 district "simply by virtue of their location in the immediate vicinity of Interstate 90 and Highway 83." Because C-4 districts were established "to 'provide districts on major roads in the immediate vicinity of freeway interchanges to serve the needs of the motoring public[,]' " BP believes it should be permitted to construct its gasoline service station. BP further asserts that "unless the R-2 parcel is assembled with the two C-2 parcels, development of all the parcels is unlikely for any economic return."

The city argues that the zoning ordinances advance the legitimate governmental health, safety, and welfare concerns by, inter alia, maintaining the appearance and character of the French Creek District, and by minimizing traffic congestion. The city presented evidence which showed that the French Creek District was established to preserve the city's central district as a blend of residential and small retail and business establishments, because the area's historically rural atmosphere was quickly vanishing. Section 1287.01 of the French Creek District Codified Ordinances states that the purposes of the French Creek District are to:

> Maintain and enhance the distinctive character of a designated District to safeguard the heritage of the City; to stabilize and improve property values; to make the City more attractive to prospective residents and visitors and to secure the same as a support and stimulus to business and to industry in the community; and to strengthen the economy of the City.

Maintain and further enhance the FCD identity through architectural unity, streetscape and citizen review of any improvements in the District.

Provide for relief from certain zoning regulations as necessary to achieve the aforementioned goals. (Ord. 112-93. Passed 12-27-93.)

BP has failed to prove beyond fair debate that the zoning regulations are clearly arbitrary and unreasonable and without substantial relation to the public health, safety, morals, or general welfare of the community, or that there is no rational relationship between the regulations and their purpose. *See Desenco, Inc. v. Akron*, 706 N.E.2d 323 (Ohio 1999) (explaining the state and federal due process standards upon which an enactment may be challenged). The Supreme Court of Ohio has held that "there is a legitimate governmental interest in maintaining the aesthetics of the community and, as such, aesthetic considerations may be taken into account by the legislative body in enacting zoning legislation." (Citation omitted.) *Franchise Developers, Inc. v. Cincinnati*, 505 N.E.2d 966 (Ohio 1987), paragraph two of the syllabus. Accordingly, this Court finds that the trial court did not err in finding the provisions constitutional.

BP's sole assignment of error is overruled.

Judgment affirmed.

NOTES AND QUESTIONS

1. *Zoning and planning.* Up to this point in Chapter 3, the cases have demonstrated zoning primarily as a nuisance mediator — as a method to keep incompatible uses apart or to regulate density. Zoning thus employed becomes a way for the municipality to mediate marginal transitions in use and density. The *Avon* case shows that zoning can be used in a more imaginative way to create a development framework for an entire downtown. Under the usual "as-applied" rules explored earlier in this chapter, the landowner might very well have won. Do you see why? Was the thoroughness and coherence of the city's plan essential to persuading the court in its favor? The use of zoning ordinances to implement a long-range development plan is not limited to small municipalities such as Avon. For a description of careful development-based zoning changes in a New York City neighborhood, see Osner, *Rezoning, and Redefining, Park Slope*, N.Y. Times, sec. 11 (Real Estate), p.1 (Sunday, Dec. 28, 2003).

2. *Zoning and aesthetics.* The city's defense of its rezoning rests explicitly on preserving the "appearance" of the French Creek district. For further discussion of the aesthetics issues presented by zoning ordinances, see Chapter 9, *infra*.

The case that follows provides a sharp contrast with *Avon* on how to handle the use issue in commercial districts and deals with the problem of big box retail:

LORETO DEVELOPMENT CO., INC. v. VILLAGE OF CHARDON

695 N.E.2d 1151 (Ohio App. 1996)

MAHONEY, J., (EDWARD)

This is an appeal from an order of the Geauga County Court of Common Pleas that (1) reversed the decision of the Chardon Board of Zoning Appeals ("board") that denied appellee's application for a conditional use permit to construct a Wal-Mart store and (2) entered a declaratory judgment that the applicable zoning restriction was unconstitutional. We reverse.

On April 14, 1994, appellee, Loreto Development Co., Inc., filed an appeal, pursuant to R.C. Chapter 2506, in the Geauga County Court of Common Pleas from the denial of its application for a conditional use permit for a Wal-Mart store in the village of Chardon ("appellant"). Appellee owns an eighty-five acre parcel of land in the village of Chardon, of which twenty-three acres were zoned "C-1," and the balance was zoned "R-2" (residential). It is the "C-1" zoning that is the primary focus of this dispute. A C-1 district allows "local retail business" as a conditional use, requiring the approval of the board. The zoning code defines "local retail business" to include retail and service establishments that normally employ less than ten people, such as drugstores, beauty salons, barber shops, carry-outs, dry cleaners, and grocery stores "if less than 10,000 square feet of floor area." It was the position of Loreto that this square footage restriction and the restriction on the number of employees was unconstitutional.

On May 6, 1994, appellee filed a separate declaratory judgment action in the Geauga County Court of Common Pleas. The complaint requested that the court construe the zoning ordinances of the village of Chardon with respect to the denial of the proposed Wal-Mart store. The trial court consolidated the declaratory judgment action with the R.C. 2506 appeal.

After a trial on the issue, the common pleas court determined that restricting businesses to less than ten employees and less than ten thousand square feet of floor area bore no rational relationship to the public health, safety, or general welfare, and deprived appellee of the economically feasible use of its land. Therefore, the trial court concluded that the zoning ordinance was unconstitutional, and ordered appellant to grant appellee a conditional use permit to build the proposed Wal-Mart store.

Appellant timely appealed, asserting the following as error: . . .

[The first two assignments of error, and the court's discussion of them, are omitted. — Eds.]

> "3. The trial court erred in finding the existing zoning code on the subject property unconstitutional.
>
> "4. To the extent the trial court's judgment constituted a rezoning of the subject property, the trial court erred in not returning the matter to the village for an opportunity to rezone the property."

. . . .

In its third assignment of error, appellant argues that the trial court erred in holding that the less than ten thousand square feet or ten employees limitation of the existing zoning ordinance is unconstitutional. It is well settled in Ohio, that a party challenging the constitutionality of a zoning ordinance "must prove, beyond fair debate, both that the enactment deprives him or her of an economically viable use and that it fails to advance a legitimate governmental interest." *Gerijo, Inc. v. Fairfield*, 638 N.E.2d 533 (Ohio 1994). We apply this test bearing in mind that there is a strong presumption that a zoning ordinance is valid as enacted. *Id.* at 226. "The party challenging an ordinance bears, at all stages of the proceedings, the burden of demonstrating that the provision is unconstitutional." *Id.*

The trial court held that these zoning restrictions deprived appellee of an economically viable use of its property and that they failed to advance a legitimate governmental interest.

As to the economic viability of the property as currently zoned, appellee presented evidence that the zoning code's concept of local retail business is outdated. The modern trend in retail, according to appellee's experts, is to have a large anchor store surrounded by smaller stores. The fact that the existing zoning is not in tune with the modern trend or that it is does not allow the most profitable retail development, however, will not invalidate the existing zoning. *See Gerijo, supra*, at 228. A zoning ordinance is considered to be impermissibly restrictive only when it denies an owner all uses of the property except those which are highly unlikely or practically impossible under the circumstances. *Central Motors Corp. v. Pepper Pike*, 653 N.E.2d 639 (Ohio 1995).

Appellee failed to establish, beyond fair debate, that the zoning restrictions deprived it of the use of its property. In fact, there was evidence that appellee could profitably develop the property as it is currently zoned. Appellee had also received an offer to purchase the residential section of the property for $300,000 more than it paid for the entire parcel. Therefore, appellee failed to establish, and the trial court erred in concluding, that the zoning restrictions deprived appellee of an economically viable use of the property.

The second prong to test the constitutionality of the zoning ordinance is whether it advances a legitimate governmental interest. The appellant's determination that its zoning action would serve certain governmental interests must be given great deference. Recognizing that "the legislative, not the judicial, authority is charged with the duty of determining the wisdom of zoning regulations, . . . the judicial judgment is not to be substituted for the legislative judgment in any case in which the issue or matter is fairly debatable." *Ketchel v. Bainbridge Twp.*, 557 N.E.2d 779 (Ohio 1990).

According to the explicit terms of the zoning code, the local retail business restrictions are intended to prevent traffic congestion, excessive noise, and "other objectionable influences." There was also evidence that the large retail businesses were permitted elsewhere in Chardon, but that the appellant had attempted to preserve the residential, small town character of this part of town. This was clearly a legitimate interest to be advanced by this zoning. "[A] municipality may properly exercise its zoning authority to preserve the character of designated areas in order to promote the overall quality of life within the city's boundaries." *Central Motors, supra.*

Appellant had no burden to prove that these interests would, in fact, be advanced by the zoning ordinance. It was the burden of appellee to prove that none of the purported interests nor any other legitimate governmental interests would be advanced by the appellant's zoning ordinance. *See Central Motors, supra.*

Appellant conceded that the restrictions on the number of employees in a local retail business establishment does not, in and of itself, advance a legitimate governmental interest. Therefore, this restriction fails the second prong of the test.

The floor size restriction, according to appellee, likewise fails to advance the purported interests. Appellee has contended all along that, because the total area of retail space is the same whether there are nine small stores or one large store, there is no difference in the noise and traffic generated by the larger store. Our review of the evidence in the record, however, supports a contrary conclusion.

Appellee had presented a booklet of "community comments," in an apparent attempt to convince the village that a Wal-Mart store would have a positive impact on the community and bolster the local economy. The booklet, entitled "Working Together in our Hometown," included over one hundred letters from various chambers of commerce around the country, many of which praised Wal-Mart for its ability to draw business from surrounding communities, in effect creating a new economic hub in the area. This evidence only supported appellant's concern that such a large store would cause noise and traffic congestion and would destroy the existing character of the area.

Even though no legitimate governmental interest is advanced by the zoning restriction on the number of employees in a local retail business, the restriction did not fail both prongs of the *Genjo* test. Because appellee failed to present competent, credible evidence that the local retail business restrictions both deprived it of any economically viable use of its property and failed to advance a legitimate governmental interest, the trial court erred in finding these zoning restrictions unconstitutional. The third assignment of error is well taken.

In appellant's fourth assignment of error, it is argued that the trial court erred in failing to allow appellant the opportunity to rezone the property. In light of our disposition of the third assignment of error, this argument has been rendered moot and need not be addressed. *See* App. R. 12(A)(1)(c).

The judgment of the trial court is reversed, and this cause is remanded to the trial court to enter judgment in favor of the appellant.

NOTES AND QUESTIONS

1. *Districting problems.* Zoning districts for commercial and industrial uses present classification problems, just as do zoning districts that separate single-family and multi-family residential uses. In the principal case, as well as in *Avon, supra,* the courts adopted a deferential stance towards the township's decision to exclude the unwanted type of business. Courts generally uphold commercial and industrial districts if they find the distinctions between uses excluded and included defensible. *Tidewater Oil Co. v. Mayor & Council,* 209 A.2d 105 (N.J. 1965) (industrial zoning); *State ex rel. American Oil Co. v. Bessent,* 135 N.W.2d 317 (Wis. 1966) (filling stations excluded from retail commercial district). Do you see differences between the two cases? Should it matter, for instance, that the Village of Chardon utilized a conditional use procedure that gave it individualized review of each development proposed in the village business district, or that the application it was considering was for a particularly large store, a "big box" Wal-Mart? Might it have approved the gasoline station proposed for the city of Avon? (Issues involving "big box" retail are considered in Note on "Big Box" Retail Zoning, *infra*; conditional uses are explored further in Chapter 6.)

2. *Arbitrariness.* What if a zoning ordinance prohibits a convenience store from including liquor in the goods it sells for off-site use, but permits separate liquor stores and sale of liquor by restaurants for on-site consumption? The court thought this restriction had no reasonable relationship to zoning purposes in *Gas 'N Shop, Inc. v. City of Kearney,* 539 N.W.2d 423 (Neb. 1995). On this question, compare the *Baker* case, reproduced *supra,* which invalidated a restriction on the number of unrelated people who could live together and suggested other means of dealing with the problem they might present. Are there other ways to deal with the liquor problem? With the big box problem considered in *Manalapan* (see the Note on "Big Box," *infra*)? (The concurring justice in *Manalapan* cites *Baker.*)

Strip development is a nagging commercial use problem. One commercial use on a busy thoroughfare usually leads to others and a commercial strip is the result. What if a municipality attempts to stop strip development by limiting commercial uses on thoroughfares to intersections? See *City of Phoenix v. Fehlner*, 363 P.2d 607 (Ariz. 1961) (held constitutional under "fairly debatable" rule); *Jarvis Associates, LLC v. Charter Township of Ypsilanti*, 2008 Mich. App. LEXIS 2362 (Mich. App. 2008) (no substantive due process violation and no taking for denying, to prevent strip commercial development, rezoning from industrial to commercial).

3. *Formula businesses.* "Big box" stores are only one part of the problem. Many national merchandise chains, as well as restaurants, hotels and service businesses, have standardized products for sale with impersonal service, standardized buildings and signs, and (in the view of critics) a mind-numbing sameness that deprives shopping districts of their vitality. A growing number of communities restrict these so-called "formula businesses." To protect its tourist-oriented commercial district, for instance, Carmel, California totally prohibits "formula food establishments" in a prime location, Ocean Avenue. City of Carmel-by-the-Sea Mun. Code § 17.56.020. It defines "formula food establishment" as "A business that (1) is required by contractual or other arrangements to offer standardized menus, ingredients, food preparation, employee uniforms, interior decor, signage or exterior design; or (2) adopts a name, appearance or food presentation format that causes it to be substantially identical to another restaurant regardless of ownership or location." *Id.* § 17.70.010. Other definitions are broader, such as that of another California municipality: "'Formula business' means an eating and drinking establishment that maintains any of the following features in common with more than four other establishments in the nine Bay Area counties: standardized array of services and/or merchandise, trademark, logo, service mark, symbol, sign, decor, uniform, menu, or other similar standardized feature." City of Benicia Mun. Code § 17.12.030 http://www.codepublishing.com/ca/benicia.

How does one make the case for the legality of these restrictions? More generally, is there a problem with local ordinances that target national chains, thereby arguably burdening interstate commerce in violation of the Dormant Commerce Clause implications of U.S. Const. Art. I, § 8? See *Island Silver & Spice, Inc. v. Islamorada*, 542 F.3d 844 (11th Cir. 2008) (finding Commerce Clause violation); *City of New Rochelle v. Town of Mamaroneck*, 111 F. Supp. 2d 353 (S.D.N.Y. 2000) (denying motion to dismiss Commerce Clause claim); Shoemaker, *The Smalling of America?: Growth Management Statutes and the Dormant Commerce Clause*, 48 Duke L.J. 891 (1999) (discussing susceptibility of state anti-super-store statutes to dormant Commerce Clause challenges).

See generally Salkin, *Municipal Regulation of Formula Businesses: Creating and Protecting Communities*, 58 Case W. Res. L. Rev. 1251 (2008), www.governmentlaw.org/files/MuniRegofFormBus.pdf; Svete, *Combating "Sameness" with a Formula Business Ordinance*, Zoning News, March, 2003. A website, www.newrules.org/retail/rules/formula-business-restrictions, serves as a clearinghouse for information useful to those opposed to the proliferation of formula businesses. See D. Botwinick, J. Effron & J. Huang, *Saving Mom And Pop: Zoning And Legislating For Small And Local Business Retention*, 18 J.L. & Pol'y 607 (2010).

4. *Duplicate buildings.* A variation on the formula business regulation is one such as that contained in the Sarasota County, Florida, zoning regulations, § 7.7.3, which regulates the building rather than the business. A "duplicate building" is defined, in part, as "(1) A building design that is commonly associated with a specific tenant or user; (2) A building design that uses the building or architectural elements as advertising for the specific business located in that building; (3) A building that is stylized in an attempt to use the building or elements of the building as advertising. This may include items of trade dress such as exterior decorations or

colors; (4) A building that is not appropriately designed for the specific site; (5) A building that makes little or no attempt to blend into the existing surrounding architectural context, or makes no significant architectural contribution to the surrounding area." http://library.municode.com/index.aspx?clientId=11511&stateId=9&stateName=Florida or http://tinyurl.com/2vugvu5. Is this approach more or less preferable to the ordinances described in Note 3, *supra*?

5. *Non-cumulative or "exclusive" zoning.* Modern zoning ordinances are almost always non-cumulative, or exclusive. Each district is limited to the uses permitted as-of-right or as a conditional use. An argument can be made that non-cumulative zoning, especially for the more intensive uses such as commercial and industrial uses, is unconstitutional. It does not recognize the hierarchical "compatibility" principle established by the *Euclid* case. This principle would seem to authorize restrictions on land use only to protect the less intensive from the more intensive uses. Do industrial uses need protection from residential uses?

Non-cumulative zoning was held constitutional in a leading case, *People ex rel. Skokie Town House Bldrs., Inc. v. Village of Morton Grove*, 157 N.E.2d 33 (Ill. 1959), where the court held that the exclusion of incompatible uses from all zoning districts would ensure a "better and more economical use of municipal services." The developer wanted to build townhouses in a non-cumulative industrial district. See also *Kozesnik v. Township of Montgomery*, 131 A.2d 1 (N.J. 1957) (upholding industrial district restricted to single use). But see *Katobimar Realty Co. v. Webster*, 118 A.2d 824 (N.J. 1955) (invalidating light industrial district excluding all retail uses because uses held not incompatible). See Note, *Industrial Zoning to Exclude Higher Uses*, 32 N.Y.U. L. Rev. 1261 (1957). It has been argued that the noncumulative, exclusive industrial district is a concept that should be abandoned. R. Hills & D. Schleicher, *The Steep Costs of Using Noncumulative Zoning to Preserve Land for Urban Manufacturing*, George Mason Law & Economics Research Paper No. 10-02, U. Chi. L. Rev., Vol. 77, No. 1 (2010), http://papers.ssrn.com.

Although (or perhaps because) non-cumulative zoning has won the day, "mixed use" developments have attracted attention in recent years as a better planning alternative.

6. *Buffers.* A consequence of non-cumulative zoning is that it creates relatively sharp (and potentially discordant) boundaries between different uses. One way of handling the problem of incompatible uses in close proximity is to provide for a buffer zone. A general residential district in which apartments are permitted is often used as a buffer between single-family districts and commercial districts. See, e.g., *Evanston Best & Co. v. Goodman*, 16 N.E.2d 131, 132 (Ill. 1938) (approving the use of this technique "to prevent an impact between the intensity of the use to which commercial areas are put with the quiet and cleanliness which are essential to property devoted to higher type residential uses."). Accord *Stampfl v. Zoning Board of Appeals*, 599 N.E.2d 646 (Mass. App. 1992) (upholding 75–foot buffer between industrial and residential use); *Carlson v. City of Bellevue*, 435 P.2d 957 (Wash. 1968) (district allowing multi-family housing and non-retail business may be used as buffer between "prime residential" and industrial areas). As the *Krause* case, *supra*, pointed out, however, it makes little sense to place apartments next to noncommercial uses because apartments have a higher density of residential use than single-family dwellings. See also *Seminary Galleria, LLC v. Dulaney Valley Improvement Ass'n, Inc.*, 995 A.2d 1068 (Md. Spec. App. 2008) (higher density residential zone as buffer for commercial uses). Alternative ways of buffering include landscaped strips, see, e.g., *State v. Gallop Bldg.*, 247 A.2d 350 (N.J. App. Div. 1968) (20-foot screen belt of trees required for every business use adjacent to a residential district), and using streets as dividing lines between zoning districts. See *Perron v. Village of New Brighton*, 145 N.W.2d 425 (Minn. 1966).

7. *Total exclusion.* Some courts have invalidated residential exclusionary zoning in suburban municipalities. See Chapter 5. Most courts have not invalidated commercial and industrial exclusions. *Town of Los Altos Hills v. Adobe Creek Properties, Inc.*, 108 Cal. Rptr. 271 (Cal. App. 1973) (commercial); *Town of Beacon Falls v. Posick*, 563 A.2d 285 (Conn. 1989) (exclusion of landfill); *Duffcon Concrete Prods., Inc. v. Borough of Cresskill*, 64 A.2d 347 (N.J. 1949) (upholding industrial exclusion because other industrial sites available in region).

Pennsylvania has long held that a total exclusion of a commercial use shifts the burden to justify the exclusion to the municipality. See *Borough Council v. Pagal, Inc.*, 460 A.2d 1214 (Pa. Commw. 1983). The court held invalid the total exclusion of restaurants from a municipality. It refused to accept arguments in support of the exclusion that the community was historically residential and that surrounding communities had readily accessible restaurants. The Michigan courts also have struck down total exclusions of nonresidential uses. See *Ottawa County Farms, Inc. v. Township of Polkton*, 345 N.W.2d 672 (Mich. App. 1983) (sanitary landfill). Compare *Wrigley Properties, Inc. v. City of Ladue*, 369 S.W.2d 397 (Mo. 1963) (regional shopping needs do not invalidate residential zoning prohibiting commercial use).

8. *As-applied problems.* Commercial developers prohibited from developing their property by residential zoning may make the usual claim that the residential zoning is unconstitutional "as applied." In many of these cases, the residential area already has been invaded by commercial uses. What if the commercial uses already in the residential area were allowed by the municipality? Although most courts do not hold municipalities bound by their prior zoning actions, a court occasionally takes the opposite view. *City of Birmingham v. Morris*, 396 So. 2d 53 (Ala. 1981). Why did the commercial developer lose in the *City of Avon* case, *supra*?

9. *Industrial performance zoning.* This is a zoning technique that became popular in the 1960s. It is intended to provide an alternative or a supplement to traditional zoning for industrial uses. The zoning ordinance adopts performance standards applicable to noise, vibrations, smoke, odors, and air pollutants. The idea has caught on to some extent, although the adoption of strict pollution standards in the national Clean Air Act of 1970 has somewhat undercut industrial zoning performance standards.

In *DeCoals, Inc. v. Board of Zoning Appeals*, 284 S.E.2d 856 (W. Va. 1981), the court upheld an industrial performance zoning ordinance that included an absolute "no dust" prohibition. It cited air pollution cases to hold that the technology-forcing "no dust" standard was valid and that any technical infeasibility or economic hardship in complying with the standard need not be considered. See also *State v. Zack*, 674 P.2d 329 (Ariz. App. 1983) (ordinance prohibiting "offensive vibration" not unconstitutionally vague). Contra *Lithonia Asphalt Co. v. Hall County Planning Comm'n*, 364 S.E.2d 860 (Ga. 1988). For discussion, see J. Schwab, *Industrial Performance Standards for a New Century*, American Planning Association, Planning Advisory Serv. Rep. No. 444 (1993); Duerksen, *Modern Industrial Performance Standards: Key Implementation and Legal Issues*, 18 Zoning & Plan. L. Rep. 33 (1995); Performance Zoning (Minnesota Local Planning Assistance Center, undated) at http://www.lpa.state.mn.us/pdf/infopackets/PerformanceZoning.pdf.

A NOTE ON "BIG BOX" RETAIL ZONING

The *Village of Chardon* case, *supra*, exemplifies the tensions that arise as courts struggle to adapt traditional Euclidean zoning principles to marketplace innovations. One such shift occurred after World War II when downtown retail shopping gave way to larger stores in shopping malls strategically located at interchanges on the new interstate highways. Another such shift has occurred more recently with the evolution of so-called "big box" superstores. They are targeted by all kinds of opponents:

- The National Trust for Historic Preservation, which regards them as a threat to older downtown commercial districts (and ugly to boot), has mounted a vigorous campaign of opposition. See C. Beaumont & L. Tucker, *Big-Box Sprawl (and How to Control It)*, reprinted and widely distributed by the Trust from 43 Municipal Lawyer No. 2, Mar.-Apr. 2002 at 7, at

  www.preservationnation.org/issues/smart-growth/additional-resources/big_box_sprawl.pdf.

- Small "mom and pop" competitors, often anchoring traditional downtown shopping districts, see the big boxes (with good reason) as "category killers," because of the competitive pricing edge that their enormous size (represented in the accompanying drawing) gives them. "Control of competition" issues are raised by the *City of Hanford* case, reproduced and discussed in the next section.

- Unions frequently oppose zoning for big box stores because they tend not to be unionized. See, e.g., Lefcoe, *The Regulation of Superstores: The Legality of Zoning Ordinances Emerging from the Skirmishes Between Wal-Mart and the United Food and Commercial Workers Union*, 58 Ark. L. Rev. 833 (2006). Economically-motivated attempts to derail a competitor's regulatory approval, including land use applications, can raise antitrust problems but are usually protected by the *Noerr-Pennington* doctrine. This problem is discussed briefly in the section on Antitrust, *infra*.

Defining "big box." The term has become virtually synonymous with "Wal-Mart," the retail giant that pioneered this business model. See, e.g., Zelinsky, *Maryland's "Wal-Mart" Act: Policy And Preemption*, 28 Cardozo L. Rev. 847 (2006). This rough-and-ready approach will not suffice for a legal definition in a statute or ordinance, of course, and one survey found that planners' definitions varied widely. J. Evans-Cowley, *Meeting the Big Box Challenge: Planning, Design and Regulation Strategies*, American Planning Ass'n, Planning Advisory Serv. Rep. No. 537 (2006), at 7. Professor Evans-Cowley attempted a synthesis:

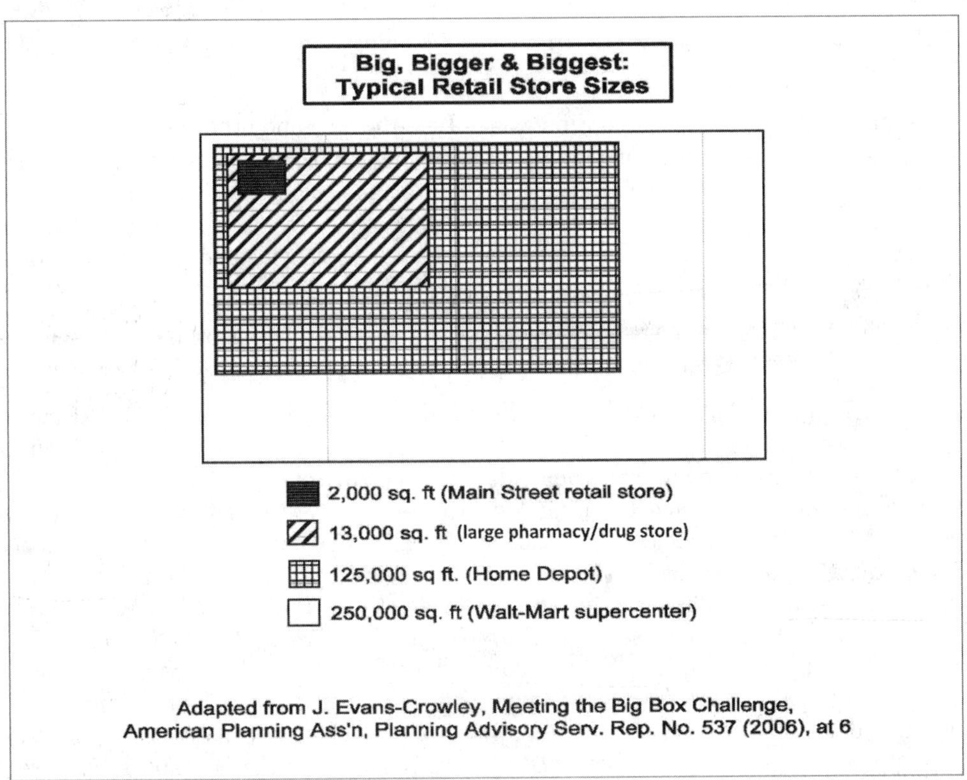

A big-box retail store is typically a one-story warehouse building with a height of 30 feet or more, simple and rectangular in construction, made of corrugated metal, concrete block or brick-faced walls, and ranging in size from 20,000 to 260,000 square feet. It is generally a stand-alone building with a large parking lot or part of a larger shopping center. In describing the "function" of a big-box retailer, planners said they delivered inexpensive goods. [*Id.*]

Size. Most land use regulations use size criteria to separate big box businesses from other, similar uses in a zone. In *Village of Chardon, supra*, the zone was limited to businesses with fewer than ten employees and less than ten thousand square feet of floor area. The Maine Informed Growth Act, Me. Rev. Stat. tit. 30-A § 4365, adopted in June 2007, defines "large scale retail development" as "any retail business establishment having a gross floor area of 75,000 square feet or more in one or more buildings at the same location, and any expansion or renovation of an existing building or buildings that results in a retail business establishment having a gross floor area of 75,000 square feet or more in one or more buildings, except when the expansion of an existing retail business is less than 20,000 square feet."

Regulating the big box. A federal district court took a more skeptical view of size limitations than did the *Chardon* court, refusing to dismiss a complaint claiming that the distinction between sizes of stores served no zoning purpose, that it restricted "the public's ability to take advantage of the product selection and price advantages offered by superstores," and that it served the economic interests of existing businesses by protecting them from competition. *A&P v. Town of East Hampton*, 997 F. Supp. 340 (E.D.N.Y. 1998). See also Shigley, *Big Box Regulations Sweep Across the State*, California Planning and Development Report, Jan. 3, 2004:

> Recently adopted or proposed ordinances in Los Angeles [and other California cities] specifically limit stores of a certain size, usually about 100,000 square feet, to no more than 5% to 10% of floor area devoted to non-taxable goods [such as groceries]. A Wal-Mart supercenter is usually 180,000 to 230,000 square feet, and groceries fill more than one-third of the stores." [excerpts available at goliath.ecnext.com/coms2/gi_0199-76942]

Is the "big box" problem an example of market economics operating properly (in which case zoning obstacles might be viewed with suspicion), or market failure?

Merriam, *Breaking Big Boxes: Learning from the Horse Whisperers*, 6 Vt. J. Envtl. L. 7 (2004-05), http://www.vjel.org/journal/VJEL10029.html, opposes stonewalled opposition to big box retail and believes they can be accommodated in the environment. He points out that "the 'over-our-dead-bodies' approach to siting big box retail only raises the ire and resolve of developers. Media attention exacerbates the strong feelings on both sides and creates a gestalt of winning by attrition, not reason. The winner of the contest is the one who gives up the most and spends the most, much like the semi-myth of the potlatch Indians." *Id.* at 16. He draws on a seminal report by Chris Duerksen, *Site Planning for Large-Scale Retail Stores*, PAS Memo (American Planning Ass'n, Apr. 1996), to suggest the following regulations for integrating big box retail into the landscape: regulate the architectural character of the building so it looks smaller; mandate color and material to get away from the cheaply constructed appearance of the typical big box; make the big box relate better to surrounding uses and spaces; require design that makes it pedestrian friendly; and limit front-field parking to get the big boxes to relate better to the street.

Standing. When the big box store's development application is denied, it obviously has standing to appeal, but who has standing to challenge a decision in favor of the superstore? Competitor standing generally is addressed *infra*. With specific reference to "big box" stores, see *Barton v. City of Lebanon*, 88 P.3d 323 (Ore. App. 2004) (small grocery store owner had standing to challenge Wal-Mart approval); *Jenkins v. City of Gallipolis*, 735 N.E.2d 44 (Ohio 2000) (commercial land owner lacked standing; no individualized injury). For an anti-big box advocate's perspective, see A. Norman, *Sprawl and the Coercive Force of Zoning Law: Fear & Loathing*, 6 Vt. J. Envtl. L. 7 (2004-2005), http://www.vjel.org/journal/VJEL10025.html. See *Save Our Springs Alliance v. City of Dripping Springs*, 304 S.W.3d 871 (Tx. App. 2010) (illustrative of difficulty of opposition groups proving harm and having standing); *Concerned Citizens for the Preservation of Watertown, Inc. v. Planning and Zoning Commission of the Town of Watertown*, 984 A.2d 72 (Conn. App. 2009) (group has no standing to challenge big box store), http://www.jud.ct.gov/external/supapp/Cases/AROap/AP118/118ap56.pdf.

Targeted exclusion. With the *Avon* and *Chardon* cases, *supra*, compare *Manalapan Realty, L.P. v. Township of Manalapan*, 658 A.2d 1230 (N.J. 1995). The New Jersey court upheld an ordinance that permitted retail stores, shops and markets "including establishments engaged in the selling of paint, glass, wallpaper, or hardware items for household use, but not including any establishment engaged in the sale of lumber or building materials or storing, displaying, or selling materials outside a completely enclosed building." The ordinance was specifically adopted to exclude a Home Depot "big box" home improvement store from a proposed regional shopping center development. The lower courts found the ordinance arbitrary and capricious, but the Supreme Court went to some lengths to defend the reasonableness of the municipality's choice in relationship to a master plan calling for "mixed uses" in the commercial district. "Mixed" does not signify that any and all uses need to be permitted, the court held.

The Glynn County Island Planning Commission addressed this issue of prohibiting some high traffic generating uses in 2009 in considering a planned development ("ZM1464 (I) Island Professional Park"). Go to http://www.glynncounty.org/DocumentView.aspx?DID=7612 or http://tinyurl.com/2e2t52r.

Beyond land use regulation. Sometimes, land use objectives can be accomplished indirectly without land use regulation. Opponents, hoping to create an unfavorable climate for the big box model, have persuaded several states to mandate that large businesses (but not others) provide expensive employee benefits. See, e.g., Maryland Fair Share Health Care Fund Act, Md. Code Ann., Lab. & Empl. §§ 8.5-101 to -107, discussed in Zelinsky, *supra*. Available at http://tinyurl.com/2fzc5gd. A related approach ties land use approval to the preparation of an "economic impact analysis," as a result of which the applicant might be required to agree to mitigate any adverse impacts. See Los Angeles, Cal. Mun. Code §§ 12.24(U)(14)(d)(1) through (d)(3) available at http://tinyurl.com/2dvuvv; Lefcoe, *supra*, 58 Ark L. Rev. at 846-47.

Sources. "Small Town America in an Era of Big Box Development," a symposium presented at Vermont Law School, is published at 6 Vt. J. Envtl. L. 1 (2005), www.vjel.org/journal/VJEL10030.html. For a comprehensive website addressing local business preservation, see www.newrules.org/retail. See also S. Mitchell, Big-Box Swindle: The True Cost of Mega-Retailers and the Fight for America's Independent Businesses (2006) (strong critique); Bianco, *Wal-Mart's Midlife Crisis*, Business Week, Apr. 30, 2007, at 46, available at http://www.businessweek.com/magazine/content/07_18/b4032001.htm.

A NOTE ON INCENTIVE ZONING AND SPECIAL DISTRICTS IN DOWNTOWN AND COMMERCIAL AREAS

Incentive zoning. Incentive zoning is a land use regulatory technique that enlists market forces by trading valuable density increases for site improvements that are thought to benefit the general public. The city may permit the building to be taller or bulkier, creating more rentable space, for instance, or expensive requirements such as on-site parking may be relaxed, reducing costs. As Professor Kayden notes, "When the value of an incentive exceeds the cost of providing an amenity, then developers may find it in their self-interest to engage in such public-private transactions." Kayden, *Market-Based Regulatory Approaches: A Comparative Discussion of Environmental and Land Use Techniques in the United States*, 19 B.C. Envtl. Aff. L. Rev. 565, 568 (1992). Professor Kayden has noted a number of problems with incentive zoning, however, including the difficulty of accurately "pricing" the value of what the city gains for what it gives up, equity consequences that favor the large developers who are in the best position to take advantage of incentives, and potential distortion of the land use plan if regulators uncritically approve undesirable projects in order to obtain "free" benefits for the city. *Id.* at 571. See *Municipal Art Soc'y v. City of New York*, 522 N.Y.S.2d 800 (N.Y. 1987) (development agreement violated principles of incentive zoning scheme); *Tribe v. Central Puget Sound Growth Management Hearings Board*, 235 P.3d 812 (Wash. Ct. App. 2010) (uncertain that the density incentive complies with Growth Management Act). For additional reading, see J. Getzels & M. Jaffe, *Zoning Bonuses in Central Cities*, American

Planning Association, Planning Advisory Rep. No. 410 (1988); M. Morris, *Incentive Zoning: Meeting Urban Design and Affordable Housing Objectives*, American Planning Association, Planning Advisory Rep. No. 494 (2000); Morris, *Using Zoning Bonuses for Smart Growth Development*, Am. Plan. Ass'n Zoning News, July 2000 (discusses programs in several cities).

Special Districts. The *City of Avon* case, *supra*, utilized an innovative zoning technique known as a "special district" to regulate its downtown area. A special district takes the place of the set of underlying zoning regulations that would otherwise apply zone-by-zone within the targeted area. This way, the special district can include area-specific land use regulations and standards, and can also use the discretionary review of new development to ensure that district requirements will be met. New York has an extensive special district program in Manhattan. *Franchise Developers, Inc. v. City of Cincinnati*, 505 N.E.2d 966 (Ohio 1987), held that standards contained in an Environmental Quality District were not unconstitutionally vague. See also *Bell v. City of Waco*, 835 S.W.2d 211 (Tex. App. 1992), holding the standards contained in a Neighborhood Conservation District were reasonable, and that the district was authorized by the zoning statute. For discussion, see R. Babcock & W. Larsen, Special Districts (1990); Ziegler, *Shaping Megalopolis: The Transformation of Euclidean Zoning by Special Zoning Districts and Site-Specific Development Review Techniques*, 15 Zoning & Plan. L. Rep. 57 (1992). A related technique, known as an "overlay zone," is discussed *infra*, sec. E, because it is often used in connection with environmental regulation. See H. Wiseman, *Public Communities, Private Rules*, 98 Georgetown L.J. 697 (2010); University of Tulsa Legal Studies Research Paper No. 2010-03 available at http://papers.ssrn.com. Special districts for downtown and other areas may also be used as the basis for urban design plans, discussed in Chapter 9.

[b.] Control of Competition as a Zoning Purpose

The districting problems explored in the preceding section generally turn on issues of policy and planning, as to which the courts predictably give municipalities generous room for discretion. Commercial zoning can also raise legitimacy of purpose issues, however, because a zoning decision can favor one competitor over another. (Legitimacy issues in residential zoning are explored in Chapter 5.) This section considers the control of competition problem as it is handled in state law, and the next section considers whether and how federal antitrust law applies.

HERNANDEZ v. CITY OF HANFORD

41 Cal. 4th 279, 59 Cal. Rptr. 3d 442, 159 P.3d 33 (2007)

George, C.J.:

This case involves a constitutional challenge to a zoning ordinance enacted by the City of Hanford in 2003. In order to protect the economic viability of Hanford's downtown commercial district — a prominent feature of which is a large number of regionally well-regarded retail furniture stores — the challenged ordinance generally prohibits the sale of furniture in another commercial district in Hanford (currently designated the Planned Commercial or PC district) that contains a large shopping mall in which several department stores as well as other retail stores are located. At the same time, the ordinance creates a limited exception to the general prohibition on the sale of furniture in the PC district, permitting large department stores (those with 50,000 or more square feet of floor space) located within that district to sell furniture within a specifically prescribed area (occupying no more than 2,500 square feet of floor space) within the department store. . . .

I

In 1989, the City of Hanford amended its general plan to provide for a new commercial district in the vicinity of 12th Avenue and Lacey Boulevard. This new district originally was designated the "Regional Commercial" district but later was renamed the Planned Commercial or PC district. The district encompassed several hundred acres of land and was intended to accommodate the location of malls, large "big box" stores, and other retail uses.

At trial, Jim Beath, the city's community development director, testified . . . "that when the city was considering the creation of the new district in 1989, it was concerned that the extent of anticipated commercial development in the proposed district might well have a negative effect on the city's downtown commercial district. In light of that concern, the city council appointed the Retail Strategy Development Committee (the Committee) "made up of people from the mall area as well as the downtown district and other citizens." The Committee was asked to propose land use rules for the new district that would "provide for the large box and other kinds of retail use that the City . . . had grown to need and yet still make sure that [the new district] didn't have a negative impact on the downtown district."

The Committee ultimately recommended that certain designated uses generally not be permitted in the new district, and Beath testified that those uses "were ones that were already established in the downtown district that they didn't want to see removed from the downtown district and relocate[d] out at the planned commercial district, and those were car dealerships, banks, professional offices, and furniture stores." . . . Accordingly, as relevant here, the 1989 ordinance included department stores and the sale of home furnishings within the list of permitted uses within the new district, but did not include furniture stores or the sale of furniture as a permitted use. . . .

In the fall of 2002, more than a decade after establishment of the PC district, plaintiffs Adrian and Tracy Hernandez leased space in a building located in the PC district with the intent to establish a new business at that location to be called Country Hutch Home Furnishings and Mattress Gallery (hereafter Country Hutch Home Furnishings). [They intended to sell furniture but Mr. Beath informed plaintiffs that they would not be permitted to sell furniture.]

[P]laintiffs opened the Country Hutch Home Furnishings store. Soon thereafter a city inspector, citing plaintiffs for violating the zoning ordinance by offering furniture for sale in their new store, instructed them to remove all of the furniture from the store. Plaintiffs thereafter sent a letter to the members of the Hanford City Council, complaining that the zoning code was being applied in a discriminatory fashion because numerous department stores in the PC district were selling furniture and had not been cited by the city, while plaintiffs were cited for engaging in the same conduct.

On March 4, 2003, one week after receiving plaintiffs' letter, the city council held a "study session" to consider the issues raised by plaintiffs' letter. Plaintiffs, as well as representatives of the downtown furniture stores and representatives of the PC district department stores, attended and participated in the study session. . . . During the next four months, [t]he various alternatives were debated vigorously by the directly affected businesses, with representatives of the downtown business district emphasizing the critical importance for the city's overall general welfare of preserving the economic viability of that district, and representatives of the large department stores located in the PC district observing that their stores had offered some furniture for sale for the past decade without having a negative impact on Hanford's downtown furniture stores,[a] that virtually all of their sister stores in other locations contained furniture departments, and that the elimination of furniture departments in the department stores in Hanford could result in a substantial reduction of revenue for the city (by virtue of lost sales tax receipts) as well as for the individual stores. . . . Ultimately, on July 15, 2003, the city council adopted the amendment to the city zoning provisions relating to the sale of furniture in the PC district that is challenged in this case, Hanford Ordinance 03-03 (Ordinance No. 03-03). . . . [T]the ordinance in question generally prohibits the sale of furniture in the PC district, but at the same time creates a limited exception permitting a large department store within the PC district to display and sell furniture within a single location in the store measuring no more than 2,500 square feet.

Shortly after the ordinance was enacted, plaintiffs filed the present action against the city, challenging the validity of the ordinance . . . .

II

Before reaching the equal protection issue upon which the Court of Appeal based its decision, we turn first to the more general (and more sweeping) contention that plaintiffs raised below and upon which they continue to rely in this court — that the zoning ordinance at issue is invalid because the "primary purpose" of the ordinance's general prohibition of the sale of furniture in the PC district assertedly was to "regulat[e] economic competition." Although neither the trial court nor the Court of Appeal found the ordinance invalid on this basis, as we shall see, plaintiffs' claim that the city exceeded its authority under the police power by enacting a zoning ordinance that regulates or restricts economic competition apparently is based upon some ambiguous and at least potentially misleading language that appears in a number of zoning decisions of the Courts of Appeal. As we shall explain, despite some arguably ambiguous language the decisions in these cases plainly do not support plaintiffs' challenge to the validity of the zoning ordinance here at issue, and we shall attempt to clarify the language in question to avoid possible confusion in the future.

Van Sicklen v. Browne, 92 Cal. Rptr. 786 (1971) (*Van Sicklen*), is the earliest in the series of relevant Court of Appeal decisions. In *Van Sicklen*, the petitioner landowners applied for a conditional use permit to construct an automobile service station, but the city denied the application on the ground, among others, that a proliferation of service stations already existed in the area and thus that there was no demonstrated need for an additional service station at that location at that time. On appeal, the landowners claimed the city had denied the use permit "for economic rather than planning considerations resulting in an invalid attempt to regulate competition through zoning laws." In analyzing this contention, the court in *Van Sicklen* stated: "Although cities may not use zoning powers to regulate economic competition [citing three out-of-state decisions], it is also recognized that land use and planning decisions cannot be made in any community without some impact on the economy of the community. . . . Taking cognizance of this concept we perceive that planning and zoning ordinances traditionally seek to maintain property values, protect tax revenues, provide

---

[a] The record indicates that the number of retail furniture stores in Hanford's downtown business district had increased from five stores in 1989 to 13 stores in 2003.

neighborhood social and economic stability, attract business and industry and encourage conditions which make a community a pleasant place to live and work. Whether these be classified as 'planning considerations' or 'economic considerations,' we hold that so long as the primary purpose of the zoning ordinance is not to regulate economic competition, but to subserve a valid objective pursuant to a city's police powers, such ordinance is not invalid even though it might have an indirect impact on economic competition." The court in *Van Sicklen* then went on to uphold the city's denial of the use permit, concluding that "[i]ntensity of land use is a well-recognized and valid city concern and relates to both health and safety factors and to proper zoning practice" and "encompasses within its purview the degree of saturation in a particular area of land devoted to automobile service stations."

The passage from *Van Sicklen* quoted above correctly recognized many of the numerous factors and interests, including economic considerations, that a municipality properly may take into account in fashioning zoning ordinances and making zoning decisions, and we agree with the court's determination upholding the particular zoning action challenged in that case. We believe, however, that some of the language in the above quoted passage from *Van Sicklen* is at least potentially misleading. First, the initial general statement that "cities may not use zoning powers to regulate economic competition" is quite clearly overbroad. As one leading zoning treatise accurately observes: "[A]ll zoning has some impact on competition. The simple division of the community into districts has an inherent and profound effect on the real estate market, because some land is withdrawn from the commercial market and placed in the residential market. . . . Some competitive impact results from nearly every provision of the original zoning ordinance, and from each amendment. Accordingly, competitive impact alone cannot invalidate a zoning ordinance. A zoning ordinance which serves some established purpose of zoning is not necessarily invalid simply because it has the additional effect of limiting competition." (1 Anderson's American Law of Zoning (4th ed. 1996) § 7.28, p. 807.)

Second, we believe that the additional statement in the quoted passage — that "so long as the primary purpose of the zoning ordinance is not to regulate economic competition, but to subserve a valid objective pursuant to [the] city's police powers, such ordinance is not invalid even though it might have an indirect impact on economic competition" also is ambiguous and at least potentially misleading. That language could be interpreted to suggest that a zoning ordinance is valid *only* when the ordinance has merely an "indirect impact" on economic competition, and *never* when the regulation of economic competition is a direct and intended effect of the ordinance, even in instances in which a zoning ordinance uses the regulation of competition simply as a means or tool to achieve an authorized and valid *public* purpose — such as the preservation of an existing downtown commercial district — rather than to serve an impermissible *private* anticompetitive purpose or interest — such as securing a financial advantage or monopoly position for the benefit of a favored business or individual or imposing a disadvantage on an unpopular business or individual. As so interpreted, the language would be inaccurate. . . . [T]he more recent decisions have upheld zoning actions even when regulation of economic competition reasonably could be viewed as a direct and intended effect of a challenged zoning action, so long as the primary purpose of the zoning action — that is, its principal and ultimate objective — is to achieve a valid *public* purpose such as furthering a municipality's general plan for controlled growth or for localized commercial development, rather than simply to serve an impermissible anticompetitive *private* purpose such as investing a favored private business with monopoly power or excluding an unpopular company from the community. . . .

The more recent case of *Wal-Mart Stores, Inc. v. City of Turlock*, 41 Cal. Rptr. 3d 420

(2006) (*Wal-Mart*), provides another apt example. In *Wal-Mart*, the City of Turlock enacted a zoning ordinance that, while permitting the operation of traditional "big box" discount stores in a designated district, prohibited the development, anywhere in the city, of so-called discount superstores — defined generally as large discount stores that include a full-service grocery department. In explaining the rationale underlying the restriction on discount superstores, the ordinance set forth a series of facts or findings, stating in part that (1) " 'the Turlock General Plan . . . establishes locational requirements for the [regional and neighborhood] retail centers: encouraging a number of neighborhood centers equally dispersed throughout the city while encouraging a concentration of regional shopping centers along the Highway 99/ Countryside Drive corridor' " (2) the city's " 'General Plan policies promote and encourage vital neighborhood commercial districts that are evenly distributed throughout the city so that residents are able to meet their basic daily shopping needs at neighborhood shopping centers' " (3) " 'discount superstores compete directly with existing grocery stores that anchor neighborhood-serving commercial centers' " (4) " 'the establishment of discount superstores in Turlock is likely to negatively impact the vitality and economic viability of the city's neighborhood commercial centers by drawing sales away from traditional supermarkets located in these centers' " and (5) " 'smaller stores within a neighborhood center rely upon the foot traffic generated by the grocery store for their existence and in neighborhood centers where the grocery store closes, vacancy rates typically increase and deterioration takes place in the remaining center.' "

[T]he Court of Appeal in *Wal-Mart* stated: "With respect to Wal-Mart's claim of anticompetitive purpose, we agree with the trial court that, while the Ordinance likely will have an anticompetitive effect on the grocery business in [the City of Turlock], that incidental effect does not render arbitrary an Ordinance that was enacted for a valid purpose. [Citing *Van Sicklen, supra.*] While zoning ordinances may not legitimately be used to control economic competition, they may be used to address the urban/suburban decay that can be its effect. [Citing cases.]" The appellate court in *Wal-Mart* concluded: "In summary, the police power empowers cities to control and organize development within their boundaries as a means of serving the general welfare. [The City of Turlock] legitimately chose to organize the development within its boundaries using neighborhood shopping centers dispersed throughout the city. The Ordinance is reasonably related to protecting that development choice." . . .

Our court has not previously had occasion to address the question whether a municipality, in order to protect or preserve the economic viability of its downtown business district or neighborhood shopping areas, may enact a zoning ordinance that regulates or controls competition by placing limits on potentially competing commercial activities or development in other areas of the municipality. . . . As the circumstances underlying the decisions in [an earlier case] and *Wal-Mart*, *supra*, demonstrate, even when the regulation of economic competition reasonably can be viewed as a direct and intended effect of a zoning ordinance or action, so long as the primary purpose of the ordinance or action — that is, its principal and ultimate objective — is not the impermissible *private* anticompetitive goal of protecting or disadvantaging a particular favored or disfavored business or individual, but instead is the advancement of a legitimate *public* purpose — such as the preservation of a municipality's downtown business district for the benefit of the municipality as a whole — the ordinance reasonably relates to the general welfare of the municipality and constitutes a legitimate use of the municipality's police power. . . . To the extent that any language in *Van Sicklen* or

Wal-Mart Stores may be interpreted as inconsistent with this conclusion, such an interpretation is disapproved.

In the present case, it is clear that the zoning ordinance's general prohibition on the sale of furniture in the PC district — although concededly intended, at least in part, to regulate competition — was adopted to promote the legitimate public purpose of preserving the economic viability of the Hanford downtown business district, rather than to serve any impermissible private anticompetitive purpose. Furthermore, as in *Ensign Bickford* [*Realty Corp. v. City Council*, 68 Cal. App. 3d 467, 137 Cal. Rptr. 304 (1977)], *supra*, here the zoning ordinance's restrictions are aimed at regulating "*where*, within the city" a particular type of business generally may be located, a very traditional zoning objective. Under these circumstances, we agree with the lower court's conclusion that the zoning ordinance cannot be found invalid as an improper limitation on competition.

III

As noted above, although the Court of Appeal agreed that the challenged zoning ordinance's general prohibition on the sale of furniture in the PC district is permissible, that court concluded the ordinance in question violates the equal protection clause by limiting the exception created by the ordinance to only the sale of furniture by large department stores, and not making the exception available to other retail stores wishing to sell furniture within the same amount of square footage permitted for furniture sales by large department stores. . . . [T]he Hanford ordinance challenged here clearly was intended to serve multiple purposes. The city desired to protect the economic viability of its downtown business district, but at the same time it did not wish to diminish the financial benefits of the PC district for the large department stores that it wanted to attract and maintain in that district. Because the city viewed large department stores as particularly significant elements of the PC district, and because the management of those stores had made clear the importance to them of retaining their ability to offer furniture sales that typically were offered by their sister stores in other locations, it was rational for the city to decide to provide an exception from the general prohibition on furniture sales in the PC district for such large department stores and only such stores. The circumstance that the city also decided to limit the exemption afforded to department stores by placing a square-foot limit on the area within each store in which furniture could be displayed does not in any manner detract from the rationality of limiting the exception to large department stores. . . .

We conclude that the ordinance's differential treatment of large department stores and other retail stores is rationally related to one of the legitimate legislative purposes of the ordinance — the purpose of attracting and retaining large department stores within the PC district. The Court of Appeal's resolution of this issue, which would have required the city to extend the ordinance's 2,500-square-foot exception for furniture sales to *all* retail stores within the PC district, would have undermined the ordinance's overall objective of permitting the sale of furniture in the PC district only to the extent such activity is necessary to serve the city's interest in attracting and retaining large department stores in that district.

NOTES AND QUESTIONS

1. *Control of competition.* In the principal case, the court declares flatly that *all* zoning regulations have competitive effects. Do you agree? If so, in what sense is it then meaningful to have a rule that "control of competition is not a legitimate purpose of land use regulation"? Might the relative ease with which the "control of competition" rule can be avoided (as the principal case demonstrates) explain why there are relatively few modern cases on this issue, despite the prevailing rule? Consider *Ensign Bickford*, for instance, which is discussed in the principal case. The land in issue was zoned for residential use and a rezoning was sought. What if the city had explained its denial of the shopping center rezoning on the ground that it was inconsistent with adjacent residential uses? This is a standard reason for denying commercial rezonings, and the reasoning is usually sustainable under the "debatable question" standard of review discussed earlier in this chapter. Would this raise a control of competition problem? What if the proposed rezoning had been for a multi-family development in a residential area and the council denied it? See the *Krause* case, *supra*. Would this raise a control of competition problem? Why might motive be an issue in a "control of competition" zoning case but not in other zoning cases?

2. *Motive and purpose.* At various points in the *City of Hanford* opinion, Chief Justice George contrasts a "valid" public purpose, such as zoning for "preservation of an existing downtown commercial district," with an "impermissible private anticompetitive purpose," such as conferring economic benefit on a "favored business or individual." How is a court to know which of these purposes was at work? Suppose, for instance, that plaintiffs in the principal case had been longstanding political opponents of the majority party in Hanford? Had complained repeatedly to the press about perceived abuses of the zoning power by the Planning Board? In an omitted part of the opinion, the court rejected an arbitrariness claim based on *Village of Willowbrook v. Olech*, *supra* Chapter 2. Plaintiffs alleged that the ordinance had been amended in retaliation for their complaint about non-enforcement of the furniture sale rule against large department stores, but the court found no evidence of hostility towards them. In thinking about this, review the facts of the principal case. Notice the emphasis that the court places on the inclusive and transparent process employed by the city, involving all interested parties and extending over many months, before adopting the challenged rule. Does this help convince the court that no "impermissible" purpose was involved?

Are motive and purpose different? Consider the following:

> But the "motive" of preventing competition in [*Ensign Bickford*] does not refer to some underlying subjective explanation for the city council's behavior. Rather the "motive" at issue is the immediate legislative objective of the ordinance — to protect certain commercial enterprises by regulating their competition out of the geographical market. This is the same kind of "motive" which, . . . using the term "purpose," the Supreme Court struggles with in *Arlington Heights*. When state courts dismiss this sort of "motive" inquiry as inappropriate, they are in substantive disagreement with courts permitting such inquiries but using the terminology of purpose. [Brownstein, *Illicit Legislative Motive in the Municipal Land Use Regulation Process*, 57 U. Cin. L. Rev. 1, 124 (1988).]

Arlington Heights, a U.S. Supreme Court decision holding that a legitimate zoning purpose could overcome allegations of discriminatory racial motivations, is discussed further in Chapter 5.B. If the zoning purpose is found to be "legitimate," does that preclude inquiry into anticompetitive motive? The Court of Appeal in *Ensign Bickford* thought so. Does *City of*

Hanford call into question this conclusion in any way?

The land use approval process is often the battle ground for market competitors. Consider this recent front page story in the Wall Street Journal:

> MUNDELEIN, Ill. — Robert Brownson long believed that his proposed development here, with its 200,000-square-foot Wal-Mart Supercenter, was being held hostage by nearby homeowners.
>
> He had seen them protesting at city hall, and they had filed a lawsuit to stop the project.
>
> What he didn't know was that the locals were getting a lot of help. A grocery chain with nine stores in the area had hired Saint Consulting Group to secretly run the antidevelopment campaign. Saint is a specialist at fighting proposed Wal-Marts, and it uses tactics it describes as "black arts."
>
> As Wal-Mart Stores Inc. has grown into the largest grocery seller in the U.S., similar battles have played out in hundreds of towns like Mundelein. Local activists and union groups have been the public face of much of the resistance. But in scores of cases, large supermarket chains including Supervalu Inc., Safeway Inc. and Ahold NV have retained Saint Consulting to block Wal-Mart, according to hundreds of pages of Saint documents reviewed by The Wall Street Journal and interviews with former employees.
>
> Saint has jokingly called its staff the "Wal-Mart killers." P. Michael Saint, the company's founder, declines to discuss specific clients or campaigns. When read a partial list of the company's supermarket clients, he responds that "if those names are true, I would say I was proud that some of the largest, most sophisticated companies were so pleased with our success and discretion that they hired us over the years."
>
> Supermarkets that have funded campaigns to stop Wal-Mart are concerned about having to match the retailing giant's low prices lest they lose market share. Although they have managed to stop some projects, they haven't put much of a dent in Wal-Mart's growth in the U.S., where it has more than 2,700 supercenters — large stores that sell groceries and general merchandise. Last year, 51% of Wal-Mart's $258 billion in U.S. revenue came from grocery sales. . . . For the typical anti-Wal-Mart assignment, a Saint manager will drop into town using an assumed name to create or take control of local opposition, according to former Saint employees. They flood local politicians with calls, using multiple phones to make it appear that the calls are coming from different people, the former employees say.
>
> They hire lawyers and traffic experts to help derail the project or stall it as long as possible, in hopes that the developer will pull the plug or Wal-Mart will find another location.
>
> "Usually, clients in defense campaigns do not want their identities disclosed because it opens them up to adverse publicity and the potential for lawsuits," Mr. Saint wrote in a book published by his firm.

A. Zimmerman, *Rival Chains Secretly Fund Opposition to Wal-Mart*, Wall Street Journal (June 7, 2010) available at http://tinyurl.com/254lb8h. What do you think of this often sub rosa activity?

3. *Competitor standing.* The rule that control of competition is not a legitimate function of zoning has led many courts to state as a corollary that competitors lack standing to challenge a decision favoring a competitor, unless they can assert a basis other than loss of competitive advantage. See, e.g., *Center Bay Gardens*, sec. B1, *supra* (finding a showing of "particularized harm). Why was standing not an issue in the principal case? If plaintiffs had remained in their downtown store, rather than moving to the mall, would they have had standing to challenge this same zoning amendment, giving their department store competitors' favorable treatment? Compare *Tyson v. City of Sunnyvale*, 920 F. Supp. 1054 (N.D. Cal. 1996) (denial of rezoning for single-family homes upheld by court; claim that other residential rezoning applications treated more favorably dismissed).

The basis for the no-standing rule is explained in *Circle Lounge & Grille, Inc. v. Board of Appeal*, 86 N.E.2d 920 (Mass. 1949). Circle Lounge was held not to have standing to challenge a variance permitting the construction of a restaurant across the street in a residential zoning district. The court said that the purpose of zoning is to ensure the compatibility of uses. Residential owners in the residential zone could challenge the variance, but a commercial use in an adjacent commercial zone could not, even though the new commercial use was located in a residential zone. Accord *Nautilus of Exeter v. Town of Exeter*, 656 A.2d 407 (N.H. 1995); *Sun-Brite Car Wash, Inc. v. Board of Zoning & Appeals*, 508 N.E.2d 130 (N.Y. 1987). Compare *Swain v. County of Winnebago*, 250 N.E.2d 439 (Ill. App. 1969) (downtown business merchants denied standing to challenge a regional shopping center rezoning some distance from the downtown in the adjacent county), with *Westgate Shopping Village v. City of Toledo*, 639 N.E.2d 126 (Ohio App. 1994) (rival mall had standing to challenge a competitor's rezoning two miles distant because it might reduce the property value of plaintiff's mall). Is this a subterfuge for granting competitor standing? Compare *DePetro v. Wayne Planning Bd.*, 842 A.2d 266, 273 (N.J. App. Div. 2004) ("Indeed, a competitor may be particularly well equipped to frame the challenge and to provide the background that will illuminate its merits and faults."). Is the *DePetro* rationale more pertinent to the facts of the principal case than that of *Circle Lounge, supra*? If control of competition is the legitimate purpose of the ordinance, rather than the traditional quasi-nuisance rationale of separating incompatible uses such as the homes and restaurant at issue in *Circle Lounge*, does it follow that competitors ought to have standing on the basis of competitive injury alone? What do you think of this recent conclusion by an appellate court: "We conclude that plaintiff's interest in thwarting competition from a nearby restaurant business, even assuming that such prospective competition constitutes an 'actual' and not merely 'conjectural' or 'hypothetical' injury, is not a 'legally protected interest' sufficient to establish standing." *Miller Apple Limited Partnership v. Emmet County*, 2010 Mich. App. LEXIS 285 (Mich. Ct. App. 2010).

4. *Examples of control of competition problems.*

(a) *Distance requirements.* Municipalities commonly adopt distance requirements for gasoline filling stations, liquor stores and other similar uses, requiring that they be separated by a minimum distance. The original justification in the case of filling stations, that proximity increases the risk of fire and other hazards, has not prevailed. See *Exxon Co., U.S.A. v. Township of Livingston*, 199 N.J. Super. 470, 489 A.2d 1218 (App. Div. 1985). The Court in *Stone v. City of Maitland*, 446 F.2d 83 (5th Cir. 1971), upheld a 350-foot distance requirement because "[a]bsent these requirements, the probability of business failure in this highly competitive area is high. The result is abandoned stations." *Id.* at 89. The court added that abandoned stations detract from the quality of the aesthetic environment. Are these rationales consistent with the principal case? A spacing requirement as to liquor stores was rejected in

Costco Wholesale Corp. v. Orange County, 780 So. 2d 198 (Fla. App. 2001). In *Pawn America Minnesota, LLC v. City of St. Louis Park*, 787 N.W.2d 565 (Minn. 2010), the court upheld an interim ordinance to implement a recommendation of "a distance separation requirement between pawnshops, gun shops, liquor stores, and certain other businesses, prohibit[ing] pawnshops from being located within 350 feet of residentially zoned property . . . ." When commercial uses enjoy First Amendment protection, distance requirements require additional analysis. See sec. 5, *infra*.

(b) *The "need" cases.* In *Van Sicklen*, discussed in the principal case, the court upheld the denial of a filling station because no need for the station was shown. By applying a "need" standard, the municipality avoids the potentially arbitrary application of distance requirements, but is the underlying rationale the same, that is, avoidance of destructive competition that will blight the community? Compare *Cardinal Props. v. Borough of Westwood*, 547 A.2d 316 (N.J. App. Div. 1988) (invalidating need standard for storage yards as improper). In *Technical & Prof. Serv., Inc. v. Board of Zoning Adjustment*, 558 S.W.2d 798 (Mo. App. 1977), the court upheld a board decision denying a conditional use for a cemetery. The ordinance required, inter alia, that the board find that the use would not "seriously injure the appropriate use of neighboring property." The court held that the board weighed the need for a cemetery with this factor "and concluded that the scales tipped heavily in favor of the latter." *Id.* at 802. See *DF Land Development, LLC v. Charter Township Of Ann Arbor*, 2010 Mich. App. LEXIS 1333 (Mich. Ct. App. 2010) (upheld denial of rezoning to commercial use where there was little or no commercial zoning and no need).

(c) *Protection of existing businesses.* In *Zaehring v. Long Beach Twp.*, 151 A.2d 425 (N.J.L. Div. 1959), the municipality zoned as marine commercial all lots in residential districts on which nonconforming marine commercial uses existed, but other lots suitable for marine commercial use were not rezoned for this use. The court struck down the rezoning, noting it was "adopted to solve the economic and competitive problems of particular individuals." *Id.* at 430. Is this an example of the "impermissible private purposes" condemned by the principal case? Can you pinpoint why? The question of unfair zoning treatment may come up as an equal protection claim, as in *Reget v. City of La Crosse*, 595 F.3d 691 (7th Cir. 2010) (claims dismissed).

In *Saddle Brook Realty v. Township of Saddle Brook*, 906 A.2d 454 (N.J. App. Div. 2006), a "medium size suburban town," totally prohibited fast food restaurants, but three existing restaurants were protected as non-conforming uses. The court reversed the grant of a variance for a new fast food restaurant in a strip mall on the grounds that it impaired the intent and purpose of the zoning ordinance banning this use. How is this different from *Zaehring*, *supra*, where the court invalidated protecting the existing uses? Compare *Fogg v. City of South Miami*, 183 So. 2d 219 (Fla. App. 1966) (ordinance prohibiting drive-in retail businesses in a commercial district invalid). The court admitted the city could prohibit drive-in businesses that create excess noise or traffic or the "gathering of unsavory elements," but concluded that the drive-in store excluded by the ordinance was not in this category. Is it relevant that *Saddle Brook* and *Fogg* were decided forty years apart? Drive-through bans are a hot topic today in the war against obesity. G. Goodale, *Birthplace of the Drive-Thru Bans Them to Curb Obesity*, Christian Science Monitor, August 2, 2010, available at http://tinyurl.com/29xma5q. Is the prevention of obesity a proper purpose of zoning?

5. *Related uses.* In the cases discussed thus far, there was a sharp distinction that could be seen between the uses permitted and the use excluded. A more difficult problem arises when a community attempts to determine the retail character of a district by drawing a line between different but similar retail uses. One example is the exclusion of drive-in businesses to encourage walk-in trade. In *Board of Supvrs. v. Rowe*, 216 S.E.2d 199 (Va. 1975), the court held unconstitutional a commercial district that permitted hotels but not banks and that permitted restaurants but not drive-in restaurants. The court held that the excluded commercial uses were legitimate and no more detrimental than the uses included. This seems sensible, but on what constitutional basis do you suppose the court relied? The *Manalapan* court emphasized that the commercial developers before it had no "fundamental right" to the zoning they sought. Chapter 4 addresses the problem of exclusionary residential zoning. Is there a principled basis for treating commercial developers differently? Recall that in the *Avon* case, *supra*, the protected downtown district permitted both residential and commercial uses. For an unusual example of an excluded use, see *Midrash Sephardi, Inc. v. Surfside*, 366 F.3d 1214 (11th Cir. 2004), rejecting the town's argument that it could exclude houses of worship from its business district, while allowing social clubs and other secular organizations, in order to encourage "retail synergy" among uses. First Amendment issues presented by this type of case are explored *infra*. But see the recent RLUIPA decision in *River of Life Kingdom Ministries v. Village of Hazel Crest*, 611 F.3d 367 (7th Cir. 2010) (upheld denial of zoning approval for a church in a commercial area).

6. *Providing a conceptual basis for the control of competition cases.* Mandelker, *Control of Competition as a Proper Purpose in Zoning*, 14 Zoning Dig. 33, 34 (1962), suggests that these cases can be divided into proximity and market-demand cases. Another commentator notes that both questions are present in many cases. In a proximity case, an existing entrepreneur objects to a new market entrant because his market share is threatened. In a market-demand case, the argument is "that entrants must be regulated because the market cannot absorb them." Existing entrepreneurs argue that a failure to regulate will cause severe economic dislocations, such as bankruptcies and property tax losses caused by underutilized or abandoned land. "The sophisticated protectionist may even argue that regulation of market entry . . . [prevents] one decision maker from shifting external costs to non-decision makers — the most traditional basis for public regulation of land use." Tarlock, *Not in Accordance With a Comprehensive Plan: A Case Study of Regional Shopping Center Location Conflicts in Lexington, Kentucky*, 1970 Urb. L. Ann. 133, 175. Do you agree with this "sophisticated" argument?

7. For additional reading, see Strom, *Land Use Controls: Effects on Business Competition I*, 3 Zoning & Plan. L. Rep. 33 (1980); *II*, *id.*, at 41; Weaver & Duerksen, *Central Business District Planning and the Control of Outlying Shopping Centers*, 14 Urb. L. Ann. 57 (1977).

PROBLEM

You are the city attorney for the town of Rustic Hills, a small rural town that is a shopping center for surrounding agricultural areas. However, the town's business district has been declining. A city council member received a call from a friend of his who is in real estate advising that a Big Box retail company was planning to buy a large site on the edge of town for a Big Box store. The site is zoned residential but is adjacent to a state highway.

What would you recommend? (1) A ten-month moratorium on all commercial retail development so the town can study the problem? (2) Stringent design standards for the Big Box retail store? (3) A cap of 10,000 square feet on all new retail stores? The cap would not affect existing stores, all of which are under this size. (4) A quota relating commercial retail space to population? The quota would be set low enough so that it would exclude any new Big

Box stores. (5) A requirement that all new Big Box stores prepare an economic statement detailing the effect they would have on existing retail stores in the town? Any legal problems? See Walters, *Blocking the Big Box*, Governing, July, 2000, at 48.

[c.] Antitrust Problems

Reconsider the facts in the *Ensign Bickford* case, reproduced *supra*. Do they raise a possibility of municipal liability under the Sherman Antitrust Act? Section 1 of the Act, 15 U.S.C. § 1, provides:

> Every . . . conspiracy, in restraint of trade or commerce among the several States, . . . is hereby declared to be illegal.

Section 2, 15 U.S.C. § 2, provides:

> Every person who shall monopolize, or attempt to monopolize, or combine or conspire with any other person or persons, to monopolize any part of the trade or commerce among the several States . . . shall be deemed guilty of a felony.

In *Parker v. Brown*, 317 U.S. 341 (1943), the Court construed the Sherman Act to contain a "state action" exemption that excused, on principles of intergovernmental comity, *state*-approved anticompetitive behavior. It was assumed that the *Parker v. Brown* exemption also applied to local governments, until the Court held that it did not in *City of Lafayette v. Louisiana Power & Light Co.*, 435 U.S. 389 (1978). In a series of subsequent cases, the Supreme Court applied antitrust liability to local governments but it then effectively restored the exemption for land use cases. Here are the important cases:

Community Communications Co. v. City of Boulder, 455 U.S. 40 (1982). In a case challenging a moratorium on new cable television licenses, the Court held a city's home rule status did not afford it immunity under the state action doctrine. The Court confirmed the rule adopted in *Lafayette* that municipal immunity from the antitrust law requires clearly and affirmatively expressed state policy to displace competition. The Court held the constitutional home rule authority under which the city adopted the moratorium did not confer immunity under this test.

Town of Hallie v. City of Eau Claire, 471 U.S. 34 (1985). Four unincorporated townships adjacent to the city brought an antitrust action against the city. They claimed they were potential competitors of the city and that the city used its monopoly power over sewage treatment to gain an unlawful monopoly over the provision of sewage collection and transportation services. The Court upheld the district court's dismissal of the complaint.

Wisconsin statutes gave cities the authority to construct sewerage systems and to determine the area to be served. The Court held that the statutes evidenced "a 'clearly articulated and affirmatively expressed' state policy to displace competition with regulation in the area of municipal provision of sewerage services." The Court held it was enough if these statutes contemplated that the city might engage in anticompetitive conduct, and that such conduct was "a foreseeable result of empowering the City to refuse to serve unannexed areas." It was not necessary for the state legislature to state explicitly that it expected the City to engage in anticompetitive conduct. *Lafayette* means only it is enough if "the statutes authorized the City to provide sewage services and also to determine the areas to be served. We think it is clear that anticompetitive effects logically would result from this broad authority to regulate." *Id.* at 42. The Court also held it was not necessary to show that the state "compelled" the city to act.

In *City of Columbia v. Omni Outdoor Advertising Co.*, 499 U.S. 365 (1991), the Court held that state action immunity protected a municipality from antitrust liability claimed to arise from an ordinance restricting the size, location and spacing of billboards. These restrictions, especially those on spacing, benefitted an existing billboard company that controlled 95% of the local market, because they already had billboards in place, and severely hindered a potential competitor that was trying to enter the market.

The Court held that state action immunity was conferred by the city's "unquestioned zoning power over the size, location and spacing of billboards" that the state zoning act, which was based on the Standard Act, authorized. The Court rejected a defense that state action immunity did not apply if a municipality exercises its delegated authority in a substantively or procedurally defective manner. This defense would undercut the "very interests of federalism" the state action doctrine was designed to protect. This holding means immunity is available even if a state court holds a zoning regulation invalid because it is an improper control of competition.

The Court next held the "clear articulation" rule was "amply met here" because "[t]he very purpose of zoning regulation is to displace unfettered business freedom in a manner that regularly has the effect of preventing normal acts of competition, particularly on the part of new entrants." An ordinance restricting the size, location and spacing of billboards, which the Court characterized as "a common form of zoning," necessarily protects existing billboards from new competition. The Court also rejected a conspiracy exception to state action immunity and held that bribery and misconduct would not make state action immunity unavailable.

NOTES AND QUESTIONS

1. *Local government liability today.* The Court's decision in *Omni* almost totally protects local government land use actions from antitrust liability. See also *Jacobs, Visconsi & Jacobs Co. v. City of Lawrence*, 927 F.2d 1111 (10th Cir. 1991) (immunity found when city refused suburban shopping center zoning to implement plan designating downtown as primary retail area). But see *Kentuckiana Med. Ctr. LLC v. Clark County*, 2006 U.S. Dist. LEXIS 3298 (S.D. Ind. 2006) (moratorium on hospital construction to protect county hospital not authorized by state law; no immunity).

What about home rule municipalities? *Omni* did not discuss *Boulder*, which held that state action immunity does not apply to a home rule municipality. Can a home rule municipality claim antitrust immunity by relying on statutory rather than home rule powers to carry out land use controls?

2. *Noerr-Pennington doctrine.* This doctrine, which is based on two Supreme Court cases, provides a First Amendment antitrust defense for competitors who petition to influence governmental action. *United Mine Workers v. Pennington*, 381 U.S. 657 (1965); *Eastern R.R. Presidents Conference v. Noerr Motor Freight Co.*, 365 U.S. 127 (1961). The doctrine is important in land use cases, like *Omni*, where an entity uses political advocacy to influence the adoption of a regulation that hinders a competitor. The Court held in *Omni* that there is no conspiracy exception to the *Noerr-Pennington* doctrine.

There is also a "sham" exception to the doctrine, but in *Professional Real Estate Investors, Inc. v. Columbia Pictures Indus., Inc.*, 508 U.S. 49 (1993), the Court held the sham exception requires objective proof and cannot be based on the subjective intent of the parties. *Columbia Pictures* substantially restricts opportunities to prove a sham exception. See *VIM, Inc. v.*

Somerset Hotel Ass'n, 19 F. Supp. 2d 422 (W.D. Pa. 1998), *aff'd without opinion*, 187 F.3d 627 (3d Cir. 1999). Defendants defeated a claim that they had impeded the construction of plaintiff's hotel, which eventually was built, by interposing patently meritless legal challenges to plaintiffs' positions before the local zoning and planning commissions, and before the courts. Accord, *Empress L.L.C. v. City and County of San Francisco*, 419 F.3d 1052 (9th Cir. 2005) (effort by low income housing advocate to prevent conversion of residential hotel to tourist use). State courts have followed suit. *Anderson Dev. Co. v. Tobias*, 116 P.3d 323 (Utah 2005). For recent illustrations of the protection afforded by *Noerr-Pennington*, see *Mercatus Group LLC v. Lake Forest Hosp.*, 695 F. Supp. 2d 811 (N.D. Ill. 2010) (no antitrust violation resulting from hard-pitched zoning battle between medical services competitors) and *Mosdos Chofetz Chaim, Inc. v. Village of Wesley Hills*, 701 F. Supp. 2d 568 (S.D.N.Y. 2010) (*Noerr-Pennington* protects villages' right to petition under the First Amendment).

3. *Private liability.* What is left of antitrust liability after *Omni*? Private party liability in land use cases is still a possibility. Consider, for example, how private party liability might arise on the facts of the *Omni* case. The Court addressed private party liability under the antitrust laws in *FTC v. Ticor Title*, 504 U.S. 621 (1992), in which six large title insurance companies were charged with price-fixing. For private entities to claim antitrust immunity under the state action doctrine, the Court held, they must show that the state "has played a substantial role in determining the specifics of supervision." The mere potential for state supervision is not enough. Nor is it enough, as in *Ticor*, that the state retained the right to reject proposed rates for thirty days, after which rates become final. Land use regulation does not meet the *Ticor* test except in states which have active state land use control programs. Thus, private antitrust liability remains a possibility. But see *Jackson Hill Road Sharon Ct., LLC v. Town Of Sharon*, 2010 U.S. Dist. LEXIS 62908 (D. Conn. 2010) (neighbors protected by *Noerr-Pennington* in opposing development).

4. *The Local Government Antitrust Act of 1984.* Even before *Omni*, this statute had taken much of the sting out of antitrust actions against local governments by prohibiting awards of damages and attorney's fees against municipalities. 15 U.S.C. § 34-36. Injunctive and declaratory judgment relief remains available. Had the antitrust laws otherwise remained an attractive source of law for plaintiffs, it is unclear whether the limitation of remedies would have diminished the incentive to bring such suits. It is likely that it would have diminished the incentive for municipalities to settle antitrust cases. (Consider the parallel to the "damages" issue in *First English*, *supra* ch. 2.)

5. *State immunity legislation.* Some states have granted their local governments an exemption from federal antitrust liability. Some of this legislation is limited to specific functions, such as public transportation and water and sewage systems, but some statutes are broad enough to cover zoning. Consider the following:

> All immunity of the state from the provisions of the Sherman Antitrust Act . . . is hereby extended to any city or city governing body acting within the scope of the grants of authority [contained in statutes granting authority to municipalities]. When acting within the scope of the grants of authority . . . a city or city governing body shall be presumed to be acting in furtherance of state policy. [N.D. Cent. Code § 40-01-22.]

Can a *state* alter the meaning of federal law this way? Remember that the state action exemption is the result of the *federal court's* construction of *Congress'* intent. There are no cases.

6. For discussion of *Omni*, see *The Supreme Court, 1990 Term: Leading Cases*, 105 Harv. L. Rev. 177, 361 (1991); Note, *Municipal Antitrust Immunity After City of Columbia v. Omni Outdoor Advertising, Inc.*, 67 Wash. L. Rev. 479 (1992). See also Sullivan, *Antitrust Regulation of Land Use: Federalism's Triumph Over Competition, The Last Fifty Years*, 3 Wash. U. J.L. & Pol'y 473 (2000). See generally P. Rohan, originally, and E. Kelley, editor, Federal Antitrust Laws in Land Use Controversies (2010).

[4.] Districting and Nonconforming Uses

A NOTE ON THE HISTORY OF NON-CONFORMING USES

The nonconforming use problem. When a zoning ordinance is enacted for the first time, undeveloped areas in the municipality can be divided into districts in which, initially at least, all new development will be required to conform to the district regulations. But this may be impossible when a zoning ordinance is enacted for the first time in an area that is already substantially or entirely developed. As one of our most perceptive zoning commentators has observed:

> One of the most troublesome problems which faces the planners and administrators of zoning ordinances is where to draw the boundary lines of use districts. The haphazard growth of our cities and villages has resulted in an inter-larding of strips of residential areas with stores, gas stations, and even heavy industrial properties. To superimpose a use map upon an established urban area must inevitably result in creating large numbers of nonconforming uses and, in many cases, in establishing dividing lines between use districts which will offend those who own property on or near the border line. [Babcock, *The Illinois Supreme Court and Zoning: A Study in Uncertainty*, 15 U. Chi. L. Rev. 87, 94 (1947).]

Whether a zoning ordinance will create nonconforming uses often becomes a strategic question that affects the drawing of district boundaries. This point is often overlooked in discussions of the nonconforming use problem, which typically start with the assumption that land use mixtures are evil and should be eliminated. Look again at the sample zoning map and accompanying text in § A, *supra*, or at the zoning map of your own community. Can you spot areas where the map makers probably drew a use district boundary line around uses that were already there?

The Standard Act approach. The drafters of the Standard State Zoning Enabling Act omitted any reference to nonconforming uses, and most of the early zoning legislation (including the pioneering New York legislation) was as silent as the Standard Act on this point. The omission of any reference to the problem of nonconforming uses was apparently largely based on political considerations; the drafters of the early enabling statutes feared that state legislatures would not enact them if they expressly authorized the elimination of nonconforming uses without payment of compensation. Thus, Bassett states that

> [d]uring the preparatory work for the zoning of Greater New York fears were constantly expressed by property owners that existing nonconforming buildings would be ousted. The demand was general that this should not be done. The Zoning Commission went as far as it could to explain that existing nonconforming uses could continue, that zoning looked to the future, and that if orderliness could be brought about in the future the nonconforming buildings would to a considerable extent be

> changed by natural causes as time went on. It was also stated by the Commission that the purpose of zoning was to stabilize and protect lawful investments and not to injure assessed valuations or existing uses. This has always been the view in New York. No steps have been taken to oust existing nonconforming uses. Consideration for investments made in accordance with the earlier laws has been one of the strong supports of zoning in that city. [E. Bassett, Zoning 113 (rev. ed. 1940).]

Whether the United States Supreme Court, in the 1920s, would have upheld zoning regulations requiring termination of lawfully established nonconforming uses without compensation is far from clear. *Hadacheck* and *Reinman, supra,* would certainly have supported termination requirements applicable to "nuisance" types of land use, but would not necessarily have supported termination requirements where the nonconforming use, though "incompatible" with surrounding land uses, was not close to being a "nuisance." Moreover, the *Pennsylvania Coal Co.* case, *supra,* could have been adduced against any termination requirement in cases where the capital value of the nonconforming use was substantial. In any case, many state courts could have been expected to take a strict view of the limits of the police power and to hold that elimination of nonconforming uses without compensation was an unconstitutional "taking" of private property. That is in fact the position that state courts generally take today. An early leading case is *Jones v. City of Los Angeles,* 295 P. 14 (Cal. 1930).

The modern approaches to non-conforming uses. Many states prohibit or limit the termination of nonconforming uses. E.g., Ky. Rev. Stat. § 100.253; Utah Code Ann. § 10-9-408. When a state's zoning enabling act was silent on the subject of nonconforming uses, the early zoning ordinances almost invariably provided expressly that lawfully established nonconforming uses might continue, although many ordinances contained a wide variety of restrictive regulations which were meant to hasten their disappearance. Such provisions are still a feature of almost all local zoning ordinances. Typically, they prohibit or severely restrict the physical extension of nonconforming uses, impose limitations on the repair, alteration, or reconstruction of nonconforming structures, and prohibit the resumption of nonconforming uses after "abandonment" or "discontinuance." See the Model Zoning Ordinance, *supra.*

Two competing philosophies dominate the cases on the validity of these restrictions. One, following the views of the City Beautiful reformers of the early 20th century, takes an expansive view of the police power to favor the gradual elimination of nonconforming uses for the public welfare. The other is more restrictive and views restrictions on nonconforming uses as a "taking" of rights vested under the zoning ordinance. Which view predominates in the following case?

CONFORTI v. CITY OF MANCHESTER

677 A.2d 147 (N.H. 1996)

HORTON, J. The plaintiff, Andrew Conforti, and the intervenors, Orion Theatre, Inc. and Robert A. Howe, appeal a ruling of the Superior Court (O'Neill, J.) that the Zoning Board of Adjustment (ZBA) of the City of Manchester (city) correctly concluded that the city zoning ordinance did not permit live entertainment on the property owned by the plaintiff and leased to the intervenors, and that live entertainment was not a preexisting, nonconforming use of the property, which, at the time of enactment of the ordinance, was used only as a movie theater. We affirm.

The plaintiff owns the Empire Theater in Manchester. The theater, erected as a movie house in 1912, is located in what is now a B-1 zoning district. The plaintiff leased the property to Orion Theatre, Inc., who in turn subleased it to Robert Howe. In 1990, the city granted a building permit for interior renovations of the theater, recognizing that, although the use of property as a movie theater was not allowed in a B-1 zoning district, the use of the Empire Theater to show movies was a preexisting, nonconforming use.

Following the 1990 renovations, Howe began arranging for live concerts to be performed at the Empire Theater. Approximately sixty live shows, mostly rock concerts, were performed before the city buildings department notified the plaintiff that use of the theater for purposes other than showing movies violated the city zoning ordinance. The plaintiff appealed this decision to the ZBA, which denied both his appeal and motion for a rehearing. Pursuant to RSA 677:4 (1986) (amended 1994), the plaintiff appealed to superior court. Orion Theatre, Inc. and Howe subsequently intervened in this action. The trial court upheld the ZBA's decision, and this appeal followed. . . .

[The court concluded that the ordinance prohibited live concerts. — Eds.]

The plaintiff and intervenors next contend that the trial court erred in concluding that holding live performances at the Empire Theater is an expansion of a preexisting, nonconforming use. We "will uphold the decision of the superior court unless that decision is not supported by the evidence or is legally erroneous." *Ray's Stateline Market v. Town of Pelham*, 665 A.2d 1068, 1071 (N.H. 1995) (quotation omitted). A zoning ordinance does not apply to structures or uses of the property that existed at the time the ordinance was enacted. *See* RSA 674:19 (1986). An ordinance, however, "shall apply to any alteration of a building for use for a purpose or in a manner which is substantially different from the use to which it was put before alteration." *Id.*

"The policy of zoning law is to carefully limit the enlargement and extension of nonconforming uses. The ultimate purpose of zoning regulations contemplates that nonconforming uses should be reduced to conformity as completely and rapidly as possible." *New London Land Use Assoc. v. New London Zoning Board*, 543 A.2d 1385, 1389 (N.H. 1988) (citations, quotation, brackets, and ellipses omitted). "The burden of establishing that the use in question is fundamentally the same use and not a new and impermissible one is on the party asserting it." *New London v. Leskiewicz*, 272 A.2d 856, 860 (N.H. 1970).

> In deciding whether the particular activity is within the scope of the established or acquired nonconforming use consideration may be given to, among others, the following factors: (1) to what extent does the use in question reflect the nature and purpose of the prevailing nonconforming use; (2) is it merely a different manner of utilizing the same use or does it constitute a use different in character, nature and kind; (3) does this use have a substantially different effect on the neighborhood. [272 A.2d at 860.]

The question in this case, therefore, is whether the trial court erred in concluding that the use of the Empire Theater for live performances is substantially different in character, nature, or kind than the use of the theater to show movies. *See* RSA 674:19. The plaintiff argues that the purpose of the Empire Theater is to provide entertainment in a theater setting. The trial court rejected this broad characterization of the theater's purpose. In order to determine the nature of the facility's permissible nonconforming use, we must look to the use of the property at the time the ordinance giving rise to the nonconforming use was enacted. *See Ray's Stateline Market*, 665 A.2d at 1071. The ordinance at issue was adopted in 1965. Although live music accompanied the early silent movies, with the introduction of the "talkies," the performance of live music at the Empire Theater largely ended in the 1950s. The record contains no evidence that the Empire Theater was used for any purpose other than to show movies at the time the ordinance was enacted. The plaintiff cannot establish a permitted expansion of a nonconforming use by simply showing that the new use is "generically the same as the old." 1 Anderson's American Law of Zoning § 6.37, at 603 (K. Young ed., 4th ed. 1995). Such an approach would run counter to the policy of zoning law, which is "to carefully limit the enlargement and extension of nonconforming uses." *New London Land Use Assoc.*, 543 A.2d at 1389.

Whether a different use of the property is a substantial change in the nature or purpose of the nonconforming use turns on the facts and circumstances of the particular case. *See Town of Hampton v. Brust*, 446 A.2d 458, 461 (N.H. 1982). The record supports the trial court's conclusion that live entertainment differs substantially from showing movies. There was testimony that when bands perform live at the theater they bring their own lighting and occasionally sound equipment. There was also evidence that the noise levels were higher during live performances than when movies were shown. In fact, the buildings department initially was made aware that live music was being performed at the theater by complaints of the noise during the concerts. Accordingly, we conclude that the trial court's decision was neither unsupported by the evidence nor legally erroneous. *See Ray's Stateline Market*, 665 A.2d at 1072.

Affirmed.

NOTES AND QUESTIONS

1. *Expansion and change of nonconforming use.* Expansion and change in nonconforming businesses occur all the time. The question is whether this results in a loss of nonconforming use status. How would you state the "test" of the principal case? Does the court give you a workable basis for advising a client that an expansion or change of a nonconforming use is or is not legal? (Note that in *Conforti*, the theater owners began offering live entertainment soon after renovating the building, presumably with this plan in mind.) Suppose, instead of switching to live entertainment, the Empire Theater now proposes to offer adult movies. Compare *Trip Assoc. v. Mayor and Council*, 824 A.2d 977 (Md. App. 2003) (nonconforming adult entertainment club; expansion of hours not permitted). See also *Severance v. Town of Epsom*, 923 A.2d 1057 (N.H. 2007), holding that simply using a seasonal structure for year-round use did not impermissibly expand the property's nonconforming use. The court noted that the actual footprint of the building had not changed and held that merely increasing the amount or intensity of the nonconforming use did not unlawfully expand that use. Why is this case different from the principal case?

In *Belleville v. Parrillo's, Inc.*, 416 A.2d 388 (N.J. 1980), a nonconforming restaurant was located in a residential zone. The facts were described by the trial court as follows:

> The business was formerly advertised as a restaurant; it is now advertised as a "disco". It was formerly operated every day and now it is open but one day and three evenings. The primary use of the dance hall was incidental to dining; now it is the primary use. The music was formerly provided by live bands and now it is recorded and operated by a so-called "disc-jockey" . . . . Formerly there was but one bar; now there are several.

> During the course of the testimony it was admitted that the business is operated as a "disco". Normal lighting in the premises was altered to psychedelic lighting, colored and/or revolving, together with mirrored lighting. The premises were crowded and there were long lines waiting to enter. There are now fewer tables than the prior use required and on one occasion there were no tables. The music was extremely loud and the premises can accommodate 431 persons legally. There have been numerous complaints from residents adjacent to the area. During the course of the testimony "disco" dancing was described by the owners as dancing by "kids" who "don't hold each other close". The bulk of the prior business was food catering; now there is none. The foods primarily served at the present time are "hamburgers" and "cheeseburgers", although there are other selections available to people who might come in earlier than the "disco" starting time. [416 A.2d at 390–91.]

The change from restaurant to "disco" was disallowed. Note that each element of the former legal nonconforming use (food service, dancing, music) was continued in the new use. The court found error in a lower court's separate review of each component of the old and new operation. "The analysis . . . should have been qualitative. Put differently, the focus in cases such as this must be on the quality, character and intensity of the use, viewed in their totality and with regard to their overall effect on the neighborhood and the zoning plan." 416 A.2d at 390. Is this the same standard as used by the New Hampshire court in the principal case? How important is it, in any of the cases described here, that the expansion or change was to a use that had more nuisance-like qualities? Would the New Jersey court have been as skeptical if the restaurant had been converted to a ballroom dancing establishment for senior citizens who, unlike the "kids" in *Parrillo*'s, "hold each other close"?

Sometimes, it is difficult to determine if a change in use is an expansion which may affect the standard for decision making. As the court concluded in *Saadala v. E. Brunswick Zoning Bd.*, 991 A.2d 866 (N.J. App. Div. 2010):

> This appeal requires us to determine whether an application for a use variance for establishment of a combined convenience store and retail gasoline station, to replace two separate nonconforming uses for a convenience store and gasoline station, constitutes an expansion of a nonconforming use, which is subject to the more liberal standards for a use variance set forth in Burbridge v. Township of Mine Hill, [117 N.J. 376, 568 A.2d 527 (1990)], rather than the restrictive standards applicable to a use variance for creation of a new use set forth in Medici v. BPR Co. We conclude that such a redevelopment plan constitutes the creation of a new use, which is subject to the Medici standards, and that those standards were not satisfied in this case.

A change of use within a building also can present problems. Compare *DiBlasi v. Zoning Bd. of Appeals*, 624 A.2d 372 (Conn. 1993) (change of use to probation office does not change nonconforming status), with *Philm Corp. v. Washington Township*, 638 A.2d 388 (Pa. Commw. 1994) (addition of go-go dancers to restaurant changes nonconforming status). Physical changes may lead to a loss of nonconforming use status. An example is the addition of an automated car wash to a nonconforming filling station. *Anderson v. Board of Adjustment*, 931 P.2d 517 (Colo. App. 1996). *Baxter v. City of Preston*, 768 P.2d 1340 (Idaho 1989), provides an extensive review of the case law on the change and expansion of nonconforming uses and adopts a flexible, case-by-case approach in holding that a nonconforming use of land for grazing livestock could not be converted to a year-round feed lot. Often, these controversies have an overlay of abandonment or discontinuance, discussed below. See *Herres v. Harrison Twp. Bd.*

of Trustees, 2010 Ohio 3909 (Ohio Ct. App. 2010) (upheld township enforcement action where nonconforming use had been abandoned and new use established).

2. *Physical expansion or change.* The cases in Note 1 involve change of use within an existing building. Problems can also arise when it is the structure, rather than the use, that undergoes transformation. In *Parrillo's*, for instance, suppose the cuisine at the original nonconforming restaurant became so popular that the "mom'n pop" proprietors proposed to build a new wing and triple the number of tables? See *Bjorklund v. Zoning Bd.*, 878 N.E.2d 915 (Mass. 2008) (increasing the size of the house fivefold increases the nonconforming nature of the building; court noted that many municipalities do not appreciate the "mansionization" trend). *City of Marion v. Rapp*, 655 N.W.2d 88 (S.D. 2002) (replacing nonconforming mobile home with larger one not allowed). Compare *Conway v. City of Greenville*, 173 S.E.2d 648 (S.C. 1970) (prior operation of a construction business justified the use of the entire property for construction of a shopping center). Contra *Stuckman v. Kosciusko County Bd. of Zoning Appeals*, 506 N.E.2d 1079 (Ind. 1987) (nonconforming automobile graveyard; clearing and smoothing additional land to increase the number of cars stored disallowed). Or suppose the owner of a building that is nonconforming because it violates setback lines proposes to expand vertically by adding an additional floor or floors? Compare *Nettleton v. Zoning Bd. of Adjustment*, 828 A.2d 1033 (Pa. 2003) (two-floor addition permitted), with *Munroe v. Zoning Bd. of Appeals*, 818 A.2d 72 (Conn. App. 2003) (disallowed).

Note how the rules on change and expansion of nonconforming uses can "solve" the nonconforming use problem that worried the drafters of the SSZEA. If the choice is between continuing a nonconforming use that cannot be changed or expanded, or relinquishing nonconforming status to better exploit the property, this "voluntary" choice eliminates any takings claim. This can be considered an alternative to amortization, which is considered *infra*.

3. *Repair, alteration and reconstruction.* The relationship between the zoning ordinance, governing land use, and building codes, governing safety, can be difficult. In *In re O'Neal*, 92 S.E.2d 189 (N.C. 1956), the nonconforming use was a small nursing home. Its owners were notified that the building must be torn down because it was not fireproof and because it violated the institutional provisions of the building code. The owners wished to reconstruct a fireproof nursing home on their premises. The court noted that the new home could not exceed the capacity of the old, but held that the applicants were entitled to rebuild their building. The protection of preexisting "lawful" uses referred to the zoning ordinance and not the building code, and protected any use that was lawful under the zoning regulations. A reasonable construction of the zoning regulations required that a balance be struck between the impairment of neighborhood character and the restriction of an existing use of land by means of new regulations. This ordinance did not contain a prohibition on "structural alterations" and, in addition, the new construction was imposed involuntarily under the building code. Accord *Money v. Zoning Hearing Bd.*, 755 A.2d 732 (Pa. Commw. 2000) (deteriorated garage/chicken coop).

In *Granger v. Board of Adjustment*, 44 N.W.2d 399 (Iowa 1950), a manufacturer of burial vaults was allowed to replace the brick and frame walls and roof of his nonconforming building with concrete and steel. The court held that the work could be categorized as a reasonable repair rather than as a structural alteration. Contra *Selligman v. Von Allmen Bros.*, 179 S.W.2d 207 (Ky. 1944). Ky. Rev. Stat. § 100.253 restricts the enlargement or extension of nonconforming use "beyond the scope and area of its operation at the time of the regulation." Drawing a line between what is a repair and what is an alteration or replacement where the local regulations make such a distinction can be difficult. See how this conflict played out in *Players Pizza & Pub, LLP v. City of Oshkosh*, 788 N.W.2d 384 (Wis. Ct. App. 2010) (reconstruction of a nonconforming asphalt parking lot is a permitted repair). See also, *Lamar Outdoor Advertising-Lakeland v. Florida Department of Transportation*, 17 So. 3d 799 (Fl. Dist. Ct. 2009) (Florida Department of Transportation did not have the authority to revoke the license for a sign when the owner increased its height above ground).

4. *Abandonment and discontinuance.* Nonconforming uses are compatible with the overall scheme of zoning because, in theory, they will gradually disappear over time and be replaced by conforming uses. To achieve this end, most zoning ordinances (and some enabling statutes) provide that once discontinued, a nonconforming use may not be resumed, but this leads to considerable problems of interpretation. If the discontinuance is not voluntary on the owner's part (if it occurs because of a fire or storm, for instance), constitutional problems may arise. See, e.g., *Bruce L. Rothrock Charitable Foundation v. Zoning Hear'g Bd.*, 651 A.2d 587 (Pa. Comm. 1994). To avoid problems, most ordinances are interpreted to require voluntariness, i.e., an intent to abandon accompanied by some overt act of abandonment. See, e.g., *Town of West Greenwich v. A. Cardi Realty Assoc.*, 786 A.2d 354 (R.I. 2001); *City of Myrtle Beach v. Jual P. Corp.*, 543 S.E.2d 538 (S.C. 2001); *City of University Place v. McGuire*, 30 P.3d 453 (Wash. 2001). But see *Estate of Cuomo v. Rush*, 708 N.Y.S.2d 695 (App. Div. 2000) (opening nightclub for one night out of the year does not prevent abandonment). *Boles v. City of Chattanooga*, 892 S.W.2d 416 (Tenn. App. 1994), reviews the cases, and *Berkeley Square Ass'n, Inc. v. Zoning Bd. of Adjustment*, 981 A.2d 127 (N.J. App. Div. 2009), explains the burden of proof.

Some ordinances, however, will presume an intent to abandon from a failure to exercise a nonconforming use; under these provisions, mere nonuse for the stated period of time is sufficient to terminate the nonconforming use. See, e.g., *Miller v. City of Bainbridge Island*, 43 P.3d 1250 (Wash. App. 2002); *Snake River Brewing Co. v. Town of Jackson*, 39 P.3d 397 (Wyo. 2002). Sometimes a presumptive time period, often very short, is established. See, e.g., *McKenzie v. Town of Eaton*, 917 A.2d 193 (N.H. 2007) (one year, held constitutional).

Close questions abound. See, e.g., *Ansley House, Inc. v. City of Atlanta*, 397 S.E.2d 419 (Ga. 1990) (temporary nonuse because of revocation of prior owner's rooming house license insufficient to constitute abandonment); *Cizek v. Concerned Citizens of Eagle River Valley*, 41 P.3d 140 (Alaska 2002) (abandonment found despite sporadic use of airport). But see *Caster v. West Valley City*, 29 P.3d 22 (Utah App. 2001) (nonconforming auto junk yard; storage of 5 or 6 vehicles for past 10–15 years constitutes continuing use). The court in *State ex rel. Eberts v. Inland Prods.*, 2010 Ohio 4510, 2010 Ohio App. LEXIS 3810 (Ohio Ct. App. 2010), concluded that an accessory or ancillary use may need to be considered as part of the overall use in determining abandonment.

Some statutes deal with these problems. Neb. Rev. Stat. § 19-904.01 (nonconforming use terminates if "discontinued" for 12 months); R.I. Gen. Laws § 45-24-39 (overt act or failure to act required; involuntary interruption such as by fire or catastrophe does not terminate nonconforming use).

Nonconforming signs will more easily disappear if the municipality can remove them once a business the nonconforming sign advertised has closed. The question is whether the abandonment of the business is an abandonment of the nonconforming sign. See *Camara v. Board of Adjustment*, 570 A.2d 1012 (N.J. App. Div. 1990) (holding yes), though the cases are divided. Compare contra, *Motel 6 Operating Ltd. Partnership v. City of Flagstaff*, 991 P.2d 272

(Ariz. App. 1999) (business did not close but wanted to replace nonconforming signs with new sign faces). See Strauss & Geise, *Elimination of Nonconformities: The Case for Voluntary Discontinuance*, 25 Urb. Law. 159 (1993).

5. *Change of ownership or development of land.* It is generally held that nonconforming uses "run with the land" and therefore are unaffected by a change in ownership. This rule undercuts the premise that nonconforming uses will disappear over time; in some circumstances it may actually enhance the staying power of the nonconforming use, because the nonconforming use is legally protected against market competition from new entrants in the same business or activity, and that degree of monopoly power has value than can be transferred from owner to owner.

In *Village of Valatie v. Smith*, 632 N.E.2d 1264 (N.Y. 1994), the New York court held that the municipality could, by ordinance, terminate the nonconforming use of mobile homes when there is a change of ownership. The owner argued (correctly) that this approach had nothing to do with recouping her financial investment in the mobile home, but the court found that it was not irrational for the village to consider the nonfinancial interests of individual owners of nonconforming uses, particularly in the case of residential uses where occupying the property may be more important to the owner than its investment value. Balancing the interests of the nonconforming user with those of the public, the court emphasized that the owner's interest in possession was eliminated by a decision to sell. It also held that the ordinance did not violate the principle that zoning can only regulate land use, not ownership, so long as an individual owner was not singled out for different treatment. (The Valatie ordinance applied to six mobile homes.) The court cited, but did not discuss, the contrary case of *O'Connor v. City of Moscow*, 202 P.2d 401 (Idaho 1949). See the recent typical decision in *City of Clear Lake v. Kramer*, 2010 Iowa App. LEXIS 865 (Iowa Ct. App. 2010) (nonconforming use runs with the land; pasture use dating back to 1936 may continue after a change in ownership).

Outdoor Systems, Inc. v. City of Mesa, 997 F.2d 604 (9th Cir. 1993), upheld ordinances requiring the removal of nonconforming signs when vacant land is developed. The court held there was a "simple and clear" nexus between this requirement and the interest of the cities in removing nonconforming signs. Accord, *Adams Outdoor Adv., L.P. v. Zoning Hearing Bd.*, 909 A.2d 469 (Pa. Commw. 2006).

The most controversial technique for eliminating nonconforming uses and structures is "amortization" — a technique considered in the next principal case.

CITY OF LOS ANGELES v. GAGE

127 Cal. App. 2d 442, 274 P.2d 34 (1954)

VALLEE, JUSTICE:

. . . In 1930 Gage acquired adjoining lots 220 and 221 located on Cochran Avenue in Los Angeles. He constructed a two-family residential building on lot 221 and rented the upper half solely for residential purposes. He established a wholesale and retail plumbing supply business on the property. He used a room in the lower half of the residential building on lot 221 as the office for the conduct of the business, and the rest of the lower half for residential purposes for himself and his family; he used a garage on lot 221 for the storage of plumbing supplies and materials; and he constructed and used racks, bins, and stalls for the storage of such supplies and materials on lot 220. [Gage's business became non-conforming in 1941 when the zoning was changed to residential. In 1946, Ordinance 90,500 was passed. As applied to Gage's property, it required discontinuance of his non-conforming use within five years. On the City's suit to enjoin further operation of his business, Gage contended that the ordinance was unconstitutional.]

[The trial court found that] the business conducted by Gage on the property has produced a gross revenue varying between $125,000 and $350,000 a year. If he is required to abandon the use of the property for his business, he will be put to the following expenses: "(1) The value of a suitable site for the conduct of its business would be about $10,000; which would be offset by the value of $7,500 of the lot now used. (2) The cost incident to removing of supplies to another location and construction of the necessary racks, sheds, bins and stalls which would be about $2,500. (3) The cost necessary to expend to advertise a new location. (4) The risk of a gain or a loss of business while moving, and the cost necessary to reestablish the business at a new location, the amount of which is uncertain."

The noise and disturbance caused by the loading and unloading of supplies, trucking, and the going and coming of workmen in connection with the operation of a plumbing business with an open storage yard is greater than the noise and disturbance that is normal in a district used solely for residential purposes. . . .

The court concluded: Gage became vested with the right to use the property for the purpose that it was used; insofar as the Los Angeles Municipal Code purports to require the abandonment of the use of the building on Lot 221 as an office for the plumbing and plumbing supply business or the use of Lot 220 for the open storage of plumbing supplies in the manner that it has been and is being used by Gage, it is void and of no legal effect . . . in that it deprives him of a vested right to use the property for the purpose it has been used continuously since 1930 and deprives him of property without due process of law. Judgment was that plaintiff take nothing. Plaintiff appeals . . . .

The right of a city council, in the exercise of the police power, to regulate or, in proper cases, to prohibit the conduct of a given business, is not limited by the fact that the value of investments made in the business prior to any legislative actions will be greatly diminished. A business which, when established, was entirely unobjectionable, may, by the growth or change in the character of the neighborhood, become a source of danger to the public health, morals, safety, or general welfare of those who have come to be occupants of the surrounding territory. . . .

No case seems to have been decided in this state squarely involving the precise question presented in the case at bar. Until recently zoning ordinances have made no provision for any systematic and comprehensive elimination of the nonconforming use. The expectation seems to have been that existing nonconforming uses would be of little consequence and that they would eventually disappear. It is said that the fundamental problem facing zoning is the inability to eliminate the nonconforming use. The general purpose of present-day zoning ordinances is to eventually end all nonconforming uses. There is a growing tendency to guard against the indefinite continuance of nonconforming uses by providing for their liquidation within a prescribed period. It is said, "The only positive method of getting rid of nonconforming uses yet devised is to amortize a nonconforming building. That is, to determine the normal useful remaining life of the building and prohibit the owner from maintaining it after the expiration of that time." Crolly and Norton, *Termination of Nonconforming Uses*, 62 Zoning Bulletin 1, Regional Plan Ass'n, June 1952. . . .

The theory in zoning is that each district is an appropriate area for the location of the uses which the zone plan permits in that area, and that the existence or entrance of other uses will tend to impair the development and stability of the area for the appropriate uses. . . . The presence of any nonconforming use endangers the benefits to be derived from a comprehensive zoning plan. Having the undoubted power to establish residential districts, the legislative body has the power to make such classification really effective by adopting such reasonable regulations as would be conducive to the welfare, health, and safety of those desiring to live in such district and enjoy the benefits thereof. There would be no object in creating a residential district unless there were to be secured to those dwelling therein the advantages which are ordinarily considered the benefits of such residence. It would seem to be the logical and reasonable method of approach to place a time limit upon the continuance of existing nonconforming uses, commensurate with the investment involved and based on the nature of the use; and in cases of nonconforming structures, on their character, age, and other relevant factors.

Exercise of the police power frequently impairs rights in property because the exercise of those rights is detrimental to the public interest. Every zoning ordinance effects some impairment of vested rights either by restricting prospective uses or by prohibiting the continuation of existing uses, because it affects property already owned by individuals at the time of its enactment. In essence there is no distinction between requiring the discontinuance of a nonconforming use within a reasonable period and provisions which deny the right to add to or extend or enlarge an existing nonconforming use, or which deny the right to substitute new buildings for those devoted to an existing nonconforming use — all of which have been held to be valid exercises of the police power.

The distinction between an ordinance restricting future uses and one requiring the termination of present uses within a reasonable period of time is merely one of degree, and constitutionality depends on the relative importance to be given to the public gain and to the private loss. Zoning as it affects every piece of property is to some extent retroactive in that it applies to property already owned at the time of the effective date of the ordinance. The elimination of existing uses within a reasonable time does not amount to a taking of property nor does it necessarily restrict the use of property so that it cannot be used for any reasonable purpose. Use of a reasonable amortization scheme provides an equitable means of reconciliation of the conflicting interests in satisfaction of due process requirements. As a method of eliminating existing nonconforming uses it allows the owner of the nonconforming use, by affording an opportunity to make new plans, at least partially to offset any loss he might suffer. The loss he suffers, if any, is spread out over a period of years, and he enjoys a monopolistic position by virtue of the zoning ordinance as long as he remains. If the amortization period is reasonable the loss to the owner may be small when compared with the benefit to the public. Nonconforming uses will eventually be eliminated. A legislative body may well conclude that the beneficial effect on the community of the eventual elimination of all nonconforming uses by a reasonable amortization plan more than offsets individual losses.

We have no doubt that Ordinance 90,500, in compelling the discontinuance of the use of defendants' property for a wholesale and retail plumbing and plumbing supply business, and for the open storage of plumbing supplies within five years after its passage, is a valid exercise of the police power. Lots 220 and 221 are several blocks from a business center and it appears that they are not within any reasonable or logical extension of such a center. The ordinance does not prevent the operation of defendants' business; it merely restricts its location. Discontinuance of the nonconforming use requires only that Gage move his plumbing business to property that is zoned for it. Such property can be found within a half mile of Gage's property. The cost of moving is $5,000, or less than 1% of Gage's minimum gross business for five years, or less than half of 1% of the mean of his gross business for five years. He has had eight years within which to move. The property is usable for residential purpose. Since 1930 lot 221 has been used for residential purposes. All of the land within 500 feet of Gage's property is now improved and used for such purposes. Lot 220, now unimproved, can be improved for the same purposes.

We think it apparent that none of the agreed facts and none of the ultimate facts found by the court justify the conclusion that Ordinance 90,500, as applied to Gage's property, is clearly arbitrary or unreasonable, or has no substantial relation to the public's health, safety, morals, or general welfare, or that it is an unconstitutional impairment of his property rights. . . .

The judgment is reversed. . . .

NOTES AND QUESTIONS

1. *Constitutional issues. Gage* held that a zoning ordinance that amortizes nonconforming uses is facially constitutional, and also held the amortization period constitutional as applied to the property. An overwhelming majority of the courts now uphold amortization as a constitutional zoning technique, although the courts so holding do not always accept the *Gage* rationale that the distinction between prospective zoning and elimination of lawfully established nonconforming uses is only a matter of degree. See D. Mandelker, Land Use Law § 5.85 n.6 (5th ed. 2003) (citing cases). Are these due process or taking cases? To the extent that taking law is involved, is *Lucas* or *Penn Central* the relevant starting point?

Some courts take a middle ground and hold amortization constitutional only if applied to nonconforming uses that constitute nuisances. E.g., *Loundsbury v. City of Keene*, 453 A.2d 1278 (N.H. 1982); *Northern Ohio Sign Contrs. Ass'n v. City of Lakewood*, 513 N.E.2d 324 (Ohio 1987). See also *Stoner McCray Sys. v. City of Des Moines*, 78 N.W.2d 843 (Iowa 1956) (indicating it would uphold amortization if period reasonable and nonconforming use endangered health, safety and welfare). *Sed quaere* why nonconforming uses that amount to nuisances or endanger health and safety cannot be summarily terminated, without allowing any "amortization" period. In Missouri, the supreme court held that "amortization" is unconstitutional as applied to open land storage uses, but later held that "amortization" of billboards was constitutional. *Hoffmann v. Kinealy*, 389 S.W.2d 745 (Mo. 1965) (open land storage); *University City v. Diveley Auto Body Co.*, 417 S.W.2d 107 (Mo. 1967). For a recent case holding that a nuisance finding is not required, see *Cioppa v. Apostol*, 755 N.Y.S.2d 458 (App. Div. 2003) ("Bottoms Up" Tavern; 30-day amortization period "quite contracted" but extensions may be granted).

2. *Unconstitutional.* In *Harbison v. City of Buffalo*, 152 N.E.2d 42 (N.Y. 1958), where two judges embraced the "amortization" theory but the other two judges who joined to make up a majority only concurred in the result, Judge Van Voorhis, in dissent, said:

> This theory [amortization] to justify extinguishing nonconforming uses means less the more one thinks about it. . . . [T]he term "amortization," as thus employed, has not the same meaning which it carries in law or accounting. . . . It is just a catch phrase, and the reasoning is reduced to argument by metaphor. Not only has no effort been made in the reported cases . . . to determine what is the useful life of the structure, but almost all were decided under ordinances or statutes which prescribe the same

> time limit for many different kinds of improvements. This demonstrates that it is not attempted to measure the life of the particular building or type of building, and that the word "amortization" is used as an empty shibboleth. . . . [*Id.* at 54.]

This view, which is distinctly the minority position, has nonetheless gained some prominent adherents in recent years, with both Georgia and Pennsylvania now holding that amortization is an unconstitutional zoning technique. *Lamar Advertising of South Georgia, Inc. v. Albany*, 389 S.E.2d 216 (Ga. 1990); *PA Northwest Distribs., Inc. v. Zoning Hearing Board*, 584 A.2d 1372 (Pa. 1991). These courts took the absolutist position that property is property and cannot be "taken" without compensation. As the Pennsylvania court said, "[i]t is clear that if we were to permit the amortization of nonconforming uses in this Commonwealth, any use could be amortized out of existence without just compensation." See J. Borden, Note, *Derailing Penn Central: A Post-Lingle, Cost-Basis Approach to Regulatory Takings*, 78 Geo. Wash. L. Rev. 870 (June, 2010).

3. *The amortization period.* The courts rarely make it clear just what is being "amortized" when they consider the validity of zoning ordinance provisions authorizing the "amortization" of nonconforming uses. This makes it difficult for courts to formulate a test for determining the reasonableness of "amortization" provisions. Some zoning ordinances set out the factors to be considered in determining the length of the "amortization" period. *County of San Diego v. 1560 N. Magnolia Ave., LLC*, 2009 Cal. App. Unpub. LEXIS 1198 (Cal. Ct. App. 2009) (3½-year amortization period).

In *Metromedia, Inc. v. City of San Diego*, 610 P.2d 407 (Cal. 1980), *rev'd on other grounds*, 453 U.S. 490 (1981), the court upheld a provision requiring "amortization" of nonconforming signs in one to four years, depending on the "adjusted market value" of a particular sign, defined as the sign's original cost less ten percent of the original cost for each year the sign was in place prior to the effective date of the ordinance. But what is the rational basis for assuming that the market value of all signs decreased at the rate of ten percent of original cost per year?

In *Metromedia, supra*, the court said that the constitutionality of "amortization" provisions as applied to nonconforming structures depends in part on facts peculiar to particular structures, including, in the case of billboards, "the cost of the billboard, its depreciated value, remaining useful life, the length and remaining term of the lease under which it is maintained, and the harm to the public if the structure remains standing beyond the prescribed amortization period." The highest New York court approved similar factors in *Modjeska Sign Studios, Inc. v. Berle*, 373 N.E.2d 255 (N.Y. 1977), where the court said:

> Whether an amortization period is reasonable is a question that must be answered in the light of the facts of each particular case. Certainly, a critical factor is the length of the amortization period in relation to the investment. Similarly, another factor considered significant by some courts is the nature of the nonconforming activity prohibited; generally a shorter period may be provided for a nonconforming use as opposed to a nonconforming structure. The critical question, however, . . . is whether the public gain achieved by the exercise of the police power outweighs the private loss suffered by the owners of nonconforming uses. While an owner need not be given that period of time necessary to recoup his investment entirely, the amortization period should not be so short as to result in a substantial loss. In determining what constitutes a substantial loss, the court should look to, for example, such factors as: initial capital investment, investment realization to date, life expectancy of the investment, and the existence or nonexistence of a lease obligation as well as a

contingency clause permitting termination of the lease. Generally, most regulations requiring the removal of nonconforming billboards and providing a reasonable amortization period should pass constitutional muster. [*Id.* at 262.]

Courts sometimes place emphasis on particular factors, such as whether the nonconforming use has been amortized for tax purposes. *National Adv. Co. v. Monterey County*, 464 P.2d 33 (Cal. 1970) (billboards deemed "fully amortized" on basis of Internal Revenue Service rules as to "amortization" for tax purposes). Another question is whether courts should consider whether a nonconforming use has remaining physical life. See *La Mesa v. Tweed & Gambrell Planing Mill*, 304 P.2d 803 (Cal. App. 1957) (5-year "amortization" period invalid as applied to 20-year-old building with remaining useful life of 21 years). However, in *AVR, Inc. v. City of St. Louis Park*, 585 N.W.2d 411 (Minn. App. 1998), the court refused to consider whether a nonconforming cement mixing plant had a remaining "economic" life because its owners had recovered 560% on their investment and it was fully depreciated for tax purposes. Otherwise, the court said, the owner of a nonconforming use could extend its life by replacements or improvements. Accord, e.g., *City of University Park v. Benners*, 485 S.W.2d 773, 777 (Tex. 1972).

4. *Amortization post-Lucas.* The *Metromedia* approach survived the 1987 Supreme Court takings trilogy, but the analysis can be complicated. For example, in *Outdoor Graphics v. City of Burlington*, 103 F.3d 690 (8th Cir. 1996), the court upheld a five-year amortization period for a nonconforming sign. It first considered plaintiff's argument that there was a per se taking under *Lucas*. Plaintiff owned the land that the sign was on, and a real estate appraiser testified that because of the irregular shape of the parcels, they would be marketable only to adjacent landowners for a fraction of their value as billboard sites. Instead of deciding whether this amounted to a total deprivation of use, however, the Eighth Circuit concluded that the owner had no "legitimate investment backed expectations" of billboard use because the sites had been purchased after the billboard restrictions were put in place. But see the Supreme Court's decision in *Palazzolo*, reprinted *supra*, Chapter 2, holding that acquisition of land after enactment of a restriction does not per se eliminate investment-backed expectations. The court then proceeded under *Penn Central* to "weigh[] such factors as whether the land has any other economic use, the depreciation and life expectancy of the billboards, the income from the billboards during the amortization or grace period, the salvage value of the billboards and whether any amortization period is reasonable." See also *Tahoe-Sierra*, *supra* Chapter 2.

In *Georgia Outdoor Advertising, Inc. v. City of Waynesville (II)*, 900 F.2d 783 (4th Cir. 1990), the court attempted to reconcile amortization and takings principles by holding that an amortization clause neither validates nor invalidates a removal ordinance, but is merely one factor to consider in deciding whether there is a taking; the court remanded for trial, noting that summary judgment is rarely proper in such a case.

5. *Statutory authority.* Statutory authority is another major problem. Most courts have found an implied authority to amortize when express authority is not provided. See *Mayor & Council v. Rollins Outdoor Adv., Inc.*, 475 A.2d 355 (Del. 1975). Many states now prohibit amortization for billboards located on federal highways to comply with provisions in the federal Highway Beautification Act that require compensation for their removal. See Chapter 9. Other states prohibit amortization for all nonconforming uses. See Minn. Stat. Ann. § 394.21(1a), adopted in reaction to the *AVR* case, *supra*, which exempts from protection "adults-only bookstores, adults-only theaters, or similar adults-only businesses."

The American Planning Association's Growing Smart Legislative Guidebook, 2002 Edition at pp. 8-118 through 8-123, surveys state statutes and caselaw, noting that there is specific statutory authorization for amortization in only eight states, although others find authority in other ways. The APA's model legislation authorizes amortization in a zoning ordinance. *Id.* § 8-502(4) (2000). It does not attempt to specify the factors that should govern amortization but provides two alternative methods. A zoning ordinance may "state a period of time after which nonconforming land uses or structures, or designated classes of nonconforming land uses or structures, must terminate." In the alternative, it may provide "criteria" that the local planning or code enforcement agency "may apply to provide a period of time after which a nonconforming land use or structure must terminate." Do you see the advantage of this approach? The *AVR* case, *supra*, held that the adoption of an amortization period by applying criteria was not a quasi-judicial action.

The model legislation also authorizes amortization only if a local government adopts a comprehensive plan and amortization "implements an express policy contained in the plan." § 8-502(5). The requirement will compel municipalities to decide where amortization can be useful, and should support its constitutionality by specifying the benefits that amortization can bring. The APA model also "highly recommends," but does not require, that municipalities prepare an inventory of nonconforming uses as a basis for registration and regulation of such uses. *Id.* § 8-502(1). Such an inventory would be useful were some of the techniques discussed in the Note on Alternative Strategies for Eliminating Nonconforming Uses, *infra*, to be adopted.

6. *Does amortization work?* In 1971, the American Society of Planning Officials polled its membership to determine the extent to which amortization was being used to eliminate nonconforming uses. Out of 489 cities and counties responding, 159 reported that they had zoning ordinances providing for amortization, but only 27 municipalities reported use of the amortization technique against buildings. The report indicated that amortization has most frequently been used against billboards and other uses involving a small capital investment. Most of the zoning administrators who responded expressed dissatisfaction with the amortization technique. R. Scott, The Effect of Nonconforming Land-Use Amortization (American Soc'y of Planning Officials, Planning Advisory Service Rep. No. 280, May 1972).

7. For further discussion of amortization, see Cobb, *Amortizing Nonconforming Uses*, Land Use L. & Zoning Dig., Vol. 37, No. 1, at 3 (1985); Durden, *Sign Amortization Laws: Insight Into Precedent, Property, and Public Policy*, 35 Cap. U. L. Rev. 891 (2007); D. Menthe, *Reconciling Speech and Structural Elements in Sign Regulation*, Gonzaga L. Rev., Vol 44, No 2 (2008); Michaels, *Amortization and the Constitutional Methodology for Terminating Nonconforming Uses*, 41 Urb. Law. 807 (2009); Peterson & McCarthy, *Amortization of Legal Land Use Nonconformities as Regulatory Takings: An Uncertain Future*, 35 Wash. U. J. Urb. & Contemp. L. 37 (1989); Reynolds, *The Reasonableness of Amortization Periods for Nonconforming Uses — Balancing the Private Interest and the Public Welfare*, 34 Wash. U. J. Urb. & Contemp. L. 99 (1988); Comment, *Looking Back: The Full-Time Baseline in Regulatory Takings Analysis*, 24 B.C. Envt'l Aff. L. Rev. 199 (1996).

NOTE ON ALTERNATIVE STRATEGIES FOR ELIMINATING NONCONFORMING USES

The legal treatment of nonconforming uses reflects fundamental conflict. Preferring the planned uniformity of the "city beautiful," the drafters of early zoning ordinances barely concealed their contempt for nonconforming uses, reflected in the often-harsh rules on expansion, rebuilding and abandonment canvassed in the notes following the *Conforti* case, *supra*. Conversely, the rise of property-rights thinking in recent years has led some courts (notably Pennsylvania's) to protect nonconforming uses no matter what the consequences, an approach also reflected in the many zoning enabling acts that prohibit forced discontinuance of these uses (which, in turn, stimulates the strict limitations on nonconformities). Is there a better way?

In an article in the American Planning Association's *Zoning News*, the zoning director for the City of Rochester, New York, says that there is:

> Whether a particular nonconformity is a negative influence on a neighborhood is much more of a contextual issue than one of inherent problems with the nonconformity itself. It has been acknowledged that, even though a nonconformity may be thought of as a nuisance, it may simply be the right thing in the wrong place. In a more contemporary view of what creates a sense of place, nonconformities may now be considered the right thing for many places. Hence, they should be dealt with on a case-by-case basis rather than by general requirements that seek to extinguish them. Selective removal rather than blanket elimination is a concept that should underlie nonconformity regulations if zoning codes are to evolve in the direction of promoting good urban form, diversity, activity, and creating quality mixed-use urban neighborhoods. [Ientilucci, *Pigs in the Parlor or Diamonds in the Rough? A New Vision for Nonconformity Regulation*, Zoning News, April, 2003, at 3.]

He goes on to suggest that bulk or "area" variances can be a useful way to introduce flexibility and a positive attitude into the regulation of nonconforming uses, because they permit the municipality and the neighbors to carefully weigh whether the nonconforming physical structure actually "promot[es] good urban form, diversity, activity, and . . . quality mixed-use urban neighborhoods." Use variances, by contrast, typically generate much greater community opposition because they run with the land and raise concerns about future unknowns. Special use permits present an attractive alternative to use variances, because they can be tailored to the specific building and neighborhood, and reviewed over time as the use or user changes. Variances and special (or "conditional") uses are presented in Chapter 5, *infra*.

What about a negotiated remediation of the nonconforming use, in which the municipality would agree to convert the use to conforming status in exchange for the owner eliminating those aspects of the nonconformity that are most injurious to the municipality's overall regulatory scheme? Writing with particular reference to the problem of nonconforming signs, a frequent target of amortization programs, Professor Mandelker cautions that the bargaining solution may give too much standardless discretion to the municipality, or might be seen by a court as an illegal bargaining away of the municipality's legislative power. D. Mandelker, *Street Graphics and the Law Revised*, Am. Plan. Ass'n, Plan. Advisory Serv. Rep. No. 527 (2004). See *Chesapeake Outdoor Enterprises, Inc. v. Baltimore*, 597 A.2d 503 (Md. App. 1991) (settlement agreement held invalid). These issues are also discussed in Chapter 6, *infra*. For a comprehensive discussion of recent developments, see P. Salkin, *Abandonment, Discontinuance and*

Amortization of Nonconforming Uses: Lessons for Drafters of Zoning Regulations, 38 Real Estate L.J. 482, Albany Law School Research Paper No. 48 (Spring 2010), available at http://papers.ssrn.com.

How would these strategies apply, if at all, to the nonconforming issues in *Conforti* and *Gage*? Can you think of other strategies?

[5.] Uses Entitled to Special Protection

[a.] Free Speech-Protected Uses: Adult Businesses

Supreme Court decisions in the mid-1970s applied free speech doctrine to zoning ordinances regulating land uses that affect free speech. This change occurred because the Court brought commercial speech within the protection of the Free Speech Clause. See *Bigelow v. Virginia*, 421 U.S. 809 (1975) (newspaper advertisement for abortion services). Free speech review of zoning ordinances applies to a limited number of land uses. It applies to zoning for adult sex businesses, such as adult book stores and cinemas. This problem is discussed in this section. Sign regulation is also entitled to free speech protection. See Ch. 9, *infra*. Free speech protection has produced a revolution in the judicial review of land use controls. The courts substantially reverse the usual presumption of constitutionality and review more intensively the justifications for zoning restrictions.

How much is commercial speech protected? The Supreme Court stated its tests for the review of commercial speech in *Central Hudson Gas & Elec. Corp. v. Public Serv. Comm'n*, 447 U.S. 557 (1980) (invalidating regulation prohibiting electricity promotion advertising). The Court adopted a three-part test for commercial free speech review; this is the test now applied to adult businesses. The *Central Hudson* tests require the court to determine: (1) whether the "asserted governmental interest" in regulation is "substantial," (2) whether the regulation "directly advances the governmental interest asserted," and (3) whether "it is not more extensive than is necessary" to serve that interest. *Id.* at 563. The Court has moderated the last requirement of the *Central Hudson* test to permit more extensive regulation so long as there is a reasonable "fit" between the legislature's ends and the means chosen to accomplish them. See *Board of Trustees v. Fox*, 492 U.S. 469 (1989).

Another principle in free speech law that affects land use regulation is the requirement that regulation of speech must be content-neutral, not content-based. One example of a content-neutral regulation is a time, place and manner regulation, such as a zoning ordinance that regulates adult businesses. These principles are explained as applied to adult use regulation in the Supreme Court's *Renton* case, which is reproduced *infra*, and there is additional discussion in the section on sign regulation in Chapter 9. First, it is necessary to look at Supreme Court adult use regulation cases that precede *Renton.*

The Supreme Court adult business cases. The first two Supreme Court adult business decisions, *Young v. American Mini Theatres, Inc.*, 427 U.S. 50 (1976), and *Schad v. Borough of Mt. Ephraim*, 452 U.S. 61 (1981), provided some guidance on how free speech doctrine applies to zoning regulations affecting these businesses, but they were plurality decisions that left many questions unanswered. *Young v. American Mini Theatres, Inc.* considered the constitutionality of a dispersal zoning strategy adopted by the City of Detroit. The zoning ordinance required a distance of 1000 feet between adult businesses. This requirement applied to a number of other businesses, such as hotels and bars. The ordinance also prohibited any of these businesses from locating within 500 feet of a residential area. Operators of two adult movie theaters brought an action challenging the constitutionality of both requirements on free speech grounds. Justice Stevens wrote a plurality opinion upholding the ordinance, in which Justice Powell concurred.

Justice Stevens first noted that the Free Speech Clause did not absolutely prohibit the dispersal ordinance. The ordinance did not regulate free speech because of its point of view, and he would not give adult sexual expression the same protection under the Free Speech Clause that he would give to political debate. He then found a factual basis for concluding that the zoning ordinance would have its desired effect of preserving the character of city neighborhoods. "[T]he city's interest in attempting to preserve the quality of urban life is one that must be accorded high respect."

Justice Powell agreed with the plurality, although he would give adult sexual expression the same protected status as political debate. He upheld the ordinance as an "incidental" interference with First Amendment concerns. Noting that the Court had upheld innovative zoning techniques, he indicated that the Detroit ordinance was constitutional because it only controlled the "secondary effects" of "adult" expression on neighborhoods.

The plurality and concurring opinions in *Mini Theatres* do not indicate how far a municipality may go in restricting adult businesses within a city. In an important footnote, Justice Stevens indicated that the situation "would be quite different" if the ordinance had suppressed or greatly restricted access to lawful speech.

In *Schad v. Borough of Mount Ephraim*, a suburban municipality in New Jersey adopted a zoning ordinance that the Court interpreted to exclude all live entertainment, including nude dancing. An adult book store owner installed glass booths in which customers could observe nude dancers perform. He brought an action challenging the ordinance as a violation of free speech.

The actual holding in the case was quite narrow. The Court wrote five opinions, including a plurality opinion signed by three Justices. The seven Justices whose opinions made up a majority could only agree that the ordinance was facially overbroad and that the municipality had not justified it. The municipality claimed that the exclusion of the adult business was justified because the ordinance allowed businesses that met only local needs. The plurality rejected this justification, noting that the ordinance did allow other businesses that met nonlocal needs. The plurality also held that the live entertainment businesses excluded by the ordinance did not present any more parking, police or other problems than the businesses the ordinance permitted.

The borough also claimed that the ordinance was a reasonable "time, place and manner" regulation of free speech. This refers to First Amendment doctrine that permits regulation that advances a governmental interest and does not have as its primary purpose the suppression of speech. The Court rejected this justification because the borough did not offer evidence that live entertainment was basically incompatible with normal uses in commercial districts. It was on this point that five of the Justices in other concurring opinions disagreed, so a majority of the court actually held that a community could ban adult businesses under appropriate circumstances.

The issues left unresolved in *Mini Theatres* and *Schad* were resolved to a considerable extent in the *Renton* decision, which follows. You may note that the Court relies for its free speech doctrine on the Supreme Court's decision in *O'Brien v. United States* rather than

Central Hudson. However, the principles adopted in the two cases are, for all practical purposes, identical.

CITY OF RENTON v. PLAYTIME THEATRES, INC.

475 U.S. 41 (1986)

JUSTICE REHNQUIST delivered the opinion of the Court:

This case involves a constitutional challenge to a zoning ordinance, enacted by appellant, the city of Renton, Washington, that prohibits adult motion picture theaters from locating within 1,000 feet of any residential zone, single- or multiple-family dwelling, church, park, or school. Appellees, Playtime Theatres, Inc., and Sea-First Properties, Inc., filed an action in the United States District Court for the Western District of Washington seeking a declaratory judgment that the Renton ordinance violated the First and Fourteenth Amendments and a permanent injunction against its enforcement. The District Court ruled in favor of Renton and denied the permanent injunction, but the Court of Appeals for the Ninth Circuit reversed and remanded for reconsideration. 748 F.2d 527 (1984). We noted probable jurisdiction, and now reverse the judgment of the Ninth Circuit.

In May 1980, the Mayor of Renton, a city of approximately 32,000 people located just south of Seattle, suggested to the Renton City Council that it consider the advisability of enacting zoning legislation dealing with adult entertainment uses. No such uses existed in the city at that time. Upon the Mayor's suggestion, the City Council referred the matter to the city's Planning and Development Committee. The committee held public hearings, reviewed the experiences of Seattle and other cities, and received a report from the City Attorney's Office advising as to developments in other cities. The City Council, meanwhile, adopted Resolution No. 2368, which imposed a moratorium on the licensing of "any business . . . which . . . has as its primary purpose the selling, renting or showing of sexually explicit materials." The resolution contained a clause explaining that such businesses "would have a severe impact upon surrounding businesses and residences."

In April 1981, acting on the basis of the Planning and Development Committee's recommendation, the City Council enacted Ordinance No. 3526. The ordinance prohibited any "adult motion picture theater" from locating within 1,000 feet of any residential zone, single- or multiple-family dwelling, church, or park, and within one mile of any school. The term "adult motion picture theater" was defined as "[a]n enclosed building used for presenting motion picture films, video cassettes, cable television, or any other such visual media, distinguished or characteri[zed] by an emphasis on matter depicting, describing or relating to 'specified sexual activities' or 'specified anatomical areas' . . . for observation by patrons therein."

In early 1982, respondents acquired two existing theaters in downtown Renton, with the intention of using them to exhibit feature-length adult films. The theaters were located within the area proscribed by Ordinance No. 3526. At about the same time, respondents filed the previously mentioned lawsuit challenging the ordinance on First and Fourteenth Amendment grounds, and seeking declaratory and injunctive relief. While the federal action was pending, the City Council amended the ordinance in several respects, adding a statement of reasons for its enactment and reducing the minimum distance from any school to 1,000 feet. In November 1982, the Federal Magistrate to whom respondents' action had been referred recommended the entry of a preliminary injunction against enforcement of the Renton ordinance and the denial of Renton's motions to dismiss and for summary judgment. The District Court adopted the Magistrate's recommendations and entered the preliminary injunction, and respondents began showing adult films at their two theaters in Renton. Shortly thereafter, the parties agreed to submit the case for a final decision on whether a permanent injunction should issue on the basis of the record as already developed.

The District Court then vacated the preliminary injunction, denied respondents' requested permanent injunction, and entered summary judgment in favor of Renton. . . . Relying on *Young v. American Mini Theatres, Inc.*, 427 U.S. 50 (1976), and *United States v. O'Brien*, 391 U.S. 367 (1968), the court held that the Renton ordinance did not violate the First Amendment.

The Court of Appeals for the Ninth Circuit reversed. . . .

In our view, the resolution of this case is largely dictated by our decision in *Young v. American Mini Theatres, Inc., supra.* There, although five Members of the Court did not agree on a single rationale for the decision, we held that the city of Detroit's zoning ordinance, which prohibited locating an adult theater within 1,000 feet of any two other "regulated uses" or within 500 feet of any residential zone, did not violate the First and Fourteenth Amendments. 427 U.S., at 72-73 (plurality opinion of Stevens, J., joined by Burger, C.J., and White and Rehnquist, JJ.); *id.*, at 84 (Powell, J., concurring). The Renton ordinance, like the one in *American Mini Theatres*, does not ban adult theaters altogether, but merely provides that such theaters may not be located within 1,000 feet of any residential zone, single- or multiple-family dwelling, church, park, or school. The ordinance is therefore properly analyzed as a form of time, place, and manner regulation. *Id.*, at 63, and n.18; *id.*, at 78–79 (Powell, J., concurring). Describing the ordinance as a time, place, and manner regulation is, of course, only the first step in our inquiry. This Court has long held that regulations enacted for the purpose of restraining speech on the basis of its content presumptively violate the First Amendment. *See Carey v. Brown*, 447 U.S. 455, 462–463, and n.7 (1980); *Police Dept. of Chicago v. Mosley*, 408 U.S. 92, 95, 98–99 (1972). On the other hand, so-called "content-neutral" time, place, and manner regulations are acceptable so long as they are designed to serve a substantial governmental interest and do not unreasonably limit alternative avenues of communication.

At first glance, the Renton ordinance, like the ordinance in *American Mini Theatres*, does not appear to fit neatly into either the "content-based" or the "content-neutral" category. To be sure, the ordinance treats theaters that specialize in adult films differently from other kinds of theaters. Nevertheless, as the District Court concluded, the Renton ordinance is aimed not at the *content* of the films shown at "adult motion picture theatres," but rather at the *secondary effects* of such theaters on the surrounding community. The District Court found that the City Council's "*predominate* concerns" were with the secondary effects of adult theaters, and not with the content of adult films themselves (emphasis added). But the Court of Appeals, relying on its decision in *Tovar v. Billmeyer*, 721 F.2d 1260, 1266 (9th Cir. 1983), held that this was not enough to sustain the ordinance. According to the Court of Appeals, if "*a motivating factor*" in enacting the ordinance was to restrict respondents' exercise of First Amendment rights the ordinance would be invalid, apparently no matter how small a part this motivating factor may have played in the City Council's decision. 748 F.2d, at 537 (emphasis in original). This view of the law was rejected in *United States v. O'Brien*, 391 U.S. 367, 382–386 (1968), the very case that the Court of Appeals said it was applying:

> "It is a familiar principle of constitutional law that this Court will not strike down an otherwise constitutional statute on the basis of an alleged illicit legislative motive. What motivates one legislator to make a speech about a statute is not necessarily what motivates scores of others to enact it, and the stakes are sufficiently high for us to eschew guesswork." *Id.*, at 383–384.

The District Court's finding as to "predominate" intent, left undisturbed by the Court of Appeals, is more than adequate to establish that the city's pursuit of its zoning interests here was unrelated to the suppression of free expression. The ordinance by its terms is designed to prevent crime, protect the city's retail trade, maintain property values, and generally "protec[t] and preserv[e] the quality of [the city's] neighborhoods, commercial districts, and the quality of urban life," not to suppress the expression of unpopular views. As Justice Powell observed in *American Mini Theatres*, "[i]f [the city] had been concerned with restricting the message purveyed by adult theaters, it would have tried to close them or restrict their number rather than circumscribe their choice as to location." 427 U.S., at 82, n.4.

In short, the Renton ordinance is completely consistent with our definition of "content-neutral" speech regulations as those that "are *justified* without reference to the content of the regulated speech." *Virginia Pharmacy Board v. Virginia Citizens Consumer Council, Inc.*, 425 U.S. 748, 771 (1976) (emphasis added). The ordinance does not contravene the fundamental principle that underlies our concern about "content-based" speech regulations: that "government may not grant the use of a forum to people whose views it finds acceptable, but deny use to those wishing to express less favored or more controversial views." *Mosley, supra*, at 95–96. It was with this understanding in mind that, in *American Mini Theatres*, a majority of this Court decided that, at least with respect to businesses that purvey sexually explicit materials, zoning ordinances designed to combat the undesirable secondary effects of such businesses are to be reviewed under the standards applicable to "content-neutral" time, place, and manner regulations. Justice Stevens, writing for the plurality, concluded that the city of Detroit was entitled to draw a distinction between adult theaters and other kinds of theaters "without violating the government's paramount obligation of neutrality in its regulation of protected communication," 427 U.S., at 70, noting that "[i]t is th[e] secondary effect which these zoning ordinances attempt to avoid, not the dissemination of 'offensive' speech," *id.*, at 71, n.34. Justice Powell, in concurrence, elaborated:

> "[The] dissent misconceives the issue in this case by insisting that it involves an impermissible time, place, and manner restriction based on the content of expression. It involves nothing of the kind. We have here merely a decision by the city to treat certain movie theaters differently because they have markedly different effects upon their surroundings. . . . Moreover, even if this were a case involving a special governmental response to the content of one type of movie, it is possible that the result would be supported by a line of cases recognizing that the government can tailor its reaction to different types of speech according to the degree to which its special and overriding interests are implicated." *Id.*, at 82, n.6.

The appropriate inquiry in this case, then, is whether the Renton ordinance is designed to serve a substantial governmental interest and allows for reasonable alternative avenues of communication. It is clear that the ordinance meets such a standard. As a majority of this Court recognized in *American Mini Theatres*, a city's "interest in attempting to preserve the quality of urban life is one that must be accorded high respect." 427 U.S., at 71 (plurality opinion); *see id.*, at 80 (Powell, J., concurring) ("Nor is there doubt that the interests furthered by this ordinance are both important and substantial"). Exactly the same vital governmental interests are at stake here.

The Court of Appeals ruled, however, that because the Renton ordinance was enacted without the benefit of studies specifically relating to "the particular problems or needs of Renton," the city's justifications for the ordinance were "conclusory and speculative." 748 F.2d, at 537. We think the Court of Appeals imposed on the city an unnecessarily rigid burden of proof. The record in this case reveals that Renton relied heavily on the experience of, and studies produced by, the city of Seattle. In Seattle, as in Renton, the adult theater zoning ordinance was aimed at preventing the secondary effects caused by the presence of even one such theater in a given neighborhood. *See Northend Cinema, Inc. v. Seattle*, 585 P.2d 1153 (Wash. 1978). The opinion of the Supreme Court of Washington in *Northend Cinema*, which was before the Renton City Council when it enacted the ordinance in question here, described Seattle's experience as follows:

> "The amendments to the City's zoning Code which are at issue here are the culmination of a long period of study and discussion of the problems of adult movie theaters in residential areas of the City. . . . [T]he City's Department of Community Development made a study of the need for zoning controls of adult theaters . . . . The study analyzed the City's zoning scheme, comprehensive plan, and land uses around existing adult motion picture theaters. . . ." *Id.*, at 1155.
>
> "[T]he [trial] court heard extensive testimony regarding the history and purpose of these ordinances. It heard expert testimony on the adverse effects of the presence of adult motion picture theaters on neighborhood children and community improvement efforts. The court's detailed findings, which include a finding that the location of adult theaters has a harmful effect on the area and contribute to neighborhood blight, are supported by substantial evidence in the record." *Id.*, at 1156.
>
> "The record is replete with testimony regarding the effects of adult movie theater locations in residential neighborhoods." *Id.*, at 1159.

We hold that Renton was entitled to rely on the experiences of Seattle and other cities, and in particular on the "detailed findings" summarized in the Washington Supreme Court's *Northend Cinema* opinion, in enacting its adult theater zoning ordinance. The First Amendment does not require a city, before enacting such an ordinance, to conduct new studies or produce evidence independent of that already generated by other cities, so long as whatever evidence the city relies upon is reasonably believed to be relevant to the problem that the city addresses. That was the case here. Nor is our holding affected by the fact that Seattle ultimately chose a different method of adult theater zoning than that chosen by Renton, since Seattle's choice of a different remedy to combat the secondary effects of adult theaters does not call into question either Seattle's identification of those secondary effects or the relevance of Seattle's experience to Renton.

We also find no constitutional defect in the method chosen by Renton to further its substantial interests. Cities may regulate adult theaters by dispersing them, as in Detroit, or by effectively concentrating them, as in Renton. "It is not our function to appraise the wisdom of [the city's] decision to require adult theaters to be separated rather than concentrated in the same areas. . . . [T]he city must be allowed a reasonable opportunity to experiment with solutions to admittedly serious problems." *American Mini Theatres, supra*, at 71 (plurality opinion). Moreover, the Renton ordinance is "narrowly tailored" to affect only that category of theaters shown to produce the unwanted secondary effects, thus avoiding the flaw that proved fatal to the regulations in *Schad v. Mount Ephraim*, 452 U.S. 61 (1981), and *Erznoznik v. City of Jacksonville*, 422 U.S. 205 (1975).

Respondents contend that the Renton ordinance is "under-inclusive," in that it fails to regulate other kinds of adult businesses that are likely to produce secondary effects similar to those produced by adult theaters. On this record the contention must fail. There is no evidence that, at the time the Renton ordinance was enacted, any other adult business was located in, or was contemplating moving into, Renton. In fact, Resolution No. 2368, enacted in October 1980, states that "the City of Renton does not, at the present time, have any business whose primary purpose is the sale, rental, or showing of sexually explicit materials." That Renton chose first to address the potential problems created by one particular kind of adult business in no way suggests that the city has "singled out" adult theaters for discriminatory treatment. We simply have no basis on this record for assuming that Renton will not, in the future, amend its ordinance to include other kinds of adult businesses that have been shown to produce the same kinds of secondary effects as adult theaters. *See Williamson v. Lee Optical Co.*, 348 U.S. 483, 488–489 (1955).

Finally, turning to the question whether the Renton ordinance allows for reasonable alternative avenues of communication, we note that the ordinance leaves some 520 acres, or more than five percent of the entire land area of Renton, open to use as adult theater sites. The District Court found, and the Court of Appeals did not dispute the finding, that the 520 acres of land consists of "[a]mple, accessible real estate," including "acreage in all stages of development from raw land to developed, industrial, warehouse, office, and shopping space that is criss-crossed by freeways, highways, and roads."

Respondents argue, however, that some of the land in question is already occupied by existing businesses, that "practically none" of the undeveloped land is currently for sale or lease, and that in general there are no "commercially viable" adult theater sites within the 520 acres left open by the Renton ordinance. The Court of Appeals accepted these arguments, concluded that the 520 acres was not truly "available" land, and therefore held that the Renton ordinance "would result in a substantial restriction" on speech. 748 F.2d, at 534.

We disagree with both the reasoning and the conclusion of the Court of Appeals. That respondents must fend for themselves in the real estate market, on an equal footing with other prospective purchasers and lessees, does not give rise to a First Amendment violation. And although we have cautioned against the enactment of zoning regulations that have "the effect of suppressing, or greatly restricting access to, lawful speech," *American Theatres*, 427 U.S., at 71, n.35 (plurality opinion), we have never suggested that the First Amendment compels the Government to ensure that adult theaters, or any other kinds of speech-related businesses for that matter, will be able to obtain sites at bargain prices. *See id.*, at 78 (Powell, J., concurring) ("The inquiry for First Amendment purposes is not concerned with economic impact"). In our view, the First Amendment requires only that Renton refrain from effectively denying respondents a reasonable opportunity to open and operate an adult theater within the city, and the ordinance before us easily meets this requirement.

In sum, we find that the Renton ordinance represents a valid governmental response to the "admittedly serious problems" created by adult theaters. *See id.*, at 71 (plurality opinion). Renton has not used "the power to zone as a pretext for suppressing expression," *id.*, at 84 (Powell, J., concurring), but rather has sought to make some areas available for adult theaters and their patrons, while at the same time preserving the quality of life in the community at large by preventing those theaters from locating in other areas. This, after all, is the essence of zoning. Here, as in *American Mini Theatres*, the city has enacted a zoning ordinance that meets the goals while also satisfying the dictates of the First Amendment. The judgment of the Court of Appeals is therefore

Reversed.

JUSTICE BLACKMUN concurs in the result.

JUSTICE BRENNAN joined by JUSTICE MARSHALL, dissenting:

Renton's zoning ordinance selectively imposes limitations on the location of a movie theater based exclusively on the content of the films shown there. The constitutionality of the ordinance is therefore not correctly analyzed under standards applied to content-neutral time, place, and manner restrictions. But even assuming that the ordinance may fairly be characterized as content-neutral, it is plainly unconstitutional under the standards established by the decisions of this Court. Although the Court's analysis is limited to cases involving "businesses that purvey sexually explicit materials," and thus does not affect our holdings in cases involving state regulation of other kinds of speech, I dissent. . . . [Most of Justice Brennan's dissent is omitted, but the following paragraphs illustrate his views on the impact of the Free Speech Clause on the allocation of land for adult businesses under zoning ordinances:]

Finally, the ordinance is invalid because it does not provide for reasonable alternative avenues of communication. The District Court found that the ordinance left 520 acres in Renton available for adult theater sites, an area comprising about five percent of the city. However, the Court of Appeals found that because much of this land was already occupied, "[l]imiting adult theater uses to these areas is a substantial restriction on speech." 748 F.2d, at 534. Many "available" sites are also largely unsuited for use by movie theaters. Again, these facts serve to distinguish this case from *American Mini Theatres*, where there was no indication that the Detroit zoning ordinance seriously limited the locations available for adult businesses. *See American Mini Theaters, supra*, at 71 n.35 (plurality opinion) ("The situation would be quite different if the ordinance had the effect of . . . greatly restricting access to, lawful speech"); *see also Basiardanes v. City of Galveston*, 682 F.2d 1203, 1214 (5th Cir. 1982) (ordinance effectively banned adult theaters by restricting them to " 'the most unattractive, inaccessible, and inconvenient areas of a city' "); *Purple Onion, Inc. v. Jackson*, 511 F. Supp. 1207, 1217 (N.D. Ga. 1981) (proposed sites for adult entertainment uses were either "unavailable, unusable, or so inaccessible to the public that . . . they amount to no locations").

Despite the evidence in the record, the Court reasons that the fact "that respondents must fend for themselves in the real estate market, on an equal footing with other prospective purchasers and lessees, does not give rise to a First Amendment violation." However, respondents are not on equal footing with other prospective purchasers and lessees, but must conduct business under severe restrictions not imposed upon other establishments. The Court also argues that the First Amendment does not compel "the government to ensure that adult theatres, or any other kinds of speech-related businesses for that matter, will be able to obtain sites at bargain prices." However, respondents do not ask Renton to guarantee low-price sites for their businesses, but seek only a reasonable opportunity to operate adult theaters in the city. By denying them this opportunity, Renton can effectively ban a form of protected speech from its borders. The ordinance "greatly restrict[s] access to lawful speech," *American Mini Theatres, supra*, at 71, n.35 (plurality opinion), and is plainly unconstitutional.

NOTES AND QUESTIONS

1. *Renton* resolved many of the questions left open by earlier Supreme Court adult business zoning cases, but commentators have criticized the Court's handling of the free speech issues:

> The Renton ordinance was content-based regulation of the first order. The ordinance identified speech of a certain content and, on the theory that such speech caused undesirable effects, restricted its exercise. Precisely this sort of content-regarding ordinance, under the Court's prior holdings, demands the strictest scrutiny. . . .
>
> The Court's analysis of the facial underinclusiveness of the ordinance also departed from precedent. [The Court held that the ordinance was constitutional even though it singled out adult theaters for regulation but not businesses causing similar problems].
>
> This reasoning marks a startling break with traditional first amendment jurisprudence. Although the Court has held that, in the field of economic regulation, a legislature can address one evil at a time without offending the equal protection clause, the Court's underinclusiveness doctrine has not been so permissive when the first amendment is involved. [*The Supreme Court, 1985 Term*, 100 Harv. L. Rev. 1, 195, 196 (1986).]

Nevertheless, the Court's treatment of what is essentially a hybrid regulation — one that regulates content while at the same time regulating the secondary effects of a business — stands.

For additional commentary on *Renton*, see Stein, *Regulation of Adult Businesses Through Zoning After Renton*, 18 Pac. L.J. 351 (1987); Ziegler, *City of Renton v. Playtime Theatres, Inc.: Supreme Court Reopens the Door for Zoning of Sexually Oriented Businesses*, 9 Zoning & Plan. L. Rep. 33 (1986).

2. *Current practice.* So-called concentration ordinances, that concentrate adult uses in one area of a community, are no longer common. The "Boston Combat Zone," for example, is practically gone. See Gilmore, *Zoned Out: A New Take on Regulating Adult Businesses*, Planning, Feb. 1999, at 15. Some ordinances also set a minimum distance between adult businesses, as well as a minimum distance between adult uses and vulnerable areas and uses, such as residential areas. Which methods of control are used has an important effect on the courts' decisions. See *VIP of Berlin, LLC v. Town of Berlin*, 593 F.3d 179 (2d Cir. 2010) (250-foot separation from residential uses; definition of sexually-oriented business not vague).

3. *Proving secondary effects.* A showing of secondary effects from adult businesses is critical to litigation success, but proof of secondary effects is more difficult after *City of Los Angeles v. Alameda Books, Inc.*, 535 U.S. 425 (2002), a plurality opinion signed by four of the Justices. To close a loophole in its ordinance, the city amended it to prohibit more than one adult business in the same building. The Court accepted the city's argument that negative secondary effects from adult uses occur whether they are separate establishments or in one building. It then repeated its *Renton* holding that a city could rely on studies "reasonably believed to be relevant" but could not get away with "shoddy data or reasoning." If a plaintiff casts doubt on a city's justification, the city has the burden to supplement the record with additional evidence to "fairly support the municipality's rationale for its ordinance." Justice Kennedy concurred, and while agreeing with the plurality's statement of the municipal evidentiary burden, added that the critical inquiry is the effect on speech and that a "city may not assert that it will reduce secondary effects by reducing speech in the same proportion."

The adult business industry has used the Kennedy concurrence to attack adult use ordinances. They find support in an article arguing that secondary effect studies showed no correlation between adult businesses and secondary effects. Paul, Linz & Shafer, *Government Regulation of "Adult" Businesses Through Zoning and Anti-Nudity Ordinances: Debunking the Legal Myth of Negative Secondary Effects*, 6 Comm. L. & Pol'y 355 (2001). The Seventh Circuit has relied on studies by Professor Linz submitted by plaintiffs to strike down adult use ordinances for lack of evidence on secondary effects. *Annex Books, Inc. v. City of Indianapolis*, 581 F.3d 460 (7th Cir. 2009). See McCleary & Weinstein, *Do "Off-Site" Adult Businesses Have Secondary Effects? Legal Doctrine, Social Theory, and Empirical Evidence*, 31 Law & Pol'y 217 (2009).

Other courts are more deferential. *Doctor John's v. G. Blake Wahlen (III)*, 542 F.3d 787 (10th Cir. 2008) (rejecting Linz study and noting Supreme Court rejection); *Baby Dolls Topless Saloons, Inc. v. City of Dallas*, 295 F.3d 471 (5th Cir. 2002) (studies showing sex crimes three to five times more frequent in study area met "reasonable belief" standard necessary to justify proof of secondary effects). Studies supporting secondary effects can justify isolation in an industrial area. *Tollis Inc. v. County of San Diego*, 505 F.3d 935 (9th Cir. 2007). Another example of deferential treatment is *Flanigan's Enterprises, Inc. v. Fulton County*, (11th Cir. 2010) ("[T]he County relied on ample statistical, surveillance, and anecdotal evidence, the live testimony of the chief of police and the chief judge of the juvenile court, among others, and dozens of foreign studies, all of which support the County's efforts to curb the negative secondary effects of alcohol and live nude dancing in its communities."). See Hanna, *Exotic Dance Adult Entertainment: A Guide for Planners and Policy Makers*, 10 J. Plan. Lit. 116 (CPL Bibliography 375, 2005) (reviewing studies, claimed to be done by industry experts, showing no secondary effects). One observer commented anonymously to one of the authors "that most, if not all, of the studies of 'deterioration' are flawed — on both sides — by the difficulties in finding well-matched pairs, plus the inability to control for extraneous factors, such as overall real estate market conditions, or new development beyond the study and/or control boundaries. The more recent crime studies do seem to find an association between adult businesses and increased crime."

4. *Providing an adequate number of sites. Renton* caused a revolution by requiring an adequate number of sites for adult businesses. This is a market share approach unknown in other areas of land use regulation. The inquiry first requires consideration of the relevant market and the availability of land in that market for adult uses. *D. Russo, Inc. v. Romankow*, 2010 N.J. Super. Unpub. LEXIS 2272 (N.J. App. Div. 2010) (determination of market area essential).

Woodall v. City of El Paso (II), 959 F.2d 1305 (5th Cir. 1992) (per curiam), adopted a narrow rule of availability that is usually applied: Land is unavailable only when cities allocate "land that is completely unsuitable from a legal or physical standpoint for adult business use." This test excludes economic considerations. Distance and spacing requirements can reduce the number of sites available and result in a court decision that available sites are inadequate. *Renton* did not provide guidance on the adequacy issue beyond accepting the percentage of land available as adequate. The cases usually balance a number of factors to determine adequacy, including "geographical size, the number of acres available to adult entertainment establishments as a percentage of that size, where the sites are located, the number of adult entertainment establishments currently in existence . . . , and the number of adult entertainment establishments wanting to operate." *Boss Capital, Inc. v. City of Casselberry*, 187 F.3d 1251, 1254 (11th Cir. 1999). The ratio of sites to population is considered important by some courts. *Executive Arts Studio, Inc. v. City of Grand Rapids*, 227 F. Supp. 2d 731 (D. Mich. 2002). There is no requirement that a specific proportion of a municipality be available for adult businesses. *D.H.L. Assocs., Inc. v. O'Gorman*, 199 F.3d 50 (1st Cir. 1999).

Some courts adopted a "supply and demand" test. Under this test, there must be more "reasonable" sites available than adult businesses with demands for them. See *Lakeland Lounge v. Jackson*, 973 F.2d 1255 (5th Cir. 1992). Other courts have not adopted this bright line rule but place a heavy emphasis on meeting supply and demand. E.g., *Buzzetti v. City of New York*, 140 F.3d 134 (2d Cir. 1998) (all existing adult uses must be allowed to continue at current or relocated sites); *North Ave. Novelties, Inc. v. City of Chicago*, 88 F.3d 441 (7th Cir. 1996) (must be no evidence that adult use was prevented from opening). Isn't a supply and demand test inconsistent with the holding in *Renton* that market issues are not important? See *Young v. City of Simi Valley*, 216 F.3d 807, 816 (9th Cir. 2000) (rejecting rule).

Keep in mind that a distance requirement reduces the number of sites available, despite the amount of land zoned, because it limits the number of adult uses that can locate close to each other. One way to monitor this problem is to identify all sites and areas protected by a distance requirement and then map the availability of adult use sites using this requirement. This will give you a graphic depiction of site availability. See *Fly Fish, Inc. v. City of Cocoa Beach*, 337 F.3d 1301 (11th Cir. 2003) (discussing this issue and invalidating an ordinance that zoned out an existing adult business). For discussion of the various tests in an article favoring the supply and demand test, see Comment, *A Matter of Arithmetic: Using Supply and Demand to Determine the Constitutionality of Adult Entertainment Ordinances*, 52 Emory L.J. 319 (2002).

5. *Sites outside the municipality. Schad* suggested that the availability of sites in nearby areas outside the city might be sufficient. The problem can be especially serious for small municipalities, some of whom can argue they should not be required to tolerate adult businesses at all. Courts have been lenient when a municipality was small in area and had a small population. See *421 Northlake Blvd. Corp. v. Village of North Palm Beach*, 753 So. 2d 754 (Fla. App. 2000) (two sites and population ratio of 1/6100). See also Cal. Gov't Code § 65850.4(d) (authorizing local governments to cooperate in the regulation of adult businesses); *Township of Saddle Brook v. A.B. Family Center*, 722 A.2d 530 (N.J. 1999) (interprets statute to authorize consideration of sites outside municipality). To the contrary, a New Jersey court decided more recently that sites outside the municipality should not be considered. *Sayreville v. 35 Club, LLC*, 3 A.3d 1268 (N.J. App. Div. 2010) ("The abridgment of constitutionally protected speech, no matter how seemingly unpopular or morally undesirable it may be, cannot be sustained when the alternative suitable sites for the expression of that speech are located outside the electoral reach of the people affected by such abridgement."). A concurring and dissenting opinion in *Sayerville* addresses the apparent inconsistency.

The issue has not yet been decided, but is it reasonable to let municipal lines decide the free speech issue? As the Seventh Circuit noted, "[t]he constitutional rule is that a person have adequate opportunity to speak, not that the land be in one polity (the City of Marshall) rather than another (Clark County)." *Illinois One News, Inc. v. City of Marshall*, 477 F.3d 461, 463 (7th Cir. 2007). The court did not resolve this issue but held that the availability of one site was enough.

6. *Site acceptability.* What makes an adult use site acceptable? *Hickerson v. City of New York*, 146 F.3d 99 (2d Cir. 1998), held that municipalities need only identify general areas, not exact sites. Nor is there a free speech violation if the cost of relocating to a designated site puts the adult use out of business. *Holmberg v. City of Ramsey*, 12 F.3d 140 (8th Cir. 1993). *Vincent v. Broward County*, 200 F.3d 1325 (11th Cir. 2000), reviews the cases and summarizes the rules. The court held that 1) there has to be "a genuine possibility that a site will become available for new commercial uses within a reasonable time"; (2) a site is available if it is reasonably accessible to the public; (3) a site "in a manufacturing zone with infrastructure such as roads, sidewalks, and lights" is available; (4) a site for relocation "must be appropriate for some commercial business" but "does not have to suit the particular needs of adult businesses"; and (5) "commercially zoned plots are considered available." *Id.* at 1334, discussing *Topanga Press, Inc. v. City of Los Angeles*, 989 F.2d 1524, 1532–33 (9th Cir. 1993).

The courts have also applied the rule that adult businesses must fend for themselves in the real estate market. *Vincent, supra*, for example, held that it does not matter "that the real estate market may be tight and sites currently unavailable for sale or lease, or that property owners may be reluctant to sell to an adult venue." *Id.* A California case upheld an ordinance requiring location in a shopping center to escape a distance requirement, even though the three existing shopping centers might not accommodate or be feasible for adult businesses. *City of National City v. Wiener*, 12 Cal. Rptr. 2d 701 (Cal. App. 1992). See also *Mag Realty, LLC v. City of Gloucester City*, 2010 U.S. Dist. LEXIS 82035 (D.N.J. 2010) (toxic waste site not an adequate alternative; court considers standard of 12 sites or 1% of land area as minimum required). Note the interplay between the acceptability of designated sites and the adequacy issue. An adult business can win a case by eliminating enough sites as unacceptable to reduce acceptable sites to an inadequate number. How would you guard against this problem?

7. *The prior restraint problem.* It is usual, as Chapter 6 explains, for zoning ordinances to authorize some uses as "conditional" uses in their districts; these are uses that, even though permitted by the ordinance, require the site-specific approval of a zoning agency. A requirement that an adult business cannot operate unless it obtains a conditional use permit creates a "prior restraint" problem. Originally developed as a response to official censorship of time-sensitive speech, such as a news article or an artistic performance, the doctrine prohibits "prior restraints" and places the burden on the government to persuade a court that the material is not protected under the First Amendment before it can be suppressed. *Freedman v. Maryland*, 380 U.S. 51 (1965). However, when this principle was applied to regulation of adult businesses as conditional uses in *FW/PBS, Inc. v. Dallas*, 493 U.S. 215, 227 (1990) (plurality opinion), the Court accepted the legitimate and customary role that licensing plays in land use law, and the weaker inference that censorship was involved. For adult uses, it applied only two of the three *Freedman* requirements, which it described as the "core" of prior restraint doctrine: that "the licensor must make the decision whether to issue the license within a specified and reasonable time period during which the status quo is maintained, and there must be the possibility of prompt judicial review in the event that the license is erroneously denied." It did not apply the third *Freedman* factor, that the government bear the burden of seeking judicial review or the burden of persuasion before the court, reasoning that adult businesses had a sufficient economic stake to pursue their First Amendment claims if they chose to do so, compared to the more ephemeral interest of the movie distributor in *Freedman*. Do you agree with this distinction? See *H.D.V.-Greektown, LLC v. City of Detroit*, 2010 U.S. Dist. LEXIS 93382 (E.D. Mich. 2010) (adoption of "Procedures and Criteria for Michigan

Liquor Control Commission Activity Permits" which includes consideration of zoning not prior restraint).

Thomas v. Chicago Park Dist., 534 U.S. 316, 322 (2002), a case involving a content-neutral time, place and manner regulation of large scale events in city parks, subsequently introduced doctrinal confusion by holding that "We have never required that a content-neutral permit scheme regulating speech in a public forum adhere to the procedural requirements set forth in *Freedman*." Recall that the *Renton* case, *supra*, was premised on the adult uses zoning ordinance being a content-neutral time, place and manner regulation of the "secondary effects" of adult businesses, which would suggest that none of the *Freedman* factors should be applied in the adult uses context, *FW/PBS* notwithstanding. The *Thomas* Court explicitly distinguished *FW/PBS*, however, describing it as a regulation that "targeted businesses purveying sexually explicit speech," *id.* at n.2, and noting that *FW/PBS* imposed two of the three *Freedman* factors. It is not clear why the sexually "targeted . . . speech" was content-neutral in *Renton* but content discriminatory in *FW/PBS*. For a recent decision analyzing the issues, see *Richland Bookmart, Inc. v. Knox County*, 555 F.3d 512 (6th Cir. 2009) (zoning regulations content-neutral).

Doctrinal confusion aside, however, two additional considerations provide guidance in the land use context. First, even in the "content-neutral" context of *Thomas*, the Court required (on an as-applied basis) that the regulation must "contain adequate standards to guide the official's decision and render it subject to effective judicial review" because where an official has unduly broad discretion there is a risk he will "favor or disfavor speech based on its content." *Id.* at 323. Second, two years after *Thomas*, in *Littleton v. Z.J. Gifts D-4, L.L.C.*, 541 U.S. 774 (2004), the Court explicitly applied the prompt judicial review requirement of *FW/PBS* to an adult licensing ordinance, albeit in a somewhat watered-down way. It held that statutory procedures for judicial review are adequate if the courts are sensitive to the need to prevent First Amendment harms and act accordingly. It also found the objective standards contained in the ordinance did not authorize an improper use of discretion. Thus, a safe conclusion for land use lawyers is that the courts will require more detailed standards for conditional uses than they do when the Free Speech Clause is not implicated, although the burden rests with the speech claimant to pursue this result. See *Lady J. Lingerie, Inc. v. City of Jacksonville*, 176 F.3d 1358 (11th Cir. 1999) (virtually any amount of discretion beyond the ministerial is suspect); Carter & Clark, *Death of Procedural Safeguards: Prior Restraint, Due Process and the Elusive First Amendment Value of Content Neutrality*, 11 Comm. L. & Pol'y 225 (2006).

8. *Amortization.* The plurality opinion in *Mini Theatres* left open the constitutionality of an amortization period for adult businesses. 427 U.S. 50 at 71 n.35. However, most courts have held that zoning provisions amortizing adult businesses are constitutional. See *Ambassador Books & Video, Inc. v. City of Little Rock*, 20 F.3d 858 (8th Cir. 1994); *Lydo Enters. v. City of Las Vegas*, 745 F.2d 1211 (9th Cir. 1986); *Independence News, Incorporated v. City of Charlotte*, 568 F.3d 148 (4th Cir. 2009) (eight year amortization period to meet separation requirement).

9. *Statutory regulation.* Legislation in some states authorizes the regulation of adult businesses. California, for example, authorizes ordinances that advance a substantial governmental interest, do not unreasonably restrict avenues of communication and are based on "narrow, objective, and definite standards." It also authorizes reliance on the experience of other local governments and court case findings "in establishing the reasonableness of the ordinance and its relevance to the specific problems it addresses," including the "harmful secondary effects" of the businesses on a community. Cal. Gov't Code § 65850.4. See also N.C.

Gen. Stat. § 160A-181.1 (contains findings on the adverse secondary effects of adult businesses and authorizes zoning and other regulations). Tex. Local Gov't Code §§ 243.001-243.011 (similar and authorizing inspections, fees and enforcement). Are these statutes consistent with the Supreme Court decisions?

10. *Sources.* J. Gerard & S. Bergthold, Local Regulation of Adult Businesses (2009); Baradaran-Robison, *Viewpoint Neutral Zoning of Adult Entertainment Businesses*, 31 Hastings Const. L.Q. 447 (2004); Clay & Richards, *Stripping Away First Amendment Rights: The Legislative Assault on Sexually Oriented Businesses*, 7 N.Y.U. J. Legis. & Pub. Pol'y 287 (2004); Fee, *The Pornographic Secondary Effects Doctrine*, 60 Ala. L. Rev. 291 (2009); Kelly, *Current and Critical Issues in Regulating Sexually Oriented Businesses*, Planning & Envtl. L., July 2004, at 3; Ryder, *The Changing Nature of Adult Entertainment Districts: Between a Rock and a Hard Place*, 41 Urb. Studies 1659 (2004) (noting suburbanization of industry); Note, *Sex But Not the City: Adult-Entertainment Zoning, The First Amendment, and Residential and Rural Municipalities*, 46 B.C. L. Rev. 625 (2005).

[b.] Religious Uses

The conflict between the demands of religious institutions whose members exercise their religious beliefs in many different ways through various institutional activities, and the requirements of zoning ordinances that may limit religious activities to protect community well-being, is an especially dynamic area of land use law. In addition to state legislation and constitutional protection, the regulation of religious uses is governed by the federal Constitution and a relatively new federal act, the Religious Land Use and Institutionalized Persons Act (RLUIPA). The location and expansion of religious institutions and their accessory uses in residential areas and in downtown redeveloping areas are a source of much controversy. This section examines state and federal court approaches to issues created by religious uses.

The problem. Churches and their accessory uses often face substantial opposition when they attempt to get necessary approvals in the zoning process. This opposition may often be concentrated on new and fundamentalist denominations, not part of the mainstream religious community. One study found, for example, that while minority religions constitute about nine percent of the general population, they were litigants in over forty-nine percent of the cases concerning the location of a religious building, and over thirty-three percent of the cases where approval of accessory uses was the issue. Keetch & Richards, *The Need for Legislation to Enshrine Free Exercise in the Land Use Context*, 32 U.C. Davis L. Rev. 725 (1999).

These findings suggest that religious discrimination is a factor in some of the opposition to zoning for religious uses. Consider that one group of cases holds that churches should not be allowed in residential areas because they generate traffic, see *State v. Cameron*, 445 A.2d 75, 80 (N.J.L. Div. 1982) (collecting cases on traffic problems associated with churches), *rev'd on other grounds*, 498 A.2d 1217 (N.J. 1985), while another group holds they should not be allowed in commercial areas because they do not generate enough traffic, see *International Church of the Foursquare Gospel v. City of Chicago Heights*, 955 F. Supp. 878, 881 (N.D. Ill. 1996). Other reasons for community concerns may result from the changing nature of religious institutions, in the rise of "megachurches" that conduct continuous activities in large or campus-like settings unlike the traditional "parish church" of old. See Schwab, *Faith-Based Planned Developments: Sorting Out the Uses*, Zoning News, June 2003; Note, *Super-Sized with Fries: Regulating Religious Land Use in the Era of Megachurches*, 88 Minn. L. Rev. 416-47 (2003). The question is whether the law as it now stands strikes a proper balance between religious and community needs, as expressed through zoning restrictions.

State cases. State courts traditionally apply a substantive due process analysis to zoning restrictions, but the cases are divided. The majority-view cases accord special protection to religious uses and frequently reverse the presumption of constitutionality accorded to zoning ordinances. See *Jehovah's Witnesses Assembly Hall v. Woolwich Twp.*, 532 A.2d 276 (N.J.L. Div. 1987) (citing cases); *State ex rel. Lake Shore Drive Baptist Church v. Village of Bayside Bd. of Trustees*, 108 N.W.2d 288 (Wis. 1961). Courts in these states strike down zoning ordinances excluding churches from residential districts. Courts following the majority view may uphold site development regulations with which a church can reasonably comply. See *Board of Zoning Appeals v. Decatur, Ind. Congregation of Jehovah's Witnesses*, 117 N.E.2d 115 (Ind. 1954) (invalidating parking requirement but upholding setback requirement).

A minority of courts take an opposite view. California leads this group. In *Corporation of Presiding Bishop of Church of Jesus Christ of Latter-Day Saints v. City of Porterville*, 203 P.2d 823 (Cal. 1949), the court accepted traffic congestion and property value arguments to uphold the exclusion of churches from residential districts. Accord, *Seward Chapel, Inc. v. City of Seward*, 655 P.2d 1293 (Alaska 1982).

New York, which was once a leading state adopting the majority view, no longer follows it. The highest New York court in *Cornell Univ. v. Bagnardi*, 503 N.E.2d 509 (N.Y. 1986), adopted a balancing approach that illustrates the difficulties of reconciling the conflicting claims of religious institutions and zoning objectives. The case actually considered the zoning problems of educational as well as religious institutions. The following paragraphs summarize the court's views on how to handle zoning disputes. After stating its earlier holdings "that the total exclusion of such institutions from a residential district serves no end that is reasonably related to the morals, health, welfare and safety of the community," the court continued:

> These general rules, however, were interpreted by some courts to demand a full exemption from zoning rules for all educational and church uses. The result has been to render municipalities powerless in the face of a religious or educational institution's proposed expansion, no matter how offensive, overpowering or unsafe to a residential neighborhood the use might be. Such an interpretation, however, is mandated neither by the case law of our State nor common sense. . . .
>
> The controlling consideration in reviewing the request of a school or church for permission to expand into a residential area must always be the over-all impact on the public's welfare. Although the special treatment afforded schools and churches stems from their presumed beneficial effect on the community, there are many instances in which a particular educational or religious use may actually detract from the public's health, safety, welfare or morals. In those instances, the institution may be properly denied. There is simply no conclusive presumption that any religious or educational use automatically outweighs its ill effects. The presumed beneficial effect may be rebutted with evidence of a significant impact on traffic congestion, property values, municipal services and the like. . . .
>
> A special permit may be required and reasonable conditions directly related to the public's health, safety and welfare may be imposed to the same extent that they may be imposed on noneducational applicants. Thus, a zoning ordinance may properly provide that the granting of a special permit to churches or schools may be conditioned on the effect the use would have on traffic congestion, property values, municipal

services, the general plan for development of the community, etc. The requirement of a special permit application, which entails disclosure of site plans, parking facilities, and other features of the institution's proposed use, is beneficial in that it affords zoning boards an opportunity to weigh the proposed use in relation to neighboring land uses and to cushion any adverse effects by the imposition of conditions designed to mitigate them. [*Id.* at 514–16.]

Why is a conditional use permit a "more balanced approach than total exclusion"? Would a conditional use requirement be an unconstitutional "burden" on religious exercise? See, e.g., *Konikov v. Orange County*, 410 F.3d 1317 (11th Cir. 2005) (requirement to apply for a conditional use permit is not in itself a substantial burden); *Tran v. Gwinn*, 554 S.E.2d 63 (Va. 2001) (conditional use permit necessary for use of home as a place of worship). The facts of the particular case, of course, may be influential. Compare *Kali Bari Temple v. Board of Adjustment*, 638 A.2d 839 (N.J. App. Div. 1994) (use of home in residential area; any adverse effect on neighborhood reduced by conditions), with *Macedonian Orthodox Church v. Planning Bd.*, 636 A.2d 96 (N.J. App. Div. 1994) (proposal to more than double the size of existing church). For more on conditional uses see Chapter 6, *infra*. For the difficult problem of applying historic preservation laws to religious structures, see Chapter 9, *infra*.

The courts have recognized that a wide variety of uses are acceptable as accessory uses to religious institutions, especially in those majority states granting religious uses special protection. *City of Richmond Heights v. Richmond Heights Presbyterian Church*, 764 S.W.2d 647 (Mo. 1989) (day care center); *Solid Rock Ministries Int'l v. Board of Zoning Appeals*, 740 N.E.2d 320 (Ohio Ct. App. 2001) (home for pregnant unwed teenage girls). But see *First Assembly of God v. Collier County*, 20 F.3d 419 (11th Cir. 1994) (homeless shelter not an accessory use to church).

The court's interpretation of the free exercise clause of the particular state's constitution, and sometimes special legislation mandating religious preferences, are also important in the outcome of state court review. For example, the Indiana court has held that churches must be allowed in residential districts to satisfy its constitutional provision for religious freedom, in *Church of Christ in Indianapolis v. Metropolitan Bd. of Zoning Appeals*, 371 N.E.2d 1331 (Ind. App. 1978). In Massachusetts, a state law known as the Dover Amendment prohibits local governments from regulating religious uses except in relation to parking and square footage restrictions. Because of the law, in *Martin v. Corporation of Presiding Bishop of Church of Jesus Christ of Latter Day Saints*, 747 N.E.2d 131 (Mass. 2001), the town of Belmont was prohibited from applying height limitations of its code to the temple's proposed eighty-three-foot-high steeple.

State Religious Freedom Restoration Acts. These are modeled after the federal Religious Freedom Restoration Act, which was struck down so far as it applied to state and local governments as beyond the powers of Congress in *City of Boerne v. Flores*, 521 U.S. 507 (1997). Like the original federal act, the state acts provide more protection than the federal or state constitutions. The state acts require that if religious exercise is "substantially burdened" by government regulation, the government must demonstrate that the regulation is narrowly tailored to achieve a compelling state interest. Oftentimes the acts provide specifically that regulations that are generally applicable are subject to the compelling state interest test, as well as providing for recovery of attorney's fees if a plaintiff is successful in a claim under the act. E.g., Fla. Stat. Ann. § 761.03; 775 Ill. Comp. Stat. 35/15 to 35/25; R.I. Gen. Laws. §§ 42-80.1-1 to 42-80.1-4. The "little RFRAs" to date, however, have not generally been interpreted broadly in favor of religious uses. For instance, the denial of a special exception permit for expansion of a church school in a residential area was found not to be a violation of the Florida RFRA where traffic safety concerns outweighed any burden on religious expression in *First Baptist Church of Perrine v. Miami Dade County*, 768 So. 2d 1114 (Fla. App. 2000); see also *City of Chicago Heights v. Living Word Outreach Full Gospel Church & Ministries, Inc.*, 707 N.E.2d 53 (Ill. App. 1999) (upholding special use requirement for church under Illinois act); C. Laneri, Comment. *The Texas Religious Freedom Restoration Act: Does It Really Work?* 16 Tex. Wesleyan L. Rev. 457 (Spring, 2010).

RLUIPA. Land use restrictions on religious uses also are subject to attack under federal law, most recently the Religious Land Use and Institutionalized Persons Act (RLUIPA), as well as federal constitutional claims based on equal protection or the Free Exercise Clause. RLUIPA was adopted by Congress in 2000 after the Supreme Court had invalidated RFRA and, unlike the earlier statute, applies directly to land use regulation. RLUIPA had strong legislative and administrative support, and Congress intended to compel the courts to apply a strict scrutiny standard of review to the land use regulation of religious uses that the Supreme Court had rejected. RLUIPA cases have proliferated, attracting advocates on all sides who either participate as "friends of the court" or represent parties in RLUIPA challenges. Because successful plaintiffs under the Act can recover attorney's fees, governments have a significant incentive to conform their land use regulations and behavior to the Act's requirements, or perhaps go beyond what RLUIPA requires. The following case illustrates one application of RLUIPA:

CIVIL LIBERTIES FOR URBAN BELIEVERS, CHRIST CENTER, CHRISTIAN COVENANT OUTREACH CHURCH v. CITY OF CHICAGO

342 F.3d 752 (7th Cir. 2003), *cert. denied*, 541 U.S. 1096 (2004),
Noted, 23 Pace Envtl. L. Rev. 263 (2006)

BAUER, CIRCUIT JUDGE:

. . . .

The [Chicago Zoning Ordinance or "CZO"] broadly divides the city into R, B, C, and M zones for residential, business, commercial, and manufacturing uses, respectively. Each zone, in turn, is subdivided into numbered districts and subdistricts. A majority of Chicago land available for development is zoned R. The CZO's stated purposes include the following: (i) "to promote and to protect the public health, safety, morals, comfort, convenience, and the general welfare of the people," and (ii) "to protect the character and maintain the stability for residential, business, commercial, and manufacturing areas within the City, and to promote the orderly and beneficial development of such areas." *See* 17 Mun. Code Chi. § 2(1), (3) (2001). Churches are permitted uses as of right in all R zones, but are termed Variations in the Nature of Special Uses ("Special Use") in all B zones as well as C1, C2, C3, and C5 districts. All Special Uses, whether of a religious or nonreligious nature, require approval by the Zoning Board of Appeals ("ZBA") following a public hearing. *See id.* §§ 7.3-1(4), 8.4, 9.4, & 11.10. Special Use approval is expressly conditioned upon the design, location, and operation of the proposed use consistent with the protection of public health, safety, and welfare, and the proposed use must not substantially injure the value of neighboring property. *See id.* § 11.10-4. Factoring such expenses as application, title search, and legal fees, as well as appraisal and neighbor notification costs, the aggregate cost of obtaining Special Use approval approaches $5000. Before a church may locate in a C4 district or an M zone, the Chicago City Council must vote in favor of a Map Amendment, effectively rezoning the targeted parcel. *See id.* §§ 9.4-4, 10, & 11.9. Development for church use of land consisting of two or more acres (necessary for congregations exceeding roughly 500 members) requires approval by City Council vote of a Planned Development. *See id.* §§ 11.11-1(a) & 11.11-3.

Civil Liberties for Urban Believers ("CLUB") is an unincorporated association of 40 to 50 Chicago-area religious or not-for-profit Illinois corporations ranging in size from 15 to 15,000 congregants. Five of these individual member churches joined CLUB as plaintiffs in an action challenging the validity of the CZO. [Chicago later amended the CZO, after plaintiffs initially brought suit, to require that not only churches but all assembly uses in the referenced zoning districts undergo special use approval, and exempted churches from the showing that the use was necessary for public convenience.] . . . Appellants argue that the CZO violates RLUIPA's substantial burden provision, which requires land-use regulations that substantially burden religious exercise to be the least restrictive means of advancing a compelling government interest, *see* 42 U.S.C. § 2000cc(a), as well as its nondiscrimination provision, which prohibits land-use regulations that either disfavor religious uses relative to nonreligious uses or unreasonably exclude religious uses from a particular jurisdiction, *see* 42 U.S.C. § 2000cc(b).

. . . In order to prevail on a claim under the substantial burden provision, a plaintiff must first demonstrate that the regulation at issue actually imposes a substantial burden on religious exercise. RLUIPA defines "religious exercise" to encompass "any exercise of religion, whether or not compelled by, or central to, a system of religious belief," including "the use, building, or conversion of real property for the purpose of religious exercise." 42 U.S.C. § 2000cc-5(7). This definition reveals Congress's intent to expand the concept of religious exercise contemplated both in decisions discussing the precursory RFRA and in traditional First Amendment jurisprudence. Although the text of the statute contains no similar express definition of the term "substantial burden," RLUIPA's legislative history indicates that it is to be interpreted by reference to RFRA and First Amendment jurisprudence. *See* 146 Cong. Rec. 7774-01, 7776 ("The term 'substantial burden' as used in this Act is not intended to be given any broader interpretation than the Supreme Court's articulation of the concept of substantial burden or religious exercise"). Chicago cites a decision of this Court which held that, within the meaning of RFRA, a substantial burden on religious exercise "is one that forces adherents of a religion to refrain from religiously motivated conduct, inhibits or constrains conduct or expression that manifests a central tenet of a person's religious beliefs, or compels conduct or expression that is contrary to those beliefs." *Mack v. O'Leary*, 80 F.3d 1175, 1179 (7th Cir. 1996) (vacated on other grounds). Substituting RLUIPA's broader definition of religious exercise, which need not be "compelled by or central to" a particular religion, for that articulated in *Mack*, the meaning of "substantial burden on religious exercise" could be read to include the effect of any regulation that "inhibits or constrains the use, building, or conversion of real property for the purpose of religious exercise." Such a construction might lend support to Appellants' contention that the CZO, insofar as it contributes to other existing constraints upon the use of specific parcels as churches, substantially burdens religious exercise. However, this cannot be the correct construction of "substantial burden on religious exercise" under RLUIPA. Application of the substantial burden provision to a regulation inhibiting or constraining any religious exercise, including the use of property for religious purposes, would render meaningless the word "substantial," because the slightest obstacle to religious exercise incidental to the regulation of land use — however minor the burden it were to impose — could then constitute a burden sufficient to trigger RLUIPA's requirement that the regulation advance a compelling governmental interest by the least restrictive means. We therefore hold that, in the context of RLUIPA's broad definition of religious exercise, a land-use regulation that imposes a substantial burden on religious exercise is one that necessarily bears direct, primary, and fundamental responsibility for rendering religious exercise — including the use of real property for the purpose thereof within the regulated jurisdiction generally — effectively impracticable.

Appellants contend that the scarcity of affordable land available for development in R zones, along with the costs, procedural requirements, and inherent political aspects of the Special Use, Map Amendment, and Planned Development approval processes, impose precisely such a substantial burden. However, we find that these conditions — which are incidental to any high-density urban land use — do not amount to a substantial burden on religious exercise. While they may contribute to the ordinary difficulties associated with location (by any person or entity, religious or nonreligious) in a large city, they do not render impracticable the use of real property in Chicago for religious exercise, much less discourage churches from locating or attempting to locate in Chicago. Significantly, each of the five individual plaintiff churches has successfully located within Chicago's city limits. That they expended considerable time and money so to do does not entitle them to relief under RLUIPA's substantial burden provision. Otherwise, compliance with RLUIPA would require municipal governments not merely to treat religious land uses on an equal footing with nonreligious land uses, but rather to favor them in the form of an outright exemption from land-use regulations. Unfortunately for Appellants, no such free pass for religious land uses masquerades among the legitimate protections RLUIPA affords to religious exercise.

NOTES AND QUESTIONS

1. *Substantial burden under RLUIPA.* The *CLUB* case is typical in treating the financial expense of locating a religious use where the zoning allows it, albeit through special review procedures, as an inconvenience and not the "substantial burden" required to find a RLUIPA violation. Has the court adopted a correct interpretation of "substantial burden"? Recall that it holds that a substantial burden is imposed if it "necessarily bears direct, primary, and fundamental responsibility for rendering religious exercise . . . effectively impracticable." See also *Vision Church v. Village of Long Grove*, 468 F.3d 975 (7th Cir. 2006) (denial of special use permit for 100,000 square foot church complex was not a substantial burden where zoning code allows 55,000 square feet, but rather an "incidental" burden where the size would enable the church to grow). If not, what interpretation should it adopt?

Living Water Church of God v. Charter Twp. Meridian, 258 Fed. Appx. 729, 735, 736 (6th Cir. 2007), has described the meaning of "substantial burden" adopted by other circuits:

> [T]he Eleventh Circuit, addressing a challenge to a city zoning ordinance that required the plaintiffs to relocate their synagogues to another part of the city, concluded that a substantial burden
>
>> must place more than an inconvenience on religious exercise; a "substantial burden" is akin to significant pressure which directly coerces the religious adherent to conform his or her behavior accordingly. Thus, a substantial burden can result from

> pressure that tends to force adherents to forego religious precepts or from pressure that mandates religious conduct.
>
> *Midrash Sephardi, Inc. v. Town of Surfside*, 366 F.3d 1214, 1227 (11th Cir. 2004). In *San Jose Christian College v. City of Morgan Hill*, 360 F.3d 1024 (9th Cir. 2004), the Ninth Circuit held that a " 'substantial burden' on 'religious exercise' must impose a significantly great restriction or onus upon such exercise." 360 F.3d at 1034 (challenging the city's denial of the college's rezoning application). The Fourth Circuit has announced that it "likewise follow[s] the Supreme Court's guidance in the Free Exercise Clause context and conclude[s] that, for RLUIPA purposes, a substantial burden on religious exercise occurs when a state or local government, through act or omission, 'put[s] substantial pressure on an adherent to modify his behavior and to violate his beliefs.' " *Lovelace v. Lee*, 472 F.3d 174, 187 (4th Cir. 2006) (inmate's RLUIPA action).

The court noted that it had not "expressly defined" substantial burden. Would the result in the *Club* case have been different under any of these tests?

Does the presence of apparent bad faith action on the part of the government influence the court's assessment of whether there is a substantial burden? Compare *CLUB* with *Sts. Constantine and Helen Greek Orthodox Church, Inc. v. City of New Berlin*, 396 F.3d 895 (7th Cir. 2005) (denial of a planned unit development approval, and consequent delay, expense and uncertainty if church were to reapply for a different permit is a substantial burden, especially on the facts where there is a "whiff" of bad faith by city actors). Similarly, see the district court's comparison of facts in *Guru Nanak Sikh Society of Yuba City v. County of Sutter*, 456 F.3d 978 (7th Cir. 2006) (history behind two conditional use permits and the inconsistent and vague reasons for ultimately denying the permits found to be violation), with the facts in *Hillcrest Christian School v. City of Los Angeles*, 2007 U.S. Dist. Lexis 95925 (C.D. Cal. 2007) (approval, with conditions for operation and location of school's expansion, after several earlier expansions allowed with conditions, not a substantial burden for RLUIPA or constitutional purposes).

2. *Common themes.* K. Chaffee & D. Merriam, *Six Fact Patterns of Substantial Burden in RLUIPA: Lessons for Potential Litigants*, 2 Alb. Gov't L. Rev. 437 (2009), note some common themes in the substantial burden cases: (1) financial hardship does not automatically result in a substantial burden. (2) "Since the ability to worship together is crucial for many, some courts seem reluctant to grant summary judgment to local governments defending decisions to limit or deny churches' requests to build or expand in order to accommodate a growing congregation." Decisions on expansion are fact-intensive, however. (3) "[C]ourts may look to the availability of other suitable properties or building sites when considering whether the institution is substantially burdened." (4) "The courts are fairly uniform in holding that religious institutions must show more than a 'mere inconvenience' to establish a substantial burden." (5) "[I]n most cases, a court's substantial burden analysis is likely to be influenced by the presence or absence of discriminatory treatment." (6) "When issues of fairness are not at play, and it is likely that a local government will grant an applicant's request after some modification, courts tend not to find a substantial burden."

3. *Least restrictive means to further a compelling governmental interest.* Where the religious use under RLUIPA can prove a substantial burden, then it is up to the government to show that it is using the "least restrictive means" to further a "compelling governmental interest." In the *Cottonwood Christian Center v. Cypress Redev. Agency*, 218 F. Supp. 2d 1203

(C.D. Cal. 2002), the city and Redevelopment Agency argued that their interest was to prevent blight and generate revenue for the city, but the court disagreed, finding that the church could have helped to eliminate any blight that might exist, as well as to generate a market for surrounding commercial developments. It noted that the city had not demonstrated that there was no other way to provide revenue without taking the church property and preventing it from building in that location. Another example of a city's violation of RLUIPA is found in the case of *Murphy v. Zoning Comm'n*, 289 F. Supp. 2d 87 (D. Conn. 2003), *vacated on ripeness grounds*, 402 F.3d 342 (2d Cir. 2005). There, a residential homeowner who held weekly Sunday afternoon prayer meetings was found to be substantially burdened by a city's code enforcement requirement that limited the number of persons who could attend the meeting. The court held that the enforcement action had a chilling effect on attendance at prayer meetings and thus defeated the religious purpose of the meetings to help those in need of prayer. The court also found that the city could have used a less restrictive means to protect its recognized compelling interest in code enforcement, such as limiting the associated traffic or on-street parking rather than the number of persons. See also *Lighthouse Cmty. Church of God v. City of Southfield*, 382 F. Supp. 2d 937 (E.D. Mich. 2005) (denial of a parking variance a substantial burden; resulting outright prohibition of the use is not the least restrictive means). But see *New Life Worship Center v. Town of Smithfield Zoning Board*, 2010 R.I. Super. LEXIS 101 (RI Super. Ct. 2010) (denial of special permit for a commercial fitness center in a private relgious high school was the least restrictive means to protect students). Could the city in the *Cottonwood* case have used a more narrowly tailored restriction on religious uses to further its zoning and redevelopment interests?

4. *Equal treatment under RLUIPA*. RLUIPA also requires that religious uses not be treated on less than equal terms with a nonreligious assembly: "no government shall impose or implement a land use regulation in a manner that treats a religious assembly or institution on less than equal terms with a nonreligious assembly or institution." § 2000cc(b)(1). In *CLUB*, the federal court found that Chicago's later amendment to the zoning code, to require that both churches and other types of assembly uses go through the conditional use process, avoided a violation under this requirement. The courts have disagreed on how the equal terms provision should be applied. The Third Circuit Court of Appeals held that a plaintiff claiming a violation of RLUIPA's Equal Terms Clause does not need to establish that the regulation substantially burdens religious exercise, agreeing with the Eleventh and Seventh Circuits on that point. However, unlike the Eleventh and Seventh Circuits, the Third Circuit held that a plaintiff claiming a violation of the Equal Terms Clause must identify a similarly-situated secular counterpart that is better treated under the regulatory objectives. The Third Circuit also deviated from the Eleventh Circuit by applying a strict liability standard under the Equal Terms Clause rather than strict scrutiny. See *Lighthouse Inst. for Evangelism, Inc. v. City of Long Branch*, 510 F.3d 253 (3d Cir. 2007); *see also Digrugilliers v. Consol. City of Indianapolis*, 506 F.3d 612 (7th Cir. 2007) (holding that plaintiff need not prove substantial burden of religious exercise for Equal Terms claim). The Seventh Circuit en banc established its own test in *River of Life Kingdom Ministries v. Village of Hazel Crest*, 611 F.3d 367 (7th Cir. 2010), distinguishing it from that of the Third Circuit: "The problems that we have identified with the Third Circuit's test can be solved by a shift of focus from regulatory purpose to accepted zoning criteria. The shift is not merely semantic. 'Purpose' is subjective and manipulable, so asking about 'regulatory purpose' might result in giving local officials a free hand in answering the question 'equal with respect to what?' 'Regulatory criteria' are objective — and it is federal judges who will apply the criteria to resolve the issue." To what extent do

these interpretations reflect judicial interpretation of the constitutional Equal Protection Clause?

5. *The constitutionality of RLUIPA.* Much debate resulted after the passage of RLUIPA as to whether it would be upheld as constitutional as applied to the states. The predecessor act was found unconstitutional as applied to the states in *City of Boerne v. Flores*, 521 U.S. 507 (1997). RLUIPA was found constitutional by a unanimous Supreme Court as not in violation of the Establishment Clause, as applied to prisoners, in *Cutter v. Wilkinson*, 544 U.S. 709 (2005). Most lower federal courts have held the Act to be constitutional, as in *Guru Nanak Sikh Society of Yuba City v. County of Sutter*, 456 F.3d 978 (7th Cir. 2006), and *Westchester Day School v. Village of Mamaroneck*, 504 F.3d 338 (2d Cir. 2007). See the debate between Anthony R. Picarello, Jr. (Beckett Fund for Religious Liberty) and Marci A. Hamilton (Benjamin N. Cardozo School of Law) in Planning & Envtl. L., April 2004, at 3-13.

6. *Free Exercise Clause of the United States Constitution.* In the principal case, the churches also claimed that Chicago's zoning ordinance violated the protections granted the free exercise of religion under the First Amendment of the U.S. Constitution, the "Free Exercise Clause." Before RLUIPA was enacted, this clause was often the basis of actions by religious groups seeking protection from land use restrictions, with mixed results that led to the attempt to provide more protection under RLUIPA.

CLUB, *Murphy*, *Guru Nanak* and similar cases have held the two claims to be virtually identical. Under the Free Exercise Clause, a substantial burden of the exercise of religion must be justified by a compelling state interest, a test otherwise known as the "strict scrutiny" test. *Sherbert v. Verner*, 374 U.S. 398 (1962). However, the U.S. Supreme Court cases have held that the strict scrutiny test under the Free Exercise Clause does not apply to a law of "general applicability." In *Employment Division v. Smith*, 494 U.S. 872 (1990), the Court upheld the firing of a drug counselor for using a controlled substance as part of a Native American ritual, because the law applied was one of "general applicability." No Supreme Court case has considered a land use regulation under the Free Exercise Clause. Zoning ordinances are laws of general applicability to the extent that they apply to all uses and divide municipalities into different zoning districts. RLUIPA can be argued to have codified earlier free exercise law except to the extent that it repealed the "laws of general applicability" rule.

Prior to *Smith*, the federal circuit courts had evolved a three-part balancing test to determine if the Free Exercise Clause is violated, as explained in *Grosz v. City of Miami Beach*, 721 F.2d 729 (11th Cir. 1983): "First, the government regulation must regulate religious conduct, not belief. Second, the law must have a secular purpose and a secular effect. Third, once these two thresholds are crossed, the court engages in a balancing of competing governmental and religious interests. On the free exercise side of the balance weighs the burden that Appellees bear of conducting their services in compliance with applicable zoning restrictions or relocating in a suitably zoned district. Countering on the government's side is the substantial infringement of the City's zoning policy that would occur were the conduct allowed to continue . . . ."

In *Grosz*, the court found that the balancing favored the city's zoning code, and thus decided that the code constitutionally restricted the conduct of religious services in a remodeled garage accessory to a residence, where the zoning code prohibited religious congregations in the single-family district. Accord *Lakewood, Ohio Congregation of Jehovah's Witnesses, Inc. v. City of Lakewood*, 699 F.2d 303 (6th Cir. 1983) (upholding prohibition against building church in residential district). Does RLUIPA change this balancing equation? If so, how?

Courts will, of course, strike down the exclusion of a religious edifice when there is blatant discrimination. *Islamic Center of Mississippi, Inc. v. City of Starkville*, 840 F.2d 293 (5th Cir. 1988) (Muslims only worshipers denied exception to prohibition of churches in residential zone). But see *Christian Gospel Church, Inc. v. San Francisco*, 896 F.2d 1221 (9th Cir.), *cert. denied*, 498 U.S. 999 (1990).

7. *Individualized assessment. Smith* left undisturbed the application of the strict scrutiny test when the law contains a "system of individualized exceptions," or where the government makes an individualized assessment in a discretionary decision-making process. Land use regulations commonly include procedures that make "individualized assessments," such as in the granting of variances, special use permits, certificates of appropriateness for historic preservation purposes, and the like. Cases before and after *Smith* continue to apply strict scrutiny to land use cases where individualized assessments are involved. See, e.g., *Cottonwood Christian Center, supra* Note 3 (city's finding of necessity to condemn church property); *Christian Gospel Church, Inc. v. City and County of San Francisco*, 896 F.2d 1221 (9th Cir. 1990) (pre-*Smith* case applying strict scrutiny to denial of a conditional use permit); *First Covenant Church v. City of Seattle*, 840 P.2d 174 (Wash. 1992) (post-*Smith* case applying strict scrutiny to historical landmark decision); *Rocky Mountain Christian Church v. Bd. of County Comm'rs*, 612 F. Supp. 2d 1163 (D. Colo. 2009) ("[T]he substantial burden 'jurisdictional hook' concerning land use regulations imposed via individualized assessments is applicable in this case."). Since many land use decisions are made in "individualized assessment" proceedings, this is an important exception to the *Smith* rule. Chapter 6 considers variances and other administrative remedies in zoning regulations.

8. *The "Establishment" Clause*. This is the converse of the "free exercise" problem. The Establishment Clause provides that "Congress shall make no law respecting the establishment of religion." U.S. Const. Amend. I. An Establishment Clause problem can arise when a zoning ordinance gives a preferred status to a religious use.

Larkin v. Grendel's Den, Inc., 459 U.S. 116 (1982), *noted*, 28 Vill. L. Rev. 1000 (1982-83), upheld a claim that a Massachusetts statute providing that liquor licenses could not be issued if vetoed by a church or school located within 500 feet of the licensed premises violated the Establishment Clause. A church vetoed a liquor license under this provision.

The Court held that the statutory veto violated the Establishment of Religion Clause of the federal Constitution. Similar veto provisions are contained in many zoning regulations. The Court applied its separation of church and state line of authority. It held that the usual deference due zoning ordinances was not warranted because the delegation was to a private entity. The veto violated the three Establishment Clause criteria adopted in *Lemon v. Kurtzman*, 403 U.S. 602 (1971). The regulation must have a secular purpose. The purpose was secular here because the veto would protect churches and schools from disturbances from liquor outlets. The regulation also must not primarily advance or inhibit religion. This test was not met because the standardless veto authorized by the statute could be used by churches for religious purposes. Finally, the regulation must not foster excessive government entanglement with religion. This test was not met because the statute "enmeshes churches in the process of government" and could create political fragmentation on religious lines. *Id.* at 127.

Justice Rehnquist dissented. He would have upheld the statute as "a quite sensible Massachusetts liquor zoning law." *Id.* at 128. He noted that a flat ban on liquor stores within a certain radius of churches, "which the majority concedes is valid, is more protective of churches and more restrictive of liquor sales than the present [statute]." *Id.* He concluded that "[t]he State can constitutionally protect churches from liquor for the same reasons it can protect them from fire, noise, and other harm." *Id.* at 130.

Establishment Clause issues may become more important as states and municipalities seek to provide favorable treatment for religious uses. See Colo. Rev. Stat. § 29-1-1202 (prohibiting local governments from limiting when or how frequently individuals may meet in private residences to pray or worship). In *Ehlers-Renzi v. Connelly School of the Holy Child*, 224 F.3d 283 (4th Cir. 2000), the court upheld an ordinance exempting religious uses from the requirement to obtain conditional use approval, as not being a violation of the Establishment Clause. Similarly, the California Supreme Court upheld a state law which allowed religious organizations to exempt themselves from the application of local historic landmarking ordinances in *East Bay Asian Local Dev. Corp. v. California*, 13 P.3d 1122 (Cal. 2000). See *Rocky Mountain Christian Church v. Bd. of County Comm'rs*, 612 F. Supp. 2d 1163 (D. Colo. 2009) ("equal terms, substantial burden, and unreasonable limitations provisions of RLUPA, as applied in this case, do not violate the Establishment Clause.").

9. *Sources.* Evans-Cowley & Pearlman, *Six Flags over Jesus: RLUIPA, Megachurches, and Zoning*, 21 Tul. Envtl. L.J. 203 (2008); Galvan, *Beyond Worship: The Religious Land Use and Institutionalized Persons Act of 2000 and Religious Institutions' Auxiliary Uses*, 24 Yale L. & Pol'y Rev. 207 (2006); Lennington, *Thou Shalt Not Zone: The Overbroad Applications and Troubling Implications of RLUIPA's Land Use Provisions*, 29 Seattle L. Rev. 805 (2006); Salkin & Lavine. *The Genesis of RLUIPA and Federalism: Evaluating the Creation of a Federal Statutory Right and its Impact on Local Government*, 40 Urb. Law. 195 (2008); Weinstein, *How to Avoid a "Holy War" — Dealing with Potential RLUIPA Claims*, Planning & Envtl. L., March 2008, at 3; A. Lavine & P. Salkin, *God and the Land: A Holy War Between Religious Exercise and Community Planning and Development*, Albany Gov't L. Rev., Vol. 2 (2009) available at http://papers.ssrn.com; A. MacLeod, *A Non-Fatal Collision: Interpreting RLUIPA Where Religious Land Uses and Community Interests Meet*, The Urban Lawyer (2010).

E. MIXED-USE ZONING, FORM-BASED ZONING, AND TRANSIT-ORIENTED DEVELOPMENT

Nowhere is the Euclidean hybrid form of zoning more apparent than in new zoning techniques that depart substantially from the Euclidean model to introduce new forms of urban development. These techniques are characterized by regulations encouraging a mixture of uses rather than the separation of uses, and by a form-based zoning approach to land development that does away with use distinctions altogether.

[1.] Mixed-Use Development

Mixed-use development (MXD) is just that. It can include a mix of residential building types and can also add retail and commercial uses. MXD requires special treatment in the zoning ordinance, which divides communities into districts in which only one use is permitted. One option is the planned unit development, discussed in Chapter 6, which can authorize mixed uses in the development plan. Large-scale master-planned communities include a variety of mixed-use neighborhoods and centers.

Here is a typical expression of what an MXD is intended to do: "The purpose of the RD3 Riverfront Mixed-Use Zoning District is to promote a mix of residential, commercial and light industrial uses that are compatible with uses along the river, including housing and commercial buildings; preserve and adaptively reuse existing mill-type structures; promote variations in the siting of structures and amenities; and to enhance view corridors to the river." *City of Pawtucket v. Pawtucket Zoning Board of Review*, 2010 R.I. Super. LEXIS 71 (R.I. Super. Ct. 2010).

MXD is also common in infill development in downtown or suburban centers, and typically includes high density housing. As one report explained, "[i]n a town center or infill development downtown, mixed use can succeed within each building. It may mean offices or apartments over shops along the town square, or a hotel over shops downtown. Mixing uses in each building or in adjacent buildings works best when design guidelines ensure that the buildings will be consistent in height and size, regardless of use." [California] Local Government Comm'n, Creating Great Neighborhoods: Density in Your Community 33 (2003). Birch, Who Lives Downtown (Brookings Institution, 2005), presents an interesting survey of downtown populations. Here is a prescription for town centers:

> The keys to a successful town center . . . are numerous high-density mixed uses and an appealing public realm designed especially for pedestrians and their activities. It needs to have good connections to neighborhoods and the region so that people can come and enjoy it, and it must have a mix of activities so it is full of life not only in the day, but also during evening and weekends. [Sheridan, *Centering Towns*, Urban Land, April, 2005, at 90, 92.]

How should this kind of development be zoned? One approach for allowing MXD as infill is discretionary review, usually done through the approval of a planned unit development for an MXD. A community can also adopt an MXD district that contains land use regulations specially tailored for mixed use development. What is required may depend upon the purpose of the MXD. The ordinance may require minimum densities and floor area ratios in order to achieve desired residential and commercial densities for a high-density MXD. At the other end of the spectrum, for a mid-scale MXD in an existing downtown or other center, the MXD ordinance may impose maximum parking ratios and limitations on square footage to prohibit Big Box retail and other large developments that might overwhelm the neighborhood. See Tillett, *Retrofitting the Suburbs: The Gresham Civic Neighborhood*, PAS Memo, Nov. 1995.

The Fort Collins, Colorado, Medium Density Mixed-Use Neighborhood District is an example. It is "intended to be a setting for concentrated housing within easy walking distance of transit and a commercial district." Its list of permitted uses includes single- and multi-family residential and limited commercial and retail uses, with more intensive uses permitted through special review. Land use standards require "an overall minimum average density of twelve units per acre of residential land," a mix of housing types, access to a park, buildings facing the street, and "development as a series of complete blocks bounded by streets." Land Use Code, Div. 4.5. Here is another approach:

> Silver Spring, Maryland, is approaching mixed use by "districting" — that is, by assigning each building to a single use, whether office or residential (most buildings do, however, include ground-floor retail), and grouping the buildings together around a central plaza or strategic institutions so that a district is created in which live, work, and play uses are within short distances of each other. [Kozloff, *Refning Mixed Use*, Urban Land, Feb. 2005, at 92, 95.]

For discussion of MXD, see Baers, *Zoning Code Revisions to Permit Mixed Use Development*, 7 Zoning & Plan. L. Rep. 81 (1984); Gosling, *Patterns of Association*, Urb. Land, Oct. 1998, at 42 (discussing MXDs in various cities); Jenkins, *Housing That Works*, Builder, Sep. 1998, at 133 (live/work neighborhoods); Schutz & Kline, *Getting to the Bottom of Mixed Use*, Planning, Jan., 2004, at 16 (mixed retail use). For an illustration of the general acceptance of this form of development, see *Gyrodyne Co. of Am., Inc. v. State*, 2010 NY Slip Op 51129, 2010 N.Y. Misc. LEXIS 2791 (NY Ct. of Cl., 2010) (mixed use district possibility used to prove value in eminent domain case).

[2.] Transit-Oriented Development

What it is. Transit-oriented development, or TOD, is a specialized form of mixed-use development that takes advantage of public transit to develop mixed-use communities around transit stops and stations. These can include bus stops as well as light rail. The difference is that TOD requires special attention to the connectivity with the transit that is available. Two planners have identified the 3Ds of TODs — density, which requires a sufficiently high density near transit stops; design; and diversity. Tumlin & Millard-Ball, *How to Make Transit-Oriented Development Work*, Planning, May, 2003, at 14. The following definition of TOD in the transportation planning rules of the Oregon Land Conservation and Development Commission captures the idea:

> Transit-Oriented Development (TOD)" means a mix of residential, retail and office uses and a supporting network of roads, bicycle and pedestrian ways focused on a major transit stop designed to support a high level of transit use. The key features of transit oriented development include:
>
> (a) A mixed use center at the transit stop, oriented principally to transit riders and pedestrian and bicycle travel from the surrounding area;
>
> (b) High density residential development proximate to the transit stop sufficient to support transit operation and neighborhood commercial uses within the TOD;
>
> (c) A network of roads, and bicycle and pedestrian paths to support high levels of pedestrian access within the TOD and high levels of transit use. [Oregon Admin. R. § 660-012-005(28).]

The inclusion of essential services and conveniences close to the transit station is also recommended so they can be accessed by pedestrians. What do you think this kind of development would look like? For a statute authorizing municipalities to cooperate with public transportation agencies to establish districts to achieve transit-oriented development and redevelopment, see Pa. Stat. Ann. tit. 73, § 850.101 et seq.

Table 2: TOD Types and Characteristics

TOD TYPE	Land-Use Mix	Minimum Housing Density	Regional Connectivity	Frequencies	Examples
Urban Downtown	• Office Center • Urban Entertainment • Multifamily Housing • Retail	>60 units/acre	High *Hub of Radial System*	<10 Minutes	• LoDo, Denver • Printer's Row, Chicago • Embarcadero, San Francisco
Urban Neighborhood	• Residential Retail • Class B Commercial	>20 units/acre	Medium *Access to Downtown* *Subregional Circulation*	10 Minutes Peak 20 Minutes Off-peak	• Mockingbird Station, Dallas • Wicker Park, Chicago • Barrio Logan, San Diego
Suburban Center	• Primary Office Center • Urban Entertainment • Multifamily Housing • Retail	>50 units/acre	High *Access to Downtown* *Subregional Hub*	10 Minutes Peak 10–15 Off-peak	• Arlington Heights, Ill. • Addison Circle, Addison, Tex. • Downtown Plano, Plano, Tex. • Rosslyn Ballston Corridor, Arlington County, Va.
Suburban Neighborhood	• Residential • Neighborhood Retail • Local Office	>12 units/acre	Medium *Access to Suburban Centers and Access to Downtown*	20 Minutes Peak 30 Minutes Off-peak	• Maplewood, N.J. • Ohlone Chenoweth, Santa Clara County, Calif. • The Crossings, Calif.
Commuter Town Center	• Retail Center • Residential	>12 units/acre	Low *Access to Downtown*	Peak Service Demand-Responsive	• Prairie Crossing, Ill. • Suisun City, Calif.

Source: From Dittmar, Transit-Oriented Development, Planning Practice, August, 2004, at 4.

TOD requires a transit-oriented and pedestrian-friendly site design that includes convenient paths and connections to transit stops and other destinations, and a continuous network of streets and pathways to minimize travel distances. The pedestrian environment should be improved through measures such as security, lighting and heightened visibility; protection from traffic; adequate space for pedestrians and bicycles; weather protection; and transit shelters. See M. Morris, ed., *Creating Transit-Supportive Land-Use Regulations* ch. 1, American Planning Association, Planning Advisory Serv. Rep. No. 468 (1996). The report also discusses other aspects of TOD, such as appropriate parking design, reduction of parking spaces to discourage automobile use, mixed-use development, and density increases to support transit. Parking is a critical issue. Excessive parking interferes with the integrated and accessible kind of development necessary for a successful TOD. See also The New Transit Town (H. Dittmar & G. Ohland eds., 2003); California Dep't of Transp., Statewide Transit-Oriented Development Study (2002).

Robert Freilich explains what should be contained in a TOD ordinance:

> TOD regulations govern the amount of development because they tend to permit higher densities of development proximate to transit stations. TOD regulations govern the type of development by permitting a richer variety of land-uses within a given area. TOD regulations are spatial in that they attempt to minimize the distance between intensive land uses and public transit facilities, thereby encouraging persons living or working in the area to utilize transit facilities. TOD regulations are relational in that they use innovative urban design guidelines to insure not only compatibility between mixed land uses, but also that those land uses relate functionally to the transit system. [*The Land-Use Implications of Transit-Oriented Development: Controlling the Demand Side of Transportation Congestion and Urban Sprawl*, 30 Urb. Law. 547, 551 (1998).]

What land use regulations would you adopt or modify to implement these objectives?

Washington County, Oregon's Community Development Code § 375-7(c)) states that "[c]ommercial uses shall be permitted in . . . [certain TOD districts] only if (1) It can be demonstrated they primarily serve adjacent residences and offices; (2) The proposed site is located [at specified major intersections]; and (3) They are located on the first floor of a multi-story building." What is the reason for this type of regulation? A requirement for minimum rather than maximum densities?

Effect on travel mode. Whether TOD actually decreases automobile travel is another issue. One study of San Francisco found that living within a half-mile of transit station did not affect transit travel. Only 18 percent of station area residents used public transit. Niles & Nelson, Measuring the Success of Transit-Oriented Development, available at http://globaltelematics.com/apa99.htm. Crane, *The Influence of Urban Form on Travel: An Interpretive Review*, 15 J. Plan. Lit. 3 (2000), also reviewed several studies of the relationship between transportation and land use and found that any definite conclusions are problematic. A more recent study, however, Bento et al., *The Effects of Urban Spatial Structure on Travel Demand in the United States*, 87 Rev. Econ. & Statistics 466 (2006), concludes that population centrality, jobs-housing balance, city shape, and road density have a significant effect on annual household vehicle miles traveled.

Challenges and problems. One recent study finds that much needs to be learned about what makes TODs work and how they should be developed. They note a number of challenges to TODs, including lack of clarity about what TOD is, a failure to obtain a functional integration between transit and surrounding uses, and the lack of good development guidelines. In addition, they found that synergy among different uses and functions was lacking, the regulatory and policy environment was fragmented, and market conditions may not be supportive. Belzer & Autler, Transit-Oriented Development: Moving From Rhetoric to Reality Ch. II.B (Brookings Institution, 2002). They suggest active and cooperative roles for local governments, transit agencies, lenders and developers and, on the planning side, recommend adoption of transit-oriented development area plans around all transit stations. TODs show how good urban development requires more than planning, but the authors note:

> The demand for more "urban style" development will likely increase over the next several years. Whether in revitalizing cities like Washington, D.C., outer-ring suburbs like Lenexa, Kansas, or the increasingly dense "boomburg" suburbs of Orange County, California, places with proximity to fixed-guideway transit systems will become increasingly valuable development sites in any region dealing with growth. TOD can help address the urban growth problems of these places if it is recognized as a mainstream development product. The challenge is to recognize the full extent of the opportunity offered by such sites and push for real transit-oriented development, rather than settling for sub-optimal projects that will provide considerably fewer benefits over the long run. [*Id.* at 28.]

The disposition of land around stations can result in new types of disputes. See, e.g. *Greenbelt Ventures, LLC v. Washington Metropolitan Area Transit*, 2010 U.S. Dist. LEXIS 90345 (D. Md. 2010).

[3.] New Urbanism, Neotraditional Development, Form-Based (and Smart) Codes

What it is. New Urbanism is an umbrella term that includes new development forms such as transit-oriented development but also includes traditional neighborhood development (TND) and neotraditional development. The New Urbanism takes inspiration from one of the most influential planning books of the 20th century — The Death and Life of Great American Cities (1961), in which Jane Jacobs applied meticulous techniques of observation to conclude that the "life" of urban places lies in their unplanned spontaneity of diverse uses. It is a reaction to urban sprawl with its low densities and reliance on the automobile, and attempts to create new urban forms at higher densities with mixed uses that are not so completely car-dependent.

A frequent complaint of the "new urbanists" is that conventional zoning makes it difficult, if not impossible, to achieve TNDs. Nor, they say, does it help to allow neotraditional developments as an alternative to conventional zoning, using techniques such as conditional use permits or planned unit developments, if conventional developments can be built "as of right." They believe the planned unit development process is too open and negotiable to produce the kind of development the prefer. Here is what two of the leaders of the New Urbanism movement say about traditional zoning:

> It is legally difficult to build good urban places in the United States. . . . Our current codes are based on a theory of urbanism that is decidedly anti-urban. They separate land uses, decrease densities, and increase the amount of land devoted to car travel, prohibiting the kind of urbanism that typifies our most beloved urban places. [Duany & Talen, *Growth: Making the Good Easy: The Smart Code Alternative*, 29 Fordham Urb. L.J. 1445 (2002).]

What do New Urbanists want? The New Urbanist charter contains a number of principles stretching from the region through the town to the individual building, but the application of New Urbanist principles at the neighborhood level is most familiar. Robert Sitkowski has noted six basic tenets of New Urbanism as applied to create traditional neighborhood development (TND). New Urbanism: Legal Considerations 3-5 (2004) (unpub. ms. on file with authors). These are:

- A focus on building types and a vertical and horizontal mix of uses. This tenet reflects a basic criticism of zoning, that it is based on a separation of uses considered no longer appropriate under New Urbanism, which promotes the integration of home, work and recreation with an emphasis on building types as opposed to use. New Urbanism TND ordinances are prescriptive rather than prohibitive. This is an important feature.
- A focus on design character. New Urbanism promotes features such as "build to" lines rather than setbacks, on-street parking, front porches, and architecture that respects local building traditions.
- A focus on the public realm. Zoning does not give serious consideration to public spaces. TND requires a regulation of the form of urban spaces with the center of each neighborhood defined by a public space and increased emphasis on the street as a design element.
- The street grid and connectivity. TND equally favors the pedestrian and the automobile and prefers a modified street grid with narrower streets and greater connectivity

through multiple avenues to a destination. Garages and parking areas are to be at the rear of buildings to increase "curb appeal."

- Increased density with a mix of uses and a pedestrian orientation. Neighborhood size should require only a five to ten minute walk to the center.

- A sense of community created by walkability, increased density, public spaces, and a mix of uses.

The Congress for the New Urbanism has a charter with 27 statements available at http://www.cnu.org/charter.

Much in TND incorporates design principles featured in mixed-use and transit-oriented development, with the difference that TND design principles require very specific design and architectural requirements. See R. Arendt, *Crossroads, Hamlet, Village, Town*, American Planning Ass'n, Planning Advisory Serv. Rep. No. 523/524 (2004).

Form-based codes. This is one type of land use regulation that is used to implement New Urbanist concepts. The Form-Based Code Institute provides the following definition:

> Form-based codes address the relationship between building facades and the public realm, the form and mass of buildings in relation to one another, and the scale and types of streets and blocks. The regulations and standards in form-based codes, presented in both diagrams and words, are keyed to a *regulating plan* that designates the appropriate form and scale (and therefore, character) of development rather than only distinctions in land-use types. This is in contrast to conventional zoning's focus on the segregation of land-use types, permissible property uses, and the control of development intensity through simple numerical parameters (e.g., FAR, dwellings per acre, height limits, setbacks, parking ratios). [Available at www.formbasedcodes.org.]

The Institute also describes the elements of form-based codes:

- *Regulating Plan.* A plan or map of the regulated area designating the locations where different building form standards apply, based on clear community intentions regarding the physical character of the area being coded.

- *Building Form Standards.* Regulations controlling the configuration, features, and functions of buildings that define and shape the public realm.

- *Public Space/Street Standards.* Specifications for the elements within the public realm (e.g., sidewalks, travel lanes, street trees, street furniture, etc.).

- *Administration.* A clearly defined application and project review process.

- *Definitions.* A glossary to ensure the precise use of technical terms.

Here is a definition of a regulating plan from Farmers Branch, Texas: "The regulating plan is the coding key for the Station Area form-based code. The regulating plan shows how each lot relates to public spaces (streets, civic greeens, pedestrian pathways,etc.) and the surrounding neighborhood."

Form-based codes can be adopted as an independent code, as a code parallel to the conventional zoning ordinance or as a floating overlay zone. The City of Miami has recently revised its zoning ordinance to incorporate form-based code concepts. For the city website with the zoning code posted, and information about the public participation process and the history of the effort see www.miami21.org. A summary is available on www.1000friendsofflorida.org/planning/Miami21.asp.

Smart codes. Another variety of New Urbanism regulation is the Smart Code, Developed by Duany Plater-Zyberk & Company, which is described as follows:

> The Smart Code is based on the transect concept. A transect is a geographic cross-section of a region that can be used to identify a continuum of habitats, ranging from rural to urban, that vary by their level and intensity of urban character. The continuum of the transect lends itself to the creation of different zoning categories, from rural preserve to urban core. [Duany & Talen, *supra*, at 1453.]

The Smart Code format includes a regional-scale planning code that generally regulates where development can occur, articles regulating horizontal development aspects, such as block sizes, thoroughfare assemblies and open spaces for projects in greenfield and infill areas, and an article regulating the vertical elements of a development, such as building use and configuration, landscaping, signage and a limited amount of architectural detail. For a web site and model smart code see www.smartcodecentral.org.

Over 100 communities have adopted some type of TND or Smart Code regulation. Some have revised all or parts of their ordinances, while others created special TND districts. These may either be permissive and applied through floating zones, or mandatory and mapped. Another technique is the specific or "regulating" plan, which has maps as well as text that includes the development regulations, and is similar to the urban design plan discussed in the next chapter. *Congress for the New Urbanism, Codifying New Urbanism: How to Reform Municipal Land Use Regulations*, American Planning Ass'n, Planning Advisory Serv. Rep. No. 526 (2004), describes several examples of New Urbanist codes.

The Central Petaluma Specific Plan and Smart Code, available at http://cityofpetaluma.net/cdd/cpsp.html, is a good example of a New Urbanist land use regulation. *Id.* at 60–63. The plan and code replace conventional zoning for a 400-acre infill site and include mixed-use zones for the General Urban, Urban Center and Urban Core sectors of the transect. "Block perimeter, lot coverage, building placement, building heights (minimum and maximum), parking location, and street types are all coded based upon historical urban fabric, walkability, and community preferences." *Id.* at 60.

NOTES AND QUESTIONS

1. *Legal and implementation issues.* New Urbanist codes have legal and implementation issues. The prescriptive standards contained in these codes may prove too inflexible and require the same kind of modification through variances that is typical of traditional zoning. Is mandatory prescription of development standards preferable to the flexibility provided through site plan, planned unit development and other flexible review techniques discussed in Chapter 9? The design review required in New Urbanist codes also raises due process, void for vagueness, and free speech problems.

Restigouche, Inc. v. Town of Jupiter, 59 F.3d 1208 (11th Cir. 1995), upheld an ordinance for a highway corridor that included New Urbanist principles against a substantive due process challenge:

> To further the goal of creating a traditional main street, the Town sought to encourage retail uses along Indiantown Road which would serve the everyday needs of nearby

> residents, promote pedestrian traffic, and have a character consistent with the neighboring residential developments. The Town could have reasonably believed that the purchase of an automobile is not an everyday need, that the typically large lot of an automobile dealership might break up the pedestrian flow between retail establishments, and that such dealerships might disrupt the planned residential character of the street with bright lights, red flags and flashy signage. Thus, we readily conclude that the prohibition of car dealerships could rationally further the Town's legitimate aesthetic purposes and its goal of creating a traditional downtown. [*Id.* at 1214.]

Highly prescriptive ordinances may create problems, however. In *Dallen v. City of Kansas City*, 822 S.W.2d 429 (Mo. App. 1991), owners of a gas station and car wash wanted to rebuild their station, which was a permitted use in the base zoning district. The city also adopted a corridor overlay district incorporating New Urbanist principles that included a 10-foot build-to line for all buildings in the corridor. The court held the additional requirements in the overlay district were a "modification" of the underlying zoning district, which was prohibited by the overlay ordinance:

> The underlying zoning for respondents' property is C-3a2, allowing for an unrestricted use of that property so long as the requirements set forth in C-3a2 are complied with. Ordinance 59380 adds additional requirements restricting the manner in which respondents can use their property above and beyond those requirements of the C-3a2 zone.
>
> Some of these requirements include the mandatory ten foot setback, the regulation of building materials, the parking regulations and the restrictions applying to signs, building entrances and windows. All of these requirements are confiscatory and unconstitutional. The trial judge was correct in setting aside the whole MSSRD for these reasons alone . . . . [*Id.* at 434.]

How would you remedy these problems in a TND ordinance?

2. *Legislation for New Urbanist development.* States are beginning to adopt legislation authorizing New Urbanist developments such as TND. A Connecticut statute authorizes a zoning district with design objectives similar to those for TND. Conn. Gen. Stat. § 8-2j. A Wisconsin statute mandates all local governments with a population over 12,500 to adopt New Urbanist regulations within two years. Wis. Stat. § 66.1027. The legislation defines a "traditional neighborhood development" as "a compact, mixed-use neighborhood where residential, commercial and civic buildings are within close proximity to each other." What image of TND does this statute contemplate? The statute called for the preparation of a model ordinance, available at www.wisc.edu/urpl/people/ohm/index.html. For discussion of the Wisconsin statute, see Ohm, *Reforming Land Planning Enabling Legislation at the Dawn of the 21st Century: The Emerging Influence of Smart Growth and Livable Communities*, 32 Urb. Law. 181 (2000).

Pennsylvania, following the recommendations of a gubernatorial 21st Century Environment Commission, also enacted a statute authorizing TND, Pa. Stat. Ann. tit. 53, § 10701-A, which comprehensively includes TND tenets. Section 10706-A specifies the required standards for a TND. The APA model legislation contains a brief section authorizing TND as a "zoning use" or "overlay" district and defines the standards for a TND in the usual manner. American Planning Association, Growing Smart Legislative Guidebook: Model Statutes for Planning and Management of Change § 8-201(5) (S. Meck ed., 2002)

3. *Is New Urbanism exclusionary?* Two Florida towns, Seaside and Celebration (the latter sponsored by Walt Disney Company as an outgrowth of its Orlando ventures) are exemplars of the New Urbanism model. Two books on Celebration are critical. D. Frantz & C. Collins, Celebration USA: Living in Disney's Brave New Town (1999); A. Ross, The Celebration Chronicles: Life, Liberty and the Pursuit of Property Values in Disney's New Town (1999). Critics uniformly note that for a model that embraces diversity as a value, New Urbanist communities like Seaside and Celebration have made little, if any, progress towards either racial or economic integration.

4. *Sources.* A. Duany & E. Plater-Zyberk, Suburban Nation: The Rise of Sprawl and the Decline of the American Dream (2000) (with Jeff Speck); C. Emerson, The Smart Code Solution to Sprawl (2007); Emerson, *Making Main Street Legal Again: The Smart Code Solution to Sprawl*, 71 Mo. L. Rev. 637 (2006); Garvin & Jourdan, *Through the Looking Glass: Analyzing the Potential Legal Challenges to Form-Based Codes*, 23 J. Land Use & Envtl. L. 395 (2008); Parolek, Parolek & Crawford, Form-Based Codes: A Guide for Planners, Urban Designers, Municipalities, and Developers (2008); Innis, *Back to the Future: Is Form-Based Code an Efficacious Tool for Shaping Modern Civic Life*?, 11 J.L. & Soc. Change 75 (2007-2008); Katz, *Form First*, Planning, Nov. 2004, at 16; Lewyn, *New Urbanist Zoning for Dummies*, 58 Ala. L. Rev. 257 (2006); Madden & Spikowski, *Place Making with Form-Based Codes*, Urban Land, Sept. 2006, at 174; Sitkowski *The Influence of New Urbanism on Local Ordinances: The Twilight of Zoning?*, 35 Urb. Law. 783 (2003); White & Gourdan, *Neo-Traditional Development: A Legal Analysis*, Land Use L. & Zoning Dig., Aug., 1997, at 3; Note, *Sprawl and the New Urbanist Solution*, 89 Va. L. Rev. 447 (2003) (New Urbanists do not have regional plan). For a fact sheet on form-based codes, go to http://tinyurl.com/2ehm9va. The Congress for New Urbanism site is www.cnu.org.

Chapter 4

ENVIRONMENTAL AND AGRICULTURAL LAND USE REGULATIONS

This chapter covers the topics of land and environmental protection and preservation. The chapter begins by discussing the impact of development and urbanization on agricultural lands and discusses various tools used to protect and preserve agricultural resources, including differential tax assessments, agricultural zoning districts, the purchase of development rights, and the enactment of right to farm laws to protect existing farming operations. The chapter also discusses the regulation of agricultural uses through zoning and the constitutionality of agricultural zoning. The latter half of the chapter addresses the more traditional environmental topics of wetlands, floodplains, ground and surface waters, steep slopes, and coastal zone management and ends with a discussion of sustainability and climate change in the context of land use regulation.

A. PRESERVING AGRICULTURAL LAND

[1.] The Preservation Problem

Sprawl excessively consumes agricultural land. Growth management, discussed in Chapter 8, can help diminish the impact of urban development on agricultural land, but must contain regulatory and other programs that can prevent conversion of agricultural land to urban uses and interfering with agricultural production. The other reason for agricultural preservation is the greater fear (which some say is unfounded) that America's farmlands are under attack, and are disappearing at so alarming a rate that the production of food to feed the nation's population is threatened.

Agricultural land preservation is a major policy problem that gained national prominence with the publication of the Final Report of the National Agricultural Lands Study in 1981. This massive, interagency, federally funded study found a crisis in the conversion of agricultural land: Nearly three million acres of agricultural land had been converted from 1967 to 1975, about 75 percent to urban and transportation uses. A subsequent study confirmed that farmland loss remains a serious problem. A. Sorenson, R. Green & K. Russ, American Farmland Trust, Farming on the Edge (1997). The study found that four million acres of prime farmland were converted from 1982 to 1992, and that a substantial amount of the best farmland was under significant development pressure. A worst case scenario predicted this country would become a net importer of food within 60 years. *Id.* at 2. The National Resources Conservation Service now carries out an annual National Resources Inventory. Its 2007 inventory found an average rate of development between 2002 and 2007 of 1.5 million acres per year. The inventories are available at: nrcs.usda.gov.

There are dissenters. The Reason Public Policy Institute claims that farmland loss has moderated significantly since the 1960s, that cropland has remained stable for decades despite farmland loss, that only about 26% of cropland loss is caused by urbanization, and that land accounts for only 18% of agricultural productivity with that figure declining. S. Staley, The "Vanishing Farmland" Myth and the Smart-Growth Agenda (Policy Brief No. 12, Jan. 2000). See also Lockeretz, *Secondary Effects on Midwestern Agriculture of Metropolitan Development and Decreases in Farmland*, 65 Land Econ. 205 (1989) (studies fail to support conclusion that metropolitan expansion has adverse effect on farmland).

NOTES AND QUESTIONS

1. *Urban sprawl and agriculture.* Urban sprawl with leap frog development among farm uses has the expected problems. A study in the Chicago suburbs found that scattered development that fragmented agricultural areas did not pay enough taxes to pay for education costs and road maintenance. Extending water and sewer services to this kind of development was risky because buildout at sufficiently rapid rates was not assured. A. Sorensen & J. Esseks, Living on the Edge: The Costs and Risks of Scatter Development (American Farmland Trust, 1999).

2. *The structure of American farming.* Changes in the size of farms and the character of American farming have an important impact on agricultural preservation programs. The number of farms continues to decline, and their average size continues to increase. Data from the 2007 Census of Agriculture shows that small farms producing under $10,000 annually (about 60% of all farms) account for about 1% of total farm sales, while farms that produce over $500,000 annually (about 5% of all farms) account for about 75% of total farm sales. Only 3.6% of all farms are over 2,000 acres. The trend is toward fewer small farms and more large farms. Many agricultural preservation programs appear concentrated on saving the "family farm." Does this make sense in view of these statistics? Could it be that the recent increasing interest in home grown organic food will slow or reverse this trend? Should there be a concern with preserving large contiguous areas of farm land? The Census is accessible at: agcensus.usda.gov.

3. *A market solution?* Classic market theorists make another argument against interventionist programs that seek to retard farmland conversion. They argue that competition for land in the open market will prevent the excessive withdrawal of farmland, presumably because the demand price for agricultural land will be sufficiently high to bid it away from potential urban users. This argument overlooks a set of externalities that occur when agricultural land is withdrawn from production. Fewer acres will be farmed, and maximizing production on a reduced agricultural acreage may lead to negative environmental impacts such as soil erosion and compaction, declining groundwater supplies, and a loss of wildlife habitat. It also overlooks the problem of distributional equity inherent in reliance on the mechanism of price. How likely is it that agricultural users will outbid urbanizers? Is there, in effect, a ceiling price on agricultural land, determined by how much less-affluent consumers can afford to pay for the food grown on that land? How would an economist solve this problem?

Intergenerational problems are also disregarded in the classic market calculus. Because we value the consumption needs of future generations less than our own, we are not likely to take the agricultural land needs of future generations into account. Market economists sometimes concede this difficulty, but argue that technological innovation will compensate for declining agricultural resources. See *Book Review*, 48 J. Am. Planning A. 112 (1982).

[2.] Programs for the Preservation of Agricultural Land

The key issues in agricultural land preservation programs are determining what farmland will be subject to preservation and deciding on what programs to adopt. The decision on what farmland to preserve is made in establishing and changing urban growth boundaries, as in Oregon, that divide urban from agricultural land. The decision on what land to protect can be more difficult when there is no clear cut boundary decision.

Church, *Farmland Conversion: The View From 1986*, 1986 U. Ill. L. Rev. 521, notes that the uncertain rate of agricultural land conversion suggests a number of criteria for agricultural land preservation programs. They should concentrate on the direction rather than the quantity of conversion, should not provide cropland protection for only a temporary period because this will only divert conversion elsewhere, and should concentrate on areas not now under pressure. *Id.* at 559–60. Even without an urban growth boundary, of course, an agricultural land preservation program becomes a de facto growth control to the extent that it prohibits urban development on reserved land.

The federal government plays a limited role in the preservation of agricultural land. The following article describes state and local programs:

Cordes, *Takings, Fairness and Farmland Preservation*,
60 Ohio St. L.J. 1033, 1045–1049 (1999)

[*Property Tax Relief*]

One of the earliest and most common techniques for farmland preservation is state programs providing various types of tax-relief to owners of agricultural land. Today all fifty states have some form of tax relief provisions for agricultural land. The most common of these are preferential-assessment statutes, which assess land at a reduced value when used for agriculture, and deferred taxation programs, which provide lower assessment for farmland but require partial or total repayment of tax savings if the land is later converted to other uses. The obvious purpose of both types of legislation is to provide financial incentives for farmers to offset the financial pressures posed by conversion. [See, e.g., Ariz. Rev. Stat. Ann. §§ 42-12004, 42-15004; Iowa Code Ann. § 441.21; W. Va. Code § 11-1A-10. — Eds.]

[*Right-to-Farm Laws*]

A second type of farmland preservation program, also found in all fifty states, are right-to-farm laws. These statutes provide farmers protection against certain nuisance actions, typically in "coming to the nuisance" situations, where development has moved out to agricultural areas and created conflicting uses. Slightly less than half the states also provide protection against local government efforts to zone out existing agricultural uses, again typically in "coming to the nuisance" scenarios. They do not permit expansion of existing uses, but provide protection for the level of agricultural activity in existence when development arrived. These right-to-farm statutes do not guarantee preservation, but provide protection to farmers who desire to continue farming in the face of approaching development. [See, e.g., Ala. Code § 6-5-127; 740 Ill. Comp. Stat. Ann. §§ 70/1 to 5; Ind. Code Ann. § 32-30-6-9. — Eds.]

[*Agricultural Districting*]

A third and less common type of preservation program is agricultural districting. Currently recognized in approximately fifteen states, agricultural districting involves the voluntary creation of special agricultural districts, which require that the land be used for agricultural purposes. Districts are established for a limited period of time, such as five to ten years, which can then be renewed. In exchange for the requirement that the land stay agricultural, landowners receive a number of benefits, depending on the particular authorizing statute. Some are similar to benefits conferred by other statutes, such as differential tax assessments and right-to-farm provisions. Others are more unique to the district, and might include [purchase of development rights] provisions, limitations on the exercise of eminent domain against farm property, and restrictions on special assessments and government annexations. [See, e.g., Md. Code Ann., Agric. §§ 2-501 to 516; Minn. Stat. Ann. §§ 473 H.01-473 H.18; N.J. Stat. Ann. §§ 4:1C- 1 to 55; Utah Code Ann. §§ 17-41-101 to 406. — Eds.]

. . . [T]he voluntary nature of all of the above programs significantly limits their effectiveness. Right-to-farm laws are only effective in preventing involuntary conversion against a landowner's wishes; they provide little basis to preserve farmland when a farmer desires to convert. Although tax incentives and agricultural districting can both provide some temporary relief from conversion pressures, neither is sufficient to offset the financial incentive of conversion when significant development pressure exists. Indeed, in some instances they simply help subsidize farmland while waiting for development. Such programs play an important role in a comprehensive preservation program, but by themselves will often be ineffective in establishing long-term farmland preservation.

[*Agricultural Zoning*]

For that reason, effective farmland preservation programs will need to restrict a landowner's ability to convert by relying on techniques that place decision-making authority elsewhere, most notably the government. The most common and least expensive way this can be done is by some type of public restriction placed on the land, typically in the form of agricultural zoning. Fourteen states currently have statutes which specifically address and authorize particular forms of "agricultural protection zoning," but as a practical matter agricultural zoning clearly falls within local government's general zoning power, even in the absence of a special statute. Because it can preclude conversion of farmland even when significant financial incentives exist, zoning is a widely and increasingly used farmland preservation technique at the local government level. [For statutes authorizing agricultural zoning, see, e.g., Ky. Rev. Stat. Ann. § 100.187; Or. Rev. Stat. § 215.203; Vt. Stat. Ann. tit. 24, §§ 4301-4496. — Eds.]

NOTES AND QUESTIONS

1. *Differential property tax assessment.* The following excerpt explains how differential property tax assessments work:

> Differential assessment laws are usually categorized as falling into one of three categories: preferential assessment, deferred taxation, and restrictive agreement. Preferential assessment laws produce an abatement of taxes by authorizing assessors simply to assess eligible land on the basis of farm use value, rather than on market

value. Deferred taxation laws add an additional feature and impose a sanction requiring owners of eligible land who convert it to non-eligible uses to pay some or all the taxes which they were excused from paying for a number of years prior to conversion. Restrictive agreement laws include both preferential assessment and, in all states except Vermont, a sanction in the form of a payment of back taxes. In addition, they require the owner to sign a contract spelling out his rights and duties, and preventing him from converting the land to an ineligible use for a specified term of years. [Keene, *Differential Assessment and the Preservation of Open Space*, 14 Urb. L. Ann. 11, 14 (1977).]

Critics claim that the differential tax programs simply make it easier for speculators to buy and hold farmland until it can be developed because the tax reduction reduces holding costs. The following commentary provides some insight into this problem:

> Differential assessment operates primarily on one of the supply factors, by reducing the income squeeze which farmers in rural-urban fringe areas experience as a result of rising property taxes. It has a secondary impact on the demand side because it permits farmer-buyers, speculators and developers either to offer somewhat more for the land or to buy more land at the same price because their carrying costs are reduced. This latter effect is difficult to appraise, but it is likely to be marginal because the buyer will normally be simply exchanging tax costs on the land for interest costs on the money he has to borrow either to pay the higher price or to buy additional land. [Council on Environmental Quality, Untaxing Open Space 77–78 (1976).]

Differential property tax assessment increases the price of farmland because the lower tax is capitalized in the selling price, providing a windfall to farmland owners at the time the assessment goes into effect. The lower tax burden may not reduce the land costs for new farmers. Future farmer-buyers, as the excerpt indicates, may find reduced taxes offset by the higher carrying costs of purchasing farmland. The property tax reduction is lost when farmland is converted to urban use, depressing the price of farmland for urban development. Agricultural zoning may moderate these equity effects by keeping differentially taxed farmland in agricultural use. For additional discussion, see Property Tax Preferences for Agricultural Land (N. Roberts & H. Brown eds., 1980).

Another criticism is that voluntary differential property tax assessment programs do not achieve the preservation of agricultural land in urbanizing areas close to cities. A study reported in Note, *Farmland and Open Space Preservation in Michigan: An Empirical Analysis*, 19 U. Mich. J.L. Reform 1107 (1986), reaches similar conclusions. The study found that the program was successful in enrolling a substantial amount of farm acreage in the state but was not successful in attracting enrollment near urban areas, where development pressures are the greatest. See also Comment, *The State of Agricultural Land Preservation in California in 1997: Will the Agricultural Land Stewardship Program Solve the Problems Inherent in the Williamson Act?*, 7 San Joaqin Agric. L. Rev. 135 (1998); *Evaluating the Effectiveness of Use-Value Programs*, 7 Prop. Tax J. 157 (1988) (program slowed rate of farm conversion in three of four Virginia counties studied); Sullivan & Eber, *The Long and Winding Road: Farmland Protection in Oregon 1961 -2009*, 18 San Joaquin Ag. L. Rev. 1 (2008-2009).

2. *Agricultural districts.* Sixteen states have agricultural district legislation. See Safran, *Contracting for Preservation: An Overview of State Agricultural District Programs*, Zoning & Plan. L. Rep., July/Aug., 2004, at 1. A review of agricultural district programs in New York state shows they can be helpful in preserving farmland but have their limits. White, *Beating*

Plowshares Into Townhomes: The Loss of Farmland and Strategies For Slowing Its Conversion to Nonagricultural Uses, 28 Envtl. L. 113 (1998). As of 1996, 8.48 million acres of land were protected in 411 districts. About two-thirds of this acreage was being used for agricultural production. Nevertheless, farmland loss in New York has been substantial, over half of the state's agricultural production land is within developing areas, and the districts have very little effect on local zoning. Farmland conversions may occur incrementally within a district, which will allow a county to terminate it under the law because its character has changed. See also Nolon, *The Stable Door is Open: New York's Statutes to Protect Farm Land*, 67 N.Y. St. B.J. 36 (1995). A Long Island county has supplemented the district program with a purchase of development rights program. These are discussed *infra.* For discussion of agricultural districts, preferential assessment and a model statute, see American Planning Association, Growing Smart Legislative Guidebook: Model Statutes for Planning and Management of Change 10-75 to 10-90 (S. Meck ed., 2002). For a favorable report, see American Farmland Trust, North Carolina Voluntary Districts: A Progress Report (2004).

3. *The Federal Farmland Policy Protection Act.* In response to the agricultural conversion problems identified by the National Agricultural Lands Study, Congress enacted the Farmland Policy Protection Act, 7 U.S.C. §§ 4201-4209 (1981). The Department of Agriculture, in cooperation with other federal agencies, is to "develop criteria for identifying the effects of Federal programs on the conversion of farmland to nonagricultural uses." 7 U.S.C. § 4202(a). The Act then provides:

> Departments, agencies, independent commissions, and other units of the Federal Government shall use the criteria established under subsection (a) of this section, to identify the quantity of farmland actually converted by Federal programs, and to identify and take into account the adverse effects of Federal programs on the preservation of farmland; consider alternative actions, as appropriate, that could lessen such adverse effects; and assure that such Federal programs, to the extent practicable, are compatible with State, unit of local government, and private programs and policies to protect farmland. [7 U.S.C. § 4202(b).]

Federal agencies must review their policies and regulations to determine whether they are consistent with the Act and must develop "proposals for action" to bring their "programs, authorities, and administrative activities" into compliance with the Act. 7 U.S.C. § 4203.

All of this sounds quite formidable, but the Act expressly declares that it does "not authorize the Federal Government in any way to regulate the use of private or non-Federal land, or in any way affect the property rights of owners of such land." 7 U.S.C. § 4208(a). Regulations of the Department of Agriculture indicate the Act is not an absolute bar to development. 7 C.F.R. § 658.3(c). A federal agency need only take any adverse effects on farmland into account and develop alternative actions that could mitigate these effects. It is not required to disapprove a development if its effects on agricultural land are adverse. *Id.* See Johnson & Fogleman, *The Farmland Protection Policy Act: Stillbirth of a Policy?*, 1986 U. Ill. L. Rev. 563. But see *Eagle Found., Inc. v. Dole*, 813 F.2d 798 (7th Cir. 1987) (Act requires Secretary of Transportation to consider impact on agriculture when approving highway route).

4. *Sources.* For additional discussion of agricultural land preservation programs, see Alterman, *The Challenge of Farmland Preservation: Lessons From a Six-Nation Comparison*, 63 J. Am. Plan. Ass'n 220 (1997); Duncan, *Agriculture as a Resource: Statewide Land Use Programs for the Preservation of Farmland*, 14 Ecology L.Q. 401 (1987); Pope, *A Survey of Governmental Response to the Farmland Crisis: States' Application of Agricultural Zoning,*

11 U. Ark. Little Rock L.J. 515 (1988-89). For a comprehensive analysis of Oregon's EFU program that offers preferential treatment for land in "farm use" and "zoned exclusively for farm use" zones, see Sullivan & Eber, *The Long and Winding Road: Farmland Protection in Oregon 1961-2009*, 18 San Joaquin Ag. L. Rev. 1 (2008-2009). Taking the position that existing agricultural preservation policies have failed because they are not comprehensive enough is Cremer, *Tractors Versus Bulldozers: Integrating Growth Management and Ecosystem Services to Conserve Agriculture*, 39 ELR 10542 (2009). A general resource for agricultural land preservation approaches can be found at www.csrees.usda.gov/nea/nre/in_focus/ere_if_preserve.html.

A NOTE ON PURCHASE OF DEVELOPMENT RIGHTS AND EASEMENT PROGRAMS

How they work. Professor Cordes' article briefly mentions the purchase of development rights as an agricultural preservation program. Many states have purchase of development rights programs. See, e.g., Cal. Pub. Res. Code §§ 10200 to 10277; Conn. Gen. Stat. Ann. §§ 22-26aa to 26jj; N.Y. Gen. Mun. L. § 247; Miller & Krieger, *Purchase of Development Rights: Preserving Farmland and Open Space*, Planning Commissioners Journal, Winter 2004, at 1 (www.pcj.typepad.com/planning_commissioners_jo/2010/02/140b.html). In these programs, a government entity buys the development rights on agricultural land, and pays the difference between the land's value for development and its value when restricted to agricultural uses. Often the conveyance of a temporary or permanent easement restricting the development of the land is required in return for the development rights payment.

At the federal level, purchase of development rights programs are included in federal farm legislation. These programs are usually available to owners of agricultural land who agree to carry out conservation or preservation measures in compliance with approved plans. Examples are the Wetland Reserve Program, 16 U.S.C. §§ 3837 et seq., which provides funding for the conveyance of permanent or thirty-year easements, and restoration cost agreements, for wetlands protection. Another program, the Conservation Reserve Program, most commonly relies on contractual provisions rather than easements to protect environmentally sensitive land. 16 U.S.C. §§ 3831 et seq. It has removed millions of acres of highly erodible and other sensitive cropland from production for ten-year periods. The 2008 farm bill increased the funds available for conservation to $24 billion. For discussion, see Davidson, *The Federal Farm Bill and the Environment*, Natural Resources & Env't, Summer, 2003, at 3.

For discussion of purchase of development rights and easement programs, see Protecting the Land: Conservation Easements Past, Present and Future (J. Gustanski & R. Squires eds., 2000); Morisette, *Conservation Easements and the Public Good*, 41 Nat. Resources J. 373 (2001); White, *Beating Plowshares Into Townhomes*, *supra*, at 140–144 (1998) (noting fairly high expense of preserving a limited number of acres in one county); Comment, *Conservation Easements: Now More Than Ever — Overcoming Obstacles to Protect Private Lands*, 34 Envtl. L. 247 (2004). A Uniform Conservation Easement Act proposed in 1984 has been adopted by several states, and the APA model legislation references this Act and contains provisions for purchase of development rights and conservation easement programs. See American Planning Association, Growing Smart Legislative Guidebook: Model Statutes for Planning and Management of Change 7-64 to 7-67 (S. Meck ed., 2002) (www.planning.org/growingsmart/guidebook/print/pdf/chapter7.pdf).

Purchase vs. regulation. This casebook has concentrated on regulation as the method of implementing land use policies. The purchase of easements and development rights are an alternative. Which is preferable? Some commentators claim that easement purchase problems will have negative impacts on regulatory programs:

> However, there are several important drawbacks to such programs. First, from a regulatory standpoint, direct payments to landowners may establish a troublesome compensation precedent. Such a precedent, if firmly established, would create an atmosphere of entitlement and redefine the concept of property rights in a much more protective manner than is currently accepted. A political atmosphere that precluded regulatory mechanisms could negatively impact biodiversity preservation and other goals of current regulatory programs. Moreover, government resources are too limited to turn easement acquisitions and cooperative agreements into the sole methods of regulating land-use. [Comment, *Biodiversity and Federal Land* Ownership, 25 Ecology L.Q. 229, 293 (1998).]

Other commentators claim the assumption that easements offer permanent protection is illusory, a claim borne out by a Wisconsin study. Ohm, *The Purchase of Scenic Easements and Wisconsin's Great River Road*, 66 J. Am. Plan. Ass'n 177 (2000) (requests for variances from easement restrictions have increased, but state agency requires landowners to buy back development rights before granting variances). Early reports from a nationwide survey of easement programs also note that easement programs seldom complement regulation. Two authors challenge these arguments, claiming in part that easement programs will facilitate a transition from a rights-oriented to a responsibility-oriented view. Cheever & McLaughlin, *Why Environmental Lawyers Should Know (and Care) About Land Trusts and Their Private Land Conservation Transactions*, 34 Envtl. L. Rep. 10223, 10228 (2004). They also argue that conservation easements lower land prices, but a recent study in Maryland contradicts this claim. Nickerson & Lynch, *The Effect of Farmland Preservation Programs on Farmland Prices*, 83 Am. J. Agric. Econ. 341 (2001) (http://agnr.umd.edu/departments/AREC/LibComp/AREClib/Publications/Working-Papers-PDF-files/99-08.pdf).

Eminent Domain as a Technique to Preserve Farmland. In the case *In the Matter of Aspen Creek Estates Ltd. v. Town of Brookhaven*, 47 A.D.3d 267, 848 N.Y.S.2d 214 (N.Y.A.D. 2 Dept., 2007), a New York appellate court upheld the Town of Brookhaven's decision to exercise its power of eminent domain to condemn property in the "Manorville Farmland Protection Area" for the purpose of preserving its use as farmland. The protection area is an approximately 500-acre working farm belt that is a high priority preservation target for the Town. Regarding the issue of whether the condemnation serves a public purpose, the court concluded that the Town's stated reasons — preserving farmland, maintaining open space and scenic vistas — are all legitimate public purposes. The court noted that the preservation of farmland "confers a benefit upon the public, since it enables residents of the Town to enjoy locally grown produce and scenic views." The court also found that the preservation of farmland is consistent with the public policy of the state to "promote, foster, and encourage the agricultural industry," and "preservation of open space and enhancement of natural resources." Lastly, the court noted that the Town residents demonstrated that protection of open spaces and natural resources is important because they overwhelmingly supported a $20 million bond act of such purpose in 2002 and a bond act of up to $100 million in 2004 for preservation of open space, farmland and wildlife habitats.

As to Aspen Creek's claim that the condemnation was unconstitutional because the true purpose was to bestow a private benefit on certain individuals (e.g., farmers), the court found that this allegation had no factual support in the record and was insufficient to demonstrate bad faith. The court said that "the mere fact that the condemnation will provide incidental benefits to private individuals does not invalidate the condemnor's determination as long as the public purpose is dominant." Further, the court maintained that since the land had been continuously farmed for more than a century prior to the Aspen Creek purchase, "allowing farming to continue on the property is fully consistent with the purpose of the condemnation, the fact that one or more individuals may benefit is merely incidental, and does not render the public benefit to be achieved by condemnation illusory." The Court concluded that a comprehensive development plan was not required pursuant to *Kelo v. City of New London*, 545 U.S. 469 (2005), because that condemnation was based upon the public purpose of economic development, and here the public purpose was farmland and open space protection.

Do you agree with the *Brookhaven* court that the greater good is served by condemning one private individual's land to allow another private individual to farm it? Is this a public or private benefit?

Mutual Impact Easements as a Preservation Tool. In *Coffey v. County of Otoe*, 274 Neb. 796 (2008), the Nebraska Supreme Court considered a challenge to a zoning ordinance that prohibited the construction of single-family dwellings in general agricultural districts within a one-half mile radius of certain animal feeding facilities unless the owner of the dwelling grants an impact easement to the owner of the facility and the facility owner agrees to the easement. The zoning law provides that if a homeowner grants an impact easement to the owner of a confined or intensive animal feeding use or waste handling facility, dwelling units associated with the land on which any such easement has been granted shall not be included in the specified minimum distance measurements. Prior to the adoption of the ordinance, Coffey purchased 195 acres of land adjacent to a hog confinement facility owned by Kreifels. Approximately 192 of these acres fall within the one-half mile distance separation requirement. Coffey subdivided his land and entered into an agreement to sell one parcel for the construction of a home. Acknowledging the need to obtain an impact easement, he had one drafted and sent to Kreifels, who refused to sign or return the easement. Without the easement, the property owners could not obtain a building permit and Coffey was denied a conditional use permit and a variance to enable the construction. Coffey filed suit, alleging that the zoning regulations are unlawful because the impact easement requirement constitutes "an unlawful delegation of the county's governmental regulatory power to private individuals." The court upheld the mutual impact easement requirement, finding that it did not constitute an unconstitutional delegation of legislative authority, and it therefore did not violate due process.

Where does this leave us? A Brookings Institution study that included federal lands and programs found a significant increase in open space protection programs in recent years but that information about them was scanty, and that they were not well integrated with growth management programs. Hollis & Fulton, Open Space Protection: Conservation Meets Growth Management (2002). Participation is another matter. Purchase of development rights programs only work if there is adequate participation. A Maryland study found variable participation rates with the likelihood of participation increasing with farm size, growing crops, a child that plans to continue farming, eligibility and share of income from farming. Landowners closer to urban areas were less likely to participate. Lynch & Lovell, *Participation in Agricultural Land Preservation Programs*, 79 Land. Econ. 259 (2002) (study also included transfer of development rights programs). What do you think lies behind these variations? What might you do to increase participation?

[3.] Agricultural Zoning

Limitations in programs like preferential tax assessment and agricultural districts that rely on incentives to preserve farmland indicate that direct regulation through zoning may be necessary as an additional program. Professor Cordes describes how agricultural zoning works:

Cordes, *Takings, Fairness and Farmland Preservation*,
60 OHIO ST. L.J. 1033, 1047–1048 (1999)

Fourteen states currently have statutes which specifically address and authorize particular forms of "agricultural protection zoning," but as a practical matter agricultural zoning clearly falls within local government's general zoning power, even in the absence of a special statute. Because it can preclude conversion of farmland even when significant financial incentives exist, zoning is a widely and increasingly used farmland preservation technique at the local government level. [For statutes authorizing agricultural zoning, see, e.g., Ariz. Rev. Stat. Ann. § 9-462.01; Neb. Rev. Stat. §§ 19-903 to 916; Or. Rev. Stat. § 215.203. — Eds.]

Agricultural zoning can take several basic forms. On the one hand, local governments can impose what is often referred to as "exclusive agricultural zoning," which prohibits any use other than agricultural. Even this type of zoning will permit certain compatible or accessory buildings, such as barns, on the property; fundamentally, however, exclusive agricultural zoning is designed to limit the property to agricultural use only.

A more common approach to agricultural zoning is to permit non-farm uses, most notably residential, but in effect to establish agricultural restrictions through severe density limitations. This is often done through large minimum-lot size requirements, where the minimum lot size typically corresponds to "the minimum size of commercial farms . . . in the area." Thus, minimum lot sizes might range from one house per 40 acres to one house per 160 acres. The obvious effect is to limit the property to agricultural use. Agricultural zoning might also impose density restrictions but permit small lot "clustering" of actual development on the property. This permits a greater overall density level, such as one dwelling per ten acres, but leaves a significant area of land to be completely free for farming.

Whatever its form, agricultural zoning serves the purpose of significantly limiting development on farmland property, thus preserving the property's farmland status. Importantly, by placing public restrictions on the property the landowner is not free to sell the land for nonagricultural use when development pressure and attendant financial incentives become great. The result is to place the cost of preservation as reflected in diminution in land value on the restricted landowner.

NOTES AND QUESTIONS

1. *Agricultural zoning as a preservation technique.* Agricultural zoning seems to be most widespread in Pennsylvania, Maryland, parts of the midwest including Minnesota and Wisconsin, and along the Pacific Coast. Some of these states, such as Oregon and Minnesota, require communities to adopt agricultural zoning. For discussion, see American Farmland

Trust, Saving American Farmland: What Works (1997).

Is it effective? Cordes, *Agricultural Zoning: Impacts and Future Directions*, 22 N. Ill. U. L. Rev. 419 (2002), reports an unpublished study in Wisconsin finding that agricultural zoning did not have a significant impact on farmland preservation but notes it has been effective where there is a strong commitment to making it work. He recommends that agricultural preservation should occur as part of comprehensive planning and a reasonable plan to manage growth (including urban growth boundaries), and that it needs to coordinate with other preservation techniques, such as development rights purchase. How agricultural zoning is done can also be important. Large lot agricultural zoning, for example, may simply produce sprawl. Thompson, *"Hybrid" Farmland Protection Programs: A New Paradigm for Growth Management?*, 23 Wm. & Mary Envtl. L. & Pol'y Rev. 831 (1999), discusses examples where regulation has been successfully used with other programs. The American Farmland Trust (2009) has extensive information on farmland preservation at www.farmland.org.

Karen Jordan, in *Perpetual Conservation: Accomplishing the Goal Through Preemptive Federal Easement Programs*, 43 Case W. Res. L. Rev. 401, 435–438 (1993), identifies problems. She claims the productivity costs of regulation, (i.e., the costs of production), are difficult to assess because productivity varies annually, and because costs may also be offset by gains from regulation that protect the ecological quality of farms. She argues that farmers may not be able to pass the costs of regulation on to consumers because agricultural producers cannot set prices, which are determined by the marketing chain. She also claims that regulation impairs competition in agriculture. Farmers are not equally affected by regulation because the distribution of environmentally-sensitive agricultural lands varies geographically. Are these appropriate factors to consider in a regulatory program?

2. *The Oregon program.* Oregon has one of the most comprehensive agricultural land preservation programs in the country. State land use Goal 3 requires in part that agricultural lands "shall be preserved and maintained for farm use, consistent with existing and future needs for agricultural products . . . and open space," and includes factors local governments must consider before agricultural land can be converted to urbanizable land. This goal made mandatory a program for Exclusive Farm Use (EFU) Zones the legislature had authorized earlier. Land in EFU zones can be used only for farming. New farm and nonfarm dwellings are regulated, minimum lot sizes of 80 acres are mandatory, and land classified EFU must meet exacting statutory criteria before it can be reclassified. Land in EFU zones receives preferential property tax assessment. For the lot size requirement, see Ore. Rev. Stat. § 215.780.

The EFU program is extensive. Half the private land in the state is in an EFU zone, and most of the 16 million acres of agricultural land is also in the property tax abatement program. A fact sheet from One Thousand Friends of Oregon on its website www.friends.org, notes that:

> [o]f the 2 million acres in farm zones in the Willamette Valley, only 4,070 acres, or 2/10 of 1%, was lost between 1987 and 1999, either by being added to urban growth boundaries or by being rezoned from farm use to rural development. During the same period, the population of the valley increased by nearly 23%, to 2,268,200. (For comparison purposes, California's Central Valley is losing 15,000 acres of farmland every year.) . . . Yet every year, Oregon counties continue to approve the construction of over 1000 houses on farmland, in addition to dozens of other nonfarm uses.

Another problem is the extensive list of nonfarm uses permitted in EFU zones, which includes several types of dwelling units. See, e.g., Ore. Rev. Stat. § 215.203. Other uses include greyhound kennels, golf courses, and solid waste disposal sites. A state Land Conservation and Development Commission rule provides more stringent requirements for nonfarm uses than the statute does. The supreme court upheld the rule in *Lane County v. Land Conservation & Dev. Comm'n*, 942 P.2d 278 (Ore. 1997). The court of appeals also strengthened the minimum lot size requirement by holding it prevented the division of farm land into parcels that violate the minimum. *Dorvinen v. Crook County*, 957 P.2d 180 (Ore. App. 1998). See also *Still v. Board of County Comm'rs*, 600 P.2d 433 (Ore. App. 1979) (nonfarm residential development not allowable in an EFU zone if it violates the state's statutory agricultural preservation policy, even if it is economically unfeasible to farm the land, and even if it does not interfere with farming on adjacent land, without considering "the policy ramifications of the proposed nonfarm residential use"). Is this a taking? For discussion, see Rasche, *Protecting Agricultural Lands in Oregon: An Assessment of the Exclusive Farm Use Zone System*, 77 Or. L. Rev. 993 (1998); White, *Beating Plowshares Into Townhomes: The Loss of Farmland and Strategies For Slowing Its Conversion to Nonagricultural Uses*, 28 Envtl. L. 113, 118–125 (1998); Sullivan & Eber, *The Long and Winding Road: Farmland Protection in Oregon 1961-2009*, 18 San Joaquin Ag. L. Rev. 1 (2008-2009).

3. *Quarter/quarter zoning.* Quarter/quarter zoning is a density-based zoning technique which is most appropriate in rural areas with large farming operations, moderate growth pressures, and where average parcel sizes generally exceed 40 acres. "Quarter/quarter zoning" refers to a quarter of a quarter section of land (1/16 of 640 acres, or 40 acres) where a limited number of non-farm homes are allowed for every 40 acres of land. The non-farm splits are usually regulated by minimum and maximum sizes, e.g., no less than 1 acre and not greater than 2 acres. They are often required to be contiguous to one another to avoid breaking up farmland into smaller or odd-shaped sizes. A variation of this method is to establish a density of homes within each section of land. Once that density is reached, further residential or other development is prohibited. A discussion of quarter/quarter zoning and other tools for preserving farmland can be found at http://planningtoolkit.org/agriculture/protecting_agricultural_lands.pdf

4. *Planning for agricultural preservation?* Agricultural preservation programs can be much improved if comprehensive plans contain an agricultural preservation element. The APA model legislation contains a provision for an optional agricultural element, that includes forest preservation and can be extended to scenic preservation. American Planning Association, Growing Smart Legislative Guidebook: Model Statutes for Planning and Management of Change § 212 (S. Meck ed., 2002). The element "calls for the local government to map such areas, prioritize them, and proposed a program of action that would preserve and protect such lands" as well as promote their continuance through "joint marketing efforts and grant and loan programs, among other initiatives." *Id.* at 7-154. The model law authorizes agricultural zoning along with other programs, such as conservation easements and tax abatement, to implement this element. The next case addresses the constitutional problems presented by a hybrid program of this type.

GARDNER v. NEW JERSEY PINELANDS COMMISSION

125 N.J. 193, 593 A.2d 251 (1991)

The opinion of the Court was delivered by HANDLER, J.

The central issue in this case is whether the application of state regulations that limit the use of land in an environmentally-sensitive area constitutes an unconstitutional taking of private property. The regulations strictly limit residential development on such land and require that all remaining undeveloped acreage be subject to a recorded deed restriction limiting it to agriculture and related uses. A farmer contends that the application of this regulatory scheme to his farm effects a partial taking of his property without compensation.

Hobart Gardner lived and worked for almost seventy years on a 217-acre farm that had been owned by his family since 1902. The farm is located in Shamong Township, Burlington County, a part of the pinelands region subject to the regulations. Gardner, now deceased, and his son, who lives on the farm today, cultivated sod and grain. The farm includes a two-family house, barns, and out-buildings. . . . .

[Gardner brought an inverse condemnation action claiming the regulations an unlawful taking, and also claimed the regulations were an unlawful exaction and a denial of equal protection. All actions were brought under the New Jersey Constitution. The trial court granted summary judgment for defendants on plaintiff's inverse condemnation claim and the appellate division affirmed.]

I

The value of the unique ecological, economic, and cultural features of the New Jersey Pine Barrens, or Pinelands, has been recognized for decades. Protection of the area, however, did not begin in earnest until Congress enacted the National Parks and Recreation Act of 1978, establishing over one-million acres as the Pinelands National Reserve. . . .

[The court described the Pinelands as a wilderness of pine-oak forests and wild and scenic rivers that overlies a major aquifer.] There has been very little development within the Pinelands; there are no major retail centers, and developed property comprises only one to two percent of the land in most areas. Agriculture in the Pinelands, especially the cultivation of cranberries and blueberries, is particularly important both nationally and locally.

In recent years, anxiety over the loss of farming and the fragile ecology of the Pinelands has produced increasingly stringent federal and state regulation. Both the federal and the implementing state legislation make clear that conservation, preservation, and protection are the principal ends of governmental regulation of land use in the Pinelands. . . .

[The court described the creation of the New Jersey Pinelands Commission and its mandate "to develop a 'comprehensive management plan' (CMP) to serve as the land-use blueprint for the region." Counties and municipalities are required to conform their master plans and zoning ordinances to the CMP and to have such plans and ordinances approved by the Commission. If plans and ordinances do not conform, the Commission will exercise direct control over local land use.]

Reflecting the aims of the federal and state statutes, the goals of the CMP include the "continuation and expansion of agricultural and horticultural uses." N.J.S.A. 13:18A-9(b)(3).

The original CMP, adopted by the Commission in November 1980, stressed that agriculture contributes both to the unique characteristics of the Pinelands and to the environment "by creating open space, terrestrial and aquatic habitats, and wild-life feeding areas." It also stated that suburban development contributes to "an unfavorable economic environment for farmers through escalating taxes, enactment of inhibiting local ordinances, and increased trespassing and vandalism." Consequently, the original CMP called for several programs to accomplish the objective of agricultural preservation. It identified eight "Pinelands Management Areas" of varying ecological sensitivity, including a Preservation Area District, Forest Areas, Agricultural Production Areas, and Regional Growth Areas.

The original CMP restricted residential development in Agricultural Production Areas, reserving them primarily for farm and farm-related purposes. Section 5-304 of the plan allowed residential units on lots with 3.2 acres as long as the applicant met certain stringent conditions. The original CMP also permitted ten-acre residential zoning, that is, one residential unit per ten acres, "provided that the dwelling unit is accessory to an active agricultural operation, and is intended for the use of the owners or employees of the agricultural operation."

The Commission further created a development-rights transfer program, under which it would award Pinelands Development Credits (PDCs) to landowners for recording permanent deed restrictions on their property limiting the land to specific uses set forth in the CMP. The PDC program seeks to channel development by permitting holders of PDCs to transfer them to owners who wish to increase densities in specially-designated Regional Growth Areas. PDCs may be sold privately at market prices; according to the Assistant Director for Development Review at the Commission, Burlington County has a PDC bank that routinely pays $10,000 per credit. A landowner in an Uplands Agricultural Production Area — the designation that apparently includes the Gardner farm — receives two PDCs per thirty-nine acres.

In the fall of 1987, Gardner explored the possibility of subdividing his property into fourteen to seventeen ten-acre "farmettes" in accordance with the CMP option allowing one farm-related residential unit per ten acres of land. Before the application was submitted, the Commission completed a periodic revision and amendment of the CMP, as required by the Act. The Commission determined, according to an affidavit submitted by its Assistant Director for Development Review, that the ten-acre farm option had deteriorated into a ten-acre subdivision requirement with no guarantee that the land actually would be used for farming, and had led in some situations "to the cessation of agricultural operations," "effectively eliminating existing agricultural uses, and threatening significant agricultural use of adjoining areas."

The revised CMP permits only three options for residential development of farmland in Agricultural Production Areas: (1) second-generation Pinelands residents or persons whose livelihood depends on traditional Pinelands economic activities may build homes on 3.2-acre lots; (2) a home may be constructed on a ten-acre lot for an operator or employee of the farm, but that option may be exercised only once every five years; or (3) homes may be constructed at a density of one unit per forty acres, but only if the residences are clustered on one-acre lots and the remaining thirty-nine acres allocated to each residence are permanently dedicated to agricultural use by a recorded deed restriction. The restriction of residential development to forty-acre tracts prompted the filing of Gardner's complaint.

II

Land use regulations span a wide spectrum, from conventional zoning, to particularized restrictions on property with special characteristics, [citing *Penn Central*]. The Pinelands Protection Act virtually fills the entire spectrum. It imposes comprehensive and complex regulatory land-use controls over an extensive geographic region with distinctive natural, economic, cultural, and historic characteristics. . . .

[The court held "the Pinelands scheme is fundamentally a regime of zoning," discussed federal takings law, and concluded:] Essentially, then, application of takings principles requires a fact-sensitive examination of the regulatory scheme, focusing on whether it substantially advances a legitimate public purpose and whether it excessively interferes with property rights and interests.

A

There is not the slightest quarrel that the Act substantially advances several interrelated legitimate and important public purposes. . . . [The court noted the legislative declaration of purpose to protect the Pinelands, and added that the comprehensive management plan] reiterates that purpose, recognizing especially the importance of agriculture because of its capacity to contribute to the special character of the Pinelands and to the environment "by creating open space, terrestrial and aquatic habitats, and wildlife feeding areas," as well as adding "to the cultural, historical, social, visual, and economic characteristics of the Pinelands." . . .

The preservation of agriculture and farmland constitutes a valid governmental goal. N.J. Const. art. VIII, § 1, para. 1(b) (lands used for agriculture or horticulture entitled to favorable tax treatment). The Act and the land-use regulations directly advance agricultural preservation, particularly through the limitation of residential development by large-tract requirements and complementary deed restrictions on undeveloped, nonresidential land. Cf. *Barancik v. County of Marin*, 872 F.2d 834, 837 (9th Cir. 1988) (upholding county plan that restricts housing density to one residence per sixty acres in a valley used for agriculture); *Gisler v. County of Madera*, 112 Cal. Rptr. 919 (Cal. App. 1974) (upholding ordinance providing for exclusive agricultural use and prohibiting sales of parcels less than eighteen acres); *Wilson v. County of McHenry*, 416 N.E.2d 426 (Ill. App. 1981) (upholding 160-acre minimum lot size in agricultural zones); *Codorus Township v. Rodgers*, 492 A.2d 73 (Pa. Commw. 1985) (upholding ordinance prohibiting division of productive farmland into tracts of less than fifty acres).

The Act further advances a valid public purpose by preventing or reducing harm to the public. That is exemplified most dramatically by its measures to safeguard the environment and protect the water supply by severely limiting development. The Legislature specifically determined that "pressures for residential, commercial and industrial development" and the "current pace of random and uncoordinated development" pose an "immediate threat" to a region of vital public importance. N.J.S.A. 13:18A-2.

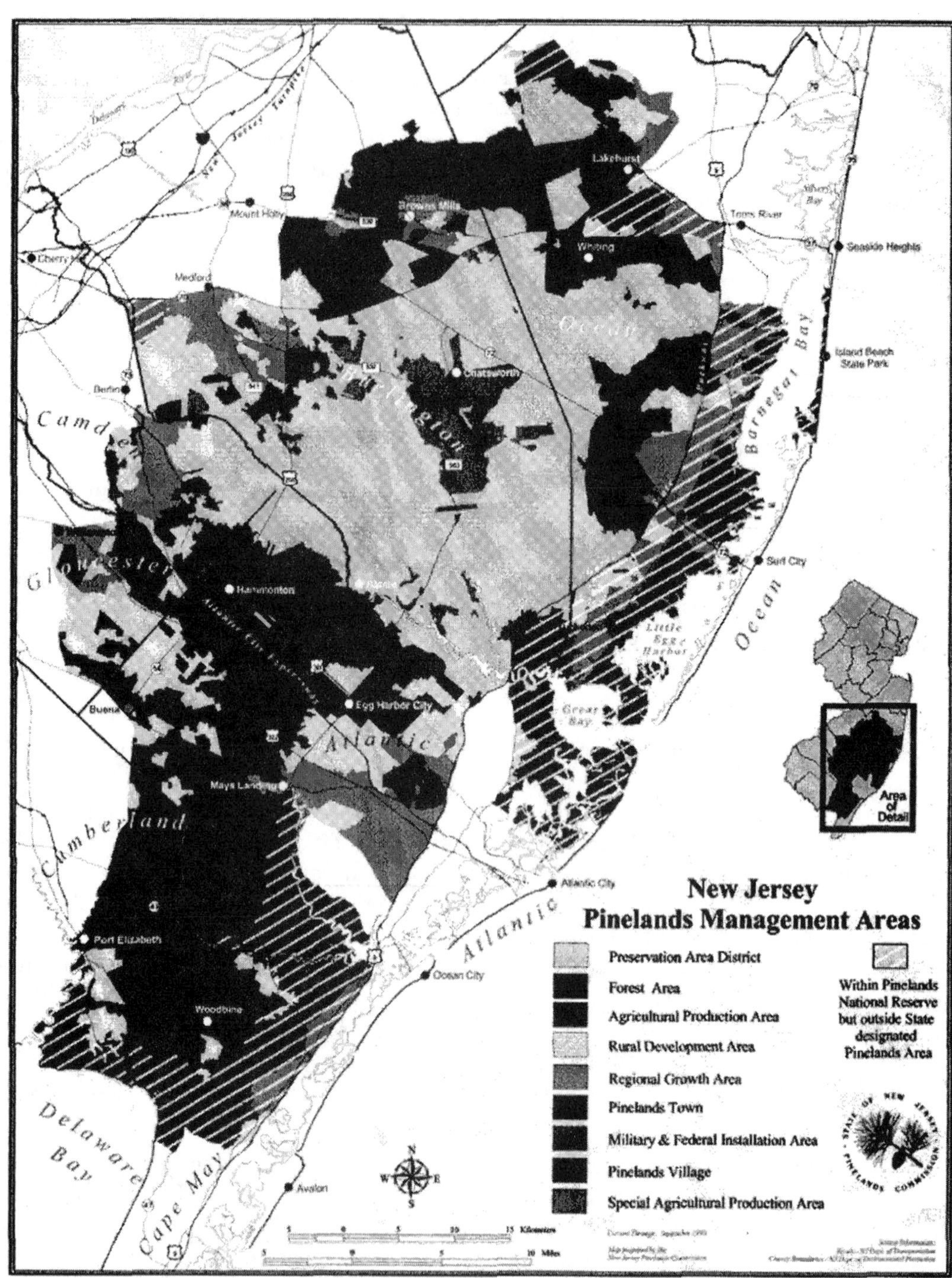

The health, safety and morals or general welfare may be promoted by prohibiting certain uses of land.

That land itself is a diminishing resource cannot be overemphasized. Environmentally-sensitive land is all the more precious. Hence, a proposed development that may constitute only a small insult to the environment does not lessen the need to avoid such an offense. The cumulative detrimental impact of many small projects can be devastating. . . .

B

The critical remaining question is whether the regulations impair to an impermissible degree valuable property rights and interests. . . . A regulatory scheme will be upheld unless it denies "all practical use" of property, or "substantially destroys the beneficial use of private property," or does not allow an "adequate" or "just and reasonable" return on investment. [Citing cases] Significantly, our courts have applied the standard that focuses on the beneficial or economic uses allowed to a property owner in the context of particularized restraints designed to preserve the special status of distinctive property and sensitive environmental regions, such as the Pinelands.

Plaintiff acknowledges that preserving agriculture is a legitimate governmental objective that can be achieved through land-use regulation. He contends, nonetheless, that the land-use regulations, including the required deed restrictions of the revised CMP, interfere to an intolerable degree with his right and freedom to use and enjoy his farmland property. The response to that contention is found in *Penn Central.* [The court discussed *Penn Central*]. . . .

Plaintiff's claim fails under the *Penn Central* analysis. The CMP does not change or prohibit an existing use of the land when applied to plaintiff's farm. Like Penn Central, plaintiff may continue the existing, admittedly beneficial use of the property. Further, although whether Penn Central could again make use of all of its property, particularly the airspace over its terminal, was unclear, plaintiff may gainfully use all of his property, including the right to build five homes clustered together on the restricted land. There also is no showing that the economic impact of the regulations interferes with distinct investment-backed expectations. In addition, Penn Central could offset its loss by transferring valuable property rights to other properties, even if such transfers did not fully compensate it. Plaintiff possesses the similar right to offsetting benefits; it may receive Pinelands Development Credits in return for recording the deed restrictions. Finally, there is no invidious or arbitrary unfairness in the application of the regulatory scheme. Gardner's neighbors in Uplands Agricultural Areas are burdened by exactly the same restrictions, and other landowners in the Pinelands must abide by comparable regulations as part of an integrated comprehensive plan designed to benefit both the region and the public. . . .

In sum, plaintiff retains several viable, economically-beneficial uses of his land under the revised CMP. That those uses do not equal the former maximum value of the land in a less- or un-regulated state is not dispositive, for there exists no constitutional right to the most profitable use of property. We conclude that the restriction on lands to farmland and related uses, given the distinctive and special characteristics of the Pinelands, does not deprive plaintiff of the economic or beneficial use of all or most of his property, sufficiently diminish the value or profitability of his land, or otherwise interfere with his ownership interest to constitute a taking of property without just compensation.

III

Plaintiff contends that the regulations constitute a form of illegal "exaction," in effect requiring Pinelands farmers to pay the costs of zoning benefits for the public at large. . . .

On a conceptual level, applying the nexus requirement that governs responsibility for off-site improvements in connection with a single private development to a comprehensive environmental protection scheme that limits the use of land is difficult, if not impossible. Moreover, in the exactions cases, the development constitutes a lawful, permitted use; in that situation, the critical issue is the validity of imposing on the permissible development the costs for off-site improvements or for overcoming burdens occasioned by the development. In contrast, regulations that lawfully impose land-use constraints on an ecologically-sensitive area can validly disallow the development itself. If, in that context, the developer could not claim that the regulation effects an unlawful taking, it cannot claim that it constitutes an unlawful exaction.

Furthermore, unlike exactions for off-site improvements that unfairly or disproportionately penalize a developer and benefit the general public, the uniform land-use restrictions in the CMP are part of a comprehensive scheme. The CMP creates eight areas within the vast Pinelands region, prescribing different land uses according to the environmental, ecological, economic, and cultural characteristics of the respective areas. The CMP distributes and allocates the economic burdens among all property owners in order to promote the public good. Thus, plaintiff and his neighbors within the Uplands Agricultural Production Area are subject to identical development restrictions; that the impact of such a broad scheme may affect particular property differently does not impugn the scheme. Plaintiff and his neighbors, as well as the general public, also share the benefits from the preservation of the natural environment and the protection of the water supply. . . .

STEIN, J., concurring. [Omitted.]

NOTES AND QUESTIONS

The constitutionality of agricultural zoning. The agricultural zoning program upheld in the *Gardner* decision is an example of a hybrid program implementing a comprehensive plan, and including a transfer of development rights (TDR) option that helped support its constitutional validity. The court's "all practical use" test is consistent with *Lucas*, and the availability of economically viable agricultural uses should make most agricultural zoning survive the *Lucas* per se takings test. Notice the one-sentence comment on investment-backed expectations. *Palazzolo* would seem to require more attention to this problem. The TDR program also helped save the Pinelands program. TDR programs are discussed in the Note following the *Tonter* case, *infra*, and their constitutionality is considered in Chapter 9. Note also how the court handled the exactions argument. Did it adopt a version of the reciprocity of advantage rule toward the end of the opinion?

Most courts have upheld exclusive agricultural zoning that requires large lots. For a case upholding 20-acre agricultural zoning, see *Mays v. Board of Trustees of Miami Township.*, 2002 Ohio App. Lexis 3347 (Ohio App., June 28, 2002). Landowners may also claim that agricultural zoning is an as-applied taking. Several courts have decided these cases by applying the same multifactor test the Illinois courts have used with as-applied challenges to zoning restrictions. See *Racich v. County of Boone*, 625 N.E.2d 1095 (Ill. App. 1993) (no taking, and upholding rating system that determined when agricultural land should be developed). Contra *Pierson v. Henry County*, 417 N.E.2d 234 (Ill. App. 1981).

Local governments must be careful to provide reasonable and justifiable restrictions in their agricultural zoning, however. In *C&M Developers v. Bedminster Township Zoning*

Hearing Bd., 820 A.2d 143 (Pa. 2002), an ordinance covering 90 percent of the township required a landowner to restrict 50 percent of prime farm land on his property to agricultural use. The ordinance further restricted development on the remaining area to single-family homes on a minimum lot size of one acre in areas free of watercourses, floodplain soils, wetlands, lakes, or ponds. The court held the lot size requirement arbitrary and capricious, noting it was selected because it was a "good number" that would prevent large houses from being built on small lots. It upheld the set-aside requirement. *Proesch v. Canyon County Bd. of Comm'rs*, 44 P.3d 1173 (Idaho 2002), also indicates that courts will be sensitive to the need for agricultural preservation. The court upheld a conditional use allowing a subdivision for homes on rocky land that had not been successfully farmed in an area where other residential development existed. Reconsider the APA proposal for an agricultural element in comprehensive plans. How could it deal with the problems presented in each of these decisions? For a case finding an impermissible downzoning, or decrease in density, to preserve land for agricultural development in a developed area, see *In re Realen Valley Forge Greenes Assocs.*, 838 A.2d 718 (Pa. 2003). See also Gottlieb & Adelaja, *The Impact of Down-Zoning on Land Values: A Theoretical Approach*, 69 Ag. Fin. Rev. 2 (2009).

The following case addresses a challenge that a county's agricultural restrictions were *ultra vires* and void as applied to plaintiffs' lots because the restrictions prohibited residential development on agriculturally zoned property.

Beyond the scope of its powers

TONTER INVESTMENTS v. PASQUOTANK COUNTY
681 S.E.2d 536 (N.C. App. 2009)

ELMORE, JUDGE.

This case concerns three separate tracts of land in Pasquotank County (defendant) that were purchased by Tonter Investments, Inc. (plaintiff), in March and July 2007. Soon thereafter, defendant passed several ordinances that resulted in plaintiff not being able to build residences on any of the lots. Defendant argues that this particular application of defendant's zoning power is an attempt to circumvent certain exemptions given by the State Legislature to tracts of land that exceed ten acres, and, as such, defendant's ordinances are *ultra vires* and not valid. The trial court issued summary judgment in favor of defendant, finding that the ordinances were within defendant's zoning power. We affirm the trial court's decision.

In March 2007, plaintiff purchased a 136-acre tract of land (Tract 1) that has approximately 1,665 feet of frontage along a state-maintained highway known as Sandy Road. Later that same month, plaintiff purchased a 75.7 acre tract of land (Tract 2) that has approximately 2,751 feet of frontage on Sandy Road. Plaintiff also owns a 26-acre tract of land (Tract 3) with approximately 800 feet of frontage on Sandy Road. All three tracts are located in Pasquotank County.

Tracts 1 and 2 are zoned by defendant as A-2, Agricultural District, which permitted residential structures at the time that plaintiff purchased the tracts. However, on 6 August 2007, defendant passed an ordinance (the August Amendment) prohibiting all residential uses for A-2 districts, thus preventing plaintiff from turning Tracts 1 and 2 into subdivided residential developments as planned. Meanwhile, Tract 3 is zoned as A-1, Agricultural, a designation which has permitted residential structures since the time of plaintiff's purchase. However, defendant passed another ordinance on 4 September 2007 (the September Amendment) requiring that, unless an exception is granted by defendant,

> [n]o building or structure shall be established on a lot recorded in the Pasquotank County Registry after September 4, 2007[,] which does not meet the following requirements:
>
> (A) Lots shall contain a minimum of 25 feet of frontage on a state maintained road or a road that has been approved in accordance with the Pasquotank County Subdivision Ordinance; and
>
> (B) Lots shall be located within 1,000 feet of a public water supply.

All three tracts have proper amounts of road frontage, but none of the three tracts is located within 1,000 feet of a public water supply, meaning that plaintiff cannot build any structures on the tracts without an exception granted by defendant. On 28 September 2007, plaintiff filed a complaint alleging that the August and September Amendments were beyond defendant's zoning power. On 10 March 2008, defendant rejected plaintiff's request for an exception to the August and September Amendments. The case was then heard before the Honorable W. Russell Duke, Jr., on 9 June 2008 at the Pasquotank County Superior Court. On 19 June 2008, Judge Duke granted defendant's motion for summary judgment, effectively ruling that the August and September Amendments were within defendant's zoning power. Plaintiff appeals to this Court.

Plaintiff argues that the August and September Amendments are *ultra vires* and thus void as applied to lots in excess of ten acres. We disagree. . . .

It is well established that "[c]ounties are creatures of the General Assembly and have no inherent legislative powers. They are instrumentalities of state government and possess only those powers the General Assembly has conferred upon them." . . . The General Assembly has authorized counties to adopt ordinances regulating land subdivisions, which is defined to include "all divisions of a tract or parcel into two or more lots, building sites, or other divisions when any one or more of those divisions are created for the purpose of sale or building development[.]" N.C. Gen. Stat. § 153A-335(a) (2007). However, counties are not authorized to regulate all types of subdivisions. N.C. Gen. Stat. § 153A-335(a) specifically exempts "division of land into parcels greater than 10 acres" from "regulations enacted pursuant to [section 153A-335]." N.C. Gen. Stat. § 153A-335(a)(2) (2007). That is, counties cannot adopt subdivision ordinances where the lots are greater than ten acres in size. Both parties to the present litigation agree that plaintiff had already subdivided some of the tracts — and had plans to subdivide the remaining tracts — into lots that were all at least ten acres in size. As such, defendant clearly has no ability to impose subdivision regulations on plaintiff's lots greater than ten acres.

However, the August and September Amendments were both passed by defendant as zoning ordinances, not subdivision ordinances. With respect to counties' authority to create zoning regulations, the General Assembly has provided:

> For the purpose of promoting health, safety, morals, or the general welfare, a county may adopt zoning and development regulation ordinances. These ordinances may be adopted as part of a unified development ordinance or as a separate ordinance. A zoning ordinance may regulate and restrict the height, number of stories and size of

> buildings and other structures, the percentage of lots that may be occupied, the size of yards, courts and other open spaces, the density of population, and the location and use of buildings, structures, and land for trade, industry, residence, or other purposes. . . .

Plaintiff argues that defendant passed the August and September Amendments under the guise of zoning ordinances because defendant knew that it could not use subdivision ordinances to regulate plaintiff's large lots. As such, plaintiff argues, the August and September Amendments are *ultra vires* and designed to circumvent the General Assembly's intent to exempt lots greater than ten acres from regulation by counties. As such, plaintiff's argument is that lots greater than ten acres in size are exempt from all county zoning regulations, not just subdivision regulations. . . .

[Court upheld the September Amendment as a valid exercise of the county's zoning power.]

Plaintiff then argues that the August Amendment, which prohibits any residential structures from being built on lots zoned "A-2, Agricultural," is also *ultra vires* because it is inconsistent with the General Assembly's exemption of ten-acre lots from regulatory control. In particular, plaintiff argues that the General Assembly never intended to allow a county to completely prevent single-family homes from being constructed on lots greater than ten acres.

At the hearing for the August Amendment, Planning Director Shelley Cox stated:

> the purpose [of the August Amendment] is to prevent future residential development in this area. She said there has been some interest in dividing ten-acre parcels in the Sandy Road area and plats have been brought to her office that contain 31 ten-acre lots that have been cut up in this area. Ms. Cox stated that the county is very concerned about this[.]

Plaintiff interprets this language to mean that defendant's sole purpose in enacting the August Amendment was to prevent plaintiff from developing ten-acre lots near Sandy Road. However, the August Amendment applies to all lots zoned A-2, not just ten-acre lots. Additionally, the General Assembly has provided that a county may divide its jurisdiction into "districts of any number, shape, and area that it may consider best suited to carry out the purposes of [zoning]," and within each district, the county is authorized to regulate and restrict the "use of buildings, structures, or land." N.C. Gen. Stat. § 153A-342 (2007). Plaintiff has not cited any authority tending to show that counties must allow residences in all zoning districts. . . .

Additionally, as stated above, a zoning regulation will be struck down only if it has no foundation in reason and bears no substantial relation to the public health, morals, safety, or welfare. . . . According to Rodney Bunch, the Assistant County Manager, the August Amendment was passed based on: (1) the remote nature and lack of improved roads within most of the A-2 district, (2) the potential strain on the County's ability to provide essential public services to residents in this district, (3) the fact that only five residences currently exist in the entire A-2 district, and (4) the aerial application of pesticides within a large part of the district. As such, there was a clear relationship between preventing residences from being built in the A-2 zone and public health and safety; the County would be unable to provide essential public services to the new residences, and the residences would also be subject to safety concerns from aerial pesticide spraying. Plaintiff is not deprived of all uses of the land, since the August Amendment prohibits only residences in zone A-2, leaving intact the other uses of the land approved by defendant.

The Amendment had a rational basis founded on a relationship to protect the public safety in zone A-2; as such, it was within defendant's zoning power, and plaintiff's argument is overruled.

The August and September Amendments both had rational bases for their creation, namely that their requirements had a strong relationship to public safety and health. Additionally, the fact that lots greater than ten acres are exempted from subdivision regulations imposed by a county does not mean that the lots are not still subject to a county's zoning power. To hold otherwise would fly in the face of zoning authority specifically granted to counties by the General Assembly for the purpose of promoting public health by regulating the location and use of structures and land. As such, we hold that defendant's August and September Amendments were both valid exercises of defendant's zoning power granted to it by the General Assembly and were not *ultra vires*. Plaintiff's arguments are overruled.

Affirmed.

Judges CALABRIA and GEER concur.

NOTES AND QUESTIONS

1. *Presumption of Validity.* In *Tonter*, the plaintiffs argued that the zoning ordinance that prohibited all residential structures from property zoned agricultural was *ultra vires* because it was inconsistent with a state law that exempted 10 acre lots from regulatory control. The court disagreed, holding that the state law preempted *subdivision* authority but not zoning authority. According to the court, the challenged zoning ordinances were valid exercises of the county's zoning power and were not, therefore, *ultra vires*. The test used by the court was that a zoning regulation would not be struck down unless it "has no foundation in reason and bears no substantial relation to the public health, morals, safety, or welfare."

Zoning ordinances are generally afforded a "presumption of validity" that makes them difficult to successfully challenge even where they exclude otherwise lawful uses such as residential dwellings. For example, a New York court upheld a local zoning ordinance that prohibited the development of a housing subdivision in an agricultural district, finding that the ordinance did not exceed the town's authority to regulate open spaces, density and location and use of buildings for the general welfare. The plaintiffs in *Schlossin v. Town of Marilla*, 852 N.Y.S.2d 515 (App. Div. 2008), sought to rezone property located in an agricultural district to rural-residential in order to construct single family homes. The town denied the rezoning request, finding that it was inconsistent with the comprehensive plan, which sought to preserve open space and the agricultural integrity of the town. In upholding the town's denial, the court found that the agricultural zoning restrictions were within the town's zoning power and that preserving the agricultural integrity of the town was a legitimate governmental interest.

2. *Area-based allocation zoning.* This is an alternate form of agricultural zoning that allows landowners to build one dwelling for each specified unit of land that they own. The dwelling allowance can be fixed to build at some density, say one dwelling unit for 40 acres on lots of limited size, usually less than 3 acres. This low-density, small-lot approach leaves larger areas open for agricultural use. Some area-based allocation ordinances use a sliding scale in which density decreases as farm size increases. Smaller farms are allowed more units on the theory that smaller acreage is more difficult to farm.

Defenders of area-based allocation zoning consider it more defensible because it allows some development, but these systems have been challenged. In *Hopewell Township Bd. of Supervisors v. Golla*, 452 A.2d 1337 (Pa. 1982), the Pennsylvania Supreme Court struck down an ordinance that allowed only five dwelling units on prime agricultural land whatever the size of the farm. It held the ordinance arbitrary and discriminatory because the dwelling cap had the effect of allowing a greater percentage of land for housing on smaller tracts. The court believed that a straight linear scale would not preserve agricultural land properly. See also *Codorus Township v. Rodgers*, 492 A.2d 73 (Pa. 1985) (agricultural zoning provisions that precluded subdivision of farmland into less than 50 acres constitutional).

Three years later, the court upheld a similar ordinance with a nonlinear sliding scale that allowed more dwelling units on smaller parcels. The ordinance also imposed a maximum of two dwellings on prime farm land no matter what the size of the parcel, but the court upheld this limitation as part of the broader scheme. *Boundary Drive Assocs. v. Shrewsbury Township Bd. of Supervisors*, 491 A.2d 86 (Pa. 1985). Do you think that area-based allocation zoning really is more defensible legally than exclusive agricultural zoning? For discussion, see Hartzell, *Agricultural and Rural Zoning in Pennsylvania — Can You Get There From Here?*, 10 Vill. Envtl. L.J. 245 (1999); Pivo, Small & Wolfe, *Rural Cluster Zoning: Survey and Guidelines*, Land Use L. & Zoning Dig., Sept., 1990, at 3.

A NOTE ON THE TRANSFER OF DEVELOPMENT RIGHTS AS A TECHNIQUE FOR PROTECTING AGRICULTURAL AND NATURAL RESOURCE AREAS

As the *Gardner* case indicates, transfer of development rights (TDR) programs can be a helpful supplement to agricultural land preservation programs. The objective is to avoid taking of property problems and achieve a fairer distribution of the burdens and benefits of regulation. In addition to the Pinelands, a highly successful TDR program that helps implement an agricultural preservation program is in effect in Montgomery County, Maryland, adjacent to Washington, D.C. The text that follows reviews these programs. Takings and other problems in TDR programs are discussed in the section on historic preservation in Chapter 9.

Montgomery County. The county adopted a plan for the preservation of agriculture and rural open space land, which it implemented through a downzoning of 91,591 acres in an agricultural reserve area by increasing the minimum lot size from five to 25 acres. This large minimum lot size was considered necessary to sustain farming on a cash crop basis. One development right for residential development can be transferred in the TDR program for every five acres of land, so that five times as much development can occur if development rights are transferred — one house could be built on 25 acres and four development rights sold to a developer and used elsewhere. The county has designated receiving sites for transferred development rights in nine communities. The preserved sending areas are in the northern part of the county, while the receiving areas are in the southern part adjacent to Washington, D.C., where there is a demand for housing.

Zoning at the receiving sites has two maximum densities, one for development without TDR and one for development in which transferred development rights are used. A developer is not guaranteed the maximum density because the Planning Board can require a lower density if there are site constraints and environmental limitations. There is a minimum density of at least two-thirds of the allowable density increase. This requirement was adopted to prevent developers from building at reduced densities on large sites. Site plan review at the receiving site is required to provide greater assurance that it will not be overwhelmed by the transferred density, and that it will not cause problems for adjacent properties. Easements with land use restrictions must be placed on the transfer site. The county initially established but then terminated a TDR fund for buying development rights. As of 2003, the county had saved about one-half of the land zoned as farmland through the TDR program. See R. Pruetz, Beyond Takings and Givings 208–212 (2003). Though the Montgomery County program has been successful, one problem is that development has leapfrogged the sending areas into adjacent counties. A recent study also finds the county is running out of receiving areas, TDR prices are falling, and residents in some receiving areas oppose TDR transfers that increase densities. J. Cohen & I. Preuss, An Analysis of Equity Issues in the Montgomery County (MD) Transfer of Development Rights Program (2002) (www.smartgrowth.umd.edu/research/pdf/CohenPreuss_TDREquity_DateNA.pdf). See also A. Nelson et. al., The TDR Handbook: Designing and Implementing Successful Transfer of Development Rights Programs (2010).

The Pinelands. — The *Gardner* decision contains a brief description of the Pineland Development Credits (PDC) program. It was created for areas in the Pinelands covered by severe development restrictions, and the plan also contemplates the public acquisition of one-tenth of the Pinelands area through the use of federal and state funds. Once conservation easements have been created, owners of land in the protected areas can transfer development rights to Regional Growth Areas. The number of PDCs allocated to a sending area depends on its development potential and the environmental sensitivity of the land. Four dwelling units can be built in a growth area for every development credit transferred from a protected area. Applications for PDC transfer are submitted to the Pinelands Commission first and then to the receiving community. A New Jersey Pinelands Development Credit Bank acts as a buyer of last resort and has been active in purchasing and holding PDCs. It may sell PDCs only if there is sufficient demand to justify a sale, and only if the sale would not impair the private sale of PDCs. The bank has been assisted since 2000 by a state Special Development Credit Purchase Program supported by state funding.

To be certain there would be enough land to receive transferred credits, the Pinelands plan designated receiving areas capable of receiving twice the number of PDCs available. In each receiving community, the zoning code designates the extra density available when PDCs are used, and these are available as a matter of right. As of April 1, 2010, 2713 PDCs or 10,852 transferable development rights had been severed and 58,900 acres had been preserved. See www.state.nj.us/pinelands/infor/fact/PDCfacts.pdf.

NOTES AND QUESTIONS

1. *Montgomery County.* In *West Montgomery County Citizens Ass'n v. Maryland-Nat'l Capital Park & Planning Comm'n*, 522 A.2d 1328 (Md. 1987), the court invalidated the original Montgomery County TDR program. The court held that the zoning ordinance amendment adopting the TDR program improperly delegated unlimited authority concerning land to be designated as receiving parcels and the increased density to be assigned to these parcels to the planning board. The ordinance failed because the board did not have the necessary zoning authority to carry out this function:

> What appears to have been contemplated by the District Council in its attempts to implement the receiving area prong of the TDR concept is the creation of zoning

> subclassification systems within the designated single family zones. These subclassifications would contain the properties approved as TDR receiving areas, grouped according to the density level assigned. . . . Proper implementation of that structure would result in uniformity of zones, and informative identification of the precise classification of the property on the zoning map. [*Id.* at 1337.]

The system was subsequently amended to incorporate the district concept.

2. *The New Jersey Pinelands.* A county development bank program in the Pinelands was upheld by a trial court in *Matlack v. Board of Chosen Freeholders*, 466 A.2d 83 (N.J.L. Div. 1983). The trial judge upheld the price set by the county for a PDC, and reviewed and approved the PDC program.

3. *Sources.* For additional discussion of the Montgomery County and Pinelands programs, see Beetle, *Are Transferable Development Rights a Viable Solution to New Jersey's Land Use Problems?: An Evaluation of TDR Programs within the Garden State*, 34 Rutgers L.J. 513 (2003); Johnston & Madison, *From Landmarks to Landscapes: A Review of Current Practice in the Transfer of Development Right*, 63 J. Am. Plan. Ass'n 365 (1997). See also Juergensmeyer, Nichols & Leebrick, *Transferable Development Rights and Alternatives After Suitum*, 30 Urb. Law. 441 (1998); Pruetz & Standridge, *What Makes Transfer of Development Rights Work?* 75 J. Am. Plan. Ass'n 78 (2009); A. Nelson et. al., The TDR Handbook: Designing and Implementing Successful Transfer of Development Rights Programs (2010).

[4.] Right-To-Farm Laws

Right-to-farm laws, which have been adopted in all 50 states, are a popular attempt to preserve agricultural land by modifying the law of nuisance. The most popular version of these laws provides that a farming operation shall not be or become a public or private nuisance if it was not a nuisance at the time it began operation, even though conditions change in the surrounding area. Usually, the agricultural use must have been in place for at least one year. Some laws protect the agricultural use even if it changes, but some remove the statutory protection once there is a change or expansion.

This type of law is an attempt to protect farming from disruptive nuisance suits filed by invading residential neighbors. It does so by legislating the "coming to the nuisance" rule that some courts apply in private nuisance suits. See Chapter 2. The rule means that a plaintiff may not successfully sue to prevent a nuisance if the nuisance was in existence when the plaintiff purchased her property. The effect of the statute is that a preexisting agricultural use acquires an implicit negative easement that prohibits development on surrounding property, because it prevents adjacent property owners suing to prohibit the use as an agricultural nuisance.

Here is a description of the other requirements in these laws and how they vary among the states:

> State RTF laws differ considerably on the activities that are covered by the statutory nuisance protection. While some laws specifically delineate coverage to farms and farming operations, other laws cover roadside markets and the manufacturing of animal feed. Generally, RTF laws cover the growing and harvesting of crops, the feeding, breeding, and management of livestock, and other agricultural and horticultural uses.

Prerequisites concerning location and practices also restrict RTF laws' coverage of agricultural operations. Many RTF laws only apply to commercial activities so that hobbyists or non-farmers do not qualify for the nuisance protection. Some states require agricultural producers to be in an agricultural district before they can qualify for the nuisance protection. A law may require that the activity at issue be a sound agricultural practice before it qualifies for legal protection. Other provisions say that improper and negligent agricultural activities are not protected. . . .

Provisions in most of the RTF laws do not affect other causes of action in tort or obviate the requirements of other statutes. Agricultural producers remain subject to zoning ordinances, building codes, and local and state laws. RTF laws do not impact environmental laws or pollution legislation, thus, producers must comply with legislation governing clean water and the disposal of animal manure. Further, the RTF laws do not offer protection to the operation or the operator if the activities or actions constitute negligence or trespass or violate other legal provisions. For causes of action for negligence, many of the RTF laws specifically provide that any negligent or improper operation at an agricultural facility is not protected. Other provisions in RTF laws may state that the laws do not affect any other right to sue for damages. [Centner, *Anti-Nuisance Legislation: Can the Derogation of Common-Law Nuisance Be a Taking?*, 30 Envtl. L. Rep. 10253, 10254 (2000).]

An initial question under right-to-farm laws is when is an agricultural activity protected from nuisance litigation, as considered in the next case:

BUCHANAN v. SIMPLOT FEEDERS LIMITED PARTNERSHIP

134 Wash. 2d 673, 952 P.2d 610 (Wash. 1998)

DOLLIVER, J. The certified question in this case stems from the Buchanans' federal lawsuit against Defendants Simplot Feeders Limited Partnership (Simplot) and IBP, Inc. (IBP). The lawsuit complains of manure dust, flies, and odors allegedly emanating from Defendants' feedlot and meat processing plant adjacent to the Buchanans' farm.

Our summary of the facts behind this lawsuit is based solely on the parties' motions and pleadings. The following summary should not be construed as an endorsement of any of the parties' factual claims. The Buchanans own and operate a 320-acre farm near Pasco, Washington. They have farmed and lived on the land since 1961. When they purchased the property, the adjacent properties were primarily used as rangeland. In approximately 1969, a small cattle feeding operation opened on land to the southeast of the Buchanan farm. The Buchanans allege Simplot purchased the feedlot in fall 1992. The Simplot operation now allegedly covers over 580 acres of pens and holds over 40,000 cows. The Buchanans allege Simplot's operation of the lot since 1992 has resulted in a significant increase of flies and foul and obnoxious odors.

The Buchanans allege a small meat processing plant began operation on property to the southeast of the Buchanan farm on or about 1970. They allege IBP purchased and has operated the facility since 1976. The Buchanans claim IBP has significantly expanded its meat processing and rendering plant since 1993, adding a new, large wastewater storage lagoon, a new, large storage pond for brine, and several new "cookers." The Buchanans allege this expansion has resulted in a significant increase in foul and obnoxious odors crossing onto the Buchanans' farm and residence.

The Buchanans sued Simplot and IBP in federal court, alleging nuisance, trespass and negligence. Under the trespass action, the Buchanans complained of flies and manure dust which were damaging the Buchanans' crops. Under the nuisance claim, they complained of the foul and obnoxious odors.

As to the nuisance claim, Simplot and IBP argued to the federal court that their operations were exempt from nuisance suits under RCW 7.48.305, a "right-to-farm" statute. RCW 7.48.305 declares certain agricultural activities do not constitute a nuisance under certain conditions.

The Buchanans disputed Defendants' reliance on RCW 7.48.305. They argued to the federal court that the statute cannot apply since the Buchanan farm allegedly was in operation before Defendants' activities. . . . [The federal court certified a question concerning an interpretation of the law, but the state court decided it must first determine whether the law was available as defense in this case.]

During the 1970s and early 1980s, every state except South Dakota enacted what are generally referred to as right-to-farm statutes. Right-to-farm statutes were created to address a growing concern that too much farmland was being overtaken by urban sprawl. As more urban dwellers moved into agricultural areas, nuisance lawsuits by those urbanites threatened the existence of many farms. Nuisance suits frustrated farming operations and encouraged farmers to sell to developers, continuing the cycle.

Most of the right-to-farm statutes adopted across the country codified the common law defense of "coming to the nuisance." Plaintiffs who purchase or improve property, after the establishment of a local nuisance activity, have "come to the nuisance." While this fact did not absolutely bar the plaintiff's nuisance action, it was one factor to be considered in whether to grant the plaintiff relief. Restatement (Second) of Torts sec. 840D (1977).

The Washington State Legislature embraced the right-to-farm issue in 1979, when it passed an act entitled "Agricultural Activities-Protection from Nuisance Lawsuits." Laws of 1979, ch. 122 (codified at RCW 7.48.300-.310 &.905). We will refer to this legislation as the Right-to-Farm Act, or the Act. . . .

The Right to Farm Act was intended to protect existing farms from the pressures associated with urbanization. Urbanization is not at issue in this case. Instead, it is the Buchanan family farm that is being forced out by the expanding cattle feedlot and industrial-like beef processing facility. The Right to Farm Act neither expressly nor impliedly applies to this situation.

The Buchanans further argued RCW 7.48.305 applies only to the following situation:

> If a farm or agricultural activity pre-exists at a particular location and then a non-farm activity, such as a residential community, moves into the area, the non-farm activity is precluded from bringing an action for nuisance against the pre-existing farm.

Since the Buchanan farm allegedly does not constitute "encroaching urbanization," and since the Buchanans' farm was allegedly in operation before Defendants' activities giving rise to the nuisance, the Buchanans argued the Defendants should not be able to raise RCW 7.48.305 as a defense.

In their memoranda submitted to the federal court, Simplot and IBP argued they can rely on RCW 7.48.305. They claimed the only time a farm is not exempt from a nuisance suit under

the statute is if the farm locates in preexisting urban areas. Simplot and IBP assert their activities were established before any surrounding nonagricultural activities, allowing them to rely on RCW 7.48.305 as a defense. The record shows no indication of any nonagricultural activities existing in the area. . . .

As written, RCW 7.48.305 is not very structured. The statute provides:

> Notwithstanding any other provision of this chapter, agricultural activities conducted on farmland and forest practices, if consistent with good agricultural and forest practices and established prior to surrounding nonagricultural and nonforestry activities, are presumed to be reasonable and shall not be found to constitute a nuisance unless the activity has a substantial adverse effect on the public health and safety.
>
> If those agricultural activities and forest practices are undertaken in conformity with all applicable laws and rules, the activities are presumed to be good agricultural and forest practices not adversely affecting the public health and safety for purposes of this section and RCW 7.48.300. An agricultural activity that is in conformity with such laws and rules shall not be restricted as to the hours of the day or days of the week during which it may be conducted.
>
> Nothing in this section shall affect or impair any right to sue for damages.

Three conditions can be derived from this statute. An agricultural activity is presumed to be reasonable and shall not constitute a nuisance when: (1) the activity does not have a substantial adverse effect on public health and safety; (2) the activity is consistent with good agricultural practices, laws, and rules; and (3) the activity was established prior to surrounding nonagricultural activities. The Legislature itself has read RCW 7.48.305 in a similar way. See 52d Wash. State Leg., 1991 Final Legislative Report 133 (describing the Right-to-Farm Act as allowing nuisance immunity when those three circumstances are present).

The third condition requires the challenged agricultural activity to have been established prior to surrounding nonagricultural activities before the nuisance exemption applies. This condition also suggests an established farm may not be able to institute a new or radically expanded "activity" and maintain nuisance immunity, because the language of the statute focuses on agricultural activity that has been established prior to the urban encroachment. Cf. *Payne v. Skaar*, 900 P.2d 1352, 1355 (Idaho 1995) (Idaho Right-to-Farm Act does not protect an established feedlot from nuisance suits if the nuisance arises because of expansion of the agricultural activity). This third condition presents an ambiguity within the structure of RCW 7.48.305: One would assume the statute's nuisance exemption is limited to situations where the nuisance suit arises *because of* the subsequent surrounding nonagricultural activities, since the Legislature expressly states the statute is designed to protect farms "*in urbanizing areas*" from nuisance suits. RCW 7.48.300 (emphasis added). The language of the statute, however, does not explicitly make this connection between the nuisance suit and the urbanization.

Since the statute contains an ambiguity, this court must look to legislative intent when applying the statute. When analyzing the ambiguous language in RCW 7.48.305 along with the Legislature's finding and purpose in RCW 7.48.300, it becomes clear the nuisance immunity should be allowed just in those cases where the nuisance suit arises because of urban encroachment into an established agricultural area.

Our ability to interpret and apply the Right-to-Farm Act is enhanced by the Legislature's express statement of findings and purpose. See RCW 7.48.300. The first sentence of the statute clearly connects the design of the Act to protecting farms in urbanizing areas:

> The legislature finds that agricultural activities conducted on farmland and forest practices in urbanizing areas are often subjected to nuisance lawsuits, and that such suits encourage and even force the premature removal of the lands from agricultural uses and timber production.

RCW 7.48.300. The second sentence of the statute, however, offers a more sweeping statement:

> It is therefore the purpose of RCW 7.48.300 through 7.48.310 and 7.48.905 to provide that agricultural activities conducted on farmland and forest practices be protected from nuisance lawsuits.

RCW 7.48.300. This second sentence broadly offers nuisance protection for all agricultural activities. In their arguments to the federal court, Defendants focused on this second sentence.

When determining the legislative intent of the nuisance exemption, we cannot blindly focus on the second sentence — we must read it in context with the first sentence. . . . The Legislature is concerned farmlands in urbanizing areas are prematurely being closed to agricultural use because of nuisance lawsuits in those urbanizing areas. This first sentence expresses the specific problem the Legislature intended to address. We read the second sentence in a narrow sense as responding to the specific problem of farming operations being threatened by urbanization.

The Legislature's stated purpose of the Right-to-Farm Act supports a narrow interpretation of RCW 7.48.305. A narrow reading is also supported by the legislative history of the statute, which is an important tool to ascertain intent. The Senate floor debate concerning passage of the Right-to-Farm Act clearly shows RCW 7.48.305 was intended to protect farms in urbanizing areas from nuisance suits.

Senator Rasmussen, who was the only senator to vote against passage of the law, posed several hypothetical situations in the attempt to criticize the bill. In defense of the bill, Senator Gaspard stated:

> "We are really trying to state a policy that farm lands are disappearing from this Puget Sound region and those farm lands that have been established *before urban areas and suburban areas have surrounded them* are having a very difficult time staying where they are. I think that it is more a statement of policy by the state than anything else." 46th Wash. State Leg., Senate Journal 514 (1979) (emphasis added).

Senator Bottiger also stated:

> "An answer that Senator Gaspard didn't give, and that I think turns the case against Senator Rasmussen, is the question *who was there first*. If the dog kennel was there first and you chose to come with your subdivision and build all around it, then you bought with the dog kennel next door to you and you can't bring a nuisance action to get rid of them. . . ."

Id. at 515 (emphasis added). Senator Bottiger's statement supports finding Washington's Right-to-Farm Act codifies the coming to the nuisance defense, and it justifies a narrow application of the nuisance exemption. . . .

The express legislative purpose and the legislative history behind the Right-to-Farm Act support this court's reading the phrase "established prior to surrounding nonagricultural . . . activities" as including the premise that the only nuisance suits barred by RCW 7.48.305 are those which arise because of subsequent nonagricultural development and which are filed by one of those nonagricultural activities referenced in the language of the statute. This narrow reading of the ambiguous condition serves the narrowly tailored legislative intent of protecting farms "in urbanizing areas" from nuisance lawsuits which arise because of the encroaching urbanization.

Additionally, we find public policy considerations urge a narrow application of the Act. The protection afforded by the nuisance exemption is similar to a prescriptive easement. When a farm establishes a particular activity which potentially interferes with the use and enjoyment of adjoining land, and urban developments subsequently locate next to the farm, those developers presumably have notice of those "farm" activities. The Right-to-Farm Act gives the farm a quasi easement against the urban developments to continue those nuisance activities.

A farm obtains this quasi easement much more easily under the Act than if the farm was required to meet the strict requirements for a prescriptive easement. See *Bradley v. American Smelting & Refining Co.*, 709 P.2d 782 (Wash. 1985) (prescriptive easement claimant must show (1) open, notorious, uninterrupted use for 10 years which is (2) adverse to the title owner, and (3) the owner was aware of the adverse use and had the opportunity to enforce the owner's rights). The Right-to-Farm Act does not even set a minimum time period for which a farm activity must be established in order to be exempt from nuisance suits. Compare *Payne v. Skaar*, 900 P.2d 1352, 1355 (Idaho 1995) (Idaho Right-to-Farm Act requires the agricultural activity to be "in operation for more than one (1) year" before nuisance exemption applies); see also Neil D. Hamilton & David Bolte, *Nuisance Law and Livestock Production in the United States: A Fifty-State Analysis*, 10 J. Agric. Tax'n & L. 99, 101 (1988) (most right-to-farm statutes require the challenged agricultural activity predates changes in the neighborhood by at least one year). Just as prescriptive rights are difficult to obtain, and are not favored in law, we hold the nuisance protection afforded by the Right-to-Farm Act must be applied cautiously and narrowly. RCW 7.48.305 should not be read to insulate agricultural enterprises from nuisance actions brought by an agricultural or other rural plaintiff, especially if the plaintiff occupied the land before the nuisance activity was established. See Neil D. Hamilton, *Right-To-Farm Laws Revisited: Judicial Consideration of Agricultural Nuisance Protections*, 14 J. Agric. Tax'n & L. 195, 217 (1992) ("A right-to-farm law does not give farmers the power to inflict any hardship on neighbors just because an agricultural facility is involved, especially when the neighbors are there first.").

We have commented on the issue of who may raise RCW 7.48.305 as a defense only because we find no case law clarifying the ambiguous statute. We are unprepared to rule on the merits of Defendants' reliance on the statute in this case, nor does the certified question ask for such a ruling. Our analysis is solely intended to aid the federal court in deciding the question when the federal proceedings resume. . . .

ALEXANDER, J. (dissenting) [Omitted.]

NOTES AND QUESTIONS

1. *What does the right-to-farm law protect?* The *Simplon* case raises some important questions about the protection offered by a right-to-farm (RTF) law. Do you agree with the holding that the law only protects against "urbanization"? If so, what is "urbanization"? What about a neighboring "martini ranch" — a term coined by John DeGrove, a noted growth management expert who used it to describe Florida small hobby farms of, say 5–10 acres which are more residential than agricultural? Notice that the court does not really consider the factual situation in the case, which would have prevented the application of the statute because the defendant's use had changed. For a case taking the contrary view under a similar statute it held to be unambiguous, see *Souza v. Lauppe*, 69 Cal. Rptr. 2d 494 (Cal. App. 1997).

The court takes the position that the application of the law must be based on fairness. Note, however, that the Washington law did not require a farm to be in existence for a designated period of time before it was protected from a nuisance suit. Is this fair? Some RTF laws require this. See *Holubec v. Brandenberger*, 111 S.W.3d 32 (Tex. 2003). Does legislating the coming to the nuisance rule make the law fair? To what extent, under the interpretation in the *Simplon* case, is an RTF law a kind of rural zoning? RTF statutes usually require the protected agricultural use to be a specified distance from nonagricultural uses. Mich. Comp. Laws § 286.473(2) (within one mile).

2. *Change and expansion.* Notice that the Washington law does not protect a farm use once it changes or expands. See *Trickett v. Ochs*, 838 A.2d 66 (Vt. 2003) (applying similar provision). This is a serious limitation, because change and expansion occur in agricultural uses as they do in any use. This type of law will probably protect an agricultural use only for a limited period of time if change and expansion are inevitable. It may actually have a negative effect on agricultural activities if farmers avoid changes in operations because they know that such actions will remove the protection of the law. The rules on change and expansion are similar to those applied to nonconforming uses but seem inconsistent with the intent of RTF law, which is to protect existing agriculture.

Some RTF laws allow expansion of an agricultural use. E.g., Or. Rev. Stat. § 30.936(3). A change may not be allowed if the change will be a nuisance. See also Fla. Stat. Ann. § 823.14(4) ("act shall not be construed to permit an existing farm operation to change to a more excessive farm operation with regard to noise, odor, dust, or fumes where the existing farm operation is adjacent to an established homestead or business on March 15, 1982").

3. *Zoning.* Many of the RTF laws provide that zoning and other local ordinances cannot make a protected farm a nuisance. Ala. Code § 6-5-127(c). Alabama's provision does not preempt zoning ordinances. *Ammirata v. Zoning Bd. of Appeals*, 782 A.2d 1285 (Conn. App. 2001). Some laws, however, explicitly preempt the application of zoning ordinances. N.J. Stat. Ann. § 4:1C-9. When zoning ordinances apply, they can limit the protection afforded by the RTF law. See *Wellington Farms, Inc. v. Township of Silver Spring*, 679 A.2d 267 (Pa. Commw. 1996) (poultry slaughterhouse not protected by RTF law). What are the arguments pro and con for preempting zoning ordinances?

4. *The takings issue.* The *Simplon* case referred to the protection provided by the RTF law as a quasi-easement. In *Bormann v. Board of Supervisors*, 584 N.W.2d 309 (Iowa 1998), the court held the statutory immunity from nuisance suits conferred by an RTF law was a taking without compensation. It created an easement over the land of others that allowed protected agricultural uses to carry out activities that would otherwise be a nuisance. The court noted the *Lucas* per se takings rule, and held a nontrespassory invasion could be a per se taking. How is the statutory immunity's effect on property value any different from the effect of a zoning ordinance that restricts the use of land?

Unlike other RTF laws, the Iowa law conferred protection from nuisance suits even if the agricultural activity expanded, and did not require the protected use to follow sound agricultural practices. For a trial court case refusing to apply *Bormann* because the RTF law applied only when a state agency found that an agricultural practice is sound, see *Pure Air & Water, Inc. v. Davidsen*, No. 2690-97 (N.Y. Sup. Ct. May 25, 1999), *appeal dismissed*, 719 N.E.2d 928 (N.Y. 1999). For discussion of *Bormann*, see Centner, *Governments and Unconstitutional Takings: When Do Right-To-Farm Laws Go Too Far?*, 33 B.C. Envtl. Aff. L. Rev. 87 (2006); Pearson, *Immunities as Easements as "Takings": Bormann v. Board of Supervisors*, 48 Drake L. Rev. 53 (1999).

The Indiana Right to Farm Act, which limits nuisance suits against agricultural operations, was upheld against a takings challenge in *Lindsey v. DeGroot*, 898 N.E.2d 1251 (Ind. App. 2009). The owners of property located near a dairy farm claimed that the Act amounted to a taking by awarding the farm an easement over their property. The property owners relied on *Bormann v. Board of Supervisors*, 584 N.W.2d 309 (Iowa 1998), discussed *supra*. The Indiana court, however, followed decisions in Idaho (*Moon v. North Idaho Farmers Ass'n*, 96 P.3d 637 (Idaho 2004)) and Texas (*Barrera v. Hondo Creek Cattle Co.*, 132 S.W.3d 544 (Tex. App. 2004)), rejecting the claim that the right to maintain a nuisance is an easement.

A Maine law authorizes the registry of farmland in local registers, and provides that "No owner of abutting land may undertake or allow any inconsistent development upon or use of land within 100 feet of properly registered farmland." The statute also prohibits the issuance of building permits for development prohibited under this section. Me. Rev. Stat. Ann. tit. 7, § 56. Any taking problems?

In *Gacke v. Pork Xtra, L.L.C.*, 684 N.W.2d 168 (Iowa 2004), the Iowa Supreme Court, citing *Bormann* as controlling, held that a RTF law that purported to provide nuisance immunity to animal feeding operations violated the Iowa constitution "to the extent it deprives property owners of a remedy for the taking of their property resulting from a nuisance created by an animal feeding operation." The court also held that the RTF law violated the Iowa constitution as an unreasonable exercise of the state's police power.

5. *Best management practices*. As noted above, farms can be serious contributors to environmental pollution. Some RTF statutes authorize nuisance actions against agricultural uses that pollute streams or other bodies of water that cross a plaintiff's property. See Ark. Code Ann. § 2-4-106. Another remedy for this problem is to limit the protection of an RTF law to agricultural operations that comply with generally accepted agricultural and managerial practices. Mich. Comp. Laws § 286.473(1) provides that the state Department of Agriculture shall review accepted practices annually. It may also conduct an investigation of a complaint about a farm or farm operation involving "the use of manure and other nutrients, agricultural waste products, dust, noise, odor, fumes, air pollution, surface water or groundwater pollution, food and agricultural processing by-products, care of farm animals and pest infestations." The Department may investigate and require the farm to "resolve or abate" these problems if they exist. *Id.* § 286.474. This type of provision turns an RTF law into a regulatory program. See also Minn. Stat. Ann. § 561.19(1) ("An agricultural operation is not and shall not become a private or public nuisance after two years from its established date of operation as a matter of law if the operation: "(1) is located in an agriculturally zoned area; (2) complies with the provisions of all applicable federal, state, or county laws, regulations, rules, and ordinances and any permits issued for the agricultural operation; and (3) operates according to generally accepted agricultural practices. A farm or farm operation shall not be found to be a public or private

nuisance if the farm or farm operation alleged to be a nuisance conforms to generally accepted agricultural and management practices according to policy determined by the Michigan commission of agriculture."). Is this desirable?

6. *Good or bad?* Whether RTF laws are good or bad social policy is contested. Farmers, of course, claim that these laws are essential to protect them from disruptive nuisance litigation. A student Note, *The Right to Farm: Hog-Tied and Nuisance-Bound*, 73 N.Y.U. L. Rev. 1694 (1998), takes a different view. The author argues that RTF laws assume that those who come to a nuisance are to blame for their troubles. He then argues that protected uses may be operators that do not contribute to the goals of RTF laws, that typical plaintiffs are not new residents in the area, that the number of nuisance suits is exaggerated and that some protected agricultural uses can be environmental polluters. Finally, he notes the shift to larger farms, and claims that larger farm units can remedy nuisance-creating activity, and are able to provide buffers between their offensive land uses and neighbors because their farms are bigger.

How would you draft a right-to-farm law to deal with these criticisms? How would your evaluation of nuisance law, discussed in Chapter 2, affect your recommendations? What about bargaining between neighbors as an alternative, as recommended in the classic Coase article discussed in Chapter 1?

7. *Sources.* For additional discussion of RTF Laws, see Burgess-Jackson, *The Ethics and Economics of Right-to-Farm Statutes*, 9 Harv. J.L. & Pub. Pol'y 481 (1986); Grossman & Fischer, *Protecting the Right to Farm: Statutory Limits on Nuisance Actions Against the Farmer*, 1983 Wis. L. Rev. 95; Hand, *Right-to-Farm Laws: Breaking New Ground in the Preservation of Farmland*, 45 U. Pitt. L. Rev. 289 (1984); Comment, *Michigan's Right to Farm Act: Have Revisions Gone Too Far?*, 2002 L. Rev. M.S.U.-D.C.L. 213; Krasnow, *Farm Wars*, Next American City, Issue 8, April 2005 (http://americancity.org/magazine/article/farm-wars-krasnow/); Onsted, *Farming on the Fringe*, Next American City, Issue 11, Summer 2006 (http://americancity.org/magazine/article/farming-on-the-fringe-onstead/). For an interesting discussion of the issue of state preemption and right to farm laws, see Bussell, *As Montville, Maine Goes, so Goes Wolcott, Vermont? A Primer on the Local Regulation of Genetically Modified Crops*, 43 Suffolk U. L. Rev. 727 (2010) (http://www.law.suffolk.edu/highlights/stuorgs/lawreview/documents/Bussell_Formatted.pdf).

A NOTE ON THE INDUSTRIALIZATION AND ENVIRONMENTAL IMPACTS OF AGRICULTURE

The other side of agriculture. Agriculture is often not an entirely benign use of land. Ruhl, *Farms, Their Environmental Harms, and Environmental Law*, 27 Ecology L.Q. 263 (2000), identifies environmental harms caused by agriculture: habitat loss and degradation, soil erosion and sedimentation, water resources depletion, soil and water salinization, agrochemical releases, animal waste, nonpoint source water pollution through runoff from fields and livestock operations, and chemical air pollution. He then points to a number of "safe harbors" for agriculture in federal environmental laws, such as the agricultural exemptions in the Clean Water Act. There are some exceptions, such as the regulation of Concentrated Animal Feeding Operations, or CAFOs, under the Clean Water Act. Among other recommendations, he suggests that "if a sector-based approach is used to identify farming operations that exhibit high-impact polluting effects, such as CAFOs and large-scale crop operations, conventional prescriptive regulation can yield significant environmental benefits at manageable administrative cost levels." *Id.* at 337. Agricultural pollution problems may arise under right-to-farm laws which protect agricultural activity from nuisance suits, and which may require farms to engage in good agricultural practices as a condition to protection.

Proliferation of CAFOs? According to a study by the Institute of Science, Technology and Public Policy, although Iowa produces roughly the same amount of pork it did a century ago, the number of hog farmers in the state has declined 83% — from 59,134 farms in 1978 to 10,205 farms in 2002. The reason? Most of the 17 million Iowa hogs today are raised in CAFOs, where thousands of hogs are contained before being shipped to the meatpacking plant. For a full copy of the Institute's Report, see istpp.org/pdf/istpp_cafo.pdf. For general information about CAFOs, visit the Environmental Protection Agency's website at cfpub.epa.gov/npdes/afo/info.cfm.

Anticipatory Nuisance Claims. The Supreme Court of Iowa, in *Simpson v. Kollasch*, 749 N.W.2d 671 (Iowa 2008), held that the neighbors of two proposed hog confinement facilities (CAFOs) failed to meet their burden of proof for a cause of action in anticipated nuisance. On the issue of anticipatory nuisance, the court stated, "an anticipated nuisance will not be enjoined unless it clearly appears a nuisance will necessarily result from the act . . . it is sought to enjoin. Relief will usually be denied until a nuisance has been committed where the thing sought to be enjoined may or may not become such, depending on its use or other circumstances." The court stated that the standard is "clear and convincing evidence." Applying this standard, the court held that with careful and diligent operation, the CAFO facility need not be a nuisance. The district court had allowed the applicant for the CAFO to present evidence of compliance with DNR standards and regulations. Although compliance with the standards and regulations is not a defense to a nuisance claim, the court held that the evidence was relevant to show that a nuisance would not necessarily result from the operation.

Preemption of Local CAFO Restrictions. In *Richland Township. v. Kenoma, LLC*, 284 S.W.3d 672 (Mo. App. S.D., 2009), the owner of approximately 30 acres began construction of a 2,400-head hog operation at about the same time that the township adopted a zoning ordinance. The Township's new zoning code prohibited concentrated livestock operations with more than 800 animals and imposed setbacks and screening requirements on smaller operations. The Township unsuccessfully sought an injunction and the appeals court affirmed, based on state statute in Missouri that prohibits townships from zoning "so as to impose regulations or to require permits with respect to land used or to be used for the raising of crops . . . or with respect to the erection, maintenance . . . of farm buildings or farm structures." The court invalidated that portion of the zoning code that regulates farm structures that would be used for concentrated livestock operations. See also *Board of Supervisors of Crooks Township v. Valadco*, 504 N.W.2d 267 (Minn. App. 1993) (striking down a township ordinance regulating feedlots because it was preempted by comprehensive state laws that regulated activities that could contaminate ground water or the environment).

An example of a state law restricting local regulation of livestock facilities is Wisconsin's Livestock Facility Siting Law. This statute establishes procedures that local governments must follow if they decide to issue conditional use or other local permits for siting livestock facilities. The statute limits the exclusion of livestock facilities from agricultural zoning districts. It also created a livestock facility siting review board to hear appeals concerning local permit decisions. The law requires local governments to determine whether a proposed facility meets certain criteria set forth in the statute, such as:

- Property line and road setbacks

- Management and training plans
- Odor management
- Nutrient management
- Manure storage facilities
- Runoff management

Wis. Stat. § 93.90. For a more detailed description of Wisconsin's law, see datcp.state.wi.us/arm/agriculture/land-water/livestock_siting/siting.jsp.

California voters took matters in their own hands with Proposition 2, approved in 2008. Proposition 2 provides as follows: "Shall certain farm animals be allowed, for the majority of every day, to fully extend their limbs or wings, lie down, stand up and turn around?" According to the California Attorney General, beginning January 1, 2015, this measure would prohibit, with certain exceptions, the confinement on a farm of pregnant pigs, calves raised for veal, and egg-laying hens in a manner that does not allow them to turn around freely, lie down, stand up, and fully extend their limbs. Violators of the law would be guilty of a misdemeanor, punishable by a fine of up to $1,000 and/or imprisonment in county jail for up to six months. The measure passed with 63.4% of the voters in favor. See www.smartvoter.org/2008/11/04/ca/state/prop/2/. In Ohio, the state entered into an agreement with major agricultural organizations to address various livestock and other animal issues. The agricultural organizations agreed to these restrictions in exchange for the Human Society's agreement not to pursue a ballot initiative similar to Proposition 2 in California. For more information about the Ohio agreement, see www.governor.ohio.gov/Default.aspx?tabid=1719.

Sources. J. Aiken, *The Nebraska Hog Wars*, 10 No. 1 ABA Agric. Mgmt. Comm. Newsl. 21 (2005); J. Becker, *Promoting Agricultural Development Through Land Use Planning Limits*, 36 Real Prop. & Tr. J. 619 (2002) (interesting discussion of the emergence of industrialized agriculture); Zande, *Note, Raising A Stink: Why Michigan CAFO Regulations Fail To Protect The State's Air And Great Lakes And Are In Need Of Revision*, 16 Buff. Envtl. L.J. 1 (2008-2009).

B. ENVIRONMENTAL LAND USE REGULATION

The environmental movement has produced new land use programs intended to preserve natural resource areas that are separate from local planning and land use regulation. The appearance of these new regulatory programs is not surprising. Though zoning can address environmental concerns, it has usually accepted the inevitability of converting land to development and has only tried to manage the process.

Environmental land use regulation has a number of distinguishing features. One is an important federal and state presence. Federal legislation often encourages and may even mandate environmental land use regulation, as may state legislation. Environmental land use regulation also differs from traditional land use controls because it is resource-driven and protects defined natural resource areas that are vulnerable to development. These programs usually require the issuance of permits for development that satisfies permit standards. They do not use the districting technique typical of zoning, and they usually do not require a comprehensive plan.

There is also an erratic distribution of governmental responsibility. Environmental land use regulation programs do not provide a coordinated response to the problems of resource protection, but were enacted piecemeal as environmental land use issues attracted public attention. Because their objective is preservation, they also place substantial limits on new development rather than allowing it to occur when it complies with regulatory requirements.

This section will introduce you to some of the important environmental land use programs. Its purpose is to outline how they work and to highlight the differences between these and traditional land use programs. For an interesting view of these issues, see Spyke, *The Land Use-Environmental Law Distinction: A Geo-Feminist Critique*, 13 Duke Envtl. L. & Pol'y F. 55 (2002).

NOTES AND QUESTIONS

1. *Environmental elements in comprehensive plans.* A number of state land use planning statutes require planning elements, either mandatory or discretionary, that must address environmental concerns. Statutes requiring the consideration of natural resources are most common. The California statute, for example, requires the following mandatory element:

> A conservation element for the conservation, development, and utilization of natural resources including water and its hydraulic force, forests, soils, rivers and other waters, harbors, fisheries, wildlife, minerals, and other natural resources. The conservation element shall consider the effect of development within the jurisdiction, as described in the land use element, on natural resources located on public lands, including military installations. [Cal. Gov't Code § 65302(d).]

The statute also authorizes the conservation element to include other measures, such as the regulation of land use in stream channels; the prevention, control, and correction of the erosion of soils, beaches, and shores; the protection of watersheds and flood control. Like several other states, California also requires an open space plan, *id.* §§ 65560-65568, including an action plan. See also Fla. Stat. Ann. § 163.3177(6)(d) (conservation element). California and Florida require land use controls to be consistent with the comprehensive plan. For discussion of state planning statutes with environmental elements, see Breggin & George, *Planning for Biodiversity: Sources of Authority in State Land Use Laws*, 22 Va. Envtl. L.J. 81 (2003).

The APA model legislation contains an extensive Critical and Sensitive Areas Element for comprehensive plans. American Planning Association, Growing Smart Legislative Guidebook: Model Statutes for Planning and Management of Change § 7-209 (S. Meck ed. 2002). The purposes of this element include establishing "thresholds at which the identified areas begin to decline in value as a resource," and identifying "mitigating measures that may need to be taken in such areas to offset or accommodate the impacts of development."

2. *Carrying capacity analysis.* This planning technique is a method for evaluating the capacity of environmental resources to accept new development, and is an analytic technique often used in planning and regulating environmental areas. The American Planning Association Guidebook recommends using carrying capacity analysis in environmental planning:

> [Carrying capacity] analysis is an assessment of the ability of a natural system to absorb population growth as well as other physical development without significant degradation. Understanding the carrying capacity or constraints of natural resources (particularly ground and surface water systems) provides local governments with an

> effective method for identifying which portions of the community or region are most suitable sites for new and expanded development. Similarly, knowledge of carrying capacity limitations allows local government residents and officials to make more rational and defensible decisions regarding how and where development may occur. [*Id.* at 7-136.]

The Guidebook gives the following example: "[D]etermining the carrying capacity of a water surface water body with respect to nitrogen or phosphorus loading requires a thorough understanding of the dynamics of the water body, the sources of nitrogen or phosphorus in the watershed, and the level at which nitrogen or phosphorus is assimilated by the water resource." *Id.* at 7-136. The carrying capacity determination can then be translated into limitations on residential density. The Guidebook notes that "by providing a factual basis for specialized land development regulations that may need to be enacted to protect the critical and sensitive areas against harm or degradation, this plan element may avert or minimize a taking claim when development must be severely restricted." *Id.* at 7-137.

Some object to a planning approach that relies on physical determinants. D. Schneider, D. Godschalk & N. Axler, *The Carrying Capacity Concept as a Planning Tool*, 9 American Planning Ass'n, Planning Advisory Serv. Rep. No. 338 (1978) ("The danger lies in not recognizing the tenuousness of carrying capacity conclusions and mistaking them for finite limits or thresholds rather than estimates or ranges."). See also Witten, *Carrying Capacity and the Comprehensive Plan: Establishing and Defending Limits to Growth*, 28 B.C. Envtl. Aff. L. Rev. 583 (2001).

3. *Intergovernmental roles.* Problems with regulatory programs at the state and local level, fragmented jurisdictions, and uneven regulation led initially to a strategy that placed primary responsibility for environmental regulation with the federal government. States and local governments implement federal laws under federal standards, though some federal programs, such as the coastal zone management program, give states more discretion in implementing federal requirements. But see *Symposium of the Advent of Local Environmental Law*, 20 Pace Envtl. L. Rev. 1 (2002) (discussing local programs). The programs discussed in this section vary considerably in the roles assigned to each governmental level. States have become increasingly active in growth management programs, discussed in Chapter 8.

4. *Disaster mitigation planning.* The Disaster Mitigation Act of 2000 is an example of a coordinated federal, state and local program for disaster mitigation planning, which has received increased attention since Hurricane Katrina. The Act requires state, tribal and local governments to submit, as a condition of an increased share of federal hazard mitigation assistance, a "mitigation plan that outlines processes for identifying the natural hazards, risks, and vulnerabilities of the area under the jurisdiction of the government." 42 U.S.C. § 5165(a). Local and tribal plans shall "(1) describe actions to mitigate hazards, risks, and vulnerabilities identified under the plan; and (2) establish a strategy to implement those actions." *Id.* § 5165(b). The Boulder Valley [Colorado] Comprehensive Plan is an example of a plan containing a disaster mitigation element. The plan delineates hazardous areas and contains policies for the control or mitigation of development in those areas. It is available at bouldercolorado.gov. For discussion of the Boulder plan and the federal statute, see Nolon, *Disaster Mitigation Through Land Use Strategies, in* Losing Ground: A Nation on Edge Ch. 1 (J. Nolon & D. Rodriguez eds., 2007), and Salkin, *Sustainability at the Edge, The Opportunity and Responsibility of Local Governments to Most Effectively Plan for Disaster Mitigation, in id.*, Ch. 4. Dean Salkin discusses a number of measures that can be used for disaster mitigation, including overlay

zones, hillside protection regulations and critical environmental areas that are discussed later in this section.

[1.] Wetlands

Wetlands, usually found at the intersection of land and bodies of water but sometimes isolated, have important ecological functions. Wetlands can be either coastal or inland. They include salt and freshwater marshes, swamps, wet meadows, bogs, fens and potholes. They are typified by poorly-drained soils, periodic inundation of water, and the capability of supporting plants which grown mainly in wetland areas. Many wetlands, both coastal and inland, are in attractive locations, which makes them ideal for residential and recreational development. Coastal wetlands also are coincident with development that is water-dependent, such as port and industrial uses.

Wetlands have critical environmental functions. They can reduce floodpeaks by storing and conveying stormwater, they are important in groundwater recharge, and they are essential to fish and wildlife that are wetland-dependent. Wetlands also improve the quality of water that flows over and through them by temporarily retaining pollutants, such as toxic chemicals, and disease-causing micro-organisms. Their ecological importance and sensitivey were highlighted once more as a result of the 2010 BP oil spill in the Gulf of Mexico.

The loss of wetlands through land development has been dramatic. Development in wetlands usually requires a process known as "dredging and filling." Wetlands are dredged to provide artificial waterways, and soil removed in the dredging process or brought in from elsewhere is used to build up the wetlands so they can be developed. Regulatory programs in wetland areas attempt to control this process by prohibiting or limiting dredge and fill activities.

Many states have wetlands statutes. Most of these simply rely on the water quality standards of the Clean Water Act to protect wetlands and federal statutory authority to enforce them. Others, however, have permit programs, require local wetland protection measures, or have non-regulatory programs such as educational programs. Some of the state regulatory statutes are modeled on the federal program, but some go beyond it by regulating more than dredge and fill activities and by including a protective buffer strip around wetlands areas. See *In re Freshwater Wetlands Protection Act Rules*, 852 A.2d 1083 (N.J. 2004). A typical state law creates a state agency to administer the program or confers administrative authority on an existing agency, such as an environmental agency. It defines covered wetlands or authorizes the state agency to designate them. It then provides that no person shall carry out any designated activities in wetlands, such as dredging and filling or development that may impair the wetlands, without obtaining a state permit. Activities that are not harmful to wetlands may be permitted, such as recreation, grazing, and farming. Administrative and judicial appeals and enforcement authority are authorized. A study by the Environmental Law Institute has profiled the state programs in detail in a series of reports available at www.eli.org.

State statutes may also authorize the adoption of "land use regulations" in wetland areas specifying permitted uses. See N.Y. Envtl. Conserv. Law § 25-0302(1). The statute provides that "[i]n preparing such regulations the commissioner shall be guided by factors including, but not limited to, the public policy set forth in this act as well as the present and potential value of the particular wetland for marine food production, as a wildlife habitat, as an element of flood and storm control, and as a source of recreation, education and research." An alternate but similar regulatory technique authorizes the state agency to adopt orders "regulating, restricting or prohibiting dredging, filling, removing or otherwise altering, or polluting" coastal wetlands. N.J. Stat. Ann. § 13:9A-2.

State statutory standards for permits differ from federal standards. Several statutes contain general standards authorizing consideration of the "public interest" or the "policy" of the wetlands law. Other statutes contain more specific "factors" for consideration in permit review, such as the environmental impact of the proposed development and its suitability for the area in which it is proposed. These statutes vary, but the North Carolina statute is a typical example:

> The Department may deny an application for a dredge or fill permit upon finding: (1) that there will be significant adverse effect of the proposed dredging and filling on the use of the water by the public; or (2) that there will be significant adverse effect on the value and enjoyment of the property of any riparian owners; or (3) that there will be significant adverse effect on public health, safety, and welfare; or (4) that there will be significant adverse effect on the conservation of public and private water supplies; or (5) that there will be significant adverse effect on wildlife or fresh water, estuarine or marine fisheries. [N.C. Gen. Stat. § 113-229(e).]

Some state wetlands laws also require compliance with local regulations, and a number require local governments to adopt wetlands regulations consistent with the state statute and subject to the approval of the state agency. The state agency may be authorized to adopt regulations for the local government if it fails to enact them. See N.Y. Envtl. Conserv. Law § 24-0903 (also authorizes more restrictive local regulation). If the state law is silent on local regulation, a local government may adopt one if the regulatory system adopted at the state level is not preemptive. A local ordinance can provide local policies for wetlands protection, and can fill gaps in the state law if the state law is limited to large wetlands areas and to a limited number of activities. Some state legislation in the Midwest requires local regulation of shoreland areas, which include wetlands, and also requires local adoption of regulatory programs subject to state approval. *Cherry v. Town of Hampton Falls*, 846 A.2d 508 (N.H. 2004), upheld a denial of a permit for a subdivision road under a local wetlands ordinance even though a state permit had been obtained because there had been no consideration of whether an alternative route was feasible, as required by the ordinance.

NOTES AND QUESTIONS

1. *The Federal Wetlands Protection Program of the Clean Water Act.* Section 404 of the Clean Water Act, 33 U.S.C. § 1344, presents complicated jurisdictional issues that affect the coverage of the statute. Wetlands adjacent to bodies of water are clearly covered, but isolated wetlands are more problematic. The Court addressed the jurisdiction issue in *Rapanos v. United States*, 547 U.S. 715 (2006), *noted*, 32 Colum J. Envtl. L. 141 (2007). The case involved wetlands filling near ditches that eventually emptied into navigable waters, and a divided Court (4-1-4) held they did not fall within the jurisdiction of the act. The plurality opinion would assert jurisdiction over a water body not a traditional navigable water if it is relatively permanent because it flows year-round or at least seasonally, and over wetlands adjacent to such water bodies if they "directly abut" the water body. Justice Kennedy's concurring opinion would assert jurisdiction on a case-by-case basis only over waters that have a "significant nexus" with waters that are or were navigable in fact or that could reasonably be made so.

Two years after the Supreme Court's murky *Rapanos* opinion interpreting the Clean Water Act, the U.S. Environmental Protection Agency ("EPA") and the Army Corps of Engineers ("Corps") issued guidance on protecting waters under the Clean Water Act. The agencies will assert jurisdiction over waters that the courts determine to be navigable-in-fact, waters that are currently used or have historically been used for commercial navigation, or waters that could realistically be used for commercial navigation in the future. The guidance also states that a protected, adjacent wetland must have an unbroken hydrologic connection to jurisdictional waters, a beam or similar barrier must separate the waters from the wetland, or the wetland must be reasonably close to a jurisdictional water. See *Clean Water Act Jurisdiction Following the U.S. Supreme Court's Decision in Rapanos v. United States & Carabell v. United States* (epa.gov/owow/wetlands/pdf/CWA_Jurisdiction_Following_Rapanos120208.pdf). See also Klein et al., *Where's Waldo? Finding Federal Wetlands After the Rapanos Decision*, 29 Zoning and Plan L. Rep. 1 (2006).

2. *Decisional Hierarchy*. The hierarchy of the Army Corps of Engineers's goals in the area of wetland regulations can be summarized in the following priority order: (1) avoidance of wetlands; (2) minimization of impact to wetlands; and (3) then, and only then, mitigation of wetlands, discussed in the following note.

3. *Mitigation*. Mitigation of wetlands loss caused by development can be achieved through the creation, restoration, enhancement or preservation of wetlands. This program is controversial because the viability of restoration or creation measures is doubtful. A report by the National Research Council found that the record on mitigation is mixed. Compensating for Wetland Losses Under the Clean Water Act (2001). The ratio of wetland replacement to wetland loss was 1.8 to 1.0, but it was not clear that all of the wetlands required as mitigation had actually been provided. On March 31, 2008, the EPA and the U.S. Army Corps of Engineers issued revised regulations governing compensatory mitigation for authorized impacts to wetlands, streams, and other waters of the U.S. under Section 404 of the Clean Water Act. Information about the final rule can be found at http://water.epa.gov/lawsregs/guidance/wetlands/wetlandsmitigation_index.cfm. Commentators suggest, however, that the cost of mitigation usually makes it more cost-effective to mitigate wetlands impacts by avoiding or minimizing the impacts of wetlands development. P. Cylinder et al., Wetlands, Streams, and Other Waters 146 (2004).

Mitigation banks are another option. They are created by developers, either singly or jointly, to create or restore wetlands and "bank" them for future projects. For discussion of mitigation, see M. Dennison, Wetland Mitigation: Mitigation Banking and Other Strategies for Development and Compliance (2007); Mitigation Banking: Theory and Practice (J. DeGrove et al. eds., 1996); Comment, *Paving the Road to Wetlands Mitigation Banking*, 27 B.C. Envtl. Aff. L. Rev. 161 (1999); Comment, *Federal Conservation of Wetlands Runs Amuck with Wetland Mitigation Banking*, 31 Ohio N.U. L. Rev. 177 (2005); J. Wilkinson, In-Lieu Fee Mitigation: Model Instrument Language and Resources (Wetlands Ecol. Mgmt. 2009); J. Wilkinson, et. al., The Status and Character of In-Lieu Fee Mitigation in the United States (Envtl. L. Inst. 2006); R. Bendick & B. McKenney, The Nature Conservancy, *The Next Generation of Mitigation: Linking Current and Future Mitigation Programs with State Wildlife Action Plans and Other State and Regional Plans* (2009).

4. *The takings issue*. The taking problem could be troublesome since the Supreme Court's *Lucas* decision, reproduced *supra* in Chapter 2, which held a *per se* taking occurs when a landowner is denied all economically viable use of her land. Most courts, however, have avoided

this result. *Cooley v. United States*, 324 F.3d 1297 (Fed. Cir. 2003) (no taking under *Lucas* though 98.8% reduction in value). When a wetlands is only part of a site on which development is proposed, the whole parcel rule from *Penn Central* may avoid a takings claim if a reasonably productive use is possible on the upland portion. See *Giovanella v. Conservation Comm'n of Ashland*, 857 N.E.2d 451 (Mass. 2006) (discussing cases). A takings claim under the "default" *Penn Central* test may also fail. See *Cherry v. Town of Hampton Falls*, 846 A.2d 508 (N.H. 2004) (rejecting a takings claim against a local wetlands ordinance and finding that none of the *Penn Central* factors supported the landowner). See also *Gove v. Zoning Bd. of Appeals*, 831 N.E.2d 865 (Mass. 2005) (property had value of $23,000 for open space and rejecting *Penn Central* claim though 88% reduction in value).

5. *Sources.* W. Want, Law of Wetlands Regulation; David Salvesen, Wetlands: Mitigating and Regulating Development Impacts (2d ed. 1994). Wetlands Law and Policy: Understanding Section 404 (K. Connelly, S. Johnson & D. Williams eds., ABA 2005), is an excellent collection of chapters including discussion of the alternatives and mitigation requirements. The site of the American Society of Wetlands Managers at www.aswm.org is an excellent source of material on wetlands regulation. See also *Land Use and Wetlands: A Local Decision Makers' Guide to Wetland Conservation* (wisconsinwetlands.org/LocalDecisionMakersGuide_screen.pdf); USDA/NRCS Wetland Conservation Provisions (nrcs.usda.gov/programs/compliance/wcindex.html). The site of the Environmental Law Institute's Wetlands Program at http://www.eli.org/program_areas/wetlands.cfm is also a comprehensive site for wetlands publications.

[2.] Floodplain Regulation

Between seven and ten percent of our land is floodplain. About 90 percent of all losses from natural disasters are caused by floods, and economic losses from floods are astronomic, reaching $6 billion annually in recent years. These facts provide strong support for programs that can prevent flood losses. Though flood loss can be prevented through dams, reservoirs, river channeling, and similar structural measures, land use regulation in floodplains is an important alternate loss avoidance technique. This is called the nonstructural approach to flood damage prevention and minimization.

Source: American Soc'y of Planning Officials, Regulations for Flood Plains, Fig. 17, p. 45 (Planning Advisory Service Rep. No. 277 (1972).

Floodplain is defined by FEMA as "any land susceptible to being inundated by flood waters from any source." Areas covered by floodplain regulation include the floodway and the floodway fringe. The floodway is defined as an area subject to a 100-year flood, which means the statistical chance that a flood will occur is one percent in any one year. All structural development in the floodplain channel is usually prohibited. Structural uses are allowed in the floodway fringe subject to requirements that will avoid flood losses, such as requirements that structures be elevated or floodproofed. The figure illustrates a typical floodplain and the land use regulations usually applied.

FLOODPLAIN DISTRICT REGULATION

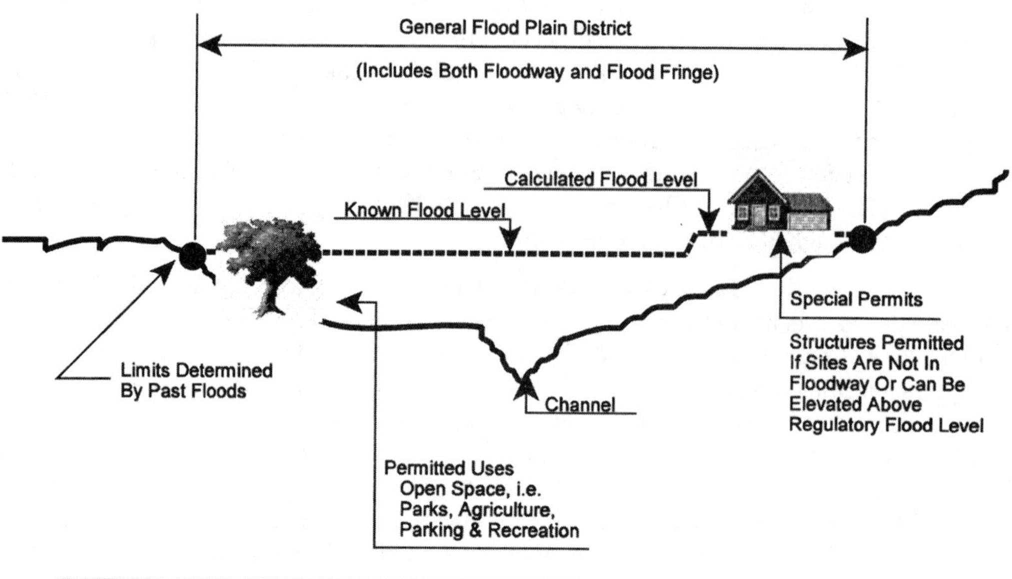

Adapted from: American Soc'y of Planning Officials, Regulations for Flood Plains, Fig. 17, p.45 (Planning Advisory Service Rep. No. 277 (1972).

A "Regulatory Floodway" means the channel of a river or other watercourse and the adjacent land areas that must be reserved in order to discharge the base flood without cumulatively increasing the water surface elevation more than a designated height. Communities must regulate development in these floodways to ensure that there are no increases in upstream flood elevations. For streams and other watercourses where FEMA has provided Base Flood Elevations (BFEs), but no floodway has been designated, the community must review floodplain development on a case-by-case basis to ensure that increases in water surface elevations do not occur, or identify the need to adopt a floodway if adequate information is available.

THE FEDERAL ROLE AND THE FEDERAL FLOOD INSURANCE PROGRAM

The federal role in flood management is substantial and includes participation by many federal agencies. Dam and levee construction by the Corps of Engineers to contain flooding and prevent flood damage is an important part of federal efforts. They are uncoordinated, however, and the massive midwest flood of 1993 called into question the federal strategy of flood containment. The report of a federal committee established after the flood recommends an improved federal flood management strategy that includes measures for reducing flood loss by avoiding inappropriate uses of floodplains. Sharing the Challenge: Floodplain Management Into the 21st Century, Report of the Interagency Floodplain Management Review Committee (1994).

The Flood Insurance Program. Congress enacted a national Flood Insurance Program (NFIP) in 1968 to make flood insurance more affordable and increase the number of insured structures. Insurance can be issued by the Federal Emergency Management Agency (FEMA), which administers the program, or from private "Write Your Own" insurers. Participation in the program was originally voluntary, but in 1973 Congress amended the program to include a "Mandatory Purchase Requirement" which makes flood insurance mandatory on loans from private financial institutions regulated or insured by the federal government and for the receipt of direct federal financial assistance. 42 U.S.C. § 4012a.

A federally-sponsored report states that about 50% of single family homes in mapped floodplain areas have flood insurance. Final Report, Evaluation of the National Flood Insurance Program 25 (2006). Amendments to the program in 1994 strengthened the requirements for participation. See Bernstein, Myers & Steen, *Flood Insurance "Reform" Act Engulfs Mortgage Lenders*, 48 Consumer Fin. L.Q. Rep. 304 (1994). The NFIP is not directly subsidized, but homes existing before the program receive a premium subsidy that is made up by charging new homeowners coming into the program, a concession that has increasingly been questioned. Participation by private insurers also remains low despite incentives to participate, including significant commission payments.

Low participation rates have put the program substantially in debt. Budgeting issues, repetitive claims, and the rebuilding of properties in floodplains despite a federal rule prohibiting rebuilding when a property incurs a 50% loss, are other major problems. See General Accounting Office, Challenges Facing the Federal Flood Insurance Program (2003). See also Scales, *A Nation of Policyholders: Governmental and Market Failure in Flood Insurance*, 26 Miss. C. L. Rev. 3 (2006/2007). The courts have rejected takings claims against the program. See *Adolph v. Federal Emergency Mgt. Agency*, 854 F.2d 732 (5th Cir. 1988).

The NFIP requires communities to adopt flood hazard regulations to make the community eligible for federal flood insurance and enable homeowners to buy insurance. As administrator of the federal program, FEMA is to adopt "comprehensive criteria" for the adoption of adequate state and local measures which, to the maximum extent feasible, will:

(1) constrict the development of land which is exposed to flood damage where appropriate,

(2) guide the development of proposed construction away from locations which are threatened by flood hazards,

(3) assist in reducing damage by floods, and

(4) otherwise improve the long-range land management and use of flood-prone areas. . . . [42 U.S.C. § 4102(c).]

The following report explains how the National Flood Insurance (NFIP) program works:

Missouri Coalition for the Environment, The State of Missouri's Floodplain Management Ten Years After the 1993 Flood 9-11 (2003)

NFIP — Federal Role

The primary role of the federal government in the NFIP is to make flood insurance available to participating communities. FEMA issues the general rules for implementing the NFIP, including those governing community eligibility, available policies, property eligibility, insurance application procedures and rate determinations.

FEMA also has the responsibility of identifying flood hazard areas throughout the country. This responsibility includes publication of flood hazard boundary maps (FHBM) and flood insurance rate maps (FIRM). The maps form the basis of the risk zones that are used to determine insurance rates and show the boundaries of special flood hazard areas (SFHA). The FHBM and FIRM delineate the hazard zones that must be regulated by communities in order to participate in the NFIP. . . .

The FIRM usually shows the base flood elevations (BFE). The BFE is the elevation of the water during a flood that has a one-percent chance of being exceeded in any year, commonly referred to as the "100-year flood." . . .

Development is precluded inside the floodway if it would cause any increase in flood heights. Developments outside the floodway, but inside the flood hazard areas, must obtain a permit from the local authority and be protected from the base flood.

NFIP — State Role

Each state designates an agency to act as liaison between FEMA and local governments and to coordinate the NFIP within the state. The state coordinating agency assists communities in developing and adopting the specific floodplain management measures required for NFIP participation. In most states, the department of natural resources (DNR) is responsible for floodplain management and coordination of NFIP activities. . . . [Some states also have floodplain legislation. — Eds.]

NFIP — Local Role

Cities and counties have primary responsibility for implementing the NFIP. Participating communities must adopt and enforce floodplain management ordinances that regulate new construction and substantial improvement of existing structures in flood hazard areas. Under the NFIP, the regulatory floodway is defined as the area required to convey floodwaters with no more than a one-foot rise in the base flood [elevation]. The flood fringe is the area outside the floodway that is inundated during the 100-year flood. . . . [The boundaries of the floodway are determined by computer simulation that "squeezes" the BFE until a one-foot rise occurs. — Eds.]

Local ordinances must prohibit any development in the floodway that would increase flood heights above the one-foot rise contemplated when defining the floodway. The ordinance must also require that all new construction or substantial improvements construct the lowest floor above the base flood level. Participating communities must regulate and keep records of all development in the 100-year floodplain. It is the responsibility of local communities to issue floodplain development permits and elevation certificates for properties in designated flood hazard areas. FEMA requires each community that participates in the NFIP to complete a biennial report of floodplain development permits and enforcement actions. The report must be submitted to FEMA and the state coordinating agency. [A copy of the report can be found at http://www.moenviron.org/pdf/FloodingForgotten.pdf]

NOTES AND QUESTIONS

1. *Has the federal program been effective?* Almost all eligible communities participate in the program, and the amount of insurance has doubled in recent years. Whether the insurance program has helped to prevent flood loss is another question. A study by FEMA claimed that buildings built to NFIP minimum standards sustained 71% less loss than buildings not built to these standards. Sarmiento & Miller, *Costs and Consequences of Flooding and the Impact of the National Flood Insurance Program* 36 (2006) (http://www.fema.gov/library/viewRecord.do?id=2577&fromSearch=fromsearch). Some critics claim, however, that the availability of insurance in floodplain areas has encouraged development by providing an assurance that losses will be paid if flooding occurs. Repetitive payments for the loss of the same building are common. Two percent of the policies held under the program have accounted for 32% of the losses and 38% of the payments. Neither have federal regulations served as a barrier to development in floodprone areas, since development is allowed when structure elevation or other protective measures can avoid or mitigate flood damage. Existing development in areas where it is prohibited under the regulations has also been a problem. For a summary of FEMA regulatory and design standards for floodplain regulation, see http://www.fema.gov/plan/prevent/fhm/gs_main.shtm.

The Final Report on the National Flood Plain Insurance Program, *supra*, contains extensive recommendations for program reform. On the floodplain development issue, the report notes that "Traditional mapping allows a large floodplain fringe to be developed because the floodway delineation is based on the area needed to discharge the base flood without cumulatively increasing the water surface elevation more than one foot. This results in a relatively narrow floodway in which most development is excluded." *Id.* at 14. There are no other provisions for keeping floodplains clear, even in environmentally sensitive areas. Neither are there provisions limiting the siting of public facilities in floodplains. The report concludes that the program should do more to guide development away from floodplain areas worthy of protection. *Id.* at 16. See also a report by the Association of State Floodplain Managers, National Flood Programs and Policies in Review — 2007, which argues for strong state programs. Legislation to reform the FIP has been introduced in Congress but has not yet passed.

In addition, in November of 2010, FEMA sent notice soliciting comments on its proposed "NFIP Reform Effort." The effort is comprised of three phases. See 75 Fed. Reg. 69096. Addition information can be found at http://www.fema.gov/business/nfip/nfip_reform.shtm.

2. *State legislation.* Half the states have state-level floodplain laws. Minimal state laws may only require local adoption of federal NFIP standards, though some may give permitting authority to the state over certain designated floodways. E.g., Ill. Comp. Stat. Ann. 615 § 5/18g. Other statutes set state floodplain standards but leave implementation to local governments. See Minn. Stat. Ann. § 103A.207, which authorizes the state agency to impose the state standards on local governments if they do not adopt them. The state agency may also be authorized to set and implement the state standards. The New Jersey legislation is typical. It authorizes the state agency

> to adopt . . . rules and regulations and to issue orders concerning the development and use of land in any delineated floodway which shall be designed to preserve its flood carrying capacity and to minimize the threat to the public safety, health and general welfare. [N.J. Stat. Ann. § 58:16A-55(a).]

State floodplain legislation may authorize more extensive controls over existing uses and new development than the federal statute. Some also authorize the review of new subdivisions. State legislation can also be more stringent than the federal requirements by allowing a smaller increase in the Base Flood Elevation, which is one foot under the federal regulations. For a discussion of local options, see Schwab, *Zoning for Flood Hazards*, Zoning News, Oct. 1997, at 1. Clustering, which locates development on uplands and out of floodplain areas, is one option when land includes both floodplain and upland areas. For discussion, see Note, *How*

Quickly We Forget: The National Flood Insurance Program and Floodplain Development in Missouri, 19 Wash. U. J.L. & Pol'y 365 (2005); J. Schwab, *Hazard Mitigation: Intergrating Best Practices into Planning*, American Planning Ass'n, Planning Advisory Serv. Rep. No. 560 (2010) (http://wyohomelandsecurity.state.wy.us/pubs/haz_mit_png_best_practices.pdf).

In 2010, Illinois enacted legislation that defined the term "100-year flood plain" in several state statutes and added certain safeguards against flooding for critical facilities. 415 ILCS 5/3.102 and 103. The law, amending various provisions of the Illinois Environmental Protection Act, was designed to fix what was a practical problem with a previously issued executive order by then-Governor Blagojevich that "critical facilities" could not be built in a 100-year floodplain, including roads, bridges, police stations and a wide range of other public and private facilities and programs.

3. *The "no adverse impact" proposal.* Concern over the limitations of the federal program has led to a "no adverse impact" proposal by the Association of State Floodplain Managers (ASFM). They believe flood fringe areas are rapidly being filled in many areas of the country, but that there is no requirement to consider the impact this increase in water surface will have on flooding problems. New development in the floodplains creates more stormwater runoff and is displacing land area that rivers naturally use to store storm waters. Larson & Plamencia, *No Adverse Impact: A New Direction in Floodplain Management Policy*, Natural Hazards Rev., Nov. 2001, at 167.

The ASFM defines the "no adverse impact" approach as follows:

> "No Adverse Impact Floodplain Management" is a managing principle that is easy to communicate and from a policy perspective tough to challenge. In essence, No Adverse Impact floodplain management is where the action of one property owner does not adversely impact the rights of other property owners, as measured by increased flood peaks, flood stage, flood velocity, and erosion and sedimentation. No Adverse Impact floodplains could become the default management criteria, unless a community has developed and adopted a comprehensive plan to manage development that identifies acceptable levels of impact, appropriate measures to mitigate those adverse impacts and a plan for implementation. No Adverse Impact could be extended to entire watersheds as a means to promote the use of retention/detention or other techniques to mitigate increased runoff from urban areas. [Available at floods.org/NoAdverseImpact/whitepaper.asp.]

Does this proposal remedy the problems created by the narrow geographic scope of floodplain controls?

4. *Floodplain Executive Order.* President Carter issued a Floodplain Management Order, Exec. Order No. 11,988, 13 Weekly Comp. Pres. Doc. 803 (May 24, 1977), which is similar to the Executive Order for wetlands. The order requires federal agencies to "provide leadership and . . . take actions to reduce the risk of flood losses, to minimize the impact of floods on human safety, health and welfare, and to restore and preserve the natural and beneficial values served by floodplains." Federal agencies proposing actions in floodplains must consider "alternatives to avoid adverse effects and incompatible development in the floodplains." Federal structures and facilities constructed in floodplains must also be consistent with criteria imposed by the flood insurance program.

5. *Takings and other issues.* A number of cases upheld floodplain regulations against takings attacks prior to the Supreme Court's *Lucas* decision, whose *per se* takings rule could conceivably threaten floodplain regulation. *Maple Leaf Investors, Inc. v. State*, 565 P.2d 1162 (Wash. 1977), is a leading case. Other leading cases included *Turner v. County of Del Norte*, 101 Cal. Rptr. 93 (Cal. App. 1972), and *Turnpike Realty Co. v. Town of Dedham*, 284 N.E.2d 891 (Mass. 1972).

Grenier v. Zoning Bd. of Appeals, 831 N.E.2d 865 (2005), is instructive on how courts can handle takings claims against floodplain regulations under recent Supreme Court doctrine. The court found the denial of a permit to build a house in a coastal floodplain was not a taking. It did not find a taking under *Lucas* because, applying the Supreme Court's decision in *Palazzolo*, discussed in Chapter 2, it found the property had a residual value of $23,000 not including other uses allowed under the regulation. It did not find a taking under *Penn Central* because the property owner did not have reasonable investment-backed expectations to develop the property after the regulation was passed. The economic loss was not outside the "range of normal fluctuation in the value of coastal property," and the character of the regulation was the prevention of a harmful land use that had always been upheld. Applying the deferential substantive due process test adopted in *Lingle*, the court found the regulation advanced legitimate governmental interests, such as the ability of the town to respond to natural disasters. See also *Zanghi v. Board of Appeals*, 807 N.E.2d 221 (Mass. App. 2004) (no categorical taking applying whole parcel rule; landowner purchased before ordinance adopted and could use land for forestry, agriculture and conservation uses as well as cluster development).

Takings attacks on floodplain regulations are offset to some extent in floodway fringe areas because regulations in these areas do not prohibit development absolutely; development above the 100-year base flood height elevation usually is allowed. This option substantially mitigates the regulatory burden, and may prevent facial taking attacks by landowners who have not exhausted the possibilities for development that does not interfere with floodway flow. See *Vartelas v. Water Resources Comm'n*, 153 A.2d 822 (Conn. 1959).

The Federal Emergency Management Agency ("FEMA") has been criticized for failing to protect endangered species when granting insurance for new development under the National Flood Insurance Act ("NFIA"). In *Florida Key Deer v. Paulison*, 522 F.3d 1133 (11th Cir. 2008), FEMA was enjoined from issuing insurance for development in the Florida Keys where FEMA's administration of NFIA had jeopardized several endangered species. The Eleventh Circuit Court of Appeals held that Section 7(a)(1) of the Endangered Species Act applies to FEMA's administration of NFIA and requires FEMA to develop programs to protect endangered species.

6. *Sources.* The web site of the Association of State Floodplain Managers, floods.org, contains useful publications and information on floodplain regulation and the NFIP. See also Note and Commentary, *The Future of the National Flood Insurance Program in the Aftermath of Hurrican Katrina*, 12 Conn. Ins. L.J. 629 (2005/2006); Burby et al., *Unleashing the Power of Planning to Create Disaster-Resistant Communities*, 65 J. Am. Plan. Ass'n 247 (1999); Asmus, *The Growing Complexity of Stormwater Management*, Land Development, Spring 2010 at 14; Thomas & Bowen, *Preventing Human Caused Disasters*, Natural Hazards Observer (Nov. 2009), at 1 (http://www.colorado.edu/hazards/o/archives/2009/nov_observerweb.pdf); Thomas & Medlock, *Mitigating Misery: Land Use and Protection of Property Rights Before the Next Big Flood*, 9 Vt. J. Envtl. L. 155 (2008).

A NOTE ON OVERLAY ZONES

> An overlay is a zone that is placed on the zoning map "over" traditional zoning districts. Overlay zoning was born of the necessity to add an additional dimension to land use control to the zoning map for some special public purpose that does not coincide with the boundaries of the current zoning. Overlay zoning has been in use since the 1960s, although its application to a wide variety of public interests, particularly protection of environmentally sensitive areas, historic sites, . . . and viewshed protection, are of more recent origin. [Maryland Office of Planning, Overlay Zones 2 (1995).]

An overlay zone provides flexibility to meet special regulatory needs by adding additional requirements to the underlying zoning ordinance. Overlay zones are often used for environmental land use regulations, such as floodplain regulations, and for other zoning purposes, such as the protection of historic districts. The Maryland report provides several examples, including a Residential Conservation and Highway Corridor overlay zone. Each zone contains a statement of purpose and standards to be applied within the zone through discretionary review of development applications. For example, the statement of purpose for the Annapolis, Maryland Residential Conservation Overlay District provides:

> The purpose of the . . . district is to preserve patterns of design and development in residential neighborhoods characterized by a diversity of styles and to ensure the preservation of a diversity of land uses, together with the protection of buildings, structures or areas the destruction or alteration of which would disrupt the existing scale and architectural character of the neighborhood. [*Id.* at 19–20.]

Four additional standards are then provided, directed to preservation of architectural and neighborhood scale, compatibility and encouragement of existing land uses. In a variant of this approach, the ordinance may provide for the adoption of a neighborhood plan, which then becomes the basis on which new development is reviewed. This type of overlay zone can be useful in environmental regulation, such as floodplain regulation, where it can integrate flood control requirements with conventional zoning regulations.

Coordination between the review standards in the overlay district and the underlying ordinance is essential. See *Dallen v. Kansas City*, 822 S.W.2d 429 (Mo. App. 1991), holding that a setback requirement in a Main Street Special Review District was a modification of the underlying zoning that violated a provision in the city's zoning ordinance that prohibited such modifications. The decision contains the text of the special district ordinance.

For a discussion of how zoning regulations can mitigate the risk of flood damage, such as through overlay zones, setbacks, open space zones, density controls and nonconforming use regulations, see Roths, *Using Zoning to Reduce Flood Damages*, Zoning Practice, Mar. 2008, at 2. Roths emphasizes that local governments should always engage in risk analysis when preparing comprehensive plans and suggests that municipalities are underutilizing the land use tools available to mitigate the risk of flood damage.

[3.] Groundwater and Surface Water Resource Protection

Groundwater is a major source of water supply, and at least half of the country depends on groundwater aquifers. Groundwater quality protection is a major environmental concern as it is difficult to clean up groundwater, yet there is still no fully coordinated intergovernmental groundwater protection strategy. Federal controls are limited, and the most extensive programs are at the local level. Protecting the watersheds of surface waters such as streams, lakes and other sources of water from pollution that can damage water sources is also a critical problem.

Federal legislation. The federal Clean Water Act contains extensive provisions to protect surface waters from pollution, in part by requiring private and public sources of water pollution to obtain discharge permits from the federal Environmental Protection Agency or from state environmental agencies if they have been delegated this function. The courts are split, however, on whether the Clean Water Act applies to sources that pollute groundwater. See Commentary, *Reevaluating "Isolated Waters": Is Hydrologically Connected Groundwater "Navigable Water" under the Clean Water Act?* 54 Ala. L. Rev. 159 (2002); Student Comment, *Regulating Point-Source Discharges to Groundwater Hydrologically Connected to Navigable Waters*, 5 Barry L. Rev. 95 (2005).

Several other federal programs include groundwater protection elements, though they are limited. The Resource Conservation and Recovery Act, 42 U.S.C. §§ 6901-6991i, protects groundwater that is threatened by waste disposal facilities. The Safe Drinking Water Act has a program that protects underground water aquifers by prohibiting federal assistance for development over groundwater sources. 42 U.S.C. § 300h-3(e). Amendments to this statute in 1996 expanded its water source protection program. A key program provides federal assistance to states "for the development and implementation of a State program to ensure the coordinated and comprehensive protection of ground water resources within the State." *Id.*, § 300h-8(a). For a report on this program, see EPA, Safe Drinking Water Act: Groundwater Report to Congress (1999). EPA also adopted a groundwater strategy, Protecting the Nation's Groundwater: EPA's Strategy for the 1990s (1991).

The 1996 amendments also require states to prepare a Source Water Assessment Program for approval by EPA that covers all drinking water sources, including groundwater. This is a major undertaking in geological analysis. The program must delineate the source water assessment area, conduct an inventory of potential sources of contamination, determine the susceptibility of the water supply to contamination, and provide the assessment results to the public. *Id.*, § 300j-14. The statute does not mandate source water protection measures, but EPA encourages governments to use the Program to develop protection measures, such as land use regulations and the purchase of conservation easements. For discussion, see Cox, *Evolution of the Safe Drinking Water Act: A Search for Effective Quality Assurance Strategies and Workable Concepts of Federalism*, 21 Wm. & Mary Envtl. L. & Pol'y Rev. 69 (1997).

State programs. State programs include a number of controls to protect water resources such as discharge permits, controls on pollution sources, the implementation of best management practices to control pollution, policies to prevent the degradation of water supply sources, and the adoption of water quality standards. The EPA groundwater report, *supra*, contains examples of state programs. See also Vance, *Total Aquifer Management: A New Approach to Groundwater Protection*, 30 U.S.F. L. Rev. 803 (1996). State programs do not usually include land use controls. For examples of state legislation authorizing the consideration of local groundwater and watershed protection in planning and zoning, see Conn. Gen. Stat. § 8-2(a) (zoning to consider protection of drinking water supplies); Fla. Stat. Ann. § 163.3177(6)(c) (local comprehensive plan to include groundwater recharge element and protection requirements). For a critique of groundwater control strategies, see George, *Is*

Groundwater Regulation Blindman's Bluff?, 3 J. Plan. Lit. 231 (1988).

Local groundwater and watershed protection programs. Local land use regulation can play an important role in protection ground and surface water resources. The following excerpt explains the problem and how local ordinances can deal with it:

> Source water protection involves preventing the pollution of the groundwater, lakes, rivers, and streams that serve as sources of drinking water for local communities. Source water protection ordinances help safeguard community health and reduce the risk of contamination of water supplies. When drafting an ordinance aimed at protecting these sources, the drinking water supplies can be divided into two general sources; aquifers and wells (groundwater) and lakes and reservoirs (surface water). Wellhead Protection (WHP) Zones and Aquifer Protection Areas are two examples of source water protection ordinances that seek to protect groundwater sources. Water Supply Watershed Districts and Lake Watershed Overlay Districts are examples of local management tools that provide protection to surface water supplies by restricting land uses around a reservoir used for drinking water.
>
> Communities may take for granted that a plentiful supply of high quality drinking water will be available. However, drinking water sources, whether they be from ground water, or surface water, or both, are a vulnerable natural resource that needs to be protected. To ensure that these drinking water sources are protected most effectively, an ordinance should contain several basic concepts. First, source water planning should be done on a scale that ensures protection of the whole recharge zone for that source water. For surface waters, communities may wish to create overlay zoning districts that have boundaries large enough to protect both the source water resource and the tributaries and streams that contribute to the resource. . . . Second, an ordinance should have language specifying allowable and prohibited land uses within the source water protection zone. For example, many source water protection ordinances limit or forbid the storage of hazardous materials and place restrictions on the location of businesses that use these materials within the overlay district. An ordinance should also include procedures for review of proposed projects within a source water protection district to verify that the project is consistent with the ultimate goal of the ordinance. This might include requiring applicants to submit geotechnical and hydrological analyses to determine the potential impacts to water quality and the submission of spill control plans for businesses performing potentially contaminating activities. Finally, language explaining the mechanisms for enforcement of the requirements of the ordinance, including the civil and criminal penalties that may apply for failure to obey, should be included. [U.S. Environmental Protection Agency, Model Ordinances to Protect Local Resources: Source Water Protection, available at: epa.gov/owow/nps/ordinance/mol7.htm.]

The delineation of zones of protection can be determined by the travel time of groundwater sources — how long it takes the water entering the earth to make its way to its final location of natural storage. The site that has the EPA report includes model ordinances and the ordinances of selected communities to illustrate different approaches. The following article explains how these ordinances are drafted:

> The regulated area is typically depicted with overlay mapping. After the resource area is delineated, it is laid over the zoning districts. This is the recommended approach because it would be extremely difficult to conform underlying zoning

> districts to the haphazard shapes of watershed and water resources. . . .
>
> The text establishing the rules for the overlay district varies depending upon the resource being protected: Some regulations prohibit most uses deemed a threat to water resources, others use "performance based" criteria. Most water resource protection regulations list uses that are prohibited because they are deemed a threat to water systems. In some cases, this list is extensive, in others only the allowed uses are listed. [Witten, *Water Resource Protection and the Takings Issue*, Land Use L. & Zoning Dig., Vol. 50, No. 5, at 3 (1998).]

Some ordinances provide for conditional uses and contain approval criteria that require consideration of the impact of the conditional use on the water resource. *Id.* at 3–4. See also Tarlock, *Prevention of Groundwater Contamination*, 8 Zoning and Planning Law Report 121, 125–26 (1985). State legislation may require land use regulations to protect water supplies from degradation by development. N.J. Stat. Ann. § 40:55(D)-38(b)(13). See also Pa. Stat. Ann. tit. 53, § 10603(d) (zoning ordinances may contain provisions to assure availability of reliable, safe and adequate water supplies).

NOTES AND QUESTIONS

1. *Regulatory models.* Water resource protection ordinances often require the adoption of a series of concentric protected zones surrounding a groundwater resource, such as a stream. The Wake County, North Carolina zoning ordinance, § 1-1-131 is an example. It establishes a number of buffer zones around drinking water sources. For perennial streams, for example, there is an inner 50-foot buffer zone and a contiguous outer 50-foot buffer zone. Only listed expressly allowed passive activities are permitted within these zones, though grading, revegetating, lawns and landscaping are also allowed in the outer zone. The listed activities do not include permanent development of any kind but include activities such as driveways for single-family dwellings, utility lines, pedestrian and bikeway trails and vegetation management. Even these activities must be carried out to minimize impervious surface coverage, diffuse stormwater flow, and use best management practices to minimize adverse water quality impacts. The EPA site contains models of aquatic buffer ordinances. Note that water resource protection overlay zones can overlap other overlay zones, such as floodplain and wetlands zones and create a multiple veto problem. The regulatory requirements of these different zones can also vary.

A water resource protection ordinance can also limit density and surface coverage, as in the Stratham, New Hampshire ordinance contained on the EPA site. This ordinance adopts lot sizes provided in the underlying zone, but "[l]arger lot sizes may be required depending on the soil-based lot sizing standards found within the Stratham subdivision regulations." See http://www.epa.gov/owow/NPS/urbanmm/pdf/urban_ch01.pdf. The ordinance limits impervious site coverage to no more than 20 percent of the site, but this coverage can be exceeded if protective performance standards are met. Conditional uses are authorized subject to criteria requiring protective measures.

The Pekin, Illinois Groundwater Protection Ordinance is an example of a permit system. It requires a permit for all "facilities" in protected areas and authorizes the issuance of a permit only if "adequate plans, specifications, test data, and/or other appropriate information has been submitted by the owner and/or operator showing that the proposed design and construction of the facility meets the intent and provisions of this Ordinance and will not impact the short term, long term on cumulative quantity or quality of groundwater." § 7(A)(3).

A Model Aquifer Protection Bylaw prepared by the Cape Cod Commission has similar and more extensive requirements. It authorizes the designation of Aquifer Protection Overlay Districts and prohibits uses within those districts that can damage groundwater sources; and requires a special permit for development such as subdivisions of more than ten lots, the construction of ten or more dwelling units and retail uses 40,000 square feet in size or greater. The criteria for permit approval contain design and operating guidelines such as criteria for the containment of hazardous substances and the reporting of spills.

West Virginia passed a law establishing criteria for a state water resources management plan and authorizing regional water resources management plans. *See* S.B. 641 (W. Va. 2008).

Low impact development ("LID") can be utilized in urban areas to manage storm water and protect surface water resources. LID allows the built environment to act as a forested site by capturing rain and slowly returning it to the ground, reducing runoff on impervious surfaces and consequently reducing pollutants carried to local water resources. For more information on how LID management practices work, see http://www.nrdc.org/water/pollution/storm/chap12.asp.

As water resources become increasingly scarce, especially in the face of climate change, some local governments have initiated water conservation efforts through land use regulations. For example, Bernalillo County, New Mexico adopted an ordinance that requires all new developments to have water conservation measures and significantly restricts water use for landscaping, irrigation and recreation. *See* Bernalillo County, N.M., Water Conservation Ordinance (2007). For a compelling argument that linking land use law to water policy would most effectively conserve natural resources and prepare communities for climate change, see Hirokawa, *The Relevance of Land Use Law to Climate Change Preparedness: The Case of Sustainable Water Practices*, Trends, May/June 2009, at 6 (http://papers.ssrn.com/sol3/papers.cfm?abstract_id=1577853).

2. *The legality issue. Manzo v. Mayor & Twp. Council*, 838 A.2d 534 (N.J.L. Div.), *aff'd on the basis of the trial court opinon*, 838 A.2d 463 (N.J. App. Div. 2003), upheld a stream corridor protection ordinance enacted to protect a reservoir. The ordinance required reduced densities that varied by zone, and also allowed cluster development as a way to have less land disturbance and less opportunity for stormwater runoff from residential development that can carry pollution. Cluster development achieves this objective by clustering housing in one part of the project while preserving the rest as open space. The court had no difficulty finding water resource protection is a valid regulatory purpose and upheld the cluster development option as a way of reducing water pollution.

3. *The takings issue.* The cases have usually upheld groundwater and watershed protection ordinances against takings objections, but none have considered problems raised by ordinances with highly restrictive controls. Low density restrictions requiring large lot zoning have been upheld post-*Lucas* because they did not deny all economically beneficial or productive use of the land. *Security Mgt. Corp. v. Baltimore County*, 655 A.2d 1326 (Md. App. 1995) (five acres). For pre-*Lucas* cases in accord, see *Moviematic Industries Corp. v. Board of County Commissioners of Metropolitan Dade County*, 349 So. 2d 667 (Fla. App. 1977) (five acres); *Ketchel v. Bainbridge Township*, 557 N.E.2d 779 (Ohio 1990) (three acres). *Connecticut Resources Recovery Auth. v. Planning & Zoning Comm'n*, 626 A.2d 705 (Conn. 1993), upheld a prohibition on solid waste disposal in an aquifer protection zone. *Lucas* apparently prevents consideration of the environmental purposes of groundwater and watershed protection if the regulation does not allow any economically beneficial or productive use. Is there a way out? See *Jones v. Zoning Hearing Bd.*, 578 A.2d 1369 (Pa. Commw. 1990) (upholding buffer yards adopted to preserve woodlands, streams and steep slopes).

4. *Sources.* M. Jaffe & F. DiNovo, Local Groundwater Protection 49-54 (1987); DiNovo & Jaffe, *Local Regulations for Groundwater Protection Part I: Sensitive-Area Controls*, 36 Land Use L. & Zoning Dig., No. 5, at 6, 12, 13 (1984); Malone, *The Necessary Interrelationship Between Land Use and Preservation of Groundwater Resources*, 9 UCLA J. Envtl. L. & Pol'y 1 (1990); Marsh & Hill-Rowley, *Water Quality, Stormwater Management, and Development Planning in the Urban Fringe*, 36 Wash. U. J. Urb. & Contemp. L. 3 (1989) (discussing Austin, Tx.); Porter, *Fixing Our Drinking Water: From Field and Forest to Faucet*, 23 Pace Envtl. L. Rev. 389 (2006); Reading & MacDonald, *Meeting Potable Water Needs*, 49 Water & Wastes Digest 11 (2009) (http://www.biggrower.com/Meeting-Potable-Water-Needs-article11231).

[4.] Protecting Hillsides

[a.] The Problem

Steep slopes on hillsides are attractive places for development and can command high prices because people like home sites with vistas. Development on steep slopes, however, presents a number of environmental problems. Landslides are one. See Andrews, *Shifting Sands, Sliding Land*, Planning, June, 1999 at 4 (discussing landslides in Laguna Beach, California). Hillside development can also increase the risk of fire, as fires beginning in remote areas of a hill can be fanned uphill by winds and spread out of control. Erosion and drainage problems are intensified because the removal of vegetation for development increases impervious surface that accelerates water runoff. Communities may also want to regulate the view from hillsides or protect their natural features by prohibiting development on hillside crests. The same problems occur on mountains, and the discussion that follows also applies to them.

The following study explains the reasons for hillside regulation:

> Safety — Structures built on a hillside are subject to gravity in a way that other structures simply are not. Early hillside planning focused on limiting the risk from poorly engineered buildings and from landslide through grading regulations. Newer rules have also focused on limiting danger of landslide by a series of flexible rules that vary with the underlying geology of the slope. Fire is another safety concern with hillsides, fire travels faster uphill. Narrow streets in hillside communities can make access for firefighters difficult and water can be limited or insufficient in pressure.
>
> Environment — Hillsides can be areas of special environmental concern. Issues of erosion and run-off are closely linked to landslide concerns, but are also environmental issues. Unique habitats can exist on hillsides that require special protection.
>
> Aesthetic — Hillsides are areas of special concern to many communities because they are frequently associated with a community's sense of place and their high visibility means that unattractive hillside development can literally hang over an entire community. Aesthetic reasons are the most common in enabling legislation. [R. Olshansky, *Planning for Hillside Development*, American Planning Association, Planning Advisory Service Rep. No. 466 (1996).]

Land disturbance is a major issue in hillside development. Placing level structures on sloping surfaces creates inherent problems. Building structures inevitably creates land disturbance. Disturbed surfaces create loose materials that tend to move downhill, and structures will also experience a gravitational force that creates downhill movement. *Id.* at 9. Hillside regulations provide a variety of measures for controlling land disturbance.

The following selection explains some of the regulatory alternatives:

> A jurisdiction might choose to encourage development while emphasizing public safety, thus requiring extensive mass regrading and re-engineering of hillsides to provide high-quality roadways that allow quick access for public safety vehicles. Or a jurisdiction might require selective grading and improvements of hillsides for safety concerns, while imposing development standards (e.g., setbacks from ridgelines, restrictions on removal of native vegetation) to protect important natural features. A third approach could be to prohibit hillside development altogether. [C. Duerksen & M. Goebel, *Aesthetics, Community Character, and the Law*, American Planning Association, Planning Advisory Service Rep. Nos. 489–90 (1999).]

Approval as a conditional use or through a permit procedure may also be required. Some statutes authorize hillside regulation. Utah Code Ann. § 17-27a-403(3)(a)(ii).

[b.] Regulations for Hillside Protection

Here are some common examples of hillside protection ordinances. They are often included in overlay zones:

Grading regulations. These are the most common. They are usually incorporated into the building code, like this regulation from King County, Washington:

> Cuts and fills shall conform to the following provisions unless otherwise approved by the director.
>
> 1. Slope. No slope of cut and fill surfaces shall be steeper than is safe for the intended use and shall not exceed two horizontal to one vertical, unless otherwise approved by the director.
>
> 2. Erosion control. All disturbed areas including faces of cuts and fill slopes shall be prepared and maintained to control erosion in compliance with subsection A. [This subsection contains requirements for erosion and sedimentation control.] [Building and Construction Standards, § 16.82.100(B).]

Grading ordinances can also include minimum standards for height, gradient, drainage terraces, structural setbacks for cut and fill slopes and a maximum steepness ratio. A maximum steepness ratio of two horizontal to one vertical for both cut and fill slopes has become standard.

Erosion and sedimentation controls. These controls can help avoid erosion and runoff problems caused by grading and road construction. The EPA site noted above that contains Model Ordinances for Resource Protection includes a model erosion and sedimentation control ordinance. It requires an erosion and sediment control plan and includes design requirements, grading, erosion and sediment control practices. The ordinance should also provide for the proper collection and transportation of stormwater runoff in a pipe or other approved manner.

Slope/density reduction regulations. This type of regulation limits development by decreasing allowable development density as average slope increases. The assumption is that steeply sloped hillsides are unsuitable for intense development. The following table from the Palmdale, California Zoning Ordinance, § 100.09(A) is an example:

Slope Category	***Allowable Density***	***Equivalent Number of Units Per Acre***
0-10 percent	Upper Limit of the Applicable General Plan Density Range	Same
10-25 percent	.57 du/ac	1 unit/1-3/4 acres
25-50 percent	.40 du/ac	1 unit/2-1/2 acres
Greater then 50 percent	.025 du/ac	1 unit/40 acres

Cluster development. Density reductions can limit the dangers from hillside development, but they can mean more roads and grading and increase utility infrastructure costs because fewer homes occupy more space. Ordinances that encourage cluster housing development are a partial answer to these problems. They are not a perfect solution, as clustering can increase the visual impact of development. The following ordinance from the Santa Clara County, California is an example of a clustering ordinance.

> A cluster permit is required for the division of land into lots of less than 160 acres. A cluster arrangement of structures shall achieve economy of land use and efficiency of access, while avoiding or minimizing impact to the natural environment to the extent feasible. Defined development areas shall include no more than 10% of the total land area subject to the land division, with at least 90% of the remaining land area preserved in permanent open space by means of dedication of development rights which prevents future subdivision of such lands. Such open space area is not required to be contiguous to the development area but must be located within the Open Space/Field Research district. This dedicated open space shall be located in a medium-high or high visibility zone as determined through use of the OS/F viewshed analysis (§ 2.50.040(B)), or an area of environmental significance, as determined by the County. [Santa Clara County Code § 5.45]

Land disturbance regulations. These regulations attempt to avoid hillside erosion by limiting the amount of land disturbance. The Paradise Valley, Arizona Hillside Development Regulations, for example, contain a table that specifies how much land disturbance is allowed at the slope level for each building site. Zoning Ordinance Article XXII, § 2207(III), Table I. At a ten per cent building site slope level, for example, a land disturbance of 60% is allowable. The amount of land disturbance allowed decreases as the building site slope increases. At a 30% slope it is 10.62%. At a 95% slope it is 4.50%. Another effect of this regulation is to reduce the amount of impervious surface that is created for each building site, which reduces runoff.

Fire safety regulations. Density reductions and land disturbance limitations may increase danger from fire because the unchecked growth of vegetation in open areas can create fire control difficulties. San Bernardino County addressed fire safety issues by establishing a fire safety overlay district. See San Bernardino County, California, Fire Safety (FS) Overlay District § 82.13.

Aesthetic regulations. Communities may also want to protect the visual appearance of hillsides by limiting or prohibiting ridge line development, as in the following ordinance from Paradise Valley, Arizona:

> At and above an elevation of 1500 feet mean sea level, no Development shall occur which will Alter the Mountain Top Ridge Lines. Further, no structure may extend above a plane that originates on the primary ridge line and angles downward from the primary ridge line by twenty degrees. [Hillside Dev. Reg., Article XXII, § 2207(I)(A).]

Setback regulations are another alternative. Glare from reflective glass can be a problem, and can be controlled by limitation on reflective glass that reduce its visibility and glare potential. An ordinance can also contain special design criteria. They can include a requirement that maximum use be made of building materials, such as rock and stone, that are compatible with the hillside environment.

How would you resolve the conflicting objectives in hillside regulation ordinances to create a hillside protection program for your community? Notice that some controls regulate how development is carried out, and other controls regulate density and location. See http://www.dca.ga.gov/development/PlanningQualityGrowth/programs/downloads/MtHillsideOrdinance.pdf for an example of a comprehensive hillside protection ordinance.

Comprehensive steep slope regulations. Lake Forest, Illinois enacted a steep slope ordinance that comprehensively regulates development in and around ravines and bluffs along the shore of Lake Michigan. See http://www.cityoflakeforest.com/cs/cdev/cs_cd2f6.htm. The City also requires site plan review for all construction near a protected ravine area. A portion of the City's steep slope ordinance is reprinted below:

> Sec. 46-15. Steep Slope Ordinance
>
> (A) PURPOSE.
>
> The provisions contained herein are adopted to protect public and private property from damage or destruction resulting from natural erosion processes occurring within the ravines and bluffs along the shore of Lake Michigan, or abnormal or accelerated ravine and bluff erosion resulting from land development and construction activities occurring on adjacent or nearby properties, and to protect the fragile ravine and bluff ecosystem from unwarranted damage or destruction caused by land development and construction activities.
>
> (B) APPLICABILITY.
>
> The provisions contained herein shall apply to all land development and construction activities on all properties abutting ravines and bluffs as delineated by hashed lines (or shaded areas) on Exhibit A, a copy of which is attached hereto and made a part hereof.
>
> (C) REQUIREMENTS AND RESTRICTIONS.
>
> (1) Building Setbacks:
>
> (a) From Ravines

All building construction shall be on Table Land, but in no case shall any structure or building foundation be located closer than twenty (20) feet to the Ravine Area.

(b) From Bluffs

All building construction shall be on Table Land, but in no case shall any structure or building foundation be located closer than seventy-five (75) feet to the Bluff Area.

(2) Construction Activity:

(a) Adjacent to Ravines

All construction activity, i.e., grading, excavating, filling, terracing, tree removal, stockpiling of excavated material, is prohibited within twenty (20) feet of the Ravine Area, except as may be necessary to provide site drainage improvements, as may be approved and/or required by the City Engineer.

(b) Adjacent to Bluffs

All construction activity, i.e., grading, excavating, filling, terracing, tree removal, stockpiling of excavated material, is prohibited within fifty (50) feet of the Bluff Edge, except as may be necessary to provide site drainage improvements, as may be approved and/or required by the City Engineer. . . .

Sources. For discussions of local programs see the discussion of the Foothills and Canyons Overlay Zoning District adopted in Salt Lake County, Utah in Duerksen & Gobel, *supra* at 48–49. The Andrews article, cited above, discusses the hillside protection program in Seattle, Washington. For a detailed review, see R. Olshansky, *Planning for Hillside Development*, American Planning Association, Planning Advisory Service Rep. No. 466 (1996). See also Fox, Land-Use Controls for Hillside Preservation in the City of Pittsburgh (Allegheny Land Trust, 2004), available at alleghenylandtrust.org/; Schwab, *Regulating Hillside Development*, Zoning News, March, 1992, at 1. In California, a special purpose entity called a Geologic Hazard Abatement District can be created under Cal. Pub. Res. Code §§ 26500-26654 to address landslide hazards. Examples of hillside development permit application checklists can be found at http://www.tucsonaz.gov/dsd/hdz.pdf and www.ci.concord.ca.us/pdf/permits/planning/appscheck/plng-hillsidedevplan.pdf.

[c.] Takings and Other Legal Issues

Hillside protection ordinances have usually not had difficulties in court. The cases have upheld the purposes of this type of regulation. *In re Interim Bylaw, Waitsfield*, 742 A.2d 742 (Vt. 2003); *Terrazas v. Blaine County*, 207 P.3d 169 (Idaho 2009). The Waitsfield ordinance prohibited one- and two-family dwellings above 1700 feet in a forest reserve district, and the court also found it did not deny all economically beneficial use because it allowed several uses, including agricultural and forestry uses. *Girton v. City of Seattle*, 983 P.2d 1135 (Wash. App. 1990), upheld an ordinance restricting slope coverage to 28 percent, noting that "[t]he public has a significant interest in controlling the harmful effects of erosion, not just in avoiding 'significant injury' to property or the environment." It also found the plaintiff did not suffer an economic loss. He could still build his three-story house, the loss of view was negligible, and he should have anticipated the regulation, which was passed after he bought the land. See also *NJD, Ltd. v. City of San Dimas*, 2 Cal. Rptr. 3d 818 (2003) (rejecting facial takings claim and noting a variance was available to mitigate any harshness imposed by hillside development restrictions); *Sellon v. City of Manitou Springs*, 745 P.2d 229 (Colo. 1987) (upholding purpose of ordinance and rejecting vagueness challenge). Contra *Corrigan v. City of Scottsdale*, 720 P.2d 528 (Ariz. App. 1985), *vacated on other grounds*, 720 P.2d 513 (Ariz. 1986) (easement or dedication required). But see *Monks v. City of Rancho Palos Verdes*, 167 Cal. App. 4th 263, 84 Cal. Rptr. 3d 75 (2008) (city's ban on residential construction in landslide area violated state takings clause because it deprived landowners of all economically beneficial use).

[5.] Coastal Zone Management

The nation's coastal areas are a valuable but threatened environmental resource. More than 75 percent of the population lives in coastal areas or nearby, and this proportion is increasing. Like other environmental land use programs, coastal management is resource-driven, but with a difference. Coastal areas differ widely in character, and can include developed urban as well as natural resource areas, such as wetlands and agricultural areas. For this reason, they require a variety of different land use programs.

Congress responded to concern about coastal areas by enacting the Coastal Zone Management Act of 1972 (CZMA), a program of federal assistance to the states for the development of state coastal management programs. Congress adopted the program because it found that "present state and local institutional arrangements for planning and regulating land and water uses in such areas are inadequate." 16 U.S.C. § 1451(a). When first adopted, the CZMA did not include substantive policies for coastal protection. Congress remedied this problem in 1980 by enacting a set of protective statutory policies for state coastal management that to some extent answered claims that the program lacked an articulate purpose. The states have considerable flexibility, however, in setting coastal management policies. The CZMA is at 16 U.S.C. §§ 1451-1466. References in this discussion are to the section numbers of the original legislation as adopted by Congress.

The three "means" of control include, either separately or in combination: (1) state criteria and standards for local implementation, subject to state review; (2) direct state planning and regulation; or (3) state administrative review of state and local plans, projects, and regulations to determine consistency with the state coastal program. There must also be a method for assuring that state and local coastal zone regulations "do not unreasonably restrict or exclude land and water uses of regional benefit." Another related section affecting state review of land development requires "adequate consideration of the national interest" in the planning and siting of facilities, including energy facilities, that "meet requirements which are other than local in nature." § 306(d)(12).

NOTES AND QUESTIONS

1. *The scope and future of coastal management.* Programs funded by the CZMA address many issues, including habitat preservation, energy and government facility siting, coastal hazards, ocean resources, public access and water quality. For this and other objectives the CZMA provides a flexible format:

> As a voluntary program, the states have been given flexibility over how to design a coastal program to address existing and emerging concerns. This flexibility allows states to tailor their coastal program to the different resources, land and water use issues, and organizational, legal, and regulatory structures that exist within each state. The flexibility in implementing the CZMA has encouraged participation by almost all coastal states. However, the broad scope and diversity of approaches has raised

> questions regarding how this collection of efforts adds up to demonstrable improvement in any one area of concern. Some question whether adequate resources are available to CZMA programs in order to address all the existing issues, let alone take on any new or emerging concerns. [NOAA, Current and Future Challenges for Coastal Management 27 (2006).]

This report guides an envisioning program sponsored by NOAA and the Coastal States Organization that is expected to produce suggestions for change. Interviews with program managers found that growth and development was the key coastal issue, and that increased political will and support was needed for program success. See Envisioning the Future of Coastal Management: Key Findings of Manager Issues (2007) (http://coastalmanagement.noaa.gov/czm/media/Visioning2findings.pdf). See also Envisioning the Future of Coastal Management: Land Use (2007) (http://coastalmanagement.noaa.gov/czm/media/LandUse.pdf). The envisioning program implements two recent reports that suggested changes in coastal management: Pew Oceans Comm'n, America's Living Oceans: Charting a Course for Sea Change (2003), and the U.S. Commission on Ocean Policy, An Ocean Blueprint for the 21st Century (2004). The Ocean Blueprint report recommended that "The CZMA can be strengthened by developing strong, specific, measurable goals and performance standards that reflect a growing understanding of ocean and coastal environments, the basic tenets of ecosystem-based management, and the need to manage growth in regions under pressure from coastal development."

2. *The role of state and local coastal plans.* The following excerpt summarizes state and local participation in coastal management:

> The current CZMA program is focused primarily at the state level, but does provide for a local role if the state desires local participation. However, only seven state CZMA programs have full blown local coastal programs and a little more than one half of the programs have local implementation of one or more program elements. Some state programs have broad permitting authority, a few states have comprehensive planning at the state level, but fewer have formal input into local land use decisions. [Current and Future Challenges for Coastal Management, *supra*, at 9 (2006).]

An important issue is what the statutory requirement for a "management program" contemplates for state coastal plans. *American Petr. Inst. v. Knecht*, 456 F. Supp. 889 (C.D. Cal. 1978), *aff'd*, 609 F.2d 1306 (9th Cir. 1979), interpreted the federal statutory requirements that determine the content of state coastal plans. The question was whether the California coastal management plan lacked the specificity Congress intended to enable landowners in the coastal zone to "predict with reasonable certainty" whether their activities were consistent with the management plan. The court held Congress did not intend states to establish such detailed criteria that private users will be able to rely on them as predictive devices for determining the fate of projects without interaction between the relevant state agencies and the user. 456 F. Supp. at 919. The management plans have become the focus of debate in coastal wind power projects. Note & Comment, *Offshore Wind Energy in the United States: Regulations, Recommendations, and Rhode Island*, 15 Roger Williams U.L. Rev. 217 (2010).

3. In *Stop the Beach Renourishment, Inc. v. Florida Department of Environmental Protection*, 130 S. Ct. 2592 (2010), the U.S. Supreme Court held that the land under the water at a Florida shoreline continued to belong to the state even after the state added new sand, extending the beach and interrupting property owners' exclusive access to the water. By a vote of eight to zero, the Court upheld a decision by the Florida Supreme Court which had held that the state's ownership of newly created land at the shoreline was not an unconstitutional taking.

4. *Sources.* T. Beatley, D. Brower & A. Schwab, An Introduction to Coastal Zone Management (2d ed. 2002); Dennison, *State and Local Authority to Regulate Coastal Land Use Practices Under the Coastal Zone Management Act*, 15 Zoning & Plan. L. Rep. 65 (1992); Jones, *The Coastal Barrier Resources Act: A Common Cents Approach to Coastal Protection*, 21 Envtl. L. 1015 (1991); Kalen, *The Coastal Zone Management Act of Today: Does Sustainability Have a Chance?*, 15 Southeastern Envtl. L.J. 191 (2006); Comment, *Louisiana and The Coastal Zone Management Act in the Wake of Hurricane Katrina: A Renewed Advocacy for a More Aggressive Use of the Consistency Provision to Protect and Restore Coastal Wetlands*, 12 Ocean & Coastal L.J. 133 (2006); *No Adverse Impact Coastal Handbook*, Association of State Floodplain Managers (May 2007) (http://www.floods.org/CNAI/index.asp).

[6.] Sustainability

A NOTE ON LAND USE PLANNING AND SUSTAINABILITY

What it is. Sustainability of the natural environment as an environmental goal has attracted international and national attention. The Brundtland Commission's seminal report on sustainability to the United Nations defined sustainable development as follows:

> Sustainable development is development that meets the needs of the present without compromising the ability of future generations to meet their own needs. It contains within it two key concepts:
>
> the concept of 'needs', in particular the essential needs of the world's poor, to which overriding priority should be given; and
>
> the idea of limitations imposed by the state of technology and social organization on the environment's ability to meet present and future needs. [Our Common Future, Report of the World Commission on Environment and Development 43 (1987).]

Later, in 1992, the Earth Summit meeting in Rio de Janeiro issued an *Agenda 21* whose central goal is "to halt and reverse the environmental damage to our planet and to promote environmentally sound and sustainable development in all countries on earth."

To implement the goals of the Brundtland Commission, President Clinton appointed a President's Council on Sustainable Development. Their final report, *Towards a Sustainable America* (1999), contains recommendations for sustainable community development. (clinton2.nara.gov/PCSD/Publications/tsa.pdf.)

> An earlier report in 1996 on *Sustainable Development* had this recommendation:
>
> Sustainable building design and community planning make efficient use of existing infrastructure, energy, water, materials, and land. Not only does such use save money, it also safeguards public health and the environment and conserves natural resources. Building codes can shape how much energy, water, and materials a building consumes in its construction and operation. Zoning ordinances frequently influence decisions on the construction, design, and siting of buildings and developments. Efficient land use protects vulnerable environmental areas that provide important benefits to society. For example, coastal areas, watersheds, and floodplains absorb the forces unleashed by nature. And preserved wetlands can filter water far more cheaply than expensive

> water treatment facilities. In contrast, development in these areas exposes people and their investments to unnecessary risks and natural hazards. [*Id.* at 92.]

See clinton2.nara.gov/PCSD/Publications/TF_Reports/amer-top.html.

What this means for planning. Many will conclude that achieving sustainability simply embraces many of the goals of good planning. For example, Goal 6 of the *Sustainable Development* report states:

> SUSTAINABLE COMMUNITIES
>
> Encourage people to work together to create healthy communities where natural and historic resources are preserved, jobs are available, sprawl is contained, neighborhoods are secure, education is lifelong, transportation and health care are accessible, and all citizens have opportunities to improve the quality of their lives. [*Id.* at 12.]

How sustainability issues can be used in local planning is indicated in K. Krizek & J. Power, A Planners Guide to Sustainable Development, American Planning Ass'n, Planning Advisory Serv. Rep. No. 46 (1996). The authors point out that sustainability originally was a "green" environmental movement but has expanded to include a new way of thinking that places equal weight on environmental, economic and social issues. In Chapter 3, they explain that planning for sustainability recognizes the limits to development, approaches matters based on their natural and geographic characteristics, is oriented to the means of obtaining sustainable development rather than concentrating on functional planning areas and is holistic and interconnected. Many of the environmental programs discussed in this chapter, such as wetlands, floodplain and agricultural preservation, have a place in a planning program based on sustainability.

Sustainability concerns also influence site and building design. A. Pitts, Planning and Design Strategies for Sustainability and Profit (2004), for example, has design recommendations that help achieve solar access. She states:

> The prime need in terms of environmental design of individual buildings is to focus on climate sensitivity, both in terms of reducing impact on global climate and in recognizing the effect of climate on the environments in and around the building. In practice terms it is necessary to design appropriate building forms, including location, size and type of openings in the building envelope, so as to exploit advantageous solar heat gain. [*Id.* at 81.]

The LEED-ND Program. In February, 2007 a pilot program in Leadership in Energy and Environmental Design for Neighborhood Development was launched by the U.S. Green Building Council, the Congress for New Urbanism and the Natural Resources Defense Council. The report was funded by the U.S. Environmental Protection Agency. LEED ratings for new building construction have previously been available, but the ND program extends these ratings to project development. The LEED program is a rating system that awards credit for good design and certifies projects that have achieved a required number of credits. LEED-ND is available at: www.usgbc.org.

Many of the recommendations in LEED-ND relate to wetland and agricultural protection and floodplain avoidance, but they also contain recommendations for neighborhood design that reflect New Urbanism principles:

> Intent

Conserve land. Promote livability, transportation efficiency, and walkability.

Requirements

Build any residential components of the project at an average density of seven or more dwelling units per acre of buildable land available for residential uses;

AND

Build any non-residential components of the project at an average density of 0.50 FAR or greater per acre of buildable land available for non-residential uses. [*Id.* at 50.]

Several pilot projects have been accepted into the program and revision as experience is gained is expected. The program was updated, for example, in June, 2007.

Sources. Report of the World Commission on Environment and Development: Our Common Future, Chapter 2: Towards Sustainable Development (www.un-documents.net/wced-ocf.htm); *Sustainable Justice: Reconciling Economic, Social And Environmental Law*, Marie-Claire Cordonier Segger (Editor), C. G. Weeramantry (Editor). More sources are available at: www.attra.ncat.org/publication.html.

[7.] Climate Change

Recent statutory land use reforms in many states have focused on climate change, green house gas emissions and green development, as well as linking those sustainability techniques to regional planning, transportation and affordable housing. For example, California is spearheading the charge against greenhouse gas emissions through land use planning. Senate Bill 375, passed in 2008, requires regional targets for greenhouse gas emissions and regional plans (called sustainable communities strategies) to meet those targets. Regional transportation and housing decisions, including funding, must be made according to the strategies. It remains to be seen how effective the sweeping legislation will be as the regional strategies are not yet developed, and S.B. 375 will not be fully implemented until 2011. See S.B. 375 (Cal. 2008); Shigley, *California's Aerial Combat: The State Tries a First-in-the-Nation Approach to Attacking Climate Change*, Planning, Feb. 2009, at 10.

Other states are following California's lead. For example, Florida now requires local governments to include climate change initiatives in comprehensive plans, such as reductions in greenhouse gas emissions and energy conservation measures. See C.S./H.B. 697 (Fla. 2008). Also in 2008, the Washington Legislature passed a bill acknowledging that it is in the public interest to reduce the state's dependence on foreign oil and that land use development patterns affect greenhouse gas emissions and consumption of foreign oil. The bill mandates that the Department of Community, Trade and Economic Development provide local governments with mechanisms for responding to climate change and work with the Department of Transportation to reduce greenhouse gas emissions. See S.B. 6580 (Wash. 2008). For an overview of 2008 legislation addressing climate change and sustainability through land use, see Salkin, *Zoning and Land Use Planning: Linking Land Use with Climate Change and Sustainability Topped State Legislative Land Use Reform Agenda in 2008*, 37 Real Estate L.J. 336 (2009).

Some states are encouraging alternative energy use through land use regulations and permitting requirements. New Hampshire, for example, adopted a law prohibiting municipalities from unreasonably limiting the development of renewable energy systems such as solar and wind systems through their zoning powers. See H.B. 310 (N.H. 2008). As another example, new legislation in Hawaii prohibits the issuance of building permits for single family homes that do not have a solar water heating system as of January 1, 2010. See S.B. 644 (Haw. 2008).

Executive or legislative commissions have also been established to examine the possible consequences of climate change for a state and the costs and benefits associated with addressing them, and develop recommendations for appropriate policies. Examples of states that have established commissions include Alaska, Arkansas, Arizona, Kansas, and North Carolina.

At least 36 states have completed comprehensive climate action plans, or are in the process of revising or developing one. The plans detail steps that the states can take to reduce their contribution to climate change. The process of developing a climate action plan can identify cost-effective opportunities to reduce greenhouse gas (GHG) emissions that are relevant to the state. The individual characteristics of each state's economy, resource base, and political structure provide different opportunities for dealing with climate change.

Courts are also beginning to recognize the potential link between green house gases and climate change. In the first climate change case before the U.S. Supreme Court, *Massachusetts v. E.P.A.*, 549 U.S. 497 (2007), the Court ruled that the EPA has authority under the Clean Air Act to regulate greenhouse gas emissions from motor vehicles. In this case, a coalition of 12 states, along with three major cities, American Samoa, and many environmental groups, challenged the federal EPA's refusal to regulate greenhouse gases under the Clean Air Act. The EPA had concluded that it had no authority under existing law to regulate greenhouse gases, and that, for a variety of policy reasons, it would not use that authority even if it possessed it.

The Court ruled that states have standing to challenge the EPA's decision not to regulate CO_2 and other greenhouse gases from the transportation sector. The Court found that the EPA's refusal to regulate CO_2 has led to "actual" and "imminent" harm to the state of Massachusetts, mainly in the form of rising sea-levels along the state's coast. The ruling also noted that "the harms associated with climate change are serious and well recognized." The Court also found that "given EPA's failure to dispute the existence of a causal connection between man-made greenhouse gas emissions and global warming, its refusal to regulate such emissions, at a minimum, contributes to Massachusetts' injuries." Finally, while acknowledging that regulating greenhouse gases from motor vehicles alone will not reverse global warming, the Court found that lawsuits such as the one brought by Massachusetts against the EPA can play a role in slowing or reducing warming.

The Court held that the agency could not refuse to use that authority based on the agency's policy preferences. Instead, the EPA would have to decide, based on the science, whether it believed that greenhouse gas emissions were posing dangers to public health or welfare. If the agency determined that endangerment was occurring, the agency would have to start the process of setting emission standards for greenhouse gases. In late 2007, EPA officials sent a proposed endangerment determination to the White House as an e-mail attachment, but White House officials refused to open the document, and former EPA Administrator Stephen Johnson refused repeated requests to make the document public.

As noted in the following case, there is a potential for conflict between a state government's interest in encouraging alternative energy systems and a local government's interest in preserving and protecting its residents from alleged adverse impacts created by alternative energy sources.

ECKER BROS. v. CALUMET COUNTY

321 Wis. 2d 51, 772 N.W.2d 240 (2009)

Brown, C.J.

We read the Wisconsin statutes to say that our legislature favors alternative energy systems, such as the proposed wind energy system at issue in this case. We also read the statutes to disfavor wholesale local control which circumvents this policy. Instead, localities may restrict a wind energy system only where necessary to preserve or protect the public health or safety, or where the restriction does not significantly increase the cost of the system or significantly decrease its efficiency, or where the locality allows for an alternative system of comparable cost and efficiency. This determination must be made on a case-by-case basis where the local governing arm first hears the specifics of the particular wind system and then decides whether a restriction is warranted. But here, Calumet County promulgated an ordinance in which it arbitrarily set minimum setback, height and noise requirements for any wind system that might want to exist in Calumet County. We hold that this "one size fits all" scheme violates the legislative idea that localities must look at each wind system on its own merits and decide, in each specific case, whether the wind system conflicts with public health or safety. We reverse and remand with directions that the circuit court strike the County's ordinance as ultra vires.

The relevant facts are undisputed. The Ecker Brothers are farmers with one wind turbine on their farm. They wanted to build more wind turbines on their property to generate energy to sell back to the power company. So, they began seeking funding to do so. Part of the funding they needed was in the form of a grant, and that grant required an acknowledgement letter from Calumet County and the town of Stockbridge that the Ecker Brothers did not need a permit to build wind turbines. The town sent the letter, but the County did not. Instead, the County passed a moratorium on further wind turbines, and, eventually, it passed a wind turbine ordinance restricting all wind energy systems uniformly based on a system's classification as a large or small system. Under the new ordinance, the Ecker Brothers had to apply for a permit and their proposed wind turbines had to meet the ordinance's restrictions. So, the Ecker Brothers filed a declaratory judgment action claiming, inter alia, that the County's wind energy ordinance was ultra vires because the County exceeded its authority under Wis. Stat. § 66.0401 (2007-08). [footnote omitted]

Both parties moved for summary judgment. The County argued that the Ecker Brothers' claim was barred by Wis. Stat. § 893.80 because they failed to serve the County with the proper written notice of circumstances and claim. The circuit court agreed with the County and dismissed the case. The Ecker Brothers appealed.

[Discussion of notice of claims argument omitted.]

Now we can get to the substantive issue, which concerns the scope of the State's delegation of authority to its political subdivisions to restrict wind energy systems. [footnote omitted] Wisconsin Stat. § 66.0401(1) is the primary statute governing this issue. This statute is a state legislative restriction that expressly forbids political subdivisions from regulating solar and wind energy systems. . . . The scope of this preemption, however, expressly allows some local control insofar as they satisfy one of three conditions. . . .

> (1) AUTHORITY TO RESTRICT SYSTEMS LIMITED. No county, city, town, or village may place any restriction, either directly or in effect, on the installation or use of a wind energy system, as defined in s. 66.0403(1)(m), unless the restriction satisfies one of the following conditions:
>
> (a) Serves to preserve or protect the public health or safety.
>
> (b) Does not significantly increase the cost of the system or significantly decrease its efficiency.
>
> (c) Allows for an alternative system of comparable cost and efficiency.

Thus, a political subdivision's consideration of a wind energy system must be in light of the conditions placed on local regulation by this section . . . A "wind energy system" is "equipment that converts and then stores or transfers energy from the wind into usable forms of energy." . . .

In this case, Calumet County enacted an ordinance to restrict wind energy systems pursuant to Wis. Stat. § 66.0401. The County's ordinance divides the systems into two categories, small and large, and a set of uniform, across-the-board restrictions controls each category. These restrictions are based on the County's policy decision that in all situations, wind energy systems must be bound by the same set of restrictions. . . .

The Ecker Brothers contend that the local restrictions cannot be the same for *all* systems and cannot be created before the fact without knowledge of the facts of an individual project. Instead, the Ecker Brothers assert that the statutory scheme allows political subdivisions to restrict systems only on a case-by-case basis through conditional use permits. Thus, this argument boils down to the proper method for restricting wind energy systems: (1) a conditional use permit procedure that restricts systems as needed on a case-by-case basis, or (2) an ordinance creating a permit system with across-the-board regulations based on legislative policy-making. . . .

At oral argument, Calumet County agreed that its ordinance was the product of legislative facts. The legislative facts it "found" were that the restrictions in its ordinance are always needed to preserve or protect the public health or safety in all situations, do not significantly increase the cost or significantly decrease the efficiency of any wind system at any time, at any place, in any circumstance, or that an alternative system of comparable cost and efficiency will always, *ipso facto*, be available. In other words, the County has decided that its restrictions will never conflict with Wis. Stat. § 66.0401, no matter what system they are applied to. And, in the rare instance that a landowner thinks the ordinance does violate § 66.0401, the County posits that the landowner has the burden of contesting the application of the ordinance based on the facts of that situation.

The County asserts that Wis. Stat. § 66.0401 permits this approach because the legislature delegated the authority to political subdivisions to make policy decisions within the three conditions. And, it contends, so long as the policy decision is related to those conditions, the legislature does not dictate the processes political subdivisions may use to restrict wind energy systems. Taking the County's argument to its fullest, we interpret this argument as saying that the County may as a matter of local policy disfavor wind energy systems, even severely restrict them, so long as the policy is tied to one of the three conditions in § 66.0401(1). This argument requires us to read the statutes to say that the legislature actually authorized localities to make their own policy regarding alternative energy systems.

We do not buy this argument. Counties have no inherent power to govern. . . . Whatever power of local, legislative or administrative power they have is delegated to political subdivisions by the legislature. . . . Administrative powers involve the interpretation or application of law, and require the authority to carry a law into execution or implementation. . . . Powers of an administrative character do not allow political subdivisions to make policy. . . . The true difference between powers that are strictly legislative and those that are administrative and merely relate to the execution of the statutory law, "is between the delegation of power to make the law, which necessarily involves a discretion as to what it shall be, and conferring authority or discretion as to its execution, to be exercised under and in pursuance of the law."

Here, the legislature already made the policy decision that it favors wind energy systems. It created a scheme wherein owners of the systems can apply for permits that protect their ability to harness wind. And, it restricted the political subdivisions' ability to contravene this policy. However, the legislature did allow political subdivisions to place restrictions on a wind energy system if, and only if, the restriction "[s]erves to preserve or protect the public health or safety," *or* it "[d]oes not significantly increase the cost of the system or significantly decrease its efficiency," *or* it "[a]llows for an alternative system of comparable cost and efficiency." Sec. 66.0401(1)(a)-(c).

Because the legislature did not delegate legislative powers to localities, the County cannot make findings of legislative fact. The County thus exceeded its authority under Wis. Stat. § 66.0401 when it created its wind energy ordinance. We therefore hold the ordinance to be *ultra vires*. We reverse and remand with directions that the circuit court reconsider the Ecker Brothers' declaratory judgment action given that the ordinance is *ultra vires*.

By the Court. — Judgment reversed and cause remanded with directions

NOTES AND QUESTIONS

1. *Conflict between state and local governments*. Should state governments be permitted to "trump" local control over aesthetics, as well as public health, safety, and welfare? What happens to local jurisdiction over zoning and siting of energy facilities?

2. *Climate change and alternative energy litigation*. At least one court has upheld a county-wide ban on all commercial wind farms. *Zimmerman v. Wabaunsee County*, 218 P.3d 400 (Kan. 2009). For a chart showing climate change litigation, see www.climatecasechart.com.

3. *Survey of Climate Change Initiatives*. A complete survey of all of the myriad state, regional, and local initiatives and policies on climate change could fill multiple volumes. Instead, the following is intended to provide a "sampling" of some recent climate change activities taking place at the state and regional levels.

Stringent building code for new buildings: In 2010, the California Building Standards Commission approved what is being heralded as the most environmentally stringent building code in the United States for new commercial buildings, hospitals, schools, shopping malls, and homes. The new code, named Cal Green, requires builders to install a number of environmentally friendly features in new buildings, including plumbing to cut indoor water use, efficient heaters and air conditioners, and requires them to divert 50 percent of construction waste to recycling. (www.documents.dgs.ca.gov/bsc/documents/2010/Draft-2010-CALGreenCode.pdf)

School Wind and Solar Generation Program: The State of Illinois recently adopted a school wind and solar generation program, authorizing the funding through the Finance Authority Act for low-interest loans to school districts and community college districts for engineering studies, feasibility studies, research studies, and construction costs for wind and solar generation projects. (www.ilga.gov/legislation/publicacts/96/PDF/096-0725.pdf)

Green Buildings Act: In an effort to promote energy efficiency in state government buildings, the Illinois General Assembly enacted the Green Buildings Act, requiring all new state-funded building construction and renovations to seek LEED, Green Globes or equivalent certification, and further requiring that all projects receive the highest level of certification practical within the project budget. (www.ilga.gov/legislation/publicacts/96/PDF/096-0073.pdf)

Wind Energy Systems: Effective January 2010, new legislation in New Jersey restricts how municipalities can regulate wind energy systems, and prohibits municipalities from unreasonably limiting the installation of such systems designed primarily for on-site consumption. Unreasonable limits or hindrances to performance include the following:

- Prohibiting small wind energy systems in all districts within the municipality
- Restricting tower height or system height through application of a generic ordinance or regulation on height that does not specifically address allowable tower height or system height of a small wind energy system
- Requiring a setback from property boundaries for a tower that is greater than 150 percent of the system height. In a municipality that does not adopt specific setback requirements for small wind energy systems, any small wind energy system shall be set back from the nearest property boundary a distance at least equal to 150 percent of the system height; provided, however, that this requirement may be modified by the zoning board of adjustment upon application in an individual case if the applicant establishes the conditions for a variance under this act
- Setting a noise level limit lower than 55 decibels, as measured at the site property line, or not allowing for limit overages during short-term events such as utility outages and severe wind storms
- Setting electrical or structural design criteria that exceed applicable State, federal or international building or electrical codes or laws. [www.njleg.state.nj.us/2008/Bills/PL09/244_.PDF]

Alternative Energy as Inherently Beneficial Use: The New Jersey Municipal Land Use Law was amended to expand the definition of Inherently Beneficial Use to include a wind, solar or photovoltaic energy facility or structure. The statute now provides: "Inherently beneficial use means a use which is universally considered of value to the community because it fundamentally serves the public good and promotes the general welfare. Such a use includes, but is not limited to, a hospital, school, child care center, group home, or a wind, solar or photovoltaic energy facility or structure." (www.njleg.state.nj.us/2008/Bills/PL09/146_.PDF). See also Merriam, *Regulating Backyard Wind Turbines*, 10 Vermont J. Env. Law 291 (2009) (http://www.vjel.org/journal/pdf/VJEL10091.pdf).

Reduction of Emissions From Large Buildings: In 2009, New York City enacted four bills (Local Laws 84, 85, 87 and 88) designed to implement the City's plans to improve energy efficiency in existing buildings. These include the following:

- Creation of a New York City Energy Code that existing buildings will have to meet whenever they make renovations (nyc.gov/html/dob/downloads/pdf/ll85of2009.pdf)
- Requirements that large buildings owners make an annual benchmark analysis of energy consumption so that owners, tenants, and potential tenants can compare buildings' energy consumption (nyc.gov/html/dob/downloads/pdf/ll84of2009.pdf)
- Requirements that large commercial buildings (over 50,000 square feet) upgrade their lighting and sub-meter tenant spaces over 10,000 square feet (nyc.gov/html/dob/downloads/pdf/ll88of2009.pdf)
- Requirements that large private buildings conduct energy audits once every decade and implement energy efficient maintenance practices. Also, all city-owned buildings over 10,000 sq ft will be required to conduct audits and complete energy retrofits that pay for themselves within 7 years (www.nyc.gov/html/dob/downloads/pdf/ll87of2009.pdf)

Climate Change and Transportation Legislation: In 2010, Oregon Governor Ted Kuglonoski signed legislation that lays the groundwork for sustainable and cost-effective transportation systems. (www.leg.state.or.us/10ss1/measpdf/sb1000.dir/sb1059.en.pdf)

Sources. Environmental Law Institute, Lasting Landscapes: Reflections on the Role of Conservation Science in Land Use Planning (2007); J. McElfish, Nature-Friendly Ordinances (2004); M. Roseland, Toward Sustainable Communities (rev. ed. 2005); B. Murillo & S. Vargas, *Green Neighborhood Design*, Urban Land, Aug. 2007, at 138; Hing Wong, *Address Climate Change through Land Use*, San Francisco Chronicle, 1/29/08 (www.articles.sfgate.com/2008-01-29/opinion/17149079_1_greenhouse-gas-emissions-tons-of-carbon-dioxide-american-planning-association-s-california); Brian Stone, Jr., *Land Use as Climate Change Mitigation*, Environmental Science and Technology, Vol. 43, No. 24, pp. 9052–9056 (www.pubs.acs.org/doi/pdf/10.1021/es902150g); Scherr & Sthapit, *Mitigating Climate Change Through Food and Land Use*, 2009 (www.ecoagriculture.org/documents/files/WWR179.pdf); Tappendorf, *Climate Change and Land Use, ALI-ABA Land Use Institute*, August 25-28, 2010; Ziegler, *The Case for Megapolitan Growth Management in the 21st Century: Regional Urban Planning and Sustainable Development in the United States*, 41 Urb. Law. 147 (2009); Andriano, *The Power of Wind: Current Legal Issues in Siting for Wind Power*, Planning & Envtl. L., May 2009, at 3; Kozlowski, Note, *Dams and Levees Are Not Enough: The Case for Recognizing a Cause of Action Against Non-Complying NFIP Communities*, 32 Wm. & Mary Envtl. L. & Pol'y Rev. 245-271 (2007); Schach, *Stream Buffer Ordinances: Are Municipalities on the Brink of Protecting the Health of Streams or Opening the Floodgates of Takings Litigation?*, 40 Urb. Law. 73-94 (2008); *Recent Developments in the Law of Standing in Court Cases Challenging Land Use Permits*, 39 Urb. Law. 711–722 (2007); J. Nolan, *Creating a Local Environmental Law Program*, Zoning and Land Use Planning 350 (2007).

Chapter 5

EQUITY ISSUES IN LAND USE: "EXCLUSIONARY ZONING" AND FAIR HOUSING

Scope of Chapter

"Exclusionary zoning" is the use of zoning ordinances, usually by suburban municipalities, to exclude housing that is affordable to lower-income households. It is part of a larger issue of the persistence of discrimination — racial and otherwise — in land use. As a rough generalization, "affordable housing" and other income-related land use issues have been dealt with (if at all) primarily by state courts and legislatures, and other forms of discrimination have been best addressed under federal law although, as you will see, these categories are far from mutually exclusive. Section A will consider these problems of equity in land use from the state law perspective, and then Section B will cover some of the same ground from the federal perspective, and introduce new issues under federal law.

A. EXCLUSIONARY ZONING AND AFFORDABLE HOUSING: STATE LAW

[1.] The Problem

The statement of facts that follows is taken from the first *Mount Laurel* case. It describes the conditions which, collectively, have come to be known as "exclusionary zoning." Various techniques for dealing with the problems described by Justice Hall will be set out later in this chapter. (Some details have been omitted from the statement of the facts without noting each omission separately, and some relevant footnote material has been incorporated into the text.) Keep in mind that townships have been given planning and land use powers by statute.

SOUTHERN BURLINGTON COUNTY NAACP v. TOWNSHIP OF MOUNT LAUREL (I)

67 N.J. 151, 336 A.2d 713 (1975) *appeal dismissed & cert. denied*, 423 U.S. 808 (1975)

Hall, J.

Mount Laurel is a flat, sprawling township, 22 square miles in area, on the west central edge of Burlington County. It is about seven miles from the boundary line of the city of Camden and not more than 10 miles from the Benjamin Franklin Bridge crossing the river to Philadelphia. In 1950, the township had a population of 2817, only about 600 more people than it had in 1940. It was then, as it had been for decades, primarily a rural agricultural area with no sizeable settlements or commercial or industrial enterprises. After 1950, as in so many other municipalities similarly situated, residential development and some commerce and industry began to come in. By 1960 the population had almost doubled to 5249 and by 1970 had more than doubled again to 11,221. These new residents were, of course, "outsiders" from the nearby central cities and older suburbs or from more distant places drawn here by reason of employment in the region. The township is now definitely a part of the outer ring of the South Jersey metropolitan area, which area we define as a semicircle having a radius of 20 miles or so from the heart of Camden city. And 65% of the township is still vacant land or in agricultural use.

The growth of the township has been spurred by the construction or improvement of main highways through or near it. This highway network gives the township a most strategic location from the standpoint of transport of goods and people by truck and private car. There is no other means of transportation. The location and nature of development has been, as usual, controlled by the local zoning enactments. Under the present ordinance, 29.2% of all the land in the township, or 4,121 acres, is zoned for industry. . . . At the time of trial no more than 100 acres were actually occupied by industrial uses. They had been constructed in recent years, mostly in several industrial parks, and involved tax ratables of about 16 million dollars. The rest of the land so zoned has remained undeveloped. If it were fully utilized, the testimony was that about 43,500 industrial jobs would be created, but it appeared clear that, as happens in the case of so many municipalities, much more land has been so zoned than the reasonable potential for industrial movement or expansion warrants. At the same time, however, the land cannot be used for residential development under the general ordinance.

[A small amount of land is zoned for retail business, near the turnpike interchange and in a handful of neighborhood commercial districts. There is no concentrated retail commercial area — "downtown" — in the township.] The balance of the land area, almost 10,000 acres, has been developed until recently in the conventional form of major subdivisions. The general ordinance provides for four residential zones, designated R-1, R-1D, R-2 and R-3. All permit only single-family, detached dwellings, one house per lot — the usual form of grid development. Attached townhouses, apartments (except on farms for agricultural workers) and mobile homes are not allowed anywhere in the township under the general ordinance. The dwellings are substantial; the average value in 1971 was $32,500 and is undoubtedly much higher today.

The general ordinance requirements, while not as restrictive as those in many similar municipalities, nonetheless realistically allow only homes within the financial reach of persons of at least middle income. The R-1 zone requires a minimum lot area of 9,375 square feet, minimum lot width of 75 feet at the building line, and a minimum dwelling floor area of 1,100 square feet if a one-story building and 1,300 square feet if one and one-half stories or higher. Most of the subdivisions have been constructed within it so that only a few hundred acres remain. The R-2 zone, comprising a single district of 141 acres in the northeasterly corner, has been completely developed. While it only required a minimum floor area of 900 square feet for a one-story dwelling, the minimum lot size was 11,000 square feet; otherwise the requisites were the same as in the R-1 zone.

The general ordinance places the remainder of the township, outside of the industrial and commercial zones and the R-1D district (to be mentioned shortly), in the R-3 zone. This zone comprises over 7,000 acres — slightly more than half of the total municipal area — practically all of which is located in the central part of the township extending southeasterly to the apex of the triangle. The testimony was that about 4,600 acres of it then remained available for housing development. Ordinance requirements are substantially higher, however, in that the minimum lot size is increased to about one-half acre (20,000 square feet). (We understand that sewer and water utilities have not generally been installed, but, of course, they can be.) Lot width at the building line must be 100 feet. Minimum dwelling floor area is as in the R-1 zone. Presently this section is primarily in agricultural use; it contains as well most of the municipality's substandard housing.

[The court described the R-1D District, which permitted clustering on smaller lots but with overall low density requirements roughly comparable to the R-3 zone, and the R-4 District, which permitted retirement communities with amenities unaffordable to lower income seniors.]

A variation from conventional development has recently occurred in some parts of Mount Laurel, as in a number of other similar municipalities, by use of the land use regulation device known as "planned unit development" (PUD). . . . While multi-family housing in the form of rental garden, medium rise and high rise apartments and attached townhouses is for the first time provided for, as well as single-family detached dwellings for sale, it is not designed to accommodate and is beyond the financial reach of low and moderate income families, especially those with young children.

A few details will furnish sufficient documentation. . . . The approvals also sharply limit the number of apartments having more than one bedroom. Further, they require that the developer must provide in its leases that no school-age children shall be permitted to occupy any one-bedroom apartment and that no more than two such children shall reside in any two-bedroom unit. . . . In addition, low density, required amenities, such as central air conditioning, and specified developer contributions help to push rents and sales prices to high levels. These contributions include fire apparatus, ambulances, fire houses, and very large sums of money for educational facilities, a cultural center and the township library. . . .

All this affirmative action for the benefit of certain segments of the population is in sharp contrast to the lack of action, and indeed hostility, with respect to affording any opportunity for decent housing for the township's own poor living in substandard accommodations, found largely in the section known as Springville (R-3 zone).The continuous official reaction has been rather a negative policy of waiting for dilapidated premises to be vacated and then forbidding further occupancy. In 1968 a private non-profit association sought to build subsidized, multi-family housing in the Springville section with funds to be granted by a higher level governmental agency. Advance municipal approval of the project was required. The Township Committee responded with a purportedly approving resolution, which found a need for "moderate" income housing in the area, but went on to specify that such housing must be constructed subject to all zoning, planning, building and other applicable ordinances and codes. This meant single-family detached dwellings on 20,000 square foot lots. (Fear was also expressed that such housing would attract low income families from outside the township.) Needless to say, such requirements killed realistic housing for this group of low and moderate income families.

There cannot be the slightest doubt that the reason for this course of conduct has been to keep down local taxes on property (Mount Laurel is not a high tax municipality) and that the policy was carried out without regard for nonfiscal considerations with respect to people, either within or without its boundaries. This policy of land use regulation for a fiscal end derives from New Jersey's tax structure, which has imposed on local real estate most of the cost of municipal and county government and of the primary and secondary education of the municipality's children. The latter expense is much the largest, so, basically, the fewer the school children, the lower the tax rate. Sizeable industrial and commercial ratables are eagerly sought and homes and the lots on which they are situate are required to be large enough, through minimum lot sizes and minimum floor areas, to have substantial value in order to produce greater tax revenues to meet school costs. Large families who cannot afford to buy large houses and must live in cheaper rental accommodations are definitely not wanted, so we find drastic bedroom restrictions for, or complete prohibition of, multi-family or other feasible housing for those of lesser income. One incongruous result is the picture of developing municipalities rendering it impossible for lower paid employees of industries they have eagerly sought and welcomed with open arms (and, in Mount Laurel's case, even some of its own lower paid municipal employees) to live in the community where they work.

[Justice Hall then noted the postwar exodus of population and jobs from the inner cities, such as Camden, and noted that low-income employees could not reach outlying centers of employment and needed cheaper housing than the suburbs provided.]

NOTES AND QUESTIONS

1. *Some history.* The *Mount Laurel* decision emerged as the Warren Court era ended and the U.S. Supreme Court changed directions. The Court held that housing was not a fundamental right, *Lindsey v. Normet*, 405 U.S. 56 (1972), that poverty was not a suspect class, *San Antonio Independent School District v. Rodriguez*, 411 U.S. 1 (1973), and that exclusionary zoning plaintiffs lacked federal standing, *Warth v. Seldin*, 422 U.S. 490 (1975), effectively leaving the zoning issue to the state courts. Nor was New Jersey the early leader. As described in the Note on Exclusionary Zoning in Other States, *infra*, the *National Land* case in Pennsylvania struck down a large-lot zoning ordinance in 1965. New Jersey, by contrast, upheld numerous ordinances with exclusionary features all through the post-war years, culminating in a 1962 decision affirming the total exclusion of mobile homes from a town, *Vickers v. Gloucester Township*, 181 A.2d 129 (N.J. 1962). *Vickers*, however, drew a vigorous dissent from Justice Frederick Hall, who argued that exclusionary zoning failed to serve the "general welfare," by which he meant the welfare of the entire region, and the *Vickers* dissent eventually eclipsed the majority opinion. One noted commentator, Richard Babcock, said that it "should be required reading for every planning student and every member of a municipal plan commission or legislature." The Zoning Game 181 (1966). Several years later, an influential article documented exclusionary zoning practices in the northern New Jersey suburbs. Williams & Norman, *Exclusionary Land Use Controls: The Case of North-Eastern New Jersey*, 22 Syracuse L. Rev. 475, 486–87 (1971). The first *Mount Laurel* decision soon followed.

2. *The Mount Laurel "Doctrine."* After reciting the facts set out above, the New Jersey Supreme Court concluded that the Mount Laurel zoning ordinance was unconstitutional under the New Jersey Constitution. It held that if a "developing community" regulates land uses (as, of course, all developing communities do), it must use its delegated zoning power so as to afford a "realistic opportunity for the construction of its fair share of the present and prospective regional need for low and moderate income housing." The subsequent doctrinal history of the *Mount Laurel* doctrine is considered below. The social history of the *Mount Laurel* litigation itself is engagingly told in D. Kirp et al., Our Town: Race, Housing and the Soul of Suburbia (1995).

3. *Exclusionary zoning and class.* All zoning restrictions have some exclusionary effects. Indeed, the essence of any zoning ordinance is the exclusion of certain uses, densities, and building types from particular districts. But the term "exclusionary zoning" describes local land use controls that exclude most low-income and many moderate-income households from suburban communities and, indirectly, most members of minority groups as well. The generally accepted approach is to define low-income households as earning less than 50% of the regional median income and moderate-income groups as earning between 50–80% of median. To be nonexclusionary, there must be housing opportunities for each group.

In the *Mount Laurel I* opinion, Justice Hall also adverted to the presumptive obligation of municipalities to "make realistically possible an appropriate variety and choice of housing." 336 A.2d 713, 724 (N.J. 1975). In 1983, however, the second *Mount Laurel* case (reproduced *infra*) limited enforcement of the *Mount Laurel* doctrine only to creation of low and moderate income housing opportunities, reasoning that upper and middle income households had at least some opportunities available to them. Had the "variety and choice" phraseology been pursued, would the consequence have been to "open up" individual suburbs to households of all economic strata, including lower middle class households that are priced out of market housing in many municipalities but are not eligible for the housing created under the *Mount Laurel* doctrine? See Fishman, *"Variety and Choice": Another Interpretation of the Mount Laurel Decisions*, 5 J. Plan. Hist. 162 (2006). On the use of zoning and affordability to segregate on the basis of economic class, see Iglesias, *Our Pluralist Housing Ethics and the Struggle for Affordability*, 42 Wake Forest L. Rev. 511, 553–69 (2007); McFarlane, *Redevelopment and the Four Dimensions of Class in Land Use*, 22 J. L. & Politics 33 (2006). Data on increasing class stratification in metropolitan areas is collected and analyzed in J. Booza, J. Cutsinger & G. Galster, Where Did They Go? The Decline of Middle-Income Neighborhoods in Metropolitan America (Brookings Institution 2006) (noting use of inclusionary zoning as a potential solution). See also Lubell, *Zoning to Expand Affordable Housing*, Zoning Practice, Dec. 2006.

4. *Exclusionary zoning and race.* The litigation against Mount Laurel Township was brought on behalf of minority plaintiffs by the NAACP, but Justice Hall does not ever mention race. As will be explored in § B, *infra*, racial discrimination is intimately related to housing discrimination; was Justice Hall's decision to sidestep race "audacious," see C. Haar, Suburbs Under Siege: Race, Space and Audacious Judges 23 (1996), or was it shortsighted? The court undoubtedly thought that its ruling would benefit all poor households, white and non-white alike, while minimizing the chance of a doctrinally unfriendly review in the U.S. Supreme Court. But there are many more poor white households in New Jersey than there are non-white, even though non-white households are disproportionately poor, creating a risk that white families would dominate any remedial efforts, particularly if the number of new affordable units fell far short of the need (as indeed was to be the case). Before too long, the minority community began sounding the alarm. See Holmes, *A Black Perspective on Mount Laurel II: Toward a Black "Fair Share,"* 14 Seton Hall L. Rev. 944 (1984). See also Boger, *Toward Ending Residential Segregation: A Fair Share Proposal for the Next Reconstruction*, 71 N.C. L. Rev. 1573 (1993); Note, *Racial Diversity in Residential Communities: Societal Housing Patterns and a Proposal for a "Racial Inclusionary Ordinance,"* 63 S. Cal. L. Rev. 1151 (1990). In addition, many minority politicians regard the attack on exclusionary zoning as a threat to their hard-won ascendance in urban city halls, seeing a dilution of their constituent base and a diminution of their ability to "bargain" politically for that constituency, as public choice theory would have them do.

Professor Schuck, while agreeing that poor people can individually benefit by moving to the suburbs, criticizes the *Mount Laurel* cases for valuing diversity as an end in itself, rather than as instrumental of other social goals. He commends the voucher-based housing mobility program as a better alternative because it facilitates individual choice rather than imposing government regulation. *Judging Remedies: Judicial Approaches to Housing Segregation*, 37

Harv. C.R.-C.L. L. Rev. 289 (2002); see also Been, *Residential Segregation: Vouchers and Local Government Monopolists*, 23 Yale L. & Pol. Rev. 33 (2005). McUsic, Symposium, *Brown at Fifty: The Future of Brown v. Board of Education: Economic Integration of the Public Schools*, 117 Harv. L. Rev. 1334, 1369–74 (2004), suggests one response to Professor Schuck's criticism. Professor McUsic argues that the economic integration promoted by zoning cases such as *Mount Laurel* might eventually produce the educational benefits that have mostly eluded school integration under *Brown.*

Sources: Rutgers University maintains a compendium of decisions related to *Mount Laurel* at: njlegallib.rutgers.edu/mtlaurel/opinions.php.

A NOTE ON ZONING, REGULATION AND MARKETS

A major premise of the legal campaign against "exclusionary zoning" was that municipalities were misusing their land use regulatory powers to drive up the cost of housing and therefore to exclude poorer families who could not pay market prices. Justice Hall thought that it was virtually self-evident that this was what Mount Laurel Township was doing in the 1960s. Review his description of the Mount Laurel ordinances, *supra.* Do you agree? Which ordinance provisions are exclusionary? Do the same with the various zoning techniques presented in Chapter 3, *supra.*

The cost of housing. For economists, the relationship between housing price and regulation is more complicated. Standing alone, individual land use regulations may have relatively little impact on the cost of housing. The real issue is whether they have a significant exclusionary effect on housing costs when taken together. Unfortunately, the components that determine the price of housing are complex and not well understood, making it difficult to draw unambiguous conclusions. Nonetheless, it is generally assumed that regulation does exert upward pressure on price, and some empirical studies support this conclusion. See, e.g., L. Sagalyn & G. Sternlieb, Zoning and Housing Costs: The Impact of Land Use Controls on Housing Price (Center for Urban Policy Research, Rutgers Univ. 1972); Pollakowski & Wachter, *The Effects of Land-Use Constraints on Housing Prices*, 66 Land Econ. 31 (1990). One commentator has added that exclusionary zoning segregates the tax base into wealthy suburban and poor urban components, and encourages the concentration of poverty. Dietderich, *An Egalitarian's Market: The Economics of Inclusionary Zoning Reclaimed*, 24 Fordham Urb. L.J. 23, 31–33 (1996).

In a widely-noted 2002 paper, economists Edward Glaeser and Joseph Gyourko offered a fresh perspective on these questions. Glaeser & Gyourko, *Zoning's Steep Price*, Regulation, Fall 2002, at 24. (The cited article is an abridged version of a more technical paper, *Building Restrictions on Housing Affordability*, published in the Federal Reserve Bank of New York's Economic Policy Review.) Glaeser and Gyourko posited three components of the cost of housing — actual construction cost, the cost of land, and the cost of compliance with land use regulations. They reasoned that the final cost to a purchaser could not normally be less than the cost of producing the housing unit, and that the more actual sales prices diverged from actual construction costs in a community, the greater the likelihood that high housing prices are caused either by high land prices or by "artificial limits on construction created by the regulation of new housing." *Id.* at 26. Finally, using complex statistical methods, they concluded that variations in land values played a less important role than excessive regulation (including zoning regulations requiring large lots, which increase the land component of the final product) in explaining high home prices.

Applying their model, Glaeser and Gyourko concluded that there was no national affordability "crisis." In much of the country, where housing prices hewed reasonably closely to construction costs, there are households unable to pay the actual economic cost of shelter, but this is a function of their poverty, not of arbitrary inflation of prices, and the solution may well be in poverty-alleviation rather than in zoning reform. Only in parts of the Northeast and on the West Coast did the authors find evidence of "excessive" housing prices where unnecessary regulation might be the culprit and "zoning reform" the solution. Notice, in the material that follows, that most of the legal attention to "exclusionary zoning" is concentrated in New England, the mid-Atlantic states, and the Pacific coast.

Exclusionary zoning and markets. In Chapter 1, we noted briefly that communities may compete with each other to provide different packages of goods and services (at different levels of local taxation), resulting in an efficient pattern of land uses by giving people an opportunity to "shop" for what they value most highly. See Tiebout, *A Pure Theory of Local Expenditures*, 64 J. Pol. Econ. 416 (1956). One possible consequence of this theory, of course, is that housing will be more expensive in some communities than in others. Is "exclusionary zoning" simply an example of the Tiebout hypothesis at work? Or is exclusionary zoning an example of market failure, wherein the delegation of zoning authority to small suburban communities gives them monopoly power to distort an efficient distribution of land uses? For a vigorous argument that exclusionary zoning can be justified neither by the Tiebout hypothesis nor by microeconomic theory in general, see Dietderich, *supra*, at 31–33.

Does zoning give municipalities monopoly power, as Dietderich contends? One study supported a hypothesis that when fiscal community costs are proportional to the density of development, a community does have an incentive to adopt a zoning monopoly. This incentive decreases in jurisdictions where suburban governments are geographically small because no single jurisdiction can capture the benefits of monopoly zoning power. Hamilton, *Zoning and the Exercise of Monopoly Power*, 5 J. Urb. Econ. 116 (1978). Another study found that towns with monopoly power tend to have higher housing prices, but that there is no evidence they used their power to limit the production of new housing. Thorson, *An Examination of the Monopoly Zoning Hypothesis*, 72 Land Econ. 43 (1996). For an argument that price levels for housing in suburbs are a function of the degree of competition in the local housing market and that this is determined by the extent to which the market erects barriers to entry through land use controls, see Landis, *Land Regulation and the Price of New Housing: Lessons From Three California Cities*, 52 J. Am. Plan. Ass'n 9 (1986). Additional discussion of the effect of land use regulation on housing markets can be found in Chapter 8, *infra*.

Redistribution of wealth. Opponents of exclusionary zoning argue that opening up the suburbs is justified because it positively redistributes wealth to the lower-income households that move to suburban areas, for instance, by providing better housing and better schools. An influential statement of the general argument is A. Downs, Opening Up the Suburbs (1973). Metzger bitterly attacked Downs and other advocates of "deconcentration" strategies, however, contending that such policies (and even the advocacy of such policies) hastens the decline of potentially viable urban neighborhoods and worsens the plight of those left behind. He advocates community reinvestment and other neighborhood revitalization strategies. Metzger, *Planned Abandonment: The Neighborhood Life-Cycle Theory and National Urban Policy*, 11 Hous. Pol'y Debate 7 (2000); see also Downs, *Comment on John T. Metzger's "Planned Abandonment: The Neighborhood Life-Cycle Theory and National Urban Policy," id.* at 41 (2000); D. Troutt, *Mount Laurel and Urban Possibility: What Social Science Research Might Tell the Narratives of Futility*, 27 Seton Hall L. Rev. 1471 (1997) (linking

Mount Laurel Doctrine to urban revitalization).

Modern studies consistently find that many fully-employed low-wage households are "cost burdened" with respect to housing, that is, they must allocate more than 30% of their income to shelter. See, e.g., National Housing Conference, Paycheck to Paycheck: Wages and the Cost of Housing in America (2003) (janitors and retail clerks priced out of all 60 large housing markets studied). See Delaney, *Addressing the Workforce Housing Crisis in Maryland and Throughout the Nation: Do Land Use Regulations That Preclude Reasonable Housing Opportunity Based upon Income Violate the Individual Liberties Protected by State Constitutions?*, 33 U. Balt. L. Rev. 153 (2004). On workforce housing, see Urban Land Institute, Workforce Housing, Barriers, Solutions, Model Programs (2004). A separate movement has evolved to address middle income needs. In 2006, for instance, Montgomery County, Maryland, supplemented its pioneering inclusionary zoning program with a Workforce Housing Ordinance. Montgomery County Code, Art. V, § 25B.23 *et seq.*; *id.* § 59-A-6.18.2(a). In addition to moderately priced dwelling units (MPDU), builders must now set aside 10% of larger developments (35 units or more) affordable up to 120% of regional median income. The older MPDU program is described *infra.*

Jobs and housing. The spatial mismatch between jobs and housing has figured prominently in arguments about exclusionary zoning. Early commentators claimed that jobs were in the suburbs, the poor were in the older central cities, public transportation to suburban jobs was nonexistent, and that an end to exclusionary zoning would end these problems. M. Danielson, The Politics of Exclusion 23-24 (1976). See especially Kain, *The Spatial Mismatch Hypothesis: Three Decades Later*, 3 Hous. Pol'y Debate 371 (1994).

Today these issues are much more complicated. Locating jobs close to housing is an important strategy in growth management programs, where it figures as a method of reducing commuting times and traffic congestion and improving air quality. See Chapter 8. One study showed, however, that this strategy may not necessarily have these effects but that affordable housing at higher densities would be attractive to low- to medium-income single-worker households. See Levine, *Rethinking Accessibility and Jobs-Housing Balance*, 65 J. Am. Plan. Ass'n 133 (1998). But see Arnott, *Economic Theory and the Spatial Mismatch Hypothesis*, 35 Urb. Studies 1171 (1998) (questioning theory and assumption that job dispersal to suburbs causes low rates of employment and wages for African-Americans in inner cities).

A. Downs, Still Stuck in Traffic: Coping with Peak-Hour Traffic Congestion 228–44 (2004), concludes that changing the jobs-housing balance could have desirable social benefits, such as housing opportunities for lower-income workers, a better suburban labor pool, and more diverse communities. He argues, however, that political obstacles and individual preferences would make change difficult to achieve, and that insofar as the traffic problem is concerned, policymakers would be better advised to expend their limited political capital on such direct congestion-management strategies as peak-hour road pricing. See also Blumenberg & Manville, *Beyond the Spatial Mismatch: Welfare Recipients and Transportation Policy*, 19 J. Plan'g Lit. 182 (2004). The authors agree that the spatial mismatch hypothesis has merit, but they argue that a more comprehensive approach to the problem of connecting low-income households to jobs is needed. The article contains extensive citations to the spatial mismatch literature. *The Affordability Index: A New Tool for Measuring the True Affordability of a Housing Choice*, published by the Urban Markets Initiative of the Brookings Institution (Jan. 2006), integrates shelter and transportation costs of different neighborhood locations in metropolitan Minneapolis-St. Paul into a single "affordability index" as a policymaking tool.

The study concluded that only central city neighborhoods were "affordable" to low-income families. What policy guidance might be drawn from this conclusion?

The federal role and the Regulatory Barriers Commission. A 1991 Report by an Advisory Commission on Regulatory Barriers to Affordable Housing, *"Not in My Back Yard": Removing Barriers to Affordable Housing*, examined a variety of land use issues and made a number of proposals for reform. The Commission identified growth controls, exclusionary zoning, impact fees, and environmental regulations as among the primary contributors to excessive housing costs. The Removal of Regulatory Barriers to Affordable Housing Act, 42 U.S.C. §§ 12705a-12705d, implements the Commission's recommendations. It provides grants to state and local governments to pursue barrier removal strategies and establishes a Regulatory Barriers Clearinghouse, both as recommended by the Commission. Section 12705b excludes rent controls from the definition of "regulatory barriers." Also excluded are "policies that have served to create or preserve . . . housing for low- and very low-income families, including displacement protections, demolition controls, replacement housing requirements, relocation benefits, housing trust funds, dedicated funding sources, waiver of local property taxes and builder fees, inclusionary zoning, rental zoning overlays, long-term use restrictions, and rights of first refusal." The excluded policies and techniques are ineligible for grant funding under the Act. The Clearinghouse created under the Act, which can be found at: www.regbarriers.org, has proven to be a useful tool for those interested in regulatory reform.

A problem with the regulatory barriers approach, and indeed with many discussions of housing affordability, is the failure to differentiate between barriers that affect the cost of all housing, from luxury to basic, and those barriers that particularly affect low- and moderate-income housing. A hypothetical 20% reduction attributable to the relaxation of regulations might reduce the price of a $500,000 house to $400,000, which would be a boon to the aspiring upper middle class but irrelevant to the poor. Nor will the poor benefit from a 20% reduction in a $150,000 house to $120,000. This is not to say that elimination of wasteful regulation is wrong, but care must be taken not to eliminate useful regulations solely on the appealing argument that low- and moderate-income needs will be served. It is also necessary to balance affordability gains against other policy losses when a regulation is relaxed. Open space preservation may reduce the supply of land and put pressure on prices, for instance, but it is at least a debatable question whether the affordability cost ought to be accepted in light of the environmental gain. In this connection, Professors Glaeser and Gyourko's distinction between an affordability problem and a poverty problem, noted *supra*, is worth recalling.

For a useful collection of papers on the Regulatory Barriers Commission report, see Downs, *The Advisory Commission on Regulatory Barriers to Affordable Housing: Its Behavior and Accomplishments*, 2 Hous. Pol'y Debate 1095 (1991), together with comments by William Fischel, Chester Hartman and Bernard Siegan, *id.* 1139–78. The 1991 Report has been updated: *"Why Not in Our Community?" Removing Barriers to Affordable Housing*, U.S. Dept. of Hous. & Urb. Dev. (2005). Professor Salsich examines affordability and economic segregation problems through the lens of federal policy and recommends new legislation that would "elevat[e] affordable housing for low- and moderate-income households to a level of national concern similar to national policies [such as environmental protection]" and providing for a federal mechanism to override incompatible local laws. Salsich, *Toward a Policy of Heterogeneity: Overcoming a Long History of Socioeconomic Segregation in Housing*, 42 Wake Forest L. Rev. 459, 465 (2007).

G. Knapp et al., *Zoning as a Barrier to Multifamily Housing Development*, American Planning Ass'n, Planning Advisory Serv. Rep. No. 548 (2007), is a report on barriers in several metropolitan areas. The authors conclude, inter alia, that zoning appears to impede the development of high-density housing in some jurisdictions, that no single indicator provides unambiguous evidence of regulatory barriers, that ample high-density and multifamily housing is neither necessary nor sufficient to produce affordable housing, and that this type of housing is not always affordable while low-density housing is not always costly. Some of these conclusions may seem counterintuitive, but should be kept in mind as you read. For instance, as will be discussed *infra*, Pennsylvania requires zoning for different housing "types," including multifamily, but does not address affordability. A New Jersey court, on the other hand, required a municipality to *reduce* the minimum density on a site designated for an "inclusionary" development in order to create a "realistic opportunity" as determined by demand for market-rate housing. *Toll Bros., Inc. v. West Windsor Twp.*, 803 A.2d 53 (N.J. 2002).

Sources. There is an extensive literature on housing affordability. For a comprehensive survey, with extensive citations to the literature, see B. Katz & M. Austin Turner, Rethinking Local Affordable Housing Strategies: Lessons from 70 Years of Policy and Practice (2003). Nguyen, *Does Affordable Housing Detrimentally Affect Property Values? A Review of the Literature*, 20 J. Plan. Lit. 15 (2005), summarizes what is known about neighborhood impacts. T. Iglesias & R. Lento, eds., The Legal Guide to Affordable Housing Development (ABA Sec. on Local Gov't L. 2005), is a succinct and useful practice-oriented guide. *A Place to Call Home? Affordable Housing Issues in America*, 42 Wake Forest L. Rev. No. 2 (2007), is a recent symposium issue devoted to these problems. Market-oriented housing affordability studies, including those critical of growth management and inclusionary zoning mandates, can be found at: reason.org/areas/topic/housing-and-mortgages.

[2.] Redressing Exclusionary Zoning: Different Approaches

The first *Mount Laurel* decision gave no attention to remedies for exclusionary zoning and simply ordered the municipality to comply. In later cases, the court approved weak remedies that inadvertently encouraged municipal intransigence. Finally, in 1980, the court assembled six appeals that presented a full range of remedial issues, heard four full days of oral argument, and then retired to ponder the problem for more than two years before issuing *Mount Laurel II*. The story is told in Payne, *Housing Rights and Remedies: A "Legislative" History of Mount Laurel II*, 14 Seton Hall L. Rev. 889 (1984). The court helpfully supplied its own summary of the key rulings, which is presented here.

SOUTHERN BURLINGTON COUNTY NAACP v. TOWNSHIP OF MOUNT LAUREL (II)

92 N.J. 158, 456 A.2d 390 (1983)

The opinion of the Court was delivered by WILENTZ, C.J.:

This is the return, eight years later, of *Southern Burlington County N.A.A.C.P. v. Township of Mount Laurel (Mount Laurel I)*. We set forth in that case, for the first time, the doctrine requiring that municipalities' land use regulations provide a realistic opportunity for low and moderate income housing. The doctrine has become famous. The *Mount Laurel* case itself threatens to become infamous. After all this time, ten years after the trial court's initial order invalidating its zoning ordinance, Mount Laurel remains afflicted with a blatantly exclusionary ordinance. Papered over with studies, rationalized by hired experts, the ordinance at its core is true to nothing but Mount Laurel's determination to exclude the poor. Mount Laurel is not alone; we believe that there is widespread non-compliance with the constitutional mandate of the original opinion in this case. . . .

This case is accompanied by five others, heard together and decided in this opinion. All involve questions arising from the *Mount Laurel* doctrine. They demonstrate the need to put some steel into that doctrine. The deficiencies in its application range from uncertainty and inconsistency at the trial level to inflexible review criteria at the appellate level. The waste of judicial energy involved at every level is substantial and is matched only by the often needless expenditure of talent on the part of lawyers and experts.

I

. . . .

B. *Constitutional Basis for Mount Laurel and the Judicial Role*

The constitutional basis for the *Mount Laurel* doctrine remains the same. The constitutional power to zone, delegated to the municipalities subject to legislation, is but one portion of the police power and, as such, must be exercised for the general welfare. When the exercise of that power by a municipality affects something as fundamental as housing, the general welfare includes more than the welfare of that municipality and its citizens: it also includes the general welfare — in this case the housing needs — of those residing outside of the municipality but within the region that contributes to the housing demand within the municipality. Municipal land use regulations that conflict with the general welfare thus defined abuse the police power and are unconstitutional. In particular, those regulations that do not provide the requisite opportunity for a fair share of the region's need for low and moderate income housing conflict with the general welfare and violate the state constitutional requirements of substantive due process and equal protection. . . .

It would be useful to remind ourselves that the doctrine does not arise from some theoretical analysis of our Constitution, but rather from underlying concepts of fundamental fairness in the exercise of governmental power. The basis for the constitutional obligation is simple: the State controls the use of land, all of the land. In exercising that control it cannot favor rich over poor. It cannot legislatively set aside dilapidated housing in urban ghettos for the poor and decent housing elsewhere for everyone else. The government that controls this land represents everyone. While the State may not have the ability to eliminate poverty, it cannot use that condition as the basis for imposing further disadvantages. And the same applies to the municipality, to which this control over land has been constitutionally delegated.

The clarity of the constitutional obligation is seen most simply by imagining what this state could be like were this claim never to be recognized and enforced: poor people forever zoned out of substantial areas of the state, not because housing could not be built for them but because they are not wanted; poor people forced to live in urban slums forever not because suburbia, developing rural areas, fully developed residential sections, seashore resorts, and other attractive locations could not accommodate them, but simply because they are not wanted. It is a vision not only at variance with the requirement that the zoning power be used for the general welfare but with all concepts of fundamental fairness and decency that underpin many constitutional obligations. . . .

While *Mount Laurel I* discussed the need for "an appropriate variety and choice of housing," the specific constitutional obligation addressed there, as well as in our opinion here, is that relating to low and moderate income housing. All that we say here concerns that category alone; the doctrine as we interpret it has no present applicability to other kinds of housing. It is obvious that eight years after *Mount Laurel I* the need for satisfaction of this doctrine is greater than ever. Upper and middle income groups may search with increasing difficulty for housing within their means; for low and moderate income people, there is nothing to search for.

C. *Summary of Rulings*

. . . .

The following is a summary of the more significant rulings of these cases:

(1) *Every* municipality's land use regulations should provide a realistic opportunity for decent housing for at least some part of its resident poor who now occupy dilapidated housing. The zoning power is no more abused by keeping out the region's poor than by forcing out the resident poor. In other words, each municipality must provide a realistic opportunity for decent housing for its indigenous poor except where they represent a disproportionately large segment of the population as compared with the rest of the region. This is the case in many of our urban areas.

(2) The existence of a municipal obligation to provide a realistic opportunity for a fair share of the region's present and prospective low and moderate income housing need will no longer be determined by whether or not a municipality is "developing." The obligation extends, instead, to every municipality, any portion of which is designated by the State, through the SDGP [the State Development Guide Plan] as a "growth area." This obligation, imposed as a remedial measure, does not extend to those areas where the SDGP discourages growth — namely, open spaces, rural areas, prime farmland, conservation areas, limited growth areas, parts of the Pinelands and certain Coastal Zone areas. The SDGP represents the conscious determination of the State, through the executive and legislative branches, on how best to plan its future. It appropriately serves as a judicial remedial tool. The obligation to encourage lower income housing, therefore, will hereafter depend on rational long-range land use planning (incorporated into the SDGP) rather than upon the sheer economic forces that have dictated whether a municipality is "developing." Moreover, the fact that a municipality is fully developed does not eliminate this obligation although, obviously, it may affect the extent of the obligation and the timing of its satisfaction. The remedial obligation of municipalities that consist of both "growth areas" and other areas may be reduced based on many factors, as compared to a municipality completely within a "growth area."

There shall be a heavy burden on any party seeking to vary the foregoing remedial consequences of the SDGP designations.

(3) *Mount Laurel* litigation will ordinarily include proof of the municipality's fair share of low and moderate income housing in terms of the number of units needed immediately, as well as the number needed for a reasonable period of time in the future. "Numberless" resolution of the issue based upon a conclusion that the ordinance provides a realistic opportunity for *some* low and moderate income housing will be insufficient. Plaintiffs, however, will still be able to prove a *prima facie* case, without proving the precise fair share of the municipality, by proving that the zoning ordinance is substantially affected by restrictive devices, that proof

creating a presumption that the ordinance is invalid.

The municipal obligation to provide a realistic opportunity for low and moderate income housing is not satisfied by a good faith attempt. The housing opportunity provided must, in fact, be the substantial equivalent of the fair share.

(4) Any future *Mount Laurel* litigation shall be assigned only to those judges selected by the Chief Justice with the approval of the Supreme Court. The initial group shall consist of three judges. . . . Since the same judge will hear and decide all *Mount Laurel* cases within a particular area and only three judges will do so in the entire state, we believe that over time a consistent pattern of regions will emerge. Consistency is more likely as well in determinations of regional housing needs and allocations of fair share to municipalities within the region. . . . While determinations of region and regional housing need will not be conclusive as to any municipality not a party to the litigation, they shall be given presumptive validity in subsequent litigation involving any municipality included in a previously determined region.

(5) The municipal obligation to provide a realistic opportunity for the construction of its fair share of low and moderate income housing may require more than the elimination of unnecessary cost-producing requirements and restrictions. Affirmative governmental devices should be used to make that opportunity realistic, including lower-income density bonuses and mandatory set-asides. Furthermore, the municipality should cooperate with the developer's attempts to obtain federal subsidies. For instance, where federal subsidies depend on the municipality providing certain municipal tax treatment allowed by state statutes for lower income housing, the municipality should make a good faith effort to provide it. Mobile homes may not be prohibited, unless there is solid proof that sound planning in a particular municipality requires such prohibition.

(6) The lower income regional housing need is comprised of both low and moderate income housing. A municipality's fair share should include both in such proportion as reflects consideration of all relevant factors, including the proportion of low and moderate income housing that make up the regional need.

(7) Providing a realistic opportunity for the construction of least-cost housing will satisfy a municipality's *Mount Laurel* obligation if, and only if, it cannot otherwise be satisfied. . . .

(8) Builder's remedies will be afforded to plaintiffs in *Mount Laurel* litigation where appropriate, on a case-by-case basis. Where the plaintiff has acted in good faith, attempted to obtain relief without litigation, and thereafter vindicates the constitutional obligation in *Mount Laurel*-type litigation, ordinarily a builder's remedy will be granted, provided that the proposed project includes an appropriate portion of low and moderate income housing, and provided further that it is located and designed in accordance with sound zoning and planning concepts, including its environmental impact. . . .

We reassure all concerned that *Mount Laurel* is not designed to sweep away all land use restrictions or leave our open spaces and natural resources prey to speculators. Municipalities consisting largely of conservation, agricultural, or environmentally sensitive areas will not be required to grow because of *Mount Laurel.* No forests or small towns need be paved over and covered with high-rise apartments as a result of today's decision.

As for those municipalities that may have to make adjustments in their lifestyles to provide for their fair share of low and moderate income housing, they should remember that they are not being required to provide more than their *fair* share. No one community need be concerned that it will be radically transformed by a deluge of low and moderate income developments. [The court held that trial judges could phase new housing over a period of years to avoid too-rapid change.] Nor should any community conclude that its residents will move to other suburbs as a result of this decision, for those "other suburbs" may very well be required to do their part to provide the same housing. Finally, once a community has satisfied its fair share obligation, the *Mount Laurel* doctrine will not restrict other measures, including large-lot and open area zoning, that would maintain its beauty and communal character.

. . . [A]ny changes brought about by this opinion need not be drastic or destructive. Our scenic and rural areas will remain essentially scenic and rural, and our suburban communities will retain their basic suburban character. But there will be *some* change, as there must be if the constitutional rights of our lower income citizens are ever to be protected. That change will be much less painful for us than the status quo has been for them. . . .

D. *Meeting the Mount Laurel Obligation*

1. Removing Excessive Restrictions and Exactions

In order to meet their *Mount Laurel* obligations, municipalities, at the very least, must remove all municipally created barriers to the construction of their fair share of lower income housing. Thus, to the extent necessary to meet their prospective fair share and provide for their indigenous poor (and, in some cases, a portion of the region's poor), municipalities must remove zoning and subdivision restrictions and exactions that are not necessary to protect health and safety. . . .

2. Using Affirmative Measures

Despite the emphasis in *Mount Laurel I* on the affirmative nature of the fair share obligation, the obligation has been sometimes construed . . . as requiring in effect no more than a theoretical, rather than realistic, opportunity. As noted later, the alleged realistic opportunity for lower income housing in *Mount Laurel II* is provided through three zones owned entirely by three individuals. There is absolutely no assurance that there is anything realistic in this "opportunity": the individuals may, for many different reasons, simply not desire to build lower income housing. They may not want to build any housing at all, they may want to use the land for industry, for business, or just leave it vacant. It was never intended in *Mount Laurel I* that this awesome constitutional obligation, designed to give the poor a fair chance for housing, be satisfied by meaningless amendments to zoning or other ordinances. "Affirmative," in the *Mount Laurel* rule, suggests that the municipality is going to do something, and "realistic opportunity" suggests that what it is going to do will make it realistically possible for lower income housing to be built. Satisfaction of the *Mount Laurel* doctrine cannot depend on the inclination of developers to help the poor. It has to depend on affirmative inducements to make the opportunity real.

It is equally unrealistic, even where the land is owned by a developer eager to build, simply to rezone that land to permit the construction of lower income housing if the construction of other housing is permitted on the same land and the latter is more profitable than lower income housing. One of the new zones in *Mount Laurel* provides a good example. The developer there intends to build housing out of the reach of the lower income group. After creation of the new zone, he still is allowed to build such housing but now has the "opportunity" to build lower income housing to the extent of 10 percent of the units. There is absolutely no reason why he should take advantage of this opportunity if, as seems apparent, his present housing plans will result in a higher profit. There is simply no inducement, no reason, nothing affirmative, that makes this opportunity "realistic." For an opportunity to be "realistic" it must be one that is at least sensible for someone to use.

Therefore, unless removal of restrictive barriers will, without more, afford a realistic opportunity for the construction of the municipality's fair share of the region's lower income housing need, affirmative measures will be required. . . .

(i) Mandatory Set-Asides

[An] effective inclusionary device that municipalities must use if they cannot otherwise meet their fair share obligations is the mandatory set-aside.[1] According to the Department of Community Affairs, as of 1976 there were six municipalities in New Jersey with mandatory set-aside programs, which varied from a requirement that 5 percent of developments in a certain zone be composed of low and moderate income units (Cherry Hill, Camden County) to a requirement that between 15 and 25 percent of all PUDs be reserved for low and moderate income housing (East Windsor, Mercer County). Apparently, judging from [sources] and from responses to our inquiries at oral argument, lower income housing is in fact being built pursuant to these mandatory requirements. . . .

As several commentators have noted, the problem of keeping lower income units available for lower income people over time can be a difficult one. Because a mandatory set-aside program usually requires a developer to sell or rent units at below their full value so that the units can be affordable to lower income people, the owner of the development or the initial tenant or purchaser of the unit may be induced to re-rent or re-sell the unit at its full value.

This problem, which municipalities must address in order to assure that they continue to meet their fair share obligations, can be dealt with in two ways. First, the developer can meet its mandatory quota of lower income units with lower cost housing, such as mobile homes or "no-frills" apartments, which may be affordable by lower income families at close to the units' market value. The other, apparently more common, approach for dealing with the re-sale or re-rent problem is for the municipality to require that re-sale or re-rent prices be kept at lower income levels. . . .

In addition to the mechanisms we have just described, municipalities and trial courts must consider such other affirmative devices as zoning substantial areas for mobile homes and for other types of low cost housing and establishing maximum square footage zones, i.e., zones

---

[1] Mandatory set-asides do not give rise to the legal issues treated in *Property Owners Ass'n of North Bergen v. Township. of North Bergen*, 378 A.2d 25 (N.J. 1977). We held in that case that rent control ordinances that exempted units occupied by senior citizens from future rent increases were confiscatory as to the landlord, unfair as to the tenants, and unconstitutional on both grounds. No one suggests here that units created by mandatory set-asides be exempt thereafter from rent increases under a rent control ordinance. Such increases, one aspect of an inflationary economy, generally parallel increases in the median income of lower income families. They would not ordinarily result in rentals beyond the lower income range. As for confiscation, the builder who undertakes a project that includes a mandatory set-aside voluntarily assumes the financial burden, if there is any, of that condition. There may very well be no "subsidy" in the sense of either the landlord or other tenants bearing some burden for the benefit of the lower income units: those units may be priced low not because someone else is subsidizing the price, but because of realistic considerations of cost, amenities, and therefore underlying values.

where developers cannot build units with more than a certain footage or build anything other than lower income housing or housing that includes a specified portion of lower income housing. In some cases, a realistic opportunity to provide the municipality's fair share may require over-zoning, i.e., zoning to allow for more than the fair share if it is likely, as it usually is, that not all of the property made available for lower income housing will actually result in such housing.

Although several of the defendants concede that simply removing restrictions and exactions is unlikely to result in the construction of lower income housing, they maintain that requiring the municipality to use affirmative measures is beyond the scope of the courts' authority. We disagree. . . . The contention that generally these devices are beyond the municipal power because they are "socio-economic" is particularly inappropriate. The very basis for the constitutional obligation underlying *Mount Laurel* is a belief, fundamental, that excluding a class of citizens from housing on an economic basis (one that substantially corresponds to a socio-economic basis) distinctly disserves the general welfare. That premise is essential to the conclusion that such zoning ordinances are an abuse of the zoning power and are therefore unconstitutional.

E. *Judicial Remedies*

If a trial court determines that a municipality has not met its *Mount Laurel* obligation, it shall order the municipality to revise its zoning ordinance within a set time period to comply with the constitutional mandate; if the municipality fails adequately to revise its ordinance within that time, the court shall implement the remedies for noncompliance outlined below; and if plaintiff is a developer, the court shall determine whether a builder's remedy should be granted.

1. Builder's Remedy

Builder's remedies have been one of many controversial aspects of the *Mount Laurel* doctrine. Plaintiffs, particularly plaintiff-developers, maintain that these remedies are (i) essential to maintain a significant level of *Mount Laurel* litigation, and the only effective method to date of enforcing compliance; (ii) required by principles of fairness to compensate developers who have invested substantial time and resources in pursuing such litigation; and (iii) the most likely means of ensuring that lower income housing is actually built. Defendant municipalities contend that even if a plaintiff-developer obtains a judgment that a particular municipality has not complied with *Mount Laurel*, that municipality, and not the developer, should be allowed to determine how and where its fair share obligation will be met.

. . . We hold that where a developer succeeds in *Mount Laurel* litigation and proposes a project providing a substantial amount of lower income housing, a builder's remedy should be granted unless the municipality establishes that because of environmental or other substantial planning concerns, the plaintiff's proposed project is clearly contrary to sound land use planning. We emphasize that the builder's remedy should not be denied solely because the municipality prefers some other location for lower income housing, even if it is in fact a better site. Nor is it essential that considerable funds be invested or that the litigation be intensive.

Other problems concerning builder's remedies require discussion. Care must be taken to make certain that *Mount Laurel* is not used as an unintended bargaining chip in a builder's negotiations with the municipality, and that the courts not be used as the enforcer for the builder's threat to bring *Mount Laurel* litigation if municipal approvals for projects containing no lower income housing are not forthcoming. Proof of such threats shall be sufficient to defeat *Mount Laurel* litigation by that developer.

NOTES AND QUESTIONS

1. *Remedies. Mount Laurel II* is a case about remedies. The two most important (and controversial) remedies embraced by the court are "inclusionary zoning" and the "builder's remedy." Inclusionary zoning is explored later in this section. The builder's remedy, which Charles Haar described as "one of the court's bolder and most politically savvy moves," Haar, Suburbs Under Siege: Race, Space and Audacious Judges 44–45 (1996), was especially bold because, as noted in Chapter 3, *supra*, courts do not usually give specific relief in zoning cases. The builder's remedy was heavily used after *Mount Laurel II*. See Mallach, *The Tortured Reality of Suburban Exclusion: Zoning, Economics and the Future of the Berenson Decision*, 4 Pace Envtl. L. Rev. 37, 119 (1986) (more than 100 builders suits against 70 New Jersey municipalities between 1983 and 1986).

Builders' remedies turned out to be a double-edged sword, however. The flood of lawsuits noted by Mallach resulted in much new affordable housing, but the pre-emptive approvals the builder-plaintiffs claimed, and their inevitable preference to build "inclusionary" developments, raised public concern about "sprawl" and environmental degradation, despite *Mount Laurel II*'s insistence on sound planning criteria. See Payne, *Book Review: Lawyers, Judges and the Public Interest*, 96 Mich. L. Rev. 1685, 1691-1702 (1998). These concerns fueled public and political opposition to *Mount Laurel*. The New Jersey Fair Housing Act, discussed *infra*, sought to replace the builder's remedy with incentives for voluntary municipal compliance, but in practice, municipalities complied "voluntarily" only when they thought themselves susceptible to builders' litigation.

2. *Regional need and fair share. Mount Laurel I* had offered virtually no guidance on how to determine regional need or fair share, and two years later, in *Oakwood at Madison v. Madison Township*, 371 A.2d 1192 (N.J. 1977), the court approved a "numberless" approach, leaving litigants to slug it out in endless trial proceedings. To "put some steel" into the *Mount Laurel* doctrine, *Mount Laurel II* reversed course and required the three specially appointed trial judges to develop an objective methodology that would result in each municipality knowing, in advance of litigation, exactly what its presumptive fair share number was. See *AMG Realty Co. v. Warren Township*, 504 A.2d 692 (N.J.L. Div. 1984), defining housing regions, accepting an estimate of present and prospective housing need, and approving a fair share allocation formula. Can you glean from the *Mount Laurel I* and *II* opinions what the components of a fair share formula should be? Is a formula capable of incorporating considerations such as the "suitability" of the municipality for lower income housing, as the plaintiff's expert argued in *Mount Laurel II*?

3. *The State Development Guide Plan (SDGP).* Another of *Mount Laurel II*'s bold innovations was to rescue from obscurity a document called the State Development Guide Plan and use it as the basis for allocating fair share obligations. In 1986, the legislature mandated the creation of a completely new State Development and Redevelopment Plan (SDRP), described *infra*, which has now replaced the older plan as a guide for *Mount Laurel* allocations. The SDRP was last updated in 2001, and, as of 2010, was undergoing a revision. It may be downloaded at: www.state.nj.us/dca/divisions/osg/plan/

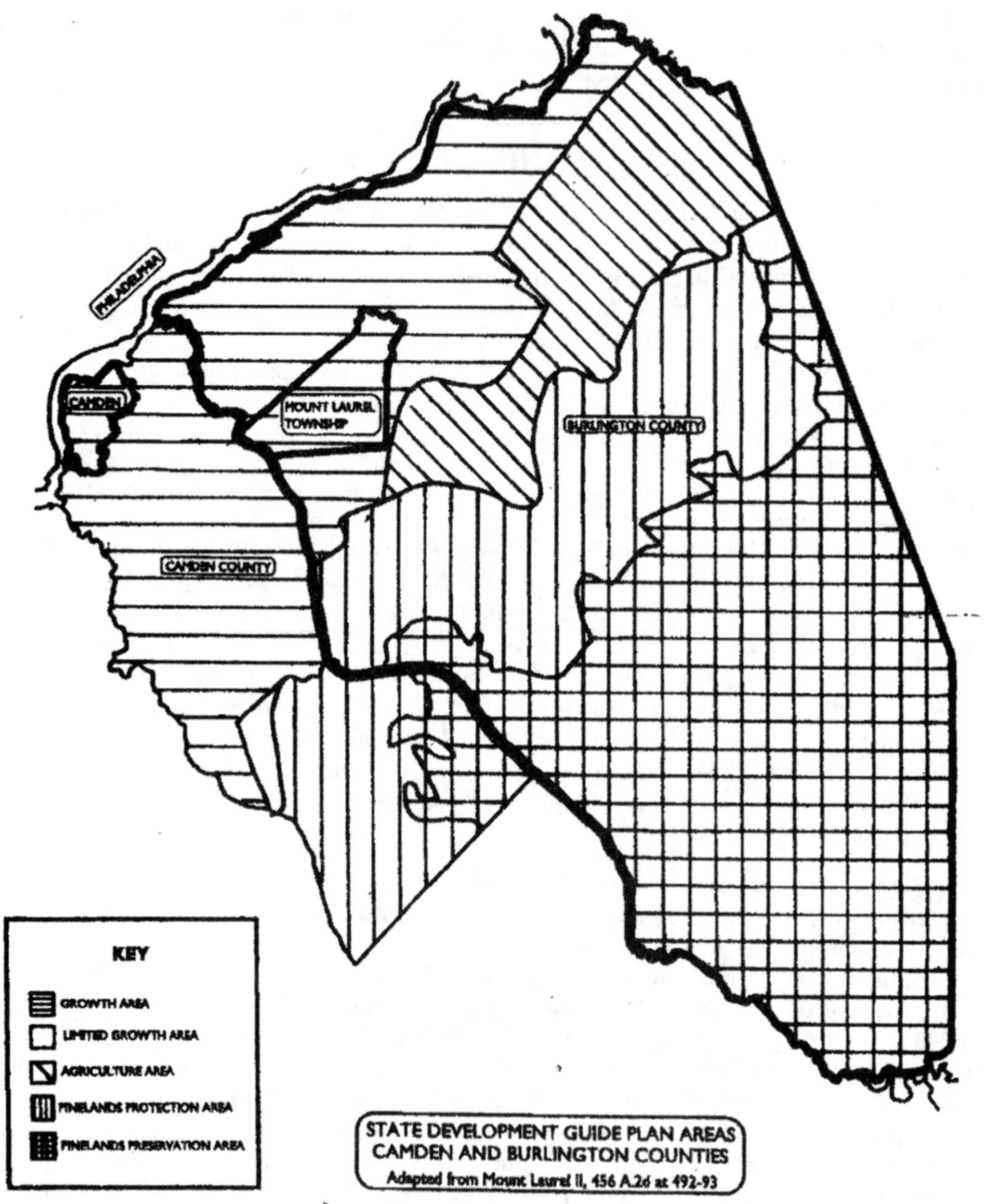

4. *Presumption of validity.* As we have seen elsewhere, courts normally give substantial deference to governmental decision making in land use matters. See, e.g., *Krause v. Royal Oak*, reproduced *supra* in Chapter 3. This is what the *Mount Laurel II* court had to say about the presumption of validity:

> Mount Laurel's actions in this matter, . . . require a modification of the rule that attaches presumptive validity to municipal ordinances. Its actions not only make such a presumption inappropriate, but, given the importance of the constitutional obliga-

tion, require just the reverse, namely, that the burden be cast on Mount Laurel to prove that its ordinances are valid. [456 A.2d at 422.]

A municipality's ordinance can be found to be presumptively invalid on either of two grounds: that the municipality, *in fact*, has not met its fair share obligation; or that the ordinance, on its face, contains features preventing or discouraging the creation of low and moderate income housing. The municipality must satisfy a "heavy burden" to overcome the presumption.

challenge to ordinane

5. *Following New Jersey's lead.* The *Mount Laurel II* opinion is a leading case without a following. New Hampshire came closer than any other state, in *Britton v. Town of Chester*, 595 A.2d 492 (1991), but ultimately it stopped short. The court held that Chester's ordinance was exclusionary, relying in part on *Mount Laurel I*, but without delineation of housing regions, explicit rejection of a numerical fair share, and on statutory rather than constitutional grounds. It permitted a "builder's remedy," following a conventional rule followed in some other states, rather than the expansive remedy announced in *Mount Laurel II*. *Britton* has been followed. *Community Resources for Justice, Inc. v. City of Manchester*, 949 A.2d 681 (N.H. 2008) (holding that trial court properly awarded a builder's remedy to plaintiff, which successfully challenged a zoning ordinance that prevented it from operating a halfway house for federal prisoners). See the discussion of zoning remedies in Chapter 3, *supra*. Payne, *From the Courts: Exclusionary Zoning and the "Chester Doctrine,"* 20 Real Est. L.J. 366, 370–72 (1992), argues that *Chester* may be an astute repackaging of *Mount Laurel*, noting that the court relied on an existing state plan that assigned the town a "fair share" of 90 lower-income units. See Blaesser et al., *Advocating Affordable Housing in New Hampshire*, 40 Wash. U. J. Urb. & Contemp. L. 3, 20 n.50 (1991).

6. *Standing to sue.* New Jersey has taken a liberal approach to standing to sue, relying in part on a statute granting standing in land use cases to nonresidents, N.J. Stat. Ann. § 40:55D-4. The court has at various times granted standing to a trade organization; "the public," represented by the New Jersey Public Advocate; and several advocacy organizations. It found they had "a sufficient stake and real adversariness" to achieve "individual justice, along with the public interest," without "procedural frustrations." See, e.g., *Home Bldrs. League v. Township of Berlin*, 405 A.2d 381, 384 (N.J. 1979); *Urban League v. Mayor & Council*, 359 A.2d 526 (N.J. Ch. Div. 1977); *Urban League v. Township of Mahwah*, 370 A.2d 521 (N.J. App. Div. 1977). New York has also granted standing to a wide variety of individuals and groups. See *Suffolk Hous. Serv. v. Town of Brookhaven*, 397 N.Y.S.2d 302 (Sup. Ct.), *aff'd as modified*, 405 N.Y.S.2d 302 (App. Div. 1978).

7. *Achieving fair share.* If a municipality achieves its fair share of affordable housing, that is no guarantee that it need not accept any more. In *Homes of Hope, Inc. v. Eastampton Tp. Land Use Planning Bd.*, 976 A.2d 1128 (N.J. App. Div. 2009), an appeals court held that a municipality's compliance with the Fair Housing Act (FHA) by meeting its fair share obligation does not impact affordable housing's inherently beneficial use status — a provision in the state's municipal land use law that is a positive criterion for a variance — for purposes of obtaining a use variance under N.J. Stat. Ann. § 40:55D-70(d)(2). Because affordable housing is an inherently beneficial use under state law and because the state's public policy "has long been that persons with low and moderate incomes are entitled to affordable housing," even if the fair share obligation has been satisfied, there may still be a need for affordable housing. 976 A.2d at 1132. Compare with *Zoning Bd. of Appeals of Canton v. Housing Appeals Committee*, 923 N.E.2d 114 (Mass. App. 2010), *review denied*, 928 N.E.2d 950 (Mass. 2010), discussed *infra*.

Do you agree with the reasoning in these cases? If the numbers are guidelines rather than absolute upper limits, why have them?

For an appraisal of progress under *Mount Laurel II* from a symposium at Princeton University, see *Mount Laurel II* at 25: The Unfinished Agenda of Fair Share Housing (T.N. Castano & D. Sattin, eds., 2008), available at: wws.princeton.edu/research/prior-publications/conference-books/mt-laurel-complete-final.pdf

A NOTE ON POLICY AND PLANNING ISSUES

The constitutional basis for Mount Laurel II. Art. I, par. 1, of the New Jersey Constitution, in language similar to most state constitutions, provides that "All persons are by nature free and independent, and have certain natural and unalienable rights, among which are those of enjoying and defending life and liberty, *of acquiring, possessing, and protecting property*, and of pursuing and obtaining safety and happiness." (Emphasis added.) The *Mount Laurel I* court reasoned that this provision guarantees substantive due process and equal protection of the laws, and operates as a restriction on the police power of the state to legislate.

Reread the "Constitutional Basis" section of *Mount Laurel II, supra.* Does the court adequately explain its major shift from the passive remedies of *Mount Laurel I* to the mandatory use of inclusionary zoning? Professor Payne has suggested three justifications for the shift: that affirmative remedies were necessary to undo past discrimination, that the state's monopoly over control of land imposes an obligation of fairness on it, and that individuals have a "right to shelter" that gives them a claim to public assistance. See Payne, *Reconstructing the Constitutional Theory of Mount Laurel II*, 3 Wash. U. J.L. & Policy 555 (2000). The first justification is inconsistent with the requirement that *all* municipalities implement the *Mount Laurel* doctrine, the second is plausible but doesn't distinguish land use controls from the many other fields in which regulation interferes with the private market, leaving the third, which adequately explains the case even if it flies in the face of conventional wisdom about social welfare rights.

The state plan. Mount Laurel II's reliance on the State Development Guide Plan not only solved a judicial process problem (how to choose appropriate sites for compliance without making "legislative" decisions), but it also served to underscore the court's insistence that providing affordable housing opportunities was consistent with principles of sound planning. The Guide Plan, however, had not been written with the *Mount Laurel* doctrine in mind and, primarily in response to the *Mount Laurel II* decision, the legislature adopted a State Planning Act authorizing a State Planning Commission to prepare a new State Development and Redevelopment Plan (SDRP). N.J. Stat. Ann. §§ 52:18A-196 to 52:18A-207. The Plan is required to provide a coordinated, integrated and comprehensive strategy for the growth, development, renewal and conservation of the state and its regions, identifying areas for growth, agriculture, open space conservation and other appropriate designations. § 52:18A-199(a). The SDRP, initially adopted in the early 1990s after an extensive "cross acceptance" process of negotiation with local communities and since revised, adopts a weak form of Oregon's growth boundary approach, see Chapter 8, *infra*, by encouraging higher density growth where development and infrastructure already exist and setting aside extensive agricultural and conservation areas, but also permitting new centers of compact growth in rural areas. How are these policies, if followed (compliance with the Plan is not mandatory), likely to affect the *Mount Laurel* process, which has relied so heavily on large-scale inclusionary developments?

A role for the state? Does the new emphasis on state and regional planning described above have implications for the *Mount Laurel* obligation of the state itself, as opposed to individual municipalities? The "general welfare" concept on which the *Mount Laurel* doctrine rests applies not just to local governments but to other units of government including the state itself. Shortly after the decision in *Mount Laurel II*, the state agency responsible for regulating coastal development in New Jersey imposed an inclusionary set aside in approving a large building project, and this was upheld by the Supreme Court. *In re Egg Harbor Associates (Bayshore Centre)*, 464 A.2d 1115 (N.J. 1983). After that, however, *Mount Laurel* law developed solely in the context of local compliance, but this may be changing. In *In the Matter of Adoption of N.J.A.C. 19:3*, 922 A.2d 852, 858 (N.J. App. Div. 2007), the court "perceive[d] no sound basis for concluding that when, as here, the State entrusts one of its agencies [the Meadowlands Development Commission] with complete control over the planning and zoning of a vast amount of land, approximately 21,000 acres, the agency is free to exercise its authority without taking affirmative steps to ensure adequate affordable housing." How would *Mount Laurel* compliance differ at the state level from the rules and techniques that have been applied to municipalities? See Payne, *Fairly Sharing Affordable Housing Obligations: The Mount Laurel Matrix*, 22 W. N.E. L. Rev. 365 (2001). See also *In re Adoption of the 2003 Low Income Housing Tax Credit Qualified Allocation Plan*, 848 A.2d 1 (N.J. App. Div. 2004) ("consistency" with *Mount Laurel* required of state agency allocating tax credits).

Sources. Additional commentary on *Mount Laurel II* includes Anglin, *Searching for Justice: Court-Inspired Housing Policy as a Mechanism for Social and Economic Mobility*, 29 Urb. Aff. Quarterly 432 (1994) (negative appraisal); *Mount Laurel Housing Symposium*, 27 Seton Hall L. Rev. 1268 (1997); Patrick, Gilbert & Wheeler, *Trading the Poor: Intermunicipal Housing Negotiation in New Jersey*, 2 Harv. Negotiation L. Rev. 1 (1997); Symposium, *Twists in the Path from Mount Laurel*, 30 B.C. Envtl. Aff. L. Rev. No.3 (2003); Note, *Promoting the General Welfare: After Nearly Thirty Years of Influence, Has The Mount Laurel Doctrine Changed the Way New Jersey Citizens Live?* 3 Geo. J.L. & Pub. Pol'y 295 (2005); Note, *Special Masters in State Court Complex Litigation: An Available and Underused Case Management Tool*, 31 Wm. Mitchell L. Rev. 1299 (2005) (role of special masters). Barron, *Reclaiming Home Rule*, 116 Harv. L. Rev. 2255 (2003), places exclusionary and inclusionary zoning within the broader context of local government theory. For an appraisal of progress under *Mount Laurel II* from a symposium at Princeton University, see *Mount Laurel II* at 25: The Unfinished Agenda of Fair Share Housing (T.N. Castano & D. Sattin, eds., 2008), *available at:* wws.princeton.edu/research/prior-publications/conference-books/mt-laurel-complete-final.pdf

A NOTE ON EXCLUSIONARY ZONING DECISIONS IN OTHER STATES

Pennsylvania. Nationally, the first significant limitation on exclusionary land use practices came in *National Land & Investment Co., Inc. v. Kohn*, 215 A.2d 597 (Pa. 1965), which held invalid a four-acre minimum lot size requirement. See also *Appeal of the Township of Concord*, 268 A.2d 765 (Pa. 1970) (same, 2-3 acre zoning). Five years later, the same court held in *Appeal of Girsh*, 263 A.2d 395 (Pa. 1970), that every municipality must zone at least some of its land for multi-family dwellings. In the middle 1970s, the Pennsylvania Supreme Court seemed to be aligning itself with the "fair share" approach to lower income housing that was evolving next door in New Jersey, see *Township of Willistown v. Chesterdale Farms*, 341 A.2d 466 (Pa. 1975), but in *Surrick v. Zoning Hearing Board*, 382 A.2d 105 (Pa. 1977), the court reduced any "fair share" concept to the status of a non-binding "general precept."

Finally, in *BAC, Inc. v. Millcreek Township*, 633 A.2d 144 (Pa. 1993), the court held that only restrictions on uses of property, not classes of people, were covered by the Pennsylvania rules. It concluded that the unmet needs of lower-income households in the community were irrelevant to whether adequate provision for mobile homes had been made. The *BAC* case would seem to erode the modest holding of *Fernley v. Board of Supervisors*, 502 A.2d 585 (Pa. 1985), which held invalid a total exclusion of multi-family housing, placing it squarely on "use" rather than "user" grounds. For an evaluation of the Pennsylvania cases prior to *Fernley* that questions the simplicity of the Pennsylvania rules, see Hyson, *Pennsylvania Exclusionary Zoning Law: A Simple Alternative to Mount Laurel II?* Land Use L. & Zoning Dig., Sept. 1984, at 3. See also Comment: *Anti-Exclusionary Zoning in Pennsylvania: A Weapon for Developers, A Loss for Low-Income Pennsylvanians*, 80 Temp. L. Rev. 1271 (2007).

New York. In 1975, the same year as New Jersey's *Mount Laurel I* and Pennsylvania's *Williston* decisions, New York jumped into the fray with *Berenson v. Town of New Castle*, 341 N.E.2d 236 (N.Y. 1975), involving a total exclusion of multiple dwelling units. Denying the Town's motion for summary judgment, the Court of Appeals established a two-part test that the municipality would have to satisfy in order to prevail:

> The first branch of the test, then, is simply whether the board has provided a properly balanced and well ordered plan for the community. . . . Secondly, in enacting a zoning ordinance, consideration must be given to regional needs and requirements. . . . [New Castle may have enough multi-family units to satisfy its present and future population, but] residents of [surrounding] Westchester County, as well as the larger New York City metropolitan region, may be searching for multiple-family housing in the area to be near their employment or for a variety of other social and economic reasons. There must be a balancing of the local desire to maintain the status quo within the community and the greater public interest that regional needs be met. [*Id.* at 249.]

Although the New York court has never expressly repudiated the more adventurous implications of *Berenson*, neither has it found an opportunity to pursue them. The *New Castle* case itself was resolved without building low income housing. See *Blitz v. Town of New Castle*, 463 N.Y.S.2d 832 (1983). See also *Continental Bldg. Co. v. Town of North Salem*, 625 N.Y.S.2d 700 (1995) (ordinance failed *Berenson* test). Subsequently, in *Suffolk Housing Services v. Town of Brookhaven*, 511 N.E.2d 67 (N.Y. 1987), brought by a low-income advocacy organization specifically to test the implications of *Berenson*, the Court of Appeals denied relief, emphasizing that no identified lower-income households had been shown to have been denied housing, and expressing concern that to order a broad rezoning of the Town would be to invade the province of the legislature. In effect, the court limited *Berenson* to site-specific challenges brought by developers. See also *Asian Americans for Equality v. Koch*, 527 N.E.2d 265 (N.Y. 1988) (no *Berenson* issue in claim that a special New York City zoning district adopted for Chinatown would displace lower-income housing, because lower-income housing was available elsewhere in the entire city). For a contemporaneous comment on the New York cases, see Mallach, *The Tortured Reality of Suburban Exclusion: Zoning, Economics and the Future of the Berenson Doctrine*, 4 Pace Envtl. L. Rev. 37 (1986); see also Nolon, *A Comparative*

Analysis of New Jersey's Mount Laurel Cases with the Berenson Cases in New York, 4 Pace Env. L. Rev. 3 (1986).

The New York Supreme Court, Appellate Division, has held that new zoning restrictions, enacted pursuant to the comprehensive plan and two local laws, which eliminated the multifamily (RM-1) zoning district, constituted exclusionary zoning. *In re Land Master Montg I, LLC v. Town of Montgomery*, 862 N.Y.S.2d 292 (App. Div. 2008). See the trial court case at 821 N.Y.S.2d 432 (N.Y. 2006) for more details of the litigation.

A Pennsylvania appeals court has upheld a zoning ordinance's two-acre minimum lot restriction, finding it rationally related to an open space purpose and, thus, was not invalid. The challenge was brought under the curative amendment provisions in the Pennsylvania Municipalities Planning Code (MPC) (53 P.S. §§ 10609.1, 10916.1) and involved a community some 20 miles from Philadelphia. The court noted that the MPC permits density restrictions, and no minimum acreage requirement has been found to be per se unconstitutional. The court applied a three-part test used by the Pennsylvania courts in deciding whether an ordinance is exclusionary: (1) whether the community in question is a logical area for population growth and development; (2) if the community is in the path of growth, the present level of development; and (3) if the community is in the path of growth but is not already highly developed, whether the ordinance has the practical effect of unlawfully excluding the legitimate use in question. Here the court record and the provisions of the ordinance itself did not support a finding that the ordinance was exclusionary. *Keinath v. Twp. of Edgmont*, 964 A.2d 458 (Pa. Commw. 2009).

Resources: For an examination using both qualitative and quantitative techniques of how communities, through restrictive zoning policies, limit the supply of multifamily housing, a major source of affordable housing, see G. Knaap et al., Zoning as a Barrier to Multifamily Housing Development, American Planning Ass'n Planning Advisory Serv. Rep. No. 548 (2007), *available at:* www.huduser.org/Publications/pdf/zoning._MultifmlyDev.pdf; *see also* NAHB Research Center, *Study of Subdivision Requirements as Regulatory Barrier* (2007), *available at* www.huduser.org/Publications/pdf/subdiv_report.pdf; for an analysis of regulatory barriers in a Florida county, see Casella & Meck, *Removing Regulatory Barriers to Affordable Housing in Development Standards, Density Bonuses, and the Processing of Permits in Hillsborough County, Florida*, 11 Cityscape No. 2, 61-82 (2009), *available at:* www.huduser.org/portal/periodicals/cityscpe/vol11num2/ch3.pdf.

[3.] Affordable Housing Legislation

The *Mount Laurel* doctrine has been highly controversial in New Jersey, in part because of a widespread perception that it was inappropriate for the courts to "intrude" into legislative policy matters. See Kirp et al., *supra*, at 123-25. It is no surprise, therefore, that the few states that have addressed affordable housing issues directly have done so through legislation rather than litigation. As you consider the legislative responses described below, ask yourself whether they are likely to be more or less effective than the *Mount Laurel* approach. See generally Note, *Democratizing the American Dream: The Role of a Regional Housing Legislature in the Production of Affordable Housing*, 37 U. Mich. J.L. Ref. 599 (2004).

An empirical study published by the Lincoln Institute of Land Policy, Ingram et al., *Smart Growth Policies: An Evaluation of Programs and Outcomes* (2007), *available at* www.lincolninst.edu/pubs/smart-growth-policies.aspx, examined, among other areas, the impact of state smart growth programs on housing affordability for the period 1990-2000. The study compared Florida, New Jersey, Maryland and Oregon against Colorado, Indiana, Texas and Virginia. The specific indicator for affordability (or its lack thereof) is the share of households in a community whose housing cost burden exceeds 30% of household income, and how that share changed over the decade by each county (i.e., if the figure is 10% in 1990 and 15% in 2000, then the affordability problem is worsening). The study noted:

> Statistical regressions were used to analyze the determinant of change in the shares of cost-burdened owners and renters. . . . Smart growth programs were associated with increased shares of cost-burdened households. Additional regressions that allowed each state to have an independent effect found that the shares of the cost-burdened owners and renters increased the most in Oregon and the least in Texas. But New Jersey and Florida — smart growth states that both require affordable housing elements in local plans — performed better than Oregon and Maryland for owners, and better than Oregon, Maryland, Virginia, and Colorado for renters. [*Id.* at 142–143.]

Elected legislatures have the authority to address policy issues much more freely and flexibly than do courts. It follows that affordable housing legislation can range far and wide into areas that courts can address, if at all, only in reaction to some initiative that the political branches have taken first. We summarize some of these legislative initiatives in this section. These initiatives break down, roughly speaking, into procedural and substantive approaches, but as is always the case with this particular classification, the categories are far from mutually exclusive. We begin with discussion of the broad decision making structures that legislatures have erected to deal with affordable housing issues, borrowing the American Planning Association's classification of these processes as the "top down," "bottom up," and "appeals board" approaches. Following this is an inventory of various substantive programs and tools that legislatures have at their command to see that affordable housing is actually produced.

[a.] Decision Making Structures

A NOTE ON STATE AND LOCAL APPROACHES TO PLANNING FOR AFFORDABLE HOUSING NEEDS

The "housing element" of local comprehensive plans. All fifty states authorize local planning, but almost half (24) do so only in weak language derived from the Standard City Planning Enabling Act of the 1920s. Of the 26 states that have modernized their planning statutes at least to some degree, 25 have legislation requiring a housing element in the local comprehensive plan. See, e.g., Conn. Gen. Stat. § 8-23; Fla. Stat. Ann. § 163.3177(6); N.Y. Town Law § 277-a(3)(h); R.I. Gen. Laws § 45-22.2-6(C); Vt. Stat. Ann. tit. 24, § 4302(C)(11). Some of these statutes are brief and may only require provision for the housing needs of the municipality's own residents. See the Rhode Island planning law reproduced *supra* in Chapter 1. The state statutes are collected and analyzed in American Planning Association, Growing Smart Legislative Guidebook: Model Statutes for Planning and Management of Change pp. 7-277 through 7-281 and Table 7-5 (S. Meck, gen. ed., 2002).

Professor Mandelker has described the role of the housing element of a comprehensive plan, with particular reference to the *Mount Laurel* cases, which he describes as a "preemptive strike" on the *process* of planning:

> [T]he comprehensive plan is the overall guide to zoning and the development of land within a community. It provides general policies for carrying out development in a community and balances different needs within the community against each other: the need for housing, the need for environmental protection, the need for growth, and, in some cases, the need for restriction. . . . [S]tatutes always require what we call "elements" to be included in the comprehensive plan document. All states require a land use element and a transportation element. The housing element is a newer idea. . . . What is different about the housing element, as compared with the other comprehensive plan elements, is that the other elements the statutes prescribe must include a policy on a particular issue, such as transportation, but the statute does not tell municipalities what that policy should be. The housing element tells municipalities what their housing policy should be, and so it is what we call a "substantive planning element" and not an element that simply requires a planning process. For that reason, there can be a conflict between what the housing element requires for housing and what the rest of the comprehensive plan requires for other problems in the community. [Mandelker, *The Affordable Housing Element in Comprehensive Plans*, 30 B.C. Envtl. Aff. L. Rev. 555, 557–58 (2003).]

He argues that the housing element of a comprehensive plan should not be "one dimensional," but rather part of an overall planning strategy that "balances competing needs within a community properly." *Id.* at 564. How well do the statutory approaches described below measure up?

State and regional housing plans. The Growing Smart Legislative Guidebook, *supra*, points out that housing elements in local plans often work best in conjunction with state or regional housing plans. Professor Salsich explains:

> State planning programs that fully assess housing trends and needs on a broader base than local plans are critical components of an effective national housing strategy. Housing markets vary from state to state, as well as within areas of particular states. Because of the dynamics of these markets, assessments of housing needs tend to be more accurate if they are made from a perspective that is broader than a local perspective but narrower than a national one. [Salsich, *Urban Housing: A Strategic Role for the States*, 12 Yale L. & Policy Rev. 93 (1994).]

For a description of state housing plans, see Growing Smart Legislative Guidebook, *supra*, 4-59 to 4-60; for regional plans, see *id.*, at 6-61. Housing elements in comprehensive plans are especially helpful in states that require land use controls to be consistent with the comprehensive plan. Cf. *Low Income Housing Inst. v. City of Lakewood*, 77 P.3d 653 (Wash. App. 2003) (consistency with state housing goals). For an imaginative proposal that addresses the tension between statewide housing policies and local control of the land use regulatory process, see Iglesias, *Housing Impact Assessments: Opening New Doors for State Housing Regulation While Localism Persists*, 82 Ore. L. Rev. 433 (2003). Housing elements are also used in conjunction with Housing Appeals Board processes, discussed, *infra* § (d).

The American Planning Association's Model Act, Growing Smart Legislative Guidebook: Model Statues for Planning and Management of Change § 4-208, (S. Meck, gen. ed., 2002), presents two alternative approaches to implementing a statewide affordable housing strategy. One of its two models is based on the New Jersey Fair Housing Act, but with the significant modification that under the model act, the Council would have both its own enforcement power and the power to enforce its orders through the courts. The second model is a variant on the housing appeals board procedure, in which the council would have the power to hear appeals from inclusionary developers who are denied approvals by municipalities that do not have housing plans approved by the Council. These models, as well as the housing element approach, are considered in this section.

[i.] "Top Down": The New Jersey Fair Housing Act

The aftermath of Mount Laurel II. The forceful remedies imposed by *Mount Laurel II* worked as the court had intended. Beginning in 1984 with *AMG Realty v. Warren Township, supra*, orders to rezone specific parcels of land began to issue from the specially-designated *Mount Laurel* trial judges, and municipalities began clamoring for the legislative solution that the Supreme Court had said it preferred. Is it fair to conclude that the stringent *Mount Laurel II* remedies were designed to back the legislature into a corner and force it to act?

The result was the Fair Housing Act of 1985, N.J. Stat. §§ 52:27D-301 *et seq.*, adopted as a legislative response to *Mount Laurel II*. The Act explicitly confirms the "fair share" concept as legislative policy, but provides new procedures. A state agency was established, the Council on Affordable Housing (COAH), with "primary jurisdiction for the administration of housing obligations in accordance with sound regional planning considerations." *Id.* § 304. Before being sued by a developer seeking a builder's remedy, a municipality can voluntarily present a *Mount Laurel* compliance plan to COAH and, if COAH finds that the plan "make[s] the achievement of the municipality's fair share of low and moderate income housing realistically possible," it can grant "substantive certification." *Id.* §§ 313, 314. If there is objection to the plan, a "mediation and review process" is provided for, rather than litigation. *Id.* § 315. Once "substantively certified," a municipality's fair share plan is presumed constitutional if there is subsequent litigation, rebuttable only on a "clear and convincing evidence" standard. For additional discussion of the New Jersey Fair Housing Act, see Franzese, *The New Jersey Supreme Court's Judicious Retreat*, 18 Seton Hall L. Rev. 30 (1988).

How does one reconcile the voluntary features of the Act with the mandatory obligation to comply with the constitution? Review the features described above and identify the incentives for municipalities to submit to COAH's jurisdiction. In a unanimous decision, the New Jersey Supreme Court held that the Act was facially constitutional. *Hills Dev. Co. v. Township of Bernards*, 510 A.2d 621 (N.J. 1986) ("*Mount Laurel III*"). A particular concern of the Legislature in creating COAH was to minimize, if not altogether eliminate, the builder's remedy. The Act contained a temporary and largely symbolic "moratorium" on judicial award of builder's remedies, see N.J. Stat. Ann. § 52:27D-328, but it did not explicitly prohibit COAH from granting a builder's remedy. COAH's regulations initially provided that a builder's remedy would be awarded only in "extraordinary situations," N.J. Admin. Code § 5:91-3.6, and its current regulation, *id.* § 5:95-3.8, essentially prohibits builder's remedies altogether so long as a municipality remains in good standing in the COAH process. This does not mean, however, that developers offering sites for inclusionary zoning are without influence in the COAH process. They routinely appear as "objectors" when a municipality petitions for substantive certification, and they are presumptively entitled to "site specific relief" when certain planning criteria have been met. See N.J. Admin. Code § 5:93-13.1, *et seq.*

Municipalities can still be sued if they fail to obtain "substantive certification," and some have been. In *Hills*, however, the Supreme Court instructed trial courts to act "consistently" with the COAH rules. 510 A.2d at 640. As a practical matter, this has meant that the COAH regulations govern in either forum. In *Toll Bros. Inc. v. West Windsor Twp.*, 803 A.2d 53 (N.J.

2002), the municipality allowed its substantive certification to lapse and was thereafter sued. The Supreme Court upheld the award of a builder's remedy against the township, a result that would have been very unlikely in a COAH proceeding. *Toll* is discussed in Note, *The New Jersey Supreme Court Reaffirms The Builder's Remedy As The Solution To Mount Laurel Litigation*, 34 Rutgers L.J. 1277 (2003).

The standard of review. It will be recalled that *Mount Laurel II* shifted to municipalities the burden of demonstrating that they were in compliance with the *Mount Laurel* doctrine. After the New Jersey Fair Housing Act shifted the focus on compliance to COAH, and vested the Council with power to adopt fair share regulations, a question arose as to the standard of review to be applied when COAH rules were challenged. Well-settled principles of administrative law in New Jersey and elsewhere give substantial deference to agencies when acting within their expertise and this would normally apply to complex issues of housing policy. However, COAH is implementing a constitutional as well as a statutory mandate. Does this require a different standard of review? Initially, in *Hills, supra*, COAH was accorded virtually unreviewable deference — perhaps the New Jersey Supreme Court wanted to give the new experiment some time to mature. A more restrictive standard was subsequently articulated in *In re Warren Twp., supra*, requiring a "searching" examination to insure that the regulations were methodologically sound and internally consistent. A recent intermediate court opinion, *In re N.J.A.C. 5:94*, to be discussed *infra*, is unclear about the proper standard of review and inconsistent in its approach, giving some issues the "searching" examination required by *Warren* but deciding others solely on the basis of deference to COAH's expertise. In a companion case, however, the same court unequivocally gave full deference to COAH on an issue of constitutional importance: whether some *Mount Laurel* opportunities must be created for households earning below 40% of median income. See *In re Adoption of Uniform Housing Affordability Controls*, 914 A.2d 402, 409 (N.J. App. 2007) ("heavy burden" to overcome "presumption of reasonableness"). The New Jersey Supreme Court has not clarified the matter.

Success or failure? There has been surprisingly little systematic study of the actual results of *Mount Laurel II* and the New Jersey Fair Housing Act. Earlier work is summarized in Payne, *Norman Williams, Exclusionary Zoning and the Mount Laurel Doctrine: Making the Theory Fit the Facts*, 20 Vt. L. Rev. 665, 669–73 (1996). After roughly ten years of implementation of *Mount Laurel II*, it was estimated that about 13,500 low and moderate income housing units had been constructed or rehabilitated, a number which has continued to grow. A more recent study focuses on the occupants of *Mount Laurel* housing, rather than on the number of units. See Wish & Eisdorfer, *The Impact of Mount Laurel Initiatives: An Analysis of Applicants and Occupants*, 27 Seton Hall L. Rev. 1268 (1997). They concluded that most of the beneficiaries of the *Mount Laurel* process already lived in the suburbs, that whites were more successful than minorities in obtaining a *Mount Laurel* unit, and that in order to obtain a unit, some minority households relocated from a suburb to an urban location.

The most accurate current numbers are based on monitoring reports submitted to COAH by municipalities that elected to be part of the affordable housing program and summarized on its website. As of August 24, 2010, COAH estimated that approximately 109,264 new units had been proposed or completed, and of that, 58,991 had actually been completed; in addition, 24,866 units had been proposed or completed for rehabilitation, and, of that, 14,402 had been completed. New Jersey Council on Affordable Housing, Proposed and Completed Affordable Units (2010), *available at:* www.state.nj.us/dca/affiliates/coah/reports/units.pdf. This is either a remarkable achievement because most of those units would not have been created otherwise, or an abject failure because there remain hundreds of thousands of households eligible for *Mount Laurel* units that have not been created.

A NOTE ON RECENT *MOUNT LAUREL* DEVELOPMENTS

In *Hills, supra*, the New Jersey Supreme Court found the Fair Housing Act facially constitutional, but it cautioned that the process set up by the Act might fail "as applied" if COAH did not achieve compliance with the constitutional mandate. Despite this assurance, it was virtually a given that the court would not interfere for quite a while, see Payne, *Politics, Exclusionary Zoning and Robert Wilentz*, 49 Rutgers L. Rev. 689 (1997), and it did not. For the next fifteen years, the court handed COAH only one significant setback, holding that municipalities could not be authorized to establish residency preferences, so that those who already lived or worked in the town would have priority for any *Mount Laurel* units built. *In re Warren Twp.*, 622 A.2d 1257 (N.J. 1993).

COAH and its critics. COAH's enforcement of the *Mount Laurel* doctrine has drawn increasing criticism over the years, most vocally from affordable housing advocates but also from inclusionary developers and even from municipalities. Numerous appeals failed, however. See, e.g., *Calton Homes, Inc. v. Council*, 582 A.2d 1024 (N.J. App. Div. 1990). The affordable housing constituencies complain that the governing COAH regulations are unnecessarily complex and that its administrative processes are both slow and ineffective. Some basis for this can be found in the facts and procedures described in *Fair Share Hous. Ctr. v. Twp. of Cherry Hill*, 802 A.2d 512 (N.J. 2002), where the municipality's fair share plan for the period 1986-1992 was not resolved (by a combination of court and COAH actions) until 1994 and was still in controversy almost a decade later. The other broad complaint, heard mostly from housing advocates, is that COAH has tried to minimize, rather than maximize, the actual amount of affordable housing built in the suburbs, either by manipulating the fair share formula to produce smaller numbers or by looking past problems in municipal compliance plans, all in an effort to encourage voluntary municipal participation in the COAH process. As to the latter, for instance, see *In re for Substantive Certification, Township of Southampton*, 768 A.2d 233, 239–41 (N.J. App. Div. 2001). The court rejected a COAH-approved municipal housing element and fair share plan, holding that the Council's "passive" and "perfunctory" "paper review" completely ignored abundant evidence that the crucial compliance site was unbuildable, thus violating the "realistic opportunity" standard of *Mount Laurel.*

Housing advocates made a concerted effort in 2002 to persuade the New Jersey Supreme Court to consider the "as applied" failures of the Fair Housing Act. While the court fully reaffirmed the *Mount Laurel* doctrine, *Toll Bros., Inc. v. West Windsor Twp., supra*, it rejected a request by various *amici* to review and restate the remedial process in light of the experience gained after two decades of trial and error under *Mount Laurel II*. *Amici* argued that the COAH rules did not provide housing opportunities for the poorest households, those falling below 40% of median income, that they overemphasized the use of inclusionary zoning, and that they discouraged participation by public interest plaintiffs, whose interests are different from those of inclusionary developers. The court held, two Justices dissenting, that these issues were "not ripe" because they had been raised by *amici* rather than the parties. Would either the builder-plaintiff or the municipal defendant in a case such as *Toll Brothers* ever have a reason to raise such issues?

Matters came to a head in late 2004 when, after extensive delays that advocates characterized as a moratorium on compliance, see *In re Six Month Extension of N.J.A.C.*

5:91-1 et seq., 855 A.2d 582 (N.J. App. Div. 2004) (delay "dramatic and inexplicable"), COAH adopted new regulations to govern compliance through 2014. See N.J.A.C. 5:94-1 *et seq.* Nominally heeding the criticism that the fair share formula was too complex and ineffective, COAH adopted a weak version of the "growth share" methodology described *supra*, but the new methodology was itself extremely complex and it appeared to substantially reduce the housing obligations of many municipalities without providing a clear methodological basis for doing so, reinforcing complaints that COAH was too deferential to municipal interests. This broader context is described in Payne, *The Paradox of Progress: Three Decades of the Mount Laurel Doctrine*, 5 J. Plan. Hist. 126 (2006). Housing advocates who had lobbied for growth share for many years objected to the new COAH approach and in early 2007 the regulations were invalidated. *In the Matter of the Adoption of N.J.A.C. 5:94 and 5:95*, 914 A.2d 348, 372 (N.J. App. Div. 2007) (the methodology "defies comprehension"). The issues of methodology raised by this litigation require more detailed explanation than can be presented here, but the *N.J.A.C. 5:94* opinion provides a succinct and useful summary. *Id.* at 356–65.

In 2008, the New Jersey legislature undertook a major overhaul of the 1985 Fair Housing Act that created the administrative structure to manage the state's affordable housing program. The amendments eliminated the controversial regional contribution agreement (RCA), which had permitted a municipality to contract with another municipality to transfer (and pay for) up to 50% of its fair share of affordable housing. Critics of the RCAs maintained that they permitted wealthier communities to buy their way out of *Mount Laurel* obligations. In addition, the legislation established a statewide 2.5% nonresidential development fee to be used for affordable housing purposes. Another change was a requirement that 13% of a municipal fair share obligation be restricted to very low-income households (30% or less of median household income). The amendments establish a state housing commission and charge the commission with preparing an annual strategic housing plan for the state. A set of special requirements applies to areas of the state that are subject to comprehensive management plans (the Highlands, Meadowlands, Pinelands and the Fort Monmouth area), where at least 20% of the residential units constructed are to be reserved for low- and moderate-income households, "to the extent this is economically feasible." Public Laws of New Jersey, 2008, Ch. 46, *available at* www.njleg.state.nj.us/2008/Bills/PL08/46_.PDF. One amendment authorized regional planning entities to identify and coordinate opportunities for housing on a regional basis. N.J.S.A. § 52:27D-329.9. For a discussion of the interaction between the Council on Affordable Housing and the Highlands Council, the regional planning body that oversees development in the northwest part of New Jersey (discussed in Chapter 1 *supra*) in order to protect drinking water sources, see *Heritage at Independence, LLC v. State of New Jersey*, 2010 N.J. Super. Unpub. LEXIS 2025 (App. Div. 2010).

Apart from the legislation itself, the Council on Affordable Housing, under court directives, enacted new rules in 2008 for the third round of the program that established a growth share formula for the determination of the individual municipal obligation. Under the growth share formula, the municipal obligation is tied to actual residential and nonresidential growth. The rules, which revise previously issued growth share ratios, update the affordable housing requirement for municipalities based on the latest available data.

Below is a summary of the major changes:

- The use of a growth share approach is continued, with affordable housing need measured as a percentage of residential and non-residential growth from 2004 to 2018.

- New ratios are 1 affordable unit among 5 units and 1 affordable unit for every 16 jobs (previously ratios were 1 among 9 units and 1 for every 25 jobs).
- New affordable housing need for the state is 115,000 affordable units (an increase from 52,000 units in previous adoption). The administrative rules establish payment in lieu standards (cost of constructing an affordable unit) averaging $161,000 per affordable unit. N.J. Admin. Code § 5:96 (procedural rules), *available at* www.state.nj.us/dca/affiliates/coah/regulations/thirdroundregs/596.pdf, and N.J. Admin. Code § 5:97 (substantive rules), *available at* www.state.nj.us/dca/affiliates/coah/regulations/thirdroundregs/597.pdf.

The consultants' reports that document the methodology behind these rules appear at N.J. Admin. Code § 5:97 — Appendix F, *available at:*

www.state.nj.us/dca/affiliates/coah/regulations/thirdroundregs/597f.pdf.

The idea for growth share was that of the late Professor John Payne of the Rutgers School of Law in Newark, New Jersey, one of the original editors of this casebook. The concept was initially discussed in Payne, *Remedies for Affordable Housing: From Fair Share to Growth Share*, Land Use & Zon. L. Dig., June 1997, at 3. Growth share implicitly links compliance to capacity rather than need. Is this inconsistent with the "regional need" basis of the *Mount Laurel* doctrine? Cf. *Alliance for Metropolitan Stability v. Metropolitan Council*, 671 N.W.2d 905, 918 (Minn. App. 2003) (plan based on negotiated "goals" rather than "need").

The Third Round rules were invalidated for a second time by an appeals court (the first time was in 2007), and COAH was given five months to try again. *In re Adoption of N.J.A.C. 5:96 & 5:97*, 6 A.3d 445 (N.J. App. Div. 2010).

The appeals court held that the growth share methodology for determining a municipality's share of the prospective regional need for affordable housing set forth in the revised Third Round rules was invalid. The court also invalidated N.J.A.C. 5:97-3.2(a)(4)(iv), which authorizes a municipality to obtain substantive certification of a compliance plan that proposes to construct municipally-funded affordable housing without any specifics regarding the location of the site or source of funding; those parts of the Third Round rules that fail to provide sufficient incentives for the construction of inclusionary developments. Likewise, N.J.A.C. 5:97-3.5, which governs rental bonuses for prior round obligations, was invalidated, as was N.J.A.C. 5:97-3.18, which authorizes compliance bonuses for affordable housing units approved during the period from December 20, 2004 to June 2, 2008.

What is interesting about the October 2010 decision is that the court, in remanding the matter to COAH, directed it to adopt new Third Round rules that use a methodology for determining prospective need similar to the methodologies used in the First and Second Rounds — no more growth share. The court noted that the determination should be made on the basis of the most up-to-date available data.

At the same time (October 2010), the New Jersey Legislature is considering abolishing the Council on Affordable Housing, eliminating substantive certification by an administrative agency, and dramatically altering the manner in which housing goals are calculated, and by the next update of this casebook, it is likely that the Fair Housing Act will have been amended once more.

[ii.] "Bottom Up": The California Housing Element Requirement

The statutory framework. California requires that each municipality adopt a comprehensive plan, which must include a detailed housing element. See Cal. Gov't Code §§ 65580-65589.8. The housing element, which must be revised every five years, contains six statutorily-mandated parts: a review of progress under the prior plan; an assessment of existing and projected needs for lower income housing, as further described below; a resource inventory; identification of public and private constraints on providing affordable housing; quantified housing objectives; and a description of housing programs to implement the plan. *Id.* § 65583.

The key portions of this approach are the assessment of housing needs and the establishment of quantified goals, and these aspects of the planning process are largely removed from the municipality's control. Regional Councils of Government (COGs), in concert with the California Department of Housing and Community Development (HCD), make these determinations on the basis of data compiled by the state. Although the COGs nominally make these calculations independently, they are subject to state review for consistency with statewide housing needs. Once the regional allocation of need has been agreed upon, the COGs then determine each county's or city's share of the calculated need. The statute gives criteria for how this allocation is to be made, and permits HCD to give "advice," but it does not specify any allocation formula. Draft allocations undergo local public hearings and further revised before finally being incorporated into the local housing element. *Id.* § 65584. See generally Field, *Why Our Fair Share Housing Laws Fail*, 34 Santa Clara L. Rev. 35 (1993). How does this "fair share" process differ from that adopted in New Jersey? Does the California approach solve any of the problems that have been noted in New Jersey?

Under an earlier version of the statute, the five-year housing program incorporated into the housing element was required to identify "adequate sites which will be made available through appropriate zoning and development standards and with public services and facilities needed" for "the development of a variety of types of housing for all income levels" and to "[a]ddress and, where appropriate and legally possible, remove governmental constraints to the . . . development of housing." The zoning of "sufficient vacant land for residential use with appropriate standards . . . to meet housing needs as identified in the general plan" is required. *Id.* § 65913.1. In 2004, however, the statute was amended to require that the plan:

> . . . [i]dentify *actions* that will be taken to make sites available *during the planning period* of the general plan with appropriate zoning and development standards and with services and facilities to accommodate that portion of the city's or county's share of the *regional housing need* for each income level that could not be accommodated *on sites identified in the inventory* [required by another section of the statute]. (Emphasis added)

The importance of this change, making the planning requirement action-oriented, is indicated by *Fonseca v. City of Gilroy*, 56 Cal. Rptr. 3d 374 (Cal. App. 2007), which upheld a plan under the earlier version of the statute against a claim that it failed to comply with statutory requirements as to an inventory of available land, identification of suitable sites, and proper zoning. The court intimated that the result might have been different if the amended statute had been in force.

Local governments submit their comprehensive plans, including the housing element, to HCD, which reviews it for compliance with the statute. *Id.* § 65585. However, a local government may adopt a housing element despite HCD's objections if it makes findings that the element "substantially complies" with the statute. *Id.* § 65583(f)(2). HCD has no powers of enforcement, and this has limited the effectiveness of the statute. Enforcement is through private litigation, which is nominally a powerful weapon because the statute authorizes a hold on the issuance of building permits until an approved housing element is produced. *Id.* § 65587. California permits transfer of fair share obligations for a county and cities within a county, but without any requirement for financial provisions among local governments. Cal. Gov't. Code § 65584.07; cf. *Shea Homes L.P. v. County of Alameda*, 2 Cal. Rptr. 3d 739 (Cal. App. 2003).

Enforcement. For the most part, private litigation to enforce the local housing plan has mostly proven ineffective. The courts have invoked the usual presumptions of validity and deference to the local determination that the housing element "substantially complies" with the statute, thus avoiding consideration of the merits of the plan. See *Hernandez v. City of Encinitas*, 33 Cal. Rptr. 2d 875 (Cal. App. 1994) (rejecting plaintiff's argument as an attack on the merits where housing element appeared to contain all statutorily required elements). While this judicial deference confers considerable discretion on the local government in deciding how to comply with the statute, the threat of litigation has encouraged some local governments to adopt inclusionary housing programs, discussed *infra*. See also *Shea Homes L.P. v. County of Alameda*, 2 Cal. Rptr. 3d 739 (Cal. App. 2003), holding that these planning provisions were not violated by adoption of a wide-ranging initiative measure that removed substantial developable land from the urban growth boundary.

In an important judicially-crafted exception to the deferential approach, some courts have given substantive review to the provision of the law requiring identification of "adequate" sites for affordable housing, if the court finds that the sites provided do not meet statutory requirements. *Hoffmaster v. City of San Diego*, 64 Cal. Rptr. 2d 684 (Cal. App. 1997) (sites not "adequate" because development standards constrained their potential for development).

What remedies are available to a developer if sites are not adequately specified? Recall from Chapter 3 that most courts will not require the rezoning of land to a more intensive use to comply with the policies in a comprehensive plan. Does this rule apply to the "adequate sites" policy?

Given the amount of state and regional involvement in calculating housing needs in California, is it truly accurate to describe it as a "bottom-up" system? The APA's commentary on the California approach somewhat blurs the categories, describing "bottom-up" as "a collaborative effort between regional planning agencies and local governments under state supervision." American Planning Association, Growing Smart Legislative Guidebook: Model Statutes for Planning and the Management of Change 4-146 (S. Meck, gen. ed., 2002).

Court review of general plan housing elements in California focuses on whether the requirements of the statute are satisfied and does not question the wisdom of the particular set of policies that have been selected. *St. Vincent's School for Boys, Catholic Charities CYO* v. *City of San Rafael*, 75 Cal. Rptr. 3d 213 (Cal. App. 2008) (finding that the housing element substantially complied with housing element law, and that the city "tailored its regulatory activities and zoning controls to *maximize* the potential for housing development at identified sites, not to frustrate development" [emphasis in original]). The California Court of Appeals in *City of Irvine v. S. Cal. Ass'n of Gov't*, 96 Cal. Rptr. 3d 78 (Cal. App. 2009) held that courts have no jurisdiction to review the allocation of a region's share of affordable housing. The only remedy for a municipality to challenge the allocation determination is through the administrative procedure established under the Government Code. The court found that that nature and scope of a general plan's housing element removed the allocation process from judicial review.

Occasionally, litigation challenging the housing element is successful. See *Urban Habitat Program v. City of Pleasanton*, Case No. RG06-293831 (Cal. Sup. Ct. Alameda Cty, March 12, 2010) (order granting petition for writ of mandate and finding that Pleasanton was in "clear violation" of California housing element law, least cost housing law, and regional housing needs allocation, in part because of a voter-approved housing cap of 29,000 homes). See *Pleasanton Tosses Housing Cap to Settle Lawsuit*, Washington Examiner, August 19, 2010, *available at*: www.washingtonexaminer.com/local/ap/pleasanton-tosses-housing-cap-to-settle-lawsuit-101092049.html. The California Attorney General intervened in this case in 2009 on behalf of the plaintiffs.

Resources: Baer, *California's Fair-Share Housing: 1967-2004: The Planning Approach*, 7 J. Plan. Hist. 48 (2008) (highly recommended); Lewis, *Can State Review of Local Housing Plans Increase Housing Production?* 16 Hous. Pol'y Debate 173–200 (2004) (finding that although the California housing element law gives the state of California the power to review local plans for compliance with statutory requirements, a multivariate analysis indicates that the compliance status of California municipalities in 1994 did not predict the number of single-family or multifamily housing permits issued from 1994 to 2000); S. Meck, R. Retzlaff & J. Schwab, *Regional Approaches to Affordable Housing*, American Planning Ass'n, Planning Advisory Serv. Rep. No. 513/514, at 42-67 (2003) (presents data and a thorough critique of the California legislation). See also Landis & LeGates, *Housing Planning and Policy*, in the Practice of Local Government Planning ch. 10 (C. Hoch, L. Dalton & F. So eds., 3d ed. 2000); Calavita et al., *Inclusionary Housing in California and New Jersey: A Comparative Analysis*, 8 Hous. Pol'y Debate 109 (1997). Oregon has affordable housing legislation in its state land use program, which is discussed in Chapter 8, *infra*. For an empirical analysis of the impacts of inclusionary zoning in California, see Bento et al., *Housing Market Effects of Inclusionary Zoning*, 11 Hous. Pol'y Debate No. 2, 7-26 (2009) (finding that, consistent with economic theory, inclusionary zoning policies had measurable effects on housing markets in jurisdictions that adopt them — the price of single-family houses increases and the size of single-family houses decreases — and that, although the cities with such programs did not experience a significant reduction in the rate of single-family housing starts, they did experience a marginally significant increase in multifamily housing starts), *available at*: www.huduser.org/portal/periodicals/cityscpe/vol11num2/ch1.pdf.

[iii.] Housing Appeals Boards

The statutory framework. The "appeals" approach to planning for affordable housing needs involves a considerably simpler structure than either the New Jersey or California statutes, and it gives considerably more deference to local initiative in making land use decisions. This approach was pioneered by Massachusetts in 1969, before even the first *Mount Laurel* decision. Mass. Gen. L. Ch. 40B §§ 20-23 (2010). It has been adopted more recently in two neighboring states, Connecticut, Conn. Gen. Stat. Ann. Ch. 126a, § 8-30(g) (2010), and Rhode Island, R.I. Gen. L. Ch. 53 § 45-53-1 *et seq.*, and has spread beyond New England. See 310 Ill. Comp. Stat. 67/1.

As described by the drafters of the APA Model Statutes, "affordable housing appeals statutes are not planning statutes per se; they require no planning framework at the state, regional or local levels." American Planning Association, Growing Smart Legislative

Guidebook: Model Statutes for Planning and the Management of Change 4-152 (S. Meck, gen. ed., 2002). Instead, they:

> . . . provide for a direct appeal and override of local decisions which reject or restrict proposals for low- or moderate-income housing. They have each established a procedure by which an appeals board (in Massachusetts and Rhode Island) or a court (in Connecticut) can set aside local zoning decisions blocking housing developments that receive federal or state assistance. . . . These statutes tend, either explicitly or implicitly, to reverse or shift the burden of proof. The local government must now justify its exclusion of the affordable housing project, or the conditions that make the project economically infeasible, whereas before, developers had the burden of showing why they should be granted relief from zoning requirements. [*Id.*]

In concept, a housing appeals system can function without any numerical housing goal being stated. In practice, however, the statutes furnish an incentive to voluntary compliance by exempting local decisions from appeal if the municipality already has provided a minimum threshold percentage of lower income housing.

How does the housing appeals approach differ from the New Jersey and California models? Is the 10% threshold preferable to the fair share approaches used in those two states? With respect to the shifted burden of proof, are the appeals statutes closer to the APA's "top-down" or "bottom-up" model? Is it accurate to describe the New England statutes as more deferential to local control, given their very premise that local decisions are subject to review by a state agency or a court? Is it possible to defer to local decisionmaking and still achieve meaningful progress towards provision of lower income housing?

Board or agency? Note that the Massachusetts and Rhode Island systems provide for a specialized Housing Appeals Board, whereas Connecticut permits appeals under the statute to be carried into the regular court system. Is one mechanism preferable to the other? The evidence is mixed.

In *West Hartford Interfaith Coalition, Inc. v. Town of West Hartford*, 636 A.2d 1342 (Conn. 1994), a case of first impression, the court gave the statute a sympathetic reading. It held that under the statute, the trial court could order a requested zone change and approve a special development district designation. Later decisions held that a court can approve an affordable housing application even though it does not comply with local zoning, *Wisniowski v. Planning Comm'n*, 655 A.2d 1146 (Conn. 1995), and that traffic and environmental problems did not justify denial of an affordable housing application, *Kaufman v. Zoning Comm'n*, 653 A.2d 798 (Conn. 1995). After this initial flurry of favorable decisions, however, the Connecticut Supreme Court held in *Christian Activities Council, Congregational v. Town of Glastonbury*, 735 A.2d 231 (Conn. 1999), that a town's denial of an affordable housing developer's application should be based on a deferential standard of review. It took the report of a Blue Ribbon Commission and an act of the Legislature, Conn. Pub. Act. 00-206 (2000), to overrule this decision. See *Quarry Knoll II Corp. v. Town of Greenwich*, 780 A.2d 1, 20n.14, 28-39 (Conn. 2001).

Municipal concerns about the impact of an affordable housing project must be more than speculative for a court to give them weight under the Connecticut housing appeals law. A Connecticut appeals court held that there was insufficient evidence in the record to support a planning and zoning commission's decision approving a zoning amendment with modifications, but denying a zone change and site plan approval for a 100-unit luxury apartment complex when 30% of the units would be designated as affordable rental units. The stated bases were of inadequate gaps in traffic to allow drivers to exit from the proposed development safely, inadequate recreational space, and safety concerns associated with a bus stop. *Avalonbay Communities, Inc. v. Plan. & Zoning Comm'n*, 930 A.2d 793 (Conn. App. 2007). *See also CMB Capital Appreciation v. Planning and Zoning Commission of the Town of North Haven*, 4 A.3d 1256 (Conn. App. 2010) (holding that planning and zoning commission was required to grant application for site plan approval for affordable housing on the condition that developer obtain approval of sewer connection and that evidence was insufficient to support denial on the basis of inadequate provision for emergency services).

For discussion of experience under the law, see Tondro, *Connecticut's Affordable Housing Appeals Statute: After Ten Years of Hope, Why Only Middling Results?*, 23 W. New Eng. L. Rev. 115 (2001). Professor Tondro describes the Appeals Act after a combination of judicial interpretations and the 2000 amendments as making the statute more difficult for towns to evade, more focused on the "truly poor," more dependent on deep public subsidies as a result, and more complicated for developers to invoke. *Id.* at 160-64. Importantly, the act does not extend to wetlands regulation or state regulatory approvals. Could this adversely affect its curative impact?

In Massachusetts and Rhode Island (Rhode Island is discussed in more detail in the next section), which utilize a specialized non-judicial board, the role of the courts has been, until recently, largely limited to upholding the constitutionality of their respective statutes, see *Curran v. Church Community Hous. Corp.*, 672 A.2d 453 (R.I. 1996) (upholding grant of approval), and providing occasional interpretive guidance. In 2007, however, the Massachusetts Supreme Judicial Court took a potentially important interpretive step, holding under its statute that a municipality could override local zoning regulations to approve a low and moderate income development, *even though* the town had already achieved compliance with the statutory 10% minimum for affordable housing, based on an assessment of regional need. *Boothroyd v. Zoning Bd. of Appeals*, 868 N.E.2d 83 (Mass. 2007). Objectors had argued that the development should have been reviewed under conventional (and more restrictive) variance standards. See also *Zoning Bd. of Appeals of Canton v. Housing Appeals Committee*, 923 N.E.2d 114 (Mass App. 2010). Here, while an appeal of the permit application in question was pending, the Canton Zoning Board of Appeals (ZBA) approved construction of additional affordable units. Approval of both applications would increase the town's affordable housing stock to 12.6 percent. The ZBA argued that 12.6 percent was an "unreasonable overage" as compared with the 10 percent minimum set forth in Mass. Gen. Laws ch. 40B, § 20. It also claimed that HAC's determinations as to the projected traffic impacts of the project were not supported by substantial evidence. The court found, *inter alia*, that attainment of the 10 percent did not necessarily demonstrate that the town's need for affordable housing had been satisfied. Chapter 40B authorized the HAC to issue a permit for a project where the completion of the contemplated units would exceed the 10 percent requirement by a reasonable number. Based on its expertise in deciding similar cases, the court ruled, HAC was entitled to find that, even if there was increased congestion that resulted in an "inconvenience," it did not rise to the level of "a sufficiently high safety concern to outweigh the regional need for affordable housing." *Id.* at 119.

Chapter 40B limits the ability of local boards to impose conditions that render an affordable housing project uneconomic. For an interesting case involving Chapter 40B, where the local zoning board imposed *94 conditions* (including subconditions) on an affordable housing project, ranging from typical zoning issues, such as construction, density, and bedroom limitations, to nonzoning restrictions, such as land acquisition values and allowable profit, regulatory documents, and marketing, see *Zoning Bd. of Appeals v. Hous. Appeals Comm.*, 2010 Mass. LEXIS 604 (2010). Here, the Massachusetts Supreme Court ruled a local zoning board's power to impose conditions is not all encompassing, but is limited to the types of conditions that the various local boards in whose stead the local zoning board acts might impose, such as those concerning matters of building construction and design, siting, zoning, health, safety, environment, and the like. It further concluded that in reviewing a developer's appeal from a comprehensive permit approved with conditions, the Housing Appeals Committee is authorized in the first instance to review and strike conditions that were not within the board's power to impose, even though such conditions may not render the project "[u]neconomic" as that term is defined in Chapter 40B.

In Massachusetts, where the law is better established by far than in either Connecticut or Rhode Island, the results are measurable. Krefetz, *The Impact and Evolution of the Massachusetts Comprehensive Permit and Zoning Appeals Act: Thirty Years of Experience with a State Legislative Effort to Overcome Exclusionary Zoning*, 22 W. New Eng. L. Rev. 381 (2001), surveyed the data and found that, over time, municipalities have become more accommodating of affordable housing developers, thus reducing appeals, because the developers had a very high rate of success before the Housing Appeals Board. Simultaneously, she reports, the Board has encouraged mediated, rather than adjudicative, decisions, in order to further reduce controversy. At least until recently, that approach appears to have dampened controversy. Might it also be relevant that, unlike in New Jersey, for-profit developers are not part of the process?

For a discussion of the arguments for and against Chapter 40B, see Regnante & Haverty, *Compelling Reasons Why the Legislature Should Resist the Call to Repeal Chapter 40B*, 88 Mass. L. Rev. No. 2, (2003) available at: http://www.massbar.org/publications/massachusetts-law-review/2003/v88-n2/compelling-reasons-why-the-legislature. For a critical assessment of the Massachusetts statute, see Witten, *The Cost of Developing Affordable Housing: At What Price?*, 30 B.C. Envtl. Aff. L. Rev. 509, 525–46 (2003).

As of April 2010, 242,976 low- and moderate-income units, 9.6% of the state's total of year-round housing units (as of the 2000 census) had been built. Massachusetts Department of Housing and Community Development, Chapter 40B Subsidized Housing Inventory (SHI), April 1, 2010, *available at:* www.mass.gov/Ehed/docs/dhcd/hd/shi/shiinventory.htm.

A referendum question was certified in Massachusetts, looking to repeal that state's housing appeals law in the November 2010 election, but Massachusetts voters rejected the repeal. Those who wanted to save Chapter 40B won 58 percent of the total vote, while those who wanted to repeal the law garnered 42 percent. Littlefield & Conway, *Chapter 40B survives ballot test; housing law upheld*, The Enterprise, November 3, 2010, http://www.enterprisenews.com/features/x4796441/Chapter-40B-survives-ballot-test.

Under the Rhode Island Low and Moderate Income Housing Act, R. I. Gen. L. § 45-53-1 *et seq.*, a developer proposing to building affordable housing "may submit to the local review board [either the planning board or zoning board] a single application for a comprehensive permit to build that housing" in lieu of separate permits from other municipal boards. R.I. Gen. L. Ch. 53, § 45-53-4(a); see *Town of Smithfield v. Churchill & Banks Companies*, 924 A.2d 796, n.1 (R.I. 2007) (characterizing the comprehensive permit application process as "one stop shopping" for developers). As in Massachusetts, denials of comprehensive permits and approvals with conditions and requirements that make the construction or operation of the housing "infeasible" may be appealed to the state housing appeals board. The statute provides that local land use regulations are non-exclusionary, and decisions under them are not subject to review if they provide opportunities for affordable housing "consistent with local needs," which the statute defines as providing low- and moderate-income housing in excess of 10% of all the housing units in the community. R.I. Gen. L. Ch. 53, § 45-53-3(b). In addition, any municipality that has an affordable housing plan approved by the state and "that is meeting local housing needs" within the meaning of the statute may by ordinance limit the number of housing units in a comprehensive permit application to "an aggregate of one percent . . . of the total number of year-round housing units in the town[.]" *Id.* § 45-53-3(10), -4(a)(4)(xii). This limitation applies to applications from for-profit developers only. See *Sand Trace LLC v. Rossi*, 2010 R.I. Super. LEXIS 4 (2010) (interpreting R.I. Gen Law Ch. 53, § 45-53-4(a)(4)(xii)). The statute has been construed to authorize the local review board to grant "comprehensive permit applications requiring variances or waivers upon a finding that 'local concerns' related to the granting of the variances or waivers 'do not outweigh the state and local need for low and moderate income housing.' " *Jagolinzer v. Kennedy*, 2008 R.I. Super. LEXIS 168 (2010).

Illinois, the first state outside New England to adopt the housing appeals approach, has moved very cautiously. Although the new appeals board became operational in 2006, it may not formally reverse a local decision until 2009. 310 Ill. Comp. Stat. 67/25(a), 30. Hoch, *How Plan Mandates Work*, 73 J. Am Plan. Ass'n 86 (2007), found "grudging compliance" in wealthy Illinois suburbs with the minimum statutory requirements for preparing a housing plan, but he found that many of the plans failed to acknowledge past exclusionary practices or propose specific solutions, and he predicted that the unpopularity of the mandate would slow progress towards meaningful compliance. Does this experience suggest that there is no meaningful difference as to political controversy between the court-mandated approach in New Jersey and the legislative approach pioneered in Massachusetts? Developments in Illinois can be followed at the state Housing Development Authority's website, www.ihda.org. For a description and critique of the Illinois legislation, see Golz, *Breaking Into Affluent Illinois Suburbs: An Analysis of the Illinois Affordable Housing Planning and Appeal Act*, 15 J. Aff. Hsg. 181 (2006).

Sources. For a comprehensive empirical evaluation of the impacts of Massachusetts, Connecticut, and Rhode Island laws, see Cowan, *Anti-Snob Land Use Laws, Suburban Exclusion, and Housing Opportunity*, 28 J. Urb. Aff. 295 (2006) (finding that "adoption of an anti-snob law can result in the creation of significantly more affordable housing in exclusionary municipalities than would have been created if the law had not been enacted"). All three statutes, and New Jersey, are surveyed, with data, in Symposium, *Increasing Affordable Housing and Regional Housing Opportunities in New England*, 23 W. New Eng. L. Rev. (2001). See also American Planning Association, Growing Smart Legislative Guidebook: Model Statutes for Planning and the Management of Change § 4-208 (Alternative 2) (S. Meck, gen. ed., 2002) (derived from the three New England statutes).

[iv.] Approaches in New Hampshire, New York, Rhode Island, and North Carolina

A New Hampshire law requires municipalities that enact land use ordinances to provide "reasonable and realistic opportunities for the development of workforce housing, including rental multi-family housing." Its stated purpose is the clarification of the requirements of *Britton v. Town of Chester*, 595 A.2d. 492 (N.H. 1991), an anti-exclusionary zoning decision interpreting the zoning enabling act. It defines "workforce housing" as "housing which is intended for sale and which is affordable to a household with an income of no more than 100 percent of the median income for a 4-person household for the metropolitan area or county in which the housing is located as published annually by the United States Department of Housing and Urban Development" (HUD). The term also "means rental housing which is affordable to a household with an income of no more than 60 percent of the median income for a 3-person household for the metropolitan area or county in which the housing is located as published annually by HUD."

The New Hampshire legislation contains a procedure by which developers of workforce housing can appeal a local land use board's denial of a permit or approval with conditions or restrictions that are alleged to have "a substantial adverse effect on the viability of the proposed workforce housing development." The appeal is heard by the Superior Court, which may appoint a referee to oversee the case upon request by either of the parties. The court or referee can reverse the local decision or modify or waive the conditions or restrictions and can require that the municipality and developer negotiate in good faith to ensure that the project be maintained as workforce housing for the long term. N.H. Rev. Stat. Ann. §§ 674:59 to 674:61.

New York's legislation, which applies to Nassau and Suffolk Counties on Long Island, also addresses workforce housing. Under this law, when a developer makes an application to a local government to build five or more residential units in those two counties, the local government shall require one of the following in exchange for a density bonus of at least 10% or other incentives: (a) the set aside of at least 10% of those units for "affordable workforce housing," defined as housing for individuals or families at or below 130% of Long Island's median income; (b) the construction of the required affordable units on other land within the same municipality; or (c) the payment of a fee for each affordable unit that the developer would have been required to construct. The law sets the fee as equal to two times the median income for a family of four on Long Island. It provides that in cases where the fee exceeds the appraised value of the building lot, the fee shall equal the appraised value of the lot. The law gives the local government various options on how to use the fees, including turning the funds over to another local government within the same county subject to an intermunicipal agreement or the Long Island Housing Partnership to buy land for affordable housing or construct or rehabilitate affordable housing units. There are no specific duration requirements for affordability; the law only specifies that local governments "shall ensure that all affordable housing units created pursuant to this article remain affordable." N.Y. Gen. Mun. Law Art. 16-A.

Rhode Island has adopted procedures that attempt to expedite permitting for affordable housing through a state-level review of a "housing project of critical concern." Such a project is defined as "an eligible affordable housing project designated by the housing resources commission to be significant, in its operational stage, by its ability to advance affordable goals set forth in duly approved plans for affordable housing and to help alleviate affordable housing shortages in Rhode Island." Such housing projects contain at least 25% of the housing units for low- and moderate-income households and must remain affordable for at least 30 years from initial occupancy. The procedure is aimed at accelerating review by state agencies, not local governments, flagging to the agency the importance of affordable housing.

A person may apply to the Rhode Island Housing Resources Commission and request that a project be classified as a project of critical housing concern. If the project is found to be a housing project of critical concern, which involves a review by a state planning official for "probable consistency" with state plans pertaining to affordable housing development, the Rhode Island Housing Resources Commission may issue a certificate of critical housing concern. This certificate expires two years from the date of issuance. A person must then submit the certificate of critical concern with the appropriate state agency that has licensing or permitting authority over the project at the time of filing the necessary permit application(s) required for the project with the state agency. The state agency must give priority to the project of critical concern in the handling and processing of the application. However, the issuance and filing of a certificate of critical housing concern do not constitute, and are not to be considered, a waiver of any element, rule, regulation or statute upon which the license or permit is granted.

The statute requires the state agency to render a written status report to the applicant within three months of the submission of a "substantially complete application." The report must contain information that will enable the person to make "a sound business decision as to whether or not to pursue the application." If the state agency does not issue a permit for the project, the agency must complete status reports on the project for the next three months, and then must deliver monthly status reports to the Commission and the Associate Director on the application until a decision to accept or reject the application has been made. R.I. Gen. Laws Tit. 42, ch. 128.2.

A North Carolina law makes it illegal to discriminate in land-use decisions or permitting of developments based on race, color, religion, sex, national origin, handicapping condition, familial status, or where the development contains affordable housing for families or individuals below 80% of area median income. The law provides that it is not a violation if the land use decision or permitting is based on high concentrations of affordable housing or where there was a bona fide legitimate governmental interest. N.C. Gen. Stat. §§ 41A-4 to 41A-5.

[b.] Techniques for Producing Affordable Housing

[i.] Inclusionary Zoning

"Inclusionary zoning" is indelibly associated with the *Mount Laurel* decisions, but the New Jersey court did not invent this technique. By endorsing it and insuring that it would be widely used under court order, however, *Mount Laurel II* stimulated wider legislative use elsewhere. See, e.g., Cal. Gov't Code §§ 65915, 65915.5; Md. Ann. Code Art. 66B, § 12.01; N.H. Rev. Stat. § 674:21; N.Y. Town Law § 261-b. Examples of recent adoptions of local inclusionary zoning ordinances include Highland Park, Illinois; San Diego, California; and Madison, Wisconsin. Recent studies of affordable housing strategies make clear, however, that without the impetus of a mandate such as that found under the *Mount Laurel* doctrine and its implementing state statute, relatively little inclusionary housing gets built. See Meck, Retzlaff & Schwab, *Regional Approaches to Affordable Housing*, American Planning Ass'n, Planning Advisory Serv. Rep. No. 513/514 (2003); Katz & Turner, Rethinking Local Affordable Housing Strategies: Lessons from 70 Years of Policy and Practice (2003) (discussion paper for Brookings Institution Center on Urban and Metropolitan Housing).

The premise of inclusionary zoning is simple: in exchange for a profitable increase in allowable density of residential development, the builder is required to "set aside" a portion of the units to be sold or rented to low- and moderate-income households with deed restrictions requiring controlled, "affordable" prices for a period of years, although in some cases, the inclusion of affordable housing may be a mandate, without any compensating benefits. The ordinance can also relax site development requirements, provide for the provision of affordable housing off-site or in-lieu cash payments, and it may give a public agency an option to purchase units to operate as "public housing." *Mount Laurel II* held that a "minimum" of 20% of the units had to be "affordable" for the project to be considered "inclusionary." It is generally agreed that inclusionary zoning programs must be mandatory to work under most circumstances. Meck et al., *supra*, at 45; Katz & Turner, *supra*, at 74. There is a planning cost to providing affordable housing opportunities through inclusionary developments, however. Using the 20% set-aside, for example, every unit of lower-cost housing approved also requires approval of four units of market-rate housing. Does this promote "sprawl"? Can inclusionary housing be developed consistent with sound planning principles? On the relationship between affordable housing and environmental goals, see *Symposium: Twists in the Path of Mount Laurel*, 30 B.C. Envtl. Aff. L. Rev. 437, 487, 581 (2003).

The inclusionary ordinance. Lubell, *Zoning to Expand Affordable Housing*, Zoning Practice, Dec. 2006, at 6-7, describes the typical format of an inclusionary zoning program:

> Inclusionary zoning generally involves a requirement or an incentive for developers to include a modest percentage of affordable homes within newly created developments. This is one way of harnessing the power of the market to produce affordable homes. The nation's first inclusionary zoning law [in Montgomery County, Md., described *infra*] specified that in any new housing development including 50 or more homes, at least 12.5 to 15 percent must be made affordable to families with incomes at or below 65 percent of the area median income. In exchange for this requirement, developers received a density bonus allowing them to build up to 22 percent more homes than otherwise permitted. The affordable homes were required to remain affordable for 20 years.

Other jurisdictions vary the specifics but the structure is essentially the same. In New Jersey, where inclusionary zoning is a key component of implementing *Mount Laurel*, COAH regulations have established a range of 15–20% affordable ("set aside") units, N.J.A.C. 5:96-5.3(b)(2), equally divided between low (less than 50% of median income) and moderate income (50–80%), *id.* § 7.2, a presumptive density of at least 4-6 dwelling units per acre, *id.* § 5.6(b)(2), and affordability controls for at least 30 years. *Id.* § 9.2. Note a significant difference between the Montgomery County and New Jersey programs: Lubell describes a density *bonus* — "up to 22% *more* homes than otherwise permitted" — whereas New Jersey specifies "presumptive" densities that may or may not exist in the current zoning. Unlike other aspects of a typical affordable housing program, such as the calculation of "fair share," there is no quasi-objective methodology for calculating density bonuses. Where a town's existing zoning is "exclusionary," i.e., only low density development is permitted, a substantial "bonus" is a necessity so that the new, higher density makes it economically attractive to build a mix of market-rate and "affordable" units. As blatant exclusionary zoning wanes, it becomes a closer question whether the existing zoning will suffice, so that all that is required is to make inclusionary development mandatory, or whether a density "bonus" is still required. The practical solution is for municipalities and potential developers to bargain to find a density that all can agree on (recall the discussion of markets in Chapter 1). Each party has an incentive to conceal its true position so as to increase profit (in the case of the developer) or political acceptability (in the case of the municipality). Where inclusionary zoning is part of the remedy in a lawsuit, or a proceeding before an agency such as COAH, the supervision of a court-appointed master or a mediator can serve to keep the bargaining within bounds. So can COAH's "presumptive" densities. Do you see how? The relationship between density bonuses and presumptive densities is explored further in the Note on Inclusionary Zoning and Regulatory Takings, *infra*.

Programs vary as to whether the affordable units must be built on site or can be off site. When units are provided on site, practice also varies from either scattering the units throughout the development or clustering them in one particular location. What are the policy implications of these alternatives? Which one is a developer more likely to prefer, or will that vary according to circumstances? Policies also vary with respect to whether those who live or work in a community have a priority claim to affordable units constructed in that community.

New Jersey's Council on Affordable Housing maintains an informative website, written in accessible language, that explains many of the components of operating an inclusionary zoning program. It can be found, with links to related sites, under the caption *Administration of Affordable Units, available at:* http://www.state.nj.us/dca/affiliates/coah/resources/adminresources.html ("*Resources*"). The description that follows is based on this source; although practices will vary from state to state, New Jersey's well-developed procedures are representative. Once eligibility for occupying an affordable housing unit is determined using the median income guidelines described *supra*, the actual price that a purchaser or renter pays requires a complex calculation, at the base of which is a policy that no more than about 30% of household income should be devoted to shelter. However, in order to simplify the process, the 30% rule of thumb is not applied to *actual* household income but is based on statistical artifacts of median households within the income range. Thus, a family can actually pay more or less than 30% of income. *Resources, supra*, contains sample calculations.

When new units become available, either the municipality or the developer administers the selection process. "Affirmative marketing" by the developer is required in an attempt to assure that all eligible households know to apply. While these efforts often fall short (can you see why?), invariably, many more families apply than there are units, and so various priority systems, including first-come, first-serve and lottery, are used. When units are vacated by the original occupants, the new rent or sales price is controlled; typical provisions permit an upward adjustment only to account for capital improvements or inflation. A particular problem arises when units are released from inclusionary controls after a fixed period, such as the 20-year period mentioned by Lubell. To prevent a windfall profit to the last occupant, ordinances often provide for full or partial "recapture" of any "excess" profit, with the recaptured amount returned to the production of new affordable housing. Does this present any takings problems?

The provisions described here (and many more detailed ones) are typically set forth initially in an ordinance and then written into the conveyancing documents for individual properties so that they can be recorded and enforced reliably against subsequent purchasers. *Resources, supra*, has links to a variety of deed forms.

Montgomery County. With the exception of New Jersey, discussed earlier in this chapter, probably the most successful inclusionary effort in the country is that of Montgomery County, Maryland, the Moderate-Priced Dwelling Unit Program. Its proponents might argue that it is more successful (although implemented on a county-wide, rather than state-wide, basis) because it has generated less controversy. Montgomery County summarizes its law on its website:

> The law presently requires that between 12.5 and 15 percent of the total number of units in every subdivision or high-rise building of 20 or more units be moderately

priced. The law is applicable to property zoned one-half acre or smaller. Subdivisions which are not served by public water and sewer are exempt from the requirement because higher densities are difficult to achieve when installing well and septic systems. The zoning ordinance allows a density increase of up to 22 percent above the normal density permitted under the zone. The ordinance also allows some attached housing in single-family zoning classifications so that optimum development of the property can be achieved and less costly housing can be constructed. The density bonus, in effect, creates free lots upon which the MPDUs are constructed. The builder normally obtains some additional market rate units equal to the difference between the density bonus and the MPDU requirement. Because of physical constraints of the land, the full density bonus cannot always be obtained; the MPDU requirement, therefore, falls within a range of from 12.5% to 15.0% based on the actual bonus density achieved.

The County imposes certain resale and occupancy restrictions on the MPDUs when the completed units are sold. Because of changes in the law over time, this control period varies according to when the unit was initially sold. For this reason, the control period can be either 10, 15, or 30 years. The price for which the unit can be resold is controlled during this period, and the unit must be resold through the MPDU program to another MPDU certificate holder. The County has the right of first refusal to purchase any MPDU put up for sale, and almost all units that are sold during the control period are purchased by the County or HOC [Housing Opportunities Commission, the county's housing authority]. . . .

A recent change in the MPDU Law which took effect on April 1, 2005 lengthened the control period for sales units to 30 years (which will renew each time the MPDU is sold within the existing control period). Under this law, the control period for rental MPDUs was extended to 99 years. Another change in the law reduced the number of units within a development that trigger the requirement to provide MPDUs. Previously, developments with thirty or more units were required to provide MPDUs; this has been reduced to developments with 20 or more units. [Montgomery County, Maryland, "History of the MDPU Program in Montgomery County" available at: www.montgomerycountymd.gov/dhctmpl.asp?url=/content/dhca/housing/housing_P/mpdu/history.asp]

Montgomery County itself contends there are three limitations to the program. First, it relies on a favorable housing market; affordable housing is only constructed in connection with market rate housing. Second, the program loses an owner-occupied, affordable house at the end of the 10-year price control period (for those units sold before March 1, 2002). However, the law was amended to require that half the "excess" or "windfall" profit made when the MPDU is sold at the fair market price after the control period expires be paid into a Housing Initiative Fund (HIF). The fund is used to produce future affordable housing projects. Third, little rental housing except for those projects with low-income tax credits or tax-exempt bond financing has been constructed. The county observes that the bonus density does not provide enough incentive to construct apartment projects. To solve this problem, Montgomery County has offered construction and permanent financing through the HIF to nonprofit housing sponsors to purchase and renovate existing apartment houses and to build new rental projects. *Id.*

As of the end of 2009, the program had produced 12,963 units since 1976, with 9,067 in home ownership and 3,896 as rental. Of that number, 1,550 are for-sale units and 1,261 are rental in private ownership, units not controlled by the County or its public housing authority. Montgomery County, Maryland, "Number of MPDUs Produced Since 1976" (2010), *available at*: www.montgomerycountymd.gov/dhctmpl.asp?url=/content/dhca/housing/housing_P/mpdu/Number_of_MPDUs_Produced.asp.

For an evaluation of the Montgomery County ordinance, see Student Note, *A Tale of Two Cities: Examining the Success of Inclusionary Zoning Ordinances in Montgomery County, Maryland and Boulder, Colorado*, 13 J. Gender Race & Just. 753 (2010).

California. Calavita & Grimes, *Inclusionary Housing in California: The Experience of Two Decades*, 64 J. Am. Plan. Ass'n 159 (1998), report some 24,000 inclusionary units built in that large state over the period surveyed. Compare to that, however, the more than 10,000 units produced in one Maryland county. In addition, California makes inclusionary units available to households well above 80% of regional median income, the typical benchmark set in New Jersey and elsewhere. This may be justified on policy grounds by the notoriously high cost of housing in California, but it does little to meet the needs of lower-income households. Moreover, as noted above, California's affordable housing planning legislation is weak at the enforcement level, which works against the effectiveness of the inclusionary technique. Meck et al., *supra*, at 45, conclude that while California may be providing *opportunities* for inclusionary zoning, "these opportunities may not be translating into the actual construction of affordable housing units." Nonetheless, local governments appear to be adopting inclusionary ordinances with increasing frequency. Updated information can be found in Talbert & Costa, *Inclusionary Housing Programs: Local Governments Respond to California's Housing Crisis*, 30 B.C. Envtl. Aff. L. Rev. 567 (2003).

Interpreting the state's density bonus statute, a California appeals court ruled that a city had discretion to award a density bonus for affordable housing that was higher than the maximum amount set forth in the applicable statute. The municipality had granted the developer a 40% density bonus for affordable housing, and a citizen's group challenged the bonus on the grounds that it exceeded a maximum in the statute of 35%. Examining the legislative history of the statute, the court concluded:

> Because the statute imposes a mandatory duty on local governments, and provides a means for developers to enforce this duty through civil proceedings (Cal. Gov. Code. § 65915, subd. (d)(3)), it is clear that 35 percent represents the maximum amount of bonus a city is *required to provide*, not the maximum amount a developer can ever obtain. The entire aim of Section 65915 is to provide incentives to developers to construct housing for seniors and low income families. [*Friends of Lagoon Valley v. City of Vacaville*, 65 Cal. Rptr. 3d 251, 266 (2007).]

The City's approval of a 40.5 percent density bonus was based on the project's construction of a 100-unit age-restricted townhouse community for senior citizens and 75 units of housing for moderate-income households, and its provision of several other amenities, such as the creation of a neighborhood park, the building of a new fire station, and the addition of over 70 acres to a community park. *Id.*

New Hampshire. As discussed earlier in this chapter, New Hampshire's *Britton* decision is the only state court decision nationally to rely on the *Mount Laurel* doctrine to require revision of a local zoning ordinance. While Meck et al., *supra*, and his colleagues found an admirable level of attention to affordable housing assessments in local and regional housing elements, they report that only one New Hampshire municipality, Portsmouth, had adopted an inclusionary mandate, and only for one specific site. *Id.* at 87. To put this in perspective, however, they also note that only 95 of New Hampshire's 234 communities have adopted any form of zoning regulation.

Other jurisdictions. A county ordinance in Maui, Hawaii requiring a set-aside of affordable housing withstood federal due process and equal protection challenges. The federal district court found the ordinance clearly addressed a legitimate governmental objective for purposes of facial substantive due process and equal protection; its stated purpose was to provide affordable housing to median and gap group workforce households in order to alleviate a shortage of workers and resulting downward pull on the local economy. Further, the court held that in order to consider a facial takings claim — whether under the state or federal constitution — the plaintiff must first seek state compensation under *Williamson. Kameole Pointe Dev. LP v. County of Maui*, 573 F. Supp. 2d 1354 (D. Haw. 2008).

Although the Twin Cities region of Minnesota has extensive guidelines for the production of affordable housing, it, like New Hampshire, relies on incentives and voluntary compliance to produce inclusionary housing rather than on mandatory programs. Meck *et al.*, *supra*, at 88. Likewise, the Portland, Oregon, metropolitan area, which is celebrated (and much studied) for its statewide planning process incorporating regional fair share goals, and for its stringent urban growth boundary regulations, relies more on growth management tools and provisions for a variety of densities and housing types within the urban growth boundary than on formal regulatory programs such as inclusionary zoning. Indeed, at the behest of the state's building industry, in 1999, the legislature *prohibited* cities, counties and the Portland Metro from adopting mandatory set-asides for affordable housing in sales (but not rental) developments. Meck et al., *supra*, at 68. Concern has also been expressed that by restricting the land available for development, the growth boundary system creates an artificial scarcity that will drive up housing costs.

Local programs. Most of the programs described here have been mandated by state legislation and have statewide application. Housing conditions vary widely, however, as do political attitudes, and in many states, it may be difficult or impossible to forge a statewide consensus supporting the use of aggressive techniques such as inclusionary zoning. In this situation, a number of local governments have stepped into the breach, creating local housing programs on their own.

Even where inclusionary zoning is mandated by the state, it is implemented through the local zoning code, so there is nothing inherently difficult about a municipality following the many model codes available and choosing a form that suits its needs. Local programs appear to be more controversial and more vulnerable to challenge than those originated or enforced at the state level, however. One explanation lies in the political geography. Comparing inclusionary programs adopted in San Diego and Berkeley, California, one commentator noted the "more aggressive, conservative building industry" in San Diego compared to a different culture encouraging a search for consensus between housing advocates and developers in the Bay Area. Morley, *Inclusionary Zoning in San Diego: Secure at Last?*, Zoning Practice, Sept. 2006, at 7. After four years of controversy and a trial court ruling that the San Diego ordinance was unconstitutional, *Building Industry Association of San Diego County v. City of San Diego*, Case No. GIC817065 (Cal. Sup. Ct., San Diego County, May 24, 2006), a settlement was finally negotiated permitting the ordinance to be readopted on terms favorable to the building industry. *Id.* The ordinance is available at: www.housingsandiego.org/documents/

SettlementReport-Ordinance7-25-06.pdf. Another risk that local initiatives face is conflict and preemption under state law. In *Apartment Ass'n of S. Cent. Wis., Inc. v. City of Madison*, 722 N.W.2d 614 (Wis. App. 2006), for instance, the city's ordinance requiring that 15% of the units in certain newly-constructed rental developments be affordable was found to be preempted by a state statute prohibiting rent control, notwithstanding that other state statutes required the city to address its affordable housing needs. Accord, *Town of Telluride v. Lot Thirty-Four Venture, LLC*, 3 P.3d 30 (Colo. 2000). Apart from technical issues of state preemption law, is the flaw in the Madison ordinance that it targets a narrow segment of the housing market, rather than the market as a whole? Or, on the contrary, is its virtue that as a local ordinance it can be shaped to address specific local problems, such as rents in a college town like Madison?

Sources. The APA PAS Report (Meck *et al.*) and the Brookings Discussion Paper (Turner et al.), *supra*, contain extensive bibliographies, including numerous sources describing individual local programs. The most comprehensive discussion of the design of an inclusionary program, still valuable despite its age, is A. Mallach, Inclusionary Housing Programs: Policies and Practices (1984). See also Padilla, *Reflections on Inclusionary Zoning and a Renewed Look at its Viability*, 23 Hofstra L. Rev. 539 (1995); Span, *How the Courts Should Fight Exclusionary Zoning*, 32 Seton Hall L. Rev. 457 (2001); Comment, *In Defense of Inclusionary Zoning: Successfully Creating Affordable Housing*, 36 U.S.F. L. Rev. 971 (2002); Note, *Breaking the Exclusionary Land Use Regulation Barrier: Policies to Promote Affordable Housing in the Suburbs*, 82 Geo. L.J. 2039 (1994). The APA has collected many of its affordable housing resources at one accessible site, http://myapa.planning.org/affordablereader/. See also Rifkin, Comment, *Responsible Development? The Need for Revision to Seattle's Inclusionary Housing Plan*, 32 Seattle U. L. Rev. 443 (2009); Schuetz et al., *31 Flavors of Inclusionary Zoning: Comparing Policies From San Francisco, Washington, DC, and Suburban Boston*, 75 J. Am. Plan. Ass'n. 441(2009); Comment: *Cracking the Foundation: Highlighting and Criticizing the Shortcomings of Mandatory Inclusionary Zoning Practices*, 37 Pepp. L. Rev. 1039 (2010).

For an empirical analysis of the impacts of inclusionary zoning in California, see Bento et al., *Housing Market Effects of Inclusionary Zoning*, 11 Hous. Pol'y Debate 7 (2009) (finding that, consistent with economic theory, inclusionary zoning policies had measurable effects on housing markets in jurisdictions that adopt them — the price of single-family houses increases and the size of single-family houses decreases — and that, although the cities with such programs did not experience a significant reduction in the rate of single-family housing starts, they did experience a marginally significant increase in multifamily housing starts), *available at:* www.huduser.org/portal/periodicals/cityscpe/vol11num2/ch1.pdf.

Local legislators may attempt to structure inclusionary zoning ordinances so that current residents or local employees, rather than those seeking to move into the community but have no prior connection to it, obtain preference for the affordable units that are created. For a discussion of the pitfalls to this approach, see Norquist, Note, *Local Preferences in Affordable Housing: Special Treatment for Those Who Live or Work in a Community?* 36 B.C. Envtl. Aff. L. Rev. 207 (2009). Norquist argues that preferences are threatened by three chief legal principles: (1) the potential for such preferences to be viewed by the courts as a penalty on nonresidents' fundamental right to interstate travel and migration; (2) the potential that such preferences are motivated by local legislators' desire to exclude a protected class of persons, leading to the conclusion that the preferences violate the Equal Protection Clause; and (3) the potential that local resident and employee preferences can violate the Federal Fair Housing Act by creating or perpetuating discriminatory racial impacts. These latter violations require no proof of discriminatory intent on behalf of legislators. Norquist recommends that local governments should structure their affordable housing programs as broadly and inclusively as possible, offering multiple methods for an applicant to receive preference — such as preferences based on bona fide residency, employment, and expanded geographic areas — and by limiting the scope and duration of the preferences.

A now-dated critique of inclusionary zoning argued that inclusionary zoning is an "irony" because it provides very few "winners," while inefficiently raising housing prices everywhere else in the community, which makes it even more impossible for the far larger group of low-income "losers" to find affordable shelter. Ellickson, *The Irony of Inclusionary Zoning*, 54 S. Cal. L. Rev. 1167 (1981). For a convincing rebuttal of this argument, see Dietderich, *supra*, 24 Fordham Urb. L.J. at 39-45. In turn, Dietderich's economic analysis is vigorously disputed in Powell & Stringham, *"The Economics of Inclusionary Zoning Reclaimed": How Effective Are Price Controls?*, 33 Fla. St. U. L. Rev. 471 (2005). See also M. Morris, *Incentive Zoning: Meeting Urban Design and Affordable Housing Objectives Pt. 3*, American Planning Association, Planning Advisory Rep. No. 494 (2000).

For a model affordable housing density bonus zoning ordinance, see Morris, gen. ed., Smart Codes: Model Land-Development Regulations, American Planning Ass'n, Planning Advisory Serv. Rep. No. 556, ch. 4.4 (2009); Cresswell, *Model Density Bonus Ordinance* (California Department of Housing and Community Development, Office of Housing Policy Development, 1996), *available at*: www.hcd.ca.gov/hpd/hrc/bonus.pdf. For an excellent analysis of the impact of density bonuses for affordable housing on the rate of return on investment in a housing project using alternative assumptions, see R.W. Burchell & S. Mukerji, *Comment — Smart Growth and Affordable Housing*, in Growth Management and Affordable Housing: Do They Conflict 106-116 (A. Downs, ed., 2004). See also, Mukhija, Regus, Slovin, & Das, *Can Inclusionary Zoning Be and Effective an Efficient Housing Policy? Evidence from Los Angeles and Orange Counties*, 23 J. Urb. Aff. 228 (2010) (finding no statistically significant evidence of inclusionary zoning's adverse affect on housing supply in cities with inclusionary mandates and concluding that critics underestimate the affordable housing productivity of such a program, and overestimate its adverse effect on housing supply).

A NOTE ON INCLUSIONARY ZONING AND REGULATORY TAKINGS

Does a mandatory set-aside requirement pose any constitutional problems as a regulatory taking? *Mount Laurel II* thought not. In a footnote reproduced *supra*, Chief Justice Wilentz reasoned that "the builder who undertakes a project that includes a mandatory set-aside voluntarily assumes the financial burden, if there is any, of that condition." 456 A.2d at 446 n.30. An earlier Virginia case, *Board of Supervisors v. DeGroff Enters.*, 198 S.E.2d 600 (Va. 1973), disagreed in a very narrow opinion holding that "rental or sale prices not fixed by a free market" violated the just compensation clause of the Virginia Constitution. *DeGroff* has not been followed. However, both *Mount Laurel II* and *DeGroff* were decided before the U.S. Supreme Court's 19787 "takings trilogy," *supra* Chapter 2, and the later decision in *Dolan*, *infra* Chapter 7, which collectively expanded property rights protection under the Takings Clause.

Surprisingly, there have been relatively few cases even in recent years, and those have not been favorable to developers. In *Home Builders Ass'n v. City of Napa*, 108 Cal. Rptr. 2d 60 (Cal. App. 2001), the court addressed the takings issue squarely and held that a 10% mandatory set aside regulation was not facially invalid under *Nollan* and *Dolan*. Although the ordinance imposed significant burdens on developers, the court noted that they were also granted significant benefits, including expedited processing and density bonuses. In addition, the ordinance contained a waiver provision and allowed alternate ways to meet the 10% requirement (such as payment of an in-lieu fee). (The court also emphasized that provision of affordable housing advanced legitimate state interests, although that issue has now been largely eliminated from takings doctrine by the more recent U.S. Supreme Court decision in *Lingle, supra* Chapter 2.) See also *Action Apartment Ass'n v. City of Santa Monica*, 166 Cal. App. 4th 456 (2008) (finding two-pronged *Nollan/Dolan* test does not apply to facial challenge of inclusionary zoning ordinance). The *Napa* case is discussed in Talbert & Costa, *Inclusionary Housing Programs: Local Governments Respond to California's Housing Crisis*, 30 B.C. Envtl. Aff. L. Rev. 567 (2003); Note, *California Court of Appeal Finds Nollan's and Dolan's Heightened Scrutiny Inapplicable to Inclusionary Zoning Ordinance*, 115 Harv. L. Rev. 2058 (2002); Burling & Owen, *The Implications of Lingle on Inclusionary Zoning and other Legislative and Monetary Exactions*, 28 Stan. Envtl. L.J. 397 (2009).

Do you agree with the *Mount Laurel II* court that inclusionary developers are "volunteers" who have waived any takings claim? Where the inclusionary development is optional — for instance, where the ordinance gives the developer a choice between building single-family homes at a lower density or an inclusionary development with a density "bonus" — the concept of "volunteer" makes sense. If the zoning *mandates* inclusionary development, however, doesn't that by definition contradict the notion of voluntarism? Stripped of its voluntarism camouflage, is the answer that a mandatory program is not a taking if, but only if, profitable development is possible under the terms of the ordinance? Note that in *Napa*, the court held out the possibility that an as-applied challenge could conceivably succeed even though a facial challenge did not. If a carefully drawn ordinance permits reduction (or even elimination) of the affordable units in order to preserve the viability of the development, can an as-applied challenge ever succeed?

Some of these questions were addressed, *inter alia*, by the New Jersey court in *In re Adoption of N.J.A.C. 5:94 & 5:95*, 914 A.2d 348 (N.J. App. Div. 2007). COAH authorized, and many municipalities adopted, "growth share" ordinances requiring *all* developers to provide a set-aside for affordable housing or pay an in-lieu fee. Without reaching the challengers' takings claim, the court held that the ordinances were invalid under the *Mount Laurel* doctrine unless "compensating benefits" were made available to developers. 914 A.2d at 389. The court reasoned that without such incentives, the zoning did not provide a "realistic opportunity" as defined in *Mount Laurel II*. Does this mean that additional benefits over and above whatever the existing zoning allows are *always* required, i.e., a density *bonus*, or would it suffice that the project remained economically viable under the existing zoning even with the new set-aside requirement added? Do you see how it would matter, in considering this question, whether a "takings" or a "realistic opportunity" standard is used? The court has not clarified its holding to date.

[ii.] Funding Mechanisms

Inclusionary zoning is a purely regulatory program. While the designers of such programs must always keep practical economic considerations in mind if the program is to succeed (such as by insuring the developer's right to build at sufficiently high densities so that it is feasible to "set aside" the lower income units), no money changes hand. Instead, the developer provides affordable units "in kind" as part of the overall development.

A different approach, which can be used alone or in concert with inclusionary zoning, is to generate funds for a Housing Trust Fund, out of which the government can direct subsidies to construct new units or reduce mortgage payments and rent. A number of states and local governments earmark specific revenue sources to build up a trust fund. These are described generally in Meck et al., *supra* Chapter 5. They include Vermont, which has a statewide fund supported by periodic appropriations and 50% of the state's real estate transfer tax; King County (Seattle), Washington, a regional fund supported by municipalities' contribution of their federal Community Development Block Grant awards plus appropriations and linkage fees (discussed below); Columbus/Franklin County, Ohio (similar sources plus earmarked hotel and motel tax); and Montgomery County, Ohio (earmarked sales tax). For a national overview of housing trust funds, see the website maintained by the Center for Community Change: www.communitychange.org/our-projects/htf.

The programs just described operate independently of the system of land use regulation that is our primary concern in this casebook. They touch zoning and planning matters only to the extent that, in providing a funding source in support of affordable housing, they indirectly offset any negative consequences that land use regulations may have. A funding mechanism directly tied to the land use system, by contrast, is the practice of charging a housing "linkage" fee on new development, such as King County does. The New Jersey Supreme Court has held that mandatory development fees for affordable housing imposed on commercial and non-inclusionary residential development are authorized by the Fair Housing Act as a *Mount Laurel* compliance device. *Holmdel Bldrs. Ass'n v. Township of Holmdel*, 583 A.2d 277 (N.J. 1990). The Fair Housing Act also permits residential developers to make a cash payment in lieu of constructing *Mount Laurel* units. Should they be treated interchangeably? The court held no in *Bi-County Development of Clinton, Inc. v. High Bridge*, 805 A.2d 433 (N.J. 2002) (unless developer constructs units, preferential access to regional infrastructure not appropriate); see Note, *Refining Municipal Obligations Under Mount Laurel, the New Jersey Supreme Court Hints at a New Conception of Regional Responsibility*, 116 Harv. L. Rev. 1541(2003). "Linkage fees" are a form of exaction, raising a more general set of problems that are explored in Chapter 7, *infra*.

[iii.] Other Tools

In the PAS Report, *Regional Approaches to Affordable Housing, supra*, at 195, Meck, Retzlaff & Schwab catalogue "a full toolbox of techniques" to produce affordable housing. In addition to inclusionary zoning, linkage fees, and housing trust funds, they note that local governments should have procedures to monitor the local land market to insure that there is an adequate supply of land for affordable housing needs; be authorized to waive permit and other fees for affordable housing, and to otherwise remove regulatory barriers; and be authorized or required to permit accessory dwelling units (discussed in Chapter 3, *supra*). They also emphasize the obligations of the states with respect to local governments: to provide clear planning enabling legislation insuring an analysis of housing needs, establish measurable goals, and a concrete plan of implementation; to create regional institutions; to provide both funding and technical assistance to local efforts to plan effectively, create subsidy programs, rehabilitate housing stock, and remove regulatory barriers; and, most importantly, to be the "strongest actor" in dealing with the problem of affordable housing. *Id.* at 189–95.

The PAS Report is also quite specific about what will not work: "aspirational regional planning" that is not linked to the local comprehensive plan and to local land development regulations; a planning approach that emphasizes study and analysis of housing problems without a commitment to housing production; and inadequate financial support for effective planning, particularly if linked to sanctions for failure to comply with planning mandates that effectively penalize those most committed to providing affordable housing. *Id.* at 188–89. Ultimately, the authors conclude with advice to both governments and housing advocates. As to public officials, "the most important element in ensuring the provision of affordable housing on a regional basis is political will and leadership." As to housing advocates, two admonitions: first, understand housing markets and how a variety of market forces continuously change the nature of the problem; and second, "reframe the need for affordable housing as a market inefficiency to be corrected rather than as charity or welfare for the poor or less deserving." *Id.*

In the large frame of reference provided by the PAS Report, review the materials presented thus far in this chapter. Do you agree that there is an affordable housing problem? Is the system of land use controls wholly or partially responsible for the problem, e.g., by analogy, what would happen to the price of automobiles if owners or manufacturers of expensive automobiles could prevent the production of less costly, less luxurious automobiles? Is land use law capable of addressing the problem? Can the problem be solved? Is it glib or insightful to say that the problem is that some people don't have enough money to compete successfully for decent housing?

B. DISCRIMINATORY ZONING UNDER FEDERAL LAW

[1.] The Problem

Race-conscious housing and zoning policies were certainly high on the Kerner Commission's list of wrongs to be righted when it famously declared "Our nation is moving toward two societies, one white, one black — separate and unequal." National Advisory Commission on Civil Disorders, Report of the National Advisory Commission on Civil Disorders 1 (1968). As we have seen in Sec. A, *supra*, many states have adopted legal tools to deal directly with the inequitable operation of land use controls, usually with an emphasis on economic rather than racial diversity and fairness. Federal law has taken a different approach, focusing on the discriminatory consequences of state and local land use decisions, rather than directly on the structure of land use controls. This has resulted in an emphasis on racial discrimination in housing, augmented more recently by a rapidly expanding body of law on disability discrimination and group homes.

This is not to suggest, however, that the federal government bears no responsibility for the problem of housing segregation. While local governments largely controlled the zoning process, the federal government subsidized an array of related programs ranging from urban renewal to single-family home mortgages to the highways that opened up the suburbs, and there is no doubt about the race-conscious approach that the federal authorities took:

> The juxtaposition of the Supreme Court's decision in the school desegregation cases and the passage of a new housing act in the spring and summer of 1954 forced a reexamination of national policy. Urban renewal's sweeping mandate to rehabilitate downtown business districts and "save" threatened neighborhoods had to be carried out in the context of powerful demographic and civil rights currents. The growing minority presence in the urban core, the emergence of largely white suburbs, and the persistent demand for more and better housing in the face of entrenched homeowner

> resistance to racial change led to an eager official advocacy of a racially dual housing market and separate development. The Eisenhower administration . . . offered to supply a modicum of new African-American housing as long as it facilitated the economic development of the central city and did not challenge existing racial patterns. Family public housing increasingly became a minority relocation program locked in the urban core, while government subsidies brought homeownership and suburban mobility within reach of the white middle class. In terms of national housing programs, *Brown* [the Supreme Court's school desegregation case — Eds.] brought a renewed commitment not to "separate but equal," but to an admitted, lower standard of "separate and adequate." [Hirsch, *A Racial Agenda for the Housing Acts of 1949 and 1954*, 11 Hous. Pol'y Debate 393, 431 (2000).]

The scholarly literature on race, zoning and housing is too complex and extensive to readily summarize. For a comprehensive current bibliography, see Medford, *Housing Discrimination in U.S. Suburbs: A Bibliography*, 18 J. Plan'g Lit. 399 (2004). Chused, *Euclid's Historical Imagery*, 51 Case W. Res. L. Rev. 597, at 613 (2001), declares that the Supreme Court's validation of zoning "gave us a picture of an 'apartment' that 'politely' — that is, without the overt use of racial and ethnic slurs — called forth the most negative, stereotypical imagery of New York tenement house districts." Chused argues that, notwithstanding *Buchanan v. Warley*, 245 U.S. 60 (1917) (racial zoning unconstitutional), the Court assumed that single-family suburban zones could be kept all-white by resort to restrictive covenants, which were not declared unconstitutional until twenty years later in *Shelley v. Kraemer*, 334 U.S. 1 (1948). Wiggins, *Race, Class and Suburbia: The Modern Black Suburb as a "Race-Making Situation,"* 35 U. Mich. J. L. Reform 749 (2002), explores why all-black suburbs have not evolved in the same way that all-white suburbs did a generation or two ago. Bell & Parchomovsky, *The Integration Game*, 100 Colum. L. Rev. 1965 (2000), apply game theory to analyze the behavior of individual suburban homeowners and suggest, *inter alia*, that regional growth controls, directed towards the creation of new suburbs could have an integrative effect. See also McFarlane, *Operatively White?: Exploring the Significance of Race and Class Through the Paradox of Black Middle-Classness*, 72 Law & Contemp. Probs. 168 (2010) (discussing the role of class in the racialized structure of land use); Godsil, *Viewing The Cathedral from Behind the Color Line: Property Rules, Liability Rules, and Environmental Racism*, 53 Emory L.J. 1807, 1862–63 (noting that existing black residential areas were often classified as industrial districts with the least protection from uses incompatible with residential use).

Is racial segregation still a problem? A report by the U.S. Department of Housing and Urban Development found little improvement in minority homeownership from 1994 to 2001. Barriers to Homeownership (2002), available at hud.gov/news/releasedocs/barriers.cfm#top. See also Selmi, *Race in the City: The Triumph of Diversity and the Loss of Integration*, 22 J. L. & Politics 49 (Winter, 2006), discussing housing segregation in our major cities and arguing that "diversity is celebrated at every turn, while the lack of integration is widely ignored and accepted as a social condition that, if not inevitable, no longer seems particularly problematic."

[2.] Federal "Standing" Rules

It is now clear that the only private plaintiffs who have standing to challenge allegedly exclusionary land use control in federal court are developers of subsidized housing seeking site-specific relief from zoning and/or other land use restrictions. Any broad challenge by civil rights organizations or low-income housing sponsors on the ground that the general, overall effect of the land use restrictions is exclusionary is practically foreclosed by the decision of the United States Supreme Court in *Warth v. Seldin*, 422 U.S. 490 (1975).

In *Warth*, suit was brought in Federal District Court against Penfield, a suburb of Rochester, New York, alleging that its zoning ordinance, by its terms and as enforced, effectively excluded persons of low and moderate income from living in the town, in violation of petitioners' constitutional rights and of 42 U.S.C. §§ 1981, 1982, and 1983. Plaintiffs and intervenors included local housing advocacy groups, individual Rochester taxpayers, several Rochester area residents with low or moderate incomes who are also members of minority racial or ethnic groups, and the Rochester Home Builders Association. The Supreme Court affirmed holdings below that none of these parties had standing under Article III's "case and controversy" doctrine.

The taxpayers and advocacy groups were denied standing on prudential grounds, in that they suffered little or no direct injury and thus were within the "normal" rule barring third party standing to assert the rights of others. The builder's organization lacked standing because it also suffered no injury, and the possible injury to its members would be peculiar to each case, requiring in effect that an actual builder with an actual project be in court before a claim could be evaluated. Why might a developer, even one with a relatively strong claim, prefer to have the Builder's Association conduct the litigation? Might there be a "free rider" problem in going it alone?

Given the Court's reluctance to let third parties, even those with some stake in the outcome, represent the interests of the lower income persons with the primary constitutional and statutory claims, the most surprising aspect of *Warth* is its holding that these plaintiffs also lacked standing. Their problem, the Court held, was that they might not actually benefit from a revision of Penfield's ordinance, because they still might not find or be able to afford a home or apartment in Penfield. Justice Powell described one plaintiff, Ms. Reyes, who earned $14,000 per year, which put her over the eligibility limit for a subsidized development that Penfield had turned down. "There is no indication that in nonsubsidized projects, removal of the challenged zoning restrictions — in 1971 — would have reduced the price on new single-family residences to a level that petitioner Reyes thought she could afford." 422 U.S. at 507, n.17. Inclusionary zoning is not mentioned in *Warth*. Especially after *Mount Laurel II*, how might Ms. Reyes have answered Justice Powell's disposition of her standing claim? For commentary on *Warth v. Seldin*, see Note, *Alternatives to Warth v. Seldin: The Potential Resident Challenger of an Exclusionary Zoning Scheme*, 11 Urb. L. Ann. 223 (1976). See also *Hope, Inc. v. County of DuPage*, 738 F.2d 797 (7th Cir. 1984) (denying standing to nonresident individuals and a low-cost housing sponsor who had not formulated a concrete, site-specific low-cost housing project).

Courts grant standing to developers and organizations who complain of discrimination directed to a specific parcel of land. *ACORN v. County of Nassau*, 2006 U.S. Dist. LEXIS 50217 (E.D.N.Y. 2006). Compare *Taliaferro v. Darby Twp. Zoning Bd.*, 458 F.3d 181 (3d Cir. 2006), noted, 120 Harv. L. Rev. 1105 (2006), where the city granted a variance for nonresidential development. Plaintiffs challenged the variance, claiming there was a conspiracy to limit the African-American vote by blocking residential housing on the site. The court found that the plaintiffs lacked standing because the injury was too generalized. For a thorough discussion of standing under the federal Fair Housing Act, see *Human Res. Research & Mgmt Group v. County of Suffolk*, 687 F. Supp. 2d 237, 248–249 (E.D.N.Y. 2010) (holding that standing under the FHA is "coextensive with Article III [of the Constitution]" and citing *Havens Realty Corp. v. Coleman*, 455 U.S. 363, 372 (1982)).

[3.] The Federal Court Focus on Racial Discrimination

[a.] The Constitution

Zoning is "state action," but federal constitutional doctrine is not hospitable to the economic discrimination theory used in *Mount Laurel II*, see *San Antonio Independent School District v. Rodriguez*, 411 U.S. 1 (1973), nor to housing as a "fundamental right," see *Lindsey v. Normet*, 405 U.S. 56 (1972). Where exclusionary zoning claims have been successful in the federal courts, it has been on the theory that restrictive land use controls violate equal protection by indirectly discriminating against blacks and other minorities by excluding low-income and moderate-income households from the suburbs. See generally McUsic, Symposium, *Brown at Fifty: The Future of Brown v. Board of Education: Economic Integration of the Public Schools*, 117 Harv. L. Rev. 1334, 1367 (2004).

The first barrier to implementing this approach originates in *Washington v. Davis*, 426 U.S. 229 (1976), an employment discrimination case where the Court held that proof of discriminatory intent is essential to the success of a racial discrimination claim under the Fourteenth Amendment. In the course of its opinion, the Court said:

> [V]arious Courts of Appeals have held in several contexts . . . that the substantially disproportionate impact of a statute or official practice standing alone and without regard to discriminatory purpose, suffices to prove racial discrimination violating the Equal Protection Clause absent some justification going substantially beyond what would be necessary to validate most other legislative classifications. . . . [T]o the extent that those cases rested on or expressed the view that proof of discriminatory racial purpose is unnecessary in making out an equal protection violation, we are in disagreement. [*Id.* at 244–45.]

In a footnote to this passage, the Court cited, among other cases, the Seventh Circuit decision in *Arlington Heights*, an exclusionary zoning case in which it had recently granted certiorari. With this daunting preview, counsel for the low income housing developer then tried to convince the Court that Arlington Heights' disapproval of a subsidized, racially integrated housing development was racially motivated.

VILLAGE OF ARLINGTON HEIGHTS v. METROPOLITAN HOUSING DEVELOPMENT CORP.

429 U.S. 252 (1977)

JUSTICE POWELL delivered the opinion of the Court

In 1971 respondent Metropolitan Housing Development Corporation (MHDC) applied to petitioner, the Village of Arlington Heights, Ill., for the rezoning of a 15-acre parcel from single-family to multiple-family classification. Using federal financial assistance, MHDC planned to build 190 clustered townhouse units for low and moderate income tenants. The Village denied the rezoning request. [MHDC, joined by other plaintiffs, sued in district court. The court found for the village after a bench trial, and the plaintiffs appealed. The Seventh Circuit reversed, finding that the "ultimate effect" of the denial was racially discriminatory and a violation of the Fourteenth Amendment.]

I

Arlington Heights is a suburb of Chicago, located about 26 miles northwest of the downtown Loop area. Most of the land in Arlington Heights is zoned for detached single-family homes, and this is in fact the prevailing land use. The Village experienced substantial growth during the 1960s, but, like other communities in northwest Cook County, its population of racial minority groups remained quite low. According to the 1970 census, only 27 of the Village's 64,000 residents were black.

The Clerics of St. Viator, a religious order (the Order), own an 80-acre parcel just east of the center of Arlington Heights. Part of the site is occupied by the Viatorian high school, and part by the Order's three-story novitiate building, which houses dormitories and a Montessori school. Much of the site, however, remains vacant. Since 1959, when the Village first adopted a zoning ordinance, all the land surrounding the Viatorian property has been zoned R-3, a single-family specification with relatively small minimum lot size requirements. On three sides of the Viatorian land there are single-family homes just across a street; to the east the Viatorian property directly adjoins the back yards of other single-family homes. . . . [MHDC and the Order entered into a 99-year lease and contract of sale covering a 15-acre site in the southeast corner of the Viatorian property, contingent upon obtaining zoning clearances from the Village and § 236 housing assistance from the federal government.]

MHDC engaged an architect and proceeded with the project, to be known as Lincoln Green. The plans called for 20 two-story buildings with a total of 190 units, each unit having its own private entrance from outside. One hundred of the units would have a single bedroom, thought likely to attract elderly citizens. The remainder would have two, three or four bedrooms. A large portion of the site would remain open, with shrubs and trees to screen the homes abutting the property to the east. . . . MHDC consulted with the Village staff for preliminary review of the development. The parties have stipulated that every change recommended during such consultations was incorporated into the plans.

During the Spring of 1971, the Plan Commission considered the proposal at a series of three public meetings, which drew large crowds. Although many of those attending were quite vocal and demonstrative in opposition to Lincoln Green, a number of individuals and representatives of community groups spoke in support of rezoning. Some of the comments, both from opponents and supporters, addressed what was referred to as the "social issue" — the desirability or undesirability of introducing at this location in Arlington Heights low and moderate income housing, housing that would probably be racially integrated.

Many of the opponents, however, focused on the zoning aspects of the petition, stressing two arguments. First, the area always had been zoned single-family, and the neighboring citizens had built or purchased there in reliance on that classification. Rezoning [to R-5] threatened to cause a measurable drop in property value for neighboring sites. Second, the Village's apartment policy, adopted by the Village Board in 1962 and amended in 1970, called for R-5 zoning primarily to serve as a buffer between single-family development and land uses thought incompatible, such as commercial or manufacturing districts. Lincoln Green did not meet this requirement, as it adjoined no commercial or manufacturing district.

At the close of the third meeting, the Plan Commission adopted a motion to recommend to the Village's Board of Trustees that it deny the request. The motion stated: "While the need for low and moderate income housing may exist in Arlington Heights or its environs, the Plan Commission would be derelict in recommending it at the proposed location." Two members voted against the motion and submitted a minority report, stressing that in their view the change to accommodate Lincoln Green represented "good zoning." The Village Board . . . denied the rezoning by a 6-1 vote. . . .

A divided Court of Appeals reversed [a District Court holding in favor of the village]. It first approved the District Court's finding that the defendants were motivated by a concern for the integrity of the zoning plan, rather than by racial discrimination. Deciding whether their refusal to rezone would have discriminatory effects was more complex. The court observed that the refusal would have a disproportionate impact on blacks. Based upon family income, blacks constituted 40% of those Chicago area residents who were eligible to become tenants of Lincoln Green, although they comprised a far lower percentage of total area population. The court reasoned, however, that under our decision in *James v. Valtierra*, 402 U.S. 137 (1971), such a disparity in racial impact alone does not call for strict scrutiny of a municipality's decision that prevents the construction of the low-cost housing.

There was another level to the court's analysis of allegedly discriminatory results. Invoking language from *Kennedy Park Homes Association v. City of Lackawanna*, 436 F.2d 108, 112 (2d Cir. 1970), *cert. denied*, 401 U.S. 1010 (1970), the Court of Appeals ruled that the denial of rezoning must be examined in light of its "historical context and ultimate effect."[6] Northwest Cook County was enjoying rapid growth in employment opportunities and population, but it continued to exhibit a high degree of residential segregation. The court held that Arlington Heights could not simply ignore this problem. Indeed, it found that the Village had been "exploiting" the situation by allowing itself to become a nearly all white community. The Village had no other current plans for building low and moderate income housing, and no other R-5 parcels in the Village were available to MHDC at an economically feasible price.

Against this background, the Court of Appeals ruled that the denial of the Lincoln Green proposal had racially discriminatory effects and could be tolerated only if it served compelling interests. Neither the buffer policy nor the desire to protect property values met this exacting standard. The court therefore concluded that the denial violated the Equal Protection Clause of the Fourteenth Amendment.

II

At the outset, petitioners challenge the respondents' standing to bring the suit. It is not clear that this challenge was pressed in the Court of Appeals, but since our jurisdiction to decide the case is implicated, we shall consider it. . . .

A

[The Court held that MHDC had standing because its proposed project was "detailed and specific." Even though the contingent nature of its lease spared it from major economic loss, it had expended a considerable amount of money pursuing its application, and it had also suffered non-economic harm to its social objectives.]

---

(6) This language apparently derived from our decision in *Reitman v. Mulkey*, 387 U.S. 369, 373 (1967) (quoting from the opinion of the California Supreme Court in the case then under review).

B

Clearly MHDC has met the constitutional requirements and it therefore has standing to assert its own rights. Foremost among them is MHDC's right to be free of arbitrary or irrational zoning actions. [Citing *Euclid, Nectow* and *Belle Terre.*] But the heart of this litigation has never been the claim that the Village's decision fails the generous *Euclid* test, recently reaffirmed in *Belle Terre*. Instead it has been the claim that the Village's refusal to rezone discriminates against racial minorities in violation of the Fourteenth Amendment. As a corporation, MHDC has no racial identity and cannot be the direct target of the petitioners' alleged discrimination. In the ordinary case, a party is denied standing to assert the rights of third persons. *Warth v. Seldin*, 422 U.S., at 499. But we need not decide whether the circumstances of this case would justify departure from that prudential limitation and permit MHDC to assert the constitutional rights of its prospective minority tenants. For we have at least one individual plaintiff who has demonstrated standing to assert these rights as his own.[9]

Respondent Ransom, a Negro, works at the Honeywell factory in Arlington Heights and lives approximately 20 miles away in Evanston in a 5-room house with his mother and his son. The complaint alleged that he seeks and would qualify for the housing MHDC wants to build in Arlington Heights. Ransom testified at trial that if Lincoln Green were built he would probably move there, since it is closer to his job.

The injury Ransom asserts is that his quest for housing nearer his employment has been thwarted by official action that is racially discriminatory. If a court grants the relief he seeks, there is at least a "substantial probability," *Warth v. Seldin*, 422 U.S., at 504, that the Lincoln Green project will materialize, affording Ransom the housing opportunity he desires in Arlington Heights. His is not a generalized grievance. Instead, as we suggested in *Warth, id.*, at 507, 508 n.18, it focuses on a particular project and is not dependent on speculation about the possible actions of third parties not before the court. *See id.*, at 505; *Simon v. Eastern Kentucky Welfare Rights Org.*, 426 U.S., at 41–42. Unlike the individual plaintiffs in *Warth*, Ransom has adequately averred an "actionable causal relationship" between Arlington Heights' zoning practices and his asserted injury. *Warth v. Seldin*, 422 U.S., at 507. We therefore proceed to the merits.

III

Our decision last Term in *Washington v. Davis*, 426 U.S. 229 (1976), made it clear that official action will not be held unconstitutional solely because it results in a racially disproportionate impact. "Disproportionate impact is not irrelevant, but it is not the sole touchstone of an invidious racial discrimination." *Id.*, at 242. Proof of racially discriminatory intent or purpose is required to show a violation of the Equal Protection Clause. Although some contrary indications may be drawn from some of our cases, the holding in *Davis* reaffirmed a principle well established in a variety of contexts.

Davis does not require a plaintiff to prove that the challenged action rested solely on racially discriminatory purposes. Rarely can it be said that a legislature or administrative body operating under a broad mandate made a decision motivated solely by a single concern,

[9] Because of the presence of this plaintiff, we need not consider whether the other individual and corporate plaintiffs have standing to maintain the suit.

or even that a particular purpose was the "dominant" or "primary" one. In fact, it is because legislators and administrators are properly concerned with balancing numerous competing considerations that courts refrain from reviewing the merits of their decisions, absent a showing of arbitrariness or irrationality. But racial discrimination is not just another competing consideration. When there is proof that a discriminatory purpose has been a motivating factor in the decision, this judicial deference is no longer justified.

Determining whether invidious discriminatory purpose was a motivating factor demands a sensitive inquiry into such circumstantial and direct evidence of intent as may be available. The impact of the official action — whether it "bears more heavily on one race than another," *Washington v. Davis*, 426 U.S., at 242 — may provide an important starting point. Sometimes a clear pattern, unexplainable on grounds other than race, emerges from the effect of the state action even when the governing legislation appears neutral on its face. The evidentiary inquiry is then relatively easy. But such cases are rare. Absent a pattern as stark as that in *Gomillion* [364 U.S. 339 (1960)] or *Yick Wo* [118 U.S. 356 (1886)] impact alone is not determinative, and the Court must look to other evidence.[15]

The historical background of the decision is one evidentiary source, particularly if it reveals a series of official actions taken for invidious purposes. The specific sequence of events leading up to the challenged decision also may shed some light on the decisionmaker's purposes. For example, if the property involved here always had been zoned R-5 but suddenly was changed to R-3 when the town learned of MHDC's plans to erect integrated housing,[16] we would have a far different case. Departures from the normal procedural sequence also might afford evidence that improper purposes are playing a role. Substantive departures too may be relevant, particularly if the factors usually considered important by the decisionmaker strongly favor a decision contrary to the one reached.[17]

The legislative or administrative history may be highly relevant, especially where there are contemporary statements by members of the decisionmaking body, minutes of its meetings, or reports. In some extraordinary instances the members might be called to the stand at trial to testify concerning the purpose of the official action, although even then such testimony frequently will be barred by privilege.

The foregoing summary identifies, without purporting to be exhaustive, subjects of proper inquiry in determining whether racially discriminatory intent existed. With these in mind, we now address the case before us.

---

[15] In many instances, to recognize the limited probative value of disproportionate impact is merely to acknowledge the "heterogeneity" of the nation's population.

[16] *See, e.g., Progress Development Corp. v. Mitchell*, 286 F.2d 222 (7th Cir. 1961) (park board allegedly condemned plaintiffs' land for a park upon learning that the homes plaintiffs were erecting there would be sold under a marketing plan designed to assure integration); *Kennedy Park Homes Association, Inc. v. City of Lackawanna*, 436 F.2d 108 (2d Cir. 1970), *cert. denied*, 401 U.S. 1010 (1971) (town declared moratorium on new subdivisions and rezoned area for park land shortly after learning of plaintiffs' plans to build low income housing). To the extent that the decision in *Kennedy Park Homes* rested solely on a finding of discriminatory impact, we have indicated our disagreement. *Washington v. Davis*, 426 U.S., at 244–245.

[17] *See Dailey v. City of Lawton*, 425 F.2d 1037 (10th Cir. 1970). . . .

IV

[The Court discussed the decisions below.] . . .

We also have reviewed the evidence. The impact of the Village's decision does arguably bear more heavily on racial minorities. Minorities comprise 18% of the Chicago area population, and 40% of the income groups said to be eligible for Lincoln Green. But there is little about the sequence of events leading up to the decision that would spark suspicion. The area around the Viatorian property has been zoned R-3 since 1959, the year when Arlington Heights first adopted a zoning map. Single-family homes surround the 80-acre site, and the Village is undeniably committed to single-family homes as its dominant residential land use. The rezoning request progressed according to the usual procedures.[19] The Plan Commission even scheduled two additional hearings, at least in part to accommodate MHDC and permit it to supplement its presentation with answers to questions generated at the first hearing.

The statements by the Plan Commission and Village Board members, as reflected in the official minutes, focused almost exclusively on the zoning aspects of the MHDC petition, and the zoning factors on which they relied are not novel criteria in the Village's rezoning decisions. There is no reason to doubt that there has been reliance by some neighboring property owners on the maintenance of single-family zoning in the vicinity. The Village originally adopted its buffer policy long before MHDC entered the picture and has applied the policy too consistently for us to infer discriminatory purpose from its application in this case. Finally, MHDC called one member of the Village Board to the stand at trial. Nothing in her testimony supports an inference of invidious purpose.[20]

In sum, the evidence does not warrant overturning the concurrent findings of both courts below. Respondents simply failed to carry their burden of proving that discriminatory purpose was a motivating factor in the Village's decision.[21] This conclusion ends the constitutional inquiry. The Court of Appeals' further finding that the Village's decision carried a discriminatory "ultimate effect" is without independent constitutional significance.

---

[19] Respondents have made much of one apparent procedural departure. The parties stipulated that the Village Planner, the staff member whose primary responsibility covered zoning and planning matters, was never asked for his written or oral opinion of the rezoning request. The omission does seem curious, but respondents failed to prove at trial what role the Planner customarily played in rezoning decisions, or whether his opinion would be relevant to respondents' claims.

[20] Respondents complain that the District Court unduly limited their efforts to prove that the Village Board acted for discriminatory purposes, since it forbade questioning Board members about their motivation at the time they cast their votes. We perceive no abuse of discretion in the circumstances of this case, even if such an inquiry into motivation would otherwise have been proper. Respondents were allowed, both during the discovery phase and at trial, to question Board members fully about materials and information available to them at the time of decision. In light of respondents' repeated insistence that it was effect and not motivation which would make out a constitutional violation, the District Court's action was not improper.

[21] Proof that the decision by the Village was motivated in part by a racially discriminatory purpose would not necessarily have required invalidation of the challenged decision. Such proof would, however, have shifted to the Village the burden of establishing that the same decision would have resulted even had the impermissible purpose not been considered. If this were established, the complaining party in a case of this kind no longer fairly could attribute the injury complained of to improper consideration of a discriminatory purpose. In such circumstances, there would be no justification for judicial interference with the challenged decision. But in this case respondents failed to make the required threshold showing. *See Mt. Healthy City School Dist. Bd. of Education v. Doyle*, 429 U.S. 274.

V . . .

[The Court remanded the case to the Court of Appeals to consider a statutory claim under the Fair Housing Act, which it had not considered.]

Reversed and remanded.

[The opinion of Justice Marshall, joined by Justice Brennan, concurring in part and dissenting in part, is omitted, as is the dissenting opinion of Justice White. Justice Stevens took no part in the consideration or decision of this case. — Eds.]

NOTES AND QUESTIONS

1. *Is proof of intent realistically possible?* The implicit holding of the case is that a zoning decision is not racially discriminatory if it is supported by "normal" zoning factors. Professor Mandelker offers this critique:

> The Supreme Court's decision in *Arlington Heights* has foreclosed a finding of racially discriminatory intent in all but the most blatant cases. Unless a municipality has historically discriminated against zoning proposals for subsidized housing, or unless the municipality abruptly changes a zoning classification or otherwise acts affirmatively to frustrate the construction of a subsidized housing development, no opportunity for proving the existence of racially discriminatory intent appears present. Moreover, none of these events is likely to surface. Developers facing a hostile municipality are unlikely to challenge that municipality's zoning to any great extent, so that no "clear pattern" of discrimination is likely to emerge. [Mandelker, *Racial Discrimination and Exclusionary Zoning: A Perspective on Arlington Heights*, 55 Tex. L. Rev. 1217, 1239 (1977).]

Reconsider the "but for" test explained by the Court in footnote 21. How does this test make proof of racial discrimination in zoning difficult? Since the Court said that "[s]ometimes a clear pattern, unexplainable on grounds other than race," will support a finding of racial discrimination, why wasn't the refusal to zone held to be racially discriminatory considering the nearly all-white character of the village's population? Could circumstantial evidence allow such a conclusion? See *The Inclusive Communities Project, Inc. v. The Town of Flower Mound, Texas*, 2010 U.S. Dist. LEXIS 64193 at * 2 (E.D. Tx. 2010), quoting *Simms v. First Gibraltar Bank*, 83 F.3d 1546, 1556 (5th Cir. 1996), where the court, in applying a standard for discriminatory intent under the Age Discrimination in Employment Act from *Simms*, approved the use of " 'circumstantial evidence' that 'would allow a rational fact finder to make a reasonable inference' that race was a motivating factor in Fair Housing Act cases."

2. *Segregation in urban areas.* Most cities, unlike most suburbs, do not totally exclude subsidized housing, but they often handle siting and occupancy in a racially discriminatory way, as a number of courts have found. The best known case finding intentional discrimination is *United States v. Yonkers Bd. of Educ.*, 624 F. Supp. 1276 (S.D.N.Y. 1985) (extensive findings of fact). The different fact pattern in the urban discrimination cases underscores Professor Mandelker's conclusion about the unlikelihood of proving intent in suburban zoning cases. The *Yonkers* case reached the Supreme Court in *Spallone v. United States*, 493 U.S. 265 (1990), where the issue was the scope of the district court's contempt power, rather than the merits of the housing claims.

3. *Segregative intent.* Housing discrimination cases since *Arlington Heights* have usually involved zoning disputes. Most such cases have not found equal protection violations. See, e.g., *Hallmark Developers, Inc. v. Fulton County*, 466 F.3d 1276 (11th Cir. 2006); *Orange Lake Assocs. v. Kirkpatrick*, 21 F.3d 1214 (2d Cir. 1994) (no racial discrimination when downzoning prevented construction of high-priced dwellings). The disappearance of federal subsidies for housing construction makes discriminatory intent more difficult to find and prove because federally-subsidized housing has a nondiscrimination requirement that made proof of discrimination easier because minority applicants had to be accepted in that housing. The typical argument now is that zoning restrictions such as the exclusion of multifamily development and the requirement of large lot zoning discriminate against minorities because they have lower incomes that require multifamily housing and development on smaller lots. See *Dews v. Town of Sunnyvale*, 109 F. Supp. 2d 526, 570–73 (N.D. Tex. 2000), *decree modified*, 2001 U.S. Dist. LEXIS 13086 (Aug. 24, 2001), where the court used the *Arlington Heights* factors to conclude that plaintiffs had established intentional racial discrimination. Sunnyvale, a "beautiful, rural Texas town" of 11,000 acres and 2,000 inhabitants, only twelve miles from Dallas, had used its zoning powers to "preserve [its] rural lifestyle," including an outright ban on apartments and minimum one-acre zoning. *Id.* at 529.

4. *Standing.* Is the Court's holding on standing in *Arlington Heights* consistent with its holding in *Warth*, discussed *supra*? How likely is it that the black plaintiff in *Arlington Heights* would actually be offered a dwelling unit in the project if it were built? Professor Sager claims that "In adjudging [the private plaintiff's] injury [in *Arlington Heights*] to be sufficient under the *Warth* test, the Court ignored both the possibility that the housing might not in fact be constructed and the remoteness of the likelihood that any one applicant would obtain housing amid the brisk competition for the units which would develop if they were completed." Sager, *Questions I Wish I Had Never Asked: The Burger Court in Exclusionary Zoning*, 11 Sw. U. L. Rev. 509, 517 n.25 (1979). Cases since *Arlington Heights* have granted standing to developers to challenge zoning claimed to be racially discriminatory. See *Scott v. Greenville County*, 716 F.2d 1409 (4th Cir. 1983) (if standing not granted to developer, local officials could destroy a project at an early stage before occupancy could be determined).

5. For additional discussion of the constitutional and standing issues raised by *Arlington Heights*, see B. Blaesser & A. Weinstein, Federal Land Use Law & Litigation §§ 11:2-11:15 (2010); Daye, *The Race, Class and Housing Conundrum: A Rationale and a Proposal for a Legislative Policy of Suburban Inclusion*, 9 N.C. Cent. L.J. 37 (1977); *Developments in the Laws — Zoning*, 91 Harv. L. Rev. 1427, 1666–79 (1978). See also Note, *Community and Democracy: The Case for Race-Conscious Remedies in Residential Segregation Suits*, 107 Colum. L. Rev. 1195 (2007).

[b.] Fair Housing Legislation

The Federal Fair Housing Act, 42 U.S.C. §§ 3601-3617, generally forbids racial discrimination in housing. 42 U.S.C. § 3604(a) provides in part that "it shall be unlawful . . . [t]o make unavailable or deny . . . a dwelling to any person because of race, color, religion, or national origin." The statute is primarily concerned with rooting out individual acts of discrimination by sellers, landlords, real estate agents, and banks, and it does not explicitly mention zoning, but the courts have held that discrimination in zoning ordinances makes housing "unavailable" under the statute. There is increasing recognition that enforcement of anti-discrimination laws one complaint at a time is inefficient and ineffective. See Abravanel, *Public Awareness of Fair Housing Laws: Does it Protect Against Housing Discrimination?*, 13 Hous. Pol'y Debate 469

(2003). For this reason, using fair housing laws against zoning ordinances and other broad-based regulations that have discriminatory consequences is important, in order to attack market-wide distortions. Much of the exclusionary zoning litigation in the federal courts has been based on allegations that local land use controls, as applied, violate the Fair Housing Act.

Arlington Heights after remand. Upon the Supreme Court's remand in *Arlington Heights*, the court of appeals held that "at least under some circumstances a violation of section 3604(a) can be established by a showing of discriminatory effect without a showing of discriminatory intent." 558 F.2d 1283 (7th Cir. 1977). The rationale of this holding is stated in the following excerpt from the court's opinion:

> The major obstacle to concluding that action taken without discriminatory intent can violate section 3604(a) is the phrase "because of race" contained in the statutory provision. The narrow view of the phrase is that a party cannot commit an act "because of race" unless he intends to discriminate between races. By hypothesis, this approach would excuse the Village from liability because it acted without discriminatory intent. The broad view is that a party commits an act "because of race" whenever the natural and foreseeable consequence of that act is to discriminate between races, regardless of his intent. Under this statistical, effect-oriented view of causality, the Village could be liable since the natural and foreseeable consequence of its failure to rezone was to adversely affect black people seeking low-cost housing and to perpetuate segregation in Arlington Heights. [*Id.* at 1288.]

In order to determine whether Arlington Heights had violated § 3604(a), the Seventh Circuit panel said that four factors must be weighed: (1) "how strong is the plaintiff's evidence of discriminatory effect"? (2) "is there evidence of discriminatory intent, though not enough to satisfy the constitutional standard of *Washington v. Davis*"? (3) "what is the defendant's interest in taking the action complained of"? (4) "does the plaintiff seek to compel the defendant to affirmatively provide housing for minority groups or merely to restrain the defendant from interfering with individual property owners who wish to provide such housing"? Consideration of these factors led the court to conclude that "this is a close case" and that "whether the Village's refusal to rezone has a strong discriminatory effect because it effectively assures that Arlington Heights will remain a segregated community is unclear from the record."

The court then remanded the case to the district court with directions to determine whether the case was moot; whether, absent a subsidy under § 236 of the National Housing Act, alternative subsidies would be available, and whether the project would be racially integrated. The court also put on the defendant "the burden of identifying a parcel of land within Arlington Heights which is both properly zoned and suitable for low-cost housing under federal standards. If defendant fails to satisfy this burden, the district court should conclude that the Village's refusal to rezone effectively precluded plaintiffs from constructing low-cost housing within Arlington Heights, and should grant plaintiffs the relief they seek." *Id.* at 1295.

The settlement in Arlington Heights. The district court never resolved the question whether Arlington Heights had violated the Civil Rights Act of 1968. After the case was remanded, Arlington Heights annexed an unincorporated tract — presumably owned or controlled by MHDC — abutting the nearby Village of Mount Prospect, and then agreed both to rezone this tract to allow multi-family and commercial uses and to exempt it from most subdivision exactions. MHDC agreed to build 190 units of subsidized rental housing on the tract, and to give residents of Arlington Heights preference in renting these units to the extent permitted by federal law. Both the Village of Mount Prospect and nearby landowners intervened and objected to this proposed resolution of the suit against Arlington Heights, but the district court approved it and entered a consent judgment dismissing the suit. 469 F. Supp. 836 (E.D. Ill. 1979), *aff'd*, 616 F.2d 1006 (7th Cir. 1980).

In a footnote, the Seventh Circuit panel observed "that Lincoln Green would conform with the standard set by the Village's multiple zoning classification," and hence that it "need not reach the question of whether plaintiffs would have been entitled to relief if Lincoln Green had been out of conformance with the Village's multiple family zoning classification as well as its single family zoning classification." Suppose the latter had been the case, but that the Village's multi-family zoning classification required a density so low as to preclude construction of any low-cost housing?

Why should it be relevant, in a case where discriminatory intent need not be proved, to determine whether there is "evidence of discriminatory intent"? Did the final settlement of the *Arlington Heights* case result in satisfaction of the Village's obligation under 42 U.S.C. § 3604(a) not to "make unavailable or deny . . . a dwelling to any person because of race, color, religion, or national origin"?

For a critical analysis of the Seventh Circuit's formula, see Clamore, *Fair Housing and the Black Poor*, 18 Clearinghouse Rev. 606, 646–50 (1984).

A series of actions taken by the Village of Farmingdale, New York, against Latino day laborers, including the preparation and implementation of a redevelopment plan that included an apartment complex that was the plaintiffs' former residence, were sufficient to support plausible disparate impact and disparate treatment claims under the Fair Housing Act (FHA), a federal district court has determined. Although only 12.6% of the population of the Village was Latino, the proposed redevelopment area had a Latino population of 56.2%; a population that requires low-cost housing. The redevelopment plan was expected to displace 21% of the Village's Latinos while only displacing 1.2% of the Village's White residents. The private redeveloper of the apartment complex took steps to renovate the building and terminated the leases of all of its tenants and the plaintiffs were forced to move into new housing in the Village with higher rental rates and less space. Other Village actions claimed to be FHA violations to curb the activities of day laborers included, among other things, fencing in day laborer hiring sites and enacting traffic ordinances aimed at preventing contractors from picking up day laborers. *Rivera Inc. v. Vill. of Farmingdale*, 571 F. Supp. 2d 359 (E.D.N.Y. 2008).

The Eleventh Circuit has held that it would be a "reasonable accommodation" under the FHA to allow the owner of four halfway houses for recovering substance abusers to locate within zones that already permitted unlimited turnover in multifamily dwellings surrounding those properties. By contrast, it would not be a "reasonable accommodation" to require the city to allow high turnover of the two halfway houses located within zones that allowed only single family residential dwellings and forbade tourist dwellings, the court said. However, the property owner presented no evidence of disparate treatment of, or disparate impact on, handicapped persons. *Schwarz* v. *City of Treasure Island*, 544 F.3d 1201 (11th Cir. 2008). See also *Budnick v. Town of Carefree*, 518 F.3d 1109 (9th Cir. 2008) (holding that potential residents of a senior retirement community do not presently qualify as disabled under the FHAA simply because some of them will become disabled as they age; the court commented that "being old is not, *per se*, equivalent to being disabled"); *Quad Enterprises Co. LLC v. Town of Southold*, 369 Fed. Appx. 202 (2d Cir. 2010) (plaintiffs alleged that town density restrictions and building type restrictions in zoning code prevented them from building multifamily development for the elderly, thus limiting access of handicapped to desired types of housing; while plaintiffs had identified facially neutral policy, evidence that number of handicapped people in town was larger than number of handicapped-accessible housing units was insufficient to show that zoning restrictions caused disproportionate impact).

Resources: Seicshnaydre, *Is the Road to Disparate Impact Paved with Good Intentions?: Stuck on State of Mind in Antidiscrimination Law*, 42 Wake Forest L. Rev. 1141 (2007); de Leeuw et al., *The Current State of Residential Segregation and Housing Discrimination: The United States' Obligations under the International Convention on the Elimination of All Forms of Racial Discrimination*, 13 Mich. J. Race & L. 337 (2008).

There have been several other cases applying the Fair Housing Act to claims of racial discrimination. The following case is one of the most important of these decisions. Note how it modifies the *Arlington Heights* test.

HUNTINGTON BRANCH, NAACP v. TOWN OF HUNTINGTON

844 F.2d 926 (2d Cir. 1988)

KAUFMAN, CIRCUIT JUDGE:

. . . .

The Huntington Branch of the National Association for the Advancement of Colored People (NAACP), Housing Help, Inc. (HHI), and two black, low-income residents of Huntington appeal from an adverse judgment of the United States District Court for the Eastern District of New York (Glasser, J.), following a bench trial, in their suit against the Town of Huntington (the Town) and members of its Town Board. Appellants allege that the Town violated Title VIII by restricting private construction of multi-family housing to a narrow urban renewal area and by refusing to rezone the parcel outside this area where appellants wished to build multi-family housing. Specifically, appellants sought to construct an integrated, multi-family subsidized apartment complex in Greenlawn/East Northport, a virtually all-white neighborhood. The Town's zoning ordinance, however, prohibited private construction of multi-family housing outside a small urban renewal zone in the Huntington Station neighborhood, which is 52% minority. Thus, appellants petitioned the Town to revise its code to accommodate the project. When the Town refused, appellants brought this class-action to compel the change under Title VIII. . . . [The court reversed the district court and granted site-specific relief.]

Huntington is a town of approximately 200,000 people located in the northwest corner of Suffolk County, New York. In 1980, 95% of its residents were white. Blacks comprised only 3.35% of the Town's population and were concentrated in areas known as Huntington Station and South Greenlawn. [Additional racial data is repeated later in the opinion.] . . .

Although a disproportionate number of minorities need low-cost housing, the Town has attempted to limit minority occupancy in subsidized housing projects. . . .

In response to the great need for subsidized housing in the Town, HHI decided to sponsor an integrated housing project [Matinecock Court] for low-income families. HHI determined that the project could foster racial integration only if it were located in a white neighborhood outside the Huntington Station and South Greenlawn areas. . . . [The only vacant property available for multifamily housing was located in an urban renewal area.]

After a lengthy search, HHI determined that a 14.8 acre parcel located at the corner of Elwood and Pulaski roads in the Town was well suited for a 162-unit housing project. This flat, largely cleared and well-drained property was near public transportation, shopping and other services, and immediately adjacent to schools.

Ninety-eight percent of the population within a one-mile radius of the site is white. HHI set a goal of 25% minority occupants. The district court found that "a significant percentage of the tenants [at Matinecock Court] would have belonged to minority groups." *Huntington*, 668 F. Supp. at 785. HHI officials determined that the property was economically feasible and offered a lengthy option period. . . .

[Miness, a local planning official, assured HHI that zoning would not be an obstacle if the town supported the project. HHI obtained an option to purchase the Elwood-Pulaski parcel on January 23, 1980. Miness stated, when asked, that he was familiar with the property and believed it was a good location for development.]

Throughout 1980, HHI sought to advance its project by gaining the approval of the Town Board to rezone the property to R-3M from its R-40 designation. . . .

When the proposal became public, substantial community opposition developed. . . . [A petition with 4,100 signatures was submitted to the Town Board, and a protest meeting drew 2,000 persons.] Matinecock Court came before the Town Board at a meeting on January 6, 1981. The Board rejected the proposed zoning change and adopted the following resolution [which concluded that]: . . .

> "THE TOWN BOARD finds that although favoring housing for the senior citizens and others, in appropriate areas, that the location referred to herein is not an appropriate location due to lack of transportation, traffic hazard and disruption of the existing residential patterns in the Elwood area and requests that the Department of Housing and Urban Development (HUD) reject the application by HOUSING HELP, INC."

The district court based its refusal to order rezoning on three alternative grounds: (1) appellants never formally applied for rezoning; (2) even if they had applied, they failed to make the requisite prima facie showing of discriminatory effect; and (3) even if they had demonstrated discriminatory effect, the city had rebutted it by articulating legitimate, non-pretextual justifications. We now consider each ground separately. . . .

[The court held that exhaustion of remedies was not required.]

In its second holding, the court adopted the four-prong disparate impact test set out in [the Seventh Circuit's decision in *Arlington Heights* on remand from the Supreme Court, which is discussed *supra*,] and concluded that, even if appellants applied for a rezoning change, they had failed to make out a prima facie case. . . . [The court quoted the "four-prong" test adopted by the Seventh Circuit and discussed the district court's holding.]

In its third rationale, the court applied the test set forth in *McDonnell Douglas Corp. v. Green*, 411 U.S. 792 (1973), as a final determination on the merits for Title VII disparate treatment cases. . . .

We find it convenient to discuss Judge Glasser's second and third holdings together. In considering them, we start by pointing out that this case requires what has been called "disparate impact" or "disparate effects" analysis, not "disparate treatment" analysis. A disparate impact analysis examines a facially-neutral policy or practice, such as a hiring test or zoning law, for its differential impact or effect on a particular group. Disparate treatment analysis, on the other hand, involves differential treatment of similarly situated persons or groups. The line is not always a bright one, but does adequately delineate two very different kinds of discrimination claims. . . .

Under disparate impact analysis, as other circuits have recognized, a prima facie case is established by showing that the challenged practice of the defendant "actually or predictably results in racial discrimination; in other words that it has a discriminatory effect." *United States v. City of Black Jack*, 508 F.2d 1179, 1184–85 (8th Cir. 1974), *cert. denied*, 422 U.S. 1042 (1975). . . . [The court held that the purpose of the act, legislative history and the parallel between Title VII and Title VIII supported their conclusion that "a Title VIII violation can be established without proof of discriminatory intent."]

Once a prima facie case of adverse impact is presented, as occurred here, the inquiry turns to the standard to be applied in determining whether the defendant can nonetheless avoid liability under Title VIII. [The court decided to "refine" the standard adopted in *Arlington Heights* and in *Resident Advisory Bd. v. Rizzo*, 564 F.2d 126 (3d Cir. 1977), *cert. denied*, 435 U.S. 908 (1978).]

In considering the defendant's justification, we start with the framework of Title VII analysis. When an employer's facially neutral rule is shown to have a racially disproportionate effect on job applicants, that rule must be shown to be substantially related to job performance. In a zoning case, the facially neutral rule is the provision of the zoning ordinance that bars the applicant and, in doing so, exerts a racially disproportionate effect on minorities. The difficulty, however, is that in Title VIII cases there is no single objective like job performance to which the legitimacy of the facially neutral rule may be related. A town's preference to maintain a particular zoning category for particular sections of the community is normally based on a variety of circumstances. The complexity of the considerations, however, does not relieve a court of the obligation to assess whatever justifications the town advances and weigh them carefully against the degree of adverse effect the plaintiff has shown. Though a town's interests in zoning requirements are substantial, they cannot, consistently with Title VIII, automatically outweigh significant disparate effects. . . .

A district court's findings of fact may not be set aside "unless clearly erroneous." Fed. R. Civ. P. 52(a). . . . We review Judge Glasser's findings in two areas: the strength of the discriminatory effect and the import of the Town's justifications.

The discriminatory effect of a rule arises in two contexts: adverse impact on a particular minority group and harm to the community generally by the perpetuation of segregation. In analyzing Huntington's restrictive zoning, however, the lower court concentrated on the harm to blacks as a group, and failed to consider the segregative effect of maintaining a zoning ordinance that restricts private multi-family housing to an area with a high minority concentration. Yet, recognizing this second form of effect advances the principal purpose of Title VIII to promote, "open, integrated residential housing patterns." *Otero v. New York Housing Authority*, 484 F.2d 1122, 1134 (2d Cir. 1973).

Seventy percent of Huntington's black population reside in Huntington Station and South Greenlawn. Matinecock Court, with its goal of 25% minorities, would begin desegregating a neighborhood which is currently 98% white. Indeed, the district court found that a "significant percentage of the tenants" at Matinecock Court would belong to minority groups. The court, however, failed to take the logical next step and find that the refusal to permit projects outside the urban renewal area with its high concentration of minorities reinforced racial segregation in housing. This was erroneous. Similarly, the district court found that the Town has a shortage of rental housing affordable for low and moderate-income households, that a "disproportionately" large percentage of the households using subsidized rental units are minority citizens, and that a disproportionately large number of minorities are on the waiting lists for subsidized housing and existing Section 8 certificates. [The certificates are a federal subsidy. — Eds.] But it failed to recognize that Huntington's zoning ordinance, which restricts private construction of multi-family housing to the largely minority urban renewal area, impeded integration by restricting low-income housing needed by minorities to an area already 52% minority. We thus find that Huntington's refusal to amend the restrictive zoning ordinance to permit privately-built multi-family housing outside the urban renewal area significantly perpetuated segregation in the Town.

On the question of harm to blacks as a group, the district court emphasized that 22,160 whites and 3,671 minorities had incomes below 200% of the poverty line, a cutoff close to the Huntington Housing Authority's qualification standards. Thus, the district court focused on the greater absolute number of poor whites compared with indigent minorities in Huntington. The district court, however, did not analyze the disproportionate burden on minorities as required by *Griggs v. Duke Power Co.*, 401 U.S. 424 (1971). By relying on absolute numbers rather than on proportional statistics, the district court significantly underestimated the disproportionate impact of the Town's policy. Thus, the district court perceived facts through a misapprehension of the applicable law and we must make our own findings at least as to the significance of the undisputed underlying facts.

The parties have stipulated that 28% of minorities in Huntington and 11% of whites have incomes below 200% of the poverty line. What they dispute is the meaning of these statistics. Judge Glasser found that, as the Town contends, there is no showing of discriminatory effect because a majority of the victims are white. We disagree for reasons analogous to those the Supreme Court enumerated in *Griggs*. The disparity is of a magnitude similar to that in *Griggs*, where the Court found discriminatory an employer's policy of hiring only high school graduates because 12% of black males in North Carolina had high school diplomas while 24% of white males were high school graduates. But the plaintiffs presented even stronger evidence reflecting the disparate impact of preventing the project from proceeding. Under the Huntington HAP [This was a plan required by the federal agency as a basis for federal community development assistance. — Eds.] for 1982-1985, 7% of all Huntington families needed subsidized housing, while 24% of the black families needed such housing. In addition, minorities constitute a far greater percentage of those currently occupying subsidized rental projects compared to their percentage in the Town's population. Similarly, a disproportionately high percentage (60%) of families holding Section 8 certificates from the Housing Authority to supplement their rents are minorities, and an equally disproportionate percentage (61%) of those on the waiting list for such certificates are minorities. Therefore, we conclude that the failure to rezone the Matinecock Court site had a substantial adverse impact on minorities.

In sum, we find that the disproportionate harm to blacks and the segregative impact on the entire community resulting from the refusal to rezone create a strong prima facie showing of discriminatory effect . . . . Thus, we must consider the Town's asserted justifications.

The *Rizzo* approach has two components: (1) whether the reasons are bona fide and legitimate; and (2) whether any less discriminatory alternative can serve those ends. For analytical ease, the second prong should be considered first. Concerns can usually be divided

between "plan-specific" justifications and those which are "site-specific." "Plan-specific" problems can be resolved by the less discriminatory alternative of requiring reasonable design modifications. "Site-specific" justifications, however, would usually survive this prong of the test. Those remaining reasons are then scrutinized to determine if they are legitimate and bona fide. By that, we do not intend to devise a search for pretext. Rather, the inquiry is whether the proffered justification is of substantial concern such that it would justify a reasonable official in making this determination. Of course, a concern may be non-frivolous, but may not be sufficient because it is not reflected in the record.

Appellants challenge both the ordinance which restricts privately-built multi-family housing to the urban renewal area and the Town Board's decision to refuse to rezone the Elwood-Pulaski site. All the parties and the district court judge, however, focussed on the latter issue. Indeed, appellees below simply relied on the existence of the Housing Assistance Plan and the zoning ordinance and failed to present any substantial evidence indicating a significant interest in limiting private developers to the urban renewal area. On appeal, appellees now contend that the ordinance is designed to encourage private developers to build in the deteriorated area of Huntington Station. Although we believe that the Town's failure to raise this argument below precludes its consideration here, we briefly address this contention. The Town asserts that limiting multi-family development to the urban renewal area will encourage restoration of the neighborhood because, otherwise, developers will choose to build in the outlying areas and will by-pass the zone. The Town's goal, however, can be achieved by less discriminatory means, by encouraging development in the urban renewal area with tax incentives or abatements. The Town may assert that this is less effective, but it may actually be more so.

Developers are not wed to building in Huntington; they are filling a perceived economic void. Developments inside the urban renewal area and outside it are not fungible. Rather, developers prevented from building outside the urban renewal area will more likely build in another town, not the urban renewal area. Huntington incorrectly assumes that developers limit their area of interest by political subdivision. In fact, the decision where to build is much more complex. Hence, if the Town wishes to encourage growth in the urban renewal area, it should do so directly through incentives which would have a less discriminatory impact on the Town.

We turn next to the Town's reasons rejecting the Elwood-Pulaski site. . . . [The court held that only the traffic and health hazard objections were site-specific.]

At trial, however, none of Huntington's officials supported these objections. Butterfield, for example, was primarily concerned that the Matinecock Court project would "torpedo" the Town's plan to develop the site at Broadway and New York Avenue in the urban renewal area in Huntington Station. (Testimony of Kenneth C. Butterfield.) Moreover, Huntington's only expert, planner David Portman, set forth entirely different problems than were contained in Butterfield's letters. Specifically, he noted sewage concerns, lack of conformity with the low density of the surrounding neighborhood, and inaccessibility of the site to public transportation (Testimony of David J. Portman). Once during his testimony, he did mention "the relationship [of the site] to the power station." Never, however, did he raise any concern about a health hazard from the proximity to the substation. Indeed, appellees do not broach this issue in their brief to this court. Accordingly, we find the reasons asserted are entirely insubstantial.

The sewage problem was first raised at trial by appellees' expert Portman. Appellees now advance it as an additional concern. The district court, however, chose not to consider it. We agree. Post hoc rationalizations by administrative agencies should be afforded "little deference" by the courts, and therefore cannot be a bona fide reason for the Town's action. Moreover, the sewage concern could hardly have been significant if municipal officials only thought of it after the litigation began. If it did not impress itself on the Town Board at the time of rejection, it was obviously not a legitimate problem. In sum, the only factor in the town's favor was that it was acting within the scope of its zoning authority, and thus we conclude that the Town's justifications were weak and inadequate. . . .

Appellees argue that we should deny site-specific relief because there are 64 "community development" sites available for low-cost multi-family housing in Huntington. [The court rejected this argument and held that "there is only one site, not 64 sites, zoned and available for private low-cost multi-family housing."] However, even as to the one site — the MIA site in Huntington Station — by the time of trial, HUD had determined it was in an area with a high concentration of minorities and therefore an inappropriate location for a federally subsidized housing development.

Ordinarily, HHI would not be automatically entitled to construct its project at its preferred site. The Town might well have legitimate reasons for preferring some alternative site to the one preferred by HHI. On the other hand, the Town would not be permitted to select a site that suits the Town's preference if that site imposed undue hardships on the applicant, such as distance from public transportation or other services. Thus, we would ordinarily remand this case to the district court to afford the appellees an opportunity to identify an alternative site, outside the urban renewal area, that would be appropriate for HHI's project and eligible for the same financial arrangements and assistance available at the Matinecock Court site. If the Town identified such a site, it would then have the burden of persuading the district court that there were substantial reasons for using its preferred site and that those reasons did not impose undue hardships on the appellants. If the district court was not persuaded on balance of the benefits of an alternative site, it would then enter an appropriate judgment to enable HHI to proceed with its project at the Matinecock Court site. . . .

This case, however, is not ordinary. [The court granted site-specific relief to rezone the plaintiff's property to R-3M zoning because of the protracted nature of the litigation, because the Town had demonstrated little good faith, and because "the other 63 parcels outside the urban renewal area are not presently zoned for multi-family housing."]

NOTES AND QUESTIONS

1. *Subsequent history.* The judgment of the Court of Appeals in the principal case was affirmed (per curiam). 488 U.S. 15 (1988). Thereafter, Huntington rezoned the site for affordable housing, but the State of New York denied Housing Help's application for funding, apparently because of community opposition to the project. Housing Help again sued, naming various public and private persons, the Town, and the state financing agency. After the district court refused to dismiss key claims, see *Housing Help, Inc. v. Town of Huntington*, Fair Housing-Fair Lending Reporter ¶ 16,308 (E.D.N.Y., Doc. No. CV-97-3430, Sept. 10, 1998), both Huntington and the state settled, in 2000 and 2002 respectively. More than 30 years after Housing Help first attempted to build in Huntington, the affordable housing project, named "Martinecock Court" with 155 units, 50% rental and 50% sale, still has not been constructed, as of 2010. For the Town of Huntington's explanation, see A.J. Carter, Some Facts About Matinecock Court, March 12, 2010, *available at*: town.huntington.ny.us/newsdetails.cfm?id=1761.

2. *How settled is the effects standard?* By taking a somewhat strained view of the procedural posture of the *Huntington* case on appeal, the Supreme Court was able to avoid deciding whether proof of "disparate impact," without proof of "discriminatory intent," satisfies the Fair Housing Act. The Court's entire discussion of the question was as follows: "Without endorsing the precise analysis of the Court of Appeals, we are satisfied on this record that disparate impact was shown, and that the sole justification proffered to rebut the prima facie case was inadequate." 488 U.S. at 18. When Congress substantially amended the Fair Housing Act in 1988, it did not address the discriminatory impact question, but President Reagan, in signing the bill into law, asserted his understanding ("executive history"?) that it embodied an intent standard. Senator Kennedy, the Act's principal sponsor, promptly replied, noting that all of the federal courts of appeals had accepted the impact test. 134 Cong. Rec. S12449 (Sept. 14, 1988). Thus the matter stands.

The *Black Jack* decision, discussed in the principal case, held that once a discriminatory effect was shown, the government must defend the challenged zoning (exclusion of multi-family housing, in a community in the heavily segregated St. Louis metropolitan area) by showing a "compelling" interest. How does this differ from *Huntington*? Which approach is preferable?

3. *Later cases.* The effects test applied under the Fair Housing Act has allowed courts to grant summary judgment or refuse to dismiss complaints in cases claiming discrimination under zoning ordinances. *Summerchase Ltd. Partnership I v. City of Gonzales*, 970 F. Supp. 522 (M.D. La. 1997) (granting summary judgment); *Homeowner/Contractor Consultants, Inc. v. Ascension Parish Planning & Zoning Comm'n*, 32 F. Supp. 2d 384 (M.D. La. 1999) (refusing to grant motion to dismiss). Other cases refused to find violations of the statute when developers claimed a denial of zoning approval was discriminatory. E.g., *Jackson v. City of Auburn*, 41 F. Supp. 2d 1300 (M.D. Ala. 1999) (denial of conditional use permit). Merely asserting a race-based allegation, arguing that a prohibition against low-income housing would have a disproportionately adverse impact on monitoring groups absent evidentiary support, does not form the basis for an FHA violation. *White Oak Property Development, LLC v. Washington Township, Ohio*, 606 F.3d 842, 851 (6th Cir. 2010), citing and quoting *United States v. City of Parma*, 661 F.2d 562 (6th Cir. 1981).

Note that the court in *Huntington* determined whether there had been a disparate impact by examining the proportionate impact of the zoning denial on minorities. This differed from the approach used by the district court, which determined disparate impact by looking at the absolute number of whites and minorities affected by the zoning denial, an approach that precludes a finding of disparate impact because minority status necessarily means smaller numbers. The *Huntington* approach is consistent with the Title VII employment discrimination cases. Later cases have accepted the *Huntington* approach. *Hallmark Developers, Inc. v. Fulton County*, 466 F.3d 1276 (11th Cir. 2006).

Following *Huntington* does not guarantee success for plaintiffs, however. *Hallmark* held a zoning denial for a housing project was not a violation of the statute because the cost and rent of similar existing housing near the proposed project was speculative evidence of disparate impact. People living in such housing would not necessarily purchase housing in the proposed project. In the majority of cases where disparate impact has been found, the court held, there was a waiting list for affordable housing or a shortage of housing for which only a defined group qualified. Compare *Dews v. Town of Sunnyvale*, 109 F. Supp. 2d 526, 570–73 (N.D. Tex. 2000) (exclusion of homes costing less than $150,000 evidence of disparate impact because number of African-Americans who could buy housing in excess of that amount was disproportionately low). For discussion of these issues, see Note, *Making Exclusionary Zoning Remedies Work: How Courts Applying Title VII Standards to Fair Housing Cases Have Misunderstood the Housing Market*, 24 Yale. L. & Pol'y Rev. 437 (2006).

4. *The state role.* Because of the close links between race and poverty, state housing subsidy programs can play a crucial role in the elimination of housing segregation. A Brookings Institution study of the federal Low Income Housing Tax Credit program (administered by the states) documents the positive impact that subsidy programs can have in promoting racial and economic diversity, while at the same time noting that minority households continue to cluster disproportionately in subsidy neighborhoods. Center on Urban and Metropolitan Policy, Siting Affordable Housing: Location and Neighborhood Trends of Low Income Housing Tax Credit Developments in the 1990s (2004). But what if the state fails to cooperate, as was the case in *Housing Help, supra* note 1? In *In re Adoption of the 2003 Low Income Housing Tax Credit Qualified Allocation Plan*, 848 A.2d 1 (N.J. Super. 2004), the court held that a state housing finance agency had a duty under Title VIII to "affirmatively further" integration in administering the federal tax credit program. In *Housing Help*, the federal court had to thread through a maze of Eleventh Amendment immunity rules to hold the state agency liable; more recent decisions of the Supreme Court have broadened the scope of this constitutional immunity, although none deals directly with housing issues. Cf. *University of Alabama v. Garrett*, 531 U.S. 356 (2001).

5. *Application to zoning.* For discussion of the application of the Fair Housing Act to zoning, see Federal Land Use Law, *supra*, §§ 11:16, 11:17; Johnson, *Race-Based Housing Importunities: The Disparate Impact of Realistic Group Conflict*, 8 Loy. J. Pub. Int. L. 97 (2007); Schwartz, *The Fair Housing Act and "Discriminatory Effect": A New Perspective*, 11 Nova L.J. 71 (1987); Ford, *The Boundaries of Race: Political Geography in Legal Analysis*, 107 Harv. L. Rev. 1841, 1894-97 (1994).

6. *Westchester County, N.Y. settlement.* Administered by the U.S. Department of Housing and Community Development, the federal Community Development Block Grant (CDBG) program provides annual grants on a formula basis to entitled cities and counties to carry out a wide range of community development activities directed toward revitalizing neighborhoods, economic development, and providing improved community facilities and services. The program is authorized under Title 1 of the Housing and Community Development Act of 1974, Public Law 93-383, as amended; 42 U.S.C. § 5301 *et seq.* Communities develop their own programs and funding priorities. However, grantees must give maximum feasible priority to activities which benefit low- and moderate-income persons. A grantee may also carry out activities which aid in the prevention or elimination of slums or blight. Additionally, grantees may fund activities when the grantee certifies that the activities meet other community development needs having a particular urgency because existing conditions pose a serious and immediate threat to the health or welfare of the community where other financial resources are not available to meet such needs. CDBG funds may not be used for activities which do not meet these broad national objectives. U.S. Department of Housing and Urban Development, Community Development Block Grant Entitlement Communities Grants, *available at:* www.hud.gov/offices/cpd/communitydevelopment/programs/entitlement/

Federal law requires CDBG recipients to conduct an "analysis of impediments" to fair housing choice within their jurisdictions, and outline appropriate actions to overcome those impediments." 24 C.F.R. § 91.425(a)(1)(i). Recipients of the grants are required to make certifications to the Secretary of Housing and Urban Development including certifications that "the grant will be conducted and administered in conformity with the Civil Rights Act of 1964, 42 U.S.C. §§ 2000a *et seq.*, and the Fair Housing Act, 42 U.S.C. §§ 3601 *et seq.*, that the grantee will affirmatively further fair housing," and that "the projected use of funds has been developed so as to give maximum feasible priority to activities which will benefit low- and moderate-income families or aid in the prevention or elimination of slums or blight." 42 U.S.C. § 5304(b)(2), (3). In 2009, Westchester County entered into a settlement agreement with the U.S. Departments of Justice and Housing and Urban Development as a result of a lawsuit brought by an antidiscrimination advocacy and litigation group under the federal False Claims Act, 31 U.S.C. §§ 3729 *et seq.* The suit said that when Westchester applied for federal grants for affordable housing and other projects, it lied by claiming to have complied with mandates to encourage fair housing through the impediments analysis. *United States ex rel. Anti-Discrimination Center of Metro New York, Inc. v. Westchester County, New York*, 495 F. Supp. 2d 375 (S.D.N.Y. 2007); *United States ex rel. Anti-Discrimination Center of Metro New York, Inc. v. Westchester County*, No. Case 1:06-cv-02860-DLC, Opinion and Order (S.D.N.Y. April 24, 2009).

Under the settlement, agreed to in August 2009, Westchester County is required to spend $51.6 million over seven years to develop the affordable housing. Specifically it must build or acquire 750 homes or apartments, 630 of which must be provided in towns and villages where black residents constitute three percent or less of the population and Hispanic residents make up less than seven percent. The 120 other spaces must meet different criteria for cost and ethnic concentration. In the agreement, Westchester County also agrees that it has the authority to challenge zoning rules in villages and towns that in many cases implicitly discourage affordable housing by setting minimum lot sizes, discouraging higher-density developments or appropriating vacant property for other purposes. Westchester agreed to "take legal action to compel compliance if municipalities hinder or impede the county" in complying with the agreement. Roberts, *Westchester Adds Housing to Desegregation Pact*, N.Y. Times, August 10, 2009, available at:

> www.nytimes.com/2009/08/11/nyregion/11settle.html?_r=1&sq=westchester%20housing%20spano&st=cse&adxnnl=1&scp=6&adxnnlx=1265926401-M0UZ25fpSXt+nM/2ogbPFg.

For a copy of the agreement, see

> www.antibiaslaw.com/sites/default/files/files/SettlementFullText.pdf.

Westchester County has created a website where it posts all documents related to the settlement including the implementation plan, *available at:*

> http://homes.westchestergov.com/index.php?option=com_content&task=view&id=2592&Itemid=4485

For the current status of actions by Westchester County in this case from the perspective of the plaintiffs, see http://www.antibiaslaw.com/westchester-false-claims-case.

This case signals an important change in direction of the enforcement of the Fair Housing Act under the administration of President Barack Obama as it applies to the CDBG program. For a discussion of the case and the settlement, see Allen, *No Certification, No Money: The Revival of Civil Rights Obligations in HUD Funding Programs*, 78 Planning Comm'rs J. 12 (2010). For an overview of federal enforcement efforts, see Remarks as Prepared for Delivery by Assistant Attorney General for Civil Rights Thomas E. Perez at the National Fair Housing

Policy Conference, July 20, 2010, *available at:* http://www.justice.gov/crt/speeches/perez_fairhousingpolicyconf_speech.php.

C. DISCRIMINATION AGAINST GROUP HOMES FOR THE HANDICAPPED

Congress in 1988 amended the Fair Housing Act to prohibit discrimination against group homes for the handicapped. The amendments prohibit a number of discriminatory practices in the sale or rental of housing, but they also apply to discrimination in zoning ordinances. By adopting the case-by-case approach to zoning discrimination against group homes, Congress opened up a Pandora's box of litigation that has not clarified community responsibility under the Act. Below are some of the major features of the Act. The important question is the effect the amendments have on zoning restrictions and the zoning process. It is an important example of a congressional override on local zoning, and has prompted calls for revision from local government organizations.

Definition of handicap. The Act does not apply to all group homes, only to homes for the handicapped. Congress explicitly adopted the definition used in the Rehabilitation Act of 1973. 29 U.S.C. § 794. The statute defines "handicap" as a "physical or mental impairment which substantially limits one or more of such person's major life activities." 42 U.S.C. § 3602(h). The definition includes alcoholism, drug addiction and persons with AIDS. See *Bragdon v. Abbott*, 524 U.S. 624 (1998) (persons with AIDS). It does not cover all of the group homes that often are subject to discriminatory restrictions under zoning law. Discrimination in zoning against these group homes has been litigated under other statutes, such as the Americans with Disabilities Act (discussed in Note 7 after *Larkin, infra*).

Application to zoning. The Act does not explicitly include zoning, but it includes language borrowed from elsewhere in the Act that prohibits acts that "otherwise make unavailable or deny" a dwelling because of a handicap. 42 U.S.C. § 3604(f)(1). The courts have made it clear in racial discrimination cases that this phrase includes zoning, and the House Judiciary Committee report on the group home amendments makes it clear they are to apply to "zoning decisions and practices." These include special requirements and conditional and special use permits "that have the effect of limiting the ability of such individuals to live in the residence of their choice in the community." H.R. Rep. No. 711, 100th Cong., 2d Sess. 24 (1988). The legislative history indicates courts are to apply an effects test to discrimination against the handicapped by zoning ordinances.

The Act also includes as discrimination the refusal to make reasonable accommodations in rules, policies and practices when such accommodations are necessary to afford handicapped persons an opportunity to use and enjoy a dwelling. 42 U.S.C. § 3604(f)(3)(B). This provision is limited to this part of the Fair Housing Act, and could be a powerful requirement as applied to zoning.

Facial vs. as-applied attacks. State statutes and local zoning ordinances can violate the Fair Housing Act in two ways: they may be facially in conflict with the Act, or they may violate the Act as applied. One example of a requirement that may conflict facially with the Act are zoning ordinances and statutes that contain density, spacing and quota requirements for group homes. The presence of provisions of this type in group home statutes and ordinances raises important questions about the use of quotas in land use regulation. Similar quotas for the spacing of housing based on racial occupancy are unthinkable. The following case considers the validity of this type of requirement under the Fair Housing Act ("as-applied" cases are discussed in Note 5 after *Larkin*, *infra*).

LARKIN v. STATE OF MICHIGAN DEPARTMENT OF SOCIAL SERVICES

89 F.3d 285 (6th Cir. 1996)

ALDRICH, DISTRICT JUDGE. . . .

I.

Geraldine Larkin sought a license to operate an adult foster care (AFC) facility which would provide care for up to four handicapped adults in Westland, Michigan. The Michigan Adult Foster Care Licensing Act (MAFCLA), M.C.L. §§ 400.701 et seq., governs the issuance of such licenses. It prevents the issuance of a temporary license if the proposed AFC facility would "substantially contribute to an excessive concentration" of community residential facilities within a municipality. M.C.L. § 400.716(1). Moreover, it requires compliance with section 3b of the state's zoning enabling act, codified as M.C.L. § 125.583b. M.C.L. § 400.716(3). Section 3b of the zoning act provides in part:

> At least 45 days before licensing a residential facility [which provides resident services or care for six or fewer persons under 24-hour supervision], the state licensing agency shall notify the council . . . or the designated agency of the city or village where the proposed facility is to be located to review the number of existing or proposed similar state licensed residential facilities whose property lines are within a 1,500-foot radius of the property lines of the proposed facility. The council of a city or village or an agency of the city or village to which the authority is delegated, when a proposed facility is to be located within the city or village, shall give appropriate notification . . . to those residents whose property lines are within a 1,500-foot radius of the property lines of the proposed facility. A state licensing agency shall not license a proposed residential facility if another state licensed residential facility exists within the 1,500-foot radius of the proposed location, unless permitted by local zoning ordinances or if the issuance of the license would substantially contribute to an excessive concentration of state licensed residential facilities within the city or village.

M.C.L. § 125.583b(4). MAFCLA also requires notice to the municipality in which the proposed AFC facility will be located. M.C.L. § 400.732(1).

Michigan Department of Social Services (MDSS) notified Westland of Larkin's application in accordance with MAFCLA. Westland determined that there was an existing AFC facility within 1,500 feet of the proposed facility and so notified MDSS. It also notified MDSS that it was not waiving the spacing requirement, so that MDSS could not issue a license to Larkin. When MDSS informed Larkin of Westland's action, Larkin withdrew her application. . . .

[On cross-motions for summary judgment, the district court ruled that the Michigan statutes were preempted by the Fair Housing Act and violated the federal Equal Protection Clause. The department appealed.]

III.

. . . [The court reviewed the provisions of the federal act.]

A. Preemption

. . . [The court noted that "[i]n this case, the FHAA [the Fair Housing Act] expressly provides that any state law 'that purports to require or permit any action that would be a discriminatory housing practice under this subchapter shall to that extent be invalid.'" 42 U.S.C. § 3615. It thus treated the case as one of express preemption and actual conflict between the federal and state law.]

B. Discrimination

This brings us to the crux of the case: whether the statutes at issue discriminate against the disabled in violation of the FHAA. The district court held that two different aspects of MAFCLA violate the FHAA: (1) the 1500-foot spacing requirement of M.C.L. § 125.583b(4); and (2) the notice requirements of M.C.L. §§ 125.583b(4) & 400.732(1). . . . [The court noted that most courts applying the Fair Housing Act have analogized it to Title VII of the Civil Rights Act, and have concluded a violation can be shown through disparate treatment or disparate effect.]

Here, the challenged portions of MAFCLA are facially discriminatory. The spacing requirement prohibits MDSS from licensing any new AFC facility if it is within 1500 feet of an existing AFC facility. The notice requirements require MDSS to notify the municipality of the proposed facility, and the local authorities to then notify all residents within 1500 feet of the proposed facility. By their very terms, these statutes apply only to AFC facilities which will house the disabled, and not to other living arrangements. As we have previously noted, statutes that single out for regulation group homes for the handicapped are facially discriminatory. Accordingly, this is a case of intentional discrimination or disparate treatment, rather than disparate impact.

MDSS argues that the statutes at issue cannot have a discriminatory intent because they are motivated by a benign desire to help the disabled. This is incorrect as a matter of law. The Supreme Court has held in the employment context that "the absence of a malevolent motive does not convert a facially discriminatory policy into a neutral policy with a discriminatory effect." [*International Union, United Auto. Aerospace & Agricultural Implement Workers v.*] *Johnson Controls*, 499 U.S. [187] at 199 (1991). Following *Johnson Controls*, all of the courts which have considered this issue under the FHAA have concluded the defendant's benign motive does not prevent the statute from being discriminatory on its face. MDSS relies on *Familystyle of St. Paul, Inc. v. City of St. Paul*, 728 F. Supp. 1396 (D. Minn. 1990), *aff'd*, 923 F.2d 91 (8th Cir. 1991), for the proposition that proof of a discriminatory motive is required for a finding of discriminatory intent. However, both decisions in *Familystyle* preceded the Supreme Court's opinion in *Johnson Controls*. Thus, they have been implicitly overruled by *Johnson Controls* in this regard.

Because the statutes at issue are facially discriminatory, the burden shifts to the defendant to justify the challenged statutes. However, it is not clear how much of a burden shifts. MDSS urges us to follow the Eighth Circuit and rule that discriminatory statutes are subject to a rational basis scrutiny, i.e., they will be upheld if they are rationally related to a legitimate government objective. *See Familystyle*, 923 F.2d at 94. Plaintiffs urge us to reject the rational basis test and adopt the standard announced by the Tenth Circuit, which requires the defendant to show that the discriminatory statutes either (1) are justified by individualized safety concerns; or (2) really benefit, rather than discriminate against, the handicapped, and are not based on unsupported stereotypes. *Bangerter* [*v. Orem City Corp.*], 46 F.3d [1491] at 1503–04 [(10th Cir. 1995)].

Although we have never explicitly decided the issue, we have held that in order for special safety restrictions on homes for the handicapped to pass muster under the FHAA, the safety requirements must be tailored to the particular needs of the disabled who will reside in the house. *Marbrunak* [*v. City of Stowe*], 974 F.2d [43] at 47 [(6th Cir. 1992)]. We rejected the ordinances at issue in that case because they required

> nearly every safety requirement that one might think of as desirable to protect persons handicapped by any disability — mental or physical; and all the requirements applied to all housing for developmentally disabled persons, regardless of the type of mental condition that causes their disabilities or of the ways in which the disabilities manifest themselves.

Id. Therefore, in order for facially discriminatory statutes to survive a challenge under the FHAA, the defendant must demonstrate that they are "warranted by the unique and specific needs and abilities of those handicapped persons" to whom the regulations apply. *Id.*

MDSS has not met that burden. MDSS claims that the 1500-foot spacing requirement integrates the disabled into the community and prevents "clustering" and "ghettoization." In addition, it argues that the spacing requirement also serves the goal of deinstitutionalization by preventing a cluster of AFC facilities from recreating an institutional environment in the community.

As an initial matter, integration is not a sufficient justification for maintaining permanent quotas under the FHA or the FHAA, especially where, as here, the burden of the quota falls on the disadvantaged minority. The FHAA protects the right of individuals to live in the residence of their choice in the community. *Marbrunak*, 974 F.2d at 45. If the state were allowed to impose quotas on the number of minorities who could move into a neighborhood in the name of integration, this right would be vitiated.

MDSS argues that the state is not imposing a quota because it is not limiting the number of disabled who can live in a neighborhood, it is merely limiting the number of AFC facilities within that neighborhood. However, as we have previously noted, disabled individuals who wish to live in a community often have no choice but to live in an AFC facility. Alternatively, if the disabled truly have the right to live anywhere they choose, then the limitations on AFC facilities do not prevent clustering and ghettoization in any meaningful way. Thus, MDSS's own argument suggests that integration is not the true reason for the spacing requirements.

Moreover, MDSS has not shown how the special needs of the disabled warrant intervention to ensure that they are integrated. MDSS has produced no evidence that AFC facilities will cluster absent the spacing statute. In fact, this statute was not enforced from 1990 to 1993, and MDSS has offered no evidence that AFC facilities tended to cluster during that period.

Instead, MDSS simply assumes that the disabled must be integrated, and does not recognize that the disabled may choose to live near other disabled individuals. The result might be different if some municipalities were forcing the disabled to segregate, or cluster, in a few small areas. However, Michigan already prohibits such behavior:

> In order to implement the policy of this state that persons in need of community residential care shall not be excluded by zoning from the benefits of a normal residential surroundings, a state licensed residential facility providing supervision or care, or both, to 6 or less persons shall be considered a residential use of property for purposes of zoning and a permitted use in all residential zones, including those zoned for single family dwellings, *and shall not be subject to a special use or conditional use permit or procedure different from those required for other dwellings of similar density in the same zone.*

M.C.L. § 125.583b(2) (emphasis added). The only clustering or segregation that will occur, then, is as the result of the free choice of the disabled. In other words, the state's policy of forced integration is not protecting the disabled from any forced segregation; rather, the state is forcing them to integrate based on the paternalistic idea that it knows best where the disabled should choose to live.

In contrast, deinstitutionalization is a legitimate goal for the state to pursue. However, MDSS does not explain how a rule prohibiting two AFC facilities from being within 1500 feet of each other fosters deinstitutionalization in any real way. Two AFC facilities 500 feet apart would violate the statute without remotely threatening to recreate an institutional setting in the community. In fact, the spacing requirement may actually inhibit the goal of deinstitutionalization by limiting the number of AFC facilities which can be operated within any given community.

MDSS relies again on *Familystyle*, where both the district court and the Eighth Circuit found that the goal of deinstitutionalization justified facially discriminatory spacing requirements. However, *Familystyle* is distinguishable from the present case. In *Familystyle*, the plaintiff already housed 119 disabled individuals within a few city blocks. The courts were concerned that the plaintiffs were simply recreating an institutionalized setting in the community, rather than deinstitutionalizing the disabled.

Here, however, Larkin seeks only to house four disabled individuals in a home which happens to be less than 1500 feet from another AFC facility. The proposed AFC facility, and many more like it that are prohibited by the spacing requirement, do not threaten Michigan's professed goal of deinstitutionalization. Because it sweeps in the vast majority of AFC facilities which do not seek to recreate an institutional setting, the spacing requirement is too broad, and is not tailored to the specific needs of the handicapped. . . .

MDSS also has failed to provide an adequate justification for the notice requirements. MDSS merely offers the same justifications for the notice requirements as it offers for the spacing requirements, i.e., integration and deinstitutionalization. Notifying the municipality or the neighbors of the proposed AFC facility seems to have little relationship to the advancement of these goals. In fact, such notice would more likely have quite the opposite effect, as it would facilitate the organized opposition to the home, and animosity towards its residents. Furthermore, MDSS has offered no evidence that the needs of the handicapped would warrant such notice. We find that the notice requirements violate the FHAA and are preempted by it.

By this holding, we in no way mean to intimate that the FHA, as amended by the FHAA, prohibits reasonable regulation and licensing procedures for AFC facilities. As was stated in *Marbrunak*, "the FHAA does not prohibit the city from imposing *any* special safety standards for the protection of developmentally disabled persons." *Marbrunak*, 974 F.2d at 47 (emphasis in original). Rather, it merely prohibits those which are not "demonstrated to be warranted by the unique and specific needs and abilities of those handicapped persons." *Id.* . . .

For the foregoing reasons, the judgment of the district court is

Affirmed.

NOTES AND QUESTIONS

1. *When zoning conflicts.* Compare the court's view of the statutory requirements in the *Larkin* case with the court's analysis of the zoning denial in the *Huntington* case, reproduced *supra.* In what ways are they similar? Different? The court in *Larkin* finds a deinstitutionalization policy in the federal law and then applies it to invalidate the state statutes. Compare that policy with the desegregation policy implicit in *Huntington.* Do the courts treat the burden of proof issue the same way in both cases?

2. *Spacing requirements.* The *Larkin* court held the spacing requirements were a facial violation of the Fair Housing Act, and distinguished *Familystyle* on factual grounds not actually relied on in that decision. Accord *Horizon House Developmental Services, Inc. v. Township of Upper Southhampton*, 804 F. Supp. 683 (E.D. Pa. 1992) (1000-foot spacing requirement facially invalid). *Oconomowoc Residential Programs, Inc. v. City of Milwaukee*, 300 F.3d 775, 787 (7th Cir. 2002), invalidated a 2500-foot spacing requirement. The court said, "Because the spacing ordinance draws a nearly half mile circle around each existing group home, it currently precludes new group homes from opening in most of the [city]." 300 F.3d at 787. *Harding v. City of Toledo*, 433 F. Supp. 2d 867 (D. Ohio 2006), distinguished both of these cases because the spacing requirement was only 500 feet. Should this be a factual issue? Is this a "fair share" problem like *Mount Laurel*? See also *Nevada Fair Hous. Ctr., Inc v. Clark County*, 2007 U.S. Dist. LEXIS 12800 (D. Nev. 2007) (invalidating 1500-foot requirement). In that case, the state statute mandated a spacing requirement. In the *Toledo* case, the statute authorized but did not require spacing requirements.

Even an approval procedure that has no expressly stated spacing requirement may be suspect. In *Human Res. Research & Mgmt Group v. County of Suffolk*, 687 F. Supp. 2d 237 (E.D.N.Y. 2010), the plaintiffs, an organization that established substance abuse recovery houses and individuals who participated in substance abuse recovery programs, alleged that a local law regulating substance abuse recovery houses violated the United States Constitution, the Fair Housing Act (FHA), the Americans With Disabilities Act, and state law. Among other things, it challenged a site-selection provision that established a notice requirement and approval procedure to assess the desirability of the proposed substance abuse house in the area under consideration. The procedure, in the County's words, was aimed at ensuring that " 'there be some level of uniformity and dispersal of these substance abuse houses, so that one neighborhood's resources and facilities are not unduly drained while others are unaffected.' " *Id.* at 57. Reviewing other federal decisions on spacing and dispersal, including *Larkin* and *Oconomowoc*, the district court concluded, under a heightened scrutiny analysis, that Suffolk County failed to show that it has a legitimate interest in uniform dispersal of substance abuse houses. The court observed that the law permits a community where a substance abuse house was proposed to object on the simple basis that there is no "need" for the facility in the municipality or in the area. "Under the plain terms of the law, then, a municipality can object to the location of a substance abuse home in a particular community even if there are no such establishments in the community at all, based on an assessment that the house is not needed.

This extremely vague and flexible standard for municipal objections is in direct conflict with the overarching goal of the FHA to allow protected individuals — including disabled persons — to 'live in the residence of their choice in the community.' " *Id.* at 61–62.

3. *Occupancy and other potentially discriminatory requirements.* Occupancy limits are critical for group homes because restrictive limits can make a group home impracticable. Chapter 3 considered a similar issue concerning limitations in zoning ordinances on the number of unrelated people who can live together. Occupancy limitations in zoning ordinances that apply to group homes also present a problem of facial conflict with the federal Act.

Oxford House-C v. City of St. Louis, 77 F.3d 249 (8th Cir. 1996), upheld an ordinance that allowed eight unrelated persons in a group home and only three unrelated persons in a single family dwelling. This limitation effectively prohibited group homes that had to have more than eight residents to be financially successful. The court relied on the Supreme Court's *Belle Terre* case, reproduced *supra*, to hold that the legitimate goals of decreasing traffic, congestion and noise in residential areas justified the ordinance. Is this case contrary to *Larkin*, at least in spirit? Some district courts disagree with the *St. Louis* case. *Children's Alliance v. City of Bellevue*, 950 F. Supp. 1491 (W.D. Wash. 1997) (invalidating ordinance limiting group home to six residents, not more than two caretakers, plus minor children of residents and caretakers).

Courts have invalidated limitations and requirements they find discriminatory. They have invalidated ordinances that exclude group homes from residential areas, for example, either through the definition of "family," *Oxford House, Inc. v. Town of Babylon*, 819 F. Supp. 1179 (E.D.N.Y. 1993), or by adopting onerous restrictions that have the effect of excluding group homes, *Children's Alliance, supra.* A discriminatory application to group homes of zoning requirements such as a certification requirement also violates the act. *Community Hous. Trust v. Department of Consumer & Regulatory Affairs*, 257 F. Supp. 2d 208 (D.D.C. 2003), *noted*, 21 J. Contemp. Health L. & Pol'y 205 (2005).

4. *Statutory exemption for reasonable occupancy restrictions.* The statute contains an exemption that permits "reasonable . . . restriction[s] regarding the maximum number of occupants permitted to occupy a dwelling." 42 U.S.C. § 3607(b)(1). In *City of Edmonds v. Oxford House, Inc.*, 514 U.S. 725 (1995), the city's zoning ordinance defined "family" as a household either "related by genetics, adoption or marriage," or consisting of no more than five unrelated persons; this definition blocked a group home. The city argued that the ordinance definition was permitted by § 3607(b)(1) as a reasonable occupancy restriction.

The Court disagreed. Justice Ginsburg distinguished between *occupancy limits*, normally found in a housing code, which restrict the number of persons who may live in a dwelling, and *use restrictions*, such as the limitation to single-family use at issue before the court. The definition of family, she held, was ancillary to this *use restriction*, and thus not covered by the exemption applicable to occupancy limits. Congress provided the occupancy limit exemption, the Court held, because in another provision of the 1988 Amendments, it had prohibited discrimination against families with children, and it did not want to leave municipalities unable to prevent overcrowding. The Edmonds ordinance exactly inverted this concern, permitting families of any number but limiting unrelated groups.

True occupancy restrictions are permitted by the exemption. *Fair Hous. Advocates Ass'n v. City of Richmond Heights*, 998 F. Supp. 825 (N.D. Ohio 1998) (upholding occupancy restriction based on number of square feet in unit). The exception does not apply when there is discriminatory enforcement. *Valdez v. Town of Brookhaven*, 2005 U.S. Dist. LEXIS 36713

(D.N.Y. 2005) (discriminatory enforcement against Latinos).

5. *Exceptions and variances.* Zoning ordinances may require group homes to obtain exceptions or conditional use permits, or variances. These zoning techniques, which are discussed in the next chapter, require some (usually discretionary) approval from a zoning agency. A refusal to grant a variance or exception is a potential as-applied violation of the federal Act.

Regional Economic Community Action Program, Inc. (RECAP) v. City of Middleton, 294 F.3d 35 (2d. Cir. 2002), illustrates how discretionary decisionmaking can raise questions under the Act. The city denied special use permits for a half-way house for recovering alcoholics, and the district court granted summary judgment in the city's favor. The Second Circuit panel concluded that recovering alcoholics were a protected class, but it drew sharp distinctions between plaintiffs' disparate treatment, disparate impact and reasonable accommodations theories. On the evidence presented, the court found that a jury could find that the city's reasons for denying the permits were pretextual and that it was motivated wholly or in part by animus towards the class. On the disparate impact claim, however, it upheld the grant of summary judgment because the plaintiffs only challenged the denial of their own permits and made no effort to show that the facially neutral special permit requirement, which applied to a variety of uses in the zones in question, had a disproportionate impact on plaintiffs as opposed to other groups. The court also upheld summary judgment on plaintiffs' reasonable accommodation claim. But see *Baxter v. City of Belleville*, 720 F. Supp. 720 (S.D. Ill. 1989) (refusal to grant special use permit for a hospice for terminally ill AIDS patients; refusal had a discriminatory impact on people with AIDS because it was based on fear of AIDS). Compare *Cleburne, reproduced supra*, Ch. 3. In light of *Baxter*, could plaintiffs in *RECAP* successfully restate their disparate impact claim?

Courts will uphold a denial of a variance or exception when there is a legitimate reason for the denial. See *Gamble v. City of Escondido*, 104 F.3d 300 (9th Cir. 1997) (proposed building too large for lot and did not conform in size and bulk with neighborhood structures). An interesting question is the extent to which the Fair Housing Act modifies the usual rules for exceptions and variances. One court held a proposed group home was not entitled to a special exception in a business zone when traditional homes would also have been denied an exception in this zone. *Forest City Daly Hous., Inc. v. Town of North Hempstead*, 175 F.3d 144 (2d Cir. 1999). Compare Hovsons, Inc. v. Township of Brick, 89 F.3d 1096 (3d Cir. 1996) (refusal to grant variance in residential area violated reasonable accommodation requirement when group homes for handicapped were not allowed in these areas as-of-right).

Challenging individual denials of special uses and other land use approvals is a time-consuming, expensive and uncertain strategy, however. Could it be argued that the very requirement of a special use or other approval facially violates the Act because of the stigma it attaches to group homes for the handicapped? The court thought not in *United States v. Village of Palatine*, 37 F.3d 1230 (7th Cir. 1994):

> In this case the burden on the inhabitants of [the group home] imposed by the public hearing — which they need not attend — does not outweigh the Village's interest in applying its facially neutral law to all applicants for a special use approval. Public input is an important aspect of municipal decision making; we cannot impose a blanket requirement that cities waive their public notice and hearing requirements in all cases involving the handicapped. [*Id.* at 1234.]

A few cases, however, have held that requiring a group home to go through the variance process is not a reasonable accommodation because of the burden it places on the entity seeking a variance. See *Horizon House, supra.* You might consider, after you finish the next chapter, whether there is a reason for distinguishing a variance from a special exception.

6. *Reasonable accommodation.* The "reasonable accommodation" requirement is unique to the group home provisions in Title VIII. In addition to "reasonableness," the statute requires that the accommodation be "necessary" to afford a person with a disability an "equal opportunity to use and enjoy a dwelling." *Advocacy Center for People With Disabilities, Inc. v. Woodlands Estates Ass'n., Inc.*, 192 F. Supp. 2d 1344 (M.D. Fla. 2002), explains:

> The determination of whether an accommodation is reasonable is highly fact-specific and determined on a case-by-case basis. For example, an accommodation is reasonable if it does not impose "undue financial and administrative burdens" or "changes, adjustments, or modifications to existing programs that would be substantial, or that would constitute fundamental alterations in the nature of the program." In determining whether a requested accommodation is necessary, "the overall focus should be on 'whether waiver of the rule would be so at odds with the purposes behind the rule that it would be a fundamental and unreasonable change.'" Courts generally balance the burdens imposed on the defendant by the contemplated accommodation against the benefits to the plaintiff. [*Id.* at 1348 (citations omitted).]

The courts have divided on which party has the burden of proof as to both "reasonableness" and "necessity." See *Lapid-Laurel L.L.C. v. Zoning Bd. of Adj.*, 284 F.3d 442 (3d Cir. 2002) (different for different issues); *Groner v. Golden Gate Gardens Apts.*, 250 F.3d 1039 (6th Cir. 2001) (plaintiff).

In the typical situation, the municipality is asked to provide a reasonable accommodation to modify a limitation in the ordinance that makes it impossible to locate a group home. One example is a reasonable accommodation to modify a spacing requirement. *New Hope Fellowship, Inc. v. City of Omaha*, 2005 U.S. Dist. LEXIS 39174 (D. Neb. 2005) (requiring 94% modification in requirement; no concentration of group homes found). Another is a reasonable accommodation to modify a limitation on occupancy. *Dr. Gertrude A. Barber Ctr., Inc. v. Peters Twp.*, 273 F. Supp. 2d 643 (D. Pa. 2003) (accommodation required). One way for a municipality to make "reasonable accommodation" is to provide for variances and special exceptions, as discussed in Note 5, *supra*. The typical situation is one in which a variance or special exception has been sought and denied, and the group home argues that the municipality has refused to make a "reasonable accommodation." See *Dr. Gertrude A. Barber Center, supra*, where the court held the exception would not "fundamentally alter" the zoning scheme.

An even more difficult problem is whether the "reasonable accommodation" provision requires a municipality to amend its zoning ordinance to allow for a group home. See *Smith & Lee Assocs. v. City of Taylor (II)*, 102 F.3d 781 (6th Cir. 1996) (rezoning required, but density limited). Recall the discussion in *City of Richmond v. Randall, supra* Chapter 3, about the reluctance of courts to interfere in the "legislative" act of rezoning. In *Hemisphere Bldg. Co. v. Village of Richton Park*, 171 F.3d 437 (7th Cir. 1999), the court refused to require a rezoning to the highest density found anywhere in the zoning district in question.

7. *The Americans with Disabilities and Rehabilitation Acts.* Group homes not covered by the Fair Housing Act may be able to bring suits claiming zoning discrimination under these acts. Both statutes prohibit municipalities denying disabled persons the benefits of "services, programs or activities." See 42 U.S.C. § 12132 (ADA). *Innovative Health Systems, Inc. v. City of White Plains*, 117 F.3d 37 (2d Cir. 1997), held that this language included zoning, and held the plaintiff stated a claim that these statutes had been violated by a refusal to issue a building permit for an alcohol- and drug-dependent treatment center based on "stereotypes and generalized fears." The courts have applied these acts to strike down restrictions on group homes. *New Directions Treatment Servs. v. City of Reading*, 2007 U.S. App. LEXIS 14025 (3d Cir. 2007) (reviewing cases and invalidating statute prohibiting location of home within 500 feet of residential areas and other structures).

8. *Some final comments.* The Fair Housing Act amendments that cover group homes for the handicapped have had a substantial effect on zoning practices. Do you agree with the balance the courts have struck? How does the impact of the Fair Housing Act on zoning for group homes compare with the impact of exclusionary zoning rules on zoning for affordable housing? HUD has declined to issue regulations interpreting the group homes provision in the Fair Housing Act, leaving its interpretation to the courts on a case-by-case basis. If you were to recommend regulations, what should they provide?

9. *Sources.* For additional discussion, see Elliott, *The Fair Housing Act's "Reasonable Accommodation" Requirement*, Land Use L. & Zoning Dig., April 2000, at 3; Everly, *A Reasonable Burden: The Need for a Uniform Burden of Proof Scheme in Reasonable Accommodation Claims*, 29 Dayton L. Rev. 37 (2003); Sampson, *Pygmy Goats, Child Molesters, Fire Bugs, and Drug Addicts: The Land-Use Variance as Reasonable Accommodation Under the Fair Housing Amendments Acts*, Municipal Lawyer, May/June 2007, at 6; Schonfeld, *"Reasonable Accommodation" Under the Federal Fair Housing Amendments Act*, 25 Fordham Urb. L.J. 413 (1998); Note, *Not In My Backyard: The Disabled's Quest For Rights in Local Zoning Disputes Under the Fair Housing, the Rehabilitation, and the Americans with Disabilities Acts*, 33 Val. U. L. Rev. 581 (1999); Note and Comment, *The Role of Exhaustion and Ripeness Doctrines in Reasonable Accommodations Denial Under the Fair Housing Amendments Act*, 24 BYU J. Pub. L. 347 (2010).

Chapter 6

THE ZONING PROCESS: EUCLIDEAN ZONING GIVES WAY TO FLEXIBLE ZONING

A. THE ROLE OF ZONING CHANGE

We have so far considered the traditional, or Euclidean, zoning system, so named for the U.S. Supreme Court case that upheld the constitutionality of zoning by districts. Euclidean zoning contemplates the division of the community into districts, in which land uses are allowed as-of-right. The administrative process should be quite simple:

> The originators of zoning anticipated a fairly simple administrative process. They thought of the zoning regulation as being largely "self-executing." After the formulation of the ordinance text and map by a local zoning commission and its adoption by the local governing body, most administrations would require only the services of a building official who would determine whether proposed construction complied with the requirements. This official was not expected to exercise discretion or sophisticated judgment. Rather, he was to apply the requirements to the letter. In the case of new construction, he was to compare the builder's plans with the requirements governing the particular land and either grant or deny a permit. Even today, this nondiscretionary permit process is at the heart of zoning administration. [Building the American City 202 (Report of the Nat'l Comm'n on Urban Problems, 1968).]

The Standard Zoning Act also provided for discretionary administrative procedures as well as a process through which the zoning ordinance could be amended, as the following article points out. Some of these procedures were intended to provide relief from the land use restrictions of the zoning ordinance.

Mandelker, *Delegation of Power and Function in Zoning Administration*, 1963 Washington University Law Quarterly 60, 61–63

As elsewhere in public administration, the basic problem in zoning is to achieve as clear a differentiation as possible between policy-making and policy-application. On this score the Standard State Zoning Enabling Act, on which a majority of the state statutes are modeled, failed to make tenable distinctions. Policy-making was confided to the governing body of the locality, which was given the authority to adopt the zoning ordinance. Administration was given to the zoning administrator, often the building inspector, who has the power to issue zoning permits. But ambiguity comes in the introduction of two agencies, the plan commission and the board of adjustment, known also as the board of zoning appeals. Both the commission and the board exercise functions that are partly legislative and partly administrative.

The plan commission is to advise on the enactment and amendment of the original ordinance. In theory, zoning amendments are to be made in response to substantial changes in environmental conditions or in other instances in which a policy change is indicated. Instead, amendments have often been employed to take care of limited changes in use, usually confined to one lot, a technique that has disapprovingly been called "spot zoning." Spot zoning for one parcel, vigorously opposed by adjacent neighbors, takes on adversary characteristics that give it a distinctly adjudicative cast.

The agency originally intended to provide a safety valve from the zoning ordinance is the board of adjustment. This board was authorized to grant both variances and [special] exceptions. . . . The variance is an administratively authorized departure from the terms of the zoning ordinance, granted in cases of unique and individual hardship, in which a strict application of the terms of the ordinance would be unconstitutional. The grant of the variance is meant to avoid an unfavorable holding on constitutionality.

By way of contrast, an exception is a use permitted by the ordinance in a district in which it is not necessarily incompatible, but where it might cause harm if not watched. Exceptions are authorized under conditions which will insure their compatibility with surrounding uses. Typically, a use which is the subject of a special exception demands a large amount of land, may be public or semi-public in character and might often be noxious or offensive. Not all of these characteristics will apply to every excepted use, however. Hospitals in residential districts are one example, because of the extensive area they occupy, and because of potential traffic and other problems which may affect a residential neighborhood. A filling station in a light commercial district is another example because of its potentially noxious effects.

NOTES AND QUESTIONS

1. This chapter covers moratoria or interim development controls, which are important tools for delaying the effectiveness of zoning controls while a jurisdiction considers changes to its zoning ordinance. It then addresses the variance, special exception and zoning amendment, which are the traditional statutory techniques through which landowners secure a change in the zoning restrictions applicable to their property. It also covers the floating zone and contract zoning, which are newer forms of flexible zoning, and the role of site-plan review and the comprehensive plan in the zoning process. A concluding section considers the role of the initiative and referendum in zoning, and SLAPP suits, or Strategic Lawsuits Against Public Participation. For a discussion of the zoning process and wait-and-see zoning, see Krasnowiecki, *Abolish Zoning*, 31 Syracuse L. Rev. 719 (1980).

2. Try to work out as clearly as you can the difference between a zoning amendment, a variance, and a special exception. The difficulty is that the owner of a small lot who wishes to have the applicable zoning restrictions changed as they apply to his property might conceivably make use of any of these techniques. He can ask the governing body for a map amendment to apply a different zoning classification. He might also be able to ask for a variance. He can also apply for a special exception if the use he proposes is listed as a special exception use in the zoning district in which his land is located. Under what circumstances might any or all of these alternatives be available? This is the problem addressed by the materials in this chapter.

The nature of the zoning change problem also varies with the nature of the area in which the landowner's property is located. In built-up areas, his property is likely to be an "infill" piece of vacant property surrounded by developed uses. The question is whether his proposed use fits in with this built-up land use environment. In suburban and developing areas, the problem is different. Here the surrounding area is likely to be undeveloped or sparsely developed. The landowner may own a substantial piece of land on which he plans to build a major development, such as a shopping center or a large residential development.

In suburban and developing areas, as *Building the American City* pointed out, the community may not intend its zoning ordinance to guide future development. Typically, such land use is zoned just below what it is anticipated that the market will demand, requiring all developers to come before a local zoning body to request some kind of zoning change. This type of zoning was called "wait-and-see" zoning, *id.* at 206; the zone is often referred to as a "holding zone," in that the municipality is holding open its options. Under a wait-and-see zoning system, all land development requires some type of permission, and zoning becomes a discretionary decisionmaking process rather than a system in which land uses are permitted as-of-right. Are the "taking" cases an impediment to this approach? Do you see other potential constitutional problems? Is this system of zoning administration rational? Well-organized? The American Planning Association has proposed model legislation that provides a major overhaul of the zoning administration process. American Planning Association, Growing Smart Legislative Guidebook: Model Statutes for Planning and Management of Change, Ch. 10 (S. Meck ed., 2002). Similarly, the American Bar Association adopted a model land use procedures code drafted by a Joint Task Force of the State and Local Government section with the cooperation of the Administrative Law and Regulation section. The ABA procedures are based significantly on the procedures proposed by the Growing Smart Legislative Guidebook. See http://law.wustl.edu/landuselaw/ModelLandUseCode.pdf.

3. The administration of the zoning process may involve the participation and expertise of various persons. The process can vary from a single zoning administrator in a small municipality, who may also be responsible for related tasks such as subdivision approval, community development, building permits and inspection and the like. In large metropolitan areas, the administration is necessarily more complex. The following example of an organizational chart from the City of Portland is one illustration of a complex administration that reflects the varied and sophisticated parts of the approval process.

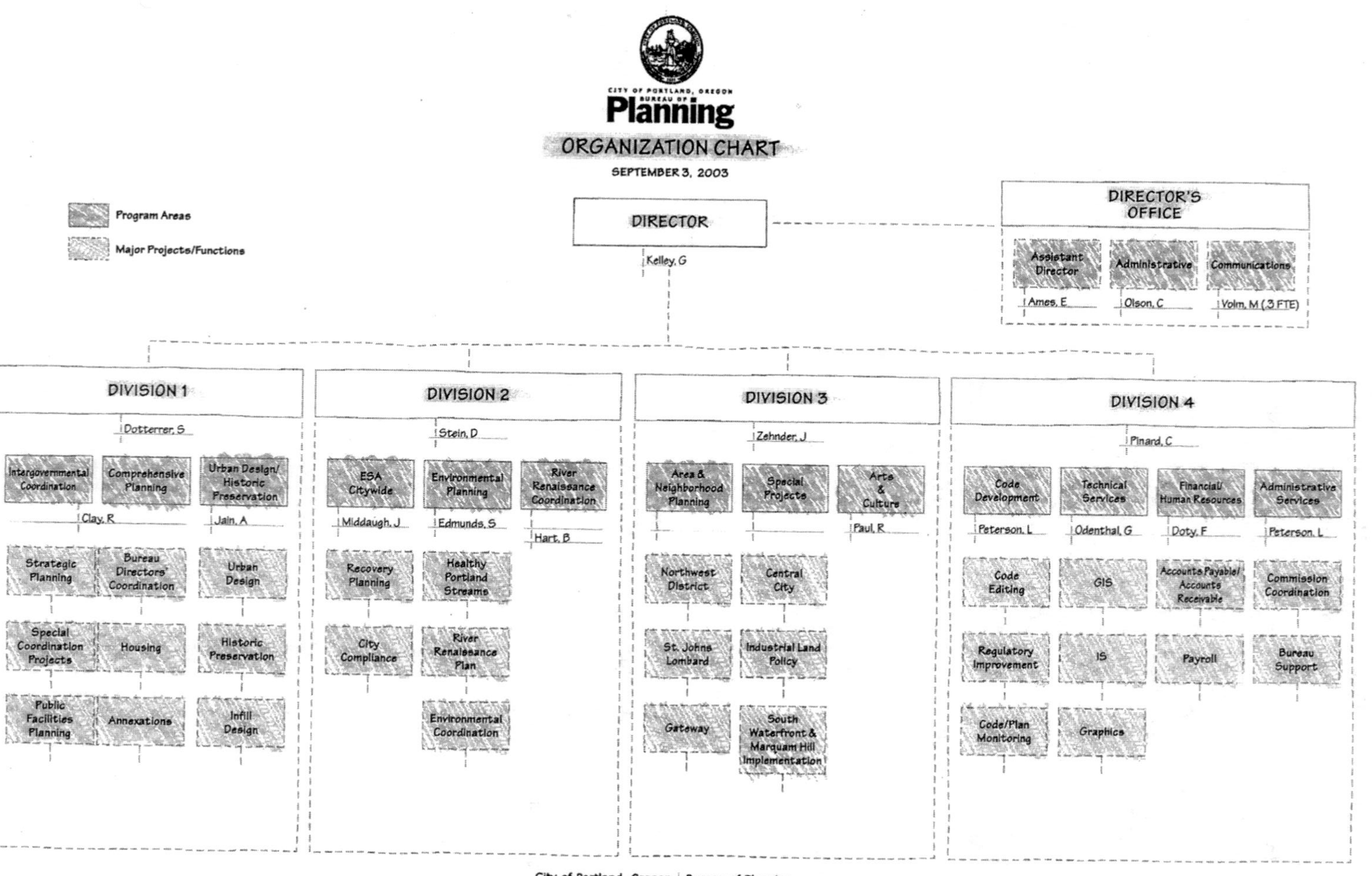
CITY OF PORTLAND, OREGON
BUREAU OF
Planning
ORGANIZATION CHART
SEPTEMBER 3, 2003
Program Areas
Major Projects/Functions
DIRECTOR
Kelley, G
DIRECTOR'S OFFICE
Assistant Director
Administrative
Communications
Ames, E
Olson, C
Volm, M (.3 FTE)
DIVISION 1
Dotterrer, S
Intergovernmental Coordination
Comprehensive Planning
Urban Design/ Historic Preservation
Clay, R
Jain, A
Strategic Planning
Bureau Directors' Coordination
Urban Design
Special Coordination Projects
Housing
Historic Preservation
Public Facilities Planning
Annexations
Infill Design
DIVISION 2
Stein, D
ESA Citywide
Environmental Planning
River Renaissance Coordination
Middaugh, J
Edmunds, S
Hart, B
Recovery Planning
Healthy Portland Streams
City Compliance
River Renaissance Plan
Environmental Coordination
DIVISION 3
Zehnder, J
Area & Neighborhood Planning
Special Projects
Arts & Culture
Paul, R
Northwest District
Central City
St. Johns Lombard
Industrial Land Policy
Gateway
South Waterfront & Marquam Hill Implementation
DIVISION 4
Pinard, C
Code Development
Technical Services
Financial/ Human Resources
Administrative Services
Peterson, L
Odenthal, G
Doty, F
Peterson, L
Code Editing
GIS
Accounts Payable/ Accounts Receivable
Commission Coordination
Regulatory Improvement
IS
Payroll
Bureau Support
Code/Plan Monitoring
Graphics
City of Portland, Oregon | Bureau of Planning
1900 S.W. 4th Avenue | Suite 4100 | Portland, OR 97201
503-823-7700 | FAX 503-823-7800
www.planning.ci.portland.or.us

4. The zoning process is one of several that any development may need to go through in order to be finally built. Large developments on vacant land may require not only rezoning, but also subdivision approval, comprehensive plan changes, site plan approval, and building plan approvals before building permits can be issued, construction completed and ultimately the structures can be inspected and certificates of occupancy issued. The chart below demonstrates the various stages and approval requirements for the development process of the City of Austin, Texas. The chart is helpful to developers and citizens alike, and is posted on the city website. Keep this in mind as context while studying this chapter.

	Development Assessment (Optional) →	**Zoning** →	**Subdivision** →	**Site Plan** →	**Building Plan** →	**Inspection**
Regulation Review Elements	**Pre-Application Review** **Explanation of Procedures and Requirements for all Processes** **Fee Estimates** **Potential Issues** **Exemptions** **Corrections** **Land Status**	**Land Use Appropriateness** **Development** Intensity Density Height **Traffic Impact** **Environmental Impact**	**Park Land** **Design** Layout Lot/Tract Size Circulation Street Drainage/Grading Flood Plain **Environmental** Water Quality Tree/Vegetation Habitat Critical Features **Utilities** Transmission Distribution Service	**Design** Intensity Density Height Setbacks Compatibility **Transportation** Driveways Parking/Circulation Traffic Impact **Construction** Drainage Grading Flood Plan **Environmental** Landscaping/Tree Water Quality **Utility (Service)** **Fire (Site)**	**Health** **Taps** **Electric Service** **Industrial Waste** **Construction** Occupancy Access/Exiting Structural Mechanical Electrical Plumbing Energy Fire Zoning Review **Signs** **Barricades** **Underground Tanks**	**Site & Building Plan Compliance** **Code Enforcement of existing structures**
Notice		Property Owners within 300', Registered Neighborhood Organizations, Sector Groups at time of Application, and for Public Hearings • **Signs Posted** • **Newspaper Ads**	Property Owners within 300', Registered Neighborhood Organizations, Sector Groups at time of Application, and for Public Hearings (Preliminary Only)	Property Owners within 300', Registered Neighborhood Organizations, Sector Groups at time of Application, and for Public Hearings (If any...)		
Approval Authority		City Council	• **Zoning & Platting Commission** • **Watershed Protection & Development Review** Final w/o Prelim. < 4 lots Amended Plats	• **Watershed Protection & Development review** • **Zoning & Platting Commission** Conditional Use, Hill Country	**Watershed Protection & Development Review**	**Watershed Protection & Development Review** **Neighborhood Planning & Zoning**
Appeal			**Watershed Variances to City Council**	**Waivers to Planning Commission w/Appeals to City Council** **Zoning & Platting Commission Approval w/Appeal to City Council**	**Building Official** **Trade Boards** **Zoning Variances to Board of Adjustment** **Sign Variances to SRB**	**Building Official** **Trade Boards**
Product	**Assessment Report**	**Zoning Ordinance**	**Preliminary Plan** **Final Plat**	**Released Site Plan**	**Building Permit**	**Certificate of Occupancy**

Proceedings before zoning boards lack the formality and controls of a judicial proceeding. The following fictitious transcript of a zoning variance hearing, written by the late R. Marlin Smith, illustrates how this process works. Marlin claimed that every statement made in this hearing was based on an actual occurrence!

PROCEEDINGS BEFORE THE PLANNING AND ZONING BOARD OF THE CITY OF SAN CIBOLA

THE DOCKET

Case No. 80-V-8: Application of Bullion Bank & Trust for a variance for a drive-up banking window.

The Members of the Board:

Wilbert Wawfull, Chairperson

Greta Greenbelt Grotheplanne

Oliver Oldmoney

Preston Pettefogg

Mark Multilist

[The chairperson called the proceedings to order and immediately recognized Mr. Giltedge, who rose to speak:]

Giltedge: I'm Gilbert Giltedge, President of Bullion Bank & Trust. You've got our variation application at the very end of the agenda and I know it's not going to be controversial. On the other hand it looks like some of the matters tonight are going to take a long time and I don't see why we can't get my simple little variation out of the way and let me go home.

Wawfull: That seems reasonable to me.

Grotheplanne: Mr. Chairman, that seems to me to be highly irregular. The bank's application for a variance was filed only a little more than two weeks ago and it is the last item on the agenda.

Wawfull: That doesn't really matter. It's the Chairman's prerogative to take these things up in the order he thinks best, and there's just no sense to making an important person like Mr. Giltedge sit here through all these other matters.

Grotheplanne: Well, I've only been on this Board for eight months and no one has given me a copy of the rules yet, but I can't believe that they permit you to decide to hear cases out of order without the consent of the Board.

Wawfull: But we don't really have any rules. We just try to do what's fair and it doesn't seem fair to me to ask Mr. Giltedge to wait when his matter won't take very long.

Grotheplanne: How do you know that?

Wawfull: Why, he told me all about it when we had dinner before the meeting.

Giltedge: This is a very simple matter. We want to build a drive-up teller window in the parking lot alongside our bank on Main Street. We applied for a building permit, but the Zoning Administrator gave us some foolishness about drive-ins not being a permitted use and he said we would have to get a variance from this Board. I've got some plans here showing how we propose to do it. If you look at the plans, you'll see that we would put the drive-up facility along the west side of the bank. Cars would still enter the existing parking lot from Main Street, and then they could proceed either to a parking place or to the drive-up window. There would still be two exits, one on Central Avenue and one on Main Street. Most banks have these drive-up facilities now, and we're just trying to stay abreast of the times and provide modern conveniences for our customers.

Pettefogg: I don't know whether we've got any rules, but if we have let's waive them.

Oldmoney: I agree.

Wawfull: It's settled then, we'll hear Mr. Giltedge.

Giltedge: This new drive-up window will be architecturally harmonious with the rest of the bank and we think it will be a credit to the downtown area.

Wawfull: That sounds like a fine idea, Mr. Giltedge. Anybody got any questions or objections?

Multilist: I don't seem to have a copy of the application.

Wawfull: That's because we just received it tonight.

Grotheplanne: Then how could the zoning administrator prepare the notice? There was a notice published, wasn't there?

Wawfull: Oh yes. Mr. Codebook just took down the information for the notice from Mr. Giltedge.

Multilist: (Puzzled) I'm looking at the notice now and it appears to me the legal description is not right. It refers to Lot 5 in the River Trails Subdivision.

Giltedge: That fool Codebook must've copied from the wrong piece of paper.

Wawfull: Well, that's just a little technical problem. The street address is right and everybody knows where the Bullion Bank is.

Pettefogg: I agree. We can't let technicalities stand in the way of progress.

Grotheplanne: Your idea sounds fine, Mr. Giltedge, but I wonder if you are aware of the standards in the zoning ordinance for variances?

Giltedge: Codebook gave me some forms, but I didn't have time to pay much attention to a lot of bureaucratese.

Grotheplanne: Well, to be specific the ordinance requires that you establish five points to the satisfaction of this Board showing that the restrictions in the ordinance cause you an unnecessary hardship.

Wawfull: Greta, if you are in one of your technical moods, we're going to be here all night.

Grotheplanne: Don't be snide, Wilbert. Now as I was saying, there are five standards. First, the property cannot yield a reasonable return if it can be used only in accord with the regulations in the zoning district. Second, the plight of the owner is due to unique circumstances. Third, the variance will not serve merely as a convenience to the applicant, but will alleviate some demonstrable and unusual hardship. Fourth, the alleged hardship has not been created by anyone presently having a proprietary interest in the property. Fifth, the proposed variance will not alter the essential character of the area, cause congestion in the streets, injure the value of nearby property, or adversely affect the health, safety, or welfare of the public. I don't recall, Mr. Giltedge, that anything you said dealt with any of those matters.

Oldmoney: Really, Greta, you'd think Mr. Giltedge was a newcomer to our town. Why that bank has been in his family for three generations. My own family has done business with them since Mr. Giltedge's grandfather founded it. Surely you don't believe a Giltedge would do anything that would not be good for San Cibola?

Grotheplanne: (Somewhat waspishly) I don't see anything in the zoning ordinance that says Giltedges are exempt from it.

Giltedge: (Placatingly) Now, Ms. Grotheplanne, I think that I can set your mind at ease. There won't be any traffic congestion because there won't be any additional traffic. We will have the same customers, but some will use the drive-up window. The bank is in the downtown business district and our drive-up window will be just another commercial use. There will not be any injurious effect on the value of any nearby property. After all, our bank is the closest property and we would not want to injure the value of our own property. The variance is not a convenience for us, it's a convenience for our customers. Our bank didn't create this hardship; it was created by the changing nature of the banking business. You could say our situation is unique because you've already given the Fourth Bank and Trust and Fidelity Savings & Loan variances for drive-up windows. And if you want to talk about a reasonable rate of return, let me tell you that if we can't stay competitive, we're not going to be able to stay in the downtown area very long.

Wawfull: Maybe we had better vote.

Bill Bottomline: Doesn't the public get a chance to say anything? I thought that this was supposed to be a public hearing.

Wawfull: Sure you do. What would you like to say?

Bottomline: My name is Bill Bottomline. I'm the Chief Accountant at the San Cibola plant of Bliteland Metals. You folks let the Fourth Bank and Trust Co. put in a drive-up window last year and it created a terrible mess on Front Street because the cars stack up in the street waiting to get in to the drive-up window. Some mornings it can take 10 minutes to go one block on Front Street. You are going to have the same kind of traffic jam if you let the Bullion Bank do the same thing on Main Street. Why can't you make them close the entrance on Main and enter from Central Avenue, which is the side street? Then there would be room for cars to line up on the parking lot and if some backed up into the street, it still would not create as much of a problem.

Giltedge: We couldn't do that — Central is a one-way street and people coming from the east would have to drive all the way to Bluff Boulevard and then come back to turn into Central. Besides, that would make it difficult for cars to get into and out of parking spaces and it wouldn't be energy efficient.

Grotheplanne: I am a little concerned that the exhaust from cars standing in line may have more pollutants in it than moving vehicles do. I think that we should have some air quality information before we act upon this variance application.

Wawfull: Well, I don't know about that. It would just delay the bank and we like to move these matters along. I think we're ready to vote.

Multilist: Aren't we going to have any discussion?

Wawfull: Sure, Mark. What did you want to say?

Multilist: I think that this Board ought to know that people from Bullion Bank & Trust have been in my real estate office to inquire about available land out near the new regional shopping mall. It seems to me that if Bullion Bank & Trust are not allowed to put in their drive-up window downtown, then they may move their main banking facilities out to the mall and build the drive-up facility out there.

So if we don't want to see businesses moving out of downtown and deterioration set in, we should not be too fussy about a little modernization that will benefit the City.

Wawfull: Any more discussion? (Pause) I'll entertain a motion based on the findings of fact to grant the variance.

Grotheplanne: What findings of fact?

Wawfull: That there is unnecessary hardship.

Grotheplanne: There isn't anything resembling evidence of hardship.

Wawfull: When Mr. Giltedge says our zoning ordinance creates a hardship for him, I believe him. It's not his fault that the ordinance does not list drive-in banks as a permitted use.

Multilist: I move we grant the variance.

[Oldmoney seconded the motion and all voted in favor except Grotheplanne.]

NOTES AND QUESTIONS

1. *Due process?* This variance proceeding raises both substantive and procedural problems. What procedural problems do you see? Variances and their substantive requirements are discussed in the next section. What if the zoning ordinance required drive-in teller windows to be approved as a special exception? Would this be constitutional? Would the bank be entitled to a special exception? Could this problem be handled through an amendment to the zoning ordinance? How? Consider this question as you study special exceptions and zoning amendments later in this section. Also consider, when you review the material on site plans, *infra*, whether a site plan would help resolve the problems raised by the bank's application.

2. *The parties to land use litigation.* In most of the cases studied so far, either a landowner or a third party in interest, such as a housing organization, has brought the case to court. Landowners can appeal denial of a requested zoning change, but if the change is granted, the neighbors may appeal. This type of case raises somewhat different problems, so at this point it will be helpful to make some distinctions in the way in which zoning cases get to court and who the real parties in interest are. Professor Williams' discussion of the "three parties in interest" in land use litigation makes the point:

> Zoning litigation arises when a developer wishes to do something which requires a change in the rules, or perhaps an interpretation of them. The normal starting point for a zoning case is therefore a request for relaxation of some of the restrictions applying to the land in question. If the municipal authorities refuse to authorize such a relaxation, the developer may either accept this decision, or challenge it by suing the municipality. In the latter instance, the result is the first type of zoning case — often referred to below as a "developer's case." The question in such a case is whether the municipal decision has unreasonably restricted the developer's property right to make use of his land. In the opposite situation, if the municipality decides to go along with a relaxation of the preexisting rules, neighboring landowners may (and often do) object, and may bring an action challenging this decision to relax the rules; and the result is a "neighbors' case." In such a case the plaintiff is a neighboring landowner, and the real defendant is the developer; in this instance the municipality ends up siding

with the developer. In one sense, therefore, the municipality is not a separate party in interest in land use conflicts, but merely the ally of one or the other of two primary parties in interest.

> In many states the courts handle these two types of cases quite differently, either explicitly (by different doctrine) or implicitly (by a markedly different pattern of decisions). As for the latter, the states vary sharply in their attitude towards claims by developers; but in almost all states the neighbors usually lose, with a few striking exceptions. [1 N. Williams, American Land Planning Law § 2:1 (Rev. ed. 2010).]

Professor Williams also states that the legal issues in developer cases are "fairly well defined," and that it is in these cases that the states "split sharply." In neighbor cases "the legal technology is relatively primitive," with no clearly established rules nationwide. He adds that the major zoning states have used a good deal of ingenuity in applying various doctrines to give neighbors some standing to raise issues in court. *Id.* at § 2:2.

The next group of cases primarily considers neighbors who have challenged zoning changes the municipality has granted a developer. When reviewing the materials in this section, consider whether the distinctions Professor Williams makes between developer and neighbor cases are correct.

Who are the third party interests in zoning litigation? Professor Williams refers to these third party interests as "third-party nonbeneficiaries of the entire system." Their interests may be severely affected, but they "rarely appear in the case law." An example is the racial and economic minorities often excluded from a community by exclusionary zoning, who were considered in the last chapter.

PROBLEM

Excellent views of the snow-covered Del Pedro Mountains are available from all parts of Metro City. Proposals by developers to build several high-rise office buildings on the outskirts of Metro City threaten to spoil these views for Metro City residents. To prevent this from happening, the Metro City Council amended its comprehensive plan to include View Protection Guidelines (VPG) for areas of the city where view-threatening development is imminent. The VPG recommend as limits a 100-foot height and a 100-foot width for any new buildings in the area covered by the VPG. The State of Metro Zoning Act, which is modeled on the Standard Zoning Enabling Act, authorizes Metro City's zoning regulations.

Mesa Development Company owns a vacant block in an area covered by the VPG which is zoned C-N Commercial. The C-N Commercial district allows commercial (but not office) uses subject to a height limit of 40 feet and 35-foot front, rear and side setbacks. The four-block area surrounding the Mesa site is also zoned C-N Commercial and is almost fully developed with commercial buildings that conform to the height and setback restrictions. Mesa has applied for a rezoning from the C-N Commercial to the O-2 Office District, which allows office buildings without any height or setback restrictions. Mesa plans a 200 foot high office building, to be built to the lot lines.

(1) Assume the Metro City Council grants Mesa's rezoning application without restriction. The planning commission report recommending the rezoning states it is needed to help fill a growing demand for office space in the city. An owner of an adjacent commercial building has sued to have the rezoning declared invalid. What result? Now assume that the O-2 Office District has the same setbacks as the C-N Commercial District. Mesa now applies for a

variance from the setback requirements so it can build to the lot lines. Should the variance be granted?

(2) Now assume that after Mesa applied for the rezoning, the city planning department informed Mesa the city council would grant the rezoning if Mesa agreed to record an easement on its property that would limit the building's height to 100 feet and its width to 100 feet. Mesa accepted the planning department's recommendation and recorded the easement. The city council then rezoned the Mesa site to O-2. Is the rezoning valid?

(3) Now assume an office building is a conditional use in the C-N zone. The height and setback restrictions of the C-N zone apply to any approved conditional use. The Zoning Board of Adjustment is authorized by the code to approve a conditional use if it finds the use is compatible with adjacent and permitted uses, will have adequate off-street parking and loading facilities, and will be adequately served by public facilities. The Board holds a hearing and decides Mesa's conditional use meets all of these requirements except the compatibility requirement. The Board denies the conditional use and Mesa appeals to a state court. What result?

B. MORATORIA AND INTERIM CONTROLS ON DEVELOPMENT

A moratorium is a regulation that temporarily prohibits new development. It can also be called an interim development control. Municipalities often adopt moratoria in order to forestall inappropriate development while they are considering a new growth management program, which may include a revision of the comprehensive plan and the zoning ordinance, the adoption of new growth management techniques, or a combination of these measures. A community may also adopt a development moratorium to prohibit development so it can remedy deficiencies in public facilities. Development moratoria can use a number of land use control techniques. They can include a temporary halt, reduction or quota restrictions on:

- The extension of public facilities to new areas.
- New connections to utilities.
- Building permits.
- Subdivision approvals.
- Rezonings to higher densities.

The terms "moratorium" or "interim development controls (IDC)" (or "interim zoning") are often used interchangeably, or at least are interrelated. Each may be used in different ways. A municipality can enact a freeze on new development that shuts down the development permit and land use approval processes and prohibits any new development during the moratorium period. Another alternative is to limit the development freeze to selected developments, such as major developments that are likely to have an adverse effect on a new plan or growth management program. A moratorium or IDC may also be limited to certain areas of the municipality where planning or public facility problems are critical. A recent study found moratoria in use in 3.6% of jurisdictions in the largest metropolitan areas covering 6.5% of the land area. R. Pendall et al., From Traditional to Reformed: A Review of the Land Use Regulations in the Nation's 50 Largest Metropolitan Areas 11 (2006).

NOTES AND QUESTIONS

1. *The takings issue.* Development moratoria clearly raise important takings problems. Prior to the Supreme Court's 1987 trilogy of takings cases, the courts had pretty much accepted the constitutionality of moratoria when they had a legitimate public purpose and when they were not unreasonably long. The 1987 cases raised some new issues, especially because *First English* considered a moratorium that prohibited development in a floodplain. It held that temporary takings are compensable but did not reach the validity of the moratorium under the Takings Clause. At the same time, dictum in *First English* seemed to support moratoria, at least of limited duration, because the Court said that "normal delays" caused by the processing of applications for development approval are not compensable. Cases after *First English* upheld development moratoria. The following case indicates the usual favorable view courts adopted on moratoria in this period:

> Assuming that the municipality has the legislative authority to adopt such [interim] ordinances, and assuming that such an ordinance or resolution is of limited duration for a period of time that is reasonable under the circumstances and has been enacted in good faith and without discrimination, such ordinances have generally been upheld, . . . so long as the purpose is to study and to develop a comprehensive zoning plan which does in fact proceed promptly, culminating in the expeditious adoption of appropriate zoning ordinances when the study is completed. [*State ex rel. SCA Chem. Waste Serv., Inc. v. Konigsberg*, 636 S.W.2d 430, 435 (Tenn. 1982).]

In this case, a county adopted an interim ordinance prohibiting the issuance of building permits for hazardous waste treatment plants to preserve the status quo until a previously adopted zoning ordinance could take effect. For other cases upholding the reasonableness of time periods in moratoria, see *Guinnane v. City & County of San Francisco*, 241 Cal. Rptr. 787 (Cal. App. 1987) (more than one year); *Tocco v. New Jersey Council on Affordable Housing*, 576 A.2d 328 (N.J. App. Div. 1990) (18-month development moratorium).

2. The takings landscape changed with the Court's 1992 decision in *Lucas*, which held a per se taking occurs when a land use regulation denies a landowner all economically beneficial use of his land, even though the regulation serves a legitimate governmental purpose. There was the possibility that development moratoria would be vulnerable under *Lucas* because they prohibit all development during the moratorium period, even if justified by the need to gain time to remedy public facility plans or develop a new plan or land use ordinance. In *Tahoe-Sierra Regional Preservation Council, Inc. v. Tahoe Regional Planning Agency*, 535 U.S. 302 (2002), however, the Court held a moratorium on land development was not a per se taking of a property interest during the moratorium period. The case is reproduced in Chapter 2. *Tahoe* also held that the takings tests adopted by the *Penn Central* decision, also reproduced in Chapter 2, are the "default" rule in takings cases.

The *Tahoe* case endorsed the importance of moratoria in the planning process, but did not provide any guidance for determining when a moratorium would be a taking beyond suggesting that a moratorium lasting more than one year would be suspect. The case that follows indicates how courts have handled the constitutionality of a moratorium after the *Tahoe* decision:

ECOGEN, LLC v. TOWN OF ITALY

438 F. Supp. 2d 149 (W.D.N.Y. 2006)

David G. Larimer, U.S. District Judge.

The development of wind power projects, which convert wind energy into electricity, seems to be on the upswing in this country, but that growth has not been universally welcomed. *See, e.g.*, Felicity Barringer, *Debate Over Wind Power Creates Environmental Rift*, N.Y. Times, June 6, 2006, at A18. As in *Don Quixote*, where one person sees a windmill, another sees a "monstrous giant" looming over the countryside.[1] This case involves one such proposed project that has met with local opposition.

Plaintiff, Ecogen, LLC ("Ecogen"), commenced this action under 42 U.S.C. § 1983, seeking relief from a moratorium ("the Moratorium") enacted by the Town of Italy (N.Y.) Town Board ("the Board"), which, for the duration of the moratorium prohibits the "construction or erection of wind turbine towers, relay stations and/or other support facilities in the Town of Italy." Ecogen has moved for an order preliminarily enjoining defendants from enforcing or continuing the Moratorium insofar as it relates to the construction and operation of an electrical substation within the Town of Italy. Defendants, who include the Town of Italy ("the Town" or "Italy"), the Town supervisor, and the Board, have moved to dismiss the complaint for lack of subject matter jurisdiction pursuant to Rule 12(b)(1) of the Federal Rules of Civil Procedure, and under Rule 12(b)(6) for failure to state a claim upon which relief may be granted.

BACKGROUND

Ecogen is an independent power producer engaged in the development of wind-energy projects (sometimes referred to as "wind farms") in New York State. Wind farms produce electrical energy through the use of wind turbines, which are windmill-like structures that use a wind-driven rotor mounted on a tower to create electricity through the use of a generator. According to plaintiff, only certain types of areas are suitable for the construction of wind farms. In particular, wind farms should ideally be located in areas with strong winds and nearby electrical transmission lines.

In 2001, Ecogen identified certain ridge tops in the contiguous Towns of Prattsburgh and Italy as viable spots for wind energy projects ("the Prattsburgh Project" and "the Italy Project"). Ecogen determined that it would be feasible to build about 30 wind turbines in Prattsburgh, and another 23 in Italy. None have been built to date.

One important feature of these ridge tops is their proximity to an electrical transmission line that runs, in part, through Italy. For the project to succeed, in either Prattsburgh or Italy, a substation would have to be built to connect with that line, and according to plaintiff, the best location for the substation, from an engineering standpoint, would be somewhere in Italy.

---

[1] At this point they came in sight of thirty or forty windmills that are on that plain, and as soon as Don Quixote saw them he said to his squire, "Fortune is arranging matters for us better than we could have shaped our desires ourselves, for look there, friend Sancho Panza, where thirty or more monstrous giants present themselves, all of whom I mean to engage in battle and slay . . . ."

Miguel de Cervantes Saavedra, Don Quixote, pt. 1, Chapter VIII (John Ormsby, trans.), available at http://www.online-literature.com/cervantes/don_quixote/.

Plaintiff states that the substation would be roughly 150 feet square, surrounded by a fence of about 200 by 300 feet, noiseless, and would be set well back from the nearest road or other property. Apparently, the chosen site is about one mile from the Italy-Prattsburgh town line.

In anticipation of the Prattsburgh and Italy Projects, Ecogen has acquired property rights and easements to an assemblage of properties in both towns. The Town of Prattsburgh has allegedly welcomed the Prattsburgh Project, and Ecogen has been proceeding with that project, but it cannot be completed until the substation is built.

The Town of Italy Board was apparently less receptive to the project for that town, however. On June 8, 2004, the Board passed a "local law Establishing a Moratorium on Construction or Erection of Wind Turbine Towers, Relay Stations and/or other support facilities in the Town of Italy." The stated purpose of the Moratorium is to prohibit the construction of such structures "for a reasonable time pending the completion of a plan for control of construction of such structures in the Town of Italy as part of the adoption of comprehensive zoning regulations . . . ." *Id.* § 3(A). The Board also stated that it took this action "to protect the value, use and enjoyment of property in the Town" by its citizens. *Id.* § 3(B). Specifically, the Board stated that "a principal concern is the scenic and aesthetic attributes of the Town of Italy as they relate to the use of land in the Town for residential, recreational and tourism purposes," and that "the installation of wind turbine facilities in the Town of Italy may have an adverse affect [sic] upon the scenic and aesthetic attributes of the Town of Italy and a correspondingly detrimental influence upon residential and recreational uses as well as real estate values in the Town of Italy, unless properly controlled through zoning regulations." *Id.* § 3(C).

To fulfill these stated objectives, the Board decreed that "[f]or a period of six (6) months from and after the effective date of this Local Law, no construction or erection of wind turbine towers, relay stations and/or support facilities shall be permitted within the geographical limits of the Town of Italy," nor could any permits for such facilities be filed during that period. *Id.* § 4. The Moratorium became effective upon its filing with the New York Secretary of State on June 15, 2004. *Id.* at 1.

The Moratorium also contains a provision, entitled "Alleviation of Extraordinary Hardship," which provides that the Board "may authorize exceptions to the moratorium imposed by this Law when it finds, based upon evidence presented to it, that deferral of action on an application for facility construction, or the deferral of approval of the application for the duration of the moratorium would impose an extraordinary hardship on a landowner or applicant." *Id.* § 5(A). To apply for such an exception, the applicant must pay a fee of $500, together with a recitation of the relevant facts and supporting documentation. A public hearing on the application is to be held by the Board "no later than forty-five (45) days after the complete application for hardship exception has been filed with the Town Clerk." *Id.* § 5(C). The Moratorium provides that "[a]t the conclusion of the public hearing and after reviewing the evidence and testimony placed before it, the Town Board shall act upon the application," but it does not provide a time period within which the Board must issue a decision. *Id.* § 5(E).

As stated, the original duration of the Moratorium was six months. However, the Board has renewed the Moratorium several times since its original passage. It most recently did so on March 29, 2006, and the Moratorium, which has now been in effect for about two years, is currently scheduled to expire — if it is not again renewed — in October 2006.

Because of the Moratorium, then, Ecogen has been unable to erect any wind turbines or related facilities within the Town of Italy, including the substation. Ecogen claims that this is holding up not only the Italy Project but also the Prattsburgh Project, which requires completion of the substation. Ecogen also contends that it has been unable to take certain procedural steps that are necessary to both projects (such as the completion of environmental impact studies), and that it is in jeopardy of losing certain tax credits, which are contingent upon the Prattsburgh Project's completion by December 31, 2007.

Ecogen has not applied for a hardship exception as provided for in the Moratorium, but through its attorneys it has written a number of letters to various Town officials objecting to the inclusion of the substation in the Moratorium. These letters generally set forth Ecogen's position that, given the aesthetic concerns that were the stated impetus behind the Moratorium, there was no rational reason to include the relatively unobtrusive, and also explained the adverse consequences to Ecogen of not being able to proceed with the construction of the substation in Italy. All these letters went unanswered.

Ecogen commenced this action on March 29, 2006. The complaint purports to assert six causes of action. The first alleges that defendants have deprived plaintiff of due process of law, in violation of the Fourteenth Amendment to the United States Constitution, by enacting and perpetuating the Moratorium, especially as it relates to the substation, thereby denying plaintiff the "use of property based on an illegal, irrational and unconstitutional motivation." The second cause of action seeks a judgment pursuant to 28 U.S.C. § 2201 declaring that the Moratorium is unconstitutional or otherwise unenforceable. The third cause of action alleges a "violation of 42 U.S.C. § 1983." The fourth cause of action seeks injunctive relief, and the final two causes of action assert claims under state law.

I. Defendants' Motion to Dismiss

A. Facial or As-Applied Challenge?

[The court finds the case ripe for review on a facial substantive due process challenge to the Moratorium.]

B. Facial Challenge

Plaintiff alleges that insofar as the Moratorium relates to the proposed substation, defendants' actions in passing and renewing the Moratorium have denied plaintiff the use of property without due process of law, in violation of the Fourteenth Amendment. Defendants respond that the Moratorium is a valid exercise of the Town's police and zoning powers.

In the context of land use regulation, the constitutional guarantee of substantive due process protects a person with an interest in property from arbitrary or irrational governmental action depriving the person of that interest. In order to prevail on its substantive due process claim, Ecogen must establish that the Moratorium, at least insofar as it prohibits Ecogen's construction of a substation, bears no rational relationship to any legitimate governmental purpose.

In undertaking that analysis, the Court is mindful that "federal courts are not to be turned into zoning boards of appeals." Nevertheless, if a property owner's constitutional rights are infringed by a municipality's actions, the Court's "duty to protect the constitutional interest is clear."

As stated, facial challenges are difficult to mount successfully, and that holds true in the context of zoning and land use regulation as well. "Generally a municipal zoning ordinance is presumed be valid, and will not be held unconstitutional if its wisdom is at least fairly debatable and it bears a rational relationship to a permissible state objective." *Greene v. Town of Blooming Grove*, 879 F.2d 1061, 1063 (2d Cir. 1989) (citing *City of Cleburne v. Cleburne Living Center*, 473 U.S. 432, 440 (1985)). In applying those principles here, defendants' subjective motivation in enacting the Moratorium is irrelevant.

While the Court certainly may consider whether the Moratorium is rationally related to its stated purpose, that is ultimately not determinative, and in fact it is not necessary for defendants to enunciate any purpose for the Moratorium. "Because legislatures are not required to articulate reasons for the enactment of a statute, 'it is entirely irrelevant for constitutional purposes whether the conceived reason for the challenged distinction actually motivated the legislature' ") (quoting *F.C.C. v. Beach Communications, Inc.*, 508 U.S. 307 (1993)) footnote omitted). Instead, "the proper inquiry is concerned with the existence of a conceivably rational basis, not whether that basis was actually considered by the legislative body." *Haves v. City of Miami*, 52 F.3d 918, 922 (11th Cir. 1995). Plaintiff thus has the heavy burden "to negative every conceivable basis which might support" the Moratorium. *Heller v. Doe*, 509 U.S. 312, 320 (1993).

Applying these standards to the case at bar, I find that plaintiff has not stated a valid claim that the Moratorium is invalid on its face. Whatever its shortcomings, I am not able to say that it is so arbitrary or irrational as to violate plaintiff's substantive due process rights.

First, I note that, at least for purposes of the pending motions, plaintiff does not appear to dispute that in general the Town has an interest in preserving its aesthetic character. See, e.g., *Sprint Spectrum L.P. v. Willoth*, 176 F.3d 630, 645 (2d Cir. 1999) ("Aesthetics is generally a valid subject of municipal regulation and concern"); *Cellular Tel. Co. v. Town of Oyster Bay*, 166 F.3d 490, 495 ("In New York, aesthetics can be a valid ground for local zoning decisions"). Plaintiff contends, though, that the modest substation presents no aesthetic concerns.

The question, then, is whether the Moratorium's prohibition of the construction of "wind turbine towers, relay stations and/or other support facilities" is rationally related to that interest. Again, I am unable to say that it is not. Assuming that the Town has a legitimate concern in restricting the construction of wind towers, the Moratorium is not completely irrational. If the aim is to prevent wind towers from being built in Italy, certainly it makes some sense to prohibit the construction of wind tower support facilities, such as substations, as well.

Plaintiff's contention that the substation itself would have no adverse aesthetic impact, and that it makes no sense to single out substations related to wind power projects, therefore miss the mark. Prohibiting the construction of wind power substations is not an end in itself, but a means to an end: prohibiting (for the duration of the Moratorium, a matter which is further discussed below) the construction of wind farms in Italy.

It may be that defendants' means of attaining that end are not the most efficacious, wisest or fairest possible, but that is not the standard by which they are to be judged by this Court, especially at this stage of the litigation. "A classification does not fail rational-basis review because it is not made with mathematical nicety or because in practice it results in some inequality") (internal quotation marks omitted); *Rojas-Reyes v. I.N.S.*, 235 F.3d 115, 123 (2d Cir. 2000) (legislative acts "need not result in the most just or logical result in every case to pass constitutional muster"); *Richmond Boro Gun Club, Inc. v. City of New York*, No. 92 CV 0151 (E.D.N.Y. Feb. 23, 1994) ("In a challenge to a law's rationality, the court is precluded from weighing the wisdom, need, or utility of the law," and "is also not allowed to speculate on a better method for remedying the problems sought to be regulated").

Courts "will not strike down a law as irrational simply because it may not succeed in bringing about the result it seeks to accomplish, because the problem could have been better addressed in some other way, or because the statute's classifications lack razor-sharp precision." *Beatie v. City of New York*, 123 F.3d 707, 712 (2d Cir. 1997) (citations omitted). "This is the standard of review because the judicial system has long recognized that '[t]he problems of government are practical ones and may justify, if they do not require, rough accommodations — illogical, it may be, and unscientific.' " *Rojas-Reyes*, 235 F.3d at 124 (quoting *Heller*, 509 U.S. at 321).

As the Second Circuit has explained, "[s]ubstantive due process is an outer limit on the legitimacy of governmental action. It does not forbid governmental actions that might fairly be deemed arbitrary or capricious and for that reason correctable in a state court lawsuit seeking review of administrative action. Substantive due process standards are violated only by conduct that is so outrageously arbitrary as to constitute a gross abuse of governmental authority." *Natale v. Town of Ridgefield*, 170 F.3d 258, 263 (2d Cir. 1999).

In support of its position, Ecogen cites New York case authority to the effect that a municipality may exercise its police power only where there is a "dire necessity" to act and where the municipality's actions are "reasonably calculated to alleviate or prevent the crisis condition." See *Matter of Belle Harbor Realty Corp. v. Kerr*, 35 N.Y.2d 507, 512, 364 N.Y.S.2d 160, 323 N.E.2d 697 (1974). That may indeed be the law of New York, but it is not the test for determining whether one's due process rights under the United States Constitution have been violated. See *Harlen Associates*[, *Inc. Vill. of Mineola*], 273 F.3d [494], at 505 [(2d Cir. 2001)] (stating that plaintiff's "arguments rely heavily on New York cases arising out of Article 78 appeals of local zoning decisions which raise no federal constitutional issue"); *Natale*, 170 F.3d at 262 ("Arbitrary conduct that might violate zoning regulations as a matter of state law is not sufficient to demonstrate conduct so outrageously arbitrary as to constitute a gross abuse of governmental authority that will offend the substantive component of the Due Process Clause"). I believe, therefore, that plaintiff's facial challenge must fail.

C. As-Applied Challenge

[The court finds that the as-applied substantive due process claim is not ripe for review.]

D. Duration of the Moratorium

Although I find that the Moratorium is facially valid, and that Ecogen's as-applied challenge to the Moratorium is not yet ripe, I also recognize that to pass constitutional muster, a moratorium must be of reasonable duration, and that at some point, a so-called "moratorium" can amount to an unconstitutional taking or violation of a property owner's due process rights. See *Bronco's Entm't v. Charter Twp. of Van Buren*, 421 F.3d 440, 453 (6th Cir. 2005) (upholding moratorium on submission of rezoning petitions in part because moratorium "was of a reasonably short duration"); *ASF, Inc. v. City of Seattle*, 408 F.Supp.2d 1102,

1108–09 (W.D. Wash. 2005) (finding seventeen-year moratorium on issuance of new adult entertainment licenses unconstitutional); *Q.C. Constr. Co. v. Gallo*, 649 F.Supp. 1331, 1337 (D.R.I. 1986) (noting that "[a]pproved moratoriums have also been either temporary or of reasonable or limited duration") (collecting cases), *aff'd*, 836 F.2d 1340 (1st Cir. 1987). A municipality may not use a "moratorium" as a de facto means of achieving a desired legislative purpose.

Whether a given moratorium is unreasonably lengthy depends upon the surrounding circumstances. In land use cases, the critical question is often how much time the municipality needs to study the situation before it and develop a comprehensive zoning plan or other response to the situation. See, e.g., *Phillips v. Borough of Keyport*, 107 F.3d 164, 181 (3d Cir. 1997) ("if a public official authorized by local law to impose a moratorium on the issuance of permits imposed such a moratorium for the purpose of allowing the municipality a reasonable opportunity to consider whether the secondary effects of adult entertainment uses required additional zoning regulation, any resulting delay could not constitute a substantive due process violation"); *Q.C. Constr.*, 649 F.Supp. at 1337 ("Moratoriums have been approved when they form a part of a comprehensive plan to remedy a problem situation"); *Smoke Rise, Inc. v. WSSC*, 400 F.Supp. 1369, 1383 (D.Md. 1975) (reasonableness of sewer moratoria was to be judged by their purpose and duration).

There is, then, no bright-line rule as to how long a moratorium can remain in effect without treading upon constitutional rights, see *Tahoe-Sierra Pres. Council, Inc. v. Tahoe Regional Planning Agency*, 535 U.S. 302, 342 (2002). Though the Supreme Court has commented that "[i]t may well be true that any moratorium that lasts for more than one year should be viewed with special skepticism," *id.* at 341, it also held in *Tahoe-Sierra* that a thirty-two-month moratorium on development was not such an extraordinary delay as to amount to a compensable taking. *Id.* at 341–42. Under the circumstances here, it does seem curious and suspicious that a two-year period is needed to adopt a zoning plan for wind turbines.

In the case at bar, defendants contend that the moratorium is needed to maintain the status quo while the Town, which has no comprehensive zoning plan, develops such a plan. They also contend that they are nearing completion of that plan, and that it will likely be issued in the near future. At oral argument on this motion, counsel for the Town represented that the moratorium should end in October, 2006.

Plaintiff asserts that it has heard such promises before. Plaintiff claims that further delay in construction of the substation will jeopardize Ecogen's chances of obtaining millions of dollars in tax credits, which are contingent upon the Prattsburgh Project being completed no later than December 31, 2007. In that regard, I note that there is some authority that significant hardships occasioned by governmental delay in acting can warrant judicial intervention, even if the plaintiff has not obtained a final decision on its application. See *Gilbert v. City of Cambridge*, 932 F.2d 51, 61 (1st Cir. 1991) ("There may be a further facet of the futility exception, applicable where the degree of hardship that would be imposed by waiting for the permit process to run its course is so substantial and severe, and the prospects of obtaining the permit so unlikely, that the property may be found to be meaningfully burdened and the controversy concrete enough to warrant immediate judicial intervention").

Mindful of the competing interests of the Town in preserving the status quo pending completion of a comprehensive zoning plan, and of Ecogen in obtaining a prompt decision on its proposal to build a substation in Italy to service its project in Prattsburgh, I deny plaintiff's motion for a preliminary injunction at this time, but with the added provision that defendants must either: (1) enact a comprehensive zoning plan within ninety days of the date of issuance of this Decision and Order; or (2) render a decision on plaintiff's application for a hardship exception within ninety days of its filing. If defendants fail to do either of these things, plaintiff may again seek injunctive relief in this Court.

NOTES AND QUESTIONS

1. *The constitutionality of moratoria post-Tahoe.* The principal case indicates that courts are likely to uphold moratoria of reasonable length after the *Lake Tahoe* decision. Other post-*Tahoe* cases have upheld moratoria. See *Sheffield Dev. Co. v. City of Glenn Heights*, 140 S.W.3d 660 (Tex. 2004) (downzoning; no taking); Amand & Merriam, *Defensible Moratoria: The Law Before and After the Tahoe-Sierra Decision*, 43 Nat. Resources J. 703 (2003), available at http://papers/ssrn.com. The length of time is a critical issue, however, as the principal case illustrates. Compare *Bronco's Entertainment v. Charter Twp. of Van Buren*, 421 F.3d 440, 453 (6th Cir. 2005) (upholding 182-day moratorium on accepting site plans for adult uses), with *Bill Salter Advertising, Inc. v. City of Brewton*, 486 F. Supp. 2d 1314 (D. Ala. 2007) (holding plaintiff showed substantial likelihood of success on the merits on claim against 22-month moratorium on new billboards after hurricane). Refer to the discussion of substantive due process in Chapter 2. Does this case fall within the standard review criteria? See also the discussion of aesthetic regulation in Chapter 9.

2. *Inadequate public facilities.* Public facility problems are often a reason for growth management programs, and when facilities are inadequate, a local government may adopt a moratorium to allow time to remedy the problem. The cases recognize this as a sufficient reason for adopting a moratorium, but require that it be limited in time and that inadequacies be remedied during the moratorium period. *Smoke Rise, Inc. v. Washington Suburban Sanitary Comm'n*, 400 F. Supp. 1369 (D. Md. 1975), is a leading case, decided pre-*Lucas*, that upheld a moratorium on sewer hook-ups in an area of rapid growth around Washington, D.C. The court held there was no indication the moratorium was intended to prevent the area from accepting a fair share of the region's growth while plans were being implemented to improve facility capacity, and the moratorium was reasonable in length. See also the California court's decision on remand from the Supreme Court in *First English II*, 258 Cal. Rptr. 893 (Cal. App. 1989), which upheld the moratorium because its purpose was to protect public safety; *Kaplan v. Clear Lake City Water Auth.*, 794 F.2d 1059 (5th Cir. 1986); and *Cappture Realty Corp. v. Board of Adjustment*, 313 A.2d 624 (N.J. L. Div. 1993), *aff'd*, 336 A.2d 30 (N.J. App. Div. 1995).

The cases usually invalidate public facilities moratoria when there is no necessity for it. See *Lockary v. Kayfetz*, 917 F.2d 1150 (9th Cir. 1990) (no water shortage); *Q.C. Constr. Co. v. Gallo*, 649 F. Supp. 1331 (D.R.I. 1986), *aff'd without opinion*, 836 F.2d 1340 (1st Cir. 1987) (invalidating sewer moratorium when no remedial measures planned); *Tisei v. Town of Ogunquit*, 491 A.2d 564 (Me. 1985) (temporary moratorium on development must be justified by service emergency). What if a municipality consistently refuses to budget funds to improve sewer facilities and then imposes a moratorium on development because the facilities are inadequate? Would a court invalidate? See Note, *Sometimes There's Nothing Left to Give: The Justification for Denying Water Service to New Consumers to Control Growth*, 44 Stan. L. Rev. 429 (1992).

3. *Equal protection and pretext.* A moratorium can raise equal protection problems if a community adopts it to stall plans by a specific developer. See *Mont Belvieu Square, Ltd. v. City of Mont Belvieu*, 27 F. Supp. 2d 935 (S.D. Tex. 1998) (moratorium adopted to block

lower-income housing developer). However, in *Kaplan v. Clear Lake City Water Auth., supra* Note 2, a water and sewer district adopted a moratorium on sewer connections because capacity was inadequate and refused service to a proposed multi-family development. The court applied deferential federal doctrine to reject due process and equal protection objections. See also *Pawn America Minnesota, LLC v. City of St. Louis Park*, 787 N.W.2d 565 (Minn. 2010) (pawnshops). Does the subject of the moratorium make a difference? Compare *Morales v. Haines*, 349 F. Supp. 684 (N.D. Ill. 1972) (one-year suspension of building permits for subsidized housing held to violate equal protection); *Begin v. Inhabitants of Town of Sabattus*, 409 A.2d 1269 (Me. 1979) (slow-growth ordinance applicable only to mobile homes held to violate equal protection), and *Pritchett v. Nathan Rodgers Constr. & Realty Co.*, 379 So. 2d 545 (Ala. 1979) (invalidating refusal to connect to sanitary sewer when tap-ins denied on an arbitrary, case-by-case basis).

4. *Downzoning during moratorium.* When a moratorium is adopted in response to a specific development proposal the municipality does not like, and the community then downzones the developer's property during the moratorium period to lower density, she may have a successful as-applied claim even if all of the requirements for a zoning estoppel are not met, if the court is impressed with the equities of the landowner's case. The cases pro and con are collected in Annot., 30 A.L.R.3d 1196, 1235–50 (2009).

A NOTE ON STATUTES AUTHORIZING MORATORIA AND INTERIM ZONING

Authority to adopt. Most courts have found an implied authority to adopt moratoria and interim zoning ordinances under zoning statutes based on the Standard Act, even though it does not expressly authorize moratoria. See *Droste v. Board of County Comm'rs*, 159 P.3d 601 (Colo. 2007); *Arnhold Bernhard & Co. v. Planning & Zoning Comm'n*, 479 A.2d 801 (Conn. 1984); *Collura v. Town of Arlington*, 329 N.E.2d 733 (Mass. 1975) (citing cases). But see *Naylor v. Township of Hellam*, 773 A.2d 770 (Pa. 2000) (no statutory authority to adopt moratorium). Municipalities sometimes use procedural shortcuts when they adopt moratoria because development proposals they want to stop may be imminent. When that happens, a court will invalidate the moratorium if the municipality adopted it without following the formal notice and hearing requirements of the zoning statute. See *Deighton v. City Council*, 902 P.2d 426 (Colo. App. 1995).

Statutes authorizing moratoria. Concern about how moratoria can affect development opportunities and the supply of affordable housing have led a number of states to adopt statutes that specify when and for how long a moratorium can be in place. Examples are Cal. Gov't Code § 65858 (limiting the duration of the ordinance and prohibiting uses that may be in conflict with contemplated zoning when there is a threat to health, safety and welfare); Minn. Stat. Ann. § 394.34 (one year when revision in comprehensive plan or land use regulations pending and one year renewal); Mont. Code Ann. § 76-2-206 (counties; one year with one year extension); Utah Code Ann. § 17-27a-504 (counties, six-month interim ordinance; two six-month extensions possible); cf. Wash. Rev. Code Ann. § 36.70.790 (no time limit).

Some statutes authorize development moratoria but limit the authorization to threats to public health. For example, N.J. Stat. Ann. § 40:55D-90 authorizes a six-month moratorium, but only when there exists "a clear imminent danger to the health of the inhabitants." The statute modifies prior case law on moratoria. See *Toll Bros. v. West Windsor Twp.*, 712 A.2d 266

(N.J. App. Div. 1998) (ordinance authorizing timed growth controls held to be a moratorium prohibited by the statute). A California statute provides that a quota on residential development is presumed to have an impermissible effect on the regional housing supply, but exempts from this limitation "a moratorium, to protect the public health and safety, on residential construction for a specified period of time." Cal. Evid. Code § 669.5. *Pawn America Minnesota, LLC v. City of St. Louis Park, supra*, is a recent case applying Minnesota Stat. Ann. § 462.355(4)(a) (requiring the city to conduct a study prior to adoption).

Do these limitations address takings problems or other constitutional concerns? If so, which ones? Do they effectively preclude a constitutional attack? The statutory proposal for moratoria in the APA's Legislative Guidebook provoked considerable controversy and objections from developer representatives on the advisory committee that moratoria are often an excuse to stop development. A compromise includes three alternatives. The narrowest is limited to shortfalls in public facilities and other compelling needs, a second adds limited moratoria for preparing plans and regulations and includes the general welfare in compelling needs, and the broadest authorizes planning and regulatory moratoria on a broader basis and a full range of compelling needs. Moratoria are limited to six months with one six-month extension. American Planning Association, Growing Smart Legislative Guidebook: Model Statutes for Planning and Management of Change § 8-603 (S. Meck ed., 2002).

The most extensive statutory restrictions on development moratoria have been adopted in Oregon. The statute authorizes a moratorium only "to prevent a shortage of public facilities which would otherwise occur during the effective period of the moratorium." Or. Rev. Stat. § 197.520. A moratorium not justified by a shortage of facilities must be justified by a demonstration of "compelling need." For land within urban growth boundaries this demonstration requires the following:

> (A) That application of existing development ordinances or regulations and other applicable law is inadequate to prevent irrevocable public harm from development in affected geographical areas;
>
> (B) That the moratorium is sufficiently limited to ensure that a needed supply of affected housing types and the supply of commercial and industrial facilities within or in proximity to the city, county or special district are not unreasonably restricted by the adoption of the moratorium;
>
> (C) Stating the reasons alternative methods of achieving the objectives of the moratorium are unsatisfactory;
>
> (D) That the [local government] . . . has determined that the public harm which would be caused by failure to impose a moratorium outweighs the adverse effects on other affected local governments, including shifts in demand for housing or economic development, public facilities and services and buildable lands, and the overall impact of the moratorium on population distribution; and
>
> (E) That the [local government] proposing the moratorium has determined that sufficient resources are available to complete the development of needed interim or permanent changes in plans, regulations or procedures within the period of effectiveness of the moratorium. [Or. Rev. Stat. § 197.520(3).]

To what extent does this statute remedy the problems with moratoria identified in the case law? See *Davis v. City of Bandon*, 805 P.2d 709 (Ore. App. 1991) (moratorium justified by need to preserve valuable wildlife habitat). *Gisler v. Deschutes County*, 945 P.2d 1051 (Ore. App. 1997), held that denial of a subdivision application because it did not meet local approval standards was not a moratorium as defined by the statute.

C. THE ZONING VARIANCE

PURITAN-GREENFIELD IMPROVEMENT ASSOCIATION v. LEO

7 Mich. App. 659, 153 N.W.2d 162 (1967)

LEVIN, JUDGE:

Defendant-appellant John L. Leo claims the circuit judge erred in setting aside a use variance granted by the Detroit Board of Zoning Appeals.

Leo owns a one-story, one-family dwelling at the northwest corner of Puritan avenue and Prest avenue, located in the northwest section of Detroit in an R-1 (single family residence) zoning district. On application and after hearing, the board granted Leo a variance to permit the use of the property as a dental and medical clinic (an RM-4 use) and to use the side yard for off-street parking on certain conditions.

The order of the board states that immediately to the west of the westerly boundary of Leo's property is a gasoline service station (at the corner of Puritan and Greenfield); that there was testimony Leo had not received any offers from residence-use buyers during the period of over a year the property had been listed and offered for sale; and, in the event a variance was granted, it was intended to preserve the present exterior of the building without significant alteration so that it would continue to appear to be a one-family dwelling.

The appeal board's dominant finding was:

> "That the board found unnecessary hardship and practical difficulty because of the heavy traffic and the closeness to the business section immediately to the west."

The board also found that the proposed use would not alter the essential character of the neighborhood, would not be injurious to the contiguous property, would not be detrimental to the surrounding neighborhood, and would not depreciate property values.

Plaintiff-appellee, Puritan-Greenfield Improvement Association, filed a complaint with the circuit court which was treated by the court as one for superintending control. The matter was heard by the circuit judge on the record made before the board. The circuit judge reversed the decision of the board, stating *inter alia* that it had not been shown the land could not yield a reasonable return or be put to a proper economic use if used only for a purpose allowed by existing zoning and that such showing of hardship as had been made was of "self-created" hardship attributable to the character of the structure thereon.

The applicable enabling act provides for a board of zoning appeals authorized to grant a variance upon a showing of practical difficulties or unnecessary hardship. The Detroit ordinance requires evidence of special conditions and unnecessary hardship or practical difficulties.

. . . The minimum constitutional standard establishes the scope of review. The circuit judge and we are required by the Michigan constitution to determine whether the findings of the board and its order are authorized by law and whether they are supported by competent, material, and substantial evidence on the whole record.

Although there has been a great deal of judicial effort expended in Michigan in considering challenges to the reasonableness or constitutionality of zoning as applied to individual properties, we find no Michigan appellate decisions construing the words "unnecessary hardship or practical difficulties."

The first modern zoning regulations were adopted by the city of New York and the phrase "practical difficulties or unnecessary hardship" was fashioned as the applicable standard to guide New York's board of appeals in considering applications for variances. A comparison of the relevant language of the applicable Michigan enabling act with that of the original New York city legislation shows that the Michigan provision authorizing the vesting in a board of zoning appeals the authority to grant variances parallels the corresponding New York city provision.

It appears that most State enabling acts, and ordinances based thereon, use "unnecessary hardship" as the governing standard. In those States (like Michigan and New York) where the applicable standard is "unnecessary hardship *or* practical difficulties," the phrase "practical difficulties" had been regarded as applicable only when an area or a dimension variance is sought, and in determining whether a use variance will be granted the decisive words are "unnecessary hardship." In the light of this history, we have turned for guidance to decisions of other States applying the "unnecessary hardship" standard.

A text writer, Rathkopf, states that courts have held, variously, that a property owner seeking a variance on the ground of "unnecessary hardship" must show credible proof that the property will not yield a reasonable return if used only for a purpose allowed by the ordinance or must establish that the zoning gives rise to hardship amounting to virtual confiscation or the disadvantage must be so great as to deprive the owner of all reasonable use of the property. He concedes that the showing required "is substantially equivalent to that which would warrant a court in declaring the ordinance confiscatory, unreasonable, and unconstitutional in its application to the property involved." 2 Rathkopf, The Law of Zoning and Planning, p. 45-14.

These principles also find expression in the frequently stated generalizations that variances should be sparingly granted, that it is not sufficient to show that the property would be worth more or could be more profitably employed if the restrictions were varied to permit another use, and that the board of appeals, being without legislative power, may not in the guise of a variance amend the zoning ordinance or disregard its provisions.

The judicial attitudes so expressed could well have been influenced by the early history of the boards of zoning appeal and the need to declare more precise standards than the somewhat nebulous "unnecessary hardship." When zoning was in its infancy it was thought by some that without a board of zoning appeals the individual declarations of zoning ordinance invalidity would be so numerous it would become necessary to declare the legislation void as a whole and, thus, "the chief value of the board of appeals in zoning is in protecting the ordinance from attacks upon its constitutionality." That view of the purpose of the board of zoning appeals has been said to require a standard related to the reasonableness of the zoning:

> "The hardship contemplated in this legislation has constitutional overtones, and it is the purpose of the variance to immunize zoning legislation against attack on the ground that it may in some instances operate to effect a taking of property without just

compensation." *R.N.R. Associates v. City of Providence Zoning Board of Review*,210 A.2d 653, 654 (R.I. 1965).

It has been said that the function of a board of zoning appeals is to protect the community against usable land remaining idle and it is that purpose which gives definition to "unnecessary hardship."

> "Since the main purpose of allowing variances is to prevent land from being rendered useless, 'unnecessary hardship' can best be defined as a situation where in the absence of a variance no feasible use can be made of the land." 74 Harv. L. Rev. p.1401 (1961).

Whatever the rationale may be, it has been held that a variance should not be granted until it appears the property cannot be put reasonably to a conforming use; or the application of the ordinance is so unreasonable as to constitute an arbitrary and capricious interference with the basic right of private property; or that the property cannot be used for a conforming purpose.

> "An unnecessary hardship exists when all the relevant factors taken together convince that the plight of the location concerned is unique in that it cannot be put to a conforming use because of the limitations imposed upon the property by reason of [its] classification in a specific zone." *Peterson v. Vasak*, [76 N.W.2d at 426 (Neb. 1956)].

The authors of a number of scholarly studies appear to agree that an applicant desiring a variance must show

> "(a) that if he complies with the provisions of the ordinance, he can secure no reasonable return from, or make no reasonable use of, his property; (b) that the hardship results from the application of the ordinance to his property; (c) that the hardship of which he complains is suffered by his property directly, and not merely by others; (d) that the hardship is not the result of his own actions; and (e) that the hardship is peculiar to the property of the applicant." Green, *The Power of the Zoning Board of Adjustment to Grant Variances from the Zoning Ordinance* (1951), 29 N.C. Law Rev. 245, 249.

The New York Court of Appeals has stated:

> "Before the Board may exercise its discretion and grant a [use] variance upon the ground of unnecessary hardship, the record must show that (1) the land in question cannot yield a reasonable return if used only for a purpose allowed in that zone; (2) that the plight of the owner is due to unique circumstances and not to the general conditions in the neighborhood which may reflect the unreasonableness of the zoning ordinance itself; and (3) that the use to be authorized by the variance will not alter the essential character of the locality." *Otto v. Steinhilber* (1939), 282 N.Y. 71, 24 N.E.2d 851.

The *Otto* definition has been adopted by other courts.

We find overwhelming support for the proposition — expressed in *Otto* — that the hardship must be unique or peculiar to the property for which the variance is sought. . . .

Under these definitions even if the land cannot yield a reasonable return if used only for a purpose permitted by existing zoning, a use variance may not be granted unless the landowner's plight is due to unique circumstances and not to general conditions in the neighborhood that may reflect the unreasonableness of the zoning.

This limitation on the board's powers is related to the third limitation expressed in *Otto* — that a use authorized by a variance shall not alter the essential character of the locality. In this connection we note that the Detroit ordinance prohibits a variance that would be contrary to the public interest or inconsistent with the spirit of the ordinance.

> "If it [the hardship] affects a whole area, then his remedy lies in seeking an amendment to the zoning ordinance. This is true even where the applicant's property is situated in an area where none of the properties can be put to any reasonable beneficial use owing to zoning restrictions. It is not for the board in these circumstances to bestow liberties upon one single member of this group of property holders. The legislature must be the body to make decisions of this sort even in cases where the most severe hardship can be shown." Pooley, Planning Zoning in the United States, [Michigan Legal Publications, Ann Arbor, Michigan (1961)].

The Rhode Island Supreme Court has stated that once the right to a variance becomes established the only matter remaining is the scope and character of the relief to be granted, which must be effectuated in a manner consistent with the public interest; but if a considerable number of property owners are similarly affected, it might well appear contrary to the spirit of the ordinance to grant relief to one while denying it to another, and in such a case it has been said that relief should be withheld until it can be decreed by the governing body or, if necessary, by the courts.

While we have discussed the foregoing statements that the hardship must be unique and that there are limitations on a zoning appeal board's power to frame a remedy when the hardship is shared with others — such statements being so inextricably a part of judicial, text and scholarly definitions of "unnecessary hardship" that the construction of that term could not accurately be discussed without reference to those statements — we do not here express our views thereon, as it is not necessary to do so in order to decide this case. We limit our holding to that expressed in the next paragraph.

Our review of the authorities leads us to hold that a use variance should not be granted unless the board of zoning appeals can find on the basis of substantial evidence that the property cannot reasonably be used in a manner consistent with existing zoning. In *Otto* the New York Court of Appeals stated that one seeking a variance must show that the land in question cannot yield a *reasonable return* if used only for a purpose allowed in the relevant zoning district. It will be noted that we have used the word "property" (i.e., including improvements) rather than "land," reserving to a later day the decision whether we wish to adopt that aspect of the *Otto* definition. It will also be noted that our holding speaks in terms of "reasonable use" rather than "reasonable return." Whether property usable in trade or business or held for the production of income can reasonably be used for a purpose consistent with existing zoning will, no doubt, ordinarily turn on whether a reasonable return can be derived from the property as then zoned. While any property, including a single family residence, may be made to produce income if a tenant can be found therefor, it would in our opinion be unrealistic as to all properties (without regard to their varying utility) to resolve the question solely on the basis of the return that can be derived from the property.

In the case of Leo's property, we perceive the question to be whether the property can continue reasonably to be used as a single family residence. The appeal board made no determination in that regard, resting its finding of unnecessary hardship solely on the "heavy traffic and the closeness to the business section immediately to the west."

Leo's property has been used for some time as a single family residence. While the board found there was "testimony" that Leo had not received any offers from residence-use buyers during the period of over a year the property had been listed and offered for sale, the asking price for the house and adjoining lot was $38,500 in a neighborhood where, according to the only record evidence, houses generally sell for $20,000 to $25,000. There was no evidence of efforts to sell the property at any price lower than $38,500; indeed, there was no testimony at all as to the extent of the sales effort or the income that could be derived from the property as zoned.

Testimony that the house and lot could not be sold for $38,500 in a neighborhood where houses generally sell for substantially less than that amount does not, in our opinion, constitute any evidence that the property could not continue reasonably to be used as a single family residence.

Thus there was not only a failure to find that the property could not reasonably be used in a manner consistent with existing zoning, but, as we read the record, there was no evidence upon which such a finding could have been based. In this connection, it should be remembered that the fact that the property would be worth more if it could be used as a doctor's clinic and that the corner of Puritan and Prest has disadvantages as a place of residence does not authorize the granting of a variance. Heavy traffic is all too typical of innumerable admittedly residential streets. Adjacency to gasoline stations or other commercial development is characteristic of the end of a business or commercial district and the commencement of a residential district. "A district has to end somewhere." *Real Properties, Inc. v. Board of Appeal of Boston* (Mass. 1946), 65 N.E.2d 199, 201.

It can readily be seen that unless the power of the board of zoning appeals to grant a use variance is defined by objective standards, the appeal board could [and we do not in any sense mean to suggest this would be deliberate] rezone an entire neighborhood — a lot or two lots at a time. The variance granted in response to one "hardship" may well beget or validate another claim of hardship and justify still another variance. If it is a hardship to be next to a gasoline station, it could be a hardship to be across from one, to be behind one, or diagonally across from one. If heavy traffic is a valid basis, variances might become the rule rather than the sparingly granted exception.

We do not wish to be understood as challenging the judgment of the board of zoning appeals. A doctor's office with the appearance of a single family residence on a busy street which already has other commercial uses may very well be a logical, sensible and unobjectionable use. However the question before us is not whether the board of zoning appeals has acted reasonably, but whether on the proofs and findings the board could grant a variance on the ground of unnecessary hardship. We have concluded that neither the proofs nor the findings justified the variance granted.

We have given careful consideration to the considerable number of cases we found where the result was based on the reviewing court's conclusion that the appeal board had not abused the discretion confided to it. If there is substantial evidence to support the necessary findings, such a decision is, indeed, the correct one. However, there must be such evidence and such findings.

We have considered and rejected appellee's contention that a board of zoning appeals may not grant a use variance. We have also considered appellee's contention that the board's action should be reversed because the hardship alleged by Leo was "self-created." However, the hardship found by the board in this case could not be said to have been self-created — Leo neither created the traffic conditions on Puritan nor the gasoline station immediately to the west of his property.

Affirmed. Costs to appellee.

NOTES AND QUESTIONS

1. *The role of variances.* The Standard Zoning Act provided a single standard for variances, but over time a distinction has grown up between so-called "use" variances, in which a change in the use permitted in the district is sought, and "area" variances, in which relaxation of physical requirements (lot size, setbacks, height, etc.) is sought. Area variances are described, *infra.*

The principal case adopts and applies the usual tests that are used to review use variances. What are they? How would you define a "use" variance? For an extensive discussion of the role of use variances, see *Cromwell v. Ward*, 651 A.2d 424 (Md. App. 1995).

What effect does the granting of a variance have on the property and on the underlying zoning? Although the personal circumstances of the applicant affected the court's decision in the principal case, it is clear that personal need cannot be the basis for a variance. *Larsen v. Zoning Bd. of Adjustment*, 543 Pa. 415 (Pa. 1996) (variance requested to provide play area for children). Moreover, a variance runs with the land and is not personal to the applicant who receives one, because zoning deals with the use, not the users. Although the granting of a variance does not change the applicable zoning restrictions, a new owner can continue to rely on the terms of the variance. See *Stop & Shop Supermarket Co. v. Board of Adjustment of Springfield*, 744 A.2d 1169 (N.J. 2000) (variance for parking in residential zone). Under what conditions might the underlying zoning be applied?

Some of the requirements for a use variance are the result of judicial interpretation, not explicit statutory language. The authority to grant variances derives from § 7 of the Standard Zoning Act, which most states have adopted. The Standard Act is reproduced in Chapter 3, Section A.2. Some states have adopted standards for variances that are more detailed than the Standard Act. E.g., Pa. Stat. Ann. tit. 53, § 10910.2. New Jersey authorizes a "special reasons" variance, which is more like a special exception because hardship is not required. N.J. Stat. § 40:55D-70(d). Note also that the statute and court-adopted standards impose a multi-factor test, and that all elements of the test must be met if a variance is to be granted.

Although the courts may interpret the statutory criteria, most courts hold that the statutory criteria for a variance may not be modified by the zoning ordinance. See *Nelson v. Donaldson*, 50 So. 2d 244 (Ala. 1951); *Cohen v. Board of Appeals*, 795 N.E.2d 619 (N.Y. 2003) (undue hardship/practical difficulty standard of local ordinance is preempted by state statute requiring a balancing test). Indeed, an ordinance provision that any variance granted must be the minimum variance necessary to provide the landowner with a reasonable return on his investment has been held invalid as an additional standard not included in the statute. See *Celentano, Inc. v. Board of Zoning Appeals*, 184 A.2d 49 (Conn. 1962); *Coderre v. Zoning Bd. of Review*, 230 A.2d 247 (R.I. 1967). But where the statute is unambiguous in adopting this standard, the municipality may not vary from it. See *Krummenacher v. City of Minnetonka*, 783 N.W.2d 721 (Minn. 2010).

2. *Variance standards. Otto v. Steinhilber*, cited and quoted in the principal case, is undoubtedly the leading case on standards for granting zoning variances. In *Steinhilber*, the court distinguished situations where a variance should be granted from those where zoning regulations as applied to a substantial area should be held invalid, as follows:

> The object of a variance granted by the Board of Appeals in favor of property owners suffering unnecessary hardship in the operation of a zoning law, is to afford relief to an individual property owner laboring under restrictions to which no valid general objection may be made. Where the property owner is unable reasonably to use his land because of zoning restrictions, the fault may lie in the fact that the particular zoning restriction is unreasonable in its application to a certain locality or the oppressive result may be caused by conditions peculiar to a particular piece of land. In the former situation, the relief is by way of direct attack upon the terms of the ordinance. . . . In order to prevent the oppressive operation of the zoning law in particular instances, when the zoning restrictions are otherwise generally reasonable, the zoning laws usually create a safety valve under the control of a Board of Appeals, which may relieve against "unnecessary hardship" in particular instances. [24 N.E.2d at 852.]

Some states have codified the uniqueness rule. Cal. Gov't Code § 65906.

Most courts follow the New York decisions and refuse to approve a variance if it appears that the variance is based on conditions general to the neighborhood. *Nance v. Town of Indialantic*, 419 So. 2d 1041 (Fla. 1982); *Priest v. Griffin*, 222 So. 2d 353 (Ala. 1969); *Boyer v. Zoning Hearing Board*, 987 A.2d 219 (Pa. Commw. 2010). Compare *Wolfman v. Board of Appeals*, 444 N.E.2d 943 (Mass. App. 1983) (soil conditions justified variance to avoid height increase). Of course, when "unnecessary hardship" is a result of conditions general to the neighborhood, it would be proper for the local governing body to amend the ordinance, either on its own initiative or on the request of the landowners in the neighborhood.

Otto v. Steinhilber also states that the use allowed by a variance should not "alter the essential character of the locality." Some courts have adopted this limitation, and refer to it as the negative criterion. See *Commons v. Westwood Zoning Bd. of Adjustment*, 410 A.2d 1138 (N.J. 1980). How should this requirement be applied? Is it redundant? In *Medici v. BPR Co.*, 526 A.2d 109 (N.J. 1987), the court expanded on this approach by requiring an "enhanced quality of proof" in use variance cases: "Such proofs and findings must satisfactorily reconcile the grant of a use variance with the ordinance's continued omission of the proposed use from those permitted in the zone." Approval of a four-story motel in an industrial zone was overturned. However, the New Jersey court does not apply the enhanced *Medici* proof where an "inherently beneficial use" requests a use variance. See *Sica v. Board of Adjustment*, 603 A. 2d 30 (N.J. 1991) (trauma rehabilitation center). A use variance cannot be granted just because it is less intensive than uses permitted by the zoning ordinance. *Klein v. Hamilton County Bd. of Zoning Appeals*, 716 N.E.2d 268 (Ohio App. 1998) (insurance office).

The Standard Act requirement, that the spirit of the ordinance be observed and "substantial justice" done, has not received much attention in the cases. But see *Belanger v. City of Nashua*, 430 A.2d 166 (N.H. 1966). However, statutes and ordinances often include this requirement as one factor to consider in deciding whether to grant a variance.

3. *No reasonable return.* What is the significance of the distinction drawn by Judge Levin, in the principal case, between proof that the land in question "cannot yield a *reasonable return* if used only for a purpose allowed in the relevant zoning district" and proof that no reasonable use of the property can be made unless a variance is granted? This distinction is rarely made in the variance cases from other states, and courts seem to use the two formulas interchangeably. Typical of judicial statements with respect to the "unnecessary hardship" test is the following language from *MacLean v. Zoning Bd. of Adjustment*, 185 A.2d 533 (Pa. 1962), where the court affirmed the board's refusal to grant a variance to permit construction of a gasoline service station in a residential area:

> [T]he real owner of this property, testified that the "best use" of this property would be as a gasoline service station, [so] it is obvious that his definition of "best use" is that use which would be most productive of economic profit. An examination of this record clearly shows that the request for a variance is not based upon any lack of feasibility of the use of this property for residential purposes but rather upon the expectation that the property will be productive of greater financial gain if used as a gasoline service station. This is the type of "economic hardship" which time and again we have stated does not constitute an "unnecessary hardship" sufficient to justify the grant of a variance. [*Id.* at 536.]

See also *State v. Winnebago County*, 540 N.W.2d 6 (Wis. App. 1995) (variance cannot be granted to maximize value of the property). Compare *North Bethlehem Neighbors Group v. Zoning Bd.*, 822 A.2d 840 (Pa. Commw. 2003) (gas station met unnecessary hardship standard in office district where property could not be developed at all without a use variance).

4. *What about Lucas?* Is the *Puritan-Greenfield* case consistent with the Supreme Court's *Lucas* decision, which held a taking occurs per se when a land use regulation denies a property owner all economically productive use of his land? Is the variance standard adopted in that case, though it does not use the same terminology, virtually the same test? Presumably, if the *Lucas* test is met, a variance should follow automatically. See *Village Bd. v. Jarrold*, 423 N.E.2d 385 (N.Y. 1981), holding pre-*Lucas* that the "no reasonable return" rule applied in variance cases is similar to the rule applied to takings claims. The post-*Lucas* case *Blair v. Department of Conservation and Recreation*, 932 N.E.2d 267 (Mass. 2010), considered whether the denial of a variance was a regulatory taking, and viewing the effect of the denial on the whole parcel, decided that it was not. See also the discussion in Chapter 2, Note 5 following, regarding *Tahoe-Sierra*, on *Tahoe-Sierra*'s impact on the *Lucas* test. Note that a takings claim is not "ripe" for adjudication in federal court unless the property owner has asked for and been denied a variance, pursuant to *Williamson County Reg'l Planning Comm'n v. Hamilton Bank*, 473 U.S. 172, 186–188 (1985), reproduced in Chapter 2. The variance thus acts as an important "safety valve" for takings claims. See Mixon & Waggoner, *The Role of Variances in Determining Ripeness in Takings Claims Under Zoning Ordinances and Subdivision Regulations of Texas Municipalities*, 29 St. Mary's L.J. 765 (1998).

5. *Efforts to sell.* The court's concern in the principal case about the landowner's efforts to sell the property reflects the rule adopted in *Forrest v. Evershed*, 164 N.E.2d 841 (N.Y. 1959), that a landowner applying for a variance must show that he made diligent efforts to sell his property without success. Should this rule be part of variance law? Isn't the value of the property dependent on conditions in the neighborhood, not on the unique circumstances of the land? If so, isn't the "attempt to sell" rule inconsistent with the uniqueness requirement? In *Valley View Civic Ass'n v. Zoning Bd. of Adjustment*, 462 A.2d 637 (Pa. 1983), the court rejected this rule but noted that evidence of inability to sell "has unquestionable probative value."

6. *Self-inflicted hardship.* If the landowner's hardship is "self-inflicted," courts will set aside any variance granted on the ground of hardship. Hardship is clearly self-inflicted if a landowner or developer proceeds to build in willful or accidental violation of the zoning ordinance and the municipal authorities insist that the violation be corrected. Hardship is also self-inflicted when it is "manufactured" — e.g., where the landowner or developer has torn down a residential structure and then claims that his property cannot profitably be put to residential use, or where he has deliberately carved a triangular lot out of a larger tract and then claims that development for residential use is not feasible. *Baker v. Connell*, 488 A.2d 1303 (Del. 1985). Similarly, when a developer pays a premium price for land, and then seeks a variance on the ground of financial hardship, the hardship has been held to be self-inflicted. *Josephson v. Autrey*, 96 So. 2d 784 (Fla. 1957).

Some courts also have held that the purchase of property with knowledge of the zoning restrictions gives rise to self-inflicted hardship even if, arguably, the vendor could have established sufficient hardship to justify a variance. See *Sanchez v. Board of Zoning Adjustments*, 488 So. 2d 1277 (La. App. 1986). Such a broad rule is difficult to justify, since it results in a requirement that any landowner who has a legitimate claim to a hardship variance must himself obtain the variance before selling his property, even though he has no intention of developing the property himself; otherwise, the purchaser will be barred from obtaining a variance and, presumably, must attempt to have the zoning restrictions declared invalid as applied to his property if no reasonable return on a conforming use is possible.

Other courts have rejected the rule that purchase alone is self-created hardship. *Spence v. Board of Zoning Appeals*, 496 S.E.2d 61 (Va. 1998), *Wilson v. Plumstead Twp. Zoning Hearing Bd.*, 936 A.2d 1061 (Pa. 2007); *Lamb v. Zoning Bd. of Appeals*, 923 N.E. 2d 1078 (Mass. Ct. App. 2010). Cf. *Sam's East v. United Energy Corp., Inc.*, 927 N.E.2d 960 (Ct. App. Ind. 2010). Others hold that it is only one factor to consider. *Ifrah v. Utschig*, 774 N.E.2d 732 (N.Y. 2002). See Reynolds, *Self-Induced Hardship in Zoning Variances: Does a Purchaser Have No One But Himself to Blame?*, 20 Urb. Law 1 (1988).

7. *Use variances.* So-called "use" variances have been recognized as valid in the great majority of states, and the litigated cases on variances usually involve use variances. See *Matthew v. Smith*, 707 S.W.2d 411 (Mo. 1986). In a few states, however, the courts have refused to recognize the validity of use variances on the ground that to grant a variance that changes the uses permitted in a zoning district is, in substance, to amend the zoning ordinance, and thus to usurp the legislative power of the local governing body. *Josephson v. Autrey*, 96 So. 2d 784 (Fla. 1957); *Bray v. Beyer*, 166 S.W.2d 290 (Ky. 1942); *Leah v. Board of Adjustment*, 37 S.E.2d 128 (N.C. 1946). The California zoning enabling act also prohibits use variances: "[a] variance shall not be granted for a parcel of property which authorizes a use or activity which is not otherwise expressly authorized by the zone regulation governing the parcel of property." Cal. Gov't Code § 65906.

8. *Conditions.* Most courts hold that the zoning board of adjustment (or appeals) has the power to attach appropriate conditions to the grant of any variance, although the Standard State Zoning Enabling Act and enabling statutes modeled on it do not expressly confer such power. It is arguable that the power to impose conditions can be implied from the final phrase in the Standard Act's authorization for the granting of variances — "so that the spirit of the ordinance shall be observed and substantial justice be done." Municipal zoning ordinances often expressly authorize the board of adjustment (or appeals) to impose conditions upon the grant of a variance, and in some cases the courts have considered this authorization to be significant. See also *Town of Burlington v. Jencik*, 362 A.2d 1338 (Conn. 1975) (conditions alleviate possible harm from use allowed by variance).

Not all conditions will be upheld. Conditions affecting the development of the site, such as conditions requiring landscaping, paving and access, are usually upheld. *Wright v. Zoning Bd. of Appeals*, 391 A.2d 146 (Conn. 1978). See also *Cornell v. Board of Appeals of Dracut*, 906 N.E.2d 334 (Mass. 2009) (time limitation). What about a condition terminating a variance if there is a change in the person using the property? See *St. Onge v. Donovan*, 522 N.E.2d 1019 (N.Y. 1988) (held invalid). Why not allow this condition?

9. *Findings.* Should boards of adjustment be required to make formal findings in variance cases? A few statutes require findings, e.g., 65 Ill. Comp. Stat. Ann. 5/11-13-11. Even without a statutory requirement, some courts require formal findings in order to provide for effective judicial review. A leading case is *Topanga Ass'n for a Scenic Community v. County of Los Angeles*, 522 P.2d 12 (Cal. 1974), noted, 1975 Urb. L. Ann. 349.

10. *Abuse.* The variance was initially considered an important "safety valve" in the administration of zoning ordinances. However, because of lack of expertise, political influence, and — in some of the larger cities — far too heavy a caseload, many zoning boards of adjustment (or appeals) have long shown a regrettable tendency to ignore the standards prescribed by statute and by judicial decision for the granting of variances, as the drive-in bank case at the beginning of this section illustrates. Substantial empirical studies of variance procedures have concluded that the boards in the communities under study did not, in a majority of cases, insist that the statutory and case law standards for variances be satisfied. See Dukeminier & Stapleton, *The Zoning Board of Adjustment: A Case Study in Misrule*, 50 Ky. L.J. 273 (1962); Comment, 50 Cal. L. Rev. 101 (1962); Contemporary Studies Project, *Rural Land Use in Iowa: An Empirical Analysis of County Board of Adjustment Practices*, 68 Iowa L. Rev. 1083 (1983). The non-profit Municipal Art Society, which advocates for urban planning in New York City, has conducted a study of the city variance process and applications in 2001-2002, and found that most variances are approved, and questioned whether the process is being used to by-pass underlying zoning. The Municipal Art Society of New York, *Zoning Variances and the New York City Board of Standards and Appeals* (March 2004), available at http://mas.org. But see Johannessen, *Zoning Variances: Unnecessarily an Evil*, 41 Land Use L. & Zoning Dig., No. 7, at 3 (1989).

11. *Sources.* See Reynolds, *The "Unique Circumstances" Rule in Zoning Variances — An Aid in Achieving Greater Prudence and Less Leniency*, 31 Urb. Law. 127 (1999); Comment, *A Constitutional Safety Valve: The Variance in Zoning and Land-Use Based Environmental Controls*, 22 B.C. Envtl. Aff. L. Rev. 307 (1995).

A NOTE ON AREA OR DIMENSIONAL VARIANCES

Much of the preceding material on zoning makes it clear that area, bulk and density regulations are often more important to the land developer than use regulations. This is especially so with residential district regulations. Most communities have several residential zones, and the distinctions between the zones are usually based on density rather than use. Density, in turn, may be controlled in a variety of ways, often used in combination: limitations on the number of dwelling units per acre, height limitations, restrictions on the percentage of lot that can be covered, and provisions requiring a minimum amount of open space for each residential unit. A developer can obtain a modification of these regulations through what are known as dimensional, area or site variances.

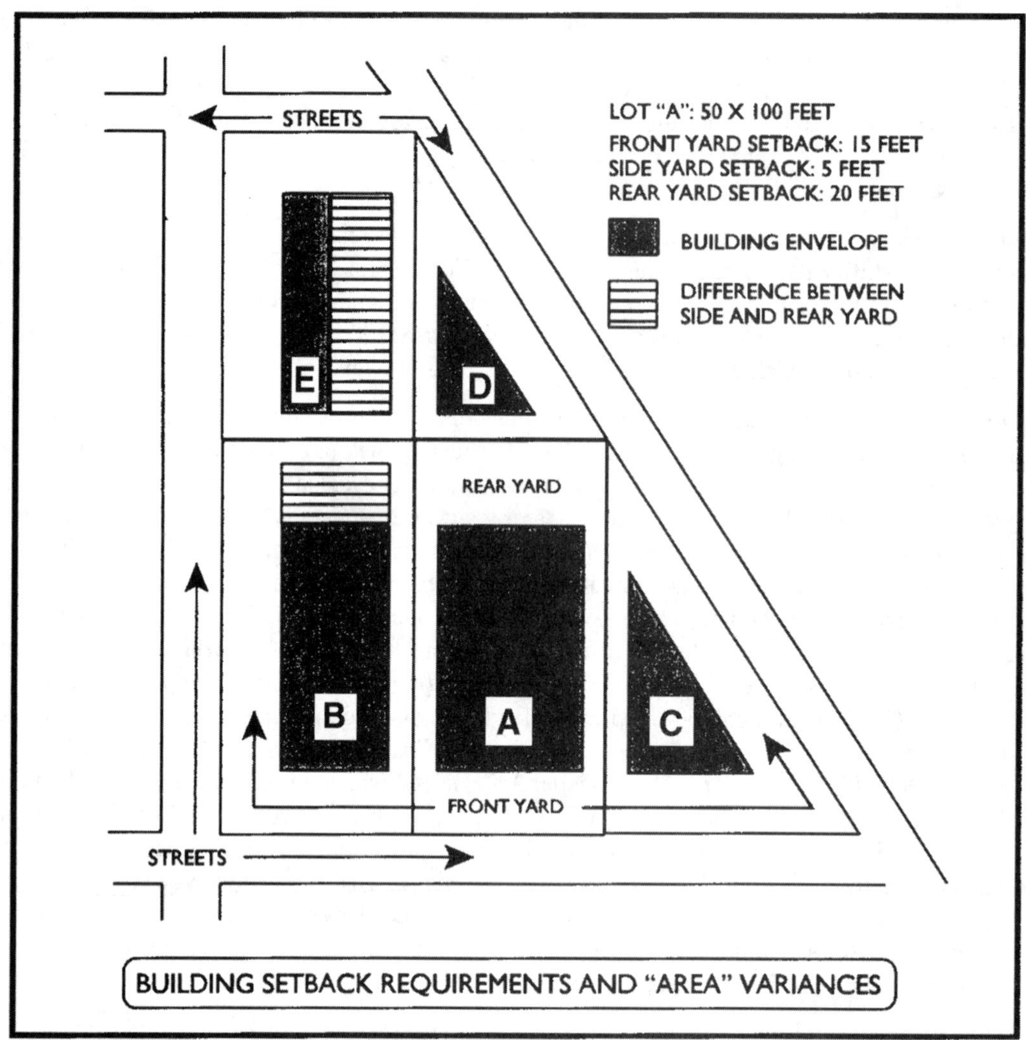

A developer may request a dimensional variance for a number of reasons. She may need only a minor adjustment in a setback regulation. She may also seek a more fundamental increase in density. A density increase is important to the developer because it increases her return.

The Standard Zoning Act provided a single "unnecessary hardship" test for all variances. A number of zoning statutes and ordinances have modified the Standard Act by providing that a variance may be granted for "practical difficulties" as well as for unnecessary hardship. Many cases hold that this type of statute does not create a dual standard and apply the unnecessary hardship test and other tests to both use and area variances. *City & Borough of Juneau v. Thibodeau*, 595 P.2d 626 (Alaska 1979), is a leading decision. Accord *Cochran v. Fairfax County Bd. of Zoning Appeals*, 594 S.E.2d 571 (Va. 2004). Other statutes apply only a "practical difficulties" test for area variances. Me. Rev Stat. tit. 30-A, § 4353(4).

Why should the standards for an area variance be less restrictive than those for a use variance? Consider the following case:

ZIERVOGEL v. WASHINGTON COUNTY BOARD OF ADJUSTMENT

676 N.W.2d 401 (Wis. 2004)

SYKES, JUSTICE:

We are called upon in this case to reconsider the legal standard by which zoning boards of adjustment measure "unnecessary hardship" when determining whether to grant area zoning variances. The legislature has by statute vested local boards of adjustment with broad discretionary power to authorize variances where the strict enforcement of zoning regulations results in unnecessary hardship to individual property owners. "Unnecessary hardship," however, is not defined in the statute. It has fallen to courts to give meaning to the term. . . .

We now conclude that the distinctions in purpose and effect of use and area zoning make the perpetuation of a single, highly-restrictive "no reasonable use of the property" standard for all variances unworkable and unfair. Use zoning regulates fundamentally how property may be used, in order to promote uniformity of land use within neighborhoods or regions. Area zoning regulates lot area, density, height, frontage, setbacks, and so forth, in order to promote uniformity of development, lot, and building size.

Restricting the availability of variances to those property owners who would have "no reasonable use" of their property without a variance may be justifiable in use variance cases, given the purpose of use zoning and the substantial effect of use variances on neighborhood character. But applying the same strict "no reasonable use" standard to area variance applications is unjustifiable. The "no reasonable use" standard is largely disconnected from the purpose of area zoning, fails to consider the lesser effect of area variances on neighborhood character, and operates to virtually eliminate the statutory discretion of local boards of adjustment to do justice in individual cases. . . .

Richard Ziervogel and Maureen McGinnity ("petitioners") own a 1.4 acre parcel of property on Big Cedar Lake in the Town of West Bend in Washington County. The property has 200 feet of lake frontage and a 1600-square-foot house with a legal nonconforming setback of 26 feet from the ordinary high water mark of the lake. A public roadway bisects the lot along the side of the house opposite the lake, and the remainder of the lot on the other side of roadway is in a floodplain.

The petitioners purchased the property in 1996 and have used it as a summer home. They now wish to live in the house year-round, and would like to construct a ten-foot vertical addition to the structure consisting of two bedroom-bathroom suites and an office. In 1996, such an addition would have been permissible under the applicable shoreland zoning ordinance. However, in 2001 Washington County amended its ordinance to prohibit any expansion of any portion of an existing structure within 50 feet of the ordinary high-water mark of the lake. Accordingly, the petitioners need a variance to go ahead with their plans. . . . [The petitioners were denied an area variance by the Washington County Board of Adjustment, and on petition for writ of certiorari, the circuit court upheld the Board, which was affirmed on appeal.] . . .

By definition, all variances depart from the purpose of the zoning ordinance and implicate the public interest, because they permit something that is otherwise strictly prohibited. But they do so to varying degrees and levels of acceptability, depending on the type of variance requested and the nature of the zoning restriction in question. As such, courts have long recognized a distinction between use variances, which permit a landowner to put property to an otherwise prohibited use, and area variances, which provide exceptions from such physical requirements as setbacks, lot area, and height limits. . . . Use zoning regulates fundamentally how property may be used, in order to promote uniformity of use within neighborhoods and regions. Area zoning, on the other hand, regulates density, setbacks, frontage, height, and other dimensional attributes, in order to promote uniformity of development, lot size, and building configuration and size.

Use and area variances thus threaten the integrity of zoning ordinances in qualitatively different ways, and generally to a different extent. Use variances by their nature have the potential to bring about great changes in neighborhood character, but area variances usually do not have this effect. While area variances provide an increment of relief (normally small) from a physical dimensional restriction such as building height, setback, and so forth, use variances permit wholesale deviation from the way in which land in the zone is used. Accordingly, the measure of unnecessary hardship for use and area variances is different. . . .

Application of the "no reasonable use" standard to area variances overwhelms all other considerations in the analysis, rendering irrelevant any inquiry into the uniqueness of the property, the purpose of the ordinance, and the effect of a variance on the public interest. . . . For the statutory discretionary authority to be meaningful, boards of adjustment must have the opportunity to distinguish between hardships that are unnecessary in light of unique conditions of the property and the purpose of the ordinance, and hardships that do not warrant relief, either because they are inconsequential or not unique or because a variance would unduly undermine the purpose of the ordinance or the public interest. Boards of adjustment must "have some very real flexibility in granting variances." Under the "no reasonable use" standard, however, boards of adjustment are effectively prohibited from considering the graduated nature of intrusions upon the strict letter of area restrictions. The "no reasonable use" standard, therefore, leaves boards of adjustment with almost no flexibility and empties the concept of "discretion" of any real meaning.

Kenosha County's adoption of the "no reasonable use" standard for area variances generally precludes any property owner currently using his property from ever getting a variance, regardless of the merits of the application or the type, size, and nature of the variance requested. This "unreasonably prevents private property owners from making even highly beneficial, completely legal improvements to their property," if doing so requires a variance to legalize even the slightest nonconformity. Almost all variance applicants — certainly all applicants who are putting their property to some use at the time of application — will flunk the "no reasonable use" test, divesting the board of any real discretion. . . .

We therefore reinstate [an earlier caselaw] formulation of unnecessary hardship for area variance cases: " 'whether compliance with the strict letter of the restrictions governing area, set backs, frontage, height, bulk or density would unreasonably prevent the owner from using the property for a permitted purpose or would render conformity with such restrictions unnecessarily burdensome.' " [This formulation] also emphasized that variance requests are always evaluated in light of the purpose of the zoning ordinance and the public interests at stake. Accordingly, whether the [formulation] is met in individual cases depends upon a consideration of the purpose of the zoning restriction in question, its effect on the property, and the effect of a variance on the neighborhood and larger public interest. The established requirements that the hardship be unique to the property and not self-created are maintained, and the burden of proving unnecessary hardship remains on the property owner. [The court reversed the court of appeal decision that upheld the denial of the variance, and remanded the case for further proceedings consistent with the modified standard of "unnecessary hardship" for area variances.]

NOTES AND QUESTIONS

1. *Tests for area variances.* How would you summarize the tests the court adopted in the principal opinion for area variances? How do these tests adopted by the principal opinion differ from the tests courts apply to use variances? Courts have adopted a variety of tests for area variances when they do not apply the unnecessary hardship test. They indicate that the difference between the tests for use and area variances is a matter of degree, but emphasize that the test for area variances is less stringent. Courts usually apply a set of factors to determine when the practical difficulties test justifies an area variance. These usually include the significance of the economic injury, the magnitude of the variance sought, whether the difficulty was self-created, and whether other feasible alternatives could avoid the difficulty. Statutes and ordinances may also contain different standards, such as requiring only "adverse impact," and may also impose a "uniqueness" requirement. See *Cromwell v. Ward*, 651 A.2d 424 (Md. App. 1995) (summarizing the cases).

In re the Matter of the Decision of County of Otter Tail Board of Adjustment, 754 N.W.2d 323 (Minn. 2008) (en banc), provides an excellent history of the use of the standard for "particular hardship" applied to use variances, and "practical difficulty" applied to area variances, beginning with the 1916 New York City Building Zone Resolution. The court concludes that the standard for an area variance is less stringent than that of a use variance, and should consider equitable factors including "(1) how substantial the variation is in relation to the requirement; (2) the effect the variance would have on government services; (3) whether the variance will effect a substantial change in the character of the neighborhood or will be a substantial detriment to neighboring properties; (4) whether the practical difficulty can be alleviated by a feasible method other than a variance; (5) how the practical difficulty occurred, including whether the landowner created the need for the variance; and (6) whether, in light of all of the above factors, allowing the variance will serve the interests of justice" (footnote omitted).

The APA model legislation prohibits use variances and recommends the following legislative standards for area variances: "(3) provide that the variance requested is required by exceptional or unique hardship because of: (a) exceptional narrowness, shallowness, or shape of a specific piece of property; or (b) exceptional topographic conditions or physical features uniquely affecting a specific piece of property; (4) require a showing that there are no other reasonable alternatives to enjoy a legally permitted beneficial use of the property if the variance is not granted." American Planning Association, Growing Smart Legislative Guidebook: Model Statutes for Planning and Management of Change § 10-503 (S. Meck ed., 2002). How do these judicial and statutory tests compare with those adopted in the principal case?

Husnander v. Town of Barnstead, 660 A.2d 477 (N.H. 1995), illustrates a typical situation in which courts will uphold an area variance. The court upheld a setback variance under a statutory provision similar to the Standard Act that contained an unnecessary hardship requirement. The building envelope allowed by the permitted setback was an elongated, curved strip roughly seventy feet long. One end was approximately thirty feet wide, but more than half of the strip was only fifteen feet wide. The owner conceded the allowable building envelope contained adequate square footage to construct a dwelling of the same size even if she did not get a variance, but contended that "the odd-shaped result from such construction would make the living space dysfunctional." The court found sufficient evidence of unnecessary hardship. For a similar case, see *Lang v. Zoning Bd. of Adjustment*, 733 A.2d 464 (N.J. 1999) (variance for in-ground pool).

Hertzberg v. Zoning Bd. of Adjustment, 721 A.2d 43 (Pa. 1998), upheld an area variance to allow the owner of a dilapidated vacant building in a rundown area to convert it to a homeless shelter. The court held that courts may consider factors in deciding whether to grant area variances that include "economic detriment if the variance is denied, financial hardship created by work necessary to bring a building into strict zoning compliance, and the character of the surrounding neighborhood." Any other standard, it found, would prohibit a variance that would allow the rehabilitation of a dilapidated building. Subsequent lower court cases have limited this holding. See, e.g., *Cardomone v. Whitpain Township Zoning Hearing Bd.*, 771 A.2d 103 (Pa. Commw. 2001) (subdivision of lot into two lots that do not meet frontage standards for driveway properly denied even applying relaxed standard for unnecessary hardship, as resulting lots not compatible with the neighborhood and owner seeks to obtain funds to improve her current residence).

The financial viability of the use without the area variance is increasingly viewed by courts more sympathetically to the landowner. See *Amurrio v. Zoning Appeals Board*, 59 Va. Cir. 170 (2002) (take-out restaurant was a permitted use, but property required eight area variances in order to make it financially viable for commercial use); *Boccia v. City of Portsmouth*, 855 A.2d 516 (N.H. 2004) (stating a more liberal test for unnecessary hardship when considering an area variance, including whether the variance was needed to enable the applicant's proposed use of the property and whether the benefit could be achieved by some other method); *Matter of Long Island Affordable Homes, Inc. v. Board of Appeals of Town of Hempstead*, 57 A.D.3d 996 (N.Y. App. Div. 2008) (overturning town's denial of a variance for an oversized residential lot and street frontage requirement, where the value of the property without the variance was $5,000 and with the variance was $60,000 where evidence was that neighbors did not want to lose what they considered vacant land). But courts also continue to "hold the line" in applying the unnecessary hardship standard. See, e.g., *Michler v. Planning and Zoning Bd. of Appeals*, 2010 Conn. App. LEXIS 385 (Aug. 10, 2010) (change in the regulations that effectively reduces the lot area by thirty-four percent and renders the lot nonconforming as to area is not in itself an unnecessary hardship).

2. *Area versus use variances.* It is not always clear what the courts mean when they speak of an area variance, which matters if the area standard is more permissive than the use standard. For instance, the New York court has held that a variance is an area variance even though it results in an increase in density for apartments. *Wilcox v. Zoning Bd. of Appeals*, 217 N.E.2d 633 (N.Y. 1966). Other courts have not been as lenient. *O'Neill v. Zoning Bd. of Adjustment*, 254 A.2d 12 (Pa. 1969). Here the property was located in an apartment zone, but the developer secured a variance permitting him to increase the floor space in his building by two and one-half times. While admitting that it might be willing to relax its rules for space variances, the court held that a change of this magnitude had to be made legislatively. The variance was set aside. Of similar import is *Mavrantonis v. Board of Adjustment*, 258 A.2d 908 (Del. 1969), where the court set aside a variance which would have reduced the side yard for

a 12-story apartment building. The court noted that there were "sound reasons" for side yards.

If a court does not take this view and is willing to treat "density" variances like "area" variances for the purpose of applying the "practical difficulties" standard rather than the "unnecessary hardship" standard, it seems likely that it would treat height and similar variances in the same manner. However, in *Taylor v. District of Columbia Bd. of Zoning Adjustment*, 308 A.2d 230 (D.C. 1973), the landowner was denied a variance from height, side yard, court and lot occupancy requirements which would have allowed him to build twenty-seven townhouses instead of ten detached single-family dwellings on his property. The court noted that "while the requested variance may not be a use variance in its 'purest form,' it was a hybrid variance which would drastically alter the character of the zoned district" and could be characterized as "a use-area variance." *Id.* at 233.The New Hampshire court in *Schroeder v. Town of Windham*, 965 A.2d 1081 (N.H. 2008) explained, in a case involving location of a garage in a setback, that "[t]he critical distinction between area and use variances is whether the purpose of the particular zoning restriction is to preserve the character of the surrounding area and thus is a use restriction."

This problem can arise in other contexts. *Jenney v. Durham*, 707 A.2d 752 (Del. Super.), *aff'd*, 696 A.2d 396 (Del. 1997), held a variance from a steep slope ordinance to allow the building of two homes was a use variance, because the ordinance did not allow residences as a permitted use in the prohibitive steep slope district in which the proposed homes would be located.

What policy factors in the administration of zoning ordinances appear to control these cases? How could a zoning ordinance deal with these important problems?

D. THE SPECIAL EXCEPTION, SPECIAL USE PERMIT, OR CONDITIONAL USE

COUNTY v. SOUTHLAND CORP.

224 Va. 514, 297 S.E.2d 718 (1982)

RUSSELL, J., delivered the opinion of the Court:

In this zoning case, we must decide whether a local zoning ordinance may constitutionally distinguish "quick-service food stores" from other grocery stores and similar retail uses. The Southland Corporation brought a motion for declaratory judgment against the Board of Supervisors of Fairfax County, seeking an adjudication that certain parts of the Fairfax County Zoning Ordinance were unconstitutional and void as applied to it. The trial court, after hearing the evidence ore tenus, in a written opinion found for Southland. It held that the ordinance, as applied to Southland, violates the due process and equal protection provisions of the Virginia and United States Constitutions, as well as Code § 15.1-488, which requires the uniform application of zoning laws within zoning districts.

Southland operates a nationwide chain of retail food and convenience stores known as "7-Eleven." These are typically located in free-standing buildings containing less than 5000 square feet, on small parcels of land fronting on heavily traveled roads, and feature drive-in parking immediately in front of the entrance. The majority of the stores contain 2500 square feet of net floor area.

language The Fairfax County Zoning Ordinance, art. 20, § 20-300 classifies "any building which contains less than 5000 square feet of net floor area and which is used for the retail sale of food and other items" as a "quick-service food store." Quick-service food stores are permitted in free-standing buildings as a matter of right in three zoning districts: planned development housing (PDH), planned development commercial (PDC), and planned residential community (PRC), but these in turn require a development plan individually approved by the Board of Supervisors. Such stores are also permitted as a matter of right in certain shopping centers (in C-6, C-7, and C-8 districts), but only if they are located under the roof of a shopping center which contains at least six other stores and meets certain highway access criteria. They are permitted in free-standing buildings in C-5, C-6, C-7, C-8, I-5, and I-6 commercial and industrial districts, but only if they obtain a special exception from the Board. They share this special exception requirement with twenty-two other uses classified as "Commercial and Industrial Uses of Special Impact." *Id.* art. 9, § 9-500, 501. These are defined as uses "which by their nature or design can have an undue impact upon or be incompatible with other uses of land within a given zoning district." *Id.* art. 9, § 9-001. The Board reserves the right to deny any application for a special exception for one of these uses if it deems such use to be incompatible with existing or planned development in the district. The Board may also impose such "conditions and restrictions" as it thinks proper to insure that such a use will be homogeneous with the neighborhood. *Id.*

langage and as applied w/ which Southland takes issue

Southland points out that the effect of these provisions is to deny it the right to construct or operate a free-standing quick-service food store in any commercial district in Fairfax County. It contends that the special exception process to which it is thus subjected costs about $4,000.00 in application fees, attorneys fees, engineering and other costs for each site, increases construction costs substantially, and delays each store's opening for nine to twelve months. As Southland says, many other commercial uses, permitted by right, are exempt from the special exception process. Among these are grocery stores over 5000 square feet in floor area, restaurants, retail stores, shopping centers, banks, theaters, churches, hotels, motels, and schools. Southland argued, and the trial court found, that quick-service food stores of the "7-Eleven" type would have less adverse impact upon neighboring properties, the environment, and traffic than would some uses permitted by right, and that the ordinance was therefore an unreasonable classification as applied to Southland. [The court held that it had jurisdiction under the declaratory judgment statute to decide this attack on the ordinance.] . . .

unfair as applied to Southland

authority

We now turn to the merits. The power to regulate the use of land by zoning laws is a legislative power, residing in the state, which must be exercised in accordance with constitutional principles. This power may be delegated to the political subdivisions of the state. Code § 15.1-486 authorizes the governing bodies of Virginia counties to adopt local zoning ordinances. Section 15.1-491(c) authorizes such governing bodies to reserve unto themselves the right to issue "special exceptions under suitable regulations and safeguards."

The terms "special exception" and "special use permit" are interchangeable. Both terms refer to the delegated power of the state to set aside certain categories of uses which are to be permitted only after being submitted to governmental scrutiny in each case, in order to insure compliance with standards designed to protect neighboring properties and the public. The legislature may require certain uses, which it considers to have a potentially greater impact upon neighboring properties or the public than those uses permitted in the district as a matter of right, to undergo the special exception process. Each site is to be examined by public officials, guided by standards set forth in the ordinance, for the impact the use will have if carried out on that site. Although the uses in such special exception categories are permissible under the ordinance,[2] such permission is to be granted subject to such limitations and conditions as public officials may impose in order to reduce the impact of the use upon neighboring properties and the public to the level which would be caused by those uses permitted as a matter of right.

Whether a legislative body has reserved unto itself the power to grant or deny special exceptions or use permits, or has delegated the power to a Board of Zoning Appeals, we have consistently held the exercise of that power to be a legislative, rather than an administrative act.[3] A fortiori, the decision of the legislative body, when framing its zoning ordinance, to place certain uses in the special exception or conditional use category, is a legislative action. It involves the same balancing of the consequences of private conduct against the interests of public welfare, health, and safety as any other legislative decision.

The parameters of the judicial review of legislative zoning decisions are well settled. The action of the local governing body in enacting or amending its zoning ordinance is presumed to be valid. Inherent in the presumption of legislative validity is a presumption that the classification that the ordinance contains, and the distinctions which it draws, are not arbitrary, not capricious, but reasonable. Where such presumptive reasonableness is challenged by probative evidence of unreasonableness, the ordinance cannot be sustained unless the governing body meets the challenge with some evidence of reasonableness. But the governing body is not required to go forward with evidence sufficient to persuade the fact-finder of reasonableness by a preponderance of the evidence. The burden is less stringent. If evidence of reasonableness is sufficient to make the question "fairly debatable," the ordinance must be sustained.

Applying the foregoing principles to the evidence before us, we conclude that the County was entitled to a presumption of legislative validity, which Southland challenged by probative evidence tending to show unreasonableness. Although the evidence touched upon such problems as glare from night lighting and run-off from storm drainage, the principal dispute was the relative amount of highway traffic congestion caused by quick-service food stores, compared to that caused by the uses permitted by right. It is unnecessary to review the evidence in detail, except to observe that it was sufficient to overcome the County's initial presumption of legislative validity. It is self-evident, for example, that large shopping centers and supermarkets generate more total traffic than 2500 square foot convenience stores.

The County, however, responds with evidence of two countervailing considerations. First, actual traffic counts showed that the peak hours of vehicle activity entering and leaving quick-service food stores tended to coincide with the peak hours of traffic on the adjacent roads, particularly the morning rush hour. The peak hours in the larger commercial uses permitted by right tended to occur in mid-morning, or at other times when the roads were less congested. Second, the intensity of traffic activity in relation to land area was far greater in the case of small convenience markets. They were found to generate 506 "trips" per 1000 square feet, while neighborhood shopping centers generated only 65 such "trips." A "trip" was

---

[2] This distinguishes the special exception from the variance. The latter authorizes a use which would otherwise be prohibited by the ordinance. Zoning ordinances usually delegate to public officials the power to grant variances where literal enforcement would result in unnecessary hardship. Code § 15.1-495(b). Public officials, passing upon requests for variances, act in an administrative, rather than a legislative, capacity.

[3] This appears to be a minority view.

defined as a vehicle either entering or leaving the site between 7:00 a.m. and 7:00 p.m.

This might have little significance in itself, but it was coupled with the fact that the small convenience markets, situated on much smaller parcels of land, had little flexibility in the location of entrances and "curb cuts." If such a store were to be sited at the corner of a busy intersection, for example, it would precipitate a substantial amount of traffic directly into the most congested part of the traffic pattern, at the most congested hours. While entrances and "curb cuts" may be reasonably regulated in the exercise of the police power, access may not be entirely denied, absent a "taking" for public use and the resulting constitutional necessity for the payment of just compensation.

Larger shopping centers and supermarkets, by contrast, being located on larger tracts of land, may be subjected to far more traffic control before the point of confiscatory regulation is reached. Their greater size permits more flexibility in providing service roads, deceleration lanes, and other means of access control. Even if they are to be provided only with simple entrances, these may more readily be kept away from congested intersections and other danger points by reason of the greater land area involved.

We shall not undertake to resolve the controversy posed by the foregoing arguments because they demonstrate that the question whether quick-service food stores should be required to obtain a special exception is "fairly debatable." "Given the human tendency to debate any question, an issue may be said to be fairly debatable when the evidence offered in support of the opposing views would lead objective and reasonable persons to reach different conclusions." *Fairfax County v. Williams*, 216 S.E.2d 33, 40 (Va. 1975). Thus the County has presented evidence sufficient to render the reasonableness of the ordinance "fairly debatable," and it must therefore be sustained. . . .

NOTES AND QUESTIONS

1. *What they are.* The issue of what uses can be classified as special exceptions has surprisingly not received extensive consideration in the courts. Compare this statement in a leading case with the holding in the principal case:

> [C]ertain uses, considered by the local legislative body to be essential or desirable for the welfare of the community . . . , are entirely appropriate and not essentially incompatible with the basic uses in any zoning . . . , but not at every or any location . . . or without conditions being imposed by reason of special problems the use . . . presents from a zoning standpoint . . . . [*Tullo v. Millburn Twp.*, 149 A.2d 620, 624, 625 (N.J. App. Div. 1959).]

Could the drive-in bank that was the subject of a variance application in the hypothetical hearing, sec. A *supra*, be classified as a conditional use? What about a landfill? See *Bierman v. Township of Taymouth*, 383 N.W.2d 235 (Mich. App. 1985) (can classify junkyards but not landfills as special exceptions in agricultural district). Contra *Ackman v. Board of Adjustment*, 596 N.W.2d 96 (Iowa 1999). See Blaesser, *Special Use Permits: The "Wait-and-See" Weapon of Local Communities*, 21 Zoning & Plan. L. Rep. 69 (1998).

It is clear that the zoning pioneers did not intend the "special exception" to be anything more than a supplement to the basic technique of "pre-zoning" a municipality into a number of different use and density districts. *Rockhill v. Chesterfield Twp.*, 128 A.2d 473 (N.J. 1956), makes it clear that the special exception technique, combined with low density and "wait-and-see" zoning, cannot be used as the primary method by which a municipality controls its growth and development. Accord *Town of Rhine v. Bizzell*, 751 N.W.2d 780 (Wis. 2008) (no justification exists for precluding all uses as of right and doing so is a substantive due process violation).

2. *Who may create the special exception standards?* Note that the Standard Zoning Act, § 7, largely left to the governing body the decision on what standards to adopt for special exceptions. It provides:

> [T]he . . . board of adjustment may, in appropriate cases and subject to appropriate conditions and safeguards, make special exceptions to the terms of the ordinance in harmony with its general purpose and intent and in accordance with general or specific rules contained therein.

Many states have adopted this language verbatim. Compare the present New Jersey statute, which authorizes the zoning ordinance to allow the planning board to grant special exceptions "according to definite specifications and standards which shall be clearly set forth with sufficient certainty and definiteness to enable the developer to know their limit and extent." N.J. Stat. Ann. § 40:55D-67(a). Why do you suppose the legislature made this change? See also Idaho Code § 67-6512(e) (government may require social, economic, fiscal and environmental studies prior to granting).

As Judge (later Justice) Hall said in *Tullo*, "special use" or "special use permit" would be a more accurate term than "special exception" to describe the uses specified in the zoning ordinance as permitted in a given district with the approval of a designated local zoning board or agency. The term "conditional use" or "conditional use permit" is sometimes used in zoning enabling acts and local zoning ordinances. See Cal. Gov't Code § 65901(a).

3. *Which agency?* Zoning ordinances often delegate the authority to grant special exceptions to the planning commission or local governing body, probably because these agencies almost always will receive advice on the special exception from the planning staff. See the model zoning ordinance, Chapter 3, *supra*. In states that have adopted the Standard Zoning Act § 7, the courts hold this arrangement impermissible, because of the specific delegation to the board of adjustment. See *Holland v. City Council*, 662 N.W.2d 681 (Iowa 2003). Delegation to these bodies is allowable when the statute leaves open the authority to grant special exceptions. See *Kotrich v. County of Du Page*, 166 N.E.2d 601 (Ill. 1960).

The planning commission is authorized by statute to grant special exceptions in some states. See Neb. Rev. Stat. § 19-929(3) (council may also retain power). Some states allow more than one agency to grant special exceptions. Cal. Gov't Code § 65902 (board of adjustment or zoning administrator). A state that authorizes hearing examiners may give them the authority to grant special exceptions. Nev. Rev. Stat. Ann. § 278.265(3).

4. *Delegation of power.* Because it acts to apply the legislatively created standards, most courts have held that a zoning board of adjustment (or appeals) acts "administratively" when it grants or denies a special exception, special use permit, or conditional use. Moreover, where the final decision is made by the local governing body upon recommendation of the board of adjustment (or appeals), the courts have generally held that the governing body acts "administratively" rather than "legislatively." The principal case is contra, and a distinct minority. Thus, in theory, the zoning ordinance should contain standards that are adequate to guide the exercise of administrative discretion by the board of adjustment (or appeals). Judicial treatment of ordinance standards for special exceptions, special use permits, and conditional

uses is summarized as follows in American Law Institute, Model Land Development Code, Tentative Draft No. 2, Note to § 2-207 (1970):

> Mandelker's review of cases shows that "nuisance standards" — negatively phrased standards directing that uses will not be allowed as exceptions if they create nuisance type external costs — have been approved overwhelmingly. Ordinances without any standards — simply authorizing an administrative board to issue an exception — generally have been held to delegate legislative authority invalidly. But most zoning ordinances provide general welfare standards and here judicial reaction is mixed. (Usually the ordinance allows the board to permit any of the enumerated special uses if such action would be in accord with the purposes and intent of the ordinance and be conducive to the general welfare.) Many cases sustain such standards without any critical comment. Some courts attempt to evaluate such standards and conclude that they are certain enough in view of the technological complexities of zoning administration. A number of cases hold such standards unconstitutional or ultra vires. Confusingly, courts in the same jurisdiction, and even the same courts, render inconsistent opinions on similar standards in different cases. The problems raised by exceptions are like those raised by variances. At base it is the fear that without somewhat concrete standards landowners will be vulnerable to discrimination. In addition, there is the desire to have policy made by a representative body and to assure neighborhood status quo. And as with variances, courts have not been able to take solace in procedural regularity because enabling acts and ordinances have not required administrative agencies to state in detail the reasons for granting or denying exceptions.

"Mandelker's review of cases" can be found in Mandelker, *Delegation of Power and Function in Zoning Administration*, 1963 Wash. U. L.Q. 60.

5. *Discretion to deny or approve.* How much discretion does a local zoning agency have to grant or deny a special exception use? As is discussed further in the next set of notes and questions, the standards for special exceptions can be quite broad, e.g., in the general welfare or public interest. Consider the following from *Archdiocese of Portland v. County of Wash.*, 458 P.2d 682 (Or. 1969):

> [T]he ordinance itself reveals the legislative plan forecasting the likelihood that certain specified uses will be needed to maximize the use of land in the zone for residential purposes. The Board's discretion is thus narrowed to those cases in which an application falls within one of the specified uses. The fact that these permissible uses are pre-defined and have the legislative endorsement of the governing body of the county as a tentative part of the comprehensive plan for the area limits the possibility that the Board's action in granting a permit will be inimical to the interests of the community. The suspicion which is cast upon the approval of a change involving an incompatible use . . . is not warranted where the change has been anticipated by the governing body. Therefore, unlike the spot zoning cases the granting of permits for conditional uses is not likely to cause the "erosive effect upon the comprehensive zoning plan" described in *Smith v. County of Washington* [406 P.2d 545 (Or. 1965)]. [*Id.* at 686.]

Does this analysis suggest that zoning boards have limited discretion to deny a special exception?

The following case indicates how courts review decisions by zoning boards on special exception applications:

CROOKED CREEK CONSERVATION AND GUN CLUB, INC. v. HAMILTON COUNTY NORTH BOARD OF ZONING APPEALS

677 N.E.2d 544 (Ind. App. 1997)

SULLIVAN, JUDGE

Appellant Crooked Creek Conservation & Gun Club, Inc. (Crooked Creek) sought a special exception from appellee Hamilton County North Board of Zoning Appeals (BZA) in order to build a trap and skeet shooting range in Hamilton County. Following a public hearing during which remonstrators opposed Crooked Creek's plans, the BZA refused to grant the special exception. Crooked Creek petitioned the trial court for a writ of certiorari and the trial court affirmed the BZA's decision.

Crooked Creek now appeals, presenting the following restated issues for our review:

(1) Did the trial court err in affirming the BZA's refusal to grant the special exception? . . .

Crooked Creek has operated a trap and skeet shooting club in Marion County for over 45 years. Concerned with the increased urbanization of the area in which its present facilities are located, Crooked Creek found what it believed to be a more suitable parcel of land upon which to conduct its activities in rural Hamilton County. The property is zoned "A-2," a designation which contemplates agricultural, large-lot residential, and flood plain uses. The Hamilton County Zoning Ordinance (HCZO) provides that gun clubs may be permitted in A-2 districts as special exceptions to the above-delineated uses. Hamilton Co. Zoning Ord. (hereinafter HCZO) Art. 15(B) § 1. A special exception is simply a use permitted under a zoning ordinance upon the showing of certain criteria set forth in the ordinance. The HCZO provides that the BZA must determine that the specially excepted use will fulfill three separate requirements before the BZA may grant the exception. As HCZO Art. 15(A) § 2 states:

> Upon hearing, in order for a special exception to be granted, the board must find, in writing, that:
>
> a. The establishment, maintenance, or operation of the special exception will not be injurious to the public health, safety, morals, or general welfare of the community;
>
> b. The special exception will not affect the use and value of other property in the immediate area in a substantially adverse manner;
>
> c. The establishment of the special exception will be consistent with the character of the district (particularly that area immediately adjacent to the special exception) and the land use permitted therein.

In March, 1994, Crooked Creek applied to the Hamilton County North Board of Zoning Appeals for a special exception for its trap and skeet shooting operation. On April 26, 1994, the Hamilton County North Board of Zoning Appeals convened to review and take public comments upon Crooked Creek's application. Crooked Creek presented testimonial evidence and submitted a comprehensive package of documentary evidence in support of its application.

Crooked Creek's evidence generally supported its assertion that its shooting operation would satisfy the three above-mentioned requirements for the granting of a special exception. The remonstrators, however, presented evidence, both documentary and testimonial, which suggested, among other things, that Crooked Creek's trap and skeet shooting activities would be detrimental to public health and would decrease property values in the area. After both sides completed their presentations, the BZA tabled the matter so that the board members could consider the documentary evidence supporting and opposing Crooked Creek's application. The BZA indicated that it would come to a conclusion at the following meeting to be held May 24, 1994.

When the BZA reconvened on May 24, Crooked Creek asked the BZA to consider additional documentary evidence compiled by Crooked Creek assertedly rebutting the evidence presented by the remonstrators at the April 26 meeting. The BZA refused to consider this additional evidence, indicating that the time for submission of evidence ended upon the adjournment of the April 26 meeting, and then voted three to one to deny Crooked Creek's application. The BZA members voting against the application found, generally, that the lead shot used in trap and skeet shooting presented potential public health hazards, and that gun noise could adversely impact property values in the otherwise bucolic surroundings.

When reviewing a decision of a zoning board, an appellate court is bound by the same standard of review as the certiorari court. Under this standard, a reviewing court, whether at the trial or appellate level, is limited to determining whether the zoning board's decision was based upon substantial evidence. The proceeding before the certiorari court is not intended to be a trial de novo, and neither that court nor the appellate court may reweigh the evidence or reassess the credibility of witnesses; rather, reviewing courts must accept the facts as found by the zoning board.

I.

Crooked Creek argues that the trial court erred in failing to reverse the BZA's decision to deny Crooked Creek's application. Crooked Creek first contends that since it presented substantial evidence to show that it would comply with the three criteria for special exceptions, the BZA was required to grant the exception. Crooked Creek also argues that the remonstrators presented insufficient evidence to support the BZA's conclusion that the trap and skeet shooting operations would not meet the special exception criteria.

Crooked Creek claims that the award of a special exception is mandatory upon the applicant's presentation of evidence that its proposed use satisfies the statutory prerequisites set forth in the zoning ordinance. It is often true, as Crooked Creek notes, that if a petitioner for a special exception presents sufficient evidence of compliance with relevant statutory requirements, the exception must be granted. *Town of Merrillville Bd. of Zoning Appeals v. Public Storage, Inc.*, 568 N.E.2d 1092, 1095 (Ind. App. 1991), trans. denied. However, the *Town of Merrillville* case was careful to note that while some special exception ordinances are regulatory in nature and require an applicant to show compliance with certain regulatory requirements (e.g. structural specifications), providing the zoning board with no discretion, some special exception ordinances provide a zoning board with a discernable amount of discretion (e.g. those which require an applicant to show that its proposed use will not injure the public health, welfare, or morals). *Id.* at n.3. Crooked Creek's position that a board of zoning appeals must grant a special exception upon the applicant's submission of substantial evidence of compliance with the relevant criteria is true only as to ordinances falling within the former category. In other words, when the zoning ordinance provides the board of zoning appeals with a discernable amount of discretion, the board is entitled, and may even be required by the ordinance, to exercise its discretion. When this is the case, the board is entitled to determine whether an applicant has demonstrated that its proposed use will comply with the relevant statutory requirements.

The ordinance implicated in the present case confers upon the Hamilton County North Board of Zoning Appeals a significant amount of discretion. The ordinance requires the board to find a variety of facts before issuing a special exception. For example, the board must find that the specially excepted use "will not be injurious to the public health, safety, morals, or general welfare of the community" and that the use "will not affect the use and value of other property in the immediate area in a substantially adverse manner; . . ." HCZO Art. 15(A) § 2. It is clear that these criteria, having no absolute objective standards against which they can be measured, involve discretionary decision making on the part of the board. Thus, the BZA was entitled to determine whether Crooked Creek satisfied the requirements for the grant of a special exception.

Crooked Creek nevertheless maintains that the evidence presented by the remonstrators was not sufficiently substantial to support the BZA's determination. We must note here that the burden of demonstrating satisfaction of the relevant statutory criteria rests with the applicant for a special exception. This court has accordingly been cautious to avoid the imposition upon remonstrators of an obligation to come forward with evidence contradicting that submitted by an applicant. Crooked Creek bore the burden to show that its trap and skeet shooting operation would comply with the three above-mentioned criteria. Neither those opposed to Crooked Creek's application, nor the BZA, were required to negate Crooked Creek's case.

Since remonstrators need not affirmatively disprove an applicant's case, a board of zoning appeals may deny an application for a special exception on the grounds that an applicant has failed to carry its burden of proving compliance with the relevant statutory criteria regardless of whether remonstrators present evidence to negate the existence of the enumerated factors.[(1)] However, since the BZA determined that Crooked Creek was not entitled to a special exception, and based its determination upon evidence presented by the remonstrators, we will determine whether the BZA's decision was based upon substantial evidence by examining the sufficiency of the evidence presented by the remonstrators.

When determining whether an administrative decision is supported by substantial evidence,

---

[(1)] This court previously noted the apparent dilemma thus presented for boards of zoning appeals. A zoning board may in its discretion determine that an applicant has not presented substantial evidence to demonstrate that its proposed use will comply with statutory requirements even in the absence of contrary evidence submitted by remonstrators. The difficulty arises when the zoning board attempts to support its determination. This court has indicated that it would be inappropriate to require the board to provide a detailed explanation as to why the criteria have not been met, for to do so would either force those who object to the exception to come forward with specific evidence in opposition, or would compel the board to explain how the criteria should or could have been met. Both options, we have noted, improperly remove the burden from the applicant to affirmatively prove compliance with the criteria. This dilemma is not squarely before us because the remonstrators presented evidence that Crooked Creek's proposed use would not meet the criteria set forth in the zoning ordinance, and because the BZA expressly rested its conclusion on this evidence. However, in the event that boards of zoning appeals deny applications for special exceptions upon grounds that the applicant has failed to carry its burden to show compliance with relevant statutory criteria, boards would be well advised to at least state as much in their findings and to point out what they see as any deficiency in the applicant's evidence. Boards should be able to perform this task without improperly assuming the burden of negating the applicant's case.

the reviewing court must determine from the entire record whether the agency's decision lacks a reasonably sound evidentiary basis. Thus, we have noted that evidence will be considered substantial if it is more than a scintilla and less than a preponderance. In other words, substantial evidence is such relevant evidence as a reasonable mind might accept as adequate to support a conclusion. We think that the certiorari court's conclusion that the BZA's determination was supported by substantial evidence was not error.

The remonstrators presented substantial evidence that the lead shot used in trap and skeet shooting presents a public health hazard, and that noise from gunfire could impair local property values. The remonstrators submitted a letter signed by Thomas F. Long, described in the letter and by the letterhead as a Senior Toxicologist with the Environmental Toxicology Section of the Illinois Department of Public Health, explaining the effects of lead shot used in target shooting upon human health. The letter stated that when lead shot is discharged from a shotgun into a target, "it tends to be pulverized into a fine dust." This dust, according to the letter, "tends to be mobile and moves easily in the environment on wind or in water." Finally, the letter concluded that lead is a very dangerous, although often subtle, poison absorbed by the gut and lung. In humans, lead primarily attacks the nervous system with children being at highest risk. Children exposed to excessive levels of lead can suffer damage as subtle as a loss of IQ and developmental delays or as serious as mental retardation and death. Adults may also experience nervous system damage as a result of lead exposure although it is generally not as devastating as is seen in children. Additionally, lead will attack the digestive system, the blood, the kidneys, and the reproductive system. Since lead can damage both male and female reproduction and will cross the placenta, miscarriage and birth defects can result. The opinion of Mr. Long constitutes sufficient evidence to justify the Board's conclusion in this regard.

The remonstrators also presented testimony from a qualified and experienced real estate appraiser who gave his opinion that the location of a gun club in the community would reduce demand for the property, thereby decreasing its value. Another remonstrator, a builder and developer of a local subdivision, testified that one individual made an offer to purchase one of the builder's properties upon the condition that Crooked Creek's plans were denied. The builder also stated his belief that the presence of a gun club would negatively impact property values in the area. Moreover, many of the remonstrators who testified at the April 24 meeting expressed their concern with respect to the noise level of Crooked Creek's activities, expressing the fear that the noise of gunfire would take away from the quiet, rural character which attracted them to the area. Crooked Creek's own real estate appraisal expert testified that the value of property is driven by the demand for that property. Substantial evidence was adduced at the April 26 meeting to support the BZA's conclusion that a gun club could reduce the value of land in the area by taking away its only apparent attraction, the peace and quiet of the rural neighborhood.

Crooked Creek disputes these contentions and submitted evidence to the effect that the lead involved in trap and skeet shooting poses no threat to human health in its normal usage, and that the presence of the gun club would not tend to reduce property values in the area. However, the zoning board was under no obligation to give the evidence presented by Crooked Creek more weight than that of the remonstrators. As we have noted, a board of zoning appeals has the discretion to deny a special exception if the board determines that the applicant has not met the relevant criteria. Moreover, when both the applicant and remonstrators present substantial evidence in support of their respective positions, it is the function of the board of zoning appeals, with its expertise in zoning questions, to determine which side shall prevail.

Since the board's determination in either case would be supported by substantial evidence, it should not be disturbed upon appeal.

The remonstrators presented evidence to support the BZA's conclusion that the lead discharged during trap and skeet shooting posed a public health hazard, and that the gun club would negatively impact local property values. The BZA, as it was entitled to do, credited that evidence and determined that Crooked Creek was not entitled to a special exception because it found that the lead shot used in target shooting could be hazardous to human health and that property values could be negatively impacted by the existence of a gun club in the area. . . . The decision of the trial court affirming the BZA is affirmed.

NOTES AND QUESTIONS

1. *Judicial review of conditional use decisions.* The *Crooked Creek* case makes an important distinction between standards that confer discretion on zoning boards and those that do not. This distinction has an important effect on judicial review. What do you think of this distinction? In the *Merrillville* case, which is discussed in *Crooked Creek*, the board denied a conditional use for a public storage facility when neighbors objected. The court reversed because it found the use complied with the criteria contained in the ordinance.

The Merrillville board found the use would violate a requirement that it not have an adverse effect on property values. Opponents to the use had expressed fears on this issue but did not present evidence. The court held that was not the point: "Once a petitioner has established its right to a special exception by presenting sufficient evidence of compliance with relevant statutory requirements, the exception must be granted." *Id.* at 1095. The court also held the use would not violate an ordinance requirement that it would not impede the development of the area, which was a mixed-use urban strip. The board had again relied only on remarks by objectors to find that the development of the area would be impeded. How does the evidence in *Crooked Creek* differ?

Objections by neighbors to conditional use applications are common, especially when the proposed use is considered undesirable. Why were the fears of neighbors acceptable in *Crooked Creek* but not in *Merrillville*? How should courts distinguish between legitimate neighbor concerns and spurious objections? In *Washington State Dep't of Corrections v. City of Kennewick*, 937 P.2d 1119 (Wash. App. 1997), the court held that whereas in nuisance cases the fears of neighbors were a factor in finding the existence of a nuisance, the rule did not apply in zoning cases; the court reversed a decision to deny a conditional use for a work release facility. Compare *Jesus Fellowship, Inc. v. Miami-Dade County*, 752 So. 2d 708 (Fla. App. 2000) (quashing denial of church expansion for private school and day care center), with *First Baptist Church of Perrine v. Miami Dade County*, 768 So. 2d 1114 (Fla. App. 2000) (upholding the denial of an expansion of a church school). See also *Amoco Oil Co. v. City of Minneapolis*, 395 N.W.2d 115 (Minn. App. 1986) (reversing denial of conditional use for 24-hour gas station and grocery store; restrictions to minimize late night noise, glare and traffic held sufficient despite residential neighbors' objections). The cases illustrate the general rule, that courts will reverse a denial of a special exception when all of the standards in the ordinance have been met.

2. *What if?* Given the court's treatment of the evidence in the principal case, can you imagine any state of facts under which the gun club could have prevailed? (Both it and the court seem to assume that lead shot is the only ammunition available.) If not, what point is there in listing gun clubs as a "special exception"?

3. *The standards issue.* The typical conditional use case is concerned with "compatibility," the ability of the "special" use to harmonize with its neighbors. See *McDonald v. City of Concord*, 655 S.E.2d 455 (N.C. Ct. App. 2008), discussing how a correctional facility conforms to the character of the neighborhood. Most courts have upheld a "compatibility" standard, but it could be subject to criticism that it is too vague. In *Rolling Pines Limited Partnership v. City of Little Rock*, 40 S.W.3d 828 (Ark. App. 2001), the city code allowed conditional uses if "the proposed land use is compatible with and will not adversely affect other property in the area where it is proposed to be located." The city planning commission denied the location of manufactured homes in a single family district as incompatible, and the applicant challenged the standard as unconstitutionally vague. Without further defining what it believed to be the meaning of "compatibility," the court found that the term has a "well-defined meaning and is not so vague as to leave an applicant guessing as to its import or meaning." *Id.* at 835. Do you agree? If the compatibility standard is met, a board cannot deny a proposed conditional use because it is more intensive than a previous use on the property. *State ex rel. Presbyterian Church v. City of Washington*, 911 S.W.2d 697 (Mo. App. 1995). Does this make sense?

Although the *Crooked Creek* case held that ordinance standards can confer discretion on zoning boards, courts may find them vague if they confer too much discretion and will not uphold a board decision denying an exception that relies on them. In *C.R. Invs., Inc. v. Village of Shoreview*, 304 N.W.2d 320 (Minn. 1981), the court reversed the denial of a special exception for nineteen "quad" apartments to be built adjacent to single-family homes located across a road. It relied for reversal on policies in its comprehensive plan, but the court reversed and held the policies were "unreasonably vague" and "unreasonably subjective." The plan standards required an applicant to demonstrate that the proposed use was "an improvement on the plan and consistent with the plan's general intent and purpose" and that the proposed use was "equal to or better than, single-family usage." How do these policies compare with the ordinance standards in *Crooked Creek*?

4. *Evidentiary matters and findings.* The *Crooked Creek* case applies the accepted rule, that the applicant carries the burden of proof in conditional use cases. Do you agree with the court's suggestions on burden of proof in footnote 1? Do they contradict the ordinance requirement that the board must make findings of fact?

Must local zoning agencies make findings of fact when they grant or deny special exceptions? *Tullo, supra*, said yes. *Flathead Citizens for Quality Growth, Inc. v. Flathead County Board of Adjustment*, 175 P.3d 282 (Mont. 2008), explains the importance of findings of fact to demonstrate that the board of adjustment's decision is not arbitrary. But compare *Archdiocese of Portland, supra*, in which the court held that its function was to determine only whether the zoning agency acted arbitrarily or capriciously. "The basis for that action need not be found in 'evidence' as we use that term in connection with the trial of cases before a court." In *Kotrich, supra*, the court held there was no need for "written findings of fact" when a legislative rather than an administrative body grants a special exception. In such a case, "judicial review is had in an independent action on a new record made in court." Does this make sense? Are "written findings of fact" more or less important in special exception than in variance cases? Note that the courts are divided on whether standards are required when a legislative body exercises administrative functions under the zoning ordinance, such as the review of special exceptions. See *State v. Guffey*, 306 S.W.2d 552 (Mo. 1957) (standards required). Should the decision on standards affect the court's view on whether findings of fact are required? Of course, the enabling statute or the ordinance itself may require that the board make written findings of fact. See, for example, *County Council v. Brandywine Enterprises,*

711 A.2d 1346 (Md. 1998) (state statute requiring written findings and conclusions could not be changed by ordinance providing for summary denial).

5. *Reforming procedures.* Draft Chapter 10 of the American Planning Association model legislation provides a carefully scripted application and hearing process for administrative decisions on conditional use and other similar remedies, such as variances. An application for any of these remedies must be considered complete by the local government before it can be processed. If the local government requires a record hearing, the notice of the hearing must state the land development regulations and comprehensive plan elements that apply to the application. Detailed findings and a decision by the hearing board are required. Section 10-615(d) authorizes the court to reverse the decision if it "is not supported by evidence that is substantial when viewed in light of the record before the court." The American Bar Association model, *supra* Section A, is very similar. Would the model laws have required a different result in *Crooked Creek*? For discussion, see Mandelker, *Model Legislation for Land Use Decisions*, 35 Urb. Law. 635 (2003).

6. *Conditions.* The Standard Zoning Act, and the state zoning acts that follow it, expressly authorize conditions on special exceptions. Should this affect the discretion of the zoning agency under a special exception provision? The law on special exception conditions is similar to the law on variance conditions. Compare *Water Dist. No. 1 v. City Council*, 871 P.2d 1256 (Kan. 1994) (upholding condition on operation of sludge lagoon), with *Sandbothe v. City of Olivette*, 647 S.W.2d 198 (Mo. App. 1983) (invalidating conditions restricting hours of operation and prohibiting drive-through facility for fast food restaurant). The conditions may be defined by the enabling statute or ordinance, but in any event must relate to the conditional use itself. See *BP Oil Company v. City of Dayton*, 672 N.E.2d 256 (Ohio App 1996) (conditions on remodeling of gas station and convenience store). What additional conditions could be validly imposed in the *Amoco* case, *supra* Note 1, where the business included a car wash, large trucks deliver gasoline to the site, customers' cars arrive with headlights on and (the facts established) there was another 24-hour convenience store in the same block?

E. THE ZONING AMENDMENT

The zoning amendment is probably the most straightforward way in which a landowner can secure a change in zoning that will allow a land use not permitted by the existing zoning classification. Indeed, the drafters of the Standard Zoning Act appear to have considered the zoning amendment as the principal method for making changes in the land use classifications in the zoning ordinance. Reread the provisions in the Standard Act, reproduced in Chapter 3 *supra*, on the zoning amendment. Note that the Act provides no standards for zoning amendments. Why do you suppose this was done?

The zoning amendment can be used to make comprehensive changes in the zoning ordinance, including a comprehensive revision of the zoning text or map or a revision affecting a substantial part of the community. In the more usual case, the landowner seeks only a map amendment for his tract of land, which may be as small as a quarter-acre city lot or smaller. He usually requests a map amendment to make a textual zoning classification applicable to his land that will permit a more intensive land use. In this discussion, this type of zoning amendment will be called an upzoning. (A downzoning, by contrast, moves the site towards a less intense permitted use.)

The distinction between a comprehensive zoning ordinance amendment and a tract or "spot" amendment is important, as these materials will indicate. Note also that the spot upzoning amendment accomplishes the same result as a variance or special exception. Consider the differences between these zoning techniques when you study these materials.

[1.] Estoppel and Vested Rights

Assume a developer buys a tract of land zoned for multi-family use. He plans to build a multi-family project, enters into contracts for site plans and architectural drawings, and begins preliminary site preparation. Neighborhood opposition develops and the city council, in response, downzones his land to single-family use. Is the developer protected from this downzoning change?

The answer to this question lies in a doctrine known variously as the "estoppel" or "vested rights" doctrine, although most courts use these terms interchangeably and the two doctrines do not always produce different results. Estoppel and vested rights problems have become increasingly important as disputes over land use have become aggravated in many communities. The following case indicates how the courts apply estoppel and vested rights theories to protect developers from zoning change.

WESTERN LAND EQUITIES, INC. v. CITY OF LOGAN

617 P.2d 388 (Utah 1980)

STEWART, JUSTICE:

Defendants appeal from a ruling of the district court that the City of Logan unlawfully withheld approval of plaintiff's proposed residential plan and was estopped from enforcing a zoning change that prohibits plaintiffs' proposed use. We affirm the trial court's order. . . .

[Plaintiffs planned to build a moderately priced single-family housing project on 18.53 acres of land zoned M-1, in which both manufacturing and single-family development was allowed. The planning commission rejected a proposed subdivision of the land after going on record in opposition of single-family development in M-1 zones. The plaintiffs unsuccessfully appealed the planning commission's decision to the municipal council and then filed a complaint in the trial court. The court granted and then lifted a restraining order prohibiting the city from amending the zoning ordinance. After the order was lifted, the council adopted a zoning amendment prohibiting single-family development in M-1 zones.]

. . . It is established that an owner of property holds it subject to zoning ordinances enacted pursuant to a state's police power. With various exceptions legislative enactments, other than those defining criminal offenses, are not generally subject to the constitutional prohibitions against retroactive application. The legality of retroactive civil legislation is tested by general principles of fairness and by due process considerations.[1]

. . .

[T]he rule generally accepted in other jurisdictions [is] that an applicant for a building permit or subdivision approval does not acquire any vested right under existing zoning

---

[1] See discussion of retroactive legislation in Cunningham and Kremer, *Vested Rights, Estoppel, and the Land Development Process*, 29 Hastings L.J. 623, 660 *et seq.* (1978).

regulations prior to the issuance of the permit or official approval of a proposed subdivision. Generally, denial of an application may be based on subsequently-enacted zoning regulations.

However, for the reasons discussed below, we are of the view that the majority rule fails to strike a proper balance between public and private interests and opens the area to so many variables as to result in unnecessary litigation. We hold instead that an applicant for subdivision approval or a building permit is entitled to favorable action if the application conforms to the zoning ordinance in effect at the time of the application, unless changes in the zoning ordinances are pending which would prohibit the use applied for, or unless the municipality can show a compelling reason for exercising its police power retroactively to the date of application.

In the present case, the trial court found that plaintiffs had acquired a vested development right by their substantial compliance with procedural requirements and that the city was estopped from withholding approval of the proposed subdivision. The court used the language of zoning estoppel, a principle that is widely followed.[2] That principle estops a government entity from exercising its zoning powers to prohibit a proposed land use when a property owner, relying reasonably and in good faith on some governmental act or omission, has made a substantial change in position or incurred such extensive obligations or expenses that it would be highly inequitable to deprive the owner of his right to complete his proposed development.[3]

The focus of zoning estoppel is primarily upon the conduct and interests of the property owner. The main inquiry is whether there has been substantial reliance by the owner on governmental actions related to the superseded zoning that permitted the proposed use. The concern underlying this approach is the economic hardship that would be imposed on a property owner whose development plans are thwarted. Some courts hold that before a permit is issued no action of the owner is sufficient reliance to bar application of changes in zoning ordinances because there has been no governmental act sufficient to support an estoppel. Accordingly, a landowner is held to have no vested right in existing or anticipated zoning. *Avco Community Developers, Inc. v. South Coast Regional Comm'n*, 553 P.2d 546 (Cal. 1976). Other courts consider any substantial change of position in determining the estoppel issue. This Court in *Wood v. North Salt Lake*, 390 P.2d 858 (Utah 1964), held a zoning ordinance change requiring larger lots unenforceable because water mains and sewer connections had already been provided for lots that conformed in size to a previous ordinance. The Court stated that enforcement of the new ordinance in those circumstances would be unfair and inequitable.

Generally, "substantial reliance" is determined by various tests employed by the courts — for example, the set quantum test, the proportionate test, and a balancing test. The set quantum test, used by the majority of courts, determines that an owner is entitled to relief from new, prohibitory zoning if he has changed his position beyond a certain point, measured quantitatively. A related test is the proportionate test, which determines the percentage of money spent or obligations incurred before the zoning change as compared with the total cost. The problem with both of these tests is that there is no predictable point short of adjudication

---

(2) See *People v. County of Cook*, 206 N.E.2d 441 (Ill. App. 1965); Heeter, *Zoning Estoppel: Application of the Principles of Equitable Estoppel and Vested Rights to Zoning Disputes*, 1971 Urban L. Ann. 63.

(3) These requirements are discussed in Heeter, *supra* n.2, and Delaney and Kominers, *He Who Rests Less, Vests Best: Acquisition of Vested Rights in Land Development*, 23 St. Louis U. L.J. 219 (1979).

which separates reliance that is less than "substantial" from the reliance sufficient to result in a vested right or to support an estoppel.

The balancing test, although likely to produce a more fair outcome in a particular case, also results in little predictability. The test weighs the owner's interest in developing his property and the reasonableness of his proposed use against the interests of public health, safety, morals, or general welfare. If the gain to the public is small when compared to the hardship that would accrue to the property owner, the actions of the owner in preparation for development according to a formerly permitted use may be seen as sufficiently substantial to justify the issuance of a permit or continuation of development despite an amendment to the zoning ordinances. See *Nott v. Wolff*, 163 N.E.2d 809 (Ill. 1960).

An additional requirement generally considered in zoning estoppel cases is that of the existence of some physical construction as an element of substantial reliance. Preconstruction activities such as the execution of architectural drawings or the clearing of land and widening of roads are not sufficient to create a vested right, nor generally are activities that are not exclusively related to the proposed project.

If the substantial reliance requirement of zoning estoppel were applied to the facts of the present case, we could not agree with the trial court that plaintiffs' "substantial compliance" with procedural requirements justified the estoppel of the city's enforcement of a new zoning ordinance. Although plaintiffs allege they proceeded with subdivision plans and incurred significant costs with the encouragement of certain city officials, they had not yet received official approval of their plan, and their expenditures were merely for surveying and preliminary plans. The record indicates that plaintiffs spent $1,335 for a boundary survey and $890 for the preparation of a preliminary subdivision plat. The boundary survey has value regardless of the city's approval or disapproval of the plaintiffs' proposal. The expenditure of $890 for the plat is not significant in relation to the size of the parcel and is not substantial enough to justify an estoppel with regard to the enforcement of valid zoning ordinances that became effective before official approval of plaintiffs' proposed subdivision.

In rejecting the zoning estoppel approach in this matter, we are not prepared to state that it would never be relevant to a determination of the validity of the retroactive application of a zoning ordinance. We are of the view, however, that the relevant public and private interests are better accommodated in the first instance by a different approach.

A number of other approaches have been followed or suggested as alternatives to zoning estoppel in an effort to promote fairness and consistency. . . .

Courts in several states have adopted the view . . . that an application for a building permit creates a vested right as of the time of application. Pennsylvania, one of these states, initially followed the general rule that a vested right accrued when an owner could show substantial reliance, made in good faith, on a validly issued permit.[(4)] *Schechter v. Zoning Board of Adjustment*, 149 A.2d 28 (Pa. 1959). . . . At the present time Pennsylvania follows what is termed the "pending ordinance rule." This rule provides that an application for a permitted use cannot be refused unless a prohibiting ordinance is pending at the time of application. *Boron Oil Co. v. Kimple*, 284 A.2d 744 (Pa. 1971), stated the applicable test as follows:

---

(4) The Pennsylvania experience with the vested zoning rights issue is analyzed in Keiter, *Emerging from the Confusion: Zoning and Vested Rights in Pennsylvania*, 83 Dickinson L. Rev. 515 (1979).

> [A]n ordinance is pending when a Borough Council has resolved to consider a particular scheme of rezoning and has advertised to the public its intention to hold public hearings on the rezoning. The pending ordinance rule reflected the court's attempt to . . . balance the interest of the municipality in effecting a change in its zoning laws free from the perpetuation of nonconforming uses against the interest of the individual property owner to be free from lengthy restraints upon the use of his property.

The court in *Boron Oil Co.*, also imposed a duty of good faith on the part of the municipality:

> [I]t is to be emphasized that the various governmental authorities charged with the responsibility of proposing, promulgating and administering local zoning and planning laws are under a basic duty to act reasonably. In sum, a building permit may be properly refused in situations such as the one at bar *only* when the municipality acts initially in good faith to achieve permissible ends and thereafter proceeds with reasonable dispatch in considering the proposed rezoning.

The Pennsylvania cases do not indicate whether an owner need show substantial reliance on the permitted zoning prior to the advertisement of a zoning change as an element of acquiring a vested development right. Nor is there a time limit on an owner's right to develop in accordance with a superseded use pursuant to the pending ordinance rule. . . .

The State of Washington has also refused to follow the general rule that building permits are not protected against revocation by subsequent zoning change unless a permittee has gained a vested right through a substantial change in position in reliance on the permit. As stated in *Hull v. Hunt*, 331 P.2d 856, 859 (Wash. 1958):

> Notwithstanding the weight of authority, we prefer to have a date certain upon which the right vests to construct in accordance with the building permit. We prefer not to adopt a rule which forces the court to search through (to quote from . . . [an earlier Washington case], "the moves and countermoves of . . . parties . . . by way of passing ordinance and bringing actions for injunctions" — to which may be added the stalling or acceleration of administrative action in the issuance of permits — to find that date upon which the substantial change of position is made which finally vests the right. The more practical rule to administer, we feel, is that the right vests when the party, property owner or not, applies for his building permit, if that permit is thereafter issued. This rule, of course, assumes that the permit applied for and granted be consistent with the zoning ordinances and building codes in force at the time of application for the permit.

The court met the argument that its rule would result in speculation in building permits by noting that the cost of preparing plans and meeting permit requirements was such that an applicant would generally have a good faith expectation of proceeding according to his application, and, furthermore, that the city building code renders a permit null and void if work authorized by the permit does not commence within 180 days.

A "rule of irrevocable commitment" was suggested as an appropriate standard in an extensive treatment of the vested development rights problem in Cunningham and Kremer, *Vested Rights, Estoppel, and the Land Development Process, supra*, n.1. This approach would protect from new laws any project to which the developer has made a "reasonable and irrevocable commitment of resources." The scope of the protection granted would be determined by a detailed analysis of the resources committed, the planned objectives of the project, and the concerns of the general welfare. If the investment made in the project prior to passage of a new prohibitory zoning regulation could be utilized for another legitimate use, there would be less need to protect the developer's right to proceed than if significant expenditures were uniquely related to the original project. . . .

A vested right in a particular development scheme may be created by statute. For example, in Pennsylvania, § 508(4) of the Municipalities Planning Code confers a vested right on property owners who have previously received approval of a subdivision plan in which the lots are too small to conform to the requirements of a newly-enacted ordinance. This vested right has a three-year duration. . . .

In our view the tests employed by most other jurisdictions tend to subject landowners to undue and even calamitous expense because of changing city councils or zoning boards or their dilatory action and to the unpredictable results of burdensome litigation. The majority rule permits an unlimited right to deny permits when ordinances are amended after application and preliminary work. It allows government in many cases broader power with regard to land regulation than may be justified by the public interests involved. A balancing test, though geared toward promoting fairness, must be applied on a case-by-case basis and offers no predictable guidelines on which landowners can intelligently base their decisions regarding extensive development projects. Tests currently followed by the majority of states are particularly unsatisfactory in dealing with the large multistage projects. The threat of denial of a permit at a late stage of development makes a developer vulnerable to shifting governmental policies and tempts him to manipulate the process by prematurely engaging in activities that would establish the substantial reliance required to vest his right to develop when inappropriate.

The economic waste that occurs when a project is halted after substantial costs have been incurred in its commencement is of no benefit either to the public or to landowners. In a day when housing costs have severely escalated beyond the means of many prospective buyers, governmental actions should not be based on policies that exacerbate a severe economic problem without compelling justification. Governmental powers should be exercised in a manner that is reasonable and, to the extent possible, predictable.

On the other hand, a rule which vests a right unconditionally at the time application for a permit is made affords no protection for important public interests that may legitimately require interference with planned private development. If a proposal met zoning requirements at the time of application but seriously threatens public health, safety, or welfare, the interests of the public should not be thwarted.

The above competing interests are best accommodated in our view by adopting the rule that an applicant is entitled to a building permit or subdivision approval if his proposed development meets the zoning requirements in existence at the time of his application and if he proceeds with reasonable diligence, absent a compelling, countervailing public interest. Furthermore, if a city or county has initiated proceedings to amend its zoning ordinances, a landowner who subsequently makes application for a permit is not entitled to rely on the original zoning classification.

This rule . . . is intended to strike a reasonable balance between important, conflicting public and private interests in the area of land development. A property owner should be able to plan for developing his property in a manner permitted by existing zoning regulations with some degree of assurance that the basic ground rules will not be changed in midstream. Clearly it is desirable to reduce the necessity for a developer to resort to the courts. An applicant for approval of a planned and permitted use should not be subject to shifting policies that do not reflect serious public concerns.

At the same time, compelling public interests may, when appropriate, be given priority over individual economic interests. A city should not be unduly restricted in effectuating legitimate policy changes when they are grounded in recognized legislative police powers. There may be instances when an application would for the first time draw attention to a serious problem that calls for an immediate amendment to a zoning ordinance, and such an amendment would be entitled to valid retroactive effect. It is incumbent upon a city, however, to act in good faith and not to reject an application because the application itself triggers zoning reconsiderations that result in a substitution of the judgment of current city officials for that of their predecessors. Regardless of the circumstances, a court must be cognizant of legitimate public concerns in considering whether a particular development should be protected from the effects of a desirable new law.

In the present case, the zoning of the property in question was found by the trial court to have permitted the proposed use at the time of the application. The owners had received encouragement from city officials, although no official approval was rendered. After the application, the city council members decided to reexamine the pertinent zoning regulation and thereafter voted to amend or "clarify" the zoning ordinance to disallow subdivisions in an M-1 zone and permit residences only by special permit. Their actions may have had a reasonable basis. It was argued that fire protection would be undermined because of limited access roads, but it does not appear the problem would be any less serious if the unarguably-permitted manufacturing facilities were erected instead of single-family houses. Objections as to inadequate sidewalks and other problems can be handled by requiring modification of specifications that do not meet city subdivision requirements. Indeed, the order of the trial court stated that the developers must comply with all the reasonable requirements of the city's subdivision ordinance.

We do not find the reasons given by the city for withholding approval of plaintiffs' proposed subdivision to be so compelling as to overcome the presumption that an applicant for a building permit or subdivision approval is entitled to affirmative official action if he meets the zoning requirements in force at the time of his application.

NOTES AND QUESTIONS

1. *The issues.* The principal case reviews the competing rules and policy considerations applied and considered by the courts in estoppel and vested rights cases. The rule of the principal case, that rights can vest even though no building permit has been issued, is a minority view. Note the varying views the courts take, and the extent to which they put the parties at the risk of uncertain judicial interpretations. The Utah court has refused to apply its rule broadly, beyond the facts in the principal case. See *Patterson v. Am. Fork City*, 67 P.3d 466, 474 (Utah 2003): "Nothing in *Western Land Equities* suggests that the 'entitlement' to a building permit in the face of an amended zoning ordinance would extend beyond the facts in that case. Otherwise, the ability of the City to protect the public interest in specific land development cases would be supplanted by a rule that mere adherence to formal requirements always entitles a developer to approval, whatever the countervailing public interests might be." What does this decision indicate about how the court now evaluates the competing interests in vested rights cases?

What are the real issues in these cases? As the article by Heeter, which is cited in the principal case, points out, the theory on which relief is awarded to the landowner is not entirely clear:

> The defense of estoppel is derived from equity, but the defense of vested rights reflects principles of common and constitutional law. Similarly their elements are different. Estoppel focuses on whether it would be inequitable to allow the government to repudiate its prior conduct; vested rights upon whether the owner acquired real property rights which cannot be taken away by governmental regulation. [1971 Urban L. Ann. at 64–65.]

Do these doctrines isolate the issues courts should consider in cases of this type? Did the principal case cut through both doctrines and consider policy issues that are more important in these cases? If so, what policy issues did the court consider? What other policy issues should it have considered? Do you agree with the rule the court adopted? Do you see a relationship between vested rights doctrine and the protection courts provide to nonconforming uses?

As the principal case indicates, the long-term trend in the decisions has been toward greater protection for the landowner and consideration of the "equities." See *Tremarco Corp. v. Garzio*, 161 A.2d 241 (N.J. 1960). The court found an estoppel, noting that the municipality changed its zoning regulations only after neighborhood residents protested and that there were no zoning reasons that justified the change. See also *Geisler v. City Council of the City of Cedar Falls*, 769 N.W.2d 162 (Iowa 2009), describing the "bad faith" exception to the general vested rights rule, where a city enacts an ordinance to prohibit development which meets all of the code requirements.

2. *A majority rule?* The estoppel-vested rights rule is usually stated as follows:

> A court will preclude a municipality from changing its regulations as they apply to a particular parcel of land when a property owner in good faith, upon some act or omission of the government, has made a substantial change in position or has incurred such extensive obligations and expenses that it would be highly inequitable and unjust to destroy the right he acquired. [*Florida Cos. v. Orange County*, 411 So. 2d 1008, 1010 (Fla. App. 1982).]

The act or omission requirement has been the biggest stumbling block for developers. As the principal case indicates, the majority rule requires a building permit as the governmental "act." *Avco Community Builders*, cited in the principal case, is a leading decision on this point. As the *Avco* court noted, protecting a developer who has not been issued a building permit would impair the right of government to "control land use policy." Why? Does the principal case convince you that a building permit should not be required?

Some cases take an intermediate view and find estoppel when a landowner relies on some government act other than a building permit. In *Town of Largo v. Imperial Homes Corp.*, 309 So. 2d 571 (Fla. App. 1975), the town knew "that the purchase of the land by Imperial was contingent upon obtaining multiple-family zoning." The town rezoned to the developer's satisfaction, the developer purchased the land, and the court held that the town was estopped from a subsequent downzoning to a restrictive single-family classification. A subdivider's diligent effort to go through the pre-permit process has been found to estop the application of a new setback restriction in *In re 244.5 Acres of Land v. Delaware Agricultural Lands Foundation*, 808 A.2d 753 (Del. 2002). Is it enough if the developer makes informal inquiries at the zoning office and is told to "go ahead"? Compare *Nemmers v. City of Dubuque*, 716 F.2d

1194 (8th Cir. 1983) (estoppel found when city made road improvements to serve development and was receptive to development proposal), with *Colonial Inv. Co. v. City of Leawood*, 646 P.2d 1149 (Kan. App. 1982) (contra, when developer relied on advice from planning staff). What policy reason is there for requiring a building permit as the basis for an estoppel?

3. *Substantial reliance.* As the principal case indicates, the courts disagree on how much "substantial reliance" by the developer is required. The Maryland court has a high threshold. "[T]he work done must be recognizable, on inspection of the property by a reasonable member of the public, as the commencement of a building for a use permitted under the then current zoning." *Sterling Homes Corp. v. Anne Arundel County*, 695 A.2d 1238, 1249 (Md. App. 1997) (marina bathhouse and parking lot; grading, bulkhead and revetment construction not enough). *Maryland Reclamation Assocs. v. Harford County*, 994 A.2d 842 (Md. App. 2010), notes that "substantial reliance" is "the one which most often determines the outcome of the [zoning estoppels] cases." *Id.* at 874. It reiterates Maryland's strict stance, stating "[l]and developers must understand that, to a *limited* extent, the local government will meander, and before they incur significant expense without final permitting, they must carefully assess the risk that the government will shift course. On the other hand, there may be situations in which the developer's good faith reliance on government action in the pre-construction stage is so extensive and expensive that zoning estoppel is an appropriate doctrine to apply." *Id.* at 875. Preliminary expenditures may not be enough unless the developer enters into preliminary contractual obligations. See *County Council v. District Land Corp.*, 337 A.2d 712 (Md. 1975). The courts divide on whether site excavation is enough, *Prince George's County v. Sunrise Dev. Ltd. Partnership*, 623 A.2d 1296 (Md. 1993), and the purchase of land is usually not sufficient. Compare *Tremarco, supra*, rejecting a quantitative rule and applying a test that balances the interests of the developer against the interests of the municipality. See also *Clackamas County v. Holmes*, 508 P.2d 190 (Or. 1973) (relaxed substantial reliance test and applied equitable factors); *Even v. City of Parker*, 597 N.W.2d 670 (S.D. 1999) (finding reliance when a person of humble means spent a small amount on a building). Does the equitable nature of estoppel suggest that equitable "balancing" is the better rule?

4. *Good faith.* The principal case did not have much to say on the "good faith" requirement. The courts apply either an objective or a subjective good faith test, with the objective courts more likely to find good faith. Obviously, a developer who rushes to complete his project knowing that a zoning change may be made runs a serious risk that he will be found in bad faith. Note how the Pennsylvania cases discussed in the principal case handled the good faith problem when an ordinance proposing a zoning change was pending. The courts also have held that a developer may still claim good faith reliance even when there is an expectation of a political change to the city commission that will bring about a revision of the zoning ordinance. See *Sakolsky v. City of Coral Gables*, 151 So. 2d 433 (Fla. 1963).

5. *Illegal building permit.* What if the municipality issues a building permit but it turns out later that the building permit was illegally issued because the project violates the zoning ordinance? May the municipality later revoke the permit? Some courts distinguish between permits that were issued based on mistakes of law, and mistakes of fact. See, e.g., *Branca v. City of Miramar*, 634 So. 2d 604 (Fla. 1994) (estoppel only applies to erroneous representations of fact, not of law). There are competing policy considerations in these cases. The developer may have been "innocent," yet the zoning ordinance theoretically embodies the "general welfare," and the common good arguably should be allowed to prevail. Note the qualified nature of both these statements. A sophisticated developer (as opposed to an amateur home remodeler) may be as capable of reading the relevant ordinances as a clerk in the building

department. Most ordinances, in truth, embody only one of many solutions to the "general welfare." Is it possible to state a categorically "fair" rule? Most courts allow revocation in this situation. See, e.g., *Parkview Assocs. v. City of New York*, 519 N.E.2d 1372 (N.Y. 1988). Contra, *Town of West Hartford v. Rechel*, 459 A.2d 1015 (Conn. 1983).

6. *Phased developments.* Very large residential projects, usually known as planned unit developments (PUDs), are usually completed in phases over a period of time. What if a municipality issues building permits for Phase I of a PUD, the developer completes Phase I, but the municipality then refuses to issue building permits for Phase II even though it had approved the plans for the entire project earlier? *Avco, supra*, is a PUD case indicating that preliminary approvals such as the approval of project plans are not enough, and that rights do not vest until the municipality issues a building permit. Contra, *Village of Palatine v. LaSalle Nat'l Bank*, 445 N.E.2d 1277 (Ill. App. Ct. 1983):

> We regard Palatine's approval of the original site plan, the issuance of building permits for Phase I, and the continuing treatment of [the project] as a PUD "in fact" as the type of affirmative acts of public officials upon which a landowner is entitled to rely. [*Id.* at 1283.]

Is this decision correct, or should the multi-phase developer be "at risk" until he receives building permits for each phase of his project? Some states provide statutory protection in this situation. See "A Note on Development Agreements," *infra*. For discussion of PUDs, see Chapter 7, Section C. The ripeness problems raised by a phased development are reviewed in the Supreme Court's *Hamilton Bank* case, reproduced in Chapter 2, *supra*. What about the case of a proposed residence for which the owners have received multiple permits preliminary to the final building permit? See, e.g., *Pingitore v. Town of Cave Creek*, 981 P.2d 129 (Ariz. App. 1999) (town was estopped from enforcing the ridge line restrictions of a new zoning district where homebuilders had received variances, driveway permits, sewer and water permits and had begun construction). Are the equities any different when one residence, rather than multiple residences, is involved?

7. *The developer's dilemma.* One court, discussing a rule making building permits revocable, saw the problem this way:

> The permittee could win immunity from such "ex post facto" revocation only by constructing a substantial portion of the structure authorized by his permit in good faith reliance upon the prior law. A permittee who delayed construction in the face of an impending amendment to the zoning laws might find that he had not progressed far enough in time to qualify for immunity; one who proceeded with unseemly haste ran the risk that his conduct might bear the stigma of bad faith. No facile formula informed the permittee how to strike the delicate balance which would afford the desired immunity. [*Russian Hill Imp. Ass'n v. Board of Permit Appeals*, 423 P.2d 824, 828–29 (Cal. 1967).]

The court enforced a revocation based on a newly enacted height limit.

8. *Statutory and ordinance protection.* Several states have adopted statutes enacting vested rights protection. Most of them follow the Washington rule, now codified by statute, that confers protection as of the date an application is filed. The Oregon statute states it simply:

> If the application [e.g., for a permit or zone change] was complete when first submitted or the applicant submits the requested additional information within 180 days of the

> date the application was first submitted and the city has a comprehensive plan and land use regulations acknowledged under [the state land use law], approval or denial of the application shall be based upon the standards and criteria that were applicable at the time the application was first submitted. [Ore. Rev. Stat. § 227.178(3).]

Note that the statute requires a "complete" application. This is designed to preclude vesting based on vague proposals, hastily drafted to beat a change in the law. For the Washington law, see Wash. Rev. Code Ann. § 19.27.095. See Overstreet & Kircheim, *The Quest for the Best Test to Vest: Washington's Vested Rights Doctrine Beats the Rest*, 23 Seattle U.L. Rev. 1043 (2000). See also N.J. Stat. Ann. 40:55D-10.5 (effective May 6, 2011). What are the benefits of dating vested rights protection from the time an application is submitted? Does this tip the scales too much in favor of developers? Such legislation in Texas has been upheld against constitutional challenge. See *City of Austin v. Garza*, 124 S.W.3d 867 (Tex. App. 2003) (Tex. Loc. Gov't Code Ann. § 245.002(d), allowing subdivider to choose to develop under law in effect at the time of application or at the time of final approval is not an unconstitutional delegation of power to private parties).

Other statutes provide protection from the time of submission of applications for site plan, subdivision or similar approvals. E.g., Cal. Gov't Code §§ 66498.1 to 66498.3; Colo. Rev. Stat. § 24-68-102.5; Conn. Gen. Stat. § 8-2h(a); Mass. Gen. Laws Chapter 40A, § 6. A Virginia statute codifies the court-made law of vested rights. Va. Code § 15.2-2307. Some of these statutes specify the regulations covered by the vested rights protection, and some have time limits. For a review of statutes and an argument for the need for legislation, see Hall, *State Vested Rights Statutes: Developing Certainty and Equity and Protecting the Public Interest*, 40 Urb. Law. 451 (2008). The American Planning Association has developed state model vesting legislation, recognizing that vested rights law common law and statutory law is quite varied throughout the states. See American Planning Association Growing Smart Legislative Guidebook: Model Statutes for Planning and Management of Change, § 8-501 (S. Meck ed., 2002). The model legislation contains two alternatives. One is the standard vesting rule requiring reliance on a building permit. The other is the rule that vests at the time of application.

The economic downturn beginning in 2007 created legislative sympathy for developers who had obtained permits in earlier times but were unable to begin or complete construction. States and local governments enacted legislation to extend the time frame of permits, effectively granting vested rights. See, e.g., California SB 1185, adding Government Code section 66452.21 to the Subdivision Map Act. Any tentative subdivision map that (a) had not expired prior to July 15, 2008 and (b) otherwise would expire before January 1, 2011, and any state agency approval pertaining to the subdivision maps, is extended by two years. The law also applies to vesting maps and to parcel maps that require a tentative map. Likewise, in 2010, the Florida legislature extended certain state permits, Developments of Regional Impact, and local government "development orders" with expiration dates between 9/1/08 and 1/1/12, and their phasing dates, for two years after its previous date of expiration. (Chapter 2010-147, Laws of Florida.) Virginia in 2008 amended its zoning enabling law to vest nonconforming buildings from local zoning ordinances that might require their removal, as long as the use obtained building permits and a certificate of occupancy after construction, and has paid property taxes on the structure for 15 years. The structure must come into conformity with the Uniform Statewide Building Code. See § 15.2-2307 of the Code of Virginia, amended by H.B. No. 1078. Do the permit extensions strike an appropriate balance, or tilt too heavily toward developers?

9. *Sources.* Delaney, *Vesting Verities and the Development Chronology: A Gaping Disconnect*, 3 Wash. U. J.L. & Pol'y 603 (2000); Delaney & Vaias, *Recognizing Vested Development Rights as Protected Property in Fifth Amendment Due Process and Taking Claims*, 49 J. Urb. & Contemp. L. 27 (1996); Dennison, *Estoppel as a Defense to Enforcement of Zoning Ordinance*, 19 Zoning & Plan. L. Rep. 69 (1996); Pelham, Lindgren & Weil, *"What Do You Mean I Can't Build?" A Comparative Analysis of When Property Rights Vest*, 31 Urb. Law. 901 (1999).

A NOTE ON DEVELOPMENT AGREEMENTS

The development agreement is an alternative to a reliance on judicially protected vested rights. It removes uncertainty in the development process by providing the developer with an assurance that development regulations that apply to his project will not change. A number of states have now adopted statutes that authorize development agreements, beginning with California as a response to the *Avco* decision, *supra*, and as an alternative to legislation providing greater protection for vested rights. Cal. Gov't Code §§ 65864-65869.5. See also, e.g., Fla. Stat. Ann. §§ 163.3220 to 163.3243; Hawaii Rev. Stat. §§ 46-121 to 46-132; Nev. Rev. Stat. §§ 278.0201 to 278.0207.

> The statutes . . . authorize local governments to enter into agreements with developers and to make local land use and development regulations in place at the time of the agreement a part of the contract. The statutes direct the local government to hold public hearings prior to approving an agreement or making subsequent modifications. They also require periodic review of the development project and allow the governing body to modify or terminate the agreement if the developer is unable to comply with its terms. The governing body may also modify the agreement if circumstances arise which threaten the public interest. Unless the statute provides a special remedy for the enforceability of the agreement, the parties may use common law contract remedies. [Moore, *A Comparative Analysis of Development Agreement Legislation in Hawaii, Nevada and Florida*, 11 Newsl. of the Plan. & L. Div. of the Am. Plan. Ass'n, No. 3, at 19 (1987).]

The "approval freeze" is an important element of development agreements because it prevents the local government from making changes in development regulations that apply to the project. Here is what the Florida statute provides:

> (2) A local government may apply subsequently adopted laws and policies to a development that is subject to a development agreement only if the local government has held a public hearing and determined: (a) They are not in conflict with the laws and policies governing the development agreement and do not prevent development of the land uses, intensities, or densities in the development agreement; (b) They are essential to the public health, safety, or welfare, and expressly state that they shall apply to a development that is subject to a development agreement; (c) They are specifically anticipated and provided for in the development agreement; (d) The local government demonstrates that substantial changes have occurred in pertinent conditions existing at the time of approval of the development agreement; or (e) The development agreement is based on substantially inaccurate information supplied by the developer. [Fla. Stat. Ann. § 163.3233.]

Without an "approval freeze," a municipality is free to disregard an agreement and downzone property that is subject to an agreement. *Spenger, Grubb & Assocs., Inc. v. City of Hailey*, 903 P.2d 741 (Idaho 1995).

The "approval freeze" provisions of development agreement statutes are their most critical feature but raise a number of constitutional questions. The most important is whether the statutes authorize an unconstitutional bargaining-away of the police power. Compare *Buckhorn Ventures v. Forsyth County*, 585 S.E.2d 229 (Ga. App. 2003) (settlement agreement allowing continuation of mining in district and preventing future restrictions on mining nullified because it illegally binds future county commissioners on a legislative matter), and *Morgran v. Orange County*, 818 So. 2d 640 (Fla. App. 2002) (development agreement stating that county would support rezoning was unenforceable contract zoning), with *Stephens v. City of Vista*, 994 F.2d 650 (9th Cir. 1993) (city can guarantee development density while retaining review of the design features of a development without surrendering control of its land use powers). In an analogous situation, the courts have upheld agreements in which a landowner agrees to annex to a municipality in return for a municipality's promise to provide public services. See *Morrison Homes Corp. v. City of Pleasanton*, 130 Cal. Rptr. 196 (Cal. App. 1976). While cases may uphold similar provisions in development agreements, a freeze on existing zoning restrictions is more doubtful. Compare *City of Louisville v. Fiscal Court*, 623 S.W.2d 219 (Ky. 1981) (annexation agreement in which city agreed to cooperate in rezoning held invalid), with *Mayor & City Council v. Crane*, 352 A.2d 786 (Md. 1976) (city bound by agreement providing for density increase in exchange for developer's donation of land to city), and *Santa Margarita Residents Together v. San Luis Obispo County*, 100 Cal. Rptr. 2d 740 (Cal. App. 2000) (five year zoning freeze valid when agreement required development consistent with general plan and approval of detailed building permits).

Development agreements may also require improvements from the developer and can be used to impose exactions, a practice which has been approved in some states. See Crew, *Development Agreements After Nollan v. California Coastal Commission*, 22 Urb. Law. 23 (1990). See also *Nicolet Minerals Co. v. Town of Nashville*, 641 N.W.2d 497 (Wis. App. 2002) (state statute created authority for agreements incorporating zoning and land use permits in exchange for payments from mining companies).

NOTES AND QUESTIONS

1. *How much certainty?* A development agreement statute is not an "open sesame" to guaranteed protection against changes in land use regulations. For one thing, developer performance of the agreement is essential. For another, statutes require very specific details on the development the developer plans to carry out. For example, the Florida statute requires details as to "the development uses permitted on the land, including population densities, and building intensities and height; a description of public facilities that will service the development, including who shall provide such facilities; the date any new facilities, if needed, will be constructed; and a schedule to assure public facilities are available concurrent with the impacts of the development; a description of any reservation or dedication of land for public purposes." Fla. Stat. Ann. § 163.3227. This is typical. Exaction requirements are subject, of course, to the exaction tests discussed in Chapter 7, *infra*.

Here's the dilemma: In the large, long-term projects for which development agreements are most suited, changes in the project and marketing possibilities may make the original development agreement obsolete. An amendment is then necessary, and it is not guaranteed.

Similar problems arise in planned unit developments. See Chapter 7, Section C, *infra*.

Nor do development agreement statutes guarantee that no change can occur in existing regulations. Note the provisions in the Florida law authorizing the application of subsequent laws to a development agreement. For a California case upholding the adoption of ordinances under the health and safety exception that rescinded a development agreement, see *216 Sutter Bay Associates v. County of Sutter*, 68 Cal. Rptr. 2d 492 (Cal. App. 1997). On balance, how do development agreements compare with relying on vested rights doctrine?

2. *Bargaining and the comprehensive plan.* Development agreements are an example of bargaining over land development regulations. Conditional zoning, which is discussed later in this chapter, is another example. How does this kind of bargaining compare with the bargaining over land use restrictions that is reviewed in Chapter 1, *supra*? In answering that question, keep in mind that many of the development agreement statutes require agreements to be consistent with the comprehensive plan. See Haw. Rev. Stat. § 46-129. Consider how effective this control might be after you review the materials on consistency of zoning with the comprehensive plan later in this chapter. Likewise, development contributions agreed to by development agreement may still be further restricted by state statute. See *Toll Bros., Inc. v. Board of Chosen Freeholders*, 944 A.2d 1 (N.J. 2008) (agreement is only a tool to establish the conditions of approval, and does not provide an independent contractual basis for requiring obligations that go beyond the costs as governed by the state statute). See also *Neighbors in Support of Appropriate Land Use v. County of Tuolumne*, 68 Cal. Rptr. 3d 882 (Cal. Ct. App. 2007) (development agreement cannot be a substitute for rezoning to allow a use not permitted by the zoning ordinance).

3.

Sources. See D. Callies, D. Curtin & J. Tappendorf, Bargaining for Development (2003); Curtin & Edelstein, *Development Agreement Practice in California and Other States*, 22 Stetson L. Rev. 961 (1993); Delaney, *Development Agreements: The Road from Prohibition to "Let's Make a Deal!"*, 25 Urb. Law. 49 (1993); Taub, *Development Agreements*, Land Use L. & Zoning Dig., Vol. 42, No. 10, at 3 (1990); Wegner, *Moving Toward the Bargaining Table: Contract Zoning, Development Agreements, and the Theoretical Foundations of Government Land Use Deals*, 65 N.C. L. Rev. 957 (1987).

[2.] "Spot" Zoning

KUEHNE v. TOWN OF EAST HARTFORD

136 Conn. 452, 72 A.2d 474 (1950)

MALTBIE, C.J.:

. . . . [A substantial part of the opinion is omitted. — Eds.]

Main Street in East Hartford runs substantially north and south. The petitioner before the town council, Langlois, owned a piece of land on the east side of it which he had been using for growing fruit and vegetables, and he has had upon it a greenhouse and a roadside stand for the sale of products of the land. The premises, ever since zoning was established in East Hartford in 1927, had been in an A residence district. Langlois made an application to the town council to change to an A business district a portion of the tract fronting on Main Street for about 500 feet and extending to a depth of 150 feet. He intended, if the application was granted, to erect upon the tract a building containing six or eight stores, apparently in the nature of retail stores and small business establishments calculated to serve the needs of residents in the vicinity. Starting at a business district to the north and extending for almost three miles to the town boundary on the south, the land along Main Street and extending to a considerable depth on each side of it has been, ever since zoning was established in the town, in an A residence district, with certain exceptions hereinafter described. Seven hundred feet north of the Langlois property is a small business district lying on both sides of Main Street; the land on the east side is used for a fruit and vegetable stand, a milk bar and a garage and gas station; and the land on the west side, with an area a little larger than the Langlois tract in question, is now unoccupied. About 500 feet south of the Langlois property is another small business district in which is located a grill and restaurant, a drugstore, a cleaning and dyeing business and a large grocery and meat market. Formerly the land about the tract in question was used quite largely for agricultural purposes, but within the last few years a large residential community, comprising some one thousand houses, has grown up in the vicinity.

The application to the town council was based upon the claim that residents in the vicinity need the stores and services which could be located in the building Langlois proposed to erect. There was, for example, a petition filed with the council in support of the application signed by fifty-one of those residents which asked it to allow such a change as might be necessary to permit for their benefit a shopping center on the property. None of the signers, however, owned property on Main Street or in the immediate vicinity of the Langlois property. On the other hand, the application was opposed by the owner of property directly opposite the tract in question and by the owners of the two properties fronting on Main Street immediately south of the Langlois land.

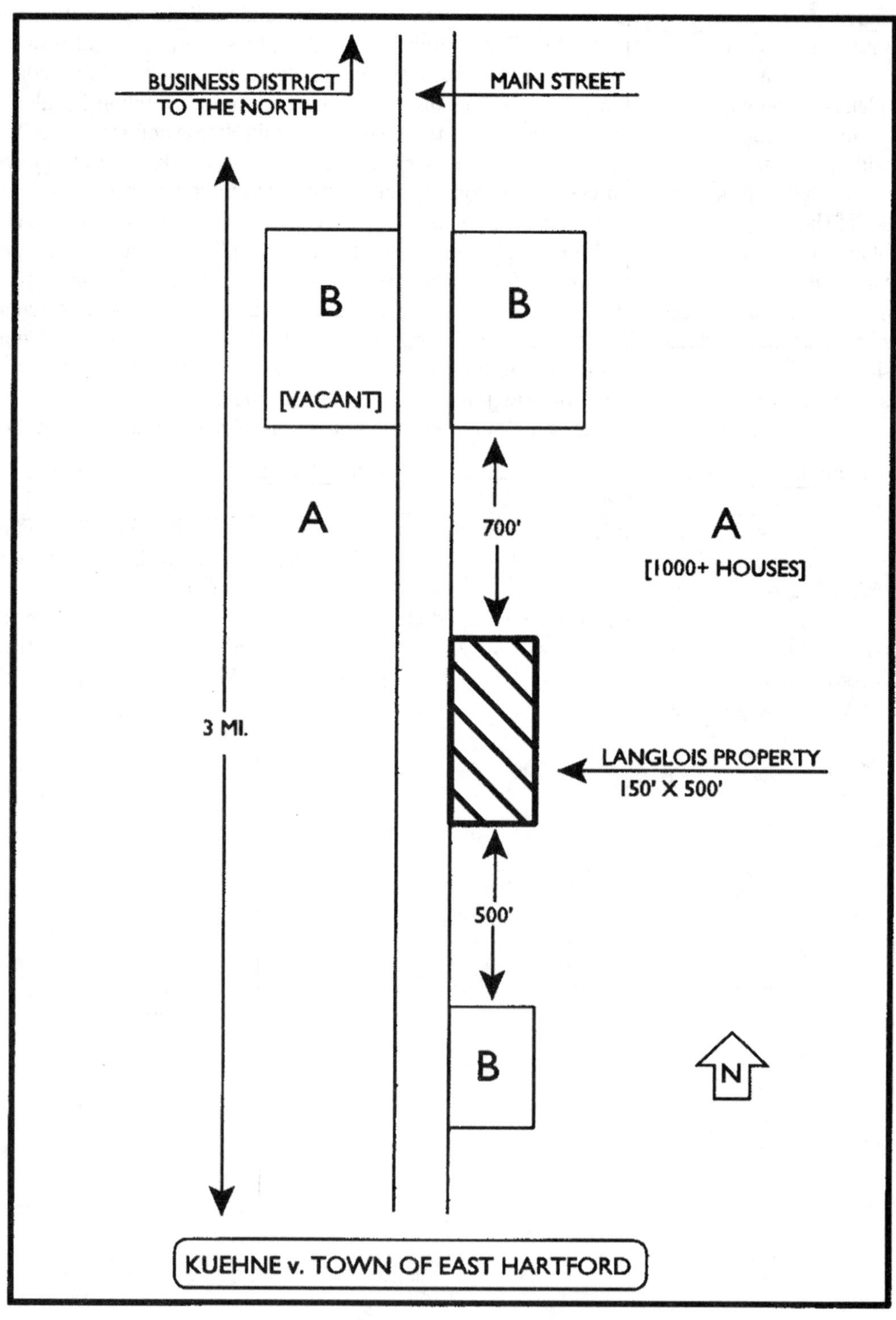
BUSINESS DISTRICT
TO THE NORTH
MAIN STREET
B
[VACANT]
B
A
700'
A
[1000+ HOUSES]
3 MI.
LANGLOIS PROPERTY
150' X 500'
500'
B
N
KUEHNE v. TOWN OF EAST HARTFORD

The council voted that the application "be granted for the general welfare and the good of the town in that section." In *Bartram v. Zoning Commission* (Conn.), 68 A.2d 308, we recently had before us an appeal from the granting by a zoning commission of an application to change a lot in Bridgeport even smaller than the tract here in question from a residence to a business zone, and we sustained the action of the commission. We said: "A limitation upon the powers of zoning authorities which has been in effect ever since zoning statutes were made applicable generally to municipalities in the state is that the regulations they adopt must be made 'in accordance with a comprehensive plan.' 'A "comprehensive plan" means "a general plan to control and direct the use and development of property in a municipality or a large part of it by dividing it into districts according to the present and potential use of the properties.' " Action by a zoning authority which gives to a single lot or a small area privileges which are not extended to other land in the vicinity is in general against sound public policy and obnoxious to the law. It can be justified only when it is done in furtherance of a general plan properly adopted for and designed to serve the best interests of the community as a whole. The vice of spot zoning lies in the fact that it singles out for special treatment a lot or a small area in a way that does not further such a plan. Where, however, in pursuance of it, a zoning commission takes such action, its decision can be assailed only on the ground that it abused the discretion vested in it by the law. To permit business in a small area within a residence zone may fall within the scope of such a plan, and to do so, unless it amounts to unreasonable or arbitrary action, is not unlawful." It appeared in that case that the change was granted by the commission in pursuance of a policy to encourage decentralization of business in the city and to that end to permit neighborhood stores in outlying districts. It is true that we said in that opinion that if the commission decided, "on facts affording a sufficient basis and in the exercise of a proper discretion, that it would serve the best interests of the community as a whole to permit a use of a single lot or small area in a different way than was allowed in surrounding territory, it would not be guilty of spot zoning in any sense obnoxious to the law." We meant by that statement to emphasize the fact that the controlling test must be, not the benefit to a particular individual or group of individuals, but the good of the community as a whole, and we did not mean in any way to derogate from our previous statement that any such change can only be made if it falls within the requirements of a comprehensive plan for the use and development of property in the municipality or a large part of it.

In the case before us it is obvious that the council looked no further than the benefit which might accrue to Langlois and those who resided in the vicinity of his property, and that they gave no consideration to the larger question as to the effect the change would have upon the general plan of zoning in the community. In fact, the controlling consideration seems to have been that Langlois intended to go ahead at once with his building rather than any consideration of the suitability of the particular lot for business uses, because there is no suggestion in the record that the council considered the fact that only some 700 feet away was a tract of land already zoned for business which, as appears from the zoning map in evidence, was more easily accessible to most of the signers of the petition than was the Langlois land.

In *Strain v. Mims*, (Conn.), 193 A. 754, we said "One of the essential purposes of zoning regulation is to stabilize property uses." In this case it is significant that the change was opposed by the owners of three properties so situated as to be most affected by it, while those who supported it were the owner of the tract and residents who did not live in its immediate vicinity. It should also be noted that the petition they signed contained a provision that it should not be construed as supporting permission for the use of the premises as a liquor outlet, but at the hearing before the council the attorney for Langlois in effect conceded that the zoning regulations permitted such a use in an A business district; and if that is so and the change were granted, it is quite possible that the premises would be sooner or later converted to such a use.

The action of the town council in this case was not in furtherance of any general plan of zoning in the community and cannot be sustained. . . .

There is error, the judgment is set aside and the case is remanded to be proceeded with according to law. . . .

NOTES AND QUESTIONS

1. *The problem.* The principal case is a typical spot zoning decision. Notice how a rezoning differs from a variance or conditional use. Statutory standards govern variances, while standards in the zoning ordinance govern the conditional use. No such statutory or ordinance standards govern a rezoning, which is a legislative act in most states. But what is spot zoning? One court defined spot zoning as

> descriptive of the process of singling out a small parcel of land for a use classification different and inconsistent with the surrounding area, for the benefit of the owner of such property and to the detriment of the rights of other property owners. [*Burkett v. City of Texarkana*, 500 S.W.2d 242, 244 (Tex. Civ. App. 1973).]

Well and good, but what is the constitutional basis for attacking spot zoning? Substantive due process? Equal protection? Why?

The principal case makes the point that spot zoning violates the statutory requirement that rezoning be "in accordance with" a comprehensive plan. This requirement comes from the Standard Zoning Act, § 3, and has been adopted in most states. Note that the principal case finds the "comprehensive plan" in the policies of the zoning ordinance. What is there in the opinion that supports this conclusion? A minority of states now require the adoption of a comprehensive plan and the consistency of zoning with that plan. See sec. H *infra*. Consistency with the plan, however, does not necessarily defeat a spot zoning claim, though consistency is a factor in considering the claim. See *Griswold v. City of Homer*, 925 P.2d 1015 (Alaska 1996). Should it be?

The cases sometimes emphasize that spot zoning rules are flexible and that "spot zoning" is merely a descriptive term. The ultimate test is the reasonableness of the zoning as determined by a number of factors such as compatibility with adjacent uses and consistency with the comprehensive plan. *Chrismon v. Guilford County*, 370 S.E.2d 579 (N.C. 1988); *Smith v. Town of St. Johnsbury*, 554 A.2d 233 (Vt. 1988). But courts vary somewhat in how they state spot zoning rules, which leads to inconsistent decisions.

2. *An erratic rule?* Was the Connecticut court persuasive in distinguishing the principal case from *Bartram v. Zoning Comm'n* on the ground that, in *Bartram*, "the change was granted by the commission in pursuance of a policy to encourage decentralization of business in the city and to that end to permit neighborhood stores in outlying districts"? Perusal of the *Bartram* opinion indicates that only one commission member testified that the commission had adopted such a policy; the court, however, said, "nowhere in the record is there any suggestion that this testimony is not true," and apparently gave significant weight to it. Assuming that the zoning commission, in fact, had formulated such a policy in *Bartram*, does it rise to the dignity of "a comprehensive plan" within the meaning of the Standard State Zoning Enabling Act and the Connecticut zoning statute? The *Bartram* opinion does not indicate that the zoning commission had adopted any standards or guidelines to be applied when landowners sought rezoning to permit establishment of business uses in areas zoned for residential use. The zoning commission justified the business rezoning in *Bartram* as follows:

> 1. The location is on Sylvan Avenue, a sixty-foot street, and there is no shopping center within a mile of it. To the north of this tract there is a very large development but only small nonconforming grocery stores to serve people. 2. There is practically only one house, adjacent to this tract on the north, which will be directly affected by this change of zone. 3. Business Zone No. 3 regulations, with their thirty-foot setback and liquor restrictions, were designed to meet conditions like this and help alleviate the great congestion in the centralized shopping districts.

Do any of these findings demonstrate that the land rezoned was, in fact, the best location for a new neighborhood shopping center in the general area involved in the case? Would a refusal to rezone be an improper use of zoning to control competition?

Courts sometimes say they are applying the fairly debatable rule in spot zoning cases. *MC Props., Inc. v. City of Chattanooga*, 994 S.W.2d 132 (Tenn. App. 1999); *Childress v. Yadkin Co.*, 650 S.E.2d 55, 59 (N.C. App. 2007) ("Spot zoning is not invalid *per se* in North Carolina so long as the zoning authority made 'a clear showing of a reasonable basis for such distinction.' "). Are they? Of course, in states where zoning is not considered "legislative" but is instead "quasi-judicial," the fairly debatable standard will not apply. See section 3, *infra*.

3. *Rezoning for commercial use.* The differing results in the Connecticut cases indicate the ad hoc nature of spot zoning and the often ad hoc way in which courts consider spot zoning claims. The difficulty is that a spot zoning is necessarily piecemeal and at odds with a comprehensive planning and zoning regime for a municipality.

Spot commercial rezonings illustrate this point. In *Griswold, supra*, for example, the city, having agonized for years over whether to allow auto sales lots in its central business district, passed a zoning ordinance prohibiting them in this area, but then adopted a rezoning for this use on 13 lots, primarily to help out a lot owner who lost his "grandparented" rights to such a business. The court upheld the rezoning, citing tax, employment, infill and convenience benefits. Likewise, in *Durand v. IDC Bellingham*, 793 N.E.2d 359 (Mass. 2003), the court upheld the rezoning of a parcel from agriculture and suburban use to industrial, where the town was in need of industrial development and the developer of a power plant promised to contribute eight million dollars to the town for municipal projects, including a school. See also *Scalambrino v. Town of Michiana Shores*, 904 N.E.2d 673 (Ind. Ct. App. 2009) (rezoning city property to allow cell phone tower lease and revenues therefrom not spot zoning but rationally related to town's welfare). Not all courts recognize tax benefits, e.g., *Little v. Winborn*, 518 N.W.2d 384 (Iowa 1994). Why should they?

The issues are tougher when a commercial zoning is in a residential district on a small lot. Some courts see this as zoning anathema and invalidate the rezoning. *Bossman v. Village of Riverton*, 684 N.E.2d 427 (Ill. App. 1997). Other courts are impressed with the tax and job gain and uphold the rezoning. *Rando v. Town of North Attleborough*, 692 N.E.2d 544 (Mass. App. 1998).

4. *Rezoning of large tracts.* The courts usually acknowledge that the size of a rezoned tract is an important factor in spot zoning cases, but they caution that it is not determinative. With this comment in mind, consider the following cases:

(a) *Chrobuck v. Snohomish County*, 480 P.2d 489 (Wash. 1971). The county rezoned 635 acres out of a 7680-acre tract of land located in a prime residential and recreational area to allow the construction of an oil refinery. The court invalidated the rezoning. The county based the rezoning on the potential tax revenue of the project and the reluctance of the oil refinery company to consider another site. The planning department's report recommended against the rezoning and noted that the refinery site was in the "wrong place." It was located "in the midst of an outstanding residential area without adequate road or rail access and could possibly have an effect on water and land resources." But see *Save Our Rural Env't v. Snohomish County*, 662 P.2d 816 (Wash. 1983) (upholding business park rezoning partly because it would broaden the industrial base of the region and produce energy and travel savings for employees).

(b) *Little v. Winborn*, 518 N.W.2d 384 (Iowa 1994). The court invalidated a rezoning of 223 acres from an A-1 to an A-2 agricultural district to permit the construction of two uninhabited structures and a shooting club. The tract was surrounded by agricultural land, and there was no reason for the rezoning other than the benefit to the club members. The A-1 district was adopted to prevent the intrusion of non-agricultural uses in agricultural areas, while the A-2 zone was a holding zone adopted as a transition to urban development.

(c) *Save Our Forest Action Coalition, Inc. v. City of Kingston*, 675 N.Y.S.2d 451 (App. Div. 1998). The court upheld a rezoning of 107 acres in a residential district to industrial use. "[T]he primary motivation for the zoning amendment was to support local economic development through retention of the City's largest employer and to reap associated economic and tax benefits in connection with the development of a business park." The court also noted the zoning was adopted after an extensive review that considered the impact on adjoining residential areas, consistency with existing zoning plans, alternative sites and environmental concerns. Why didn't the city just carry out a comprehensive rezoning for industrial uses? See also *Willott v. Village of Beachwood*, 197 N.E.2d 201 (Ohio 1964) (court applied fairly debatable rule to uphold rezoning of 80-acre tract in residential area for a shopping center, even though objectors claimed no change in conditions, "drastic depreciation" in the value of their homes, and dangers from traffic, noise and other nuisances).

(d) *Greater Yellowstone Coalition, Inc. v. Board of County Comm'rs*, 25 P.3d 168 (Mont. 2001). A property owner was granted a rezoning of a 323-acre parcel from a low density residential district permitting 323 single family homes, to a Planned Unit Development zone, allowing a variety of residential and commercial uses. The parcel was part of a larger, 13,280 acre area planned by the county as the Hebgen Lake Zoning District, and separated from Yellowstone National Park by a strip of U.S. Forest Service land. After applying an accepted three-part test for spot zoning (comparison with prevailing use in the area; size of the area or number of owners benefited; benefit to the public/accordance with a comprehensive plan), the court reversed the county rezoning. The PUD benefited only one owner, did not benefit the public or the significant wildlife in the area, and conflicted with the plan, which designated other areas for commercial development.

5. *Purpose and need.* In some cases in which a rezoning from single-family to multi-family use has been granted, the courts rely on a need for multi-family housing to justify the rezoning. See *Lee v. District of Columbia Zoning Comm'n*, 411 A.2d 635 (D.C. 1980), holding that rezonings of this kind are "not disturbed . . . when a need for housing exists and injury to the land is minimal." Accord *City of Pharr v. Tippitt*, 616 S.W.2d 173 (Tex. 1981), holding that evidence of a need for multi-family housing was "evidence that rezoning would benefit and promote the general welfare of the community." Is this view consistent with the definition of spot zoning in Note 1 *supra*?

6. *The change-mistake rule.* The courts in spot zoning cases often give weight to whether a change in conditions has occurred that justifies the rezoning. See *Pierrepont v. Zoning Comm'n*, 226 A.2d 659 (Conn. 1967) (rezoning for apartments). Compare *Zoning Comm'n v. New Canaan Bldg. Co.*, 148 A.2d 330 (Conn. 1959), invalidating a downzoning from multi-family to single-family use. The court noted that no change in conditions had occurred that justified the rezoning and that "[t]hose who buy property in a zoned district have the right to expect that the classification made in the ordinance will not be changed unless a change is required for public good."

Maryland has gone one step farther. In that state, a rezoning must be justified either by an original mistake in the zoning ordinance or by a change in conditions. See *Wakefield v. Kraft*, 96 A.2d 27 (Md. 1953). The rule does not apply to a comprehensive rezoning. A few states have adopted the change-mistake rule, e.g., *Lewis v. City of Jackson*, 184 So. 2d 384 (Miss. 1966), but other states have expressly rejected it. See *King's Mill Homeowners Ass'n v. City of Westminster*, 557 P.2d 1186 (Colo. 1976); *Palermo Land Co. v. Planning Comm'n*, 561 So. 2d 482 (La. 1990) (citing to states that reject the rule). Maryland has codified the rule. Md. Ann. Code art. 66B, § 4.05.

Unless there was a mistake in the original zoning ordinance, the change-mistake rule requires the court to find some change in conditions in the surrounding area that justifies the zoning amendment. This determination requires the courts to make planning judgments. In apartment zoning cases, for example, the Maryland courts have had to determine whether apartments are appropriate as buffer zones between residential and nonresidential districts, and whether a new highway or improved public facilities are changes in conditions that justify an apartment rezoning. For a review of the Maryland apartment rezoning change-mistake cases, see D. Mandelker, The Zoning Dilemma 87-105 (1971). Is the change-mistake rule based on a misunderstanding of the planning process or is it desirable because it encourages municipalities to do comprehensive rezoning? Note that in Washington, the change-mistake rule does not apply when rezoning implements the comprehensive plan. See *Bjarnson v. Kitsap County*, 899 P.2d 1290 (Wash. App. 1995). Are there cases where piecemeal change in the zoning ordinance is justified?

7. *Sources.* For discussion of the zoning amendment, see Burke, *The Change-Mistake Rule and Zoning in Maryland*, 26 Am. U. L. Rev. 631 (1976); Reynolds, *"Spot Zoning"-A Spot That Could Be Removed from the Law*, 48 Wash. U. J. Urb. & Contemp. L. 117 (1995).

[3.] Quasi-Judicial Versus Legislative Rezoning

Some observers of the zoning process believe it is an error to characterize the rezoning decision as legislative because it does not grant enough protection to due process concerns and reduces the ability of the courts to review the process or substance of the zoning hearing. One way to deal with this problem is to recharacterize the zoning process as quasi-judicial, which both changes the procedures at the local level and allows courts to modify the usual standards of judicial review. The Florida case that follows is an example of this approach:

BOARD OF COUNTY COMMISSIONERS OF BREVARD COUNTY v. SNYDER

627 So. 2d 469 (Fla. 1993)

GRIMES, J.:

. . . Jack and Gail Snyder owned a one-half acre parcel of property on Merritt Island in the unincorporated area of Brevard County. The property is zoned GU (general use) which allows construction of a single-family residence. The Snyders filed an application to rezone their property to the RU-2-15 zoning classification which allows the construction of fifteen units per acre. The area is designated for residential use under the 1988 Brevard County Comprehensive Plan Future Land Use Map. Twenty-nine zoning classifications are considered potentially consistent with this land use designation, including both the GU and the RU-2-15 classifications.

After the application for rezoning was filed, the Brevard County Planning and Zoning staff reviewed the application and completed the county's standard "rezoning review worksheet." The worksheet indicated that the proposed multifamily use of the Snyders' property was consistent with all aspects of the comprehensive plan except for the fact that it was located in the one-hundred-year flood plain in which a maximum of only two units per acre was permitted. For this reason, the staff recommended that the request be denied.

At the planning and zoning board meeting, the county planning and zoning director indicated that when the property was developed the land elevation would be raised to the point where the one-hundred-year-flood plain restriction would no longer be applicable. Thus, the director stated that the staff no longer opposed the application. The planning and zoning board voted to approve the Snyders' rezoning request.

When the matter came before the board of county commissioners, Snyder stated that he intended to build only five or six units on the property. However, a number of citizens spoke in opposition to the rezoning request. Their primary concern was the increase in traffic which would be caused by the development. Ultimately, the commission voted to deny the rezoning request without stating a reason for the denial.

The Snyders filed a petition for certiorari in the circuit court. Three circuit judges, sitting *en banc*, reviewed the petition and denied it by a two-to-one decision. The Snyders then filed a petition for certiorari in the Fifth District Court of Appeal.

The district court of appeal acknowledged that zoning decisions have traditionally been considered legislative in nature. Therefore, courts were required to uphold them if they could be justified as being "fairly debatable." Drawing heavily on *Fasano v. Board of County Commissioners*, 507 P.2d 23 (Or. 1973), however, the court concluded that, unlike initial zoning enactments and comprehensive rezonings or rezonings affecting a large portion of the public, a rezoning action which entails the application of a general rule or policy to specific individuals, interests, or activities is quasi-judicial in nature. Under the latter circumstances, the court reasoned that a stricter standard of judicial review of the rezoning decision was required. The court went on to hold: . . .

[The court below held "that the governmental agency (by whatever name it may be characterized) applying legislated land use restrictions to particular parcels of privately owned lands, must state reasons for action that denies the owner the use of his land and must make findings of fact and a record of its proceedings, sufficient for judicial review." The court also held the landowner has the burden to show that his proposal "complies with the reasonable procedural requirements of the ordinance and that the use sought is consistent with the applicable comprehensive zoning plan." At this point "the landowner is presumptively entitled to use his property in the manner he seeks unless the opposing governmental agency asserts and proves by clear and convincing evidence that a specifically stated public necessity requires a specified, more restrictive, use." If this showing is made, the landowner has the burden to show that this more restrictive use is a taking of his property.]

Applying these principles to the facts of the case, the court found (1) that the Snyders' petition for rezoning was consistent with the comprehensive plan; (2) that there was no assertion or evidence that a more restrictive zoning classification was necessary to protect the health, safety, morals, or welfare of the general public; and (3) that the denial of the requested zoning classification without reasons supported by facts was, as a matter of law, arbitrary and unreasonable. The court granted the petition for certiorari. . . .

Historically, local governments have exercised the zoning power pursuant to a broad delegation of state legislative power subject only to constitutional limitations. Both federal and state courts adopted a highly deferential standard of judicial review early in the history of local zoning. In *Village of Euclid v. Ambler Realty Co.*, 272 U.S. 365 (1926), the United States Supreme Court held that "if the validity of the legislative classification for zoning purposes be fairly debatable, the legislative judgment must be allowed to control." 272 U.S. at 388. This Court expressly adopted the fairly debatable principle in *City of Miami Beach v. Ocean & Inland Co.*, 3 So. 2d 364 (1941).

Inhibited only by the loose judicial scrutiny afforded by the fairly debatable rule, local zoning systems developed in a markedly inconsistent manner. Many land use experts and practitioners have been critical of the local zoning system. Richard Babcock deplored the effect of "neighborhoodism" and rank political influence on the local decisionmaking process. Richard F. Babcock, *The Zoning Game* (1966). Mandelker and Tarlock recently stated that "zoning decisions are too often ad hoc, sloppy and self-serving decisions with well-defined adverse consequences without off-setting benefits." Daniel R. Mandelker and A. Dan Tarlock, *Shifting the Presumption of Constitutionality in Land-Use Law*, 24 Urb. Law. 1, 2 (1992).

Professor Charles Haar, a leading proponent of zoning reform, was an early advocate of requiring that local land use regulation be consistent with a legally binding comprehensive plan which would serve long range goals, counteract local pressures for preferential treatment, and provide courts with a meaningful standard of review. Charles M. Haar, *"In Accordance With A Comprehensive Plan,"* 68 Harv. L. Rev. 1154 (1955). In 1975, the American Law Institute adopted the Model Land Development Code, which provided for procedural and planning reforms at the local level and increased state participation in land use decisionmaking for developments of regional impact and areas of critical state concern.

Reacting to the increasing calls for reform, numerous states have adopted legislation to change the local land use decisionmaking process. As one of the leaders of this national reform, Florida adopted the Local Government Comprehensive Planning Act of 1975. Ch. 75-257, Laws of Fla. This law was substantially strengthened in 1985 by the Growth Management Act. Ch. 85-55, Laws of Fla.

Pursuant to the Growth Management Act, each county and municipality is required to prepare a comprehensive plan for approval by the Department of Community Affairs. The adopted local plan must include "principles, guidelines, and standards for the orderly and balanced future economic, social, physical, environmental, and fiscal development" of the local government's jurisdictional area. § 163.3177(1), Fla. Stat. (1991). At the minimum, the local plan must include elements covering future land use; capital improvements generally; sanitary sewer, solid waste, drainage, potable water, and natural ground water aquifer protection specifically; conservation; recreation and open space; housing; traffic circulation; intergovernmental coordination; coastal management (for local government in the coastal zone); and mass transit (for local jurisdictions with 50,000 or more people). *Id.* at § 163.3177(6).

Of special relevance to local rezoning actions, the future land use plan element of the local plan must contain both a future land use map and goals, policies, and measurable objectives to guide future land use decisions. This plan element must designate the "proposed future general distribution, location, and extent of the uses of land" for various purposes. *Id.* at § 163.3177(6)(a). It must include standards to be utilized in the control and distribution of densities and intensities of development. In addition, the future land use plan must be based on adequate data and analysis concerning the local jurisdiction, including the projected population, the amount of land needed to accommodate the estimated population, the availability of public services and facilities, and the character of undeveloped land. *Id.* at § 163.3177(6)(a).

The local plan must be implemented through the adoption of land development regulations that are consistent with the plan. *Id.* at § 163.3202. In addition, all development, both public and private, and all development orders approved by local governments must be consistent with the adopted local plan. *Id.* at § 163.3194(1)(a). Section 163.3194(3), Florida Statutes (1991), explains consistency as follows:

> (a) A development order or land development regulation shall be consistent with the comprehensive plan if the land uses, densities or intensities, and other aspects of development permitted by such order or regulation are compatible with and further the objectives, policies, land uses, and densities or intensities in the comprehensive plan and if it meets all other criteria enumerated by the local government. . . .

Because [under the statute] an order granting or denying rezoning constitutes a development order and development orders must be consistent with the comprehensive plan, it is clear that orders on rezoning applications must be consistent with the comprehensive plan.

The first issue we must decide is whether the Board's action on Snyder's rezoning application was legislative or quasi-judicial. A board's legislative action is subject to attack in circuit court. However, in deference to the policy-making function of a board when acting in a legislative capacity, its actions will be sustained as long as they are fairly debatable. On the other hand, the rulings of a board acting in its quasi-judicial capacity are subject to review by certiorari and will be upheld only if they are supported by substantial competent evidence.

Enactments of original zoning ordinances have always been considered legislative. . . .

It is the character of the hearing that determines whether or not board action is legislative or quasi-judicial. Generally speaking, legislative action results in the formulation of a general rule of policy, whereas judicial action results in the application of a general rule of policy. In *West Flagler Amusement Co. v. State Racing Commission*, 165 So. 64, 65 (1935), we explained:

> A judicial or quasi-judicial act determines the rules of law applicable, and the rights affected by them, in relation to past transactions. On the other hand, a quasi-legislative

> or administrative order prescribes what the rule or requirement of administratively determined duty shall be with respect to transactions to be executed in the future, in order that same shall be considered lawful. But even so, quasi-legislative and quasi-executive orders, after they have already been entered, may have a quasi-judicial attribute if capable of being arrived at and provided by law to be declared by the administrative agency only after express statutory notice, hearing and consideration of evidence to be adduced as a basis for the making thereof.

Applying this criterion, it is evident that comprehensive rezonings affecting a large portion of the public are legislative in nature. However, we agree with the court below when it said:

> Rezoning actions which have an impact on a limited number of persons or property owners, on identifiable parties and interests, where the decision is contingent on a fact or facts arrived at from distinct alternatives presented at a hearing, and where the decision can be functionally viewed as policy application, rather than policy setting, are in the nature of . . . quasi-judicial action . . . .

Therefore, the board's action on Snyder's application was in the nature of a quasi-judicial proceeding and properly reviewable by petition for certiorari.

We also agree with the court below that the review is subject to strict scrutiny. In practical effect, the review by strict scrutiny in zoning cases appears to be the same as that given in the review of other quasi-judicial decisions. See *Lee County v. Sunbelt Equities, II, Ltd. Partnership*, 619 So. 2d 996 (Fla. 2d DCA 1993) (The term "strict scrutiny" arises from the necessity of strict compliance with comprehensive plan.). This term as used in the review of land use decisions must be distinguished from the type of strict scrutiny review afforded in some constitutional cases.

At this point, we depart from the rationale of the court below. In the first place, the opinion overlooks the premise that the comprehensive plan is intended to provide for the future use of land, which contemplates a gradual and ordered growth. See *City of Jacksonville Beach*, 461 So. 2d at 163, in which the following statement from *Marracci v. City of Scappoose*, 552 P.2d 552, 553 (Or. Ct. App. 1976), was approved:

> [A] comprehensive plan only establishes a long-range maximum limit on the possible intensity of land use; a plan does not simultaneously establish an immediate minimum limit on the possible intensity of land use. The present use of land may, by zoning ordinance, continue to be more limited than the future use contemplated by the comprehensive plan.

Even where a denial of a zoning application would be inconsistent with the plan, the local government should have the discretion to decide that the maximum development density should not be allowed provided the governmental body approves some development that is consistent with the plan and the government's decision is supported by substantial, competent evidence.

Further, we cannot accept the proposition that once the landowner demonstrates that the proposed use is consistent with the comprehensive plan, he is presumptively entitled to this use unless the opposing governmental agency proves by clear and convincing evidence that specifically stated public necessity requires a more restricted use. We do not believe that a property owner is necessarily entitled to relief by proving consistency when the board action is also consistent with the plan. . . .

This raises a question of whether the Growth Management Act provides any comfort to the landowner when the denial of the rezoning request is consistent with the comprehensive plan. It could be argued that the only recourse is to pursue the traditional remedy of attempting to prove that the denial of the application was arbitrary, discriminatory, or unreasonable. Yet, the fact that a proposed use is consistent with the plan means that the planners contemplated that that use would be acceptable at some point in the future. We do not believe the Growth Management Act was intended to preclude development but only to insure that it proceed in an orderly manner.

Upon consideration, we hold that a landowner seeking to rezone property has the burden of proving that the proposal is consistent with the comprehensive plan and complies with all procedural requirements of the zoning ordinance. At this point, the burden shifts to the governmental board to demonstrate that maintaining the existing zoning classification with respect to the property accomplishes a legitimate public purpose. In effect, the landowners' traditional remedies will be subsumed within this rule, and the board will now have the burden of showing that the refusal to rezone the property is not arbitrary, discriminatory, or unreasonable. If the board carries its burden, the application should be denied.

While they may be useful, the board will not be required to make findings of fact. However, in order to sustain the board's action, upon review by certiorari in the circuit court it must be shown that there was competent substantial evidence presented to the board to support its ruling. . . .

[The court quashed the decision below but allowed the landowners an opportunity to file a new application for rezoning.]

BARKETT, C.J., and OVERTON, MCDONALD, KOGAN and HARDING, J.J., concur. SHAW, J., dissents.

NOTES AND QUESTIONS

1. *Snyder* made several major changes in the rules governing judicial review of the zoning process. The presumption of constitutionality is reversed, the burden of proof is shifted to the municipality, and the plan becomes the standard under which the zoning amendment is judged. Of course, a court could adopt the quasi-judicial approach to zoning amendments, yet at the same time not require the amendment to be judged against the zoning ordinance or some other standard. See *Woodland Hills Conserv., Inc. v. City of Jackson*, 443 So. 2d 1173 (Miss. 1983) (change-mistake and public need tests applied in that state make rezoning quasi-judicial). The point is that there must be a standard or policy that communities can apply in the zoning process.

You should note the influence of the mandatory planning requirement on the court's decision. This subject is taken up in detail in Section H, *infra*. In a departure from usual practice, Florida (as the court notes) characterizes decisions on land use applications as "development orders." This is consistent with administrative practice in state agencies.

2. *Why should zoning be quasi-judicial?* The *Fasano* case, which is discussed in *Snyder*, adopted this view because it believed the zoning process was controlled by developers who pressured municipalities into rezonings that impaired the comprehensive plan. Characterizing the zoning process as quasi-judicial and reversing the presumption of constitutionality is a way to control this problem. Richard Babcock described the problem:

> The roots of this judicial restlessness lie in the mess of local zoning administration. In those zoning jurisdictions where the final local zoning decisions are legislative, . . . the courts are torn between their traditional judicial reluctance to explore the motives of legislators and their suspicion that, as one appellate judge put it, "there's a lot of hanky-panky we suspect but cannot find in the record." [R. Babcock, The Zoning Game 104 (1966).]

Yet, as one report pointed out:

> The private citizen probably stands to gain the most from the quasi-judicial approach. As a party, a citizen has the right of full participation in the hearing. . . . Well armed with the facts, the citizen can be quite effective against the most sophisticated developer. [Housing for All Under Law 272 (Report of the American Bar Ass'n Advisory Comm'n on Housing & Urban Growth, R. Fishman ed., 1978).]

The article by Professors Mandelker and Tarlock, which is quoted in the *Snyder* decision, builds a case for presumption-shifting based in part on developer capture of the local government zoning process.

3. *Other reasons for adopting the quasi-judicial view.* The Idaho Supreme Court provided a different reason in *Cooper v. Board of County Comm'rs*, 614 P.2d 947 (Idaho 1980):

> The great deference given true legislative action stems from its high visibility and widely felt impact, on the theory that the appropriate remedy can be had at the polls. . . . This rationale is inapposite when applied to a local zoning body's decision as to the fate of an individual's application for rezon[ing]. Most voters are unaware or unconcerned that fair dealing and consistent treatment have been sacrificed. [*Id.* at 950.]

The Idaho court based its rationale in part on the following description of the political process:

> . . . [P]olitical judgments are a product of informal negotiation, conciliation, and compromise with a variety of end goals in mind which may or may not be canonized in something described, for that matter, as a "plan" or "regulation." Such a process is admirably suited to broadly-based decisions in which the general feeling of the populace is deciphered. When such a process determines what a particular owner may or may not do, whether an adjoining owner's expectation will be compromised, whether a community will accommodate legitimate housing needs, we may question its essential fairness. The combination of broad authority exercised on an ad hoc basis by local laymen and political officials has been described by some as chaotic [citing Smith, *Judicial Review of Rezoning Discretion: Some Suggestions for Idaho*, 14 Idaho L. Rev. 591, 599 (1978)].

What kind of "remedy at the polls" is the court talking about? Voting out the council members? A referendum on a zoning ordinance? On the use of referenda in zoning, see section I, *infra*. Note the trade-off here. Only local legislative actions are subject to referendum, so that a holding that a rezoning is quasi-judicial means that a referendum on the rezoning is not available. But see *Margolis v. District Court*, 638 P.2d 297 (Colo. 1981) (rezoning held quasi-judicial for purposes of judicial review but legislative for purposes of referendum). Is this a good compromise?

Other states have adopted the quasi-judicial view. See, e.g., *Tate v. Miles*, 503 A.2d 187 (Del. 1986); *Golden v. City of Overland Park*, 584 P.2d 130 (Kan. 1978); *Fleming v. City of Tacoma*, 502 P.2d 327, 331 (Wash. 1972) (rezonings without areawide significance are quasi-judicial).

4. *Is every rezoning quasi-judicial?* As the *Snyder* case held, a rezoning is quasi-judicial only when the local governing body *applies* policy through the rezoning ordinance. Would a rezoning covering a substantial tract of land be legislative because the area is so large that the rezoning amounts to a change in land use policy for the municipality?

The Oregon Supreme Court considered this question in *Neuberger v. City of Portland*, 603 P.2d 771 (Or. 1979). The city rezoned a 601-acre parcel of land for a development of more than 1000 single-family homes at a more intensive density. The court indicated when and why a land use decision would be held quasi-judicial:

> [O]ur land use decisions indicate that when a particular action by a local government is directed at a relatively small number of persons, and when that action also involves the application of existing policy to a specific factual setting, the requirement of quasi-judicial procedures has been implied. [*Id.* at 775.]

The court stated that quasi-judicial procedures are necessary when relatively few individuals are involved to provide "the safeguards of fair and open procedures." When pre-existing criteria are applied, quasi-judicial procedures are necessary "in order to assure that factual determinations will be made correctly."

The court then considered whether the rezoning was a "free choice among competing policies" or the "application of existing policy." Both types of decisionmaking were present. The rezoning required a policy decision because the development was so large that it would have a major impact on municipal services and other local government jurisdictions. Yet the rezoning also was quasi-judicial because it required the application of statutory rezoning criteria and the state planning goals. The court concluded that the action was quasi-judicial, but that the municipality had met its burden; the rezoning was upheld. Compare *Albuquerque Commons P'ship v. City Council of City of Albuquerque*, 184 P.3d 411 (N.M. 2008) (adoption of uptown sector plan which downzoned small portion of uptown sector is quasi-judicial and must be justified by mistake or change in surrounding community).

Is the amendment of a comprehensive plan quasi-judicial? In *Martin County v. Yusem*, 690 So. 2d 1288 (Fla. 1997), the Florida Supreme Court reaffirmed *Snyder* as applied to the type of zoning at issue in that case, but held that amendments to the comprehensive plan are legislative. It held that an amendment to the plan "required the County to engage in policy reformulation of its comprehensive plan and to determine whether it now desired to retreat from the policies embodied in its future land use map for the orderly development of the County's future growth." What about an amendment to a comprehensive plan that only affects a small tract? That, too is legislative, according to the Florida court in *Coastal Development v. City of Jacksonville Beach*, 788 So. 2d 204 (2001), in part so that the courts would have a "bright line" rule to follow. See also *Stuart v. Board of County Comm'rs*, 699 P.2d 978 (Colo. App. 1985) (plan amendment held legislative when the development and its impact authorized by the plan was not known).

5. *The quasi-judicial view rejected.* Several courts refused to follow *Fasano*'s holding that a rezoning map amendment is quasi-judicial. See, e.g., *Wait v. City of Scottsdale*, 618 P.2d 601 (Ariz. 1980); *Hall Paving Co. v. Hall County*, 226 S.E.2d 728 (Ga. 1976); *State v. City of Rochester*, 268 N.W.2d 885 (Minn. 1978). The most elaborate rejection of *Fasano* came in *Arnel*

Dev. Co. v. City of Costa Mesa, 620 P.2d 565 (Cal. 1980), although the court did not expressly mention *Fasano.* Voters had adopted an initiative ordinance downzoning land on which a developer planned to build a moderate-income housing development that was allowable under the zoning ordinance before the initiative was passed. The California court said in part:

> The factual setting of the present case illustrates the problems courts will face if we abandoned past precedent and attempted to devise a new test distinguishing legislative and adjudicative decisions. The Court of Appeal, for example, found here that the instant initiative was an adjudicative act because it rezoned a "relatively small" parcel of land. It is not, however, self-evident that 68 acres is a "relatively small" parcel; some cities have entire zoning classifications which comprise less than 68 acres. The size of the parcel, moreover, has very little relationship to the theoretical basis of the Court of Appeal holding — the distinction between the making of land-use policy, a legislative act, and the asserted adjudicatory act of applying established policy. The rezoning of a "relatively small" parcel, especially when done by initiative, may well signify a fundamental change in city land-use policy.
>
> Plaintiffs alternatively urge that the present initiative is adjudicatory because it assertedly affects only three landowners. But this is a very myopic view of the matter; the proposed construction of housing for thousands of people affects the prospective tenants, the housing market, the residents living nearby, and the future character of the community. The number of landowners whose property is actually rezoned is as unsuitable a test as the size of the property rezoned. Yet without some test which distinguishes legislative from adjudicative acts with clarity and reasonable certainty, municipal governments and voters will lack adequate guidance in enacting and evaluating land-use decisions.
>
> In summary, past California land-use cases have established generic classifications, viewing zoning ordinances as legislative and other decisions, such as variances and subdivision map approvals, as adjudicative. This method of classifying land-use decisions enjoys the obvious advantage of economy; the municipality, the proponents of a proposed measure, and the opponents of the measure can readily determine if notice, hearings, and findings are required, what form of judicial review is appropriate, and whether the measure can be enacted by initiative or overturned by referendum. [*Id.* at 572.]

The court also held that adopting the quasi-judicial view was not necessary to protect the public interest in "orderly land use planning," noting that California requires consistency with the land use plan and that the California court adopted a "regional general welfare" rule that limits exclusionary zoning. Absent these two safeguards, would you agree with the court's conclusions?

6. *Sources.* For discussion of the Florida cases and problems of quasi-judicial decision making in zoning, see Lincoln, *Executive Decisionmaking by Local Legislatures in Florida: Justice, Judicial Review and the Need for Legislative Reform*, 25 Stetson L. Rev. 627 (1996); Sullivan & Kressel, *Twenty Years After: Renewed Significance of the Comprehensive Plan Requirements*, 9 Urb. L. Ann. 33 (1975); Note, *Trying to Fit an Elephant in a Volkswagen: Six Years of the Snyder Decision in Florida Land Use Law*, 52 Fla. L. Rev. 217 (2000).

A NOTE ON PROCEDURAL DUE PROCESS IN LAND USE DECISIONS

Due process requirements under state law. The procedural responsibilities of zoning agencies are not well-developed in state law. The Standard Zoning Act and most state acts provide rudimentary procedural requirements, such as requirements for notice and a hearing before legislative and administrative bodies, but this is usually about all. What state statutory requirements are provided, however, must be followed closely or the result may be to nullify the zoning decision. Failure to give adequate notice can be fatal. See, e.g., *American Oil Corp. v. City of Chicago*, 331 N.E.2d 67 (Ill. App. 1975). A failure to provide an opportunity for a hearing is also fatal, e.g., *Bowen v. Story County Bd. of Supervisors*, 209 N.W.2d 569 (Iowa 1973). There generally are no requirements for the adequacy of a hearing in states that classify a rezoning as legislative, but see *Pendley v. Lake Harbin Civic Ass'n*, 198 S.E.2d 503 (Ga. 1973) (post-midnight hearing inadequate). State statutes, again, must be followed, as for example when the statute requires that a hearing take place at a certain time. See, e.g., Fla. Stat. Ann. § 166.041(3)(c)2.a, requiring certain zoning map applications to be heard after 5 p.m. on a weekday. Generally, state statutes will provide more specific and greater procedural protection than any protection afforded under federal constitutional law. The rights are not unlimited, however, and the extent of the process that must be afforded will depend on the totality of the circumstances. See, e.g., *Crispin v. Town of Scarborough*, 736 A.2d 241 (Me. 1999) (where statute required "adequate opportunity to be heard in the preparation of a zoning ordinance," limitation of initial comments to three minutes was reasonable in light of number of people at hearing, an opportunity to speak a second time at the end of initial comments, acceptance by the council of prior written submissions, and participation by attorney representing the speakers).

When a hearing is administrative or quasi-judicial, courts may require that the local government grant the parties in the proceeding (the applicant and objectors) the right to present evidence, the right to cross-examine witnesses, the right to respond to written submissions, the right to counsel and a decision on the record with stated reasons. States vary considerably however, in regard to how "judicial" the proceedings may be. Compare *Petersen v. Chicago Plan. Comm.*, 707 N. E.2d 150 (Ill. App 1998) (cross-examination not required), with *Coral Reef Nurseries, Inc. v. Babcock Co.*, 410 So. 2d 648 (Fla. App 1982) (right to cross-examination). Some states have developed detailed procedural safeguards for quasi-judicial and administrative proceedings. See, e.g., Or. Rev. Stat. § 197.763; Fla. Stat. Ann. § 163.3215(4) (local government which adopts minimum specified procedures under special master will have judicial challenge to decision reviewed by writ of certiorari).

Complainants may find it difficult to sustain claims of procedural violations. Litigants may have to defeat the presumption that local authorities performed their duties properly, prove that they were prejudiced by the authorities' failure to follow certain processes, *White v. Town of Hollis*, 589 A.2d 46 (Me. 1991), and preserve their rights by objecting to procedural violations at the hearing level.

Courts will not usually allow the taking of ex parte evidence by an administrative board, *Rodine v. Zoning Bd. of Adjustment*, 434 N.W.2d 124 (Iowa 1988). See also *Blaker v. Planning & Zoning Comm'n*, 562 A.2d 1093 (Conn. 1989) (rezoning and special permit; receipt of ex parte evidence shifts burden of proof); *Jennings v. Dade County*, 589 So. 2d 1337 (Fla. App. 1995) (ex parte communication creates presumption of bias). Site visits can be a problem; adequate notice of the meeting must be provided. *Nazarko v. Conservation Comm'n*, 717 A.2d

853 (Conn. App. 1998) (notice inadequate). See Comment, *Ex Parte Communications in Local Land Use Decisions*, 15 B.C. Envtl. Aff. L. Rev. 181 (1987).

As noted earlier, neighborhood opposition is often a factor in the denial of applications for rezonings, conditional uses and the like. Courts often set aside a zoning decision if they believe that neighborhood opposition tainted the zoning action with an improper motive or purpose. *Chanhassen Estates Residents Ass'n v. City of Chanhassen*, 342 N.W.2d 335 (Minn. 1984), is a leading case. See Ellis, *Neighborhood Opposition and the Permissible Purposes of Zoning*, 7 J. Land Use & Envtl. L. 275 (1992).

Open meetings. All states have open meeting laws, which usually apply to planning commissions and boards of adjustment. A closed meeting can void a zoning decision if one is required. *Town of Palm Beach v. Gradison*, 296 So. 2d 473 (Fla. 1974) (comprehensive rezoning void because citizens advisory committee appointed by a town board to assist with ordinance held closed meetings); *Alderman v. County of Antelope*, 653 N.W.2d 1 (Neb. App. 2002) (evidence from meeting held in violation of open meetings law cannot be considered). Exchange of emails among council members prior to a final hearing was found to be a violation of the state open meetings act in *Johnston v. Metro. Gov't of Nashville & Davidson County*, 2009 Tenn. App. LEXIS 832 (Dec. 10, 2009), but the court found that the full discussion at the subsequent open meeting made it unnecessary to void the decision. All of the meeting must be open. A board cannot hold an evidentiary hearing and then go into closed session to make a decision. *Beck v. Crisp County Zoning Bd. of Appeals*, 472 S.E.2d 558 (Ga. App. 1996). See Note, *The Changing Weather Forecast: Government in the Sunshine in the 1990s — An Analysis of State Sunshine Laws*, 71 Wash. U. L.Q. 1165 (1993).

Federal law. The federal law on procedural due process requirements is better developed and at the same time more flexible. *Cloutier v. Town of Epping*, 714 F.2d 1184 (1st Cir. 1983), is an example of a federal decision in which procedural due process problems were raised. There, the developers of a mobile home park argued successfully in state court that the town had illegally revoked a sewer permit, but the federal court refused to find a federal due process violation because the local informal proceedings, coupled with state court proceedings were sufficient. Like the state courts, the federal courts apply procedural due process requirements only to administrative actions, but beyond that, the federal law varies:

> Procedural due process requirements apply only to an entitlement to a property interest, not to an expectancy. A landowner has an entitlement:
>
> a. if he has a vested right in a particular use of his land; or
>
> b. if his land use is permitted at the time he makes an application for a permit or requests development approval, and the land use agency does not have the discretion to deny the permit or request for approval. . . .
>
> The federal courts apply a balancing test [based on *Mathews v. Eldridge*, 424 U.S. 319 (1976),] to administrative decision-making to determine whether an administrative decision violates procedural due process. . . . [T]hey consider:
>
> a. the private interest affected by the official action;
>
> b. the risk of an erroneous deprivation of such an interest through the procedures used [and]

c. the government's interest, including the function involved and [burdens] that the additional or substitute procedures require. [Land Use and the Constitution 40–41, 43 (B. Blaesser & A. Weinstein eds., 1989).]

Most of the federal cases have not found procedural due process violations, as in *Cloutier v. Town of Epping, supra.* As stated in *Coniston Corp. v. Hoffman Estates*, 844 F.2d 461, 468 (7th Cir. 1988), "[t]he Constitution does not require legislatures to use adjudicative-type procedures, to give reasons for their enactments, or to act 'reasonably' in the sense in which courts are required to do; as already noted, legislatures can base their actions on considerations — such as the desire of a special-interest group for redistributive legislation in its favor — that would be thought improper in judicial decision-making." But see *Herrington v. County of Sonoma*, 834 F.2d 1488 (9th Cir. 1987), upholding jury determination that notice and hearing for a subdivision denial were inadequate. Failure to follow state statutory procedures is not in itself generally a federal due process violation. See, e.g., *Chongris v. Board of Appeals*, 811 F.2d 36 (1st Cir. 1987).

NOTES AND QUESTIONS

1. *An example.* Review the proceedings in the drive-in bank variance application in the hypothetical hearing, *supra.* Are there procedural due process violations under state law? Under federal law? Since under federal law there must be an entitlement in order to trigger procedural due process requirements, and since under state law most land use approvals are discretionary, will the application of federal procedural due process be limited? Which land use approval techniques are likely to create "entitlements" under federal law? See *Yale Auto Parts, Inc. v. Johnson*, 758 F.2d 54 (2d Cir. 1985) (junkyard permit discretionary).

The Supreme Court took a somewhat different view of distinguishing legislative from administrative actions in a case in which it held that legislative bodies were immune from suit under § 1983. In *Bogan v. Scott-Harris*, 523 U.S. 44 (1998), the Court held that whether an act is legislative turns not on the motive of the legislators, but on whether the act was "formally legislative" and within the "traditional sphere of legislative activity." In this case, an ordinance terminating an employee position was legislative because it was a "discretionary, policymaking decision" that could well have prospective effect.

2. *Bias and conflict of interest.* The law of bias and conflict of interest developed by the state courts also provides a control on decision making in the zoning process, but is generally applied only to administrative decisions. States have also adopted legislation on this problem that attempts to codify the common law rules. E.g., N.J. Stat. Ann. § 40:55D-23b. Board members are disqualified for bias when they make outspoken public statements on matters they subsequently hear, *Lage v. Zoning Bd. of Appeals*, 172 A.2d 911 (Conn. 1961), or make statements at the hearing indicating that they have prejudged the matter before them, e.g., *Barbara Realty Co. v. Zoning Bd. of Cranston*, 128 A.2d 342 (1957). But see *Lane Construction Corp. v. Town of Washington*, 942 A.2d 1202 (Me. 2008) (no bias despite chairman's public statements). Prior involvement in trying to resolve a conflict among parties can indicate bias when the person becomes a decision maker. See *Armstrong v. Turner County Bd. of Adjustment*, 772 N.W.2d 643 (S.D. 2009). Campaign statements are an exception. *City of Farmers Branch v. Hawnco, Inc.*, 435 S.W.2d 288 (Tex. Civ. App. 1968). Disclosure may also cure a presumption of bias arising from ex parte contacts. *Idaho Historic Preservation Council v. City Council*, 8 P.3d 646 (Idaho 2000); Fla. Stat. Ann. § 286.0115 (procedures to reverse presumption of bias resulting from ex parte contacts).

Pecuniary interest based on the ownership of property is the typical conflict of interest case. See *Griswold v. City of Homer*, 925 P.2d 1015 (Alaska 1996), where the court found a conflict of interest when a council member owned one of 13 lots in a central business district that was rezoned to allow auto sales. Compare *Copple v. City of Lincoln*, 274 N.W.2d 520 (Neb. 1979) (council member's vote for comprehensive plan designation distinguished from abstention on vote for rezoning for property he owned). Is ownership of property in the municipality enough to disqualify from voting on a plan amendment eliminating a proposed floating zone for mining? *Segalla v. Planning Bd.*, 611 N.Y.S.2d 287 (App. Div. 1994), held no, because everybody in the municipality is equally affected and any benefit from the rezoning is speculative. Location of the property is the more critical factor. See *Clark v. City of Hermosa Beach*, 56 Cal. Rptr. 2d 223 (Cal. App. 1996) (council member who lived one block away from a housing project he opposed was disqualified).

Close business or personal relationships can also create a conflict of interest. A board member was disqualified when his nephew was a member of the law firm that represented the applicant. *Kremer v. City of Plainfield*, 244 A.2d 335 (N.J. 1968). Accord *Dick v. Williams*, 452 S.E.2d 172 (Ga. App. 1994). A planning board member's personal relationship with an engineering firm principal that represented the board created a conflict of interest in *Randolph v. City of Brigantine Planning Bd.*, 963 A.2d 1224 (N.J. App. Div. 2009). Should the board member resign in this instance? What if a commissioner's wife was occasionally employed by an applicant who received a site plan approval which the commissioner opposed and voted against? The court found no problem in *Petrick v. Planning Bd.*, 671 A.2d 140 (N.J. App. Div. 1996), because the conflict was too remote and speculative. Past title work for an applicant disqualified the mayor from voting on a zoning and master plan in *Mountain Hill, L.L.C. v. Township Comm. of the Twp. of Middletown*, 958 A.2d 1 (N.J. Super. Ct. App. 2008). Was there bias or a conflict of interest in the hypothetical drive-in bank variance hearing?

An effective solution for the bias and conflict of interest problems is elusive. Individual residents of a community may own property, have well-defined views on land use issues, and relatives employed in a variety of occupations. Should they be disqualified from serving on zoning agencies, and if they serve, should they be disqualified when apparent conflict or bias emerges?

For discussion, see Baker, *Ethical Limits on Attorney Contact with Represented and Unrepresented Officials: The Example of Municipal Zoning Boards Making Site-Specific Land Use Decisions*, 31 Suffolk U. L. Rev. 349 (1997); Dyas, *Conflicts of Interest in Planning and Zoning Cases*, 17 J. Legal Prof. 219 (1993); Tarlock, *Challenging Biased Zoning Board Decisions*, 10 Zoning & Plan. L. Rep. 97 (1987); Vietzen, *Controlling Conflicts of Interest in Land Use Decisions*, 38 Land Use L. & Zoning Dig., No. 1, at 3 (1986).

3. *The hearing process.* Oregon legislation provides some useful insights on how the quasi-judicial procedural "revolution" affects the land use decision making process. Ore. Rev. Stat. § 197.763. Detailed requirements are included for giving notice. The notice must "explain the nature of the application and the proposed use or uses which could be authorized, [and] list the applicable criteria from the ordinance and the plan that apply to the application at issue." This limits the basis for the hearing.

All documents and evidence submitted by the applicant must be available to the public. "Any staff report used at the hearing shall be available at least seven days prior to the hearing." A statement must be made at the commencement of the hearing that lists the applicable substantive criteria and "states that failure to raise an issue accompanied by statements or evidence sufficient to afford the decision maker and the parties an opportunity to respond to the issue precludes appeal to the board based on that issue." The statute also provides for continuances. See also Sullivan & Richter, *Out of the Chaos: Towards a National System of Land-Use Procedures*, 34 Urb. Law. 449 (2002).

4. *The APA Model.* The Model Statute of the APA Growing Smart project recommends procedures for development permit hearings that include notice at least 20 days before the hearing, going beyond the typical notice to include information regarding the land development regulations and comprehensive plan policies that apply to the application, an explanation of the conduct of the hearing, documents that are available for inspection, and identification of other governmental units with jurisdiction of the project. Only one hearing is required. Before the hearing, the staff report and application materials on which the evidence will be based must be disclosed, and the officer presiding at the hearing has powers, like a judge, to compel discovery, issue subpoenas, compel witness attendance and production of relevant evidence under oath and subject to cross-examination. Ex parte contacts are regulated. The government is responsible for providing a verbatim recording of the hearing. There must be a decision following the record hearing that includes a written statement of the facts, the basis for the decision, and how it is "based on" the development regulations and the policies and other elements of the comprehensive plan. See §§ 10-205-10-210. The local government must adopt record hearing rules, as part of its unified land development code, that include these procedures at a minimum. See Mandelker, *Model Legislation for Land Use Proceedings*, 35 Urb. Law. 635 (2003).

The Florida statutes provide an option to local governments that adopt minimum statutory procedures for quasi-judicial hearings, that allows a subsequent court challenge to the government decision to proceed on the record established in the hearing, rather than as a full evidentiary "de novo" proceeding in court. See Fla. Stat. Ann § 163.3215(4). The statute applies only to challenges that may be brought on the basis that the approved development order is inconsistent with the adopted comprehensive plan. It was intended to provide an incentive to local governments to adopt more formal proceedings for review of development orders, as judicial review on the record made at the local hearing can be more speedy and less costly, and the judicial review standard favors the local government decision if there is "substantial competent evidence" in the record below to support the decision. Is this incentive enough to encourage local governments to formalize their proceedings? Does it benefit the applicant? Objectors?

A NOTE ON BRIBERY AND CORRUPTION IN ZONING

Conflict of interest and bias problems are only part of a larger problem of bribery and corruption in the zoning process. The following comment, which especially applies to land use regulation, shows why this issue is important:

> A major strand in thinking about corruption is curtailing the role of special interest groups within the political and governmental process. Susan Rose-Ackerman's landmark study of corruption provides a helpful framework. [Corruption: A Study in Political Economy (1978).] She describes our system of making allocative choices as a "mixed" one in which "both market and nonmarket mechanisms clearly have important allocative roles to play." The democratic political system is the preferred mechanism for allocating public goods. However, "wealth and market forces can undermine whatever dividing line has been fixed. Thus, political decisions that are made on the

> basis of majority preferences may be undermined by wide use of an illegal market as the method of allocation." The result is political corruption. [Brown, *Putting Watergate Behind Us — Salinas, Sun-Diamond, and Two Views of the Anticorruption Model*, 74 Tul. L. Rev. 747, 752 (2000).]

Corruption in zoning was the subject of a multi-volume study by the Stanford Research Institute, Corruption in Land Use and Building Regulation (1978). Bribery was the major culprit, as the study of Fairfax County, Virginia indicates. The county is part of the Washington, D.C. metropolitan area.

> In the 1960s, some developers and their lawyers apparently began to work together with several of the members of the Board of Supervisors in order to ensure that rezonings needed for high-profit development were approved by the Board of Supervisors. Subsequent investigations during this period indicated that lawyers representing some developers provided money to supervisors to rezone a factory site, approve sites for apartment complexes, and approve a shopping center complex. . . . Some members of the county planning staff were also involved in some deals. . . . It appears that the loosely run land-use regulatory system existing in the county during this time encouraged these abuses; the practices continued until the land-use system was overhauled after scandals surfaced. [Vol. I, An Integrated Report of Conclusions 41 (1978).]

The Fairfax County example illustrates the heavy involvement of developers and construction interests in local politics, and the cooperative relationship that can emerge between these interests and local decision makers. For a detailed account of this kind of symbiotic relationship in a Long Island, New York suburb, see M. Gottdiener, Planned Sprawl: Private and Public Interests in Suburbia (1977). These problems have not disappeared with time. For some successful prosecutions against local officials for accepting bribes in zoning matters, see *Evans v. United States*, 504 U.S. 255 (1992) (federal officer impersonated developer); *State v. Lefevre*, 972 P.2d 1021 (Ariz. App. 1998); *Sawyer v. State*, 583 N.E.2d 795 (Ind. App. 1991).

As Professor Brown indicates in his article, *supra*, the answer to these problems has been to tighten restrictions on public officials and step up criminal prosecutions. This approach was taken in a companion report to the corruption study, sponsored by the American Planning Association, that recommended a number of zoning reforms to reduce corruption. See J. Getzels & C. Thurow, An Analysis of Zoning Reforms: Minimizing the Incentive for Corruption (1978). Many of these reforms have been discussed in these pages, such as the use of quasi-judicial procedures and hearing examiners and a requirement that land use decisions be consistent with a comprehensive plan. One of the major themes of the Stanford corruption report was that opportunities for corruption decrease when decision making is highly visible. If this is so, then more formal and open procedures in the decision making process, as described in the American Planning Association's model legislation, should help.

Yet Professor Brown notes a reaction to heightened efforts at dealing with the "scandal" problem:

> Numerous academic and policy experts have spearheaded a formidable reaction to what they see as the excessive zeal of the post-Watergate approach. The office of independent counsel is their favorite target, but others include the overcriminalization of ethical matters, the need for greater concern about the rights of public officials, and

> the advantages of a pluralistic system in which interest groups voice their concern within a process mediated by institutions such as political parties. [*Id.* at 810.]

Consider these comments in view of the discussion of market solutions to land use conflicts in Chapter 1, and the comment there that reliance on the market may motivate some participants to try to bribe decision makers. Consider how the perception of corruption in the land use and zoning process influences the public's interest and acceptance of initiative and referenda as the better process for decision making, addressed in Section I, *infra*.

[4.] Downzoning

STONE v. CITY OF WILTON

331 N.W.2d 398 (Iowa 1983)

McGIVERIN, JUSTICE:

Plaintiffs Alex and Martha Stone appeal from the dismissal of their petition for declaratory judgment, injunctive relief and damages in an action regarding defendant City of Wilton's rezoning from multi-family to single-family residential of certain real estate owned by plaintiffs. The issues raised by plaintiffs focus on the validity of the rezoning ordinance and the trial court's striking of plaintiffs' claim for lost profits. We find no error in [the] trial court's rulings and affirm its decision.

This appeal is a zoning dispute involving approximately six acres of land in the city of Wilton, Iowa. Plaintiffs purchased the undeveloped land in June 1979 with the intent of developing a low income, federally subsidized housing project. The project was to consist of several multi-family units; therefore, feasibility of the project depended upon multi-family zoning of the tract. At the time of the purchase approximately one-fourth of plaintiffs' land was zoned R-1, single-family residential, and the remainder was zoned R-2, multi-family residential.

After the land was purchased, plaintiffs incurred expenses for architectural fees and engineering services in the preparation of plans and plats to be submitted to the city council and its planning and zoning commission. In addition, plaintiffs secured a Farmers' Home Administration (FHA) loan commitment for construction of the project.

This suit is based primarily on actions of city officials between December 1979 and June 1980. We will discuss only the most pertinent events now and will relate other facts later when we consider the issues raised by plaintiffs.

In December 1979 plaintiffs filed a preliminary plat for the project with the city clerk. In March 1980, following a public meeting, the planning and zoning commission recommended to the city council that land in the northern part of the city be rezoned to single-family residential due to alleged inadequacies of sewer, water and electrical services. The rezoning recommendation affected all of plaintiffs' property plus tracts owned by two other developers. Plaintiffs' application on May 21, 1980, for a building permit to construct multi-family dwellings was denied due to the pending rezoning recommendation.

In May 1980, plaintiffs filed a petition against the city seeking a declaratory judgment invalidating any rezoning of their property, temporary and permanent injunctions to prohibit passage of any rezoning ordinance, and in the event of rezoning, $570,000 damages for monies expended on the project, anticipated lost profits and alleged reduction in the value of plaintiffs' land. The temporary injunction was denied.

In accordance with the recommendation of the planning and zoning commission, the city council passed an ordinance rezoning the land from R-2 to R-1 in June 1980. . . .

This action proceeded to trial in November 1980. . . .

I. *Scope of Review*

[The court held the case was "best treated as one in equity" and that review was de novo.]

II. *Validity of the Rezoning Ordinance*

. . . .

Land use restrictions (such as at issue here) reasonably related to the promotion of the health, safety, morals, or general welfare repeatedly have been upheld even though the challenged regulations destroyed or adversely affected recognized real property interests or flatly prohibited the most beneficial use of the property. Hence, such laws, when justifiable under the police power, validly enacted and not arbitrary or unreasonable, generally are held not to be invalid as taking of property for public use without compensation. However, some instances of government regulation are "so onerous as to constitute a taking which constitutionally requires compensation." *Goldblatt v. Town of* [*Hempstead*], 369 U.S. 590, 594 (1962).

A.

We focus initially on the general claims which plaintiffs make concerning the validity of the rezoning. Controlling our review of the enactment's validity is the principle that the validity of a police power enactment, such as zoning, depends on its reasonableness; however, "[the Supreme Court] has often said that 'debatable questions as to reasonableness are not for the courts but for the legislature. . . .' " *Goldblatt*, 369 U.S. at 595.

The zoning ordinance at issue was passed as a general welfare measure. It affected not only Stones' proposed housing project, but also land owned by Land, Ltd. and Wilton Sunset Housing Corporation, which intended to erect multi-family housing for the elderly. The city council's stated reasons for rezoning this section of the city from R-2 to R-1 were as follows: (1) The existing zoning was no longer appropriate to the current and anticipated growth and development of the area; (2) the existing zoning would create a greater density than now appropriate; (3) the existing zoning would create a traffic and pedestrian flow too great for the existing street and sidewalk systems in the area; and (4) the city's electrical, water and sewer systems were inadequate for a concentration of multi-family dwellings in that area of town.

Plaintiffs, however, claim the above were mere pretext. They contend that the council disregarded its comprehensive plan. They further argue that the council was prompted by a desire to advance the private economic interests of a member of the planning and zoning commission and by racial discrimination against the "type" of persons who might live in plaintiffs' housing project. The trial court disagreed and so do we. "If the [city council] gave full consideration to the problem presented, including the needs of the public, changing conditions, and the similarity of other land in the same area, then it has zoned in accordance with a comprehensive plan." *Montgomery v. Bremer County Board of Supervisors*, 299 N.W.2d 687, 695 (Iowa 1980). On the record in this case, we cannot conclude that the council's stated reasons, which are recognized as valid reasons for zoning, Iowa Code §§ 414.2,.3 (1981), were mere pretext. . . .

Plaintiffs also suggested that questions concerning the "types" of tenants in the housing project were racially motivated and affected the council's decision to rezone. The evidence is clear that the Wilton city council was faced with a number of competing concerns in regard to the proper zoning of the area of the city in which plaintiffs' land was situated. It is precisely because legislative bodies, like this city council, are faced with balancing numerous competing considerations that courts refrain from reviewing the merits of their decisions if at least a debatable question exists as to the reasonableness of their action.

"But racial discrimination is not just another competing consideration. When there is a proof that a discriminatory purpose has been a motivating factor in the decision, this judicial deference is no longer justified." *Village of Arlington Heights v. Metropolitan Housing Development Corp.*, 429 U.S. 252, 265–66 (1977). We are unable to find sufficient evidence in the record to conclude that plaintiffs carried their burden of proof. We find that discriminatory purpose was not a motivating factor in the council's decision to rezone.

In sum, zoning is not static. A city's comprehensive plan is always subject to reasonable revisions designed to meet the ever-changing needs and conditions of a community. We conclude that the council rationally decided to rezone this section of the city to further the public welfare in accordance with a comprehensive plan. . . .

Affirmed

NOTES AND QUESTIONS

1. *Downzoning issues.* The principal case indicates some of the special characteristics of a downzoning amendment. The city takes away what the landowner had before, and the action looks arbitrary and capricious, and discriminatory. Yet the Iowa court applied the usual "fairly debatable" rule to uphold the downzoning and rejected the racial discrimination claim. Note that an upzoning amendment discriminates in favor of the landowner, while the downzoning amendment discriminates against the landowner. Should the courts treat these discrimination claims differently?

The downzoning cases are closely related to the vested rights cases, even though the landowner has no vested right in the continuation of a pre-existing zoning classification. When the zoning is changed after the landowner has owned the property and made other investments in the property, or has begun the permitting process, the public purposes for the downzoning may appear suspect. Should a vested rights claim strengthen the landowner's challenge to a downzoning? The court in the principal case rejected a vested rights claim made by the landowner in a portion of the decision which is not reproduced. For an account of how Virginia's vested rights statute was a response to downzoning problems, see Prichard & Riegle, *Searching For Certainty: Virginia's Evolutionary Approach to Vested Rights*, 7 Geo. Mason L. Rev. 983 (1999), and its recent application of the statute to deny a vested rights claim is found at *Hale v. Bd. of Zoning Appeals*, 673 S.E.2d 170 (Va. 2009).

Some courts do not apply the usual presumption of validity to downzonings. With the principal case compare *Trust Co. of Chicago v. City of Chicago*, 96 N.E.2d 499 (Ill. 1951). The court invalidated a downzoning of a lot from multifamily to single-family use in an area generally zoned and developed for multifamily use. The court noted that the downzoning was "not made for the public good" but "for the benefit only of those residents of the block who desired to exclude" apartments. Can you distinguish this case from the principal case? A court may also invalidate a downzoning if it appears directed at a particular developer or development project. See *A.A. Profiles, Inc. v. City of Fort Lauderdale*, 850 F.2d 1483 (11th Cir. 1988) (downzoning followed revocation of building permit). For discussion of downzoning generally, see Williamson, *Constitutional and Judicial Limitations on the Community's Power to Downzone*, 12 Urb. Law. 157 (1980).

2. *Good or bad?* "Piecemeal rezoning" is the term used for rezoning aimed at particular properties, which is not part of a comprehensive planning or zoning process. Is there anything inherently good or bad about a piecemeal downzoning? In the *Wilton* case, the downzoning was done to block a lower-income housing development. See also *Gregory v. County of Harnett*, 493 S.E.2d 786 (N.C. App. 1997), where the court reversed a downzoning done to block the extension of a mobile home park, holding that fear of crime from residents of the park was not a sufficient justification. How would the discrimination claim in *Wilton* be analyzed under *Huntington, supra* Chapter 5? (Recall that *Huntington* departs significantly from the *Arlington Heights* test, upon which the principal case relies.)

Downzoning is not always targeted at minorities or the poor, but often is supported by the local council because of pressure from residential neighbors who wish to thwart adjacent higher density residential or nonresidential development. For example, in *Pace Resources, Inc. v. Shrewsbury Township Planning Comm'n*, 492 A.2d 818 (Pa. Commw. 1985), a developer sought approval to develop an industrial park on property that had been zoned as industrial a few years earlier. During the approval process, area residents petitioned to rezone the property to an agricultural zone. The court determined that the rezoning was arbitrary and discriminatory. Similarly, in *Couch v. City of Jacksonville*, 693 So. 2d 462 (Ala. 1995), the court invalidated an ordinance that rezoned property from a district that allowed duplexes to one that only allowed single family units. The downzoning was in response to neighboring landowners who opposed a pending plan to develop duplexes on the property. See also *Kavanewsky v. Zoning Bd. of Appeals*, 279 A.2d 567 (Conn. 1971) (invalidating downzoning made as response to residents' demands to keep the city a rural community with open spaces and to keep undesirable businesses out).

Piecemail downzonings are also sometimes termed "reverse spot zoning." Compare spot zoning to increase commercial development potential discussed *supra* with *Riya Finnegan LLC v. Township Council of the Township of South Brunswick*, 962 A.2d 484 (N.J. 2008) (invalidating township downzoning of commercial zone to office professional zone in response to neighbors and inconsistent with the master plan).

Two courts have adopted rules that make it more difficult to justify piecemeal downzonings. *Parkridge v. City of Seattle*, 573 P.2d 359 (Wash. 1978), held that such downzonings were quasi-judicial actions, dropped the presumption of constitutionality, and placed the burden to prove the validity of the downzoning on the municipality. In *Board of Supvrs. v. Snell Constr. Corp.*, 202 S.E.2d 889 (Va. 1974), the court applied a variant of the Maryland change-mistake rule to piecemeal downzonings that weakened the usual presumption of constitutionality. If a piecemeal downzoning is not justified by changed circumstances, the municipality must introduce evidence of mistake, fraud, or changed circumstances sufficient to make the downzoning a reasonably debatable issue.

One commentator argues that downzoning is useful in lower-income and minority neighborhoods as a means of eliminating undesirable uses. Arnold, *Planning Milagros: Environmental Justice and Land Use Regulation*, 76 Denv. U.L. Rev. 1, 108-14 (1998). For example, in *Smith Inv. Co. v. Sandy City*, 958 P.2d 245 (Utah App. 1998), the court upheld a downzoning of 16 unused acres in a shopping center to residential use, noting it was a reasonably debatable way of limiting business concentration in an area surrounded on three sides by homes. The court also noted that the adjacent residential areas were undergoing "deteriorating housing and high turnover of owners," and that the downzoning might help stabilize the area by encouraging additional residential development. See also *Ex parte City of Jacksonville*, 693 So. 2d 465 (Ala. 1996) (upholding downzoning from multi-family to single-family residential in a neighborhood that had been developing as single family homes).

3. *Comprehensive downzonings.* As in the spot "upzoning" cases, a question to ask in the piecemeal downzoning cases is why a comprehensive downzoning was not done. A comprehensive downzoning should survive attack. A leading case is *Norbeck Village Joint Venture v. Montgomery County Council*, 254 A.2d 700 (Md. 1969). The court upheld a downzoning of fifty square miles to two-acre lots. The purpose of the downzoning was to implement a comprehensive plan based on a regional plan by creating a low density development area that would isolate a town center identified in the plan from urban sprawl. The court expressly relied on the plan as a basis for upholding the downzoning. See also *Carty v. City of Ojai*, 143 Cal. Rptr. 506 (Cal. App. 1978) (upheld downzoning of land zoned for outlying shopping center to implement plan calling for protection of downtown business district).

Downzoning is a popular method in growth management programs to reduce the zoning capacity of a community, often to bring the capacity in line with the public facility capacity. Additionally, comprehensive downzonings to very low density zones may be undertaken in an effort to protect environmentally sensitive areas or to protect farmland from urbanization. Large lot zoning has been upheld as a valid method to preserve agricultural lands from conversion to urban uses, particularly if created pursuant to a more comprehensive program. See Chapter 4, and *Gardner v. N.J. Pinelands Comm'n*, 593 A.2d 251 (N.J. 1991) (10 acre and 40 acre zoning to protect agriculture in the Pinelands special area, which is reproduced in that chapter). The effectiveness and fairness of these efforts are subject to ongoing debate. See Richardson, *Downzoning, Fairness and Farmland Protection*, 19 J. Land Use & Envtl. Law 59 (2003); Cordes, *Takings, Fairness and Farmland Preservation*, 60 Ohio St. L.J. 1033 (1999).

4. *Takings.* The court in *Norbeck, supra* Note 3, also rejected a taking claim that had been made against the downzoning, finding that the land as rezoned could be put to a reasonably profitable use. Taking claims are often made in downzoning cases. See the discussion on takings in Chapter 2, *supra*. As in cases brought to challenge any zoning restriction, the courts will consider whether the land use allowed by the downzoning is compatible with the surrounding area. Compare *Grimpel Assocs. v. Cohalan*, 361 N.E.2d 1022, 1024 (N.Y. 1977) (invalidating downzoning where the residential use would be an " 'inappropriate and unjustifiable island' surrounded by business operations and major vehicular thoroughfares"), with *McGowan v. Cohalan*, 361 N.E.2d 1025 (N.Y. 1977) (approving another part of same downzoning, where area was mix of residential, commercial and industrial uses, but Town's goal of encouraging residential use was reasonable and achievable), and *A.A. Profiles, supra* (recognizing taking claim). Of course, a court will not find a taking if the downzoning results only in a decrease in the value of the property. See *Spenger, Grubb & Assocs. v. City of Hailey*, 903 P.2d 741 (Idaho 1995).

5. *Purposes.* The principal case suggests that the purpose to be achieved by a downzoning may be an important factor bearing on its constitutionality. Courts have frequently upheld downzonings for the purpose of conforming the zoning of a site to uses compatible with the surrounding area. See *Lum Yip Kee, Ltd. v. City & County of Honolulu*, 767 P.2d 815 (Hawaii 1989); *Neuzil v. Iowa City*, 451 N.W.2d 159 (Iowa 1999) (upholding rezoning from multifamily residential to single family residential where neighboring development was single family residential).

Consider the following cases:

Mountcrest Estates v. Mayor & Twp. Comm., 232 A.2d 674 (N.J. App. Div.). The township passed a downzoning ordinance increasing lot sizes in its B residential district. Mountcrest argued that the downzoning was invalid because eighty-five percent of the lots in the B district were built upon or platted at the previous higher density. This argument did not impress the court, which upheld the downzoning. Existing uses were a factor to consider, but the plan evidenced by the zoning ordinance was mutable and a presumption of validity attached to the amended ordinance. "The municipality's problems with respect to congestion, overcrowding and inability to provide public facilities due to the population explosion will be lessened because between 180 and 250 fewer homes can be built in the B district under the amended ordinance than could have been built before the amendments — a possible difference in population of from 500 to 1,000 persons." *Id.* at 677. Accord *Chucta v. Planning & Zoning Comm'n*, 225 A.2d 822 (Conn. 1967).

Kavanewsky v. Zoning Bd. of Appeals, 279 A.2d 567 (Conn. 1971). A town doubled the minimum lot size in one of the two zoning districts into which it was divided. The court noted that the downzoning was " 'made in demand of the people to keep Warren a rural community with open spaces and keep undesirable businesses out.' We agree . . . that the reason given . . . is not in accordance with the requirements of" the purposes provision of the state zoning enabling act, which followed the Standard Act. *Id.* at 571. The downzoning was invalidated.

Sullivan v. Town of Acton, 645 N.E.2d 700 (Mass. App. 1995). The town downzoned a nine-acre parcel at the intersection of two highways which had been used since 1940 for agricultural and residential purposes, though it was zoned for general business use. The downzoning occurred after a comprehensive planning effort recommended changes for uses along the highway. Its purpose was to control strip development along the highway by restricting further commercial development; to preserve and encourage residential development; to focus new commercial growth in two defined historic "villages"; and to limit traffic growth and congestion.

The court rejected a "spot zoning" challenge, noting that several large and undeveloped parcels along the highway had been rezoned to residential use. "A comprehensive plan designed to preserve a mixture of uses over a substantial area of a municipality does not necessarily run afoul of the uniformity principle expressed in spot zoning law." The purposes for the downzoning were also reasonable. Accord on similar facts *Spenger, Grubb & Assocs. v. City of Hailey*, 903 P.2d 741 (Idaho 1995).

6. *Acquisitory intent.* In a related type of case, a municipality may plan to acquire a tract of land for a park or other public facility. It then downzones the property in order to depress its value in advance of acquisition. Courts uniformly hold this kind of zoning invalid. See, e.g., *Burrows v. City of Keene*, 432 A.2d 15 (N.H. 1981); *Rippley v. City of Lincoln*, 330 N.W.2d 505

(N.D. 1983). Can you see why these cases are consistent with the Supreme Court's 1987 taking trilogy? These cases often award compensation to the successful landowner. Is this consistent with the Supreme Court's decision in *First English*?

F. OTHER FORMS OF FLEXIBLE ZONING

[1.] With Pre-Set Standards: The Floating Zone

A "Floating Zone" is a technique by which a local government adopts the text of the zoning district, with its standards and procedures, as part of the zoning code, but does not create the district on a map until a developer applies to have the district placed on his property. The application of the zone to a particular property is a rezoning of that property. A floating zone is a flexible zoning technique that can provide a "platform" for planned unit developments, mixed-use zoning and other zoning techniques that require the exercise of discretion and the approval of a development plan as the basis for development.

An early case accepting the technique is *Rodgers v. Village of Tarrytown*, 96 N.E.2d 731 (N.Y. 1951), in which the village adopted the zone for garden apartments, by amending the zoning ordinance text to detail site and density standards for garden apartments, and requiring that the zone contain at least ten acres. The planning board was authorized to approve a zoning map amendment to place the zone on particular property, and its denial could be appealed to the village board of trustees. The neighbor of a landowner whose property was rezoned with the garden apartment zoning challenged the floating zone as arbitrary and unreasonable, and an illegal spot zone or variance. The court reasoned that the village could have simply included garden apartments as a use in the existing residential zones, according to the same standards that were in the floating zone, and accomplished in one step what it created as a two-step process. *Id.* at 735–736.

NOTES AND QUESTIONS

1. *Why use a floating zone? Tarrytown* is a classic case, and deserves careful study. What advantage was there, from the municipality's viewpoint, in using the "floating zone" amendment technique? The court may have supplied a partial answer when it said: "The mere circumstance that an owner possesses a ten-acre plot and submits plans conforming to the physical requirements prescribed by the 1947 amendment will not entitle him, *ipso facto*, to a Residence B-B classification. It will still be for the [planning] board to decide, in the exercise of a reasonable discretion, that the *grant* of such a classification accords with the comprehensive zoning plan and benefits the village as a whole." *Id.* at 734. But what standards are to guide the "exercise of a reasonable discretion"? Is it enough to say, as the New York court did, that "the board may not arbitrarily or unreasonably *deny* applications of other owners for permission to construct garden apartments on their properties"?

A floating zone has been described by one court as "[a]t the far end of the flexibility continuum of zoning categories from Euclidean zones. . . ." *Mayor & Council v. Rylyns Enters.*, 814 A.2d 469 (Md. 2002). The Standard Zoning Enabling Act does not provide for floating zones. In order to ensure that the flexibility is not a tool to circumvent the protections provided by Euclidean zoning, the court stated:

> [W]e consistently have held that the floating zone is subject to the same conditions that apply to safeguard the granting of special exceptions, i.e., the use must be compatible with the surrounding neighborhood, it must further the purposes of the proposed reclassification, and special precautions are to be applied to insure that there will be no discordance with existing uses. These precautions include such restrictions as building location and style, the percentage of the area covered by the building, minimum green area, minimum and maximum area of the use, minimum setback from streets and other uses, requirement that a site plan be approved, and a provision for revocation of the classification if the specified restrictions are not complied with. [*Id.* at 484.]

2. *Pros and cons.* One commentator has summarized the advantages of floating zones:

> The floating zone . . . can be tailored to site specific land uses, as well as performance and design objectives. It forms the host for a variety of flexible zoning districts. Moreover, it can be applied more quickly and easier than Euclidean zoning and therefore responds better to market forces and provides for more streamlined regulation. For these very reasons, however, the floating zone is viewed with suspicion by community groups and political pressure often discourages its use. [Tierney, *Bold Promises by Basic Steps: Maryland's Growth Policy in the Year 2020*, 23 U. Balt. L. Rev. 461 (1994).]

Pros

Professor Arnold has another view in his *Planning Milagros* article, *supra.* He points out that "[f]loating zones pose an uncertain threat to local residents and landowners, who do not know whether a neighboring property will be chosen for a floating zone use. . . . Furthermore, floating zones appear to be used most often for either industrial uses or high-density residential uses." *Id.* at 120. Land use attorney Brian Blaesser suggests that the comprehensive plan should contain policies to guide decisions on floating zones. Discretionary Zoning § 7.08[2] (2003). Plans could then adopt policies on location. At a minimum, a comprehensive plan can help to ensure compatibility in states where zoning must be consistent with the comprehensive plan.

3. *Other states.* Courts elsewhere have accepted the reasoning of the *Tarrytown* case and have approved floating zones. *Sheridan v. Planning Bd.*, 266 A.2d 396 (Conn. 1969); *Bellemeade Co. v. Priddle*, 503 S.W.2d 734 (Ky. 1974); *Huff v. Board of Zoning Appeals*, 133 A.2d 83 (Md. 1957) (light manufacturing zone).

A Missouri court upheld the floating zone in a sweeping decision in which land was rezoned from M-3 planned industrial to C-8 planned commercial. *Treme v. St. Louis County*, 609 S.W.2d 706 (Mo. App. 1980). The court said in part:

> We find the reasoning of the cases which have upheld the "floating zone" to be persuasive. . . . There has been no delegation of legislative authority to rezone here. Rezoning to C-8 can be accomplished only by legislative act. . . .
>
> We further find no objection to the fact that the ordinance does not spell out in detail the standards upon which a determination to rezone to C-8 is to be made. The section does provide for general standards which are to be considered by the legislative body. Rezoning cannot, by its very nature, be based upon precise and inflexible standards, for each plot of ground is different and the environment in which it lies is different. [*Id.* at 712.]

Is this case consistent with *Tarrytown?* Compare *Miami v. Save Brickell Ave., Inc.*, 426 So. 2d 1100 (Fla. App. 1983) (planned area development zoning is not constitutionally sufficient where the ordinance standards for the zone allow what is permitted in the underlying zoning district, but with broadly defined deviations as may be decided by the city council).

4. *Comparison with the special exception.* Does the floating zone have an advantage as a means for "flexible" zoning? Special exceptions are normally delineated for each zoning classification, so they can be more geographically limited than a floating zone. However, some jurisdictions provide that certain uses, such as public uses, are special exceptions in every district. Surely the special exception technique does not give any greater advance notice to landowners of the possible intrusion of a new use in an area previously restricted against such use. Nor is the expertise of the zoning board of adjustment, which normally administers the special exception procedure, likely to be greater than the combined expertise of the planning board and the local governing body, which usually administer the floating zone procedure. And it is hard to see how the standards generally held sufficient to guide the exercise of administrative discretion in special exception cases are really more definite than the statutory standards which govern the amending process. Moreover, the floating zone procedure results in a change of the zoning map to reflect the change in classification, while the special exception procedure does not. Does the landowner acquire any greater "entitlement" to have the proposed use approved under one approach or the other?

5. *Hybrids.* In *Carron v. Board of County Comm'rs*, 976 P.2d 359 (Colo. App. 1998), the ordinance created Foothills and Valley zoning districts. Initially, the boundaries of these districts were identical, and all land was presumed to be in the Valley district until a landowner applied to have his land moved to the Foothill district, which allowed more intensive development. A zoning amendment was not required. The court held the procedure was similar to that adopted for special uses and did not violate the statutory requirement that the county zoning ordinance divide the county into districts. What were the benefits of this procedure? Note that the floating zone concept is the basis for other flexible zoning techniques, such as the planned unit development, discussed in Chapter 7. See, e.g., *Martin Cerel v. Town of Natick*, 309 N.E.2d 893 (Mass. App. 1974) (planned cluster development zone upheld as a floating zone that can later be applied to a map).

[2.] Without Pre-Set Standards: Contract and Conditional Zoning

COLLARD v. INCORPORATED VILLAGE OF FLOWER HILL

52 N.Y.2d 594, 439 N.Y.S.2d 326, 421 N.E.2d 818 (1981)

JONES, JUDGE:

Where a local municipality conditions an amendment of its zoning ordinance on the execution of a declaration of covenants providing, in part, that no construction may occur on the property so rezoned without the consent of the municipality, absent a provision that such consent may not be unreasonably withheld, the municipality may not be compelled to issue such consent or give an acceptable reason for failing to do so.

Appellants now own improved property in the Village of Flower Hill. In 1976, the then owners of the subject premises and appellants' predecessors in title, applied to the village board of trustees to rezone the property from a General Municipal and Public Purposes

District to a Business District.[1] On October 4 of that year the village board granted the rezoning application by the following resolution:

"Resolved that the application of Ray R. Beck Company for a change of Zone of premises known and designated as Section 6, Block 73, Lots 9, 12 and 13 on the land and tax map of Nassau County from General Municipal and Public Purposes District be and the same hereby is granted upon the following conditions:

"(a) The Subject Premises and any buildings, structures and improvements situated or to be situated thereon, will be erected, altered, renovated, remodeled, used, occupied and maintained for the following purposes and no other:

"(i) Offices for the practice of the professions of medicine, dentistry, law, engineering, architecture or accountancy;

"(ii) Executive offices to be used solely for the management of business concerns and associations and excluding therefrom, but without limitation, retail or wholesale sales offices or agencies, brokerage offices of all types and kinds, collection or employment agencies or offices, computer programming centers or offices, counseling centers or offices and training offices or business or trade schools.

"(b) No more than four separate tenancies or occupancies are to be permitted on the subject premises or in any building, structure or improvement situated therein at any one time.

"(c) No building or structure or any portion thereof situated or to be situated on the Subject Premises is to be occupied by more than one person (excluding visitors, clients or guests of any tenant or occupant of such building or structure) for each 190 square feet of the gross floor area of such building or structure.

"(d) No building or structure situated on the Subject Premises on the date of this Declaration of Covenants will be altered, extended, rebuilt, renovated or enlarged without the prior consent of the Board of Trustees of the Village.

"(e) There will be maintained on the Subject Premises at all times, no less than twenty-six paved off-street, onsite parking spaces for automobiles and other vehicles, each such parking space to be at least 9' * 20' in dimensions and will be served by aisles and means of ingress and egress of sufficient width to permit the free movement and parking of automobiles and other vehicles.

"(f) Trees and shrubs installed on the Subject Premises pursuant to a landscape plan heretofore filed with the Village in or about 1964, will be maintained in compliance with said landscape plan."

Subsequently, appellants' predecessors in title entered into the contemplated declaration of

[1] Prior to 1964 the subject premises, then vacant, had been zoned for single-family dwellings with a minimum lot size of 7,500 square feet. In that year the then owners applied to the village board to rezone a portion of the property and place it in the General Municipal and Public Purposes District so that a private sanitarium might be constructed. Concurrently with that application a declaration of covenants restricting the use of the property to a sanitarium was recorded in the county clerk's office. The village board then granted the rezoning application, but limited the property's use to the purposes set forth in the declaration of covenants. The 1976 rezoning application, which as conditionally granted is the subject of this suit, was made because the private sanitarium had fallen into disuse and it was asserted that without rezoning the property could neither be sold nor leased.

covenants which was recorded in the office of the Clerk of Nassau County on November 29, 1976. Consistent with paragraph (d) of the board's resolution, that declaration provided that "[n]o building or structure situated on the Subject Premises on the date of this Declaration of Covenants will be altered, extended, rebuilt, renovated or enlarged without the prior consent of the Board of Trustees of the Village."

Appellants, after acquiring title, made application in late 1978 to the village board for approval to enlarge and extend the existing structure on the premises. Without any reason being given that application was denied. Appellants then commenced this action to have the board's determination declared arbitrary, capricious, unreasonable, and unconstitutional and sought by way of ultimate relief an order directing the board to issue the necessary building permits.

Asserting that the board's denial of the application was beyond review as to reasonableness, respondent moved to dismiss the complaint for failure to state a cause of action. Special Term denied the motion, equating appellants' allegation that the board's action was arbitrary and capricious with an allegation that such action was lacking in good faith and fair dealing — an allegation which it found raised triable issues of fact. The Appellate Division reversed and dismissed the complaint, holding that the allegation of arbitrary and capricious action by the board was not the equivalent of an allegation that the board breached an implied covenant of fair dealing and good faith. We now affirm.

At the outset this case involves the question of the permissibility of municipal rezoning conditioned on the execution of a private declaration of covenants restricting the use to which the parcel sought to be rezoned may be put. Prior to our decision in *Church v. Town of Islip*, (N.Y.), 168 N.E.2d 680 in which we upheld rezoning of property subject to reasonable conditions, conditional rezoning had been almost uniformly condemned by courts of all jurisdictions — a position to which a majority of States appear to continue to adhere. Since *Church*, however, the practice of conditional zoning has become increasingly widespread in this State, as well as having gained popularity in other jurisdictions.

Because much criticism has been mounted against the practice, both by commentators and the courts of some of our sister States,[3] further exposition is in order.

Probably the principal objection to conditional rezoning is that it constitutes illegal spot zoning, thus violating the legislative mandate requiring that there be a comprehensive plan for, and that all conditions be uniform within, a given zoning district. When courts have considered the issue, the assumptions have been made that conditional zoning benefits particular landowners rather than the community as a whole and that it undermines the foundation upon which comprehensive zoning depends by destroying uniformity within use districts. Such unexamined assumptions are questionable. First, it is a downward change to a less restrictive zoning classification that benefits the property rezoned and not the opposite imposition of greater restrictions on land use. Indeed, imposing limiting conditions, while benefiting surrounding properties, normally adversely affects the premises on which the conditions are imposed. Second, zoning is not invalid per se merely because only a single parcel is involved or benefited; the real test for spot zoning is whether the change is other than part of a well-considered and comprehensive plan calculated to serve the general welfare of the

---

[3] See, e. g., Comment, *The Use and Abuse of Contract Zoning*, 12 UCLA L. Rev. 897. For judicial criticism, see, e.g., *Baylis v. City of Baltimore*, (Md.), 148 A.2d 429; Hartnett v. Austin, 93 So. 2d 86 (Fla.); *Houston Petroleum Co. v. Automotive Prods. Credit Ass'n*, (N.J.), 87 A.2d 319. [Several citations are omitted. — Eds.]

community (*Rodgers v. Village of Tarrytown*). Such a determination, in turn, depends on the reasonableness of the rezoning in relation to neighboring uses — an inquiry required regardless of whether the change in zone is conditional in form. Third, if it is initially proper to change a zoning classification without the imposition of restrictive conditions notwithstanding that such change may depart from uniformity, then no reason exists why accomplishing that change subject to condition should automatically be classified as impermissible spot zoning.

Both conditional and unconditional rezoning involve essentially the same legislative act — an amendment of the zoning ordinance. The standards for judging the validity of conditional rezoning are no different from the standards used to judge whether unconditional rezoning is illegal. If modification to a less restrictive zoning classification is warranted, then a fortiori conditions imposed by a local legislature to minimize conflicts among districts should not in and of themselves violate any prohibition against spot zoning.

Another fault commonly voiced in disapproval of conditional zoning is that it constitutes an illegal bargaining away of a local government's police power. Because no municipal government has the power to make contracts that control or limit it in the exercise of its legislative powers and duties, restrictive agreements made by a municipality in conjunction with a rezoning are sometimes said to violate public policy. While permitting citizens to be governed by the best bargain they can strike with a local legislature would not be consonant with notions of good government, absent proof of a contract purporting to bind the local legislature in advance to exercise its zoning authority in a bargained-for manner, a rule which would have the effect of forbidding a municipality from trying to protect landowners in the vicinity of a zoning change by imposing protective conditions based on the assertion that that body is bargaining away its discretion, would not be in the best interests of the public. The imposition of conditions on property sought to be rezoned may not be classified as a prospective commitment on the part of the municipality to zone as requested if the conditions are met; nor would the municipality necessarily be precluded on this account from later reversing or altering its decision.

Yet another criticism leveled at conditional zoning is that the State enabling legislation does not confer on local authorities authorization to enact conditional zoning amendments. On this view any such ordinance would be *ultra vires*. While it is accurate to say there exists no explicit authorization that a legislative body may attach conditions to zoning amendments, neither is there any language which expressly forbids a local legislature to do so. Statutory silence is not necessarily a denial of the authority to engage in such a practice. Where in the face of nonaddress in the enabling legislation there exists independent justification for the practice as an appropriate exercise of municipal power, that power will be implied. Conditional rezoning is a means of achieving some degree of flexibility in land use control by minimizing the potentially deleterious effect of a zoning change on neighboring properties; reasonably conceived conditions harmonize the landowner's need for rezoning with the public interest and certainly fall within the spirit of the enabling legislation.

One final concern of those reluctant to uphold the practice is that resort to conditional rezoning carries with it no inherent restrictions apart from the restrictive agreement itself. This fear, however, is justifiable only if conditional rezoning is considered a contractual relationship between municipality and private party, outside the scope of the zoning power — a view to which we do not subscribe. When conditions are incorporated in an amending ordinance, the result is as much a "zoning regulation" as an ordinance, adopted without conditions. Just as the scope of all zoning regulation is limited by the police power, and thus local legislative bodies must act reasonably and in the best interests of public safety, welfare and convenience, the scope of permissible conditions must of necessity be similarly limited. If, upon proper proof, the conditions imposed are found unreasonable, the rezoning amendment as well as the required conditions would have to be nullified, with the affected property reverting to the preamendment zoning classification.

Against this backdrop we proceed to consideration of the contentions advanced by appellants in the appeal now before us. It is first useful to delineate arguments which they do not advance. Thus, they do not challenge the conditional zoning change made in 1976 at the behest of their predecessors in title; no contention is made that the village board was not authorized to adopt the resolution of October 4, 1976, conditioned as it was on the execution and recording of the declaration of covenants, or that the provisions of that declaration were in 1976 arbitrary, capricious, unreasonable or unconstitutional.[4] The reason may be what is apparent, namely, that any successful challenge to the adoption of the 1976 resolution would cause appellants' premises to revert to their pre-1976 zoning classification — a consequence clearly unwanted by them.

The focus of appellants' assault is the provision of the declaration of covenants that no structure may be extended or enlarged "without the prior consent of the Board of Trustees of the Village." Appellants would have us import the added substantive prescription — "which consent may not be unreasonably withheld." Their argument proceeds along two paths: first, that as a matter of construction the added prescription should be read into the provision; second, that because of limitations associated with the exercise of municipal zoning power the village board would have been required to include such a prescription.

Appellants' construction argument must fail. The terminology employed in the declaration is explicit. The concept that appellants would invoke is not obscure and language to give it effect was readily available had it been the intention of the parties to include this added stipulation. Appellants point to no canon of construction in the law of real property or of contracts which would call for judicial insertion of the missing clause. Where language has been chosen containing no inherent ambiguity or uncertainty, courts are properly hesitant, under the guise of judicial construction, to imply additional requirements to relieve a party from asserted disadvantage flowing from the terms actually used.

The second path either leads nowhere or else goes too far. If it is appellants' assertion that the village board was legally required to insist on inclusion of the desired prescription, there is no authority in the court to reform the zoning enactment of 1976 retroactively to impose the omitted clause. Whether the village board at that time would have enacted a different resolution in the form now desired by appellants is open only to speculation; the certainty is that they did not then take such legislative action. On the other hand, acceptance of appellants' proposition would produce as the other possible consequence the conclusion that the 1976 enactment was illegal, throwing appellants unhappily back to the pre-1976 zoning of their premises, a destination which they assuredly wish to sidestep.

Finally, we agree with the Appellate Division that the allegation of the complaint that the village board in denying appellants' application acted in an arbitrary and capricious manner is not an allegation that the board acted in bad faith or its equivalent.

---

(4) Inasmuch as no contention is made that the adoption of the 1976 resolution by the village board constituted impermissible spot zoning or that the action of the board at that time was otherwise unreasonable or constituted an impermissible exercise of its zoning powers, we do not reach or consider such issues.

For the reasons stated the Board of Trustees of the Incorporated Village of Flower Hill may not now be compelled to issue its consent to the proposed enlargement and extension of the existing structure on the premises or in the alternative give an acceptable reason for failing to do so. Accordingly, the order of the Appellate Division should be affirmed, with costs.

NOTES AND QUESTIONS

1. *Contract zoning.* The principal case discusses the major objections to "contract" zoning. Did the court actually decide that the rezoning in the case was valid? See footnote 4 of the opinion. The court seems to hold that a contract zoning is tested by the same rules applicable to a zoning amendment without a contract. This is a minority view. Do you agree with it? Compare *Hale v. Osborn Coal Enters.*, 729 So. 2d 853 (Ala. Civ. App. 1997) (strip mining allowed by annexation agreement, where no notice was given to the public, is invalid contract zoning), with *City of Orange Beach v. Perdido Pass Developers*, 631 So. 2d 850 (Ala. 1993) (upholding annexation and zoning agreement against contract zoning challenge where the city was extensively involved in negotiations and thereby did not abdicate its legislative responsibility). *Dacy v. Village of Ruidoso*, 845 P.2d 793 (N.M. 1992), is another extensive discussion of the rules governing contract zoning. Note that conditions applied to the property in the form of private covenants will bind future owners only if they touch and concern the land. See *City of New York v. Delafield 246 Corp.*, 662 N.Y.S.2d 286 (App. Div. 1997).

2. *Protections of the public process.* Does a public review of the contract zoning make a difference in the acceptability of the result? In the *Dacy* case, the New Mexico Supreme Court found that the alleged contract to rezone property, in exchange for a deed to property the village needed for right of way, was illegal because the village promised a rezoning before having first followed the statutory procedures.

> A contract in which a municipality promises to zone property in a specified manner is illegal because, in making such a promise, a municipality preempts the power of the zoning authority to zone the property according to prescribed legislative procedures. Our statutes require notice and a public hearing prior to passage, amendment, supplement, or repeal of any zoning regulation. NMSA 1978, § 3-21-6(B). The statutes also grant to citizens and parties in interest the opportunity to be heard at the hearing. *Id.* By making a promise to zone before a zoning hearing occurs, a municipality denigrates the statutory process because it purports to commit itself to certain action before listening to the public's comments on that action. Enforcement of such a promise allows a municipality to circumvent established statutory requirements to the possible detriment of affected landowners and the community as a whole. [*Id.* at 797.]

The court distinguished contract zoning from conditional zoning, which it determined to be legal, as where the municipality makes no promise and there is no enforceable contract until the municipality acts to rezone the property. In that case, the public process of rezoning and the availability of judicial review protect the public interest. See also *Chung v. Sarasota County*, 686 So. 2d 1358 (Fla. App. 1996) (illegal contract zoning where county entered into settlement agreement in zoning litigation, agreeing to rezone property, without first adhering to the due process and statutory/ordinance requirements for enacting zoning changes). Is this a valid distinction? Can the public process make a difference in the conditions that result? Is it a disincentive to the developer to enter into a conditional zoning process?

3. *Good or bad?* The court in the principal case does not tell us when contract zoning is invalid. The distinction often made, as in *Dacy*, is that contract zoning is invalid while "conditional" zoning is valid. Another distinction is that "bilateral" zoning is invalid while "unilateral" zoning is valid. A "bilateral" zoning contract involves reciprocal promises in which the municipality promises to zone property in a certain manner in return for a promise from the other party to the contract. A "unilateral" contract consists of a promise by only one of the contracting parties; the other party's consideration is action or forbearance rather than a promise. Consider the usefulness of these distinctions in view of the following cases, which raise typical contract zoning problems.

(a) In *Carlino v. Whitpain Investors*, 453 A.2d 1385 (Pa. 1982), a developer brought an action to restrain a municipality from conditioning a rezoning on the elimination of an access road in a buffer area. The court held that this was improper "contractually conditioned zoning" because the municipal police power cannot be subjected to agreements that condition rezoning. The court also agreed with *Houston Petroleum Co.*, cited in footnote 3 of the principal opinion, that contracts "have no place in a zoning plan." Compare *State ex rel. Zupancic v. Schimenz*, 174 N.W.2d 533 (Wis. 1970), holding valid an agreement executed between a landowner-developer and his neighbors. The court held that rezoning is not invalid contract zoning when the rezoning is motivated by land use agreements made by others.

(b) In *Bartsch v. Planning & Zoning Comm'n*, 506 A.2d 1093 (Conn. App. 1986), the commission approved a zone change conditioned on the filing of a restrictive covenant limiting the use of the premises to a medical office building and requiring the creation of a green belt buffer area. The court held that "the commission has grossly violated the statutory uniformity requirement." *Id.* at 1095.

(c) In *Cross v. Hall County*, 235 S.E.2d 379 (Ga. 1977), a rezoning resolution stated that it was passed provided the landowner resurfaced a road. The court held that conditional zoning was valid when the conditions are imposed "for the protection or benefit of neighbors to ameliorate the effects of the zoning change." When the conditional zoning is "otherwise valid," these conditions cannot be attacked by these neighbors.

(d) In *Giger v. City of Omaha*, 442 N.W.2d 182 (Neb. 1989), the court upheld a rezoning for a mixed-use development that included four agreements executed by the city and the developer that incorporated a development plan. The court found the distinction between contract and conditional zoning irrelevant and held that the critical question was whether the conditions on the rezoning advanced the public health, safety and welfare. The city was entitled to make agreements with developers concerning their plans to avoid difficult enforcement problems. The court did not find a bargaining away of the police power because the agreement required city approval of variances from the plan and because the plan was more stringent than the zoning ordinance. See also *Durand v. I.D.C. Bellingham*, 793 N.E.2d 359 (Mass. 2003).

(e) In *Old Canton Hills Homeowners Ass'n v. Mayor of Jackson*, 749 So. 2d 54 (Miss. 1999), the city approved a planned unit development contingent on twenty-three conditions for changes in the site plan such as incorporation of a pedestrian circulation plan, concurrency with infrastructure capacity, and the like. In a case of first impression regarding contract zoning, the court decided that the conditions attached to the rezoning approval did not form an enforceable contract, but were reasonable conditions that provide a public benefit, especially satisfying the concerns of residents living closest to the property. In the event the developers failed to satisfy the conditions, "the process would simply go back to point zero." *Id.* at 59.

(f) In *McLean Hosp. Corp. v. Town of Belmont*, 778 N.E.2d 1016 (Mass. App. 2002), a hospital and town negotiated a memorandum of agreement regarding the hospital's plan for rezoning of its undeveloped property. In exchange for the hospitals' agreement not to try to build houses on all the rezoned land, but to leave open space, donate a cemetery, and make other concessions, the town rezoned the land and made its own concessions, including assisting the hospital in obtaining certain tax benefits. The rezoning was challenged by neighbors, and the court held the rezoning valid because it was in the town's best interest and did not involve extraneous consideration, such as the donation of park land in another part of town.

Are any of these cases distinguishable, or do some of them conflict? What rule can you derive from these decisions?

4. *Bargaining in the zoning process.* Like development agreements, "contract" zoning is another example of bargaining in the zoning process. Unlike development agreements, however, a zoning "contract" is attached to a zoning change. Contract zoning is attractive because it provides an opportunity to tailor the requirements of a zoning ordinance more specifically to the property in question, as in *Collard.* Compare the floating zone and a conditioned special use, which permit a similar "tailoring" in the formal decision making process, without an agreement. Which is preferable?

If the justification for imposing collective decision-making on the land use process is that an "efficient" result cannot always be achieved by purely private bargaining, what (if anything) is wrong with a hybrid scheme in which the government, as representative of the collective interest, explicitly bargains with the affected private party or parties? Can you decipher this tortured sentence from the principal case, in which the court appears to be considering this question?

> While permitting citizens to be governed by the best bargain they can strike with a local legislature would not be consonant with notions of good government, absent proof of a contract purporting to bind the local legislature in advance to exercise its zoning authority in a bargained-for manner, a rule which would have the effect of forbidding a municipality from trying to protect landowners in the vicinity of a zoning change by imposing protective conditions based on the assertion that that body is bargaining away its discretion, would not be in the best interests of the public.

Are those courts which prohibit or restrict contract zoning implicitly expressing misgivings about the underlying theory of land use controls?

5. *Concomitant Agreement Zoning.* Professor Bruce M. Kramer, noting that "[t]he contract-conditional zoning dichotomy is little more than a semantic game," has suggested an alternative analysis. *Contract Zoning — Old Myths and New Realities*, 34 Land Use L. & Zoning Dig., No. 8, at 4 (1982). He suggests the approach adopted by the Washington Supreme Court, which calls this device concomitant agreement zoning, or CAZ, as in *State ex rel. Myhre v. City of Spokane*, 422 P.2d 790 (Wash. 1969):

> [T]his neutral term would allow courts to analyze the underlying validity of each CAZ rather than merely concluding that contract zoning is invalid and conditional zoning is valid. This more *ad hoc* approach would allow the courts to view what most CAZs attempt to achieve — namely, the minimization of negative externalities caused by certain types of new developments that are otherwise beneficial to the community and its neighborhood. [*Id.* at 5.]

Do you agree with this suggestion? Does it explain the cases discussed in Note 3 *supra*? Would any of these cases come out differently under Professor Kramer's test? Professor Kramer reviews all of the contract zoning cases. He notes states in which contract zoning is either per se valid or invalid, states that are "schizophrenic," and states in which there are "muddy waters."

6. *Effect of invalidity.* Suppose there is no challenge by third parties to a conditional rezoning and that the landowner later refuses to observe the land use restrictions contained in a recorded covenant because they violate the statutory mandate that all zoning regulations "shall be uniform for each class or kind of buildings throughout each district." If the court should accept this argument, would it be likely simply to hold that the added restrictions were invalid, or that the entire rezoning transaction was void so that the land would revert to its prior zoning classification? See Comment, *Contract and Conditional Zoning: A Tool for Zoning Flexibility*, 23 Hastings L.J. 825, 836 (1972), observing that, where a municipality seeks to enforce the added restrictions and the landowner resists, the courts generally either sustain the added restrictions or hold them invalid without deciding the validity of the rezoning amendment itself, although a court clearly has the discretion to invalidate both the amendment and the added restrictions. How does the principal case handle this issue?

In *Cross*, Note 3 *supra*, the court said: "The owner of the rezoned land may be estopped from objecting to the conditions by having proposed or consented to them. And the conditions may be upheld against the unestopped landowner as being sustainable under the police power." 235 S.E.2d at 383 n.2. For a case holding a developer to be estopped to challenge a rezoning as illegal contract zoning, see *City of Cedar Rapids v. McConnell-Stevely-Anderson Architects & Planners*, 423 N.W.2d 17 (Iowa 1988) (developer requested and city granted zoning change and special use permit).

7. *Statutory authority.* Some statutes confer the authority to do conditional zoning. See Ariz. Rev. Stat. Ann. § 11-832 (zoning conditioned on development schedule and specific uses; board may revoke zoning if property not developed at end of scheduled period); R.I. Gen. Laws § 45-24-53(H) (similar); Va. Code Ann. § 15.2-2298 (landowner is permitted, prior to a hearing before a governing body, to submit voluntary written proffers of "reasonable conditions" as part of the landowner's proposed amendment to the zoning ordinance). This type of statute at least deals with the uniformity problem. *Sweetman v. Town of Cumberland*, 364 A.2d 1277 (R.I. 1976), held that the statute authorized the local governing body to limit the application of the conditions imposed to those parcels which are rezoned, and that identical conditions need not be imposed on land in the same use classification but not covered by the rezoning amendment.

A Maryland statute confers a more limited power:

> On the zoning or rezoning of any land, a local legislative body may retain or reserve the power to approve or disapprove the design of buildings, construction, landscaping, or other improvements, alterations, and changes made or to be made on the land being zoned or rezoned to assure conformity with the intent and purpose of this article and of the local jurisdiction's zoning ordinance. [Md. Code Ann. Art. 66B, § 4.01.]

Mayor & Council v. Rylyns Enters., 814 A.2d 469 (Md. 2002), recognizes that this statute permits a form of conditional zoning if the zoning is accomplished in conformity with the statute. State statutes authorizing development agreements are another legislative response to the judicial decisions finding that conditions to rezoning are contract zoning. For further discussion of development agreements, see Part E, *supra*, and Schwartz, *Development*

Agreements: Contracting for Vested Rights, 28 B.C. Envtl. Aff. L. Rev. 719 (2001) (discussing development agreement legislation as authorizing a valid form of contract zoning).

8. *Reverters.* One problem with conditional zoning is that market conditions or other influences may cause the developer not to proceed as planned. Can a statute or the agreement provide that the zoning will revert if development does not begin by a stated time? In *Scrutton v. County of Sacramento*, 79 Cal. Rptr. 872 (Cal. App. 1969), the court invalidated an automatic reversion clause that provided that the land would revert to its original classification if the landowner breached any of the covenants in the conditional zoning agreement. The court held that the reversion would be a second rezoning and would violate statutory requirements that rezoning be accomplished through notice, hearing and planning commission inquiry. The automatic reversion would also violate substantive limitations on the zoning power. The court characterized the automatic reversion as a "forfeiture rather than a legislative decision on land use." Accord *Spiker v. City of Lakewood*, 603 P.2d 130 (Colo. 1979); *Super Wash, Inc. v. City of White Settlement*, 131 S.W.3d 249 (Tex. App. 2004) (automatic reversion invalid as surrendering future zoning power).

Compare *Colwell v. Howard County*, 354 A.2d 210 (Md. App. 1976). The court upheld a "use it or lose it" clause under which the property would revert to its original classification unless the property owner applied for a site plan within two years of the rezoning, applied for a building permit within one year of the approval of the site plan, and commenced substantial construction within three years of the permit's issuance. The court noted that the issuance of a building permit in Maryland does not create a vested right until substantial construction is begun. For this reason, "it does no violence to his constitutional rights to require through a generally applied, properly enacted law, that a zoning change be utilized within a reasonable time period." *Id.* at 216. Are the cases distinguishable? Are they correct?

9. Increasingly, developers are negotiating privately with neighbors to mitigate impacts of large scale projects while reducing neighborhood opposition to the proposals. The contracts that result have been termed "Community Benefit Agreements." Do such private agreements skirt the problems of contract zoning? Are they another way to satisfy the NIMBYs? Among concerns about such agreements are whether the larger community is sufficiently benefitted and whether the contracts are enforceable. See Note, *Community Benefits Agreements: Can Private Contracts Replace Public Responsibility?* 18 Cornell J.L. & Pub. Pol'y 223 (2008); Salkin & Levine, *Symposium: Community Benefits Agreements and Comprehensive Planning: Balancing Community Empowerment and the Police Power*, 18 J.L. & Pol'y 157 (2009); Wolf-Powers, *Community Benefits Agreements and Local Government*, 76 J. Am. Plan. Ass'n 141 (Spring 2010); *Community Benefits Agreements: The Power, Practice, and Promise of a Responsible Redevelopment Tool* (2007, Annie E. Casey Foundation), available at www.aecf.org. One author recommends that local governments should avoid Community Benefit Agreements unless they are subject to procedural guards to ensure transparency, representativeness, legality and enforceability. Been, Community Benefits Agreements: A New Local Government Tool or Another Variation on the Exactions Theme? (Working Paper 2010), available at http://furmancenter.org/files/publications/Community_Benefits_Agreements_Working_Paper.pdf. Extensive information about CBAs can also be found at www.communitybenefits.org.

10. *Sources.* For discussion of contract zoning, reverters and other flexible zoning devices, see 2 Ziegler, Rathkopf's Law of Zoning and Planning ch. 29A; Wegner, *Moving Toward the Bargaining Table: Contract Zoning, Development Agreements, and the Theoretical Founda-*

tions of Government Land Use Deals, 65 N.C. L. Rev. 957 (1987); Note, *Concomitant Agreement Zoning: An Economic Analysis*, 1985 U. Ill. L. Rev. 89; Note, *Yes In My Backyard: Developers, Government and Communities Working Together through Development Agreements and Community Benefit Agreements.* 42 Ind. L. Rev. 227-255 (2009).

G. SITE PLAN REVIEW

Site plan review is another technique available to land use agencies to review the details of a land development project. Site plan review may give the municipality its only opportunity to review the design specifics of a development that is a permitted use and can be built "as of right." Of course, it may also be applied to developments that require a zoning change, or a separate approval, such as a conditional use permit or a subdivision approval. Site plan review is an almost invariable feature in planned unit development (PUD) zoning provisions. See Chapter 7.

The purposes of site plan review are indicated by the following New York statute, which authorizes site plan review:

> Site plans shall show the arrangement, layout and design of the proposed use of the land on said plan. The ordinance or local law shall specify the land uses that require site plan approval and the elements to be included on plans submitted for approval. The required site plan elements which are included in the zoning ordinance or local law may include, where appropriate, those related to parking, means of access, screening, signs, landscaping, architectural features, location and dimensions of buildings, adjacent land uses and physical features meant to protect adjacent land uses as well as any additional elements specified by the town board in such zoning ordinance or local law. [New York Town Law § 274-a(2)(a).]

See also N.J. Stat. Ann. § 40:55D-41 (includes elements listed in New York law and adds preservation of existing natural resources on site and conservation of energy and use of renewable energy resources). Only a few states authorize site plan review, but in the absence of statute, most courts find this authority implied in the general terms of land use legislation. See *Y.D. Dugout, Inc. v. Board of Appeals*, 255 N.E.2d 732 (Mass. 1970); *Town of Grand Chute v. U.S. Paper Converters, Inc.*, 600 N.W.2d 33 (Wis. App. 1999).

Site plan review serves many of the same purposes as conditions attached to a rezoning to the extent that it controls the details of a development. The statute or ordinance that governs the site plan will generally lay out the technical requirements of the site plan in some detail, as the plan is a graphic representation of the site development plan. The resolution or ordinance that approves the site plan may also contain conditions or restrictions on the site development that do not appear on the plan itself, such as limitations on the buildout time, off-site improvements required, and others. In the case that follows, the site plan questions arise in the absence of specific statutory authority, but the case is otherwise typical of the concerns that local boards have.

CHARISMA HOLDING CORP. v. ZONING BOARD OF APPEALS OF THE TOWN OF LEWISBORO

266 App. Div. 2d 540, 699 N.Y.S.2d 89 (1999)

DECISION & ORDER

The petitioner Charisma Holding Corp. (hereinafter Charisma) is the owner of commercially-zoned real property in the respondent Town of Lewisboro. The property is the site of an automobile dealership and is abutted to the north and east by residentially-zoned property. In January 1988 Charisma petitioned the respondent Zoning Board of Appeals of the Town of Lewisboro (hereinafter ZBA) for various relief, including an area variance to build a 3,000 square-foot six-bay garage. One bay was to be used for washing vehicles, another for spray-painting vehicles, and the remaining four for repairs and service. Although such a garage is a permitted use of the property under the relevant zoning regulations, an area variance was needed because it would bring the developed area of the property to 69% of the total area, and the relevant regulations permit development of no more than 60%. The petitioner proposed to locate the garage on the northern end of its property. During the review process, which included three public meetings and two visits to the property, residential neighbors to the north and east voiced various objections to the location of the proposed garage. One property owner in particular noted that the proposed location would place it within 100 feet of her kitchen window and would result, inter alia, in exhaust and paint fumes, and additional noise and traffic.

Based on such concerns, the ZBA considered two alternative sites for the garage. After various inquiries, the ZBA noted a preference for what they designated as site No. 3 (hereinafter the middle lot), which they determined would create significantly less impact on the surrounding residential properties. The petitioner, asserting various additional costs and concerns in building the garage on that site, pressed its preference for the site originally proposed. By determination dated April 27, 1998, the ZBA denied the petitioner's request for an area variance for the site as proposed. The ZBA found that a grant of the area variance as requested would result in a substantial undesirable change in the character of the residential neighborhood to the north, that there would be a substantial detriment to the nearby properties, and that there was an alternative site. The ZBA found that the benefit to the petitioner if the area variance was granted as requested was outweighed by the detriment to the health, safety, and welfare of the neighborhood community (see, Town Law § 267-b). However, the ZBA granted an area variance to the petitioner based on locating the garage on the middle lot, finding no similar concerns. In the judgment appealed from, the Supreme Court directed the ZBA to grant the requested area variance as proposed by the petitioner. The court held that because the garage was a permitted use of the property and otherwise conformed with all relevant zoning restrictions, the sole issue properly before the ZBA was the development of 69%, as opposed to 60%, of the total lot area. Thus, the court held, the ZBA's denial of the variance as requested was based on a matter not relevant to its considerations, that is, the proposed use of the additional area. Accordingly, the court determined that because the ZBA implicitly found that the use of the additional area should be permitted, the variance should have been granted as requested. We reverse.

Judicial review of the denial of the area variance is limited to whether the determination was illegal, arbitrary, or an abuse of discretion. If the determination is supported by substantial evidence and has a rational basis, it will not be disturbed. Here, review of the record reveals that the ZBA properly considered and weighed the relevant statutory criteria, and that its determination was supported by substantial evidence and had a rational basis (see, Town Law § 267-b). We disagree with the Supreme Court that the relevant statutory balancing test can be properly applied without consideration of the proposed use. Accordingly, the respondents' denial of the area variance as requested is confirmed.

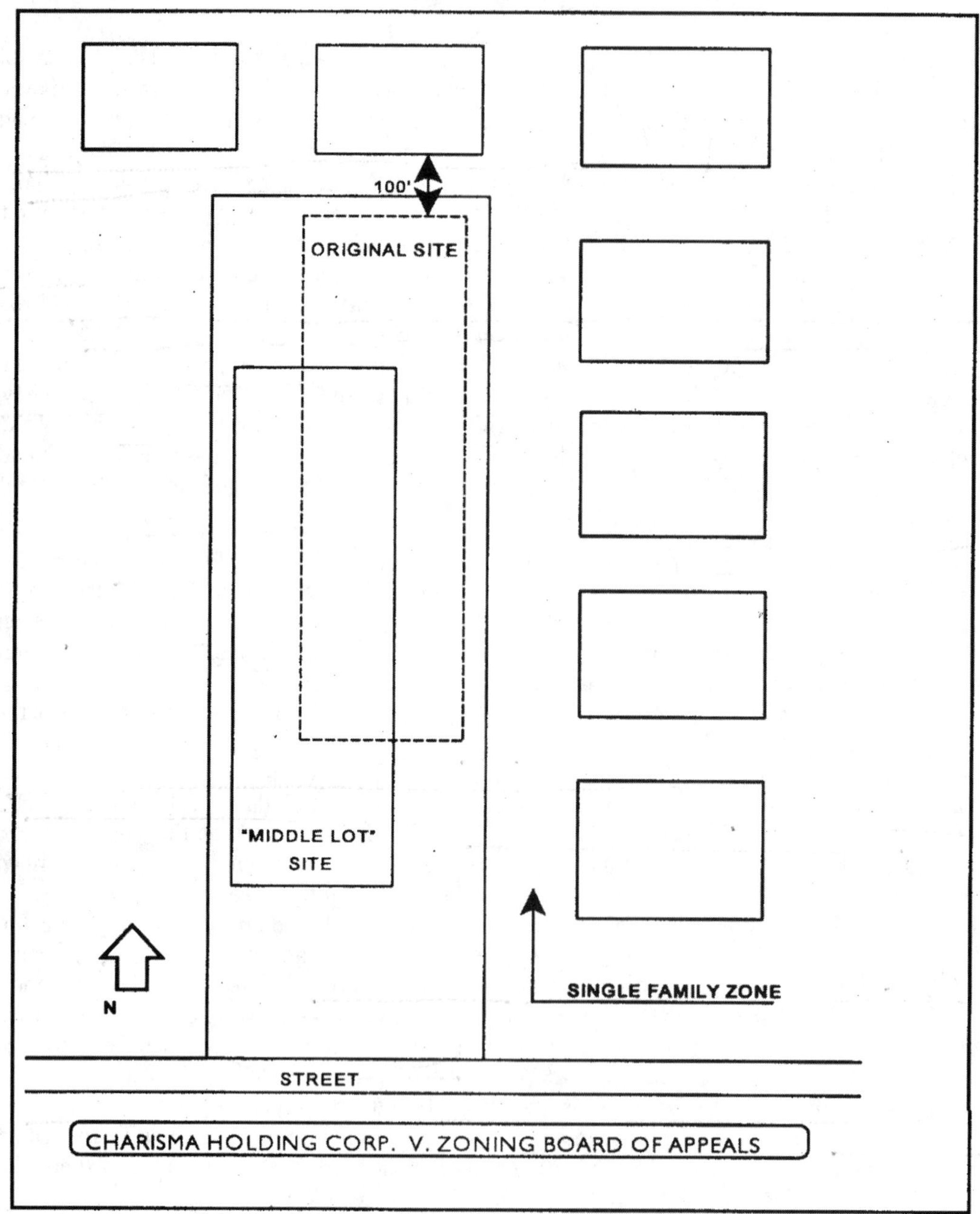

The petitioner, characterizing the determination of the ZBA as a grant of the requested area variance with a condition that the garage be built on an alternative site, argues that the ZBA usurped the role of the Planning Board by considering the location of the garage. The petitioner argues that the authority to consider the placement of buildings is vested solely with the Planning Board pursuant to its authority to approve a site plan, which includes consideration of "parking, means of access, screening, signs, landscaping, architectural features, *location and dimensions of buildings,* adjacent land uses and physical features meant to protect adjacent land uses" (see Town Law § 274-a[2] [emphasis supplied]). However, even accepting the petitioner's characterization of the ZBA's determination as correct, the determination may nonetheless be upheld. In granting use and area variances, the ZBA is expressly authorized to impose "such reasonable conditions and restrictions as are directly related to and incidental to the proposed use of the property" that are "consistent with the spirit and intent of the zoning ordinance or local law" and that shall minimize "any adverse impact such variance may have on the neighborhood or community" (Town Law § 267-b[4]). The petitioner has not cited, and research does not reveal, any case law which holds that there may be no overlap between matters that might be properly considered by a Planning Board on review of a site plan and conditions that might be properly imposed by a zoning board in granting an area variance. Rather, the conclusion to be drawn from the case law is to the contrary. The Court of Appeals has held that conditions imposed by a zoning board in granting a variance or special permit "might properly relate 'to fences, safety devices, landscaping, screening and access roads relating to period of use, screening, outdoor lighting and noises, and enclosure of buildings and relating to emission of odors, dust, smoke, refuse matter, vibration noise and other factors incidental to comfort, peace, enjoyment, health or safety of the surrounding area' " (*Matter of St. Onge v Donovan*, 522 N.E.2d 1019.) Further, the Court of Appeals has held that the rezoning of property for commercial uses had been properly conditioned on the requirement that the owners thereof "execute and record restrictive covenants relating to the maximum area to be occupied by buildings, the erection of a fence, and the planting of shrubbery" (*Matter of St. Onge v Donovan, supra*, citing *Church v Town of Islip*.) Such conditions both implicitly and expressly overlap with considerations relevant to review of a site plan (see, Town Law § 274-a[2]). [The court cited appellate division cases holding a variance for a fence was properly granted on conditions that a portion of the fence be located five feet from the property line and that certain specified green plantings be maintained; that a use variance was properly granted on condition that there be no change to the exterior design or appearance of the building; and that variances were properly granted on condition, inter alia, that petitioner remove a shed on the property and return the area to green space.] Accordingly, here, the ZBA did not exceed its authority in considering the location of the petitioner's proposed garage in rendering a determination on the requested area variance.

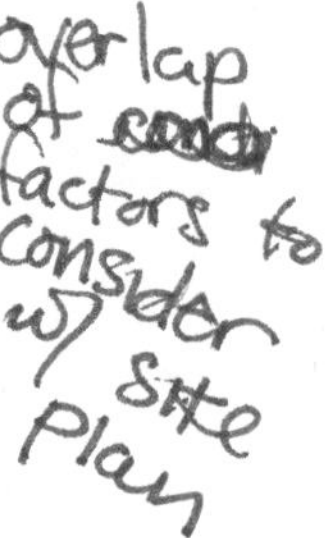

NOTES AND QUESTIONS

1. *Authority to review.* As indicated in the principal case, New York authorizes site plan review but assigns it to a different body than the one that reviews the appropriateness of the use for the property. Suppose the court had upheld the denial of the variance as initially proposed but then held that site plan issues were beyond the ZBA's jurisdiction. The applicant could have presented the "middle lot" site plan to the planning board, but that proposal also required a variance, which the planning board could not grant. Are the town and the applicant doomed to the failure of a land use proposal that, in the end, was satisfactory to both? The court's actual holding permits an efficient and equitable outcome. Some modern statutes allow boards to exercise each other's jurisdiction under some circumstances so that the application

can be considered in a single proceeding. See, e.g., N.J.S.A. § 40:55D-76.

2. *Permitted uses as a site plan issue.* In *Sherman v. City of Colorado Springs Planning Comm.*, 680 P.2d 1302 (Colo. App. 1983), the parties stipulated that a proposed 14-story residential building was in all respects a permitted use in the district under the zoning code. The site plan application was denied because of neighborhood opposition based on height and traffic. The court held that

> Where, as here, the zoning body has determined that the health, safety, and general welfare are best promoted by zoning land for residential high-rise purposes with specified set back, height, and bulk limitations, that body may not thereafter attempt to reserve to itself the discretion to decide which of the complying land uses will be permitted. To interpret this development plan ordinance as giving the city the power to deny a lawful use of property runs contrary to the requirement of adequate standards. [*Id.* at 1304.]

Other courts agree. See *Kosinski v. Lawlor*, 418 A.2d 66 (Conn. 1979) (retail complex rejection as a "poor use of the site" reversed); *S.E.W. Friel v. Triangle Oil Co.*, 543 A.2d 863 (Md. App. 1988) (cannot disapprove site plan because permitted use is not compatible with surrounding area). If this were not the general rule, would there be any difference between site plan review and the special permit approach? The distinction is not always obvious. See *A. Aiudi & Sons v. Planning & Zoning Comm'n*, 837 A.2d 748 (Conn. 2003) (town code explicitly allowed the removal of sand and gravel from the applicant's property, but subjected removal to numerous conditions and standards. Upholding the town's denial of the application, the court determined that the application was not for site plan approval, but for a special exception which could be denied for general health, safety and welfare reasons.) Why do you suppose municipalities try to use site plan review to block projects permitted by the zoning ordinance? Compare *City of Colorado Springs v. Securecare Self Storage, Inc.*, 10 P.3d 1244 (Colo. 2000) (interpreting zoning ordinance to allow rejection of use in site plan review that is authorized by the zoning ordinance).

3. *Off-site conditions.* Site plan review is intended as a review of conditions arising on the site. This does not mean that conditions off-site are irrelevant to the site plan. See *Coscan Washington, Inc. v. Maryland-National Capital Park & Planning Comm'n*, 590 A.2d 1080 (Md. App. 1991) (building materials may be regulated in new subdivision to be compatible to the adjacent historic district); *Derry Senior Dev., LLC v. Town of Derry*, 951 A.2d 170 (N.H. 2008). It is typically the case that landscaping or buffering requirements for the site will take into consideration the adjacent uses. In *Lionel's Appliance Center, Inc. v. Citta*, 383 A.2d 773 (N.J.L. Div. 1978), the reason given for rejection of an office complex site plan was, as is often the case, off-site traffic congestion. The court held that off-site traffic problems were a proper factor for consideration in the approval of variances and special exceptions, but not in site plan review. A site plan could be denied "only if the ingress and egress proposed by the plan creates an unsafe and inefficient vehicular condition." The court also held that the site plan statute authorized a contribution from the developer for off-site improvements. Accord *PRB Enters., Inc. v. South Brunswick Planning Bd.*, 518 A.2d 1099 (N.J. 1987); *Moriarty v. Planning Bd.*, 506 N.Y.S.2d 184 (App. Div. 1986) (inadequate fire protection a matter for fire inspector, not the planning board).

Attorney Brian Blaesser argues that site plan review "should not address off-site conditions except to the extent that on-site conditions affect off-site conditions." Discretionary Zoning, *supra*, at § 5.03[4]. A number of courts support this position. *Southland Corp. v. Mayor & City*

Council, 541 A.2d 653 (Md. App. 1988) (can deny site plan because of traffic hazards). However, isn't a consideration of off-site conditions an implicit reconsideration of the status of a project as a permitted use under the zoning ordinance? Note that the New York statute, reproduced *supra*, authorizes site plan elements "meant to protect adjacent land uses." How should this provision be interpreted?

This issue also arises under subdivision control ordinances. See Chapter 7. Compare *Robbins Auto Parts, Inc. v. City of Laconia*, 371 A.2d 1167 (N.H. 1977) (followed subdivision control cases to hold that site plan review may require contribution for facilities needed by subdivision), with *Riegert Apartments Corp. v. Planning Bd.*, 441 N.E.2d 1076 (N.Y. 1982) (contra). In both cases, the courts and statutes have developed restrictions on the extent to which local governments can require conditions or "exactions" as part of approvals, a matter more extensively discussed in Chapter 7.

4. *The trend toward discretionary approval.* Professor Kenneth Silliman argues that the site plan process, an original scheme for examining a narrow range of developments with reference to preset standards, has been expanded over the years to encompass a case-by-case review of a broad range of development proposals. It thus functions much like subdivision controls for properties that otherwise would not undergo platting. Silliman, *Risk Management for Land Use Regulations: A Proposed Model*, 49 Clev. St. L. Rev. 591 (2001). He points out that this expansion of the site plan review process works well, especially in well-staffed communities, to respond to unique site issues and to implement more sophisticated criteria such as design guidelines. He warns, however, that this often comes at a cost of delay in the approval process, and less predictability for the developer. What other advantages or disadvantages might there be with a more discretionary approval process?

H. THE ROLE OF THE COMPREHENSIVE PLAN IN THE ZONING PROCESS

Although the Standard Zoning Act and many state acts that follow it provide that zoning must be "in accordance with a comprehensive plan," most courts do not give this requirement its literal meaning. The leading case is *Kozesnik v. Montgomery Twp.*, 131 A.2d 1 (N.J. 1957). The court held that this requirement did not require a comprehensive plan in some "physical form" outside the zoning ordinance. The court held that the intent of this requirement was to prevent a capricious exercise of the zoning power. The court noted that

> "plan" connotes an integrated product of a rational process and "comprehensive" requires something beyond a piecemeal approach, both to be revealed by the ordinance considered in relation to the physical facts and the [statutory] purposes. [*Id.* at 7.]

Most courts still take this position. See *Sasich v. City of Omaha*, 347 N.W.2d 93 (Neb. 1984). But see *Largent v. Zoning Bd. of Appeals*, 671 S.E.2d 794 (W. Va. 2008) (statute requires that a comprehensive plan be adopted as a condition to zoning ordinance, invalidating zoning ordinance where town had not adopted a comprehensive plan). The first judicial break with this traditional interpretation came in an Oregon case, *Fasano v. Board of County Comm'rs*, 507 P.2d 23 (Or. 1973), which held that any zoning change must be consistent with the comprehensive plan. *Fasano* is considered in connection with the *Snyder* case, *supra*. Oregon later adopted legislation establishing a state planning program that requires planning by local governments and the consistency of zoning with an adopted and state-approved plan.

A number of states now mandate comprehensive planning by statute and some also require that zoning be consistent with the plan. New Jersey legislation, N.J. Stat. Ann. § 40:55D-62, which partially overruled *Kozesnik* is an example. It requires elements of a formal plan and consistency unless this requirement is set aside by a majority vote of the full membership of the local governing body:

> [The zoning] ordinance shall be adopted after the planning board has adopted the land use plan element and the housing plan element of a master plan, and all of the provisions of such zoning ordinance or any amendment or revision thereto shall either be substantially consistent with the land use plan element and the housing plan element of the master plan or designed to effectuate such plan elements . . . [except if inconsistency is authorized] only by affirmative vote of a majority of the full authorized membership of the governing body, with the reasons of the governing body for so acting set forth in a resolution and recorded in its minutes when adopting such a zoning ordinance . . . .

California is another early and a leading example. It mandates planning and requires zoning ordinances to be consistent with the comprehensive plan. Consistency is defined to mean that

> [t]he various land uses authorized by the [zoning] ordinance are compatible with the objectives, policies, general land uses and programs specified in such a plan. [Cal. Gov't Code § 65860(a)(2).]

Florida legislation provides a more comprehensive definition. It is stated in the *Snyder* case, reproduced *supra.* The *Snyder* decision gave weight to the comprehensive plan by making the presumption of constitutionality of a zoning change depend on the plan.

Why consistency? Note how the consistency requirement changes the rules under which the zoning ordinance and zoning changes are judicially reviewed. Without a consistency requirement, for example, a rezoning amendment is subject to the ad hoc rules that govern spot zoning. See Section E2, *supra.* With a consistency requirement, a rezoning will be governed by the policies of the plan. Why this change?

One answer has been provided by the Minnesota Supreme Court:

> The essence of constitutional zoning with no due process or equal protection problems is generally recognized to be demonstrated by the existence of a plan which uniformly, without discrimination and without unreasonable restrictions, promotes the general welfare. [*Amcon Corp. v. City of Eagan*, 348 N.W.2d 66, 74 (Minn. 1984).]

What does the court mean by "due process and equal protection" problems? One answer is that the court is concerned with the "fundamental fairness" in land use decision-making which is demanded by these constitutional limitations. Note that Minnesota is one of the majority states that do not mandate comprehensive planning, so that its courts interpret a comprehensive plan that has nevertheless been adopted by a city as "advisory and the city is not unalterably bound by its provisions. However, the recommendations should be entitled to some weight . . ." and a refusal to rezone to the plan's designation is evidence of arbitrariness. *Id.* at 74–75.

This "fundamental fairness" point is made in Mandelker, *Should State Government Mandate Local Planning? . . . Yes*, 44 Planning, No. 6, at 14 (1978). The article notes two aspects of the problem. One is the need to prevent arbitrary decisionmaking in the land use process, a concern dominant in the Oregon cases mandating consistency with the plan. The other is the need to resolve the "conflicting societal pressures" that land use programs make on the use of land. The article concludes that

> the courts prefer the advance statement of principle for land use decisions [through plans] to the ad hoc adjustments that commonly take place when these principles are not provided. [*Id.* at 16.]

Planning Professor Lawrence Susskind took the opposing view in this debate. *Should State Government Mandate Local Planning? . . . No*, 44 Planning, No. 46, at 17. Susskind argued that attempts to mandate local planning would fail because difficulties in winning support for planning are not taken into account and because planning is not adequately funded. He also argued that state planning standards cannot take community differences into consideration, that the planning profession cannot agree on what constitutes a good plan, and that it is "almost impossible" to ensure consistency among the elements of the plan and between a plan and subsequent zoning decisions.

NOTES AND QUESTIONS

1. *Who won the planning debate?* Many of the arguments against mandatory planning concentrate on the inadequacies of the plan and the planning process. See J. DiMento, The Consistency Doctrine and the Limits of Planning 48-51 (1980) (author favors mandatory planning). Consult Chapter 1 for a discussion of the strengths and weaknesses of planning. For more detailed arguments supporting mandatory planning and the consistency requirement, see Mandelker, *The Role of the Comprehensive Plan in Land Use Regulation*, 74 Mich. L. Rev. 899 (1976). For discussion of the reasons behind the language used in the Standard Act and a review of statutory consistency requirement, see Meck, *The Legislative Requirement that Zoning and Land Use Controls Be Consistent with an Independently Adopted Comprehensive Plan*, 3 Wash. U. J.L. & Pol'y 295 (2000).

2. *A middle view.* Some courts, like the Minnesota court quoted above, give presumptive weight to the plan if one exists, although not adopting the view that consistency with the plan is required. *Udell v. Haas*, 235 N.E.2d 897 (N.Y. 1968), is a leading case. A small suburban village downzoned a property from commercial to residential uses after it became apparent that the owner of the property intended to build commercially. The village had consistently zoned this property commercial. The court invalidated the downzoning and held that local zoning authorities must pay more than "mock obeisance" to the statutory "in accordance with the comprehensive plan" requirement. The plan was not to be defined as "any particular document," and rezonings "should not conflict with the fundamental land use policies and development plans of the community." The court noted that these policies could be found in the comprehensive plan of the community if one has been adopted. See *Palatine Nat'l Bank v. Village of Barrington*, 532 N.E.2d 955 (Ill. App. 1988) (the existence of a comprehensive plan indicates the community has given careful consideration to the orderly utilization of the property within its borders; a comprehensive plan should be considered in determining the reasonableness of a proposed use) Accord *West Bluff Neighborhood Ass'n v. City of Albuquerque*, 50 P.3d 182 (N.M. App. 2002).

A few courts also have held that the presumption of validity usually accorded zoning is shifted or weakened in the absence of a comprehensive plan. See *Forestview Homeowners Ass'n v. County of Cook*, 309 N.E.2d 763 (Ill. App. 1974) (rezoning for apartments held invalid). However, in *First Nat'l Bank v. Village of Vernon Hills*, 371 N.E.2d 659 (Ill. App. 1977), the court held the relevant issue was whether the municipality had given "care and consideration to the use and development of the land within its boundaries, not whether it had a piece of paper in the form of a comprehensive plan." Where does this leave us?

3. *Takings.* The *Amcon* case, in the excerpt quoted in the text *supra*, did not make reference to the role of the plan as a defense to taking of property objections. For a case relying on a local plan to reject taking objections to a local growth-management program, see the *Ramapo* case, reproduced *infra*, Chapter 7.

How is a court likely to interpret the consistency requirement when there is an apparent conflict between the comprehensive plan and a zoning amendment? Will the court require a better consistency when the state statute has a more explicit "consistency" requirement than the traditional "in accordance with a comprehensive plan" standard? Consider the following case from Arizona, which has adopted a legislative mandate for comprehensive planning and zoning consistency.

HAINES v. CITY OF PHOENIX

151 Ariz. 286, 727 P.2d 339 (1986)

HATHAWAY, CHIEF JUDGE:

Appellant contests the trial court's granting of summary judgment in affirmance of the City of Phoenix's (city) authority to rezone the parcel in controversy. Appellees cross-appeal and challenge the trial court's finding that the city has adopted a general or specific plan of urban development. We agree with the trial court on both counts and affirm.

On January 1, 1974, Arizona's Urban Environment Management Act (act) became effective. The act requires municipalities to adopt long-range, general plans for urban development. A.R.S. § 9-461.05(A). The act also authorizes specific plans. A.R.S. § 9-461.08. The act requires municipal zoning ordinances be consistent with the general plans. § 9-462.01(E). On July 3, 1979, the city adopted two plans — the Phoenix Concept Plan 2000 and the Interim 1985 Plan. It is disputed whether these plans are general or specific plans as defined by the statute.

This action arose from the Phoenix City Council's granting of a "height waiver" for a highrise office project that is proposed to be constructed by appellee Adams Group on 14.48 acres of land on Central Avenue between Glenrosa and Turney avenues in Phoenix. The property was zoned C-2H-R (intermediate commercial highrise) and subject to a 250-foot highrise limitation. The 1985 plan also limits to 250 feet buildings in the area in which this parcel is located.

On July 29, 1983, the Adams Group submitted an application to amend the city zoning ordinance to permit a building on the parcel in excess of the 250-foot height limitation. The rezoning application was heard by the planning commission on November 16, 1983. That body recommended denial by a 3 to 2 vote. Pursuant to § 108-J.1 of the city zoning ordinance the Adams Group requested the city council to hold a public hearing on the application and not to adopt the planning commission's recommendation. Two hearings were held, on December 19, 1983 and February 6, 1984. On February 6, the city council approved a rezoning which allowed the Adams Group to erect a 500-foot building. Appellant then filed this action alleging the city council's action is inconsistent with the general or specific plans and therefore is in violation of A.R.S. § 9.462.01(E). Appellees argue that the city had not adopted either a general or specific plan at the time of the city council action and the only issue before the city council was whether there was compliance with § 412-B.2-F(1) of the Phoenix Zoning Ordinance, permitting height amendments.

It is without dispute that the city council complied with § 412-B.2-F(1). The trial court, on August 17, 1984, granted appellant partial summary judgment finding that the city had adopted a general or specific plan. On November 26, 1984, however, the trial court entered summary judgment finding that the city council's action did not violate A.R.S. § 9-462.01(E), and therefore dismissed appellant's complaint. Appellant appealed and appellees cross-appealed.

Appellant raises one issue on appeal: The trial court erred in finding that the rezoning was in compliance with A.R.S. § 9-462.01(E). Appellees raise two issues on appeal: (1) Phoenix has not adopted a general or specific plan and is not subject to the limitations of § 9-462.01(E) and (2) in any event, the actions of the city council were in compliance with both the Concept Plan 2000 and the 1985 plan.

I. *Has the City Adopted a General or Specific Plan?*

. . . .

A.R.S. § 9-461(1) states a general plan means: ". . . [A] municipal statement of land development policies, which may include maps, charts, graphs and text which set forth objectives, principles and standards for local growth and redevelopment enacted under the provisions of this article or any prior statute." A.R.S. § 9-461(5) states a specific plan means: ". . . [A] detailed element of the general plan enacted under the provisions of this article or a prior statute."

It is clear that both the Concept Plan 2000 and the Interim Plan 1985 meet the definition for a general plan. Additionally, Interim Plan 1985 could be viewed as a specific plan for the implementation of the general plan pronounced in Concept Plan 2000. Concept Plan 2000 establishes the policy of dividing the city into villages, each containing a core, gradient and periphery. Interim Plan 1985 establishes specific criteria for the implementation of that policy in the Encanto Area in which this dispute occurred. Additionally, there is not any evidence that these two plans were not adopted under the provisions of the article pursuant to A.R.S. § 9-461.06. The real debate concerns A.R.S. § 9-461.05, which enunciates the scope of a general plan.

A.R.S. § 9-461.05(C) and (D) require the general plan to contain nine distinct elements. Those elements are:

1. A land use element.
2. Circulation element.
3. Conservation element.
4. Recreation element.
5. Public services and facility element.
6. Public buildings element.
7. Housing element.

8. Conservation rehabilitation and redevelopment element.

9. Safety element.

A review of the two plans establishes that some of the above required elements have not been addressed by either the Concept Plan 2000 or the Interim Plan 1985. . . . [We hold that] the missing elements . . . are irrelevant to the existence of a plan. . . .

While these plans are probably not satisfactory in their completeness, they are clearly plans according to the statutory definition. Appellees' reasoning would permit the city to perpetually avoid urban planning by leaving out any element or any subdivision of an element defined in § 9-461.05. This would produce the untenable result of the slightest omission causing the city to have no plan. . . .

II. *Was the Rezoning in Conformity with the Plan?*

A. *Applicability of A.R.S. § 9-462.01(E).*

A.R.S. § 9-462.01(E) states: "All zoning ordinances or regulations adopted under this article shall be consistent with the adopted general or specific plans of the municipality. . . ."

We must consider whether an amendment to a rezoning ordinance, such as we have in the current situation, falls under the mandate of this statute which only specifically states it applies to "zoning ordinances or regulations." While there are no Arizona decisions on point, other jurisdictions have held the requirement of conformity to the general plan is applicable to amendments as well as to the original zoning ordinance. [The decisions cited included *Udell v. Haas*, discussed *supra.*] The above decisions [reason] that the legislature intended to protect landowners in the populace from arbitrary and impulsive use [of] the zoning power and that such a safeguard would be meaningless unless applied to amendments of the ordinance. Other jurisdictions have held, however, that where the amendment itself constitutes a change in the comprehensive plan the limiting statute is not applicable. The current situation is controlled by the first line of cases inasmuch as the record supports no such intention by the city council. Therefore, the present amendment is valid only if it is consistent with the general and specific plans. . . .

B. *Is the amendment consistent with the general and specific plan?*

Normally the level of judicial review of a zoning ordinance or amendment is the rational basis test. This test is utilized because zoning or rezoning is a legislative act not a quasi-judicial act. Under the rational basis test if the court can hypothesize any rational reason why the legislative body made the choice it did, the statute or ordinance is constitutionally valid. This test validates statutes even if the legislative body did not consider the reasons articulated by the court. The reason for the adoption of the rational basis test was to prevent courts from sitting as super-legislatures and thereby prevent infringement upon the separation of powers. Of course, when fundamental constitutional liberties are at stake, courts will use a higher level of scrutiny.

If we were to apply the rational basis review to the current situation, we would presume the rezoning to be valid and would uphold its validity if we could hypothesize any reason why the city council may have believed the rezoning was consistent with the general plan. Some courts have taken this approach to deciding whether a zoning amendment is consistent with a general plan. Appellant argues, however, that the passage of § 9-462.01(E) vitiates the above normal level of review. He argues that if rational basis review is utilized, the legislative mandate requiring consistency between zoning and the general plan is without any force. Appellant argues instead that, due to the statute, there be no presumption of legislative validity and the city council be required to make written findings and articulate reasons for any deviation from the general plan. There is support for this approach.

We, however, reject both of the above approaches. By the enactment of § 9-462.01(E), the legislature has provided a standard by which to review zoning decisions in addition to the usual constitutional standard. That standard is consistency with the general plan. In our review, however, we will not substitute our judgment for that of the duly elected legislative body, the city council. Therefore our review will consist of viewing the record that was before the city council and determining if, from that evidence, the council could have decided that despite the deviation from the letter of the plan there was consistency. The burden of proof will still be on the plaintiff to show inconsistency.

Consistency has been defined as "basic harmony." J. Di Mento, The Consistency Doctrine and the Limits of Planning (1980). Therefore in the current situation if from the evidence before it the city council could have determined that the rezoning was in basic harmony with the general plan, the rezoning is valid. Of course in cases where the rezoning does not deviate from the general plan, rational basis review will still be utilized.

This rezoning did deviate from the general plan in that it surpassed by a large margin the 250-foot height restriction. The plan, however, has other goals for that area. The plan does provide that gradient areas where this proposed building lies will have some concentrations of land use in sub cores. Also there is a provision for commercial development of the Central Avenue corridor. The building height restrictions are only stated in precatory language. Additionally, the plan provided for open space in the gradient, encouragement of landscaping, areas for people to enjoy and commercial development. The city council had before it evidence that this building would be commercially beneficial, would provide open spaces and recreational areas, landscaping, etc. The council also heard testimony that the developer could build two 20-story buildings which would leave less open space and less potential recreational areas. In viewing the above evidence, we cannot say the city council was wrong in finding the rezoning in basic harmony with the general plan. We do not need specific findings by the council to come to this conclusion since we have viewed the same evidence the council viewed. Certainly written findings would be preferable, but they are not mandatory.

C. *Spot zoning.*

Although not argued by appellant, the issue of spot zoning must be addressed. Spot zoning is not per se invalid and validity turns on the circumstances of the particular situation. Courts have held that there is not illegal spot zoning when the zoning ordinance is in accordance with the general or comprehensive plan designed to promote general welfare. As we have held above, the amendment granted by the city council was in compliance with the general plan of the city. Therefore this amendment did not constitute illegal spot zoning.

Affirmed.

HOWARD, P.J., Specially Concurring. [Omitted.]

NOTES AND QUESTIONS

1. *The consistency issue.* Do you agree with the court's interpretation of the plan in the principal case? Under accepted rules of statutory interpretation, if the plan is ambiguous and requires judicial interpretation, the court and not the local government will determine what the planning policy really is. Does this displacement of authority provide the fundamental fairness that advocates of the consistency requirement demand? One way out of this dilemma is to require more specific plans. The plan would then resemble the zoning ordinance. Is this much specificity in plans desirable? Compare the case of *Pinecrest Lakes, Inc. v. Shidel*, 802 So. 2d 486 (Fla. App. 2001). Mrs. Shidel challenged a county approval for an apartment development on property adjacent to her single family neighborhood, on the basis that the county comprehensive plan required that new residential development proposals have "comparable density and compatible dwelling unit types" to their neighbors. The court found that there was no ambiguity in the plan and that, under the "strict scrutiny" standard adopted by the Florida courts, the approval was inconsistent with the plan. The local government interpretation was given no deference, and the court ordered the demolition of the apartments that the developer had built and rented while the case was proceeding. What if the plan had a different, more broadly phrased policy regarding comparability of uses?

As seen above, the judicial review standard courts apply in their review of the consistency requirement has a major effect on the outcome of a consistency case. This issue is discussed in the principal case, which appeared to apply the usual presumption in favor of the municipality, and in the *Pinecrest Lakes* case. See also *Fritz v. Lexington-Fayette Urban County Gov't*, 986 S.W.2d 456 (Ky. App. 1998) (applying presumption in favor of the municipality). Should the consistency requirement alter the traditional "fairly debatable" standard?

2. *Interpreting plans.* The presumption courts apply in favor of municipalities usually allows local zoning agencies considerable discretion in the interpretation of comprehensive plans. See *Greenebaum v. City of Los Angeles*, 200 Cal. Rptr. 237 (Cal. App. 1984) (accepting contention by city that land use decisions need only be in agreement or harmony with the plan). Courts also find consistency when the plan is amorphous and gives the municipality more discretion. *Sequoyah Hills Homeowners Ass'n v. City of Oakland*, 29 Cal. Rptr. 2d 182 (Cal. App. 1993). What does this say about plan drafting?

For an example of the importance of plan drafting, consider the following case. In *GATRI v. Blane*, 962 P.2d 367 (Haw. 1998), the court reviewed a special management area permit application for a restaurant use in an area on the island of Maui, where zoning permitted the use, but which was designated as "single-family" in the Kihei-Makena Community plan. The court found that the community plan was sufficiently specific regarding the single family use designation so that the proposed restaurant was inconsistent with the county general plan. It noted that the community plan's avowed purpose is to "provide a relatively detailed scheme for implementing [the General Plan] objectives and policies relative to the Kihei-Makena region," and contrasted the specificity of the Maui plan with that of the Honolulu plan. *Id.* at 374.

The court's interpretation of the Maryland statute that requires that zoning "conform" to a comprehensive plan to require only a "harmony" and not strict compliance, led directly to statutory changes requiring closer adherence. *Trail v. Terrapin Run, LLC*, 943 A.2d 1192 (Md. 2008), involved the approval of a planned development of 4,300 residences, a shopping center, equestrian center and community facilities. The court extensively reviewed the legislative history of the enabling statute, Md. Ann. Code art. 66B, and found that it did not mandate that the zoning of property strictly conform to the plan unless the local jurisdiction requires it. The use of the word "conform" in the statute does not change the intent of the law that a zoning board was not required to strictly adhere to the comprehensive plan, because the plan was merely advisory, unless it had been codified as an ordinance. In response, the Maryland legislature adopted The Smart and Sustainable Growth Act of 2009, which requires certain local actions (special exceptions, zoning ordinances, annexations, and others) to be "consistent with" the adopted plan. Actions that are "consistent with" or have "consistency with" a comprehensive plan are actions that further, and are not contrary to, the plan policies: timing of rezoning, development and implementation of the plan; development patterns; land uses; and densities or intensities. Does the legislation fix the problem caused by the *Terrapin Run* decision?

3. *Consistency not found.* Courts may sometimes find an inconsistency, especially where there is a clear conflict between the plan and the land use decision. See *Families Unafraid to Uphold Rural Eldorado County v. Board of Supervisors*, 74 Cal. Rptr. 2d 1 (Cal. App. 1998) (conflict with growth management policy as stated in the comprehensive plan).

In *Gillis v. City of Springfield*, 611 P.2d 355 (Or. App. 1980), the plan called for medium-density residential development. The rezoning allowed predominantly commercial development, though at the same density. The court held that comparability in intensity of use did not make the rezoning consistent with the plan. Should the use make any difference if the density is the same? Compare *Alluis v. Marion County*, 668 P.2d 1242 (Or. App. 1983) (density policy in plan did not mandate minimum lot size requirement in zoning ordinance), with *Board of Supvrs. v. Jackson*, 269 S.E.2d 381 (Va. 1980) (upholding interpretation of ambiguous residential infill policy in plan).

In *Mira Dev. Co. v. City of San Diego*, 252 Cal. Rptr. 825 (Cal. App. 1988), a proposed rezoning was consistent with the land use designation in the plan but violated a planning policy requiring adequate public facilities. The city denied the rezoning and the court affirmed. Is this correct? See also *Philipi v. City of Sublimity*, 662 P.2d 325 (Or. 1983) (court upheld denial of residential development in area zoned residential because plan favored retention of productive farm land in this area until it was needed for development). Some courts require specific findings as the basis for judicial review of consistency. *Love v. Board of County Comm'rs*, 671 P.2d 471 (Idaho 1983). Consider the debate between the Florida Justices regarding the importance of factual findings in *Broward County v. G.B.V. Int'l, Ltd.*, 787 So. 2d 838 (Fla. 2001), where the majority rejects the necessity to have written findings, and the dissent argues that they are necessary to improve the quality of local decisionmaking as well as appellate review of the process.

4. *Effect on zoning.* To what extent does the consistency requirement limit the discretion of a local government in the zoning process? To some courts, the comprehensive plan is simply a guide and the real standards are in the zoning ordinance. See *Nestle Waters N. Am., Inc. v. Town of Fryeburg*, 967 A.2d 702 (Me. 2009) (comprehensive plan is simply a guide; the adopted zoning ordinances have the regulatory effect). In *Baker v. City of Milwaukie*, 533 P.2d 772 (Or. 1975), the court ordered a downzoning to compel compliance with a density policy in the plan. Does this mean a court can order an upzoning? The court thought not in *Marracci v. City of Scappoose*, 552 P.2d 552 (Or. App. 1976). The court held that a plan's designation of a more intensive future land use did not require a rezoning to allow that use.

In *Bone v. City of Lewiston*, 693 P.2d 1046 (Idaho 1984), the city refused to rezone the plaintiff's land from a residential use to a commercial use shown on the comprehensive plan. The plaintiff brought an action in mandamus to compel the city to rezone its property in accordance with the comprehensive plan. The court held the action would not lie:

> It is illogical to say that what has been projected as a pattern of projected land uses is what a property owner is entitled to have zoned today. The land use map is not intended to be a map of present zoning uses, nor even a map which indicates what uses are presently appropriate. Its only purpose is that which [the statute] mandates — to indicate "suitable projected land uses." Therefore, we hold that a city's land use map does not require a particular piece of property, as a matter of law, to be zoned exactly as it appears on the land use map. [*Id.* at 1052.]

The court added that the statutory "in accordance with a comprehensive plan" requirement does not allow governing bodies to ignore their comprehensive plan when adopting or amending zoning ordinances. They must determine as a matter of fact whether a requested zoning ordinance or amendment reflects the goals of the plan and takes the plan into account in light of the factual circumstances surrounding the request. The court indicated that an aggrieved landowner could appeal this factual decision. On what basis could a court review a factual decision not to rezone to a more intensive use shown on the plan? Compare *Nova Horizon, Inc. v. City Council*, 769 P.2d 721 (Nev. 1989) (council decision refusing to rezone in accordance with plan held improper). See also *Board of Supervisors v. Allman*, 211 S.E.2d 48 (Va. 1975) (refusal to upzone invalid where similar development nearby and comprehensive plan anticipates greater density at the location).

5. *Conditional uses.* Must conditional uses be consistent with the plan in states that have a consistency requirement? This issue was considered in *Neighborhood Action Group v. County of Calaveras*, 203 Cal. Rptr. 401 (Cal. App. 1984). Although the statute did not require conditional use permits to be consistent with the plan, that requirement could be implied "from the hierarchical relationship of land use laws." The court reasoned that zoning ordinances must be consistent with the plan and that the validity of conditional use permits, which are governed by the zoning regulations, depends derivatively on "the general plan's conformity with statutory criteria." *Id.* at 407. For an Oregon case contra, see *Kristensen v. City of Eugene Planning Comm'n*, 544 P.2d 591 (Or. App. 1976).

Are there policy reasons for exempting conditional uses from compliance with the comprehensive plan? Conditional uses are similar to those in the district in which they are allowed, and are approved subject to standards in the zoning ordinance. If so, isn't it enough that the zoning ordinance complies with the plan? What about floating zones? And subdivision controls? See Cal. Gov't Code § 65567 (subdivision map must be consistent with plan). Note that the Florida statute requires that all "development orders," as broadly defined, must be consistent with the comprehensive plan. See Fla. Stat. Ann. § 163.3194. The APA's model legislation similarly requires consistency between the plan and land development regulations defined broadly as "any zoning, subdivision, impact fee, site plan, corridor map, floodplain or stormwater regulations, or other governmental controls that affect the use and intensity of land." See American Planning Association, Growing Smart Legislative Guidebook: Model Statutes for Planning and Management of Change, §§ 7.201 and 3.301 (S. Meck ed., 2002).

6. *Judicial review of plan adequacy.* To what extent will the courts review a comprehensive plan to determine whether it meets the statutory requirements? This will depend on part on the statutory scheme for review, if any, of the plan's adequacy. The California courts require "actual compliance" with the planning statute but hold a plan inadequate only if the local government acted arbitrarily. See *Twain Harte Homeowners Ass'n v. County of Tuolumne*, 188 Cal. Rptr. 233 (Cal. App. 1983) (reviewing the cases). The court found the land use element of the plan inadequate because it did not express densities in terms of population and the circulation element inadequate because transportation facilities were not correlated with land use. The analysis of housing needs in the housing element was held adequate. See also *Bownds v. City of Glendale*, 170 Cal. Rptr. 342 (Cal. App. 1980) (housing element need not contain action program for condominium conversion). Judicial review of plans in California should be deferential under the statute providing that the adoption of a plan is a legislative act. *DeVita v. County of Napa*, 889 P.2d 1019 (Cal. 1995) (citing Cal. Gov't Code § 65301.5). Recall that the amendment of a plan is legislative in Florida. See also *Section 28 Partnership, Ltd. v. Martin County*, 772 So. 2d 616 (Fla. App. 2000) (upholding county's refusal to amend the comprehensive plan against claims of substantive due process and takings challenges). In Florida, local plans and amendments to the plan are reviewed for adequacy ("compliance" with the planning statute) under an administrative review process, which results are then reviewable at the appellate court level. Fla. Stat. Ann. § 163.3184. Does this system make more sense than allowing the courts to determine "adequacy" of the plan?

Some states attempt to deal with internal conflicts in plans by statute. Cal. Gov't Code § 65300.5 requires a plan to "comprise an integrated, internally consistent and compatible statement of policies." For a case applying this provision to hold a plan internally inconsistent, see *Concerned Citizens of Calaveras County v. Calaveras County Bd. of Supvrs.*, 212 Cal. Rptr. 273 (Cal. App. 1985). Compare *Shea Homes Ltd. Partnership v. County of Alameda*, 2 Cal Rptr. 3d 739 (Cal. App. 2003) (plan policies, but not the plan objectives within the policies, by statute must be internally consistent). Internal conflicts in a plan may also support a decision that a zoning change is inconsistent with the plan. See *Bridger Canyon Property Owners' Ass'n v. Planning & Zoning Comm'n*, 890 P.2d 1268 (Mont. 1995).

7. *Spot planning.* What if a municipality amends the zoning ordinance to allow a land use and at the same time amends the comprehensive plan for the affected property to make the plan consistent with the rezoning? This is called spot planning. The courts have been willing to accept spot planning in states that do not have a consistency requirement. See *Cheney v. Village No. 2 at New Hope, Inc.*, 241 A.2d 81 (Pa. 1968). Compare *Dalton v. City & County of Honolulu*, 462 P.2d 199 (Hawaii 1969). The court invalidated a contemporaneous rezoning and plan amendment for medium-density housing. It held that plan amendments must be accompanied by studies showing the need for the housing, that the housing should be located at the site, and that the chosen location was the "best site."

A state may also limit the number of times a plan may be amended during any one year. See Cal. Gov't Code § 65358(b) (four times a year with some exceptions); Fla. Stat. Ann. § 163.3187(1) (twice a year for large scale amendments, with certain exceptions). This limitation should allow the municipality to consider together any plan amendments that affect a particular area in the community.

8. *Does the consistency requirement work?* E. Netter & J. Vranicar, *Linking Plans and Regulations*, American Planning Ass'n, Planning Advisory Serv. Rep. No. 363 (1981), reports field studies of six jurisdictions in two states, California and Florida, that have consistency requirements. The study found that some communities satisfied the consistency requirement by adopting detailed land use plans with land use districts identical to those contained in the zoning ordinance. Some jurisdictions had more general plans that permitted considerable flexibility in interpreting the consistency requirement. Other communities adopted detailed subarea plans in addition to a general community plan and relied on the subarea plans as the basis for requiring consistency. This technique helps preserve the general policy nature of the

comprehensive plan while allowing the adoption of subarea plans as needed to provide more planning guidance.

The report concluded:

> [T]he political pressures and concerns that developers and citizens previously brought on the zoning ordinance seems to have shifted to the plan itself. . . . [With one exception] the experiences of the six communities . . . do not appear to be inspiring communities to break new ground in resolving the tension between planning and regulation. . . . Even with a consistency requirement, there will always be a struggle to achieve a reasonable, workable balance between flexibility and predictability when land-use decisions are made. [*Id.* at 21.]

The American Planning Association model land use legislation requires local planning agencies to prepare an advisory report on whether proposed land use actions, such as zoning amendments, are consistent with the comprehensive plan and whether the proposal should be approved, denied or changed. § 8-104(2) (2002). In his article, *supra*, Stuart Meck, who was the director of the model legislation project, argues that this proposal introduces a process that can substantially improve the application of the consistency requirement.

9. *Sources.* See Cobb, Mandatory Planning: An Overview, (Am. Plan. Ass'n, PAS Memo, Feb. 1994); Stach, *Zoning — To Plan or Protect?*, 2 J. Plan. Lit. 472 (1987); Sullivan *The Evolving Role of the Comprehensive Plan*, 32 Urb. Law. 813 (2000); Comment: *Re-Building New Orleans: How the Big Easy Can Be The Next Big Example*, 55 Loy. L. Rev. 353 (2009).

A NOTE ON SIMPLIFYING AND COORDINATING THE DECISION MAKING PROCESS

This is probably a good place to discuss this problem. You will have noticed the Standard Act and statutes that follow it do not provide for one single permit that can authorize a development project. A mixed use project may require a rezoning for a zoning map amendment, a conditional use permit for some of its uses, and a variance if setback and other requirements are troublesome. As a result, the review of a proposed development is not a point-to-point process but a series of single-issue reviews. See the *Charisma* decision, reproduced *supra*.

There have been many proposals for some time to modify this process to make it more coordinated because delay and lack of coordination are expensive, both for the developer and the municipality. The model legislation proposed by the American Planning Association and the American Bar Association model code remedy this problem by authorizing a single development permit that covers all of the approvals a development requires. See Chapter 10 (2002) and Section 208 (authorizing a "master permit"), respectively. This follows Florida practice. See Fla. Stat. Ann. § 163.3164(8). The model legislation includes rezoning in the development permit in states where a rezoning is quasi-judicial rather than legislative. A single permit requirement can eliminate multiple hearings on single-issue problems, such as whether a variance is needed.

In addition, the model legislation authorizes a Consolidated Permit Review Process under which an applicant can apply at one time for all of the development permits or zoning map amendments required for a project. § 10-208. The advantage of this process is that it includes zoning map amendments in states where they are legislative. Appointment of a permit coordinator is authorized, and she is authorized to issue a master permit for the development. See also Ore. Rev. Stat. § 215.416(2); Wash. Rev. Code § 36.70B.120.

Additional changes can be made in the decision making process to simplify it and make it more coordinated. See Bassert, *Streamlining the Development Approval Process*, Land Development, Vol. 12, No. 4, at 14 (1999); McClendon, *Simplifying and Streamlining Zoning*, Inst. on Plan. Zoning & Eminent Domain 45, 76-95 (1982). Ms. Bassert, as a planning professional with the National Association of Homebuilders, makes a number of proposals, such as a central information desk and one-stop permitting, clearly stated submittal requirements, approval process checklists and flow charts, time limits on decisions, fast-tracking for simple projects, and combined inspections.

Unified development codes. Some municipalities have experimented with combining all their land use ordinances into one unified development code. See M. Brough, A Unified Development Ordinance (1985). The advantage of a unified code is that it provides consistency of standards for all advisory and governing bodies and simplifies the development review process. One important feature is the combination of zoning with subdivision ordinances, discussed in the next chapter, so that the code applies even though a subdivision is not required. For discussion, with examples from several cities, see Morris, *Zoning and Subdivision Codes Unite! Lessons from Four Communities with Unified Development Codes*, Planning, Vol. 59, No. 11, at 12 (1993). Florida legislation requires that land development regulations be adopted in a unified code. Fla. Stat. Ann. § 163.3202.

The application process. Section 10-202 of the American Planning Association model law requires local governments to specify the contents of development applications in detail, while § 10-203 requires a completeness determination, which has time limits and is carefully described. For example, if a local government finds an application incomplete it must specify in detail what will make it complete. For similar requirements, see Cal. Gov't Code §§ 65943 et seq.

Time limits. The model legislation also has other time limits, such as those limiting time for decisions following hearings, § 10-210. See also N.J. Stat. Ann. 40:55D-61 (120-day period for planning board actions). Under this kind of provision, a project not approved within the statutory time limit is deemed approved. One problem with this kind of approach is that more complex projects may take longer to consider. To deal with the problem, the model law provides that the time limits will not run during any period, which is suggested not to exceed 30 days, "in which a local government requests additional studies or information concerning a development permit application."

Project hierarchies. Local governments in Oregon have adopted project hierarchies that divide proposed developments according to their complexity. The simpler projects are fast-tracked, while the more complex projects require a full hearing.

For additional suggestions, see J. Vranicar, W. Sanders & D. Mosena, Streamlining Land Use Regulation: A Guidebook for Local Governments (1980). This kind of tightening in the land use process obviously works a major change over current practice in most states. What are the downsides?

A NOTE ON ALTERNATIVE DISPUTE RESOLUTION

A Typical Scenario. Zoning and land use disputes are often appropriate candidates for alternative dispute resolution processes that involve collaborative decision-making. Zoning proposals may involve issues of public importance, capturing the attention of citizen groups with different and strongly felt interests, and a very public process involving local elected or appointed officials. Consider the typical scenario: The developer of a multi-family affordable housing project wishes to locate in a growing suburb where land prices are relatively low and agricultural land is available for development. The developer needs rezoning and site plan approval in order to build the project, which is assisted by use of state grant funds. The neighbors are concerned about increased density, the nascent environmental group wishes to preserve open space and stop the increasing development of the community, and the public officials have never had to address the issue before, although they have been worrying out loud in public meetings about the lack of housing to attract teachers, police and other public employees to the community.

The developer is interested in a resolution that is speedy and results in an economically viable project. Not only an adversarial public hearing process, but the threat of litigation or a referendum or initiative process, can be costly to the project in time and in project viability, perhaps threatening the state grant. Alternatives to the adversarial process can offer the developer advantages in accelerating the approval process, decreasing costs and reducing future legal challenges. The public officials may avoid unpleasant and lengthy disputes and may be able to satisfy multiple interest groups while improving the accessibility of housing in the growing community. The citizens may find a more active role in making substantive changes to the project that meet their interests. This scenario illustrates why alternative dispute resolution has become a well-accepted and desirable part of the zoning process in many communities. When this is the case, ADR becomes an early and integral part of the zoning process. Moreover, once litigation is filed, many courts as a matter of routine, in a wide variety of civil suits including zoning litigation, now require that parties pursue mediation before the case may go to trial.

Lampe & Kaplan, Resolving Land-Use Conflicts Through Mediation: Challenges and Opportunities (Lincoln Institute of Land Policy, 1999), conclude that mediation can be successful in resolving land use disputes, provided that the disputants are motivated to resolve the issue and commit themselves to good-faith efforts to do so, using whatever ADR process is invoked. Motivation is present when the parties perceive either that they have no option, or that they stand to gain more than could be assured by conflict or adversarial process. Initial legal rules, as Coase would predict, often contribute to increasing the necessary motivation. In general, parties to land use dispute resolution find the process less costly and more personally satisfying than formal alternatives.

Forms of Dispute Resolution. There are many forms of alternative dispute resolution that provide options to the classical adjudication and administrative decision-making process. *Arbitration* allows the parties to voluntarily turn over the decision to an individual or set of individuals that have expertise in the subject area, conduct the proceedings in private, and generally provide a speedy and final decision. This alternative is not used as frequently as *mediation,* in which voluntary negotiations between parties are carried out with assistance of a neutral party, whose task is to assess the conflict, encourage information sharing and brainstorming, and suggest and negotiate potential solutions while not making the final decision. The alternative of *facilitation* also involves the assistance of a neutral party who helps the parties communicate with one another to effectively identify the important issues in the conflict and needs of the parties, so that an acceptable solution may be found. Both mediation and facilitation may be held in public or private settings, and often includes a mix of both public and private sessions. For a more complete typography of the options, see S. Goldberg et al., Dispute Resolution: Negotiation, Mediation and Other Processes (1992); The Consensus Building Institute, *Using Dispute Resolution Techniques to Address Environmental Justice Concerns: Case Studies*, U.S. Environmental Protection Agency, Office of Environmental Justice (2003).

Case Studies. Studies indicate that the use of assisted negotiation in land use disputes can play a crucial or important role in solving those disputes. See, e.g., The Consensus Building Institute, *Using Assisted Negotiation to Settle Land Use Disputes: A Guidebook for Public Officials*, Lincoln Institute of Land Policy (1999). The study interviewed mediators across the country regarding disputes that took place between 1985 and 1997. Nearly two-thirds of the disputes were settled, but in the unsettled cases, 64 percent of participants viewed the process as having helped the parties make progress toward an acceptable solution. The authors of the study are well recognized advocates of ADR, and they provide a description of a number of the case studies and the key lessons learned from them. The study also describes some of the risks of ADR, such as that the process make take considerable time; resulting decisions may also need to be approved through a formal decision-making process; training for all participants is important; organizations must be committed to the process; and professional neutrals must be chosen with care. Another set of case studies and manual for public consensus-building was prepared by The Urban Land Institute, in Pulling Together: A Planning and Development Consensus-Building Manual (1994). It describes techniques not only for alternative dispute resolution, but also for citizen participation processes such as "visioning" activities, and "meeting management" for presentations ranging in their purposes to include public information, formal hearings, workshops, focus groups and consensus building.

For a description of several examples of informal dispute resolution, see Susskind et al., *Resolving Disputes the Kindler, Gentler Way*, Planning, May 1995, at 16. In one example, a Virginia city proposed a new east-west gateway connector road in its comprehensive plan to serve the northern, less-developed part of the city and relieve congestion on a heavily traveled primary road. Residents of the area rose up in arms, and the city agreed with neighborhood demands to put a hold on the new road until a consensus was reached, and to open up the road proposal for discussion. However, neighborhood leaders also agreed to join the planning staff in a training program on collaborative problem solving.

The training process was held, and after all participants agreed on a process, a consensus committee met for a year to develop a new plan. The result was a linear park that preserves the right-of-way for the connector road. The road will be built once traffic on the primary connector reaches capacity. What problems do you see here? The negotiation process was over a plan, and the question is whether negotiation is the proper way to resolve the public interest questions a plan raises. Compare this negotiation issue with the zoning dispute describe at the beginning of this Note. How do they differ, and in what way might the zoning dispute require a different resolution process?

Problems. The concept of zoning as resulting from a deal-making process is antithetical to many as harkening back to the days where back-room deals between landowners and local government were all too common. These days are entertainingly described in R. Babcock, The

Zoning Game (1966), and R. Babcock & C. Siemon, The Zoning Game Revisited (1985). Is the process a better one when more parties, including neighbors and public interest groups, are involved? See E. Ryan, *Zoning, Taking, and Dealing: The Problems and Promise of Bargaining in Land Use Planning Conflicts*, 7 Harv. Negotiation L. Rev. 337 (2002). Does a requirement for the results of a negotiation to be adopted subsequently by the formal public zoning process obviate concerns that the public interest may be compromised by negotiation? Note that in some states, like Florida, a recommendation or agreement resulting from the alternative dispute resolution process subsequently must be adopted by the government in its normal processes. Fla. Stat. Ann. § 70.51(21) (private property rights dispute before a special magistrate); see also Fla. Stat. Ann. §§ 163.3184(16) (negotiation of compliance agreements for state approval of local comprehensive plans must proceed in public and agreement must be adopted at public hearing). Does the negotiation process necessarily result in a better project, or might it result in the "lowest common denominator" of a project plan?

Legislation. The United States Congress has authorized negotiated rule-making for agencies such as the Environmental Protection Agency, which is conducted before institution of formal procedures, at 5 U.S.C. § 581, The Negotiated Rulemaking Act. State legislatures have also adopted similar statutes. See Neb. Rev. Stat. §§ 84-919.01 et seq.; Or. Rev. Stat. § 183.502. Mediation in land use disputes is encouraged in some state legislation, such as Cal. Gov't Code §§ 66030 et seq.; and Pa. Stat. Ann. tit. 53, § 10908.1. The American Planning Association model statute provides for a process by which a landowner may request mediation if he has been denied a development permit, or granted a permit subject to conditions, which he believes imposes an undue hardship on his development and use of the land. The local government then has 30 days to decide whether or not there will be mediation. The goal of the mediation is to enter into a development agreement, although other remedies and measures may be considered. However, the only duty of the landowner and the local government is to participate and negotiate in good faith. Therefore, no remedy can be imposed by the mediator, and failure to reach an agreement is not a reviewable land-use decision. Growing Smart Legislative Guidebook: Model Statutes for Planning and Management of Change § 10-504 (S. Meck ed., 2002).

Sources. Menkel-Meadow, *Introduction: Symposium on ADR*, 44 UCLA L. Rev. 1613 (1997); Netter, *Mediation in a Land Use Context*, 1995 Inst. on Plan. Zoning & Eminent Domain; M. Fulton, *Reaching Consensus in Land Use Negotiations*, Am. Plan. Ass'n, Plan. Advisory Serv. Rep. No. 417 (1989); L. Susskind, P. Levy & J. Thomas-Larmer, Negotiating Environmental Agreements (Island Press 2000).

I. INITIATIVE AND REFERENDUM

Early in the twentieth century, many states began to adopt constitutional and statutory provisions authorizing the initiative and referendum. This reform reflected the dominant populism of the period, which favored a number of changes that would return government to the people. It also reflected a serious concern over the domination of state legislatures by interest groups and lobbyists. Today, almost all states have constitutional provisions authorizing the referendum at the state and local level, while about half the states have constitutional provisions authorizing the initiative at both governmental levels. Initiatives and referenda may also be authorized by statute or by local charters.

For many years, citizens in particular have expressed interest in the initiative and referendum as part of the local zoning process. The reasons for this interest, and the pros and cons of the initiative and referendum as it applies to zoning, were summarized in 1977 in the following student note:

> Heightened community sensitivity to the quality of the environment and increasing voter skepticism of the judgment of public officials provide much of the impetus for referenda. Moreover, such popular decisionmaking is consistent with the cardinal principle of our democratic system that decisions be made with the consent of the governed.
>
> At the same time, however, the use of the referendum to override the rezoning decisions of public bodies carries with it certain disadvantages. An individual landowner who seeks a rezoning may not be able to rely upon the electorate to make a reasoned decision that takes into account all the relevant information concerning the proposal and its impact on the municipality. Moreover, communities recognize now more than ever before the importance of planning coordinated and rational land use decisions, a goal that may be inconsistent with the referendum process. [Note, *The Proper Use of Referenda in Zoning*, 29 Stan. L. Rev. 819 (1977).]

Interest has not waned over the years, nor has the debate regarding the usefulness of the referendum and initiative processes. A more recent article finds the processes to be problematic but valuable, particularly for broad policy matters:

> By skirting procedural devices, such as public hearings and planning commission review of proposals, direct democracy does sacrifice information and process values inherent in the means by which plans are adopted and land use decisions made. Furthermore, the use of direct democracy in the land use context is at its most dubious when automatically triggered and when focused on land use decisions that have no policy aspects to them. At the same time, however, not all of the objections to direct democracy in the land use context are well taken. For example, the objections that land use decisions are too "complex" for voters and impair the "flexibility" of the land use system are unconvincing. Land use questions involving broad policy determinations in the planning context are suitable for decision by the electorate. [Selmi, *Reconsidering the Use of Direct Democracy in Making Land Use Decisions*, 19 UCLA J. Envtl. L. & Pol'y 293 (2001-2002).]

As applied to the zoning process, a referendum follows a zoning action by the legislative body and may either be mandatory or permissive. If the referendum is permissive, a zoning ordinance will not be submitted to popular vote unless a voter petition for a referendum is filed. In some states, the legislative body may also propose a referendum. Frequently, the referendum is used to block zoning amendments that provide for a more intensive use of a single piece of property; in some communities, it has developed a distinctive anti-growth bias. Referenda have also been used to block subsidized, low-income and moderate-income housing projects.

A zoning initiative is a voter-initiated zoning proposal which in some states is placed directly on the ballot following submission of a petition carrying the required number of voters' signatures. Under a variant of this process, the legislative body is first given an opportunity to accept or reject the measure before the election is held. Although it is unlikely that something as comprehensive as community-wide rezoning would be proposed through an initiative, this process has been used to propose specific zoning amendments such as height restrictions and growth moratoria. In many cases, the initiative is also used as a substitute for the referendum, which is possible in most states. If the legislative body enacts a zoning amendment which the voters wish to challenge, an initiative proposal may be filed calling for the repeal of the amendment and reinstatement of the prior zoning. This approach may be used if the period of time for filing a referendum is limited, as it may not be possible to collect all the signatures necessary for a referendum in the time provided.

The kinds of zoning actions that are subject to the initiative and referendum are about as broad as the zoning process itself, with the limitation that only legislative and not administrative zoning actions may be subject to electoral review. This limitation will restrict the use of the initiative and referendum in states in which the zoning amendment has been characterized as a quasi-judicial and not a legislative action. Even if a court does not go quite this far, the detailed notice and hearing procedures which the zoning enabling legislation requires prior to the enactment of any zoning measure may be viewed as a bar to the availability of the initiative and referendum. The case that follows considers the validity of a zoning referendum under state law.

TOWNSHIP OF SPARTA v. SPILLANE

125 N.J. Super. 519, 312 A.2d 154 (1973),
petition for certification denied,
64 N.J. 493, 317 A.2d 706 (1974)

CARTON, P.J.A.D.:

The issue to be resolved in these appeals is whether the referendum procedure provided for in the Faulkner Act applies to an amendment to the zoning ordinance of a municipality which has adopted the provisions of that act. The Township of Sparta and Township of Mount Olive cases involve this identical issue. Consequently they will be considered together, although they have not been formally consolidated.

Sparta has operated since 1960 under the Council-Manager Plan B of the Faulkner Act, N.J.S.A. 40:69A-99 et seq. On April 12, 1972 the township council adopted an amendment to its zoning ordinance authorizing a Planned Unit Development (P.U.D.) pursuant to N.J.S.A. 40:55-55 to 67. The plans for the P.U.D. were originally proposed by a subsidiary of a large corporation owning about 2,000 acres in Sparta.

The amendatory ordinance was referred to and acted upon favorably by the planning board after extended public hearings. Thereafter defendants in the Sparta action filed a petition with the municipal clerk seeking a referendum pursuant to N.J.S.A. 40:69A-185. The petition was found sufficient by the township clerk to comply with N.J.S.A. 40:69A-187, whereupon Sparta Township sought a declaratory judgment to determine whether the referendum provisions of the Faulkner Act were applicable to amendments of a zoning ordinance. The trial judge granted the township's motion for summary judgment, holding that such provisions were not applicable.

Mount Olive Township operated under the Mayor and Council Plan E of the Faulkner Act, N.J.S.A. 40:69A-68 to 73. On August 25, 1972 the township council, over strong opposition, adopted an ordinance amending the township zoning ordinance by establishing a new zone denominated C-R (Commercial-Recreational). Permissible uses in this zone included permanent year-round or seasonal amusement parks. Two of the defendants in the Mount Olive case own about two-thirds of the land in the newly created C-R zone on which they intend to construct and operate a major amusement park. The lands in question are located near Interstate Route 80 and were originally zoned for industrial uses.

The amendment was approved by the mayor after its passage by the council. On September 18 the plaintiffs in the Mount Olive case filed a petition with the township clerk for a referendum on the amendatory ordinance. This petition was found to comply with the statutory requirement.

As in the Sparta action, a declaratory judgment was sought by the municipality as to the applicability of the referendum procedures to the ordinance. The trial judge ruled in this case, as did the trial judge in the Sparta litigation, that the referendum procedure was not applicable.

The issue raised here presents a question not directly decided before in New Jersey. The Faulkner Act, in pertinent part, provides:

> The voters shall also have the power of referendum which is the power to approve or reject at the polls any ordinance submitted by the council to the voters or any ordinance passed by the council, against which a referendum petition has been filed as herein provided. No ordinance passed by the municipal council, except when otherwise required by general law or permitted by the provisions of section 17-32(b) of this act, shall take effect before twenty days from the time of its final passage and its approval by the mayor where such approval is required. . . . [N.J.S.A. 40:69A-185]

A companion section of the statute (N.J.S.A. 40:69A-184) provides a slightly different procedure for expressing public participation in municipal government through the initiative process:

> The voters of any municipality may propose any ordinance and may adopt or reject the same at the polls, such power being known as the initiative. . . .

The Faulkner Act was adopted in order to encourage public participation in municipal affairs in the face of normal apathy and lethargy in such matters. The act gave municipalities the option of choosing one form or another of local government best suited to its needs. It was a legislative demonstration of the democratic ideal of giving the people the right of choosing the form of government they preferred and the opportunity to exercise the powers under that form to the furthest limits. Some 76 of the 567 municipalities of this State have adopted one form or another of the forms of government authorized under the Faulkner Act.

The initiative and referendum processes authorized by the act comprise two useful instruments of plebiscite power and provide a means of arousing public interest. Ordinary rules of construction would, of course, dictate that such provisions should be liberally construed. See 5 McQuillin, Municipal Corporations, § 16.48 at 199–200 (1969), where the author advocates that these procedures should be respected and given wide use if possible. It should be noted, however, that he adds a caveat that any grant of the power of initiative and referendum and its exercise are subject to and must be construed with governing constitutional and statutory provisions. 5 McQuillin, *supra* at § 16.50.

Undeniably, zoning issues often are of great public interest and some, as in the present case, may concern the entire population of the municipality involved. In both the cases before us it has been argued forcefully that the proposed ordinances change or alter the complexion of the municipalities. Thus, the ultimate question is whether major decisions should be made by the planning boards and governing bodies, with only voiced public approval or dissent as prescribed in the Zoning Act, or whether they should be open to a final decision by the vote of the entire population. This issue pits the philosophy of comprehensive zoning planned by a panel of experts and adopted by elected and appointed officials, against the philosophy of a wider public participation and choice in municipal affairs.

Other states faced with similar problems of referendum provisions have arrived at conflicting determinations. However, the decisions of other states furnish little aid here since the laws of the states involved differ in substantial respects from the New Jersey statutes.

Our consideration of the applicability of the referendum provided for in the Faulkner Act to the zoning procedure logically should begin with an examination of the treatment accorded by our courts to the companion process of the initiative. *Smith v. Livingston Tp.*, 256 A.2d 85 (Ch. Div. 1969), *aff'd o.b.* 257 A.2d 698 (1969), held that the initiative was not applicable to amendatory zoning ordinances. In so holding, Judge Mintz found that the zoning statutes represented an exclusive grant of power by the Legislature to municipalities generally and was not impliedly superseded by the later adopted Faulkner Act. He noted that the Zoning Act is specific in detailing the manner in which zoning ordinances may be amended; that steps in the zoning procedure include consideration by the municipal planning board, the opportunity of property owners to object, and approval by the governing body. He also pointed out that in the event of objection by the property owners involved, a vote of two-thirds of the governing body is required to effect a change in the zoning ordinance (N.J.S.A. 40:55-34 to 35). He likewise observed that the initiative and referendum provisions in the Faulkner Act contain no specific reference to zoning. He concluded that if the initiative procedure were allowed to be applied to zoning matters, it would "disregard the valuable expertise of the planning board, and permit the electorate to defeat the beneficent purpose of the comprehensive zoning ordinance."

Appellants argue that a referendum is sufficiently dissimilar to an initiative as to justify treating it differently. They stress the fact that a referendum merely adds an additional stage which follows the governing body's approval and does not, as in the case of the initiative, provide a substitute for legislative action by the governing body. Consequently, they reason, a proposed zoning change should no more than any other legislative act be immune from further public examination. They point also to the fact that the planning board would not be altogether by-passed as in the case of initiative since a referendum begun by a petitioner would not occur until after the adoption of the zoning amendment and such adoption could not occur until the planning board had reviewed the amendment and made its recommendation. N.J.S.A. 40:55-35 and N.J.S.A. 40:69A-185.

These arguments have some cogency. However, we conclude that essentially the same considerations which bar application of the initiative process to zoning ordinance amendments apply in the case of the referendum.

Zoning is intended to be accomplished in accordance with a comprehensive plan and should reflect both present and prospective needs of the community. Among other things, the social, economic and physical characteristics of the community should be considered. The achievement of these goals might well be jeopardized by piecemeal attacks on the zoning ordinances if referenda were permissible for review of any amendment. Sporadic attacks on a municipality's comprehensive plan would tend to fragment zoning without any overriding concept. That concept should not be discarded because planning boards and governing bodies may not always have acted in the best interest of the public and may not, in every case, have demonstrated the expertise which they might be expected to develop.

The spirit and thrust of *Smith v. Livingston Tp.* requires treatment of both processes in the same fashion in their relation to the zoning procedure. Such considerations stem from the exclusivity and uniqueness of the Zoning Act itself (and the related Planning Act) and the Legislature's evident intention of providing uniformity of procedure for all municipalities in the State in zoning matters.

Thus, the Legislature has authorized governing bodies of municipalities to establish administrative agencies to assist them in the performance of functions in this area and has laid down very specific and detailed procedure to be followed by all governmental bodies in carrying out such functions. Such comprehensive and precise treatment demonstrates the special concern of the Legislature in this important area of municipal regulation.

Moreover, certain aspects of the zoning statute seem inherently incompatible with the referendum process. N.J.S.A. 40:55-35 provides three avenues by which an amendment to a zoning ordinance may be effected; first, following approval by the planning board the governing body passes the amended ordinance; second, upon rejection by the planning board the amended ordinance may be approved by two-thirds of the governing body; third, should at least 20% of the landowners directly or contiguously affected by the proposed amendment object, the governing body must pass the amended ordinance by a two-thirds vote. A zoning ordinance amendment does not become operative unless the planning board and governing body have acted. Whether the referendum stems from a submission of an ordinance by the governing body directly to the voters or by a referendum petition filed by the necessary number of voters, the so-called veto power of the planning board or protesting landowners would be rendered meaningless. A simple majority of the voters would be all that was necessary to approve or disapprove the ordinance.

We are not satisfied that the publicity which might accompany the referendum campaign and the exposure and discussion of the issues generated thereby justify disregarding these procedural requirements. In this connection we note that the zoning statute requires public notice of proposed zoning changes (N.J.S.A. 40:55-34). Moreover, from common experience we know that zoning amendments of a controversial nature, especially those which may greatly affect the entire population of the community, are often widely discussed and vigorously debated at the public hearings prior to adoption. . . .

Both judgments appealed from are affirmed.

NOTES AND QUESTIONS

1. *Referendum.* The principal case details most of the objections state courts have to allowing the use of the referendum in zoning. New Jersey has now exempted zoning ordinances and amendments from both the initiative and referendum. N.J. Stat. Ann. § 40:55D-62b. For a case agreeing with the principal case on statutory conflict grounds and reviewing cases elsewhere, see *I'On, L.L.C. v. Town of Mt. Pleasant*, 526 S.E.2d 716, 721 (S.C. 2000), which holds that allowing referenda "could nullify a carefully established zoning system or master plan developed after debate among many interested persons and entities, resulting in arbitrary decisions and patchwork zoning with little rhyme or reason." See also *Nordmarken v. City of Richfield*, 641 N.W.2d 343, 349 (Minn. App. 2002) ("Whereas the [planning statutes] provide for a comprehensive, orderly, and uniform process, referendum by its very nature is a narrow, piecemeal device that encourages sporadic and fragmented land development and use.").

The New Jersey court did not consider possible due process objections to the referendum which might arise because the referendum, by definition, precludes observance of the notice and hearing requirements contained in zoning enabling legislation. Since the referendum occurs after the zoning amendment has been enacted by the legislative body following the statutory notice and hearing, most state courts have either not perceived or have not found a due process violation on this account. See *City of Ft. Collins v. Dooney*, 496 P.2d 316 (Colo. 1972), upholding the application of a referendum to a zoning map amendment and noting that "[t]he fact that due process requirements may be met in one manner when the change is by council action does not preclude other procedures from meeting due process requirements. . . ." *Id.* at 319. Quoting from another case, the court then added that " '[t]he election campaign, the debate and airing of opposing opinions, supplant a public hearing prior to the adoption of an ordinance by the municipal governing body.' " *Id.* How realistic is this assumption?

The *Ft. Collins* case relied on the nature of the referendum as a "fundamental right" of the people in holding that a home rule charter provision allowing a referendum on "all" ordinances could not be construed to exempt zoning amendments. The court added that its holding was not intended to strip the property owner of his constitutional rights. "We can conceive of situations where the court might hold that the action of the electorate was arbitrary and capricious." *Id.*

For other cases holding that zoning is subject to referendum on zoning map amendments, see *Queen Creek Land & Cattle Corp. v. Yavapi County Bd. of Supvrs.*, 501 P.2d 391 (Ariz. 1972) (noting that the referendum does not change the zoning as an initiative does and that the notice and hearing process is accomplished prior to the referendum); *Cook-Johnson Realty Co. v. Bertolini*, 239 N.E.2d 80 (Ohio 1968) (upholding a permissive referendum and noting that the only effect of a successful referendum is to restore the zoning to what it was before the map amendment was requested); *Taylor Props. v. Union County*, 583 N.W.2d 638 (S.D. 1998) (noting national trends); and *Florida Land Co. v. City of Winter Springs*, 427 So. 2d 171 (Fla. 1983) (rejecting due process objections on the authority of *Eastlake*, reproduced *infra*). See also *State ex rel. Wahlmann v. Reim*, 445 S.W.2d 336 (Mo. 1969) (rejecting the statutory conflict argument and upholding a referendum on a newly enacted comprehensive zoning ordinance though noting that it might not be available on "isolated amendments").

For a more general critique of referenda and initiative, see Article: *The Emperor's New Clothes: Exposing the Failures of Regulating Land Use Through the Ballot Box*, 84 Notre Dame L. Rev. 1453 (2009).

2. *Legislative vs. administrative.* Referenda are available only for legislative, not administrative actions. Thus, it is critical for state law purposes whether the zoning action is considered quasi-judicial or administrative, or is considered legislative. See *State ex rel. Srovnal v. Linton*, 346 N.E.2d 764 (Ohio 1976), holding that a special exception is administrative, and thus not subject to referendum under the Ohio constitution; *State ex rel. Committee v. Norris*, 792 N.E.2d 186 (Ohio 2003), *infra* Chapter 7 (ordinances creating planned community development zoning district and adopting the district for certain property are legislative, but ordinances adopting final development plans and plats for the zoned area are administrative). But see *Kirschenman v. Hutchinson County*, 656 N.W.2d 330 (S.D. 2003) (conditional use is legislative and subject to referendum). As explained *supra*, the adoption of a comprehensive plan is a legislative act. *DeVita v. County of Napa*, 889 P.2d 1019 (Cal. 1995).

What about a zoning map amendment? Recall that most courts hold a zoning map amendment a legislative act. See *Greens at Fort Missoula v. City of Missoula*, 897 P.2d 1078

(Mont. 1995); *PH, LLC v. City of Conway*, 2009 Ark. LEXIS 689 (October 22, 2009). In *Fritz v. City of Kingman*, 957 P.2d 337 (Ariz. 1998), the question was whether a zoning map amendment that allowed four dwelling units to the acre was administrative because it implemented very specific policies in the comprehensive plan that provided a density range of one to four units per acre for the parcel. The court held no. Because the plan was an advisory document only, and not a legislative act, rezonings that implemented the plan were not administrative, but legislative policy setting. Compare *Redelsperger v. City of Avondale*, 87 P.3d 843 (Ariz. App. 2004) (conditional use approval is administrative and not subject to referendum). Utah has a statute that expressly exempts "individual property zoning decisions" from referenda. Utah Code Ann. § 20A-7-101(12)(b). The Utah court adopted a multi-factor test to apply the exemption that considers whether there was sufficient notice so that voters would know they could ask for a referendum, whether there was a material variance from the basic zoning law, and whether the zoning change implicated a policy-making decision amenable to voter control. *Citizen's Awareness Now v. Marakis*, 873 P.2d 1117 (Utah 1994), noted, 1995 Utah L. Rev. 325. Would these tests be helpful even without such a statute? Note that in a recent decision, the Utah court has decided that adopting a new zoning classification is *per se* legislative. *Friends of Maple Mt., Inc. v. Mapleton City*, 228 P.3d 1238 (Utah 2010). How does the decision on whether a zoning map amendment is subject to referendum differ from whether the amendment is quasi-judicial for purposes of judicial review?

3. *Initiative.* Most cases have held the initiative is not available to enact a zoning ordinance. Unlike the referendum, which follows legislative adoption of a zoning measure in which statutory notice and hearing requirements have been observed, a successful initiative will result in the enactment of a zoning measure without the statutory notice and hearing. For this reason, courts may find that the zoning initiative violates the statutory notice and hearing procedures, and some courts have found a denial of procedural due process as well. See, e.g., *Transamerica Title Ins. & Trust v. City of Tucson*, 757 P.2d 1055 (Ariz. 1988) (charter amendment to establish open space buffer zones around Saguaro National Monument and other parks; citing cases throughout the states); *Kaiser Hawaii Kai Dev. Co. v. City & County of Honolulu*, 777 P.2d 244 (Hawaii 1989) (downzoning by initiative); *Gumprecht v. City of Coeur D'Alene*, 661 P.2d 1214 (Idaho 1983) (building height restrictions); *Griswold v. City of Homer*, 186 P.3d 558 (Alaska 2008) (attempt to bypass advisory planning commission invalid). Most of these cases considered the use of the initiative as a means of repealing a zoning amendment applicable to single parcels of land, and this fact may have led these courts to emphasize notice and hearing problems. Some courts have approved the use of the referendum in the zoning process but disapprove the use of the initiative. Can you see why? But see *Sevier Power Co., LLC v. Board of Sevier County Comm'rs*, 196 P.3d 583 (Utah 2008), finding that the statutory limitation on use of the initiative for land use ordinances violates the state constitution (also finding amendment to the zoning code conditional use provisions to be legislative in nature).

4. *The initiative in California. Associated Homebuilders, Inc. v. City of Livermore*, 557 P.2d 473 (Cal. 1976), upheld an initiative ordinance that enacted a growth moratorium for the city. It held that the initiative procedure did not conflict with the notice and hearing and other provisions of the zoning enabling act on the ground that no such conflict was intended. The court noted the right to the initiative was reserved in the constitution, and that the zoning act might be unconstitutional if it were construed to bar the initiative. *Id.* at 479–80. It also referenced a constitutional provision authorizing the initiative as "[d]rafted in light of the theory that all power of government ultimately resides in the people." *Id.* at 477. Accord *State ex rel. Hickman v. City Council*, 690 S.W.2d 799 (Mo. App. 1985); *Garvin v. Ninth Judicial*

Dist. Court, 59 P.3d 1180 (Nev. 2002) (sustainable growth measure).

The availability of the initiative in zoning has led to an explosion of voter-initiated measures adopting growth management controls as well as other restrictions in California communities, often over the objections of council and planning staff. In *Devita v. County of Napa*, 889 P.2d 1019 (Cal. 1995), the court held the initiative is available to amend a general plan. In that case, the voters had amended the plan to substantially prevent any development of land in agricultural areas for 30 years without approval by the vote of the people. Has the court gone too far? What happens to planning in this kind of political environment? See Alperin & King, *Ballot Box Planning: Land Use Planning Through the Initiative Process in California*, 21 Sw. U. L. Rev. 1 (1992).

5. *Good or bad?* Some critics of the initiative and referendum claim that voter control of zoning will lead to excesses that will escape judicial review. Consider the case of *Ranjel v. City of Lansing*, 417 F.2d 321 (6th Cir. 1969), where the federal court overturned an injunction so as to allow a referendum to go forward on a low income housing project that had been approved by the city council. The court held that it was better to allow the referendum to go forward and, if necessary after the vote, consider any claims of discrimination. David Broder, a leading political commentator, has suggested that the initiative process threatens to subvert the American system of government, in part because of the extraordinary influence of well-financed special interest groups in the voting process. See David S. Broder, Democracy Derailed (2000). Compare the arguments for the initiative and referendum in the following student note:

> The initiative process contains adequate safeguards against arbitrary decision-making; the open process of a political campaign is likely to reveal to the voters adequate information upon which to make an intelligent decision. Even if some prejudice may be suffered by individual property owners, courts should consider the unique educational and participatory values represented by the initiative. Moreover, the protection of property owners may be accomplished by means other than categorically prohibiting the initiative's use. Courts should consider the possibility of heightened judicial scrutiny of the substance of initiative measures which seem to focus on an individual parcel rather than on broad community objectives; this type of review would be in accord with the close judicial scrutiny of "spot-zoning" discussed above. Courts concerned about forcing property owners to wage both a political campaign and a subsequent legal challenge may wish to consider relaxing the traditional judicial reluctance to rule on the validity of an initiative measure prior to passage. [Comment, *The Initiative and Referendum's Use in Zoning*, 64 Calif. L. Rev. 74, 93 (1976).]

In *Arnel Dev. Co. v. City of Costa Mesa*, 178 Cal. Rptr. 723 (Cal. App. 1981), the court held invalid an initiative that repealed a zoning amendment for moderate-income housing. The court subjected the initiative to the same tests applicable to a municipally adopted zoning ordinance. It found no change in conditions or circumstances that justified the repeal by initiative and held it was adopted for the sole and specific purpose of defeating the housing development. Neither did the initiative accommodate the regional interest in the provision of moderate-income housing, as required in California. But see *Northwood Homes, Inc. v. Town of Moraga*, 265 Cal. Rptr. 363 (Cal. App. 1989) (distinguishing *Arnel*).

6. *The legislative role.* Professor Selmi argues that the state legislature may act as a brake on the procedural concerns related to initiative and referenda by, for example, requiring a higher percentage of signatures from voters before a measure will qualify for the ballot, or designing state land use laws that are inconsistent and pre-emptive of the initiative and referendum processes. See Selmi, *supra*. He points out that many courts have held that redevelopment statutes preempt the initiative and referenda processes. This role is particularly effective where statutes, rather than the state constitution, regulate initiative and referenda. See also P. Dubois & F. Feeney, Lawmaking by Initiative: Issues, Options and Comparisons (1998). How willing do you think the state legislature is to restrict "direct democracy"?

7. *Sources*. See Callies, Neuffer & Calibaoso, *Ballot Box Zoning: Initiative, Referendum and the Law*, 39 Wash. U. J. Urb. & Contemp. L. 53 (1991); Freilich & Guemmer, *Removing Artificial Barriers to Public Participation in Land-Use Policy: Effective Zoning by Initiative and Referenda*, 21 Urb. Law. 511 (1989); Ziegler, *Limitations on Use of Initiative and Referendum Measures in Controlling Land Use Disputes*, 13 Zoning & Plan. L. Rep. 17 (1990); Comment, *Land Use By, For, and of the People: Problems With the Application of Initiatives and Referenda to the Zoning Process*, 19 Pepp. L. Rev. 99 (1991); M. Waters, Initiative and Referendum Almanac (2003); Student Note: *New Reactions to Old Growth: Land Use Law Reform in Florida*, 34 Colum. J. Envtl. L. 191 (2009).

The previous case considered the validity of a zoning referendum under state law. Constitutional objections to the initiative and referendum may also be raised in federal courts. They were given consideration in the following Supreme Court decision, which deals with a mandatory zoning referendum. When reading this decision, remember that it does not preclude a different view of either the referendum or the initiative in a state court.

CITY OF EASTLAKE v. FOREST CITY ENTERPRISES, INC.
426 U.S. 668 (1976)

CHIEF JUSTICE BURGER delivered the opinion of the Court:

The question in this case is whether a city charter provision requiring proposed land use changes to be ratified by 55% of the votes cast violates the due process rights of a landowner who applies for a zoning change.

The city of Eastlake, Ohio, a suburb of Cleveland, has a comprehensive zoning plan codified in a municipal ordinance. Respondent, a real estate developer, acquired an eight-acre parcel of real estate in Eastlake zoned for "light industrial" uses at the time of purchase.

In May 1971, respondent applied to the City Planning Commission for a zoning change to permit construction of a multifamily, high-rise apartment building. The Planning Commission recommended the proposed change to the City Council, which under Eastlake's procedures could either accept or reject the Planning Commission's recommendation. Meanwhile, by popular vote, the voters of Eastlake amended the city charter to require that any changes in land use agreed to by the Council be approved by a 55% vote in a referendum.[1] The City

---

[1] As adopted by the voters, Art. VIII, § 3, of the Eastlake City Charter provides in pertinent part: "That any change to the existing land uses or any change whatsoever to any ordinance . . . cannot be approved unless and until it shall have been submitted to the Planning Commission, for approval or disapproval. That in the event the city council

Council approved the Planning Commission's recommendation for reclassification of respondent's property to permit the proposed project. Respondent then applied to the Planning Commission for "parking and yard" approval for the proposed building. The Commission rejected the application, on the ground that the City Council's rezoning action had not yet been submitted to the voters for ratification.

Respondent then filed an action in state court, seeking a judgment declaring the charter provision invalid as an unconstitutional delegation of legislative power to the people. While the case was pending, the City Council's action was submitted to a referendum, but the proposed zoning change was not approved by the requisite 55% margin. Following the election, the Court of Common Pleas and the Ohio Court of Appeals sustained the charter provision.

The Ohio Supreme Court reversed. Concluding that enactment of zoning and rezoning provisions is a legislative function, the court held that a popular referendum requirement, lacking standards to guide the decision of the voters, permitted the police power to be exercised in a standardless, hence arbitrary and capricious manner. Relying on this Court's decisions in *Washington ex rel. Seattle Trust Co. v. Roberge*, 278 U.S. 116 (1928), *Thomas Cusack Co. v. Chicago*, 242 U.S. 526 (1917), and *Eubank v. Richmond*, 226 U.S. 137 (1912), but distinguishing *James v. Valtierra*, 402 U.S. 137 (1971), the court concluded that the referendum provision constituted an unlawful delegation of legislative power.

We reverse.

I

The conclusion that Eastlake's procedure violates federal constitutional guarantees rests upon the proposition that a zoning referendum involves a delegation of legislative power. A referendum cannot, however, be characterized as a delegation of power. Under our constitutional assumptions, all power derives from the people, who can delegate it to representative instruments which they create. See, e.g., Federalist Papers, No. 39 (Madison). In establishing legislative bodies, the people can reserve to themselves power to deal directly with matters which might otherwise be assigned to the legislature. *Hunter v. Erickson*, 393 U.S. 385, 392 (1969).

The reservation of such power is the basis for the town meeting, a tradition which continues to this day in some States as both a practical and symbolic part of our democratic processes. The referendum, similarly, is a means for direct political participation, allowing the people the final decision, amounting to a veto power, over enactments of representative bodies. The practice is designed to "give citizens a voice on questions of public policy." *James v. Valtierra*, *supra*, at 141.

In framing a state constitution, the people of Ohio specifically reserved the power of referendum to the people of each municipality within the State.

---

should approve any of the preceding changes, or enactments, whether approved or disapproved by the Planning Commission it shall not be approved or passed by the declaration of an emergency, and it shall not be effective, but it shall be mandatory that the same be approved by a 55% favorable vote of all votes cast of the qualified electors of the City of Eastlake at the next regular municipal election, if one shall occur not less than sixty (60) or more than one hundred and twenty (120) days after its passage, otherwise at a special election falling on the generally established day of the primary election. . . ."

"The initiative and referendum powers are hereby reserved to the people of each municipality on all questions which such municipalities may now or hereafter be authorized by law to control by legislative action. . . ." Ohio Const., Art. II, § 1f.

To be subject to Ohio's referendum procedure, the question must be one within the scope of legislative power. The Ohio Supreme Court expressly found that the City Council's action in rezoning respondent's eight acres from light industrial to high-density residential use was legislative in nature.(7) Distinguishing between administrative and legislative acts, the court separated the power to zone or rezone, by passage or amendment of a zoning ordinance, from the power to grant relief from unnecessary hardship. The former function was found to be legislative in nature.(9)

II

The Ohio Supreme Court further concluded that the amendment to the city charter constituted a "delegation" of power violative of federal constitutional guarantees because the voters were given no standards to guide their decision. Under Eastlake's procedure, the Ohio Supreme Court reasoned, no mechanism existed, nor indeed could exist, to assure that the voters would act rationally in passing upon a proposed zoning change. This meant that "appropriate legislative action [would] be made dependent upon the potentially arbitrary and unreasonable whims of the voting public." 324 N.E.2d, at 746. The potential for arbitrariness in the process, the court concluded, violated due process.

Courts have frequently held in other contexts that a congressional delegation of power to a regulatory entity must be accompanied by discernible standards, so that the delegatee's action can be measured for its fidelity to the legislative will. Assuming, *arguendo*, their relevance to state governmental functions, these cases involved a delegation of power by the legislature to regulatory bodies, which are not directly responsible to the people; this doctrine is inapplicable where, as here, rather than dealing with a delegation of power, we deal with a power reserved by the people to themselves.(10)

In basing its claim on federal due process requirements, respondent also invokes *Euclid v.*

---

(7) The land use change requested by respondent would likely entail the provision of additional city services, such as schools and police and fire protection. Cf. *James v. Valtierra*, 402 U.S. 137, 143 n. 4 (1971). The change would also diminish the land area available for industrial purposes, thereby affecting Eastlake's potential economic development.

(9) The power of initiative or referendum may be reserved or conferred "with respect to any matter, legislative or administrative, within the realm of local affairs. . . ." 5 E. McQuillan, Municipal Corporations § 16.54, p. 208 (3d ed. 1969). However, the Ohio Supreme Court concluded that only land use changes granted by the City Council when acting in a legislative capacity were subject to the referendum process. Under the court's binding interpretation of state law, a property owner seeking relief from unnecessary hardship occasioned by zoning restrictions would not be subject to Eastlake's referendum procedure. For example, if unforeseeable future changes give rise to hardship on the owner, the holding of the Ohio Supreme Court provides avenues of administrative relief not subject to the referendum process.

(10) The Ohio Supreme Court's analysis of the requirements for standards flowing from the Fourteenth Amendment also sweeps too broadly. Except as a legislative history informs an analysis of legislative action, there is no more advance assurance that a legislative body will act by conscientiously applying consistent standards than there is with respect to voters. For example, there is no certainty that the City Council in this case would act on the basis of "standards" explicit or otherwise in Eastlake's comprehensive zoning ordinance. Nor is there any assurance that townspeople assembling in a town meeting, as the people of Eastlake could do, will act according to consistent standards. The critical constitutional inquiry, rather, is whether the zoning restriction produces arbitrary or capricious results.

Ambler Realty Co., but it does not rely on the direct teaching of that case. Under *Euclid*, a property owner can challenge a zoning restriction if the measure is "clearly arbitrary and unreasonable, having no substantial relation to the public health, safety, morals, or general welfare." If the substantive result of the referendum is arbitrary and capricious, bearing no relation to the police power, then the fact that the voters of Eastlake wish it so would not save the restriction. As this Court held in invalidating a charter amendment enacted by referendum:

> "The sovereignty of the people is itself subject to those constitutional limitations which have been duly adopted and remained unrepealed." *Hunter v. Erickson*, 393 U.S., at 392.

But no challenge of the sort contemplated in *Euclid v. Ambler Realty* is before us. The Ohio Supreme Court did not hold, and respondent does not argue, that the present zoning classification under Eastlake's comprehensive ordinance violates the principles established in *Euclid v. Ambler Realty*. If respondent considers the referendum result itself to be unreasonable, the zoning restriction is open to challenge in state court, where the scope of the state remedy available to respondent would be determined as a matter of state law, as well as under Fourteenth Amendment standards. That being so, nothing more is required by the Constitution.

Nothing in our cases is inconsistent with this conclusion. Two decisions of this Court were relied on by the Ohio Supreme Court in invalidating Eastlake's procedure. The thread common to both decisions is the delegation of legislative power, originally given by the people to a legislative body, and in turn delegated by the legislature to a *narrow segment* of the community, not to the people at large. In *Eubank v. City of Richmond*, the Court invalidated a city ordinance which conferred the power to establish building setback lines upon the owners of two-thirds of the property abutting any street. Similarly, in *Washington ex rel. Seattle Title Trust Co. v. Roberge*, the Court struck down an ordinance which permitted the establishment of philanthropic homes for the aged in residential areas, but only upon the written consent of the owners of two-thirds of the property within 400 feet of the proposed facility.

Neither *Eubank* nor *Roberge* involved a referendum procedure such as we have in this case; the standardless delegation of power to a limited group of property owners condemned by the Court in *Eubank* and *Roberge* is not to be equated with decision-making by the people through the referendum process. The Court of Appeals for the Ninth Circuit put it this way:

> "A referendum, however, is far more than an expression of ambiguously founded neighborhood preference. It is the city itself legislating through its voters — an exercise by the voters of their traditional right through direct legislation to override the views of their elected representatives as to what serves the public interest." *Southern Alameda Spanish Speaking Organization v. City of Union City, California*, 424 F.2d 291, 294 (1970).

Our decision in *James v. Valtierra*, upholding California's mandatory referendum requirement, confirms this view. Mr. Justice Black, speaking for the Court in that case, said:

> "This procedure ensures that *all the people* of a community will have a voice in a decision which may lead to large expenditures of local governmental funds for increased public services. . . ." 402 U.S., at 143 (emphasis added).

Mr. Justice Black went on to say that a referendum procedure, such as the one at issue here, is a classic demonstration of "devotion to democracy. . . ." *Id.*, at 141. As a basic instrument of democratic government, the referendum process does not, in itself, violate the Due Process Clause of the Fourteenth Amendment when applied to a rezoning ordinance.[13] Since the rezoning decision in this case was properly reserved to the people of Eastlake under the Ohio Constitution, the Ohio Supreme Court erred in holding invalid, on federal constitutional grounds, the charter amendment permitting the voters to decide whether the zoned use of respondent's property could be altered.

The judgment of the Ohio Supreme Court is reversed, and the case is remanded for further proceedings not inconsistent with this opinion.

Reversed and remanded.

JUSTICE POWELL, dissenting:

There can be no doubt as to the propriety and legality of submitting generally applicable legislative questions, including zoning provisions, to a popular referendum. But here the only issue concerned the status of a single small parcel owned by a single "person." This procedure, affording no realistic opportunity for the affected person to be heard, even by the electorate, is fundamentally unfair. The "spot" referendum technique appears to open disquieting opportunities for local government bodies to bypass normal protective procedures for resolving issues affecting individual rights.

JUSTICE STEVENS, with whom JUSTICE BRENNAN joins, dissenting:

[Most of Justice Stevens' dissent is omitted, but his views on the zoning process and the fair procedures required in that process are of interest.]

The expectancy that particular changes consistent with the basic zoning plan will be allowed frequently and on their merits is a normal incident of property ownership. . . .

The fact that an individual owner (like any other petitioner or plaintiff) may not have a legal right to the relief he seeks does not mean that he has no right to fair procedure in the consideration of the merits of his application. The fact that codes regularly provide a procedure for granting individual exceptions or changes, the fact that such changes are granted in individual cases with great frequency, and the fact that the particular code in the record before us contemplates that changes consistent with the basic plan will be allowed, all support my opinion that the opportunity to apply for an amendment is an aspect of property ownership protected by the Due Process Clause of the Fourteenth Amendment. . . .

[W]hen the record indicates without contradiction that there is no threat to the general public interest in preserving the city's plan — as it does in this case, . . . I think the case should be treated as one in which it is essential that the private property owner be given a fair

[13] The fears expressed in dissent rest on the proposition that the procedure at issue here is "fundamentally unfair" to landowners; this fails to take into account the mechanisms for relief potentially available to property owners whose desired land use changes are rejected by the voters. First, if hardship is occasioned by zoning restrictions, administrative relief is potentially available. Indeed, the very purpose of "variances" allowed by zoning officials is to avoid "practical difficulties and unnecessary hardship." 8 E. McQuillan, Municipal Corporations § 25.159, p. 511 (3d ed. 1965). As we noted, remedies remain available under the Ohio Supreme Court's holding and provide a means to challenge unreasonable or arbitrary action.

The situation presented in this case is not one of a zoning action denigrating the use or depreciating the value of land; instead, it involves an effort to *change* a reasonable zoning restriction. No existing rights are being impaired; new use rights are being sought from the City Council. Thus, this case involves an owner's seeking approval of a new use free from the restrictions attached to the land when it was acquired.

opportunity to have his claim determined on the merits. . . .

NOTES AND QUESTIONS

1. *Federal issues.* The *Eastlake* case put to rest the federal constitutional objections to a zoning referendum. The Supreme Court's view of the referendum process was the decisive factor. How does it contrast with the view of state courts that zoning referenda are undesirable? Should the Supreme Court have held that a referendum denies due process because it results "in arbitrary decisions and patchwork zoning with little rhyme or reason," as the South Carolina Supreme Court holds? Or is it really a procedural due process question, as Justice Stevens' dissent suggests?

Would the court's disposition of *Eastlake* have been aided by acknowledging the debate in state courts over whether zoning amendments are "legislative" or "quasi-judicial"? Or does the Ohio Supreme Court's labeling dispose of that issue? Does the Supreme Court adequately answer the objection to the process by explaining that the landowner has a substantive opportunity to overturn a zoning restriction that is unconstitutionally applied to him? Could he do so in a variance proceeding, as Chief Justice Burger suggests? See accord *Taylor Props.*, (nonmandatory referendum), *supra*.

The Supreme Court had an opportunity to review the legislative/administrative distinction in the review of constitutional issues raised by a referendum in *City of Cuyahoga Falls v. Buckeye Community Hope Foundation*, 538 U.S. 188 (2003). The *Buckeye* case involved a citizen-initiated referendum to repeal city approval of a site plan authorizing a low-income housing project. The city refused to issue building permits while the referendum was being held, and the referendum later passed. The Ohio Supreme Court invalidated the referendum on the basis that the site plan approval was administrative, and thus not subject to referendum. *Buckeye Community Hope Foundation v. Cuyahoga Falls*, 697 N.E.2d 181 (Ohio 1998). The nonprofit housing foundation brought suit in federal court on claims that the city violated equal protection and substantive due process protections by allowing the referendum to go forward and denying the building permits.

The Supreme Court found that the distinction drawn by the Ohio Supreme Court, between legislative and administrative referenda, was not relevant for federal purposes, and that the placing of the site plan approval on the ballot was not *per se* arbitrary government conduct in violation of due process. It reiterated the *Eastlake* endorsement of the referendum process as a basic instrument of democratic government. While the results of a referendum may be invalid if arbitrary and capricious, the city could not be found in violation of the constitution by carrying out the referendum process. The Court also held that there was no equal protection violation, as there was not sufficient evidence of discriminatory intent by the city acting pursuant to the charter referendum requirements. "In fact, by adhering to charter procedures, city officials enabled public debate on the referendum to take place, thus advancing significant *First Amendment* interests." *Id.* at 196 (emphasis in original). The Court added that the private views of citizens as they affected decision makers could be considered when determining whether a referendum that was adopted was discriminatory.

2. *Further criticisms of mandatory referenda.* For discussion of the *Eastlake* decision, see Note, *The Proper Use of Referenda in Zoning*, 29 Stan. L. Rev. 819, 825-44 (1977). The student Note makes a series of criticisms of the use of mandatory referenda such as that in *Eastlake* in the zoning process. Voters are likely to be uninformed about the zoning proposal, and so

incapable of making an informed choice. If the referendum result is judicially reviewed, the court will not have a record of any kind on which it can base its decision. Recall *Ranjel, supra,* in which the court refused to upset an unfavorable referendum on a zoning change which would have allowed a subsidized housing project. It suggested that judicial review of the referendum "would entail an intolerable invasion of the privacy that must protect an exercise of the franchise." 417 F.2d at 324.

The student Note also suggests that developers forced to face a mandatory referendum will bypass the local legislative body entirely and seek an electoral zoning change directly through the initiative. If this occurs, there will be no opportunity for the mutual bargaining between the municipality and the developer which is often necessary to adjust the developer's proposal. Mandatory referenda also delay the development process, interfere with comprehensive planning and frustrate attempts by the municipality to zone for regional needs. What is your evaluation of these criticisms? Would they be entirely eliminated if the referendum were made permissive and not mandatory, as the student Note also suggests?

3. *A racial discrimination perspective.* Earlier Supreme Court cases considering claims of racial discrimination in the referendum process can provide a better perspective on *Eastlake* and *Buckeye:*

Hunter v. Erickson, 393 U.S. 385 (1969). The city of Akron, Ohio, enacted a fair housing ordinance that prohibited discrimination in the sale or rental of housing. After plaintiff filed a complaint under the ordinance, the city charter was amended to require a referendum on any ordinance of this type. The city also had a long-standing referendum procedure under which a referendum could be had on almost any city ordinance following the filing of a petition by ten percent of the electors.

The charter provision mandating a referendum on fair housing ordinances was held unconstitutional, as it was "an explicitly racial classification treating racial housing matters differently from other racial and housing matters." *Id.* at 389. The court noted that while the law applied on its face to both majority and minority groups, its impact fell on the minority. *Id.* at 391. Because the mandatory referendum was based on a racial classification it bore a heavier burden of justification than other classifications. It was not justified by "insisting that a State may distribute legislative power as it desires and that the people may retain for themselves the power over certain subjects . . . [as there is a violation of] the Fourteenth Amendment." *Id.* at 392. The concurring opinion noted that the optional referendum procedure was grounded upon "general democratic principle," and that procedures of this type "do not violate the Equal Protection clause simply because they occasionally operate to disadvantage Negro political interests." *Id.* at 394.

James v. Valtierra, 402 U.S. 137 (1971). The Court upheld an amendment to the California state constitution that mandated a referendum on all local public housing projects. These projects are built by local agencies and governments and receive federal subsidies. The Court distinguished *Hunter* because the amendment "requires referendum approval for any low-rent public housing project, not only for projects which will be occupied by a racial minority." There was no support in the record for "any claim that a law seemingly neutral on its face is in fact aimed at a racial minority." *Id.* at 141.

Justice Black also noted that California had provided extensively for mandatory referenda on a variety of subjects, and that there was justification for mandating the referendum in this case because localities in which public housing projects are located might be subject to large expenditures for public services needed by these projects. In a footnote, Black noted that public housing projects were exempt by federal law from local property taxation and that in-lieu payments required as a substitute for local taxation were ordinarily less than the taxes that otherwise would have been levied. Was the Court correct in ignoring the racial impact of the referendum in *Eastlake*? For discussion of these cases, see Comment, *Restoring Accountability at the Municipal Level: The "Save Miami Beach" Zoning Referendum*, 53 U. Miami L. Rev. 541 (1999).

Referenda on zoning and on proposed subsidized housing projects have been invalidated under the Fair Housing Act, which requires only proof of racially discriminatory effect rather than intent. *United States v. City of Birmingham*, 727 F.2d 560 (6th Cir.1984); *United States v. City of Parma*, 494 F. Supp. 1049 (N.D. Ohio 1980) (restrictive land use regulations). Note that these cases were as-applied rather than facial attacks. Does this suggest a strategy for attacking the referendum requirement in *Eastlake*? Note that in *Buckeye*, the housing organization initially brought a Fair Housing Act claim, but later abandoned it.

4. *Delegations to neighbors. Eubank* and *Roberge* hold that a delegation to neighbors, a "narrow segment" of the community, to establish land use rules is unconstitutional. Does *Eastlake* convince you that a referendum is qualitatively different from this type of delegation? The third case in the *Eubank-Roberge* trilogy, *Cusak*, cited but not discussed in the principal case, held that a similar delegation to *waive* restrictions in an ordinance established legislatively (there, a flat prohibition against billboards) is constitutional.

The legislative/waiver dichotomy in these old cases has defied scholarly attempts at reconciliation. For a sophisticated tour over this terrain, see Michelman, *Political Markets and Community Self-Determination*, 53 Ind. L.J. 145, 164-77 (1977-78). Notwithstanding these doubts, state courts sometimes flirt with the distinction. See *Howard Twp. Bd. of Trustees v. Waldo*, 425 N.W.2d 180 (Mich. App. 1988) (approving in principle a requirement of neighborhood consent for waiver of mobile home prohibition, citing *Eastlake*, but disapproving specific ordinance because consent of 100 percent of neighbors required). Accord *Cary v. City of Rapid City*, 559 N.W.2d 891 (S.D. 1997) (invalidating statute giving veto power to landowners); *Minton v. Ft. Worth Planning Comm'n*, 786 S.W.2d 563 (Tex. App. 1990) (consent provision of platting statute is unlawful delegation of power to neighbors).

Instead of the referendum procedure approved in *Eastlake*, could the municipality have required the applicant to have sought a waiver and subjected that process to neighborhood approval? See *Rispo Inv. Co. v. City of Seven Hills*, 629 N.E.2d 3 (Ohio App. 1993) (upholding charter requiring approval of zoning change by voters in ward in which property was located).

5. *The Eastlake model.* The mandatory referendum required in *Eastlake* is unusual and controversial. An Ohio court upheld a city charter provision authorizing mandatory referenda for zoning. *Kure v. City of North Royalton*, 517 N.E.2d 1016 (Ohio App. 1986). For discussion of this practice in Ohio, see Rosenburg, *Referendum Zoning: Legal Doctrine and Practice*, 53 U. Cin. L. Rev. 381 (1984).

The extra-majority requirement in *Eastlake* is also somewhat unusual, although it is often used in bond issue elections. The Supreme Court held that an extra-majority voting requirement for municipal bond elections did not violate the Court's one person-one vote rule. *Gordon v. Lance*, 403 U.S. 1 (1971).

J. STRATEGIC LAWSUITS AGAINST PUBLIC PARTICIPATION (SLAPP SUITS)

TRI-COUNTY CONCRETE COMPANY v. UFFMAN-KIRSCH

2000 Ohio App. LEXIS 4749 (2000)

Patricia Ann Blackmon, J.:

Appellee-Cross Appellant Tri-County Concrete Company (Tri-County) appeals the trial court's decision granting appellant-cross appellee Lisa Uffman-Kirsch's (Uffman-Kirsch) motion for summary judgment on its complaint alleging libel and tortious interference with the constitutional right to petition government for redress of grievances.

. . . .

In 1994, Lisa Uffman-Kirsch, together with other residents of the city of North Royalton, formed the North Royalton Residents Involvement Committee (NRRIC). NRRIC formed to support an initiative to establish a rural residential zoning district in North Royalton.

Tri-County Concrete Company operated a concrete plant in Twinsburg, Ohio. Tri-County decided to expand its operation and acquired property in North Royalton for this purpose. On April 10, 1996, Tri-County received a use variance from the city of North Royalton to construct a batch plant and concrete recycling plant on its North Royalton property. Tri-County's use variance was subject to eighteen conditions or restrictions. The use variance specifically stated, "failure to comply with any of the restrictions hereinafter enumerated shall be considered grounds for revocation of the use variance." Additionally, the use variance indicated authority to determine what constituted a violation belonged to the city's Building Commissioner, Carl Gawelek.

On July 1, 1996, Carl Gawelek, together with City Engineer Charles Althoff, sent a written memorandum to the city's law director informing him of Tri-County's failure to comply with several conditions of its use variance. Gawelek and Althoff generated the memorandum following Althoff's inspection of the Tri-County site. The memorandum notified the law director that a stop work order would be issued on the Tri-County site effective July 2, 1996, and requested advice on stopping the Tri-County operation pending review by the Planning Commission.

On July 2, 1996, the city posted stop work orders on the Tri-County site. Despite the stop work order, Tri-County attempted to continue its operations on July 3, 1996.

On July 5, 1996, the law director sent a letter to the mayor of North Royalton recommending the mayor refer the matter of Tri-County's use variance to the Board of Zoning Appeals (BZA) for the purpose of reconsideration. The law director expressed concern regarding Tri-County's violations of several conditions of its use variance, Tri-County's apparent failure to meet EPA requirements, and Tri-County's disregard of the stop work order issued by the city. The law director attached a list of eight violations, reported by Gawelek and Althoff, to his letter.

In addition to failing to comply with the stop work order, the listed violations included failure to comply with erosion control practice, stockpiling concrete slabs without permit and/or permission, and allowing the dumping of broken asphalt. In his letter, the law director also recommended holding a public hearing on the issue with public notice to area residents to allow "Tri-County a forum to fully address all violations and allow the Board of Zoning Appeals to decide whether the violations warrant revocation or continued validity of the use variance.

On July 9, 1996, the city issued Tri-County an order to correct violations. The city gave Tri-County fifteen days to comply with the order.

On July 22, 1996, Uffman-Kirsch sent a letter to the Planning Commission expressing her concerns regarding Tri-County's use variance. In paragraph seven of her letter Uffman-Kirsch stated:

> Last, but perhaps most importantly, I feel we must consider long and hard the risks involved in approving any applications and/or plans for an organization that has a record of total disregard to the laws, restrictions, standards and requirements of the municipality in which it operates. Tri-County's performance history with the city of Twinsburg should serve as clear forewarning of this company's lack of community responsibility. In short, any organization that operates in complete defiance of a City's requirements *while it is trying to gain approval* should cause us to give serious thought to their probable performance after approval is given. (Emphasis in original.)

Uffman-Kirsch provided a copy of her letter to City Engineer Charles Althoff and Building Commissioner Carl Gawelek.

On July 25, 1996, representatives of the Ohio Environmental Protection Agency (Ohio EPA) inspected the Tri-County site. As a result of the inspection, the Ohio EPA cited Tri-County for violations of its Ohio EPA permit. Following notice of the Ohio EPA's action, the city revoked Tri-County's use variance on July 31, 1996. However, the city reinstated Tri-County's variance after determining the revocation to be premature, as it did not afford Tri-County an opportunity to correct the violations cited by the Ohio EPA.

On September 18, 1996, Tri-County filed a complaint against Lisa Uffman-Kirsch, NRRIC, and one hundred unknown NRRIC members. The complaint alleged defamation and malicious interference with the constitutional right to petition government for redress of grievances. On November 20, 1996, Uffman-Kirsch filed a separate answer to the complaint, together with a counterclaim alleging abuse of process and violation of her first amendment right to free speech against Tri-County. The trial court dismissed the unknown NRRIC members and the NRRIC from the action on January 31, 1997 and June 30, 1998, respectively. The case proceeded with the two remaining parties.

[Summary judgment was granted at the trial level to Uffman-Kirsch on all claims asserted in Tri-County's complaint, and was granted to Tri-County on the counterclaim by Uffman-Kirsch. Both parties appealed. After setting forth the standard of review, the court next addresses Tri-County's appeal, which is based on the adverse decision regarding its libel claim against Uffman-Kirsch and its claim for malicious interference. The court explains the standards for a libel claim.]

Uffman-Kirsch argues her statements to the Planning Commission represented her opinions, and thus receive protection under both the First Amendment of the United States Constitution and Section 11, Article I, of the Ohio Constitution. Pure opinion statements are not actionable under defamation lawsuits. *Milkovich v. Lorain Journal Co.* (1990), 497 U.S. 1. A pure opinion statement exists when it does not state a fact that can objectively be proven false. Conversely, a statement objectively capable of being proven false may be actionable in a suit for defamation. Whether a statement is pure opinion or opinion reasonably interpreted as stating actual fact is a question of law. When determining whether speech is protected opinion, a court must consider the totality of the circumstances. "Specifically, a court should consider: the specific language at issue, whether the statement is verifiable, the general context of the statement, and the broader context in which the statement appeared." [Citing case.]

Applying the totality of circumstances approach to the instant case, we conclude Uffman-Kirsch's statements represented her opinion based on the general context of the statement and the broader context in which it appeared. Uffman-Kirsch resides in the city of North Royalton. She sent her letter as a follow-up to a public meeting of the North Royalton Planning Commission held to consider granting Tri-County a conditional use variance. She expressed her concern regarding Tri-County's effect on the community in which she resides. At the time Uffman-Kirsch sent her letter, the city considered Tri-County to be operating in violation of several of the conditions of its use variance. Further, correspondence between Tri-County and the city of Twinsburg demonstrates that Tri-County experienced similar compliance issues with that city. Under the circumstances, we conclude Uffman-Kirsch's statements that Tri-County "has a record of total disregard for laws, restrictions standards and requirements of the municipality and operates in complete defiance of a City's requirements" express her opinion regarding Tri-County's compliance record. Consequently, her statements are not actionable as defamatory speech. Having so concluded, we find it unnecessary to address Tri-County's arguments regarding falsity or malice. Accordingly, we overrule Tri-County's first assignment of error.

In its second assignment of error, Tri-County argues the trial court erred in granting Uffman-Kirsch summary judgment on its malicious interference with the night to petition government for redress claim based on the existence of material disputed facts. Because we conclude Tri-County failed to produce evidence sufficient to meet its burden of production on this claim, we affirm the trial count's judgment.

The Ohio Court of Appeals for the Second District recognizes the tort of malicious interference with the constitutional right to petition the government for redress of grievances. The Second District defines the tort as follows:

> The tort of malicious interference with the constitutional right to petition the government for redress of grievances (protected by Section 3, Article I of the Ohio Constitution, and by the First Amendment to the United States Constitution) occurs when a third party, without a privilege to do so, knowingly and maliciously makes a false statement for the purpose of inducing a public body to act or to fail to act, when the act, or failure to act, adversely affects the injured party.

Singer v. City of Fairborn (Ohio App. 1991), 598 N.E.2d 806, 814.

The *Singer* court went on to clarify its holding by stating:

> We do not go so far as to hold, however, that a mere omission may give rise to liability, since that would have an unduly chilling effect upon the speaker's exercise of his rights of free speech. To speak at all would give rise to a substantial risk that, in the heat of the moment, and perhaps, also, in the give and take of debate, some material fact would be omitted. If that, alone, could give rise to an inference of malice and the liability resulting therefrom, there would be too strong a disincentive to speak out at all concerning any controversial subject.

Id. In the instant case, Tri-County argues Uffman-Kirsch's made two false statements — "total disregard" and "complete defiance." As we concluded above, these statements represented Uffman-Kirsch's opinion of Tri-County's compliance record and as such, receive protection under both the Federal and Ohio Constitution. Further, even assuming Uffman-Kirsch's statements were not protected, Tri-County failed to meet its burden of establishing Uffman-Kirsch made the statements maliciously.

To establish actual malice in connection with Uffman-Kirsch's statements, Tri-County needed to prove Uffman-Kirsch made the statements with knowledge the statements were false or with reckless disregard as to their truth or falsity. Tri-County alleges Uffman-Kirsch acted in reckless disregard of the truth because she failed to reflect in her statements the fact that Tri-County acted to resolve its differences with the City of Twinsburg. However, mere omissions do not give rise to liability. "Rather, the party seeking relief must present evidence that defendant[] knew the statements were false, entertained serious doubts about whether they were false, or disregarded a high probability that they were false." *Wall* [*v. Ohio Permanete Group, Inc.*,] 695 N.E.2d 1233 [Ohio App. 1997]. Tri-County failed to demonstrate any of these alternatives applied to Uffman-Kirsch. Therefore, we conclude the trial court correctly granted Uffman-Kirsch summary judgment on Tri-County's claim. Accordingly, we overrule Tri-County's second assignment of error.

In her sole assignment of error, Uffman-Kirsch argues the trial court erred in granting Tri-County summary judgment on her counterclaim. In her counterclaim filed with the trial count on November 20, 1996, Uffman-Kirsch stated two causes of action against Tri-County — abuse of process and violation of the right to petition government, assemble, and free speech. However, Uffman-Kirsch abandoned those causes of action and does not argue for relief under either one in her brief on appeal. Instead, Uffman-Kirsch argues for relief under a cause of action not yet recognized in Ohio or any other state — SLAPP BACK.

SLAPP stands for strategic lawsuit against public participation. The Supreme Court of New Hampshire describes a SLAPP suit as follows:

> Strategic lawsuits against public participation (SLAPPs) are civil lawsuits filed against non-governmental individuals and groups, usually for having communicated with a government body, official, or the electorate, on an issue of some public interest or concern. SLAPPs are filed in response to a wide range of political activities including zoning, land use, taxation, civil liberties, environmental protection, public education, animal rights, and the accountability of professionals and public officials.
>
> SLAPPs seek to retaliate against political opposition, attempt to prevent future opposition and intimidate political opponents, and are employed as a strategy to win an underlying economic battle, political fight, or both. The SLAPP plaintiff's goal is not necessarily to "win" the lawsuit, but rather to deter public participation in the democratic process by chilling debate on public and political issues. This goal is realized by instituting or threatening multimillion-dollar lawsuits to intimidate citizens into silence.
>
> Identifying SLAPPs, which typically appear as ordinary lawsuits, presents difficulties. Objective factors for identifying SLAPPs have, however, been suggested. These factors include: the defendant's activity implicates the constitutional rights of free speech and to petition for the redress of grievances; the type of legal claim is generally a claim for defamation, tortious interference with business or contract, civil conspiracy

> or abuse of process, constitutional on civil rights violations, or nuisance; and SLAPP filers are typically real estate developers, property owners, police officers, alleged polluters, and state or local government agencies.

Opinion of the Justices, 641 A.2d 1012, 1013–1014 (N.H. 1994) (citations omitted).

As Uffman-Kirsch points out in her brief, a number of state legislatures have chosen to enact anti-SLAPP laws. See Mass. Gen. L. 231, Section 59H (1992), Cal. Civil Proc. 425.16. Generally, such legislation provides a special procedure making plaintiff's complaint subject to a motion to strike, unless the court determines the plaintiff has established a probability that plaintiff will prevail on its claim. Defendants who prevail on such special motions are entitled to recover attorney's fees and costs. The Ohio General Assembly has not yet chosen to enact anti-SLAPP legislation, and this count is constrained from recognizing such an action at this time. Beside, any party faced with this kind of lawsuit may avail herself of the frivolous lawsuit statute, which affords to the grievant ample relief including attorney fees.

Judgment affirmed.

NOTES AND QUESTIONS

1. *The problem.* Professors George Pring and Penelope Canan at the University of Denver coined the term SLAPP suit in early and influential publications describing the problem of suits that are filed to intimidate public opposition to development projects or other enterprises that raise public concerns. The typical suit is filed against ad hoc groups of local citizens or individuals who have communicated opposition to a government body, and who do not have either the financial resources or the will to defend against the suit. The filer hopes that the defendants will either drop their opposition completely or enter into a settlement agreeable to the filer that permits a modified development. As in the principal case, the litigation is brought as a tort action on claims such as defamation, abuse of process or tortuous interference with business, with conspiracy added to make all of the defendants liable as joint tortfeasors. See, e.g., Canan & Pring, *Studying Strategic Lawsuits Against Public Participation: Mixing Quantitative and Qualitative Approaches*, 22 Law & Soc'y Rev. 385 (1988). SLAPP suits chill public participation and move a public and political battle into the courtroom, with no attempt to resolve the dispute at hand but rather to distract and intimidate the public. As one court noted with some alarm,

> [T]he ripple effect of such suits in our society is enormous. Persons who have been outspoken on issues of public importance targeted in such suits or who have witnessed such suits will often choose in the future to stay silent. Short of a gun to the head, a greater threat to First Amendment expression can scarcely be imagined.

Gordon v. Marrone, 590 N.Y.S.2d 649 (Sup. Ct. 1992), *aff'd*, 616 N.Y.S.2d 98 (App. Div. 1994).

2. *The First Amendment.* SLAPP suits are like other lawsuits, which are subject to court sanctions if found to be frivolous, but they are distinguished from frivolous suits by their implications for the First Amendment rights of the citizens who are targeted. See *Protect Our Mountain Env't, Inc. v. District Court*, 677 P.2d 1361 (Colo. 1984) (en banc), where a citizens group lost a suit against a county commission which rezoned agricultural lands to a planned development zone, and who were then sued by the developer for abuse of process and economic harm. Based on the citizens' defense of the SLAPP suit as chilling their First Amendment right to petition the government, the Colorado supreme court fashioned a heightened standard of review for SLAPP suits. This standard requires the plaintiff to show that the defendant's petitioning was not protected because: (1) the asserted petition rights lacked a reasonable factual basis or cognizable legal basis; (2) the primary purpose of the petition was improper; and (3) the petitioning activity was capable of adversely affecting the legal interest of the plaintiff. The standard allows for more speedy resolution of the suit and places a greater burden on the plaintiff to have a legitimate complaint. See also *Franchise Realty Interstate Corp. v. San Francisco Local Joint Executive Bd. of Culinary Workers*, 542 F.2d 1076 (9th Cir. 1976) (requiring heightened pleading). The *Noerr-Pennington* doctrine, discussed *supra* in Chapter 2, also provides protection for SLAPP targets. What other protections should there be for public participants? What about the rights of the developer to be free from harassment by NIMBY ("Not in my backyard") groups? See *Florida Fern Grower's Ass'n, Inc. v. Concerned Citizens of Putnam County*, 616 So. 2d 562 (Fla. App. 1993) (reversing dismissal of complaint).

3. *Legislative solutions.* More than twenty states have adopted anti-SLAPP legislation. See Coover, *Pennsylvania Anti-SLAPP Legislation*, 12 Penn. St. Envtl. L. Rev. 263 (2004). California was one of the first states to pass an anti-SLAPP law. See Cal. Civ. Proc. Code § 425.16 (effective Jan. 1, 1993). The more stringent statutes require that the plaintiff demonstrate that the suit is not intended to suppress the First Amendment rights of the defendant, such as that adopted by Del. Code Ann. Tit. 10, § 8137(a). The Delaware statute also grants preference for the hearings on motions for summary judgment and to dismiss, in order to resolve the cases promptly. A meaningful disincentive to SLAPP suits is provided in the Georgia legislation that requires the signature of the plaintiff verifying that the claim is not meant to suppress the right to petition or to harass. Attorney's fees are available as a sanction if the court finds that the verification was improperly made. Ga. Code Ann. § 9-11-11.1(b). A model statute is provided in G. Pring & P. Canan, SLAPPs: Getting Sued For Speaking Out (1996). See Comment, *Have I Been SLAPPed? Arkansas's Attempt to Curb AbusiveLitigation: the Citizen Participation in Government Act*, 60 Ark. L. Rev. 507-532 (2007); Note, *SLAPPing Around the First Amendment: An Analysis of Oklahoma's Anti-SLAPP Statute and its Implications on the Right to Petition*, 60 Okla. L. Rev. 419-447 (2007). For an analysis of the political realities from a citizen viewpoint, and types of SLAPP statutes and their effectiveness, see Canan & Barker, *Inside Land-Use SLAPPs: The Continuing Fight to Speak Out*, Land Use L. & Zoning Dig., July, 2003, at 3.

4. *SLAPP-back suits.* As in the principal case, some defendants file their own suits or counterclaims based, for example, on malicious prosecutions, violation of constitutional rights, infliction of emotional distress, or the like. These suits are coined "SLAPP-back" suits. Both the plaintiff and plaintiff's counsel can be subject to large damage awards where the suits are successful. The courts may require that a SLAPP-back suit not be brought until the original action is final. See *Giglio v. Delesparo* 361 N.Y.S.2d 721 (App. Div. 1974). How does this affect the participation of the public?

5. *Sources.* See Brecher, *The Public Interest and Intimidation Suits: A New Approach*, 28 Santa Clara L. Rev. 105 (1988); Cook & Merriam, *Recognizing a SLAPP Suit and Understanding its Consequences*, 19 Zoning & Plan. L. Rep. 33 (1996); Potter, *Strategic Lawsuits Against Public Participation and Petition Clause Immunity*, 31 Envtl. L. Rep. 10852 (2001); Stetson, *Reforming SLAPP Reform: New York's Anti-SLAPP Statute*, 70 N.Y.U.L. Rev. 1324 (1995).

Chapter 7

SUBDIVISION CONTROLS AND PLANNED UNIT DEVELOPMENTS

Uncontrolled development in the 1920s left a legacy of site-assembly encumbrances on locationally choice acreage that raised the cost to developers of exploiting the economies of building multiple units within a subdivision. These encumbrances included legal and transactions costs associated with land reassembly and, where poorly planned improvements had been made, the choice between demolition, removal, and site restoration costs or development within platting constraints that were uneconomic and in many respects dysfunctional. Rural land under single ownership was available, but it was less favorably situated, farther from employment opportunities or transport nodes. Although the technology of building profitable neighborhoods through coordinated, large-scale development was more widely understood by the late 1930s, recovery relied disproportionately on owners of individual plots contracting directly with builders. Only after World War II — when better roads had been built, aggregate demand had revived more strongly, and public institutional mechanisms for overcoming the transactions costs of land reassembly had been devised — did private construction revive fully.

Many abandoned subdivisions were located so far from the immediate course of metropolitan development that, even under different institutional arrangements, they would not have been profitably developed during the 1930s. Others were more favorably situated, but a variety of obstacles hindered their redevelopment. Sometimes these took the form of the costs of removing infrastructure and restoring the site to a buildable state. When street layouts and utility hookups were unusable because their layout or capacity did not match desired new configurations, the choice was between abandoning the land and tearing them out to start afresh. Although the dollar value of unutilized public improvements was substantial, the share of prematurely subdivided lots with a full complement of utilities was small, revealing the scale on which premature subdivision had occurred during the post-World War I expansion. . . .

Poorly planned development meant that the output of housing services (and perforce output in general) grew more slowly than it might otherwise have in the 1920s. By encumbering locationally choice areas with poorly planned neighborhoods, partially completed developments, and diffuse and uncertain ownership, the uncoordinated boom laid the groundwork for a collapse in construction spending, disrupted intermediation, and a prolonged depression. Had developers not been forced to choose between the often prohibitive costs of overcoming the legal and physical debris of past subdivisions and working with undeveloped rural land farther from the city center, revived building on a larger scale could have begun earlier.

A. Field, *Uncontrolled Land Development and the Duration of the Depression in the United States*, 52 J. Econ. Hist. 785–805 (Dec. 1992).

Even today, with apparently good plans and public regulation, land development efforts can fail. Paul Donsky, *Volume of "Subdivision" Vacant Lots Overwhelms Banks*, Atlanta Business News, August 8, 2009, at p. 1–4. How can we avoid such failures in land development or minimize their impacts and protect consumers and, most importantly, land purchasers who, having relied on public and private representations, bought their land and built their homes?

One important means to those ends is subdivision regulation. As we have seen, zoning focuses, or should focus, on the city as a whole and the relationship of various types of land use to a city's overall plan of development. Subdivision regulations concentrate on the design and the internal improvements of land being developed. During the Twentieth Century, two classic models for street layout became popular: the gridiron pattern of streets at right angles to one another, first popularized in original city development and renewed in the New Urbanist movement, and the curvilinear pattern of suburban streets with cul-de-sac offshoots.

Modern subdivision regulations are a product of the suburban development boom post-World War II. The vast acreage of land that was plowed under to build suburbia required equally large outlays of money to connect the new developments to streets and highways as well as sewers and water lines. While relatively rare now, newspapers in the 1950s and 1960s carried numerous stories of households in new subdivision developments coping with cracked streets, sewer back ups and bad-looking or -tasting tap water. In response, state and local governments moved aggressively to impose increasingly sophisticated requirements on new residential developments through subdivision regulation legislation.

The budget crunch and taxpayers' revolt of the 1980s, symbolized by California's Proposition 13, created serious infrastructure funding problems for local governments. As a result, municipalities moved to pass on to developers and their customers much of the cost of infrastructure required to support new development through the use of exactions: conditions attached to development approval requiring land or money to be provided for parks, roads, schools and the like.

This chapter examines the subdivision regulation system. Special emphasis is placed on the legal issues associated with exactions, particularly the constitutional takings question (Chapter 2, *supra*) these practices raise. A popular development technique, planned unit development (PUD), is also discussed. PUD regulations combine elements of zoning and subdivision controls in a review process that simultaneously considers proposed developmental design, intensity and uses at the same time. Planned unit developments can be residential only or they may include mixed uses. Large-scale PUDs are called master-planned communities and can be full-sized towns that include many neighborhoods and retail, office and entertainment centers. The following problem is designed to introduce you to these topics.

PROBLEM

The State of Metro has adopted Sections 13 and 14 of the Standard State Planning Enabling Act, which are reproduced *infra*. Metro County has adopted a subdivision control ordinance under the authority of this statute. It includes design standards for new subdivisions, including standards for the arrangement, dimension and orientation of lots, and requirements for roads and drainage and storm sewers. Sewer and water facilities must be provided in the subdivision if connection to public systems is not possible. The ordinance also authorizes the county to require the dedication of land for the widening of adjacent roads.

Ace Development Company owns 500 acres of land in an outlying area of Metro County that has been growing rapidly. A recently developed subdivision is located just to the south, but farmland borders the tract on all of its other sides. Ace has applied to the county for approval of a preliminary subdivision plat to the county with 1000 lots for single family homes. Lot sizes and densities comply with the zoning ordinance. The Ace tract is bordered on two sides by narrow two-lane county roads.

The county ordinance authorizes the planning department to review subdivision plat proposals and submit a report to the planning commission, which holds a hearing on the plat and decides whether to approve or reject it. The planning department approved the plat for the Ace subdivision and forwarded it to the planning commission, with a recommendation that Ace dedicate a 50-foot strip to the county to widen the adjacent county roads. This requirement will reduce the number of homes that Ace can build in the subdivision.

The planning commission held a hearing, and approved the preliminary plat and the dedication requirement, but with a condition that Ace redesign the subdivision "to provide a residential design compatible with the historic design features typical of Metro County." In its finding approving the subdivision, the commission noted it disapproved of the cul-de-sac design used in the subdivision, and preferred a neotraditional design that would use a gridiron street pattern.

The President of Ace has come to you for advice and has these questions: Is the design condition authorized by the statute? Is it authorized by the ordinance? Is it unconstitutional? Is the dedication requirement authorized by the statute and is it constitutional?

A. SUBDIVISION CONTROLS

[1.] In General

In addition to zoning, the early Model Acts also authorized controls over new subdivisions. In practice, subdivision controls apply in most states only to new single family residential development. Originally intended to require the provision of streets and other necessary facilities, subdivision controls in many states now reach more broadly to include environmental protection and floodplain development, and may even implement growth management programs. For example, in California, a local government may reject a subdivision if "the site is not physically suitable for the type of development," or "the site is not physically suitable for the proposed density of development." Cal. Gov't Code § 66474(c)(d).

Another important development is the use of subdivision controls to shift the cost of providing public facilities, such as roads, to developers. This occurs through exactions that require subdividers to make certain improvements on-site and off-site, dedicate land for public facilities, or pay a fee in lieu of the exaction that municipalities can use to provide the facilities themselves. Exactions have grown in importance in recent years because tax and debt limits have restricted government spending for infrastructure, and because communities see exactions as a way of shifting public facility costs away from existing residents to new residents and developers. Impact fees, imposed on developers at the time a building permit is issued, are another form of exaction. The Supreme Court's *Nollan* case, reproduced in Ch. 2, and its *Dolan* case, reproduced in this chapter, have had important effects on exaction law.

History of Subdivision Controls. The need for subdivision controls arises because raw land that is to be developed usually is held in comparatively large tracts. Before it can be developed, it must be subdivided into lots and blocks suitable for building.

Subdivision controls were first adopted in rudimentary form as land platting legislation toward the end of the nineteenth century to remedy conveyancing problems. Land had been conveyed by metes and bounds boundary descriptions. This conveyancing method requires a reference to boundary markers, distances, and directions that are in a long, confusing narrative and can lead to disputes over land ownership and titles. To avoid these problems, land developers prepared so-called plats of subdivisions on which the blocks and lots were shown. Once a plat was recorded, parcel conveyance could be by reference to blocks and lots within the plat, e.g., "Lot 5 in Block 4 of Milligan's Addition to the City of Indian Falls." The early platting laws simply required the recording of these subdivision plats in the appropriate records office, after which the conveyance of lots within the plat could be made with reference to the plat in the manner just indicated. Many of these early laws mandated the recording of subdivision plats before conveyances with reference to the plat could be made.

It soon became apparent that the subdivision control process could accomplish substantive objectives as well. Many of the early subdivisions were cursed by poor design and layout and inadequate streets and facilities. Often the subdivider would leave his development with badly constructed streets that would soon crumble, resulting in the homeowners bearing the cost of necessary street repairs. Other problems arose when subdividers planned their subdivisions independently, with the result that streets did not connect properly from one subdivision to the next.

Modern Enabling Legislation. Some states amended their subdivision platting legislation late in the nineteenth century to require subdivision streets to conform to the municipal street system plan. When the Standard State Planning Enabling Act was drafted in the 1920s, these early subdivision platting statutes were used as a model for subdivision control provisions included in the Act. The scope of public control over subdivisions contemplated at that time is indicated by the text of the Standard Act, which incorporated these early statutory requirements and added others requiring the provision of on-site facilities necessary to service the subdivision development:

> Section 13. Whenever a planning commission shall have adopted a major street plan . . . [which is on file in the office of the county recorder], then no plat of a subdivision of land . . . shall be filed or recorded until it shall have been approved by such planning commission. . . .
>
> Section 14. Before exercising . . . [subdivision control] powers . . . the planning commission shall adopt regulations governing the subdivision of land within its jurisdiction. Such regulations may provide for the proper arrangement of streets in relation to other existing or planned streets and to the master plan, for adequate and convenient open spaces for traffic, utilities, access of firefighting apparatus, recreation, light and air, and for the avoidance of congestion of population, including minimum width and areas of lots.
>
> Such regulations may include provisions as to the extent to which streets and other ways shall be graded and improved and to which water and sewer and other utility mains, piping, or other facilities shall be installed as a condition precedent to the

approval of the plat. [Standard City Planning Enabling Act (U.S. Dep't of Commerce, 1928).]

For early discussions of subdivision control legislation, which are still helpful, see Melli, *Subdivision Control in Wisconsin*, 1953 Wis. L. Rev. 389; Reps, *Control of Land Subdivision by Municipal Planning Boards*, 40 Cornell L.Q. 258 (1955); Note, *Land Subdivision Control*, 65 Harv. L. Rev. 1226 (1952); Note, *Platting, Planning and Protection, A Summary of Subdivision Statutes*, 36 N.Y.U. L. Rev. 1205 (1961). In many states, the subdivision control legislation is still based on the provisions of the Standard Act.

More modern subdivision control legislation extends substantive requirements, tending to view the act of subdividing as a triggering event for the application of controls that shape and give character to newer development in the community. In short, subdivision control has gradually evolved from a simple control over the recording of new subdivision plats to an extensive set of controls over new land development.

Newer legislation adds requirements to those of the Standard Act. More on-site improvements and facilities are required, new subdivisions have been restricted in floodplains and on environmentally sensitive land, and the phasing of new development has been controlled in connection with the provision of public facilities. In addition, many states now have legislation authorizing exactions.

The Connecticut subdivision control enabling legislation is a modern example:

Conn. Gen. Stat.

§ 8-18. *Definitions*. . . .

"Commission" means a planning commission; . . .

"subdivision" means the division of a tract or parcel of land into three or more parts or lots . . . for the purpose, whether immediate or future, of sale or building development expressly excluding development for municipal, conservation or agricultural purposes, and includes resubdivision. . . .

§ 8-25(a). *Subdivision of land.* No subdivision of land shall be made until a plan for such subdivision has been approved by the commission. . . . [A fine of $500 is imposed for any person making subdivision without approval.] . . . Before exercising the powers granted in this section, the commission shall adopt regulations covering the subdivision of land. . . . Such regulations shall provide that the land to be subdivided shall be of such character that it can be used for building purposes without danger to health or the public safety, that proper provision shall be made for water, sewerage and drainage, . . . that proper provision shall be made for protective flood control measures and that the proposed streets are in harmony with existing or proposed principal thoroughfares shown in the plan of conservation and development . . . especially in regard to safe intersections with such thoroughfares, and so arranged and of such width, as to provide an adequate and convenient system for present and prospective traffic needs.

[The statute authorizes municipalities to "exact" open space contributions from developers of up to ten percent of the value of the land being subdivided, either by transferring land or paying a fee "in lieu" of a land transfer, with the open space contributions to be shown on the subdivision plan. Open space requirements do not apply to transfers within a family or if the subdivision is for affordable housing.]

Such regulations . . . shall provide that proper provision be made for soil erosion and sediment control. . . . [Regulations shall not impose requirements on manufactured homes constructed under federal standards that are "substantially different from conditions and requirements imposed on single family dwellings and lots containing single family dwellings."] The commission may also prescribe the extent to which and the manner in which streets shall be graded and improved and public utilities and services provided [and may accept a bond in lieu of completion of such work].

(b) The regulations adopted under subsection (a) of this section shall also encourage energy-efficient patterns of development and land use, the use of solar and other renewable forms of energy, and energy conservation . . . .

A California statute gives municipalities even broader powers over subdivisions. As noted *supra*, California cities are directed to deny approval of subdivision proposals if "the site is not physically suitable for the type of development . . . [or] for the proposed density of development." Cal. Gov't Code § 66474(c) and (d). What reasons for disapproval does this statute authorize as compared with the more traditional statute? Does it authorize disapproval of a development located on a hillside subject to erosion? See *Carmel Valley View, Ltd. v. Board of Supervisors*, 130 Cal. Rptr. 249 (Cal. App. 1976) (approving rejection because site was not physically suitable for use of individual sewage disposal systems).

The APA Growing Smart project includes a model subdivision control statute. American Planning Association, Growing Smart Legislature Guidebook: Model Statutes for Planning and Management of Change § 8-301 (S. Meck ed., 2002). The model incorporates provisions from the Standard Act as well as statutes from Kentucky, New Jersey, and Rhode Island. Ky. Rev. Stats. §§ 100.273 to 100.292; N.J. Rev. Stat. Ch. 55D, art. 6; R.I. Gen. Laws, Tit. 45, Ch. 23. The model requires the adoption of a subdivision ordinance and describes both required and optional provisions for the ordinance.

NOTES AND QUESTIONS

1. *What subdivision control covers.* Note that subdivision control applies in Connecticut, as is usually the case, only when there is a subdivision of land. (Consult again the definition in the statute *supra.*) This requirement creates a regulatory gap problem. Major developments that do not require subdivision, such as multifamily projects, shopping centers, and industrial parks, are outside the subdivision control process. This gap is one reason for site plan review (described in Ch. 5) and planned unit development controls, *infra*, either of which apply a similar review process to projects on single sites and to major residential developments. The purpose requirement in statutes worded like Connecticut's can be a problem. See *Slavin v. Ingraham*, 339 N.E.2d 157 (N.Y. 1975) (no showing that developers were selling individual lots collectively for residential purposes or holding themselves out as subdividers); *Jones v. Davis*, 594 S.E.2d 235, 239 (N.C. App. 2004) (nothing in subdivision ordinance prevents owner from leasing lots in a subdivision for placement of mobile homes).

Most courts hold that a municipality may not modify the definition of a subdivision contained in the enabling act. See, e.g., *State v. Visser*, 767 P.2d 858 (Mont. 1988). For a clever (and successful) example of avoiding even a broadly worded subdivision ordinance, see *Vinyard v. St.*

Louis County, 399 S.W.2d 99 (Mo. 1966) (creation of access road through residential lots to serve landlocked apartment development).

Section 12 of the Standard Act authorized subdivision regulation over unincorporated territory located in an extraterritorial area five miles beyond the municipal limits. Most states confer extraterritorial powers. For example, the Illinois subdivision statute authorizes municipalities to regulate subdivisions both within municipal boundaries and within one and one half miles beyond the corporate boundaries, as follows:

> No map or plat of any subdivision presented for record affecting land (1) within the corporate limits of any municipality which has heretofore adopted, or shall hereafter adopt an ordinance including an official map in the manner prescribed in this Division 12, or (2) within contiguous territory which is not more than 1 1/2 miles beyond the corporate limits of an adopting municipality, shall be entitled to record or shall be valid unless the subdivision shown thereon provides for streets, alleys, public ways, ways for public service facilities, storm and flood water run-off channels and basins, and public grounds, in conformity with the applicable requirements of the ordinances including the official map; provided, that a certificate of approval by the corporate authorities, certified by the clerk of the municipality in whose jurisdiction the land is located, or a certified copy of an order of the circuit court directing the recording as provided in Section 11-12-8, shall be sufficient evidence of compliance with this section upon which the recorder may accept the plat for recording. . . .

65 ILCS § 5/11-12-12 (emphasis added); see also *Petterson v. City of Naperville*, 137 N.E.2d 371 (Ill. 1956) (upholding extraterritorial delegation).

For model subdivision ordinances in addition to the Growing Smart Legislative Guidebook discussion *supra*, see R. Freilich & M. Shultz, Model Subdivision Regulations (2d ed. 1995); D. Listokin & C. Walker, The Subdivision and Site Plan Handbook (Ordinance) (1989).

2. *Exemptions and minor subdivisions.* Most statutes contain exemptions from subdivision control. The subdivision of land for agricultural purposes is one example. N.J. Stat. Ann. § 40:55D-7 (five acres or more). Cal. Gov't Code § 66426 contains a typical list of exemptions. They include subdivisions of less than five acres when each parcel fronts on a maintained public street or highway and no dedications or improvements are required; subdivisions with parcels of 20 acres or more with access to a maintained public street or highway; and subdivisions with parcels of 40 acres or more. Exemptions of this kind make it difficult to prevent development in areas prohibited from development in growth management programs. See Chapter 8.

Another common statutory exemption covers transfers to family members as gifts or conveyances to abutting landowners so long as the transfers are not made with the intent to avoid the objectives of the statutes. Me. Rev. Stat. Ann. tit. 30-A, § 4401(4)(D); *Tinsman v. Town of Falmouth*, 840 A.2d 100, 103–04 (Me. 2004) (record established that real estate broker made numerous transfers of property within a short period of time to a corporation he owned which was an abutting landowner in order to avoid the statute); see also *Mills v. Town of Eliot*, 2008 M.E. 134 (2008) (Maine statute exempts "family subdivisions" from the subdivision requirements). The Growing Smart model statute contains no exemptions in the definition of "subdivision." § 8-101. Drafters comment that "subdivision review is an important local government function and is not to be dodged through exemptions that evade public scrutiny." American Planning Association, Growing Smart Legislative Guidebook: Model Statutes for Planning and Management of Change, p. 8-61 (S. Meck ed., 2002).

Condominiums and other common interest ownership communities originally were not considered covered by subdivision statutes because they involve the subdivision of air, not of land. As condominiums have become more popular and have been developed horizontally as well as vertically, modern subdivision statutes in some states include them. Ariz. Rev. Stat. Ann. § 9-463.02(A); Cal. Gov't Code § 66424. See *Thornton v. Flathead County*, 220 P.3d 395 (Mont. 2009) (condominium projects required to go through the subdivision review process); but c.f. *Alford Inv. v. Zoning Board of Stamford*, 920 A.2d 1000 (Conn. 2008) (common interest community not required to obtain subdivision approval prior to receiving a zoning permit).

Statutes may also provide special procedures for minor subdivisions under a certain size, such as eliminating the preliminary plat stage. N.J. Stat. Ann. § 40:55D-47.

3. *What is required?* How has the Connecticut statute expanded the subdivision control requirements contained in the Standard Act? Note the extensive environmental controls. See also Cal. Gov't Code § 66474(e) (subdivision design must not cause substantial environmental damage). For a more extensive provision, see Ariz. Rev. Stat. Ann. § 9-463.01(C)(4), which authorizes municipalities to

> Either determine that certain lands may not be subdivided, by reason of adverse topography, periodic inundation, adverse soils, subsidence of the earth's surface, high water table, lack of water or other natural or man-made hazard to life or property, or control the lot size, establish special grading and drainage requirements, and impose other regulations deemed reasonable and necessary for the public health, safety or general welfare on any lands to be subdivided affected by such characteristics.

Does this statute provide an alternative to the prohibition of development on these lands? What is it? Many subdivision control enabling acts require the adoption of subdivision regulations by the governing body in ordinance form. Some acts give the power to approve subdivision plats to the local governing body.

4. *Health and stormwater requirements.* Many states also provide authority to state health and environmental agencies to regulate on-site wells and on-site sewage disposal through septic tanks and similar facilities. E.g., Mich. Stat. Ann. § 560.105(g), requiring the approval of all subdivisions to be conditioned on compliance with the rules of the state department of environmental quality "relating to suitability of groundwater for on-site water supply for subdivisions not served by public water or to suitability of soils for subdivisions not served by public water and public sewers." N.H. Rev. Stat. Ann. § 485-A:4(IX), authorizes a state agency to specify standards, procedures and criteria for sewage or waste disposal systems in subdivisions.

Acceptability of on-site systems under these laws is usually based on the ability of the soil to handle waste disposal. See also Mich. Stat. Ann. § 560.109(a) (no approval of subdivision of less than one acre unless public water and sewer available or approved on-site alternative). Denial of a state permit will foreclose development of the site unless the developer ties in with public facilities.

Statutes also commonly establish comprehensive state stormwater management programs. E.g., N.J. Stat. Ann. §§ 40:55D-93 to -99 (Stormwater Management Act), delegating regulatory authority to the New Jersey Department of Environmental Protection. Regulations issued by the Department requiring developments near certain waters to maintain "300-foot special water resource protection area[s on both sides of the waterway] consisting of existing vegetation or vegetation allowed to follow natural succession" were upheld as within the statutory range. *In the Matter of Stormwater Management Rules*, 894 A.2d 1241 (N.J. App. Div. 2006).

The importance of these state laws in the development of new subdivisions is often neglected. Note also that the state permit law adds another approval stage to the subdivision control process.

A NOTE ON SUBDIVISION COVENANTS AND OTHER PRIVATE CONTROL DEVICES

What they are. The act of subdivision is usually the point in the development process at which the developer decides whether to restrict the newly-created lots with rights and duties other than those contained in a formal system of land use controls, such as zoning. This Note briefly explores the complex subject of easements, covenants, and equitable servitudes, full consideration of which is usually found in Property or Real Estate Transactions courses. Over the centuries, this area of the law has acquired layers of complexity, often in order to preserve (or avoid) the rigid distinction between actions at law and in equity, or to fit within the arcane pigeonholes of the common law writ system. For a useful introduction to the modern effort to simplify this law, see Restatement (Third) of the Law, Property (Servitudes), Introductory Note (2000). For a survey of the traditional rules, see W. Stoebuck & D. Whitman, The Law of Property, Ch. 8 (3d ed. 2000).

For present purposes, a few general points will suffice. To function the way a zoning ordinance or other land use regulation does, the servitudes (we use the modern collective term espoused by the Restatement, *supra*, although it has not yet found general acceptance) must survive the individual parties who create them so that they can be enforced by and against whoever holds the land in question. This is permitted if the benefits and burdens can be shown to be sufficiently related to the land itself, or to a recognized estate in land, a requirement sometimes (but not always) embodied in the familiar phrases, "running with the land," and "touching and concerning the land." As might be expected, a substantial body of law addresses these terms. See, e.g., *Ramapo River Reserve Homeowners Ass'n, Inc. v. Borough of Oakland*, 896 A.2d 459 (N.J. 2006) (development agreement by which municipality delegated to developer its statutory requirement to provide snow and ice removal services to private residential subdivision terminated once developer was required to transfer control to homeowners' association); *1515-1519 Lakeview v. Apartment Sales Corp.*, 43 P.3d 1233 (Wash. 2002) (covenant by developer exculpating city from liability for latent risk of soil movement touches and concerns the land, thus preventing homeowners from bringing suit except for city's own negligence); *Runyon v. Paley*, 416 S.E.2d 177 (N.C. 1992) (covenant restricting land to no more than two residences touches and concerns both servient and dominant estate); *Petersen v. Beekmere, Inc.*, 283 A.2d 911 (N.J.L. Div. 1971) (covenant to pay annual assessment does not "touch or concern" land because money is not required to be expended for benefit of the subdivision).

Because England did not have recording systems, the early law of covenants abounds in complex notice rules. While notice remains a requirement, in America it is normally satisfied by compliance with state recording acts. For use in modern subdivisions and condominiums, the developer usually originates elaborate covenants, which are either recorded with the subdivision plat and incorporated by reference in the individual conveyances or set out in full in each conveyance. State subdivision and condominium statutes often regulate the form and content of this process.

Finally, in order to be enforceable, covenants must be "lawful," that is to say, they must be on a subject appropriate for private parties to agree upon and they must not be contrary to public policy. Restatement (Third) of Property: Servitudes, § 3.1 (2000). The best known example of contrary to public policy is, of course, *Shelley v. Kraemer*, 334 U.S. 1 (1947) (invalidating racially restrictive covenants). See also *Hill v. Community of Damien of Molokai*, 911 P.2d 861 (N.M. 1996) (Fair Housing Act would bar enforcement of single family use covenant to prohibit location of group home for individuals with AIDs); *Smith v. Fair Employment and Housing Comm'n*, 913 P.2d 909 (Cal. 1996) (state antidiscrimination law protects unmarried cohabitants and requiring landlord to comply with law does not substantially burden her religious exercise); contra, *State by Cooper v. French*, 460 N.W.2d 2 (Minn. 1990) (interpreting state statute barring fornication). See generally Markey, *The Price of Landlord's "Free" Exercise of Religion: Tenants' Right to Discrimination-Free Housing and Privacy*, 22 Fordham Urb. L.J. 699 (1995); A. Tekle, *Safe: Restrictive Covenants and the Next Wave of Sex Offender Legislation*, 62 SMU L. Rev. 1817 (2009). The courts also recognize the constitutionally protected right to contract by enforcing the more restrictive land use provision when a conflict arises between a covenant and a zoning ordinance.

In addition, courts will prohibit subsequent parties from disputing the validity of a covenant when a predecessor party had received the benefits. *Vo-Land, LLC v. Village of Bartlett*, 919 N.E.2d 1 (Ill. App. 2009). In 1987, the previous owner had entered into a covenant with the Village that allowed it to construct 1,875 residential units on its property provided that 96 acres of the site be maintained as a golf course or other open space. Vo-Land later took ownership of the property. In 2004, Vo-Land sought to amend the zoning for the property and wanted to close the golf course, reduce the 96-acre open space mandate to 51 acres and build 350 new residential units on the remaining golf course land. The Village board denied Vo-Land's request and refused to release the restrictive covenant and also denied Vo-Land's request to have the zoning of the parcel amended. The owner brought an action asking the court to void the restrictive covenant, or, in the alternative, to force the village to allow it to apply for amended zoning — a petition for disconnection for the property from the village. The court upheld the covenant and went further to find that Vo-Land was estopped to challenge its validity. The previous owner had agreed to keep the restrictive covenants in place for 35 years in exchange for being allowed to develop portions of the property. Much like any other form of contract, Vo-Land would not have been given the zoning variance that allowed the initial construction without the open-space restrictions that benefited the village. See also *Marinelli v. Prete*, 2010 Ohio 2257, 2010 Ohio App. LEXIS 1855 (Ohio App. 6 Dist., May 21, 2010) (enforcing covenant that required owner to hire builder to construct home).

What are the potential strengths and weaknesses of a privately-organized system of controls, such as that described in this Note? If the Restatement's position on public policy limitations gains general acceptance, will it shift ultimate decisionmaking responsibility from legislative bodies to courts? For comprehensive discussions of the new Restatement, see French, *The Touch and Concern Doctrine and the Restatement (Third) of Servitudes*, 77 Neb. L. Rev. 653 (1998) (supporting new Restatement's elimination of the "touch and concern" requirement in favor of greater emphasis on public policy), and A. Dan Tarlock, *Touch and Concern is Dead, Long Live the Doctrine*, 77 Neb. L. Rev. 804 (1998) (favoring retention of "touch and concern").

Much of the complexity in this area of the law arose from the distinction between actions at law and in equity, and the consequent distinction between monetary and injunctive relief. In practice, the modern litigant seeks to enforce (or avoid) the effects of servitudes through injunctive relief, rather than damages, and the law has generally accommodated this approach without regard to labels. Review the nuisance cases in Ch. 2, particularly *Boomer* and *Spur Industries*. What do those cases suggest about the proper relationship between legal and equitable remedies in land use control cases? Reconsider also the "taking" cases in Ch. 2. Historically, the courts' approach to servitudes has varied with society's attitude towards the utility of constraints on land use. Note the parallel in the current debate over regulatory takings. Should private and public constraints on land use be viewed the same way?

Architectural controls. It is common for subdivision developers to impose private restrictions that prohibit erection of certain kinds of buildings or to alter existing buildings without the permission of a majority of the lot owners or, where a homeowners' association has been created, the permission of the association's board of directors or a committee appointed by the board. Because of their "consensual" nature, these restrictions are generally upheld by the courts, often with a loosely worded good faith qualification. See *Valenti v. Hopkins*, 926 P.2d 813 (1996) (covenant making architectural review committee the "sole judge of the suitability" of a rule created unreviewable decisions); *Goode v. Village of Woodgreen Homeowners Ass'n*, 662 So. 2d 1064, 1077 (Miss. 1995) (announcing nearly absolute rule in favor of architectural approval covenants). However, courts seem most willing to look closely at and reverse decisions by architectural control committees. See, e.g., *Riss v. Angel*, 934 P.2d 669 (Wash. 1997) (board members, in refusing to approve proposed plans for house, acted unreasonably because they failed to conduct companion study of other designs within development); *Westfield Homes, Inc. v. Herrick*, 593 N.E.2d 97 (Ill. App. 1992) (refusal to permit above ground pool was unreasonable). But see *Walker v. Sandy Pointe Homeowners Ass'n, Inc.*, 2010 S.C. App. Unpub. LEXIS 382 (unpublished opinion, S.C. 2010) (upholding architectural review board's disapproval of plans for proposed new home that would violate setback restriction in covenants). The Reporter's Note to Restatement (Third) § 6.9, Design Control Powers, includes a collection of cases on the reasonableness of design review decisions.

Changing social and judicial attitudes toward private covenants and their enforcement may lead to more judicial intervention. See Franzese, *Does It Take a Village? Privatization, Patterns of Restrictions and the Demise of Community*, 47 Vill. L. Rev. 553 (2002); Sterk, *Minority Protection in Residential Private Governments*, 77 B.U. L. Rev. 273 (1997); Brower, *Communities Within the Community: Consent, Constitutionalism, and Other Failures of Legal Theory in Residential Associations*, 7 J. Land Use & Envtl. L. 203 (1992) (arguing for judicial review that considers substantive values). However, in *Committee for a Better Twin Rivers v. Twin Rivers Homeowners' Ass'n*, 2007 N.J. LEXIS 911 (N.J. 2007), the court applied the balancing test between expressional rights and privacy interests, and held that rules and regulations enacted by the association governing the posting of signs, the use of a community room, and access to its newsletter were reasonable time, place and manner restrictions on plaintiffs' expressional activities and did not violate the state constitution's free speech clause.

For comprehensive discussions of the use of private agreements to achieve private residential governments, see Hyatt & French, Community Association Law (1998); Korngold, Private Land Use Arrangements (1990 w/annual supplements); Korngold, *The Emergence of Private Land Use Controls in Large-Scale Subdivisions: The Companion Story to Village of*

Euclid v. Ambler Realty Co., 51 Case W. Res. L. Rev. 617 (2001); Ellickson, *New Institutions for Old Neighborhoods*, 48 Duke L.J. 75 (1998); Hyatt, *Common Interest Communities: Evolution and Reinvention*, 31 J. Marshall L. Rev. 303 (1998); Reichmann, *Residential Private Governments: An Introductory Survey*, 43 U. Chi. L. Rev. 253 (1976). See also W. Stoebuck & D. Whitman, The Law of Property §§ 8.13-8.33 (3d ed. 2000). Houston, Texas, has never had a comprehensive zoning ordinance, although it has a subdivision ordinance and building and housing codes. Because the location of different land uses is not controlled by any ordinance, private restrictive covenants are extensively used in Houston, and enforced by the city. For discussion, see Siegan, *Non-Zoning in Houston*, 13 J.L. & Econ. 71, 142–43 (1970). See also Goodrich, *Private Land Restrictions in Texas: A Need for Greater Legislative Control*, 15 St. Mary's L.J. 575 (1984). Houston last rejected a zoning ordinance in 1993.

[2.] The Structure of Subdivision Controls

Meck, Wack & Zimet, Zoning and Subdivision Regulation, *in the Practice of Local Government Planning* 343, 362–369

(J. Hoch, L. Dalton & F. So eds., 2000)

The subdivision review process

Subdivision review is a two-part process requiring the submission and review of a preliminary plan and a final plat [see figure below — Northview Manor plats]. The preliminary plan (sometimes called a preliminary plat) shows (1) the initial planning and layout of streets and lots; and (2) the type, size, and placement of utilities (water, sanitary and storm sewers, gas, electric, and cable). (Some communities may ask developers to submit a sketch for informal review before beginning detailed site design.) The preliminary plan will often cover an area that is larger than the portion to be initially developed and will indicate how the subdivision will be phased in over several years.

The preliminary plan shows topographic contour lines (typically at two-foot intervals) and other site features, such as streams and ponds, large trees and other vegetation, flood hazard areas, and existing buildings. Such information is necessary for review of the preliminary plan: the topography of the site indicates whether grading changes may be necessary to ensure that lots are well drained and buildable; to determine whether streets and lots blend with the site's inherent amenities; and to determine whether utilities, such as sanitary sewers, are designed to depend on gravity to work.

Reviewing the preliminary plan

Preliminary plan review focuses on basic design issues. The planning staff and planning commission look for the following:

Information required by the subdivision regulations

Proper street width, orientation, and integration with existing streets

Intersections that are safe and that avoid doglegs (abrupt offsets)

Lots that satisfy area and other dimensional requirements of the zoning ordinance

Sound lot layout that ensures that proposed buildings will easily conform to dimensional zoning requirements

Sites dedicated or reserved for parks or other public facilities, such as schools

Proposed utility easements, such as those for electricity and gas, that are properly located and of sufficient depth

Street names consistent with the local government's policies (e.g., avoidance of street names that may be confusing to emergency service personnel)

Blocks of appropriate length (e.g., avoidance of straight, uninterrupted stretches, which encourage speeding)

Stormwater detention or retention facilities, either on-site or as part of a larger regional facility.

Thoroughfares that are consistent with the community's major thoroughfare plan.

The planning commission reviews the preliminary plan at a public meeting or hearing; listens to comments by the developer/applicant, planning staff, and interested citizens; and then recommends that the governing body approve it, approve it with conditions, or deny approval. If the planning commission denies approval, it indicates in writing what substantive changes need to be made to the preliminary plan before a recommendation for approval can go forward and the developer or applicant can proceed to the next stage.

Reviewing the final plat

. . . The final plat is a precise drawing that fixes the location of lots and streets with reference to survey markers, such as concrete monuments and iron pins driven into the ground. Information included in the final plat, measured in tenths of a foot and in angles and bearings, creates the record of legal land title for establishing lot lines. The final plat is also the means by which streets and other proposed public improvements are conveyed to and accepted by the local government after the developer has constructed them to the government's standards.

The final plat is accompanied by engineering drawings and supporting technical analyses that deal with issues such as water pressure and stormwater. The drawings describe the installation of public and private improvements and other modifications of the site, such as grading. They also show proposed vertical and horizontal profiles of streets and of water and sewer lines; the location of streetlights, fire hydrants, and sidewalks; the design of detention and retention basins; and construction specifications, such as the type of concrete or asphalt to be used and the depth of pavement and aggregate base. Some final plats may also be accompanied by descriptions of measures to control erosion and sedimentation during site development or may address special issues, such as the protection or restoration of existing wetlands. California and Washington require project-specific environmental impact reports for development under certain circumstances and also require developers to mitigate potential adverse impacts.

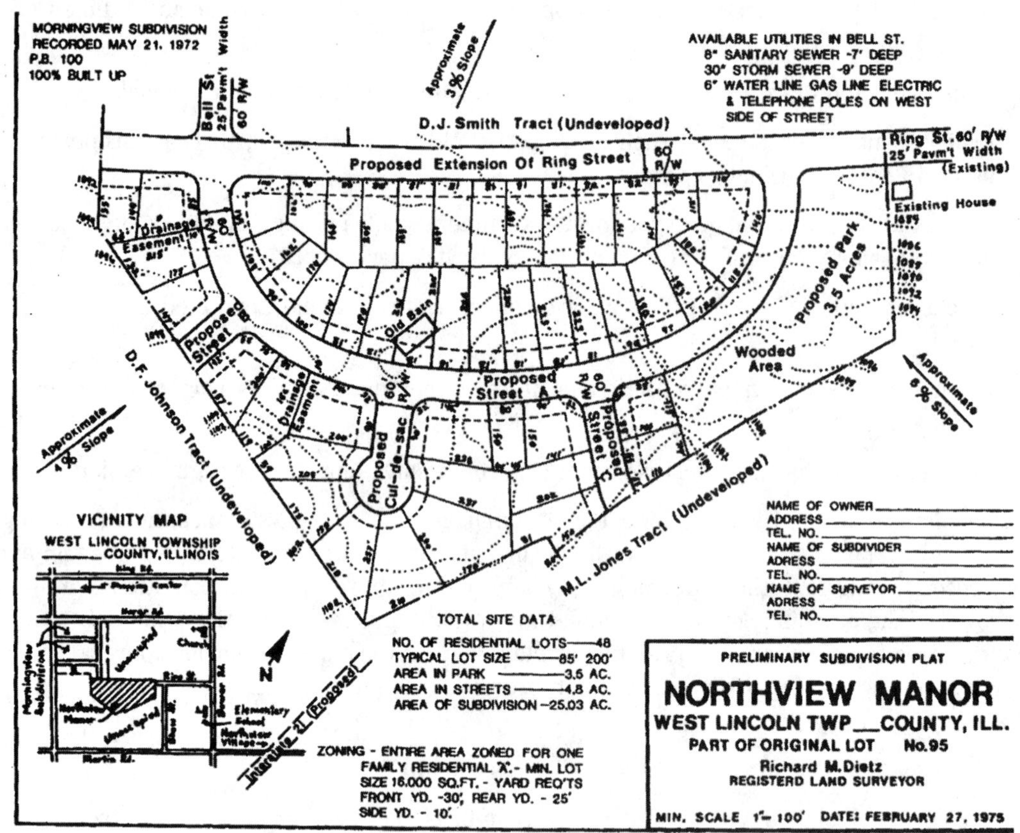

Figure 14–14 Above, a preliminary plan. At right, a portion of the same site showing the legal property descriptions allowing the final plat to be officially recorded.

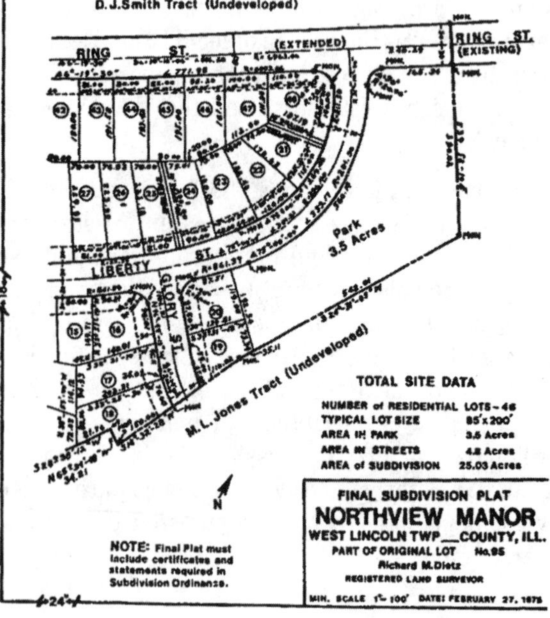

As is the case with the preliminary plan, the planning commission is the initial reviewing body, with the planning staff and other local government officials providing support as necessary. In the case of the final plat, however, the local government's engineer performs a detailed examination of the engineering drawings to ensure that the improvements are properly designed to meet the jurisdiction's engineering and construction standards.

If the final plat is consistent with the approved preliminary plan and any conditions imposed on it, the basic design and layout of the subdivision will be fixed. Still, the final plat must be checked once again against the subdivision and zoning ordinance requirements. At this point, the planning staff and planning commission may find other matters that need attention. Questions such as the following are likely to be considered:

Do sidewalks throughout the subdivision connect with other sidewalks in the area?

Are curb radii appropriate to the function of the street? (The larger the curb radius, the faster a vehicle can negotiate a turn. A smaller radius forces vehicles to move more slowly, making the intersection safer for pedestrians.)

Are streetlights provided at intersections and spaced at regular intervals?

For lots near flood hazard areas or areas with storm-water problems, are the buildable portions of the lots above the flood elevation?

Will water pressure be adequate throughout the subdivision?

Are street stubs (short lengths of street) provided to adjoining vacant tracts of land, allowing for future expansion of the internal street system?

The planning commission then reviews the final plat, sometimes along with the engineering plans, at another public meeting and recommends action on it to the governing body. . . . Once the local governing body [or the planning commission in some states] has approved the final plat and the developer has made any additional changes that may have been required, the plat is almost ready for recording. However, before the plat may be recorded, the developer must either construct the required improvements or post a performance bond to ensure that the improvements will be constructed within the next one or two years. Should the developer fail to complete the improvements within the specified period, the local government may use the performance bond, usually set at 110 to 120 percent of the estimated cost of the improvements, to pay for the installation itself.

NOTES AND QUESTIONS

1. *Vested rights.* The subdivision approval process can be long and time-consuming. At what stage in this process does the right to develop vest? A mere recording of the subdivision plat without a street dedication is probably not enough. *In re McCormick Mgt. Co.*, 547 A.2d 1319 (Vt. 1988). Neither is an approval of the preliminary plat, when the statute is silent on the effect of an approval. *Boutet v. Planning Bd.*, 253 A.2d 53 (Me. 1969). Substantial expenditure may be required. See *AWL Power, Inc. v. City of Rochester*, 813 A.2d 517 (N.H. 2002) (completion of six houses, payment of $50,000 impact fee and completion of $200,000 in public improvements under approved subdivision of 23+acre tract gave developer vested right to complete project after 10-year delay); *Union County v. CGP, Inc.*, 589 S.E.2d 240 (Ga. 2003) (no vested right to complete subdivision in violation of county flood prevention ordinance); *Gallup Westside Development, LLC v. City of Gallup*, 84 P.3d 78 (N.M. App. 2004) (expired assessment

procedure agreement for construction of public improvements did not provide basis for vested rights to continue subdivision development).

Some states require approval of the final plat if it meets the requirements imposed on the approval of the preliminary plat. Cal. Gov't Code § 66458. The approval of the final plat may then become a judicially enforceable ministerial act. *Youngblood v. Board of Supvrs.*, 586 P.2d 556 (Cal. 1979). Other states protect a finally approved subdivision for a period of time against subsequent changes in zoning and other land use regulations. See Pa. Stat. Ann. tit. 53, § 10508(4) (protection applies from time application filed); *Poirier v. Zoning Bd. of Town of Wilton*, 815 A.2d 716 (Conn. App. 2003) (statute provided vested right protection from changes in lot coverage regulations subsequent to approval of subdivision); *Toll Bros., Inc. v. Planning Board*, 820 A.2d 122 (N.J. App. 2003) (timely submission of final subdivision approval application protects developer from subsequently enacted zoning amendment). What does all this indicate about the risks and uncertainties of the subdivision approval process? What risks does a subdivider face? What changes would you recommend in subdivision enabling legislation?

2. *Variances.* The subdivision control statute may authorize variances, sometimes called deviations, waivers, or exceptions, in the subdivision context. N.J. Stat. Ann. § 40:55D-51(a). See *South E. Prop. Owners & Residents Ass'n v. City Plan Comm'n*, 244 A.2d 394 (Conn. 1968) (statutory authority required). The criteria are similar to those applicable to zoning variances. There has been little case law, but see *Baum v. Lunsford*, 365 S.E.2d 739 (Va. 1988) (assumed subdivision variance requires lesser proof than zoning variance and held variance may not be granted to prevent financial loss); *Ifrah v. Utschig*, 774 N.E.2d 732 (N.Y. 2002) (no basis for variance to construct second house on lot that was non-conforming in size for existing house); *Dupont v. Zoning Bd. of Appeals*, 834 A.2d 801 (Conn. App. 2003) (desire to subdivide was a self-created hardship not meriting a variance); *Kaywood Properties, Ltd. v. M. Cecil Forte, 892 N.Y.S.2d 182* (N.Y App. 2010) (upholding denial of subdivision application because applicant failed to meet hardship requirement).

3. *Evasion and enforcement.* Evasion is possible for the small developer who wishes to build on one lot at a time. Even the developer of a large residential subdivision can evade the ordinance by conveying through a metes and bounds boundary description. The Connecticut statute, *supra*, attempts to avoid this problem by prohibiting the sale, or offer for sale, of any land until the subdivision plat has been approved. Note the indirect sanction in the Standard Act, § 16. The Act authorizes a monetary penalty when land is sold "by reference to or exhibition" of a plat if the subdivision is not approved. Why this language?

A number of other alternatives to prevent evasion are possible:

(a) The statute provides that "no lands shall be conveyed" until the subdivision plat is "approved and recorded." But see *Kass v. Lewin*, 104 So. 2d 572 (Fla. 1958) (held unconstitutional as a restraint on alienation).

(b) The statute authorizes the denial of a building permit for buildings in unapproved subdivisions. But see *Keizer v. Adams*, 471 P.2d 983 (Cal. 1970) (may not withhold permit from innocent purchaser). Compare Wash. Rev. Code Ann. § 58.17.210 (grantee has option to void deed).

(c) The statute prohibits the issuance of a building permit except on a lot abutting a street suitably improved to the satisfaction of the municipality. See *Brous v. Smith*, 106 N.E.2d 503 (N.Y. 1952) (upheld). Why might this remedy be effective?

(d) The statute authorizes an injunction against the sale of lots in an unapproved subdivision. N.Y. Town Law § 268(2). See also *Lake County v. Truett*, 758 S.W.2d 529 (Tenn. App. 1988) (court enjoined selling of lots in unapproved subdivision but did not order subdivider to bring subdivision into compliance).

Which of these remedies do you prefer? Why? See Note, *Prevention of Subdivision Control Evasion in Indiana*, 40 Ind. L.J. 445 (1965).

4. *Preliminary plan.* Note that the preliminary plan of the Northfield Manor development shows land contours, other natural features (wooded area) and proposed streets and cul-de-sacs. How is this information relevant?

5. *Practices and attitudes of subdivision regulators.* How do local officials operate the subdivision regulation system? Have regulatory practices changed over the years? In 2002, research supported in part by the Lincoln Institute of Land Policy set out to answer these questions. A questionnaire was mailed to 500 developers and 500 public officials in areas experiencing rapid growth throughout the country. Seventeen percent of the developers (85) and about thirty two percent of the public officials (157) responded. Comparing results with a similar survey in 1976, the study author noted that the subdivision review process has increased in complexity, with more agencies involved and new requirements added. Developers and public officials disagreed sharply about the length of time to receive final approval, with public officials blaming developers for submitting incomplete plans and developers blaming officials for bureaucratic delays. While virtually all reporting jurisdictions require preliminary plat approval (92%) and final plat approval (99%) and a substantial majority impose terms and conditions to the approval (80%), only 60% required an informal sketch or concept plan to be submitted before the preliminary plat phase. E. Ben-Joseph, Subdivision Regulations: Practices & Attitudes 16-22 (2003), available from Lincoln Institute of Land Policy, http://web.mit.edu/ebj/www/LincolnWP.pdf.

GARIPAY v. TOWN OF HANOVER

116 N.H. 34, 351 A.2d 64 (1976)

GRIFFITH, JUSTICE:

This is an appeal under RSA 36:34 (Supp. 1975) [now codified as § 674:36(II)(A) — Eds.] from a decision of the planning board of the town of Hanover denying plaintiffs' agents' request for preliminary approval of a subdivision in that town. The issues were submitted to the trial court on an agreed statement of facts and transferred without ruling by Johnson, J. The planning board's denial of the request for approval of the subdivision was based on a finding that Hemlock Road, the access road connecting the proposed subdivision to the main network of town roads, would be inadequate to handle the increased traffic created by forty-nine new homes. The question presented to us is whether the planning board is authorized under RSA ch. 36 and the town ordinances to reject a subdivision proposal which intrinsically conforms to the requirements of the town zoning ordinance and regulations solely because of the inadequacy of an offsite, town-owned road.

The dangers posed by the inadequacy of Hemlock Road to accommodate increased traffic demands are discussed at length in the minutes of the planning board meetings of December 18, 1973, January 8, 1974, and January 15, 1975. The location of the proposed subdivision is on top of a hill to which Hemlock Road provides the only access. This road is described as "narrow, steep and winding, having a width of fourteen to sixteen feet, shoulders only two feet wide, a grade which at times exceeds 15%," and a course which results in "at least one horseshoe curve." Consequently, the planning board found that the road would pose "a serious danger to both pedestrian and vehicular traffic." The town police chief expressed "serious reservations about [his] department being able to respond to an emergency in this area, in the wintertime." There was evidence that in winter the steepness of the road often forces residents to leave their cars at the foot of the hill, and that while the limited available space can accommodate the present vehicles, congestion created by further abandoned cars from the subdivision could cause serious hazards.

The plaintiffs do not contest the accuracy of these findings. Their argument is that the planning board is precluded from considering offsite factors and must limit its investigation to whether the subdivision internally complies with state and town requirements. In our opinion both the state-enabling legislation and the Hanover subdivision regulations provide authority for the board's decision.

RSA 36:21 provides that town planning boards may promulgate regulations which "provide against such scattered or premature subdivision of land as would involve danger or injury to health, safety, or prosperity by reason of the lack of . . . transportation . . . or other public services, or necessitate an excessive expenditure of public funds for the supply of such services." Pursuant to this statute, Hanover has enacted article III(B) of its subdivision regulations, which uses language identical to that quoted above. These provisions plainly empower the planning board to take offsite factors into its consideration, insofar as they render subdivisions "scattered or premature."

The plaintiffs argue that the proposed subdivision cannot be deemed "scattered or premature" because there are already some eighteen homes in the area. Plaintiffs further maintain that such a finding is precluded by language on a map contained in the Hanover master plan, which designates the site "to be developed after 1970." According to this argument once an area is found not to be premature for a particular degree of development, it must be found ripe for all levels of development. In other words, where there are presently some homes in the area, the planning board may not find that an addition of forty-nine homes would be premature, regardless of the amount of public services available.

We reject this interpretation as too narrow, for prematurity is a relative rather than an absolute concept. The statute, by defining a "scattered and premature" development as one which poses a danger to the public through insufficiency of services, sets up a guide for the planning board's determination. The board must ascertain what amount of development, in relation to what quantum of services available, will present the hazard described in the statute and regulations. At the point where such a hazard is created, further development becomes premature. Thus in the instant case, although the available services suffice to meet the need of the present eighteen homes, when an additional forty-nine homes will endanger the well-being of residents both within and contiguous to the development, the statute and regulations authorize the planning board to find the subdivision premature. Thus the action of the Hanover Planning Board was within its statutory mandate.

Case law in other jurisdictions recognizes that absent specific statutory authority a planning board is authorized to reject a proposed subdivision because of an inadequate offsite access road under a general statutory mandate such as that found in RSA 36:21 "[Planning board regulations] generally may include provisions which will tend to create conditions favorable to health, safety, convenience, or prosperity." *Matter of Pearson Kent Corp. v. Bear,*

271 N.E.2d 218 (N.Y. 1971). "Subdivision controls are imposed on the supportable premise that a new subdivision is not an island, but an integral part of the whole community which must mesh efficiently with the municipal pattern of streets, sewers, water lines and other installations which provide essential services and vehicular access. . . . [O]ffsite circumstances may be considered by the reviewing board, and may provide the basis for denying approval of a plat." 3 R. Anderson, American Law of Zoning § 19.36 (1968).

Appeal dismissed.

BAKER v. PLANNING BOARD

353 Mass. 141, 228 N.E.2d 831 (1967)

KIRK, JUSTICE:

In the Superior Court the judge entered a decree that the planning board of Framingham (the board) had exceeded its authority in disapproving the definitive plan for the subdivision of approximately eleven acres of land owned by the plaintiff (Baker). The decree annulled the decision of the board and directed that it promptly take further proceedings under the subdivision control law consistent with the applicable statutes and the decree. The board's appeal brings the case to us.

. . . The only questions presented . . . are (1) whether the findings of the master are contradictory, mutually inconsistent or plainly wrong, and (2) whether the decree is within the scope of the pleadings and supported by the facts found.

We summarize the admissions made in the pleadings and the facts found by the master which, in light of the standard of review and the arguments made, are pertinent to the issues to be resolved. In December, 1934, Baker and her husband granted to the town by recorded deed an easement (ten feet wide), through land owned by them, for the purpose of constructing and maintaining a pipe drain or excavating and maintaining a ditch of "sufficient depth to permit without interruption the flow of surface water and drainage" through the Baker land. The town excavated a ditch which received water accumulating on Brook Street and channeled the water across Baker's land to land of another where it entered a fifteen inch drain controlled by the town, and thence was carried to the Sudbury River. Because of the development of land in the area since the easement was granted, including the construction of a church with a large paved parking lot, the volume of water now accumulating on Brook Street during heavy rainstorms has greatly increased. The ditch cannot carry off the increased volume of water to the drain pipe on the adjoining land, and the drain pipe, in turn, cannot carry away the water which is collected in and over the ditch. The result is that the Baker land becomes flooded for a considerable area on both sides of the ditch, and the land consequently serves as a flood control or "retention area" for the town, to the extent of 16,200 cubic feet of water, during and after heavy rains and thaws.

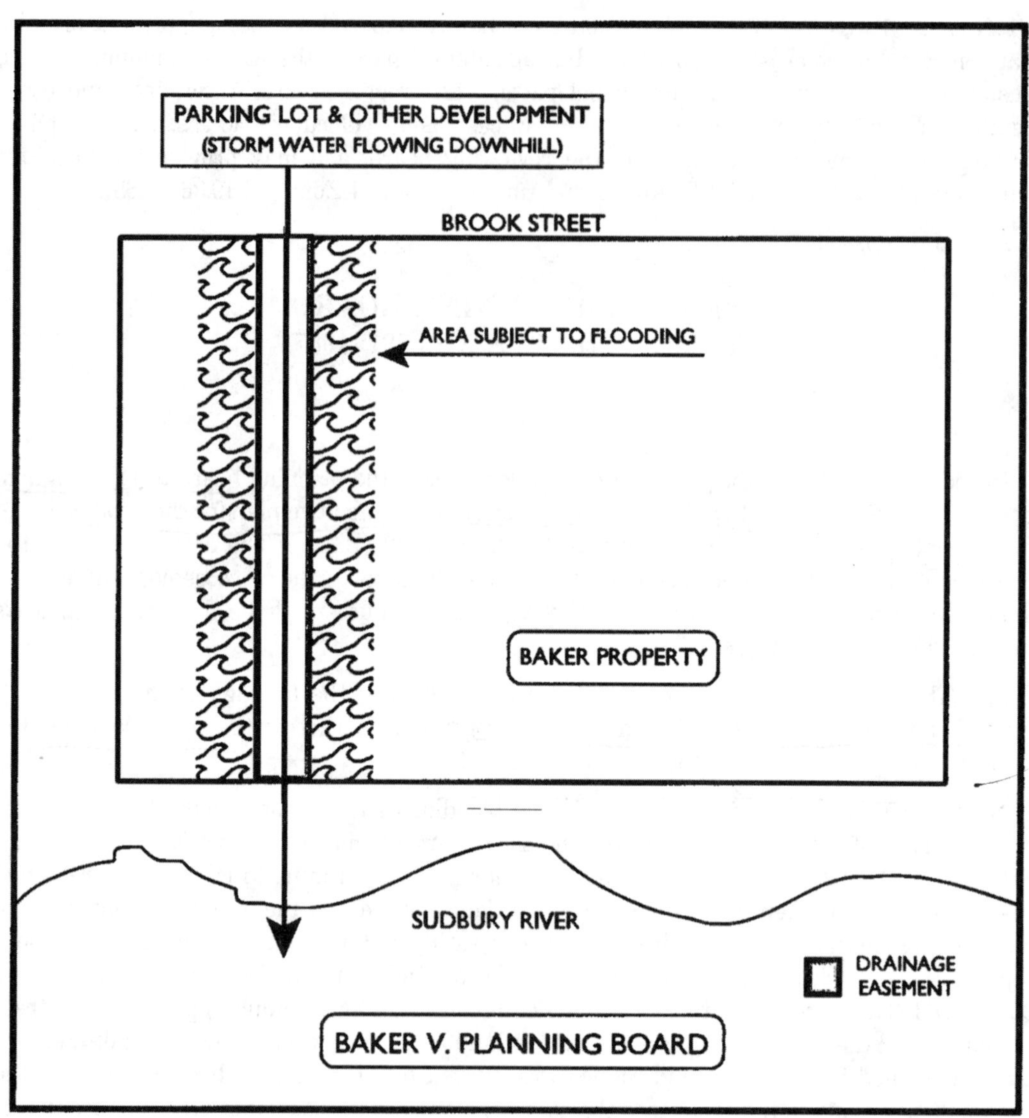

Baker's definitive plan was submitted on February 26, 1965. A preliminary plan had been submitted earlier. The board of health approved the definitive plan. G.L. c. 41, §§ 81M, 81U.(*) The planning board did not modify the definitive plan but, by majority vote, disapproved it and stated its reasons. G.L. c. 41, § 81U. In summary, the board's reasons for disapproval relate to the sewerage and water drainage systems proposed in the definitive plan. The sewerage system would require the construction and maintenance of a lift or pumping station to tie in with the

(*) Section 81M states that the legislature intends that the planning board approve a subdivision plan "if [the] plan conforms to the recommendations of the board of health and to the reasonable rules and regulations of the planning board pertaining to subdivisions of land." Section 81U states that "the planning board shall approve, or, if such plan does not comply with the subdivision control law or the rules and regulations of the planning board or the recommendations of the health board or officer, shall modify and approve or shall disapprove such plan." — Eds.

town's sewerage system, whereas the board favored a gravity system which would not require a lift station. The proposed water drainage system, although adequate for the subdivision, would deprive the town of the retention area on Baker's land and, in consequence, would overtax the downstream drainage system outside the subdivision. The board stated that neither the preliminary nor the definitive plan, as submitted, delineated the town's drainage easement across the Baker land. The board disapproved on the additional ground that "[a]pproval . . . would not be in the best interest of the Town, since it would negate the PURPOSE of section 81-M" . . . [of the subdivision control enabling act which makes] special reference to ". . . securing safety in cases of . . . flood, . . . securing adequate provision for water, sewerage, drainage and other requirements where necessary in a subdivision."

Additional findings by the master were that the majority of the board believed that they were justified in disapproving the plan because of the additional expense which the town would incur by the enlargement of the town's drainage system to compensate for the loss of use of the Baker land as a water retention area, and by the construction and maintenance of the lift station for the sewerage system. The plan with respect to the sewerage and drainage systems for the subdivision met all of the requirements of the statutes and of the rules and regulations of the board. The town already operates several lift or pumping stations in its sewerage system. The omission from the plans of the town's easement across Baker's land did not deceive and was not intended to deceive the board, but was the result of an understanding between the town engineer and Baker's engineer that the town probably would reroute its drainage system through pipes on one of the streets shown on the plans.

The master's ultimate finding was that the board "had but a single reason for disapproving the . . . [definitive] plan, namely, the extra cost to the Town of handling the sewage and surface drainage produced by the subdivision." We think that the ultimate finding of the master cannot be said to be plainly wrong and that his subsidiary findings are consistent with it.

The decree based on the master's report was right. Our decisions dealing with the powers of planning boards as clarified by G.L. c. 41 § 81M, hold that, having exercised due regard for insuring compliance with the applicable zoning by-law, approval under § 81U should be given to a plan if it complies with the recommendations of the board of health and the reasonable rules and regulations of the planning board. The zoning by-law is not an issue; the board of health has given its approval; there is no violation of, or failure to comply with, existing rules and regulations. Obviously a planning board may not exercise its authority to disapprove a plan so that a town may continue to use the owner's land as a water storage area and thereby deprive the owner of reasonable use of it. The board's action appears to be based on the assumption that it may disapprove a plan when it considers that "the best interest of the Town" or "the public interest" would be served by the disapproval of installations which meet the established requirements. This is an erroneous assumption. . . . It was beyond the board's authority to disapprove the plan.

Decree affirmed.

NOTES AND QUESTIONS

1. *The scope of controls.* Both *Baker* and *Garipay* raise questions about the use of subdivision control to monitor growth within the community, and the validity of denying subdivision approval on the basis of conditions not intrinsic to the subdivision. Would the planning commission in *Garipay* have been within the scope of its authority if the New

Hampshire statute had not specifically prohibited the "scattered or premature subdivision of land"?

In *Pearson Kent Corp. v. Bear*, 271 N.E.2d 218 (N.Y. 1971), "[t]he [planning] commission denied petitioner's development approval, not because it regarded the plan itself as intrinsically not acceptable but because the project was so located as to create danger to nearby residents in the inadequate approaches to the development from the greatly increased demands to be exerted on the existing approaches." *Id.* at 219. In a brief opinion, the court noted that while the local charter and subdivision control law were "addressed to approval or disapproval internal to the subdivision" the commission was not prevented from considering "the impact of the proposed development on adjacent territory and property within its jurisdiction. . . . These matters are the routine functions of the commission." *Id.*

Do these holdings improperly give control over new subdivisions to municipalities through the power to withhold improvements to off-site public facilities? If the developer, because of these decisions, is forced to make off-site improvements, is this a valid exercise of the subdivision control power? Was this the vice of the *Baker* case? In *North Landers Corp. v. Planning Bd.*, 416 N.E.2d 934 (Mass. 1981), the court said that all courts were in agreement "that the condition of adjacent public ways must be considered in the board's deliberations." See also *Buttermilk Farms, LLC v. Planning & Zoning Comm'n of Town of Plymouth*, 973 A.2d 64 (Conn. 2009) (Town not authorized to impose condition on approval of subdivision application to require developer to improve off-site roads).

The present version of the statute considered in *Garipay* authorizes a prematurity determination based on a lack of a number of facilities, including water supply, fire protection and schools. N.H. Rev. Stat. § 674:36(II)(a). Despite the statutory language, the court invalidated a prematurity denial based on inadequate schools in *Ettlingen Homes v. Town of Derry*, 681 A.2d 97 (N.H. 1996). It held the authority conferred by the statute was exceeded because the decision "plainly was taken to control growth."

When a municipality disapproves a subdivision because of on-site problems, the disapproval usually is upheld. In *Hamilton v. Planning Bd.*, 345 N.E.2d 906 (Mass. App. 1976), the court upheld a disapproval because of a failure to remedy flooding problems by providing adequate drainage on the subdivision site. The court distinguished the case

> from those in which a planning board had disapproved a plan adequate for the proposed subdivision solely because it would overtax existing municipal facilities or otherwise adversely affect the public interest. [*Id.* at 907, citing *Baker.*]

See also *Spinell Homes, Inc. v. Municipality of Anchorage*, 78 P.3d 692 (Alaska 2003) (city could withhold building permits from subsequent purchaser for failure of original subdivider to construct and install public improvements); *Durant v. Town of Dunbarton*, 430 A.2d 140 (N.H. 1981) (upholding disapproval based partly on potential problems with subsurface septic systems); but see *Pansy Rd., L.L.C. v. Town Plan. & Zoning Comm'n*, 926 A.2d. 1029 (Conn. 2007) (because the commission's function was administrative when reviewing a subdivision application, it could only consider off-site congestion for the purpose of addressing traffic flow within the subdivision site and entering and exiting site, and could not deny the application on the basis of off-site traffic considerations).

2. *Design and access issues.* These pose much less of a problem since they relate directly to the subdivision. The adequacy of the subdivider's plans for streets and highways is an important factor in the review process. Planning commissions will often require, as a condition

to subdivision approval, that internal streets be of sufficient width and satisfactory design, and that access be adequate.

In *Forest Constr. Co. v. Planning & Zoning Comm'n*, 236 A.2d 917 (Conn. 1967), a subdivision was denied approval because only one access was provided for 110 lots, thereby causing all traffic from the subdivision to be discharged at one intersection. The denial was found to be within the commission's authority to reject applications for development that would be hazardous to the health and welfare of the community. See also *Burke & McCaffrey, Inc. v. City of Merriam*, 424 P.2d 483 (Kan. 1967) (upholding denial of subdivision because of plan's cul-de-sac design); *Isabelle v. Town of Newbury*, 321 A.2d 570 (N.H. 1974) (upholding denial of subdivision because lot ownership pattern jeopardized access in case of fire).

3. *Stormwater runoff.* One of the significant side effects of land development is water runoff from heavy rainfall. Grading and paving land can increase the volume and rate of flow of surface water because the impervious nature of pavement eliminates the natural absorption of water by soil. Flooding caused by excessive water runoff can be handled through proper site development, such as detention ponds and ditches. Control of this problem is an important goal of subdivision regulation. For example, the St. Louis County, Missouri subdivision ordinance contains stormwater disposal standards and regulations administered by the Department of Highways and Traffic. St. Louis County Code, § 1005.185, available at www.stlouisco.com/plan/Subdivision/1005-185.pdf. The standards apply to commercial and industrial land use projects, as well as residential subdivisions. § 1005.185.2. Controlled release and storage of excess stormwater runoff may be required, as well as detention of differential runoff of stormwater through permanent detention facilities, such as dry reservoirs, ponds, or other acceptable alternatives. § 1005.185.3. Detention reservoirs or dry bottom stormwater storage areas may be designed to serve secondary purposes such as recreation, open space or other uses that will not be adversely affected by occasional flooding. § 1005.185.4. Drainage detention areas not maintained by a public authority must be conveyed as an undivided interest in common to each lot in the subdivision for maintenance purposes or conveyed to trustees with authority to perform maintenance responsibilities. § 1005.185.5.

Would a regulation such as St. Louis County's stormwater provision enable the *Baker* problem to be resolved without litigation? Problems with surface water drainage of the type considered in *Baker* also are considered in site plan review (see Chapter 6, *supra*). Substantial, but uncoordinated, federal financial and regulatory programs for flood management and groundwater protection are discussed *supra* in Chapter 4.

4. *Authority to deny or approve.* As *Baker* indicates, statutory authority questions can be serious in subdivision control cases. Subdivision control legislation is much more specific than zoning legislation, and does not provide the broad grants of authority that often allow courts to take a lenient view of scope of authority problems in zoning cases. Lack of statutory authority has limited the use of subdivision control as a basis for disapproving subdivisions because they impose an excessive burden on schools or other public facilities. *Beach v. Planning & Zoning Comm'n*, 103 A.2d 814 (Conn. 1954).

Recall that the Standard Act and most state acts require the planning commission to adopt subdivision regulations. The general enabling authority in the subdivision acts requires the commission to spell out in more detail the criteria for subdivision review. A court may hold that a municipality may not rely on the general purposes of a land use law as the basis for disapproving a subdivision but must base disapprovals on standards contained in the subdivision ordinance. See *Pizzo Mantin Group v. Township of Randolph*, 645 A.2d 89 (N.J. 1994).

Courts will reverse a subdivision denial if it is based on a reason not authorized by the statute or the subdivision regulations. See *Richardson v. City of Little Rock Planning Comm'n*, 747 S.W.2d 116, 117 (Ark. 1988) (statute did not authorize denial for "marginal development potential" because of unusual lot shapes and means for access); *PTL, LLC v. Chisago County Bd. of Commissioners*, 656 N.W.2d 567 (Minn. App. 2003) (landowner's refusal to develop in cluster format did not justify denial of preliminary subdivision plat that complied with existing zoning standards); *Interladco, Inc. v. Billings*, 538 P.2d 496 (Colo. App. 1975) (county "did not want a development of single family residences isolated from other developed urban areas"). Compare *Garipay.* Are these cases consistent? See also *Smith v. City of Mobile*, 374 So. 2d 305 (Ala. 1979) (may not disapprove subdivision because it was "out of character" with other lots in area); *Hixon v. Walker County*, 468 S.E.2d 744 (Ga. 1996) (may not base disapproval on statement of purpose to protect character and social and economic stability of county).

A court can also hold that the factual record does not support the subdivision disapproval. See *Christopher Estates, Inc. v. Parish of East Baton Rouge*, 413 So. 2d 1336 (La. App. 1982) (no proof that smaller lots in subdivision would lower property values in neighborhood). Nor may a delay in the disapproval decision help. *Norco Constr. Inc. v. King County*, 649 P.2d 103 (Wash. 1982) (county could not delay decision beyond ninety-day decision period because subdivision not in compliance with proposed plan and zoning ordinance).

Why not just put the actual criteria in the subdivision control regulations? Would there then be a problem with court approval? For example, would a court uphold a standard authorizing the disapproval of a subdivision if the development potential is marginal, as in the *Richardson* case, *supra*? In *Richardson*, the site was steep and making the Board's changes would have reduced the number of lots from 15 to 12, for which the developer "stood to lose $100,000 to $150,000." 747 S.W.2d at 119 (dissenting opinion). Do you suppose that neighborhood opposition is often a factor in subdivision disapproval in the cases cited in this Note?

Kaufman v. Planning & Zoning Comm'n, 298 S.E.2d 148 (W. Va. 1982), illustrates these problems. The commission disapproved a subdivision for subsidized housing in a decision that considered property depreciation, the project's "rental nature, [and] the economic class of the proposed occupants." The court held these factors unauthorized by a statute authorizing consideration of the harmonious development of the community, which it held too vague in the absence of more specific regulations. See Reynolds, *Local Subdivision Regulations: Formulaic Constraints in an Age of Discretion*, 24 Ga. L. Rev. 525 (1990).

5. *Zoning and the comprehensive plan.* The potential overlap between subdivision control and zoning is clear. Some subdivision statutes require compliance with the zoning ordinance. N.J. Stat. Ann. § 40:55D-38(b)(1). Can the subdivision control ordinance also include regulations commonly found in zoning ordinances? In *Wood v. City of Madison*, 659 N.W.2d 31 (Wis. 2003), the court held that the subdivision statute authorized a municipality to reject a preliminary plat based on a subdivision ordinance that considered the plat's proposed use. The statute provided that subdivision regulations were intended to "encourag[e] the most appropriate use" of land.

> Therefore, any regulation relating to the "quality" of a subdivision must necessarily consider the "most appropriate use" of land. We cannot fathom how an ordinance can consider the most appropriate use of land if it cannot consider use of land. [*Id.* at 38.]

Do you agree? See *Jones v. Davis*, 594 S.E.2d 235, 240 (N.C. App. 2004) (subdivision ordinance does not regulate land use). A municipality may reject a subdivision because it does not comply with the zoning ordinance, *Krawski v. Planning & Zoning Comm'n*, 575 A.2d 1036 (Conn. App. 1990), and may require zoning compliance in its subdivision control ordinance, *Benny v. City of Alameda*, 164 Cal. Rptr. 776 (Cal. App. 1980). How do these limitations affect the exercise of discretion in subdivision review?

For a unique twist on the relationship between zoning and subdivision regulations, see *Lord Family Windsor, L.L.C. v. Planning & Zoning Comm'n*, 954 A.2d 831 (Conn. 2008) (holding that the Planning and Zoning Commission did not have the authority to require a special use permit for subdivisions over a certain size and stating that no authority existed "for the proposition that a proposed development that satisfies a district's land use regulations governing the type and density of activity lawfully may be subject to additional regulations as a distinct 'use of land' because of its particular size").

The Standard Act required the adoption of a master street plan before a subdivision ordinance could be adopted. Some states go further and require consistency with the local comprehensive plan. Cal. Gov't Code § 66474(a). *Board of County Comm'rs v. Gaster*, 401 A.2d 666 (Md. 1979), held that the board could disapprove a subdivision not consistent with a comprehensive plan even though the subdivision complied with the zoning ordinance. See also *Lake City Corp. v. City of Mequon*, 558 N.W.2d 100 (Wis. 1997) (city plan commission may reject plat approval that is inconsistent with newly-adopted master plan). What policies should a plan on new development address? The American Planning Association's model legislation for local comprehensive plans provides that subdivision and other land development regulations are consistent with such plans when they further, "or at least do not interfere with" plan goals and policies, are "compatible with the proposed future land uses and densities and/or intensities" in the plan and carry out "any specific proposal for community facilities . . . , other specific public actions, or actions proposed by nonprofit and for-profit organizations" included in the plan. American Planning Association, Growing Smart Legislative Guidebook: Model Statutes for Planning and Management of Change 8-104(3) (S. Meck ed., 2002).

"Consistent" with the comprehensive plan does not necessarily mean "identical." In holding that a development plan was consistent with the General Plan, Policy Plan and density statutes where there were traffic concerns, increased residential development and a large density bonus, the court in *Friends of Lagoon Valley v. City of Vacaville*, 65 Cal. Rptr. 3d 251 (Cal App. 2007), explained that California law "does not require perfect conformity between a proposed project and the applicable general plan; 'rather,' to be 'consistent,' the subdivision map must be 'compatible with the objectives, policies, general land uses, and programs specified in' the applicable plan." *Id.* at 251, 259 (citations omitted).

6. *Who pays?* Lurking behind some of these cases may be an attempt by municipalities to manipulate the subdivision control process to shift their burden to provide services and facilities to the developers. Courts have held that the developer cannot be forced to resolve problems common to the community for which it is not responsible. In *Baltimore Plan Comm'n v. Victor Dev. Co.*, 275 A.2d 478 (Md. 1971), the court held that the commission could not reject the subdivision on the ground that the occupancy of apartments proposed for the subdivision would create an increase in the local population, which would in turn cause the public schools to be overcrowded. In *Warmington Old Town Assocs., L.P. v. Tustin Unified School Dist.*, 124 Cal. Rptr. 2d 744 (Cal. App. 2002), the court upheld application of a school-impact fee to a residential redevelopment construction project but required the district to refund a substantial portion of the fee assessed because the school's impact fee study did not establish the statutorily-required nexus to the redevelopment project. Impact fees are discussed *infra.*

In *Florham Park Inv. Assocs. v. Planning Bd.*, 224 A.2d 352 (N.J. L. Div. 1966), the municipality denied approval of a subdivision because the later construction of a planned highway across the subdivision would make lots in the subdivision substandard as defined by local regulations. The court reversed, noting that "[t]o deprive plaintiff of the right to use and improve its property for an indefinite time, while awaiting the final action of a third party which may come in one year or ten or never, is arbitrary and unreasonable." *Id.* at 356. The court placed some weight on the indefinite nature of the highway agency's plans for the highway. What if the route were permanently fixed and known? Would this be a reason for denial? See also *Divan Bldrs., Inc. v. Planning Bd.*, 334 A.2d 30 (N.J. 1975) (developer made to contribute to construction cost of off-site municipal drainage system as condition to subdivision approval). On the question of whether municipalities may condition development approval on the availability of municipal facilities and services, see Chapter 8.

B. DEDICATIONS, EXACTIONS, AND IMPACT FEES

> Exactions require that developers provide, or pay for, some public facility or other amenity as a condition for receiving permission for a land use that the local government could otherwise prohibit. [Been, *Exit as a Constraint on Land Use Exactions: Rethinking the Unconstitutional Conditions Doctrine*, 91 Colum. L. Rev. 473, 478–79 (1991).]

Supreme Court taking decisions have made exactions a major battleground in land use law. Exactions started quite simply. Communities asked developers only to provide streets and other internal improvements, which are facilities required by new developments. Exactions requirements soon expanded. Communities saw they could use the subdivision control process to provide for parks and schools, so park and school dedications were added. Developers were also asked to dedicate land or make cash payments for adjacent street widenings and for off-site facilities, such as sewage and drainage facilities, that served the subdivision. Cash payments, called in-lieu fees, are sometimes offered or required as an alternative to in-kind construction or dedication. A community may require a fee, for example, when a residential development creates a need for additional recreation space but there is no land within the development that can be dedicated for this purpose.

Another form of exaction is levied outside the subdivision control process as an impact fee. The fee is usually collected at the time the building permit is issued and is used to construct or improve off-site facilities, such as water and sewage facilities.

Exactions are even more important to municipalities in an age of municipal financial austerity. In California, after voter adoption of Proposition 13 amended the constitution to drastically limit local property taxes, municipalities turned to impact fees to make up the revenue shortfall. Fee increases have been substantial. Rapid growth has stimulated the widespread use of impact fees on new development in Florida. Exactions in Florida are now tied to a mandatory planning process.

All of this activity has led to substantial increases in the absolute and relative amount of exactions levied. Impact fees as high as $25,000 or more are common in some areas. This, in turn, has also led to developer protests when they believe exactions are too high. Developers believe that the legality of exactions is one of the most important legal issues in land use controls.

In the current economic climate, with a development slow-down, some municipalities are reducing impact fees in order to encourage development. For example, Collier County reduced impact fees for some new development and has waived entirely other fees for affordable housing developments. Layden, *Collier County Considers Reducing Impact Fees to Encourage Development*, January 11, 2009 (www.naplesnews.com/news/2009/jan/11/economy-having-impact-impact-fees/). See also Hogan, *Bonita Impact Fee Goes, Business Arrives*, August 27, 2010 (www.news-press.com/article/20100827/NEWS0102/100826059/Bonita-impact-fee-goes/).

Although exactions and impact fees are, in one sense, a land use control, they also raise critical questions about public responsibility for public services. Who should pay — the taxpayers, through general revenues, or new development through exactions and impact fees? Note also the equity problems. Do exactions and impact fees make an inequitable distinction between old and new residents? Between rich and poor? These questions concerning the distribution of fiscal responsibility for municipal services should be kept in mind when reviewing the materials in this section.

[1.] The Takings Clause and the Nexus Test

The Takings Clause is the legal crucible in which the legality of subdivision exactions is tested. State courts traditionally had tested the validity of exactions under a nexus test: a relationship between the exaction and some need for public facilities created by the subdivision had to be shown. For example, if a new subdivision reduced service levels by causing congestion on an adjacent road, a dedication of subdivision land to widen the road could be required.

The U.S. Supreme Court's decisions in *Nollan* and *Dolan v. City of Tigard*, 512 U.S. 374 (1994), substantially changed the law of exactions because Supreme Court precedents apply, of course, in state courts and can control state land development policies. However, recognizing that "state courts have been dealing with this question a good deal longer than we have," 512 U.S. at 389, Chief Justice Rehnquist in *Dolan* provided a useful summary of the varied approaches among the states, with which we begin:

> In some States, very generalized statements as to the necessary connection between the required dedication and the proposed development seem to suffice. *See, e.g., Billings Properties, Inc. v. Yellowstone County*, 394 P.2d 182 (Mont. 1964); *Jenad, Inc. v. Scarsdale*, 218 N.E.2d 673 (N.Y. 1966). We think this standard is too lax to adequately protect petitioner's right to just compensation if her property is taken for a public purpose.
>
> Other state courts require a very exacting correspondence, described as the "specifi[c] and uniquely attributable" test. The Supreme Court of Illinois first developed this test in *Pioneer Trust & Savings Bank v. Mount Prospect*, 176 N.E.2d 799, 802 (1961). Under this standard, if the local government cannot demonstrate that its exaction is directly proportional to the specifically created need, the exaction becomes "a veiled exercise of the power of eminent domain and a confiscation of private

property behind the defense of police regulations." *Id.*, at 802. We do not think the Federal Constitution requires such exacting scrutiny, given the nature of the interests involved.

A number of state courts have taken an intermediate position, requiring the municipality to show a "reasonable relationship" between the required dedication and the impact of the proposed development. Typical is the Supreme Court of Nebraska's opinion in *Simpson v. North Platte*, 292 N.W.2d 297, 301 (1980), where that court stated: "The distinction, therefore, which must be made between an appropriate exercise of the police power and an improper exercise of eminent domain is whether the requirement has some reasonable relationship or nexus to the use to which the property is being made or is merely being used as an excuse for taking property simply because at that particular moment the landowner is asking the city for some license or permit." Thus, the court held that a city may not require a property owner to dedicate private property for some future public use as a condition of obtaining a building permit when such future use is not "occasioned by the construction sought to be permitted." *Id.*, at 302.

Some form of the reasonable relationship test has been adopted in many other jurisdictions. [citing cases]. [512 U.S. at 389–90.]

Reread or refresh your memory of the *Nollan* case, reproduced in Ch. 2. *Nollan* reaffirmed the nexus test but indicated courts should apply it more stringently.

A NOTE ON THE PRICE EFFECTS OF EXACTIONS: WHO PAYS?

Exactions have price effects on housing markets. Dedications of land or fees are costs to developers they will have to absorb unless they can pass them on. Costs can be passed forward to buyers who purchase dwelling units in a development subject to exactions or backward to landowners who sell land to developers. Costs can also be shared among all three of these market participants.

Several studies have examined the price effects of exactions with inconclusive results. All studies agree that who finally pays for the exaction depends on how competitive the housing and land markets are and the elasticity of supply and demand. Developers will not be able to pass exaction costs on to homebuyers if there is alternative and equally attractive housing in jurisdictions that do not charge exactions. In this situation, developers can try to pass the cost of exactions back to sellers of land by offering lower prices. Sellers of land can resist price reductions in markets where they have monopoly power because the area has unique features that make it more attractive to consumers. Sellers may also resist price reductions because they do not consider the time-value of money and have a reservation price below which they will not sell.

One study notes that homebuilders' ability to make long-run market adjustments may be more important than their ability to set price. In the short run, they may not be able to add the cost of development fees to the price of their houses. But in the long run, by reducing annual production, they can force prices back up to a level that requires consumers to absorb the cost of the exactions. T. Snyder & M. Stegman, Paying for Growth 106 (1986). For other studies reaching the same conclusion, see Huffman, Nelson, Smith & Stegman, *Who Bears the Burden of Impact Fees?*, 54 J. Am. Plan. Ass'n 49 (1988); Singell & Lillydahl, *An Empirical Examination of the Effect of Impact Fees on the Housing Market*, 66 Land Econ. 82 (1990).

A review of empirical and theoretical research literature concludes that while use of development impact fees has grown, studies of the effects have not kept pace. Several possible goals for impact fees are noted: reduce tax burdens on current residents, relieve fiscal stress, enhance property values, provide adequate services and infrastructure. Planners must consider what particular goals their communities desire to pursue. Evans-Cowley & Lawhon, *The Effects of Impact Fees on the Price of Housing and Land: A Literature Review*, 17 J. Plan. Lit. 351 (2003). Professor Vicki Been, in a paper presented at a conference on regulatory barriers to affordable housing sponsored by the Department of Housing and Urban Development, drew the following conclusions:

> [A]nalysis of the existing research . . . reveals that the existing literature does not yet establish that impact fees raise the net price of housing — the price after off-setting benefits such as amenities or savings on alternative financing mechanisms are accounted for. The evidence that a transition from existing methods of financing growth to greater use of impact fees will have disproportionate effects on low- and moderate-income consumers in general, or racial minorities in particular, or otherwise lead to a "new segregation" is even thinner, because the issue has just begun to be addressed by rigorous testing and analysis. . . .
>
> Impact fees can be used to correct the myriad of market failures that have allowed inefficient development to harm the natural and built environments of our communities, often at taxpayer expense. But impact fees also can be abused, either to exclude low- and moderate-income residents or people of color from communities, or to exploit new homebuyers, who have no vote in the community. They also can be unfair to those caught in the transition from other forms of infrastructure finance. [V. Been, *Impact Fees and Housing Affordability*, Cityscape: A Journal of Policy Development and Research, 8(1), at 139, 168 (2005).]

Professor Been argues that researchers should pay "careful attention" to the following issues concerning impact fees: prices versus affordability; distributional effects; accounting for the benefits provided by impact fees; the relativity of the effect of impact fees on affordability; the relationship between impact fees and measures to increase affordability by encouraging more efficient land use, more efficient regulatory systems, or greater density; and the relationship between impact fees and programs explicitly designed to increase affordable housing ("mitigation" measures). By doing so, researchers "can help local governments seize the potential impact fees offer for promoting more efficient development patterns while minimizing any negative effects impact fees might have on the affordability of housing and the distribution of housing opportunities to all residents," she asserted. *Id.* at 168–169.

What effect should these studies have on the constitutionality of exactions? Some studies note that exactions provide a windfall to the owners of existing homes because increases in the price of new homes allow owners of existing homes to raise their prices. Should this be considered?

For additional studies of the price incidence of exactions, see Ihalanfeldt & Shaughnessy, *An Empirical Investigation of the Effects of Impact Fees on Housing and Land Markets*, 34 Reg. Sci. & Urb. Econ. 639 (2004) (one dollar impact fee increases price of new and existing housing by $1.60 and reduces price of land by $1.00); Downing & McCaleb, *The Economics of Development Exactions, in* Development Exactions 42 (J. Frank & R. Rhodes eds., 1987); Weitz, *Who Pays Infrastructure Benefit Charges: The Builder or the Home Buyer, in* The Changing Structure of Infrastructure Finance, 94 (J. Nicholas ed., 1985); Delaney & Smith,

Development Exactions: Winners and Losers, 17 Real Estate L.J. 195 (1989); Impact Fees and Housing Affordability, A Guidebook for Practitioners Prepared for U.S. Department of Housing and Urban Development Washington (2008), available at www.huduser.org/portal/publications/affhsg/impactfees.html. Yinger, *Who Pays for Development Fees? in* Local Government Tax and Land Policies in the United States, ch. 11 (H. Ladd ed., 1998), finds some of the empirical studies flawed, but agrees that the incidence of exactions is likely to fall on sellers of land in many cases.

[2.] The "Rough Proportionality" Test

DOLAN v. CITY OF TIGARD

512 U.S. 374 (1994)

CHIEF JUSTICE REHNQUIST delivered the opinion of the Court:

Petitioner challenges the decision of the Oregon Supreme Court which held that the city of Tigard could condition the approval of her building permit on the dedication of a portion of her property for flood control and traffic improvements. We granted certiorari to resolve a question left open by our decision in *Nollan v. California Coastal Comm'n*, of what is the required degree of connection between the exactions imposed by the city and the projected impacts of the proposed development.

I

. . . Petitioner Florence Dolan owns a plumbing and electric supply store located on Main Street in the Central Business District of the city. The store covers approximately 9,700 square feet on the eastern side of a 1.67-acre parcel, which includes a gravel parking lot. Fanno Creek flows through the southwestern corner of the lot and along its western boundary. The year-round flow of the creek renders the area within the creek's 100-year floodplain virtually unusable for commercial development. The city's comprehensive plan includes the Fanno Creek floodplain as part of the city's greenway system.

Petitioner applied to the city for a permit to redevelop the site. Her proposed plans called for nearly doubling the size of the store to 17,600 square feet, and paving a 39-space parking lot. The existing store, located on the opposite side of the parcel, would be razed in sections as construction progressed on the new building. In the second phase of the project, petitioner proposed to build an additional structure on the northeast side of the site for complementary businesses, and to provide more parking. The proposed expansion and intensified use are consistent with the city's zoning scheme in the Central Business District.

The City Planning Commission granted petitioner's permit application subject to conditions imposed by the city's CDC [the Community Development Code, required by Oregon's comprehensive land use management statute]. The CDC establishes the following standard for site development review approval: "Where landfill and/or development is allowed within and adjacent to the 100-year floodplain, the city shall require the dedication of sufficient open land area for greenway adjoining and within the floodplain. This area shall include portions at a suitable elevation for the construction of a pedestrian/bicycle pathway within the floodplain in accordance with the adopted pedestrian/bicycle plan." . . . The dedication required by that condition encompasses approximately 7,000 square feet, or roughly 10% of the property. In accordance with city practice, petitioner could rely on the dedicated property to meet the 15% open space and landscaping requirement mandated by the city's zoning scheme. The city would bear the cost of maintaining a landscaped buffer between the dedicated area and the new store. . . .

[Dolan's challenge to the conditions was unsuccessful in state administrative and judicial proceedings.]

II

The Takings Clause of the Fifth Amendment of the United States Constitution, made applicable to the States through the Fourteenth Amendment, *Chicago, B. & Q. R. Co. v. Chicago*, 166 U.S. 226, 239 (1897), provides: "[N]or shall private property be taken for public use, without just compensation."(5) One of the principal purposes of the Takings Clause is "to bar government from forcing some people alone to bear public burdens which, in all fairness and justice, should be borne by the public as a whole." *Armstrong v. United States*, 364 U.S. 40, 49 (1960). Without question, had the city simply required petitioner to dedicate a strip of land along Fanno Creek for public use, rather than conditioning the grant of her permit to redevelop her property on such a dedication, a taking would have occurred. *Nollan, supra*, at 831. Such public access would deprive petitioner of the right to exclude others, "one of the most essential sticks in the bundle of rights that are commonly characterized as property." *Kaiser Aetna v. United States*, 444 U.S. 164, 176 (1979).

On the other side of the ledger, the authority of state and local governments to engage in land use planning has been sustained against constitutional challenge as long ago as our decision in *Euclid v. Ambler Realty Co.*, 272 U.S. 365 (1926). "Government hardly could go on if to some extent values incident to property could not be diminished without paying for every such change in the general law." *Pennsylvania Coal Co. v. Mahon*, 260 U.S. 393, 413 (1922). A land use regulation does not effect a taking if it "substantially advance[s] legitimate state interests" and does not "den[y] an owner economically viable use of his land." *Agins v. Tiburon*, 447 U.S. 255, 260 (1980).(6)

The sort of land use regulations discussed in the cases just cited, however, differ in two relevant particulars from the present case. First, they involved essentially legislative determinations classifying entire areas of the city, whereas here the city made an adjudicative decision to condition petitioner's application for a building permit on an individual parcel. Second, the conditions imposed were not simply a limitation on the use petitioner might make of her own parcel, but a requirement that she deed portions of the property to the city. In *Nollan, supra*, we held that governmental authority to exact such a condition was circumscribed by the Fifth and Fourteenth Amendments. Under the well-settled doctrine of "unconstitutional conditions," the government may not require a person to give up a

(5) Justice Stevens' dissent suggests that this case is actually grounded in "substantive" due process, rather than in the view that the Takings Clause of the Fifth Amendment was made applicable to the States through the Fourteenth Amendment. But there is no doubt that later cases have held that the Fourteenth Amendment does make the Takings Clause of the Fifth Amendment applicable to the States, [citing *Penn Central* and *Nollan*]. Nor is there any doubt that these cases have relied upon *Chicago, B. & Q. R. Co. v. Chicago*, 166 U.S. 226 (1897), to reach that result. . . .

(6) There can be no argument that the permit conditions would deprive petitioner "economically beneficial us[e]" of her property as she currently operates a retail store on the lot. Petitioner assuredly is able to derive some economic use from her property.

constitutional right — here the right to receive just compensation when property is taken for a public use — in exchange for a discretionary benefit conferred by the government where the benefit sought has little or no relationship to the property. *See Perry v. Sindermann*, 408 U.S. 593 (1972); *Pickering v. Board of Ed. of Township High School Dist.*, 391 U.S. 563, 568 (1968).

Petitioner contends that the city has forced her to choose between the building permit and her right under the Fifth Amendment to just compensation for the public easements. Petitioner does not quarrel with the city's authority to exact some forms of dedication as a condition for the grant of a building permit, but challenges the showing made by the city to justify these exactions. She argues that the city has identified "no special benefits" conferred on her, and has not identified any "special quantifiable burdens" created by her new store that would justify the particular dedications required from her which are not required from the public at large.

III

In evaluating petitioner's claim, we must first determine whether the "essential nexus" exists between the "legitimate state interest" and the permit condition exacted by the city. *Nollan*, 483 U.S., at 837. If we find that a nexus exists, we must then decide the required degree of connection between the exactions and the projected impact of the proposed development. We were not required to reach this question in *Nollan*, because we concluded that the connection did not meet even the loosest standard. Here, however, we must decide this question.

A

We addressed the essential nexus question in *Nollan*. [The Court described the "nexus" analysis of *Nollan*.] . . . The absence of a nexus left the Coastal Commission in the position of simply trying to obtain an easement through gimmickry, which converted a valid regulation of land use into "an out-and-out plan of extortion." *Ibid.*, quoting *J.E.D. Associates, Inc. v. Atkinson*, 432 A. 2d 12, 14–15 (N.H. 1981).

No such gimmicks are associated with the permit conditions imposed by the city in this case. Undoubtedly, the prevention of flooding along Fanno Creek and the reduction of traffic congestion in the Central Business District qualify as the type of legitimate public purposes we have upheld. It seems equally obvious that a nexus exists between preventing flooding along Fanno Creek and limiting development within the creek's 100-year floodplain. Petitioner proposes to double the size of her retail store and to pave her now-gravel parking lot, thereby expanding the impervious surface on the property and increasing the amount of stormwater run-off into Fanno Creek.

The same may be said for the city's attempt to reduce traffic congestion by providing for alternative means of transportation. In theory, a pedestrian/bicycle pathway provides a useful alternative means of transportation for workers and shoppers: "Pedestrians and bicyclists occupying dedicated spaces for walking and/or bicycling . . . remove potential vehicles from streets, resulting in an overall improvement in total transportation system flow." A. Nelson, *Public Provision of Pedestrian and Bicycle Access Ways: Public Policy Rationale and the Nature of Private Benefits* 11, Center for Planning Development, Georgia Institute of Technology, Working Paper Series (Jan. 1994). *See also*, Intermodal Surface Transportation Efficiency Act of 1991, Pub. L. 102-240, 105 Stat. 1914 (recognizing pedestrian and bicycle facilities as necessary components of any strategy to reduce traffic congestion).

B

The second part of our analysis requires us to determine whether the degree of the exactions demanded by the city's permit conditions bear the required relationship to the projected impact of petitioner's proposed development. *Nollan, supra,* at 834, quoting *Penn Central,* 438 U.S. 104, 127 (1978) (" '[A] use restriction may constitute a taking if not reasonably necessary to the effectuation of a substantial government purpose' "). Here the Oregon Supreme Court deferred to what it termed the "city's unchallenged factual findings" supporting the dedication conditions and found them to be reasonably related to the impact of the expansion of petitioner's business.

The city required that petitioner dedicate "to the city as Greenway all portions of the site that fall within the existing 100-year floodplain [of Fanno Creek] . . . and all property 15 feet above [the floodplain] boundary." In addition, the city demanded that the retail store be designed so as not to intrude into the greenway area. The city relies on the Commission's rather tentative findings that increased stormwater flow from petitioner's property "can only add to the public need to manage the [floodplain] for drainage purposes" to support its conclusion that the "requirement of dedication of the floodplain area on the site is related to the applicant's plan to intensify development on the site."

The city made the following specific findings relevant to the pedestrian/bicycle pathway:

> "In addition, the proposed expanded use of this site is anticipated to generate additional vehicular traffic thereby increasing congestion on nearby collector and arterial streets. Creation of a convenient, safe pedestrian/bicycle pathway system as an alternative means of transportation could offset some of the traffic demand on these nearby streets and lessen the increase in traffic congestion."

The question for us is whether these findings are constitutionally sufficient to justify the conditions imposed by the city on petitioner's building permit. Since state courts have been dealing with this question a good deal longer than we have, we turn to representative decisions made by them. [The Court's discussion of state cases is reprinted above]

We think the "reasonable relationship" test adopted by a majority of the state courts is closer to the federal constitutional norm than either of those previously discussed. . . . But we do not adopt it as such, partly because the term "reasonable relationship" seems confusingly similar to the term "rational basis" which describes the minimal level of scrutiny under the Equal Protection Clause of the Fourteenth Amendment. We think a term such as "rough proportionality" best encapsulates what we hold to be the requirement of the Fifth Amendment. No precise mathematical calculation is required, but the city must make some sort of individualized determination that the required dedication is related both in nature and extent to the impact of the proposed development.[8]

---

[8] Justice Stevens' dissent takes us to task for placing the burden on the city to justify the required dedication. He is correct in arguing that in evaluating most generally applicable zoning regulations, the burden properly rests on the party challenging the regulation to prove that it constitutes an arbitrary regulation of property rights. Here, by contrast, the city made an adjudicative decision to condition petitioner's application for a building permit on an individual parcel. In this situation, the burden properly rests on the city. This conclusion is not, as he suggests, undermined by our decision in *Moore v. East Cleveland,* 431 U.S.494 (1977), in which we struck down a housing

Justice Stevens' dissent relies upon a law review article for the proposition that the city's conditional demands for part of petitioner's property are "a species of business regulation that heretofore warranted a strong presumption of constitutional validity." But simply denominating a governmental measure as a "business regulation" does not immunize it from constitutional challenge on the grounds that it violates a provision of the Bill of Rights. In *Marshall v. Barlow's, Inc.*, 436 U.S. 307 (1978), we held that a statute authorizing a warrantless search of business premises in order to detect OSHA violations violated the Fourth Amendment. And in *Central Hudson Gas & Electric Corp. v. Public Service Comm'n of N.Y.*, 447 U.S. 557 (1980), we held that an order of the New York Public Service Commission, designed to cut down the use of electricity because of a fuel shortage, violated the First Amendment insofar as it prohibited advertising by a utility company to promote the use of electricity. We see no reason why the Takings Clause of the Fifth Amendment, as much a part of the Bill of Rights as the First Amendment or Fourth Amendment, should be relegated to the status of a poor relation in these comparable circumstances. We turn now to analysis of whether the findings relied upon by the city here, first with respect to the floodplain easement, and second with respect to the pedestrian/bicycle path, satisfied these requirements.

It is axiomatic that increasing the amount of impervious surface will increase the quantity and rate of storm-water flow from petitioner's property. Therefore, keeping the floodplain open and free from development would likely confine the pressures on Fanno Creek created by petitioner's development. In fact, because petitioner's property lies within the Central Business District, the Community Development Code already required that petitioner leave 15% of it as open space and the undeveloped floodplain would have nearly satisfied that requirement. But the city demanded more — it not only wanted petitioner not to build in the floodplain, but it also wanted petitioner's property along Fanno Creek for its Greenway system. The city has never said why a public greenway, as opposed to a private one, was required in the interest of flood control.

The difference to petitioner, of course, is the loss of her ability to exclude others. As we have noted, this right to exclude others is "one of the most essential sticks in the bundle of rights that are commonly characterized as property." *Kaiser Aetna*, 444 U.S., at 176. It is difficult to see why recreational visitors trampling along petitioner's floodplain easement are sufficiently related to the city's legitimate interest in reducing flooding problems along Fanno Creek, and the city has not attempted to make any individualized determination to support this part of its request.

The city contends that recreational easement along the Greenway is only ancillary to the city's chief purpose in controlling flood hazards. It further asserts that unlike the residential property at issue in *Nollan*, petitioner's property is commercial in character and therefore, her right to exclude others is compromised. The city maintains that "[t]here is nothing to suggest that preventing [petitioner] from prohibiting [the easements] will unreasonably impair the value of [her] property as a [retail store]." *PruneYard Shopping Center v. Robins*, 447 U.S. 74, 83 (1980).

Admittedly, petitioner wants to build a bigger store to attract members of the public to her property. She also wants, however, to be able to control the time and manner in which they enter. The recreational easement on the Greenway is different in character from the exercise

ordinance that limited occupancy of a dwelling unit to members of a single family as violating the Due Process Clause of the Fourteenth Amendment. The ordinance at issue in *Moore* intruded on choices concerning family living arrangements, an area in which the usual deference to the legislature was found to be inappropriate. *Id.*, at 499.

of state-protected rights of free expression and petition that we permitted in *PruneYard*. In *PruneYard*, we held that a major private shopping center that attracted more than 25,000 daily patrons had to provide access to persons exercising their state constitutional rights to distribute pamphlets and ask passersby to sign their petitions. *Id.* at 85. We based our decision, in part, on the fact that the shopping center "may restrict expressive activity by adopting time, place, and manner regulations that will minimize any interference with its commercial functions." *Id.*, at 83. By contrast, the city wants to impose a permanent recreational easement upon petitioner's property that borders Fanno Creek. Petitioner would lose all rights to regulate the time in which the public entered onto the Greenway, regardless of any interference it might pose with her retail store. Her right to exclude would not be regulated, it would be eviscerated.

If petitioner's proposed development had somehow encroached on existing greenway space in the city, it would have been reasonable to require petitioner to provide some alternative greenway space for the public either on her property or elsewhere. *See Nollan*, 483 U.S., at 836 ("Although such a requirement, constituting a permanent grant of continuous access to the property, would have to be considered a taking if it were not attached to a development permit, the Commission's assumed power to forbid construction of the house in order to protect the public's view of the beach must surely include the power to condition construction upon some concession by the owner, even a concession of property rights, that serves the same end."). But that is not the case here. We conclude that the findings upon which the city relies do not show the required reasonable relationship between the floodplain easement and the petitioner's proposed new building.

With respect to the pedestrian/bicycle pathway, we have no doubt that the city was correct in finding that the larger retail sales facility proposed by petitioner will increase traffic on the streets of the Central Business District. The city estimates that the proposed development would generate roughly 435 additional trips per day.[9]

Dedications for streets, sidewalks, and other public ways are generally reasonable exactions to avoid excessive congestion from a proposed property use. But on the record before us, the city has not met its burden of demonstrating that the additional number of vehicle and bicycle trips generated by the petitioner's development reasonably relate to the city's requirement for a dedication of the pedestrian/bicycle pathway easement. The city simply found that the creation of the pathway "could offset some of the traffic demand . . . and lessen the increase in traffic congestion."[10]

As Justice Peterson of the Supreme Court of Oregon explained in his dissenting opinion, however, "[t]he findings of fact that the bicycle pathway system '*could* offset some of the traffic demand' is a far cry from a finding that the bicycle pathway system *will*, or is *likely to*, offset some of the traffic demand." 854 P.2d, at 447 (emphasis in original). No precise mathematical calculation is required, but the city must make some effort to quantify its findings in support of the dedication for the pedestrian/bicycle pathway beyond the conclusory statement that it could offset some of the traffic demand generated.

---

[9] The city uses a weekday average trip rate of 53.21 trips per 1000 square feet. Additional Trips Generated = 53.21 * (17,600 - 9720).

[10] In rejecting petitioner's request for a variance from the pathway dedication condition, the city stated that omitting the planned section of the pathway across petitioner's property would conflict with its adopted policy of providing a continuous pathway system. But the Takings Clause requires the city to implement its policy by condemnation unless the required relationship between the petitioner's development and added traffic is shown.

IV

Cities have long engaged in the commendable task of land use planning, made necessary by increasing urbanization particularly in metropolitan areas such as Portland. The city's goals of reducing flooding hazards and traffic congestion, and providing for public greenways, are laudable, but there are outer limits to how this may be done. "A strong public desire to improve the public condition [will not] warrant achieving the desire by a shorter cut than the constitutional way of paying for the change." *Pennsylvania Coal*, 260 U.S., at 416.

The judgment of the Supreme Court of Oregon is reversed, and the case is remanded for further proceedings consistent with this opinion.

JUSTICE STEVENS, with whom JUSTICE BLACKMUN and JUSTICE GINSBURG join, dissenting:

. . . .

IV

The Court has made a serious error by abandoning the traditional presumption of constitutionality and imposing a novel burden of proof on a city implementing an admittedly valid comprehensive land use plan. Even more consequential than its incorrect disposition of this case, however, is the Court's resurrection of a species of substantive due process analysis that it firmly rejected decades ago. . . .

This case inaugurates an even more recent judicial innovation than the regulatory takings doctrine: the application of the "unconstitutional conditions" label to a mutually beneficial transaction between a property owner and a city. . . . Although it is well settled that a government cannot deny a benefit on a basis that infringes constitutionally protected interests — "especially [one's] interest in freedom of speech," *Perry v. Sindermann*, 408 U.S. 593, 597 (1972) — the "unconstitutional conditions" doctrine provides an inadequate framework in which to analyze this case.[12]

Dolan has no right to be compensated for a taking unless the city acquires the property interests that she has refused to surrender. Since no taking has yet occurred, there has not been any infringement of her constitutional right to compensation.

Even if Dolan should accept the city's conditions in exchange for the benefit that she seeks, it would not necessarily follow that she had been denied "just compensation" since it would be appropriate to consider the receipt of that benefit in any calculation of "just compensation." *See Pennsylvania Coal Co. v. Mahon*, 260 U.S. 393, 415 (1922) (noting that an "average reciprocity of advantage" was deemed to justify many laws); *Hodel v. Irving*, 481 U.S. 704, 715 (1987) (such " 'reciprocity of advantage' " weighed in favor of a statute's constitutionality). Particularly in

---

[12] Although it has a long history, *see Home Ins. Co. v. Morse*, 20 Wall. 445, 451 (1874), the "unconstitutional conditions" doctrine has for just as long suffered from notoriously inconsistent application; it has never been an overarching principle of constitutional law that operates with equal force regardless of the nature of the rights and powers in question. *See, e.g.*, Sunstein, *Why the Unconstitutional Conditions Doctrine is an Anachronism*, 70 B.U. L. Rev. 593, 620 (1990) (doctrine is "too crude and too general to provide help in contested cases"); [other citations omitted]. As the majority's case citations suggest, modern decisions invoking the doctrine have most frequently involved First Amendment liberties [citations omitted]. The necessary and traditional breadth of municipalities' power to regulate property development, together with the absence here of fragile and easily "chilled" constitutional rights such as that of free speech, make it quite clear that the Court is really writing on a clean slate rather than merely applying "well-settled" doctrine.

the absence of any evidence on the point, we should not presume that the discretionary benefit the city has offered is less valuable than the property interests that Dolan can retain or surrender at her option. But even if that discretionary benefit were so trifling that it could not be considered just compensation when it has "little or no relationship" to the property, the Court fails to explain why the same value would suffice when the required nexus is present. In this respect, the Court's reliance on the "unconstitutional conditions" doctrine is assuredly novel, and arguably incoherent. The city's conditions are by no means immune from constitutional scrutiny. The level of scrutiny, however, does not approximate the kind of review that would apply if the city had insisted on a surrender of Dolan's First Amendment rights in exchange for a building permit. One can only hope that the Court's reliance today on First Amendment cases, . . . [such as *Perry v. Sindermann*], and its candid disavowal of the term "rational basis" to describe its new standard of review, do not signify a reassertion of the kind of superlegislative power the Court exercised during the Lochner era. . . .

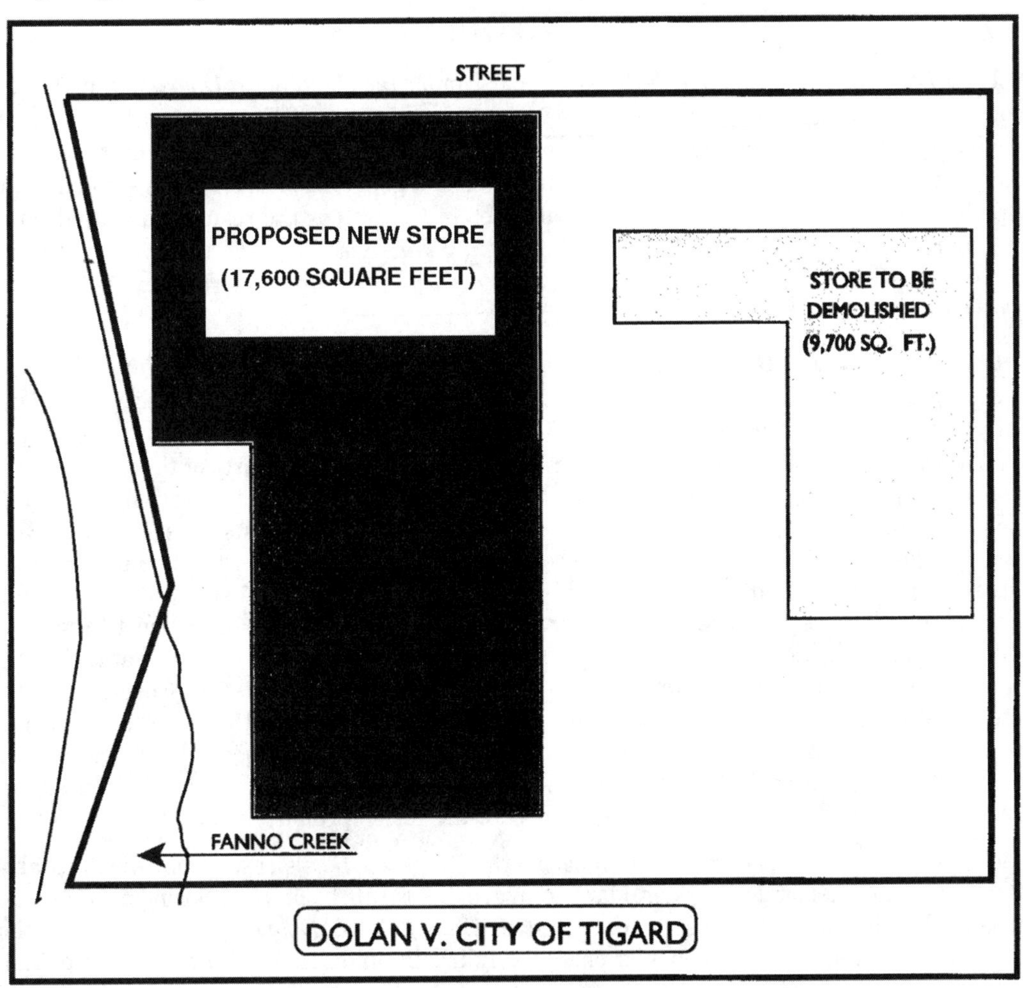

[Justice Souter's separate dissent concluded with the following paragraph:]

> "In any event, on my reading, the Court's conclusions about the city's vulnerability carry the Court no further than *Nollan* has gone already, and I do not view this case as a suitable vehicle for taking the law beyond that point. The right case for the enunciation of takings doctrine seems hard to spot."

[He amplified this conclusion by arguing there was an ample nexus between the greenway and the flood control problem, that the public's "incidental recreational use [of the greenway] can stand or fall with the bicycle path," and that the city had met its burden under *Nollan* of showing a nexus between the bikeway and the traffic congestion rationale. He appeared to agree with Justice Stevens that, *Nollan* having been satisfied, there was no need to subject the city's conditions to an additional "rough proportionality" test.]

NOTES AND QUESTIONS

1. *What does Dolan mean?* Perhaps the most important holding in *Dolan* is the decision to adopt a new "rough proportionality" rule for exactions. Professor Freilich argues that courts "would do well to avoid reading the *Dolan* test as establishing a rigid requirement, but instead interpret the circumstances of a dedication in terms of a general reasonableness standard, and applying heightened scrutiny to a dedication which is required as the result of an adjudicative or administrative determination." Freilich, *"Thou Shalt Not Take Title Without Adequate Planning": The Takings Equation After Dolan v. City of Tigard*, 27 Urb. Law. 187, 200–01 (1995). Do you agree?

In *B.A.M. Dev., L.L.C. v. Salt Lake County*, 196 P.3d 601 (Utah 2008), the Supreme Court of Utah provided further insight on the meaning of *Dolan*'s "rough proportionality" standard. The court held that "rough proportionality" analysis really means a "rough equivalency" test that compares the costs of the municipally required exaction and the costs of the impact to the developer. In deciding whether a municipally-mandated widening of a street constituted an unconstitutional taking, the *B.A.M.* court examined whether the costs to each party were roughly equivalent. Revisiting *Dolan*, the court asserted that "rough proportionality" did not mean "proportionality," because this term was used to avoid the confusion that "reasonably related" might cause to those who compare it with "rational basis." According to the Utah Supreme Court, the aim of *Dolan*'s "rough proportionality" test was to ensure that the cost of the exaction was more or less equivalent to the cost of the impact. The court overturned the determination at the trial level stating that the correct inquiry is whether the "imposition on the community of a proposed development is roughly equal to the cost being extracted to offset it." *Id.* at 604. Is the *B.A.M.* court's interpretation of the "rough proportionality" standard correct? Was the court too quick to dispense with the term "proportionality"?

The *Dolan* majority is careful to emphasize that the state nexus cases from which it takes guidance are not dispositive of federal law (compare the use of "background principles" of state nuisance law in the *Lucas* case, reproduced in Ch. 2). After *Dolan*, however, an exaction justified on a "weak" nexus theory is presumably invalid under federal law, thus essentially narrowing the range of state nexus tests to "strict" and "stricter."

2. *Unconstitutional conditions.* As noted in Chapter 2, the Court in *Lingle* concluded that *Nollan* and *Dolan* were not affected by its decision to drop the *Agins* "substantially advances" prong from its takings analysis because those two cases did not apply that test. Rather than being concerned with whether an exaction would advance "some legitimate state interest," the Court stressed that *Nollan* and *Dolan* "involve[d] the question whether the exactions advanced the *same* interests that land use authorities asserted would allow them to deny the permits altogether." 544 U.S. at 547.

> *Nollan* and *Dolan* both involved dedications of property so onerous that, outside the exactions context, they would be deemed *per se* physical takings. . . . [T]hese cases involve a special application of the "doctrine of unconstitutional conditions," which provides that "the government may not require a person to give up a constitutional right — here the right to receive just compensation when property is taken for public use — in exchange for a discretionary benefit conferred by the government where the benefit [sought] has little or no relationship to the property." [*Id.*, quoting *Dolan*, 512 U.S. at 385.]

What does *Lingle*'s emphasis on unconstitutional conditions doctrine mean for exactions? Are these statements dicta and thus open to conjecture about what the Court may do when faced with an exaction that is outside the factual parameters on *Nolan* and *Dolan*, or are they "best understood as a necessary decisional step along the decisional path to its outcome and part of its holding"? See Fenster, *Regulating Land Use in a Constitutional Shadow: The Institutional Contexts of Exactions*, 58 Hastings L.J. 729, 757 (2007) (arguing for the latter interpretation).

A leading analysis of the unconstitutional conditions doctrine offers the metaphor of a "minefield to be traversed gingerly." Sullivan, *Unconstitutional Conditions*, 102 Harv. L. Rev. 1415, 1416 (1989). Professor Sullivan recounts that the doctrine first was fashioned by the *Lochner* Court in the early 20th Century, which applied heightened scrutiny to strike down much social legislation in order to protect economic liberties of corporations, and was revived by the liberal *Warren* Court in the 1960s to "protect personal liberties of speech, association, religion, and privacy." *Id.* Over the years, application of the doctrine has been "riven with inconsistencies," *id.*, with *Nollan* highlighted as one example of the limits of the concept of germaneness. The beach access condition could further state interest in public access to the beach, the dissent's point, or be unrelated to visual access, the majority's point. *Id.* at 1474. But rather than reject the doctrine or treat it as "a second-best alternative to an unattainable constitutional ideal," Professor Sullivan argues that it "serves a limited but crucial role . . . of identif[ying] a characteristic technique by which government appears not to, but in fact does burden . . . [constitutionally preferred] liberties, triggering a demand for especially strong justification by the state." *Id.* at 1416–1419. In addition to this "state-checking function, . . . [the doctrine] bars redistribution of constitutional rights as to which government has obligations of evenhandedness . . . and prevents inappropriate hierarchy among rightholders," she concludes. *Id.* at 1506.

Aside from the *Nollan/Dolan* public easement dedication condition, what other types of land use exactions raise the "constitutional conditions" issue as Professor Sullivan has articulated it? Would a requirement to transfer development rights on 10% of a particular tract of land by means of a conservation easement in favor of the local government be subject to heightened review? What about a requirement to pay a per-lot fee to be deposited in a special fund to pay for water and sewer services necessary for the new development? For an argument that *Lingle* wisely confined the heightened judicial scrutiny triggered by the "unconstitutional conditions" doctrine to physical exactions which affect the property power to exclude because an "institutional web" of state and local elected and appointed officials, along with state courts applying state law and private landowners, "can ultimately provide better, more responsive oversight," see Fenster, 58 Hastings L.J. at 751–775. See also Been, *"Exit" as a Constraint on Land Use Exactions: Rethinking the Unconstitutional Conditions Doctrine*, 91 Colum. L. Rev. at 506–45 (arguing that "market forces are a prime candidate for an alternative to judicial scrutiny").

In *Kameole Pointe Dev. LP v. County of Maui*, 573 F. Supp. 2d. 1354 (D. Haw. 2008), the court addressed the developer's contention that a county ordinance requiring a set-aside for affordable housing was an unconstitutional condition. The court held that the developer's claim was properly a facial regulatory takings claim, not one of unconstitutional conditions. The court rejected the developer's argument that the *Nollan/Dolan* analysis applied in its case because the developer was mounting a facial challenge to the ordinance. Moreover, the developer was not alleging a physical invasion of property as was the case in *Nollan and Dolan*. The court found that *Lingle* abrogated the "substantially advances test" for takings. The only way to avoid the *Williamson County* ripeness requirement to litigate first in state court before proceeding to federal court was if the case fell under the "substantially advances test." Since this test was no longer available, the developers were required to seek damages in state court. After *Lingle*, facial takings claims are limited to the *Lucas* analysis.

3. *Is a unified theory of takings possible?* Since the revival of interest in regulatory takings doctrine in the mid-1960s, commentators have struggled to articulate a general theory that explains where the line should be drawn between compensation and no compensation for the adverse effects of regulations. Until Justice Scalia's arrival, by contrast, the Supreme Court tended to approach the problem as, in Justice Brennan's oft-quoted phrase from the *Penn Central* opinion, a series of "essentially ad hoc, factual inquiries." First with the heightened "nexus" test of *Nollan* and then with the *per se* rule of *Lucas*, Justice Scalia seemed to be guiding the court towards an objectified, property-rights theory of regulatory takings. How does *Dolan*'s "individualized determination" requirement differ, if at all, from Justice Brennan's "essentially ad hoc, factual" inquiry? Is individualized determination consistent with implementing a general theory of takings? Does *Lingle* advance a unified theory?

4. *Nexus.* Many commentators and courts interpreted *Nollan* as applying heightened scrutiny to the nexus requirement. If that is so, what does *Dolan* add? In *Nollan*, Justice Scalia concluded there was absolutely no nexus at all between the lateral beachfront easement and the loss of visual access occasioned by the new development. After *Dolan*, would it be more accurate to say that there was a nexus of sorts in *Nollan* (as Justice Brennan argued) but that it was too tenuous to satisfy the "rough proportionality" test? Or does *Nollan* mean that there is a zone of *de minimis* nexus that is tantamount to a *per se* taking? (Notice the parallel to the open question of whether *Lucas' per se* test applies in a zone where the regulation leaves the property with some residual, but *de minimis* use and value.) See Morgan, *Exactions as Takings: Tactics for Dealing with Dolan*, Land Use L. & Zoning Dig., Sep., 1994, at 3.

5. *The "right to exclude."* Both *Dolan* and *Nollan* emphasize the compulsory conveyance of a property interest to the public, the beachfront easement of passage in *Nollan*, the greenway and bikeway easements in *Dolan*. Earlier Supreme Court cases held that physical occupancy is a *per se* taking. Why is that not the end of the inquiry in *Dolan*, without going on to the nexus analysis at all, or at least to the new second step? Is there constitutional significance in the fact that Mrs. Dolan applied for a land use permit, while the property owners in the physical occupation cases did not?

6. *Dedications.* Consider the greenway and bikeway requirements separately.

a. *Greenway.* Insofar as flood control is concerned, it would appear that the city could obtain all that it is entitled to have by restricting development within the floodplain and leaving title in Dolan. Can you think of any reason why the city needed title to protect against flooding? If Dolan retained title, could she argue for a reduction in the taxable value of the land based on its unavailability for development? If the city, at a later date, condemned an easement of way through the greenbelt for the benefit of the public, could it argue that the property taken had only nominal value because of the legitimate restriction on its use? Cf. *Preseault v. ICC*, 494 U.S. 1 (1990).

On these matters, consider this additional portion of Justice Stevens' dissent:

> Given the commercial character of both the existing and the proposed use of the property as a retail store, it seems likely that potential customers "trampling along petitioner's floodplain," are more valuable than a useless parcel of vacant land. Moreover, the duty to pay taxes and the responsibility for potential tort liability may well make ownership of the fee interest in useless land a liability rather than an asset. That may explain why Dolan never conceded that she could be prevented from building on the floodplain.

b. *Bikeway.* Whatever the fate of the greenway dedication, the bikeway would be pointless without public access. But even if there is an essential nexus of appropriate nature and extent between the bikeway and traffic generated by the new stores, is there one between Dolan's traffic and recreational users of the bikeway? How far does the majority's analysis reach? Why, to pose a more typical example, can a municipality require a subdivider to dedicate internal streets and sidewalks when it is clear that many of the users will not actually be traveling to or from the properties in the subdivision? Should the landowner be able to opt for private streets if desired, and require the public to pay for any public access? The majority seems to assume that an uncompensated dedication is constitutional once the nexus is established. Is this deference to the traditional way of doing things simply a further example of the extent to which takings theory is becoming a loosely connected series of *ad hoc* rules?

7. *Burden of proof.* A very important aspect of *Dolan* is the shifting of the burden of proof to the government to justify the exaction. Why might this be so? Consider the following:

a. *Trial strategy.* Is the majority demanding of the city anything more than that it prepare its justification more carefully (avoiding soft words such as "could," for instance, when defending the bikeway requirement)? How likely is it that the "nature" and "extent" of the "essential nexus" required by the court are susceptible of proof by hard evidence? Should the city be advised that it must make formal findings of "rough proportionality" at the time the exaction is imposed? Or is it sufficient that the city be able to establish that it met that standard if and when the exaction is challenged? See *Hammer v. City of Eugene*, 121 P.3d 693, 696–97 (Ore. App. 2006) (nothing in *Dolan* requires such findings at the time an exaction is imposed). Is Justice Stevens correct when he says that "predictions on such matters [as bikeway usage] are nothing more than estimates"?

In representing the city, how would you attempt to reformulate the record on remand? Even if not many of Mrs. Dolan's customers used the bikeway, would it be sufficient to show that the bikeway reduced road usage otherwise making room for Mrs. Dolan's customers?

b. *The rights hierarchy.* In citing cases such as *Perry v. Sindermann*, does the majority mean that the Constitution protects property rights to the same extent that it protects free speech and other aspects of individual liberty? (See also Justice Scalia's footnote 3 in *Nollan*, reproduced in Chapter 2, *supra.*) Is this what justifies the shift in the burden of proof? How does this relate to the debate between the majority and Justice Stevens over substantive due process? Consider also the care the court takes to differentiate "rough proportionality" from the federal constitutional law of minimum scrutiny "rational basis" tests. Do *Nollan* and *Dolan* lay the foundation for the Court to eventually reexamine the different levels of judicial review based on the distinction between economic rights and individual liberties established by footnote four of *United States v. Carolene Products*, 304 U.S. 144 (1938)?

In their concurrence in *United States v. Carlton*, 512 U.S. 26, 41 (1994), cited in footnote 13 of Justice Stevens' dissent (not included above), Justices Scalia and Thomas are much blunter: "The picking and choosing among various rights to be accorded 'substantive due process' protection is alone enough to arouse suspicion; but the categorical and inexplicable exclusion of so-called 'economic rights' (even though the Due Process Clause explicitly applies to 'property') unquestionably involves policymaking rather than neutral legal analysis."

c. *The commercial/residential distinction.* Another way to evaluate both the "rights hierarchy" problem and the question of whether a uniform theory is possible is to consider the distinction between commercial and non-commercial exactions suggested by Justice Stevens. In writing for the majority, he notes, with a faint tinge of scorn, that he relies on a law review article for this argument. The article includes the following key language which Justice Stevens quotes:

> The subdivider is a manufacturer, processor, and marketer of a product; land is but one of his raw materials. In subdivision control disputes, the developer is not defending hearth and home against the king's intrusion, but simply attempting to maximize his profits from the sale of a finished product. As applied to him, subdivision control exactions are actually business regulations. [Johnston, *Constitutionality of Subdivision Control Exactions: The Quest for a Rationale*, 52 Cornell L.Q. 871, 923 (1967).]

How does the Chief Justice answer this point? Are separate rules for commercial regulation workable? Inescapable under *Carolene Products*? Note that if takings and free speech doctrines are indeed analogous, as the majority implies, the separate treatment of "commercial speech" has been steadily eroded by the court in recent years.

8. *Legislative vs. adjudicative.* What is the significance of characterizing the city's action as "adjudicative," rather than "legislative"? Dissenting on this point, Justice Souter said, "[T]he permit conditions were imposed pursuant to Tigard's Community Development Code. The adjudication here was of Dolan's requested variance from the permit conditions otherwise required to be imposed by the Code. This case raises no question about discriminatory, or 'reverse spot' zoning, which 'singles out a particular parcel for different, less favorable treatment than the neighboring ones.' [*Penn Central*]" Did the Court mean that every application of a legislative rule is adjudicative? Further developments on this issue are discussed in the next section.

9. *Subsequent events. Dolan* eventually was settled, but only after additional controversy. When Mrs. Dolan resubmitted building plans, the city attached an easement dedication requirement based on its analysis of traffic and storm water effects of her proposed new store. She refused to grant the easement and the family later sued in state court for damages, seeking $2.4 million for delays in construction and corresponding loss of business. After a trial court awarded compensation, the parties settled by exchanging an easement and $1.5 million. The settlement also permitted the Dolans to attach a plaque that included the words, "nor shall

private property be taken for public use without just compensation," at the entrance to the public pedestrian trail crossing their property. Murphy, *Dolan v. City of Tigard: What's Happened Since*, Planning, Dec. 2000, at 3.

[3.] *Dolan* Applied

The task of applying *Dolan* has been complicated by its failure to discuss whether the rough proportionality test applies only when a contribution of property or cash is required incident to a land use approval or whether it applies to all regulatory takings claims and also, within the category of contributions, whether it applies only to physical dedications of land. The actual case involved an "exaction," in which a property interest in the land itself was required to be dedicated to the public. Another very common technique is to require payment of a cash "impact fee," levied in the subdivision control process or at the time a building permit issues, to finance public facilities, on- or off-site, that are needed because of the new development. Or municipalities may levy an "in-lieu" fee, which is paid in cash in lieu of a dedication of land or the construction of improvements. Many important takings cases (*Penn Central, Loretto, Nollan*) have either said explicitly or implied that physical invasion under the guise of regulation will increase the likelihood of there being a taking. Is *Dolan*'s "rough proportionality" test triggered only by exactions, which "take" a property interest, or does it apply across the board?

Del Monte Dunes. The heated debate over the reach of *Dolan* was at least partially settled by the Supreme Court in *City of Monterey v. Del Monte Dunes, Ltd.*, 526 U.S. 687 (1999). *Del Monte* was an inverse condemnation case in which the claim was that the development had been rejected altogether; neither exactions nor impact fees were at issue. The Court held (without much explanation) that the "rough proportionality" test of *Dolan* did not apply:

> Although in a general sense concerns for proportionality animate the Takings Clause, we have not extended the rough-proportionality test of *Dolan* beyond the special context of exactions — land use decisions conditioning approval of development on the dedication of property to public use. The rule applied in *Dolan* considers whether dedications demanded as conditions of development are proportional to the development's anticipated impacts. It was not designed to address, and is not readily applicable to, the much different questions arising where, as here, the landowner's challenge is based not on excessive exactions but on denial of development. We believe, accordingly, that the rough-proportionality test of *Dolan* is inapposite to a case such as this one. [*Id.* at 702–03.]

Read literally, the Court would seem to mean that the *Dolan* test applies *only* when physical dedications of land are required as an exaction. As noted earlier, the Court in *Lingle* did nothing to discourage that implication. Some state courts have taken the same position. See, e.g., *City of Olympia v. Drebick*, 126 P.3d 802 (Wash. 2006) (construing state impact fee statute and concluding that Supreme Court has not extended *Nollan/Dolan* to impact fees); *McCarthy v. City of Leawood*, 894 P.2d 836 (Kan 1995); *Smith v. Town of Mendon*, 771 N.Y.S.2d 781 (App. Div. 2004) (conservation easement requirement in site plan approval is not a *Dolan* exaction, distinguishing *Grogan v. Zoning Bd. of Appeals*, 633 N.Y.S.2d 809 (App. Div. 1995)). See also Fenster, *supra*; Curtin, Gowder & Wenter, *Exactions Update: The State of Development Exactions after Lingle v. Chevron U.S.A.*, 38 Urb. Law. 641 (2006). But the Court also connects "rough proportionality" to "the development's anticipated impacts." Is there reason to apply stricter scrutiny when land, as opposed to cash, is demanded? Does *Loretto* help answer this question?

There are courts that have rejected limiting *Nollan/Dolan* to physical exactions. For example, in *St. Johns River Water Mgmt. Dist. v. Koontz*, 5 So. 3d 8 (Fla. App. 2009), the court held that requiring offsite mitigation work in exchange for a development permit effected a taking and that such an exaction was properly analyzed under the *Nollan/Dolan* test. The court rejected the District's argument that *Dolan* did not cover cases other than those involving physical dedications of property. The court stated that it would include required physical improvements in the set of exactions subject to *Nollan/Dolan* analysis. The court also dispensed with the District's argument that the fact that the developer never had to do the exacted mitigation work meant that there was no taking. The imposition of conditions requiring an exaction was enough to fall under the *Nollan/Dolan* analysis, and in this case, result in a taking. Does this case result in a line-drawing problem for courts? Is the line for possible takings properly drawn at the imposition of conditions requiring an exaction?

Impact fees and rough proportionality. Even if, for the sake of argument, one applies *Dolan* to impact fees as well as exactions, it is clear that impact fees can more easily satisfy the rough proportionality test:

> Perhaps the exactions most at risk from an attack under *Dolan* are subdivision regulations requiring the contribution of land and facilities to assure adequacy of roadways, water, wastewater and drainage (the so-called "hard services") to serve the project. Such traditional land use regulations are applied almost universally by municipalities large and small. Typically, as in *Dolan*, exactions are guided by a master plan that identifies approximate locations and dimensions of system facilities necessary to serve the community. Such location-based exactions do not readily lend themselves to proportionality tests. . . .
>
> On the other hand, demand-based exaction programs, such as impact fees, are designed to measure the impacts created by a development on community facilities and to convert such demand to a value expressed as monetary fees. "Because . . . impact fees were developed in the context of judicially crafted proportionality standards, . . . [they] should satisfy 'rough proportionality' tests from the outset.'" [Morgan, Shortlidge & Watson, *Right-of-Way Exactions and Rough Proportionality*, Mun. Law, Jan. 1999, at 28.]

Legislative vs. adjudicative. Now assume that *Del Monte* is read literally, so that *Dolan* applies only in exactions cases. Does the rough proportionality test apply only when an exaction is imposed adjudicatively (as in *Dolan* itself), or also when an exaction is imposed legislatively. A review of the cases finds that "[a] clear pattern . . . has been that legislatively designed impact fees will not be subjected to the rigors of the . . . Court's heightened scrutiny regime . . . [because courts believe that legislatively determined impact fees] will achieve significant public purposes in a uniform way and will distribute development costs in an open and fair fashion." Rosenberg, *The Changing Culture of American Land Use Regulations: Paying for Growth with Impact Fees*, 59 SMU L. Rev. 177, 255–59 (2006). But courts may still scrutinize the administration of legislatively designed programs. Compare *Curtis v. Town of South Thomaston*, 708 A.2d 657, 660 (Me. 1998) (legislative nature of exaction only one factor in applying *Dolan*), and *Schultz v. City of Grants Pass*, 884 P.2d 569 (Ore. App. 1994) (dedication imposed on a landowner is adjudicative though required by the provisions of the local ordinance), with *Ehrlich v. City of Culver City*, 911 P.2d 429, 438 (Cal. 1996) (concluding that *Nollan* and *Dolan* only apply to cases of regulatory "leveraging" where conditions are imposed on land use approvals). The *Ehrlich* Court added that "the heightened standard of scrutiny is triggered by a relatively narrow class of land use cases — those exhibiting circumstances which increase the risk that the local permitting authority will seek to avoid the obligation to pay just compensation." *Id.* at 439. Does this distinction make sense? Accord *Home Builders Ass'n of Central Arizona v. City of Scottsdale*, 930 P.2d 993 (Ariz. 1997); *Home Builders Ass'n v. City of Napa*, 108 Cal. Rptr. 2d 60 (Cal. App. 2001) (applying *Ehrlich* standard in upholding inclusionary housing ordinance with mandatory set aside provision). For a detailed discussion of the legislative-adjudicative distinction, see Baker, *Much Ado About Nollan/Dolan: The Comparative Nature of the Legislative Adjudication Distinctions in Exactions*, 42 Urb. Law. 171 (2010).

Should it make a difference whether the exaction complained of was contained in a general legislative pronouncement or was applied to a single parcel of land through a development approval condition? The Supreme Court of Texas said no in *Flower Mound v. Stafford Estates Limited Partnership*, 135 S.W.3d 620 (Tex. 2004) (discussed in [b] Impact Fees, below), but refused to decide "in the abstract whether the *Dolan* standard should apply to all 'legislative' exactions — whatever that really means — imposed as a condition of development. It is enough to say that we can find no meaningful distinction between the condition imposed on Stafford and the condition imposed on Dolan and the Nollans. All were based on general authority taking into account individual circumstances." 135 S.W.3d. at 641. Do you agree? See Reznik, *The Distinction Between Legislative and Adjudicative Decisions in Dolan v. City of Tigard*, 75 N.Y.U. L. Rev. 242, 266 (2000) ("in reality, the discretionary powers of municipal authorities exist along a continuum and seldom fall into the neat categories of a fully predetermined legislative exaction or a completely discretionary administrative determination as to the appropriate exaction"), quoted with approval in *B.A.M. Development, L.L.C. v. Salt Lake County*, 128 P.3d 1161, 1170–71 (Utah 2006) (concluding that the *Dolan* rough proportionality test, as codified by statute, applies to "all exactions, irrespective of their source").

In *Krupp v. Breckenridge Sanitation Dist.*, 19 P.3d 687 (Colo. 2001), the Supreme Court of Colorado declined to apply *Dolan* to a plant investment fee (PIF) assessed on all building projects by a special district providing wastewater services.

> Unlike the landowners in *Nollan* and *Dolan*, whose conditions for development were determined on an individualized adjudicative basis, the Krupps were charged a fee that was assessed on all new development within the district. The PIF assessment on the Krupp's development, then, is different from exactions in *Nollan* and *Dolan*, both in its creation and its reach. [*Id.* at 696, quoting with approval *Ehrlich v. City of Culver City*.]

The Colorado Court also noted that Colorado has codified the *Nollan/Dolan* test and the distinction between adjudicative and legislative determinations. Colo. Rev. Stat. § 29-20-203(1) (*Nollan/Dolan* limited to charges "determined on an individual and discretionary basis"). See also *City of Olympia v. Drebick*, 126 P.3d 802, 808–11 (Wash. 2006) (impact fee statute permits calculation of fee based on service area's improvements "as a whole" and does not require "individualized assessments" of a proposed development's "direct impact on each improvement planned in a service area"); *Greater Atlanta Homebuilders Ass'n v. DeKalb County*, 588 S.E.2d 694, 697 (Ga. 2003) (*Dolan* not applicable to a "facial challenge of a generally applicable land use regulation"). For an argument that the *Nollan/Dolan* standard should be extended to all exactions, land and monetary as well as legislative and adjudicative, and feature "an explicit analysis of the degree of burden distribution that accompanies exaction programs," see Ball & Reynolds, *Exactions and Burden Distribution in Takings Law*, 47 Wm. & Mary L. Rev. 1513, 1559–84 (2006).

For a review of the cases and commentary on the reach of the exactions decisions observing that "[l]ower federal and state courts tend to respect this adjudicative-legislative distinction and extend the nexus and proportionality tests only to individualized exactions, although some courts, with the approval of some commentators, have nevertheless applied heightened scrutiny to legislatively enacted exactions," see Fenster, *Takings Formalism and Regulatory Formulas: Exactions and the Consequences of Clarity*, 92 Cal. L. Rev. 609, 635–42 (2004). The difficulties in distinguishing between legislative and adjudicative decisions in the exactions context reflect the difficulties typically encountered in making these distinctions generally in the land use decision making process, as discussed in Chapter 5. Surveys of municipal practices show an almost even split between exactions that are formula-based, those that use a legislative standard with some flexibility, and those that are based on case-by-case adjudication. Purdum & Frank, *Community Use of Exactions: Results of a National Survey*, *in* Development Exactions 128 (J. Frank & R. Rhodes eds., 1987). Does this complicate the characterization problem? Note that in *Dolan* the dedication was imposed under the development code but was determined administratively. Would it be best to apply *Dolan* to all exactions, even though imposed legislatively?

The plaintiffs in *Action Apartment Ass'n v. City of Santa Monica*, 82 Cal. Rptr. 3d 722 (Cal. App. 2008), attempted to alter the bright-line, legislative-versus-adjudicative distinction by arguing that the city's ordinance was a facial violation of the *Nollan-Dolan* test. The ordinance required developers of multifamily housing units in multifamily residential zones to construct affordable housing on-site or elsewhere. The plaintiffs unsuccessfully argued that *Lingle* disrupted the consensus view that the *Nollan-Dolan* heightened scrutiny applied only to individual adjudicative decisions and not legislative zoning decisions. The court found that *Lingle* only held that the "substantially advances" test was no longer the only test for a regulatory taking. According to the *Action* court, *Lingle* did not open the door for the application of the *Nollan-Dolan* test to facial challenges (which essentially challenge legislative enactments). Are there other ways in which the bright-line prohibition of *Nollan-Dolan* scrutiny of legislative decisions has become blurred?

What about exactions for environmental purposes? See *Leroy Land Dev. v. Tahoe Regional Planning Agency*, 939 F.2d 696 (9th Cir. 1991) (upholding exaction to mitigate environmental impact of development); *Grogan v. Zoning Bd. of Appeals*, 633 N.Y.S.2d 809 (App. Div. 1995) (same; conservation easement required as condition to development of property); *Gardner v. New Jersey Pinelands Comm'n*, 547 A.2d 725 (N.J. Ch. Div. 1988) (upholding exaction restricting housing in agricultural area of Pinelands to agricultural use). See also Ledman, Note, *Local Government Environmental Mitigation Fees: Development Exactions, the Next Generation*, 45 Fla. L. Rev. 835 (1993).

Relationship to development. In *Paradyne Corp. v. State Dep't of Transp.*, 528 So. 2d 921 (Fla. App. 1988), the Department required Paradyne to redesign its road connection as a condition to a road connection permit. The Department also required Paradyne to provide joint access across its property for an adjacent property. The court upheld the redesign requirement but not the joint access requirement. Can you see why? See also *Surfside Colony, Ltd. v. California Coastal Comm'n*, 277 Cal. Rptr. 371 (Cal. App. 1991) (invalidating beach access requirement as condition to permission to build revetment because no showing that revetment would cause erosion).

Variations on the nexus test. The Illinois Supreme Court has adopted a test for exactions that is more stringent than the "reasonableness" test. It held that a municipality could impose an exaction on a developer only if it was "specifically and uniquely attributable" to his activity. *Pioneer Trust & Sav. Bank v. Village of Mount Prospect*, 176 N.E.2d 799 (Ill. 1961). This test has a limited following. See *Aunt Hack Ridge Estates, Inc. v. Planning Comm'n*, 273 A.2d 880 (Conn. 1970) (upholding lot fee for parks). In 2003, Illinois codified the "specifically and uniquely attributable" test in an amendment to its subdivision enabling statute:

> For purposes of implementing ordinances regarding developer donations or impact fees, and specifically for expenditures thereof, "school grounds" is defined as including land or site improvements, which include school buildings or other infrastructure necessitated and specifically and uniquely attributed to the development or subdivision in question. This amendatory Act of the 93rd General Assembly applies to all impact fees or developer donations paid into a school district or held in a separate account or escrow fund by any school district or municipality for a school district.

65 ILCS 5/11-12-5(7). This amendment was intended to address the Illinois Supreme Court's decision in *Thompson v. Village of Newark*, 768 N.E.2d 856 (Ill. 2002), invalidating an ordinance assessing impact fees for school building construction. See also *Northern Illinois Homebuilders Ass'n, Inc. v. County of Du Page*, 649 N.E.2d 384 (Ill. 1995) (applying the specifically and uniquely attributable test to road impact fees).

Are the "reasonableness" and "nexus" tests the same? Two commentators reviewed the tests the courts apply and concluded "[a]s a matter of dictionary definition, it is difficult to see any differences between them." Kayden & Pollard, *Linkage Ordinances and Traditional Exactions Analysis: The Connection Between Office Development and Housing*, 50 Law & Contemp. Probs. 127, 128 n.3 (1987). Do you agree? The *Surfside* case, *supra*, held that *Nollan* had heightened the judicial review standard for exactions.

Dedications vs. conditions. In *City of Annapolis v. Waterman*, 745 A.2d 1000 (Md. 2000), the city required a subdivider to set aside one lot for recreational space to be used by residents of the subdivision. The court held this was a condition on the subdivision subject only to regulatory taking tests, and not a dedication subject to the tests for exactions "because the proposed recreational space is not for general public use; it is intended only for the use of those residing within the Parkway development." *Id.* at 1011. See also *Clark v. City of Albany*, 904 P.2d 185 (Ore. App. 1995), where the city imposed a condition requiring a traffic-free area as part of an approval of a site plan for a fast food restaurant. The court held this was a traffic regulation, not a dedication.

Is there a relationship between these cases and cases that always uphold requirements for improvements internal to a subdivision? See *Pima County v. Arizona Title Ins. & Trust Co.*, 565 P.2d 524 (Ariz. App. 1977) (street paving); *Garvin v. Baker*, 59 So. 2d 360 (Fla. 1952) (width of streets).

Compare *Parking Ass'n v. City of Atlanta*, 450 S.E.2d 200 (Ga. 1994). A city ordinance applied to all parking lots of more than 30 spaces in downtown and midtown zoning districts, and required ten percent of the lot to be landscaped and one tree for every eight spaces. The court held the exaction tests did not apply. "Here the city made a legislative determination with regard to many landowners and it simply limited the use the landowners might make of a small portion of their lands. Moreover, the city demonstrated a 'rough proportionality' between the requirements and objectives of the ordinance." *Id.* at 203, n.3 What were the objectives? Does the *Annapolis* test apply?

The Supreme Court denied certiorari, 515 U.S. 1116 (1995), but Justices Thomas and O'Connor dissented from the denial because they believed legislative acts should be subject to the exaction tests. This issue is discussed *infra.*

Dedications in the zoning process. Courts have also upheld compulsory dedications in the zoning process. In *Bringle v. Board of Supvrs.*, 351 P.2d 765 (Cal. 1960), the court upheld a variance granted on the condition that an easement be dedicated for the widening of a street. The court held that reasonable conditions may be attached to a variance to preserve the purpose and intent of the zoning ordinance. See also *Southern Pac. Co. v. City of Los Angeles*, 51 Cal. Rptr. 197 (Cal. App. 1966) (same; building permit). As in subdivision control, the need for the improvement must be created by the development. *Bethlehem Evangelical Lutheran Church v. City of Lakewood*, 626 P.2d 668 (Colo. 1981) (condition attached to building permit). See also *Mayor & City Council v. Brookeville Tpk. Constr. Co.*, 228 A.2d 263 (Md. 1967) (may impose compulsory dedication when land annexed to municipality).

Some courts do not allow compulsory dedications outside the subdivision control process. *City of Corpus Christi v. Unitarian Church*, 436 S.W.2d 923 (Tex. Civ. App. 1968); *Board of Supvrs. v. Rowe*, 216 S.E.2d 199 (Va. 1975).

Sources. P. Salkin, Trends in Land Use Law from A to Z: Adult Uses to Zoning (2001); R. Freilich & D. Bushek, Exactions, Impact Fees, and Dedications: Shaping Land use Development and Funding Infrastructure in the Dolan Era (1995); J. Frank, Development Exactions (1987); Fenster, *Takings Formalism and Regulatory Formulas: Exactions and the Consequences of Clarity*, 92 Cal. L. Rev. 609 (2004); Ziegler, *Development and Permit Decisions: Nollan, Dolan, and Del Monte Dunes*, 34 Urb. Law. 155 (2002); Fennell, *Hard Bargains and Real Steals: Land Use Exactions Revisited*, 86 Iowa L. Rev. 1 (2000).

[a.] Dedications of Land

The following case illustrates how courts apply the rough proportionality test to dedications of land. A "short plat" in this context is a subdivision of fewer than five lots. See Wash. Rev. Code § 58.17.020(6), (8).

SPARKS v. DOUGLAS COUNTY

127 Wn. 2d 901, 904 P.2d 738 (1995)

SMITH, J.

Petitioner Douglas County seeks review of a decision by the Court of Appeals, Division Three, reversing a ruling of the Douglas County Superior Court which upheld action of the Board of Commissioners of Douglas County conditioning approval of [four] short plat applications [containing four residential lots each] by Respondents Herschel and Elizabeth Sparks upon dedication of rights of way for road improvements. We granted review. We reverse.

QUESTION PRESENTED

The question presented in this case is whether the action by Douglas County conditioning approval of the Sparkses' short plat applications upon dedication of rights of way for road improvements was arbitrary and capricious and constitutes an unconstitutional taking of property.

[The court's statement of facts is omitted. The litigation up to and including the court of appeals reversal occurred prior to the *Dolan* decision.]

DISCUSSION

. . . .

The *Dolan* Test of Constitutionality

The statement of the law by the Court of Appeals conflicts with the United States Supreme Court's recent ruling in *Dolan v. Tigard*. The Court of Appeals stated a dedication is permissible only if it "reasonably prevents or compensates for, in a specific and proportional fashion, adverse public impacts of the proposed development." *Dolan* found such exacting scrutiny unacceptable. . . . [The court then discussed the *Dolan* case.]

The approach adopted by the United States Supreme Court in *Dolan* can be applied in consonance with Washington law. RCW 82.02.020 permits dedications as a condition for subdivision approval if the local government can show the conditions are "reasonably necessary as a direct result of the proposed development or plat to which the dedication of land or easement is to apply." Reviewing agencies must consider adequacy of access to a proposed subdivision, and may condition approval on provision of adequate access. Short subdivision plats may not be approved unless the legislative body finds, among other things, that appropriate provisions are made "for the public health, safety, and general welfare and for . . . open spaces, drainage ways, streets or roads . . . ."

[The court discussed but did not decide the role of anticipated future road improvement needs in the *Dolan* analysis.] At any rate, the determinative issue in this case is not future use, but the degree of connection between the County's exaction and the impact of the developments.

Rough Proportionality

Addressing the first step of the *Dolan* test, the Sparkses have conceded that a "nexus" exists between requiring dedication of rights of way and the County's legitimate interest in promoting road safety. The next step — determining whether a reasonable relationship also exists between the dedications and the impact created by the developments — is disputed in this case.

The pivotal issue under the *Dolan* approach is whether the exactions demanded by Douglas County are roughly proportional to the impact of the Sparkses' proposed developments. Respondents Sparks argue that the determination by the Court of Appeals that the new land use has no adverse impact on road safety demonstrates an absence of rough proportionality between development impact and exactions. Respondents also claim there is no way to truly measure whether the conditions demanded by the County are proportionate to the impact of the development.

While *Dolan* disregarded precise calculations in analyzing development impacts, it ruled that local government must make some effort to quantify its findings to support its permit conditions. In this case, the findings made by the County were more than mere conclusory statements of general impact. They were the result of the kind of individualized analysis required under *Dolan*. The report prepared by the Planning Office for each of the short plats documented the deficiencies in right of way width and surfacing of the adjoining streets. Douglas County's records also reflect calculation of increase in traffic and the specific need for dedication of rights of way based upon the individual and cumulative impacts of the series of short subdivisions.

The findings upon which the County relies reflect the required rough proportionality between the exactions and the impact of the Respondents' proposed developments. It is undisputed that the developments would generate increased traffic on adjacent roads which are not adequate for safe access under county standards. The County has, in the process of individualized analysis, satisfied the final step of the *Dolan* test.

Respondents argue that the substandard conditions of the roads existed even prior to the Sparkses' plat applications and cannot therefore be caused by their proposed developments. But it has been established that the increase in traffic generated by those plats on already unsafe roads would require additional right of way and reconstruction to accommodate the overflow. Empire Avenue, in particular, has been listed in the County's six-year road improvement plan, and the county engineer testified the developments themselves necessitate upgrading of that road. The adverse impact created by the plats on adjacent roads was concluded by the trial court upon substantial evidence and need not be re-examined by this Court. . . .

We reverse the decision of the Court of Appeals which reversed the Douglas County Superior Court ruling upholding the action by Petitioner Douglas County conditioning approval of plat applications by Respondents Sparks on dedication of rights of way for road improvements.

ALEXANDER, J. (dissenting in part).

. . . Admittedly, the County's traffic predictions are detailed, scientifically based, and individualized calculations concerning the specific area surrounding the proposed developments. I am, nonetheless, satisfied that the exactions are constitutionally deficient with respect to the right-of-way along Empire Way because the County has not demonstrated that the extent of the exactions along this street are roughly proportional to the impact that it anticipates will be caused by the developments.

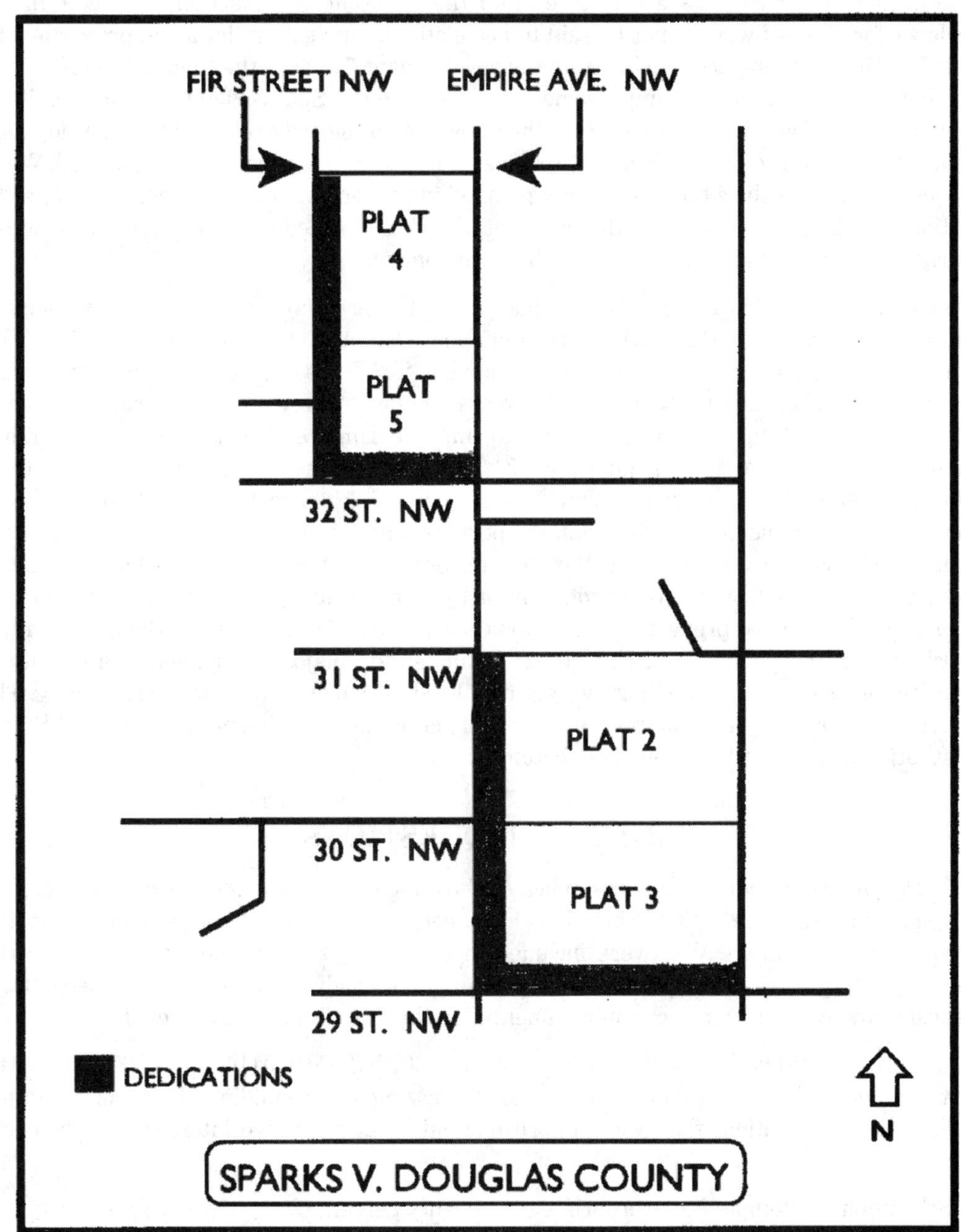

In reviewing a challenged exaction, a court must first identify the starting point from which to measure the extent of the exaction as a necessary predicate to calculating whether an exaction is proportional to an impact. In regard to Empire Way, at least, it cannot be presumed that the current condition of the roadway is the appropriate reference point for calculating the extent of the exaction. I reach this conclusion because Douglas County had previously made a formal announcement of its commitment to make certain improvements to Empire Way. Once these planned improvements are factored into the equation, the exaction of land from the developer for right-of-way cannot be said to be related in any extent, let alone proportionally related, to the traffic impacts arising from the development. Because the County has effectively said that Empire Way needed improvement, even before the Sparkses applied for permits to develop their land adjoining Empire Way, the impacts that logically relate to that development are only those that require roadway improvements in addition to those already planned. When the County failed to show that its already planned improvements could not accommodate the additional traffic generated by the development, the County failed to show that the exaction of any right-of-way is related, in extent, to the development.

The record shows that Douglas County had placed Empire Way on its six-year development plan prior to the date that either the Planning Commission or the Board of County Commissioners considered the Sparkses' plat application. It also reveals that the County had been unsuccessful in earlier attempts to obtain funding for the project. By its earlier action, the County determined that it was necessary to improve Empire Way to meet specifications contained in that plan. It is a pure fortuity that the Sparkses decided to develop their properties before the County completed these planned improvements. Had they delayed submitting their application for development permits until after the County was able to carry out its roadway improvement plan, the County, presumably, would have been required to obtain the necessary frontage by negotiation or by invoking its power of eminent domain. In either case, the affected property owners would have been compensated for their involuntary contribution to the public good. Unfortunately, under the majority's opinion, the County is rewarded for its delay, and the Sparkses are penalized for a mere happenstance of timing. The protections afforded by the due process clause of the Fifth Amendment to the United States Constitution should not hinge on such fortuities. . . .

NOTES AND QUESTIONS

1. *Defending dedications. Sparks* indicates the difficulties in defending dedications of land for roads and other facilities. Should it have been a defense to the exaction that the improvements to Empire Way were included in the county's comprehensive plan? See the article by Morgan et al., *supra.* Should planning for roadway improvements necessarily invalidate any exactions for such improvements? Is this the dissent's argument?

Compare *Amoco Oil Co. v. Village of Schaumburg*, 661 N.E.2d 380 (Ill. App. 1995), where the court invalidated the approval of a site plan for the razing and rebuilding of a gasoline station conditioned on dedications that would improve an adjacent congested intersection. The court said:

> Schaumburg attempted to expropriate over twenty percent (20%) of Amoco's property without a legitimate reason. In fact, the record is replete with evidence showing that the required dedication had little or no relationship to the anticipated impact of the proposed development. For example, in addition to the testimony cited by the circuit court, Kenneth Hemstreet also testified that Amoco's proposed improvements would have had no effect on the need to increase the number of lanes for both Golf and Roselle roads. In fact, according to Hemstreet, IDOT [the state transportation agency] recommended widening the streets notwithstanding the redevelopment of Amoco's property. [*Id.* at 388.]

See also *Isla Verde International Holdings, Inc. v. City of Camas*, 49 P.3d 867 (Wash. 2002) (30 percent "open space" set-aside condition invalidated under statute requiring demonstration of reasonable necessity "as a direct result of the proposed development," but requirement to provide secondary access road for emergency road vehicles not violative of substantive due process). In *J.C. Reeves Corp. v. Clackamas County*, 887 P.2d 360 (Ore. App. 1994), the landowner was required to provide surfacing, stormwater, curb and sidewalk improvements along an existing roadway. The court invalidated this requirement because the county did not make "the appropriate comparison . . . between the traffic and other effects of the subdivision and the subdivision frontage improvements that the county has required." *Id.* at 365. Merely stating the relationship between subdivision-generated traffic and the need for improvements is not enough.

2. *Future use and development.* In most subdivision dedication cases, the development that will occur on the subdivided land and its impact on the roadway system is clear. But that is not always the case. In *Hallmark Inns & Resorts, Inc. v. City of Lake Oswego*, 88 P.3d 284, 291–92 (Ore. App. 2004), the court held that, under *Nollan* and *Dolan*, a public pedestrian pathway dedication could be required based on use to which a building "may be put without *further applications* [for approval] *or development*" (emphasis in original).

> Hallmark's challenge is based on an artificially and erroneously restrictive view of potential development impacts to be considered in the "rough proportionality" calculus. Under *Dolan*, the temporal benchmark for determining "rough proportionality," including assessing development-related impacts, is at the time the condition is imposed — or very shortly thereafter. Given that, the inquiry is necessarily forward-looking; it properly considers reasonable projected impacts from permitted uses of the development, rather than being limited to impacts from a single permitted use. That is, "rough proportionality" is not restricted to considering the impacts of a single, particular use of the site when the development application, as approved, allows a *range* of uses reasonably generating a variety of impacts. [*Id.* (emphasis in original).]

The court distinguished *Schultz v. City of Grants Pass*, 884 P.2d 569 (Ore. App. 1994), in which the court reversed a city decision conditioning the partitioning of one lot into two with a requirement that the subdivider dedicate land for adjacent roadways because the dedication was based on a "worst-case scenario" that assumed the development of the tract to its "full development potential." See also *State by & Through Dep't of Transp. v. Altimus*, 905 P.2d 258 (Ore. App. 1995), holding in a condemnation case that the jury could consider the effect of a hypothetical dedication requirement on a condemnation award.

Goss v. City of Little Rock, 151 F.3d 861 (8th Cir. 1998), considered a similar problem when a dedication was attached to a rezoning. The court relied on the district court opinion to invalidate a rezoning to a commercial use district on condition that the landowner dedicate 22% of the land for the expansion of an adjacent roadway. The district court found that the nexus test was satisfied but not the rough proportionality test. It concluded that "Little Rock's assessment of the impact of rezoning was too speculative because that assessment was based on traffic that could, as said by the city's witness, 'conceivably' be generated at some unknown point in the future if a strip mall were erected on Goss's land, although there are no plans to build a strip mall on the property and there is no reason to expect one to be built." *Id.* at 863.

Note the difficulties this decision creates for municipalities. As Chapter 6 pointed out, an application for a rezoning amendment is an application for a zoning map change, not an application for a particular use or development. Is there a way out of this dilemma?

3. *Off-Site Exactions.* While many courts will uphold onsite dedications and improvements as reasonable, what about conditions that require a subdivider to construct offsite improvements? At least two recent decisions have struck down such exactions. As noted *supra*, in *St. Johns River Water Mgmt Dist. v. Koontz*, 5 So. 3d 8 (Fla. 2009), the court found no essential nexus under *Nollan* or any rough proportionality under *Dolan* for the District's requirement of offsite wetland mitigation work. In *Buttermilk Farms, LLC v. Planning & Zoning Comm'n of Plymouth*, 973 A.2d 64 (Conn. 2009), the court struck down a subdivision condition requiring the construction of a sidewalk adjacent to a proposed residential subdivision as exceeding the municipality's statutory authority. See also *Hillcrest Property, LLP v. Pasco County*, 2010 U.S. Dist. LEXIS 77563 (M.D. Fla., July 30, 2010) (challenging off-site road improvement requirement because need to widen road is not attributable to traffic generated by proposed development). But see *West Linn Corporate Park, LLC v. City of West Linn*, 240 P.3d 29 (Ore. 2010) (upholding condition of development that required construction of off-site road improvements under federal and state takings analysis).

[b.] Impact Fees

The Supreme Court's *Del Monte* decision seems to have held that impact fees are not subject to the *Dolan* rough proportionality test. In *Lingle*, reproduced *supra*, the Court did nothing to negate this impression, describing the *Dolan* rule as a requirement that was applied to "an adjudicative exaction requiring dedication of private property." 512 U.S. at 547. The Supreme Court of Washington so held in *City of Olympia v. Drebick*, 126 P.3d 802 (Wash. 2006) (rejecting application of *Dolan* to impact fees), as have other state courts.

Recently, the Supreme Court refused to consider the issue of whether impact fees are subject to the *Nollan/Dolan* tests in *Joy Builders, Inc. v. Town of Clarkstown*, 129 S. Ct. 2010 (2009). In *Joy Builders, Inc. v. Town of Clarkstown*, 864 N.Y.S.2d 86 (N.Y. App. 2008), the New York Supreme Court considered a challenge to Clarkstown's imposition of a fee in lieu of parkland dedication as a condition of subdivision approval of a cluster residential development. In upholding the fee, the New York court found that the planning board acted rationally when it assessed the fee, and that the board established an "essential nexus" between its recreational needs and the fee imposed and cited *Dolan* in support of its analysis. The New York Court of Appeals dismissed the petitioners' appeal, finding that no substantial constitutional question was directly involved. The petitioner then filed a writ of certiorari with the United States Supreme Court, arguing that the Town had violated the doctrine of unconstitutional conditions and that there was a split in the courts as to whether monetary payments are subject to the *Nollan/Dolan* tests. The Supreme Court denied certiorari, leaving this question unanswered.

Because of the lack of any definitive statement from the Supreme Court on this issue, other state courts have concluded that the logic of *Dolan* indicates that it should be applicable to impact fees. *Town of Flower Mound v. Stafford Estates Limited Partnership*, 135 S.W.3d 620, 635–42 (Tex. 2004) (*Dolan* standard applies to both dedicatory and non-dedicatory exactions, such as requirement to rebuild abutting public road); *Home Builders Ass'n v. City of Beavercreek*, 729 N.E.2d 349, 354–56 (Ohio 2000) (impact fee to partially fund new road projects must meet *Dolan* standard); *Ehrlich v. City of Culver City*, 911 P.2d 429, 438–439 (Cal. 1996) ($280,000 fee in lieu of construction of public tennis courts held a taking under *Dolan*); *Northern Ill. Home Builders Ass'n v. County of DuPage*, 649 N.E.2d 384, 388–89 (Ill. 1995) (applying state standard stricter than *Dolan* to road improvement impact fees).

In *Flower Mound*, the Supreme Court of Texas reasoned as follows:

The town argues that if non-dedicatory exactions are subject to the *Dolan* standard, "Texas cities will be forced to run a fierce constitutional gauntlet that will significantly erode the practical ability of cities to regulate land development to promote the public interest and protect community rights." But we are unable to see any reason why limiting a government exaction from a developer to something roughly proportional to the impact of the development — in other words, prohibiting " 'an out-and-out plan of extortion' " — will bring down the government. Pressed to defend this assertion at oral argument, counsel for the Town argued that the real problem with the "rough proportionality" standard is not the standard itself; after all, the government can hardly argue that it is entitled to exact more from developers than is reasonably due to the impact of development. The real problem, the Town argues, is that the validity of an exaction in an individual case is not presumed but must be shown by the government. We are unable to see why this burden is unduly onerous. Rather, we think the burden is essential to protect against the government's unfairly leveraging its police power over land use regulation to extract from landowners concessions and benefits to which it is not entitled. To repeat *Dolan*: "No precise mathematical calculation is required, but the city must make some sort of individualized determination that the required dedication is related both in nature and extent to the impact of the proposed development." 512 U.S 374, 391.

Finally, the Town argues that if the *Dolan* standard applies to non-dedicatory exactions, then it must "apply to *all* development requirements, including that houses be built of brick rather than of wood, and of a certain size on a certain sized lot, since these are all conditions placed on the ability to develop land." Clearly, the cited examples of routine regulatory requirements do not come close to the exaction imposed by the Town in this case. There may be other requirements that do. Determining when a regulation becomes a taking has not lent itself to bright line-drawing. But we are satisfied that the distinction between exactions and other types of regulatory requirements is meaningful and necessary.

We agree with the Supreme Court of California's decision in *Ehrlich.* For purposes of determining whether an exaction as a condition of government approval of development is a compensable taking, we see no important distinction between a dedication of property to the public and a requirement that property already owned by the public be improved. The *Dolan* standard should apply to both. [*Id.* at 639–40.]

NOTES AND QUESTIONS

1. *Ehrlich and other cases.* In *Ehrlich v. City of Culver City*, 911 P.2d 429 (Cal. 1996), after the plaintiff demolished a private recreational facility, the city approved an office building on the site subject to a condition that the plaintiff pay a recreational mitigation fee to be used for additional recreational facilities to replace those lost when the plaintiff demolished the facility. The city also required payment of an "art in public places" fee. The fees were challenged under California's Mitigation Fee Act (Act) (Cal. Gov't. Code §§ 66000-66003) which established a statutory standard of "reasonable relationship" to determine the validity of a proposed exaction. Concluding that the heightened scrutiny of *Nollan* and *Dolan* applies to regulatory "leveraging" (attaching a condition that may not be related to the particular development proposal), the court concluded that the Act's "reasonable relationship" standard "should be construed in light of *Dolan's* 'rough proportionality' test." *Id.* at 437.

The court held the discontinuance of a private use could have significant impacts justifying a monetary exaction to alleviate it. It also held the city's findings on the relationship between the monetary exaction and the withdrawal of land restrictively zoned for private recreational use satisfied the nexus test, but it remanded the case because the record did not support the amount of the fee required. That fee should be based on the loss of land reserved for recreational use, not the loss of plaintiff's facilities, which were privately owned. The court upheld the "art in public places" fee because "[t]he requirement of providing art in an area of the project reasonably accessible to the public is, like other design and landscaping requirements, a kind of aesthetic control well within the authority of the city to impose." *Id.* at 450.

In *Benchmark v. City of Battleground*, 972 P.2d 944 (Wash. App. 2000), *aff'd on other grounds*, 49 P.3d 860 (Wash. 2002), the court applied the *Nollan* and *Dolan* tests, both before and after *Del Monte Dunes*, to a permit condition requiring a development company to make half-street improvements to a street adjoining its project. Prior to *Del Monte Dunes*, the court invalidated the condition because the city failed to meet *Dolan*'s "rough proportionality" standard. Following *Del Monte Dunes*, the court refused to reconsider, citing the "similarity of exacting land and money."

> If the government in *Nollan and Dolan* had exacted money rather than land and then purchased land to solve the problems, the same question would arise: was the money exacted for and used to solve a problem connected to the proposed development? (*Nollan*) and was the amount of money exacted roughly proportional to the development's impact on the problem? (*Dolan*). [14 P.3d at 175.]

A case cited with approval in *Flower Mound* applied the *Dolan* test to uphold an impact fee for roadway improvements, but described this test as a "reasonable relationship" test and did not discuss the *Del Monte* decision. *Home Builders Ass'n of Dayton v. City of Beavercreek*, 729 N.E.2d 349 (Ohio 2000). The fee was based on an accepted methodology similar to that described in the Morgan article, *supra*. The court held the choice of methodology was primarily for the local legislature and said "a court must only determine whether the methodology used is reasonable based on the evidence presented." It then held that the decision of the trial court, which had upheld the fee, was supported by sufficient evidence in the record. The impact was contained in an ordinance, but the court did not indicate whether this qualified as a legislative action. See also *Home Builders Association of Central Arizona v. City of Goodyear*, 221 P.3d 384 (Az. App. 2009) (applying rough proportionality test to impact fees).

2. *Park and school fees.* Impact fees for parks and schools can present a more serious problem because these facilities are used by both new and old residents, and facility needs created by new developments are more difficult to identify. If the fee is not earmarked for projected needs created by new development, a court may hold it invalid. See *Weber Basin Home Bldrs. Ass'n v. Roy City*, 487 P.2d 866 (Utah 1971) (proceeds of building permit fee went into city's general fund).

In *St. John's County v. Northeast Florida Builders Ass'n*, 583 So. 2d 635 (Fla. 1991), decided after *Nollan*, the court upheld an impact fee for new schools levied on new residential development. The court required a showing of a rational nexus between the need for new schools and the population growth the subdivision generated, and between the expenditure of the fees and the benefits accruing to the subdivision. To satisfy this requirement, funds had to be earmarked to benefit residents of the subdivisions where fees would be collected. The court rejected a claim that the fee was invalid because it would be collected for homes that would never have school children. Is the fee valid after *Dolan*? Contra, *West Park Ave., Inc. v. Ocean*

Twp., 224 A.2d 1, 3–4 (N.J. 1966) (schools traditionally are the responsibility of the entire community, including undeveloped land taxed in prior years).

In *Twin Lakes Dev. Corp. v. Town of Monroe*, 801 N.E.2d 821 (N.Y. 2003), the New York Court of Appeals applied *Nollan/Dolan* to uphold a $1,500 per-lot recreation fee. The Town established an "essential nexus" through "explicit findings" of increased demand for recreational facilities, current capacity being exceeded, continued subdivision development and "upward-spiraling land costs." The "individualized consideration" standard of *Dolan* was evidenced by the town's finding that "the lot area and ownership patterns do not suit it to the development of a park suitable to meet the requirements of the site." *Id.* at 825. See also *Home Builders Assoc. of Metro. Portland v. City of West Linn*, 131 P.3d 805, 814 (Ore. 2006) (statutorily authorized park and recreation fee imposed on new developments does not effect a taking); but c.f., *Greater Franklin Developers Assoc. Inc. v. Town of Franklin*, 738 N.E.2d 750 (Mass. App. 2000) (invalidating school impact fee as an unconstitutional tax).

3. *Equalizing relative tax burdens.* For an elaborate test that requires municipalities to equalize the relative tax burdens borne by new and existing properties, see *Banberry Dev. Corp. v. South Jordan City*, 631 P.2d 899 (Utah 1981), applied and explained in *Home Builders Ass'n v. City of American Fork*, 973 P.2d 425 (Utah 1999). The test is based on an article by Professor Ellickson, *Suburban Growth Controls: An Economic and Legal Analysis*, 86 Yale L.J. 385 (1977), who argues that "if a municipality mixes special and general revenues in financing a service, the portion financed by general revenues should presumptively be distributed equally per dwelling unit." *Id.* at 460.

Could a state statute or municipal ordinance provide that the municipal contribution to facilities such as sewers should in no case be excessive, and authorize an appropriate increase in developer contributions on a case-by-case basis to avoid excessive municipal contributions? See *Land/Vest Properties, Inc. v. Town of Plainfield*, 379 A.2d 200 (N.H. 1977) (applying statute enacting this requirement). For a similar approach to park and recreation facilities, see *Home Builders Association of Metro. Portland, supra.*

4. *How to do it right.* Morgan et al., *supra*, provide a method for calculating an impact fee for roadways that meets the rough proportionality test. The objective is to measure "the consumption of vehicular capacity of the municipality's thoroughfare system by a particular development, and [convert] this demand into dollars." The first step is to determine the type of roads to be included in the network used to simulate travel demand. Total travel on the road network associated with the new development must then be estimated. This is a two-part determination involving trip generation and trip length.

"The roadway capacity consumed by a new development is the number of trips generated during a selected time period multiplied by the average trip length." The next step is to determine the value of the road capacity consumed by the proposed development. Dividing the cost of the roadway by its carrying capacity provides an average cost per thoroughfare mile-trip. This average cost is then multiplied by the number of thoroughfare mile-trips the development will generate.

The final step is to establish a value for the developer's contributions of land and facilities that are required as an exaction. The municipality can demand the exaction in full if the cost of providing the facility is equal to or greater than the value of the exaction. Morgan, at 37–38. Notice that this method requires a case-by-case adjudication of each exaction, although it would seem that an ordinance should establish the criteria for making these determinations.

How does this method fit under the *Dolan* rules? See generally Dahtastrom, *Development Impact Fees: A Review of Contemporary Techniques for Calculation, Data Collection and Documentation*, 15 N. Ill. L. Rev. 557 (1995) (emphasizing the importance of designing development impact fees that are "demand sensitive, cost sensitive, and revenue sensitive"). See also Bowles & Nelson, Impact Fees: Equity and Housing Affordability: A Guidebook for Practitioners 42-69 (2007), recommending a "persons per 1,000 square feet" standard for residential impact fees rather than a flat fee, along with a range of credits and exemptions to foster housing affordability; Callies & Sonoda, *Providing Infrastructure for Smart Growth: Land Development Conditions*, 43 Idaho L. Rev. 351, 380-407 (2007) (recommending use of land development agreements to resolve exaction issues); Pindell, *Developing Law Vegas: Creating Inclusionary Affordable Housing Requirements in Development Agreements*, 42 Wake Forest L. Rev. 419 (2007) (advocating use of developments agreements as a mechanism for including affordable housing within the "infrastructure" of a municipality).

5. *Local legislation on impact fees.* Highland Park, Illinois has enacted a comprehensive Development Impact Fee Ordinance (Chapter 160 of the City Code). The ordinance establishes procedures for the calculation, collection, maintenance and disbursement of development impact fees imposed on new residential developments to finance school, park and library site and capital improvements. Triennial needs assessment studies, which serve as the foundation for land acquisition and capital facilities plans, must be prepared.

The ordinance includes specific formulae for calculating development impact fees for school sites and their capital improvements, park sites and their capital improvements, and library capital improvements, as well as a ten percent credit for each capital improvement impact fee to account for future property tax payments and state financial aid expected to be received. The basic formula established by the ordinance is 1) the number of people (libraries and parks) or students (schools) expected to be generated by the residential development, 2) times the capital costs per resident (libraries and parks) or per student (schools) for the respective facilities as determined by the approximate triennial needs assessment, 3) adjusted for the appropriate capital improvement credit.

A Model Impact Fee Bylaw prepared for the towns of Barnstable County, Massachusetts by the Cape Cod Commission, available at capecodcommission.org/bylaws/impactfee.htm, contains the following caution:

> There are two basic rules of thumb in determining impact fees: (1) be conservative in your assumption and numbers; and (2) keep the methodology clear. Your impact fee system must be fair and reasonable. Fees are set by establishing the costs of providing capital facilities to new development and subtracting system-wide credits and then dividing these costs among expected new development based upon type of land use. . . . Most communities apply an across the board discount after calculating reasonable fees. However, be aware that significantly undercharging fees may result in a failure to acquire sufficient funds to complete the capital facility. In such a case the town may have to refund monies collected through the impact fee system. [Model Bylaw, § 06.0.]

Do these approaches comply with the *Dolan* rules?

Timing of Collection. Also significant is when during the development process a local governmental body may collect an impact fee. Cal. Gov't Code § 66007 permits local agencies to collect impact fees, except school impact fees, at the time of final inspection or issuance of a certificate of occupancy, whichever is first. The law was amended on August 1, 2008, to authorize the deferral of impact fee collection beyond the traditional time for collection (during the building permit process) in order to relieve developers of the burden of paying the impact fees and then suffering cancellations and other uncertainties during difficult economic times.

See also Raintree Homes, Inc. v. Village of Long Grove, 906 N.E.2d 751 (Ill. App. 2009), holding that the Village had abused its powers by requiring impact fees to be paid at the time that building permits were issued for residential units. Raintree Homes paid impact fees for ten years to the Village, without a formal protest. It then filed a lawsuit to invalidate the fees. The impact fees, over a period of time, increased from $4,300.00 to $7,300.00 per building permit. The court found that the fees were improper because they were collected at the time of building permit, and not at subdivision approval as authorized by state statute, and entered a judgment in the builder's favor in the amount of $114,700.00. In addition, the appellate court found that the impact fees were improperly used to pay for school district operations rather than to acquire land and that the bulk of the park fees went to the Village rather than to the park district. The court further found that the way in which Long Grove had been charging these fees and using the funds did not comply with the "specifically and uniquely-attributable" test required under Illinois' constitutional standard. The Village's appeal of the appellate court's decision was denied by the Illinois Supreme Court in 973 A.2d 64 (2009).

Refund of Unspent Fees. Some local ordinances require impact fees to be expended within a certain period of time — if they are not spent, they must be refunded to the owner. For example, West Virginia authorizes a developer to apply for a refund of impact fees that have not been spent within six years from the date of collection. W. Va. Code. § 7-20-9. See also *Anne Arundel County v. Halle Dev., Inc.* 971 A.2d 214 (Md. 2009). The Anne Arundel County ordinance provided that if fees "have not been expended or encumbered by the end of the sixth fiscal year following collection," the county must publish notice of the availability of a refund within 60 days of the end of the fiscal year. The court found that the county did not properly use $4,719,359.00 in fees collected between 1988 and 1996, and that eligible owners could sue to recover the unexpended fees. The court also struck down the publication notice as inadequate because the current owners that would be eligible for the fees were likely not the same owners who paid the fees and would have little reason to understand the significance of the published notice.

6. *Sources.* See, e.g., Bowles & Nelson, Impact Fees: Equity and Housing Affordability: A Guidebook for Practitioners (2007); Exactions, Impact Fees and Dedications (R. Freilich & D. Bushek eds., 1995); Private Supply of Public Services (R. Alterman ed., 1988); Callies & Sonoda, *Providing Infrastructure for Smart Growth: Land Development Conditions*, 43 Idaho L. Rev. 351 (2007); Reynolds & Ball, *Exactions and the Privatization of the Public Sphere*, 21 J. L. & Pol. 451 (2005); Reynolds, *Taxes, Fees, Assessment, Dues, and the "Get What You Pay For" Model of Local Government*, 56 Fla. L. Rev. 373 (2004); Stroud, *Development Exactions and Regulatory Takings — Do Monetary and Legislative Exactions Get Less Takings Clause Scrutiny than Real Property and Ad Hoc Exactions?* ALI-ABA Cont. Leg. Ed. (April 22–24, 2004); Breemer, *The Evolution of the "Essential Nexus": How State and Federal Courts Have Applied Nollan and Dolan and Where They Should Go From Here*, 59 Wash. & Lee L. Rev. 373 (2002); Saxer, *Planning Gain, Exaction, and Impact Fees: A Comparative Study of Planning Law in England, Wales, and the United States*, 32 Urb. Law. 21 (2000); Reznick, Note, *The Death of Nollan and Dolan? Challenging the Constitutionality of Monetary Exactions in the Wake of Lingle v. Chevron*, 87 B.U. L. Rev. 725 (2007); Kent, *Theoretical Tension and Doctrinal Discord: Analyzing Development Impact Fees as Takings*, 51 W.M. L. Rev. 1833 (2010).

As the following case discusses, arguments are often made that impact fees are taxes and that communities may not levy them because there is no statutory authority for a tax of this type.

THE DREES COMPANY v. HAMILTON TOWNSHIP, OHIO

2010 Ohio 3473, 2010 Ohio App. LEXIS 2939 (Ohio App. 2010)

POWELL, P.J.

Plaintiffs-appellants, The Drees Company, Fischer Single Family Homes II, LLC, John Henry Homes, Inc., Charleston Signature Homes, LLC, and the Home Builders Association of Greater Cincinnati (collectively, Builders), appeal from the decision of the Warren County Court of Common Pleas granting summary judgment in favor of defendants-appellees, Hamilton Township, Ohio, Hamilton Township Board of Trustees, Becky Ehling, Trustee, Michael Munoz, Trustee, and O.T. Bishop, Trustee (collectively, the Township), in a case regarding the authority of the Township to impose "impact fees" upon anyone who applies for a zoning certificate for new construction or redevelopment within its unincorporated areas. For the reasons outlined below, we affirm. . . .

On May 2, 2007, the Hamilton Township Board of Trustees passed Amended Resolution No. 200722120418, entitled "Amended Resolution Implementing Impact Fees Within Unincorporated Areas of Hamilton Township, Ohio for Roads, Fire and Police, and Parks," that established a fee schedule charged to anyone who applied for a zoning certificate for new construction or redevelopment within the Township's unincorporated areas. As the title indicates, the resolution includes four fee categories: a road impact fee, a fire protection impact fee, a police protection impact fee, and a park impact fee. The sum of these four fees, which varies based on the intended land use, make up the total impact fee charged to the applicant on a per unit basis and are charged as follows:

Land Use Type	Unit	Road	Fire	Police	Park	Total
Single family Detached	Dwelling	$3,964	$335	$206	$1,648	$6,153
Multi-Family	Dwelling	$2,782	$187	$115	$921	$4,005
Hotel/Motel	Room	$2,857	$160	$98	$0	$3,115
Retail/Commercial	1,000 sq. ft.	$7,265	$432	$265	$0	$7,962
Office/Institutional	1,000 sq. ft.	$4,562	$244	$150	$0	$4,956
Industrial	1,000 sq. ft.	$3,512	$153	$94	$0	$3,759
Warehouse	1,000 sq. ft.	$2,503	$97	$60	$0	$2,660
Church	1,000 sq. ft.	$2,797	$91	$56	$0	$2,944
School	1,000 sq. ft.	$3,237	$138	$85	$0	$3,460
Nursing Home	1,000 sq. ft.	$1,871	$244	$150	$0	$2,265
Hospital	1,000 sq. ft.	$7,212	$244	$150	$0	$7,606

Each of the collected fees, which are assessed "to offset increased services and improvements needed because of the development," and which must be paid before a zoning certificate will be issued, are kept in separate accounts apart from the Township's general fund. Once collected, the fees are to be used "to benefit the property by providing the Township with adequate funds to provide the same level of service to that property that the Township currently affords previously developed properties." If the fees are not spent on projects initiated within three years of their collection date, the fees are to be refunded with interest. The resolution also defines a list of projects exempt from payment and creates an extensive system of credits.

In the fall of 2007, The Drees Company, Fischer Single Family Homes II, John Henry Homes, and Charleston Signature Homes, applied for a zoning certificate with the Township, were assessed the applicable "impact fee," and paid the charge under protest. After the zoning applications were approved, Builders filed a complaint against the Township seeking injunctive relief, declaratory judgment, and damages. Builders and the Township then filed crossmotions for summary judgment. After holding a hearing on the matter, the trial court granted summary judgment in favor of the Township. . . .

Initially, Builders argue that the trial court erred by granting summary judgment to the Township because the "impact fees are really taxes" that are "not authorized by any Revised Code provision governing taxes or special assessments a township can impose." . . . In support of their claim, Builders argue that the charges are taxes because they "are intended to be spent on public infrastructure unassociated with the development, as a means to benefit the public broadly," that "the benefit is not targeted to the fee payer," and that "it is easy to envision that a property for which an impact fee is paid may never see an improvement that directly benefits it, even if every impact fee dollar is spent." However, while it may be true that money generated through taxes is "expended for the equal benefit of all the people," Builders' claim flies in the face of the parties' stipulated facts, which state, in pertinent part:

> "The purpose of the impact fee is to benefit *the property* by providing the Township with adequate funds to provide the same level of service to *that property* that the Township currently affords previously developed properties." (Emphasis added.)

To quote Builders, "[i]n order to be classified as a fee, a charge must specially benefit the property that pays the fee." Based on the parties stipulated facts, that is exactly what occurs here; namely, a payment to the Township to obtain a zoning certificate in order to build on property within its unincorporated areas so that "*that property*" can receive the same level of service provided to previously developed properties. By stipulating to these facts, Builders are now bound by their agreement. . . .

Furthermore, the collected charges are never placed in the Township's general fund, but instead, separated into individual funds to be used only for narrow and specific purposes occasioned by the Township's ever-expanding population growth. In addition, the collected charges are refunded if not spent on projects initiated within three years of their collection date. These factors, when taken together, indicate that the charges imposed by the Township are fees paid in return for the services it provides. Therefore, after a thorough review of the record, and based on the narrow and confined facts of this case, we find the charges imposed upon all applicants seeking a zoning certificate for new construction or redevelopment within the Township's unincorporated areas function not as a tax, but as a fee.

Accordingly, because the collected charges are fees, Builders' first argument is overruled.

[The discussion of counts II and III is omitted]

In light of the foregoing, we find no error in the trial court's decision granting summary judgment to the Township. Builders' sole assignment of error is overruled.

Judgment affirmed.

Ringland and Hendrickson, JJ., concur.

NOTES AND QUESTIONS

1. *Fee vs. tax.* In *Drees*, the analysis of whether the collected charges were fees or illegal taxes turned on three factors: (1) whether the charges were segregated from general funds; (2) whether the charges were refunded if not expended within a set period of time; and (3) whether the charges benefited the development that is the subject of the charge. Which factor was most important to the *Drees* court? Do you agree that the challenged impact fee was collected solely for the benefit of the development? Does it matter that the fees would benefit all township residents, not just the new property owners?

In *Hillis Homes, Inc. v. Snohomish County*, 650 P.2d 193 (Wash. 1982), two counties levied fees for waste disposal facilities, parks, roads, and sheriff's services. The court held that the characterization of the fees would turn on their primary purpose. The fees would not be taxes if they were "merely tools in the regulation of land subdivision." They would be taxes if their primary purpose was to raise money. The court held that "[t]here can be no question" that the primary purpose of the fees was to raise revenue. The fees were clearly "to be applied to offset the costs of providing specified services." No provision was made for regulating residential development. *Id.* at 195-96. Accord *Country Joe, Inc. v. City of Eagan*, 560 N.W.2d 681 (Minn. 1997). Contra, *Contractors & Builders Ass'n v. City of Dunedin*, 329 So. 2d 314 (Fla. 1976).

Is this reasoning in *Hillis Homes* helpful? Can you provide an alternative test for determining when an impact fee is a tax? Courts will also find that a fee is a tax if it produces revenue in excess of the reasonable costs of providing the services or facilities for which the fee is levied. See *Building Indus. Ass'n v. City of Oxnard*, 198 Cal. Rptr. 63 (Cal. App. 1984) (applying this reasoning to "growth requirement development fee" levied as 2.8 percent of building valuation of development). See also *J.W. Jones Cos. v. City of San Diego*, 203 Cal. Rptr. 580 (Cal. App. 1984) (upholding a facilities benefit assessment (FBA) on undeveloped property in growth areas. Though some of the facilities were remote, the FBA was levied in proportion to benefit). Washington has since enacted legislation authorizing impact fees. Wash. Rev. Code § 82.02.020, noted in *Ivy Club Investors Ltd Partnership v. City of Kennewick*, 699 P.2d 782, 785 (Wash. App. 1985); Comment, *Subdivision Exactions in Washington: The Controversy Over Imposing Fees on Developers*, 59 Wash. L. Rev. 289 (1984).

In *Richmond v. Shasta Comm. Services Dist.*, 83 P.3d 518 (Cal. 2004), the Supreme Court of California held that a capacity charge imposed as a condition for a new connection to a water system was not an assessment within the meaning of a constitutional amendment (article XIII D) requiring voter approval because it was not imposed "on identifiable parcels, but only on individuals who request a new service connection." *Id.* at 523. The court also concluded that while the capacity charge at issue was "similar to a development fee in being imposed only in response to a property owner's voluntary application to a public entity, . . . it is different in that the application may be only for a water service connection without necessarily involving any development of the property. . . . The capacity charge is neither an assessment nor a development fee under article XIII D." *Id.* at 527. Finally, the court concluded that a fire suppression charge contained in the connection fee was not a charge for general government services prohibited by article XIII D because "it results from the owner's voluntary decision to apply for [a new] connection" rather than being "imposed 'as an incident of property ownership.' " *Id.* at 528. For a review of the fee vs. tax classification issue, see Rosenberg, 59 SMU L. Rev., at 249–53.

2. *The tax option.* When statutory authority is present, a municipality can levy an impact fee for new facilities as a tax. The tax is then subject to the relaxed equal protection rules applied to non-property taxes. See *Cherry Hills Farms v. City of Cherry Hills*, 670 P.2d 779 (Colo. 1983) (service-expansion fee held to be excise tax); *Oregon State Homebuilders Ass'n v. City of Tigard*, 604 P.2d 886 (Or. App. 1979) (system development charge held to be tax reasonably related to cost of providing new services); *Paul L. Smith, Inc. v. Southern York County School Dist.*, 403 A.2d 1034 (Pa. Commw. 1979) (school privilege tax). If all this sounds too easy, keep in mind that municipal power to levy taxes is limited in many states. See *Rancho Colorado, Inc. v. City of Broomfield*, 586 P.2d 659 (Colo. 1978) (service-expansion fee held not to be valid occupation tax); Etahier & Weiss, *Development Excise Taxes: An Exercise in Cleverness and Imagination*, 42 Land Use L. & Zoning Dig., Feb. 1990, at 3.

A NOTE ON STATUTORY AUTHORITY FOR DEDICATIONS, IN-LIEU FEES AND IMPACT FEES

The statutory authority problem. The Standard Planning Act did not authorize the imposition of dedications or in-lieu fees in subdivision control, and this led some courts to hold there was no statutory authority to impose dedications. *Hylton Enters. v. Board of Supvrs.*, 258 S.E.2d 577 (Va. 1979). Other courts held to the contrary, *Divan Bldrs., Inc. v. Planning Bd.*, 334 A.2d 30 (N.J. 1975) (fee for off-site improvements), and some found the authority to require dedication in constitutional home rule powers, *City of College Station v. Turtle Rock Corp.*, 680 S.W.2d 802 (Tex. 1984).

The problem of finding sufficient authority for impact fees can also be troubling. See *Mayor & Bd. of Aldermen, City of Ocean Springs v. Homebuilders Ass'n of Miss., Inc.*, 932 So. 2d 44, 51–59 (Miss. 2006) (impact fee invalidated as illegal tax because not authorized by constitution or statute, reviewing statutes and cases); *Amherst Builders Ass'n v. City of Amherst*, 402 N.E.2d 1181 (Ohio 1980) (home rule powers confer authority to levy impact fee). Failure to comply with enabling legislation can lead to invalidation. See *Simonsen v. Town of Derry*, 765 A.2d 1033 (N.H. 2000); *Southern Nevada Homebuilders Association v. City of North Las Vegas*, 913 P.2d 1276, 1278–79 (Nev. 1996) (statutory definition of "capital improvements" does not include fee for fire and emergency medical services). Local impact fees may also be preempted by conflicting legislation authorizing the funding of public facilities. See *Albany Area Builders Ass'n v. Town of Guilderland*, 546 N.E.2d 920 (N.Y. 1989) (local transportation impact fee preempted by state highway funding law).

Fees in lieu of dedications also fall under attack as taxes not authorized by state legislation. See *Haugen v. Gleason*, 359 P.2d 108 (Or. 1961) (unauthorized tax because fees not earmarked for benefit of subdivision). In *Jenad, Inc. v. Scarsdale*, 218 N.E.2d 673 (N.Y. 1966), the court stated that fees in lieu of dedication are not taxes but are "fees imposed on the transaction of obtaining plat approval." *Id.* at 676. In *Jenad*, the fees were earmarked for park purposes but not for use within the contributing subdivision. Contra *Town of Longboat Key v. Lands End, Ltd.*, 433 So. 2d 574 (Fla. App. 1983) (in-lieu fee held a tax because not earmarked for benefit of subdivision).

Statutory authority. To resolve the statutory problem, several states have authorized dedications and in-lieu fees. E.g., Colo. Rev. Stat. § 30-28-133(4)(a) (park and school sites or fees reasonably necessary to serve subdivision); 65 ILCS § 5/11-12-5 (Illinois statute authorizes school and park in-lieu fees).

Just over half the states have also adopted legislation authorizing impact fees, and this legislation has become a major factor in the use of these fees and in litigation. Some of this legislation is brief, and merely contains enabling authority, but most of the laws contain elaborate requirements for impact fee programs. These may include the preparation of a capital improvements plan, detailed accounting requirements and time limits on the expenditure of fees collected. These statutes often codify the constitutional nexus test. See *Homebuilder's Ass'n of Central Arizona v. City of Scottsdale*, 930 P.2d 993 (Ariz. 1997); *F & W Assocs. v. County of Somerset*, 648 A.2d 482 (N.J. App. 1994) (applying a statutory rational nexus test to uphold a traffic impact fee based on trip generation studies that determined each developer's share of needed traffic improvements in the township).

The California legislation, which is typical, applies to fees imposed on "development projects," authorizes the preparation of a capital improvement plan and requires the identification of the purpose of the fee, which may refer to the plan. The municipality must find a "reasonable relationship" between the need for the public facility and the type of development project on which the fee is imposed. The fee must not exceed the reasonable cost of establishing the facility. Special accounting is required, and fees must be spent for the project for which they are collected. Unspent fees not properly accounted for must be returned to developers. Cal. Gov't Code §§ 66000-66008. The statute expressly states that its purpose is to codify existing "constitutional and decisional law." *Id.* § 66005. The type of development fees that can be charged pursuant to statutory authority is broad, provided the local government follows the statutory requirements. See *Homebuilders Ass'n of Tulare/Kern County, Inc. v. City of Lemoore*, 112 Cal. Rptr. 3d 7 (2010) (upholding fees for police equipment, garbage trucks, and a naval air museum).

Texas also has an elaborate impact fee statute. Tex. Local Gov't Code Ann. §§ 395.001-395.081. The statute enacts the nexus test by authorizing impact fees "to generate revenue for funding or recouping the costs of capital improvements or facility expansions necessitated by and attributable to . . . new development." § 395.001(4). Detailed provisions are included for calculating and assessing the fee. Before it can levy a fee, a local government must adopt findings on "land use assumptions," which are "a description of the service area and projections of changes in land uses, densities, intensities, and population in the service area over at least a 10-year period." §§ 395.001(5); 395.045. Why do you suppose the statute contains this requirement?

For additional legislation, see Ga. Code Ann. § 36-71-1 to § 36-71-13; Haw. Rev. Stat. § 46-141 to § 46-148; Me. Rev. Stat. tit. 30-A, § 4354; Rhode Island G.L. 1956, § 45-22.4; Wash. Rev. Code § 82.02.050. Some statutes exempt affordable housing from impact fees. Wash. Rev. Code § 82.02.060. Is this justified?

Here is a typical statutory statement of the standard for levying impact fees:

> County governments affected by the construction of new development projects are hereby authorized to require the payment of fees for any new development projects constructed therein in the event any costs associated with capital improvements or the provision of other services are attributable to such project. Such fees shall not exceed a proportionate share of such costs required to accommodate any such new development. Before requiring payment of any fee authorized hereunder, it must be evident that some reasonable benefit from any such capital improvements will be realized by any such development project. [W. Va. Code § 7-20-4.]

For discussion of impact fee legislation, see Rosenberg, *The Changing Culture of American Land Use Regulation: Paying for Growth With Impact Fees, supra*, 59 SMU L. Rev., at 245-49; Leitner & Schoettle, *A Survey of State Impact Fee Enabling Legislation*, 25 Urb. Law. 491 (1993); Blaesser & Kentopp, *Impact Fees: The "Second Generation,"* 38 Wash. U.J. Urb. & Contemp. L. 55 (1990). For suggested statutory language authorizing exactions and impact fees, see American Planning Association, Growing Smart Legislative Guidebook: Model Statutes for Planning and Management of Change §§ 8-601 & 8-602. For general information about impact fees, see Growth & Infrastructure Consortium, www.growthandinfrastructure-.org.

A NOTE ON OFFICE-HOUSING LINKAGE PROGRAMS

What they are. A number of cities have adopted exaction programs requiring office developers either to construct low- or moderate-income housing or pay an in-lieu fee to the city to be used for the construction of such housing. The programs are based on the assumption that new office space creates new jobs that attract new office workers who create pressures on the housing market. Programs in Boston and San Francisco are leading examples. These programs can be mandatory whenever a new office development is built, or can apply only when a developer requests a discretionary approval, such as a variance or special use. For discussion of the San Francisco program, see Goetz, *Office-Housing Linkage in San Francisco*, 55 J. Am. Plan. Ass'n 66 (1989). The program has produced a substantial number of affordable housing units.

Authority to adopt. San Francisco relied on powers derived from a municipal code section that gives the planning commission discretion to grant or deny permits. Share & Diamond, *San Francisco's Office-Housing Production Program*, 35 Land Use L. & Zoning Dig., Oct. 1983 at 4, 6. After *Bonan v. City of Boston*, 496 N.E.2d 640 (Mass. 1986), suggested the need for legislation to authorize the Boston program, the legislature passed enabling legislation specifically authorizing the program as it then existed. Mass. Gen. Laws ch. 665, §§ 15-20.

For an unusual resolution of the statutory authority issue, see *Holmdel Bldrs. Ass'n v. Township of Holmdel*, 583 A.2d 277 (N.J. 1990). Although there was no explicit state legislative authorization, the court held that approval of housing impact fees was implicit in the state's authorization to adopt inclusionary zoning ordinances. Before fees could actually be collected, however, it required that implementing regulations be adopted by the state's affordable housing agency.

However, in *San Telmo Assocs. v. City of Seattle*, 735 P.2d 673 (Wash. 1987), a city ordinance required owners of low-income housing who demolish it to convert the property to nonresidential use, give the current tenants relocation notices and assistance, and replace a specified percentage of the low-income housing with other suitable housing. The owner could contribute to a low-income housing replacement fund in lieu of providing replacement housing. The court held that the low-income housing requirements were an unauthorized tax:

> Quite simply, the municipal body cannot shift the social costs of development on to a developer under the guise of a regulation. Such cost shifting is a tax, and absent specific legislative pronouncement, the tax is impermissible and invalid. [*Id.* at 675.]

See also *Nunziato v. Planning Bd.*, 541 A.2d 1105 (N.J. App. Div. 1988), invalidating a developer's contribution for affordable housing in return for site plan approval of an office building. It held the board's action was arbitrary and capricious because the contribution was made to induce approval of the building. Without legislative standards, the possibilities for abuse in this situation were unlimited, and the free-wheeling dealing in this case was grossly inimical to sound land use regulation.

Is it an exaction? This question is moot if impact fees do not fall under *Dolan*, as *Del Monte Dunes* seems to hold. But see *Flower Mound*, discussed *supra*, in which the Texas Supreme Court concluded that *Del Monte Dunes* merely "elaborate[s] on the same distinction drawn in *Dolan* between conditions limiting the use of property and those requiring a dedication of property." 135 S.W.3d at 636. Otherwise, the tests for exactions apply. In the *San Telmo* case, *supra*, the court said:

> [T]he City may not constitutionally pass on the social costs of the development of the downtown Seattle area to current owners of low income housing. The problem must be shared by the entire city, and those who plan to develop their property from low income housing to other uses cannot be penalized by being required to provide more housing. [*Id.* at 675.]

The court also suggested the ordinance would be a taking of property because the developer would have to build a new, comparable housing project or contribute approximately $1.5 million to the low-income housing fund. The court seriously questioned whether that levy would allow the developer to make a profitable use of its property. See *Sintra, Inc. v. City of Seattle (II)*, 935 P.2d 555 (Wash. 1997) (taking found on remand).

However, in *Commercial Bldrs. of Northern California v. City of Sacramento*, 941 F.2d 872 (9th Cir. 1991), the Ninth Circuit upheld a linkage fee for building permits on noncommercial buildings. The city based the fee on a study of the need for lower-income housing, and the amount required to offset the impact of nonresidential use on such housing. The court held that the *Nollan* rule of stricter scrutiny did not apply, and that the fee was based on careful study and conservatively assessed only part of the need for lower-income housing to developers. See also *Terminal Plaza Corp. v. City & County of San Francisco*, 223 Cal. Rptr. 379 (Cal. App. 1986) (upholding affordable housing exaction on hotel owners who planned to convert residential hotels to another use).

Holmdel, supra, considered the question raised by *San Telmo* by holding that new developments consume land that could otherwise be used for affordable housing: "The scarcity of land as a resource bears on the opportunity and means to provide affordable housing." 583 A.2d at 285, citing Major, *Linkage of Housing and Commercial Development: The Legal Issues*, 15 Real Estate L.J. 328, 331 (1987). How does the dwindling supply of land specially affect the provision of affordable housing? Recall, in this connection, Chief Justice Wilentz' statement in *Mount Laurel II, supra*: "The state controls the use of land, *all* of the land." Does a diminished supply of land support development fees for other, non-housing, purposes?

Broward County recently conducted a study of housing linkage programs in Policy Issues Regarding a Potential Housing Linkage Fee Program for Broward County (2008), available at www.broward.org/Housing/Documents/housingfeereport.pdf.

Sources. For an analysis suggesting the Boston linkage program meets the subdivision exaction nexus test, see Kayden & Pollard, *Linkage Ordinances and Traditional Exactions Analysis: The Connection Between Office Development and Housing*, 50 Law & Contemp. Probs. 127 (1987). See also Inclusionary Zoning Moves Downtown (D. Merriam, D. Brower & P. Tegeler eds., 1985); Downtown Linkages (D. Porter ed., 1985); Merrill & Lincoln, *Linkage Fees and Fair Share Regulations: Law and Method*, 25 Urb. Law. 223 (1993); Schukoske,

Housing Linkage: Regulating Development Impact on Housing Costs, 76 Iowa L. Rev. 1011 (1991); *Survey of Linkage Programs in Other U.S. Cities with Comparisons to Boston*, prepared by the Boston Redevelopment Authority (May 2000).

C. PLANNED UNIT DEVELOPMENTS (PUDs) AND PLANNED COMMUNITIES

Planned Unit Development as a Zoning Concept,
in D. Mandelker, Planned Unit Developments pp. 2, 4, 5, 10–11 (Planning Advisory Service Report No. 545 (2007)

SOME HISTORY

PUD as a land use concept began in the 1950s and 1960s. Simply put, a planned unit development is a development project a municipality considers comprehensively at one time, usually in the zoning process employed to approve a development plan. A PUD proposal will contain a map and the regulations under which the project will be built. PUDs were at first primarily residential. They were a change in style from the standard residential developments common after the Second World War.

This change occurred because the standard subdivision ordinance and the accompanying zoning regulations have serious design flaws when applied to residential land use projects. Most conventional zoning ordinances do not allow single family, multifamily, and nonresidential uses in the same zoning district. They also contain site development standards for setbacks, site coverage, and the like that produce dull projects because they apply uniformly throughout each district. Subdivision control deals principally with infrastructure and lot and block layout in new subdivisions. Neither allows the review of a project on a comprehensive basis as an integrated entity, where a jurisdiction can consider its development and design details.

Allowing for effective open space was another problem inherent in standard subdivision ordinances. Building lots at the time subdivision legislation was adopted were small and located in built-up urban areas where parks were provided by the local government. As development moved to the suburbs, lots became bigger, but most of the open space surrounding single family homes was unusable. Yet there was no way under existing zoning and subdivision regulations to link the approval of new residential development with common open space that would provide recreational and other amenities for project residents.

Developers who had to comply with these zoning and subdivision regulations typically built residential projects with a sameness that led to the nickname "cookie-cutter" development. Residential lots were all the same size. The ranch house style was common, leading to what some called "cheesebox on a raft" development in which look-alike ranch homes were built on oversized lots with private open space that received little use. Nothing in the regulations required attention to design. . . .

The PUD concept was a response to these failings in residential development. It was implemented by a new set of regulations in the zoning ordinance that applied primarily to residential development and required a discretionary project review followed by the approval of a development plan that displaced zoning regulations in residential zones. In its early stages, PUD was intended to provide a comprehensive development review that could overcome the shortcomings of zoning and subdivision regulation, improve project design, and provide for common open space in return for "clustering" development elsewhere in the project at increased densities. Open space was either privately held and available only to the residents of the PUD or dedicated to the local government. Total project density was not increased. This form of PUD is usually called "cluster" development. . . .

WHAT PUD IS TODAY

The origins of PUD regulation explain what PUD is today. It has a dual character. As [an] Urban Land Institute report stated several years ago, PUD is both a physical plan and a legal concept. This definition highlights the difficulty in defining PUD, as it is both a development type and a legal process for approving a development type. . . .

PUDs can range in size from infill housing development on a few acres in a downtown area to a large master-planned community of 50 square miles in outer suburbia. This variety suggests that different kinds of regulation are required for different types of development and that no single approach to PUD regulation can fit all alternatives. Downtown sites, for example, may not have natural resources to preserve. . . . A PUD that has a variety of mixed uses is usually called a master-planned community when it is built on a large scale. The development of increasing numbers of these communities is one of the most important changes in the PUD concept in recent years, and this increase has significantly changed the way in which communities draft and apply PUD regulations. We have had master-planned communities for some time, of course — large-scale developments often with thousands of homes and divided into neighborhoods with mixed uses, including retail and employment centers. Now, especially in the west, the south, and other growing areas of the country, the master-planned community is becoming the standard method of development. Their larger scale and mix of uses may require different kinds of regulatory treatment in PUD ordinances. . . . [The report notes that design and resource preservation issues have become important in PUD regulation.]

FITTING PUD INTO THE SURROUNDING COMMUNITY

When a PUD is limited in scale, its external impacts are likely to be minimal, especially if it includes only single family residential development with no increase in density, as in cluster zoning. . . . [Major changes in housing type, use and density can have a significant effect on traffic congestion, the adequacy of public facilities and the surrounding community.]

PUD ordinances can include requirements to take these problems into account. One is a jobs/housing balance requirement that requires an adequate balance of jobs and housing to reduce effects on the community outside the project. Another is a requirement that a PUD must provide an adequate amount of affordable housing so that housing will be available for persons who cannot afford market-rate housing. Ordinances can also address the traffic problem by requiring a development to capture internally the traffic it generates. A number of communities have an adequate public facilities requirement for all new development to ensure the development will not occur unless adequate public facilities are available. PUD ordinances can also include their own adequate public facilities requirement. . . . [Adequate public facilities ordinances are discussed in Chapter 8.]

THE ROLE OF THE COMPREHENSIVE PLAN

. . . .

If a community expects to have PUDs and master-planned communities on a major scale, it needs to plan in advance to integrate them into its development and public facility policies. This can be done by providing a development framework that shows where they should be located and how the necessary public facilities and services will be supplied. The plan can also provide essential design policies, such as a design policy for project development that will ensure the development of communities that implement the plan. Densities, the mix of uses, and other design elements that will shape the character of PUDs can be further identified. The PUD ordinance can then implement the plan with more detailed standards and requirements and can require consistency with the plan.

NOTES AND QUESTIONS

1. *Planned unit development types.* There is considerable variety in planned development types. The following categories list the more common types of planned unit developments and indicate when and what changes in use and density occur. Developments become more intense as you move down the list:

a. Single family residential density or "cluster" developments with no change in density.

b. Single family residential development with an increase in density.

c. Multi-family residential development, with or without single family development and with or without an increase in density.

d. Single use nonresidential development, such as office, commercial or industrial development.

e. Mixed-use development, consisting of nonresidential uses combined with residential uses, either single family, multi-family, or both, with or without a change in density. This type of development can be done on an infill vacant or redevelopment site, or on a greenfield or vacant suburban or nonurban site.

f. Master-planned community. "A master-planned community is a PUD, usually on substantial acreage, that combines employment, office, retail, and entertainment centers with associated self-contained neighborhoods. It can include diverse housing types as well as its own retail, entertainment, and office centers. A master-planned community can also be a new town. There is a scale problem here. Master-planned communities are often required to have a minimum size between 600 and 1,000 acres. Their size and scale require a phased planning and development process." *Planned Unit Development, supra*, at 20.

Review and Approval Process. A major issue in the review and approval of planned unit developments is whether the approved development will deviate from what would otherwise be permitted by the underlying zoning. If deviations or variations from the underlying zoning requirements are permitted, the process will need to set out specific standards for approving deviations and determining which local government agency should be responsible for approving the changes. The nature of the approval process will vary, depending on the type and intensity of planned unit development

MAP 1. A COMPONENTS OF A PLANNED COMMUNITY

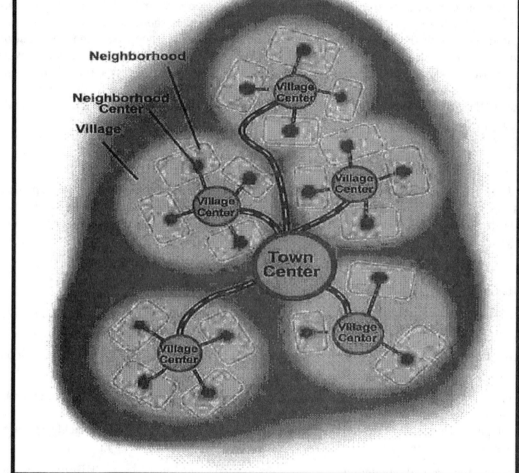

Planned Community Components
Houghton Area Master Plan, Tucson, Arizona

2. *The review process for cluster developments.* Cluster development, which does not require a change in use and may not have increased densities, can sometimes be approved administratively. Map 1 illustrates a simple density transfer planned unit residential development and the regulatory problems presented by this kind of project. What has happened is that open space areas are provided throughout the development for common use. Lot sizes are reduced for the individual lots, but this apparent increase in density is offset by the open space areas; there is no net density increase in the development.

The courts have approved administrative review for this kind of development when no change in use or density occurs. In *Prince George's County v. M&B Constr. Co.*, 297 A.2d 683

(Md. 1972), the county adopted a PUD ordinance that delegated approval of PUDs to the planning commission. Single family dwellings and townhouses were allowed in PUDs, which were a permitted use in residential zones. Reductions in lot sizes were allowed subject to a minimum lot size requirement, but existing densities and building bulk in approved PUDs were to remain the same. Town houses were permitted with a minimum square footage. The court held the approval of PUDs was properly delegated to the planning commission as part of its subdivision control powers. A provision in one of the early model planning acts authorizing density transfer PUDs has been adopted in a few states. For discussion of the New York version of this provision, see *Rouse v. O'Connell*, 353 N.Y.S.2d 124 (N.Y. Sup. 1974) (trial court).

Source: see D. Mandelker, Designing Planned Communities (2010) (www.wulaw.wustl.edu/landuselaw/BookDPC/Designing%20Planned%20Communities.pdf).

3. *The review process for changes in use and density.* A rezoning or some other zoning approval is typically required when a PUD requires a change in use or density or both. This is commonly considered a legislative change that requires a decision by the governing body, even though specific criteria control the adoption of the rezoning or zoning approval. See *Blakeman v. Planning and Zoning Comm'n*, 846 A.2d 950 (Conn. App. 2004) (new zone is created when PUD district approved); *State ex rel. Helujon, Ltd. v. Jefferson County*, 964 S.W.2d 531 (Mo. App. 1998) (change legislative even though site plan included in approval). See also *City of Waukesha v. Town Bd.*, 543 N.W.2d 515 (Wis. App. 1995) (invalidating an ordinance allowing the plan commission to approve a PUD because the ordinance did not specify where a PUD could be located and authorized a PUD approval allowing uses not authorized in the zoning district). Courts have found the approval decision legislative if the PUD accomplishes a major change in land use from what the zoning ordinance previously allowed. *Todd-Mart, Inc. v. Town Bd.*, 370 N.Y.S.2d 683 (N.Y. App. Div. 1975) (large commercial PUD). In essence, the PUD plan becomes the standards for the new zone.

Where a municipal code allows for a density increase within a PUD upon the developer's securing a conditional use permit, and where the code distinguishes between density changes that require rezoning and those that do not, a density change may not constitute a rezoning, as illustrated by the following case:

CITY OF GIG HARBOR v. NORTH PACIFIC DESIGN, INC.

210 P.3d 1096, 149 Wash. App. 159 (Wash. App. 2009)

HUNT, J.

The City of Gig Harbor appeals the City Hearing Examiner's decision to approve North Pacific Design, Inc.'s application for a conditional use permit ("CUP") allowing a density of 11.75 units per acre for a proposed residential development. The City argues that North Pacific cannot use a Planned Residential Development ("PRD") to build at this density because it conflicts with the requirements of the underlying Residential Business-2 ("RB-2") zone. The City also asks us to affirm the Hearing Examiner's decision that North Pacific cannot count perimeter setback areas toward the 30-percent "open space" calculation required for a PRD. Holding that the PRD and the underlying zoning are not mutually exclusive and that the Municipal Code's definition of "required yards" does not include perimeter setbacks, we (1) affirm the Hearing Examiner's conclusion that North Pacific's proposal falls within the density limits established for the underlying zone, and (2) reverse the Hearing Examiner's conclusion that North Pacific improperly included its perimeter setback areas in calculating the PRD 30-percent minimum open space requirement and the Hearing Examiner's order that North Pacific recalculate its open space. . . .

North Pacific Design applied for a 174-lot residential preliminary plat, a PRD, and a CUP to develop 18.8 acres of property at the northeast corner of Hunt Street and Skansie Avenue within the city limits of Gig Harbor. . . .

The City argues that North Pacific cannot (1) use a PRD to build at an increased density because it conflicts with the underlying RB-2 zone; and (2) count perimeter setback areas toward the required PRD 30-percent "open space" calculation. These arguments fail. . . .

The City's underlying RB-2 zone allowed the following maximum densities: "Eight dwelling units per acre permitted outright; 12 dwelling units per acre allowed as a conditional use." GHMC § 17.30.050(G) (Ord. 954 § 3, 2004). The Municipal Code specifically permitted the following uses in a PRD: "Those primary, accessory and conditional uses permitted in the underlying zoning district . . . ." GHMC § 17.89.050(A) (Ord. 867 § 5, 2001).

In addition to the underlying zoning regulations, developers could use PRD regulations to develop more intensely if their proposals promoted a more efficient and economical use of the land. GHMC § 17.89, which contained the PRD regulations, provided: "The intent of the PRD zone is to allow opportunity for more creative and imaginative residential projects than generally possible under strict application of the zoning regulations in order that such projects shall provide substantial additional benefit to the general community." GHMC § 17.89.010 (Ord. 867 § 1, 2001). . . .

In sum, granting a PRD application did not create a rezone because there was no conflict between GHMC § 17.30.050 and GHMC § 17.89.100. North Pacific's proposal was consistent with the RB-2 zoning requirements for obtaining a conditional use permit to increase density. It was also consistent with the PRD provision, which allowed applicants to pursue PRDs for "primary, accessory and conditional uses permitted in the underlying zoning district." GHMC § 17.89.050(A). We hold that North Pacific's proposed 11.75 per acre density met both the RB-2 *and* the PRD density requirements.

In an ancillary argument, the City contends that "density" is not a "use" for the purposes of obtaining a conditional use permit and, thus, North Pacific cannot use the phrase "conditional use" to increase Skansie Park's density. Specifically, the City argues that the City's Land Use Matrix lists all of the uses allowed in an RB-2 district, but that this list fails to include "density" as a use. This argument also fails.

Although the former Municipal Code did not list density as a "use" in the Land Use Matrix, it specifically required applicants to obtain a "conditional use permit" to increase a development's density. GHMC § 17.30.050(G) expressly provided that "12 dwelling units per acre [are] allowed as a conditional use." Thus, the City's assertion that density was not a "use" for the purposes of a obtaining a conditional use permit directly contradicts the plain language meaning of the Municipal Code.

Next, the City argues that the Hearing Examiner erred by allowing North Pacific to increase density as part of a PRD, in violation of the Municipal Code and Gig Harbor's Comprehensive Plan. Specifically, the City argues that the Hearing Examiner erred in harmonizing the RB-2 density provisions under GHMC § 17.30.050(G) with the PRD density provisions under GHMC § 17.89.100.

But as North Pacific correctly argues, these provisions do not conflict. For the RB-2 zoning regulations, GHMC § 17.30.050(G) permitted a density of up to "12 dwelling units per acre" as a conditional use. For the PRD zoning regulations, GHMC § 17.89.100(A) limited density increases to 30 percent, but only where an applicant sought to increase the density "over that *permitted* in the underlying zone." (Emphasis added). We agree with North Pacific that the City's argument asks us to ignore the plain language of GHMC § 17.30.050(G), which clearly permitted developers to build at a density of up to 12 dwelling units per acre as a conditional use in the underlying RB-2 zone.

The City also contends that PRD zoning regulations conflicted with Gig Harbor's Comprehensive Land Use Plan. Specifically, the City argues that because North Pacific's PRD was inconsistent with the Comprehensive Plan, the density in a PRD zone could not be increased over the base density allowed in an RB-2 zone. North Pacific counters, however, that the PRD zoning regulations harmonized with the "Goals" of the Comprehensive Plan, which encouraged higher densities for developments that provide open spaces, retain natural site characteristics, and allow for higher intensity residential improvement.

North Pacific's request to develop its property at a density of just under 12 dwelling units per acre was consistent with the maximum density allowed under both the Comprehensive Plan and the Municipal Code. Additionally, North Pacific's proposed development provides perimeter buffers, open space, common parks, public trails, and a natural wetland area. North Pacific also employed an innovative design that would retain the historical character of the site by providing for specific roof pitch and vertical windows. Furthermore, North Pacific intends Skansie Park to serve as a transitional buffer between high intensity commercial areas and lower intensity residential areas, and it seeks to construct a new single family neighborhood where none existed previously. In sum, North Pacific's development proposal not only complied with the City Comprehensive Plan's requirements, but it also embodied the plan's purpose to accommodate a growing population by increasing the density in residential developments and allowing for greater flexibility in land use density. . . .

The City Council imposed PRD standards to allow for increased flexibility over those otherwise authorized in the underlying zone; but there is no indication that the City Council intended for PRD regulations to displace or to supersede the underlying regulations. Instead, it appears that the City Council intended the PRD requirements to serve as supplemental regulations, which developers could follow to depart from rigid zoning requirements and to increase housing options for Gig Harbor's growing population. . . .

Holding that the Municipal Code's PRD and RB-2 provisions do not conflict, we affirm the Superior Court's decision to affirm the Hearing Examiner's approval of North Pacific's applications for a PRD, a preliminary plat, and a conditional use permit. . . .

NOTES AND QUESTIONS

1. *Consistency with local regulations.* A PUD proposal must be consistent with the zoning ordinance, *Citizens for Mount Vernon v. City of Mount Vernon*, 947 P.2d 1208 (Wash. 1997), and must comply with the comprehensive plan if the ordinance requires this, *Cathedral Park Condominium Committee v. District of Columbia Zoning Comm'n*, 743 A.2d 1231 (D.C. App. 2000). However, as noted in *Gig Harbor*, an approved planned development can, if authorized by local or state laws, deviate from the otherwise applicable requirements, including uses and density. In fact, as noted by the *Gig Harbor* court, the intent of planned developments is to "allow for increased flexibility over those otherwise authorized in the underlying zone" and the purpose was not to displace or supersede the underlying regulations, but to supplement. Do you agree with the court? Is the approved deviation from otherwise applicable density requirements a "supplemental" regulation or does the approved deviation supersede the otherwise applicable density requirements? For a case striking down an approved planned development that deviated from the underlying zoning density requirements, see *Mikell v. County of Charleston*, 687 S.E.2d 326 (S.C. 2009). In *Mikell*, Charleston County had adopted a 1999 Comprehensive Plan and 2001 Zoning and Land Development Regulations that established a base agricultural density of 1:10 (on a portion of the parcel), and allowed an increase to 1:5 using the statutory Planned Development procedure. In 2003, the County passed a Planned Development Ordinance that resulted in a density allowance of 1 unit per 2.4 acres on a portion of the property, clearly in excess of the Plan and ZLDR cap of 1:5. The Supreme Court reversed the County's approval of the planned development, finding the resulting density inconsistent with the 1:5 PD density cap contained in the County's zoning regulations.

2. *Planned development legislation.* Model legislation expressly authorizing the enactment of PUD ordinances was proposed in the mid-1960s. See Babcock, Krasnowiecki & McBride, *The Model State Statute*, 114 U. Pa. L. Rev. 140 (1965). It included a detailed adjudicatory review process and provided a detailed set of PUD approval standards. It was adopted in only a few states, where it has created problems. The American Planning Association model legislation includes a more open-ended enabling act that defines a PUD, requires consistency with the comprehensive plan and designated regulations, and authorizes approval as a conditional use or subdivision depending on the PUD's size. American Planning Association, Growing Smart Legislative Guidebook: Model Statutes for Planning and Management of Change § 8-303 (S. Meck ed., 2002). Site planning standards "may vary the density or intensity of land use" based on factors such as the provision of common open space and the physical character of the PUD, and may also authorize neotraditional neighborhood development.

Many states now have PUD enabling legislation. Many of these laws simply provide authority for the enactment of PUD ordinances. E.g., 65 Ill. Comp. Stat. 5/11-13-1.1 (authorizing planned developments as a special use). A few laws are more detailed. Some, like the Colorado and Nevada laws, require the local PUD ordinance to include provisions stating the criteria under which PUDs will be evaluated that may include density and intensity of use and design standards. The Nevada statute details the procedures that must be followed at the local level. Some statutes also contain extensive provisions for the dedication and maintenance of common open spaces. Legislative authority for PUDs can clarify the basis for local regulation and provide needed statutory direction on procedures and other issues. The state legislation is summarized in *Planned Unit Development, supra*, Ch. 6. For a chart listing planned unit development enabling statutes by state, see www.ancelglink.com/publications/PUD%20Statutes_State.pdf.

The following case considers the issue of whether a procedure for the review of PUDs is authorized under a statute modeled on the Standard Zoning Act:

CHENEY v. VILLAGE 2 AT NEW HOPE, INC.

429 Pa. 626, 241 A.2d 81 (1968)

ROBERTS, JUSTICE:

. . . [After explaining the PUD concept, the court detailed the enactment of a PUD district by the Borough of New Hope. On the same day the Borough council adopted the district, it also rezoned a large tract of land known as the Ranch Farm from low density residential to PUD. The planning commission then approved a plan for the PUD and building permits were issued. Neighboring property owners brought an action challenging the adoption of the PUD plan and the PUD rezoning, and the lower court held the ordinance invalid "for failure to conform to a comprehensive plan and for vesting too much discretion in the New Hope planning commission."

[The supreme court reversed. It held the PUD was consistent with the plan, and that it was not invalid as spot zoning. It then considered the approval procedure authorized by the PUD ordinance.]

The court below next concluded that even if the two ordinances were properly *passed*, they must fall as vesting authority in the planning commission greater than that permitted under Pennsylvania's zoning enabling legislation. More specifically, it is now contended by appellees that complete project approval by the planning commission under [the] ordinance requires that commission to encroach upon legislative territory whenever it decides where, within a particular PUD district, specific types of buildings should be placed.

In order to appreciate fully the arguments of counsel on both sides it is necessary to explain in some detail exactly what is permitted within a PUD district, and who decides whether a particular landowner has complied with these requirements. Admittedly the range of permissible uses within the PUD district is greater than that normally found in a traditional zoning district. Within a New Hope PUD district there may be: single family attached or detached dwellings; apartments; accessory private garages; public or private parks and recreation areas including golf courses, swimming pools, ski slopes, etc. (so long as these facilities do not produce noise, glare, odor, air pollution, etc., detrimental to existing or prospective adjacent structures); a municipal building; a school; churches; art galleries; professional offices; certain types of signs; a theatre (but not a drive-in); motels and hotels; and a restaurant. The ordinance then sets certain overall density requirements. The PUD district may have a maximum of 80% of the land devoted to residential uses, a maximum of 20% for the permitted commercial uses and enclosed recreational facilities, and must have a minimum of 20% for open spaces. The residential density shall not exceed 10 units per acre, nor shall any such unit contain more than two bedrooms. All structures within the district must not exceed maximum height standards set out in the ordinance. Finally, although there are no traditional "set back" and "side yard" requirements, ordinance 160 does require that there be 24 feet between structures, and that no townhouse structure contain more than 12 dwelling units.

The procedure to be followed by the aspiring developer reduces itself to presenting a detailed plan for his planned unit development to the planning commission, obtaining that body's approval and then securing building permits. Of course, the planning commission may not approve any development that fails to meet the requirements set forth in the ordinance as outlined above.

We begin with the observation that there is nothing in the borough zoning enabling act which would prohibit council from creating a zoning district with this many permissible uses. . . . Under this [act], council is given the power to regulate and restrict practically all aspects of buildings themselves, open spaces, population density, location of structures, etc., the only limitation on this power being that it be exercised so as to promote the "health, safety, morals or the general welfare" of the borough. [The same act] empowers council to adopt ordinances to govern the use of public areas, such as streets, parks, etc., again with the only limitation being that such ordinances create "conditions favorable to the health, safety, morals and general welfare of the citizens." Thus, if council reasonably believed that a given district could contain *all* types of structures, without *any* density requirements whatsoever, so long as this did not adversely affect health, safety and morals, such a district could be created. In fact, it is common knowledge that in many industrial and commercial districts just such a wide range of uses is permitted. Given such broad power to zone, we cannot say that New Hope Borough Council abrogated its legislative function by creating a PUD district permitting the mixture of uses outlined supra, especially given the density requirements.

We must next examine the statutory power of the borough planning commission to determine whether such an administrative body may regulate the internal development of a PUD district. The Act requires that all plans for land "laid out in building lots" be approved by the planning commission before they may be recorded. Thus, the traditional job of the commission has been to examine tract plans to determine whether they conform to the applicable borough ordinances. The ordinances most frequently interpreted and applied by the planning commission are those dealing with streets, sewers, water and gas mains, etc., i.e., the so-called public improvements. However, the statute contains no language which would prohibit the planning commission from approving plans with reference to ordinances dealing with permissible building uses as well. The primary reason that planning commissions have not traditionally interpreted this type of ordinance is that such regulations do not usually come into play until the landowner wishes to begin the actual construction of a particular building. By this time, the relevant subdivision plan has already been approved by the commission; thus the task of examining the plans for a particular structure to see whether it conforms to the regulations for the zoning district in which it will be erected devolves upon the local building inspector who issues the building permit.

However, in the case of PUD the entire development (including specific structures) is mapped out and submitted to the administrative agency at once. Accordingly, the requirements set forth in a PUD ordinance must relate not only to those areas traditionally administered by the planning commission, but also to areas traditionally administered by the building inspector. Therefore, quite logically, the job of approving a particular PUD should rest with a single municipal body. The question then is simply which one: Borough Council (a legislative body), the Planning Commission (an administrative body), or the Zoning Board of Adjustment (an administrative body)?

There is no doubt that it would be statutorily permissible for council itself to pass a PUD ordinance and simultaneous zoning map amendment so specific that no details would be left for any administrator. The ordinance could specify where each building should be placed, how large it should be, where the open spaces are located, etc. But what would be the practical effect of such an ordinance? One of the most attractive features of Planned Unit Development is its flexibility; the chance for the builder and the municipality to sit down together and tailor a development to meet the specific needs of the community and the requirements of the land on which it is to be built. But all this would be lost if the Legislature let the planning cement set before any developer could happen upon the scene to scratch his own initials in that cement. Professor Krasnowiecki has accurately summed up the effect on planned unit development of such legislative planning. The picture, to be sure, is not a happy one:

> "The traditional refuge of the courts, the requirement that all the standards be set forth in advance of application for development, does not offer a practical solution to the problem. The complexity of pre-established regulations that would automatically dispose of any proposal for planned unit development, when different housing types and perhaps accessory commercial areas are envisaged, would be quite considerable. Indeed as soon as various housing types are permitted, the regulations that would govern their design and distribution on every possible kind of site, their relationship to each other and their relationship to surrounding properties must be complex unless the developer's choice in terms of site, site plan, and design and distribution of housing is reduced close to zero. It is not likely . . . that local authorities would want to adopt such a set of regulations." Krasnowiecki, *Planned Unit Development: A Challenge to Established Theory and Practice of Land Use Control*, 114 U. Pa. L. Rev. 47, 71 (1965).

Left with Professor Krasnowiecki's "Hobson's choice" of no developer leeway at all, or a staggering set of legislative regulations sufficient to cover every idea the developer might have, it is not likely that Planned Unit Development could thrive, or even maintain life, if the local legislature assumed totally the role of planner.

The remaining two municipal bodies which could oversee the shaping of specific Planned Unit Developments are both administrative agencies, the zoning board of adjustment and the planning commission. As this Court views both reality and zoning enabling act, the zoning board of adjustment is not the proper body. The Act specifically sets forth the powers of a borough zoning board of adjustment. These powers are three in number, and only three. The board may (1) hear and decide appeals where there is an alleged error made by an administrator in the enforcement of the enabling act or any ordinance enacted pursuant thereto; (2) hear and decide special exceptions; and (3) authorize the grant of variances from the terms of existing ordinances. These powers in no way encompass the authority to review and approve the plan for an entire development when such plan is neither at variance with the existing ordinance nor is a special exception to it; nor does (1) above supply the necessary power since the board would not be reviewing an alleged administrative error.

Moreover, from a practical standpoint, a zoning board of adjustment is, of the three bodies here under discussion, the one least equipped to handle the problem of PUD approval. Zoning boards are accustomed to focusing on one lot at a time. They traditionally examine hardship cases and unique uses proposed by landowners. As Professor Krasnowiecki has noted: "To suggest that the board is intended, or competent, to handle large scale planning and design decisions is, I think, far fetched" Technical Bulletin 52, Urban Land Institute, p. 38 (1965). We agree.

Thus, the borough planning commission remains the only other body both qualified and statutorily permitted to approve PUD. Of course, we realize that a planning commission is not authorized to engage in actual re-zoning of land. But merely because the commission here has the power to approve more than one type of building for a particular lot within the PUD district does not mean that the commission is usurping the zoning function. Indeed, it is acting in strict *accordance* with the applicable zoning ordinance, for that ordinance *permits* more than one type of building for a particular lot. To be sure, if the commission approved a plan for a PUD district where 30% of the land were being used commercially, *then* we would have an example of illegal re-zoning by an administrator. But no one argues in the present case that appellant's plan does not conform to the requirements of [the PUD] ordinance.

Nor is this Court sympathetic to appellees' argument that [the PUD] ordinance permits the planning commission to grant variances and special exceptions. We fail to see how a development such as appellant's that meets every single requirement of the applicable zoning ordinance can be said to be the product of a variance or a special exception. The very essence of variances and special exceptions lies in their *departure* from ordinance requirements, not in their compliance with them. We therefore conclude that the New Hope Planning Commission has the power to approve development plans submitted to it under [the PUD] ordinance. . . .

NOTES AND QUESTIONS

1. *The authority problem.* Carefully review the provisions of the PUD ordinance in *Cheney;* it specified densities and uses. Does this exhaust policy making? If so, does this explain the court's decision upholding the authority of the planning commission to approve PUD plans? What if the ordinance left the determination of densities and uses to the planning commission? *Sheridan Planning Ass'n v. Board of Sheridan County Comm'rs*, 924 P.2d 988 (Wyo. 1996), held that delegation of approval of a final PUD plan to the planning commission was not an improper delegation when the plan could be approved only if it complied with a concept plan previously approved by the legislative body.

Chrinko v. South Brunswick Twp. Planning Bd., 187 A.2d 221 (N.J. App. 1963), is another case holding that PUD ordinances may be enacted under a zoning statute based on the Standard Act. The township enacted a density transfer PUD ordinance with power to approve in the planning board, which is the New Jersey term for planning commission. Although noting that the zoning act did not "in so many words" authorize PUD ordinances, the court held that the ordinance "reasonably advances the legislative purposes of securing open spaces, preventing overcrowding and undue concentration of population, and promoting the general welfare." The ordinance did not violate the requirement that uniformity of regulation is required within a zoning district because it was open to all developers. Accord on the uniformity issue, *Orinda Homeowners Comm. v. Board of Supvrs.*, 90 Cal. Rptr. 88 (Cal. App. 1970) (character of units need not be alike).

In *Rutland Envtl. Protection Ass'n v. Kane County*, 334 N.E.2d 215 (Ill. App. 1975), the court rejected an argument that the bargaining and negotiation that occurs in the PUD review process was invalid as contract zoning. The court held that "[s]ince the overall aims of . . . [PUD] zoning cannot be accomplished without negotiations and because conferences are indeed mandated by the regulating ordinance, the conduct of the . . . [county] cannot be read as contributing to contract zoning." *Id.* at 219. Krasnowiecki 114 U. Pa. L. Rev. at 102, suggests that "zoning changes granted at the request of a particular applicant can be limited by ordinance to the proposal as described in the plans and oral testimony presented by the applicant in support of his request," citing *Albright v. Town of Manlius*, 268 N.E.2d 785 (N.Y. 1971).

In *Chrinko,* the court noted the procedure was not mandatory, and in *Porpoise Point P'ship v. St. John's County*, 532 So. 2d 727 (Fla. App. 1988), the court invalidated a PUD the county adopted for a development on its own initiative. The court held that planned unit development was a voluntary procedure intended to provide development flexibility not possible under the zoning ordinance, but that it cannot be forced on a developer who simply wants a rezoning of its land.

2. *Issues in PUD regulation.* The following matrix indicates which issues come up in the drafting of PUD ordinances and the zoning options that are available:

ADOPTING PUD ZONES

DRAFTING OPTIONS	USE WHEN
As-of-Right	For established development formats, if local government believes review is unnecessary
By Review	Local government believes discretionary review of project is required
Short Form Ordinance	Maximum amount of discretion in reviewing applications is wanted and development is not expected to present complex problems
Long Form Ordinance	Development problems are complex and more than one type of planned unit development is expected
Concept Plan	Approval of basic elements of planned unit development by legislative body is desired before detailed plans are drawn
Detailed Development	Plan Approval of project detail is desired as first step in approval process
Legislative Body	Legislative decisions are required on project applications
Planning Commission	Details of project are to be approved in development plans following legislative approval
Board of Zoning Adjustment	Planned unit development is to be approved as conditional use or requires variances or special exceptions
Overlay Zone	Underlying zoning is to control project subject to modifications in the development plan
Base Zone	Planned development zone and plan replace existing zoning
Conditional Zoning	Local government wants detailed conditions governing development

Source: *Planned Unit Development, supra,* at 23.

Notice the inclusion of as-of-right PUDs. If a community knows what it wants in planned unit development and has a limited number of potential sites, it may be able to draft an ordinance that incorporates PUD design standards where they are needed. For examples see *Planned Unit Development, supra,* at 58–62. Conditional zoning, which is the last example, is discussed in Chapter 6. It, along with the concurrent adoption of a development agreement, is often used to approve PUDs in some western states.

3. *Floating zones.* A floating zone is one option for approving PUDs if a legislative decision is needed. This technique, described in Chapter 6, allows the municipality to adopt the text of a zoning district and apply it later to individual tracts of land as development proposals are made. Courts have approved this technique, and it is easily adapted for the approval of PUD zoning districts. *Campion v. Board of Aldermen,* 899 A.2d 542 (Conn. 2006), approved the adoption of PUD district under a statute based on the Standard Zoning Act. It held the planned development district was comparable to the creation of any other zone, especially floating zones, and that the lack of particular language for planned development was not determinative of the board's lack of enabling authority. The court had previously upheld floating zones as authorized by the zoning enabling legislation without specific statutory authority. It held a planned development district's lack of specific uses did not make it different from a floating zone by concluding that the differences were mostly procedural, and that the actual outcome in either case (the change of a zone's boundaries by creating a new one) was the same. Accord *Town of North Hempstead v. Village of North Hills*, 342 N.E.2d 566 (N.Y. 1975). See also *Brunswick Smart Growth, Inc. v. Town of Brunswick*, 856 N.Y.S.2d 308 (N.Y. 2008). In *Brunswick*, the court upheld a planned development district (PDD) for a 210-acre residential development, finding that the "planned development district in the Town zoning ordinance was a 'floating zone' whose boundaries were not fixed in the original ordinance, but were to be established by later amendment to the zoning map. The use of a floating zone is the common and preferred method for creating planned development districts. [citation omitted] The two-step legislative process that follows from the use of a floating zone (i.e., the initial ordinance outlines procedures for a planned development district without setting boundaries, and the second legislative act amends the zoning ordinance and/or map to place an approved district) has long been recognized as an acceptable technique."

4. *Special or conditional use.* Courts have also upheld conditional or special use, or special exception procedures, different names for the same thing, to approve PUDs. *In re Moreland*, 497 P.2d 1287 (Okla. 1972). Acting under a local PUD ordinance, the board of adjustment approved a PUD for a mobile home park and retail shopping center. The ordinance was upheld as falling within the provisions of the state zoning act allowing the board to grant special exceptions. Since the board's function was to determine whether the PUD complied with the provisions of the ordinance, it was acting in a quasi-judicial, not a legislative, capacity. No revision of the local comprehensive plan or zoning ordinance could be carried out by the board, and the ordinance required that any approved PUDs be devoted primarily to residential purposes and only secondarily to nonresidential uses. The ordinance provided a series of design standards, and also required that approved PUDs conform to the intent and purposes of the local zoning ordinance and the local and regional comprehensive plans. Accord *Chandler v. Kroiss*, 190 N.W.2d 472 (Minn. 1971) (upholding permit procedure as hybrid procedure combining variance and special exception). Compare *Lutz v. City of Longview*, 520 P.2d 1374 (Wash. 1974) (cannot give legislative function to planning commission).

5. *The scope of judicial review.* The manner of judicial review will often depend on how the decision is made, and the standards contained in the ordinance. When the decision is made by a legislative body, especially when there is a rezoning, courts will typically apply the usual deferential standard to denials and approvals. *Ford Leasing Dev. Co. v. Board of County Comm'rs*, 528 P.2d 237 (Colo. 1974) (upholding denial based on incompatibility with surrounding area); *Moore v. City of Boulder*, 484 P.2d 134 (Colo. App. 1971) (rezoning); *Home Bldg. Co. v. City of Kansas City*, 666 S.W.2d 816 (Mo. App. 1984) (refusal to rezone). A court will reverse a council's refusal to approve a PUD, however, when the application meets ordinance standards and the denial is based on personal preferences unsupported by any evidence. *South Park, Ltd. v. Council of Avon*, 2006 Ohio App. LEXIS 2683 (Ohio App. 2006).

If a PUD proposal is reviewed through a special or conditional use procedure, the usual standards of review apply. There again is no discretion to deny or impose prohibitive conditions when the approval requirements in the ordinance are specific and the applicant has met all of these requirements. *BECA of Alexandria, L.L.P. v. County of Douglas by Bd. of Comm'rs*, 607 N.W.2d 459 (Minn. App. 2000); *C.C. & J. Enters., Inc. v. City of Asheville*, 512 S.E.2d 766 (N.C.

App. 1999). There is more discretion to reject when the ordinance contains generalized health, safety and general welfare requirements. *Dore v. County of Ventura*, 28 Cal. Rptr. 2d 299 (Cal. App. 1994) (upholding denial based on safety and incompatibility findings).

6. *Defining development changes needing legislative approval.* The PUD ordinance can resolve uncertainties in the amendment process by distinguishing between minor and major changes and providing that minor changes can be made administratively. These distinctions do not necessarily bind the court. In *Foggy Bottom Association v. District of Columbia Zoning Comm'n*, 743 A.2d 578 (D.C. App. 2000), the ordinance defined a minor amendment as follows:

> (a) a two percent or smaller change in height, percentage of lot occupancy, or gross floor area of a building; (b) a two percent or smaller change in the number of rooms or gross floor area to be used for commercial or accessory purposes; (c) a two percent or smaller change in the number of parking or loading spaces; and (d) the relocation of a building within five feet of its approved location.

A minor amendment under most PUD ordinances would only require planning commission approval. See also *McCarty v. City of Kansas City*, 671 S.W.2d 790 (Mo. App. 1984) (use change requires rezoning). Bellevue, Washington also has a class of amendments the planning director can designate as exempt from review subject to express criteria. It is possible to make these distinctions qualitatively. One type of amendment exempt from review under the Bellevue ordinance is a change "that will not have the effect of significantly reducing any area of landscaping, open space, natural area or parking." Which is preferable?

7. *Decision making by the legislative body.* The characterization of decisions about PUDs in the review process arises even when the legislative body makes all the decisions. A legislative body at the local level may act both legislatively and administratively. There is no separation of powers problem. In *State ex rel. Committee for the Referendum of Ordinance No. 3844-02 v. Norris*, 792 N.E.2d 186 (Ohio 2003), the legislative body first adopted a new PUD zoning district. Then it rezoned a property to the PUD district and approved a preliminary development plan. Then, in a later ordinance, the legislative body approved final development plans and subdivision plats for part of the PUD. The court held this last ordinance was an administrative act that applied the previously approved PUD regulations and preliminary development plan. Notice that when the decision making function is with the legislative body, a conclusion that a decision is legislative may open it up to referendum. Referenda on PUDs are common in many areas. Which decisions that the council made were legislative in *Norris*? Characterizing the decision as legislative or quasi-judicial will also affect the scope of judicial review.

8. *Sources.* D. Mandelker, *Legislation for Planned Unit Developments and Master-Planned Communities*, 40 Urb. Law 419 (2008); W. Sanders, *The Cluster Subdivision: A Cost-Effective Approach*, American Planning Association, Planning Advisory Serv. Rep. No. 356 (1981); Great Planned Communities (J. Gause, ed. 2002); Growing Smarter on the Edge (Lincoln Inst. of Land Policy & Sonoranb Inst., 2005) (excellent study of planned communities in the west); A. Forsyth, Reforming Suburbia (case studies of Irvine, The Woodlands and Columbia planned communities); *A Guide to Planned Unit Development*,prepared by the NYS Legislative Commission on Rural Resources (2005) (www.dos.state.ny.us/lgss/pdfs/PUD1.pdf); Gudder, *A Primer on Planned Unit Development*, 21 Zoning & Plan. L. Rep. 18, 25 (1998); James, *Getting the Most Out of Compact Development*, Land Development, March, 2000, at 3 (reviewing cluster development design principles). R. Ewing, Best Development Practices (American Planning Ass'n, 1996), is a much-followed monograph containing recommendations

for land use, transportation, housing and other development issues that are applied in PUDs. The American Planning Association's magazine, Planning, includes a *Special Issue on Master Planned Communities* in its July 2007 edition.

A NOTE ON PUD PROJECT APPROVAL STANDARDS

The way in which PUD review standards are drafted is a critical element in the administration of a PUD ordinance. The usual problem of how to ensure flexibility while preventing arbitrary decision making again rears its head. Open-ended review standards give the reviewing agency the flexibility it needs to ensure well-done PUD projects, but may preclude effective judicial review and allow communities to use PUD review procedures to make exclusionary decisions.

The delegation of power problem. How ordinances are drafted is affected by the delegation of power issue. Delegation should not be an issue for residential developments. *Yarab v. Boardman Twp. Bd. of Zoning Appeals*, 860 N.E.2d 769 (Ohio App. 2006) (ordinance spelled out all of the elements of a project); *In re Pierce Subdivision Application*, 965 A.2d 468 (Vt. 2008) (standards for approval of planned development were not vague and town did not unlawfully delegate authority to commission). Courts have also approved ordinances that contained typical approval standards, such as compatibility, adequate public facilities, access, and design standards. *Tri-State Generation and Transmission Co. v. City of Thornton*, 647 P.2d 670 (Colo. 1982). Some standards are unacceptable. In *Soble Constr. Co. v. Zoning Hearing Bd.*, 329 A.2d 912 (Pa. Commw. 1974), the ordinance provided that "[t]he proposed developer shall demonstrate that a sufficient market exists for the type, size and character of the development proposed." The court held this requirement invalid because the market-sufficiency showing was not related to the general welfare. A municipality may not "zone or refuse to zone land for the purpose of limiting competition with existing commercial facilities."

Project approval standards. A preliminary question is whether a PUD should be approved if it satisfies use, density and other requirements in the ordinance, or whether the ordinance should also include a more generic standard to ensure that the PUD meets the design and other objectives of the ordinance. The following approval standard is an attempt to do this:

> A PUD zoning development plan may be approved by the Commission and Council, provided the following criteria are met:
>
> (1) A development pattern is proposed which is consistent with the purpose, intent and applicable standards of this Zoning Code;
>
> (2) The proposed development is in conformity with the Comprehensive Plan or portion thereof as it may apply;
>
> (3) The proposed development advances the general welfare of the City;
>
> (4) That the benefits, improved arrangement, and the design of the proposed development justify the deviation from standard residential development requirements included in this Zoning Code. [City of Hilliard Zoning Ordinance, § 1157.04.]

Do these standards raise a delegation of power problem? Vagueness? How should they be interpreted? Would you revise them?

Would you require different standards for a master-planned community? Consider the following goal for a master-planned community:

> To provide for the housing needs of the citizens of Hillsboro and surrounding community by encouraging the construction, maintenance, development and availability of a variety of housing types, in sufficient number and at price ranges and rent levels which are commensurate with the financial capabilities of the community's residents. [City of Hillsboro Zoning Ordinance, § 3 (http://www.ci.hillsboro.or.us/Planning/HTMLcompPlan/documents/Section%203.pdf).]

This standard adds a number of social criteria, such as the requirement for a variety of price ranges and rent levels for housing. Consider another social requirement of an adequate jobs-housing balance. Is that desirable? How would you determine whether the jobs-housing balance is adequate? Selecting a criterion to decide whether the balance is adequate is the critical issue. The usual measure is the ratio of jobs to housing units, but this measure is adequate only if it accurately reflects the work force. To get accuracy, communities must be able to determine the number of workers in each dwelling. See J. Weitz, *Jobs-Housing Balance*, American Planning Ass'n, Planning Advisory Serv. Rep. No. 516 (2003).

To reduce traffic congestion and trips generated by a PUD, some ordinances require that larger projects "capture" some part of their internal traffic by keeping a stated percentage of trips within the project. An adequate balance of jobs to housing can help achieve this objective, along with providing office and retail development and locating residential development near them, improving walkability and pedestrian access and implementing a traffic management program. How would you write a provision that requires these measures? How do you enforce it?

Design. Planned unit developments are expected to achieve good design, and the PUD ordinance can include design standards. One alternative is to adopt a comprehensive design program for PUDs, such as the extensive Design Standards Manual adopted by Sparks, Nevada (www.ci.sparks.nv.us/business/planning_dev/design_standards). PUD ordinances can also contain a general statement of design objectives, as in this ordinance provision from Somerville, Massachusetts:

> PUD architecture should demonstrate the cohesive planning of the development and present a clearly identifiable design feature throughout. It is not intended that buildings be totally uniform in appearance or that designers and developers be restricted in their creativity. Rather, cohesion and identity can be demonstrated in similar building scale or mass; consistent use of facade materials; similar ground-level detailing, color or signage; consistency in functional systems, such as roadway or pedestrian way surfaces, signage, or landscaping; the framing of outdoor open space and linkages, or a clear conveyance in the importance of various buildings and features on the site. [City of Somerville Zoning Ordinance, § 16.7, www.library.municode.com/index.aspx?clientId=14682&stateId=21&stateName=Massachusetts.]

This provision can be adopted as an approval standard. Compare it with the Hilliard standard at the beginning of this Note. Design issues are further explored in Chapter 9, which contains examples of building design requirements and a discussion of the legal problems raised by aesthetic regulation.

For a comprehensive analysis of the design issues related to planned communities, with a focus on larger master-planned communities, see D. Mandelker, Designing Planned Communities, *supra*.

Density. This is an important issue in the approval of PUDs. Neighbors often object, and strenuously, if density increases in a PUD. Typically, there is no overall density increase in a cluster development, and ordinances often contain a provision that density is governed by the existing zoning. Clustering does reduce lot sizes, however, and neighbors may still object even though design is improved. The PUD ordinance may also provide a density bonus above what the existing zoning authorizes. One option is to authorize a density bonus based on project features such as the provision of open space and good project design. The ordinance will usually include a cap on how much of an increase is allowable. Do you see the rationale for this kind of density bonus? Another alternative is to list the features that can justify a density bonus and then indicate how much of an increase is allowable. An ordinance can allow a two percent density increase, for example, for features such as landscaping and building design.

For other projects, there are several approaches to the density issue: the ordinance can accept the density in the existing zone, it can specify a density in the PUD ordinance, or it can authorize the zoning agency to set the density. A density decision by the zoning agency should be governed by the comprehensive plan. The ordinance can provide that the density allowed should be within the range of densities provided in the plan.

Open space. The provision of open space was an important objective in early PUD projects, and it remains an important feature of many PUDs. The PUD ordinance must be very careful to specify the requirements for common open space, its use and maintenance. Here are some questions that communities should consider: 1) What kind of open space should be included in a project? The ordinance can distinguish between common open space, which is used for active recreational purposes and can include a club house and other facilities, and open space, which consists of natural resource areas to be preserved. Floodplains and wetlands are an example. 2) Where should open space be located and should there be a minimum size? Common open space should be accessible by project residents and should be a meaningful size. 3) What uses and facilities should be allowed in common open space and open space? How will open space be preserved? 4) How will the provision of open space be coordinated with the development of a project in phases? If a development is phased, it is important to provide the open space related to each phase at the time that each phase is built. Can you draft a provision to cover each of these problems? Can you think of any other problems?

Another major issue is how open space will be maintained. The ordinance should require the formation of a homeowner's association to maintain the common open space and require measures to ensure its preservation, such as easements and conveyances. The ordinance should specify the powers the homeowner's association should have in order to maintain and preserve open space, including enforcement powers. What happens if the common open space is poorly managed? The Nevada PUD statute has an excellent enforcement provision. Nev. Rev. Stat. § 278A.180. Conveyance to a public agency by fee or easement to a public agency or private association is another option.

Vested Rights. Master-planned communities raise a vested rights problem in the approval process, an issue present for any PUD but especially serious for very large communities developed in stages. These projects can take a long time, and political changes in the governing body can lead to changes in the development plan that can make a project less attractive for a developer. As Chapter 6 indicates, however, vested rights accrue under the majority rule only when there has been substantial reliance on building permit. Though there is some support that approval of a development plan for the first stage of a PUD will vest rights in subsequent stages, *Village of Palatine v. LaSalle Nat'l Bank*, 445 N.E.2d 1277 (Ill. App. 1983), development plan approval will not vest rights in the entire project under the majority rule. See *Watergate E. Comm. Against Hotel Conversion to Co-Op Apts. v. Dist. of Columbia Zoning Comm'n*, 953 A.2d 1036 (D.C. App. 2008) (holding that owners of adjacent apartment building and members of a PUD association did not have a vested right to prevent a modification of a PUD to allow conversion of an adjacent hotel to a co-op apartment building). Some states have statutes vesting rights in approved, site-specific development plans. E.g., Ariz. Rev. Stat. §§ 9-1202, 11-1202; Colo. Rev. Stat. § 24-68-103. A developer's agreement between the municipality and the developer is an alternative where it is allowed. Otherwise, the developer is at risk.

PROBLEM

You are the city attorney of a city of 100,000 with substantial areas of undeveloped land remaining. The city operates under the standard zoning act. You have been asked by the city council to draft an ordinance authorizing the approval of planned unit developments. Based on these materials, which zoning agency would you choose to administer the PUD approval process? What kind of PUDs would you allow? What approval standards would you require? What procedures would you specify for the initial approval and subsequent amendment of PUDs?

Chapter 8

GROWTH MANAGEMENT

A. AN INTRODUCTION TO GROWTH MANAGEMENT

The Future of the San Diego Region

The San Diego region in California, which includes the city of San Diego, is an urban region on the Pacific Coast with a population over four million. By 2020, the region is likely to number well over six million. Where will these people go? While the overall historic density in the region is 7.7 housing units per acre, new construction on undeveloped land including multi-family housing is being built at only 3.7 units per acre. Low densities mean suburban sprawl.

Schools and other public facilities can't keep up with demand. The City of San Diego alone needs 2.5 billion dollars in new infrastructure. Highways are congested, but this new population will need another 1,300 lane miles of freeways because each new person adds 1.29 vehicles to the roads. This means six more freeways that will duplicate a major freeway already in place. In addition, 37 square miles of parking must be provided for each new million people added to the region.

Growth management becomes a critical issue in land use regulation when rapid growth overwhelms public facilities and services and sprawls outward, uncontrolled. This is what has happened in San Diego. Here, as in other urban areas, new development has outpaced population growth. In New Jersey, for example, the state's population grew just 1.2% in the 5 years from 2002 to 2007 while the amount of land classified as urban increased 5.3%, more than four times that rate. See J. Hasse et al., Urban Growth and Open Space Loss in New Jersey from 1986 Through 2007 (2010), available at http://gis.rowan.edu/projects/luc/. For a graphics view, go to http://science.nasa.gov/science-news/science-at-nasa/2002/11oct_sprawl/.

Defining sprawl and its problems. There is no universally accepted definition of sprawl, but it is usefully defined as "low density leap-frog development characterized by unlimited outward extension." R. Burchell et al., Transit Cooperative Research Program, The Costs of Sprawl — Revisited 2 (1998). Automobile dependency is another contributing factor, and some commentators define sprawl as low density, discontinuous, automobile-dependent development. For a comprehensive look at the issues surrounding automotive dependency, see A. Downs, Still Stuck in Traffic: Coping with Peak-Hour Traffic Congestion (2004). Discontinuous development is caused by leapfrogging, when developers pass over land in inner areas and build on cheaper, less regulated land further out, leaving vacant tracts undeveloped. See Heim, *Leapfrogging, Urban Sprawl, and Growth Management: Phoenix, 1950-2000*, 60 Am. J. Econ. & Sociology 1 (2001). Other critics have created more complex sprawl indices. See Ewing, Pendall & Chen, Measuring Sprawl and Its Impacts (2002) (sprawl index consisting of residential density, neighborhood mix, strength of activity centers and street network design); Galster et al.,

Wrestling Sprawl to the Ground: Defining and Measuring an Elusive Concept, 12 Hous. Pol'y Debate 681 (2001) (sprawl definition based on "eight distinct dimensions of land use patterns: density, continuity, concentration, clustering, centrality, nuclearity, mixed uses and proximity," sprawl represented by low numbers on one or more of these dimensions).

Sprawl, and the rapid growth that usually goes with it, create a number of problems. These include higher capital and operating costs for public facilities, higher transportation costs and traffic congestion, air pollution, the excessive conversion of agricultural and sensitive lands to new development, and an inability to provide public services and facilities as development occurs. See Johnson, *Environmental Impacts of Urban Sprawl: A Survey of the Literature and Proposed Research Agenda*, 33 Env't & Plan. 717 (2001). Some commentators claim sprawl also contributes to racial segregation and tax-base inequality. M. Orfield, American Metropolitics 61, 63 (2002) (finding these effects in regions where population density declined the most). Downs, *Some Realities About Sprawl and Urban Decline*, 10 Housing Pol'y Debate 955 (1999), concluded there was no meaningful or statistical relationship between any of the specific sprawl traits and either measure of urban decline, but that the general growth process was the likely cause of economic poverty.

Defining Growth Management. Here is a typical definition:

> Growth management is active and dynamic . . . ; it seeks to maintain an ongoing equilibrium between development and conservation, between various forms of development and concurrent provision of infrastructure, between the demands for public services generated by growth and the supply of revenues to finance these demands, and between progress and equity. [Chinitz, *Growth Management: Good for the Town, Bad for the Nation?*, 56 J. Am. Plan. Ass'n 3, 6 (1990).]

For an elaboration of this definition, see Douglas Porter's Managing Growth in America's Communities 12–13 (2d ed. 2008), hereinafter *Managing Growth*. It is important to understand that growth management addresses the rate of growth and the sequencing — where growth takes place. Also, growth management can be to encourage or stimulate growth. See the South Florida Regional Planning Council's "Eastward Ho!" program, which is designed to control the rate of growth and stimulate development of the existing urban core in the eastern end of Miami-Dade, Broward and Palm Beach counties. See www.sfrpc.com/eho.htm, and www.sfrpc.com/brwnflds/brn_corr.pdf.

Traditional zoning seems incapable of dealing with this problem. Zoning assumes that growth will occur and primarily regulates its location and intensity. Zoning does place implicit limits on growth because the density and location assignments of the zoning ordinance place a nominal cap on development in the community, but the ease with which ordinances can be amended (see Chapter 6) makes this process somewhat more theoretical than real. Zoning can also be used to implement growth-staging policies. For example, a community can hold back growth by placing land in a low-density zone or in a zone with no marketable use, e.g. heavy industry, and then rezone to permit development by shifting to more intensive or marketable uses. But traditional zoning does not include explicit growth-management controls.

> All of this means that the zoning map is not a very useful tool for planning such capital improvements as new highways, parks, and schools. Few communities are rich enough to build major roads and trunk sewer and water lines into all their undeveloped areas. Thus, to the extent that a community wants to invest in infrastructure for future needs, public officials would like to know where and when growth will occur. Because the

> zoning map does not guarantee what development will take place in what location, many communities simply wait to see what will occur before making such improvements. However, the result of that very practical policy is that such improvements are not available before development takes place. [E. Kelly, Community Growth: Policies, Techniques, and Impacts 20 (1993).]

Land use regulations can also help create sprawl. Pendall, *Do Land-Use Controls Cause Sprawl?*, 26 Envtl. & Plan. Bull. 555 (1999), concluded that public facilities programs help reduce sprawl, while low density zoning, caps on building and a heavy reliance on the property tax encourage it.

Growth management programs fill this gap by requiring planning and land use regulation programs to deal with problems of rapid growth and urban sprawl. The next selection describes commonly-used growth management techniques in more detail.

E. Kelly, Planning, Growth, and Public Facilities: A Primer for Local Officials 16

(American Planning Association, Planning Advisory Service Report No. 447, 1993)

Types of Growth Management Programs . . . .

- *Adequate public facilities programs* establish criteria to prohibit development except where adequate public facilities are available. Good programs carefully define the meaning of the term "adequate," usually using level-of-service standards to measure acceptable performance levels for traffic, school, fire, and other systems with flexible capacities. These programs directly address the availability of public facilities to serve a particular development. . . .

- *Phased-growth programs* supplement zoning controls by defining when development can take place in a particular location. The capacity of public facilities, environmental issues, and general community growth policies help to determine the phasing patterns. In addition, some communities may find that establishing adequate public facilities standards for facilities like schools can be difficult because there is no precise way to measure capacity limits. In such communities, a growth-phasing program can encourage growth in areas that generally have the most available capacity in such facilities. . . .

- *Urban growth boundary programs* attempt to regulate the shape of the community by drawing a line around it and limiting or prohibiting development outside that line. The focus of such programs is typically the elimination of "sprawl" and the protection of agricultural and other open lands. . . . [Urban service lines, that define a boundary within which urban services will be provided, are a similar technique. — Eds.]

- *Rate-of-growth programs* establish a defined growth area, either as a percentage or as a number. [Petaluma, California was a famous example of such a program. The city adopted a quota of 500 dwelling units a year which it allocated under a point system. The Petaluma plan is discussed later in the chapter. — Eds.]

NOTES AND QUESTIONS

1. *Putting it all together.* Professor Kelly provides a typology of growth management programs that can be used individually or in combination. One of the best-known is in Montgomery County, Maryland, adjacent to Washington, D.C. It includes comprehensive and special area planning based on a corridor plan concept adopted for the entire region, an adequate public facilities program, a farmland protection program, an inclusionary housing program, and a transit-oriented development program. *Managing Growth,* at 55–62 (reviewing program and finding that the county is nearing build-out). Growth management does not always come easy. For the rise and fall of growth management in Loudoun County, Virginia outside Washington, D.C., see Swope, *Rendezvous with Density,* Governing, March, 2001, at 32; *Reversing Course,* Governing, March, 2004, at 20.

2. *Sprawl's costs and its defenders.* The most extensive survey of the costs of sprawl finds significant savings from compact as compared with sprawl development from 2000 to 2025. A compact growth scenario would save over 4 million acres of land, and $126 billion or nearly 11 percent on water, sewer and road infrastructure, which translates into $2250 for each housing unit. Overall residential costs would be reduced by about $410 billion or nearly seven percent, and the average cost of a home would be eight percent lower. W. Burchell et al., Sprawl Costs: Economic Impacts of Unchecked Development (2005). Not all of the assumptions behind the different scenarios are explained, however. These conclusions are consistent with most studies, which find significant savings from compact growth that range between $5000 and $7,500 per dwelling unit. T. Litman, Understanding Smart Growth Savings 6 (Victoria Transport Policy Inst., 2004), available at www.vtpi.org/sg_save.pdf; Emrath & Liu, *The Relationship Between CO_2 and Compactness,* Land Development, Winter 2009, at 14 (gasoline development less in compact developments).

Sprawl's defenders claim a dispersed pattern of suburban development offers advantages, such as travel flexibility through use of the automobile, the privacy of low density development, quality schools and a sense of community security. Fina & Shabman, *Some Unconventional Thoughts on Sprawl,* 23 Wm. & Mary Envtl. L. & Pol'y Rev. 739 (1999). Other observers claim the sprawl index is declining, urban development does not threaten agriculture, the effect of suburban development on local government costs is exaggerated, and air quality deteriorates at higher densities. S. Staley, The Sprawling of America: In Defense of the Dynamic City (Reason Pub. Pol'y Inst. Policy Paper 251, 1999). Other critics use neoclassic economics to claim that sprawl is economically efficient and beneficial and results from increased private wealth and increased use of the automobile. Glaesser & Kahn, *Sprawl and Smart Growth,* in Handbook of Urban and Regional Economics (4) ch. 56 (J. Henderson & J. Thisse eds., 2004). How does this debate influence the legality of growth management programs? How does the data on land inventories presented in Chapter 1 bear on this debate? For a rebuttal of these criticisms, see T. Litman, Evaluating Criticism of Smart Growth (Victoria Transport Policy Inst., 2010), available at www.vtpi.org/sgcritics.pdf.

3. *Externalities and the pricing alternative.* From another perspective, the costs of sprawl are simply a market externality that free markets cannot internalize. The argument is that new residents who settle in suburban areas in sprawl developments do not pay the costs of their development, which are forced on the public sector in the form of additional highways, congestion, air pollution and the like. They should thus remedy this problem by paying for the marginal cost of their development to the community, not just the average cost of providing services and facilities.

Programs that could do this would shift the cost of new development to new residents through impact fees on new development, peak-hour road tolls on major commuting highways; and a development tax on land converted from agricultural to urban use. How practical and effective these suggestions are another matter. Anthony Downs points out that impact fees have not stopped sprawl where they are used, and that the other proposals are not likely to be adopted. Downs, *supra*, at 962. If government must intervene with growth management because the market fails to properly allocate land use, is the basis for intervention different from when government intervenes to resolve potential land use conflicts in a community through a zoning ordinance?

4. *Exclusion and motivation.* Is growth management really an example of exclusionary zoning adopted by affluent, socially-stratified suburbs? The evidence is mixed. An empirical study found that building permit caps limited the number of Hispanic residents. Other growth controls, such as urban growth boundaries, adequate public facilities ordinances and moratoria, had a more limited effect on housing types and racial distribution. Pendall, *Local Land Use Regulation and the Chain of Exclusion*, 66 Am. Plan. Ass'n J. 125 (2000). See also Pendall & Carruthers, *Does Density Exacerbate Income Segregation? Evidence from U.S. Metropolitan Areas 1980 to 2000*, 14 Hous. Pol'y Debate 4 (2003) ("both increases and decreases in density yield less segregation then stable levels of density").

What about motivation? Most studies find that broad community characteristics, such as rate of growth and whether a community emphasizes homeowner interests or economic growth, determine whether a community adopts growth controls. Belief in governmental activism and concern about government's handling of land use issues are also positively related to growth controls. See Albrecht, Bultena & Hoeberg, *Constituency of the Antigrowth Movement: A Comparison of the Growth Orientations of Urban Status Groups*, 21 Urb. Aff. Q. 607 (1986). These factors are less important in counties, and the extent of urbanization is a dominant factor in counties adopting growth controls. Steel & Lovrich, *Growth Management Policy and County Government: Correlates of Policy Adoption Across the United States*, 32 State & Local Gov't Rev. 7 (2000). A California study found greater support for growth controls among women and in higher-income counties. Minorities were also supportive. Wassmer & Lachser, *Who Supports Local Growth and Regional Planning to Deal With its Consequences?*, 41 Urb. Aff. Rev. 621 (2006) (also reviewing earlier studies). See also Logan & Zou, *The Adoption of Growth Controls in Suburban Communities*, 71 Soc. Sci. Q. 118 (1990); Neiman & Fernandez, *Local Planners and Limits on Local Residential Development*, 66 J. Am. Plan. Ass'n 295 (2000).

5. *Growth management and market monopoly.* Some critics argue that communities can impose growth controls that restrict development or make it more expensive only if there is no market substitute for the housing opportunities the community provides. See, e.g., Ellickson, *Suburban Growth Controls: An Economic and Legal Analysis*, 86 Yale L.J. 384, 425–35 (1977). See also the argument in Chapter 5, sec. A1, *supra*, that only communities with a market monopoly can engage in exclusionary zoning.

The conventional view is that monopoly is unlikely in a suburban area fragmented into numerous suburban communities. Paradoxically, suburban fragmentation and the absence of regional coordination through regional planning usually create the pressures that lead to the adoption of growth controls. See Gottdiener, *Some Theoretical Issues in Growth Control Analysis*, 18 Urb. Aff. Q. 565, 567 (1983); M. Baldassare, The Growth Dilemma 139 (1981) (small unconnected suburban governments not well organized to compete for growth). Is this a reason to support or to oppose growth management? Is it possible that numerous suburban communities, nominally in competition, hold sufficiently similar social and economic views that they act in tandem (consciously or otherwise), thus creating a de facto monopoly despite their fragmentation? A Florida study showing that growth management controls had a negative impact on construction activity may support the monopoly thesis. See Feiock, *The Political Economy of Growth Management*, 22 Am. Pol. Q. 208 (1994) (also suggesting that environmental gains may offset economic losses).

6. *Price effects.* Growth management, like exclusionary zoning, is problematic if it increases the price of housing more than would have occurred without growth management. The evidence on price impacts is conflicting. Anthony, *State Growth Management and Housing Prices*, 87 Soc. Sci. Qtly. 22 (2006), reviewed the conflicting results in the studies and found problems with study methodologies. His study identified supply side restrictions on the housing, such as restrictions on the conversion of land to urban uses, and found a "statistically significant increase in the price of single-family houses attributable to statewide growth management." In an earlier article, he concluded that the program had significantly decreased housing affordability. *The Effects of Florida's Growth Management Act on Housing Affordability*, 69 J. Am. Plan. Ass'n 282 (2004). See also Katz & Rosen, *The Interjurisdictional Effects of Growth Controls on Housing Prices*, 30 J.L. & Econ. 149 (1987) (finding 17 to 38 percent increase in housing prices in communities with growth moratoria or growth controls); R. O'Toole, The Planning Tax: The Case Against Regional Growth-Management Planning, Policy Analysis No. 606 (Cato Inst. Dec. 6, 2007) (mandatory growth management planning added $130,000 for every home sold in 2006), available at http://www.cato.org/pubs/pas/pa-606.pdf. A series of essays in Growth Management and Affordable Housing: Do They Conflict? (A. Downs ed., 2004), presents a contrary view. Nelson et al., *The Link between Growth Management and Housing Affordability: The Academic Evidence, id.* at 117, 153, review the studies and conclude that "[m]arket demand, not land constraints, is the primary determinant of housing price." The authors also note that growth management programs can increase densities, improve the housing mix, shift the housing mix to multifamily housing and promote inclusionary housing programs. Lower transportation and energy costs and better access to jobs, services and amenities can offset an increase in housing prices. Downs also notes in conclusion, *id.* at 19, that growth management can coexist with and even promote affordable housing. See also Nelson, et al., The Link Between Growth Management and Housing Affordability (2002) (both traditional land use regulation and growth management can increase housing prices; choice is between good or bad regulation to improve housing choice), available at http://smartgrowthamerica.org/growthmanag.pdf; Wassmer & Bass, *Does a More Centralized Urban Form Raise Housing Prices?*, 25 J. Pol'y Analysis & Mgt. 439 (2006) (more centralized area exhibits lower median home value and lower percentage of homes in an upper-end price category).

7. *Sources.* For additional discussion of sprawl and growth management, see Revitalizing the City: Strategies to Contain Sprawl and Revive the Core (F. Wagner et al. eds., 2005); G. Knaap, A Requiem for Smart Growth in Planning Reform in the New Century ch. 7 (D. Mandelker ed., 2004); A. Nelson & J. Duncan, Growth Management Principles & Practices (1995); Burchell & Shad, *The Evolution of the Sprawl Debate in the United States*, 5 Hastings Nw. J. Envtl. L. & Pol'y 137 (1999); Gray, *Ten Years of Smart Growth: A Nod to Policies Past and a Prospective Glimpse into the Future*, 9 Cityscape 109 (2007); Starkweather et al., *Managing Growth: Recent Legal Literature*, 18 J. Plan. Lit. 267 (CPL Bibliography 371, 2004); Yee et al., *What is "Smart Growth?" — Really?*, 19 J. Plan. Lit. 301 (2005); Note, *Putting a*

Stop to Sprawl: State Intervention as a Tool for Growth Management, 62 Vand. L. Rev. 979 (2009); Student Article, *The Constitutionality of State Growth Management Programs*, 18 Land Use & Envtl. L. 145 (2002). See also D. Hayden, A Field Guide to Sprawl (2004). T. Litman, Smart Growth Reforms (Victoria Transport Policy Inst., 2005), available at http://vtpi.org/smart_growth_reforms.pdf, contains case studies and links to resource sites.

PROBLEM

River County is a rural county that includes Metro City, a major regional center with a population of 250,000, which is located at the western edge of the county. Most of the county is undeveloped. The county consists of rolling hills and an attractive river valley along the Swimming River, for which the county is named. The county seat, River City (population 25,000) is approximately at the middle of the county. River City is served with a public sewer and water system, but the rest of the county is not. There are no other incorporated municipalities in the county and, until recently, no other areas of urban settlement.

Urban growth from Metro City is beginning to spill over into River County. There has been some scattered residential development in recent years throughout the county, and some just outside the corporate limits of Metro City. These developments are served by on-site water and sewer systems, but schools are overcrowded and county roads have become congested and are operating at lower levels of service. The state has designated a corridor in this area for a limited-access connection to an Interstate highway, but construction is not scheduled for years. The county is authorized to, but does not, provide water and sewer service.

The county planning department has asked your advice on how to prepare a growth management program for the county. The planners have told you they prefer a program that will allow moderate expansion of River City and the creation of additional growth centers at appropriate points throughout the county. It will take time to bring public facilities and services up to standard, and the planners want to avoid further scattered development that will make the provision of facilities and services inefficient. The county has a conventional zoning ordinance, but the comprehensive plan is out of date. What would you advise? How will your answer be affected by the statutory authority available for planning and land use controls?

B. GROWTH MANAGEMENT STRATEGIES

This section reviews the growth management strategies that have been adopted throughout the country. It begins with programs that adopt a quota on new development, continues with programs related to the provision of adequate public facilities and concludes with programs that directly limit areas of urban growth.

[1.] Quota Programs

[a.] How These Programs Work

The most direct control on growth is an ordinance that limits the number of dwelling units that can be built in any one year and provides a method for allocating the available units in any one annual period. These programs are not common. A survey of 1,168 communities found only 45 with rate-of-growth programs in place, and most of these were in California. *Growth Controls and Affordable Housing: Results from a National Survey*, Am. Plan. Ass'n, PAS

Memo, Jan. 1995, at 3. Here is how this type of control works:

> Each system places a carefully selected numerical limit or quota on the amount of development which will be approved during a designated time frame. Development proposals are then evaluated and ranked based upon the degree that they satisfy criteria designed to ensure consistency with the system's objectives and goals. The quota is then allocated to the developments in accordance with their ranking until all proposals are approved or the quota for the time period is exhausted. [Chinn & Garvin, *Designing Development Allocation Systems*, Land Use L. & Zoning Digest, Vol. 44, No. 2, at 3 (1992).]

Communities evaluate and rank development proposals to determine which ones will receive an allotment under the quota. Point systems are one way of doing this. Developments receive a fixed number of points for satisfying each of the ranking criteria. Quota allocations are then assigned to developments with the most points. The use of point systems seems to be declining, however, as they have proved complicated and difficult to administer. Communities more frequently use flexible systems under which development allocation awards are based on community policies or simply awarded by lottery or on a first-come, first-served basis. See Chinn & Garvin, *supra*. Some programs also include a limitation on the percentage of new dwellings that can be built in any one year, exemptions for affordable housing and credits for protecting environmental areas or providing open space. See Amherst, Mass. Zoning Bylaw, Art. 14, §§ 14.0-14.6, www.amherstma.gov/DocumentView.aspx?DID=268. These programs do not usually consider the location of new development when they make development allocations, though the Petaluma plan, described *infra*, contained geographic priorities.

[b.] Takings and Other Constitutional Issues: The *Petaluma* Case

Development quotas raise a takings issue. Assume the quota is exhausted by the time a developer applies for an allocation. He can reapply, of course, the next year. Is the one-year delay a compensable temporary taking? Ripeness is one problem. Is the case unripe because no final decision has been made on the development application and the developer can simply reapply the following year? See *Long Beach Equities, Inc. v. County of Ventura*, 282 Cal. Rptr. 877 (Cal. App. 1991) (dismissing facial takings claim against timing and quota program and holding an as-applied takings claim unripe).

The landmark case on quota programs is *Construction Industry Ass'n v. City of Petaluma*, 522 F.2d 897 (9th Cir. 1975), which considered a substantive due process challenge to a point system that allocated a quota of 500 new dwelling units per year, and was concerned primarily with the exclusionary effects of the program. The court described the allocation procedure:

> At the heart of the allocation procedure is an intricate point system, whereby a builder accumulates points for conformity by his projects with the City's general plan and environmental design plans, for good architectural design, and for providing low and moderate income dwelling units and various recreational facilities. The Plan further directs that allocations of building permits are to be divided as evenly as feasible between the west and east sections of the City and between single-family dwellings and multiple residential units (including rental units), that the sections of the City closest to the center are to be developed first in order to cause "infilling" of vacant area, and that 8 to 12 per cent of the housing units approved be for low and moderate income persons. [*Id.* at 901.]

The court found that the primary purpose of the plan was to limit Petaluma's demographic and market growth rate in housing and "the immigration of new residents." The court concluded that the plan, if adopted throughout the region, would lead to a housing shortfall that would affect housing quality and mobility and the choice of housing available to lower income families. There was no evidence, however, that these negative impacts would occur in Petaluma, especially as the plan increased the number of multifamily and low-income units, which the court said were rarely built in the days before the plan. The court then held the plan constitutional:

> Although we assume that some persons desirous of living in Petaluma will be excluded under the housing permit limitation and that, thus, the Plan may frustrate some legitimate regional housing needs, the Plan is not arbitrary or unreasonable. We agree with appellees that unlike the situation in the past most municipalities today are neither isolated nor wholly independent from neighboring municipalities and that, consequently, unilateral land use decisions by one local entity affect the needs and resources of an entire region. It does not necessarily follow, however, that the due process rights of builders and landowners are violated merely because a local entity exercises in its own self-interest the police power lawfully delegated to it by the state. If the present system of delegated zoning power does not effectively serve the state interest in furthering the general welfare of the region or entire state, it is the state legislature's and not the federal courts' role to intervene and adjust the system. . . . [T]he federal court is not a super zoning board and should not be called on to mark the point at which legitimate local interests in promoting the welfare of the community are outweighed by legitimate regional interests. [*Id.* at 906.]

NOTES AND QUESTIONS

1. *Litigation strategy.* Plaintiff's lawyers in *Petaluma* brought the case on a right-to-travel claim, which they won in the district court but lost in the court of appeal. The idea was, of course, to get the court to raise the constitutional standard of review to strict scrutiny by asserting a fundamental constitutional right. By shifting to substantive due process as applied to an economic regulation, the court was able to fall back on the deferential review of land use regulations federal courts give under the substantive Due Process Clause. The right to travel is discussed further in Note 6, *infra*.

2. *More on Petaluma.* Some additional aspects of the Petaluma Plan at the time of the decision are not covered by the court's opinion and illustrate typical components of a rate-of-growth system. McGivern, *Putting a Speed Limit on Growth*, 38 Plan. 263 (1972) (author was planning director of Petaluma). Part of the purpose of the plan was to redistribute new growth equally between an older western and a newer eastern section of the city. The council could also require that between 8 and 12 percent of each annual quota must be lower-income housing.

A Residential Development Evaluation System was utilized to determine which developers would receive the annual quota of allowable dwelling units, based on a point system. From zero to five points were awarded for each of the following public facilities factors:

1. the capacity of the water system to provide for the needs of the proposed development without system extensions beyond those normally installed by the developer;

2. the capacity of the sanitary sewers to dispose of the wastes of the proposed development without system extensions beyond those normally installed by the developer;

3. the capacity of the drainage facilities to adequately dispose of the surface runoff of the proposed development without system extensions beyond those normally installed by the developer;

4. the ability of the Fire Department of the city to provide fire protection according to the established response standards of the city without the necessity of establishing a new station or requiring addition of major equipment to an existing station;

5. the capacity of the appropriate school to absorb the children expected to inhabit a proposed development without necessitating adding double sessions or other unusual scheduling or classroom overcrowding;

6. the capacity of major street linkage to provide for the needs of the proposed development without substantially altering existing traffic patterns or overloading the existing street systems, and the availability of other public facilities (such as parks and playgrounds) to meet the additional demands for vital public services without extension of services beyond those provided by the developer.

The evaluation system was utilized to require substantial contributions from developers for citywide facilities such as water, sewer, drainage, and fire protection. Would this be constitutional under *Dolan*?

The second review category was based on site and architectural design quality and a number of developer contributions. Some of the criteria on which developers were assigned points were the following: the provision of public and/or private usable open space and/or pathways along the Petaluma River or any creek; contributions to and extensions of existing systems of foot or bicycle paths, equestrian trails, and the greenbelt provided for in the Environmental Design Plan; the provision of needed public facilities such as critical linkages in the major street system, school rooms, or other vital public facilities; the extent to which the proposed development accomplishes an orderly and contiguous extension of existing development as against "leap frog" development; and the provision of units to meet the city's policy goal of 8 percent to 12 percent low- and moderate-income dwelling units annually.

As an alternative, what about distributing development permits under a quota on a first-come, first-served basis? Is this preferable to the elaborate scoring system Petaluma used? Would it stimulate a race to propose poorly planned developments?

3. *What happened in Petaluma.* In the first several years, the Petaluma program slowed down residential growth but did not increase the number of multifamily dwellings. S. Seidel, Housing Costs & Government Regulations: Confronting the Regulatory Maze 222–28 (1978). Another study of this early period found the price of housing had increased significantly more in Petaluma than in one nearby comparison city but not in another, and that small, low-priced houses practically disappeared. Schwartz, Hansen & Green, *Suburban Growth Controls and the Price of New Housing*, 8 J. Envtl. Econ. & Mgt. 313 (1981).

Another review was critical:

> Petaluma's point system did not work well. Developers had difficulty understanding the complex point system. City staff had difficulty administering it despite a computer program designed to compute points. Projects which met minimum standards

> eventually obtained approvals. The time-consuming and costly ranking process had little impact on actual approval or denial of projects. In order to achieve minimum numbers of points, developers included in their projects some expensive features, probably not wanted by occupants or really needed by the city. As a few large developers came to dominate homebuilding in Petaluma, and as the pattern of approvals became clear, developers submitted projects which were adequate, but not excellent. In addition, it was difficult to get a majority of the evaluation committee to meet. Finally, one member could unduly skew the total points awarded and complicate the approval process by ranking a project very low or very high. [LeGates, *The Emergence of Flexible Growth Management Systems in the San Francisco Bay Area*, 24 Loyola L.A. L. Rev. 1035, 1060 (1991).]

4. *Petaluma today.* The residential Development Growth Management System with its annual quota of 500 units is still in effect, though the city has suspended the annual allocation process, but not all of the quota is typically used in any one year. A new general plan includes comprehensive land use policies for a projected buildout to 2025. City of Petaluma, General Plan 2025 (2008), available at http://cityofpetaluma.net/cdd/pdf/general-plan-may08/general-plan-may08.pdf. In early 1998, voters adopted an urban growth boundary extending to 2018 as the city neared an urban limits line established in 1969. See Lockwood, *Pioneering Petaluma*, Planning, Planning, Nov. 1998, at 16 (1998). Voters decided in the November 2010 election to extend the growth boundary limits to 2025. Much of the city's central area is vacant, but the city adopted a new Central Petaluma Specific Plan in 2003. It includes a Smart Code that incorporates New Urbanist principles. A redevelopment program is also under way.

5. *The irony of quotas.* In an essay in which he makes a plea for legitimizing quotas, land use lawyer Jan Krasnowiecki states:

> The irony of it is that while standard zoning does not approve of quotas (at least until the New York court suggested otherwise in *Ramapo*), *the easiest way to run a quota system is to employ standard zoning.* All you have to do is zone all of the undeveloped areas of the municipality at a level which is just below the level at which it is economically safe to develop. If you do the job just right, no one will be able to show that he cannot develop his property yet no one will, in fact, develop until you grant him some change. . . . Thus by employing standard zoning you can run a quota system without ever stating the principles upon which it is based. [Krasnowiecki, *Legal Aspects of Planned Unit Development in Theory and Practice*, in Frontiers of Planned Unit Development 99, 105 (R. Burchell ed., 1973) (emphasis in original).]

What do you think of his argument?

6. *The right to travel.* Because it triggers stricter scrutiny, the right to travel theory enjoyed a brief period of popularity in land use litigation, but recent decisions have followed *Petaluma* and have rejected right to travel arguments. One case had this to say about the right to travel as to the permit program of the interim California coastal act:

> It does not follow, however, that all regulations affecting travel, however indirect or inconsequential, constitute invasions of the fundamental right. The right may be invoked if the regulations "unreasonably burden or restrict" the freedom of movement. In a particular case the question is whether the travel inhibited is of sufficient importance to individual liberty to give rise to a constitutional violation. Thus far the United States Supreme Court has invoked the right to travel only in cases involving

invidious discrimination, durational residence requirements or direct restrictions on interstate or foreign travel. . . .

We fail to see how the Coastal Initiative interferes with fundamental right to travel. It is not discriminatory; it imposes no durational residence requirement; it exacts no penalty for exercising the right to travel or to select one's place of residence. In short, it has no chilling effect on an individual's freedom of movement. [*CEEED v. California Coastal Zone Conservation Comm'n*, 118 Cal. Rptr. 315, 333 (Cal. Ct. App. 1974).]

See also *Northern Ill. Home Bldrs. Ass'n v. County of Du Page*, 649 N.E.2d 384 (Ill. 1993) (no standing to assert right to travel). The U.S. Supreme Court's decision in *Saenz v. Roe*, 526 U.S. 489 (1999), which has revived constitutional interest in "right to travel" theories, was not a land use case and it does not appear to challenge the logic of state cases such as *CEEED*.

The *Petaluma* case was decided under federal constitutional law, which was deferential. A less sophisticated quota program received less favorable treatment in the following case that was brought in state court:

ZUCKERMAN v. TOWN OF HADLEY

442 Mass. 511, 813 N.E.2d 843 (2004),
noted, 20 Wash. U. J.L. & Pol'y 375 (2006),
11 Suffolk J. Trial & App. Adv. 79 (2006)

Cordy, J. This case involves a landowner's challenge to the statutory and constitutional validity of a town zoning bylaw of unlimited duration that regulates the number of building permits issued annually for the construction of single family homes. It requires us to confront more broadly the issues of duration and purpose left open in *Sturges v. Chilmark*, 402 N.E.2d 1346 (Mass. App. 1980), in which the court held that a "municipality may impose reasonable time limitations on development, at least where those restrictions are temporary and adopted to provide controlled development while the municipality engages in comprehensive planning studies." We now make explicit what was implied in the *Sturges* case, that, absent exceptional circumstances not present here, restrictions of unlimited duration on a municipality's rate of development are in derogation of the general welfare and thus are unconstitutional.

Background.

The facts of the case are largely set forth in the decision of the Land Court. At a special town meeting held in October, 1988, the town of Hadley (town) adopted a rate of development amendment (ROD amendment) to its zoning bylaws. The ROD amendment limits the rate of growth in the town by restricting the number of building permits that may be issued in any given year to a developer of lots held in common ownership, generally requiring development to be spread over a period of up to ten years.[2]

---

[2] The relevant portions of the rate of development amendment (ROD amendment) provide:

"15.0.1. Building permits for the construction of dwellings on lots held in common ownership on the effective date of this provision shall not be granted at a rate per annum greater than as permitted by the following schedule . . . .

"15.1.1. For such lots containing a total area of land sufficient to provide more than ten dwellings at the maximum density permitted for the District in which such lots are located: one tenth of the number of dwellings permitted to be constructed or placed on said area of land based on said maximum permitted density.

As articulated by the town, the bylaw was adopted for the purposes of preserving the town's agricultural land and character, and providing for a "phasing-in" of population growth, thereby allowing time for the town to plan and to expand its public services, consistent with the fiscal constraints of Proposition 2 ½.[3]

[This proposition imposes a 2 ½ percent annual limit on the increase in property tax revenue raised by a municipality. — Eds.] The ROD amendment has been in effect for fifteen years. It is undisputed that the town intends the restriction to be of unlimited duration.[4] Since adopting the ROD amendment in 1988, the town has undertaken various initiatives in response to the pressures imposed by the demands of growth. It has engaged in two planning exercises, the first culminating in 1989 with a growth management plan,[5] and the second in 1998 with an open space and recreation plan.[6] . . .[7] It has also appropriated funds to participate in the Commonwealth's agricultural preservation restriction program,[8] built a new elementary school and a public safety building, hired more full-time officials, and improved its water supply by purchasing land for aquifer protection and enhancing its water delivery system. The town has not, however, adopted many of the measures recommended in the studies that it undertook. It has not prepared or adopted a comprehensive land use plan or a community open space bylaw (as recommended in the 1998 study); it has not effected a

---

"15.2.1. For such lots containing a total area of land insufficient to provide more than ten dwellings at the maximum density permitted under these Bylaws for the District in which such lots are located: one dwelling."

(3) The preamble to the ROD amendment recites that the town is "dedicated to keep the distinction as the most agricultural community in the Commonwealth," "operates entirely with a part[-]time staff of elected officials," that the town's existing school system is operating near capacity, that its fire department is comprised solely of volunteer fire fighters and that its police department employs only three full-time officers, that fiscal constraints imposed by the requirements of Proposition 2 ½, limit the town's ability "to correct the situations which could arise by a sudden increase in population," and that a "rate of development bylaw will allow the Town of Hadley to plan for any new or expanded services required by a population increase."

(4) The town highlights what in its view is the efficacy of the ROD amendment in slowing growth, noting that, in 1987, the year before the amendment was adopted, the town issued fifty building permits, and that, in the seven years following the amendment's adoption, that number was, on average, reduced by more than one-half.

(5) The growth management plan arose from an effort by the town "to revise and update the Hadley zoning bylaw to better achieve established community goals, such as protecting community character, preserving farmland and water resources, and strengthening the local tax base." It recommended, among other measures, development of a bylaw to address commercial site plan approval; modification of the table of permitted uses; general revision and reorganization of the zoning bylaws; consideration of mechanisms for the protection of farmland; expansion of affordable housing; and preservation of historic properties.

(6) The plan "expanded . . . Hadley's previous land protection efforts to build a more comprehensive open space system," emphasizing "farmland protection[,] . . . conservation of historic resources[,] and development of new recreational opportunities." The plan specifically described five goals and objectives: protection of agricultural, natural, and historic resources; provision of recreational opportunities; and plan implementation. It also outlined a five-year schedule for its realization.

(7) In December, 1987, shortly before the adoption of the ROD amendment, the University of Massachusetts at Amherst completed a study for the town, entitled: A Preliminary Growth Management Study for Hadley, Massachusetts. Its principal recommendations were: reorganization of the town's planning process; modification of waterfront zoning rules; enhanced flood plain protection; protection of farmland through development of incentive districts, limited water and sewer service expansion, use of land trusts, and establishment of overlay districts; and revision of specified commercial and residential zoning rules to facilitate conservation.

(8) The agricultural preservation restriction program essentially buys deed restrictions to prevent farmland from being developed. Pursuant to [statute], the town also has elected to designate "agricultural incentive areas," giving it a right of first refusal to purchase farmland that otherwise would be sold or converted for nonagricultural use. As the result of these efforts, the town in 1998 was second in the Commonwealth in the number of acres of protected farmland.

major overhaul of its zoning bylaws (as recommended in the 1989 study); it has not adopted a cluster development bylaw (as recommended in the 1989 study), increased minimum lot sizes in agricultural districts to 80,000 square feet (as recommended in the 1987 study), or hired a full-time planner (also recommended in the 1987 study).

Since 1986, the plaintiff, Martha Zuckerman (or her husband), has owned an approximately sixty-six acre parcel of land located in an agricultural-residential use district within the town. The zoning bylaw applicable to such districts permits, as of right, detached one-family dwellings, agriculture, and the raising of stock. Under the subdivision control law in effect in Hadley, Zuckerman's property could accommodate a large subdivision of approximately forty single-family homes. The ROD amendment, however, limits development of her property to four units a year for ten years.

Claiming that it is not economically feasible to sequence the development of her property over a ten-year period, Zuckerman brought an action in the Land Court seeking a declaration that the ROD amendment was invalid and unconstitutional, or alternatively that it constituted a taking for which she must be compensated. The judge, ruling on cross motions for summary judgment, relied on *Sturges v. Chilmark* in concluding that "time limitations on development must be temporary and must be dependent on the completion and implementation of comprehensive planning studies."[11] Finding that the ROD amendment created a restriction on development of unlimited duration and that the town had failed to implement many of the measures recommended in the planning studies, the judge held the ROD amendment unconstitutional and entered judgment for Zuckerman. The town appealed, and we transferred the appeal to this court on our own motion.

Discussion.

As we observed in *Sturges*, "from the wide scope of the purposes of The Zoning Act it is apparent that the Legislature intended to permit cities and towns to adopt any and all zoning provisions which are constitutionally permissible," subject only to "limitations expressly stated in that act) or in other controlling legislation." Like the Land Court judge, we find no statutory bar to the adoption of the ROD amendment, and hence move directly to the constitutional question.

The classic recitation of the constitutional test is whether a zoning bylaw is "clearly arbitrary and unreasonable, having no substantial relation to the public health, safety, morals, or general welfare." [Citing *Euclid v. Ambler Realty Co.* and Massachusetts cases.] More specifically, due process requires that a zoning bylaw bear a rational relation to a legitimate zoning purpose. In our review, we make every presumption in favor of a zoning bylaw, and we measure its constitutional validity against any permissible public objective that the legislative body may plausibly be said to have been pursuing. "If its reasonableness is fairly debatable, [a zoning bylaw] will be sustained." [Citing *Sturges.*][12] In the *Sturges* case, we upheld a

---

[11] In *Sturges* the need for comprehensive planning studies was prompted by legitimate concerns over subsoil conditions that might affect water supplies and sewage disposal. In reaching its conclusion upholding the restrictions on development, the court noted that the bylaw furthered regional ("not simply local") concerns in preserving the unique and perishable qualities of the island of Martha's Vineyard, concerns that had been "articulated by the Legislature."

[12] More recent Supreme Court cases have articulated the test somewhat differently, using the more familiar language of the rational relation standard. See, e.g., *Schad v. Mount Ephraim*, 452 U.S. 61 (1981) ("Where property

restrictive rate of development zoning bylaw, adopted by the town of Chilmark to control the rate of growth for a limited period to allow time for the town to carry out various planning studies and to implement various measures necessary to protect the water supply and to ensure proper sewage disposal.[13]

Hadley asks us to expand that holding to zoning bylaws intended to control growth for an unlimited duration to assist towns in better managing their fiscal resources and in preserving their character, in this case, agricultural.

The town acknowledges that the purposes justifying the bylaw in Chilmark were short lived and specific, observes that the bylaw's relationship to those purposes depended on its temporary nature, but concludes that restraining the rate of development is a zoning tool available whenever, as in Chilmark, it bears an adequate relation to a legitimate purpose. So prefaced, the town argues that the pressures of growth justifying the ROD amendment in Hadley are indefinite in duration and substantial in their potential effect on the town's finances and character, and that the unlimited duration of the ROD amendment is therefore consistent with the purposes that motivated it. In essence, the town contends that, so long as the ROD amendment continues to limit growth over time, creating the buffer that the town considers necessary to absorb an increasing population while continuing to preserve those characteristics and to provide those public facilities that make Hadley a desirable place to live, the amendment is in the public interest and advances legitimate zoning purposes, and thus passes constitutional muster.

We recognize the enormous pressures faced by rural and suburban towns presented with demands of development, and that towns may seek to prevent or to curtail the visual blight and communal degradation that growth unencumbered by guidance or restraint may occasion. In this respect, however, Hadley is no different from other towns facing the pressures attendant to an influx of growth. Like all such towns, Hadley may, in an effort to preserve its character and natural resources, adopt any combination of zoning bylaws,[14] and participate in a wide variety of State-enacted programs,[15] that may, as a practical matter, limit growth by physically limiting the amount of land available for development. Hadley may also slow the rate of its growth within reasonable time limits as we explained in *Sturges* and *Collura*, to allow it to engage in planning and preparation for growth. What it may not do is adopt a

---

interests are adversely affected by zoning, the courts generally have emphasized the breadth of municipal power to control land use and have sustained the regulation if it is rationally related to legitimate state concerns . . ."); *Moore v. East Cleveland*, 431 U.S. 494, 498 & n.6 (1977) (plurality opinion) (requiring "rational relationship").

[13] In *Collura v. Arlington*, 329 N.E.2d 733 (Mass. 1975), we upheld an interim zoning bylaw that prohibited construction of new apartment buildings in certain districts of a town for a two-year period while the town developed a comprehensive plan, indicating that "interim zoning can be considered a salutary device in the process of plotting a comprehensive zoning plan to be employed to prevent disruption of the ultimate plan itself."

[14] Within reason, such bylaws might include, for example, either large-lot or cluster zoning, expanded frontage requirements, the development of exclusive agricultural use districts, or any other measure permitted by statute. *See generally, e.g.*, Comment, *Preserving Our Heritage*, 17 Pace L. Rev. 591, 619–623 (1997).

[15] For example, towns may seek the purchase of deed restrictions to prevent development of farmland; elect to designate agricultural incentive areas and thereby gain a right of first refusal to purchase farmland that otherwise would be sold or converted to nonagricultural use; accept the provisions of the *Community Preservation Act*, which allows communities to establish preservation funds (and to tap a State matching fund) that they may use for open space protection; and obtain zero-interest loans from the Commonwealth's Open Space Acquisition Revolving Fund to acquire land for open space. [citing statutes].

zoning bylaw for the purpose of limiting the rate of growth for an indefinite or unlimited period.[16]

Restraining the rate of growth for a period of unlimited duration, and not for the purpose of conducting studies or planning for future growth, is inherently and unavoidably detrimental to the public welfare, and therefore not a legitimate zoning purpose.[17]

Rate of development bylaws such as the one at issue here are restrictions not on how land ultimately may be used, but on when certain classes of property owners may use their land. Where classic zoning bylaws keep the pig out of the parlor, see *City of Euclid v. Ambler Realty Co.*, rate of development bylaws tell the farmer how many new pigs may be in the barnyard each year. In their intent and in their effect, rate of development bylaws reallocate population growth from one town to another, and impose on other communities the increased burdens that one community seeks to avoid. Through zoning bylaws, a town may allow itself breathing room to plan for the channeling of normal growth; it may not turn that breathing room into a choke hold against further growth. Despite the perceived benefits that enforced isolation may bring to a town facing a new wave of permanent home seekers, it does not serve the general welfare of the Commonwealth to permit one particular town to deflect that wave onto its neighbors. *Euclid v. Ambler Realty Co.* (zoning regulation invalid "where the general public interest would so far outweigh the interest of the municipality that the municipality would not be allowed to stand in the way"). As concisely stated by the Supreme Court of New Hampshire, "preventing the entrance of newcomers in order to avoid burdens upon the public services and facilities . . . is not a valid public purpose." *Beck v. Raymond*, 394 A.2d 847 (N.H. 1978).

There is little doubt that the initial adoption of Hadley's ROD amendment appropriately sought to enable the town better to plan for growth and to adopt programs and other zoning measures to preserve its agricultural resources and character. But fifteen years have passed, and the town has had more than ample time to fulfill that legitimate purpose. Neither the desire for better fiscal management nor the revenue-raising limitations imposed by Proposition 2 ½, is a proper basis on which to adopt a zoning ordinance intended to limit growth or the rate of growth in a particular town for the indefinite future. Except when used to give communities breathing room for periods reasonably necessary for the purposes of growth planning generally, or resource problem solving specifically, as determined by the

---

[16] Our holding in [*Sturges*], and our holding today, should make clear that bylaws restraining growth pass constitutional muster only where they specifically contain time limitations or where it is abundantly clear that they are temporary, because they are enacted to assist a particular planning process. Where the needs of a town to plan for an aspect of growth prove to exceed the time limits of a bylaw, the town may extend the restriction for such limited time as is reasonably necessary to effect its specific purpose.

[17] In *Home Builders Ass'n of Cape Cod, Inc. v. Cape Cod Comm'n*, 808 N.E.2d 315 (Mass. 2004), we upheld the town of Barnstable's adoption of a zoning ordinance that included a permanent building cap. We did so recognizing that the cap was adopted to protect a sole source aquifer, the integrity of which was an issue of regional importance, and that the cap was adopted through the Cape Cod regional commission, a body specifically established by the State Legislature in recognition of the "unique natural, coastal, scientific, historical, cultural, architectural, archaeological, recreational, and other values . . . threatened . . . by uncoordinated or inappropriate uses of the region's land and other resources." St. 1989, c. 716, § 1 (a). The purpose of the commission was to enable "the implementation of a regional land-use policy plan for all of Cape Cod, to recommend for designation [of] specific areas of Cape Cod as districts of critical planning concern, and to review and regulate developments of regional impact." St. 1989, c. 716, § 1 (b). The unusual circumstance that the entire town lay atop the aquifer, and that the zoning ordinance permanently restricting development was adopted by a body established to address issues of region-wide concern, presented the unusual situation in which the permanent bylaw advanced the public welfare.

specific circumstances of each case, such zoning ordinances do not serve a permissible public purpose, and are therefore unconstitutional.

The judgment of the Land Court is affirmed.

So ordered.

NOTES AND QUESTIONS

1. *Legal claims against growth quotas. Hadley* is the first case that directly confronted the issue of development quotas and found them unconstitutional. It reached a decision markedly different from what might be expected in a federal court. The Massachusetts court seems to view the restriction on development as an indefinite moratorium. What, if any, quota restriction would this court find constitutional? Would the adoption of the comprehensive plan and other recommendations made to the town have helped with the constitutional issue? Would the Petaluma program be constitutional in Massachusetts? The Land Court is a specialized lower court tribunal.

Takings claims against development quotas have been less successful. See *Del Oro Hills v. City of Oceanside*, 37 Cal. Rptr. 2d 677 (Cal. App. 1995) (rejecting facial takings claim to annual quota on residential development); *Wilkinson v. Board of County Comm'rs*, 872 P.2d 1269 (Colo. App. 1993) (upholding rejection of development proposal; takings claim not ripe). What would the takings argument be? The Nevada court held that a growth cap of 280 units per year adopted by initiative was consistent with a county's comprehensive plan. *Sustainable Growth Initiative Comm. v. Jumpers, LLC*, 128 P.3d 452 (Nev. 2006). See also *Fiore v. Town of South Kingstown*, 783 A.2d 944 (R.I. 2001) (dismissing appeal as moot but affirming trial court decision upholding 24-month building cap).

2. *Growth caps.* What about an absolute limit on growth? The *Cape Cod* case discussed in the principal decision actually raised only statutory issues, though the court in *Hadley* seemed to approve its constitutionality because of its special purpose. A Florida court invalidated a much-publicized absolute limit on population growth in *City of Boca Raton v. Boca Villas Corp.*, 371 So. 2d 154 (Fla. App. 1979). A charter amendment adopted by popular vote imposed a development cap of 40,000 dwelling units. The city council then cut the permitted densities in all multifamily districts in half. The court found that the dwelling unit limit was supported by after-the-fact studies, was not supported in trial testimony by the planning director, and was adopted without consulting the planning department. The court also found no public service inadequacies or environmental problems that would support the population limit. This litigation is said to have cost the parties $1.5 million.

3. *California legislation.* Quota programs are now limited by legislation in California. Comprehensive plans in California must contain a mandatory housing element in which communities are required to provide for their fair share of regional housing needs. In addition, these programs must meet the following statutory requirement:

> If a county or city . . . adopts or amends a mandatory general plan element which operates to limit the number of housing units which may be constructed on an annual basis, such adoption or amendment shall contain findings which justify reducing the housing opportunities of the region. The findings shall include all of the following: (a) A description of the city's or county's appropriate share of the regional need for housing. (b) A description of the specific housing programs and activities being

undertaken by the local jurisdiction to fulfill the requirements of . . . [the housing element in the plan.] (c) A description of how the public health, safety, and welfare would be promoted by such adoption or amendment. (d) The fiscal and environmental resources available to the local jurisdiction. [Cal. Gov't Code § 65302.8.]

Lee v. City of Monterey Park, 219 Cal. Rptr. 309 (Cal. App. 1985), held that a complaint challenging an annual building quota stated a cause of action under this statute and related statutes imposing similar requirements. The complaint stated the city adopted the quota without considering the housing needs of the region, that the quota did not accommodate competing municipal interests, including the need for affordable housing, and that the burden on the city's public facilities were no greater than in other cities in the region. Would a quota adopted under this statute be constitutional in Massachusetts?

[2.] Facility-Related Programs

[a.] Phased Growth Programs

The statement of purpose for the Town of Hadley development restriction cited the need to plan for new or expanded services as one reason for the ordinance, but did not tie the development restrictions to the availability of public facilities. A phased growth program is one way of achieving this objective. As Professor Kelly pointed out, it can define when public facilities are available that are adequate for development in a particular location. It does not necessarily place a limit on the rate of growth, nor does it usually place limits on the expansion of an urban area.

The highest New York court, in an early landmark case, upheld a phased growth program adopted by the Town of Ramapo, New York. The decision was all the more remarkable because at least one New York case had invalidated early forms of staged growth control. See *Albrecht Realty Co. v. Town of New Castle*, 167 N.Y.S.2d 843 (Sup. Ct. 1957) (invalidating building permit quota). When reading this decision, keep in mind that Ramapo is a New York town, a unit of local government usually limited in size that includes both unincorporated areas and incorporated villages. This type of local government is unusual and found only in a few states. Ramapo, located west of the Hudson River, had grown at an accelerated rate after construction of a thruway bridge opened up commuting to New York City and adjacent suburbs. The growth management program provided for a total build-out of the town during the growth management period, again an unusual strategy that is not possible in larger jurisdictions. It covered the entire town but included only the unincorporated area because the villages are distinct legal units.

The program included a unique special permit requirement for new residential development that linked the permit to the availability of adequate public facilities. It also included a point system and assigned points to new development based on distance from a list of public facilities. A proposed development had to have a minimum number of points before a permit could be granted.

GOLDEN v. RAMAPO PLANNING BOARD

30 N.Y.2d 359, 285 N.E.2d 291, ***appeal dismissed***, 409 U.S. 1003 (1972)

SCILEPPI, JUDGE:

Both cases arise out of the 1969 amendments to the Town of Ramapo's Zoning Ordinance. [Property owners and a builders' association brought a facial attack on the ordinance. The town planning board had denied subdivision approval for some of the property owners because they had not obtained the special development permit. The court treated the action as a facial attack and held that the alleged harm was sufficient to raise a justiciable issue concerning the validity of the ordinance.] . . .

Experiencing the pressures of an increase in population and the ancillary problem of providing municipal facilities and services,[(1)] the Town of Ramapo, as early as 1964, made application for [a federal] grant . . . to develop a master plan. [This federal program has since been terminated. — Eds.] The plan's preparation included a four-volume study of the existing land uses, public facilities, transportation, industry and commerce, housing needs and projected population trends. The proposals appearing in the studies were subsequently adopted pursuant to section 272-a of the Town Law, in July, 1966 and implemented by way of a master plan. The master plan was followed by the adoption of a comprehensive zoning ordinance. Additional sewage district and drainage studies were undertaken which culminated in the adoption of a capital budget, providing for the development of the improvements specified in the master plan within the next six years. Pursuant to section 271 of the Town Law, authorizing comprehensive planning, and as a supplement to the capital budget, the Town Board adopted a capital program which provides for the location and sequence of additional capital improvements for the 12 years following the life of the capital budget. The two plans, covering a period of 18 years, detail the capital improvements projected for maximum development and conform to the specifications set forth in the master plan, the official map and drainage plan.

Based upon these criteria, the Town subsequently adopted the subject amendments for the alleged purpose of eliminating premature subdivision and urban sprawl. Residential development is to proceed according to the provision of adequate municipal facilities and services, with the assurance that any concomitant restraint upon property use is to be of a "temporary" nature and that other private uses, including the construction of individual housing, are authorized.

The amendments did not rezone or reclassify any land into different residential or use

---

[(1)] The Town's allegations that present facilities are inadequate to service increasing demands goes uncontested. We must assume, therefore, that the proposed improvements, both as to their nature and extent, reflect legitimate community needs and are not veiled efforts at exclusion.

In the period 1940-1968 population in the unincorporated areas of the Town increased 285.9%. Between the years of 1950-1960 the increase, again in unincorporated areas, was 130.8%; from 1960-1966 some 78.5%; and from the years 1966-1969 20.4%. In terms of real numbers, population figures compare at 58,626 as of 1966 with the largest increment of growth since the decennial census occurring in the undeveloped areas. Projected figures, assuming current land use and zoning trends, approximate a total Town population of 120,000 by 1985. Growth is expected to be heaviest in the currently undeveloped western and northern tiers of the Town, predominantly in the form of submission development with some apartment construction. A growth rate of some 1,000 residential units per annum has been experienced in the unincorporated areas of the Town.

districts,[2] but, for the purposes of implementing the proposals appearing in the comprehensive plan, consist, in the main, of additions to the definitional sections of the ordinance, section 46-3, and the adoption of a new class of "Special Permit Uses," designated "Residential Development Use." "Residential Development Use" is defined as "The erection or construction of dwellings [on] any vacant plots, lots or parcels of land" (§ 46-3, as amd.); and, any person who acts so as to come within that definition, "shall be deemed to be engaged in residential development which shall be a separate use classification under this ordinance and subject to the requirement of obtaining a special permit from the Town Board" (§ 46-3, as amd.).

The standards for the issuance of special permits are framed in the terms of the availability to the proposed subdivision plat of five essential facilities or services; specifically (1) public sanitary sewers or approved substitutes; (2) drainage facilities; (3) improved public parks or recreation facilities, including public schools; (4) State, county or town roads — major, secondary or collector; and, (5) firehouses. No special permit shall issue unless the proposed residential development has accumulated 15 development points, to be computed on a sliding scale of values assigned to the specified improvements under the statute. Subdivision is thus a function of immediate availability to the proposed plat of certain municipal improvements; the avowed purpose of the amendments being to phase residential development to the Town's ability to provide the above facilities or services.

Certain savings and remedial provisions are designed to relieve of potentially unreasonable restrictions. Thus, the board may issue special permits vesting a present right to proceed with residential development in such year as the development meets the required point minimum, but in no event later than the final year of the 18-year capital plan. The approved special use permit is fully assignable, and improvements scheduled for completion within one year from the date of an application are to be credited as though existing on the date of the application. A prospective developer may advance the date of subdivision approval by agreeing to provide those improvements which will bring the proposed plat within the number of development points required by the amendments. And applications are authorized to the "Development Easement Acquisition Commission" for a reduction of the assessed valuation. Finally, upon application to the Town Board, the development point requirements may be varied should the board determine that such a variance or modification is consistent with the on-going development plan.

The undisputed effect of these integrated efforts in land use planning and development is to provide an over-all program of orderly growth and adequate facilities through a sequential development policy commensurate with progressing availability and capacity of public

---

[2] As of July, 1966, the only available figures, six residential zoning districts with varying lot size and density requirements accounted for in excess of nine tenths of the Town's unincorporated land area. Of these the RR classification (80,000 square feet minimum lot area) plus R-35 zone (35,000 square feet minimum lot area) comprise over one half of all zoned areas. The subject sites are presently zoned RR-50 (50,000 square feet minimum lot area). The reasonableness of these minimum lot requirements is not presently controverted, though we are referred to no compelling need in their behalf. . . . Under present zoning regulations, the population of the unincorporated areas could be increased by about 14,600 families (3.5 people) when all suitable vacant land is occupied. Housing values as of 1960 in the unincorporated areas range from a modest $15,000 (approx. 30%) to higher than $25,000 (25%), with the undeveloped western tier of Town showing the highest percentage of values in excess of $25,000 (41%). Significantly, for the same year only about one half of one per cent of all housing units were occupied by nonwhite families. Efforts at adjusting this disparity are reflected in the creation of a public housing authority and the authority's proposal to construct biracial low-income family housing. . . .

facilities. While its goals are clear and its purposes undisputably laudatory, serious questions are raised as to the manner in which these ends are to be effected . . . .

[The court held the power "to restrict and regulate" conferred by the Town Law, which was based on the Standard Zoning Enabling Act, included "by way of necessary implication, the authority to direct the growth of population for the purposes indicated, within the confines of the township. It is the matrix of land use restrictions, common to each of the enumerated powers and sanctioned goals, a necessary concomitant to the municipalities' recognized authority to determine the lines along which local development shall proceed, though it may divert it from its natural course." The court then rejected an argument that the program was invalid because it authorized the prohibition of subdivision, a power not delegated to the town. — Eds.]

[T]o say that the Planning Board lacks the authority to deny subdivision rights is to mistake the nature of our inquiry which is essentially whether development may be conditioned pending the provision by the municipality of specified services and facilities. Whether it is the municipality or the developer who is to provide the improvements, the objective is the same — to provide adequate facilities, off-site and on-site; and in either case subdivision rights are conditioned, not denied.(7)

Experience, over the last quarter century, however with greater technological integration and drastic shifts in population distribution has pointed up serious defects and community autonomy in land use controls has come under increasing attack by legal commentators, and students of urban problems alike, because of its pronounced insularism and its correlative role in producing distortions in metropolitan growth patterns, and perhaps more importantly, in crippling efforts toward regional and State-wide problem solving, be it pollution, decent housing, or public transportation.

Recognition of communal and regional interdependence, in turn, has resulted in proposals for schemes of regional and State-wide planning, in the hope that decisions would then correspond roughly to their level of impact. Yet, as salutary as such proposals may be, the power to zone under current law is vested in local municipalities, and we are constrained to resolve the issues accordingly. What does become more apparent in treating with the problem, however, is that though the issues are framed in terms of the developer's due process rights, those rights cannot, realistically speaking, be viewed separately and apart from the rights of others " 'in search of a [more] comfortable place to live.' "

There is, then, something inherently suspect in a scheme which, apart from its professed purposes, effects a restriction upon the free mobility of a people until sometime in the future when projected facilities are available to meet increased demands. Although zoning must include schemes designed to allow municipalities to more effectively contend with the

(7) . . . The reasoning, as far as it goes, cannot be challenged. Yet, in passing on the validity of the ordinance on its face, we must assume not only the Town's good faith, but its assiduous adherence to the program's scheduled implementation. We cannot, it is true, adjudicate in a vacuum and we would be remiss not to consider the substantial risk that the Town may eventually default in its obligations. Yet, those are future events, the staple of a clairvoyant, not of a court in its deliberations. The threat of default is not so imminent or likely that it would warrant our prognosticating and striking down these amendments as invalid on their face. When and if the danger should materialize, the aggrieved landowner can seek relief by way of an article 78 proceeding, declaring the ordinance unconstitutional as applied to his property. Alternatively, should it arise at some future point in time that the Town must fail in its enterprise, an action for a declaratory judgment will indeed prove the most effective vehicle for relieving property owners of what would constitute absolute prohibitions.

increased demands of evolving and growing communities, under its guise, townships have been wont to try their hand at an array of exclusionary devices in the hope of avoiding the very burden which growth must inevitably bring. Though the conflict engendered by such tactics is certainly real, and its implications vast, accumulated evidence, scientific and social, points circumspectly at the hazards of undirected growth and the naive, somewhat nostalgic imperative that egalitarianism is a function of growth.

Of course, these problems cannot be solved by Ramapo or any single municipality, but depend upon the accommodation of widely disparate interests for their ultimate resolution. . . . [The court rejected the alternative of striking down the Ramapo program in the "wistful" hope that state or regional planning legislation would be passed that would consider broader interests. It then held it would apply the "usual" presumption of constitutionality to the program, but added:]

Deference in the matter of the regulations' over-all effectiveness, however, is not to be viewed as an abdication of judicial responsibility, and ours remains the function of defining the metes and bounds beyond which local regulations may not venture, regardless of their professedly beneficent purposes.

The subject ordinance is said to advance legitimate zoning purposes as it assures that each new home built in the township will have at least a minimum of public services in the categories regulated by the ordinance. The Town argues that various public facilities are presently being constructed but that for want of time and money it has been unable to provide such services and facilities at a pace commensurate with increased public need. It is urged that although the zoning power includes reasonable restrictions upon the private use of property, exacted in the hope of development according to well-laid plans, calculated to advance the public welfare of the community in the future, the subject regulations go further and seek to avoid the increased responsibilities and economic burdens which time and growth must ultimately bring.

It is the nature of all land use and development regulations to circumscribe the course of growth within a particular town or district and to that extent such restrictions invariably impede the forces of natural growth. Where those restrictions upon the beneficial use and enjoyment of land are necessary to promote the ultimate good of the community and are within the bounds of reason, they have been sustained. "Zoning[, however,] is a means by which a governmental body can plan for the future — it may not be used as a means to deny the future." [Citing *National Land & Inv. Co. v. Kohn*, 215 A.2d 597, 610 (Pa. 1965).] Its exercise assumes that development shall not stop at the community's threshold, but only that whatever growth there may be shall proceed along a predetermined course. It is inextricably bound to the dynamics of community life and its function is to guide, not to isolate or facilitate efforts at avoiding the ordinary incidents of growth. What segregates permissible from impermissible restrictions depends in the final analysis upon the purpose of the restrictions and their impact in terms of both the community and general public interest. The line of delineation between the two is not a constant, but will be found to vary with prevailing circumstances and conditions.

What we will not countenance, then, under any guise, is community efforts at immunization or exclusion. But, far from being exclusionary, the present amendments merely seek, by the implementation of sequential development and timed growth, to provide a balanced cohesive community dedicated to the efficient utilization of land. The restrictions conform to the community's considered land use policies as expressed in its comprehensive plan and represent a bona fide effort to maximize population density consistent with orderly growth. True other alternatives, such as requiring off-site improvements as a prerequisite to subdivision, may be available, but the choice as how best to proceed, in view of the difficulties attending such exactions, cannot be faulted.

Perhaps even more importantly, timed growth, unlike the minimum lot requirements recently struck down by the Pennsylvania Supreme Court as exclusionary [See, e.g., *National Land & Inv. Co. v. Kohn*, 215 A.2d 597 (Pa. 1965) — Eds.] does not impose permanent restrictions upon land use. Its obvious purpose is to prevent premature subdivision absent essential municipal facilities and to insure continuous development commensurate with the Town's obligation to provide such facilities. They seek, not to freeze population at present levels but to maximize growth by the efficient use of land, and in so doing testify to this community's continuing role in population assimilation. In sum, Ramapo asks not that it be left alone, but only that it be allowed to prevent the kind of deterioration that has transformed well-ordered and thriving residential communities into blighted ghettos with attendant hazards to health, security and social stability — a danger not without substantial basis in fact.

We only require that communities confront the challenge of population growth with open doors. Where in grappling with that problem, the community undertakes, by imposing temporary restrictions upon development, to provide required municipal services in a rational manner, courts are rightfully reluctant to strike down such schemes. The timing controls challenged here parallel recent proposals put forth by various study groups and have their genesis in certain of the pronouncements of this and the courts of sister States. While these controls are typically proposed as an adjunct of regional planning, the preeminent protection against their abuse resides in the mandatory on-going planning and development requirement, present here, which attends their implementation and use.

We may assume, therefore, that the present amendments are the product of foresighted planning calculated to promote the welfare of the township. The Town has imposed temporary restrictions upon land use in residential areas while committing itself to a program of development. It has utilized its comprehensive plan to implement its timing controls and has coupled with these restrictions provisions for low and moderate income housing on a large scale. Considered as a whole, it represents both in its inception and implementation a reasonable attempt to provide for the sequential, orderly development of land in conjunction with the needs of the community, as well as individual parcels of land, while simultaneously obviating the blighted aftermath which the initial failure to provide needed facilities so often brings.

The proposed amendments have the effect of restricting development for onwards to 18 years in certain areas. Whether the subject parcels will be so restricted for the full term is not clear, for it is equally probable that the proposed facilities will be brought into these areas well before that time. Assuming, however, that the restrictions will remain outstanding for the life of the program, they still fall short of a confiscation within the meaning of the Constitution.

An ordinance which seeks to permanently restrict the use of property so that it may not be used for any reasonable purpose must be recognized as a taking: The only difference between the restriction and an outright taking in such a case "is that the restriction leaves the owner subject to the burden of payment of taxation, while outright confiscation would relieve him of that burden" (*Arverne Bay Constr. Co. v. Thatcher*, [15 N.E.2d 587 (N.Y. 1938)].) An appreciably different situation obtains where the restriction constitutes a *temporary* restriction, promising that the property may be put to a profitable use within a reasonable time. The hardship of holding unproductive property for some time might be compensated for by the ultimate benefit inuring to the individual owner in the form of a substantial increase in valuation; or, for that matter, the landowner might be compelled to chafe under the temporary restriction, without the benefit of such compensation, when that burden serves to promote the public good.

We are reminded, however, that these restrictions threaten to burden individual parcels for as long as a full generation and that such a restriction cannot, in any context, be viewed as a temporary expedient. The Town, on the other hand, contends that the landowner is not deprived of either the best use of his land or of numerous other appropriate uses, still permitted within various residential districts, including the construction of a single-family residence, and consequently, it cannot be deemed confiscatory. Although no proof has been submitted on reduction of value, the landowners point to obvious disparity between the value of the property, if limited in use by the subject amendments and its value for residential development purposes, and argue that the diminution is so considerable that for all intents and purposes the land cannot presently or in the near future be put to profitable or beneficial use, without violation of the restrictions.

Every restriction on the use of property entails hardships for some individual owners. Those difficulties are invariably the product of police regulation and the pecuniary profits of the individual must in the long run be subordinated to the needs of the community. The fact that the ordinance limits the use of, and may depreciate the value of the property will not render it unconstitutional, however, unless it can be shown that the measure is either unreasonable in terms of necessity or the diminution in value is such as to be tantamount to a confiscation. Diminution, in turn, is a relative factor and though its magnitude is an indicia of a taking, it does not of itself establish a confiscation.

Without a doubt restrictions upon the property in the present case are substantial in nature and duration. They are not, however, absolute. The amendments contemplate a definite term, as the development points are designed to operate for a maximum period of 18 years and during that period, the Town is committed to the construction and installation of capital improvements. The net result of the on-going development provision is that individual parcels may be committed to a residential development use prior to the expiration of the maximum period. Similarly, property owners under the terms of the amendments may elect to accelerate the date of development by installing, at their own expense, the necessary public services to bring the parcel within the required number of development points. While even the best of plans may not always be realized, in the absence of proof to the contrary, we must assume the Town will put its best effort forward in implementing the physical and fiscal timetable outlined under the plan. Should subsequent events prove this assumption unwarranted, or should the Town because of some unforeseen event fail in its primary obligation to these landowners, there will be ample opportunity to undo the restrictions upon default. For the present, at least, we are constrained to proceed upon the assumption that the program will be fully and timely implemented.

Thus, . . . the present amendments propose restrictions of a certain duration and founded upon estimate determined by fact. Prognostication on our part in upholding the ordinance proceeds upon the presently permissible inference that within a reasonable time the subject property will be put to the desired use at an appreciated value. In the interim assessed valuations for real estate tax purposes reflect the impact of the proposed restrictions. The proposed restraints, mitigated by the prospect of appreciated value and interim reductions in assessed value, and measured in terms of the nature and magnitude of the project undertaken, are within the limits of necessity.

In sum, where it is clear that the existing physical and financial resources of the community are inadequate to furnish the essential services and facilities which a substantial increase in population requires, there is a rational basis for "phased growth" and hence, the challenged ordinance is not violative of the Federal and State Constitutions. . . .

[Judge Breitel's dissenting opinion is omitted.]

NOTES AND QUESTIONS

1. *The issues in Ramapo.* Meck & Retzlaff, *The Emergence of Growth Management Planning in the United States: The Case of Golden v. Planning Board of Town of Ramapo and its Aftermath,* 7 J. Planning History 113 (2008), detail the history of the program, including the adoption of the master plan and the capital improvement program. There seemed to be three constitutional issues: delay as a taking, the legitimacy of the program and exclusion. Another issue, reserved for a later day, was good faith in the implementation of the program. The later day never came. How would these issues fare today?

The delay issue raises takings questions similar to those raised by a moratorium, though the delay in *Ramapo* could have been as much as 18 years, far in excess of a typical moratorium. A difference, however, is that the program offered an eventual approval of all development in the town, as it contemplated a full build-out. The present value of development to be allowed in 18 years is not very considerable. Would this be a taking of all beneficially productive use under *Lucas*? Would the notice rule help?

Should the limitation to residential development have affected the legitimacy issue? In *Petersen v. City of Decorah,* 259 N.W.2d 553 (Iowa App. 1977), the court invalidated an agricultural use district "intended to reserve areas suitable for nonagricultural use until the land is needed for development in accordance with a future land use plan." The city denied a rezoning for a shopping center because it was holding the land for future industrial development. The court noted that no industry had been attracted to the city since 1964, that the city admitted the property was suitable for a shopping center, and that the land was not suitable for agricultural purposes.

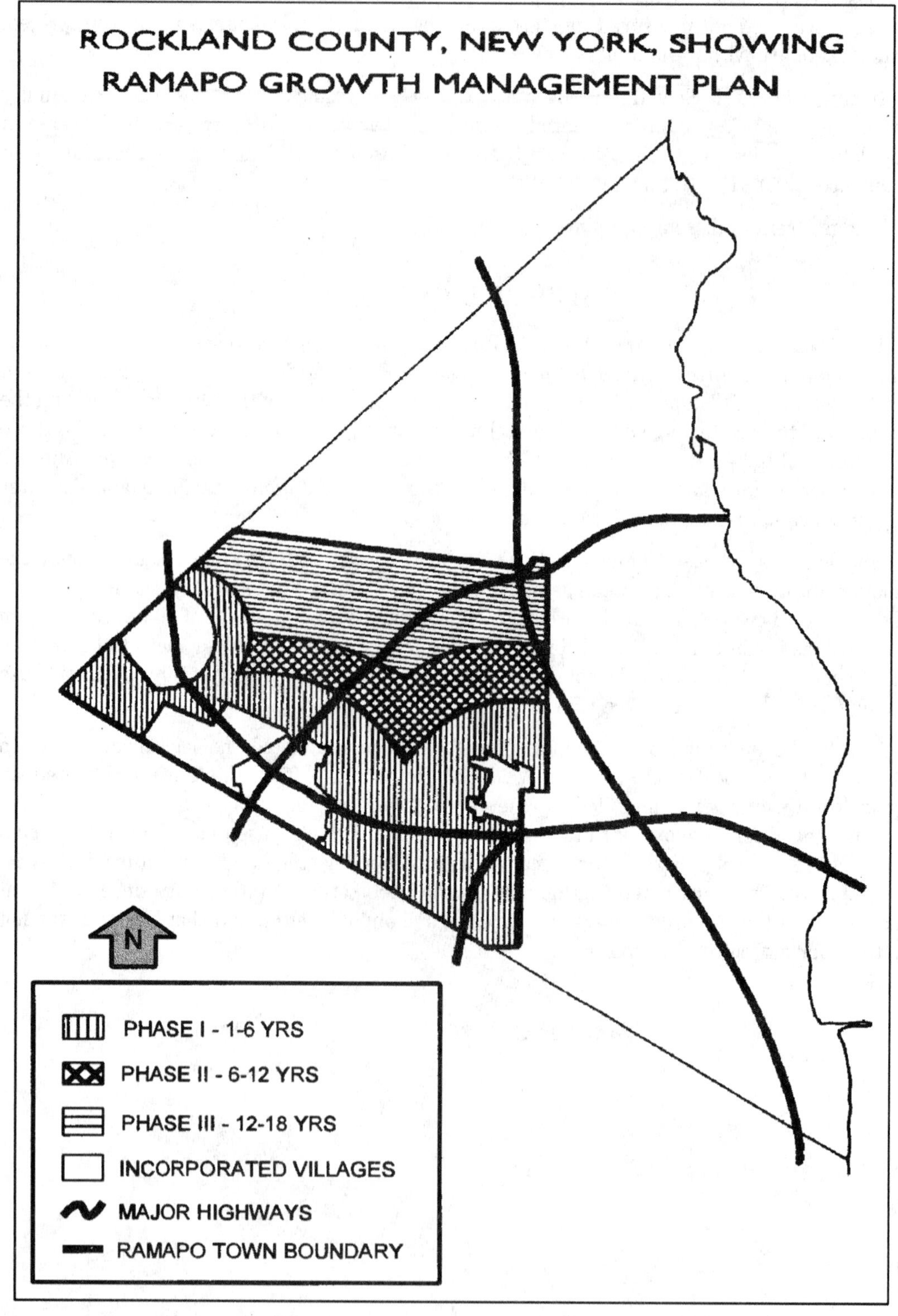
ROCKLAND COUNTY, NEW YORK, SHOWING
RAMAPO GROWTH MANAGEMENT PLAN
N
PHASE I - 1-6 YRS
PHASE II - 6-12 YRS
PHASE III - 12-18 YRS
INCORPORATED VILLAGES
MAJOR HIGHWAYS
RAMAPO TOWN BOUNDARY

2. *The commitment and good faith issues.* The Ramapo program was never attacked as-applied, but the New York court indicated how it would handle as-applied attacks on growth management programs in *Charles v. Diamond*, 360 N.E.2d 1295 (N.Y. 1977). A local ordinance required developers to connect with a village sewer system. The village authorized a connection, but the state environmental agency informed the developer that it could not connect to the system until system deficiencies were corrected. The state agency also instructed the county health department to disapprove a system connection. The developer then brought an action against the state and county agencies and the village, contending that their actions amounted to a taking of property.

Though it remanded the case for trial because the record had not been sufficiently developed to decide the constitutional issues, the court noted that temporary restrictions on development because of service difficulties were justified, but that permanent restrictions were not. It adopted a set of factors to determine how long a restriction on development for this reason could last, including the extent of the service problem, the ability of the community to raise the necessary capital, and the role of the state and federal governments. An extensive delay would be justified "only if the remedial steps are of sufficient magnitude to require extensive preparations, including preliminary studies, applications for assistance to other governmental entities, the raising of large amounts of capital, and the letting of work contracts." *Id.* at 1301.

Noting it had accepted development delays of up to eighteen years in the *Ramapo* decision, the court added that "the crucial factor, perhaps even the decisive one, is whether the ultimate cost of the benefit is being shared by the members of the community at large, or, rather, is being hidden from the public by the placement of the entire burden upon particular property owners." *Id.* at 1300. Is this statement a further extension of the court's dictum in footnote 7 of the *Ramapo* decision? Recall that *Ramapo* did not consider the growth management plan as applied to a particular property owner. The court in *Charles* also noted, again citing *Ramapo*, that a municipality "must be committed firmly to the construction and installation of the necessary improvements." *Id.* at 1301. Do *Ramapo* and *Charles* create a Catch-22 situation for a municipality attempting a growth management plan of this type? The municipality must be firmly committed to a reasonable time schedule in providing necessary public facilities, but making this commitment may be difficult if not undesirable because it locks the municipality into a rigid, long-range plan. What if the municipality commits to but does not build the necessary facilities? Can the developer compel the municipality to build them? Compel an approval of her development plan? What if the funding, say for roads and sewerage, comes from the federal and state government and is beyond local control?

3. *The exclusion issue.* H. Franklin, Controlling Growth — But for Whom? (Potomac Inst. 1973), pointed out that Ramapo was about six percent black in the 1970 census, but that ninety-one percent of the blacks lived in a village not included in the town's growth management program. Franklin also noted that very few blacks lived in Ramapo's public housing, and that sixty-five percent of the vacant land in the town was covered by large lot zoning with required minimum lot areas of 25,000 to 80,000 square feet. This large lot zoning was not challenged. Development would have been postponed until 1986 on forty-eight percent of the vacant land available under the zoning ordinance just prior to the time the Ramapo plan was adopted. The town eliminated multi-family housing from the zoning ordinance just before the growth management plan was adopted, failed to plan for any additional public housing, and lowered densities as it adopted the growth management plan. Meck & Retzlaff, *supra*, note that the very low-density development on which the program was built is a type of development

regarded as urban sprawl, and often viewed as exclusionary in places with few other development options. *Id.* at 146.

A later New York case, though noting that in *Ramapo* it had held "that a town may permissibly adopt a program for phased growth," also pointed out that in *Ramapo*, "we were careful to note that 'community efforts at immunization or exclusion' would not be countenanced." *Id.* at 241. *Berenson v. Town of New Castle*, 341 N.E.2d 236, 241 (N.Y. 1975). The New Jersey Supreme Court in *Mount Laurel I* also treated *Ramapo* cautiously. See 336 A.2d 713, 732 n.20. The New Hampshire Supreme Court, in *Beck v. Town of Raymond*, 394 A.2d 847 (N.H. 1978), stated in dictum that growth controls must be reasonable and nondiscriminatory, that they must be a product of careful study and must be reexamined constantly with a view toward relaxation or termination, and that they must be accompanied by good faith efforts to "increase the capacity of municipal services." *Id.* at 852. The court added that growth controls "must not be imposed simply to exclude outsiders, especially outsiders of any disadvantaged social or economic group." *Ibid.*

New Hampshire later codified the *Beck* holding in a statute authorizing local governments to "control the timing of development":

> Any ordinance imposing such a control may be adopted only after . . . adoption . . . of a master plan and a capital improvement program and shall be based on a growth management process intended to assess and balance community development needs and consider regional development needs. [N.H. Rev. Stat. Ann. § 674:22(I).]

See *Stoney-Brook Dev. Corp. v. Town of Fremont*, 474 A.2d 561 (N.H. 1984) (invalidating growth management program under statute that was based on a three percent growth rate); *Rancourt v. Town of Barnstead*, 523 A.2d 55 (N.H. 1986) (same, and town could not base disapproval of subdivision on master plan since it had not adopted a capital improvement program or growth management ordinance as required by the statute). Would the Ramapo plan be upheld under this statute?

The statute was amended in 2008 to require that a timing ordinance be based on "a demonstrated need to regulate the timing of development, based upon the municipality's lack of capacity to accommodate anticipated growth in the absence of such an ordinance" as shown by a study. In addition, it "shall include a termination date and shall restrict projected normal growth no more than is necessary to allow for orderly and good-faith development of municipal services," and the municipality shall adopt "a plan for the orderly and rational development of municipal services needed to accommodate anticipated normal growth." Would the Ramapo plan be upheld under this statute?

4. *Limitations and outcome of the Ramapo program.* In assessing the *Ramapo* case as a growth management decision, keep in mind that the program applied to a relatively small area, that it contemplated a total build-out of the town, and that the court did not consider the impact of the program on the excluded incorporated communities. The Ramapo program ran into trouble. Unexpected flooding resulting from hurricanes in 1971 and 1972 forced the town to appropriate $1.5 million to remedy storm damage. Much of the work scheduled on capital facilities was deferred in these years. Emanuel, *Ramapo's Managed Growth Program*, 4 Planners' Notebook, No. 5, at 1 (1974). The town gave up the program in 1983 after it abandoned the capital improvement and infrastructure funding on which the program depended. Federal funding for sewer improvements was also discontinued. This experience suggests that a commitment to capital expenditures for such a long period was unrealistic.

For discussion of the program by the person who designed it, see R. Freilich et al., From Sprawl to Sustainability ch. 3 (2010).

Marshall, *Whatever Happened to Ramapo?*, Planning, Dec., 2003, at 4, brings the Ramapo story up to date. The article states that "[s]prawling, ethnically and racially diverse, and teeming with villages, the Town of Ramapo . . . [now] is a mixture of parkland, suburban tracts, high-density enclaves, and bustling shopping centers, in different degrees of decay and renewal." Today, as compared with the late 1960s, the unincorporated area subject to the plan has shrunk from 80 to 30 percent. This has happened because the number of villages in the town doubled from six to twelve, and more village incorporations are planned. This checkerboard of incorporated communities makes planning for the entire town more difficult. Marshall quotes observers of the Ramapo scene as contending that the villages incorporated because they lost confidence in the ability of the town government to protect their neighborhoods against newcomers who opposed the constraints of the town zoning ordinance. Marshall notes there was considerable opposition to the 300 proposed units of public housing, and only 200 were actually built.

A study of the Ramapo program while it was in effect indicated it substantially reduced growth in the town, shifted development to nearby communities, and reduced the price of land not qualified for development under the point system. S. Seidel, Housing Costs & Government Regulations: Confronting the Regulatory Maze 218-22 (1978). Seidel believed the weak point was the fragmented governmental authority over the public facilities on which the point system was based. The county was responsible for the construction of interceptor sewers, and firehouses were provided by special districts formed by local residents. (The omission of facilities not controlled by the town was intentional, though a few were included). Seidel concluded the program "has proven neither useful nor accurate as a planning device, and that it has also failed to improve the township's municipal fisc." *Id.* at 222. He also noted the town's property tax had increased at a faster rate after the program was adopted than before, even though the relative increase in expenditures had declined.

5. *How fair was the Ramapo point system?* Does the Supreme Court's nexus test for exactions apply to the Ramapo program? If it does, is there a "rough proportionality" between the growth program and the points requirement, which was based on the availability of public services? The point system utilized by the ordinance was to some extent based on the distance of the required facilities from "each separate lot or plot capable of being improved with a residential dwelling." For example, points for service from fire houses were assigned as follows:

Within 1 mile	3 points
Within 2 miles	1 point
Further than 2 miles	0 points

Compare Department of Planning and Community Development: A Report of Population Growth in the City of Aurora [Colorado] 41 (1973), noting that "[t]he safety zone within which a fire station can adequately serve an area can be viewed as a diamond, with the station at the center." Fire protection, according to this report, is measured by distance from the station in time, with five minutes being the outer limit for safety purposes. Obviously, the time it takes for a fire truck to reach a fire depends on the nature of the road network and topography. Did the points for firehouses meet the "rough proportionality" requirement?

Points for drainage were based on "Percentage of Required Drainage Capacity Available." This rating was based on the capacity of the drainage system to handle peak drainage at points along the system, not on the incremental impact of a new development. The first developer in an area, in order to get the maximum number of points, had to make an improvement that provided drainage for future development in the entire area. Did this requirement satisfy the "rough proportionality" test? The entire Ramapo ordinance is reproduced in 24 Zoning Dig. 68 (1972).

6. *Statutory authority.* Statutory authority is another issue. The New York court took a generous view of this problem, but see *Beck v. Town of Raymond, supra* Note 3 (growth control ordinance enacted as a general ordinance held not a valid exercise of delegated statutory police powers); *Toll Bros., Inc. v. West Windsor Township,* 712 A.2d 266 (N.J. App. Div. 1998) (sophisticated timed growth scheme held a moratorium prohibited by state planning legislation). But see *Boulder Bldrs. Group v. City of Boulder,* 759 P.2d 752 (Colo. 1988) (growth management program including quota authorized as an exercise of home rule).

7. For discussion of the Ramapo program, see Symposium, *The 30th Anniversary of Golden v. Ramapo: A Tribute to Robert H. Freilich,* 35 Urb. Law. 15 (2003); Bosselman, *Can the Town of Ramapo Pass a Law to Bind the Whole World?,* 1 Fla. St. U. L. Rev. 234 (1973); Note, *Phased Zoning: Regulation of the Tempo and Sequence of Land Development,* 26 Stan. L. Rev. 585 (1974); Note, *A Zoning Program for Phased Growth: Ramapo Township's Time Controls on Residential Development,* 47 N.Y.U. L. Rev. 723 (1972).

[b.] Adequate Public Facility Ordinances and Concurrency Requirements

Adequate public facilities (APF) ordinances are close relatives to the Ramapo plan, because they authorize the approval of new development only if adequate public facilities are available. They may apply to the full range of public facilities or only to one or two critical facilities, such as schools and roads. They differ from the Ramapo plan, however, because that plan assumed a buildout of the town over a specified period according to a capital improvement plan. APF ordinances may or may not be based on a comprehensive plan, and may not include policies that time new development or direct it to priority areas. The typical APF ordinance authorizes a case-by-case review of new development proposals to determine if they meet criteria for adequacy contained in the ordinance. They are important as a growth management tool because "the location, quality, and timing of public facility construction strongly shapes the direction and character of community development." *Managing Growth,* at 150–151.

About one-third of the communities in the growth management survey carried out by the American Planning Association, *Growth Controls and Affordable Housing: Results from a National Survey,* Am. Plan. Ass'n, PAS Memo, Jan. 1995, *supra,* had adopted APF ordinances, and they are widely adopted in some states, *Managing Growth,* at 151. A recent survey found 1157 APF ordinances, mostly in the south and west. R. Pendall & J. Martin, Holding the Line: Urban Containment in the United States 13 (2002). The Florida and Washington state planning programs incorporate the principle of "concurrency," which is similar to an APF requirement.

[i.] Adequate Public Facilities Ordinances

How they work. The following selection describes how APF ordinances work:

> Adequate public facilities (APF) provisions require that public facilities capacities are adequate to serve proposed development before subdivision plats are approved or building permits granted. . . . Local governments spell out APF provisions in policy

statements, as separate ordinances, or as conditions of subdivision approval or issuance of permits. . . .

Ideally, facility capacity standards are keyed to communities' adoption of annual capital improvement programs (CIPs) that define a schedule of public facility construction for a multiyear period. . . . Communities usually will allow the development if facility improvements scheduled in the CIP will provide the necessary capacities, although some communities base the decision on the availability of improvements within two or three years. . . . [Some] allow approval of development only if funding for specific improvements has been authorized or appropriated in the annual budget.

Typically, the evaluation of facility adequacy is conducted during the subdivision approval process. The evaluation will determine whether facilities impacted by the proposed subdivision have capacity to support the development. If, for example, the amount of traffic generated from a proposed project will decrease the level of service of a nearby road intersection below the established standard, then the development must be postponed until (1) public programs are scheduled or funded to improve the intersection's capacity, (2) the developer promises to institute traffic management programs to reduce traffic generation to desired levels, or (3) the developer commits to funding or constructing capacity improvements to meet the standards. The de facto moratorium on further development exists until agreement is reached on one or more solutions to the congestion problem. [*Managing Growth*, at 152-155.]

Md. Code Ann. Art. 66B, § 10.01(a)(1) authorizes adequate public facilities ordinances, but this is rare, and most statutes do not include this authority. The North Carolina Court of Appeals brusquely held that the zoning and subdivision statutes did not confer the authority to adopt an APF ordinance. *Union Land Owners Ass'n v. County of Union*, 689 S.E.2d 504 (N.C. App. 2009).

NOTES AND QUESTIONS

1. *Defining adequacy.* The relative simplicity of adequate public facility ordinances hides a number of difficulty policy decisions that must be made and that require considerable judgment and discretion. One important issue is to determine whether public services are adequate. For transportation facilities, for example, decisions must be made on issues such as the study area, the facilities to be studied, trip generation rates and assumptions, data collection, project phasing and growth rates. These all require judgment, and there are no accepted criteria. Baumgaertner et al., *Leveraging Growth with APFOs*, in D. Porter, ed. Performance Standards for Growth Management 26, American Planning Association, Planning Advisory Serv. Rep. No. 461 (1996).

Defining levels of service is another problem. Adequacy is usually defined by a Level of Service, or LOS, standard:

A LOS standard is a measurement standard that describes the capacity and performance characteristic of each facility included in the APFO. The adopted LOS standard governs the rate and amount of development approvals, the quality of infrastructure, and the magnitude of capital investments for new facilities to correct existing deficiencies and to accommodate new growth. [M. White, *Adequate Public*

Facilities Ordinances and Transportation Management, 17 American Planning Association, Planning Advisory Serv. Rep. No. 465 (1996).]

The public expects more, and this affects accepted standards for levels of service. A typical LOS standard for fire and emergency medical service, for example, might state: "Respond to calls within seven minutes in 85% of cases." Compare this with the distance standard in the Ramapo plan. LOS standards for traffic are based on standard service levels for highway congestion. LOS A represents free flow, while LOS F represents forced or breakdown flow. These standards may only be crude measures. They may measure service levels at certain intersections only, and then only for peak a.m. and p.m. hours. Selection of a service level requires judgment and becomes a political decision based on local acceptance. Measuring the impacts of proposed developments on facility levels is also problematic and can only be based on estimates. *Managing Growth*, at 159–161.

2. *The impact on growth and development.* The availability of so much discretion in administering the program gives the local government considerable freedom in determining how it should be run. The result can be growth management by proxy. One study found that development was pushed into the future or indefinitely postponed, and that densities were reduced. *Leveraging Growth, supra*, at 24–25. Lower densities contribute to sprawl.

A study of a number of counties and municipalities in Maryland confirms this conclusion. Adequate Public Facilities Ordinances in Maryland: Inappropriate Use, Inconsistent Standards, Unintended Consequences (National Center for Smart Growth Research and Education, 2006), available at http://www.smartgrowth.umd.edu/research/pdf/NCSG_APFOMaryland_041906.pdf. The report notes varying adequacy standards and varying approaches to dealing with development that is not served by adequate facilities. When facilities are found inadequate, the result may be a moratorium on building until the problem is remedied. Often the only way a moratorium can be lifted is through the payment of impact fees. Another effect is that APF ordinances often deflect development away from areas designated for growth and into rural areas. The report concludes that the consistency of APF ordinances "with a local comprehensive plan is possible only if adequate funding is allocated to provide necessary infrastructure in the plan's designated areas. That, however, is often not the case." *Id.* at 4.

A study of moratoria on residential development created by APF ordinances in three Maryland counties found they reduced growth by as much as ten percent over a three-year period. The report found two adverse effects: "First, if set too strict, moratoria will translate in an excessive reduction of the new housing stock and a potential increase of housing prices; Second, because moratoria do not increase the price of providing basic public services, the growth that does not take place in the county that adopts moratoria will happen somewhere else." A. Bento, The Effects of Moratoria on Residential Development: Evidence from Harford, Howard, and Montgomery Counties 14 (2006), available at http://smartgrowth.umd.edu./research/pdf/Bento_MoratoriaResidential_042606.pdf.

3. *Problems in defining the study area.* The definition of the study area in which the adequacy determination will be made is critical. Here is one example: A suburban county adopts multiple adequacy standards for roads and highways, one for rural areas, one for urban areas, and one for its central business district. Traffic data less than six months old is not acceptable. It then adopts a fairly extensive study area for analysis for each development proposal. This decision substantially expands the number of critical intersections and roadway links to be considered, increases the competition among development proposals for available

roadway capacity, makes it more difficult to find available capacity for each additional development, and adds to the time and cost of doing traffic studies. The following case indicates how one court handled the problems that can arise:

MARYLAND-NATIONAL CAPITAL PARK AND PLANNING COMMISSION v. ROSENBERG

269 Md. 520, 307 A.2d 704 (1973)

McWilliams, J.

In this appeal, stemming from the confrontation of a landowner and the appellant (the Commission), we are asked to consider what is known in Prince George's County as the "Adequate Public Facilities Ordinance." In some jurisdictions similar enactments have been called "timing and sequential control" ordinances. They are said by professional planners to be the most important advance in planning and zoning law since *Village of Euclid v. Ambler Realty Co.* The Commission makes much of the fact that a similar ordinance has received the guarded approval of the Court of Appeals of New York. *Golden v. Planning Board of the Town of Ramapo.* While we think the Prince George's County ordinance may have an inherent deficiency which the New York court would have frowned upon, we shall assume its validity, but only in aid of resolving the difference of opinion here presented. As we see this case the single issue is whether the action of the Commission was arbitrary and capricious. We think it was. However, before we undertake to relate the facts, we shall set forth the pertinent parts of both the enabling act (Code of Public Local Laws of Prince George's County, § 59-76 (1963)), and the ordinance (Code of Ordinances and Resolutions of Prince George's County, § 3(a)16 (1967)):

[Code of Public Local Laws of Prince George's County, § 59-76 (1963):]

> ". . . The regulations may provide for . . . (5) the conservation of or production of adequate transportation, water, drainage and sanitary facilities; . . ."

[Code of Ordinances and Resolutions of Prince George's County, § 3(a)16 (1967):]

> "16. Before preliminary approval may be granted for any subdivision plat the Planning Board must find that: sufficient public facilities and services exist or are programmed for the area. It is the intent of this section that public facilities and services should be adequate to preclude danger or injury to the health, safety and welfare and excessive expenditure of public funds.
>
> > "I. The Planning Board shall give due weight to the potential of the proposed subdivision in relation to the surroundings, including the nature, extent and size of the proposed subdivision; the estimated increase in population; the anticipated timing of the development of the land proposed for subdivision; and the degree of urbanization or development within a reasonable distance of the subject property; and the following factors:
> >
> > "The availability of existing or programmed sewerage or water mains.
> >
> > "The potential effect of the proposed subdivision on the efficient and economic operation of existing or programmed public facilities.

"The distance of any necessary extension of sewerage and water facilities through unsubdivided lands which are indicated for eventual development on an approved plan.

"The location of the proposed subdivision in respect to the approved Ten Year Water and Sewerage Plan, or in any future plan which designated the timing of construction of facilities.

"The availability of access roads adequate to serve traffic which would be generated by the subdivision, or the presence of a proposal for such road(s) on an adopted Master Plan and in the current Capital Improvement Program or the State Roads Commission program.

"The availability within a reasonable distance, and the adequacy of school, fire, police, utility, and park and recreation services."

The 31 acre tract of land (the property) with which we shall be concerned abuts the northwest side of the Pennsylvania Railroad which at that point serves also as one side of an equilateral triangle; the northeast side is the Capital Beltway (Interstate Rte 495); the south side is the John Hanson Highway (U.S. Rte 50). The property lies within the development known as West Lanham Hills which is about four miles northeast of the District line. Except for the land inside the triangle one can safely say the area surrounding the property is fully developed. Since 1964 the zoning classification of the property has been R-18 (Multiple Family, Medium Density, Residential), a classification with which the owner (appellee) seems content. It is said that a six acre strip has been or will be acquired to serve as the site for the Metro's Ardmore station.

In June 1971 the appellee submitted to the Commission for its approval, as required by the subdivision regulations, a preliminary plan for the subdivision of two parcels of the property. The Commission referred the application to its staff which, in turn, sent it to various county agencies for review and comment. The Board of Education was one of the agencies whose comment was solicited. It referred the matter to its Office of Population Analysis. On 16 June the Office of Population Analysis sent a memorandum to F. Harris Allen, Principal Development Coordinator of the Commission. The memorandum indicated a "Projected Pupil Yield" of 134 for the West Lanham Hills Elementary School, the capacity of which was 640 and which, at the time, had an actual enrollment of 657.

Several weeks later there came into existence an "adequate public facilities check sheet" apparently prepared by someone on the Commission's technical staff. Allen said he used this "in the course of the review of preliminary plans." This check sheet, dated 6 July 1971, indicates that the property had a "potential" of 651 units and that, fully developed and occupied, it would yield 175.8 pupils. The Office of Population Analysis, it will be recalled, developed a figure of 134. The September 1970 enrollment at the West Lanham Hills Elementary School was stated, in the check sheet, to be 668 pupils or 11 more than the enrollment reported by the Office of Population Analysis. There appears also, in the check sheet, the following notation:

"There are no additions in the CIP [Capital Improvements Program] which would increase the capacity of this school *or any other elementary schools in the vicinity.*" (Emphasis added.)

It is conceded that the technical staff of the Commission recommended approval of the appellee's application. It was considered by the Prince George's County Planning Board of the

Commission on 9 August and disapproved the same day. A letter from Allen to the appellee, dated 13 August, states, in part:

> ". . . West Lanham Hills Elementary School which would serve this property is currently operating over its listed capacity and there are no plans for any elementary schools in the Capital Improvements Program which would relieve this situation. The property, if developed in accordance with the allowable density, would generate approximately 134 elementary school children which would further overload the existing school.
>
> "It was therefore the opinion of the Planning Board that since adequate public facilities are neither existing or programmed to serve the area the proposed subdivision should be denied."

The record seems to suggest that during the next six or eight months counsel for the appellee tried, in vain as it turned out, to persuade the Commission to recede from the position it had taken in August. In March 1972 the Commission reaffirmed its unwillingness to approve the preliminary plan. On 26 May the appellee filed her petition praying the issuance of the writ of mandamus and a mandatory injunction commanding the Commission to approve her preliminary plan. The Commission answered and on 29 November the case came on to be heard before the trial judge, Meloy, J.

The appellee produced but one witness, James Panor, who has been the Assistant Population Analyst of the Board of Education since 1962. He said the six acre parcel to be acquired for the Metro station "was not considered in the analysis or the projection of pupil yield from the [appellee's] development." The subdivision plan proposed by the appellee for her 31 acres called for the development of two parcels:

Parcel "A" — 8.13 +/− acres

Parcel "B" — 13.54 +/− acres

Panor spoke of the conversion factors he used in making his projections. In cases where R-18 zoning prevails, he said, he multiplies the number of acres by 20 to determine the maximum number of units allowable. The result here, obviously, would be 8.13 +13.54 * 20 or 433.40 units. While he did not say what factor he used to obtain the pupil yield of 134 it would seem that three units could be expected to yield about one pupil.

When he testified in the court below he said that as of 29 September 1972 the enrollment at West Lanham Hills Elementary School was 551, 106 less than shown on his memorandum of 16 June 1971 to Allen. This, he said, "would be 89 pupils under its rated capacity." He agreed that if the projected yield of 134 pupils were reduced by 89, there would be only 45 pupils over and above the rated capacity of West Lanham Hills Elementary School. It will be recalled that the June 1971 memorandum indicates the enrollment was 17 over capacity (640).

Panor went on to testify that West Lanham Hills Elementary served one of four contiguous service areas, the others being served by Margaret Brent Elementary, Woodridge Elementary, and Landover Hills Elementary. Each of these three schools is about a mile, as the crow flies, from West Lanham Hills Elementary.

Panor's reply to the question set forth below is revealing:

> "Considering the existing facilities in these adjacent service areas would there be adequate facilities to meet the projected pupil yield? A. To meet the projected pupil

yield, based on existing enrollments at the four elementary schools that I have presented here, and comparing that to the impact of the plan of subdivision and the projection, elementary pupils from the preliminary plan of subdivision, *there would be space to accommodate this number of children. . . .*" (Emphasis added.)

He went on to say that he had "totaled up the capacity of these [four] schools and it comes to 2,300; the enrollment as of September 29, 1972 is 2,049 *which means 251 children less than the capacity*." (Emphasis added.)

Asked about the boundaries of the four service areas Panor replied:

> "Well, historically I would say since I've been there and that is working for the superintendent's staff, boundaries for all schools that are involved in overcrowding are always considered for changes. . . . And I would say that we have from year to year changed literally — practically all service areas of all existing schools.
>
> "I might say when you build a school, a planned new school, to relieve a given community or a group of communities of overcrowding you must change boundaries. So for every school we have built boundaries have been changed of existing schools."

The Commission likewise produced but one witness, F. Harris Allen, identified early on as Principal Development Coordinator of the Commission. He testified the Planning Board had before it the check sheet prepared by the technical staff, but we have not found in the record any indication that the Planning Board had before it or that it considered or that it requested any other or further evidence in respect of the adequacy of school facilities. He stated unequivocally that the Board did not make "any finding other than what's recited in [his] letter [of 13 August to the appellee]." He agreed that the enrollment figure on the check sheet was "as of September 1970." He said the projected pupil yield of 175 was "the estimate of our office" and that it was based on "a potential yield of 651 units." He agreed also that a pupil yield of 175 was higher by 41 than Panor's figure. Asked to account for the difference he answered, "I can only assume that they took the entire tract [31 acres] and took no cognizance of the six acres which would have been going to Metro." Asked if what he stated in his letter of 13 August was the "only reason" for the Board's disapproval of the appellee's preliminary plan, he replied, "Correct." He agreed also that the technical staff had recommended the approval of the appellee's preliminary plan. . . .

Nothing in the record suggests the Board held any kind of a hearing and Allen's testimony makes it quite clear that the only evidence or information before the Board when it denied the appellee's application was the check sheet sent up from the technical staff. All the Board could have learned from the check sheet was that last year's (September 1970) enrollment at West Lanham Hills Elementary was 28 pupils in excess of its capacity and that the property could yield 651 dwelling units. Neither figure agreed with the information furnished by Panor, and Allen agreed the 651 figure was incorrect. Indeed in his letter of 13 August 1971 he abandoned the check sheet pupil yield of 175.8 and reverted to Panor's figure of 134. The Board could also have learned that an increase in the capacity of West Lanham Hills "*or any other elementary schools in the vicinity*" was not contemplated. What is meant by "vicinity" or which "other elementary schools" the staff had in mind is anyone's guess. We are not to be persuaded that the Board could have given "due weight . . . [to] [t]he availability within a reasonable distance, and the adequacy of school . . . services," in the light of such trivial and inaccurate evidence. . . .

The subdivision regulation does not undertake to restrict pupils to the school within the boundaries of the service area in which they reside. The only limitation is that there must be an adequate school available "within a reasonable distance." Nor do the school authorities consider the boundaries of the service areas to be static and inflexible. Panor, it will be recalled, testified that they have "from year to year changed literally — practically all service areas of all existing schools." Reflecting upon Panor's testimony that the schools in the four contiguous areas have a capacity of 2,300 pupils and that the enrollment as of September 1972 was 251 less than capacity, one need not be especially perceptive to suppose that the area boundaries could readily be adjusted to take care of the 45 pupils said to be in excess of the capacity of West Lanham Hills Elementary School. One must, of course, assume the instant development and occupancy of the appellee's project, but one need not assume that it has been in the R-18 classification since 1964. That is a fact. The regulation does not define "reasonable distance" but we do not think the Board can be heard to say that a mile, or even a mile and one-half, is not a "reasonable distance."

Since we are fully persuaded that the Board's refusal to approve the appellee's preliminary plan was arbitrary and capricious the order of the trial court will be affirmed.

Order affirmed.

NOTES AND QUESTIONS

1. *Making APF ordinances work.* The *Rosenberg* case illustrates the problems that can occur when an adequacy determination is made under an APF ordinance. Is the case limited by the failure of the county to build a really good basis for its decisions? California recently enacted a law conditioning subdivision approval of a subdivision with more than 500 units on an adequate water supply, either through a public system or through a water supply outside that system. Cal. Gov. Code § 66473.7. Does the *Rosenberg* case suggest any problems that might arise under that statute? See Tepper, *New Water Requirements for Large-Scale Developments*, 27 Los Angeles Lawyer 18 (2005).

As the principal case also indicates, problems can arise in APF programs because local governments abdicate control over the location and timing of development to the private sector, and public planning for and the provision of public facilities is reactive. This happens because an adequacy decision is made only when there is an application for a subdivision. Compare *In re Kent County Adequate Public Facililties Ordinance Litigation*, 2009 Del. Ch. LEXIS 19 (Del. Ch. Feb. 11, 2009) (rejecting a vested rights claim that would have made an APF ordinance inapplicable), with *County Comm'rs v. Forty West Builders, Inc.*, 941 A.2d 1181 (Md. App. 2008) (holding that granting of Concurrency Management Certificate to developer, who began work on subdivision, precluded additional retroactive APF requirements).

2. *How it can be done.* Doug Porter argues that local governments should remain active in planning, funding and managing APF programs so they can maintain control over the timing and planning of development. He cites Carlsbad, California, which is in the San Diego area, as an example of a city that has successfully linked its comprehensive plans, facility improvement programs and APF requirements to manage growth. *Managing Growth* at 155–157. The city adopted a growth management program that unequivocally requires adequate public facilities to be available before development can take place. Next it adopted a Citywide Facilities and Improvement Plan. The Plan —

> defined the existing and future development level of the city, specified eleven public facilities to be evaluated for adequacy and spelled out performance standards for each

> one, and identified the existing supply of facilities and future needs to accommodate existing and buildout demands. The city also delineated twenty-five zones for which more detailed plans for public facilities and financing approaches were to be completed before further development could take place within the zone.
>
> The plan also specifies performance standards for each type of facility. The city also estimated thresholds of development at which facilities would require improvement to continue meeting performance standards. The combination of standards, thresholds, and detailed zone plans provided an overall management plan for ensuring timely infrastructure improvements concurrent with development. [*Id.* at 156–157.]

Finer-grained facility analysis is required for projects under consideration for approval that considers potential facility impacts. The zone plans outline specific funding mechanisms for each facility, and funding must be provided prior to a final approval. The ordinance authorizing the program is in Ch. 21.90 of the zoning code, available at http://library.municode.com/HTML/16245/level2/T21_C21.90.html.

3. *Are APF ordinances constitutional?* There are obvious problems based on delays in development, the possibility of an unconstitutional exaction and discriminatory treatment raising equal protection problems. There are few cases. In *Schneider v. Montgomery County* (unreported), *cert. denied*, 614 A.2d 84 (Md. 1991) (table), the court upheld a denial of a subdivision plat because transportation facilities were inadequate. The denial was based on a level of service policy that allowed development in areas where traffic congestion was higher, but where the greater availability of transit services provided an alternate transportation mode. Can you see why the developer objected to this policy, and the basis for upholding it? The court rejected a takings challenge because there were alternate viable uses for the property, and the APF ordinance left open the possibility of development in the future. See also *FC Summers Walk, LLC v. Town of Davidson*, 2010 U.S. Dist. LEXIS 4393 (W.D.N.C. Jan. 20, 2010) (denying motion to dismiss claims that APF ordinance was without authority and unconstitutional); *Albany Area Builders Ass'n v. Town of Clifton Park*, 576 N.Y.S.2d 932 (App. Div. 1991) (upholding an ordinance that limited the number of building permits that could be approved in a development area to 20 percent of the total units approved for any one project to remedy congested traffic conditions).

[ii.] Concurrency

Concurrency requirements in state land planning programs are similar to APF ordinances, with the difference that they are part of a state-mandated local planning process. This means that all local governments must have a concurrency program, and that these programs must comply with state standards.

The Florida program. Florida has had a concurrency program since 1985. Local plans must contain a "capital improvements element" that includes "[s]tandards to ensure the availability of public facilities and the adequacy of those facilities including acceptable levels of service." Fla. Stat. Ann. § 163.3177(3)(a). Seven public facilities are subject to the concurrency requirement, including highways, water, sanitary sewer, solid waste and drainage facilities, and legislation in 2006 establishes a closer link between development approvals and water supply. See § 163.3180.

Here is a description of the concurrency program and recent changes to it:

Transportation concurrency is a growth management strategy aimed at ensuring that transportation facilities and services are available "concurrent" with the impacts of development. Concurrency in Florida is enacted in state growth management act provisions requiring that ". . . transportation facilities needed to serve new development shall be in place or under actual construction within 3 years after the local government approves a building permit or its functional equivalent that results in traffic generation." [Fla. Stat. Ann. § 163.3180(2)(c).]

To carry out concurrency, local governments must define what constitutes an adequate level of service for the transportation system, adopt a plan and capital improvement program to achieve and maintain adequate level of service standards, and measure whether the service needs of a new development exceed existing capacity, including capacity from scheduled improvements. If adequate capacity is not available, then the developer must provide the necessary improvements, provide a monetary contribution toward the programmed improvements, or wait until government provides the necessary improvements.

[The State Department of Community Affair's] implementing rule [Fla. Admin. Code § 9J-5.0055] establishes minimum requirements for satisfying concurrency, including a requirement for local governments to develop and implement a transportation concurrency management system. Through this system, the local government must demonstrate that the necessary transportation facilities and services to maintain the adopted level of service standards will be available and adequate to address the impacts of development within three years of issuing a building permit or its functional equivalent. Developers may satisfy the concurrency requirement through proportionate share or proportionate fair-share mitigation (pay and go) or development agreements.

In 2009, the legislature exempted "dense urban land areas" (DULAs) from transportation concurrency, with the intent of reinforcing urban growth. [These are areas that meet certain population and density thresholds.] The development of a regional impact program, which provides a process for multi-agency review of large developments, was also suspended in these areas, as was the requirement for local governments to adopt and maintain state level of service standards for the strategic intermodal system. DCA has issued the interpretation that a local government must amend its comprehensive plan to establish the [Transportation Concurrency Exemption Area.] However, a circuit court in August, 2010 invalidated the 2009 changes based on the unfunded mandates provision of the state constitution. Reenactment with the necessary majority will be attempted.

In addition, within 2 years of establishing a TCEA, local governments are required to adopt into their local comprehensive plan land use and transportation strategies to support and fund mobility within the exception area, including alternative modes of transportation. All local government comprehensive plans also must comply with [a statute] regarding reduction of GHG [greenhouse gas] emissions and energy efficient land use. This legislation requires local governments to achieve more energy efficient land use patterns in their comprehensive and long range transportation plans and to enact transportation strategies to address greenhouse gas reductions. [Fla. Dep't of Community Affairs, Evaluation of the Mobility Fee Concept: Final Report 7-8 (Nov.

2009), available at http://www.dca.state.fl.us/fdcp/dcp/MobilityFees/Files/CUTRMobilityFeeFinalReport.pdf.]

The report notes "widespread dissatisfaction" with local transportation management concurrency systems that rely on levels of service for roadways, which have created multi-lane congested roadways in urban areas that have excluded other modes. Other problems are the difficulty of maintaining LOS standards for each facility at peak traffic times, and the inequity of requiring payment only when LOS standards are exceeded. The cost of providing facilities to maintain level of service standards is often well beyond existing transportation funding mechanisms. Existing capacity is consumed by new development, which encourages sprawl, and roadway costs are inequitably placed on developers after capacity is exhausted." *Id.* at 8–9. The 2009 legislation authorized the study of mobility fees as an alternative to the concurrency program.

An urban sprawl policy adopted by the state agency attempts to deal with this problem. Fla. Admin. Code § 9J-5.006(5). The rule specifies "indicators" of urban sprawl in local comprehensive plans, such as allowance of low density development, rural development at a substantial distance from urban areas, and a "failure to make a clear separation between urban and rural areas." These indicators, in combination with an evaluation of local land uses, conditions and development controls, form the basis for determining whether a local plan must be disapproved because it "does not discourage the proliferation of urban sprawl."

Chain, *Local Governments as Policy Entrepreneurs: Evaluating Florida's "Concurrency Experiment,"* 42 Urb. APF. Rev. 505 (2007), found considerable variation in local level of service standards except for transportation, where state standards produced some uniformity. For another critical view, see Downs, *Why Florida's Concurrency Principle For Controlling New Development By Regulating Road Construction Does Not — And Cannot — Work Effectively*, Transportation Qtly., Winter 2003, at 13.

The Washington Program. The concurrency requirement in Washington's state land use program applies only to transportation facilities, but it also includes urban growth boundaries that help control urban form. Urban growth boundaries are discussed later in this chapter. The comprehensive plan must contain service levels for transportation facilities. Wash. Rev. Code § 36.70A.070(6)(a). The concurrency requirement is as follows:

> After adoption of the comprehensive plan . . . local jurisdictions must adopt and enforce ordinances which prohibit development approval if the development causes the level of service on a locally owned transportation facility to decline below the standards adopted in the transportation element of the comprehensive plan, unless transportation improvements or strategies to accommodate the impacts of development are made concurrent with the development. These strategies may include increased public transportation service, ride sharing programs, demand management, and other transportation systems management strategies. . . . "[C]oncurrent with the development" shall mean that improvements or strategies are in place at the time of development, or that a financial commitment is in place to complete the improvements or strategies within six years. [*Id.* § 36.70A.070(6)(b).]

The concurrency requirement is reinforced by requiring a capital facilities element in comprehensive plans that includes a funding requirement and a transportation element. The transportation element must evaluate land use impacts on transportation facilities, set levels of service, bring actions to bring transportation facilities and services up to established standards, and include a financing plan. *Id.* § 36.70A.070(6)(a). The statutory planning goals also include an adequate public facilities requirement for new development that applies to all public facilities. *Id.* § 36.70A.020(12). For a report on infrastructure planning, see Department of Community, Trade & Econ. Dev. (DCTED), Meeting the Growth Management Challenge in Growing Communities Pt. 1 (2008), available at www.commerce.wa.gov.

Studies by the Puget Sound Regional Council, which is the regional agency for the Seattle region, found that automobile-related programs worked well in low density suburban areas where the problem is incomplete road systems, but did not work well in denser urban areas where other forms of transportation are used or at the regional level because the concurrency program is locally focused. A high percentage of trips that leave cities for travel to other parts of a region were not usually considered in local concurrency programs. Options for Making Concurrency More Multimodal 2 (2006). The legislature now requires regional agencies to consider multimodal forms of transportation in their planning, Wash. Rev. Code § 47.80.030(1)(f), and the Council published a Multimodal Concurrency Pilot Report for the City of Bellevue. See also *id.* § 36.70A.108 (comprehensive plan may include multimodal strategies). For an earlier report by the Puget Sound Council, see Assessing the Effectiveness of Concurrency (2003). It found that the most effective programs tailored the concurrency requirement to the needs of specific areas of such urban centers by changing how they measured congestion or by reducing concurrency requirements. The reports are available at http://www.psrc.org/growth/vision2040/implementation/concurrency/. There are no exemptions in the statute. *City of Bellevue v. East Bellevue Community Municipal Corp.*, 81 P.3d 148 (Wash. App. 2003) (city cannot exempt neighborhood shopping center redevelopment projects because it believed they "would decrease traffic and provide a wide array of necessary goods and services."). For additional discussion, see Walsh & Pearce, *The Concurrency Requirement of the Washington State Growth Management Act*, 16 Puget Sound L. Rev. 1025 (1993); Note, *Halting Urban Sprawl: Smart Growth in Vancouver and Seattle*, 33 B.C. Int'l & Comp. L. Rev. 43 (2010).

A statutory proposal. The American Planning Association has proposed a model concurrency and adequate public facilities statute. Legislative Guidebook, § 8-603. The statute solves the state highway problem by requiring the state planning agency to adopt level of service standards for highways. This should also remedy the problem of inconsistent levels of service in local government jurisdictions.

PROBLEM

Review the River County Problem at the beginning of this chapter. The county administrator has asked you, as county attorney, whether you would recommend adoption of an adequate public facilities ordinance or a concurrency requirement modeled on either the Florida or Washington programs. Would you advise against this? If so, why? If you recommended a program, what would you advise? What legal problems would you see?

[c.] Tier Systems and Urban Service Areas

Tier systems and urban service areas are two related forms of growth management that are also based on the availability of public services and facilities Here is how they work:

> A principal tenet of the "tier" system involves the geographic and functional division of the planning area into subareas ("tiers"). . . . Tiers within the growth category are commonly designated "Urbanized" and "Planned Urbanizing." The tiers within the

> limited growth category would be "Rural/Future Urbanizing," "Agricultural," and "Conservation/Open Space." Each of the tiers has specific geographical boundaries and is capable of being mapped. The Urbanized tier consists of those areas which are at or near build out and served by public facilities. The Planned Urbanizing area represents the "new" growth area. The Rural/Future Urbanizing area may be a permanent rural density development area or may be a temporary "holding" zone until the growth areas are built out. The Rural/Future Urbanizing tier generally contains lands that are presently unsewered and which have a lower population density. The Agriculture tier is intended to identify those lands which should be preserved either temporarily or permanently for agricultural production. The Conservation/Open Space tier consists of lands containing natural resources or environmentally sensitive areas. [Freilich, *The Land-Use Implications of Transit-Oriented Development: Controlling the Demand Side of Transportation Congestion and Urban Sprawl,* 30 Urb. Law. 547, 559–60 (1998).]

Tier systems do not contain an explicit boundary between areas where growth can and cannot occur. They contemplate the eventual build-out of the tiered areas unless conservation and agricultural areas are permanently preserved. Here is the tier system adopted by San Diego as proposed by its consultant in the early 1970s.

> [T]he program has three growth tiers: an urbanized tier, a planned urbanizing tier, and an urban reserve tier. The consultant's proposal encouraged growth in the urbanized tier, staged growth in the planned urbanizing tier, and deferred growth for fifteen to twenty years in the urban reserve. It also included an environmental tier intended to protect the area's canyons, steep slopes and other natural resources, but the city did not adopt it. The growth management program only applies to residential development, because it assumed nonresidential development will carry its fair share of needed improvement costs and does not affect the need for schools, parks and libraries.
>
> The consultant's proposal included different policies and objectives for each tier, most of them regulatory, though it proposed other measures, such as redevelopment, where it was necessary in the urbanized tier. There was no strategy for allocating growth to designated areas within the tiers where the program allowed growth. Neither was enough attention paid to the need for capital improvements in the urbanized tier, though there was a brief discussion of a capital improvements program. In the planned urbanizing tier the city adopted a special benefits assessment, which the courts eventually upheld, that carried out the program's proposal to shift the cost of new facilities to developers. In the urban reserve the principal control was large lot zoning at a minimum of ten acres for each dwelling unit. This type of zoning protects land from urban growth because the density it allows is too low to allow development at an intensive scale. [Mandelker, *Managing Space to Manage Growth,* 23 Wm. & Mary Envtl. L. & Pol'y Rev. 801, 806, 807 (1999).]

The San Diego program succeeded in revitalizing and bringing new development to the urbanized area, though there were objections in neighborhoods where more intensive development was planned, and where some of the new development was not sensitively designed. As one observer put it, however, the system began to unravel in the 1980s, which was a period of rapid growth, and the plan was flawed from the start. It was understood from the beginning that there were serious service deficiencies in the urbanized areas. It was expected these would be remedied by general funds, but this option disappeared with the enactment in 1978 of a constitutional limitation on property taxes. Resulting deficits were substantial. For discussion of this history, see Calavita et al., The Challenge of Smart Growth: The San Diego Case in Revitalizing the City: Strategies to Contain Sprawl and Revive the Core ch. 3 (F. Wagner et al. eds., 2005).

Political pressures led to accelerated conversion of land to development in the planned urbanizing tier, though initiatives adopted by popular vote attempted to limit this. Many of the older Planned Urbanizing Tiers are built out and much of the remaining land in the Planned Urbanizing tiers is not earmarked for development. In 1997, the city council created a number of Multiple Habitat Planning Areas that are natural resource areas in which open space will be preserved. The City of San Diego General Plan (2008) includes a strategy for developing mixed-use villages throughout the city that are connected by public transit. *Id.* at LU-4. For additional discussion of tiered systems by the author of the San Diego system, see R. Freilich et al., From Sprawl to Sustainability 137–145 (2010).

Urban service areas (USAs). The USA is an area beyond which a local government will not provide basic services or invest in significant road improvements. Its primary purpose is to ensure an efficient, orderly and cost-effective delivery of services and infrastructure. Staging is achieved by timing extensions of the USA with the availability of urban public facilities. The rural area beyond the urban service limit line may be allowed to develop at densities and with uses that do not require urban services and that will not overload road capacity.

In 1958, Lexington-Fayette County, Kentucky adopted "an Urban Service Area, where development is encouraged, and a Rural Service Area, where urban-oriented activities are not permitted. Areas of future growth within the Urban Service Area were identified so that complex urban services and facilities, public and private, could be developed logically and economically." 2001 Comprehensive Plan at 1-4, Lexington's Vision of the Future. The USA has been successful in keeping growth within the urban service area limits and in protecting rural areas outside these limits. Complementary plans direct growth within the service area limits and protect the rural area through level of service standards. The 2007 Comprehensive Plan reaffirmed commitment to the urban service area concept and related growth management strategies. It decided not to expand the USA because "continuing efforts of permanent rural preservation, sustained support for infill/redevelopment, and systematic repair or inadequate community infrastructure . . . within existing neighborhoods should take priority at this time." *Id.* at 34. See From Sprawl to Sustainability, *supra*, at 326–332; Martin, Holding the Line, *supra*, at 24–28.

[3.] Growth Management in Oregon: The Urban Growth Boundary Strategy

The growth management strategies considered so far have dealt with the phasing of new development and the provision of adequate facilities but have not explicitly provided limits on where growth can occur. One important growth management strategy that can provide these limits is the urban growth boundary, or UGB. A UGB is an urbanized area boundary that marks the limits of urban growth. Development can occur within, but is not allowed outside, the boundary. It may or not include an adequate public facilities requirement. A surprising 68% of the local governments which responded to the growth management survey carried out by the American Planning Association, and which were not surrounded on all sides by other municipalities, had UGBs in place. The Brookings Institute report found that 16.4% of jurisdictions in the 50 largest metropolitan areas had an urban containment program or policy covering 37.9% of the land area. From Traditional to Reformed, *supra*, at 11.

UGB programs are also included in some state growth management programs. The best-known statewide UGB program is part of the Oregon state land use system. Washington, Tennessee and Maine also have UGB requirements in their state land use programs. Urban growth boundaries in Oregon are adopted by municipalities. They are a county responsibility in Washington and Tennessee.

Urban growth boundary programs require decisions on a number of issues. Decisions must be made on how much land to include within the growth area boundary, the shape the urban boundary should take and how to expand the boundary as growth occurs. Regulating growth just outside the boundary line to prevent future development until the boundary is extended is another problem. Development permission denials outside the growth boundary clearly raise takings problems. The article that follows outlines the basic elements of state planning and urban growth boundary program in Oregon, which has been in effect since the early 1970s:

Mandelker, *Managing Space to Manage Growth*

23 William and Mary Environmental Law and Policy Review 801, 811–17 (1999)

Oregon's state land use and urban growth boundary (UGB) programs are well-known growth management systems. A set of state planning goals adopted by the state Land Conservation and Development Commission (LCDC) are its critical elements. LCDC reviews local plans and land use regulations and approves them if they comply with the state goals. Local land use regulations and decisions must be consistent with the approved plan. A special tribunal, the Land Use Board of Appeals (LUBA), hears appeals on land use decisions after appellants exhaust all local appeals.

The principal state planning goal that mandates growth management is an urbanization goal [Goal 14] that requires incorporated municipalities to adopt urban growth boundaries. Local governments must draw a clear line between areas that can urbanize and areas that must remain nonurban. . . . Incorporated municipalities apply these factors to designate enough growth within their UGB to provide an adequate land supply for twenty years. A UGB can, and usually does, extend beyond municipal boundaries. The Portland regional planning agency [Metro] administers this program in the Portland metropolitan area and is responsible for making decisions about the boundary. The state housing goal, supplemented by legislation, requires local governments to provide needed affordable housing within UGB boundaries.

A key purpose of the state program is the preservation of the Willamette Valley in western Oregon, which has most of the state's valuable agricultural land and most of its population. [A state agricultural goal requires the preservation of agricultural land, and is reinforced by exclusive farm use zones and a required 80-acre lot size in these zones.] . . .

Observers agree that the preservation of agricultural and other natural resource areas were the primary motivation behind the urbanization goal and the UGB policy. These priorities mean that the UGB . . . is not primarily a measure to shape urban growth. The state planning goals also do not include a strategy for allocating development within a UGB. . . .

One of the reasons why higher-density development has not occurred [as expected] inside the UGBs is that opposition to this type of development has become increasingly common.

Developers became disillusioned when they could not build at the expected densities promised by the program at its adoption.

Development has continued to occur at low densities in so-called exception areas outside UGBs, often as spurious farms. [See Or. Rev. Stat. § 197.732, authorizing exceptions to the state planning goals, such as the agricultural goal.] These are areas already developed for rural residential homesites or for commercial or industrial uses, or are areas "committed" to development because of parcelization or installation of services or because surrounding development makes farming and forestry impracticable. This development is substantial and undercuts the urban growth boundary program, though it has slowed in recent years. The conversion of land contiguous to UGBs to low density development is especially troublesome because it makes the extension of UGBs difficult. If low density development occurs on land next to the UGB, it will not be available for high-density development when the boundary expands. The UGB must then expand further than it should have been, and higher-density development must leapfrog over the low-density development that is in the expansion area. This is the very type of urban sprawl the urban growth boundary program tries to prevent.

Oregon legislation [§ 195.145] now allows local governments to designate "urban reserve areas" that are next to UGBs. These areas provide for the long-term urban expansion and cost-effective provision of public facilities and services when UGB expands. Local governments are to give priority to urban reserve areas when expanding urban growth boundaries. [§ 197.298.] . . .

A significant problem in the Oregon UGB program is deciding where development should occur and at what densities. Development at low densities inside the UGBs accelerates demands for boundary expansion, which can damage the goal of preserving agricultural and forest lands. Higher densities within the UGB reduce demand for boundary expansion but create opposition from existing neighborhoods. Housing at higher densities inside the UGB can be expensive and push lower-income housing outward. Balancing these competing claims requires a carefully orchestrated strategy, which is more difficult to secure. The statutes now authorize density increases within a UGB to meet housing needs as an alternative to a boundary expansion. [§ 197.296(6)(b).]

NOTES AND QUESTIONS

1. *What the urbanization goal now provides.* The urbanization goal was amended in 2005. The goal, available at http://www.lcd.state.or.us/LCD/goals.shtml#Statewide_Planning_Goals, now has a "Land Need" factor. It states that:

> Establishment and change of urban growth boundaries shall be based on the following:
>
> (1) Demonstrated need to accommodate long range urban population, consistent with a 20-year populations forecast coordinated with affected local governments, and
>
> (2) Demonstrated need for housing, employment opportunities, livability or uses such as public facilities, streets and roads, schools, parks or open space or any combination of the need categories in this subsection (2).

Local governments must also "demonstrate that needs cannot reasonably be accommodated on land already inside the urban growth boundary." The goal also has a boundary location factor that requires consideration of alternate boundary locations. The next principal case considers this issue.

2. *Evaluating Portland.* One review notes the success of the UGB and praises Portland as "a place where the downtown has a thousand retail stores, the outlying neighborhoods are healthy and growing, and the sprawl ends at a greenbelt 20 minutes from the city line." Ehrenhalt, *The Great Wall of Portland*, Governing, May 1997, at 20. Most studies have shown that new development has occurred within UGB boundaries. Weitz & Moore, *Development Inside Urban Growth Boundaries: Oregon's Empirical Evidence of Contiguous Urban Form*, 64 J. Am. Plan. Ass'n 424, 429 tbl. 4 (1998) (substantial amount of development occurred in or near urban core). Densities and the volume of multifamily and attached housing have increased significantly in Portland, and new development averaging eight units to the acre exceeds the target in the regional 2040 plan target. LCDC requires six to ten units per acre for the Portland area on undeveloped, residentially designated lands. Or. Admin. R. 660-007-0035.

A recent study of Portland and 14 other cities concluded that "Oregon's land-use policies have excelled in protecting Portland from sprawling urban development. Person for person, new development between 1990 and 2000 in Greater Portland consumed less than half as much land as the average city in the study." Northwest Envt. Watch, The Portland Exception 21 (2004). The study found that the number of people living in low-density suburbs decreased, but also found that Portland is far less dense than many western cities of similar size, and was only average in the number of residents living in compact neighborhoods. *Id.* at 6, 7. See also Jun, *Are Portland's Smart Growth Policies Related to Automobile Dependence*?, 28 J. Plan. Educ. & Res. 100 (2008) (more diversified land use, more extensive public transit and decreased access to freeway interchanges reduced dependence).

A study of neighborhoods in one county in the Portland area found they were becoming better internally connected, more pedestrian friendly and denser, but that land uses remained relatively homogenous, Song & Knaap, *Measuring Urban Form: Is Portland Winning the War on Sprawl?*, 70 J. Am. Plan. Ass'n 210 (2004), though it was not clear that these changes were produced by the growth management program. Land use mixing and external connectivity were less apparent at the regional level. Local governments in the Portland area have also adopted provisions for mixed use and transit-oriented development that can reduce the need for automobile use while increasing densities and concentrating new development, and these developments may have contributed to improvement in neighborhood form. See also Cho et al., *Estimating Effects of an Urban Growth Boundary on Land Development*, 38 J. Ag. & Applied Econ. 287 (2006) (state-mandated urban growth boundary in Tennessee successful in causing urban revitalization).

3. *Metro's planning for the Portland metropolitan area.* Metro, a unique regional planning agency that has planning responsibility for the Portland area, has produced regional plans that provide a comprehensive planning context for the UGB. The basis for planning is the 2040 Growth Concept, which states the preferred form of regional growth and development. As summarized in a Regional Plan Framework that implements the Concept, "[t]he preferred form is to contain growth within a carefully managed Urban Growth Boundary (UGB). Growth occurs inside the UGB in the form of infill and redevelopment with higher density developed in areas where it is appropriate. Expansions of the UGB are done carefully to allow for the need for additional land." *Id.* at 1. Some of the important fundamentals to the growth concept are a "hierarchy of mixed-use, pedestrian friendly centers that are well connected by high capacity transit and corridors," a multi-model transportation system, a jobs-housing balance, and "[rural reserves that are intended to assure that Metro and neighboring cities remain separate." *Id.* The 2040 plan must be consistent with the state planning goals and local comprehensive plans, and maps must conform with the 2040 plan.

An Urban Growth Management Functional Plan is a toolbox with measures to help achieve regional growth policies, such as those in the Growth Concept and Framework Plan. It covers a wide variety of topics, including housing, employment, natural resources, neighbor cities and rural reserves. Metro does a study every five years of expected housing and forms the basis on which Metro and governments decide how to manage growth. See Urban Growth Report 2009-2020 (Jan. 2010). Metro also produced a final draft of a 2035 Regional Transportation Plan in March, 2010. Metro's planning documents can be found at http://metro-region.org. A referendum passed in 2002 provides some limits on density increases by prohibiting density increases inside the UGB but allowing density increases in areas not yet built out. This measure limits the extent to which land within the UGB can handle population increases.

4. *The push for farmland preservation.* Preserving agricultural land was a major incentive for adopting UGBs, but one observer notes: "[T]o preserve farmland, development is pushed into the hills, where it is more expensive to develop infrastructure; therefore development occurs at lower density, resulting in a larger amount of land consumed. This pattern makes it more difficult to deliver affordable housing and makes it more likely that traffic problems will be exacerbated." Chandler, *The State of Planning in Oregon*, 12 Land Development 15, 19 (2000). Portland is surrounded by hills, which creates this problem. How might similar problems arise in an area that does not have this geography? See Sullivan & Eber, *The Long and Winding Road: Farmland Protection in Oregon 1961 -2009*, 18 San Joaquin Ag. L. Rev. 1 (2008-2009).

On the hills development issue, see *Collins v. Land Conservation & Dev. Comm'n*, 707 P.2d 599 (Ore. App. 1985) (cannot include hillsides that are not urbanizable in a UGB because city wants aesthetic backdrop and wants to create area where no urbanization can occur). Does this case create a dilemma for municipalities in view of Mr. Chandler's comment? *VinCEP v. Yamhill County*, 171 P.3d 368 (Or. App. 2007), discusses a "reasons" exception for development on agricultural land.

5. *UGBs and takings.* A UGB can create takings problems because of its total restriction on development outside the boundary. Traditional zoning, such as large lot and agricultural zoning, is one way to prevent development from occurring outside the boundary. Will there be a taking if the restriction is permanent? What if the delay is temporary, which can occur on land outside a UGB in Portland? Moratoria are discussed further in chapter 6. What about the argument that a takings challenge on land a substantial distance from a boundary is not likely because a landowner may believe that "the discounted development value of her land at a future date is worth more than what she might recover as compensation in a takings suit"? *Managing Space, supra*, at 821. See *Shea Homes Ltd. Partnership v. County of Alameda*, 2 Cal. Rptr. 3d 739 (Cal. App. 2003), holding a UGB was not a taking because a number of uses were allowed, including residential and agricultural uses, and because the measure stated it would not apply if constitutional rights were violated. Jun, *The Effects of Portland's Urban Growth Boundary on Housing Prices*, 72 J. Am. Plan. Ass'n 239 (2006), found no evidence of a significant difference in housing prices inside and outside the Portland UGB.

6. *Alternate urban forms.* An urban boundary that prohibits development outside and increases densities inside the boundary contradicts the standard American development pattern, in which densities gradually slope downward as development moves out. The Oregon UGBs provide an alternate urban form, an inner urbanized area surrounded by a circular growth boundary. There are other alternatives. One consists of an urbanized core with development allowed along major corridors leading outward from the core. The corridors can contain public transit links. This is the pattern adopted for the Washington, D.C. metropolitan area in its 1965 Year 2000 Plan. A second alternative does not have corridors but complements the urbanized core with satellite nodes or centers developed at urban densities. How can either alternative be incorporated into the Oregon UGB program?

7. *Sources.* For additional discussion of UGBs and the Oregon program, see J. DeGrove, Planning Policy and Politics ch. 2 (2005); Abbott, Planning a Sustainable City: The Promise and Performance of Portland's Urban Growth Boundary in Urban Sprawl: Causes, Consequences and Policy Responses (G. Squires ed., 2002); Charles, *Lessons From the Portland Experience, in* A Guide to Smart Growth: Shattering Myths, Providing Solutions (J. Shaw & R. Utt eds., 2000); V. Easley, *Staying Inside the Lines: Urban Growth Boundaries*, American Planning Association, Planning Advisory Serv. Rep. No. 444 (1992); Lewyn, *Oregon's Growth Boundaries: Myth and Reality*, 32 Envt'l L. Rep. 10160 (2002); Lang & Hornburg, *Planning Portland Style: Pitfalls and Possibilities*, 8 Hous. Pol'y Debate 1 (1997); Liberty, *Oregon's Comprehensive Growth Management Program: An Implementation Review and Lessons for Other States*, 22 Envtl. L. Rep. 10367 (1992). A state-appointed task force published a Final Report on Land Use Planning in January, 2009, available at http://www.slartcenter.org/pageview.aspx?id=26448.

The following case examines the issues to be considered in a boundary expansion under the revised urbanization goal:

HILDEBRAND v. CITY OF ADAIR VILLAGE

217 Ore. App. 623, 177 P.3d 40 (2007)

SERCOMBE, J.

Petitioners seek judicial review of an opinion and order of the Land Use Board of Appeals (board) that remands city and county ordinances adopted to expand an urban growth boundary. Petitioners claim that the board erred in not requiring additional justification from the local governments for the urban growth boundary expansion. We conclude that the board's order is unlawful in substance because it failed to require a justification by the local governments of the quantity of land added to the area within the boundary that is necessary under Goal 14.

Respondent JT Smith, Inc., applied to the City of Adair Village and Benton County for comprehensive plan amendments to expand the city's urban growth boundary and to enact plan designations and zoning changes to accommodate the development of high-density residential housing and a school athletic field. The proposed urban growth boundary expansion area is agricultural land that is located south of the city. The city and county approved the application, expanding the urban growth boundary by 142 acres, changing the plan designation of the property from agricultural to high-density residential and open space designations, and amending the zoning for the property from an exclusive farm use zone to zoning districts for urban residential and open space uses. Petitioners appealed the approval ordinances to the board, which reviewed them in a consolidated proceeding. The ordinances included findings adopted to show compliance with state statutes and administrative rules regulating urban growth boundary changes.

Before the board, petitioners argued that the approval findings were insufficient to justify the urban growth boundary amendment in several respects, three of which are relevant to our review. First, petitioners contend that the local governments erred by "failing to demonstrate the need for housing, recreational, and schools lands, as required by Goal 14, prior to expansion of an urban growth boundary." In particular, petitioners asserted that the findings failed to comply with the requirements of Goal 14 to limit urban growth boundary expansions if there is underdeveloped or vacant land already inside the boundary that can be developed for the desired land uses.[1] Second, petitioners contended that the city and county added too much land to the expansion based on incorrect assumptions about the expected growth in city population and by understating the density of the residential development allowed in the expansion area. Third, petitioners complained about the location of the expansion area, contending that ORS 197.298 foreclosed including agricultural land within the boundary because suitable nonagricultural land was available as an alternative.

The board found that the city's and county's findings improperly discounted the availability of vacant or underdeveloped land for the desired land uses within the existing boundary, contrary to Goal 14 and its implementing rules, and remanded the ordinances to the local governments for further proceedings. But the board rejected petitioners' remaining claims of error. Petitioners seek review of the board's rulings approving the local governments' findings as to the quantity of land to be added to the urban growth boundary area and the location of the expansion.

We review the board's order to determine whether it is "unlawful in substance or procedure." ORS 197.850(9)(a). Petitioners' first assignment of error on review is that the board erred in approving the local governments' calculation of the quantity of land to be added by an urban growth boundary change. The city and county approved a 142-acre expansion to the boundary, designating 118 acres for high-density residential uses and 24 acres for open space uses. The adopted findings forecast a population increase of 1,909 persons during the relevant planning period, a likely household size of 2.75 persons, and a resulting need for 694 additional housing units. The city and county assumed that the average lot size for each housing unit would be 6,000 square feet and, based on that assumption, projected a need to expand the urban growth boundary by 118 acres to accommodate those housing and auxiliary uses. The 694 additional housing units will nearly triple the housing stock in the city from the number of existing dwelling units.

Before the board, petitioners challenged the evidentiary foundation of the finding that land designated and zoned for high-density residential uses would develop at a density of 6,000 square foot lots. Petitioners asserted: "[B]ecause the land proposed to be added to the UGB would be designated for high-density residential development, no evidence supports an 'average lot size' of 6000 square feet. Minimum lot sizes in the R-3 zone range from 1200 square feet for row houses up to 7600 square feet for duplexes (which would provide two housing units); single family homes may be constructed on lots between a minimum of 3800 square feet and a *maximum* of 6000 square feet." (Emphasis in original.)

---

[1] Statewide planning goals, adopted by the Land Conservation and Development Commission under ORS 197.040(2), apply to the adoption or amendment of city or county land use comprehensive plans, including an amendment to adopt or alter an urban growth boundary. ORS 197.175(2)(a) (obligation to adopt and amend comprehensive plans "in compliance with goals approved by the commission"). Goal 14 (Urbanization), OAR 660-015-0000(14), requires that the establishment or change of an urban growth boundary be based on a demonstrated need for additional land. Goal 14 further provides that "[p]rior to expanding an urban growth boundary, local governments shall demonstrate that needs cannot reasonably be accommodated on land already inside the urban growth boundary."

The board rejected petitioners' challenge to the adopted findings on the likely lot size:

> "[Respondent] answers that the assumptions used by the city and county are based on policies set forth in the City of Adair Village Comprehensive Plan (Plan). * * * Section 9.800 of the Plan expresses a policy of providing 'new minimum lot sizes that result in an overall average lot size of 6,000 square feet.' Those Plan policies were adopted by the city in February, 2006. It is appropriate for the city and county to rely on assumptions included in the city's acknowledged comprehensive plan policies in computing the acreage for the proposed UGB expansion. See *1000 Friends of Oregon v. City of Dundee*, 124 P.3d 1249 (2005) (an acknowledged comprehensive plan and information integrated into that plan must serve as the basis for land use decisions)."

On review, petitioners complain that the board "seems to have missed the petitioners' point." Petitioners argue that the density of residential development in the expansion area will be controlled by the likely R-3 high-density residential zoning, which sets a maximum 6,000 square foot lot allowance, and not a plan policy espousing a goal of an average lot size for the entire city. In fact, because existing lots in the city are larger than 6,000 square feet, petitioners suggest that new lots in the city must be smaller in order to comply with the plan requirement of an average citywide lot size of 6,000 square feet. Thus, petitioners conclude that the board order is "unlawful in substance" because it affirmed a critical finding for the calculation of the size of the boundary change that was not supported by substantial evidence in the local government record. . . .

We conclude that the board improperly relied on a plan policy about citywide average lot sizes to justify the likely lot size that would be developed in a smaller part of the city. . . .

The city council did not expressly interpret the meaning of the plan policy. . . .

In the absence of any city council interpretation of its plan policy to assist the board, we determine its meaning from the text and context of the policy. By its plain terms and in this context, the average lot size policy directs the content of future zoning legislation (to "provide for new minimum lot sizes"). At the very most, the policy regulates the "overall lot size" within the city. On its face, however, it does not prescribe a 6,000 square foot lot density for any particular development or part of the city.

Assuming that the plan policy on "new minimum lot sizes that will result in an overall average lot size of 6,000 square feet" applies to plan amendments (and not just to zoning legislation on minimum lot sizes), the policy arguably requires that development allowed by an urban growth boundary amendment not result in an average city lot size that is less compliant with the 6,000 square foot standard. The policy does not dictate that the average size of the lots in all new development must be 6,000 square feet. It requires that lot sizes in new development be arrayed in a way that brings the citywide average lot size closer to the 6,000 square foot standard. If the rest of the city had developed with 10,000 square foot lots, then lots smaller than 6,000 square feet would need to be added to reach an average lot size of 6,000 square feet. But that calculation was not made by the city and county. The adopted findings do not determine what residential density will be required in the expansion area in order to meet the purported plan standard. The plan policy provides no guidance for any assumed residential density without that context.

Instead, Goal 14 requires that:

"Establishment and change of urban growth boundaries shall be based on the following:

"(1) Demonstrated need to accommodate long range urban population, consistent with a 20-year population forecast with affected local governments; and

"(2) Demonstrated need for housing, employment opportunities, livability or uses such as public facilities, streets and roads, schools, parks or open space, or any combination of the need categories in this subsection (2)."

Goal 14 requires that the quantity of land added to an urban growth boundary be justified by a calculated or "demonstrated" need to add land for housing or other urban uses. How much land is needed to site 694 dwelling units is a function of how densely the land is developed, which depends, in part, on the residential density permitted by the plan designation and likely zoning. The city plans to use the urbanizing area for high-density residential uses and proposes to zone it accordingly. The necessary justification under Goal 14 of the quantity of land to be added to the urban growth boundary requires a projection of likely development under the densities allowed by the city's high-density residential zoning, the R-3 zoning district, rather than the local governments' assumption that all development will occur under the lowest density permitted by that zoning. That unsupported assumption does not constitute substantial evidence of a "demonstrated need" under Goal 14, and the board's conclusion to the contrary is unlawful in substance.

Petitioners' second assignment of error challenges the board's rulings on their assertion that the local governments insufficiently justified the location of the urban growth boundary expansion. The expansion area is land south of the city that is planned and zoned for agricultural uses. The city chose not to expand the boundary to the west to include the "Tampico Road" exception area, an area that is not designated for agricultural uses. Petitioners argued to the board that the city and county erred in adding agricultural lands to the boundary when nonagricultural land was available to be added, because ORS 197.298 expresses a preference for adding nonagricultural land.

ORS 197.298(1) sets out policies on the priority of land to be added to an urban growth boundary that apply "[i]n addition to any requirements established by rule addressing urbanization." The first priority is land designated as urban reserve land; the second priority is "an exception area," *i.e.*, land determined to be unsuitable for agricultural or forestry uses under criteria set out in Goal 2 and ORS 197.732, or "non-resource land"; the third priority is land designated as marginal land under ORS 197.247; and, if the land under the preceding priorities is "inadequate to accommodate the amount of land needed," the fourth priority is "land designated in an acknowledged comprehensive plan for agricultural or forestry, or both." ORS 197.298(1).

ORS 197.298(3) relaxes the prioritization requirements in certain circumstances. It provides:

"Land of lower priority under subsection (1) of this section may be included in an urban growth boundary if land of higher priority is found to be inadequate to accommodate the amount of land estimated in subsection (1) of this section for one or more of the following reasons:

"(a) Specific types of identified land needs cannot be reasonably accommodated on higher priority lands;

"(b) Future urban services could not reasonably be provided to the higher priority lands due to topographical or other physical constraints; or

"(c) Maximum efficiency of land uses within a proposed urban growth boundary requires inclusion of lower priority lands in order to include or to provide services to higher priority lands."

The rationale adopted by the city and county for expanding the urban growth boundary to include fourth priority lands under ORS 197.298(1) was that extension of sewer and water services to the exception area would be cost prohibitive because of the need for expensive borings under the state highway; a more efficient transportation system could be engineered on land east of the highway; and the exception area was not configured to accommodate a stated plan objective of "compact community development" and plan growth management policies favoring a " 'village center" and a transportation system disassociated from the highway. After summarizing the adopted findings, the board determined:

"ORS 197.298(3) allows the city to include resource land within the [Urban Growth Boundary (UGB)] over existing exception areas if urban services cannot reasonably be provided due to physical constraints. Highway 99W physically separates the existing UGB from the Tampico Road exception area, and the evidence in the record indicates that due to the high cost of extending urban services across the highway, those services cannot be reasonably provided to that area. Coupled with the findings that inclusion of the Tampico Road exception area within the UGB would be contrary to adopted Plan policies, we think the findings are sufficient under ORS 197.298(3) to justify the inclusion of lower-priority resource land in the UGB rather than the higher priority Tampico Road exception area."

On review, petitioners categorically contend that the board erred in allowing the addition of any lower-priority land to the urban growth area without proof that the quantity of all types of higher-priority lands was inadequate. That contention is inconsistent with the plain language of ORS 197.298(3) that sets out qualitative considerations for including lower-priority land. We rejected the same contention in *City of West Linn v. LCDC*, 119 P.3d 285 (2005). In that case, we concluded that whether there is "inadequate" land to serve a need depends on not only the constraints identified by ORS 197.298(3), but also the criteria for locating an urban growth boundary expansion under Goal 14. The "statutory reference to 'inadequate' land addresses suitability, not just quantity, of higher priority land." Thus, the ranking of land under ORS 197.298(1) is a function of its prior classification as urban reserve land, exception land, marginal land, or resource land, as well as the application of the qualitative factors under Goal 14 and ORS 197.298(3). . . . [The court held that Highway 99W was a "a 'physical constraint' to the provision of urban services" under § 197.298(3)(b), and that "urban services cannot be reasonably provided to the Tampico Road area."]

Petitioners' final contention is that the findings on plan policies about community form, growth management, and transportation needs are irrelevant to the urban growth boundary expansion decision under ORS 197.298(3), and that the local governments and the board erred in relying on that part of the justification. Petitioners' contention is incorrect. The findings are relevant to the boundary location factors in Goal 14. Goal 14 requires that the location of an urban growth boundary change be determined by "evaluating alternative boundary locations consistent with ORS 197.298" and with consideration of the following factors:

"(1) Efficient accommodation of identified land needs;

"(2) Orderly and economic provision of public facilities and services;

"(3) Comparative environmental, energy, economic and social consequences; and

"(4) Compatibility of the proposed urban uses with nearby agricultural and forest activities occurring on farm and forest land outside the UGB."

Those factors allow comparison of needed transportation improvements in the alternative expansion areas as part of the consideration of the "[o]rderly and economic provision of public facilities and services." It is likewise proper to consider the effects of an expansion on compact growth and community form in assessing the "[c]omparative * * * social consequences" of the alternative expansion areas.

Furthermore, we determined in *City of West Linn* that a higher priority of land under ORS 197.298(1) may be "inadequate" because of "the locational considerations that must be taken into account under Goal 14." 201 Ore. App. at 440.(3) For the foregoing reasons, the board did not err in upholding an urban growth boundary expansion decision justified on the qualitative factors in ORS 197.298(3), as well as those in Goal 14.

Thus, the order under review is reversed and remanded as "unlawful in substance" because the board failed to require a justification of the quantity of land needed for high-density residential use that is necessary for the urban growth boundary change to pass muster under Goal 14. The board did not err in upholding a justification of the location of the boundary change based on both *ORS 197.298* and Goal 14.

Reversed and remanded.

NOTES AND QUESTIONS

1. *The boundary expansion problem.* The principal case discusses two issues that must be considered in UGB extensions: the type of land to be included, and its location. Do the criteria for deciding these two issues overlap? Are they consistent with the UGB policy? Would you combine them? Rewrite them? Agin & Bayer, *Right-Sizing Urban Growth Boundaries*, Planning, Feb., 2003, at 22, studied UGBs nationally, found that few of the communities they surveyed had extended their UGBs and offered an eight-factor analysis to determine when expansion should occur.

2. *Reforming the boundary expansion process in the Portland metropolitan area.* Recent legislation has reformed the process for expanding the UGB in the Portland metropolitan area. Or. Rev. Stat. §§ 195.137-195.145. The process will no longer be tied to an arbitrary five-year review dependent on providing an adequate supply of land. Legislation authorizes Metro and counties in its jurisdiction to enter into agreements to designate urban and rural reserves. An urban reserve is land outside a UGB that will provide for future expansion over a long-term period and "[the] cost-effective provision of public facilities and services within the area when the lands are included within the urban growth boundary." The statute also includes a number of factors to be considered in the designation of urban reserve areas, including a finding that

(3) After we decided *City of West Linn*, Goal 14 was amended to explicitly state that the location of an urban growth boundary expansion is to be determined by applying both the Goal 14 locational factors and ORS 197.298 ("location of * * * changes to the boundary shall be determined by evaluating alternative boundary locations consistent with ORS 197.298 and with consideration of" the Goal 14 factors). The Land Conservation and Development Commission adopted OAR 660-024-0060 on October 5, 2006. . . .

public services and facilities will be adequate, that urban densities will make efficient use of public and future infrastructure investments, that sufficient land will be included suitable for a range of housing types, that sufficient development capacity will be included to a support a healthy urban economy, and that it can be designed to be walkable and serviced by a well-connected system of streets by appropriate service providers. Urban reserves must accommodate employment and population growth for up to 30 years beyond the 20-year period for which a buildable land supply has been demonstrated.

Rural reserves are "land reserved to provide long-term protection for agriculture, forestry or important landscape features that limit urban development or help define appropriate natural boundaries of urbanization, including plant, fish and wildlife habitat, steep slopes and floodplains." The statute includes a number of factors to be considered in the designation of rural reserves, including a requirement that they be in "an area that is otherwise potentially subject to urbanization, and is capable and suitable to sustaining long-term agriculture." Agreements to designate urban and rural reserves must provide for the coordinated and concurrent revision of comprehensive plans. Urban and rural reserves had been designated by the counties as of June, 2010, and will be submitted to the Land Conservation and Development Commission for approval.

3. *Oregon's affordable housing policies.* QuantEcon, Smart Growth and its Effects on Housing Markets: The New Segregation (2002), found that Portland-style land use restrictions would have increased the cost of homes in other jurisdictions by $10,000 and rent costs by six percent, but most studies do not agree. See Downs, *Have Housing Prices Risen Faster in Portland Than Elsewhere?*, 13 Hous. Pol'y Debate 1 (2002).

Affordable housing policies in the state land use program are intended to offset any impact the UGBs may have on housing prices. They include LCDC's adoption of the New Jersey fair share rule. *Seaman v. City of Durham*, 1 L.C.D.C. 283 (1978). Later LCDC issued its so-called "St. Helen's" policy, which requires communities to provide sufficient buildable land to meet housing need. LCDC also struck down building moratoria. These actions implemented the Housing Goal, No. 10, which provides:

> [P]lans shall encourage the availability of adequate numbers of housing units at price ranges and rent levels which are commensurate with the financial capabilities of Oregon households and allow for flexibility of housing location, type and density.

The legislature codified the St. Helen's policy in 1981. Or. Rev. Stat. §§ 197.295-197.314. One important provision states that approval standards, special conditions and approval procedures for needed housing must be "clear and objective and shall not have the effect, either in themselves or cumulatively, of discouraging needed housing through unreasonable cost or delay." § 197.307(6). "Needed" housing includes multi-family and manufactured housing. The purpose of this and related provisions dealing with approval standards is to prohibit the adoption of standards that can be used to deny approval to this kind of housing. See *State ex rel. West Main Townhomes, LLC v. City of Medford*, 225 P.3d 56 (Or. App. 2009); *Homebuilders Ass'n of Lane County v. City of Eugene*, 41 Or. LUBA 370 (2002).

The exclusion of any type of housing from residential zones is prohibited, and equal treatment for subsidized housing is required. § 197.312. Moratoria are strictly limited. LCDC has indicated that communities must have a formal rezoning process in which land can be rezoned to higher densities to meet the housing goal. City of Milwaukee Comprehensive Plan and Implementing Measures, Acknowledgment Order, Jan. 21, 1981. It struck down building densities as too low in an early case. *1000 Friends of Oregon v. City of Lake Oswego*, 2 L.C.D.C. 138 (1981). For a case deciding how affordable housing needs must be considered in a UGB expansion, see *Residents of Rosemont v. Metro*, 21 P.3d 1108 (Or. App. 2001). For discussion see Orfield, *Land Uses and Housing Policies to Reduce Concentrated Poverty and Racial Segregation*, 33 Fordham Urb. L.J. 877 (2006). One obstacle to affordable housing programs in Oregon municipalities, however, is a statutory prohibition on permit conditions establishing a sales price for housing or requiring the sale of a housing unit or building lot "to any particular class or group of purchasers." Or. Rev. Stat. § 197.309(1).

4. *Affordable housing in other growth management programs.* Thirty-six percent of the local government respondents to a growth management survey carried out by the American Planning Association reported they had at least one program to stimulate private sector affordable housing production. *Growth Controls and Affordable Housing, supra*, at 4. Programs included the use of city funds or staff to support nonprofit housing development agencies, assistance to local public housing authorities to build or rehabilitate housing, and inclusionary zoning. The stock of affordable housing was higher in communities with aggressive affordable housing programs.

5. *The takings measures.* In 2004, Oregon voters adopted a statute by initiative that requires either compensation or a waiver of restrictions for land use regulations that decrease property value. The initiative, popularly known as Measure 37, had a dramatic effect on Oregon land use programs. Legislation adopted in June 2007, and adopted by state voters in the fall election as Measure 49, modified Measure 37 and limited its impact. This legislation is discussed in Chapter 2, Sec. B. Martin et al., What is Driving Measure 37 Claims in Oregon?, discuss a database that collected claims filed as of March, 2007. Ninety percent of all claims are outside and within five miles of UGBs. Most have been for subdivisions on farm and forest land. The study is available at www.pdx.edu/sites/www.pdx.edu.ims/files/media_assets/ims_M37April07UAAppt.pdf. For a web site on Measure 49 see www.oregon.gov/LCD/MEASURE49/index.shtml.

6. *A statutory model for UGBs.* The American Planning Association's model legislation for UGBs notes that when UGBs are adopted by individual jurisdictions the effect may be to shift development to other communities or to the next tier of developable land, which causes sprawl. To prevent these problems, the model legislation requires adoption of UGBs by a regional agency, the provision of additional land to accommodate growth, the establishment and maintenance of a land monitoring system, and periodic five-year reviews of the boundary to ensure an adequate supply of buildable land. American Planning Association, Growing Smart Legislative Guidebook: Model Statutes for Planning and Management of Change 6-53 to 6-60 (S. Meck ed., 2002). See Land Market Monitoring for Smart Growth (G. Knaap ed., 2001).

[4.] Growth Management Programs in Other States

[a.] Washington

How it works. This state adopted a Growth Management Act (GMA) in 1990 that combines the urban growth boundary concept of the Oregon program with the concurrency requirement of the Florida program. The Act requires local governments to adopt comprehensive land use plans to guide development consistent with the statutory goals, and then implement the plan with consistent regulations. All growing counties must participate in the program, and others have opted in; 95% of the state's population is covered. The Washington program provides for local administration subject to review by a state Growth Management Hearings Board divided into three panels for different regions in the state, rather than for administrative review by a state agency, as in Oregon. (Originally there were three independent Boards). The state Department of Community, Trade and Economic Development (CTED) provides support, but it does not have rulemaking authority or the authority to approve local plans. Citizen enforcement is critical. See McGee, *Washington's Way: Dispersed Enforcement of Growth Management Controls and the Crucial Roles of NGOs*, 31 Seattle U. L. Rev. 1 (2007) (discusses legislative history). Seattle and the coastal strip are the fastest-growing areas.

Urban growth areas. The program includes three major areas: urban, rural and resource (agriculture and forestry). Counties designate Urban Growth Areas (UGAs), the equivalent of Oregon's UGBs. Development within UGAs is encouraged at "urban densities," and growth can occur outside UGAs only if it is not "urban in nature." Land must be made available within these areas to accommodate population projections made by a state agency. Land outside city limits can be included in a UGA only if it is "already characterized by urban growth," is "adjacent to" such areas, or is a "new fully contained community." § 36.70A.110(1). These requirements are intended to prevent scattered urban development in rural areas. The statute has a priority system that requires new urban growth to be located first in areas with adequate public facilities. § 36.70A.110(3). Urban growth areas must contain a green belt and open space areas.

The statute requires inclusion of "areas and densities sufficient to permit the urban growth that is projected to occur in the county or city for the succeeding twenty-year period," and "may include a reasonable land market supply factor and shall permit a range of urban densities and uses." § 36.70A.110(2). See *Thurston County v. Hearings Bd.*, 190 P.3d 38 (Wash. 2008) (statute does not authorize a bright line rule for market supply factor, which is to be upheld unless clearly erroneous); *Kitsap County v. Central Puget Sound Growth Mgmt. Hearings Bd.*, 158 P.3d 638, 643 (Wash. App. 2007) (growth policies inconsistent with actual growth).

Rural areas. For rural areas where urban growth is not allowed, the statute requires a "rural element" in comprehensive plans and contains detailed guidance for allowable development. § 36.70A.070(5)(b). "The rural element shall permit rural development, forestry, and agriculture in rural areas . . . [and] shall provide for a variety of rural densities, uses, essential public facilities, and rural governmental services needed to serve the permitted densities and uses." It must also contain measures for "[r]educing the inappropriate conversion of undeveloped land into sprawling, low-density development in the rural area." § 36.70A.070(5)(c)(iii). *Thurston, supra*, rejected a bright line rule that rural densities required a five-acre minimum lot size, holding that rural densities depended on local circumstances. *Whidbey Envtl. Action v. Island County*, 93 P.3d 885 (Wash. App. 2004), held the county could adopt alternate measures rather than downzoning to achieve rural character. These were "other innovative techniques" permitted by the statute and included "addressing visual compatibility, instituting a five percent limit on building coverage, drafting an 'excellent' Planned Residential Development ordinance, and storm water protection."

The statute authorizes the designation of new fully contained communities (FCCs) outside urban growth areas. Designation criteria include transit-oriented site planning, an affordable housing requirement and a restriction on growth in adjacent areas. Only one FCC may be designated every five years. § 36.70A.350. *Quadrant Corp. v. State Growth Mgmt. Hearings Bd.*, 81 P.3d 918 (Wash. App. 2003), *aff'd on this ground*, 110 P.3d 1132 (Wash. 2005), held a

2500-acre mixed-use development approved was an appropriate FCC. Rural residential zoning and restrictions on sewer connections prohibited growth in adjacent areas.

Natural resources, public facilities and housing. Counties must designate wetlands and other natural resource areas as "critical areas" that require protective development regulations. Wash. Rev Code §§ 36.70A.010, 36.70A060(2). See *Swinomish Indian Tribal Cmty. v. Western Wash. Growth Mgmt. Hearings Bd.*, 166 P.3d 1198 (Wash. 2007) ("no harm" standard to preserve existing conditions satisfies statutory duty to "protect" critical areas). Comprehensive plans must include a process for identifying and siting "essential public facilities" that are typically difficult to site, such as airports and correctional facilities. § 36.70A.200. They must also include a housing element, and local governments must assure that their plans and development regulations, taken collectively, shall "provide sufficient capacity of land suitable for development within their jurisdictions to accommodate their allocated housing and employment growth," consistent with the 20-year state population forecast. *Id.* § 36.70A.115. *Low Income Hous. Inst. v. City of Lakewood*, 77 P.3d 653 (Wash. App. 2001), found the city's consideration of the housing goal inadequate.

Based on the statute and court decisions, can you make a list of the statutory requirements the GMA places on counties in order to comply with the law? The statute does not prioritize its requirements. What problems does this create?

Evaluation. The Washington program's bottom-up approach, which at first had decentralized hearing boards and relies on citizen enforcement, has created compliance problems. McGee & Howell, *Washington's Way II: The Burden of Enforcing Growth Management in the Crucible of the Courts and Hearings Boards*, 31 Seattle U. L. Rev. 549 (2008) (also arguing for better delineation of proof burdens and standards of judicial review). A single state hearings board has now been created. A report by The League of Women Voters of Washington found density had increased in urban areas and infrastructure had improved. Agricultural land continued to shrink, and there was considerable variation among jurisdictions. The Growth Management Act of Washington State: Successes and Challenges (2006), available at www.seattlelwv.org/sites/default/files/GMA_study_0.pdf. Doug Porter found the program had made a worthy start, but that work was needed on several issues, including housing needs. "The central question raised by the GMA is whether Washington jurisdictions can bring off the complex balancing act of matching local planning and regulatory practices to GMA goals." Evaluation of Local Implementation of the Washington State Growth Management Act 45 (Nat'l Ass'n of Realtors, 2005).

How successful urban growth boundaries have been is another important issue. Carlson & Dierwechter, *Effects of Urban Growth Boundaries on Residential Development in Pierce County, Washington*, 59 Professional Geographer 209 (2007), found a substantial clustering of residential permits inside growth boundaries. However, Mookherjee et al., *Urban Growth and Metropolitan Sprawl in a Small Metropolitan Area*, Focus on Geography, Winter 2006, at 29, found more residential permits outside than inside the growth boundary, and a clustering of these permits in rural areas.

Sources. DeGrove, *supra*, ch. 8; Symposium, *Guidance for Growth*, 16 U. Puget Sound L. Rev. 863 (1993); Settle, *Washington's Growth Management Revolution Goes to Court*, 23 Seattle U. L. Rev. 5 (1999). The web sites of Futurewise, http://futurewise.org, an organization dedicated to supporting the growth management act, and the state Department of Community, Trade & Ecohomic Development, www.cted.wa.gov/site/375/default.aspx, are excellent resources, as is The Municipal Research and Service Center of Washington, http://mrsc.org. See also Sullivan, *Cudgels and Collaboration: Commercial Development Regulation and Support in Portland, Oregon-Vancouver, Washington Metropolitan Region*, 6 Vt. Envtl. L. 67 (2004/2005).

[b.] Vermont

How it works. Vermont's state land use law, adopted in 1970 and known as Act 250 for its chapter number, is an early state growth management program that has attracted national attention. Apart from nine small cities, the state is organized into 237 contiguous towns, New England local government units with authority over settled and rural areas within their jurisdiction. Act 250 adopted a permit requirement for major development that would be difficult to use in larger and more diverse states, but its structure and growth management elements are interesting. An attempt to adopt state planning goals failed.

State permitting. Act 250 requires a state permit in addition to local zoning for all developments and subdivisions. Vt. Stat. Ann. tit. 10, § 6081(a). Development means commercial and industrial development and development for governmental purposes on ten or more acres of land, and housing projects of ten or more units. Commercial or industrial development on one or more acres is covered in towns that do not have land use regulations. *Id.* § 6001(3). State permits are also required for subdivisions of any size. The Act creates three District Environmental Commissions that hear applications for development approvals and decide whether to issue a permit. Appeals are to a state Environmental Court, which replaced an earlier Environmental Board in 2004, and from there to the Supreme Court. *Id.* § 6089.

The Act originally contained ten criteria for permit applications that require consideration of environmental impacts, the adequacy of governmental services and consistency with local plans. *Id.* § 6086(a). See *In re Killington, Ltd.*, 616 A.2d 241 (Vt. 1992) (upholding permit denial). In 1973, the legislature added policies contained in a Land Use Capability and Development Plan for land use and development, the conservation and use of natural resources and linkages between government services and growth rates. Two of these policies have growth management implications. One requires consideration of whether a proposed development would "significantly affect" a town or region's financial capacity to "reasonably accommodate" growth. *In re Wal-Mart Stores, Inc.*, 702 A.2d 397 (Vt. 1997), noted, 54 Wash. U.J. Urb. & Contemp. L. 323 (1998), upheld a decision by the Environmental Board invalidating a permit for a Wal-Mart store under this policy. The court held the Board had properly concluded the store's impact on market competition was a relevant factor under this criterion. The court noted the project's impact on existing stores would negatively affect the tax base and thus the ability to pay for public services. The second policy requires consideration of whether the additional costs of public services and facilities caused by "scattered development" outweigh the tax revenue and other public benefits of the development, including increased employment opportunities. For discussion of District Environmental Commission and state Environmental Board cases where projects that would have created sprawl were denied, see Murphy, *Vermont's Act 250 and the Problem of Sprawl*, 9 Alb. L. Envtl. Outlook 205 (2004).

A legislative committee report on Act 250 in 2009 found the law has been effective in protecting natural resources and mitigating many of the adverse effects of rapid development. It had not been effective in addressing smart growth and sprawl. This ineffectiveness included an inability to address the cumulative impacts of development on a project-by-project basis, and the "historic lack of a land use planning framework to help guide Act 250 decision-making." Report of the Smart Growth Committee 2 (Jan. 21, 2009). The committee made a number of recommendations, which have not yet been acted on.

Legislation adopted in 2006 authorized the designation of growth centers in downtowns, villages and new towns to encourage growth in these centers through economic and regulatory incentives. Vt. Stat. Ann. tit. 24, § 2790 et seq. It is based on a detailed codification of smart growth principles and the designation of growth centers based on these principles. Problems with the program, especially the designation of oversized centers, led to changes in the program in 2010. They will streamline the application process, prevent damage to existing downtowns and village centers, and provide standards so that growth centers are planned for 20 years of growth and produce compact, mixed use areas. See Note, *Vermont's Act 183: Smart Growth Takes Root in the Green Mountain State*, 32 Vt. L. Rev. 583 (2008).

For discussion of the Vermont program, see R. Brooks, Toward Community Sustainability: Vermont's Act 250 (1996); DeGrove, *supra*, at 285-207. For updates, see the web site of Smart Growth Vermont, http://smartgrowthvermont.org.

[c.] Hawaii

Hawaii was part of the Quiet Revolution in land use controls in the 1960's and 1970's that produced the Oregon and Vermont programs, and created a statewide land use program soon after statehood in 1961. See D. Callies, Preserving Paradise (2d ed. 2010). Preservation of agricultural land was a major reason for the legislation. There is no growth management component. There is a state plan, and the statute requires amendments to the land use districts to comply with the plan, which is a set of legislatively adopted goals. See Hawaii Rev. Stat. ch. 226, § 2-5-16. Recently, the state issued an advisory Hawaii 2050 Sustainability Plan.

Professor Callies describes the statewide system:

> Land in Hawai is divided into four [state] use districts: urban, rural, agricultural, and conservation. [A state Land Use Commission] is responsible for grouping contiguous parcels of land into these districts according to the present and foreseeable use and character of the land. The urban district includes lands that are in urban use and will be for the foreseeable future. The rural district is designed for land with small farms and low-density residential. The agricultural district consists of land theoretically used for farming and ranching and after recent amendments it includes a new, statutorily defined subdistrict: "Important Agricultural Lands" (IAL). . . . Finally, the conservation district includes land in areas formerly classified as forest and water reserve zones, open spaces, water sources, wilderness, and scenic and historic areas. Land within the conservation district is further divided into five subzones: protected, limited, resource, general, and special. [*Regulating Paradise*, at 21.]

The state land use districting law acts as a growth management program. The state Land Use Commission decides where new growth and development will occur when it extends the urban district boundary. Most extensions are approved, and most are incremental additions to existing urban district land. Land use district reclassification decisions on lands of 15 acres or less are delegated to the counties, with the exception of important agricultural lands in the agricultural district. Haw. Rev. Stat. § 205-3.1. Hawaii is divided into four counties, there are no independent municipalities, and the counties regulate land development within the urban district. The counties take control of urban district land away from the Land Use Commission. Only low-density residential uses are permitted in the agricultural district, which is jointly managed by the state and the counties, and no economically beneficial use is permitted in the conservation district, which is managed by the state.

County control and influence over land use has grown, and Professor Callies comments that "as the counties and their planning and zoning departments have grown in experience, skill, and size and as their plans and ordinances have become more sophisticated, the role of the state in land use decision making not clearly involving a statewide interest is steadily diminishing." *Id.* at 4.

[5.] An Evaluation of Growth Management Programs

How have growth management programs performed? Have they lived up to their promise? The response from studies of these programs is cautious. The Lincoln Institute of Land Policy published an evaluation of growth management programs in four states. *Smart Growth Policies: An Evaluation of Programs and Outcomes* (2009), *available at* www.lincolninst.edu/pubs/PubDetail.aspx?pubid=1571. The study focused on four states with well-established smart growth programs — Florida, Maryland, Oregon and New Jersey — and compared them with four other states that use a range of other land management approaches — Colorado, Indiana, Texas and Virginia. Here are some of the conclusions:

> The evaluation reveals that the states, their policies, and their priorities are very heterogeneous; no state did well on all smart growth principles or on all performance measures, although individual states succeeded in one or more of their priority policy areas. . . .
>
> The message is clear: achieving smart growth is possible, but states have to remain focused on their key policy goals. No single approach is right for all states, and the most successful states use a variety of regulatory controls, market incentives, and institutional policies to achieve their objectives. [*Id.* at ix.]

Despite this concern, recent studies have found accomplishments:

- State growth management programs have effectively promoted compact development in terms of density and land use mixtures, and states with a higher degree of state involvement do not do better. Yin & Suan, *The Impacts of State Growth Management Programs on Urban Sprawl in the 1990s*, 29 J. Urb. Aff. 149 (2007).
- States with the strongest growth management intensity experience, such Oregon and Washington, experience consistent success in reducing urban land expansion and increasing population densities. Howell-Moroney, *Studying the Effects of the Intensity of US State Growth Management Approaches on Land Development Outcomes*, 44 Urb. Studies 2163 (2007).
- States with vertically or horizontally integrated elements were effective in reducing the square mile size of urban areas. Wassmer, *The Influence of Local Urban Containment Policies and Statewide Growth Management on the Size of United States Urban Areas*, 46 J. Reg. Sci. 25 (2006).
- Decreases in density were substantially less in growth-managed states. Anthony, *Do State Growth Management Regulations Reduce Sprawl?*, 39 Urb. APF. Rev. 376 (2004)

Doug Porter has these recommendations for growth management: aim for comprehensiveness and connectivity, which means understanding the linkages and interactions in the elements of a growth management program; expect complexity and change; and recognize regional forces and relationships. *Managing Growth*, at 299-300. How would these recommendations apply to the growth management programs reviewed in this chapter?

Sources: For additional discussion of growth management programs, see J. Weitz, Sprawl Busting: State Programs to Guide Growth (1999); Weitz, *From Quiet Revolution to Smart Growth: State Growth Management Programs, 1960 to 1999*, 14 J. Plan. Lit. 257 (CPL Bibliography 355/356/357, 1999); Salkin, *Squaring the Circle on Sprawl: What More Can We Do? Progress Toward Sustainable Land Use in the States*, 16 Widener L.J. 787 (2007). For a discussion of UGBs and other containment programs, see A. Nelson et al., The Social Impacts of Urban Containment (2008); A. Nelson & C. Dawkins, *Urban Containment in the United States*, American Planning Ass'n, Planning Advisory Serv. Rep. No. 520 (2004). Maryland has had an interesting growth management program based on priority funding areas intended to concentrate state spending in urban areas. For evaluations, see Lewis et al., *Managing Growth With Priority Funding Areas: A Good Idea Whose Time Has Yet to Come*, 75 J. Am. Plan. Ass'n 457 (2009); Knaap & Frece, *Smart Growth in Maryland: Looking Forward and Looking Back*, 43 U. Idaho L. Rev. 445 (2007).

C. CONTROLLING GROWTH THROUGH PUBLIC SERVICES AND FACILITIES

Many of the growth management strategies reviewed so far manage growth by linking the approval of new development to the availability of public services and facilities. In urban service areas, for example, the growth management program depends on the municipality's ability to refuse municipal services in areas where they are not planned to be provided. This section looks at strategies that directly manage growth through controls over public facilities and services. One strategy manages growth by limiting the availability of urban services to areas where growth is planned to occur. A second influences growth by designating corridors where land is reserved for the construction of roads and highways.

[1.] Limiting the Availability of Public Services

Several legal problems arise when local governments attempt to manage urban growth by controlling the availability of urban services:

DATELINE BUILDERS, INC. v. CITY OF SANTA ROSA

146 Cal. App. 3d 520, 194 Cal. Rptr. 258 (1983)

White, Presiding Justice:

On this appeal by Dateline Builders, Inc. (Builders) from a judgment in favor of the City of Santa Rosa (City), the major question is whether the City was required to connect its existing sewer trunk line to Builders' proposed "leap frog" housing development beyond the City's boundaries. For the reasons set forth below we have concluded that the City reasonably exercised its police power because Builders' proposed housing development was not consistent with the City's compact land use and development policy as set forth in the City and County's previously adopted General Plan.

The pertinent facts substantially as found below and revealed by the record are as follows: Builders, a California corporation, held an option on a parcel of real property located beyond the limits of the city boundary, on Todd Road in an undeveloped rural area known as the Santa Rosa Plain. The City is a charter city located in Sonora County (County).

The County Board of Supervisors determined that: (1) there was a need for development of sewer facilities in the Santa Rosa Plain; (2) it was in the public interest to avoid the proliferation of small and scattered un-unified sewer treatment facilities by a cooperative effort with the City to create a single regional facility to be owned and operated by the City. On October 17, 1964 the City and County entered into the "Plains Agreement," a mutual expression of policy and intent to exercise their police powers cooperatively for the orderly development of the Santa Rosa Plain, and to prevent a proliferation of fragment sewer districts and systems.

Paragraph 10 of the Plains Agreement provided that both the City and County would adopt a policy that the areas in the Santa Rosa Plain adaptable to urban type development, would be developed consistent with the City and County's General Plan[4] and with the development standards of the City. To implement this policy the City and County agreed to enact subdivision, building, zoning and other property development regulations "to prevent haphazard or substandard property development." Paragraph 10 further provided that any development proposal in the Santa Rosa Plain be accompanied by proof that the proposed development was consistent with the City and County's joint General Plan and consistent with the City's development standards and regulations.

To implement one of the policies of the Plains Agreement the City Council adopted a procedure that required the proponent of a development to apply for and receive a certificate of compliance (certificate) prior to the extension of new service outside the city; the certificate then served as proof of compliance with the city's development standards.

The General Plan adopted by the City and County in 1967 had as its goals, inter alia: (1) to encourage a compact growth pattern and discourage inefficient sprawl throughout the planning area; (2) to provide safe convenient traffic ways linking living areas with shopping and employment centers and recreation areas; (3) to further develop the public utility system in a manner to serve the growing metropolitan area most economically and efficiently; (4) to schedule utility extensions in a manner to help insure compact, efficient growth patterns with maximum economy; and (5) to encourage cooperation between all governmental agencies responsible for development occurring in the planning area. The Plan envisioned that utilities will be extended when it is economically feasible and "in accordance with *orderly development instead of urban sprawl.*"

Builders wanted to subdivide and develop its Todd Road property as a single family moderate and low income home tract. The Todd Road property was not contiguous with the City but was contiguous to one of the City's trunk sewer lines. Builders had obtained FHA approval for the project under a loan program for homes in communities of less than 10,000 population. The sewer hookup was not a condition for the availability of the federal funds. Builders planned to build 66 single family homes and submitted a tentative subdivision map to the County in 1971. At that time, the Todd Road property was zoned for agricultural use. On December 16, 1971, the County conditionally approved the tentative map but attached 24 conditions, including sewer hookup approval from the City and rezoning of the property to R-1

[4] The General Plan covered the 120 square mile area of the City's potential expansion.

residential use by the County.[5] For a project of the size contemplated by Builders, the County required a sewer system rather than septic tanks. After that date, Builders never performed any of these conditions or took any steps to do so. . . . [Builders was denied a certificate, and Builders appealed. The council refused to issue the certificate "as inconsistent with the City's General Plan and standards for compact development."]

On March 2, 1972, the City Council reiterated its refusal and explained that the Builders' proposed development was in conflict with the 1967 General Plan of compact growth. The staging concept would provide utility services to undeveloped and partially developed areas immediately surrounding the urban core before such services would be available to areas more removed from the urban core. The City's lack of sewer capacity was not a reason for the city's denial of the certificate. No environmental review pursuant to the state's Environmental Quality Act was prepared for the proposed development. The County's tentative approval of Builders' subdivision map expired on June 16, 1973 by operation of law. Builders commenced the instant action in May 1972.

The trial court concluded that: . . . (3) the City was not a public utility charged with providing sewer connections to the Builders proposed development; (4) the City's urban development strategy in the implementation of its General Plan, development policies and standards involved fundamental policy decisions in an exercise of the police power; (5) as a result of Builders' failure to perform any of the conditions attached to the county's approval of the tentative subdivision map, Builders were never in a position to receive any benefit from an approval of their application to the City for a certificate; (6) the City acted reasonably in determining that Builders' proposed development was inconsistent with its adopted land use plan and policies, and then denying the certificate; and (7) under the circumstances, the granting of a certificate would have been an abuse of discretion.

On appeal, the Builders argue that: . . . (2) . . . since the City was acting in its proprietary capacity as a public utility and was the only provider of utility services for the Santa Rosa Plain, the City's refusal to grant the certificate was arbitrary and constituted unjust and unlawful discrimination as a matter of law; and (3) the City had no power to act beyond its boundaries. . . .

The parties agree that the major questions here presented have not been the subject of a published opinion by a California appellate court.

Preliminarily we turn to the appropriate standard of review. After a careful review of the arguments on rehearing and the record, we are convinced there was no constitutionally suspect basis for the City's action. We hold therefore that the proper test is whether the City's action was a reasonable exercise of its police power, and whether, in fact, it bears a reasonable relationship to the public welfare. The concept of public welfare is sufficiently broad to encompass the City's desire to grow at an orderly pace and in a compact manner.

Builders rely on, and urge us to follow, *Robinson v. City of Boulder* (Colo. 1976) 547 P.2d 228 and *Delmarva Enterprises, Inc. v. Mayor and Council of the City of Dover* (Del. 1971) 282 A.2d 601. In both *Robinson* and *Delmarva, supra,* the owners of property outside of the city limits successfully argued that each city had unlawfully discriminated against them by

---

[5] The rezoning for single family residential use was contemplated by the General Plan and the property was eligible for rezoning. However, the City had no jurisdiction over zoning and could not override the County Planning Commission.

refusing to hook up their properties to the city's exclusive water and sewer services. Both the Delaware and Colorado courts reasoned that: (1) as the exclusive supplier of these services, each city acting in a proprietary capacity as a public utility, was held to the same standards as a private utility, and therefore could refuse to do so only for utility-based reasons, such as insufficient capacity; and (2) each city was bound by the rule that a municipality is without jurisdiction over territory beyond its limits in the absence of legislation. In *Boulder*, however, the court did not reach the City's argument that the rules applicable to private utilities should not apply to a governmental utility authorized to implement governmental objectives such as the adoption of a Masterplan. The City of Boulder and the county in which it was located had jointly developed and adopted a Boulder Valley comprehensive plan to provide for discretionary land use decisions. The court specifically noted that the proposed Boulder development complied with the county zoning regulations and that the county, rather than the city, had the ultimate responsibility for the approval of the proposed development.

Builders argue that the *Boulder* case, *supra*, is on all fours with the facts of the instant case. Builders, however, ignore the fact that its Todd Road project had the tentative approval of the county conditioned, inter alia, upon a change in zoning and other conditions with which Builders admittedly did not attempt to comply. However, we do not base our holding only on this factual distinction. By failing to seek rezoning from the County or meet the other 23 conditions imposed by the County in its tentative approval of the subdivision map, and then pursuing this action against the City, Builders was trying to play off against each other, the City and County who had agreed to cooperative planning. Basically, Builders argues that because a City cannot exercise its police power beyond its boundaries, the City was prevented from using the denial of the sewer hookup as a planning tool.

Builders ignores the joint policy of the City and County as expressed in the Plains Agreement, for orderly growth in conformance with the guidelines of the jointly adopted General Plan. Agreements such as that here in issue that lead to joint planning by cities and counties should and have been encouraged by the Legislature.[10]

The complex economic, political and social factors involved in land use planning are compelling evidence that resolution of the important housing and environmental issues raised here, is the domain of the Legislature. Unfortunately, the experience of many communities in this state has been that when planning is left to developers, the result is urban sprawl. The City's express and reiterated reason for denying the certificate was that Builders' proposed development violated its policy of orderly compact development from the urban core, and would result in a "leap-frog" development and "urban sprawl." A municipality cannot be forced to take a stake in the developer's success in the area. (*Cf. Reid Dev. Corp. v. Parsippany-Troy Hills Tp.* (N.J. 1954) 107 A.2d 20, at 23.) Neither common law nor constitutional law inhibits

---

[10] Around the time of the Plains Agreement, Legislature enacted many provisions encouraging the joint and cooperative planning by cities and counties and regions. For example, see Government Code sections 65061-65061.4 (Creation of Regional Planning Districts), sections 65300, 65307 (Authority and scope of General Plans). Since 1951 all cities and counties have been required to prepare and adopt a general plan. (Gov. Code, § 65300). In 1965 charter cities were exempted from some of the local planning requirements; they are not exempt from the planning elements prescribed by article 5 (commencing with Government Code section 65300) if a general plan is adopted under their charter. (Gov. Code, § 65700). Government Code section 65302 as originally enacted required a land use element (which included population density) and a circulation element. The "housing element" which shall make adequate provision for the housing needs of all economic segments of the community, was added by Statutes 1967, chapter 1658, section 1. Since then Government Code section 65302 has been amended repeatedly to require more detailed general plan elements of charter cities.

the broad grant of power to local government officials to refuse to extend utility service so long as they do not act for personal gain nor in a wholly arbitrary or discriminatory manner. (See authorities cited in *Control of the Timing and Location of Government Utility Extensions* (1974) 26 Stanford L. Rev. 945-963.)

Builders rely on the line of California authorities holding that where a municipality provides a public utility service "[g]enerally it is true that where the scope of a project transcends the boundaries of a municipality it ceases to be for a municipal purpose." . . . These authorities, of course, predate *Associated Home Builders, etc., Inc. v. City of Livermore*, [557 P.2d 473 (Cal. 1976).] We agree with the City that unlike the situation in the past, most municipalities today are neither isolated nor wholly independent from neighboring entities, and consequently, land use decisions by one local unit affect the needs and resources of the entire region. The Plains Agreement and the General Plan demonstrate that the City and County were aware of these realities.

Builders recognize that in this state, as elsewhere, publicly owned municipal utilities are not regulated by the Public Utilities Commission (PUC) or any other supervisory agency in the absence of a legislative grant of authority while privately owned utilities are. It has long been the rule in this state that when operating a municipal utility, a city retains its character as a municipal corporation. Reasons must be found for holding it liable to the same extent as a private utility corporation. Builders here argue that there were sufficient reasons here because the City was the only supplier, could not act beyond its boundaries and could not use sewer hookup as a planning device. We do not agree.

In *Associated Home Builders, etc., Inc. v. City of Livermore, supra*, our Supreme Court intimated that in California a city may enact restrictions that are effective beyond its boundaries. *Associated Home Builders* also reiterated the desirability of regional planning. As to a city's alleged inability to act beyond its boundaries, we note that Government Code section 65859 set forth below,[11] a part of the same enactment as Government Code section 65300 and 65302 . . . expressly provides otherwise.

Builders' contention that denial of the certificate could not be used as a planning device overlooks a fundamental distinction between such a decision as an improper initial use of the police power, and as here, a necessary and proper exercise of the power once the planning decision had been made. Here, of course, the adoption of the General Plan with its policy of orderly and compact growth to avoid urban sprawl was made in 1967. The policy was a proper exercise of the police power for the general welfare previously adopted by the City Council and the County. (*Cf. Golden v. Ramapo.*) Builders' argument that only zoning may be used for planning sits poorly in its mouth as they never sought to rezone the property or meet any of the County's other conditions.

The judgment is affirmed.

---

[11] § 65859. "A city *may prezone unincorporated territory adjoining the city for the purpose of determining the zoning* that will apply to such property in *the event of subsequent annexation to the city.* The method of accomplishing such prezoning shall be as provided by this chapter for zoning within the city. Such zoning shall become effective at the same time that the annexation becomes effective.

"If a city has not prezoned territory which is annexed, it may adopt an interim ordinance in accordance with the provisions of § 65858." (Emphasis added.)

NOTES AND QUESTIONS

1. *Services as a growth control.* Plans like the Ramapo plan and adequate public facilities ordinances, discussed *supra* in this chapter, link the approval of new development to facility and service adequacy. *Dateline Builders* dealt with the converse problem: the authority of a municipality to deny services as a method of controlling growth. This authority is crucial. As a practical matter, no human-use development can take place unless water and sewers can be provided at reasonable cost, either publicly or privately; conversely, once services are in place, it is usually only a matter of time before development follows, no matter what the current regulatory pattern. These implications of service provision issues are lost neither on municipalities nor developers, and resolution of service issues is often of more practical importance than is the formal zoning of the land.

2. *The precedents.* In the *Boulder* and *Delmarva* cases, relied on by the plaintiffs in the *Dateline* case, each city's refusal of service was held invalid. In both cases, the landowner was located in an area where the doctrines of "extraterritoriality" and "duty to serve," discussed below, obligated the city to provide water and sewer service. In the *Boulder* case, the proposed development was also found to be consistent with the controlling comprehensive plan, that of the county. In *Dateline Builders* the refusal to serve was also extraterritorial. Did the court successfully distinguish these cases, or was it holding that they did not apply under California law?

3. *Extraterritoriality.* Extraterritorial refusals to serve may present a problem if a municipal utility has the authority to provide service in extraterritorial areas but the local government does not have extraterritorial land use powers. This omission was fatal in the *Boulder* case because the city could not rely on its growth-management program as a basis for a service refusal in an extraterritorial area. How does the *Dateline* case resolve this problem? *County of Del Norte v. City of Crescent City*, 84 Cal. Rptr. 2d 179 (Cal. App. 1999), followed *Dateline* and upheld the city's refusal to extend water service to extraterritorial customers to implement a growth management policy. *MT Dev., LLC v. City of Renton*, 165 P.3d 427 (Wash. App. 2007), held the city could not condition the provision of utility service outside its borders on compliance with use, density and structure requirements because these constituted zoning, and the city did not have extraterritorial zoning powers. Some states have conferred statutory extraterritorial zoning powers, and these statutes have been upheld. See D. Mandelker, Land Use Law §§ 4.22-4.23 (5th ed. 2003).

4. *How much discretion?* The answer to this question depends on how a court views the duty of a publicly-owned utility to provide services. Though the distinction has been much criticized, many courts begin their analysis by asking whether the municipal public utility function is governmental or proprietary. If the function is proprietary, municipally owned utilities are subject to the duty to serve obligation imposed on private utilities. A utility may refuse to provide services under this rule only for utility-related reasons, such as economic or practicable infeasibility, insufficient expected return, or supply shortages. See *Okemo Trailside Condominiums v. Blais*, 380 A.2d 84 (Vt. 1977) (upholding rejection of extraterritorial service extension); *Reid Dev.*, cited in the principal opinion; Note, *The Duty of a Public Utility to Render Adequate Service: Its Scope and Enforcement*, 62 Colum. L. Rev. 312 (1962). What did the *Dateline* case hold on this issue?

A court may particularly hold the public utility function is proprietary in extraterritorial areas because the utility serves customers not residents of the city who do not have a political voice in public service decisions:

> [T]he consumer of utility services still cannot pick and choose his supplier of water as he does his grocer. The utility consumer is thus at the mercy of the monopoly and, for this reason, utilities, regardless of the character of their ownership, should be, and have been, subjected to control under the common-law rule forbidding unreasonable discrimination. [*City of Texarkana v. Wiggins*, 246 S.W.2d 622, 625 (Tex. 1952) (invalidating discriminatory municipal extraterritorial rates).]

Professor Tarlock has pointed out, however, that "[t]he traditional subordination of growth management to utility service ignores the fact a new public interest has been defined by local government. As more recent courts have held, a city should not be required to undermine its own growth management policy simply because it is also a water supplier." Tarlock, *Contested Landscapes and Local Voice*, 3 Wash. U. J.L. & Pol'y 513 (2000).

Some courts find statutory and constitutional authority to exercise discretion to refuse an extension of utility service. For example, in *Sunset Cay, LLC v. City of Folly Beach*, 593 S.E.2d 462 (S.C. 2004), the court upheld the city's refusal to extend utility service outside its commercial area. It held that "the decision whether to grant a sewer extension request generally must be left to the sound discretion of municipal leaders, who are charged with considering all the various factors, including financial and economic implications, aesthetic and environmental concerns, feasibility of a particular plan, and the effect of an extension on the municipality's long-range zoning, planning, or organization." *Id.* at 468. See also *Denby v. Brown*, 199 S.E.2d 214 (Ga. 1973) (extraterritorial service).

5. *Sources.* For additional discussion, see Biggs, *No Drip, No Flush, No Growth: How Cities Can Control Growth Beyond Their Boundaries by Refusing to Extend Utility Services*, 22 Urb. Law. 285 (1992); Stone, *The Prevention of Urban Sprawl Through Utility Extension Control*, 14 Urb. Law. 357 (1982).

[2.] Corridor Preservation

Corridor preservation is an important planning strategy that can preserve highway and transportation corridors from development. It is

> a concept utilizing the coordinated application of various measures to obtain control of or otherwise protect the right-of-way for a planned transportation facility. [Report of the AASHTO Task Force on Corridor Preservation 1-2 (1990).]

Corridor preservation can be an important element in planning programs such as growth management. As the Report explained, it should be applied as early as possible in the identification of a transportation corridor to prevent inconsistent development; minimize or avoid environmental, social, and economic impacts; prevent the foreclosure of desirable location options; allow for the orderly assessment of impacts; permit orderly project development; and reduce costs. *Id.*

Corridor preservation began under a very different name in the Standard Planning Enabling Act, §§ 21-25, which contained statutory authority for the adoption of an official street map by local governments. Local governments exercising this authority mapped the right-of-way for future streets, thereby keeping development out of the right-of-way until the street was completed. Two model acts published after the Standard Planning Act also included legislative authority for official maps. They differed in detail, but prohibited the development of land reserved on an official map unless the municipality granted a variance, and made the adoption of a street plan an explicit or implicit condition for the adoption of an official street map. The model acts and most state official map acts do not authorize the adoption of a time limit for an official map reservation. Official maps may also be used to reserve land for other public facilities, such as parks. Subdivision control statutes and ordinances may also authorize the reservation of land for acquisition for a public facility and prohibit the development of the land during the reservation period.

State statutes may authorize the state transportation agency to adopt maps for transportation corridors or for the location of future highway rights-of-way. They usually require the preparation and recording of official maps of the corridors, and local government referral to the state transportation agency of any application to develop land within the corridor. The state agency must negotiate with the developer either for the purchase of its land or for a modification in development plans that will protect the corridor if it finds that the development proposal has an impact on the preservation of the corridor.

NOTES AND QUESTIONS

1. *The constitutional issues.* Corridor preservation is really a type of moratorium with a clear prohibition on development within the corridor prior to land acquisition. Under the Supreme Court's *Lake Tahoe* case, this would not be a per se taking. There is the added complication, however, that corridor preservation looks a lot like the use of the police power to depress the value of land before acquisition, which is always held invalid. For example, in *People ex rel. Department of Transp. v. Diversified Props. Co. III*, 17 Cal. Rptr. 2d 676 (Cal. App. 1993), a city cooperated with the state to deny approval of development plans on property the state intended to acquire for a freeway. The court held that the delay due to these unreasonable precondemnation activities amounted to a de facto taking.

2. *More on the takings issue.* The record is mixed. In *Jensen v. City of New York*, 369 N.E.2d 1179 (N.Y. 1977), decided before the Supreme Court's recent takings cases, the court invalidated an official map reservation for streets it viewed as including all of the landowner's property. The plaintiff only wanted to sell the land, but the property was "virtually unsalable" and banks were unwilling to finance repairs because of the official map. This was "no less a deprivation of the use and enjoyment" of the property than if the plaintiff had applied for and been denied a building permit. But see *Royal v. City of New York*, 822 N.Y.S.2d 427 (Sup. Ct. 2006) (distinguishing *Jensen*). See also *Urbanizadora Versalles, Inc. v. Rivera Rios*, 701 F.2d 993 (1st Cir. 1983) (invalidating official map reservation for highway that had been in effect for 14 years); *Miller v. City of Beaver Falls*, 82 A.2d 34 (Pa. 1951) (invalidating reservation for parks and playgrounds though reservation for streets previously upheld). For a post-*Lucas* case in accord, see *Ward v. Bennett*, 625 N.Y.S.2d 609 (App. Div. 1995) (all economically viable use of property denied for 50 years).

Palm Beach County v. Wright, 641 So. 2d 50 (Fla. 1994), noted, 19 Fla. St. U.L. Rev. 1169 (1992), held a map of reservation filed in the county's thoroughfare map, which was part of its comprehensive plan, was not a per se taking. It noted the map limited development only as necessary to ensure compatibility with future land uses, and that the county had the authority to ameliorate any hardships of persons owning land within the corridor. See also *Kingston E. Realty Co. v. State*, 336 A.2d 40 (N.J. App. Div. 1975) (no taking under state highway corridor law during the time the statute stayed the building permit while the agency was allowed to consider acquisition). Contra *Lackman v. Hall*, 364 A.2d 1244 (Del. Ch. 1976). *Howard County v. JJM, Inc.*, 482 A.2d 908 (Md. 1984), upheld a reservation of land for a highway under a subdivision control statute. See Mandelker, *Interim Development Controls in Highway Programs: The Taking Issue*, 4 J. Land Use & Envtl. L. 167 (1989).

3. *Land acquisition and access management.* Mention should be made of two additional programs that can be useful in corridor preservation. Advance acquisition of land, either through condemnation or voluntary purchase, is one possibility. A federal statute, 23 U.S.C. § 108, provides federal funding for advance acquisition programs in the states. Access management is another option. A number of states have adopted access management programs. These programs regulate access points so that traffic flow is kept at acceptable levels or improved, which maintains highway capacity and helps avoid the construction of new highways. Some statutes authorize access management. See N.J. Stat. Ann. § 27:7-91.

4. *Model corridor map legislation.* The American Planning Association model land use legislation includes a model corridor map act modeled on state legislation for state highways. American Planning Association, Growing Smart Legislative Guidebook: Model Statutes for Planning and Management of Change § 7-501 (S. Meck ed., 2002). It gives the local planning agency several options in response to an application to develop land within a corridor, including a stay, a modified approval, acquisition, and compensation through a transfer of development rights. See also Thomas & Payne, *Long-Range Highway Corridor Preservation: Issues, Methods and Model Legislation*, 13 BYU J. Pub. L. 1 (1998); K. Williams & M. Marshall, Managing Corridor Development: A Municipal Handbook (Center for Urban Transp. Res., College of Engineering, Univ. S. Fla., 1996), available at www.cutr.usf.edu/pub/files/corridor.pdf.

Chapter 9

AESTHETICS: DESIGN REVIEW, SIGN REGULATION AND HISTORIC PRESERVATION

Land use regulation based on aesthetics is the focus of this chapter. They include the regulation of outdoor advertising, design review and design plans, and historic preservation. Each of these programs rests on aesthetic considerations, because each is concerned with the appearance or visual character of structures, buildings or areas of a city. Aesthetic controls have spread rapidly in recent decades and have been upheld in court. One important qualification is necessary. Free speech protection limits the regulation of outdoor advertising and qualifies the state case law that traditionally dominates this field.

A. AESTHETICS AS A REGULATORY PURPOSE

Almost a majority of courts recognize that "aesthetics alone" can be a proper regulatory purpose in land use controls, but it was not always that way. Judicial recognition of aesthetic regulation occurred in three stages. Courts early in the century held that aesthetics was not a proper basis for land use control. This early view, coming from a strict view of the police power, is illustrated by *City of Passaic v. Paterson Bill Posting, Adv. & Sign Painting Co.*, 62 A. 267 (N.J. 1905), invalidating a statute imposing setback and height restrictions on signs:

> Aesthetic considerations are a matter of luxury and indulgence rather than necessity, and it is necessity alone which justifies the exercise of the police power to take private property without compensation. [*Id.* at 268.]

Courts progressed to an intermediate view in the second stage, recognizing that aesthetics alone was not enough to justify a land use regulation but that it was sufficient if supported by other factors. A Texas case upholding the regulation of junkyards is illustrative:

> [L]eaving flammable materials in a collection of junked cars increases the possibility of fire. Wrecked cars have jagged edges of metal that are dangerous to playing children who have access to them. Leaving vehicles in a large unenclosed area facilitates theft. Because of these facts and because of the unsightliness of such operations, wrecking yards must inevitably have a depreciating effect on the value of other property in the vicinity. [*City of Houston v. Johnny Frank's Auto Parts, Inc.*, 480 S.W.2d 774, 778 (Tex. Civ. App. 1972).]

This case points to the typical "other factors" recognized in the second stage that support a land use regulation that also is motivated by aesthetic concerns. Note the reliance on health and safety problems as well as the effect on property values. The economic side of aesthetic regulation was put front and center in a leading billboard prohibition case, *United Adv. Corp. v. Borough of Metuchen*, 198 A.2d 447 (N.J. 1964):

> There are areas in which aesthetic and economics coalesce, areas in which a discordant sight is as hard an economic fact as an annoying odor or sound. We refer not to some

> sensitive or exquisite preference but to concepts of congruity held so widely that they are inseparable from the enjoyment and hence the value of property. [*Id.* at 449.]

The court added that even "the recognition of different residential districts" rests on aesthetic considerations. Why?

An important dictum by Justice Douglas in *Berman v. Parker*, 348 U.S. 26 (1954), accelerated the third and final stage in which courts accepted "aesthetics alone" as a regulatory justification. Justice Douglas said:

> [W]e emphasize what is not in dispute. . . . [T]his Court has recognized, in a number of settings, that States and cities may enact land-use restrictions or controls to enhance the quality of life by preserving the character and desirable aesthetic features of a city. . . . [*Id.* at 129.]

State v. Miller, 416 A.2d 821 (N.J. 1980), a sign ordinance case in which New Jersey moved to the third stage, illustrates the majority state court view on the acceptance of aesthetic purposes in land use control:

> Consideration of aesthetics in municipal land use planning is no longer a matter of luxury and indulgence. . . . The development and preservation of natural resources and clean salubrious neighborhoods contribute to psychological and emotional stability and well-being as well as stimulate a sense of civic pride. [*Id.* at 824.]

See also *R.H. Gump Revocable Trust v. City of Wichita*, 131 P.3d 1268 (Kan. App. 2006) (upholding rejection of permit for cellular tower); *Oregon City v. Hartke*, 400 P.2d 255 (Or. 1965) (regulation of junkyard).

Courts in all states today allow the use of aesthetic concerns in some fashion. Almost half the states accept aesthetics alone as the basis for regulation. The remaining states accept the use of aesthetics along with other factors. Some of these states have held that the use of aesthetics alone is not appropriate, some are moving toward the aesthetics alone category, and some are showing no movement in this direction. Pearlman et al., *Beyond the Eye of the Beholder Once Again: A New Review of Aesthetic Regulation*, 38 Urb. Law. 1119 (2006).

NOTES AND QUESTIONS

1. *Doubts about the second stage?* Some commentators are critical of the intermediate "other factors" view of aesthetic regulation, noting that the other factors are simply derived from the aesthetic impact. See, e.g., Rowlett, *Aesthetic Regulation Under the Police Power: The New General Welfare and the Presumption of Constitutionality*, 34 Vand. L. Rev. 603 (1981). Rowlett notes that

> the alleged economic, health, or safety benefits are often nonexistent or at least unproven. Because land use restrictions are presumed constitutional . . . , the courts rarely require proof of the "nonaesthetic" economic, health, or safety justifications. [*Id.* at 607.]

She argues that this approach to aesthetic regulation allows the courts to escape critical analysis. What does this say about the holding in *Metuchen, supra*?

2. *Defining aesthetics.* Can anyone really define what is aesthetic? Some commentators take the view that the aesthetic justification for land use regulation is really meaningless:

> [T]he words "beautiful as well as healthy" have become something of a talisman for courts forced to decide the validity of regulations that serve solely or predominantly aesthetic purposes. Rather than inquire into the nature of the individual and community interests at stake, courts have used the discretion that *Berman* [*v. Parker*] affords state and local governing bodies as a basis for upholding almost any aesthetic regulation. [Williams, *Subjectivity, Expression, and Privacy: Problems of Aesthetic Regulation*, 62 Minn. L. Rev. 1, 2 (1977).]

What about this statement?

> The utopian impulse to design and legislate public space has historically informed all inscriptions of the city, in architectural design and planning, in zoning regulation and legislation, and in literary and cinematic representations of urban scenes. Any approach to shaping the image of city spaces must reckon with ingrained cultural experiences of the image of the city — in its aesthetic, axiological, and social significance. [Amy Mandelker, *Writing Urban Spaces: Street Graphics and the Law as Postmodern Design and Ordinance*, 3 Wash. U. J.L. & Pol'y 403, 403 (2000).]

In the same vein, a provocative article by John Costonis rejects the visual beauty rationale and examines an alternate cultural stability rationale for aesthetic regulation. Costonis, *Law and Aesthetics: A Critique and a Reformulation of Policy*, 80 Mich. L. Rev. 355 (1980). Compare, Loshin, *Property in the Horizon: The Theory and Practice of Sign and Billboard Regulation*, 30 Environs Envtl. L. & Pol'y J. 101 (2006) (contrasting expressive and sensory theories of aesthetics). See also J. Costonis, *Icons and Aliens* (1989).

3. *Void for vagueness.* Though most courts may now be willing to accept aesthetics as a legitimate basis for regulation, subjectivity is again an issue when aesthetic regulations are challenged as unconstitutionally vague. Many courts use common meaning and understanding in rejecting vagueness claims. See *Carpenter v. City of Snohomish*, 2007 U.S. Dist. LEXIS 42819 (D. Wash. 2007) (regulation of murals); *Asselin v. Town of Conway*, 628 A.2d 247 (N.H. 1993) (ordinance prohibiting interior illumination of signs).

Some courts take a contrary view. In *City of Independence v. Richards*, 666 S.W.2d 1 (Mo. App. 1984), the court struck down an ordinance prohibiting the accumulation of refuse in an unsightly manner. Though conceding that regulation for aesthetic purposes is acceptable, the court held that "the ordinance term *unsightly* [does] not conjure a concept of visual incongruity so generally held that no further definition is required." Neither does the "momentary blight" of unsightly trash "concern the police power." *Id.* at 8. Vagueness problems are more serious when aesthetic regulations are challenged under the Free Speech Clause. Compare *Boyles v. City of Topeka*, 21 P.3d 974 (Kan. 2001) (upholding definition of "unsightly").

4. *Sources.* The literature on aesthetic regulation is voluminous. The classic article is still Dukeminier, *Zoning for Aesthetic Objectives: A Reappraisal*, 20 Law & Contemp. Probs. 218 (1955). See also C. Duerksen & M. Goebel, *Aesthetics, Community Character, and the Law*, Am. Plan. Ass'n, Planning Advisory Serv. Rep. No. 490 (1999); Karp, *The Evolving Meaning of Aesthetics in Land Use Controls*, 15 Colum. J. Envtl. L. 31 (1990); Saxer, Assessing RLUIPA's Application to Building Codes and Aesthetic Land Use Regulation, 2 Alb. Gov't L. Rev. 623 (2009); Stevenson, *Aesthetic Regulation: A History*, 35 Real Estate L.J. 519 (2007); Susong & Pearlman, *Regulating Beauty: A Review of Recent Law Journal Literature*, 14 J. Plan. Lit. 637 (2000); Note, *You Can't Build That Here: The Constitutionality of Aesthetic Zoning and Architectural Review*, 58 Fordham L. Rev. 1013 (1990).

B. OUTDOOR ADVERTISING REGULATION

PROBLEM

You are the city attorney of Metro City, a city of 500,000 with the usual variety of commercial, industrial and residential areas. The city council has asked your opinion on a sign ordinance it plans to adopt. The ordinance would prohibit all billboards, which are defined as signs advertising goods or services not sold or manufactured on the premises. Signs would be allowed for on-premise businesses that advertise the business being conducted on the premises. Portable signs would be prohibited. The ordinance would also regulate the size, number and location of on-premise signs. For example, each business would be allowed only one pole or other ground sign, and height and area limitations for these signs would vary depending on the zoning district in which the business is located. Temporary signs, such as "for sale signs," are allowed. Political campaign signs would be allowed 20 days before and during an election and must be removed by 30 days after an election, and more restrictive height and size regulations apply than for other temporary signs. Is the ordinance constitutional under state law? Under the Free Speech Clause of the federal Constitution? How would you define the various signs the ordinance would regulate? If the ordinance is unconstitutional for any reason, what changes would you recommend to make it constitutional?

[1.] In the State Courts

The business of outdoor advertising on a commercial basis dates from the 1880s. Under the common law, advertising posters considered offensive or dangerous were dealt with under the common law of nuisance. Prohibitory local ordinances became common from the 1890s onward, when the large-scale commercial promotion of billboard advertising became so aggressive and its methods so crude that municipal regulation was considered necessary. In the early years, the courts were generally hostile to these prohibitory ordinances and declared many of them unconstitutional. These decisions reflected the judiciary's early unwillingness to support aesthetic regulation generally.

The decision generally recognized as marking the turning point in changing judicial attitudes toward billboard regulations is *St. Louis Gunning Adv. Co. v. City of St. Louis*, 137 S.W. 929 (Mo. 1911), *appeal dismissed*, 231 U.S. 761 (1913). In a 124-page opinion, the Missouri court discussed the evolution of the law up to that time and sustained a municipal ordinance regulating the size, height, and location of billboards. In an oft-quoted passage, the court said:

> The signboards upon which this class of advertisements are displayed are constant menaces to the public safety and welfare of the city; they endanger the public health, promote immorality, constitute hiding places and retreats for criminals and all classes of miscreants. They are also inartistic and unsightly.
>
> In cases of fire they often cause their spread and constitute barriers against their extinction; and in cases of high wind, their temporary character, frail structure and broad surface, render them liable to be blown down and to fall upon and injure those who may happen to be in their vicinity. The evidence shows and common observation teaches us that the ground in the rear thereof is being constantly used as privies and the dumping ground for all kinds of waste and deleterious matters, and thereby

> creating public nuisances and jeopardizing public health; the evidence also shows that behind these obstructions the lowest form of prostitution and other acts of immorality are frequently carried on, almost under public gaze; they offer shelter and concealment for the criminal while lying in wait for his victim; and last, but not least, they obstruct the light, sunshine and air, which are so conducive to health and comfort. [*Id.* at 942.]

Although the Missouri court, in the passage set out above, expressly mentioned the fact that signboards are inartistic and unsightly, it made clear at a later point in its opinion that, in its view, aesthetic considerations alone were insufficient to justify the regulatory ordinance. *Id.* at 961. Commentators have tended to deride the public safety arguments in the *Gunning* case, and certainly the modern billboard, placed high above the ground and made of sturdy and noncombustible materials, does not match the court's description. But this line of argument can be carried too far. The day after one of the editors made this argument to a class in land use law, a young telephone operator was raped and stabbed behind a billboard in the central area of the city in which the class was held. Still, looking back today, a century later, the public safety arguments, prevention of crime and the spread of fire, seem like makeweight rationales. For a review of the aesthetic issues in sign regulation, see Note, *Judging the Aesthetics of Billboards*, 23 J. L. & Politics 171 (2007).

Modern courts are usually willing to uphold billboard prohibitions, although other non-aesthetic factors often help provide the basis for the decision. One of the best of these cases is the California Supreme Court decision in *Metromedia, Inc. v. City of San Diego*, which is reproduced next. This case was appealed to the U.S. Supreme Court, which reversed on free speech grounds that the state court found unpersuasive. The California court's holding on the aesthetic regulation issues is still important, and provides a basis for understanding the free speech implications of billboard control considered in the next section.

A note on sign types: When reading the cases and materials that follow, it is important to understand the differences between different types of signs. One distinction is between off-premise signs, usually called billboards, which are not located on the site of a business, and on-premise signs, which are located at the business site. Another distinction is between signs attached to walls and signs located on the ground, usually known as pole or ground signs, which may be either off- or on-premise. Then there are signs displayed for temporary periods of time, such as those displayed during political campaigns. Portable signs are not permanent. A ubiquitous example is the back-lit sign on a small trailer with changeable letters. Sign regulations typically regulate all of these sign types, though we will see that free speech law has eroded some of these categories and has made others questionable. So-called digital, or electronic changing message, signs can be displayed on any of these sign types.

METROMEDIA, INC. v. CITY OF SAN DIEGO

26 Cal. 3d 848, 164 Cal. Rptr. 510, 610 P.2d 407 (1980), *rev'd on other grounds*, 453 U.S. 490 (1981)

TOBRINER, JUSTICE:

The City of San Diego enacted an ordinance which bans all off-site advertising billboards and requires the removal of existing billboards following expiration of an amortization period. Plaintiffs, owners of billboards affected by the ordinance, sued to enjoin its enforcement. Upon motion for summary judgment, the superior court adjudged the ordinance unconstitutional, and issued the injunction as prayed.

We reject the superior court's conclusion that the ordinance exceeded the city's authority under the police power. We hold that the achievement of the purposes recited in the ordinance — eliminating traffic hazards and improving the appearance of the city — represent proper objectives for the exercise of the city's police power, and that the present ordinance bears a reasonable relationship to those objectives. [The court held that the ordinance did not violate the Free Speech Clause, but that it was preempted by state law to the extent it required the uncompensated removal of nonconforming billboards protected by the federal law. The court remanded for a determination of which billboards fell within the preemptive scope of the state law.] . . .

1. Summary of proceedings in the trial court.

The present case concerns the constitutionality of San Diego Ordinance No. 10795 (New Series), enacted March 14, 1972. With limited exceptions specified in the footnote[1] the ordinance as subsequently amended prohibits all off-site "outdoor advertising display signs."[2] Off-site signs are defined as those which do not identify a use, facility or service located on the premises or a product which is produced, sold or manufactured on the premises. All existing signs which do not conform to the requirements of the ordinance must be removed following expiration of an amortization period, ranging from 90 days to 4 years depending upon the location and depreciated value of the sign.

Plaintiffs, Metromedia, Inc., and Pacific Outdoor Advertising Co., Inc., are engaged in the outdoor advertising business and own a substantial number of off-site billboards subject to removal under Ordinance No. 10795. Plaintiffs filed separate actions against the city, attacking the validity of the ordinance. The actions were consolidated by stipulation. After extensive interrogatories and requests for admission had been answered all parties moved for summary judgment.

To facilitate the determination of the motion for summary judgment the parties entered into a stipulation of facts. The following portions of that stipulation are particularly pertinent to the present appeal:

(1) The original ordinance permitted the following off-site signs: Signs maintained in the discharge of a governmental function; bench advertising signs; commemorative plaques, religious symbols, holiday decorations and similar such signs; signs located within shopping malls not visible from any point on the boundary of the premises; signs designating premises for sale, rent or lease; public service signs depicting time, temperature or news; signs on vehicles conforming to city regulations; and temporary off-premises subdivision directional signs.

As originally enacted, the ordinance contained no exception for political signs. On October 19, 1977, the city counsel amended the ordinance to permit "Temporary political campaign signs, including their supporting structures, which are erected or maintained for no longer than 90 days and which are removed within 10 days after the election to which they pertain." (Ord. No. 12189 (New Series).) This amendment may have been prompted by the decision of the Ninth Circuit in *Baldwin v. Redwood City* (1976) 540 F.2d 1360, in which that court held an ordinance regulating temporary signs to be an unconstitutional restriction upon political speech.

(2) [The court noted that the ordinance did not define the term "outdoor advertising display signs," and that the exceptions did not exclude many "noncommercial signs that present no significant aesthetic blight or traffic hazard." That failure, and the failure to define the signs that were prohibited, might permit a construction of the ordinance to prohibit noncommercial signs such as political signs. To avoid that danger, which would create a "risk of constitutional overbreadth," the court adopted a narrow construction limiting the ordinance to "the intendment of the enactment," which was to prohibit commercial signs only.]

2. If enforced as written Ordinance No. 10795 will eliminate the outdoor advertising business in the City of San Diego. . . .

13. Each of the plaintiffs are the owners of a substantial number of outdoor advertising displays (approximately 500 to 800) in the City of San Diego. . . .

17. The displays have varying values depending upon their size, nature and location.

18. Each of the displays has a fair market value as a part of an income-producing system of between $2,500 and $25,000.

19. Each display has a remaining useful income-producing life in excess of 25 years.

20. All of the signs owned by plaintiffs in the City of San Diego are located in areas zoned for commercial and industrial purposes. . . .

28. Outdoor advertising increases the sales of products and produces numerous direct and indirect benefits to the public. Valuable commercial, political and social information is communicated to the public through the use of outdoor advertising. Many businesses and politicians and other persons rely upon outdoor advertising because other forms of advertising are insufficient, inappropriate and prohibitively expensive. . . .

31. Many of plaintiffs' signs are within 660 feet and others are within 500 feet of interstate or federal primary highways. . . .

34. The amortization provisions of Ordinance No. 10795 have no reasonable relationship to the fair market value, useful life or income generated by the signs and were not designed to have such a relationship.

The trial court filed a memorandum opinion stating that the ordinance was invalid as an unreasonable exercise of police power and an abridgment of First Amendment guaranties of freedom of speech and press. The court then entered judgment enjoining enforcement of the ordinance. The city appeals from that judgment.

2. The summary judgment cannot be sustained on the ground that the San Diego ordinance exceeds the city's authority under the police power.

The San Diego ordinance, as we shall explain, represents a proper application of municipal authority over zoning and land use for the purpose of promoting the public safety and welfare. The ordinance recites the purposes for which it was enacted, including the elimination of traffic hazards brought about by distracting advertising displays and the improvement of the appearance of the city. Since these goals are proper objectives for the exercise of the city's police power, the city council, asserting its legislative judgment, could reasonably believe the instant ordinance would further those objectives.

Plaintiffs cannot question that a city may enact ordinances under the police power to eliminate traffic hazards. They maintain, however, that the city failed to prove in opposition to plaintiffs' motion for summary judgment that the ordinance reasonably relates to that objective. We could reject plaintiffs' argument on the simple ground that plaintiffs, as the parties asserting the unconstitutionality of the ordinance, bear the burden of proof and cannot rely upon the city's failure of proof. To avoid unnecessary litigation upon remand of this cause, however, we have probed plaintiffs' broader argument: We hold as a matter of law that an ordinance which eliminates billboards designed to be viewed from streets and highways reasonably relates to traffic safety.

Billboards are intended to, and undoubtedly do, divert a driver's attention from the roadway. Whether this distracting effect contributes to traffic accidents invokes an issue of continuing controversy.[7] But as the New York Court of Appeals pointed out, "mere disagreement" as to "whether billboards or other advertising devices . . . constitute a traffic hazard . . . may not cast doubt on the statute's validity. Matters such as these are reserved for legislative judgment, and the legislative determination, here expressly announced, will not be disturbed unless manifestly unreasonable." (*New York State Thruway Auth. v. Ashley Motor Ct.* (1961), 176 N.E.2d 566.) Many other decisions have upheld billboard ordinances on the ground that such ordinances reasonably relate to traffic safety; we cannot find it manifestly unreasonable for the San Diego City Council to reach the same conclusion. As the Kentucky Supreme Court said in *Moore v. Ward* (1964) 377 S.W.2d 881, 884: "Even assuming [plaintiffs] could produce substantial evidence that billboard signs do not adversely affect traffic safety, . . . the question involves so many intangible factors as to make debatable the issue of what the facts establish. Where this is so, it is not within the province of courts to hold a statute invalid by reaching a conclusion contrary to that of the legislature."

We further hold that even if, as plaintiffs maintain, the principal purpose of the ordinance is not to promote traffic safety but to improve the appearance of the community, such a purpose falls within the city's authority under the police power. . . .

Because this state relies on its scenery to attract tourists and commerce, aesthetic considerations assume economic value. Consequently any distinction between aesthetic and economic grounds as a justification for billboard regulation must fail. "Today, economic and aesthetic considerations together constitute the nearly inseparable warp and woof of the fabric upon which the modern city must design its future."

[A contrary] holding also conflicts with present concepts of the police power. Most jurisdictions now concur with the broad declaration of Justice Douglas in *Berman v. Parker* (1954) 348 U.S. 26: "The concept of the public welfare is broad and inclusive. [Citation.] The values it represents are spiritual as well as physical, aesthetic as well as monetary. It is within the power of the legislature to determine that the community should be beautiful as well as healthy, spacious as well as clean, well-balanced as well as carefully patrolled." (*Id.* at p. 33.) Although Justice Douglas tendered this description in a case upholding the exercise of the power of eminent domain for community redevelopment, it has since been recognized as a correct description of the authority of a state or city to enact legislation under the police power. As the Hawaii Supreme Court succinctly stated: "We accept beauty as a proper community objective, attainable through use of the police power." (*State v. Diamond Motors, Inc.* (1967), 429 P.2d 825, 827.)

Present day city planning would be virtually impossible under a doctrine which denied a city authority to legislate for aesthetic purposes under the police power. Virtually every city in this

[7] "No matter what one's position on the sign and safety issue one can find the study to support it . . . . [D]espite the insights provided by statistical analyses, the case for the hazards of private signs rests largely upon common sense and the informed judgments of traffic engineers and other experts. The arguments are complex and sometimes highly technical, but on the whole, the courts are increasingly likely to conclude that regulation of private signs may be reasonably expected to enhance highway safety." (Dowds, *Private Signs and Public Interests, in* 1974 Institute on Planning, Zoning and Eminent Domain, p. 231.)

state has enacted zoning ordinances for the purpose of improving the appearance of the urban environment and the quality of metropolitan life. Many municipalities engage in projects of one type or another designed to beautify their communities. . . . But as the New York Court of Appeals pointed out, "Once it be conceded that aesthetics is a valid subject of legislative concern the conclusion seems inescapable that reasonable legislation designed to promote that end is a valid and permissible exercise of the police power. . . . [W]hether such a statute or ordinance should be voided should depend upon whether the restriction was 'an arbitrary and irrational method of achieving an attractive . . . community — and *not* upon whether the objectives were primarily aesthetic.' " [*People v. Stover*, 191 N.E.2d 272 (N.Y. 1963).]

In a subsequent decision, the New York Court of Appeals confirmed that aesthetic considerations may justify the exercise of the police power to ban all off-site billboards in a community. *Suffolk Outdoor Adv. Co., Inc. v. Hulse* (1977), 373 N.E.2d 263, *app. dism.*, 439 U.S. 808. "It cannot be seriously argued," the New York court said, "that a prohibition of this nature is not reasonably related to improving the aesthetics of the community." (373 N.E.2d at p. 266.) The fact that the ordinance bans billboards in commercial and industrial areas, and that it permits on-site signs, does not demonstrate that the ordinance as a whole lacks a reasonable relationship to improving community appearance. "[T]he notion that an extensively commercial or industrial area will be made more attractive by the absence of billboards is open to debate. Since the issue is debatable, however, the modern judicial presumption in favor of legislation [requires the court] to uphold the ordinance as a rational means of enforcing the legislative purpose of preserving aesthetics." (Lucking, *The Regulation of Outdoor Advertising: Past, Present and Future* (1977) 6 Environmental Aff. 179, 188.)

If the San Diego ordinance reasonably relates to the public safety and welfare, it should logically follow that the ordinance represents a valid exercise of the police power. Plaintiffs contend, however, that the police power is subject to an additional limiting doctrine: That regardless of the reasonableness of the act in relation to the public health, safety, morals and welfare[,] the police power can never be employed to prohibit completely a business not found to be a public nuisance. . . .

For the reasons we shall offer, however, we believe that this doctrine, too, conflicts with reality and with current views of the police power. The distinction between prohibition and regulation in this case is one of words and not substance. "[E]very regulation necessarily speaks as a prohibition." (*Goldblatt v. Hempstead* (1962) 369 U.S. 590, 592.) In the present case, for example, plaintiffs describe the ordinance as a *prohibition of off-site advertising*, while the city describes it as a *regulation of advertising*, one which limits advertising to on-site signs. Surely the validity of the ordinance does not depend on the court's choice between such verbal formulas.

Rather than strive to develop a logical distinction between "regulation" and "prohibition," and to find themselves embroiled in language rather than fact, courts of other jurisdictions in recent decisions have held that a community can entirely prohibit off-site advertising. These decisions fall within the general principle that a community may exclude any or all commercial uses if such exclusion reasonably relates to the public health, safety, morals or general welfare. As the Oregon Supreme Court explained in *Oregon City v. Hartke*, 400 P.2d 255, "[I]t is within the police power of the city wholly to exclude a particular use if there is a rational basis for the exclusion. . . . It is not irrational for those who must live in a community from day to day to plan their physical surroundings in such a way that unsightliness is minimized. The prevention of unsightliness by wholly precluding a particular use within the city may inhibit the economic growth of the city or frustrate the desire of someone who wishes to make the proscribed use, but the inhabitants of the city have the right to forego the economic gain and the person whose business plans are frustrated is not entitled to have his interest weighed more heavily than the predominant interest of others in the community." (400 P.2d p. 263.)

Plaintiffs stress that most of the cases upholding a community ban on billboards or other commercial uses have involved small, predominantly residential, towns or rural localities. Recently, however, the Massachusetts Supreme Judicial Court upheld an ordinance similar to the one at issue here involving a total prohibition of billboards in a densely populated town with a sizable business and industrial district. (*John Donnelly & Sons, Inc. v. Outdoor Advertising Bd.*, 339 N.E.2d 709.) The court there stated that "We believe that it is within the scope of the police power for the town to decide that its total living area should be improved so as to be more attractive to both its residents and visitors. Whether an area is urban, suburban or rural should not be determinative of whether the residents are entitled to preserve and enhance their environment. Urban residents are not immune to ugliness." (P. 720.) . . .

Nor do we perceive how we could rationally establish a rule that a city's police power diminishes as its population grows, and that once it reaches some unspecified size it no longer has the power to prohibit billboards. San Diego, for example, has already prohibited billboards within *97 percent of its limits* — a region which in area and population far surpasses most California cities. Plaintiffs claim that a ban covering 97 percent of the city is a "regulation," while the extension of that ban to the remaining 3 percent of the city is a "prohibition," but such sophistry is a mere play upon words.

Thus the validity of Ordinance No. 10795 under the police power does not turn on its regulatory or prohibitory character, nor upon the size of the city which enacted it, but solely on whether it reasonably relates to the public safety and welfare. As we have explained, the ordinance recites that it was enacted to eliminate traffic hazards, improve the appearance of the community, and thereby protect property values. The asserted goals are proper objectives under the police power, and plaintiffs have failed to prove that the ordinance lacks a reasonable relationship to the achievement of those goals. We conclude that the summary judgment cannot be sustained on the ground that the ordinance exceeds the city's authority under the police power. . . .

To hold that a city cannot prohibit off-site commercial billboards for the purpose of protecting and preserving the beauty of the environment is to succumb to a bleak materialism. We conclude with the pungent words of Ogden Nash:

"I think that I shall never see

"A billboard lovely as a tree.

"Indeed, unless the billboards fall,

"I'll never see a tree at all."

The Judgment is reversed.

CLARK, JUSTICE, dissenting:

[Omitted. Justice Clark would have held that the ordinance "unconstitutionally prohibits speech protected by the First Amendment."]

NOTES AND QUESTIONS

1. *Accepting aesthetics.* Is the principal case an acceptance of the "aesthetics alone" rule of aesthetic regulation or does it require the presence of "other factors"? What factors does the court accept, or does the court simply decide the case with presumptions? All courts have accepted a traffic safety improvement justification despite the conflicting evidence on the effect of signs on traffic safety. In *Opinion of the Justices*, 169 A.2d 762 (N.H. 1961), the court said that signs "may reasonably be found to increase the danger of accidents, and their regulation along highways clearly falls within the police power." *Id.* at 764. See also *Metro Lights v. City of Los Angeles*, 551 F.3d 898 (9th Cir. 2009).

What about tourism? Why does this factor justify a billboard prohibition? The California court quotes the New York *Stover* decision's dictum that an arbitrary and irrational method of achieving an attractive community would be unconstitutional. Can you give an example? What do you think of the court's rejection of the *prohibit* vs. *permit* distinction?

2. *The regulatory setting of billboard controls.* Exclusions from residential areas have not been a problem. See *Naegele Outdoor Adv. Co. v. Village of Minnetonka*, 162 N.W.2d 206 (Minn. 1968). The total exclusion of commercial billboards from a community is more problematic when the community has commercial and industrial areas to which the exclusion applies. In *United Adv. Corp. v. Borough of Metuchen*, 198 A.2d 447 (N.J. 1964), the court upheld a total community exclusion as applied to billboards in non-residential areas. It stressed that Metuchen was a small and primarily residential community and that the purpose of the regulation was "to achieve the maximum degree of compatibility with the residential areas." Accord *John Donnelly & Sons v. Outdoor Adv. Bd.*, discussed in the principal case. In *State of Missouri ex rel. Ad Trend v. City of Platte City*, 272 S.W.3d 201 (Mo. App. 2008), the Missouri Court of Appeals decided a case with a regulation that included a total ban on "outdoor advertising signs." but did not address the constitutionality of it. For a contrary minority view, see *Combined Commun. Corp. v. City & County of Denver*, 542 P.2d 79 (Colo. 1975), striking down a total billboard exclusion in the city. The court relied on statutory and charter provisions that authorized the city only to regulate and restrict land uses. *John Donnelly & Sons v. Mallar*, 453 F. Supp. 1272 (D. Me. 1978), upheld a total prohibition on billboards throughout the entire state against objections that it was overly broad.

What if a local government rezones land to a commercial use solely for the display of billboards? The courts have thrown this kind of zoning out when it has been challenged, though they will uphold rezoning for billboards that is part of a comprehensive rezoning. See *Kunz v. Utah Dep't of Transp.*, 913 P.2d 765 (Utah App. 1996) (rezoning held invalid).

3. *On-premise sign exemption.* The San Diego ordinance did not prohibit on-premise signs and billboards advertising the business conducted on the premises. Almost all the cases uphold this exemption, usually relying on the importance of on-premise signs to the business and disregarding problems of aesthetic uniformity in sign control. See *Metuchen, supra; City of Lake Wales v. Lamar Adv. Ass'n*, 414 So. 2d 1030 (Fla. 1982). Does the on-premise sign exemption make aesthetic sense?

4. *On-premise sign regulation.* The courts have usually upheld limitations on the size and number of on-premise signs, recognizing that their cumulative impact can have an undesirable visual effect. See *Westfield Motor Sales Co. v. Town of Westfield*, 324 A.2d 113 (N.J.L. Div. 1974) (size limits), noted, 11 Urb. L. Ann. 295 (1976); *Tunis-Huntington Dodge, Inc. v. Horn*, 290 N.Y.S.2d 7 (App. Div. 1968) (number of signs); *Capital Outdoor, Inc. v. Tolson*, 582 S.E.2d 717

(N.C. App. 2003) (height limitation). See also *Kenyon Peck, Inc. v. Kennedy*, 168 S.E.2d 117 (Va. 1969) (upholding prohibition on moving signs); *Schaffer v. City of Omaha*, 248 N.W.2d 764 (Neb. 1977) (portable signs prohibited). The last two cases relied heavily on the presumption of constitutionality. See *Outdoor Media Dimensions, Inc. v. DOT*, 132 P.3d 5 (Or. 2006) (upholding restrictions on highway signs under the Oregon free speech clause).

Regulations for on-premise signs are not usually well-drafted and may consist of an ad hoc mixture of restrictions, some of which may not make aesthetic sense. It is customary, for example, to make the size of a sign dependent on the linear footage of the premises on which a building stands. The longer the premises, the larger the sign.

Street Graphics, an aesthetically more effective method for controlling on-premise signs, was proposed in a book published in 1971, last revised as D. Mandelker, *Street Graphics and the Law Revised*, American Planning Ass'n, Planning Advisory Serv. Rep. No. 527 (2004). A number of communities have adopted a model street graphics ordinance included in the 1971 book and later revisions. The latest revision contains a legibility study done by the United States Sign Council that recommends size, height and spacing regulations for ground signs based on viewing opportunity as determined by street width, speed and traffic blockage. Wall signs are related to wall frontage and can cover only a signable wall area, defined as a certain percentage of wall frontage. There are also regulations for canopy, awning and projecting signs. Regulations for each type of sign are assigned to zoning districts.

An innovation in the model ordinance prevents communication overload by limiting the number of items of information on a sign. An item of information is defined as

> A syllable of a word, an initial, a logo, an abbreviation, a number, a symbol, or a geometric shape.

Each sign is allowed ten items of information. The amount of information contained on a sign can be increased if an "item" is defined as a word rather than a syllable. Is this restriction constitutional? Does it raise free speech problems? A local sign control ordinance based on the Street Graphics system is reproduced in an appendix to *Advertising Co. v. City of Bridgeton*, 626 F. Supp. 837 (E.D. Mo. 1985). The court rejected free speech objections to the ordinance. For an analysis of the ordinance from an urban design perspective, see Amy Mandelker, *Writing Urban Spaces, supra*. For another innovative attempt at sign regulation, see Gann, *Sign Control in Cuyahoga Falls: Regulating Outside the Box*, Zoning News, July, 2003. See also M. Morris et al. Context-Sensitive Signage Design (2001), available at www. planning.org/ research/signs/index.htm, which has chapters on aesthetics and sign ordinance issues.

5. *The takings issue.* Prior to the Supreme Court's 1987 takings trilogy, most courts held that billboard prohibitions were not restrictive enough as a limitation on land use to amount to a taking. *Inhabitants of Boothbay v. National Adv. Co.*, 347 A.2d 419 (Me. 1975); *Newman Signs, Inc. v. Hjelle*, 268 N.W.2d 741 (N.D. 1978) (applying balancing test). For example, *Jackson v. City Council*, 659 F. Supp. 470 (W.D. Va. 1987), held that an ordinance prohibiting commercial billboards was not a taking because the "only damages" were lost business opportunities and a reduction in the value of the signs. See also *New York State Thruway Auth. v. Ashley Motor Court, Inc.*, cited in the principal case, holding that the construction of a highway provides the opportunity for outdoor advertising so that a sign regulation "takes" only the value the highway added to the land. Is this holding still good law?

Since the trilogy, the courts have continued to hold that sign regulation advances legitimate governmental purposes and does not deny property owners all economically viable use. E.g.,

Summey Outdoor Adv. v. County of Henderson, 386 S.E.2d 439 (N.C. App. 1989). The Fourth Circuit adopted a multi-factor balancing test based on the Supreme Court's 1987 takings trilogy. It applied the "whole parcel" rule by looking at the area in which the company's billboards were displayed to determine whether the restriction on the company's billboards was a taking. *Naegele Outdoor Advertising, Inc. v. City of Durham*, 844 F.2d 172 (4th Cir. 1988).

What effect will the *Lucas* per se takings rule have? Could a court hold that an ordinance prohibiting billboards is a per se taking of the severable property interest in the lease or license? See *Wilson v. City of Louisville*, 957 F. Supp. 948 (W.D. Ky. 1997), holding that restrictions on the size, height and hours of display of small freestanding signs did not deprive the owner of the economically viable use of the property. The court noted that 80% of the business was outside the city, where the plaintiff could still market these signs. The court also applied dicta from *Lucas*, that the Takings Clause does not protect personal property, such as signs, from regulation. Accord *Adams Outdoor Advertising v. City of East Lansing*, 614 N.W.2d 634 (Mich. 2000) (upholding prohibition on rooftop signs). See *Lamar Corp. v. City of Longview*, 270 S.W.3d 609 (Tex. App. 2008) (no taking in requiring removal of improperly modified nonconforming billboards). For discussion, see Floyd, *The Takings Issue in Billboard Control*, 3 Wash. U. J.L. Pol'y 357 (2000).

6. *The electronic message sign and other changes in the billboard industry.* One important trend is the increasing consolidation in national and regional companies. Technology has changed, as the painted billboard has given way to vinyl manufactured off-site and attached to the sign, and to electronic message signs, which can be animated on more than one face with changing displays. There are still three standard sizes: The bulletin, which is 14x48, or 672 square feet; the poster, which is 12x25 or 300 square feet, and the junior poster, which is 6x12, or 72 square feet. Advertising for tobacco products is prohibited under the tobacco litigation settlement, and liquor advertising is not common. They have been replaced by advertisers of mainstream consumer brands.

The sign industry is converting static billboards to electronic message signs on a widespread basis. Regulating the operation of these signs is not problematic, as communities can easily limit the frequency with which messages on signs change, their brilliance, and their location. The question is whether these signs should be allowed at all. Scenic America, the national organization dedicated to sign regulation, finds that these signs present a serious safety hazard and should be prohibited. Billboards in the Digital Age: Unsafe at Any Speed (2007), available at scenic.org. Some states and communities have banned these signs, though legislation in other states permits them. See Greenblatt, *The New Digital Divide*, Governing, Feb. 2007, at 68. *Adams Outdoor Adver., L.P. v. Board of Zoning Appeals*, 645 S.E.2d 271 (Va. 2007), held that a change of copy from a static to an electric format was an unauthorized expansion of a nonconforming sign.

A NOTE ON THE FEDERAL HIGHWAY BEAUTIFICATION ACT

Federal legislation, first enacted in 1958 and strengthened in 1965, requires that states prohibit all billboards within 660 feet of the right-of-way of federal interstate and primary highways. 23 U.S.C. § 131. In rural areas, billboards must not be visible from the highway. The federal act exempts on-premise signs. It also authorizes an exemption for commercial and industrial areas under agreements between the states and the federal Secretary of Transportation. States must enact legislation that complies with the federal law, and non-complying states are subject to a penalty of ten percent of their state federal-aid highway funds. This penalty has seldom been imposed, and the federal act does not preempt state and local sign regulations. See *Markham Adv. Co. v. State*, 439 P.2d 248 (Wash. 1965). State and local governments may also adopt more restrictive regulations. See Mich. Comp. L. § 252.307a (capping billboards at present levels, approximately 16,000). The state outdoor advertising laws have all been upheld. The decisions often rely on a traffic safety rationale. See, e.g., *Moore v. Ward*, 377 S.W.2d 881 (Ky. 1964). But see *Lombardo v. Warner*, 481 F.3d 1135 (9th Cir. 2007) (Highway Beautification Act's exemption of on-premise signs from permit and fee requirements held content-based under Oregon free speech clause).

Over 127,000 legal nonconforming compensable signs have been removed, fewer than 74,000 legal nonconforming signs remain, and 750,000 illegal signs have been removed. Ninety-eight percent of all illegal signs have been removed by owners or government, and approximately 14,600 illegal signs remain to be removed. See www.outdooradvertisingexchange.com.

The federal act has always authorized the removal of nonconforming signs, but compensation is required. The federal government must share seventy-five percent of the cost, but federal funds for the removal of nonconforming billboards have not been available for years. Despite the compensation requirement, local governments continued to use amortization to remove nonconforming signs on federal highways after the federal act was adopted. See *Vermont v. Brinegar*, 379 F. Supp. 606 (D.Vt. 1974) (unsuccessful claim that compensation requirement is moot if state law permits removal without compensation). In 1978, an amendment to the federal law prohibited the use of amortization by local governments, and about half the states now prohibit local governments from amortizing nonconforming signs on federal highways; some of these laws apply to all nonconforming signs, not just signs on highways. Is it a denial of equal protection to pay compensation for nonconforming billboards on federal highways while amortizing nonconforming billboards not on federal highways? The California Supreme Court in *Metromedia* said no. For discussion of amortization, see Chapter 3, *supra*.

State outdoor advertising laws usually authorize local regulation along highways. Some courts rely on this authority to hold that the state law does not prohibit more stringent local regulation. See *City of Doraville v. Turner Commun. Co.*, 223 S.E.2d 798 (Ga. 1976) (500-foot local prohibition). Compare *Southeastern Displays, Inc. v. Ward*, 414 S.W.2d 573 (Ky. 1967) (state highway agency decision prohibiting sign preempts local ordinance under which it was permitted). For discussion of the federal Highway Beautification Act, see C. Floyd & P. Shedd, Highway Beautification (1979); Albert, *Your Ad Goes Here: How the Highway Beautification Act of 1965 Thwarts Highway Beautification*, 48 U. Kan. L. Rev. 463 (2000).

[2.] Free Speech Issues

The free speech problem. The United States Supreme Court accepted an appeal from the California Supreme Court's *Metromedia* decision, reproduced *supra*, to decide free speech issues, a development foreshadowed by Court decisions in the 1970s that brought commercial speech under the protection of the Free Speech Clause. When applying the Free Speech Clause to sign regulation, a court again considers the aesthetic and traffic safety justifications that support sign regulations but must weigh them against the constitutional interest in freedom of expression. This judicial examination is a replay of the legitimacy issues courts consider when they review sign regulations for a violation of substantive due process, except that free speech concerns are also weighed in the balance. Issues considered under the Equal

Protection Clause are also reconsidered under the Free Speech Clause when sign regulations make arguably unconstitutional distinctions between different kinds of speech, such as the distinction between ordinances regulating commercial and noncommercial speech.

Free speech law. First Amendment law protecting free speech is complicated and, to some extent, inconsistent. We cannot explore all of free speech law here, but we can study some of the major principles that determine how the law of free speech affects sign regulation. Chapter 3 considered free speech issues as they apply to adult uses. The same basic principles, with some differences, apply to sign regulation.

A major distinction in First Amendment law that affects sign regulation is the different, less rigorous protection courts give to commercial as compared with noncommercial speech. Signs with commercial messages are a form of commercial speech. In *Central Hudson Gas & Elec. Corp. v. Public Serv. Comm'n*, 447 U.S. 557 (1980), the Court adopted a four-part test for laws affecting commercial speech:

> At the outset, we must determine [1] whether the expression is protected by the First Amendment. For commercial speech to come within that provision, it at least must [a] concern lawful activity and [b] not be misleading. Next, [if the speech is protected] we ask [2] whether the asserted governmental interest is substantial. If both inquiries yield positive answers, we must determine [3] whether the regulation directly advances the governmental interest asserted, and [4] whether it is not more extensive than is necessary to serve that interest. [*Id.* at 563.]

Note how the fourth part of this test modifies the presumption of constitutionality. But see *Board of Trustees v. Fox*, 492 U.S. 469 (1989) (*Central Hudson* did not adopt a "less restrictive alternative" test; only "reasonable fit" required between ends and means). *Lorillard Tobacco Co. v. Reilly*, 533 U.S. 525 (2001), confirmed that the Court still supports the *Central Hudson* tests.

Content vs. viewpoint neutrality. This distinction has a major impact on the constitutionality of sign regulation under the Free Speech Clause. A law that regulates the subject matter of speech regulates its content. Examples are laws regulating political speech (regardless of the speaker's political position), and ordinances authorizing signs with designated messages, such as directional signs. A law is content-based even if it is a benign regulation of speech. A law regulates viewpoint if it regulates the point of view expressed, such as an ordinance prohibiting signs opposing nuclear power, but not those supporting it. Courts do not apply the *Central Hudson* tests to laws that are not content- or viewpoint-neutral. They require a compelling governmental interest to justify the law, which they hardly ever find. See *Hill v. Colorado*, 530 U.S. 703 (2000), for a discussion of content neutrality.

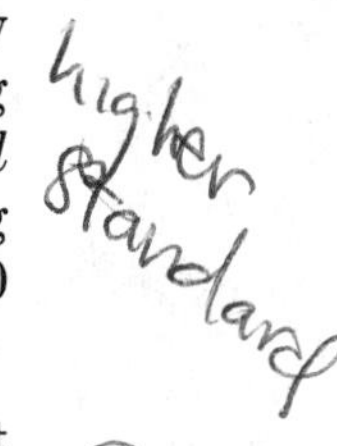

Time, place and manner regulations. These are content-neutral regulations that protect legitimate governmental interests, such as a law regulating parades to prevent traffic problems. Sign ordinances that regulate the location, number, height and size of signs also fall in this category. Time, place and manner regulations are usually given greater deference by courts than laws directly regulating speech.

Overbreadth. The overbreadth doctrine is another free speech doctrine that affects the constitutionality of sign regulations. This doctrine prevents governmental regulation from sweeping so far that it restricts protected as well as unprotected speech, such as political speech. See the discussion by the California Supreme Court in footnote 2 of its *Metromedia* opinion, reproduced *supra.*

These doctrines provide the conceptual framework for the Supreme Court's *Metromedia* decision, which is reproduced next:

METROMEDIA, INC. v. CITY OF SAN DIEGO
453 U.S. 490 (1981)

JUSTICE WHITE announced the judgment of the Court and delivered an opinion, in which JUSTICE STEWART, JUSTICE MARSHALL, and JUSTICE POWELL joined. . . .

I

Stating that its purpose was "to eliminate hazards to pedestrians and motorists brought about by distracting sign displays" and "to preserve and improve the appearance of the City," San Diego enacted an ordinance to prohibit "outdoor advertising display signs." The California Supreme Court subsequently defined the term "advertising display sign" as "a rigidly assembled sign, display, or device permanently affixed to the ground or permanently attached to a building or other inherently permanent structure constituting, or used for the display of, a commercial or other advertisement to the public." "Advertising displays signs" include any sign that "directs attention to a product, service or activity, event, person, institution or business."

The ordinance provides two kinds of exceptions to the general prohibition: onsite signs and signs falling within 12 specified categories. Onsite signs are defined as those

> "designating the name of the owner or occupant of the premises upon which such signs are placed, or identifying such premises; or signs advertising goods manufactured or produced or services rendered on the premises upon which such signs are placed."

The specific categories exempted from the prohibition include: government signs; signs located at public bus stops; signs manufactured, transported, or stored within the city, if not used for advertising purposes; commemorative historical plaques; religious symbols; signs within shopping malls; for sale and for lease signs; signs on public and commercial vehicles; signs depicting time, temperature, and news; approved temporary, off-premises, subdivision directional signs; and "[temporary] political campaign signs." Under this scheme, onsite commercial advertising is permitted, but other commercial advertising and noncommercial communications using fixed-structure signs are everywhere forbidden unless permitted by one of the specified exceptions. . . . [The Court described the outdoor advertising business and the way in which outdoor advertising is usually purchased.]

III

. . . .

[The Court noted that "at times First Amendment values must yield to other societal interests."] . . . Each method of communicating ideas is "a law unto itself" and that law must reflect the "differing natures, values, abuses and dangers" of each method. We deal here with the law of billboards.

Billboards are a well-established medium of communication, used to convey a broad range of different kinds of messages. . . . [The Court quoted from the dissenting opinion in the

California Supreme Court and the stipulation of facts, which noted that billboards convey noncommercial as well as commercial messages.]

But whatever its communicative function, the billboard remains a "large, immobile, and permanent structure which like other structures is subject to . . . regulation." 610 P.2d, at 419. Moreover, because it is designed to stand out and apart from its surroundings, the billboard creates a unique set of problems for land-use planning and development.

Billboards, then, like other media of communication, combine communicative and noncommunicative aspects. As with other media, the government has legitimate interests in controlling the noncommunicative aspects of the medium, but the First and Fourteenth Amendments foreclose a similar interest in controlling the communicative aspects. Because regulation of the noncommunicative aspects of a medium often impinges to some degree on the communicative aspects, it has been necessary for the courts to reconcile the government's regulatory interests with the individual's right to expression. . . . Performance of this task requires a particularized inquiry into the nature of the conflicting interests at stake here, beginning with a precise appraisal of the character of the ordinance as it affects communication.

As construed by the California Supreme Court, the ordinance restricts the use of certain kinds of outdoor signs. That restriction is defined in two ways: first, by reference to the structural characteristics of the sign; second, by reference to the content, or message, of the sign. Thus, the regulation only applies to a "permanent structure constituting, or used for the display of, a commercial or other advertisement to the public." 610 P. 2d, at 410, n. 2. Within that class, the only permitted signs are those (1) identifying the premises on which the sign is located, or its owner or occupant, or advertising the goods produced or services rendered on such property and (2) those within one of the specified exemptions to the general prohibition, such as temporary political campaign signs. To determine if any billboard is prohibited by the ordinance, one must determine how it is constructed, where it is located, and what message it carries.

Thus, under the ordinance (1) a sign advertising goods or services available on the property where the sign is located is allowed; (2) a sign on a building or other property advertising goods or services produced or offered elsewhere is barred; (3) noncommercial advertising, unless within one of the specific exceptions, is everywhere prohibited. The occupant of property may advertise his own goods or services; he may not advertise the goods or services of others, nor may he display most noncommercial messages.

IV

Appellants' principal submission is that enforcement of the ordinance will eliminate the outdoor advertising business in San Diego and that the First and Fourteenth Amendments prohibit the elimination of this medium of communication. Appellants contend that the city may bar neither all offsite commercial signs nor all noncommercial advertisements and that even if it may bar the former, it may not bar the latter. . . . Because our cases have consistently distinguished between the constitutional protection afforded commercial as opposed to noncommercial speech, in evaluating appellants' contention we consider separately the effect of the ordinance on commercial and noncommercial speech. . . . [The Court discussed decisions, including *Central Hudson*, indicating that commercial speech receives less protection than noncommercial speech.]

Appellants agree that the proper approach to be taken in determining the validity of the restrictions on commercial speech is that which was articulated in *Central Hudson*, but assert that the San Diego ordinance fails that test. We do not agree.

There can be little controversy over the application of the first, second, and fourth criteria. There is no suggestion that the commercial advertising at issue here involves unlawful activity or is misleading. Nor can there be substantial doubt that the twin goals that the ordinance seeks to further — traffic safety and the appearance of the city — are substantial governmental goals. It is far too late to contend otherwise with respect to either traffic safety, *Railway Express Agency, Inc. v. New York*, 336 U.S. 106 (1949), or esthetics [citing *Penn Central, Belle Terre* and *Berman v. Parker.*] Similarly, we reject appellants' claim that the ordinance is broader than necessary and, therefore, fails the fourth part of the *Central Hudson* test. If the city has a sufficient basis for believing that billboards are traffic hazards and are unattractive, then obviously the most direct and perhaps the only effective approach to solving the problems they create is to prohibit them. The city has gone no further than necessary in seeking to meet its ends. Indeed, it has stopped short of fully accomplishing its ends: It has not prohibited all billboards, but allows onsite advertising and some other specifically exempted signs.

The more serious question, then, concerns the third of the *Central Hudson* criteria: Does the ordinance "directly advance" governmental interests in traffic safety and in the appearance of the city? It is asserted that the record is inadequate to show any connection between billboards and traffic safety. . . . [The Court discussed the holding of the California court on the traffic issue.] We likewise hesitate to disagree with the accumulated, commonsense judgments of local lawmakers and of the many reviewing courts that billboards are real and substantial hazards to traffic safety. There is nothing here to suggest that these judgments are unreasonable. As we said in a different context, *Railway Express Agency, Inc. v. New York*, *supra*, at 109:

> "We would be trespassing on one of the most intensely local and specialized of all municipal problems if we held that this regulation had no relation to the traffic problem of New York City. It is the judgment of the local authorities that it does have such a relation. And nothing has been advanced which shows that to be palpably false."

We reach a similar result with respect to the second asserted justification for the ordinance — advancement of the city's esthetic interests. It is not speculative to recognize that billboards by their very nature, wherever located and however constructed, can be perceived as an "esthetic harm." San Diego, like many States and other municipalities, has chosen to minimize the presence of such structures. Such esthetic judgments are necessarily subjective, defying objective evaluation, and for that reason must be carefully scrutinized to determine if they are only a public rationalization of an impermissible purpose. But there is no claim in this case that San Diego has as an ulterior motive the suppression of speech, and the judgment involved here is not so unusual as to raise suspicions in itself.

It is nevertheless argued that the city denigrates its interest in traffic safety and beauty and defeats its own case by permitting onsite advertising and other specified signs. Appellants question whether the distinction between onsite and offsite advertising on the same property is justifiable in terms of either esthetics or traffic safety. The ordinance permits the occupant of property to use billboards located on that property to advertise goods and services offered at that location; identical billboards, equally distracting and unattractive, that advertise goods or services available elsewhere are prohibited even if permitting the latter would not multiply the number of billboards. Despite the apparent incongruity, this argument has been rejected, at least implicitly, in all of the cases sustaining the distinction between offsite and onsite commercial advertising. We agree with those cases and with our own decisions in [earlier cases].

In the first place, whether onsite advertising is permitted or not, the prohibition of offsite advertising is directly related to the stated objectives of traffic safety and esthetics. This is not altered by the fact that the ordinance is underinclusive because it permits onsite advertising. Second, the city may believe that offsite advertising, with its periodically changing content, presents a more acute problem than does onsite advertising. Third, San Diego has obviously chosen to value one kind of commercial speech — onsite advertising — more than another kind of commercial speech — offsite advertising. The ordinance reflects a decision by the city that the former interest, but not the latter, is stronger than the city's interests in traffic safety and esthetics. The city has decided that in a limited instance — onsite commercial advertising — its interests should yield. We do not reject that judgment. As we see it, the city could reasonably conclude that a commercial enterprise — as well as the interested public — has a stronger interest in identifying its place of business and advertising the products or services available there than it has in using or leasing its available space for the purpose of advertising commercial enterprises located elsewhere. It does not follow from the fact that the city has concluded that some commercial interests outweigh its municipal interests in this context that it must give similar weight to all other commercial advertising. Thus, offsite commercial billboards may be prohibited while onsite commercial billboards are permitted.

The constitutional problem in this area requires resolution of the conflict between the city's land-use interests and the commercial interests of those seeking to purvey goods and services within the city. In light of the above analysis, we cannot conclude that the city has drawn an ordinance broader than is necessary to meet its interests, or that it fails directly to advance substantial government interests. In sum, insofar as it regulates commercial speech the San Diego ordinance meets the constitutional requirements of *Central Hudson, supra.*

V

It does not follow, however, that San Diego's general ban on signs carrying noncommercial advertising is also valid under the First and Fourteenth Amendments. The fact that the city may value commercial messages relating to onsite goods and services more than it values commercial communications relating to offsite goods and services does not justify prohibiting an occupant from displaying its own ideas or those of others.

As indicated above, our recent commercial speech cases have consistently accorded noncommercial speech a greater degree of protection than commercial speech. San Diego effectively inverts this judgment, by affording a greater degree of protection to commercial than to noncommercial speech. There is a broad exception for onsite commercial advertisements, but there is no similar exception for noncommercial speech. The use of onsite billboards to carry commercial messages related to the commercial use of the premises is freely permitted, but the use of otherwise identical billboards to carry noncommercial messages is generally prohibited. The city does not explain how or why noncommercial billboards located in places where commercial billboards are permitted would be more threatening to safe driving or would detract more from the beauty of the city. Insofar as the city tolerates billboards at all, it cannot choose to limit their content to commercial messages; the city may not conclude that the communication of commercial information concerning goods and services connected with a particular site is of greater value than the communication of noncommercial messages.

Furthermore, the ordinance contains exceptions that permit various kinds of noncommercial signs, whether on property where goods and services are offered or not, that would otherwise be within the general ban. A fixed sign may be used to identify any piece of property and its owner. Any piece of property may carry or display religious symbols, commemorative plaques of recognized historical societies and organizations, signs carrying news items or telling the time or temperature, signs erected in discharge of any governmental function, or temporary political campaign signs. No other noncommercial or ideological signs meeting the structural definition are permitted, regardless of their effect on traffic safety or esthetics.

Although the city may distinguish between the relative value of different categories of commercial speech, the city does not have the same range of choice in the area of noncommercial speech to evaluate the strength of, or distinguish between, various communicative interests. With respect to noncommercial speech, the city may not choose the appropriate subjects for public discourse: "To allow a government the choice of permissible subjects for public debate would be to allow that government control over the search for political truth." *Consolidated Edison Co.* [*v. Public Service Comm'n*,] 447 U.S. [530], at 538 [1980]. Because some noncommercial messages may be conveyed on billboards throughout the commercial and industrial zones, San Diego must similarly allow billboards conveying other noncommercial messages throughout those zones.[20]

Finally, we reject appellees' suggestion that the ordinance may be appropriately characterized as a reasonable "time, place, and manner" restriction. The ordinance does not generally ban billboard advertising as an unacceptable "manner" of communicating information or ideas; rather, it permits various kinds of signs. Signs that are banned are banned everywhere and at all times. We have observed that time, place, and manner restrictions are permissible if "they are justified without reference to the content of the regulated speech, . . . serve a significant governmental interest, and . . . leave open ample alternative channels for communication of the information." *Virginia Pharmacy Board v. Virginia Citizens Consumer Council*, 425 U.S. [748], at 771 [1978]. Here, it cannot be assumed that "alternative channels" are available, for the parties stipulated to just the opposite . . . . A similar argument was made with respect to a prohibition on real estate "For Sale" signs in *Linmark Associates, Inc. v. Willingboro*, 431 U.S. 85 (1977), and what we said there is equally applicable here:

> "Although in theory sellers remain free to employ a number of different alternatives, in practice [certain products are] not marketed through leaflets, sound trucks, demonstrations, or the like. The options to which sellers realistically are relegated . . . involve more cost and less autonomy then . . . signs[,] . . . are less likely to reach persons not deliberately seeking sales information[,] . . . and may be less effective media for communicating the message that is conveyed by a . . . sign. . . . The alternatives, then, are far from satisfactory." *Id.* at 93.

---

[20] Because a total prohibition of outdoor advertising is not before us, we do not indicate whether such a ban would be consistent with the First Amendment. . . .

Similarly, we need not reach any decision in this case as to the constitutionality of the federal Highway Beautification Act of 1965. That Act, like the San Diego ordinance, permits onsite commercial billboards in areas in which it does not permit billboards with noncommercial messages. However, unlike the San Diego ordinance, which prohibits billboards conveying noncommercial messages throughout the city, the federal law does not contain a total prohibition of such billboards in areas adjacent to the interstate and primary highway systems. As far as the Federal Government is concerned, such billboards are permitted adjacent to the highways in areas zoned industrial or commercial under state law or in unzoned commercial or industrial areas. Regulation of billboards in those areas is left primarily to the States. . . .

It is apparent as well that the ordinance distinguishes in several ways between permissible and impermissible signs at a particular location by reference to their content. Whether or not these distinctions are themselves constitutional, they take the regulation out of the domain of time, place, and manner restrictions. . . .

VII

Because the San Diego ordinance reaches too far into the realm of protected speech, we conclude that it is unconstitutional on its face. The judgment of the California Supreme Court is reversed, and the case is remanded to that court.[26]

It is so ordered.

[Justice Brennan concurred in an opinion joined by Justice Blackmun. He believed the ordinance was a total ban and would uphold a total ban that sufficiently served a governmental interest when a more narrowly drawn restriction would not promote that goal. However, this ordinance was unconstitutional. There was no evidence that billboards impaired traffic safety, the city's interest in aesthetics was not sufficiently substantial in the industrial and commercial areas, and "San Diego has failed to demonstrate a comprehensive coordinated effort in its commercial and industrial areas to address other obvious contributors to an unattractive environment." Even a total ban only on commercial billboards would raise free speech problems because it would give the city the right to determine whether a proposed message was commercial or noncommercial. However, he would not read the exemption for on-site signs as limited solely to commercial speech.

[Justice Stevens dissented, though he agreed with Parts I through IV of the plurality opinion. He believed a city could totally ban all commercial and noncommercial billboards because "the essential inquiry is the same throughout the city." He believed the impact of the ordinance on signs that were on-site was speculative and need not be considered. There was no evidence of the use of on-site premises for noncommercial signs, and it was "safe to assume that such uses in the future will be at best infrequent." The exceptions for various signs contained in the ordinance were constitutional because they were viewpoint-neutral.

[Chief Justice Burger also dissented. He believed the plurality's decision had "trivialized" the First Amendment and had improperly substituted its judgment for that of the city, and that the ordinance was constitutional because it was viewpoint-neutral. The exceptions for various signs "did not remotely endanger freedom of speech," and the city was not required to allow on-site signs to display noncommercial as well as commercial speech. Justice Rehnquist agreed substantially with the other dissenting opinions, and believed that aesthetic justifications alone were enough to justify a total ban on billboards. He described the opinions in the case as a Tower of Babel.]

[26] [The Court considered whether the unconstitutional parts of the ordinance could be severed and added:] Since our judgment is based essentially on the inclusion of noncommercial speech within the prohibitions of the ordinance, the California courts may sustain the ordinance by limiting its reach to commercial speech, assuming the ordinance is susceptible to this treatment.

NOTES AND QUESTIONS

1. *What Metromedia held.* The divided Court in *Metromedia* and ambiguities in the Court's treatment of sign ordinances regulating noncommercial speech creates problems for sign regulation. However, the plurality opinion, taken with the concurring and dissenting opinions, provides a majority for the Court's holding that sign ordinances can regulate commercial speech and prohibit billboards with commercial messages. The plurality's holding on content neutrality in Part V of the opinion did not command a majority, but most federal circuits follow it. Try to decide what was fatal about the ordinance in the plurality opinion, and note how questions about content neutrality; time, place and manner regulation; and the distinction between commercial and noncommercial speech affected the plurality opinion. On remand, the California Supreme Court was unable to sever the constitutional from the unconstitutional parts of the San Diego ordinance and invalidated all of it. 649 P.2d 902 (Cal. 1982). For discussion of *Metromedia*, see Blumoff, *After Metromedia: Sign Controls and the First Amendment*, 28 St. Louis U. L.J. 171 (1984).

Metromedia came up on stipulated facts, so sign company plaintiffs argue that the justifications for sign regulation were never tried, and that studies or record evidence is needed to support sign regulation. For a case rejecting this view, see *Ackerley Communs. of the Northwest v. Krochalis*, 108 F.3d 1095 (9th Cir. 1997). Contra *Pagan v. Fruchey*, 492 F.3d 766 (6th Cir. 2007) (en banc, 6-5).

Although *Metromedia* did not consider the constitutionality of the federal Highway Beautification Act, lower federal courts have relied on aesthetic and traffic safety purposes to uphold state laws implementing the act and have rejected free speech objections. See *Lombardo v. Warner*, 353 F.3d 774 (9th Cir. 2003); *National Advertising Co. v. City of Denver*, 912 F.2d 405 (10th Cir. 1990).

2. *Commercial v. noncommercial: Discovery Network.* The Supreme Court considered and explained *Metromedia* in *City of Cincinnati v. Discovery Network, Inc.*, 507 U.S. 410 (1993). The Court invalidated an ordinance that prohibited newsracks that displayed commercial handbills, but allowed newsracks that displayed newspapers. The Court assumed the ordinance banned commercial but allowed noncommercial speech, and found there was no close fit between the regulation's goals and its purposes because this distinction bore no relationship to the purposes of the ordinance. The Court distinguished *Metromedia*:

> Unlike this case, which involves discrimination between commercial and noncommercial speech, the "offsite-onsite" distinction [in *Metromedia*] involved disparate treatment of two types of commercial speech. Only the onsite signs served both the commercial and public interest in guiding potential visitors to their intended destinations; moreover, the plurality concluded that a "city may believe that offsite advertising, with its periodically changing content, presents a more acute problem than does onsite advertising." (citation omitted) [*Id.* at 425 n.20.]

The Court in *Discovery Network* indicated its holding was narrow and that a city might be able to justify the differential treatment of commercial and noncommercial newsracks. In that case, however, the very basis for the newsrack regulation was the difference in content. For a case rejecting the application of *Discovery Network* to a sign regulation, see *RTM Media, L.L.C. v. City of Houston*, 584 F.3d 220 (5th Cir. 2009). For a case upholding a regulation of commercial signs that exempted signs at some locations, see *Clear Channel Outdoor, Inc. v. City of New York*, 594 F.3d 94 (2d Cir. 2010).

3. *The Vincent case.* A few years after *Metromedia*, in *Members of City Council v. Taxpayers for Vincent*, 466 U.S. 789 (1984), a majority of the Court upheld an ordinance prohibiting the posting of signs on public property, as applied to prevent the posting of temporary political campaign signs. The Court reaffirmed that traffic safety and aesthetic interests are sufficient to justify a sign ordinance under the Free Speech Clause, and that the ordinance in *Vincent* was a "reasonable regulation of time, place, or manner" that was no broader than necessary. Alternate methods were available to distribute the messages on these signs.

Several aspects of the *Vincent* decision help support sign regulation. The Court was willing to accept alternate means of communication as adequate, and may have indicated that sign regulations need only be viewpoint-neutral, which contradicts the *Metromedia* plurality. The Court also referred to the "substantive evil" of "visual blight . . . [as] created by the medium of expression itself" — i.e., the sign.

4. *Regulating off-premise and on-premise signs.* Regulations for these signs can prove difficult because of uncertainties in the *Metromedia* decision. Municipalities can avoid the *Metromedia* holding that ordinances may not prohibit on-premise noncommercial speech by amending their ordinances to include a substitution clause allowing any sign permitted by the ordinance to display noncommercial speech. *Outdoor Sys., Inc. v. City of Mesa*, 997 F.2d 604 (9th Cir. 1993). The ordinance can also allow noncommercial speech on premise. *Major Media of the Southeast v. City of Raleigh*, 792 F.2d 1269 (4th Cir. 1986) (no objection that owners of commercial premises would want to display only commercial signs).

The courts have followed *Metromedia* by upholding a prohibition on off-premises signs when on-premises signs are permitted. This is a distinction based on location, not content. *RTM Media, L.L.C. v. City of Houston*, 584 F.3d 220 (5th Cir. Tex. 2009) (distinguishing *Discovery* Network); *Covenant Media of S.C., LLC v. City of North Charleston*, 493 F.3d 421 (4th Cir. 2007); *Clear Channel Outdoor, Inc. v. City of Los Angeles*, 340 F.3d 810 (9th Cir. 2003). Defining off-premise signs can be difficult to do without violating content neutrality rules, however. A typical definition is that an off-premises sign is one with messages not related to business or activity on the premises, which arguably is content-related because the nature of the message defines the sign. However, *Messer v. City of Douglasville*, 975 F.2d 1505 (11th Cir. 1992), upheld an ordinance with this definition even though the city had to read the sign to determine whether it was an off-premises sign. It held the ordinance regulated signs based on location, not viewpoint. *Southlake Property Assocs., Ltd. v. City of Morrow*, 112 F.3d 1114 (11th Cir. 1998), eases the off-premise vs. on-premise problem by holding that all noncommercial speech occurs on-site. Under this view, all off-premise signs display only commercial speech. But see *Vono v. Lewis*, 594 F. Supp. 2d 189 (D.R.I. 2009) (invalidating exemption for on-premise signs in state highway beautification law). Electronic on-premises signs may be easily programmed to sneak in some revenue-generating, off-premises advertising in what Scenic America describes as "Off-premises Ad Creep." www.scenicamericablog.blogspot.com (Jan. 19, 2010). How will this be policed?

5. *Content neutrality and exemptions.* The *Metromedia* plurality's conclusion that the "ban with exemptions" approach to noncommercial billboards was unconstitutional presents another serious problem for sign regulators. Reread the exemptions. Aren't some of them necessary, such as the exemption for government signs? The plurality struck down an exemption for "For Sale" or "For Rent" signs, even though the Court had previously held that municipalities could not prohibit them. *Linmark Assocs., Inc. v. Township of Willingboro*, 431

U.S. 85 (1977). San Diego's provision exempting political signs was added after a federal court in California struck down a political sign ordinance as too restrictive. *Baldwin v. Redwood City*, 540 F.2d 1360 (9th Cir. 1976). Is the plurality saying that because some noncommercial speech must be permitted, *all* noncommercial speech must be permitted?

The *Metromedia* plurality holding on exemptions continues to be troublesome. Some courts invalidate exemptions like those in *Metromedia* by relying on the plurality opinion. E.g., *National Advertising Co. v. Town of Niagara*, 942 F.2d 145 (2d Cir. 1991). Other courts refuse to follow the *Metromedia* plurality by combining decisions by other Justices in the case that would have upheld these exemptions. E.g., *Scadron v. City of Des Plaines*, 734 F. Supp. 1437 (N.D. Ill. 1990), *aff'd mem.*, 989 F.2d 502 (7th Cir. 1993). See also *Messer, supra* (upholding exemptions because they were more limited and applied only to permit requirement); *National Adv. Co. v. Town of Babylon*, 900 F.2d 551 (2d Cir. 1990) (relying on *Linmark* to uphold exemption of "for sale" signs); *G.K. Ltd. Travel v. City of Lake Oswego*, 436 F.3d 1064 (9th Cir. 2006) (exempting certain signs from permit requirement). The Third Circuit held the *Metromedia* plurality was no longer good law, adopted its own free speech test for sign regulation, but invalidated the exemptions in the ordinance. *Rappa v. New Castle County*, 18 F.3d 1043 (3d Cir. 1994).

Content neutrality problems also arise when municipalities define the signs they want to regulate. For example, an ordinance may authorize signs providing directions on business premises, advertising the sale or rental of property, or displaying time and temperature. This kind of authorization, though benign, is unconstitutional if courts strictly apply the requirement that sign ordinances must be content-neutral. *Solantic, LLC v. City of Neptune Beach*, 410 F.3d 1250, 1264 (11th Cir. 2005), noted, 35 Stetson L. Rev. 645 (2006), applied the content neutrality requirement to strike down an ordinance authorizing signs with content. Examples were signs incorporated into machinery that advertise the service provided by the machine, memorial signs on buildings, signs guiding traffic and parking, and flags and insignia only of a "government, religious, charitable, fraternal, or other organization." *H.D.V. — Greektown, LLC v. City of Detroit*, 568 F.3d 609 (6th Cir. 2009), rejected *Solantic*:

> The *Solantic* court's classification of the sign regulations before it as content-based appears to us to reflect an overly narrow conception of the definition of content-neutral speech. The ordinances at issue in *Solantic* seem to satisfy all three of the possible independent bases for content neutrality listed by the Supreme Court in [*Hill v. State of Colorado*, 530 U.S. 703 (2000)] (i.e., (1) the regulation is not a regulation of speech, but controls only the places where the speech may occur; (2) the regulation was not adopted because of disagreement with the message that the speech conveys; or (3) the government's interests in the regulation are unrelated to the content of the affected speech). [*Id.* at 622–623.]

The content neutrality issue is a key issue in sign regulation because courts apply strict scrutiny and a presumption of unconstitutionality to sign regulations that are content-related. A critical question is whether sign ordinance provisions like those struck down in *Solantic* should be a violation of the Free Speech Clause. It is possible to write around the problem. For example, an ordinance could allow all flags to be displayed and regulate display issues such as height of flagpoles. On time and temperature signs, see *La Tour v. City of Fayetteville*, 442 F.3d 1094 (8th Cir. 2006) (approving such signs). *Complete Angler, LLC v. City of Clearwater*, 607 F. Supp. 2d 1326 (M.D. Fla. 2009), held an ordinance prohibiting a mural showing the natural habitat and waterways surrounding a bait and tackle shop was a content-based regulation of noncommercial speech.

6. *Standing and the facial attack problem.* Plaintiffs in sign regulation cases may have considerable leverage against sign ordnances under the Supreme Court's overbreadth doctrine. Under that doctrine, they can attack other provisions of the ordinance, such as restrictions on political signs, as facially unconstitutional under the First Amendment even though they are not affected by those provisions. This is an important strategic option, because a court could find the rest of the ordinance nonseverable if it holds enough provisions of the ordinance unconstitutional. Some recent decisions, however, have cut back on this doctrine in sign cases and do not allow plaintiffs to attack provisions in the ordinance that do not injure them. See *Maverick Media Group, Inc. v. Hillsborough County*, 528 F.3d 817 (11th Cir. 2008); *Prime Media, Inc. v. City of Brentwood*, 485 F.3d 343 (6th Cir. 2007) (discussing cases); *Advantage Media, L.L.C. v. City of Eden Prairie*, 456 F.3d 793 (8th Cir. 2006). On severability, see *Desert Outdoor Adver., Inc. v. City of Oakland*, 598 F.3d 1142 (9th Cir. 2010) (district court did not strike entire ordinance).

A NOTE ON FREE SPEECH PROBLEMS WITH OTHER TYPES OF SIGN REGULATIONS

Restrictions on size, height, number and method of display. These have usually been upheld as reasonable time, place and manner regulations that are not content-based. *Get Outdoors II, LLC v. City of San Diego*, 506 F.3d 886 (9th Cir. 2007). See also *City of Lake Oswego, supra*, upholding a prohibition of pole signs. The court pointed out that the pole sign restriction was not a law that favored or disfavored speech on the basis of the ideas or views expressed. *La Tour v. City of Fayetteville, supra*, upheld a prohibition of flashing, blinking, and animated signs. *Naser Jewelers, Inc. v. City of Concord*, 513 F.3d 27 (1st Cir. 2008), upheld an ordinance prohibiting electronic message, or digital, signs. The court found the ordinance was narrowly tailored to achieve the city's substantial interest in safety and aesthetics because it did not "burden substantially more speech than necessary." Since the ordinance was also content-neutral and left open reasonable alternative channels of communication by allowing static and manually changeable signs, the regulation was upheld as constitutional. See accord *Reed v. Town of Gilbert*, 587 F.3d 966 (9th Cir. 2009) (qualifying event signs); *Showing Animals Respect and Kindness v. City of West. Hollywood*, 83 Cal. Rptr. 3d 134 (Cal. App. 2008) (mobile vehicle signs); *Harnish v. Manatee County*, 783 F.2d 1535 (11th Cir. 1986) (portable signs).

Courts have also upheld regulations limiting the height, *City of Albuquerque v. Jackson*, 684 P.2d 543 (N.M. App. 1984) (26 feet), size, setback and location, *Donrey Communications Co. v. City of Fayetteville*, 660 S.W.2d 900 (Ark. 1984), and illumination of signs, *Asselin v. Town of Conway*, 628 A.2d 247 (N.H. 1993). Ordinances restricting or prohibiting price information on signs violate the Free Speech Clause. *H & H Operations, Inc. v. City of Peachtree City*, 283 S.E.2d 867 (Ga. 1981).

These cases often reflect the decision by the Supreme Court holding it does not apply the least restrictive alternative rule to regulations of commercial speech. As the Supreme Court explained:

> We have refrained from imposing a least-restrictive-means requirement — even where core political speech is at issue — in assessing the validity of so-called time, place, and

> manner restrictions. We uphold such restrictions so long as they are "narrowly tailored" to serve a significant governmental interest, a standard that we have not interpreted to require elimination of all less restrictive alternatives. . . . In requiring [government regulation of expressive conduct] to be "narrowly tailored" to serve an important or substantial state interest, we have not insisted that there be no conceivable alternative, but only that the regulation not "burden substantially more speech than is necessary to further the government's legitimate interests," *Ward v. Rock Against Racism*, 491 U.S. 781, 799 (1989). And we have been loath to second-guess the Government's judgment to that effect. [*Board of Trustees v. Fox*, 492 U.S. 469, 477, 478 (1989).]

This rule supports sign regulations that can get past the content neutrality barrier. For a case applying *Fox* and upholding a ban on signs within 200 feet of arterial roadways, see *Clear Channel Outdoor, Inc. v. City of New York*, 594 F.3d 94 (2d Cir. 2010).

Lorillard Tobacco Co. v. Reilly, supra, however, struck down a Massachusetts regulation that prohibited tobacco product advertising within 1000 feet of a school or playground. It held the regulation would vary by place and have a substantial impact on commercial speech in major metropolitan areas. It noted its decision did not apply to sign regulations that treated all signs equally.

Political and campaign signs. Temporary campaign signs are a complicated problem because they are a form of noncommercial speech. Defining these signs in an acceptable manner is almost impossible. The usual definition of a campaign sign as a "sign displaying the name of a candidate in an election" is content-based and vulnerable to challenge. Additional problems arise if the ordinance then provides more restrictive regulations for campaign than for other temporary signs. Prior to *Metromedia*, state and lower federal courts overturned a number of restrictions on campaign signs. Blumoff, *supra*, at 191–98. Restrictions limiting the amount of time a campaign sign can be displayed before an election are particularly vulnerable. *City of Painesville Bldg. Dep't v. Dworken & Bernstein Co., L.P.A.*, 733 N.E.2d 1152 (Ohio 2000) (citing cases); *Collier v. City of Tacoma*, 854 P.2d 1046 (Wash. 1993).

Whitton v. City of Gladstone, 54 F.3d 1400 (8th Cir. 1994), illustrates the tough view courts have taken on campaign sign restrictions since *Metromedia*. The court struck down an ordinance that limited the display of these signs to 30 days before an election, prohibited their external illumination, and made the candidate prima facie responsible for their erection, placement and removal. Relying heavily on *Discovery Network*, the court held that all these provisions were content-based and did not pass the strict scrutiny test required to uphold them. Accord *Beaulieu v. City of Alabaster*, 454 F.3d 1219 (11th Cir. 2006) (allowing political signs in residential areas but requiring permit in commercial areas). Can you avoid this kind of problem by adopting regulations that apply to all temporary signs and that do not identify campaign or other political signs for selective treatment? See *Sugarman v. Village of Chester*, 192 F. Supp. 2d 282 (S.D.N.Y. 2002) (upholding ordinance of this type). How would you define a "temporary" sign covered by these regulations?

Some courts uphold requirements that campaign signs must be removed within a certain time after an election. See *Messer, supra*, upholding ten-day requirement. Contra *Outdoor Systems, Inc. v. City of Merriam*, 67 F. Supp. 2d 1258 (D. Kan. 1999).

Signs on residential property: The Ladue Case. In *City of Ladue v. Gilleo*, 512 U.S. 43 (1994), an exclusive St. Louis residential suburb prohibited homeowners from displaying any signs except residence identification, "for sale," and safety hazard warning signs. However, it permitted commercial business, churches and nonprofit organizations to display signs not allowed at residences. The Court held the ordinance violated the Free Speech Clause in a case brought by a homeowner prohibited from displaying in her window an 8 ½ by 11 inch sign stating "For Peace in the Gulf." The city defended the ordinance as an attempt to improve aesthetics by limiting the number of signs in residential areas. The Court endorsed both the plurality and concurring opinions in *Metromedia*. It accepted the city's argument the ordinance was content- and viewpoint-neutral because it was aimed at the secondary effects of signs. But it held Ladue's interest in minimizing visual clutter was not a sufficiently "compelling" reason for prohibiting residential message signs completely. By limiting restrictions on signs to residential areas, the city had "diminished the credibility" of the claim that it was interested in aesthetics. Ladue had "almost completely foreclosed" a venerable, unique and important means for communicating political, religious, or personal messages.

The Court rejected Ladue's argument that the prohibition on residential message signs was a mere "time, place, or manner" regulation because residents had alternate means for conveying their messages. It held that displaying a sign from a residence carried a "quite distinct" message because it provided information about the identity of the speaker. In addition, residential signs are "an unusually cheap and convenient form of communication." Respect for individual liberty in the home, the Court concluded, has long been part of our culture and law. It suggested that Ladue could adopt "more temperate measures" to meet its regulatory needs, and noted that not every kind of sign must be permitted in residential areas.

Cases since *Ladue* have upheld reasonable regulations on signs on residential property, *Kroll v. Steere*, 759 A.2d 541 (Conn. App. 2001) (size limitation), but the case still has bite. *Cleveland Area Bd. of Realtors v. City of Euclid*, 88 F.3d 382 (6th Cir. 1996), relied on *Ladue* to strike down an ordinance prohibiting all yard signs except those displaying the residents' name and address and pertinent security information. It held the ordinance burdened substantially more speech than necessary because it completely foreclosed an inexpensive and autonomous way to communicate. Accord *Pica v. Sarno*, 907 F. Supp. 795 (D.N.J. 1995).

What about allowing one permanent six-foot square sign on each residential premise with no restrictions on what can be displayed? *Long Island Bd. of Realtors v. Incorporated Village of Massapequa Park*, 277 F.3d 622 (2d Cir. 2002), upheld an ordinance that allowed only one sign on residential property in addition to an identification sign; regulated their height, size, and duration; required existing signs to be removed when property was transferred; and prohibited off-site commercial advertising. Does this ordinance prohibit a Coca-Cola sign on residential property? A "For Sale" sign? For a case upholding restrictions on the size and location of signs on multiple family buildings see *Neighborhood Enters. v. City of St. Louis*, 2010 U.S. Dist. LEXIS 29811 (E.D. Mo. Mar. 29, 2010).

Sources. Mandelker, *Sign Regulation and Free Speech: Spooking the Doppelganger,* in Trends in Land Use Law from A to Z, Ch. 3 (American Bar Ass'n, P. Salkin ed., 2001); Mandelker, *Decision Making in Sign Codes: The Prior Restraint Barrier*, Zoning & Plan. L. Rep., Sept. 2008, at 1; Menthe, *Reconciling Speech and Structural Elements in Sign Regulation*, 44 Gonz. L. Rev. 283 (2008-2009); Brinton et al., *Deterring and Defeating the Sign Code Shakedown*, Municipal Lawyer, Jan./Feb. 2007, at 6; Gerard, *Election Signs and Time Limits*, 3 Wash. U. J.L. & Pol'y 379 (2000); Note, *Municipal Regulation of Political Signs: Balancing First Amendment Rights Against Aesthetic Concerns*, 45 Drake L. Rev. 767 (1997); Note, *Unsightly Politics: Aesthetics, Sign Ordinances, and Homeowners' Speech in City of*

Ladue v. Gilleo, 20 Harv. Envtl. L. Rev. 473 (1996); Comment, *Speech Interests Inherent in the Location of Billboards and Signs: A Method for Unweaving the Tangled Web of Metromedia, Inc. v. City of San Diego*, 2006 BYU L. Rev. 473. For a CD ROM with helpful studies of sign regulation and a photo gallery, see The Science of Sign Zoning, available from ussc.org.

C. URBAN DESIGN

Urban design deals with appearance, form and function in the urban environment. The City of Bremerton, Washington Downtown Regional Center Sub Area Plan (2007) has the following definition:

> Urban Design is the art of making safe, comfortable and inviting places for people. It includes the way places look, work and feel. Urban design includes the connections between places and buildings; the character of the built environment and the processes used for ensuring successful villages, towns and cities. [*Id.* at 3-17.]

This section considers how urban design can be used in land use regulation through design review and the adoption of design plans and policies.

[1.] Appearance Codes

Appearance codes were an early form of design review. They are often adopted in suburban or small communities, usually apply only to residential dwellings, and typically have review boards that must approve the appearance of new residences before they can be built. The following case is an early decision considering the validity of aesthetic considerations in design review under a local appearance code:

STATE ex rel. STOYANOFF v. BERKELEY
458 S.W.2d 305 (Mo. 1970)

PRITCHARD, COMMISSIONER:

. . . [The trial court issued a summary judgment ordering a writ of mandamus to compel the issuance of a building permit to the Stoyanoffs because it held the Ladue ordinance deprived the owners of their property without due process of law.] Relators' petition pleads that they applied to appellant Building Commissioner for a building permit to allow them to construct a single family residence in the City of Ladue, and that plans and specifications were submitted for the proposed residence, which was unusual in design, "but complied with all existing building and zoning regulations and ordinances of the City of Ladue, Missouri."

It is further pleaded that relators were refused a building permit for the construction of their proposed residence upon the ground that the permit was not approved by the Architectural Board of the City of Ladue. Ordinance 131, as amended by Ordinance 281 of that city, purports to set up an Architectural Board to approve plans and specifications for buildings and structures erected within the city and in a preamble to "conform to certain minimum architectural standards of appearance and conformity with surrounding structures, and that unsightly, grotesque and unsuitable structures, detrimental to the stability of value and the welfare of surrounding property, structures and residents, and to the general welfare and happiness of the community, be avoided, and that appropriate standards of beauty and conformity be fostered and encouraged." . . . [The petition claimed the ordinances were unconstitutional because "they are vague and provide no standard nor uniform rule by which to guide the architectural board," and there was no statutory authority for them.]

Relators filed a motion for summary judgment and affidavits were filed in opposition thereto. Richard D. Shelton, Mayor of the City of Ladue, deponed that the facts in appellant's answer were true and correct, as here pertinent: that the City of Ladue constitutes one of the finer suburban residential areas of Metropolitan St. Louis, the homes therein are considerably more expensive than in cities of comparable size, being homes on lots from three fourths of an acre to three or more acres each; that a zoning ordinance was enacted by the city regulating the height, number of stories, size of buildings, percentage of lot occupancy, yard sizes, and the location and use of buildings and land for trade, industry, residence and other purposes; that the zoning regulations were made in accordance with a comprehensive plan "designed to promote the health and general welfare of the residents of the City of Ladue," which in furtherance of said objectives duly enacted said Ordinances numbered 131 and 281. Appellant also asserted in his answer that these ordinances were a reasonable exercise of the city's governmental, legislative and police powers, as determined by its legislative body, and as stated in the above-quoted preamble to the ordinances. It is then pleaded that relators' description of their proposed residence as " 'unusual in design' is the understatement of the year. It is in fact a monstrosity of grotesque design, which would seriously impair the value of property in the neighborhood."

The affidavit of Harold C. Simon, a developer of residential subdivisions in St. Louis County, is that he is familiar with relators' lot upon which they seek to build a house, and with the surrounding houses in the neighborhood; that the houses therein existent are virtually all two-story houses of conventional architectural design, such as Colonial, French Provincial or English; and that the house which relators propose to construct is of ultra-modern design which would clash with and not be in conformity with any other house in the entire neighborhood. It is Mr. Simon's opinion that the design and appearance of relators' proposed residence would have a substantial adverse effect upon the market values of other residential property in the neighborhood, such average market value ranging from $60,000 to $85,000 each.

As a part of the affidavit of Russell H. Riley, consultant for the city planning and engineering firm of Harland Bartholomew & Associates, photographic exhibits of homes surrounding relators' lot were attached. To the south is the conventional frame residence of Mrs. T.R. Collins. To the west is the Colonial two-story frame house of the Lewis family. To the northeast is the large brick English Tudor home of Mrs. Elmer Hubbs. Immediately to the north are the large Colonial homes of Mr. Alex Cornwall and Mr. L. Peter Wetzel. In substance Mr. Riley went on to say that the City of Ladue is one of the finer residential suburbs in the St. Louis area with a minimum of commercial or industrial usage. The development of residences in the city has been primarily by private subdivisions, usually with one main lane or drive leading therein (such as Lorenzo Road Subdivision which runs north off of Ladue Road in which relators' lot is located). The homes are considerably more expensive than average homes found in a city of comparable size. The ordinance which has been adopted by the City of Ladue is typical of those which have been adopted by a number of suburban cities in St. Louis County and in similar cities throughout the United States, the need therefore being based upon the protection of existing property values by preventing the construction of houses that are in complete conflict with the general type of houses in a given area. The intrusion into this neighborhood of relators' unusual, grotesque and nonconforming structure would have a substantial adverse effect on market values of other homes in the immediate area. According to Mr. Riley the standards of Ordinance 131, as amended by Ordinance 281, are usually and customarily applied in city planning work and are: "(1) whether the proposed house meets the customary architectural requirements in appearance and design for a house of the particular type which is proposed (whether it be Colonial, Tudor English, French Provincial, or Modern), (2) whether the proposed house is in general conformity with the style and design of surrounding structures, and (3) whether the proposed house lends itself to the proper architectural development of the City; and that in applying said standards the Architectural Board and its Chairman are to determine whether the proposed house will have an adverse effect on the stability of values in the surrounding area."

Photographic exhibits of relators' proposed residence were also attached to Mr. Riley's affidavit. They show the residence to be of a pyramid shape, with a flat top, and with triangular shaped windows or doors at one or more corners. . . .

[On the statutory issue, the court quoted § 89.020, which is identical to § 1 of the Standard Zoning Enabling Act, reproduced in Ch. 3, sec. A, *supra.* This section authorizes the regulation of land use. The court also quoted § 89.040, which is identical to § 3 of the Standard Act, "Purposes in View." The court italicized the following language from § 3: "Such regulations shall be made with reasonable consideration . . . to the character of the district and its particular suitability for particular uses, and with a view to conserving the values of buildings and encouraging the most appropriate use of land throughout such municipality."] . . .

As is clear from the affidavits and attached exhibits, the City of Ladue is an area composed principally of residences of the general types of Colonial, French Provincial and English Tudor. The city has a comprehensive plan of zoning to maintain the general character of buildings therein. . . . [T]he italicized portion [of § 89.040] relating to the character of the district, its suitability for particular uses, and the conservation of the values of buildings therein . . . are directly related to the general welfare of the community. [The court quoted cases holding that the police power includes regulations to promote the public convenience or general welfare, and that stabilizing property values is "probably the most cogent reason" for zoning ordinances.] The preamble to Ordinance 131, quoted above in part, demonstrates that its purpose is to conform to the dictates of § 89.040, with reference to preserving values of property by zoning procedure and restrictions on the use of property. . . .

Relators say further that Ordinances 131 and 281 are invalid and unconstitutional as being an unreasonable and arbitrary exercise of the police power. It is argued that a mere reading of these ordinances shows that they are based entirely on aesthetic factors in that the stated purpose of the Architectural Board is to maintain "conformity with surrounding structures" and to assure that structures "conform to certain minimum architectural standards of appearance." The argument ignores the further provisos in the ordinance: ". . . and that unsightly, grotesque and unsuitable structures, *detrimental to the stability of value and the welfare of surrounding property, structures, and residents,* and *to the general welfare and happiness of the community,* be avoided, and that appropriate standards of beauty and conformity be fostered and encouraged." (Italics added.) Relators' proposed residence does not descend to the " 'patently offensive character of vehicle graveyards in close proximity to such highways' " referred to in the *Deimeke* [*v. State Highway Com.*], case, *supra* (444 S.W.2d 484). Nevertheless, the aesthetic factor to be taken into account by the Architectural Board is not to be considered alone. Along with that inherent factor is the effect that the proposed residence would have upon the property values in the area. In this time of burgeoning urban areas, congested with people and structures, it is certainly in keeping with the ultimate ideal of general welfare that the Architectural Board, in its function, preserve and protect existing areas in which structures of a general conformity of architecture have been erected. The area under consideration is clearly, from the record, a fashionable one. In *State ex rel. Civello v. City of New Orleans*, 97 So. 440, 444 (La.), the court said, "If by the term 'aesthetic considerations' is meant a regard merely for outward appearances, for good taste in the matter of the beauty of the neighborhood itself, we do not observe any substantial reason for saying that such a consideration is not a matter of general welfare. The beauty of a fashionable residence neighborhood in a city is for the comfort and happiness of the residents, and it sustains in a general way the value of property in the neighborhood." . . .

In the matter of enacting zoning ordinances and the procedures for determining whether any certain proposed structure or use is in compliance with or offends the basic ordinance, it is well settled that courts will not substitute their judgments for the city's legislative body, if the result is not oppressive, arbitrary or unreasonable and does not infringe upon a valid preexisting nonconforming use. The denial by appellant of a building permit for relators' highly modernistic residence in this area where traditional Colonial, French Provincial and English Tudor styles of architecture are erected does not appear to be arbitrary and unreasonable when the basic purpose to be served is that of the general welfare of persons in the entire community.

In addition to the above-stated purpose in the preamble to Ordinance 131, it establishes an Architectural Board of three members, all of whom must be architects. . . . [The court described the procedures followed by the Board in reviewing applications under the design review ordinances. Board decisions are appealable to the city council.]

Relators claim that the above provisions of the ordinance amount to an unconstitutional delegation of power by the city to the Architectural Board. It is argued that the Board cannot be given the power to determine what is unsightly and grotesque and that the standards, "whether the proposed structure will conform to proper architectural standards in appearance and design, and will be in general conformity with the style and design of surrounding structures and conducive to the proper architectural development of the City . . ." and "the Board shall disapprove the application if it determines that the proposed structure will constitute an unsightly, grotesque or unsuitable structure in appearance, detrimental to the welfare of surrounding property or residents . . . ," are inadequate. . . . Ordinances 131 and 281 are sufficient in their general standards calling for a factual determination of the suitability of any proposed structure with reference to the character of the surrounding neighborhood and to the determination of any adverse effect on the general welfare and preservation of property values of the community. Like holdings were made involving Architectural Board ordinances in *State ex rel. Saveland Park Holding Corp. v. Wieland*, 69 N.W.2d 217 (Wis.), and *Reid v. Architectural Board of Review of the City of Cleveland Heights*, 192 N.E.2d 74 (Ohio App.).

The judgment is reversed.

NOTES AND QUESTIONS

1. *Stoyanoff* is a "second stage" aesthetic regulation case. The court relied on other zoning purposes besides aesthetic purposes to uphold the ordinance. What were they? Why do you suppose the property owners' attorney moved for summary judgment? Was this wise?

What were the ordinance standards in this case? One of them required "general conformity with the style and design of surrounding structures." This is known as a similarity requirement: The proposed dwelling must be similar to surrounding dwellings. What about the mixed styles in the area surrounding the proposed dwelling in *Stoyanoff*? Or was it the point that all of the styles were traditional? *Saveland Park*, cited in the principal case, upheld a similarity ordinance intended to prevent "substantial depreciation in the property values" of neighborhoods. The court said that the protection of property values clearly fell within the police power. It was immaterial whether the ordinance was grounded solely on this objective or whether this was one of several legitimate objectives.

In *Stoyanoff*, the proposed pyramid dwelling was out of keeping with the surrounding neighborhood. *Reid*, also cited in *Stoyanoff*, was a similar case in which the property owner planned "a flat-roofed complex of twenty modules" in a residential area of "dignified, stately and conventional structures." The court upheld the ordinance, which contained generalized standards requiring a review of architectural design.

Is a similarity requirement in an appearance code simply the familiar zoning compatibility requirement in a slightly different guise? If so, is this kind of design review ordinance really so unique? Compare *Hankins v. Borough of Rockleigh*, 150 A.2d 63 (N.J. App. Div. 1959) (invalidating ordinance prohibiting flat roofs as applied in area where flat-roofed dwellings already existed).

2. *Design review procedures.* In the *Stoyanoff* case, the city created a special Architectural Board, which can also be called a Design Review Commission or Board, to administer the design review ordinance. A building permit could not issue unless the Board approved the design, and the court relied on the expert qualifications of the Board members as one basis for upholding the ordinance. The creation of a separate board to administer the ordinance is common in many design review programs and in historic preservation and historic landmark programs, which are discussed later in this chapter. Design review can also be assigned to planning commission staff, the commission, a hearing officer, or some other local official. The procedures are similar to those used in other ordinances, such as the subdivision ordinance, but are separate and distinct and apply only to the design review or historic preservation ordinance.

3. *Dissimilarity.* Another variant in appearance codes requires architectural dissimilarity. New dwellings must not be too similar to existing dwellings. What do you suppose is the reason behind the dissimilarity requirement? If a municipality disapproved the dwelling in *Stoyanoff* under a dissimilarity requirement, would a court reverse? In *Village of Hudson v. Albrecht, Inc.*, 458 N.E.2d 855 (Ohio 1984), the court upheld an ordinance that contained both a similarity and dissimilarity requirement, as well as general design review standards. The court noted that the ordinance did not rely solely on aesthetic considerations but "also reflects a concern for the monetary interests of protecting real estate from impairment and destruction of value." *Id.* at 857. The dissent claimed the building modification under review would not affect property values because it was a store located in a shopping center.

4. *Finding the right balance.* The ordinance considered in the *Stoyanoff* case had a generalized appearance standard to regulate building appearance. Another approach is to identify the elements of building appearance and adopt a code that addresses these elements. L. Kendig, Too Big, Boring or Ugly, American Planning Ass'n, Planning Advisory Serv. Rep. No. 528 (2004), discusses the objective:

> Monotony is an aesthetic term that describes one end of a continuum. At the other end of the continuum is chaos. It is a slightly unusual continuum in that both ends are undesirable while the middle condition, harmony, is desirable. Many elements of housing design provide opportunities to provide a harmonious diversity. [*Id.* at 16.]

The report includes several examples of anti-monotony regulations of this type, *Id.* at 76–82. Paola, Kansas, for example, uses the following measures to prevent monotony: floor plan, orientation, rooflines, materials, architectural features and color.

Parker, Colorado has adopted residential design standards for new residential development. The ordinance states:

> The criteria for determining whether buildings are considered similar are bundled around two general concepts: building mass and form, and building variation.
>
> ***Building mass and form.*** Building mass is the outline of the structure, which is determined by its height, width, and depth. Building form is the style of the home, such as ranch, tri-level, or two-story. If the building mass and form are similar, then both the front and rear of the house are required to meet two out of three of the building variation requirements to be considered different.
>
> ***Building variation.*** The three building variation possibilities are:
>
> ■ *Substantially different roof types.* Roof types consist of mansard, hip (full), flat, gambrel, gable, and front-to-back (shed style).
>
> ■ *Elevation plane variation.* The elevation plane is identified as the exterior wall of the structure. For an elevation plane to be considered substantially different, the secondary plane must project at least two feet from the primary plane and make up at least 30 percent of the entire elevation.
>
> ■ *Exterior surface distinctions.* Exterior surfaces include brick, stone, stucco, and siding. [As quoted in Stoll & Rossmiller, *Be Unique: A Model for Anti-Monotony in Residential Development*, Zoning News, Oct, 2003, at 2.]

The article points out that anti-monotony standards are not enough to ensure good design, and the town also has design standards for streets, parks and schools. The ordinance is at www.colocode.com/parker/parker_13.pdf. It includes a Residential Design Minimums Handbook as an appendix. See also L. Kendig & B. Keast, Community Character (2010).

5. *Free speech and vagueness issues.* Does architectural design review raise free speech problems? The dissents in *Reid* and *Village of Hudson* thought so. The first question is whether architectural expression is a form of speech. If it is, could you argue that the proposed dwelling in the *Stoyanoff* case was so intrusive on its neighbors that it justified a restriction on that expression? Would the impairment of property values justification used in *Stoyanoff* be enough to save a design review ordinance from a free speech challenge? How about an argument that a disapproved architectural style could be built elsewhere? For discussion, see Note, *Freedom of Speech and the Language of Architecture*, 30 Hastings Const. L.Q. 395 (2003).

In *Novi v. City of Pacifica*, 215 Cal. Rptr. 439 (Cal. App. 1985), the city rejected a site development permit because an ordinance prohibited approval where "there is insufficient variety in the design of the structure and grounds to avoid monotony in the external appearance." The court held the provision was not unconstitutionally vague, and that the U.S. Supreme Court's free speech decision in *Metromedia* did not require objective criteria for aesthetic land use regulation:

> The legislative intent is obvious: the Pacifica city council wishes to avoid "ticky-tacky" development of the sort described by songwriter Malvina Reynolds in the song, "Little Boxes." No further objective criteria are required. . . . [*Id.* at 441.]

See also *Breneric Assocs. v. City of Del Mar*, 81 Cal. Rptr. 2d 324 (Cal. App. 1998) (upholding denial of permit for addition to residence because inconsistent with existing structure and surrounding neighborhood). For criticism of this case, see Weinberg & McGuire, *Design Regulation and Architecture: Collision Course?*, 22 Zoning & Plan. L. Rep. 89 (1999).

[2.] Design Review

Design review goes beyond appearance codes. It requires the three-dimensional review of design, configuration and materials in a process based on design review standards contained in a design review ordinance. Design review can be applied at a number of levels. A citywide design plan can designate areas of the city for design treatment, such as commercial areas or it can be applied to a single area, such as the downtown. Design review can also be applied to entire new developments and to areas within those developments, such as town centers and residential neighborhoods. It can be an important element in the approval of planned unit developments and planned communities, which were discussed in Chapter 7. See D. Mandelker, Designing Planned Communities (2010).

Design review standards can be determinate or indeterminate. A requirement that blank building walls may be no more than 50 feet in length is an example of a determinate standard. A requirement that new development must have "harmonious visual relationships" is an example of an indeterminate standard. There is a tension here. Indeterminate standards allow flexibility in interpretation but can raise constitutional delegation of power and vagueness problems. Determinate standards may not raise constitutional problems but may be rigid and may not produce an acceptable design. Design standards can be included in zoning ordinances, in comprehensive plans, and in supplementary design manuals and guidelines. Because of their complexity, inclusion of design standards in a zoning ordinance may be difficult and may create constitutional problems if they are indeterminate. Comprehensive plans, guidelines and manuals can provide greater detail, and the zoning ordinance can make them binding in the design review process.

There is no clear, definitive case on the constitutionality of design review standards. The *Stoyanoff* case upheld design standards in a similarity ordinance applied to an existing residential neighborhood, and courts have upheld similar ordinances, like the California court in *Novi.* These ordinances may not be difficult to uphold because they require compliance with, or difference from, an established design pattern. Other courts have invalidated similar standards. *Waterfront Estates Dev. Co. v. City of Palos Hills*, 597 N.E.2d 641 (Ill. App. 1992) (inappropriateness or incompatibility with the surrounding neighborhood); *Morristown Rd. Assocs. v. Mayor & Common Council*, 394 A.2d 157 (N.J.L. Div. 1978) (design review ordinance requiring harmonious visual relationship held void for vagueness). The outcome may depend on how much a court will tolerate indeterminate delegations of power in any regulatory context.

Free-standing indeterminate design standards in zoning ordinances applied to individual dwellings in residential neighborhoods are most vulnerable, especially if they contain open-ended language with little definition. Design standards that are part of a comprehensive design or development review program, and that are more extensively specified in plans, manuals or guidelines, may receive more judicial acceptance. The following case reviews design standards applied in the approval of a cluster housing development, which is a type of planned unit development, and that were part of a comprehensive development review program. This type of development, as in this case, usually requires a waiver of existing requirements and a clustering of residential dwellings in part of the development in return for the preservation of open space elsewhere in the development. The Environmental Court is a state administrative agency that hears land use cases. The appeal is to the state supreme court.

IN RE PIERCE SUBDIVISION APPLICATION

965 A.2d 468, 184 Vt. 365 (Vt. 2008)

Burgess, J. Neighbor appeals the Environmental Court's approval of applicant's proposed Planned Residential Development (PRD) adjoining his property in Ferrisburgh, Vermont. Under the Ferrisburgh Zoning Bylaws, a qualified PRD that proposes cluster housing and preservation of open space may be authorized by the Planning Commission by waiver of the standard rules governing single-house lot development. On appeal, neighbor claims that the court erred by concluding that: . . . (3) the bylaws supply adequate standards to guide the court's discretion. . . . We affirm the project's approval.

Applicant proposed to subdivide a 113-acre portion of its property into a twenty-one lot PRD, with an additional lot reserved for common space. The bylaws define a PRD as "[a]n area of land to be developed as a single entity for a number of dwelling units, the plan for which does not conform to the zoning regulations." Zoning Bylaws for the Town of Ferrisburgh § 2.2 (as amended, March 6, 2001) [hereinafter Zoning Bylaws]. The sizes of the twenty-two lots range from under half an acre to 25.9 acres. These twenty-two lots are accessed by Pierce Woods Road, a twenty-foot-wide roadway within a sixty-foot-wide access easement.

Applicant's 113-acre parcel has varied terrain containing woods, wetlands, Lewis Creek, a stream, and steep slopes. The proposal creates a fifty-foot buffer along Lewis Creek and the stream. Applicant proposes to conserve seventy-six percent of the land in the PRD as open space through perpetual easements once the PRD is approved.

The parcel encompasses three different zoning districts: Rural Residential (RR-2), Rural Agricultural (RA-5), and Conservation (Con-25). Each district has a minimum lot size: RR-2 requires two acres, RA-5 five acres, and Con-25 twenty-five acres. *Id.* §§ 4.2(D), 4.2(C), 4.3(C). Because zoning regulations for these districts would effectively prevent applicant from clustering houses on the parcel, applicant requested six waivers of the district zoning regulations to reduce the required minimum lot size and acreage per dwelling, along with frontage, width, depth, and setback requirements.

The Planning Commission approved the proposed PRD. Neighbor appealed that decision to the Environmental Court, complaining, in pertinent part, . . . that the bylaws delegated standardless discretion to the Commission to grant waivers of the district zoning regulations . . . . The Environmental Court rejected neighbor's arguments, affirming the approval of the application. This appeal followed. . . .

III.

We now turn to neighbor's argument that §§ 5.21(C) and 5.21(D) fail to provide sufficient standards to guide the Environmental Court's exercise of discretion when evaluating the PRD. Neighbor contends that the bylaws are so vague that they do not inform applicants, courts or neighbors about what is permitted and what is prohibited. Neighbor further claims that adjoining landowners are denied due process and equal protection when challenging decisions of the Planning Commission because of the absence of standards upon which the court can review decisions.

In the context of land-use regulation, our approach to complaints of standardless, arbitrary discretion focuses on the criteria for due process and equal protection. See *In re Handy*, 764 A.2d 1226, 1235–36 (2000) ("[T]he power to grant or refuse zoning permits without standards denies applicants equal protection of the laws; and . . . due process of law.").

Zoning ordinances must "provide . . . appropriate conditions and safeguards" to guide the decisionmaker. While we will invalidate ordinances that "fail[] to provide adequate guidance" and therefore lead to "unbridled discrimination," we will uphold standards even if they are general and will look to the entire ordinance, not just the challenged subsection, to determine the standard to be applied. [Citations omitted.]

Neighbor specifically contends that the bylaw provides no standards for the Planning Commission to approve or deny the six waivers requested by applicant as part of the PRD-approval process. While it is true that § 5.21 provides no concrete standards to consider each individual modification to the zoning regulations, neighbor's argument misunderstands the nature of a PRD. The Legislature authorized PRDs to "encourage flexibility of design and development of land in such a manner as to promote the most appropriate use of land, . . . and to preserve the natural and scenic qualities of the open lands of this state." 24 V.S.A. § 4407(3) (repealed 2004).[2] In order to achieve these goals, particularly the encouragement of flexible planning, "[t]he modification of zoning regulations by the planning commission . . . may be permitted simultaneously with approval of a subdivision plan." *Id.* Such modifications, or "waivers," are part of the process of approving a PRD — a type of concentrated housing development permitted in exchange for open space which, by its very nature, does not fit the traditional zoning scheme. The consideration of these waivers, therefore, is folded into the Commission's analysis of the PRD itself. The proper inquiry is thus whether the bylaw provides the Commission with sufficient overall standards to grant a PRD permit, and whether the waivers granted comply with these standards.

Subsections (C) and (D) provide standards to guide the Commission's approval of a PRD. Some of the standards in subsection (C) are general:

1. The PRD is consistent with the municipal plan.

. . . .

---

[2] Though now repealed, § 4407(3) still applies to town ordinances written under this section until September 1, 2011. 24 V.S.A. § 4481.

> 4. The PRD is an effective and unified treatment of the development possibilities of the site and the development plan makes appropriate provision for preservation of streams, and stream banks, steep slopes, wet areas and unique natural and manmade features.
>
> 5. The development plan is proposed over a reasonable period of time in order that adequate municipal facilities and services may be provided.
>
> . . . .
>
> 8. Any open space land will be evaluated as to its agricultural, forestry and ecological quality.

Zoning Bylaw § 5.21(C). By their terms, these tend to be overall objectives and recommendations, rather than specific standards to be measured and met.

Other provisions of § 5.21(C) and (D), however, contain more specific standards for the approval of a PRD. Section 5.21(C) requires that:

> 2. The overall density of the project does not exceed the number of dwelling units which could be permitted, in the Planning Commission's judgment, if the land (excluding the area within the boundaries of any proposed road) were subdivided into lots in accordance with the district regulations and other relevant provisions of these bylaws.
>
> 3. The uses proposed for the project are residential; dwelling units may be of varied types, including one-family, two-family or multifamily construction.
>
> . . . .
>
> 7. Any modification of the zoning regulations approved under this section shall be specifically set forth in terms of standards and criteria for the design, bulk and spacing of buildings and the sizes of lots and open spaces which shall be noted on or appended to the application.

Id. § 5.21(C). In addition, § 5.21(D) requires that:

> 1. District regulations on height and spacing between main buildings shall be met.
>
> 2. To ensure adequate privacy for existing or proposed uses adjacent to the PRD, structures on the perimeter of the PRD shall be set back 50 feet and screening may be required.
>
> 3. Adequate water supply and sewage disposal facilities shall be provided.
>
> 4. Each dwelling unit shall have a minimum two acre lot exclusively associated with it and must comply with the specific standards set forth in Section 4.1 and 4.2 of these bylaws, excluding the lot depth requirement.
>
> 5. The minimum acreage for a PRD shall be 25 acres and a minimum of 60% of the total parcel shall remain undeveloped.

Id. § 5.21(D).

Thus, while some of the bylaws' objectives are general, other provisions impose specific limits to guide and check the Commission's discretion. These requirements provide restrictions on the type of units which may be allowed, the percentage of open space required in a PRD, and the timing and form of applications. As stated in *Handy*, we consider the entire ordinance when evaluating whether it provides sufficient guidance to a decision-making body. By providing both general and specific standards for PRD review, the bylaw strikes an appropriate balance between providing guidance to the Commission and avoiding inflexible requirements which would defeat the creativity and flexibility required to effectuate the goals of the PRD alternative to traditional development. The list of particular requirements set forth in § 5.21(C) and (D) provides sufficient standards for the Commission, and for the court upon review, to evaluate a proposed project's compliance with the bylaws while avoiding, as the Environmental Court put it, the "inflexibility that . . . *Handy* cautioned about."

All six waivers approved as part of the application — lot-size and acreage-per-dwelling minimums, lot frontage, width, and depth requirements, and setback rules — comply with the standards listed in § 5.21(C) and (D). In accordance with § 5.21(C)(7), the waivers were specific, establishing alternative "standards and criteria" for lot sizes, frontage, width, and depth requirements, and setbacks for the units in the PRD. The requested setback waivers did not violate § 5.21(D)(2)'s requirement that structures be set back fifty feet from the perimeter of the PRD. The waivers to minimum-lot-size and acreage-per-dwelling requirements enabled applicant to cluster dwellings in the PRD while also complying with the requirements that "[e]ach dwelling unit [] have a minimum two acre lot exclusively associated with it," *id.* § 5.21(D)(4), and that the "overall density of the project [] not exceed the number of dwelling units which could be permitted . . . if the land . . . were subdivided . . . in accordance with the district regulations," *id.* § 5.21(C)(2). The lot frontage, width, and depth waivers were similarly in accordance with the standards established by § 5.21(C) and (D). These waivers enabled the flexibility of design needed for the construction of a PRD, yet complied in full with the specific requirements established in § 5.21(C) and (D). As such, we affirm the court's approval of these waivers. . . .

Affirmed.

NOTES AND QUESTIONS

1. *Understanding constitutional problems.* The court states that "our approach to complaints of standardless, arbitrary discretion focuses on the criteria for due process and equal protection." The reference to due process is a reference to the rule that standards may not be unconstitutionally vague. The reference to equal protection means that standards must not allow arbitrary decisionmaking. The ordinance contained a design standard in its requirement that the development had to be an "effective and unified treatment of the development possibilities of the site," and the court noted that the legislature authorized planned developments to "encourage flexibility of design and development of land." Can it be said that design review with indeterminate standards has the same objectives? How did the regulatory framework for these standards convince the court that it should be upheld? See also *Tri-State Generation & Transmission Co. v. Thornton*, 647 P.2d 670 (Colo. 1982), upholding standards, including design standards, for planned communities.

The leading case striking down stand-alone design standards for individual buildings is *Anderson v. City of Issaquah*, 851 P.2d 744 (Wash. App. 1993). Design review was required for a general commercial use building in a commercial area. There were a number of indeterminate design standards such as "[e]valuation of a project shall be based on quality of its design and relationship to the natural setting of the valley and surrounding mountains." The building as presented "was to be faced with off-white stucco and was to have a blue metal roof. It was designed in a 'modern' style with an unbroken 'warehouse' appearance in the rear, and large retail-style windows in the front." The proposal went back and forth, with the Development Commission charged with applying the design standards making suggestions for revisions, but the Commission finally turned the building down because the applicant had not been "sufficiently responsive" to its concerns. The Commission held meetings but apparently no public hearings, and its decision process included one commissioner's drive up and down the street, taking notes.

The court invalidated the ordinance, both facially and as-applied, and ordered approval of the building with changes the applicant had accepted. Though the court invalidated the ordinance both facially and as applied, the design review process clearly was an important factor, and the Washington courts have not been kind to the *Issaquah* decision. *Pinecrest Homeowners Ass'n v. Glen A. Cloninger & Assocs.*, 87 P.3d 1176 (Wash. 2004), upheld design standards contained in a mixed use district ordinance, and noted that the *Issaquah* case "chronicled the repeated efforts of one developer to intuit and satisfy the shifting personal demands of members of the development commission." There were 14 design standards in the ordinance, which the court believed were more detailed than those in *Issaquah*, though one standard required the "development of integrated, mixed use communities, containing a variety of housing types arranged around an activity center (neighborhood, district, corridor); that provide a pleasant living, shopping, and working environment; that provide a sense of community; and that provide a balance of compatible retail, office, residential, recreational and public uses." *Bellevue Farm Owners Ass'n v. State Shorelines Hearings Bd.*, 997 P.2d 380 (Wash. App. 2000), upheld a shoreline management ordinance requiring the consideration of "scenic views," and distinguished *Issaquah* because it concerned "the design treatment of a building, characteristics that are relatively easy to specify." See also *Conner v. City of Seattle*, 223 P.3d 1201 (Wash. App. 2009) (upholding standards in landmark preservation ordinance against vagueness challenge and distinguishing *Issaquah*). For a case upholding an order to demolish a partly-constructed home because it violated design standards in its permit, see *Virginia City v. Estate of Olsen*, 201 P.3d 115 (Mont. 2009).

2. *Drafting design standards.* M. Hinshaw, *Design Review*, American Planning Association, Planning Advisory Serv. Rep. No. 454 (1995), makes a case for more specific design guidelines. He urges the use of visual drawings to supplement written standards, a practice that is increasingly common. He suggests that guidelines, as a minimum, should address overall site design, landscaping, building orientation and form, signage and public spaces. For suggestions on the drafting of design review ordinances, see C. Duerksen & R.M. Goebel, *Aesthetics, Community Character, and the Law* 35, American Planning Association, Planning Advisory Serv. Rep. No. 489/490 (1999).

Brindell, *Practice Design Review*, Zoning Practice, July 2009 at 2, gives examples of problematic design standards. Here is one example:

> The plan for the proposed building or structure is in conformity with good taste and design and in general contributes to the image of charm and high quality.

Brindell comments that these terms are difficult to define and apply. He suggests this alternative:

> The proposed building and landscape plans are consistent with the catalogue examples of acceptable styles, elements, materials, massing, detailing, landscaping and relation-

ships to street frontages and abutting properties and does not include the unacceptable examples in the catalogue. [*Id.* at 2, 3.]

This approach requires the creation of a catalogue of examples, either in a manual, design guidelines or similar document. Decisions on acceptable designs are then made when the catalogue is prepared.

The APA model legislation includes a legislative proposal for design review. American Planning Ass'n, Growing Smart Legislative Guidebook: Model Statutes for Planning and Management of Change § 9-301 (S. Meck ed., 2002). Commentary recommends that design review board members should have sufficient background in architecture and "related backgrounds to preclude potential due process challenges or claims of arbitrary decision making." *Id.* at 9-33.

3. *Can standards be precise?* A review of design ordinances found that roughly three-quarters used criteria such as "encourage retention of existing vegetation," "favor site-specific response to topography," and similar criteria. Lightner, *Survey of Design Review Practices*, PAS Memo, Jan. 1993, at 4. The study concluded:

> The problem with any quest for *precise* standards in design review is simply that there are some varieties of "aesthetic" regulation for which *sensible* details are impossible to prescribe without defeating the very purpose of the regulation. . . . Precise standards direct the attention of design communities to the superficialities of style instead of to the basic aspects of design that are likely to affect community life. [Introduction to Highland Park, Illinois Appearance Code, as quoted in P. Glassford, Appearance Codes for Small Communities 4 (Am. Planning Association, Planning Advisory Serv. Rep. No. 379 (1983)) (report reviews details of design review ordinances in several communities) (emphasis in original).]

The problem with imprecise standards, Brindell says, is that they require interpretation, and members of design review boards often receive no training in their decisionmaking role, and how they should approach the application of design standards to individual properties. Brindell, *supra*, at 2. Jesse Dukeminier, *Zoning for Aesthetic Objectives: A Reappraisal*, 20 Law & Contemp. Probs. 218, 226–27 (1955), argued that planners should abandon the "cry for precise criteria" and develop "a satisfactory set of operations describing what is beautiful." How should this be done?

4. *Big box retail and retail design.* Retail stores also present design problems, especially big box stores that create serious design problems because of their box-like look and sterile, windowless exterior walls. Duerksen, *Site Planning for Large-Scale Retail Stores*, American Planning Association, PAS Memo, Apr. (1996), describes design standards that can create better design. Facade treatment is an important design element. How about this design standard:

> Facades greater than one hundred (100) feet in length, measured horizontally, shall incorporate wall plane projections or recesses having a depth of at least three (3) percent of the length of the facade and extending at least twenty (20) percent of the length of the facade. No uninterrupted length of any facade shall exceed one hundred (100) horizontal feet. [Fort Collins, Colorado Land Use Code § 3.5.4(C)(1)(a)(1).]

And what about this: Building facades must include: "1. a repeating pattern that includes no less than three (3) of the following elements: a. color change; b. texture change; c. material module change; d. an expression of architectural or structural bays through a change in plane no less than twelve (12) inches in width, such as an offset, reveal or projecting rib." *Id.* § 3.5.4(C)(1)(c). What is the design theory behind these guidelines? See Merriam, *Breaking Big Boxes: Learning from the Horse Whisperers*, 6 Vt. J. Envtl. L. 7 (2005).

The Omaha, Nebraska Urban Design Handbook contains the following policy on Ground-Level Transparency:

> When a building is adjacent to a sidewalk it should provide for visual connection between the sidewalk and the first floor. This connection is necessary to link the interior functions of buildings with the sidewalk environment. Uses such as retail sales, restaurants, general services offices and entertainment are well suited for linking to the sidewalk area. . . . Long expanses of blank walls are not allowed in certain areas and will be discouraged within the district. [*Id.* at 17.]

What do you think is the design decision that led to this policy? The Handbook is available at city of omaha.org/planning/urbanplanning.

5. *Sources.* For discussion of design review, see R. Fleming, *How Corporate Franchise Design Can Respect Community Identity*, Am. Plan. Ass'n, Planning Advisory Serv. Rep. No. 503/504 (2002); Design Review: Challenging Urban Aesthetic Control (B. Scheer & W. Preiser eds., 1994); Garvin & LeRoy, *Design Guidelines: The Law of Aesthetic Controls*, Land Use L. & Zoning Dig., April, 1993, at 3; Hinshaw & Meck, *Making Your Design Review Process Defensible: A Case Study from Washington State*, Am. Plan. Ass'n, The Commissioner, Summer 2001; Note, *You Can't Build Here: The Constitutionality of Aesthetic Zoning and Architectural Review*, 58 Fordham L. Rev. 1013 (1990). See also Barnett & Hack, Urban Design in the Practice of Local Government Planning ch. 13 (C. Hoch, L. Dalton & F. So eds., 3d ed. 2000).

A NOTE ON DESIGN GUIDELINES AND MANUALS

> Design guidelines and manuals are another alternative for providing design standards. They are often adopted for downtown or historic areas or areas of the community that require design attention such as commercial corridors. Design guidelines and manuals are also adopted for certain types of development, including residential, nonresidential, and mixed use developments, and can include or be limited to planned communities. The detail provided in guidelines and manuals varies from general policy statements on design to detailed design prescriptions. . . . [*Designing Planned Communities, supra*, at 53.]

Guidelines and manuals can usefully supplement design standards in zoning ordinances by providing more detail on design criteria. Louis Colombo, former Deputy Director, Albuquerque City Council suggests, as an example, that a design standard requiring "pedestrian oriented facade design" can be supplemented with a list of elements from which a designer can choose: color palettes that include a number of allowed hues; allowed building materials that list several materials and prohibit some; frontage types that include several alternatives. Other elements can be included.

Scottsdale, Arizona is an example. It has adopted Sensitive Design Guidelines whose primary purpose is to protect the Sonoran Desert environment in which the city is located. Achieving architectural quality is another important purpose. Guideline eight, for example, states that "buildings should be designed with a logical hierarchy of masses to control the visual impact of a building's height and size [and] to highlight important building volumes and features, such as the building entry." *Id.* Architecture Design Guidelines provide additional design guidance. The statement of purpose for commercial and retail development states, for example, that their intent "is to ensure a base level of quality architecture that is responsive to its context and builds upon the aesthetic identity of the community rather than a design solution(s) that is based on a standardized formula or market prototype superimposed on the selected site." *Id.* at 53–54.

Design guidelines can also be adopted for residential development. The Residential Design Guidelines adopted by the village of Plainfield, Illinois have the following statement of purpose:

> New developments must place considerable emphasis on the relationship between buildings, streets, and dedicated open space. Neighborhoods developed under these guidelines should place significant importance on the designation of public open space and on the provision of sidewalks, footpaths, and trails in an effort to foster a pedestrian friendly community atmosphere: this is one of the key elements of good residential design that distinguishes a good neighborhood from "just another subdivision." [As quoted in *id.* at 55.]

Design manuals can provide even greater detail, such as the extensive Design Standards Manual adopted by Sparks, Nevada. The chapter on Nonresidential Design Standards, has four sections of design standards: site planning, parking and circulation, landscape, and architectural standards for compatibility and context.

> The building placement standards that are part of the site planning standards are illustrative. They require that development sites three acres or larger should have, "a minimum 15% of the total primary building frontage be located at or near the front setback line." They also require that "active building elevations with public access or windows shall face public streets." A captioned illustration states that this standard precludes blank walls. [*Id.* at 57.]

[3.] Urban Design Plans

What they are. Urban design plans are a more comprehensive application of the design concept that extends beyond design guidelines for individual buildings. They are not limited solely to visual elements, and cover the entire community or an area in which the character, form, scale, and visual attractiveness of new development is the concern. Downtown areas and retail corridors are examples.

Citywide design plans. Franklin, Tennessee has adopted a Design Concepts Plan for the entire community. An introductory statement explains its purpose:

> This plan begins with the primacy of design quality. It recognizes that a mixture of uses at a range of densities is possible if properly designed. Community character and livability are not insured simply by planning for the geographic distribution of land use and public services. Community quality of life is determined as much by the quality of development, which is a direct function of design. As a way to plan for this issue, a series of basic design approaches is established in this plan in the form of seven "Design Concepts," which are then mapped . . . . [As quoted in *Designing Planned Communities*, at 38.]

Here is what the plan does:

> The comprehensive plan maps nine large geographic areas called Character Areas, each of which has a distinctive vision, community identity, and set of design guidelines that indicate the applicable design concepts. Special subarea plans are included for each character area. These contain additional detail on issues such as streets and lot sizes. Some of the character areas are fully developed with existing uses, and plans for these areas require a continuation of the existing design character. Other character areas are available for development, and plans for these areas contain standards that indicate the type of development that should occur, including standards for planned communities. [*Id.* at 39.]

The APA model planning legislation provides for a Community Design Element whose purpose is to "assess the positive and negative factors that constitute the visual element of the community as well as the appearance and character of community gateways, business districts, neighborhoods, and other areas." American Planning Ass'n, Growing Smart Legislative Guidebook: Model Statutes for Planning and Management of Change § 7-214 (S. Meck ed., 2002).

Downtown urban design plans. Downtown areas are an important area where design is critical. Many downtowns have deteriorated in the last decades, and revitalization is needed. This often requires a public-private partnership to carry out land acquisition and funding for new development. A design plan is also needed. The problem is to create a design framework in which buildings and other elements of the downtown experience can make an acceptable design statement.

Bremerton, Washington, which is across Puget Sound from Seattle, adopted an award-winning Downtown Regional Center Sub Area Plan in 2007. The Plan has several goals. A key goal states the design intent:

> Create user-friendly development and street standards that will foster active street life, support the public realm, and add appropriate development intensity with an aim towards building a superior identity for downtown Bremerton. [*Id.* at 1-7.]

Other goals encourage "fine grained and pedestrian-oriented development," and an increase in "downtown population without sacrificing livability."

The plan also includes strategies in an Urban Design Strategy section. The policy for Street Edge Definition is an example:

> On commercial streets, good street context includes high facade transparency, facade modulation offering pedestrians pleasant places to rest or sit, and a frequency of entrances. Throughout downtown, it is preferable that new developments be comprised of shops with limited street frontage. Smaller-scaled stores offer visual diversity while large scale commercial businesses occupying a significant length of frontage are generally not appropriate within the downtown Sub Area. [*Id.* at 3-23.]

The plan is available at ci.bremerton.wa.us/display.php?id=972.

Vancouver, British Columbia has an ambitious downtown plan that encourages downtown housing. Beasley, *"Living First" in Downtown Vancouver*, Am. Plan. Ass'n, Zoning News, April 2000, available at http://vancouver.ca/commsvcs/currentplanning/living.htm. See also http://vancouver.ca/commsvcs/BYLAWS/odp/dd.pdf. The basic principles are to extend the "fabric, patterns and character of the existing city," and to develop complete mixed-use neighborhoods at the pedestrian scale. *Id.* at 2. Design guidelines complement these policies. They require thin towers with small floor plates, the separation of retail and other on-street uses to manage noise, a prohibition on blank walls, street landscaping, limited vehicle crossings of sidewalks, and underground parking. The regulatory process was then modified so that the plan is implemented through a highly discretionary regulatory framework. See J. Punter, The Vancouver Achievement (2003).

Policy alternatives. Like all plans, design plans should present alternatives. Seattle, Washington's Central Waterfront Concept Plan (2006), for a section of the Seattle waterfront, includes these alternatives for waterfront development: A linear concept that establishes a long linear axis along the waterfront; five major activity nodes with major open spaces that would be connected by a linear pedestrian promenade; and two large activity centers that dominate the northern and southern edges with an anchoring mode in the center. *Id.* at 9. The plan illustrates these alternatives with schematic maps.

Implementing the design plan. The design plan can be implemented through a variety of techniques. A design review process that applies the policies of the plan to applications for development is common. Changes may be necessary in the zoning ordinance, which can include mixed-use districts, height limitations and building bulk standards that implement the plan. An overlay district with specially tailored zoning regulations and design review process is another option. Strategies for private investment and public funding of infrastructure are also important

A New Urbanism-regulating plan is another option. The regulating plan in the New Pleasant Hill, California BART Station Property Code for transit-oriented development at the station explains: "As the principal tool for implementing the Pleasant Hill BART Station Property Codes, the regulating plan identifies the basic physical characteristics of each building site and the Building Envelope Standard (BES) assigned to it." Other useful implementation measures are incentive zoning that provides increased density in return for designated design features, historic preservation controls, and transfer of development rights programs.

Questions. Notice the different design levels these plans address. What are they? How specific and how indeterminate are they? Imagine a development proposal that you would want to make under any of these plans. What issues would you need to address? How should the plan's design policies be applied?

Sources. A. Cuthbert, The Form of Cities (2006); D. Gosling, The Evolution of American Urban Design: A Chronological Anthology (2003); T. Lassar, Carrots and Sticks: New Zoning Downtown ch. 4 (1989); J. Nasar, The Evaluative Image of the City (1998); F. Steiner et al., Planning and Urban Design Standards (2006); Urban Design Assocs., The Urban Design Handbook (2003); Madanipoor, *Roles and Challenges of Urban Design*, 11 J. Urb. Design 173 (2006); J. Punter, Design Guidelines in American Cities (1999); Puntner, *Developing Urban Design as Public Policy: Best Practice Principles for Design Review and Development Management*, 12 J. Urb. Design 167 (2007); Taylor, *Legibility and Aesthetics in Urban Design*, 14 J. Urb. Design 189 (2009). The Mayor's Institute on City Design, micd.org, is a good resource.

A NOTE ON VIEW PROTECTION

View protection is a form of aesthetic control that can be incorporated into design review or legislated as a stand-alone ordinance. Here is how it works:

> *Preserving Viewsheds.* Perhaps the most common category of view protection ordinance focuses on preserving viewsheds — those grand, scenic vistas, visible from many vantage points, that encompass a multitude of elements, both natural and man-made, and that give communities their special identity.
>
> There are two common types of viewshed ordinances. The first allows new development subject to some kind of design review [which can include height limitations]. . . . A stricter type of viewshed ordinance sharply curtails the types of new development allowed in viewsheds in order to preserve the scenic areas in a relatively undisturbed state. These ordinances require sensitive siting or screening of any buildings allowed in the viewshed. . . .
>
> *Preserving View Corridors.* . . . [V]iew corridors [are] openings in the urban fabric that allow either quick glimpses or more extended views of important constructed resources . . . or natural features. . . . View corridor regulations [can] . . . attempt to prevent shadows from falling onto important view corridors and public places. . . . View corridor regulations also may be more complex, as is the case with Denver and Austin programs that rely on mathematical formulas to calculate allowable building heights. [Duerksen & Goebel, *supra*, at 44–45.]

View protection can be carried out through discretionary design review or legislated through specific standards, which can be complex. For example, the Austin, Texas formula to protect views of the state capital "establishes height allowance in each [view] corridor defined by sightline elevations from the viewpoints to the base of the capital dome." *Id.* at 46. View protection can also be a part of hillside protection regulations. See Chapter 3, Sec. D.

View protection regulations can present a takings problem because they limit development, but a taking should not occur because only height and bulk is usually controlled. See *Landmark Land Co., Inc. v. City & County of Denver*, 728 P.2d 1281 (Colo. 1986) (ordinance served legitimate governmental purposes and was not a taking because the properties involved were still extremely valuable). See also *Echevarrieta v. City of Rancho Palos Verdes*, 103 Cal. Rptr. 2d 165 (Cal. App. 2001) (accord, tree trimming requirement).

D. HISTORIC PRESERVATION

Historic preservation is a significant issue in most of land use and planning regulation. Thousands of historic listings are on the National Register of Historic Places, federal legislation requires federal agencies to take historic resources into account, and historic preservation programs are widespread at the local level. This section reviews historic district regulation and historic landmark protection, which are the two major local regulatory programs. It also reviews the use of development rights transfers as an historic preservation technique.

What is historic? The term certainly means any building that is old, although even that limitation no longer is meaningful as buildings less than fifty years old can be listed on the National Register. A special historic architectural style is another important attribute, but a historic building may also be humble or not even architecturally interesting. The buildings in Honolulu's Chinatown are undistinguished architecturally but have important historic associations. When, if ever, is the ordinary, nondescript and commonplace worthy of preservation?

Some assistance is provided by the criteria for listing historic districts and buildings on the National Register. The criteria require a "quality of significance in American history" for districts, sites and buildings:

> (a) that are associated with events that have made a significant contribution to the broad patterns of our history; or
>
> (b) that are associated with the lives of persons significant in our past; or
>
> (c) that embody the distinctive characteristics of a type, period, or method of construction, or that represent the work of a master, or that possess high artistic values, or that represent a significant and distinguishable entity whose components may lack individual distinction; or
>
> (d) that have yielded, or may be likely to yield, information important in prehistory or history. [36 C.F.R. § 60.4.]

What is preservation? Federal regulations define "preservation" as "the act or process of applying measures to sustain the existing form, integrity, and material of a building." 36 C.F.R. § 68.2(b). For a brief summary of historic preservation law, see Callies, *Historic Preservation Law in the United States*, 32 E.L.R. 10348 (2002). For a collection of essays on the historic preservation concept, see Preservation: Of What, For Whom? (M. Tomlan ed., 1998).

NOTES AND QUESTIONS

1. *Interpreting history.* Do the federal regulations of what is historic provide a coherent rationale for historic preservation? Professor Carol Rose notes "it is a cliche among professional historians that views of 'historic significance' alter considerably with shifting social interests." Rose, *Preservation and Community: New Directions in the Law of Historic Preservation*, 33 Stan. L. Rev. 473, 476 (1981). She identifies three stages in the development of historic preservation programs. Preservation activities in the nineteenth century sought to inspire patriotism by focusing on famous individuals or events, as in the movement to save Mount Vernon. The second theme had a cultural, artistic and architectural focus on the artistic merit of buildings and the integrity of their architectural style. A third stage contains elements of the first two, is concerned about the environmental and psychological effects of preservation, and stresses a sense of place and identity; what Professor Rose terms a "community-building rationale." *Id.* at 491. "[T]he focus on community-building requires a retreat from architectural imperialism and an acceptance of community definition by community residents." *Id.* at 492.

As the historic preservation movement has evolved, tension has grown between the view of historic buildings as "documents of their time" and the view that "historic places are or ought to be living entities that can grow and accommodate change without losing their character." This tension often is manifested in controversies over the design of additions or alterations to historic buildings. Semes, *From Contrast to Continuity: A New Preservation Philosophy* (Oct. 22, 2009), http://www.planetizen.com/node/41351 (last visited July 30, 2010). For an argument that "context matters and that new buildings and additions to old buildings should be harmonious with their neighbors," see Semes, A Conservation Ethic for Architecture, Urbanism, and Historic Preservation (2009).

Compare the use of contextual standards in historic preservation with form-based codes and design review overlay zoning discussed *supra*. These techniques "propose to accomplish many of the contextual objectives of historic district designation but within the framework of conventional zoning administered by a local planning or design review commission, rather than through a specialized set of regulations administered by a local historic preservation commission under separate state enabling legislation." Email from Prof. Martin Jaffe, Dept. of Urban Planning and Policy, U. of Ill. at Chicago, to one of the authors, Aug. 3, 2010.

2. *What preservation means.* Professor Rose asks whether preservation means "maintenance, or restoration, or indeed reconstruction and adaptive alteration? . . . Does it include something new that further develops and older tradition?" 33 Stan. L. Rev. at 476, 477. Integrity may be the key word in the federal regulation quoted above. Historic preservation ordinances usually maintain integrity by preserving the historic character of building exteriors, unlike zoning ordinances, which usually only regulate land use. Preservation regulations typically also require the maintenance and rehabilitation of historic building exteriors and prohibit their demolition. Preservation of interiors occasionally is required.

A "certificate of appropriateness" is the usual requirement for demolition or a modification of a building exterior. Consider the following criteria for "inappropriateness" from the Charleston, South Carolina historic district ordinance. What view of historic preservation does it illustrate? Should it be faulted for requiring conformity?

> Among other grounds for considering a design inappropriate . . . are the following defects: Arresting and spectacular effects, violent contrasts of materials or colors and intense or lurid colors, a multiplicity or incongruity of details resulting in a restless and disturbing appearance. . . . [Charleston, South Carolina Zoning Code § 54-240(i).]

3. *Constitutional issues.* The leading takings case on historic preservation is *Penn Central Transp. Co. v. City of New York*, 438 U.S. 104 (1978), reproduced in Ch. 2. The Supreme Court upheld the designation of Grand Central Terminal as a historic landmark against objections based on substantive due process, takings of property, and equal protection. *Penn Central* settled many but not all of the legal questions raised by historic preservation. This section reviews these unsettled questions as well as the treatment of the issues considered by *Penn Central* in the state courts. On the aesthetics issue, Professor Rose states that "[t]he courts' gradual withdrawal in preservation cases from all but the most conclusory remarks on aesthetics may reflect a particularly twentieth-century sensibility about the difficulty of aesthetic judgments." *Id.* at 487. Decide, as you study these materials, whether this comment still is true.

[1.] Historic Districts

Historic district ordinances and legislation. States have enacted enabling legislation for historic districts that is separate from the Standard Zoning Act. Most of this legislation merely includes historic preservation as one of the purposes of zoning or authorizes historic districts but leaves implementation details to municipalities. See N.M. Stat. Ann. § 3-22-2; N.Y. Gen. Mun. Law § 96-a. In most municipalities, historic districts are usually established and administered separately from the zoning ordinance as a separate "overlay" district and with a separate commission.

This practice is recognized in some historic district legislation, which is more detailed and specifies the regulatory powers and procedures for historic district programs. See Mass. Gen. L. ch. 40C; Md. Ann. Code, Art. 66B, §§ 8.01-8.17; Mich. Comp. Laws Ann. §§ 399.172 to 300.215. This type of legislation authorizes local governments to establish historic district (or historic preservation) commissions, which can conduct historic area surveys and make recommendations for historic districts to the governing body, which designates historic districts. See *Casey v. Mayor & City Council*, 929 A.2d 74, 93 (Md. 2007) ("statutory scheme does not place an affirmative obligation on the Mayor and Council to consider [economic feasibility] in reaching a historic designation decision"); *Billy Graham Evangelistic Ass'n v. City of Minneapolis*, 667 N.W.2d 117 (Minn. 2003) (upholding designation of historic district); Note, *Preservation Law Survey 2001: State Preservation Law*, 8 Wid. L. Symp. J. 463 (2002).

The historic district ordinance contains standards and procedures for the designation of historic districts and creates an historic district commission or board to administer the ordinance. The most important provision requires owners of buildings within historic districts to secure a "certificate of appropriateness" from the commission for the exterior alteration or demolition of structures. (See the excerpt from the Charleston ordinance quoted above.) Owners of vacant land must secure a certificate of appropriateness for new construction. Maintenance and repair requirements may also be included. Some statutes give the commission jurisdiction over construction on nearby property that affects the district. See *Reiter v. City of Beloit*, 947 P.2d 425 (Kan. 1997) (upholding zoning change for commercial use adjacent to historic residence). See also the model legislation in American Planning Ass'n, Growing Smart Legislative Guidebook: Model Statutes for Planning and Management of Change § 9-301 (S. Meck ed., 2002).

Notice how the certificate of appropriateness requirement shapes the legal issues that arise in historic districts. Failure to seek a certificate of appropriateness before demolishing a vacant building triggered a five-year legal battle in *City of Providence v. Estate of Tarro*, 973 A.2d 597, 606 (R.I. 2009) (insufficient evidence to support finding that school building in historic district was in " 'such hazardous condition as to create an immediate danger to the public' " (quoting the statute)). Refusal to issue a certificate to allow the demolition or modification of an historic structure can raise an as-applied claim that the refusal violated the takings or some other constitutional clause. Note also how the constitutional issues change here because an existing building is affected, not a proposal to develop vacant land.

Coordination with zoning is necessary if the historic district is not part of the zoning ordinance, which is usually the case. Coordination is difficult in some communities. See *Heritage Hill Ass'n v. City of Grand Rapids*, 211 N.W.2d 77 (Mich. 1977) (variance granted to allow demolition of building in historic district). Interagency agreements are one possibility. Another approach is to place the historic district regulations in the zoning ordinance. See *City of Santa Fe v. Gamble-Skogmo, Inc.*, 389 P.2d 13 (N.M. 1964) (zoning enabling act authorized historic district controls). New Jersey's zoning enabling act mandates that local boards give notice to other boards that are involved. N.J. Stat. Ann. § 40:55D-110.

First generation districts. The first decisions considered historic districts adopted for showplace historic settlements, and the courts had no difficulty upholding their constitutionality. In *Opinion of the Justices*, 128 N.E.2d 557 (Mass. 1955), the court upheld a historic district for the town of Nantucket. It noted "the sedate and quaint appearance of the old island town [that] has to a large extent still remained unspoiled." See also *City of New Orleans v. Pergament*, 5 So. 2d 129 (La. 1941) (Vieux Carr'e); *Opinion of the Justices*, 128

N.E.2d 563 (Mass. 1955) (Beacon Hill in Boston). Charleston is another first generation district.

Second generation districts. The rationale for historic districts shifted as the historic district movement spread to include areas that were not so old, quaint, and revered. In *Bohannan v. City of San Diego*, 106 Cal. Rptr. 333 (Cal. App. 1973), the court upheld the designation of the city's "Old Town" as an historic district. The court stressed the importance of the Old Town image as "a visual story of the beginning of San Diego" and "an educational exhibit of the birth place of California." The court also stressed benefits to tourism.

A more critical view. Historic districts have not been without critics. Tipson, *Putting the History Back in Historic Preservation*, 36 Urb. Law. 289 (2004), faults historic preservation for not having a coherent theory and for favoring economics and tourism over genuine preservation efforts. He attributes this to the inclusion of tourism as well as preservation as the purpose of many ordinances. In some historic towns, he notes, downtown businesses serving local residents have been displaced by businesses serving tourists. Santa Fe is an example. He also claims some historic preservation is revisionist and not true to historic styles. Consider these criticisms when you read the following case. It illustrates the rationale courts use when the area preserved has architectural or historic merit but is neither singular nor unique:

FIGARSKY v. HISTORIC DISTRICT COMMISSION

171 Conn. 198, 368 A.2d 163 (1976)

BARBER, ASSOCIATE JUSTICE:

The plaintiffs, owners of a house and lot located within the Norwich historic district, appealed to the Court of Common Pleas from a decision of the defendant commission denying their application for a certificate of appropriateness which would permit them to demolish the house. The court rendered judgment dismissing the appeal and the plaintiffs, upon the granting of certification, have appealed to this court.

The undisputed facts of the case are as follows: The Norwich historic district, established by the city of Norwich in 1967, pursuant to §§ 7-147a through 7-147m of the General Statutes, consists of the Norwichtown Green, which dates back to colonial days, and about one hundred buildings and lots surrounding, or in close proximity to, the green. The plaintiffs' property, which they purchased in 1963, is a two-story building zoned for commercial uses and is located just inside the bounds of the district. The property faces the green but is bounded on two sides by a McDonald's hamburger stand and parking lot. The building is in need of some repairs, which the Norwich building inspector has ordered the plaintiffs to undertake. Rather than make the repairs, however, the plaintiffs would prefer to demolish the building. In August, 1972, the plaintiffs applied to the building inspector for a demolition permit. The building inspector informed the plaintiffs that before such a permit could be issued a certificate of appropriateness was required. The plaintiffs, therefore, applied to the defendant for a certificate, filing their application with the building inspector on November 29, 1972. The defendant held a public hearing on the application on January 25, 1973. The hearing was attended by more than 100 persons, none of whom, except for the plaintiffs and their attorney, spoke in favor of granting the application. On the following day, the commission voted unanimously to deny the plaintiffs' application.

The plaintiffs maintain that the costs of the repairs necessary for the building are prohibitive. The building inspector has ordered the plaintiffs to repair the foundation and replace a door sill and hall floor, and the health department has ordered the plaintiffs to tie in to a newly accessible public sewer. At the hearing before the commission, the plaintiffs offered the testimony of a local contractor to the effect that the cost of these repairs, together with the cost of reroofing the building, would amount to between $15,000 and $18,000. The plaintiffs offered no evidence of the value of the house without repairs, its value if repaired, or the value of the lot if the building were razed. Nor did the plaintiffs disclose to the commission the use which they intended to make of the lot if the building were razed.

The commission also received numerous opinions from the plaintiffs' neighbors and from the Connecticut historical commission, the southeastern Connecticut regional planning agency, and the Connecticut society of architects, as to the historic value of the premises. The consensus of these opinions was that although the building itself is of little historic value or interest, it does, by virtue of its location, perform an important screening function, separating the green from an encroaching commercial district, and its preservation is important in maintaining the character of the historic district.[1] The commission stated its reasons for denying the application as follows: "The Commission is of the opinion that the building in question significantly contributes to the importance of the Norwichtown Green as an historic landmark, and the Commission would have violated its responsibilities as defined in [§§ 7-147a to 7-147k] to have permitted its demolition. In weighing all the considerations concerning this Application, the Commission was cognizant of [§ 7-147g, pertaining to permissible variations], but concluded that the hardships presented by the Applicant were not of sufficient magnitude to warrant granting approval for demolition."

Procedure upon an appeal from any decision of a historic district commission is the same as that for appeals from zoning boards. The controlling question which the trial court had to decide was whether the historic district commission had acted, as alleged in the appeal, illegally, arbitrarily and in abuse of the discretion vested in it. Since the trial court decided the appeal solely on the record returned by the commission and made only a limited finding of facts on the issue of aggrievement, review by this court must be based on the record of the

---

[1] A communication from the state historical commission stated, in part: "Competent authority has placed the date of construction in or about 1760 and identified the owner at that period as keeping an inn where lawyers at the nearby Court of Norwich were accommodated. On the exterior at least, the structure has undergone considerable alteration over the years but still retains its essential form and proportions, wholly in keeping with the scale and appearance of numerous other old buildings that border the Green area. Aside from the house proper, its site is of historic interest as occupying the original home lot of the Reverend James Fitch, religious leader of the first settlers. It often happens that buildings forming a recognizable grouping, as around a green, may not individually be especially notable for architecture or historical association. But together as a unified whole they constitute a significant entity, no part of which can be removed without a definite and usually adverse effect upon the character and appearance of the entire area. This is the condition that obtains in Norwich town.

"The commercially zoned district south and southeast of the site under consideration exhibits the unattractive characteristics of so many such areas, with disparate structures of poor design uncoordinated with one another and obtrusive advertising signs. It stands close upon the boundaries of the local historic district. If the property at 86 Town Street were demolished, it would remove the most important screening element between these evidences of low-grade commercialism and the attractiveness of the largely unspoiled Green. State recognition of the importance of this land has recently been affirmed by the erection of a historical marker under auspices of this Commission, which details the history of early years in Norwich and the central role of the Green in that history. Nomination of the entire area has been made to the National Register of Historic Places maintained by the Office of Archeology and Historic Preservation, National Park Service, United States Department of the Interior, under the National Historic Preservation Act of 1966, Public Law 89-665."

proceedings before the commission to determine whether the commission's decision is reasonably supported by the record.

In their appeal, the plaintiffs allege that they will be forced to undergo economic hardship and loss as a result of not being permitted to demolish their building, and that the historic district commission, in denying their application for a certificate of appropriateness, acted illegally, arbitrarily and in abuse of its discretion. Several claims of law which were overruled by the trial court are assigned as error. . . .

The plaintiffs' principal claim is that the Norwich historic district ordinance, implementing the state enabling act, is unconstitutional as applied to them, and that the denial of their application for a certificate of appropriateness to demolish their building amounts to a taking of their property for public use without compensation. More specifically, they contend that the ordinance is "vague aesthetic legislation," incapable of application in accordance with mandates of due process, and that because of the denial of their application they will be forced to expend large sums in the maintenance of their property without being able to put it to any practical use.

Neither the constitution of the United States, amendments five and fourteen, nor the constitution of Connecticut, article first, § 11, deny the state the power to regulate the uses to which an owner may devote his property. . . .

[At this point the court, citing *Euclid v. Ambler Realty Co.*, stated the usual police power maxims: all property is subject to the police power; regulations restricting the use of property "to some extent" are not a taking; courts will not substitute their judgment for a fairly debatable legislative judgment. The court also quoted the dictum from *Berman v. Parker*, which endorsed aesthetic regulation.] It is apparent from the language of the enabling statute[2] that the General Assembly, in enacting those statutes, was cognizant not only of the intangible benefits to be derived from historic districts, such as an increase in the public's awareness of its New England heritage, but of the economic benefits to be reaped as well, by augmenting the value of properties located within the old sections of the state's cities and towns, and encouraging tourism within the state. In a number of recent cases, it has been held that the preservation of a historical area or landmark as it was in the past falls within the meaning of general welfare and, consequently, the police power. We cannot deny that the preservation of an area or cluster of buildings with exceptional historical and architectural significance may serve the public welfare.

The plaintiffs argue that the Norwich ordinance constitutes "vague aesthetic legislation," and point to our statement in *DeMaria v. Planning & Zoning Commission*, 271 A.2d 105, 108, that "vague and undefined aesthetic considerations alone are insufficient to support the invocation of the police power" . . . . The "aesthetic considerations" involved in the Norwich ordinance are not, however, "vague and undefined"; § 7-147f of the General Statutes, incorporated by reference into the ordinance, sets out with some specificity the factors to be considered by the commission in passing upon an application for a certificate of appropriateness.[3] Nor . . . do "aesthetic considerations alone" provide the basis for the

---

(2) "[General Statutes] § 7-147a. Historic districts authorized . . . to promote the educational, cultural, economic and general welfare of the public through the preservation and protection of buildings, places and districts of historic interest by the maintenance of such as landmarks in the history of architecture, of the municipality, of the state or of the nation, and through the development of appropriate settings for such buildings, places and districts. . . ."

(3) "[General Statutes] § 7-147f. Considerations in determining appropriateness. If the commission determines that

ordinance. . . . Although we need not directly decide the issue in the present case, we note that other jurisdictions have recognized that "aesthetic considerations alone may warrant an exercise of the police power."

Having determined that the ordinance creating the Norwich historic district constitutes a valid exercise of the state's police power, we are left with the question of whether the application of that ordinance to the plaintiffs' property amounts to an unconstitutional deprivation of their property without compensation. In this context, it has often been noted that the police power, which regulates for the public good the uses to which private property may be put and requires no compensation, must be distinguished from the power of eminent domain, which takes private property for a public use and requires compensation to the owner. The difference is primarily one of degree, and the amount of the owner's loss is the basic criterion for determining whether a purported exercise of the police power is valid, or whether it amounts to a taking necessitating the use of the power of eminent domain. See Sax, "Takings and the Police Power," 74 Yale L.J. 36. "A regulation which otherwise constitutes a valid exercise of the police power may, as applied to a particular parcel of property, be confiscatory in that no reasonable use may be made of the property and it becomes of little or no value to the owner.["]

Whether the denial of the plaintiffs' application for a certificate of appropriateness to demolish their building has rendered the Norwich ordinance, as applied to them, confiscatory, must be determined in the light of their particular circumstances as they have been shown to exist. In regulating the use of land under the police power, the maximum possible enrichment of a particular landowner is not a controlling purpose. It is only when the regulation practically destroys or greatly decreases the value of a specific piece of property that relief may be granted, provided it promotes substantial justice. "The extent of that deprivation must be considered in light of the evils which the regulation is designed to prevent."

The plaintiffs had the burden of proving that the historic district commission acted illegally, arbitrarily, in a confiscatory manner or in abuse of discretion. This the plaintiffs failed to do. The plaintiffs went no further than to present evidence that their house was unoccupied and in need of extensive repairs. There was no evidence offered that the house, if repaired, would not be of some value, or that the proximity of the McDonald's hamburger stand rendered the property of practically no value as a part of the historic district.

The Norwich historic district commission, after a full hearing, lawfully, reasonably and honestly exercised its judgment. The trial court was correct in not substituting its own judgment for that of the commission.

---

the proposed erection, construction, restoration, alteration, razing or parking will be appropriate, it shall issue a certificate of appropriateness. In passing upon appropriateness as to exterior architectural features the commission shall consider, in addition to any other pertinent factors, the historical and architectural value and significance, architectural style, general design, arrangement, texture and material of the architectural features involved and the relationship thereof to the exterior architectural style and pertinent features of other structures in the immediate neighborhood. In passing upon appropriateness as to parking, the commission shall take into consideration the size of such parking area, the visibility of cars parked therein, the closeness of such area to adjacent buildings and other similar factors. A certificate of appropriateness may be refused for any building or structure, the erection, reconstruction, restoration, alteration or razing of which, or any parking which, in the opinion of the commission, would be detrimental to the interest of the historic district."

NOTES AND QUESTIONS

1. *Average reciprocity?* In *Penn Central*, Justice Brennan indicated that historic district legislation was constitutional because it produced "an equitable distribution of benefits and burdens." This comment is an apparent reference to the "average reciprocity of advantage" that supports zoning ordinances. The theory is that even though property owners in a historic district are burdened by a restrictive zoning regulation, they benefit from the restrictions on other properties; e.g., they may not be permitted to put a window air conditioner in the front window of their 18th Century colonial home, but they also do not have to worry about their next door neighbor painting their house pink.

How does this rationale apply when, as in *Figarsky*, the land uses in a historic district are mixed? Could you argue that allowing the demolition in *Figarsky* would have an unraveling effect that would destroy the historic integrity of the district? Is the balancing test adopted by the court still good law under *Penn Central*?

Does preventing demolition confer an "average reciprocity of advantage"? What if the owner of the house in *Figarsky* had been willing to build a new building with an identical exterior facade? See Gold, The *Welfare Economics of Historic Preservation*, 8 Conn. L. Rev. 348, 368 (1976) (concluding that historic district zoning "makes sound economic sense and is justifiable on grounds analogous to ordinary zoning," but that local political units "will tend to under-preserve since localities may discount benefits that accrue to outsiders" and thus a "combination of local, regional, and national spreading of the costs seems warranted"). See also Pogrebin, *An Opaque and Lengthy Road to Landmark Status*, N.Y. Times, Nov. 25, 2008, p. A1 (describing legal battle over seven-year delay by New York City Landmarks Preservation Commission in making decision regarding proposal to extend boundaries of Park Slope Historic District in Brooklyn).

For an examination of historic district designation decisions by the New York City Landmarks Preservation Commission, see Cocks, Preserving Racism: The New York City Landmarks Preservation Commission (unpublished Masters of Science in Urban Planning thesis, Columbia University 2009), *available at* www.jamescocks.com/thesis.pdf (last visited July 27, 2010). The author studied changes in the social composition of historic districts in New York City over a 40 year period during which over 22,000 properties were included in those districts. The author created a system of measuring social indicators of land use within historic districts relative to the rest of the city, both at the time of designation and in the decades following, and evaluated five basic categories: proximity to new development, racial composition, owner occupancy by race, education by race, and income by race. The author concluded that "[a]cross nearly every measure, [historic district] designations likely to favor residents have gone to whites, while designations unlikely to favor residents have gone to minorities. Even if the landmarks commission is not intentionally discriminating, the outcome of its actions is furthering a racial divide." *Id.* at 55.

An analysis of sales of one-, two-, and three-bedroom family houses in New York City from 1975 through 2002 by the New York City Independent Budget Office concluded that historic districting tended to have a positive impact on property values. "IBO found clear evidence that after controlling for property and neighborhood characteristics, market values of properties in historic districts were higher than those outside historic districts, . . . [b]ut there is not sufficient evidence to conclude that districting itself *causes* higher prices or greater price appreciation," the study concluded. New York City Independent Budget Office, Background Paper: the Impact of Historic Districts on Residential Property Values 8 (2003), available at www.ibo.nyc.ny.us (last visited Aug. 7, 2010) (italics in original).

As *Penn Central* and related cases suggest, historic districting and landmarks preservation can be, and often is, controversial. While on vacation during August, 2010, in Saugatuck, Michigan, a resort community in the southwestern part of the state on Lake Michigan, one of the authors saw a number of signs in front yards expressing strong opposition to a proposal to establish a historic district in the community.

2. *Historic residential neighborhoods.* Additional insight on these questions is provided by *A-S-P Assocs. v. City of Raleigh*, 258 S.E.2d 444 (N.C. 1979). A declaratory judgment was brought challenging the designation as a historic district of the "only intact neighborhood . . . composed primarily of Victorian houses" in the city. The neighborhood was undergoing revitalization. Although it did not fully embrace the "aesthetics is enough" rationale, the court upheld the ordinance, relying on *Penn Central* and *Berman v. Parker.* It added to the catalog of reasons for historic preservation, noting that it could stimulate revitalization and foster architectural creativity. Why?

Plaintiffs claimed the historic district was unreasonable as applied to them because they owned a vacant lot on which they planned to construct an office building. The court replied by relying on the *tout ensemble* doctrine adopted by the Louisiana courts. This doctrine recognizes that it is important to protect the setting or scene in which historic buildings are situated. Nor were property owners prohibited from constructing new buildings. "They are only required to construct them in a manner that will not result in a structure incongruous with the historic aspects of the Historic District." *Id.* at 451. What does this say about average reciprocity?

The court dismissed an equal protection argument based on the exclusion of adjacent historic buildings from the district. It relied on the usual rational relationship standard of equal protection review. The court also found no improper delegation of power, and followed the traditional view that the required statutory comprehensive plan could be found in the zoning regulations.

Emphasizing the limited nature of the delegation of state police power to historic district preservation commissions, a North Carolina court applied *A-S-P Assocs.* in striking down a new guideline regarding building height and scale adopted by a historic district commission as "more restrictive than [what] is allowed pursuant to the authority delegated by the General Assembly." *Meares v. Town of Beaufort*, 667 S.E.2d 239, 243 (N.C. App. 2008).

3. *Value enhancement.* Compare the holding in *M & N Enters., Inc. v. City of Springfield*, 250 N.E.2d 289 (Ill. App. 1969). The city designated a four-block area around Abraham Lincoln's Springfield home as a historic district. A majority of the area was residential and was zoned residential. Plaintiffs were denied a rezoning to construct a motel prior to the adoption of the historic district. They then applied for a conditional use and variance to construct a commercial wax museum and gift shop. The city took no action on this application, even though plaintiffs said that the building would have architectural features appropriate to the district. The court held the district constitutional:

> From our review of this record, we must conclude that the enhanced value of the plaintiff's property is directly related to . . . [the creation of the historic district]. The proximity of the property to the Lincoln Home increases its value, and yet it is clear that use not in conformity with the existing zoning would be detrimental to the Lincoln Home Area and the total concept of the municipality relating to historical preservation.

> When property has an enhanced value by reason of planning and zoning for historical preservation, the zoning ordinances to implement the planning can hardly be said to be confiscatory or unreasonable or unconstitutional simply because the owners seek to use it for commercial purposes to exploit the visitors and tourists attracted, in part at least, by the creation of the Historical District. [*Id.* at 293.]

Would the Supreme Court accept this rationale?

4. *Standard of review.* The *Figarsky* court held that a reviewing court must determine whether a historic district commission's decision "is reasonably supported by the record." Does that suggest the "fairly debatable" deferential standard employed in facial challenges of "legislative" zoning decisions (*cf. Euclid v. Ambler*, reproduced in Ch. 2, *supra*) or the less deferential standard employed in as-applied challenges to "administrative" zoning decisions (*cf. Nectow v. City of Cambridge*, discussed in Ch. 3 *supra*)?

In reversing the denial of a certificate of appropriateness to repave a gravel parking area with blacktop so as to alleviate parking and traffic problems on the property, the Connecticut Supreme Court, after quoting *Figarsky*'s "reasonably supported by the record" standard, stated that "[o]ur more recent case law distinguishes . . . a land use commissions' administrative and legislative functions." The court applied the "reasonably supported by the record" standard to legislative zoning decisions and added a "substantial evidence in the record" standard for administrative zoning decisions. *Felician Sisters of St. Francis of Conn., Inc. v. Historic Dist. Comm'n of Enfield*, 937 A.2d 39, 50 (Conn. 2008). The historic district commission had denied the plaintiffs' application to pave a gravel road and parking area, finding that the "pavement diminished the historic character of the property and the surrounding area." Concluding that the commission was acting in an administrative capacity, the court held that "although the defendant had jurisdiction over the plaintiffs' parking area . . . its denial of the plaintiffs' application was not supported by substantial evidence." The city had failed to consider that the overall size of the parking area would decrease and would be farther from the view of a historic streetscape and that added vegetation would shield the parking lot from public view.

The Connecticut Supreme Court also reversed the denial of a certificate of appropriateness in *Gibbons v. Historic Dist. Comm'n*, 941 A.2d 917, 928, 931 (Conn. 2008). The plaintiffs owned property in the town's historic district and applied for a certificate of appropriateness to relocate an existing building. The historic district commission denied the plaintiffs' application, finding that the relocation of the building would damage the historical integrity of the area. The court concluded that "the commission's stated reason for its denial [while within the authority granted to it in the historic district enabling statutes — Eds.] is not supported by substantial evidence in the record . . . ." The court found no evidence documenting the historic importance of the building that was to be relocated and, thus, the commission's denial was arbitrary and unreasonable. The court also objected to the "aesthetic nature" of commissioners' concerns.

In *Figarsky*, the Connecticut court held that the commission "lawfully, reasonably and honestly exercised its judgment." What changed between 1976 and 2008? Did the commissions in 2008 fail to exercise judgment "lawfully, reasonably and honestly," or did the Connecticut court's attitude about the appropriate standard of judicial revue change during that period?

See also *Ouellette v. Town of Kingston*, 956 A.2d 286, 294 (N.H. 2008), affirming a zoning board of adjustment's *de novo* review and reversal of a historic district commission's denial of a certificate of appropriateness for a new supermarket in a historic district. "Under the *de novo* standard the ZBA is not required to give deference to the findings or rulings of the HDC; substituting its judgment for the HDC or failing to discuss evidence before the HDC, therefore, does not constitute grounds for reversal," the court concluded. In a subsequent case involving the same parties, *Saunders v. Town of Kingston*, 2010 N.H. LEXIS 87 (N.H. 2010), the court affirmed a planning board decision to grant conditional site plan approval for the supermarket project. In *Friends of Bethany Place, Inc. v. City of Topeka*, 222 P.3d 535, 540 (Kan. App. 2010), the court reversed the trial court and found that "substantial evidence existed to support the decision [of the City] to grant the Church's requested permit [to construct a parking lot on land listed on the Register of Historic Kansas Places]." In *Rocky Hill Citizens for Responsible Growth v. Planning Board of the Borough of Rocky Hill*, 967 A.2d 929, 944–945 (N.J. Super. A.D. 2009), the court emphasized that "[o]ur review of the Board's action is limited" and concluded that "[n]ot only did the Planning Board apply the appropriate standards of the ordinance while reviewing [and approving] the [development] application, but the record supports these findings."

5. *Due process/takings problems.* Here are some examples of the problems likely to arise under historic district ordinances:

(a) The property owner seeks to build or remodel a building but does not wish to conform with architectural restrictions imposed in the historic district. This problem arose in *Gamble-Skogmo, supra.* Gamble-Skogmo wished to remodel their building in the historic district of the city but did not want to comply with a requirement that window panes not exceed thirty inches square. It argued that "such a minute detail of construction is only an attempt by the city to impose its idea of an aesthetic detail of architecture." The court answered:

> They ignore the fact that the window pane requirement is only one of very many details of the historical architectural style which it is said has evolved within the City of Santa Fe from about the year 1600 to the present, which the ordinance seeks to protect and preserve. So far as the record discloses, the window design is as much a part of the Santa Fe style as are flat roofs, projecting vigas, and wooden lintels. [*Id.* at 17.]

What kind of restriction on architectural detail is justified if styles in the historic district are mixed? Cf. *Parker v. Beacon Hill Arch. Ass'n*, 536 N.E.2d 1108 (Mass. 1989) (upholding denial of additional floor on row house because it would be inimical to historic appearance of building and diminish picturesque silhouette of row houses in this location). See also *Globe Newspaper Co. v. Beacon Hill Architectural Ass'n*, 659 N.E.2d 710 (Mass. 1996) (statute held to authorize ban on street furniture on Beacon Hill); *Collins v. Historic Dist. Comm'n of Carver*, 897 N.E.2d 1281 (Mass. App. 2008) (refusal to permit construction of single-family home on one lot of 8½ acre parcel not a taking); *Conner v. City of Seattle*, 223 P.3d 1201, 1211–1213 (Wash. App. 2009) (refusal to permit construction of three contemporary homes, each larger than a landmark-designated home on the same site, not a taking because alternatives existed enabling reasonable return on investment).

(b) The historic district ordinance contains a requirement that buildings in the district must be maintained to prevent deterioration. An objection to this kind of requirement was raised in *Maher v. City of New Orleans*, 516 F.2d 1051 (5th Cir. 1975). The court simply held that "[o]nce it has been determined that the purpose of the Vieux Carre legislation is a proper one, upkeep of buildings appears reasonably necessary to the accomplishment of the goals of the ordinance. . . . It may be that, in some set of circumstances, the expense of maintenance under the [o]rdinance — were the city to exact compliance — would be so unreasonable as to constitute a taking." *Id.* at 1066–67.

(c) A property owner in a historic district is ordered to repair a building that is in a deteriorated condition. In *Lafayette Park Baptist Church v. Scott*, 553 S.W.2d 856 (Mo. App. 1977), the church owned and sought to demolish a double-entry townhouse in a historic district that was in a deteriorated condition. Permission to demolish was denied by the board of adjustment, which noted that it was feasible to restore the building. This decision was reversed in a muddled opinion, the court noting that historic district regulations were akin to zoning and that "economic considerations cannot be wholly discounted." The ordinance "must be interpreted to authorize demolition when the condition of the structure is such that the economics of restoration preclude the landowner from making any reasonable use of the property." *Id.* at 862. The court also noted that the cost of rehabilitation would exceed $50,000 and "that this cost was economically unwarranted for the end product which would result." *Id.* at 863.

On what basis does the court reach this conclusion? If all of the dwellings in the historic area are rehabilitated, is it possible that their value after rehabilitation will be more than their existing value plus the cost of repair? Accord *Keeler v. Mayor & City Council*, 940 F. Supp. 879 (D. Md. 1996) (taking when no economically feasible rehabilitation plan possible). But see *City of Pittsburgh, Historic Review Comm'n v. Weinberg*, 676 A.2d 207 (Pa. 1996) (cost of renovation would not exceed value after renovation, owner knew of historic designation when bought property and could sell it for a profit). For discussion of historic preservation in declining neighborhoods, see Gold, *supra*, at 357–61.

(d) A property owner wishes to demolish his building so that he can put his land to a more profitable use. The principal case and *Maher, supra*, considered this problem. In *Maher* the court held:

> An ordinance forbidding the demolition of certain structures, if it serves a permissible goal in an otherwise reasonable fashion, does not seem on its face constitutionally distinguishable from ordinances regulating other aspects of land ownership, such as building height, set back or limitations on use. . . . Nor did Maher demonstrate . . . that a taking occurred because the ordinance so diminished the property value as to leave Maher, in effect, nothing. In particular, Maher did not show that the sale of the property was impracticable, that commercial rental could not provide a reasonable rate of return, or that other potential use of the property was foreclosed. [*Id.* at 1066.]

Wolk v. Reisem, 413 N.Y.S.2d 60 (App. Div. 1979), overturned a denial of permission to demolish a historic house that was vacant and vandalized and was set on fire, and found by the local building official to be unsafe and dangerous. The court held that vital interests in public health and safety took precedence over aesthetic and historic concerns. But see *Casey v. Mayor & City Council*, 929 A.2d at 107 (takings claim not ripe; historic designation does not equate with denial of demolition permit); *Park Home v. City of Williamsport*, 680 A.2d 835 (Pa. 1996) (refusal to allow demolition upheld; owners did not consider sale of property as alternative).

How does the Supreme Court's decision in *Lucas* and the concept of the "categorical" taking affect the cases in this Note? *Lucas* presumably means the Court will pay no attention to regulatory objectives if there is a denial of all beneficial or productive use. In which of the cases discussed above would this be true?

6. *Delegation of power objections.* Courts have usually rejected these claims. *A-S-P Assocs., supra* Note 2, is typical. The court upheld a "congruity" standard contained in the ordinance for the review of exterior building changes. It characterized this standard as "contextual" and added that the "incongruity" standard derived its meaning from "the total physical environment of the historic district." *Id.* at 54. The architectural "melange" in the district did not make the standard meaningless. How does this holding compare with the holding in *Stoyanoff*? *Issaquah*? Accord *Mayes v. City of Dallas*, 747 F.2d 323 (5th Cir. 1984) (facade and landscape standards).

[2.] Historic Landmarks

In addition to historic districts, municipalities also commonly have programs for the designation of individual historic landmarks not located in historic districts. Some states have adopted historic landmark legislation, which may authorize historic landmark regulation in a separate ordinance, see Cal. Gov't Code §§ 25373, 37361; SDCL 1-19B-20 through 27, applied in *City of Deadwood v. M.R. Gustafson Family Trust*, 777 N.W.2d 628, 631 (S.D. 2010) (statute does not require separate ordinance designating a historic property in order for local historic preservation commission to have jurisdiction over building on both national and state historic registers), or in the zoning ordinance, see N.J. Stat. Ann. § 40:55D-65.1.

Local controls for historic landmark preservation are similar to those for historic districts. Landmark preservation ordinances and statutes authorize landmark designation and require a certificate of appropriateness from the historic preservation commission for any exterior changes and for demolition. Landmark owners may be required to keep them in good repair. To avoid takings problems, restrictions on landmarks may not apply if they do not allow the owner a reasonable return. Hardship variances may be authorized to avoid takings problems. The statutory emphasis on maintaining building exteriors may lead a court to hold there is no statutory authority to regulate building interiors. *United Artists' Theater Circuit, Inc. v. City of Philadelphia*, 635 A.2d 612 (Pa. 1994). This can create problems with historic residences, many of which have small, separated rooms not typical of modern living. If the owner of the residence guts the interior and replaces it with modern living space, which has reportedly happened in some communities, does this violate the "spirit" of historic preservation if the exterior is maintained? See Note, *"Avoiding the Disneyland Facade": The Reach of Architectural Controls Exercised by Historic Districts Over Internal Features of Structures*, 8 Wid. L. Symp. J. 323 (2002).

Most courts have also upheld historic district ordinances against delegation of power and vagueness objections. *County of Stutsman v. State Historical Soc'y*, 371 N.W.2d 321 (N.D. 1985), held that legislation authorizing the designation of sites of "historic value" was not unconstitutionally vague because these words could be given their common meaning. An involuntary historic designation ordinance, adopted to designate a house as a historic landmark, was upheld against vagueness challenges in *Kruse v. Town of Castle Rock*, 192 P.3d 591, 599 (Colo. App. 2008). In a facial analysis, the court held that the ordinance was not void for vagueness because "when the criteria for involuntary historic designation are read in conjunction with the general criteria for historic designation, the [ordinance] provides property owners with fair notice that their property may be designated a historic landmark if one or more of the criteria are satisfied." Deciding the as-applied challenge, the court found that the house met the historic designation criteria because it was one of the oldest remaining buildings in the area. *Id.* at 601-602. In *Conner v. City of Seattle*, 223 P.3d 1201 (Wash. App. 2009), a Washington court made the following point:

> Connor's argument, in its essence, is that the [landmarks preservation ordinance] is impermissibly vague because it does not tell him exactly what he can do with his property. This is not the test. The question is whether Connor can ascertain the requirements for an acceptable project. The [ordinance] contains both contextual standards and a process for clarification and guidance as to individual sites. From these, a landowner can ascertain what changes may be made. The constitution requires no more. [223 P.3d at 1211.]

Contra *Texas Antiquities Comm. v. Dallas Community College Dist.*, 554 S.W.2d 924 (Tex. 1977) (statute regulating disposition of "all . . . buildings . . . of historical . . . interest" that contains no predictable standard or safeguard is unconstitutionally vague).

In *Hanna v. City of Chicago*, 907 N.E.2d 390, 397 (Ill. App. 2009), an Illinois court held that a complaint alleging the Chicago landmark district ordinance was unconstitutionally vague on its face stated a cause of action because the city "offered no criteria by which a person of common intelligence may determine from the face of the Ordinance whether a building or district will be deemed to have value or importance . . . ." Davey, *Challenge to Landmark Law Worries Preservationists*, N.Y. Times, March 24, 2009. As noted in Chapter 3, Illinois is one of a only a few states that employ a less-deferential, and presumably pro-developer, standard of review of zoning decisions in which courts apply a multiple-factor test. The Illinois standard is discussed in Jaffe, *Zoning, Chicago-Style:* Hanna v. City of Chicago, Land Use L. & Zoning Dig., July 2001, at 6 (analyzing earlier case involving down-zoning). The Chicago landmarks ordinance challenged on vagueness grounds contained typical language tracking the criteria used by the Interior Department in administering the National Register of Historic Landmarks.

> Section 2-120-620 provides for the seven criteria the Commission should use in considering a designation. Those seven criteria are characterized as (1) critical part of the City's heritage, (2) significant historic event, (3) significant person, (4) important architecture, (5) important architect, (6) distinctive theme as a district, and (7) unique visual feature. [907 N.E.2d at 393; Email from Prof. Jaffe to one of the authors, Aug. 3, 2010.]

Is this decision merely another example of the Illinois courts' less-deferential approach to land use regulation, or does it raise more fundamental questions about the landmarks preservation process? The Illinois Supreme Court refused to hear an appeal. 910 N.E.2d 1127 (2009).

NOTES AND QUESTIONS

1. *The takings issue.* Takings questions in landmark preservation present special problems. Reciprocity of advantage may not help avoid a takings claim because historic landmarks usually are isolated and, as in *Penn Central*, surrounded by buildings that make more intensive use of the land. Historic landmark regulation may then present the classic case of a regulation that benefits the general public but concentrates burdens on a single landowner.

Penn Central Transp. Co. v. City of New York, reproduced in Ch. 2, upheld the New York City landmarks preservation law against takings objections but did not consider demolition. The Court found no taking partly because the owners of Grand Central Station could continue its use, which the owners admitted was profitable. The Court also noted that the station owners could reapply for a less intrusive building over the station, and that the opportunity to transfer development rights "undoubtedly mitigate whatever financial burdens the law has imposed . . .

and, for that reason are to be taken into account in considering the impact of regulation." 438 U.S. at 137.

An important Second Circuit case rejected "taking" and "free exercise of religion" objections to historic preservation. In *St. Bartholemew's Church v. City of New York*, 728 F. Supp. 958 (S.D.N.Y. 1989), *aff'd*, 914 F.2d 348 (2d Cir. 1990), the church challenged the New York Landmarks Commission's refusal to allow the church to demolish its seven-story "community house," located on the same lot as the church itself, and to construct a high-rise office building in its place. The church argued that the Commission's action effected a "taking" because it deprived the church of its ability to earn a "reasonable return" on its investment, and that it violated the Free Exercise Clause because it "impaired the church's ability to carry on and expand the ministerial and charitable activities that are central to its religious mission." On the takings issue, the Court of Appeals rejected the church's arguments that (1) the amount and configuration of usable space in its Community House was "insufficient to accommodate the church's various programs," and (2) that "the necessary repairs to the physically deteriorating Community House would be prohibitively expensive" and beyond the church's financial ability if it were to continue its other programs. The Court of Appeals held the church had failed to show it could no longer conduct its charitable activities or carry out its religious mission in its existing facilities. The court based this holding explicitly on *Penn Central*, where, said the Court of Appeals, the Supreme Court held that "the constitutional question is whether the land use regulation impairs the continued operation of the property in its originally expected use."

Takings objections to refusals to allow the demolition of non-religious buildings are not likely to succeed in most cases. The courts have not found a per se taking under *Lucas* or the *Penn Central* takings factors when renovation of the historic structure was economically feasible, or when there were profitable alternatives to demolition. In *City of Pittsburgh, Historic Review Comm'n v. Weinberg*, 676 A.2d 207 (Pa. 1996), for example, the court did not find a taking because the cost of renovation would not exceed the value of the property after renovation, and the owner could sell it for a profit. The court also noted that "[o]ur decision is bolstered by the fact that prior to the time of their purchase, Appellees knew that the Gateway House had been given an historic designation and were aware of the consequences of such a designation." This is the notice rule, which is not a per se block to a takings claim after *Palazzolo*. Accord *District Intown Props. Ltd. Partnership. v. District of Columbia*, 198 F.3d 874 (D.C. Cir. 1999), where the court upheld the denial of building permits to build townhouses on the site of an historic landmark. It found the property was not denied all economically beneficial use under the *Lucas* per se rule and that no taking occurred under the *Penn Central* takings factors. The court noted that at the time of purchase, the purchasers knew or should have known that the District's historic landmark laws "limited expectations of development." Contra *Keeler v. Mayor & City Council*, 940 F. Supp. 879 (D. Md. 1996) (taking when no economically feasible rehabilitation plan).

2. *Religious uses.* Landmark preservation of religious structures also raises free exercise issues. On these issues, the Court of Appeals in *St. Barholomnew's* held that the Landmarks Law was "a facially neutral regulation of general applicability within the meaning of Supreme Court decisions" which, "as applied," did not violate the Free Exercise Clause since there was no showing of discriminatory motive, coercion with respect to religious practice, or deprivation of the church's ability to carry out its religious mission in its existing facilities. Other recent cases have refused to recognize free exercise claims. See *First Church of Christ, Scientist v. Ridgefield Historic Dist. Comm'n*, 738 A.2d 224 (Super. Ct. 1998), *aff'd*, 737 A.2d 989 (Conn.

App. 1999) (upholding refusal to allow church to install vinyl clad siding in historic district).

Two earlier New York Court of Appeals cases reached somewhat inconsistent results when churches wished to demolish buildings so they could erect new buildings on the sites. In *Lutheran Church in America v. City of New York*, 316 N.E.2d 305 (N.Y. 1974), the court allowed demolition because the existing building was no longer adequate for its use. Later, in *Society of Ethical Culture v. Spatt*, 415 N.E.2d 922 (N.Y. 1980), decided after *Penn Central*, the court reached a contrary result on similar facts.

3. *State cases protecting religious uses.* In *First Covenant Church of Seattle v. City of Seattle*, 787 P.2d 1352 (Wash. 1990), the court held the church was entitled to a declaratory judgment invalidating the designation of its church as a landmark structure because, on its face, the ordinances violated the church's rights under both the First Amendment and under Washington's state constitution. The Supreme Court then granted a writ of certiorari and remanded the case to the Washington Supreme Court "for further consideration in light of *Employment Division, Dept. of Human Resources of Oregon v. Smith*, 494 U.S. 872 (1990)." *Smith* is the famous "peyote" case, where the Court held that government may constitutionally restrict certain activities associated with the practice of religion, pursuant to its general regulatory power, by a non-discriminatory, generally applicable law that happens to prohibit religiously motivated actions. (Congress' attempt to overrule the *Smith* case was declared unconstitutional in *City of Boerne v. Flores*, discussed in Chapter 3. Although *Boerne* began as an historic preservation dispute, that issue was not before the Supreme Court.)

On remand, the Washington Supreme Court, by a 4-3 vote, again struck down the landmark preservation ordinances as they affected the church in an extended set of opinions reported in 840 P.2d 174 (Wash. 1992), and distinguished both *Smith* and *St. Bartholemew's Church.* Its state constitutional provision, said the Washington court, expressly provides that "only the government's interest in peace or safety or in preventing licentious acts can excuse an imposition on religious liberty." See also *Munns v. Martin*, 930 P.2d 318 (Wash. 1997) (potential 14-month delay in issuance of building permit to demolish catholic school so pastoral house could be built held to violate free exercise); *Society of Jesus v. Boston Landmarks Comm.*, 564 N.E.2d 571 (Mass. 1990) (designation of church interior as landmark violates Free Exercise Clause when adopted to prevent renovation).

Is there a convergence in the takings and free exercise cases? Do both lines of cases turn on how courts view the "burdens" placed on religious uses by land use regulations? See Homer, *Landmarking Religious Institutions: The Burden of Rehabilitation and the Loss of Religious Freedom*, 28 Urb. Law. 327 (1996); Note, *"Their Preservation is Our Sacred Trust" — Judicially Mandated Free Exercise Exemptions to Historic Preservation Ordinances under Employment Division v. Smith*, 45 B.C. L. Rev 205 (2003). Religious use issues are covered in Chapter 3.

Statutes may protect religious organizations from landmark designation. *East Bay Asian Local Development Corp. v. State of California*, 13 P.3d 1122 (Cal. 2000), held that statutes prohibiting landmark designation without the consent of a religious organization did not violate the First Amendment Establishment Clause. Landmark preservation was a burden on religious use, and the prohibition was not an unconstitutional advancement of religion by the state just because a property could be used for a religious message. It was also irrelevant that a religious landmark owner might enjoy an economic advantage over secular owners of landmark properties. Applying *East Bay*, a California court held that San Francisco had no authority to prevent demolition of the 90-year-old First St. John's United Methodist Church by designating it a landmark. *California-Nevada Annual Conference of United Methodist Church v. City and County of San Francisco*, 94 Cal. Rptr. 3d 64, 69 (Cal. App. 2009). The statutory exemption from landmark status includes "noncommercial . . . property that is no longer used or capable of being used for a religious purpose but which may be sold and demolished for a profit," the court ruled.

4. *Incentives for historic preservation.* Regulation alone may not be enough to preserve historic resources. One alternative is the use of historic conservation easements on the exterior facade. The easement gives a private organization or a government agency the right to review any changes in the exterior building facade. More than half the states have legislation authorizing easements for conservation or historic purposes, and elsewhere, the common law of easements allows similar restrictions. Sometimes, preservation easements are donated by a public-spirited owner, in which case a federal tax deduction may be available to the donor, providing savings on federal income and estate taxes. Otherwise, the easement can be purchased just as any other property interest and compensation paid. Easements also may be used to preserve landscapes.

An important financial incentive is the federal Historic Preservation Tax Credit, I.R.C. § 47, discussed *infra*, which provides a credit against income tax of 20% of the "qualified rehabilitation expenditures with respect to any certified historic structure [listed on the National Register of Historic Places]" made by a taxpayer. I.R.C § 47(a)(2). Some states have enacted companion state historic preservation tax credits. See, e.g., Missouri Certified Historic Rehabilitation Tax Credit, R.S. Mo. §§ 253.545–253.559 (25% credit). The ability to transfer tax credits enables real estate developers to sell the credits and thereby attract private investment for rehabilitation of historic buildings.

Property tax abatements, exemptions, and assessment freezes for historic buildings also have been authorized in more than half the states. Property tax relief can offset any decline in value resulting from the landmark designation of a historic property and can avoid property tax increases resulting from rehabilitation or renovation.

The basis for property tax relief varies, and the effectiveness of tax relief programs is mixed, as there is considerable variation in the amount of tax abatement allowed. See Stockford, *Property Tax Abatement of Conservation Easements*, 17 B.C. Envtl. Aff. L. Rev. 823 (1990).

5. *Sources.* Lovelady, *Broadened Notion of Historic Preservation and the Role of Neighborhood Conservation Districts*, 40 Urb. Law. 147 (2008); Callies, *Historic Preservation Law in the United States*, 32 Envt. L. Rep. 10348 (2002); Linder, *New Directions for Preservation Law: Creating an Environment Worth Experiencing*, 20 Envtl. L. 4 (1990); Skelly, *Promoting Innovative Historic Preservation Ordinance*, Zoning News, Jan., 2002; Comment, *The Free Exercise Clause and Historic Preservation Law: Suggestions For a More Coherent Free Exercise Analysis*, 72 Tul. L. Rev. 1767 (1998); Note, *From Monuments to Urban Renewal: How Different Philosophies of Historic Preservation Impact the Poor*, 8 Geo. J. Poverty Law & Pol'y 257 (2001); Note, *Regionalism and Historic Preservation: How History is Given Greater Weight in Different Regions of the Country*, 8 Wid. L. Symp. J. 347 (2002).

A NOTE ON FEDERAL HISTORIC PRESERVATION PROGRAMS

National Historic Preservation Act. The federal government has had an interest in historic preservation for some time. Early statutes include the Historic Sites Act of 1935, 16 U.S.C. §§ 461-67, which authorizes the Department of Interior to conduct surveys and acquire property; and the Antiquities Act of 1906, 16 U.S.C. §§ 431-33, which authorizes the President to designate and implement a permit system for national monuments.

The centerpiece of federal historic preservation programs is the National Historic Preservation Act (NHPA), 16 U.S.C. §§ 470–470w, which created a National Register of Historic Places, a national Advisory Council on Historic Preservation, and a federally-funded program of state historic preservation officers to administer state programs. The act requires federal agencies to take into account the "effect" of federal "undertakings" on historic districts, sites and buildings listed on the National Register. The Act also applies to private projects that receive federal financing or permits. It establishes a National Register of Historic Places and a National Advisory Council on Historic Preservation and authorizes state historic preservation programs headed by a State Historic Preservation Officer (SHPO). Council regulations require federal agencies, with the SHPO, to identify an "area of potential effects" of any covered activity and evaluate any "adverse effect" the activity may have on historic sites within the area. 36 C.F.R. §§ 800.4, 800.5. An adverse effect includes any change in the use or physical features of an historic property that contributes to its historic significance. *Id.* § 800.5(a)(2)(iv).

If an adverse effect is found, the agency must consult with the Advisory Council and the SHPO in an attempt to minimize or avoid the adverse effect. A Memorandum of Agreement may be entered into to resolve any identified adverse effects. If no Memorandum of Agreement is reached, the Advisory Council may comment on the adverse effects on historic properties, and the agency shall take them in to account in making its decision. The agency need not adopt the Council's recommendations, however. The Act primarily provides a review process intended to improve preservation of historic properties in federal programs. It is not a regulatory process like local historic preservation ordinances. For discussion, see Note, *Federal Preservation Law: Sites, Structures & Objects*, 8 Wid. L. Symp. J. 383 (2002).

Section 4(f) of the Department of Transportation Act. This act, codified in 49 U.S.C. § 303(c), requires a review process similar to a NEPA review when a federally funded transportation project, such as a highway, crosses or affects a historic site or other designated environmental area, such as parks. The difference from the NHPA is that the Department may not approve a project affecting an historic site unless there is no feasible or prudent alternative. This is a substantive requirement that creates a legal presumption that protected areas must be avoided. *Citizens to Preserve Overton Park v. Volpe*, 401 U.S. 402 (1971). Some commentators claim, however, that judicial decisions interpreting the act have been too lenient. Gerken, *Loopholes You Could Drive a Truck Through: Systematic Circumvention of Section 4(f) Protection of Parklands and Historic Resources*, 22 Urb. Law. 121 (2000).

Income Tax Credit. The Internal Revenue Code, I.R.C. § 47, provides investment tax credits for certified rehabilitation expenses on historic buildings. The tax credit drove many historic building renovation projects until the law was amended in the 1986 Tax Reform Act by placing restrictions on who can claim the credit and by limiting the income the credit can offset. As a result, the number of rehabilitation projects using the credit has declined substantially. See Mann, Tax *Incentives for Historic Preservation: An Antidote to Sprawl?*, 8 Wid. L. Symp. J. 207 (2002).

[3.] Transfer of Development Rights as a Historic Preservation Technique

Transfer of development rights programs (TDR) are an imaginative concept that attempt to avoid takings problems by compensating landmark owners through the sale of development rights on landmark properties. Although TDR first attracted attention when the constitutionality of landmark preservation was problematic, the problem is more than constitutional, as the following comment indicates:

> Because the typical landmark building makes only partial use of the floor area allotted to its site, it often cannot compete for survival in an overheated real estate market. Intense development pressure means higher land values that present an irresistible economic temptation to owners of small parcels. Because zoning bonuses [available through incentive zoning — Eds.] can be efficiently exploited only on large parcels, developers hasten to assemble a number of smaller parcels to realize the greatest possible advantage from the system. The result . . . is inevitable: demolition of what remains of our architectural heritage. [Note, *Development Rights Transfer and Landmarks Preservation — Providing a Sense of Orientation*, 9 Urb. L. Ann. 131, 139 (1975).]

What TDR does. The TDR concept is straightforward and deceptively simple. Development rights available under the zoning ordinance on an underdeveloped historic landmark site are purchased by the owner of another site, where they may be used to supplement the development rights available under existing zoning at that site. The landmark site is called the sending site and the site to which the development rights are transferred is called the receiving or transfer site.

TDR programs may contain additional features to ensure their successful operation. The owner of a landmark on a sending site may be required to convey preservation restrictions to the city, for which the owner receives a property tax abatement. A development rights bank may be established to sell and buy development rights. The bank supports the TDR market, which may not always operate in a satisfactory manner. The development rights to be used at the receiving site may be limited to avoid excessive densities in areas where the development rights are transferred. Valuation of the development rights transferred also is a problem. For historic landmarks, one technique is to base valuation on the excess building bulk allowable at the sending site under the zoning ordinance. Whether the landmark owner must receive compensation equivalent to that which is constitutionally required under the Takings Clause is not clear.

The transaction costs — finding a buyer, paying a broker, negotiating the deal, documenting the transfer, closing the conveyance, paying lawyers — can be considerable. Also, because few rights typically are available for transfer and transfer sights tend to be limited in number, the market often is unclear and unstable.

Typical programs. New York City has had a TDR program for historic landmarks for some years, but the concept first attracted national attention when law professor John Costonis proposed a TDR program for Chicago landmarks in Space Adrift (1974). Chicago did not adopt the program, and TDR is used less often in historic preservation programs than it is in programs for the preservation of agricultural and other environmental resource areas. The use of TDR for preservation of environmentally-sensitive land is discussed in Chapter 4.

TDR programs for historic landmarks differ significantly. Under the New York program, development rights transfer is allowed from sites occupied by historic landmarks to adjacent lots, which, generally, may be contiguous lots or lots across a street. Transfers are approved by the City Planning Commission through a special permit process. An application for a transfer must include a program providing for the maintenance of the landmark, a report from the Landmarks Preservation Commission and plans for the development of the receiving site. Though there is considerable demand for increased density, most of this occurs through a zoning-lot merger process rather than through TDR, and only about a dozen TDR transfers have been made. R. Pruetz, Beyond Takings and Givings 221-24 (2003).

The San Francisco program is quite different.

> In 1985, San Francisco adopted a downtown plan which designated 253 buildings in the downtown as architecturally significant. It is very difficult to alter or destroy a historically-significant building; this gives the owners of landmarks an incentive to transfer their development rights. In addition, the 1985 plan reduced the amount of density that new buildings can achieve as a matter of right under the zoning code; this lower by-right density motivates developers to buy TDRs because there are no mechanisms, other than TDR, for exceeding these limits. Unlike many historic TDR programs, the San Francisco program allows development rights to be transferred between any lots in the same district. The approval process is ministerial and developers have come to regard it as a routine real-estate transaction. [*Id.* at 224.]

Ten historic landmarks had been preserved under the program as of 1995, and an additional one million square feet or so of development rights have been transferred or are pending transfer, making this program one of the most successful historic landmark TDR program in the country. *Id.* at 226.

Statutory authority. Although municipalities can adopt TDR programs under their zoning powers, enabling legislation for TDR can provide the necessary statutory authority, and can provide statutory guidelines to ensure that TDR will be used fairly and effectively. Some state legislation simply authorizes TDR without providing detailed implementation requirements. E.g., Idaho Code § 67-4619; S.D. Codified Laws § 1-19B-26; Wash. Rev. Code § 36.70A.090 (comprehensive plan should provide for innovative techniques, including TDRs).

Other states provide detailed guidance. For example, New York legislation for its municipalities requires that a TDR ordinance must be in accordance with a comprehensive plan, that a receiving district must have adequate public facilities and other resources to accommodate the transferred development rights, that the impact of the TDR program on affordable housing must be considered and adjusted, and that a generic environmental impact statement for the receiving area must be maintained under the state environmental review law. Sending and receiving areas must be specifically designated, and transfer procedures must be provided. An easement transferring development rights at the sending parcel and a certificate documenting the development rights transferred to the receiving parcel must be prepared and recorded. A development rights bank is authorized, and the assessed value of land affected by a TDR must be adjusted. See, e.g., N.Y. Gen. City Law § 20-f. For other detailed legislation, see, e.g., 65 Ill. Comp. Stat. Ann. §§ 5/11-48.2-1 to 48.2-7; Ky. Rev. Stat. Ann. § 100.208. The statutes usually authorize TDR programs for environmental land preservation as well as historic preservation. Consider, as you review the materials that follow, how a statute of this type can affect the constitutional issues. See Bredin, *Transfer of Development Rights: Cases, Statutes, Examples*, Am. Plan. Ass'n PAS Memo, Nov. 1998; American Planning Ass'n, Growing Smart Legislative

Guidebook: Model Statutes for Planning and Management of Change § 9-401 (S. Meck ed., 2002).

NOTES AND QUESTIONS

1. *Constitutional problems at the receiving site.* Many of the constitutional problems raised by TDR have centered on takings problems raised by the owners of sending sites. These problems are considered in the case that follows these notes. Constitutional problems also arise at the receiving site:

(a) *Uniformity.* TDR imposes a dual standard on lots in the transfer district. Developers may build at existing zoning levels without purchasing development rights, but may build more intensively only if development rights are purchased. Is there a uniformity problem? Dean Costonis argues that the uniformity objection has no merit, and relies on cases sustaining the constitutionality of PUD ordinances against uniformity objections. See Ch. 7, sec. C. "A development transfer district is, in effect, a special development district in which bulk is redistributed in accordance with the density zoning technique. It encompasses an area of the community that is unique because of the concentration there of many of the community's landmark buildings." Costonis, *The Chicago Plan: Incentive Zoning and the Preservation of Landmarks*, 85 Harv. L. Rev. 574, 623 (1972). Does this argument hold if TDR is used for purposes other than landmark preservation?

(b) *Due process and takings.* The requirement that lot owners at receiving sites purchase additional development rights in order to carry out more intensive development may raise due process and takings problems:

> If the existing zoning is sound, it may be claimed, relaxing bulk restrictions on transferee sites will overload public services and distort the urban landscape. . . . If it is too stringent, the proper course is to raise prevailing bulk limitations within the area generally and, in the process, to remove unwarranted public restrictions on the rights of property owners there. [Costonis, *supra*, at 628.]

Costonis argues against this conclusion, pointing out that "it invests the numbers in the zoning code with an aura of scientific exactitude that is largely without foundation in fact." *Id.* at 629. Therefore, "the bulk increments allotted to development rights purchasers fall within a range that is defensible in planning terms." *Id.* at 630. In other words, communities may set zoning densities within a higher and lower range. If densities are set at the lower range, so that purchase of development rights is required to build at the higher range, no constitutional problem results. For arguments that the cost of development rights to the transfer owner is justified as a way of eliminating externalities in development and as a tax on unearned increment, see Costonis, *Development Rights Transfer: Description & Perspectives for a Critique*, Urb. Land, Jan., 1975, at 5, 9.

Due process and takings problems at receiving sites may be more serious if the community must first downzone existing densities in order to create a market for the purchase of development rights at these sites. For a discussion of downzoning, see Ch. 6. How do the Supreme Court's recent takings cases affect the answer to these problems? See the discussion of the *Suitum* case in Note 4 following the next principal case.

Consider *Barancik v. County of Marin*, 872 F.2d 834 (9th Cir. 1988). A zoning ordinance required a 60-acre lot minimum in a ranching area but included a TDR program under which owners of land in the area could acquire additional development rights. A rancher wanted to build on 20-acre lots, but was unwilling to pay enough to purchase the additional rights necessary for this density. He sued after the county denied a rezoning to a 20-acre lot size. The court held the TDR program did not increase the total amount of development in the area, was rationally related to agricultural preservation, and was not an exaction falling under the *Nollan* case because payment was to a private owner, not the state.

2. *Equity issues.* Developers at receiving sites may have to pay more for development rights than their fair market value. If the excess cost is passed on to later purchasers, can TDR be faulted on equity grounds?

> [TDR] costs are even more inequitably skewed when compared to the total proportion of a given population that is beneficiary to TDR's presumed preservation services. Theoretically, a protected resource such as scenic open space or a historic mansion is a public good. That is, it is a commodity which, "if available to anyone, is equally available to all others." To be sure, in practice TDR's preserved resources are not likely to be equally accessible to *all* income or age groups in a jurisdiction. But it is just as certain that those who do have access and can visually enjoy a verdant meadow or an Italianate Victorian townhouse compose a considerably larger population than the burdened groups identified under compensatory and redistributive TDR measures. Therefore, it would seem compellingly apparent that TDR schemes of whatever stripe are likely to fail a test of equitability based on the criterion of benefits derived. [Gale, *The Transfer of Development Rights: Some Equity Considerations*, 14 Urb. L. Ann. 81, 94 (1977).]

3. *Does TDR avoid a taking?* Simulated market analysis of TDR plans casts additional light on whether the value of TDRs will fully compensate owners who are restricted from the full development of their land in TDR programs. Berry & Steiker, *An Economic Analysis of Transfer of Development Rights*, 17 Nat. Resources J. 55 (1977), examine a hypothetical TDR system in which the entire jurisdiction is subject to a TDR program and no development may occur without the purchase of development rights from landowners in areas restricted from development. The authors are skeptical that the transfer value of development rights under this kind of system will provide adequate compensation to owners of restricted land. A number of factors will determine whether exchange values for these rights will fully compensate these restricted owners, including "the revenues generated and costs associated with development, the amount of land put in the no-growth zone, and the number of development rights created." *Id.* at 73. However, if applied on a limited scale, as in site-to-site transfer situations such as those contemplated in the *French* and *Penn Central* cases, the exchange value of development rights can be expected to approach full compensation, so long as the local land market is relatively active. *Id.*

The authors also note that in order for the exchange value of development rights to yield sufficient compensation to restricted owners, the supply of those rights must be carefully managed with reference to the market demand for those rights. This kind of management requires public intervention to withhold rights from the market:

> The withholding action may be by 1) public purchase of development rights at some "parity price," 2) refusing to give out (or create) all the development rights in the first place, or 3) only the agency selling development rights and limiting sales so as to gain a high rent; the monopolist would then distribute the rents to the landowners in the no-growth zone in proportion to their losses of exchange value. All three remedies

require administrative costs and the first requires a large initial expenditure (or bond issue) before substantial revenue from sales can be obtained. [*Id.* at 64 n.23.]

Note that management problems may be serious even in a site-to-site TDR program aimed at protecting historic landmarks. As the number of landmarks protected by the program increases, the impact of the sale of development rights from these landmarks on the land market will also increase, and substantial public management may be necessary in order to guarantee full compensation to restricted landmark owners. See Conrad & LeBlanc, *The Supply of Development Rights: Results From a Survey in Hadley, Massachusetts*, 55 Land Econ. 269 (1979). The survey indicated that transferred development rights would sell at a price close to the cost of full acquisition. They suggest alternative strategies, such as acquisition with resale after the development rights have been removed. See also Thorsnes & Simons, *Letting The Market Preserve Land: The Case For a Market-Driven Transfer of Development Rights Program*, 17 Contemp. Econ. Pol'y 256 (1999); Field & Conrad, *Economic Issues in Programs of Transferable Development Rights*, 51 Land Econ. 331 (1975). For an argument that "[a] workable TDR plan would give the planning board or similar body the right of first refusal on the purchase of development rights from any owner of property in the preservation zone," see Merriam, *Making TDR Work*, 56 N.C. L. Rev. 77, 134–138 (1978).

One purpose of TDR programs is to avoid the takings objections by owners of sending sites who are restricted by landmark preservation programs. Will TDR always eliminate these objections? The following case may provide some answers.

FRED F. FRENCH INVESTING CO. v. CITY OF NEW YORK

39 N.Y.2d 587, 350 N.E.2d 381,
appeal dismissed, 429 U.S. 990 (1976)

BREITEL, CHIEF JUDGE:

Plaintiff Fred F. French Investing Co., purchase money mortgagee of Tudor City, a Manhattan residential complex, brought this action to declare unconstitutional a 1972 amendment to the New York City Zoning Resolution and seeks compensation as for "inverse" taking by eminent domain. The amendment purported to create a "Special Park District," and rezoned two private parks in the Tudor City complex exclusively as parks open to the public. It further provided for the granting to the defendant property owners of transferable development (air) rights usable elsewhere. It created the transferable rights by severing the above-surface development rights from the surface development rights, a device of recent invention. . . .

Tudor City is a four-acre residential complex built on an elevated level above East 42nd Street, across First Avenue from the United Nations in mid-town Manhattan. Planned and developed as a residential community, Tudor City consists of 10 large apartment buildings housing approximately 8,000 people, a hotel, four brownstone buildings, and two 15,000 square-foot private parks. The parks, covering about 18 1/2% of the area of the complex, are elevated from grade and located on the north and south sides of East 42nd Street, with a connecting viaduct. . . .

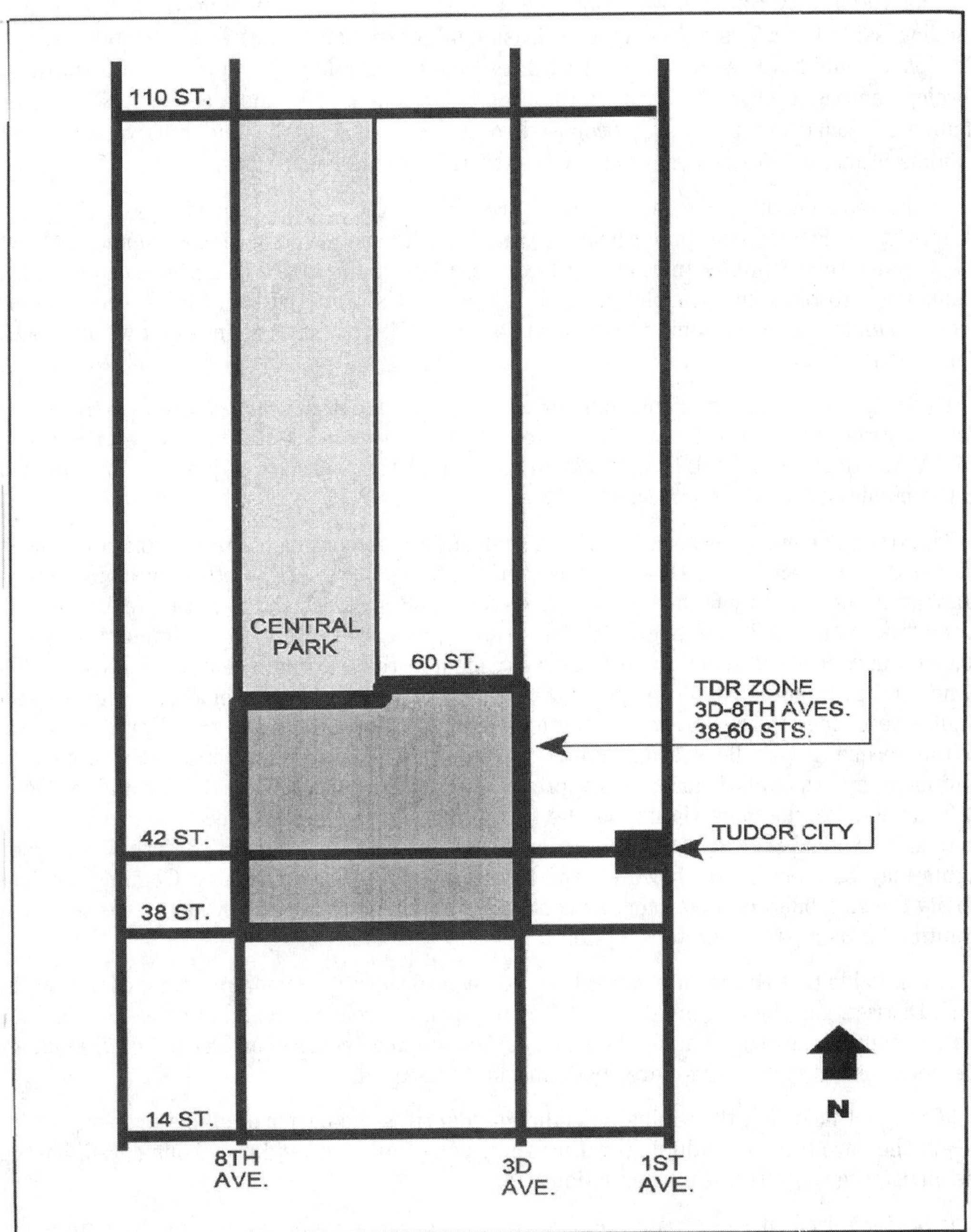

Fred F. French Investing Co. v. City of New York

Mid-town Manhattan showing Tudor City and TDR zone

[The Tudor City complex was conveyed and] the new owner announced plans to erect a building, said to be a 50-story tower, over East 42nd Street between First and Second Avenues. This plan would have required New York City Planning Commission approval of a shifting of development rights from the parks to the proposed adjoining site and a corresponding zoning change. Alternatively, the owner proposed to erect on each of the Tudor City park sites a building of maximum size permitted by the existing zoning regulations.

There was immediately an adverse public reaction to the owner's proposals, especially from Tudor City residents. After public hearings, the City Planning Commission recommended, over the dissent of one commissioner, and on December 7, 1972 the Board of Estimate approved, an amendment to the zoning resolution establishing Special Park District "P." By contemporaneous amendment to the zoning map, the two Tudor City parks were included within Special Park District "P."

Under the zoning amendment, "only passive recreational uses are permitted" in the Special Park District and improvements are limited to "structures incidental to passive recreational use." When the Special Park District would be mapped, the parks are required to be open daily to the public between 6:00 a.m. and 10:00 p.m.

The zoning amendment permits the transfer of development rights from a privately owned lot zoned as a Special Park District, denominated a "granting lot," to other areas in midtown Manhattan, bounded by 60th Street, Third Avenue, 38th Street and Eighth Avenue, denominated "receiving lots." Lots eligible to be receiving lots are those with a minimum lot size of 30,000 square feet and zoned to permit development at the maximum commercial density. The owner of a granting lot would be permitted to transfer part of his development rights to any eligible receiving lot, thereby increasing its maximum floor area up to 10%. Further increase in the receiving lot's floor area, limited to 20% of the maximum commercial density, is contingent upon a public hearing and approval by the City Planning Commission and the Board of Estimate. Development rights may be transferred by the owner directly to a receiving lot or to an individual or organization for later disposition to a receiving lot. Before development rights may be transferred, however, the Chairman of the City Planning Commission must certify the suitability of a plan for the continuing maintenance, at the owner's expense, of the granting lot as a park open to the public.

It is notable that the private parks become open to the public upon mapping of the Special Park District, and the opening does not depend upon the relocation and effective utilization of the transferable development rights. Indeed, the mapping occurred on December 7, 1972, and the development rights have never been marketed or used. . . .

[The court held that the zoning amendment "deprives the owner of all his property rights, except the bare title and a dubious future reversion of full use" and then considered whether the TDR program offset this deprivation:]

It is recognized that the "value" of property is not a concrete or tangible attribute but an abstraction derived from the economic uses to which the property may be put. Thus, the development rights are an essential component of the value of the underlying property because they constitute some of the economic uses to which the property may be put. As such, they are a potentially valuable and even a transferable commodity and may not be disregarded in determining whether the ordinance has destroyed the economic value of the underlying property.

Of course, the development rights of the parks were not nullified by the city's action. In an attempt to preserve the rights they were severed from the real property and made transferable to another section of mid-Manhattan in the city, but not to any particular parcel or place. There was thus created floating development rights, utterly unusable until they could be attached to some accommodating real property, available by happenstance of prior ownership, or by grant, purchase, or devise, and subject to the contingent approvals of administrative agencies. In such case, the development rights, disembodied abstractions of man's ingenuity, float in a limbo until restored to reality by reattachment to tangible real property. Put another way, it is a tolerable abstraction to consider development rights apart from the solid land from which as a matter of zoning law they derive. But severed, the development rights are a double abstraction until they are actually attached to a receiving parcel, yet to be identified, acquired, and subject to the contingent future approvals of administrative agencies, events which may never happen because of the exigencies of the market and the contingencies and exigencies of administrative action. The acceptance of this contingency-ridden arrangement, however, was mandatory under the amendment.

The problem with this arrangement, as Mr. Justice Waltemade so wisely observed at Special Term, is that it fails to assure preservation of the very real economic value of the development rights as they existed when still attached to the underlying property. By compelling the owner to enter an unpredictable real estate market to find a suitable receiving lot for the rights, or a purchaser who would then share the same interest in using additional development rights, the amendment renders uncertain and thus severely impairs the value of the development rights before they were severed (see Note, *The Unconstitutionality of Transferable Development Rights*, 84 Yale L.J. 1101, 1110-1111). Hence, when viewed in relation to both the value of the private parks after the amendment, and the value of the development rights detached from the private parks, the amendment destroyed the economic value of the property. It thus constituted a deprivation of property without due process of law.

None of this discussion of the effort to accomplish the highly beneficial purposes of creating additional park land in the teeming city bears any relation to other schemes, variously described as a "development bank" or the "Chicago Plan" (see Costonis, *The Chicago Plan: Incentive Zoning and the Preservation of Urban Landmarks*, 85 Harv. L. Rev. 574; Costonis, *Development Rights Transfer: An Exploratory Essay*, 83 Yale L.J. 75, 86–87). For under such schemes or variations of them, the owner of the granting parcel may be allowed just compensation for his development rights, instantly and in money, and the acquired development rights are then placed in a "bank" from which enterprises may for a price purchase development rights to use on land owned by them. Insofar as the owner of the granting parcel is concerned, his development rights are taken by the State, straightforwardly, and he is paid just compensation for them in eminent domain. The appropriating governmental entity recoups its disbursements, when, as, and if it obtains a purchaser for those rights. In contrast, the 1972 zoning amendment short-circuits the double-tracked compensation scheme but to do this leaves the granting parcel's owner's development rights in limbo until the day of salvation, if ever it comes. . . .

It would be a misreading of the discussion above to conclude that the court is insensitive to the inescapable need for government to devise methods, other than by outright appropriation of the fee, to meet urgent environmental needs of a densely concentrated urban population. It would be equally simplistic to ignore modern recognition of the principle that no property has value except as the community contributes to that value. The obverse of this principle is, therefore, of first significance: no property is an economic island, free from contributing to the welfare of the whole of which it is but a dependent part. The limits are that unfair or disproportionate burdens may not, constitutionally, be placed on single properties or their owners. The possible solutions undoubtedly lie somewhere in the areas of general taxation, assessments for public benefit (but with an expansion of the traditional views with respect to what are assessable public benefits), horizontal eminent domain illustrated by a true "taking" of development rights with corresponding compensation, development banks, and other devices which will insure rudimentary fairness in the allocation of economic burdens.

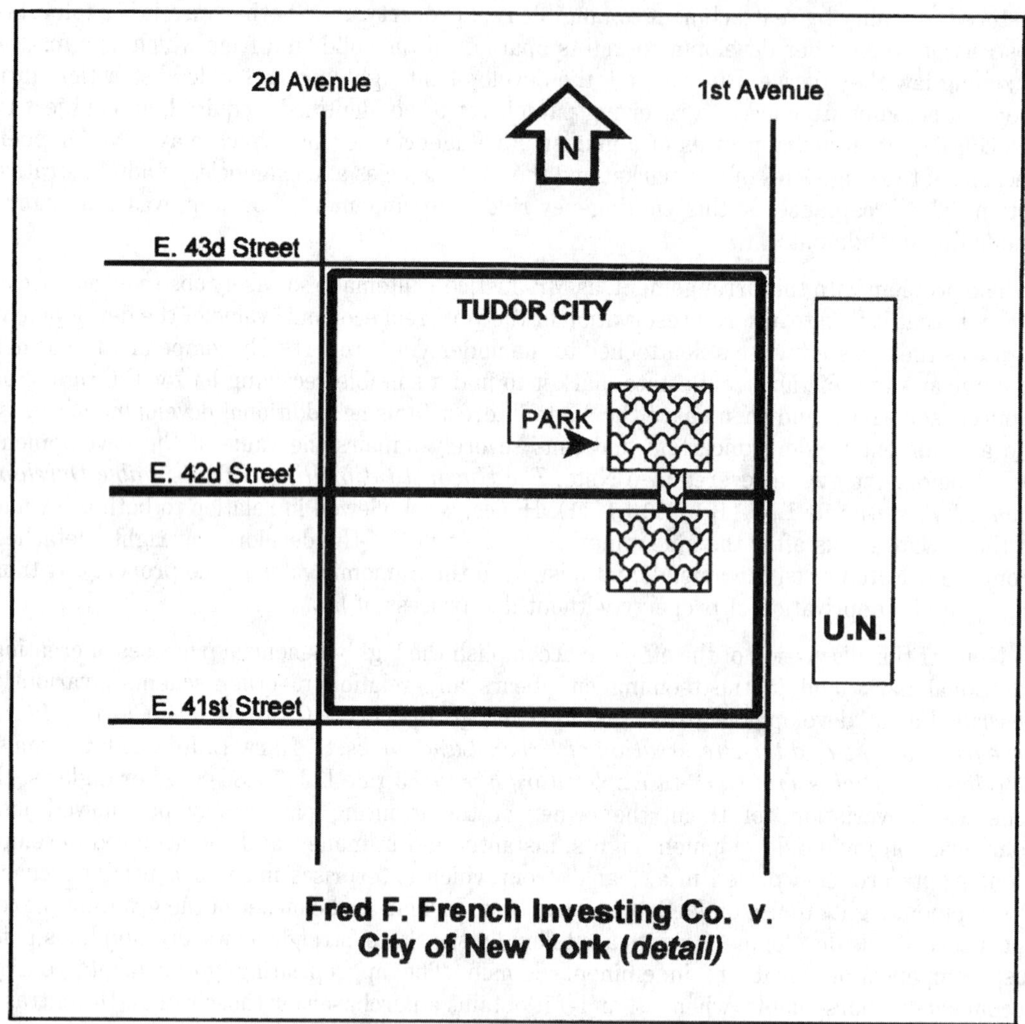

Fred F. French Investing Co. v. City of New York (*detail*)

Solutions must be reached for the problems of modern zoning, urban and rural conservation, and last but not least landmark preservations, whether by particular buildings or historical districts. Unfortunately, the land planners are now only at the beginning of the path to solution. In the process of traversing that path further, new ideas and new standards of constitutional tolerance must and will evolve. It is enough to say that the loose-ended transferable development rights in this case fall short of achieving a fair allocation of economic burden. Even though the development rights have not been nullified, their severance has rendered their value so uncertain and contingent, as to deprive the property owner of their practical usefulness, except under rare and perhaps coincidental circumstances.

The legislative and administrative efforts to solve the zoning and landmark problem in modern society demonstrate the presence of ingenuity. That ingenuity further pursued will in all likelihood achieve the goals without placing an impossible or unsuitable burden on the individual property owner, the public fisc, or the general taxpayer. These efforts are entitled to and will undoubtedly receive every encouragement. The task is difficult but not beyond management. The end is essential but the means must nevertheless conform to constitutional standards.

NOTES AND QUESTIONS

1. *Penn Central TDR upheld.* A mandatory TDR plan was also part of the landmarks designation program considered in the Supreme Court's *Penn Central* decision. The TDR program was extensively considered in the state court decision, 366 N.E.2d 1271 (N.Y. 1977), which upheld it with the following comments:

> Development rights, once transferred, may not be equivalent in value to development rights on the original site. But that, alone, does not mean that the substitution of rights amounts to a deprivation of property without due process of law. Land use regulation often diminishes the value of the property to the landowner. Constitutional standards, however, are offended only when that diminution leaves the owner with no reasonable use of the property. The situation with transferable development rights is analogous. If the substitute rights received provide reasonable compensation for a landowner forced to relinquish development rights on a landmark site, there has been no deprivation of due process. The compensation need not be the "just" compensation required in eminent domain, for there has been no attempt to take property.
>
> The case at bar, like the *French* case, fits neatly into this analysis. In *French*, the development rights on the original site were quite valuable. The regulations deprived the original site of any possibility of producing a reasonable return, since only park uses were permitted on the land. And, the transferable development rights were left in legal limbo, not readily attachable to any other property, due to a lack of common ownership of the rights and a suitable site for using them. Hence, plaintiffs were deprived of property without due process of law. The regulation of Grand Central Terminal, by contrast, permitted productive use of the terminal site as it had been used for more than half a century, as a railroad terminal. In addition, the development rights were made transferable to numerous sites in the vicinity of the terminal, several owned by Penn Central, and at least one or two suitable for construction of office buildings. Since this regulation and substitution was reasonable, no due process violation resulted. [*Id.* at 1278.]

For a discussion of the decision, see Conrad & Merriam, *Compensation in TDR Programs: Grand Central and the Search for the Holy Grail*, 56 U. Det. J. Urb. L. 1, 4-13 (1978-1979).

Little consideration was given to the TDR program in the Supreme Court because the Court held a taking had not occurred. The Court did note that the transferable development rights might not have constituted just compensation if a taking had occurred, but added that these rights mitigated whatever financial burdens the landmark designation imposed and were to be taken into account in considering the impact of this regulation. *Penn Central*, 438 U.S. at 137.

2. *Distinguishing the cases.* What further light does the *Penn Central* case shed on the "fairness" that Judge Breitel requires in TDR programs? In a speech commenting on his *French* and *Penn Central* opinions, Judge Breitel noted that in TDR programs "it becomes fairly clear that, to the extent that they [the transferable development rights] are necessary to compensate the owner of the original site, they must be either in cash, acceptable in kind, or be sufficiently translatable into cash." Breitel, *A Judicial View of Transferable Development Rights*, 30 Land Use L. & Zoning Dig., No. 2, at 5, 6 (1978). He then distinguished the two cases as follows:

> In the *Fred F. French* case, the owner at one point had been offered a tremendous price for those development rights somewhere else in mid-Manhattan. But by the time the case was decided, mid-Manhattan was terribly overbuilt and the value of the TDRs had dropped. That really isn't an accidental circumstance. This is the nature of our economy. This is the reason why the TDR transfers were found insufficient in *Fred F. French* and why, on the other hand, we found them of some value in *Penn Central*. [*Id.*]

Judge Breitel also noted, apparently with reference to *Penn Central*, that the neighboring properties were so profitable in their present use that development rights transferred to those properties would have to be heavily discounted. Nevertheless, he added that if TDR is going to be accepted "we have to abandon the fiction or pretense that we are going to give the owner of the original site full value of that part which we take away from him, let alone the full fee interest; and, . . . that the TDR is not even going to come anywhere close to the exploitative value of the air rights over his land." *Id.* at 5.

Dean Costonis does not believe the two cases can be distinguished. *The Disparity Issue: A Context for the Grand Central Terminal Decision*, 91 Harv. L. Rev. 402 (1977). He notes that both programs were mandatory and that both offered transfer districts with numerous sites suitable for development of the type desired. He states that the only difference was that the landowner in *French* did not own land within the transfer district, but that this difference did not negate the value of the transfer rights. *Id.* at 419–20. Do you agree? On the basis of these decisions, how would you formulate a TDR program for historic landmarks that would win judicial approval? How do the Supreme Court's more recent takings cases, particularly *Lucas*, affect this problem?

3. *A beachfront TDR.* The court upheld a TDR program in *City of Hollywood v. Hollywood, Inc.*, 432 So. 2d 1332 (Fla. App. 1983). A developer owned sixty-five acres of a ninety-two-acre tract on the coast. The eastern coastal portion was zoned as single family residential at seven units to the acre, for a total of 79 units. The western portion of the tract was zoned multi-family. Under the TDR plan, the coastal portion of the tract would remain open and unbuilt, but the multi-family zoning on the western portion would be intensified to allow an increase of 368 multi-family residential units.

Penn Central, the court said, required it to consider the character of the governmental action, the economic impact of the regulation and whether a taking had occurred. The court noted it had "found the government action to be proper and reasonably related to a valid public purpose." It did not disapprove of the economics of the TDR trade-off, noting that the loss of single-family units would be offset by the gain in multi-family units, that the developer owned both parcels, and that the value "of all the multifamily units will be enhanced because the buildings will have an uninterrupted ocean-front position and view." *Id.* at 1338.

What does *Hollywood* indicate about the constitutionality of a TDR program for landmark sites? For a discussion of the *Hollywood* case by the lawyer who helped design the program, see Freilich & Senville, *Takings, TDRs, and Environmental Preservation: "Fairness" and the Hollywood Beach Case*, 35 Land Use L. & Zoning Dig., Sept., 1983, at 4.

The TDR program in *Hollywood* required the developer to dedicate the beach front by deed. The court upheld this requirement as a quid pro quo for the density transfer. When there is no dedication or property restriction, a court may decide later that restrictive zoning on an historic landmark or environmental site should be lifted. See *Francis v. City & County of Denver*, 418 P.2d 45 (Colo. 1966) (landmark was vandalized and demolished).

4. *Suitum.* In *Suitum v. Tahoe Regional Planning Agency*, 520 U.S. 725 (1997), a property owner claimed that a restriction on environmentally sensitive land was a taking, even though an option to transfer development rights was available. The case was decided by the Supreme Court on a ripeness issue, but Justice Scalia examined the takings issue in a concurring opinion. He argued that the availability of TDRs can help determine the compensation due a property owner, but should not affect the question of whether a taking had occurred. Otherwise, the availability of a development rights transfer could completely eliminate a takings claim by providing enough compensation to a landowner to support an argument that substantial value remained in the property. Justice Scalia distinguished *Penn Central* because the landowner owned some of the lots to which development rights were to be transferred.

What practical effect would the Court's adoption of Justice Scalia's argument have on TDR programs? Do you agree with his attempt to distinguish *Penn Central*?

5. *Additional sources.* Bruening, *The TDR Siren Song: The Problems With Transferable Development Rights Programs and How to Fix Them*, 23 J. Land Use & Envtl. L. 423 (2008); Holloway & Guy, *The Utility and Validity of TDRs Under the Takings Clause and the Role of TDRs In the Takings Equation Under Legal Theory*, 11 Penn St. Envtl. L. Rev. 45 (2002); Johnston & Madison, *From Landmarks to Landscapes: A Review of Current Practices in the Transfer of Development Rights*, 63 J. Am. Plan. Ass'n 365 (1997); Juergensmeyer, Nicholas & Leebrick, *Transferable Development Rights and Alternatives After Suitum*, 30 Urb. Law. 441 (1998); Miller, *Transferable Development Rights in the Constitutional Landscape: Has Penn Central Failed to Weather the Storm*, 39 Nat. Res. J. 459 (1999); Note, *Banking on TDRs: The Government's Role as Banker of Transferable Development Rights*, 73 N.Y.U. L. Rev. 1329 (1998); Note, *Caught Between Scalia and the Deep Blue Lake: The Takings Clause and Transferable Development Rights Programs*, 83 Minn. L. Rev. 815 (1999); Note, *Past, Present, and Future Constitutional Challenges to Transferable Development Rights*, 74 Wash. L. Rev. 825 (1999).

A NOTE ON MAKING TDR WORK

Professor Kayden points out some of the limitations of TDR programs. *Market-Based Regulatory Approaches: A Comparative Discussion of Environmental and Land Use Techniques in the United States*, 19 B.C. Envtl. Aff. L. Rev. 565 (1992). The demand for and price of development rights are a function of a city's planning and zoning policy. Demand for rights will be created in receiving districts only if the city regulates land use in these districts tightly. Zoning must also be stable because sellers and buyers will not be willing to create a market for development rights if they do not have confidence in the stability and integrity of a city's zoning. Transaction costs are high, because time-consuming negotiation is required and the valuation of development rights is troublesome. The seller will want to receive a price equal to the capitalized value of the development foregone, while the value to the buyer depends on his site plans.

So how can TDR programs be made to work? A comprehensive analysis of the use and potential of TDR, A. Nelson et al., The TDR Handbook: Designing and Implementing Successful Transfer of Development Rights Programs (2010), reviews the economic and policy foundations of TDR; planning and design considerations; legal foundations, and case studies of effective TDR programs. The authors offer the following perspectives.

> The TDR concept originated with historic preservation but has become more popularly viewed as a way to preserve open spaces. Yet, the concept is much more robust. It can be used to protect established neighborhoods by allowing them to sell development rights that would be used in nearby urban centers. Or, it could be used to transfer development rights from antiquated subdivisions that should never have been approved in the first place, to other areas where development is more appropriate. Basically, whenever there is a need to preserve something that may be adversely impacted by growth, TDRs can be one of several tools in the quiver to achieve preservation while accommodating growth. [*Id.* at 6.]

The study by Kaplowitz, Machemer & Pruetz, *Planners' Experiences in Managing Growth Using Transferable Development Rights (TDR) in the United States*, 25 Land Use Pol'y 378 (2008), provides important lessons for overall TDR program design and implementation. First, the joint existence of a Purchase of Development Rights ("PDR") and TDR program would seem to increase the likelihood of TDR success (and maybe PDR success as well). Background studies and the formation of a TDR bank would also seem to advance success. The research also suggests that several, though perhaps not too many, advocacy groups forming a TDR coalition is important to launch TDR programs. In addition, the type of development demand in the area appears important — especially housing demand. We surmise this is important since it would be people occupying housing and they may be willing to spend more for housing in receiving areas knowing that the community has already preserved open spaces, or historic sites, or other assets that add value to the community. *Id.* at 367.

As the authors of the TDR Handbook note, several studies have examined TDR programs adopted to preserve agricultural or natural resource areas, and made recommendations for successful programs. Though meant for TDR programs that protect environmental resource areas, they also apply to programs for historic preservation. Pruetz & Standridge, *What Makes Transfer of Development Rights Work?* 75 J. Am. Plan. Ass'n 78 (2009), examined the 20 "most successful" TDR programs, based on amount of land preserved (350,000 acres) and "20 publications that list factors thought to be responsible for making TDR programs successful." They concluded that "all successful TDR programs create receiving areas that fit the community and offer development bonuses that developers actually want." *Id.* at 79.

For a series of case studies in Maryland and a proposal to enact a statewide transferable development rights program that would be administered by a state board, see J. Curtis, et al., Transferable Development Rights Legislation: A Proposal for Solving Maryland's Land Use Problems (2008). A similar study for the state of Washington was prepared by the Cascade Land Conservancy, J. Eckert, et al., Transfer of Development Rights (TDR) in Washington State: Overview, Benefits and Challenges (2008). See also Bruening, *supra*, 23 J. Land Use & Envt'l. L. at 435-436 (recommending that TDR programs require low-density rather than high-density developments to purchase development rights).

W. Fulton et al., TDRs and Other Market-Based Land Mechanisms: How They Work and Their Role in Shaping Metropolitan Growth (The Brookings Institution Center on Urban and Metropolitan Policy, 2004), recommends (1) that communities identify viable receiving areas, which may be difficult; (2) a good balance of supply and demand (as other studies have recommended; (3) sustainable sending areas where development pressures do not require high allocation rates to motivate owner participation (development pressures may be especially strong on historic landmarks); (4) strong incentives for landowner participation by allocating enough TDR rights to make them affordable in the receiving area while providing adequate compensation in the sending area; (5) a strong clearinghouse or TDR bank; (6) low transaction costs; and (7) strong community support. *Id.* at 22, 23. The report also notes that TDR programs would benefit from inclusion in a comprehensive plan where they could be part of a comprehensive planning policy.

The report suggests, as an alternative, that communities can

> combine the development or mitigation transfer idea with a more traditional notion — the development or mitigation fee. In this alternative, buyers and sellers need not find each other. Instead, applicants who either seek additional density or must provide mitigation can simply pay a "sending" fee instead of engaging in a transaction with a "receiving" landowner. . . . The fee goes to a government agency or another intermediary that then uses the resulting funds to buy the land. This approach has the advantage of lowering transaction and administrative costs and making the entire transfer system more flexible. [*Id.* at 31.]

Would this fee be an exaction? An alternative suggestion would have a developer at a receiving site pay a stated percentage of her expected profit at the site for the preservation of a sending site in order to receive a density bonus. Pruetz, Maynard & Duerksen, *TDR-Less TDR: A Transfer of Development Rights Approach that "Custom Fits" Transactions*, PAS Memo, Aug. 2002. The authors admit that the administrative complexity of their proposal is a disadvantage. Highly sophisticated TDR programs are a far cry from the common law of nuisance that began this review of land use law!

Statutory Standards. In addition to meeting constitutional standards, TDR programs must comply with state statutory standards. For example, in *KGF Development, LLC v. City of Ketchum*, 236 P.3d 1284 (Idaho 2010), the Supreme Court of Idaho struck down a TDR ordinance that allowed the purchaser of development rights to add a fourth floor to a condominium in an area that restricted building heights to 40 feet (effectively three stories). The statute authorizing TDR limited its use to preservation of open space and rural characteristics. The city ordinance authorized TDR for historic preservation and revitalization of the downtown corridor. The Idaho court concluded that the city did not have the implied power to expand its TDR power beyond preserving the rural character of the city. The court also found that the ordinance violated the uniformity provision of the Idaho Constitution in that owners of receiving sites could construct taller buildings than owners of sending sites in the same zoning district.

TABLE OF CASES

[References are to pages]

[References are to pages]

B

[References are to pages]

[References are to pages]

C

[References are to pages]

[References are to pages]

D

[References are to pages]

E

F

[References are to pages]

G

[References are to pages]

H

[References are to pages]

I

[References are to pages]

J

K

L

[References are to pages]

M

[References are to pages]

[References are to pages]

[References are to pages]

P

[References are to pages]

Q

R

[References are to pages]

S

[References are to pages]

[References are to pages]

[References are to pages]

[References are to pages]

[References are to pages]

Y

Z

INDEX

[References are to sections.]

A

C

D

[References are to sections.]

[References are to sections.]

H

I

J

L

M

N

O

P

Q

R

[References are to sections.]

[References are to sections.]